GUN TRADER'S GUIDE™

Thirty-Seventh Edition

A Comprehensive, Fully Illustrated Guide to Modern Collectible Firearms with Current Market Values

Edited by Robert A. Sado

Skyhorse Publishing

Skyhorse Publishing books may be purchased in bulk at special discounts for sales promotion, corporate gifts, fund-raising, or educational purposes. Special editions can also be created to specifications. For details, contact the Special Sales Department, Skyhorse Publishing, 307 West 36th Street, 11th Floor, New York, NY 10018 or info@skyhorsepublishing.com.

Skyhorse® and Skyhorse Publishing® are registered trademarks of Skyhorse Publishing, Inc.®, a Delaware corporation.

Visit our website at www.skyhorsepublishing.com.

10 9 8 7 6 5 4 3 2 1

Library of Congress Cataloging-in-Publication Data is available on file.

Cover design by Brian Peterson
Cover photographs courtesy Merkel USA and Henry Repeating Arms

Print ISBN: 978-1-63450-459-1
Ebook ISBN: 978-1-63450-476-8

Printed in Canada

Contents

Introduction iv
How to Use *GTG* vi
Firearms Grading xi
The Art of Gun Trading xiv
Gun Shows xv
Online Buying and Selling xvi

Handguns 14
Rifles 198
Shotguns 424
Index 581

Introduction

We at *Gun Trader's Guide* (*GTG*) take buying and selling firearms as serious business. Whether you are buying a used gun for duck hunting, trading in your old conceal carry pistol for something better, or trying to figure out the value of a wall hanger you've come into possession of, *GTG* is a valuable resource used by both professional and amateur firearms enthusiasts. *GTG* offers detailed firearms specifications as well as photographs so you can be more confident when identifying a firearm and its value.

CURRENT AND UP-TO-DATE

The *GTG* is revised annually to ensure information is both current and detailed. In the past fifty years, *GTG* has grown to over six hundred pages and more than six thousand standard firearms and their variations, evolving into one of the most complete catalogs of modern smokeless-powder rifles, shotguns, and handguns from the late 19th century, through the 20th century, to the 21st century. Every effort is made to ensure the information is current and up-to-date. Not every gun ever manufactured can be listed in a catalog of this size, but every effort has been made to include the makes and models that are most popular with American owners and collectors. Please note *GTG* does not include antique or recently manufactured blackpowder firearms.

EASY TO USE FORMAT

GTG's reference guide format is simple and straightforward. Three tabbed sections—handguns, rifles, and shotguns—makes it fast and easy to find the model in question. Entries are alphabetized by manufacturer and model with specifications that include:

- Manufacturer
- Model Name
- Model Number
- Caliber or Gauge
- Barrel Length
- Overall Length
- Weight
- Distinguishing features
- Variations of different models
- Dates of manufacture (when they can be accurately determined)
- Date of discontinuation (if applicable)
- Current value for condition
- Photos (or illustrations)

EXTENSIVE PHOTOGRAPHS

Unique to *GTG* are photographs to help identify and compare firearms. The exclusive and extensive pictorial format, along with comprehensive specifications, provide a complete resource for identifying firearms and their current value.

ACCURATE FIREARM VALUES

Values shown are based on national averages obtained by conferring with knowledgeable gun dealers, traders, collectors, online auction sites, and auctioneers around the country, not by applying an arbitrary mathematical formula that could produce unrealistic figures. The listed values accurately reflect the nationwide average at the time of publication and are updated annually. Keep in mind that the stated values are averages based on a wide spectrum of variables. No price given in any such catalog should be considered the one and only value for a particular firearm. Value is ultimately determined by the buyer and seller. Supply and demand also dictate price.

In the case of rare or one-of-a-kind items, such as the Winchester Model 1873 One of One Thousand rifle or the Parker AA1 Special shotgun in 28 gauge, where little trading takes place, active gun collectors were consulted to obtain current market values.

In researching data some manufacturers' records were unavailable and at times information was unobtainable. Some early firearms manufacturers' production records have been destroyed in fires, lost, or were simply not maintained accurately. These circumstances resulted in some minor deviations in the presentation format of certain model listings. For example, production dates may not be listed when manufacturing records are unclear or unavailable. As an alternative, approximate dates of manufacture may be listed to reflect the availability of guns from a manufacturer or d

These figures may represent disposition dates indicating when that particular model was shipped to a distributor or importer. Frequently, and especially with foreign manufacturers, production records are unavailable. Therefore, availability information is often based on importation records that reflect domestic distribution only.

This is meant to explain the procedure and policy used regarding these published dates and to establish the distinction between production dates, which are based on manufacturers' records, and availability dates, which are based on distribution records in the absence of recorded production data.

To ensure *GTG* has the most accurate information available, we encourage and solicit users to contact our research staff at Skyhorse Publishing, especially in relation to older out-of-production models.

ACKNOWLEDGMENTS

The publisher wishes to express special thanks to the many collectors, dealers, manufacturers, shooting editors, firearm firms and distributors' public relations and production personnel, research personnel, and other industry professionals who provide us with updates throughout the year. We are especially grateful for their assistance and cooperation in compiling information for this edition, as well as allowing *GTG* to reproduce photographs and illustrations of their collectible firearms. Special thanks to James D. Julia Auctioneers, Fairfield, Maine, (www.jamesdjulia.com) for the use of photos and access to information on the Elmer Keith estate.

Finally, *GTG* thanks all the dedicated readers who take the time to email us with comments, suggestions, and queries about collectible firearms. We appreciate and value your input.

Readers may send comments or suggestions to: info@skyhorsepublishing.com

---

SALES OF NOTE

Elmer Keith was legendary, a life-long firearm enthusiast, gun writer, big-game hunter, wrangler, and advocate for magnum cartridges. He was short of stature—his 10-gallon stetson made up for it—yet towered for his work with the .357 Magnum, .41 Magnum, and .44 Magnum. It was Keith tinkering with reloads for his Smith & Wesson Triple Lock that convinced Remington to create the .44 Remington Magnum, what we call today the .44 Magnum. Keith cajoled Smith & Wesson to build a revolver for the new cartridge and the iconic Model 29 was produced. Keith walked the walk, too; his everyday carry gun was a five-inch barrel S&W Model 29. Keith's knowledge and experience with rifles and handguns and reloading was unsurpassed, and aspiring gun designers like Bill Ruger visited with Keith who suggested Ruger lengthen the grip on his Blackhawk single action revolvers. Bill Ruger lengthened grip.

Over the years, Keith amassed a vast collection of firearms including the late Jim Corbett's best quality boxlock .450-400 by W. J. Jeffery & Co. Corbett was a legendary British hunter and tracker-turned-conservationist, author, and naturalist. He was famous for hunting man-eating tigers and leopards in India and wrote about his exploits in *Man-Eaters of Kumaon*.

The first ever Ithaca 10 gauge shotgun was formerly owned by another gun writer Col. Charles Askins. From custom bolt action hunting rifles to large-bore double guns and back-powder pistols, Keith had collected many guns.

In 2015, James D. Julia Auctioneers of Fairfield, Maine, held the preview of the Keith collection from March 12 through 15, and the action was held on March 15 and 16. The Keith collection sold for over $1.9 million to various bidders.

On the opening pages of the handguns, rifles, and shotguns section we have chosen what we feel is an appropriate representation for each of those three categories.—Robert A. Sadowski, ed.

Kieth's Model 29 everyday carry gun.

How to Use *GTG*

Are you planning on buying or selling a used rifle, shotgun, or handgun? Perhaps you just want to establish the value of a favorite rifle, shotgun, or handgun in your collection. No matter what your interest in collectible modern, smokeless-powder firearms, today's enthusiast inevitably turns to the *Gun Trader's Guide* (*GTG*) to determine specifications, date of manufacture, and the average value (in the United States) of a specific modern firearm.

Opening the book, the collector asks him- or herself the first obvious question: "How much is my used gun worth?" Values contained in this book should be considered retail; that is, the average price a collector anywhere in the United States may expect to pay for a firearm in similar condition. Don't leap to the conclusion that your firearm will bring top dollar! There is no right or wrong price for any collectible firearm. The listings shown here are based on national averages and may be higher or lower depending on where you live and the strength of the market in your area. There is a market for everything from folk art to Star Wars action figures, but the range of values can be extreme and only items in perfect condition will bring top dollar.

Many variables must be considered when buying or selling a used gun. Scarcity, demand, geographic location, and the buyer's position. The condition of the gun ultimately governs the selling price. Sentiment often shades the value of a particular gun in the seller's mind, but the market value of Grandpa's old .30-30 cannot be logically cataloged nor effectively marketed—except possibly to someone else in the family!

GRANDPA'S DEER GUN

To illustrate how the price of a particular gun may fluctuate, let us consider the popular Winchester Model 94 (it was discontinued in 2006, after 110 years of continuous production, then reintroduced in 2010) and see what its value might be.

The Model 1894 (or Model 94) is a lever-action, solid-frame repeater. Round or octagon barrels of twenty-six inches were standard when the rifle was first introduced in 1894. However, half-octagon barrels were offered for a slight increase in price. Various magazine lengths were also available.

Fancy grade versions in all calibers were available featuring a checkered walnut pistol grip stock and forearm.

In addition, Winchester produced this model in a carbine style with a saddle ring on the left side of the receiver. The carbine had a twenty inch round barrel and a full or half magazine. Some carbines were supplied with standard-grade barrels while others were made of nickel steel. Trapper models were also available with shorter fourteen-, sixteen-, or eighteen-inch barrels.

In later years, the Rifle and Trapper models were discontinued, and only the carbine remained. Eventually, the saddle ring was eliminated from this model and the carbine butt stock was replaced with a shotgun-type butt stock and shortened forend.

After World War II, the finish on Winchester Model 94 carbines changed to strictly hot caustic bluing; thus, prewar models usually demand a premium over postwar models.

In 1964 (a turning point for many American firearms manufacturers), beginning with serial number 2,700,000, the action on the Winchester Model 94 was redesigned for easier manufacture. Many collectors and firearms enthusiasts considered this and other design changes to be inferior to former models. Therefore, the term pre-'64 has become the watchword for collectors when it comes to setting values on Winchester-made firearms. This will likely be the case in the future, as the now-discontinued models 70, 94, and 1300 Winchester reach the collectible market.

Whether this evaluation is correct or not is unimportant. The justification for an immediate increase in the value of pre-'64 models was that they were no longer available. This diminished availability placed them in the scarce class, making them more desirable to collectors.

Shortly after the 1964 transition, Winchester began producing Model 94 commemorative models in great numbers, which added confusion to the concept of limited production. Increased availability adversely affected the annual appreciation and price stability of these commemorative models. The negative response generated by this marketing practice was increased when Winchester was sold in the 1980s. The name of this long-established American firearms manufacturer was changed to U.S. Repeating Arms Company, which manufactured the Model 94 in standard, carbine, and big-bore models until 2006. Later, the Angle-Eject model was introduced, a design change that allowed for the mounting of scope sights directly above the action. Currently the Model 94 in various con-

figurations are in production in Japan; originals were built in New Haven, Connecticut.

With the above facts in mind, let's explore *GTG* to establish the approximate value of your particular Model 94. We will assume that you recently inherited the rifle, which has "Winchester Model 94" inscribed on the barrel. Turn to the "Rifle" section of the book and look under "Winchester." The index at the back of the book is another way to locate your rifle.

This is a pre-'64 Winchester Model 94 as Grandpa would have hunted whitetails with; its condition rates fair at 70 to 75 percent.

The listings in the *GTG* are arranged within each manufacturer's entry, first by model numbers in consecutive order followed by model names in alphabetical order. At first glance, you see that there are two model designations that may apply: the original designation (Model 1894) or the revised, shorter designation (Model 94). Which of these designations applies to your recently acquired Winchester?

The next step in the process is to try to match the appearance of your model with an

illustration in the book. The photos may all look alike at first glance, but close evaluation and careful attention to detail will enable you to eliminate models that are not applicable. Further examination of your gun might reveal a curved or crescent-shaped butt plate. By careful observation of your gun's characteristics and close visual comparison of the photographic examples, you may logically conclude that your gun is the Winchester Model 94 Lever-Action Rifle. (Please note that the guns shown in the *GTG* are not always shown in proportion to one another; that is, a carbine barrel might not appear to be shorter than a rifle barrel.)

Here a pre-'64 Winchester Model 94 (left) is compared to a newer Winchester Model 94 Short Rifle (right) made in 2011. Note the differences in ejection port, hammer, thumb safety (the pre-'64 has no thumb safety), and finish.

You have now tentatively determined your model, but to be sure, you should read through the specifications for that model and establish that the barrel on the pictured rifle is twenty-six inches long and round, octagonal, or half-octagonal.

The pre-'64 Winchester Model 94 (top) has a barrel band at the muzzle and sports a front sight with removable hood (the hood is long gone from this specimen); the newer Short Rifle (bottom) has a retro-looking marbles front sight with a brass bead.

Upon measuring, you find that the barrel on your rifle is approximately twenty-six inches, perhaps a trifle under, and it is round. Additionally, your rifle is marked .38-55. The caliber offerings listed in the specifications include .38-55, so you are further convinced that this is your gun. You may read on to determine that this rifle was manufactured from 1894 to 1937. After that date, only the shorter-barreled carbine was offered by Winchester, and then only in .25-35, .30-30, and .32 Special.

At this point, you know you have a Winchester Model 94 rifle manufactured before World War II. You read the value and take the rifle to your dealer to initiate a sale.

Here is a look at some of the trades you may encounter for Grandpa's deer rifle:

SCENARIO 1
If the rifle is truly in excellent condition—that is, if it retains at least 95 percent of its original fin-

The older Winchester Model 94 (top) has a band at the end of the forearm, while the newer Winchester Model 94 (bottom) has a forearm cap.

ish on both the metal and wood and has a perfect bore—then the gun does, in fact, have a collectible value as noted. However, keep in mind that the dealer is in business to make a profit. If he pays you the full value of the gun, he will have to charge more than this when he sells it to make a reasonable profit.

Therefore, expect a reputable dealer to offer you less than the published maximum value for the gun in its present condition. The exact amount will vary for a variety of reasons. For example, if the dealer already has a dozen or so of the same model on his shelf and they do not sell well, his offer will be considerably lower. On the other hand, if the dealer does not have any of this model in stock and knows several collectors who want it, chances are his offer will be considerably higher.

SCENARIO 2
Perhaps you overestimated the true state of the rifle's condition. Suppose the gun's finish is flawed and not much of the

original bluing remains. There are several shiny, bare metal spots mixed with a brown patina over the remaining metal. Also, much of the original varnish on the wood has been worn off from extended use. Consequently, the rifle is not considered to be in excellent condition and is worth proportionately less than the Ex or Gd values shown in this book.

SCENARIO 3
Your rifle looks nearly new, as if it were just out of the box, and the rifle works perfectly. Therefore, you are convinced that the dealer should pay you the full value of the gun—less a reasonable profit of 25 to 35 percent. When the dealer offers you about half what you expect, you are shocked!

Although the rifle looks new to you, the experienced dealer has detected that the gun (or parts of it) has been refinished. Perhaps you did not notice the rounding of the formerly sharp edges on the receiver or the slight funneling of some screw holes—all dead giveaways that the rifle has been refinished. If so, your rifle is not in excellent condition as you originally assumed and is therefore worth less than high book value.

Even when a collectible firearm has been expertly refinished to excellent condition, it is no longer original, and a rule of thumb is to deduct 50 percent from the value listed in this book.

If the job is poorly done, deduct 80 percent or more.

TOP-DOLLAR OPTIONS

One alternative for getting top dollar for your gun is to advertise your item in a local newspaper or go online and list it with one of several online gun auction websites, and sell the firearm directly to a private collector. Many collectors have a special interest in certain models, manufacturers, or product lines and will happily pay full price and sometimes more for a hard-to-find piece. However, these approaches may prove time-consuming, frustrating, and expensive. Online auction websites charge fees, and you have to package and ship the firearm to your buyer's FFL dealer. In addition, there may be federal and local restrictions on the sale of firearms in your area, so be sure to check with the local police chief or sheriff before you proceed with a private sale.

STANDARDS OF CONDITION

The condition of a firearm is an important factor in determining its value. In some rare and unusual models, a variation in condition from excellent to very good can mean a value difference of 50 percent or more. Therefore, you must be able to determine the gun's condition before you can accurately evaluate the value of the firearm.

Several sets of value standards have been used in gun trading, but the National Rifle Association Standards of Condition of Modern Firearms is the most popular with the condition established as a percentage of original finish remaining on the wood and metal of the firearm.

Here's a look at how these standards are applied:

EXCELLENT

For the purpose of assigning comparative values as a basis for trading, firearms listed in this book are assumed to be in excellent (Ex) condition if they have 95 percent or more remaining original finish, no noticeable marring of wood or metal, and the bore has no pits or rust.

To the novice, this translates to meaning a practically new gun, almost as though it had just been removed from its shipping box. The trained eye, however, will see the difference between new in the box (NiB) or mint condition and merely excellent.

VERY GOOD

Any other defects, no matter how minor, diminish the value. For example, if more than 5 percent of the original finish is gone and there are minor surface dents or scratches, regardless of how small, the gun is no longer in excellent condition. Instead, it is considered to be in very good condition, provided the gun is in perfect working order. Despite the minor defects, the gun will still look relatively new to the untrained buyer.

GOOD

If the gun is in perfect working condition and functions properly but has minor wear on working surfaces (perhaps some deep scratches on the wood or metal), the gun is considered to be in good (Gd) condition, one grade below very good according to NRA standards. Again, the price shown in this book for that particular firearm must be reduced to reflect its true value.

The two remaining NRA conditions fall under the headings of fair and poor. These guns normally have little value unless they are of historical importance or an aficionado simply must have them to complete his collection. The value of such guns is then determined by the price the buyer is willing to pay.

In any case, do not sell any gun until you have researched its history and value. Many plain-looking guns have sold for thousands of dollars for a variety of reasons. Many an innocent widow has given away her deceased husband's guns without knowing that they were of extremely high value. Avoid buyers who are in a hurry to make a purchase or who quickly offer what seems to be more money than the gun is worth. Not every gun is priceless, but many of them are nearly so!

GTG offers multiplication factors to use for firearms in other than excellent condition. These factors are listed below.

Be aware that the figures given are simply another rough means of establishing value.

For guns in other-than-excellent condition, multiply the price shown in this book for the model in question by the following factors:

Multiplication Factors:

Condition	X	Factor
Mint or New (NiB)		1.25
Excellent (Ex)		1.00
Very Good (VG)		.85
Good (Gd)		.68
Fair		.45
Poor		.15

UNIQUE SERIAL NUMBERS

The serial number on a firearm can increase the value if it is unique, and consecutive serial numbers can boost value to a set of firearms.

PROVENANCE

Provenance means place or source of origin. In gun trading, it means who owned the gun and to a certain extent, when or where the gun was used. Beware of Jesse James six-shooters or else I may want to sell you the Brooklyn Bridge. Make sure the gun has documentation stating prior ownership. It can mean the difference between a really valuable firearm or a really expensive fake.

PARTING THOUGHTS

Remember, the word "guide" in *GTG* should be taken literally. This book is meant to be a reference only and is not the gospel of the collectible trade. We sincerely hope, however, that you find this publication useful when you decide to buy or sell a used collectible modern firearm.

Also, keep in mind that gun values vary from region to region. For example, lever-action deer rifles are more popular among collectors and hunters in the east, while bolt-action bean field rifles bring higher prices in the south and west. For this reason, we recommend that you attend regional gun shows, auctions, and look online to develop a better understanding of local gun values and pricing. And, whenever you travel, check the prices of guns you're familiar with to compare their values in other parts of the country. The difference can be surprising!

Finally, beware of guns that have been refinished or refurbished by amateurs or even expert gunsmiths. A century-old gun that looks brand new has probably been refinished and will actually be worth far less than a time-worn original. Every new screw, pin, or spring added to an original firearm diminishes its value—the worn, pitted original parts of a firearm enhance its value far more than modern replacements. Refinishing a gun may improve its looks and satisfy the final owner, but it will lose collectible value that will never be recovered.

ABBREVIATIONS:
ACP = Automatic Colt Pistol
Adj. = Adjustable
Auto. = Automatic
Avail. = Available
Bbl. = Barrel
C = Cylinder choke
c. = Circa
DA = Double Action
Disc. = Discontinued
Eject. = Ejector
F = Full choke
FN = Fabrique Nationale
Ga. = Gauge
H&H = Holland & Holland
IC = Improved Cylinder choke
in. = inch
L.H. = Left hand

lbs. = Pounds
LC = Long Colt
LR = Long Rifle
M = Modified choke
M&P = Military & Police
Mag. = Magnum
Mfg. = Manufactured
mm = Millimeter
NiB = New in Box
NM = National Match
O/U = Over-and-under
Reintro. = Reintroduced
Rem. = Remington
Rnd. = Round
S/N = serial number
S/S = side-by-side
SA = Single Action
SK = Skeet choke

SL = Self Loading
Spl. = Special
STW = Shooting Times Westerner
Syn. = Synthetic
TH = Target Hammer
TT = Target Trigger
UCC = Usel Caseless Cartridge
Vent. = Ventilated
VR = Vent rib
w/ = with
w/o = without
Wby. = Weatherby
Win = Winchester
WMR = Winchester Magnum
        Rimfire
WRF = Winchester Rimfire

Colt Model 1911
Semi-Automatic Pistol

Adopted by the U.S. Ordnance Department in 1911, the Colt semi-automatic pistol was originally manufactured by Colt and the government's Springfield Armory. In 1917, with the US entry into World War I, the government contracted with Colt for one million pistols and contracts were signed for the production of a total of two million more pistols with Remington-UMC, North American Arms, Savage, Winchester, National Cash Register Co., Burroughs Adding Machine, Lamston Monotype, and Caron Bros. A total of 629,000 pistols were completed by the war's end in1918. Production was resumed in 1924 with a series of design modifications introduced during the inter-war period resulting in the Model 1911 A1. From the onset of World War II until its end in 1945 Colt, Remington UMC, Remington-Rand, Ithaca, Singer, and Union Switch and Signal Company manufactured nearly 2 million M1911A1s.

NRA Perfect Condition is 100 percent original condition. This Colt 1911 has all original parts and commands the same price with or without the box. The frame and receiver are in perfect condition with no wear or damage. The checkering on the grip is in "as new" condition and the wood shows no wear, scratches, or stains.

NRA Good Condition ranges from 60 to 80 percent original condition. There are no replacement parts. This 1911 has worn, rounded edges on the frame with slight pitting and scratches. The bluing is thinning on the working surfaces and stampings show minor wear in areas. The checkering on the grips is slightly rounded with minor nicks. The wood is in good condition, not cracked or stained. A good condition pistol must be in safe working condition.

NRA Fair Condition ranges from 20 to 60 percent original condition. This Model 1911 is in well-worn condition with the frame retaining only 40 percent of its original finish. Some major and minor parts have been replaced and scratches and pitting from rust and corrosion are evident on the frame and slide. Serial numbers and other markings are shallow and difficult to identify. While the grips on this pistol are not badly scratched or soiled, they show worn checkering and several large and small dents. The gun must function and shoot properly.

Winchester Model 94

Winchester produced approximately 2,550,000 Model 94 lever action rifles between 1894 and 1962. The Model 94 was manufactured in both rifle and carbine versions with several configurations that included pistol- and straight-grip stocks, various grades of wood, and several different barrel lengths and magazine capacities. Crescent and shotgun style buttstocks and takedown barrels were also offered. The Model 94 was produced in 25-35, 30, 30-30, 32-40 and 38-55 calibers.

NRA Perfect Condition ranges from 95 to 100 percent original condition. This Model 94 shows very little use and looks in new condition with 96 percent of its original finish remaining. All parts are original and in excellent condition. There is no noticeable wear with the wood and metal showing no stains, scratches or nicks. The bluing is in near-perfect condition. The action functions smoothly and the rifle is in perfect working condition.

NRA Good Condition ranges from 60 to 80 percent original condition. There are no replacement parts. The gun has all original parts and shows no corrosive rusting or pitting. The edges of the action are slightly rounded and the bluing is beginning to wear thin on the working surfaces. The stampings show minor wear in areas. There are no broken parts and the stock fits smoothly to the metal with only minor nicking. The gun must be in safe working condition.

NRA Fair Condition ranges from 20 to 60 percent original condition. This Model 94 is in well-worn condition with some minor parts replaced or requiring restoration or adjustment. The serial numbers and descriptive stampings are shallow and hard to read. The wood is badly scratched and dented with evident repairs. There is corrosive pitting and scratches but the gun remains in safe firing condition.

Winchester Model 12

When introduced in 1912, the hammerless Model 12 slide-action shotgun was offered only in 20-gauge with a 2½-inch chamber. In 1914 12- and 16-gauge versions were introduced followed by a 28-gauge in 1937. The Model 12 was available with various chokes and with walnut, straight or pistol grip stock and forearm. Winchester sold more than 1,900,000 Model 1912s during the shotgun's 51-year history.

NRA Perfect Condition is 100 percent original condition. This Model 12 is in NIB condition and has not been previously sold at retail. The shotgun shows no signs of use and retains 100 percent of its original finish. All parts are original and in new condition.

NRA Good Condition ranges from 60 to 80 percent original condition. This gun has all original parts in good condition. There is no corrosive pitting or rusting and the action displays only slightly rounded edges. The gun retains 70 percent of its original finish with bluing beginning to wear on the working surfaces. The stock fits smoothly to the metal and has only minor nicking. The shotgun must be in good working order.

NRA Fair Condition ranges from 20 to 60 percent original condition. Showing a well-worn condition, this gun may require minor parts to be replaced or adjusted. The serial numbers and descriptive stamping are shallow and difficult to read. The wood is badly scratched and dented with evident repairs. Corrosive pitting and scratches in the metal, while considerable, do not render the gun unsafe.

The Art of Gun Trading

No matter if you are trading bottle caps, marbles, or fine firearms, there is an art and a science to the process that beginners often fail to realize and seasoned experts rely on. In other words, if you do not know what you are doing, you can expect to be burned—badly, in some cases.

GUN TRADING BASICS

As is the case when selling any collectible item, there is no substitute for research.

The first step in shrewd gun trading is to know your firearm, its condition, and its value in your market—meaning your part of the country. A Marlin .30/30 lever-action rifle, for example, will not carry as high a value in California, Georgia, or Texas as it will in Pennsylvania, Maine, New York, or elsewhere in the east, where short-range brush-country guns are most popular.

Next, study the NRA Standards of Condition (see pages xxi thru xv) and get a feel for such terms as New In Box, Excellent, and Good and what they mean to a collector.

DICKERING HOW-TO

When it comes to "horse trading" there are no rules, but the conflict is always the same: Each party wants to come out a winner.

Below are a few tips for the new gun trader to consider.

DON'T SAY TOO MUCH

Present the gun to the prospective buyer and let him or her make all the comments and ask all the questions.

DECIDE ON A PRICE

This requires a little of the poker player's panache. If you name a price and the buyer pounces on it. Set the price too high and he or she might walk away.

The right price will keep a buyer interested, which is why knowing your gun and its value is important.

DON'T LIE OR EMBELLISH

Gun collectors generally know their guns as well as anyone and are quick to spot a fraud. If your gun is not in its original condition, has been refurbished, or is not what it appears to be, be honest and say so. If you don't know the answer to an important question, take the time to find out.

KNOW WHEN TO QUIT

Trust your instincts when a buyer seems overeager to buy your gun, tells you its value is much less than you know it is worth, or tries to tell you the gun is illegal, a fake, or otherwise not what you say it is. If you feel that you are being tricked—while either buying or selling—back away, do more research, and come back with new knowledge and a different offer.

LEARN AS YOU GO

If you spend time buying and selling guns, or any collectible for that matter, you are going to make some great sales and unfortunately, you are also going to be beaten in price by a buyer or dealer who has been in the game longer than you have. Generally, the best advice is to never sell a gun for less than you paid for it. Good research will keep you from selling a $10,000 gun for $100—it happens!—or from paying thousands more than a gun is worth, which also happens.

The ultimate value of a firearm depends on the rarity of the model, the region, and the buyer's needs; rare, unusual, or one-of-a-kind guns can be worth substantially more than the standard model. It's in your best interest to find out what kind of gun you have and what it is worth before you offer it for sale.

Courtesy of NSSF.org.

Gun Shows

The best classroom for learning about the value and condition of used firearms is the weekend gun show. Dealers from the region and often across the country will attend to show, sell, buy, trade, and talk about new and used guns of every make and model. Some dealers specialize in firearms made by a specific manufacturer while some deal in just one model of firearm. Others may offer custom guns while others offer a variety of collectibles including swords, knives, and ancient weaponry.

Attending gun shows is a chance to see a wide variety of firearms, their condition, and their value at the local level. This is the place to really learn about guns and how their value is determined. Most dealers will gladly explain the nuances of gun condition, why perfectly refurbished guns are worth so much less than a rusted, beat-up original, and what makes one gun worth so much while another seemingly similar model is worth so much less.

GUN SHOW ETIQUETTE

Unless otherwise noted, all gun shows in the United States are open to the public. There are security requirements that must be met and procedures that must be followed. In general, anyone attending a gun show may bring guns for appraisal, sale, or trade. Laws vary from state to state, so be sure to check with show promoters or local law enforcement before bringing a gun.

Most guns shows are well attended, often crowded, and sales can be brisk. If a particular dealer or booth is overrun with customers, come back later to talk. There are always slow periods at gun shows, such as early in the day, lunchtime, and just before closing.

In general, do not bring a gun to a commercial show and expect to get top dollar for it. Show dealers often work in volume sales and may have a dozen or more of your model on the table.

Specialty guns, of course, will draw any dealer's attention, and once in a while you will get far more than you expected from a particular firearm. However, it is best to see what the dealer is willing to give you and compare that to the prices listed in the *GTG* and other collectible gun books. If he or she is offering you a higher price than you expected, then conduct some more research because you may have a unique and valuable model.

In most cases, there will be too much diversion to allow you to make a serious sale or trade. If you are feeling rushed or pressured, move on to another dealer. Don't be rushed into a sale.

WORK THE CROWD

While huge crowds at gun shows can be a hindrance, you can use the crowd to your advantage by carrying your locked and tagged for-sale gun with you as you move around the booths. There will be gun buyers, dealers, and fans in the crowd who may stop you to discuss your firearm. A buyer who needs a particular piece to complete his collection could easily offer you more than the gun is listed for, more than the dealer offered, and more than you ever expected to get for it.

Even if you do not make a sale, you can make valuable contacts for future transactions.

Gun shows are ongoing events that occur weekly, monthly, or annually in towns and cities around the country. Some shows are sponsored by the same organizations in the same location each time, so it is easy to keep track of them.

For a complete, updated list of gun shows near you, go to gunshows-usa.com for a listing of all the gun shows scheduled in every state. The list is updated weekly.

Online Buying and Selling

There is not a facet of our lives that isn't touched by technology. Auction websites such as gunbroker.com, gunsamerica.com, and others, as well as online dealers such as impactguns.com and galleryofguns.com offer gun buyers a vast selection of firearms you can buy and sell using your computer.

Buyers can easily search for that one rare gun to complete their collection or look for a new rifle for next deer season.

The online auction websites enable sellers to reach buyers they might not have normally reached. If you are a private individual with a gun to sell, all you need to do is create an account, type in a description, take a few digital pictures of the item, and list it. It's that simple and that easy.

All the same federal, state, and local gun laws apply when selling and purchasing a gun online as when purchasing a gun at a brick-and-mortar retailer. In fact, the transfer of the firearm is the same. When a buyer purchases a firearm on, say, gunsamerica. com, the buyer must provide the seller with a copy of their gun shop's FFL (Federal Firearms License) or arrange to have the seller ship the firearm to one of the FFL located near the buyer that is listed on the website. The

seller then ships the gun to the gun shop with the FFL holder—not directly to the buyer—and the buyer then fills out the necessary state and local paperwork to take transfer of the gun. Gun shops usually charge the buyer a fee to transfer the gun, typically $45 to $65. It is up to the buyer to be aware of state and local laws. Know your local and state laws before buying. If you bid on it and win, you own.

Auction sites charge a fee, a small percentage of the sale, to all sellers. The fee is only charged if the seller actually sells the gun through an auction. There is no charge to list a firearm. When setting up an account with online auction websites, a seller needs to provide a credit card. Once an auction closes with a sale, the fee is automatically charged to the seller's credit card.

Online gun dealers, such as galleryofguns.com, are not auction sites, but they allow users to purchase guns that are then shipped to an FFL-holding retailer in or near the buyer's zip code.

Finding a specific firearm is easy for buyers because of search functionality built into auction websites. Once a user has an account, they can click off search criteria to zero in on a specific manufacturer, model,

caliber, barrel length, magazine capacity, and other criteria. The user then has the ability to save the search and have e-mail alerts sent to their e-mail inbox with search results.

Many online auctions also offer services for after the sale with shipping profiles, FFL look up, and others tools to smoothly complete the transaction.

Most sellers and buyers online strive to ensure all parties are satisfied with the transaction. Like any aspect in a buying and selling situation, there are some who will try to take advantage. Do your due diligence and contact the seller prior to making

TYPES OF ONLINE AUCTIONS

Basic: The seller's starting price is the amount the seller is willing to take for the item.

Dutch: A seller is auctioning two or more identical items, and a buyer bids on the per-item cost. If you bid $1 and there are ten items, the total price is $10.

Absolute or Penny: Starts out at $.01 with no reserve with the item selling for the last bid after the auction closes.

Reserve: A seller has a minimum reserve price set for the item. This amount is hidden.

a bid, get as much information as you can about the item, and finally look at the seller's rating. Most sellers do their best to keep their rating high, and most will be willing to go the distance to satisfy a customer. The auction websites have a system in place to deal with buyer and seller protection. Like in anything, the old dictum "buyer beware" applies. If the deal seems too good to be true, then it probably is.

With online auctions, there is an excitement about bidding against other buyers—remember your budget, and remember what the firearm is worth. You do not want to get caught up in a bidding frenzy and overpay. On the other hand, you may be inclined to pay slightly more for an item that is rare in your geographic area or for an item that is no longer manufactured. Technology has opened up gun trading 24/7/365.

ONLINE AUCTION GLOSSARY

10- or 15-minute Rule: After the last bid activity and when an auction is ready to close, there is a time interval of 10 to 15 minutes, depending on the website, that must pass to allow any last bids to be entered. Think of it as the "going, going, gone" statement made by an auctioneer. If a bid is entered during the last 10 or 15 minutes, the 10- or 15-minute interval resets. Only when the entire 10 or 15 minutes has passed is the auction considered closed.

Auto Bid or Proxy Bid: A buyer bids the maximum amount they are willing to pay for an item, and Auto Bid automatically enters the least amount to win and continues to automatically bid to the specified maximum. For example, buyer one sets up an Auto Bid for $500, yet the current bid on the item is $450. Buyer two bids $475, and buyer one's Auto Bid bids according to the bid increment of the auction and the maximum amount specified buyer one. Once Auto Bid hits the maximum amount, it stops bidding.

Bid: Amount a buyer is willing to pay for an item.

Bid History: Shows the bids of buyers, time, and date of bid. During a live auction, the bid amounts are hidden, but after the auction closes bid amounts are shown.

Bid Increment: Amount the bid is increased by as specified by the seller.

Buy Now: Displayed price the seller is willing to accept to end the auction.

FFL: Federal Firearms License—a holder of an FFL is required to transfer a firearm from a seller to a buyer.

Feedback: Buyers and sellers can leave feedback on the auction transaction for public viewing. Both sellers and buyers are rated on a scale of how well the transaction went.

Fixed Price: An item that sells at a set price with no bidding.

Inspection Period: Some auction websites require the seller to give the buyer a set time limit, usually three days, to inspect the item. If the buyer declines the item, the buyer is entitled a full refund on the auction price. Return shipping of the item to the seller is paid for by the buyer.

Minimum Bid: Total amount of the current high bid plus the bid increment.

Reserve Price: Lowest price the seller is willing to accept; typically the reserve price is hidden.

Reserve Price Not Met/Reserve Price Met: In a reserve auction, whether the reserve price is met is indicated on a item depending on if bidding has not or has met the price.

Starting Bid: Least amount a bidder is allowed to bid; this is set by the seller.

Watch List: A buyer can use a watch list to track items they are interested in and bid or not bid on the item. Items stay in a user's watch list until deleted by a user, even if the item's auction has closed.

Handguns

The Last Word on Colt SAA Revolvers—according to Keith and Croft

Elmer Merrifield Keith (March 8, 1899 – February 14, 1984) was a horse wrangler, rancher, hunter, arsenal inspector, wildcat reloader, firearms enthusiast, and gun writer. His trademarks were a ten-gallon Stetson, chomped-on cigar, and a Model 29 strapped to his waist. Keith greatly influenced firearm and cartridge designs from the 1930s through the 1950s. He helped develop the first magnum revolver cartridges, including the .357 Magnum, .44 Magnum, and .41 Magnum, and convinced Smith & Wesson to produce the Model 29 which went on to become an iconic revolver with a little help from Clint Eastwood as Dirty Harry. The Colt SAA was a favorite revolver of Keith and the tinkerer he was, along with some help from his friend S. Harold Croft, changed a few features on the Colt to produce Old No. 5, which is perhaps the most well know of Keith's revolvers. It sold at auction in March 2014 for $80,500.

Modifications to the Colt included a reworked top strap into a flat top style, a Colt style windage adjustable rear sight, custom base pin with a ribbed hourglass shaped head that is secured with a swinging latch, hammer is Bisley style, trigger is wider and slightly longer than a standard SAA trigger, and the backstrap is an altered Bisley attached to a single action frontstrap/trigger guard.

The most famous of all Elmer Keith's handguns, a Colt single action army revolver, "THE LAST WORD – OLD NO. 5," S/N M5 in .44 Special with a 5.5-inch barrel. Finish is all blue with elaborate engraving. The muzzle is fitted with a sleeve that is mounted with a Colt double action style adjustable front sight.

No. 5 was, as its name suggests, the fifth iteration of highly modified Colt revolvers. Keith and Croft made final design changes to create what was in their minds the perfect single action revolver. The final design became No. 5, and in the April, 1929, issue of *American Rifleman* Keith titled the story "The Last Word," detailing the specifics surrounding the concept and manufacture of the revolver.

Keith was a Freemason and had the Masonic symbol added to the top strap engraving of the revolver.

The two-piece pre-ban African ivory grips are custom built to fit the frame with a raised, carved Mexican eagle on right side.

Legend has it that S. Harold Croft (left) from Philadelphia brought a suitcase full of revolvers to Oregon to meet with Elmer Keith (right); they collaborated on the design of the "Old No. 5" revolver.

Accu-Tek Model AT .380

Accu-Tek Model BL-9

Accu-Tek HC-380SS

A.A. ARMS — Monroe, North Carolina

AP-9 SERIES
Semiautomatic recoil-operated pistol w/polymer integral grip/frame design. Fires from a closed bolt. Caliber: 9mm Parabellum. 10- or 20-round magazine, 3-, 5- or 11-inch bbl., 11.8 inches overall w/5-inch bbl., Weight: 3.5 lbs. Fixed blade, protected post front sight adjustable for elevation, winged square notched rear. Matte phosphate/blue or nickel finish. Checkered polymer grip/frame. Made from 1988-99.

AP9 model
(pre-94 w/ventilated bbl., shroud) . . . NiB $445 Ex $369 Gd $267
AP9 Mini model
(post-94 w/o bbl., shroud) . . . . NiB $265 Ex $250 Gd $195
AP9 Target model
(pre-94 w/11-inch bbl.) . . . . . . NiB $550 Ex $425 Gd $315
Nickel finish, add $40

ACCU-TEK — Ontario, California (accu-tekfirearms.com)

MODEL AT-9 AUTO PISTOL
Caliber: 9mm Para. 8-round magazine, Double action only. 3.2-inch bbl., 6.25 inches overall. Weight: 28 oz. Fixed blade front sight, adj. rear w/3-dot system. Firing pin block with no External safety. Stainless or black over stainless finish. Checkered black nylon grips. Announced 1992, but made from 1995-99.
Satin stainless model . . . . NiB $347 Ex $275 Gd $210
Matte black stainless. . . . . NiB $311 Ex $250 Gd $200

MODEL AT-25 AUTO PISTOL
Similar to Model AT380 except chambered .25 ACP, 7-round magazine. Made from 1992-96.
Lightweight w/aluminum frame . . NiB $164 Ex $135 Gd $115
Bright stainless (disc. 1991) . . . . NiB $164 Ex $135 Gd $115
Satin stainless model . . . . NiB $164 Ex $135 Gd $115
Matte black stainless. . . . . NiB $164 Ex $135 Gd $115

MODEL AT-32 AUTO PISTOL
Similar to AT-380 except chambered .32 ACP. Made from 1990-2003.
Lightweight w/aluminum
Frame (disc. 1991) . . . . NiB $215 Ex $160 Gd $110
Satin stainless model . . . . NiB $215 Ex $160 Gd $110
Matte black stainless. . . . . NiB $225 Ex $170 Gd $120

MODEL AT-40 DA AUTO PISTOL
Caliber: .40 S&W. 7-round magazine, 3.2-inch bbl., 6.25 inches overall. Weight: 28 oz. Fixed blade front sight, adj. rear w/3-dot system. Firing pin block with no External safety. Stainless or black over stainless finish. Checkered black nylon grips. Announced 1992, but made from 1995-96.
Satin stainless model . . . . NiB $290 Ex $166 Gd $129
Matte black stainless. . . . . NiB $295 Ex $177 Gd $140

MODEL AT-380 AUTO PISTOL
Caliber: .380 ACP. Five-round magazine, 2.75-inch bbl., 5.6 inches overall. Weight: 20 oz. External hammer w/slide safety. Grooved black composition grips. Alloy or stainless frame w/steel slide. Black, satin aluminum or stainless finish. Made from 1992-2003.
Standard alloy frame (disc. 1992) NiB $291 Ex $165 Gd $145
AT-380II Satin stainless (Avail. 1990) NiB $291 Ex $165 Gd $145
Matte black stainless. . . . . NiB $279 Ex $188 Gd $129

MODELS BL-9, BL 380 . . . . . NiB $200   Ex $155   Gd $130
Ultra compact DAO semiautomatic pistols. Calibers: .380 ACP, 9mm
Para. 5-round magazine, 3-inch bbl., 5.6 inches overall. Weight: 24 oz.
Fixed sights. Carbon steel frame and slide w/black finish. Polymer grips.
Made 1997 to 1999.

MODELS CP-9, CP-40, CP-45
Compact, double action only, semiautomatic pistols. Calibers: 9mm
Parabellum, .40 S&W, .45 ACP, 8-, 7- or 6-round magazine, 3.2-inch
bbl., 6.25 inches overall. Weight: 28 oz. Fixed blade front sight, adj.
rear w/3-dot system. Firing-pin block with no External safety. Stainless
or black over stainless finish. Checkered black nylon grips. Made1997-
2002 (CP-9), 1999 (CP-40), 1996 (CP-45).
Black stainless model . . . . NiB $255   Ex $190   Gd $140
Satin stainless model . . . . NiB $255   Ex $190   Gd $140

MODEL HC-380 AUTO PISTOL .NiB $280   Ex $235   Gd $220
Caliber: .380 ACP. 13-round magazine, 2.75-inch bbl., 6 inches overall. Weight: 28 oz. External hammer w/slide safety. Checkered black
composition grips. Stainless finish. Made 1993 to 2003, Reintro. 2007.

ACTION ARMS — Philadelphia, Pennsylvania
*See also listings under CZ pistols. Action Arms stopped importing fire-
arms in 1994.*

AT-84S DA AUTOMATIC PISTOL .NiB $530   Ex $380   Gd $320
Caliber: 9mm Para. 15-round magazine, 4.75-inch bbl., 8 inches
overall. Weight: 35 oz. Fixed front sight, drift-adj. rear. Checkered
walnut grips. Blued finish. Made in Switzerland from 1988 to 1989.

AT-84P DA AUTO PISTOL . . . . . NiB $510   Ex $365   Gd $320
Compact version of the Model AT-84. Only a few prototypes were
manufactured in 1985.

AT-88P DA AUTO PISTOL . . . . . NiB $530   Ex $479   Gd $377
Compact version of the AT-88S w/3.7-inch bbl. Only a few prototypes
of this model were manufactured in 1985. Note: The AT-88 pistol series
was later manufactured by Sphinx-Muller as the AT-2000 series.

AT-88S DA AUTOMATIC PISTOL NiB $550   Ex $479   Gd $377
Calibers: 9mm Para. or .41 Action Express, 10-round magazine, 4.6-
inch bbl., 8.1 inches overall. Weight: 35.3 oz. Fixed blade front sight,
adj. rear. Checkered walnut grips. Imported 1989 to 1991.

ADVANTAGE ARMS — St. Paul, Minnesota

MODEL 422 DERRINGER . . . . NiB $175   Ex $115   Gd $110
Hammerless, top-break, 4-bbl., derringer w/rotating firing pin. Calibers:
.22 LR and .22 Mag., 4-round capacity, 2.5 inch bbl., 4.5 inches overall.
Weight: 15 oz. Fixed sights. Walnut grips. Blued, nickel or PDQ matte
black finish. Made from 1985 to 1987.

S. A. ALKARTASUNA FABRICA DE ARMAS — Guernica, Spain

"RUBY" AUTOMATIC PISTOL. NiB $355   Ex $283   Gd $225
Caliber: .32 Automatic (7.65mm), 9-round magazine, 3.63-inch bbl.,
6.38 inches overall. Weight: About 34 oz. Fixed sights. Blued finish.
Checkered wood or hard rubber grips. Made from 1917-22. Note: Mfd.
by a number of Spanish firms, the Ruby was a secondary standard service pistol of the French Army in World Wars I and II. Specimens made
by Alkartasuna bear the "Alkar" trademark.

**Action Arms AT-84 with
Prototype of Model
AT-84P in background**

Mateba Auto Revolver

AMERICAN ARMS — Kansas City, Missouri
*Importer of Spanish and Italian shotguns, pistols, and rifles. Acquired by
TriStar Sporting Arms, Ltd., in 2000.*

BISLEY SA REVOLVER. . . . . . NiB $490   Ex $400   Gd $315
Uberti reproduction of Colt's Bisley. Caliber: .45 LC, 6-round cylinder, 4.75-,
5.5- or 7.7-inch bbl., Case-hardened steel frame. Fixed blade front sight,
grooved top strap rear. Hammer block safety. Imported from 1997 to 1998

CX-22 CLASSIC DA AUTOMATIC PISTOL
Similar to Model PX-.22 except w/8-round magazine, 3.33-inch bbl.,
6.5 inches overall. Weight: 22 oz. Made from 1990 to 1995.
CX-22 Classic. . . . . NiB $200   Ex $145   Gd $125
**CXC-22 w/chrome
   Slide** (disc. 1990) . . . . NiB $195   Ex $140   Gd $120

EP-380 DA AUTOMATIC PISTOL NiB $410   Ex $299   Gd $160
Caliber: .380 Automatic. 7-round magazine, 3.5-inch bbl., 6.5 inches
overall. Weight: 25 oz. Fixed front sight, square notch adj. rear. Stainless
finish. Checkered wood grips. Made 1989 to 1991.

ESCORT DA AUTO PISTOL . . NiB $315   Ex $225   Gd $155
Caliber: .380 ACP, 7-round magazine, 3.38-inch bbl., 6.13 inches
overall. Weight: 19 oz. Fixed, low-profile sights. Stainless steel frame,
slide, and trigger. Nickel-steel bbl., Soft polymer grips. Loaded chamber
indicator. Made from 1995 to 1997.

MATEBA AUTO REVOLVER
Unique combination action design allows both slide and cylinder to recoil
together causing cylinder to rotate. Single or double action. Caliber: .357
Mag, 6-round cylinder, 4- or 6-inch bbl., 8.77 inches overall w/4-inch
bbl., Weight: 2.75 lbs. Steel/alloy frame. Ramped blade front sight, adjust-
able rear. Blue finish. Smooth walnut grips. Imported from 1997-99.
Mateba model (w/4-inch bbl.). NiB $1630   Ex $1130   Gd $775
Mateba model (w/6-inch bbl.). NiB $1695   Ex $1195   Gd $870

P-98 Classic DA Automatic NiB $215   Ex $140   Gd $105
Caliber: .22 LR, 8-round magazine, 5-inch bbl., 8.25 inches overall.
Weight: 25 oz. Fixed front sight, square notch adj. rear. Blued finish.
Serrated black polymer grips. Made 1989 to 1996.

**American Arms
Regulator Deluxe Model**

**American Derringer
Model 1**

**American Derringer
Model 3**

**PK-22 Classic DA
AUTOMATIC PISTOL . . . . NiB $190   Ex $145   Gd $120**
Caliber: .22 LR. 8-round magazine, 3.33-inch bbl., 6.33 inches overall. Weight: 22 oz. Fixed front sight, V-notch rear. Blued finish. Checkered black polymer grips. Made from 1989 t5o 1996.

PX-22 DA AUTOMATIC PISTOL NiB $245   Ex $177   Gd $155
Caliber: .22 LR. 7-round magazine, 2.75-inch bbl., 5.33 inches overall. Weight: 15 oz. Fixed front sight, V-notch rear. Blued finish. Checkered black polymer grips. Made from 1989-96.

PX-25 DA AUTOMATIC PISTOL NiB $255   Ex $220   Gd $190
Same general specifications as the Model PX-22 except chambered for .25 ACP. Made from 1991-92.

REGULATOR SA REVOLVER
Similar in appearance to the Colt Single-Action Army. Calibers: .357 Mag., .44-.40, .45 Long Colt. Six-round cylinder, 4.75- or 7.5-inch bbl., blade front sight, fixed rear. Brass trigger guard/backstrap on Standard model. Casehardened steel on Deluxe model. Made from 1992 to 2000.
Standard model . . . . NiB $279   Ex $210   Gd $125
Standard combo set
(45 LC/.45 ACP & .44-.40/.44 Spec.) NiB $445   Ex $375   Gd $275
Deluxe model. . . . . NiB $375   Ex $315   Gd $225

**Deluxe combo set (.45 LC/.45
   ACP & .44-40/.44 Spl.) . . . . NiB $445   Ex $389   Gd $260**
Stainless steel. . . . . NiB $425   Ex $355   Gd $250

BUCKHORN SA REVOLVER
Similar to Regulator model except chambered .44 Mag. w/4.75-, 6- or 7.7-inch bbl., Fixed or adjustable sights. Hammer block safety. Imported 1993 to 1996.
Buckhorn model (standard sights) NiB $425   Ex $315   Gd $255
w/adjustable sights, add $40

SPECTRE DA AUTO PISTOL
Blowback action, fires closed bolt. Calibers: 9mm Para., .40 S&W, .45 ACP, 30-round magazine, 6-inch bbl., 13.75 inches overall. Weight: 4 lbs. 8 oz. Adj. post front sight, fixed U-notch rear. Black nylon grips. Matte black finish. Imported 1990 to 1994.
9mm Para. . . . . NiB $545   Ex $450   Gd $260
.40 S&W (disc. 1991) . . . . NiB $515   Ex $400   Gd $300
.45 ACP . . . . NiB $560   Ex $445   Gd $315

WOODMASTER SA AUTO PISTOL NiB $300   Ex $250   Gd $195
Caliber: .22 LR. 10-round magazine, 5.88-inch bbl., 10.5 inches overall. Weight: 31 oz. Fixed front sight, square-notch adj. rear. Blued finish. Checkered wood grips. Disc. 1989.

454 SSA REVOLVER . . . . NiB $795   Ex $680   Gd $530
Umberti SSA chambered 454. 6-round cylinder, 6-inch solid raised rib or 7.7-inch top-ported bbl., satin nickel finish, adj. rear sight. Hammer block safety. Imported from 1996 to 1997.

AMERICAN DERRINGER CORPORATION — Waco, Texas (amderringer.com)

MODEL 1 STAINLESS
Single-action similar to the Remington O/U derringer, 2-shot capacity. More than 60 calibers from .22 LR to .45-70, 3-inch bbl., 4.82 inches overall, weight: 15 oz. Automatic bbl., selection. Satin or high-polished stainless steel. Rosewood grips. Made from 1980 to date.
.45 Colt, .44-40 Win., .44
   Special, .410 . . . . NiB $575   Ex $420   Gd $300
.45-70, .44 Mag., 41 Mag.,
   .30-30 Win., .223 Rem. . . . . NiB $650   Ex $550   Gd $458
.357 Max., .357 Mag., .45 Win.
   Mag., 9mm Para. . . . . NiB $655   Ex $555   Gd $460
.38 Special, .38 Super, .32 Mag.,
   .22 LR, .22 WRM. . . . . NiB $655   Ex $560   Gd $455

MODEL 2 STEEL "PEN" PISTOL
Calibers: .22 LR, .25 Auto, .32 Auto. Single-shot, 2-inch bbl., 5.6 inches overall (4.2 inches in pistol format). Weight: 5 oz. Stainless finish. Made from 1993 to 1994.
.22 LR . . . . NiB $500   Ex $430   Gd $337
.25 Auto. . . . . NiB $600   Ex $530   Gd $430
.32 Auto. . . . . NiB $650   Ex $580   Gd $480

MODEL 3 STAINLESS STEEL . . . . NiB $125   Ex $90   Gd $75
Single-shot. Calibers: .32 Mag. or .38 Special. 2.5-inch bbl., 4.9 inches overall. Weight: 8.5 oz. Rosewood grips. Made from 1984 to 1995.

MODEL 4 DOUBLE DERRINGER
Calibers: .357 Mag., .357 Max., .44 Mag., .45 LC, .45 ACP (upper bbl., and 3-inch .410 shotshell (lower bbl.). 4.1-inch bbl, 6 inches overall. Weight: 16.5 oz. Stainless steel. Staghorn grips. Made from 1984 to date. (.44 Mag.and .45-70 disc. 2003.)
.357 Mag., .357 Max . . . . NiB $789   Ex $525   Gd $345
.44 Mag., .45 LC, .45 ACP . . . . . NiB $899   Ex $555   Gd $489
Engraved, add $150

MODEL 4 ALASKAN SURVIVAL MODEL.......NiB $880 Ex $570 Gd $340
Similar specifications as Model 4 except upper bbl., chambered for .45-70 or 3-inch .410 and .45 LC lower bbl. Also available in .45 Auto, .45 LC, .44 Special, .357 Mag. and .357 Max. Made from 1985 to date.

MODEL 6 . . . . NiB $785 Ex $625 Gd $499
Caliber: .22 Mag., .357 Mag., .45 LC, .45 ACP or .45 LC/.410 or .45 Colt. Bbl.: 6 inches, 8.2 inches overall. Weight: .22 oz. Satin or high-polished stainless steel w/rosewood grips. Made 1986 to date.
Engraved, add $150

MODEL 7
Same general specifications as the Model 1 except high-strength aircraft aluminum used to reduce its weight to 7.5 oz. Made from 1986 to date. (.44 Special disc. then reintroduced in 2008.)
.22 LR, .22 WMR..........NiB $575 Ex $440 Gd $280
.44 Special, add $150

MODEL 8 . . . . NiB $920 Ex $530 Gd $280
Calibers: .45 LC/.410, 8-inch bbl., 9.8 inches overall. Weight: 24 oz. Rosewood grips. New 1997.
Engraved (Made from 1997 to 1998), add $1000

MODEL 10
Same general specifications as the Model 7 except chambered for .38 Special, .45 ACP or .45 LC with aluminum grip frame.
.38 Special or .45 ACP . . . . NiB $559 Ex $365 Gd $295
.45 LC . . . . NiB $500 Ex $395 Gd $279

Model 11 . . . . NiB $559 Ex $490 Gd $369
Same general specifications as Model 7 except with a matte gray finish only, weight: 11 oz. Made from 1980 to 2003.

25 AUTOMATIC PISTOL
Calibers: .25 ACP or .250 Mag. Bbl.: 2.1 inches, 4.4 inches overall. Weight: 15.5 oz. Smooth rosewood grips. Limited production.
.25 ACP blued
(est. production 50) . . . . .NiB $650 Ex $540 Gd $385
.25 ACP stainless
(est. production 400) . . . . .NiB $510 Ex $425 Gd $380
.250 Mag. stainless
(est. production 100) . . . . . . .NiB $675 Ex $530 Gd $407

DA 38 DOUBLE ACTION DERRINGER
Hammerless, double action, double bbl (o/u). Calibers: .22LR, .357 Mag., .38 Special, 9mm Para., .40 S&W. 3-inch bbls., satin stainless with aluminum grip frame. DA trigger, hammerblock thumb safety. Weight: 14.5 oz. Made from 1990 to date.
.22LR (1996-03),
.38 Special, 9mm Para., ...NiB $615 Ex $415 Gd $230
.357 Mag. or .40 cal. (Disc. 2012)NiB $710 Ex $445 Gd $265
Lady Derringer (faux ivory grips, made from 1992-94), add ..$40

COP DA DERRINGER . . . . . . NiB $660 Ex $510 Gd $291
Hammerless, double-action, 4-bbl., derringer. Caliber: .357 Mag. 3.15-inch bbl., 5.5 inches overall. Weight: 16 oz. Blade front sight, open notched rear. Rosewood grips. Intro. 1990, disc. 1994.

LM-5 AUTOMATIC PISTOL
Calibers: .25 ACP, .32 H&R Mag. or .380 Automatic. Bbl.: 2 inches, 3 inches overall. Weight: 15 oz. Stainless steel construction, smooth wood grips. Limited production.
.25 ACP or 32 H&R Mag. . . . . . . NiB $650 Ex $540 Gd $385
.380 Automatic (Disc. 1999). . . . NiB $425 Ex $380 Gd $300

LADY DERRINGER . . . . NiB $769 Ex $610 Gd $499
Similar specifications as Model 1 except w/custom-tuned action fitted

American Derringer
Model .38 DA

American Derringer
Lady Derringer

w/scrimshawed synthetic ivory grips. Calibers: .32 H&R Mag., .32 Special, .38 Special (additional calibers on request). Deluxe Grade engraved and highly polished w/French fitted jewelry box. Made from 1991 to date.

Deluxe Engraved (Disc. 1994) . . . NiB $699 Ex $470 Gd $355
Gold Engraved (Disc. 1994) . . . . .Rare
Lady II (aluminum frame,
made 1999-03). . . . . .NiB $400 Ex $350 Gd $255

MINI-COP DA DERRINGER . . NiB $325 Ex $200 Gd $145
Similar general specifications as the COP except chambered for .22 WMR. Made from 1990 to 1995.

SEMMERLING LM-4
Manually operated repeater. Calibers: .45 ACP or 9mm, 4-round (.45 ACP) or 6-round magazine (9mm), 3.6-inch bbl., 5.2 inches overall. Weight: 24 oz. Made from 1997 to date. Limited availability.
Blued or Stainless steel . . . . NiB $4350 Ex $3200 Gd $2020

TEXAS COMMEMORATIVE . . . . . NiB $380 Ex $350 Gd $300
Similar to Model 1 except w/solid brass frame, stainless bbls. and stag grips. Calibers: .22 LR, .32 Mag., .38 Special, .44-40 Win. or .45 LC. Made from 1991 to date.
.44-40 Win. or .45 LC . . . . NiB $800 Ex $750 Gd $695

125TH ANNIVERSARY . . . .
Same general specifications as Model 1 except w/solid brass frame, stainless bbls. and stag grips. Calibers: .38 Special, .44-40 Win. or .45 LC. Disc. 1993. Limited production.
.38 Special . . . . NiB $337 Ex $320 Gd $295
.44-40 Win. or .45 LC. . . . . NiB $400 Ex $395 Gd $375

American Derringer
Simmerling.LM-4

AMT
.45 ACP Hardballer

AMT
.45 ACP Hardballer
Long Slide

AMT (ARCADIA MACHINE & TOOL) — Trademark owed by Crusader Gun Company Houston, TX

Previously Galena Industries, Strugis, SD; and Irwindale Arms, Inc., Irwindale, CA

NOTE: *The AMT Backup II automatic pistol was introduced in 1993 as a continuation of the original .380 backup with the traditional double action function and a redesigned double safety. AMT Backup and Automag II line of handguns is currently marketed by High Standard Manufacturing, Hosuton, TX.*

45 ACP HARDBALLER . . . . NiB $545 Ex $430 Gd $345
Colt 1991 style. Caliber: .45 ACP, 7-round magazine, 5-inch bbl., 8.5 inches overall. Weight: 39 oz. Adj. or fixed sights. Serrated matte slide rib w/loaded chamber indicator. Extended combat safety, adj. trigger and long grip safety. Wraparound Neoprene grips. Stainless steel. Made 1978-2001.
Long slide conversion kit (disc. 1997), add **$315**

45 ACP HARDBALLER LONG SLIDE
Similar to the standard Hardballer except w/7-inch bbl. and slide. Also chambered for .400 Cor-Bon. Made from 1980-2001
.45 ACP long slide . . . . NiB $529 Ex $435 Gd $320
.400 Cor-Bon long slide (Intro.1998) NiB $535 Ex $425 Gd $300
5-inch conversion kit (disc. 1997), add **$315**

**45 ACP STANDARD GOVERNMENT MODEL
AUTO PISTOL** . . . . NiB $460 Ex $395 Gd $339
Caliber: .45 ACP, 7-round magazine, 5-inch bbl., 8.5 inches overall. Weight: 38 oz. Fixed sights. Wraparound Neoprene grip. Made from 1979 to date.

**AUTOMAG II
AUTOMATIC PISTOL** . . . . NiB $845 Ex $575 Gd $360
Caliber: .22 Mag., 7- or 9-round magazine, bbl. lengths: 3.38, 4.5-, 6-inch. Weight: 32 oz. Fully adj. Millett sights. Stainless finish. Smooth black composition grips. Made from 1986 to 2001, reintro 2004.

**AUTOMAG III
AUTOMATIC PISTOL** . . . . NiB $600 Ex $495 Gd $365
Calibers: .30 M1 or 9mm Win. Mag., 8-round magazine., 6.38-inch bbl., 10.5 inches overall. Weight: 43 oz. Millet adj. sights. Stainless finish. Carbon fiber grips. Made from 1992 to 2001.

**AUTOMAG IV
AUTOMATIC PISTOL** . . . . NiB $610 Ex $520 Gd $395
Calibers: 10mm or .45 Win. Mag., 8- or 7-round magazine, 6.5- or 8.63-inch bbl., 10.5 inches overall. Weight: 46 oz. Millet adj. sights. Stainless finish. Carbon fiber grips. Made from 1992-2001.

**AUTOMAG V
AUTOMATIC PISTOL** . . . . . . NiB $1000 Ex $855 Gd $775
Caliber: .50 A.E., 5-round magazine, 7-inch bbl., 10.5 inches overall. Weight: 46 oz. Custom adj. sights. Stainless finish. Carbon fiber grips. Made from 1994 to 1995.

BACKUP (SMALL FRAME) AUTOMATIC PISTOL
Caliber: .22 LR, .380 ACP, 8-round (.22LR) or 5-round (.380 ACP) magazine, 2.5-inch bbl., 5 inches overall. Weight: 18 oz. (.380 ACP). Open sights. Carbon fiber or walnut grips. Stainless steel finish. Made from 1990 to 1987.
.22 LR (disc. 1987) . . . . NiB $495 Ex $335 Gd $188
**.380 ACP (disc. 2000, reintro.
  2004, disc. 2010)**. . . . . .NiB $450 Ex $305 Gd $171

AMERICAN FIREARMS MFG. CO., INC. — San Antonio, Texas

25 AUTO PISTOL
Caliber: .25 Auto. 8-round magazine, 2.1-inch bbl., 4.4 inches overall. Weight: 14.5 oz. Fixed sights. Stainless or blued ordnance steel. Smooth walnut grips. Made from 1966 to 1974.
Stainless steel model. . . . . NiB $215 Ex $190 Gd $110
Blued steel model. . . . . NiB $200 Ex $145 Gd $110

380 AUTO PISTOL . . . . NiB $735 Ex $540 Gd $389
Caliber: .380 Auto. 8-round magazine, 3.5-inch bbl., 5.5 inches overall. Weight: 20 oz. Stainless steel. Smooth walnut grips. Made from 1972 to 1974.

BACKUP II
AUTOMATIC PISTOL . . . . NiB $300   Ex $260   Gd $200
Caliber: .380 ACP, 5-round magazine, 2.5-inch bbl., 5 inches overall.
Weight: 18 oz. Single action. Open sights. Stainless steel finish. Carbon-fiber grips. Made from 1993 to 1998.

BACKUP (LARGE FRAME) AUTO PISTOL
Calibers: .357 SIG, .38 Super, 9mm Para., .40 Cor-Bon, .40 S&W, .45 ACP. Six-round (.357 SIG, .38 Super 9mm) or 5-round (.40 Cor-Bon, .40 S&W, .45 ACP) magazine, 2.5-inch bbl., 5.75-inches overall. Weight: 23 oz. Double action only. Open fixed sights. Stainless steel finish. Carbon fiber grips. Made from 1992 to date.
.357 SIG, .38 Super, 9mm.40 S&W,
.45 ACP . . . . NiB $530   Ex $400   Gd $300
.40 Cor-Bon (disc. 2010) . . . . . . NiB $630   Ex $500   Gd $400

BULL'S EYE TARGET MODEL .NiB $695   Ex $550   Gd $415
Similar to the standard Hardballer. Caliber: .40 S&W, 8-round magazine, 5-inch bbl., 8.5 inches overall. Weight: 38 oz. Millet adjustable sights. Wide adj. trigger. Wraparound Neoprene grips. Made from 1990 to 1991.

JAVELINA . . . . NiB $695   Ex $550   Gd $420
Caliber: 10mm, 8-round magazine, 7-inch bbl., 10.5 inches overall. Weight: 48 oz. Long grip safety, beveled magazine well, wide adj. trigger. Millet adj. sights. Wraparound Neoprene grips. Stainless finish. Made from 1991 to 1993.

LIGHTNING AUTO PISTOL
Caliber: .22 LR. 10-round magazine, 5-, 6.5-, 8.5-, 10-inch bbl., 10.75 inches overall (6.5-inch bbl.). Weight: 45 oz. (6.5-inch bbl.). Millett adj. sights. Checkered rubber grips. Stainless finish. Made from 1984 to 1987.
Standard model . . . . NiB $455   Ex $315   Gd $210
Bull's-Eye model (6.5-inch bull bbl.)NiB $520   Ex $355   Gd $240

ON DUTY DA PISTOL
Calibers: .40 S&W, 9mm Para., .45 ACP. 15-round (9mm), 13-shot (.40 S&W) or 9-round (.45 ACP) magazine, 4.5-inch bbl., 7.75 inches overall. Weight: 32 oz. Hard anodized aluminum frame. Stainless steel slide and bbl., Carbon fiber grips. Made from 1991 to 1994.
9mm or .40 S&W . . . . NiB $465   Ex $316   Gd $235
.45 ACP . . . . NiB $515   Ex $400   Gd $265

SKIPPER AUTO PISTOL . . . . . NiB $465   Ex $359   Gd $325
Calibers: .40 S&W or .45 ACP, 7-round magazine, 4.25-inch bbl., 7.5 inches overall. Weight: 33 oz. Millet adj. sights. Walnut grips. Matte finish stainless steel. Made from 1990 to 1992.

ANSCHUTZ — Ulm, Germany
Mfd. by J.G. Anschutz GmbH Jagd und Sportwaffenfabrik.
Currently imported by Champion's Choice, La Vergne, TN; previously imported by Accuracy International, Boseman, MT and AcuSport Corporation, Bellefontaine, OH

MODEL 64P
Calibers: .22 LR or .22 WMR, 5- or 4-round magazine, 10-inch bbl., 64MS action w/two-stage trigger. Target sights optional. Rynite black synthetic stock. Imported from 1998 to 2003.
.22 LR . . . . NiB $490   Ex $305   Gd $225
.22 WMR . . . . NiB $515   Ex $249   Gd $195
w/tangent sights, add $100

AMT Backup

AMT Backup DAO

AMT Bull's Eye Target

AMT Skipper

Anschutz Exemplar XIV

EXEMPLAR (1416P/1451P) BOLT-ACTION PISTOL
Caliber: .22 LR, single-shot or 5-round magazine, 7- or 10-inch bbl., 19 inches overall (10-inch bbl.). Weight: 3.33 lbs. Match 64 action. Slide safety. Hooded ramp post front sight, adjustable open notched rear. European walnut contoured grip. Exemplar made from 1987-95 and 1400 series made from 1997. Disc. 1997. Note: The .22 WMR chambering was advertised but never manufactured.
Exemplar w/7- or 10-inch bbl . . . . . NiB $420   Ex $295   Gd $185

Astra Model .44 DA

Left-hand model (disc. 1997) ... NiB $535 Ex $455 Gd $365
Model 1451P (single-shot) ..... NiB $450 Ex $365 Gd $285
Model 1416P (5-round repeater) NiB $1150 Ex $869 Gd $610

EXEMPLAR HORNET ...... NiB $1015 Ex $815 Gd $700
Based on the Anschutz Match 54 action, tapped and grooved for scope mounting with no open sights. Caliber: .22 Hornet, 5-round magazine, 10-inch bbl., 20 inches overall. Weight: 4.35 lbs. Checkered European walnut grip. Winged safety. Made from 1990 to 1995.

EXEMPLAR XIV........... NiB $875 Ex $560 Gd $465
Same general specifications as the standard Exemplar bolt-action pistol except with 14-inch bbl., weight: 4.15 lbs. Made from 1989 to 1995.

ARMALITE, INC. — Genesco, IL
Formerly Costa Mesa, CA.

AR-24 AUTOMATIC PISTOL ..... NiB $550 Ex $380 Gd $300
Full size automatic, mfg. by Sarzsilmaz in Turkey. Caliber: 9mm Para, 15-round magazine, 4.67-inch bbl., 8.3 inches overall. Parkerized finish, checkered synthetic grips. Imported from 2007 to 2013.
AR-24-15C Combat Custom
  (adj. rear sight)............ NiB $630 Ex $430 Gd $375
AR-24K-13 Compact
  (3.89-inch bbl.) .... NiB $560 Ex $400 Gd $380
AR-24K-13 Combat Custom Compact (adj. rear sight, 3.89-inch
  bbl.)..................... NiB $630 Ex $430 Gd $375

ARMSCOR (Arms Corp.) — Manila, Philippines
Currently imported by Armscor Precision Int'l. Pahrump, NV. Previously Imported by K.B.I., Harrisburg, PA., 1991–95 by Ruko Products, Inc., Buffalo NY., Armscor Precision, San Mateo, CA.

MODEL M1911-A1
AUTOMATIC PISTOL .... NiB $400 Ex $320 Gd $275
Caliber: .45 ACP. Eight-round magazine, 5-inch bbl., 8.75 inches overall. Weight: 38 oz. Blade front sight, drift adjustable rear w/3-dot system. Skeletonized tactical hammer and trigger. Extended slide release and beavertail grip safety. Parkerized finish. Checkered composition or wood stocks. Imported from 1996 to 1997. Reintro. 2001 to 2008.

MODEL M1911-A1
COMMANDER .... NiB $410 Ex $300 Gd $220
Caliber: .45 ACP. Similar to M1911-A-1 except with Commander configuration and 4-inch bbl. Rear slide serrations only. Disc. 1991.

Two-tone finish, add $50
Stainless, add.................................. $95

MODEL M1911-A1 OFFICER. .... NiB $425 Ex $350 Gd $265
Caliber: .45 ACP. Similar to M1911-A-1 except with Combat configuration. Bbl.:3.5 inches. Checkered hardwood grips. Weight: 2.16 pounds. Disc. 1991.
Two-tone finish, add............................. $50
Stainless, add.................................. $95

MODEL M1911-A1
MEDALLION SERIES .... NiB $495 Ex $360 Gd $285
Caliber: 9mm Para., .40 S&W, .45ACP. Standard or Tactical, blue finish standard. Bbl.: 5 inches. Custom model with match barrel, checkered wood Pachmayr grips. Disc. 1991.
Two-tone finish (Tactical), add $200
Chrome (Tactical), add $250

MODEL200 DC/TC
DA REVOLVER ....NiB $240 Ex $160 Gd $110
Caliber: .38 Special. Six-round cylinder, 2.5-, 4-, or 6-inch bbl.; 7.3, 8.8, or 11.3 inches overall. Weight: 22, 28, or 34 oz. Ramp front and fixed rear sights. Checkered mahogany or rubber grips. Disc. 1991.

MODEL 202A REVOLVER .....NiB $165 Ex $110 Gd $95
Caliber: .38 Special. Similar to Model 200 (DC) revolver except does not have barrel shroud. Disc. 1991.

MODEL 206 REVOLVER ..... NiB $250 Ex $203 Gd $170
Caliber: .38 Special. Similar to Model 200 (DC) revolver except has a 2-7/8-inch bbl. Weight: 24 oz. Disc. 1991.

MODEL 210 REVOLVER .....NiB $219 Ex $170 Gd $135
Caliber: .38 Special. Similar to Model 200 (DC) except has a 4-inch ventilated rib bbl., adj. rear sight. Weight: 28 oz. Disc. 1991.

ASAI AG — Advanced Small Arms Industries Solothurn, Switzerland
Currently imported by Magnum Research Inc., Minneapolis, MN. See listings under Magnum Research Pistols

ASTRA — Guernica, Spain
Manufactured by Unceta y Compania.

Currently not imported to U.S., previously imported by E.A.A. Corporation, Sharpes, FL.

MODEL 357 DA REVOLVER .. NiB $385 Ex $299 Gd $230
Caliber: .357 Magnum. Six-round cylinder. 3-, 4-, 6-, 8.5-inch bbl., 11.25 inches overall (with 6-inch bbl.). Weight: 42 oz. (with 6-inch bbl.). Ramp front sight, adj. rear sight. Blued finish. Checkered wood grips. Imported from 1972 to 1988.

MODEL 44 DA REVOLVER
Similar to Astra ..357 except chambered for .44 Magnum. Six- or 8.5-inch bbl., 11.5 inches overall (6-inch bbl.). Weight: 44 oz. (6-inch bbl.). Imported from 1980 to 1993.
Blued finish (disc. 1987)....... NiB $375 Ex $290 Gd $245
Stainless finish (disc. 1993)..... NiB $395 Ex $320 Gd $255

MODEL 41 DA REVOLVER . . . . . . NiB $375 Ex $295 Gd $235
Same general specifications as Model 44 except in .41 Mag. Imported from 1980-85.

MODEL 45 DA REVOLVER . . . . . . NiB $366 Ex $275 Gd $215
Similar to Astra .357 except chambered for .45 LC or .45 ACP. Six- or 8.5-inch bbl., 11.5 inches overall (with 6-inch bbl.). Weight: 44 oz. (6-inch bbl.). Imported from 1980-87.

MODEL 200 FIRECAT
VEST POCKET AUTO PISTOL . . . . NiB $320 Ex $260 Gd $205
Caliber: .25 Automatic (6.35mm). Six-round magazine, 2.25-inch bbl., 4.38 inches overall. Weight: 11.75 oz. Fixed sights. Blued finish. Plastic grips. Made 1920 to date. U.S. importation disc. in 1968.

MODEL 202 FIRECAT
VEST POCKET AUTO PISTOL . . . . NiB $590 Ex $475 Gd $400
Same general specifications as the Model 200 except chromed and engraved w/pearl grips. U.S. importation disc. 1968.

MODEL 400 AUTO PISTOL . . . . . NiB $725 Ex $595 Gd $350
Caliber: 9mm Bayard Long (.38 ACP, 9mm Browning Long, 9mm Glisenti, 9mm Para. and 9mm Steyr cartridges may be used interchangeably in this pistol because of its chamber design). Nine-round magazine., 6-inch bbl., 10 inches overall. Weight: 35 oz. Fixed sights. Blued finish. Plastic grips. Made 1922-45. Note: This pistol, as well as Astra Models 600 and 3000, is a modification of the Browning Model 1912.
Nazis Mfg. (S/N range 92,850-98,850), add **100%**

MODEL 600 MIL./POLICE-TYPE
AUTO PISTOL . . . . NiB $565 Ex $425 Gd $300
Calibers: .32 Automatic (7.65mm), 9mm Para. Magazine: 10-round (.32 cal.) or 8-round (9mm)., 5.25-inch bbl., 8 inches overall. Weight: About 33 oz. Fixed sights. Blued finish. Checkered wood or plastic grips. Made from 1944 to 1945.
Nazis markings, add **100%**

MODEL 800 CONDOR
MILITARY AUTO PISTOL . . . . NiB $2101 Ex $1754 Gd $1512
Similar to Models 400 and 600 except has an External hammer. Caliber: 9mm Para. Eight-round magazine, 5.25-inch bbl., 8.25 inches overall. Weight: 32.5 oz. Fixed sights. Blued finish. Plastic grips. Imported from 1958 to 1965.

MODEL 2000 CAMPER
AUTOMATIC PISTOL . . . . NiB $395 Ex $279 Gd $215
Same as Model 2000 Cub except chambered for .22 Short only, has 4-inch bbl., overall length, 6.25 inches, weight: 11.5 oz. Imported from 1955 to 1960.

MODEL 2000 CUB
POCKET AUTO PISTOL . . . . NiB $363 Ex $297 Gd $214
Calibers: .22 Short, .25 Auto. Six-round magazine, 2.25-inch bbl., 4.5 inches overall. Weight: About 11 oz. Fixed sights. Blued or chromed finish. Plastic grips. Made 1954 to date. U.S. importation disc. 1968.

MODEL 3000
POCKET AUTO PISTOL . . . . NiB $1001 Ex $654 Gd $467
Calibers: .22 LR, .32 Automatic (7.65mm), .380 Auto (9mm Short). Ten-round magazine (.22 cal.), 7-round (.32 cal.), 6-round (.380 cal.). Four-inch bbl., 6.38 inches overall. Weight: About 22 oz. Fixed sights. Blued finish. Plastic grips. Made from 1947 to 1956.

MODEL 3003 POCKET AUTO PISTOL . . . . . . NiB $2420 Ex $1419 Gd $880
Same general specifications as the Model 3000 except chromed and engraved w/pearl grips. Disc. 1956.

**Astra Model
3003 Pocket**

**Astra Model
4000 Falcon**

MODEL 4000 FALCON AUTO PISTOL NiB $675 Ex $495 Gd $320
Similar to Model 3000 except has an External hammer. Calibers: .22 LR, .32 Automatic (7.65mm), .380 Auto (9mm Short). Ten-round magazine (.22 LR), 8-round (.32 Auto), 7-round (.380 Auto), 3.66-inch bbl., 6.5-inches overall. Weight: 20 oz. (.22 cal.) or 24.75 oz. (.32 and .380). Fixed sights. Blued finish. Plastic grips. Made from 1956 to 1971.

CONSTABLE DA AUTO PISTOL
Calibers: .22 LR, .32 Automatic (7.65mm), .380 Auto (9mm Short). Magazine capacity: 10-round (.22 LR), 8-round (.32), 7-round (.380). 3.5-inch bbl., 6.5 inches overall. Weight: about 24 oz. Blade front sight, windage adj. rear. Blued or chromed finish. Imported from 1965 to 1992.
Stainless finish . . . . NiB $395 Ex $290 Gd $229
Blued engraved finish . . . . NiB $605 Ex $419 Gd $297
Chrome finish (disc. 1990) . . . . . NiB $500 Ex $335 Gd $234

MODEL A-60 DA AUTO PISTOL NiB $415 Ex $285 Gd $210
Similar to the Constable except in .380 only, w/13-round magazine and slide-mounted ambidExtrous safety. Blued finish only. Imported from 1980 to 1991.

MODEL A-70 COMPACT AUTO PISTOL
Calibers: 9mm Para., .40 S&W. Eight-round (9mm) or 7-round (.40 S&W) magazine., 3.5-inch bbl., 6.5 inches overall. Blued, nickel or stainless finish. Weight: 29.3 oz. Imported from 1992 to 1996.
Blued finish . . . . NiB $414 Ex $295 Gd $210
Nickel finish . . . . NiB $424 Ex $345 Gd $229
Stainless finish . . . . NiB $593 Ex $430 Gd $372

MODEL A-75 ULTRALIGHT . . NiB $400 Ex $299 Gd $234
Similar to the standard Model 75 except 9mm only w/24-oz. aluminum alloy frame. Imported from 1994 to 1997.

Astra Cadix DA

Astra Constable DA

Auto-Ordnance 1927 A-1
Deluxe
w/drum magazine

MODEL A-80 AUTO PISTOL. . NiB $450   Ex $404   Gd $265
Calibers: 9mm Para., .38 Super, .45 ACP. 15-round or 9-round (.45 ACP). magazine. Bbl.: 3.75 inches., 7 inches overall. Weight: 36 oz. Imported from 1982 to 1989.

MODEL A-90 DA
AUTOMATIC PISTOL. . . . . . . NiB $505   Ex $400   Gd $245
Calibers: 9mm Para., .45 ACP. 15-round (9mm) or 9-round (.45 ACP) magazine, 3.75-inch bbl., 7 inches overall. Weight: about 40 oz. Fixed sights. Blued finish. Checkered plastic grips. Imported 1985 to 1990.

MODEL A-100 DA AUTO PISTOL
Same general specifications as the Model A-90 except selective double action chambered for 9mm Para., .40 S&W or .45 ACP. Imported from 1991 to 1997.
Blued finish . . . . NiB $470   Ex $310   Gd $249
Nickel finish. . . . . NiB $495   Ex $340   Gd $287
For night sights, add. $100

CADIX DA REVOLVER
Calibers: .22 LR, .38 Special. Nine-round (.22 LR) or 5-round (.38 cal.) cylinder. Four- or 6-inch bbl., Weight: About 27 oz. (6-inch bbl.). Ramp front sight, adj. rear sight. Blued finish. Plastic grips. Imported from 1960-68.
Standard model . . . . NiB $275   Ex $229   Gd $160
Lightly engraved model . . . . NiB $380   Ex $255   Gd $200
Heavily engraved model (shown) . . . . NiB $700   Ex $515   Gd $395

MODEL A-75 DECOCKER AUTO PISTOL
Similar to the Model 70 except in 9mm, .40 S&W and .45 ACP w/decocking system and contoured pebble-tExtured grips. Imported from 1993-97.
Blued finish, 9mm or .40 S&W . . . NiB $395   Ex $320   Gd $235
Nickel finish, 9mm or .40 S&W . . NiB $405   Ex $330   Gd $245
Stainless, 9mm or .40 S&W. . . . . . NiB $410   Ex $305   Gd $197
Blued finish, .45 ACP . . . . NiB $395   Ex $315   Gd $235
Nickel finish, .45 ACP . . . . NiB $405   Ex $350   Gd $275
Stainless, .45 ACP . . . . NiB $420   Ex $365   Gd $290

AUTAUGA ARMS — Prattville, Alabama

MODEL 32 (MK II)
DAO AUTOMATIC PISTOL. . . . . NiB $367   Ex $309   Gd $267
Caliber: .32 ACP. Six-round magazine, 2-inch bbl., weight: 11.36 oz.. Double action only. Stainless steel. Black polymer grips. Made from 1996 to 2000.

AUTO-ORDNANCE CORPORATION — Division of Kahr Arms, Worchester, MA
Previously West Hurley, New York.

1911 A1 GOVERNMENT AUTO . . . . NiB $515   EX $375   GD $300
Copy of Colt 1911 A1 semiautomatic pistol. Calibers: 9mm Para., .38 Super, 10mm, .45 ACP. 9-round (9mm, .38 Super) or 7-round 10mm, .45 ACP) magazine. Five-inch bbl., 8.5 inches overall. Weight: 39 oz. Fixed blade front sight, rear adj. Blued, satin nickel or Duo-Tone finish. Checkered plastic grips. Made 1983 to 1999.
1911 A1 WWII (parkerized finish) NiB $540   Ex $393   Gd $315
1911 A1 100th Anniversary (laser engraved), add 20%

1911A1 .40 S&W PISTOL . . . . NiB $498   Ex $399   Gd $309
Similar to the Model 1911 A1 except has 4.5-inch bbl., w/7.75-inch overall length. Eight-round magazine, weight: 37 oz. Blade front and adj. rear sights w/3-dot system. Checkered black rubber wraparound grips. Made from 1991 to 1999.

1911 A1 "THE GENERAL". . . . NiB $441   Ex $351   Gd $253
Caliber: .45 ACP. Seven-round magazine, 4.5-inch bbl., 7.75 inches overall. Weight: 37 oz. Blued nonglare finish. Made 1992 to 1999.

1927 A-1 DELUXE SEMIAUTOMATIC PISTOL
Similar to Thompson Model 1928A submachine gun except has no provision for automatic firing and does not have detachable buttstock. Caliber: .45 ACP, 5-, 15-, 20- and 30-round detachable box magazines. 30-round drum also available. 13-inch finned bbl., 26 inches overall. Weight: About 6.75 lbs. Adj. rear sight, blade front. Blued finish. Walnut grips. Made from 1977 to 1994.
w/box magazine. . . . . NiB $1412   Ex $1078   Gd $764
w/drum magazine, add $300

ZG-51 PIT BULL
AUTOMATIC PISTOL . . . . NiB $435   Ex $325   Gd $288
Caliber: .45 ACP. Seven-round magazine, 3.5-inch bbl., 7 inches overall. Weight: 32 oz. Fixed front sight, square-notch rear. Blued finish. Checkered plastic grips. Made from 1991 to 1999.

LES BAER — Le Claire, Iowa
Previously Hilldale, Illinois.

1911 CONCEPT SERIES AUTOMATIC PISTOL
Similar to Government 1911 built on steel or alloy full-size or compact frame. Caliber: .45 ACP. Seven-round magazine, 4.25- or 5-inch bbl. Weight: 34 to 37 oz. Adjustable low mount combat or BoMar target sights. Blued, matte black, Two-Tone or stainless finish. Checkered wood grips. Made from 1996 to date.

Concept models I & II	NiB $1402	Ex $1116	Gd $797
Concept models III, IV & VII	NiB $1556	Ex $1414	Gd $1204
Concept models V, VI & VIII	NiB $1538	Ex $1369	Gd $863
Concept models IX & X	NiB $1529	Ex $1237	Gd $1045

1911 PREMIER SERIES AUTOMATIC PISTOL
Similar to the Concept series except also chambered for .38 Super, 9x23 Win., .400 Cor-Bon and .45 ACP. 5- or 6-inch bbl. Weight: 37 to .40 oz. Made from 1996 to date.

Premier II (9x23 w/5-inch bbl.)	NiB $1760	Ex $1479	Gd $1331
Premier II (.400 Cor-Bon w/5-inch bbl.)	NiB $1540	Ex $1369	Gd $1292
Premier II (.45 ACP w/5-inch bbl.)	NiB $1446	Ex $1314	Gd $1098
Premier II (.45 ACP S/S w/5-inch bbl.)	NiB $1531	Ex $1265	Gd $875
Premier II (.45/.400 combo w/5-inch bbl.)	NiB $1749	Ex $1457	Gd $1281
Premier II (.38 Super w/6-inch bbl.)	NiB $1996	Ex $1864	Gd $1490
Premier II (.400 Cor-Bon w/6-inch bbl.)	NiB $1798	Ex $1529	Gd $1364
Premier II (.45 ACP w/6-inch bbl.)	NiB $1672	Ex $1501	Gd $1408

S.R.P. AUTOMATIC PISTOL
Similar to F.B.I. Contract "Swift Response Pistol" built on a (customer-supplied) Para-Ordance over-sized frame or a 1911 full-size or compact frame. Caliber: .45 ACP. Seven-round magazine, 5-inch bbl., weight: 37 oz. Ramp front and fixed rear sights, w/Tritium Sight insert.

SRP 1911 Government or Commanche model	NiB $2295	Ex $2084	Gd $1905
SRP P-12 model	NiB $2619	Ex $2346	Gd $2199
SRP P-13 model	NiB $2404	Ex $2178	Gd $2021
SRP P-14 model	NiB $2320	Ex $2109	Gd $1317

1911 ULTIMATE MASTER COMBAT SERIES AUTOMATIC PISTOL
Model 1911 in Combat Competition configuration. Calibers: .38 Super, 9x23 Win., .400 Cor-Bon and .45 ACP. Five- or 6-inch NM bbl., weight: 37 to 40 oz. Made from 1996 to date.

Ultimate MC (.38 or 9x23 w/5-inch bbl.)	NiB $2580	Ex $2010	Gd $1400
Ultimate MC (.400 Cor-Bon w/5-inch bbl.)	NiB $2480	Ex $1835	Gd $1300
Ultimate MC (.45 ACP w/5-inch bbl.)	NiB $2430	Ex $1910	Gd $1300
Ultimate MC (.38 or 9x23 w/6-inch bbl.)	NiB $2680	Ex $2025	Gd $1495
Ultimate MC (.400 Cor-Bon w/6-inch bbl.)	NiB $2630	Ex $2060	Gd $1450
Ultimate MC (.45 ACP w/6-inch bbl.)	NiB $2580	Ex $2010	Gd $1400
Ultimate "Steel Special" (.38 Super Bianchi SPS)	NiB $2855	Ex $2310	Gd $1661
Ultimate "PARA" (.38, 9x23 or .45 IPSC comp)	NiB $2871	Ex $2326	Gd $1650
w/Triple-Port Compensator, add			$100

Auto-Ordnance
ZG-51 Pit Bull

1911 CUSTOM CARRY SERIES AUTOMATIC PISTOL
Model 1911 in Combat Carry configuration built on steel or alloy full-size or compact frame. 4.5- or 5-inch NM bbl., chambered for .45 ACP. Weight: 34 to 37 oz.

Custom carry (steel frame w/4.24- or 5-inch bbl.)	NiB $1728	Ex $1555	Gd $1166
Custom carry (alloy frame w/4.24-inch bbl.)	NiB $2039	Ex $2029	Gd $1521

BAUER FIREARMS CORPORATION — Fraser, Michigan

.25 AUTOMATIC PISTOL . . . . . NiB $175   Ex $125   Gd $95
Stainless steel. Caliber: .25 Automatic. Six-round magazine, 2.13-inch bbl., 4 inches overall. Weight: 10 oz. Fixed sights. Checkered walnut or simulated pearl grips. Made from 1972 to 1984.

BAYARD — Herstal, Belgium
Mfd. by Anciens Etablissements Pieper.

MODEL 1908
POCKET AUTOMATIC PISTOL . . . NiB $455   Ex $300   Gd $195
Calibers: .25 Automatic (6.35mm). .32 Automatic (7.65mm), .380 Automatic (9mm Short). Six-round magazine, 2.25-inch bbl., 4.88 inches overall. Weight: About 16 oz. Fixed sights. Blued finish. Hard rubber grips. Intro. 1908. Disc. 1923.

MODEL 1923 POCKET
.25 AUTOMATIC PISTOL . . . . NiB $393   Ex $300   Gd $170
Caliber: .25 Automatic (6.35mm). 2.13-inch bbl., 4.31 inches overall. Weight: 12 oz. Fixed sights. Blued finish. Checkered hard-rubber grips. Intro. 1923. Disc. 1930.

MODEL 1923 POCKET
AUTOMATIC PISTOL . . . . NiB $429   Ex $313   Gd $218
Calibers: .32 Automatic (7.65mm), .380 Automatic (9mm Short). Six-round magazine, 3.31-inch bbl., 5.5 inches overall. Weight: About 19 oz. Fixed sights. Blued finish. Checkered hard-rubber grips. Intro. 1923. Disc. 1940.

MODEL 1930 POCKET
.25 AUTOMATIC PISTOL . . . . NiB $395   Ex $255   Gd $195
This is a modification of the Model 1923, which it closely resembles.

BEEMAN PRECISION ARMS, INC. — Santa Rosa, California

P08 AUTOMATIC PISTOL . . . . NiB $420   Ex $335   Gd $245
Luger toggle action. Caliber: .22 LR. 10-round magazine, 3.8-inch bbl., 7.8 inches overall. Weight: 25 oz. Fixed sights. Blued finish. Checkered hardwood grips. Imported from 1969 to 1991.

Benelli MP90S

Benelli MP95E

Beretta Model 21

MINI P08 AUTOMATIC PISTOL NiB $470 Ex $375 Gd $295
Caliber: Same general specifications as P08 except shorter 3.5-inch bbl., 7.4 inches overall. Weight: 20 oz. Imported 1986 to 1991.

SP METALLIC SILHOUETTE PISTOLS
Caliber: .22 LR. Single-shot. Bbl. lengths: 6-, 8-, 10- or 15-inches. Adj. rear sight. Receiver contoured for scope mount. Walnut target grips w/ adj. palm rest. Models SP made 1985-86 and SPX 1993-94.

SP Standard w/8-or 10-inch bbl.	NiB $285	Ex $235	Gd $172
SP Standard w/12-inch bbl.	NiB $330	Ex $266	Gd $191
SP Standard w/15-inch bbl.	NiB $344	Ex $286	Gd $200
SP Deluxe w/8-or 10-inch bbl.	NiB $346	Ex $276	Gd $199
SP Deluxe w/12-inch bbl.	NiB $355	Ex $291	Gd $209
SP Deluxe w/15-inch bbl.	NiB $374	Ex $306	Gd $215
SPX Standard w/10-inch bbl.	NiB $679	Ex $548	Gd $387
SPX Deluxe w/10-inch bbl.	NiB $925	Ex $744	Gd $524

BEHOLLA — Suhl, Germany
Mfd. by both Becker and Holländer and Stenda-Werke GmbH.

POCKET AUTOMATIC PISTOL NiB $272 Ex $227 Gd $191
Caliber: .32 Automatic (7.65mm). Seven-round magazine, 2.9-inch bbl., 5.5 inches overall. Weight: 22 oz. Fixed sights. Blued finish. Serrated wood or hard rubber grips. Made by Becker and Hollander 1915 to 1920, by Stenda-Werke circa 1920 to 1925. Note: Essentially the same pistol was manufactured w/the Stenda version as the "Leonhardt" by H. M. Gering and as the "Menta" by August Menz.

BENELLI — Urbino, Italy
Imported by Larry's Guns in Gray, ME since 2003. Previously imported by EEA in Sharpes, FL; Sile Dist. New York, NY; Saco, Arlington, VA.

MP90S WORLD CUP TARGET PISTOL
Semiautomatic blowback action. Calibers: .22 Short, .22 LR, .32 W.C. Five-round magazine, 4.33-inch fixed bbl. 6.75 inches overall. Weight: 36 oz. Post front sight, adjustable rear. Blue finish. Anatomic shelf-style grip. Imported from 1992 to 2001.

MP90S (.22 LR)	NiB $1430	Ex $1221	Gd $1095
MP90S (.22 Short, disc. 1995).	NiB $1314	Ex $1155	Gd $984
MP90S (.32 S&W)	NiB $1562	Ex $1364	Gd $1221
w/conversion kit, add			$80

MODEL B-76 . . . . **NiB $441 Ex $326 Gd $257**
Semi-auto, SA/DA. Cal.: 9 mm Para. Bbl.: 4.25 inches. 8-round mag. Weight: 34 oz. Disc. 1990.

MODEL B-765 TARGET . . . . . . **NiB $604 Ex $475 Gd $665**
Cal.: 9 mm Para. Similar to B-76 model but w/5.5-inch bbl., target grips, adj. rear sight. Disc. 1990.

MODEL B-77 . . . . **NiB $405 Ex $309 Gd $220**
Semi-auto, SA/DA. Cal.: 32 ACP. Bbl.: Steel, 4.25 inches. 8-round mag. Disc. 1995.

MODEL B-80 . . . . **NiB $425 Ex $315 Gd $245**
Semi-auto, SA/DA. Cal.: .30 Luger. Bbl.: Steel, 4.25 inches. 8-round mag. Weight: 34 oz. Disc. 1995.

B-80s Target, add $126

MODEL B-82 . . . . **NiB $813 Ex $551 Gd $414**
Limited production Italian police model; serial no. with "D" suffix. Cal.: .30 Luger, .32 ACP, 9 mm Ultra.

MODEL MP3S . . . . **NiB $603 Ex $467 Gd $336**
Semi-auto, target model. Cal.: 32 S&W Long Wadcutter. Bbl.: 5.5 inches. High gloss blued finish, target grips. Adj. rear sight. Disc. 1995.

MP95E SPORT TARGET PISTOL
Similar to the MP90S except with 5- or 9-round magazine, 4.25- inch bbl., Blue or chrome finish. Checkered target grip. Imported from1994 to date.

Blue MP95 (.22 LR)	NiB $892	Ex $708	Gd $467
Blue MP95 (.32 WC).	NiB $981	Ex $840	Gd $640
Chrome, add			$80

BERETTA USA CORP. — Accokeek, Maryland
Beretta firearms are manufactured by Fabbrica D'Armi Pietro Beretta S. p. A. in Gardone Val Trompia (Brescia), Italy. This prestigious firm has been in business since 1526. In 1977, Beretta U.S.A. Corp., a manufacturing and importing facility, opened in Accokeek, MD. (Previously imported by Garcia Corp., J.L. Galef & Son, Inc. and Berben Corporation.) Note: Beretta holdings also owns additional firearms manufacturing companies including: Benelli, Franchi, Sako, Stoeger, Tikka and Uberti.

MODEL 20 DA AUTO PISTOL . . . . . NiB $257 Ex $203 Gd $136
Caliber: .25 ACP. Eight-round magazine, 2.5-inch bbl., 4.9 inches overall.
Weight: 10.9 oz. Plastic or walnut grips. Fixed sights. Made 1984 to 1985.

MODEL 21 DA AUTO PISTOL
Calibers: .22 LR and .25 ACP. Seven-round (.22 LR) or 8-round (..25
ACP) magazine, 2.5-inch bbl., 4.9 inches overall. Weight: About 12
oz. Blade front sight, V-notch rear. Walnut grips. Made from 1985 to
date. Model 21EL disc. 2000.
Blued finish . . . . NiB $285 Ex $210 Gd $165
Nickel finish (.22 LR only) . . . . . . NiB $300 Ex $225 Gd $177
Model 21EL engraved model. . . . NiB $375 Ex $310 Gd $230

MODEL 70
AUTOMATIC PISTOL . . . . NiB $278 Ex $199 Gd $131
Improved version of Model 1935. Steel or lightweight alloy. Calibers: .32
Auto (7.65mm), .380 Auto (9mm Short). Eight-round (.32) or 7-round (.380)
magazine, 3.5-inch bbl., 6.5 inches overall. Weight: Steel, 22.25 oz.; alloy,
16 oz. Fixed sights. Blued finish. Checkered plastic grips. Made 1959 to
1985. Note: Formerly marketed in U.S. as "Puma" (alloy model in .32) and
"Cougar" (steel model in .380). Disc.

MODEL 70S . . . . NiB $420 Ex $288 Gd $210
Similar to Model 70T except chambered for .22 Auto and .380 Auto. Longer
bbl. guide and safety lever blocking hammer. Front blade and rear sight
fixed on breechblock. Weight: 1 lb., 7 oz. Made 1977 to 1985.

MODEL 70T
AUTOMATIC PISTOL . . . . NiB $315 Ex $231 Gd $189
Similar to Model 70. Caliber: .32 Automatic (7.65mm). Nine-round magazine, 6-inch bbl., 9.5 inches overall. Weight: 19 oz. adj. rear sight, blade
front sight. Blued finish. Checkered plastic grips. Intro. in 1959. Disc.

MODEL 71
AUTOMATIC PISTOL . . . . NiB $268 Ex $199 Gd $142
Same general specifications as alloy Model 70. Caliber: .22 LR. Six-inch
bbl., 8-round magazine, Adj. rear sight frame. Single action. Made 1959 to
1989. Note: Formerly marketed in U.S. as the "Jaguar Plinker."

MODEL 72 . . . . NiB $315 Ex $231 Gd $190
Same as Model 71 except has 6-inch bbl., w eight: 18 oz. Intro. in
1959. Disc. Note: Formerly marketed in U.S as "Jaguar Plinker."

MODEL 76 AUTO TARGET PISTOL
Caliber: .22 LR. 10-round magazine, 6-inch bbl., 8.8 inches overall.
Weight: 33 oz. adj. rear sight, front sight w/interchangeable blades.
Blued finish. Checkered plastic or wood grips. Made from 1966 to
1985. Note: Formerly marketed in the U.S. as the "Sable."
Model 76 w/plastic grips. . . . . . . NIB $393 EX $315 GD $257
Model 76W w/wood grips. . . . . . . NiB $430 Ex $357 Gd $299

MODEL 81 DA AUTO PISTOL NiB $341 Ex $247 Gd $199
Caliber: .32 Automatic (7.65mm). 12-round magazine, 3.8-inch bbl.,
6.8 inches overall. Weight: 23.5 oz. Fixed sights. Blued finish. Plastic
grips. Made principally for the European market 1975 to 1984, w/simi-
lar variations as implemented on the Model 84.

MODEL 82W DA AUTO PISTOL NiB $330 Ex $231 Gd $178
Caliber: .32 ACP. Similar to the Model 81 except with a slimmer-profile
frame designed to accept a single column 9-round magazine. Matte
black finish. Importation disc. 1984.

MODEL 84 DA AUTO PISTOL NiB $325 Ex $222 Gd $173
Same as Model 81 except made in caliber .380 Automatic w/13-round
magazine, 3.82-inch bbl., 6.8 inches overall. Weight: 23 oz. Fixed front
and rear sights. Made from 1975 to 1982.

MODEL 84B DA AUTO PISTOL NiB $335 Ex $230 Gd $184
Improved version of Model 84 w/strengthened frame and slide, and firing-pin block safety added. AmbidExtrous reversible magazine release.

Beretta Model 71

Beretta Model 72

Beretta Model 84

Beretta Model 84
Cheetah (Nickel finish)

Blued or nickel finish. Checkered black plastic or wood grips. Other
specifications same. Made circa 1982 to 1984.

MODEL 84(BB) DA AUTO PISTOL
Improved version of Model 84B w/further-strengthened slide, frame and
recoil spring. Caliber: .380 ACP. 13-round magazine, 3.82-inch bbl.,
6.8 inches overall. Weight: 23 oz. Checkered black plastic or wood
grips. Blued or nickel finish. Notched rear and blade front sight. Made
circa 1984-94.
Blued w/plastic grips . . . . NiB $393 Ex $241 Gd $152
Blued w/wood grips . . . . NiB $446 Ex $372 Gd $270
Nickel finish w/wood grips . . . . . NiB $630 Ex $493 Gd $383

Beretta Model 85

Beretta Model 85BB

Beretta Model 86 Cheetah

MODEL 84
CHEETAH SEMI-AUTO PISTOL
Similar to the Model 84 BB except with required design changes as mandated by regulation, including reduced magazine capacity (10-round magazine) and marked as 9mm short (.380) as a marketing strategy to counter increased availability of 9mm chamberings from other manufacturers. Made from 1994 to 2002, reintro. 2004.

Blued w/plastic grips	NiB $650	Ex $520	Gd $360
Blued w/wood grips	NiB $667	Ex $551	Gd $367
Nickel finish w/wood grips	NiB $735	Ex $498	Gd $372

MODEL 85
DA AUTO PISTOL . . . . NiB $660 Ex $460 Gd $330
Similar to the Model 84 except designed with a slimmer-profile frame to accept a single column 8-round magazine, no

ambidextrous magazine release. Matte black finish. Weight: 21.8 oz. Introduced in 1977 following the Model 84.

MODEL 85B DA AUTO PISTOL NiB $430 Ex $330 Gd $210
Improved version of the Model 85. Imported from 1982-85.

MODEL 85BB DA PISTOL
Improved version of the Model 85B w/strengthened frame and slide. Caliber: .380 ACP. Eight-round magazine, 3.82 inch bbl., 6.8 inches overall. Weight: 21.8 oz. Blued or nickel finish. Checkered black plastic or wood grips. Imported from 1985 to 1994.

Blued finish w/plastic grips	NiB $520	Ex $395	Gd $280
Blued finish w/wood grips	NiB $530	Ex $404	Gd $295
Nickel finish w/wood grips	NiB $582	Ex $430	Gd $315

MODEL 85 CHEETAH SEMI-AUTO PISTOL
Similar to the Model 85 BB except with required design changes as mandated by regulation and marked as 9mm short (.380) as a marketing strategy to counter increased availability of 9mm chamberings from other manufacturers. Made from 1994 to date.

Blued finish w/plastic grips	NiB $656	Ex $470	Gd $310
Blued finish w/wood grips	NiB $680	Ex $490	Gd $330
Nickel finish w/wood grips	NiB $719	Ex $525	Gd $393

MODEL 85F DA PISTOL
Similar to the Model 85BB except has re-contoured trigger guard and manual ambidExtrous safety w/decocking device. Matte black Bruniton finish. Imported in 1990 only.

plastic grips	NiB $390	Ex $315	Gd $255
wood grips	NiB $420	Ex $344	Gd $283

MODEL 86 CHEETAH
DA AUTO PISTOL . . . . NiB $628 Ex $493 Gd $278
Caliber: .380 auto. Eight-round magazine, 4.4- inch bbl., 7.3 inches overall. Weight: 23.3 oz. Bruniton finish w/wood grips. Made from 1986-89. (Reintroduced 1990 in the Cheetah series.)

MODEL 87 CHEETAH AUTOMATIC PISTOL
Similar to the Model 85 except in .22 LR w/8- or 10- round magazine (Target) and optional Extended 6-inch bbl. (Target in single action). Overall length: 6.8 to 8.8 inches. Weight: 20.1 oz. to 29.4 oz (Target). Checkered wood grips. Made from 1987 to date.

Blued finish			
(double-action)	NiB $735	Ex $550	Gd $430
Target model			
(single action)	NiB $765	Ex $580	Gd $467

MODEL 89 GOLD STANDARD TARGET
AUTOMATIC PISTOL . . . . NiB $703 Ex $556 Gd $467
Caliber: .22 LR. Eight-round magazine, 6-inch bbl., 9.5 inches overall. Weight: 41 oz. Adj. target sights. Blued finish. Target-style walnut grips. Made from 1988 to 2000.

MODEL 90 DA AUTO PISTOL NiB $325 Ex $235 Gd $195
Caliber: .32 Auto (7.65mm). Eight-round magazine, 3.63-inch bbl., 6.63 inches overall. Weight: 19.5 oz. Fixed sights. Blued finish. Checkered plastic grips. Made from 1969 to 1983.

MODEL 90-TWO TYPE F . . . . NiB $600 Ex $460 Gd $400
Similar to 92F. Caliber: 9mm Para or .40 S&W, DA/SA, 4.9-inch bbl., 8.5 inches overall. Weight: 32.5 oz. Fixed sights. Blued finish. Wrap around grip in two sizes. Accessory rail w/cover. Made from 2006-09.

MODEL 92 DA AUTO
PISTOL (1ST SERIES). . . . . NiB $824 Ex $640 Gd $445
Caliber: 9mm Para. 15-round magazine, 4.9-inch bbl., 8.5 inches overall. Weight: 33.5 oz. Fixed sights. Blued finish. Plastic grips. Initial production of 5,000 made in 1976.

MODEL 92S DA AUTO
PISTOL (2ND SERIES) . . . . **NiB $645   Ex $520   Gd $370**
Revised version of Model 92 w/ambidextrous slide-mounted safety modification intended for both commercial and military production. Evolved to Model 92S-1 for U.S. Military trials. Made from 1980 to 1985.

MODEL 92SB-P DA
AUTO PISTOL (3RD SERIES) . . **NiB $598   Ex $430   Gd $345**
Same general specifications as standard Model 92 except has slide-mounted safety and repositioned magazine release. Made 1981 to 1985.

MODEL 92D DA AUTO PISTOL . **NiB $667   Ex $470   Gd $364**
Same general specifications as Model 92F except DAO only w/bobbed hammer and 3-dot sight. Made from 1992 to 1998.
w/Tritium sights, add $100

MODEL 92F COMPACT
DA AUTOMATIC PISTOL . . . . **NiB $630   Ex $560   Gd $279**
Caliber: 9mm Para. 12-round magazine, 4.3-inch bbl., 7.8 inches over-all. Weight: 31.5 oz. Wood grips. Square-notched rear sight, blade front integral w/slide. Made from 1990-93.

MODEL 92F COMPACT L TYPE M DA AUTOMATIC PISTOL
Same general specifications as the original 92F Compact except 8-round magazine, Weight: 30.9 oz. Bruniton matte finish. Made from 1998 to 2003.
MODEL 92F
Compact L Type M . . . . **NiB $660   Ex $580   Gd $390**
Inox finish . . . . **NiB $656   Ex $583   Gd $393**
w/Tritium sights, add $100

MODEL 92F DA AUTOMATIC PISTOL
Same general specifications as Model 92 except w/slide-mounted safety and repositioned magazine release. Replaced Model 92SB. Blued or stainless finish. Made from 1992 to 1998.
Blued finish . . . . **NiB $630   Ex $493   Gd $341**
Stainless finish . . . . **NiB $619   Ex $477   Gd $325**
Model 92F-EL gold, add $200

MODEL 92FS DA AUTOMATIC PISTOL
Calibers: 9mm, 9mmx19 and .40 S&W. 15- round magazine, 4.9- inch bbl., 8.5 inches overall. Weight: 34.4 to 35.3 oz. AmbidExtrous safety/decock lever. Chrome-lined bore w/combat trigger guard. Bruniton finish w/plastic grips or Inox finish w/rubber grips. Made from 1999 to date. This model was adopted as the standard-issue sidearm by the U.S. Armed Forces in 1985 and renamed the M9.
matte black Bruniton finish . . . . . **NiB $630   Ex $520   Gd $325**
olive drab finish (made 2004), add $30
Inox finish . . . . **NiB $660   Ex $550   Gd $355**
Inox Tacical . . . . **NiB $690   Ex $470   Gd $380**
w/ checkered wood grips, add $25
w/B-lok (made 2003), add $25
470th Anniversary (made 1999)**NiB $2205   Ex $1900   Gd $1690**
"Desert Storm" edition (made 1991-92)**NiB $630   Ex $500   Gd $450**

MODEL 92FS BRIGADIER AUTOMATIC PISTOL
Similar to 92FS except w/heavier slide and rubber wrap around grips. Made from 1999-2005; reintro. 2015 to date.
Matte black Bruniton . . . . **NiB $760   Ex $556   Gd $395**
Inox. **NiB $766   Ex $630   Gd $477**

MODEL 92FS CENTURION AUTOMATIC PISTOL
Similar to 92FS except w/compact barrel/slide and full size frame. Wood or plastic grips. Made from 1999-2005; reintro. 2015 to date.
Matte black Bruniton . . . . **NiB $525   Ex $400   Gd $340**

MODEL 92FS VERTEC . . . . . . **NiB $640   Ex $450   Gd $400**
Similar to 92FS except w/straight backstrap, thin grip panels, short-reach trigger, and accessory rail. Made from 2002 to 2005.

MODEL 92G-SD . . . . **NiB $960   Ex $590   Gd $460**
Similar to 92F except w/srping loaded decocking lever, accessory rail, 10-round magazine, Tritium sights. Made from 2003-05.

MODEL 92FS BORDER MARSHAL
AUTOMATIC PISTOL . . . . **NiB $675   Ex $485   Gd $460**
Similar to 92F except commericial equivilent of I.N.S. gov't. contract pistol. Made from 1999 to 2000.

Beretta Model 92F

**Beretta Model 92
Compact L Type M**

**Beretta Model 92FS
Brigadier Inox**

MODEL 92G ELITE IA. . . . . . . NiB $730   Ex $500   Gd $360
Similar to 92FS Brigadier except w/4.7-in. stainless bbl. Made from
1999 to 2005.
Elite II (made 2000-2005) . . . . . NiB $820   Ex $540   Gd $390

Beretta Model 96
Stock

Beretta Model 949
Olimpionico

Beretta Model
950BS Jetfire

MODEL 96 DA AUTO PISTOL
Similar to Model 92F except in .40 S&W. 10-round magazine
(9-round in Compact model). Made from 1992 to 1998.
Model 96 D (DA only) . . . . NiB $475   Ex $355   Gd $300
Model 96 Centurion (compact) . . NiB $550   Ex $460   Gd $310
w/Tritium sights, add $110
w/Tritium sights system, add $115

MODEL 96 STOCK . . . . NiB $1200   Ex $870   Gd $610
Similar to Model 96 except w/frame mounted safety. Set up for
I.D.P.A. competion. Made from 1997 to 1999.

MODEL 101 . . . . NiB $270   Ex $200   Gd $155
Same as Model 70T except caliber .22 LR, has 10-round magazine,
Intro. in 1959. Disc.

MODEL 318 AUTO PISTOL. . . . . NiB $270   Ex $200   Gd $155
Caliber: .25 Automatic (6.35mm). Eight-round magazine, 2.5-inch bbl.,
4.5 inches overall. Weight: 14 oz. Fixed sights. Blued finish. Plastic
grips. Made from 1934 to c. 1939.

MODEL 418 AUTO PISTOL. . . . . NiB $270   Ex $200   Gd $155
Similar to Model 318 but with loaded chamber indicator and grip
safety. Made from 1937 to 1961.

**MODEL 949 OLYMPIC TARGET
AUTO PISTOL** . . . . NiB $708   Ex $577   Gd $456
Calibers: .22 Short, .22 LR. Five-round magazine, 8.75-inch bbl.,
12.5 inches overall. Weight: 38 oz. Target sights. Adj. bbl., weight.
Muzzle brake. Checkered walnut grips w/thumbrest. Made from 1959
to 1964.

MODEL 950B AUTO PISTOL . NiB $225   Ex $168   Gd $115
Same general specifications as Model 950CC except caliber .25 Auto,
has 7-round magazine, Made from 1959 to date. Note: Formerly marketed in the U.S. as "Jetfire."

MODEL 950B JETFIRE SA PISTOL
Calibers: .25 ACP or .22 Short (disc.1992). Seven- or 8-round magazine,
2.4- or 4- inch bbl. Weight: 9.9 oz. Fixed blade front and V-notch rear
sights. Matte Blue or Inox (Stainless) finish. Checkered black plastic grips.
Made from 1987 to 2002.
Blued finish . . . . NiB $168   Ex $99   Gd $84
Nickel finish. . . . . NiB $225   Ex $173   Gd $147
Inox finish . . . . NiB $257   Ex $204   Gd $160
w/4-inch bbl., (.22 Short) . . . . . . NiB $256   Ex $207   Gd $157

MODEL 950CC AUTO PISTOL NiB $157   Ex $126   Gd $104
Caliber: .22 Short. Six-round magazine, hinged 2.38-inch bbl., 4.75 inches overall. Weight: 11 oz. Fixed sights. Blued finish. Plastic grips. Made
from 1959 to date. Note: Formerly marketed in the U.S. as "Minx M2."

**MODEL 950CC
SPECIAL AUTO PISTOL** . . . . . . NiB $155   Ex $103   Gd $88
Same general specifications as Model 950CC Auto except has 4-inch
bbl. Made from 1959 to date. Note: Formerly marketed in the U.S. as
"Minx M4."

**MODEL 951 (1951)
MILITARY AUTO PISTOL** . . . . NiB $330   Ex $251   Gd $200
Caliber: 9mm Para. Eight-round magazine, 4.5-inch bbl., 8 inches
overall. Weight: 31 oz. Fixed sights. Blued finish. Plastic grips. Made
from 1952 to date. Note: This is the standard pistol of the Italian Armed
Forces, also used by Egyptian and Israeli armies and by the police in
Nigeria. Egyptian and Israeli models usually command a premium.
Formerly marketed in the U.S. as the "Brigadier."

MODEL 1915 AUTO PISTOL NiB $1587   Ex $1386   Gd $1087
Calibers: 9mm Glisenti and .32 ACP (7.65mm). Eight-round magazine,
4-inch bbl., 6.7 inches overall (9mm), 5.7 inches (.32 ACP). Weight: 30
oz. (9mm), 20 oz. (.32 ACP). Fixed sights. Blued finish. Wood grips. Made
1915-1922. An improved postwar 1915/1919 version in caliber .32 ACP
was later offered for sale in 1922 as the Model 1922.

MODEL 1923 AUTO PISTOL NiB $2136   Ex $2094   Gd $1669
Caliber: 9mm Glisenti (Luger). Eight-round magazine, 4-inch bbl., 6.5 inches
overall. Weight: 30 oz. Fixed sights. Blued finish. Plastic grips. Made circa
1923 to 1936.

MODEL 1934 AUTO PISTOL
Caliber: .380 Automatic (9mm Short). Seven-round magazine, 3.38-inch bbl., 5.88 inches overall. Weight: 24 oz. Fixed sights. Blued finish. Plastic grips. Official pistol of the Italian Armed Forces. Wartime pieces not as well made and finished as commercial models. Made from 1934 to 1959.

Commercial model . . . . NiB $2340 Ex $2100 Gd $1333
War model . . . . NiB $598 Ex $383 Gd $299

MODEL 1935 AUTO PISTOL
Caliber: .32 ACP (7.65mm). Eight-round magazine, 3.5-inch bbl., 5.75 inches overall. Weight: 24 oz. Fixed sights. Blued finish. Plastic grips. A roughly-finished version of this pistol was produced during WW II. Made from 1935 to 1959.

Commercial model . . . . NiB $1806 Ex $1465 Gd $1078
War model . . . . NiB $598 Ex $383 Gd $299

MODEL 3032 DA SEMIAUTOMATIC TOMCAT
Caliber: .32 ACP. Seven-round magazine, 2.45-inch bbl., 5 inches overall. Weight: 14.5 oz. Fixed sights. Blued or stainless finish. Made from 1996 to date.

Matte blue . . . . NiB $329 Ex $262 Gd $180
Polished blue . . . . NiB $386 Ex $329 Gd $252
Stainless. . . . . NiB $412 Ex $365 Gd $252

MODEL 8000/8040/8045 COUGAR DA PISTOL
Calibers: 9mm, .40 S&W and .45 Auto. Eight- or 10- shot magazine, 3.6 to 3.7- inch bbl., 7- to 7.2 inches overall. Weight: 32 to 32.6 oz. Short recoil action w/rotating barrel. Fixed sights w/3-dot Tritium system. TExtured black composition grips. Matte black Bruniton finish w/alloy frame. Made from 1995 to 2005.

8000 Cougar D (9mm DAO) . . . . NiB $715 Ex $649 Gd $400
8000 Cougar F (9mm DA) . . . . . . NiB $750 Ex $644 Gd $388
8040 Cougar D (.40 S&W DAO) . NiB $685 Ex $618 Gd $373
8040 Cougar F (.40 S&W DA) . . . NiB $685 Ex $618 Gd $373
8045 Cougar D (.45 Auto DAO) . NiB $736 Ex $637 Gd $400
8045 Cougar F (.357 Sig SA/DA) . NiB $685 Ex $536 Gd $386

MODEL 8000/8040/8045 MINI COUGAR DA PISTOL
Calibers: 9mm, .40 S&W and .45 Auto. Six- 8- or 10-round magazine, 3.6- to 3.7- inch bbl., 7 inches overall. Weight: 27.4 to 30.4 oz. Fixed sights w/3-dot Tritium system. AmbidExtrous safety/decocker lever. Matte black Bruniton finish w/anodized aluminum alloy frame. Made from 1995 to 2008.

8000 Mini Cougar D (9mm DAO) NiB $654 Ex $577 Gd $326
8000 Mini Cougar F (9mm DA) . . NiB $654 Ex $577 Gd $326
8040 Mini Cougar D (.40 S&W DAO)NiB $654 Ex $577 Gd $326
8040 Mini Cougar F (.40 S&W DA)NiB $654 Ex $577 Gd $326
8045 Mini Cougar D (.45 Auto DAO)NiB $654 Ex $577 Gd $326
8045 Mini Cougar F (.45 Auto DA)NiB $654 Ex $577 Gd $326

MODEL 9000S SUBCOMPACT PISTOL SERIES
Calibers: 9mm, .40 S&W. 10-round magazine, 3.5- inch bbl., 6.6 inches overall. Weight: 25.7 to 27.5 oz. Single/double and double-action only. Front and rear dovetail sights w/3- dot system. Chrome-plated barrel w/ Techno-polymer frame. Geometric locking system w/tilt barrel. Made from 2000 to 2005.

Type D (9mm) . . . . .NiB $432 Ex $366 Gd $304
Type D (.40 S&W) . . . . NiB $432 Ex $366 Gd $304
Type F (9mm) . . . . NiB $432 Ex $366 Gd $304
Type F (.40 S&W) . . . . NiB $432 Ex $366 Gd $304

**Beretta
Model 3032 Tomcat**

**Beretta
Model 8000 Cougar D**

**Beretta
Model 8000 Cougar F**

**Beretta
Model 8040 Mini Cougar D**

LARAMIE SA REVOLVER . . . . . . **NIB $1030 EX $760 GD $550**
Reproduction of S&W Model 1870 Schofield. Calibers: .38 Special, .45 Long Colt. 6-round cylinder, Bbl length: 5, 6.5 inches. Blued finish. Built by Uberti for Beretta from 2005 to 2008.

Beretta Stampede

STAMPEDE SA REVOLVER
Calibers: .357 Magnum, .44-40, .45 Long Colt. 6-round cylinder, Bbl length: 4.75, 5.5, 7.5 inches. Built by Uberti for Beretta from 2003–11.

Blued finish	NiB $490	Ex $345	Gd $265
Brushed nickel finish	NiB $510	Ex $355	Gd $275
Deluxe finish	NiB $520	Ex $425	Gd $325
Old west finish	NiB $515	Ex $405	Gd $305
Bisley model	NiB $510	Ex $355	Gd $275

Bernardelli Model 60 Pocket

Bernardelli Model 80 Pocket

Bernardelli Model 68

BERNARDELLI, VINCENZO S.P.A. — Gardone V. T. (Brescia), Italy

MODEL 60 POCKET
AUTOMATIC PISTOL . . . . **NiB $247 Ex $221 Gd $190**
Calibers: .22 LR, .32 Auto (7.65mm), .380 Auto (9mm Short). Eight-round magazine (.22 and .32), 7-round (.380). 3.5-inch bbl., 6.5 inches overall. Weight: About 25 oz. Fixed sights. Blued finish. Bakelite grips. Made from 1959 to 1990.

MODEL 68 AUTOMATIC PISTOL . . . . . **NiB $180 Ex $128 Gd $92**
Caliber: 6.35. Five- and 8-round magazine, 2.13-inch bbl., 4.13 inches overall. Weight: 10 oz. Fixed sights. Blued or chrome finish. Bakelite or pearl grips. This model, like its .22-caliber counterpart, was known as the "Baby" Bernardelli. Disc. 1970.

MODEL 69 AUTOMATIC
TARGET PISTOL . . . . **NiB $693 Ex $570 Gd $383**
Caliber: .22 LR. 10-round magazine, 5.9-inch bbl., 9 inches overall. Weight: 2.2 lbs. Fully adj. target sights. Blued finish. Stippled right- or left-hand wraparound walnut grips. Made from 1987 to date. This was previously Model 100; not imported to the U.S.

MODEL 80
AUTOMATIC PISTOL . . . . **NiB $204 Ex $128 Gd $92**
Calibers: .22 LR, .32 ACP (7.65mm), .380 Auto (9mm Short). Magazine capacity: 10-round (.22), 8-round (.32), 7-round (.380). 3.5-inch bbl., 6.5 inches overall. Weight: 25.6 oz. adj. rear sight, white dot front sight. Blued finish. Plastic thumbrest grips. Note: Model 80 is a modification of Model 60 designed to conform w/U.S. import regulations. Made from 1968 to 1988.

MODEL 90
SPORT TARGET . . . . **NiB $245 Ex $199 Gd $148**
Same as Model 80 except has 6-inch bbl., 9 inches overall, weight: 26.8 oz. Made from 1968 1990.

MODEL 100 TARGET
AUTOMATIC PISTOL . . . . **NiB $428 Ex $362 Gd $291**
Caliber: .22 LR. 10-round magazine, 5.9-inch bbl., 9 inches overall. Weight: 37.75 oz. Adj. rear sight, interchangeable front sights. Blued finish. Checkered walnut thumbrest grips. Made from 1969-86. Note: Formerly Model 69.

MODEL AMR AUTO PISTOL . . . . . **NiB $433 Ex $321 Gd $270**
Simlar to Model USA except with 6-inch bbl. and target sights. Imported from 1992 to 1994.

"BABY" AUTOMATIC PISTOL . . . . **NiB $321 Ex $235 Gd $179**
Calibers: .22 Short, .22 Long. Five-round magazine, 2.13-inch bbl., 4.13 inches overall. Weight: 9 oz. Fixed sights. Blued finish. Bakelite grips. Made from 1949 to 1968.

MODEL P010
AUTOMATIC PISTOL . . . . **NiB $712 Ex $520 Gd $341**
Caliber: .22 LR. Five- and 10-round magazine, 5.9-inch bbl. w/7.5-inch sight radius. Weight: 40 oz. Interchangeable front sight, adj. rear. Blued finish. TExtured walnut grips. Made from 1988 to 1992 and 1995 to 1997.

P018 COMPACT MODEL . . . . **NiB $571 Ex $461 Gd $385**
Slightly smaller version of the Model P018 standard DA automatic except has 14-round magazine and 4-inch bbl., 7.68 inches overall. Weight: 33 oz. Walnut grips only. Imported from 1987 to 1996.

P018 DOUBLE-ACTION
AUTOMATIC PISTOL
Caliber: 9mm Para. 16-round magazine, 4.75-inch bbl., 8.5 inches overall. Weight: 36 oz. Fixed combat sights. Blued finish. Checkered plastic or walnut grips. Imported from 1987 to 1996.
w/plastic grips . . . . NiB $510 Ex $405 Gd $305
w/walnut grips . . . . NiB $551 Ex $428 Gd $342

P-ONE DA AUTO PISTOL
Caliber: 9mm Para. or .40 S&W. 10- or 16-round magazine, 4.8-inch bbl., 8.35 inches overall. Weight: 34 oz. Blade front sight, adjustable rear w/3-dot system. Matte black or chrome finish. Checkered walnut or black plastic grips. Imported from 1993 to 1997.
Model P-One blue finish. . . . . . . NiB $622 Ex $525 Gd $357
Model P-One chrome finish . . . . NiB $693 Ex $556 Gd $393
w/walnut grips, add $5 0

P-ONE PRACTICAL VB AUTO PISTOL
Similar to Model P One except chambered for 9x21mm w/2-, 4- or 6-port compensating system for IPSC competition. Imported 1993 to 1997.
Model P One
  Practical (2 port) . . . . NiB $1148 Ex $1068 Gd $785
Model P One
  Practical (4 port) . . . . NiB $1259 Ex $1054 Gd $782
Model P One
  Practical (6 port) . . . . NiB $1678 Ex $1393 Gd $995
w/chrome finish, add $75

SPORTER AUTOMATIC PISTOL. NiB $332 Ex $245 Gd $133
Caliber .22 LR. Eight-round magazine, bbl., lengths: 6-, 8- and 10-inch, 13 inches overall (10-inch bbl.). weight: About 30 oz. (10-inch bbl.) Target sights. Blued finish. Walnut grips. Made 1949 to 1968.

MODEL USA AUTO PISTOL
Single-action, blowback. Calibers: .22 LR, .32 ACP, .380 ACP. Seven-round magazine or 10-round magazine (.22 LR). 3.5-inch bbl., 6.5 inches overall. Weight: 26.5 oz. Ramped front sight, adjustable rear. Blue or chrome finish. Checkered black bakelite grips w/thumbrest. Imported from 1991 to 1997.
Model USA blue finish . . . . NiB $420 Ex $330 Gd $265
Model USA chrome finish. . . . . . NiB $469 Ex $385 Gd $219

VEST POCKET
AUTOMATIC PISTOL . . . . NiB $275 Ex $199 Gd $148
Caliber: .25 Auto (6.35mm). Five- or 8-round magazine, 2.13-inch bbl., 4.13 inches overall. Weight: 9 oz. Fixed sights. Blued finish. Bakelite grips. Made from 1945 to 1968.

BERSA — Argentina
Currently imported by Eagle Imports, Wanamassa, NJ. Previously by Interarms & Outdoor Sports.

MODEL 83 DA AUTO PISTOL
Similar to the Model 23 except for the following specifications: Caliber: .380 ACP. Seven-round magazine, 3.5-inch bbl., Front blade sight integral on slide, square-notch rear adj. for windage. Blued or satin nickel finish. Custom wood grips. Imported from 1988 to 1994.
Blued finish . . . . NiB $275 Ex $201 Gd $126
Satin nickel . . . . NiB $321 Ex $271 Gd $194

MODEL 85 DA AUTO PISTOL
Same general specifications as Model 83 except 13-round magazine, Imported from 1988 to 1994.
Blued finish . . . . NiB $326 Ex $235 Gd $128
Satin nickel . . . . NiB $377 Ex $286 Gd $179

Bernardelli P010

Bernardelli P018

Bersa Model 85

www.skyhorsepublishing.com

Bersa Model 383

Bersa Thunder .380

Bersa Thunder .380 Deluxe

MODEL 86 DA AUTO PISTOL
Same general specifications as Model 85 except available in matte blued finish and w/Neoprene grips. Imported from 1992 to 1994.
Matte blued finish . . . . NiB $347 Ex $270 Gd $219
Nickel finish. . . . . NiB $362 Ex $262 Gd $199

MODEL 95 DA AUTOMATIC PISTOL
Caliber: .380 ACP. Seven-round magazine, 3.5-inch bbl., weight: 23 oz. Wraparound rubber grips. Blade front and rear notch sights. Imported from 1995 to date.
Blued finish . . . . NiB $329 Ex $214 Gd $158
Nickel finish. . . . . NiB $318 Ex $204 Gd $143

MODEL 97 AUTO PISTOL . . . . . NiB $389 Ex $332 Gd $219
Caliber: .380 ACP. Seven-round magazine, 3.3-inch bbl., 6.5 inches overall. Weight: 28 oz. Intro. 1982. Disc.

MODEL 223
Same general specifications as Model 383 except in .22 LR w/10-round magazine capacity. Disc. 1987.
Double-action . . . . NiB $243 Ex $213 Gd $143
Single-action . . . . NiB $224 Ex $168 Gd $125

MODEL 224
Caliber: .22 LR. 10-round magazine, 4-inch bbl., weight: 26 oz. Front blade sight, square-notched rear adj. for windage. Blued finish. Checkered nylon or custom wood grips. Made 1984. SA. disc. 1986.
Double-action . . . . NiB $240 Ex $204 Gd $143
Single-action . . . . NiB $204 Ex $179 Gd $122

MODEL 226
Same general specifications as Model 224 but w/6-inch bbl. Disc. 1987.
Double-action . . . . NiB $240 Ex $204 Gd $143
Single-action . . . . NiB $204 Ex $179 Gd $122

MODEL 383 AUTO PISTOL
Caliber: .380 Auto. Seven-round magazine, 3.5-inch bbl. Front blade sight integral on slide, square-notched rear sight adj. for windage. Custom wood grips on double-action, nylon grips on single action. Blued or satin nickel finish. Made 1984. SA. disc. 1989.
Double-action . . . . NiB $235 Ex $150 Gd $102
Single-action . . . . NiB $219 Ex $158 Gd $122

MODEL 622 AUTO PISTOL . . NiB $204 Ex $138 Gd $100
Caliber: .22 LR. Seven-round magazine, 4- or 6-inch bbl., 7 or 9 inches overall. Weight: 2.25 lbs. Blade front sight, square-notch rear adj. for windage. Blued finish. Nylon grips. Made from 1982 to 1987.

MODEL 644 AUTO PISTOL . . NiB $286 Ex $240 Gd $168
Caliber: .22 LR. 10-round magazine, 3.5-inch bbl., weight: 26.5 oz. 6.5 inches overall. Adj. rear sight, blade front. Contoured black nylon grips. Made from 1980 to 1988.

THUNDER 9 AUTO PISTOL . . NiB $408 Ex $272 Gd $168
Caliber: 9mm Para. 15-round magazine, 4-inch bbl., 7.38 inches overall. Weight: 30 oz. Blade front sight, adj. rear w/3-dot system. AmbidExtrous safety and decocking device. Matte blued finish. Checkered black polymer grips. Made from 1993 to 1996.

THUNDER .22 AUTO PISTOL (MODEL 23)
Caliber: .22 LR, 10-round magazine, 3.5-inch bbl., 6.63 inches overall. Weight: 24.5 oz. Notched-bar dovetailed rear, blade integral w/slide front. Black polymer grips. Made from 1988 to 1998.
Blued finish . . . . NiB $254 Ex $214 Gd $168
Nickel finish. . . . . NiB $260 Ex $220 Gd $177

THUNDER .380 AUTO PISTOL
Caliber: .380 ACP. Seven-round magazine, 3.5-inch bbl., 6.63 inches overall. Weight: 25.75 oz. Notched-bar dovetailed rear, blade integral w/slide front. Blued, satin nickel, or Duo-Tone finish. Made from 1995 to 1998.
Blued finish . . . . NiB $306 Ex $230 Gd $183
Satin nickel finish. . . . . NiB $333 Ex $255 Gd $204
Duo-Tone finish . . . . NiB $306 Ex $230 Gd $168

THUNDER .380 PLUS AUTO PISTOL
Same general specifications as standard Thunder .380 except has 10-round magazine and weight: 26 oz. Made from 1995 to 1997.
Matte finish . . . . NiB $306 Ex $230 Gd $168
Satin nickel finish. . . . . NiB $321 Ex $245 Gd $194
Duo-Tone finish, add $40

BROLIN ARMS — La Verne, California

"LEGEND SERIES" SA AUTOMATIC PISTOL
Caliber: .45 ACP. Seven-round magazine, 4- or 5-inch bbl., weight: 32-36 oz. Walnut grips. Single action, full size, compact, or full size frame compact slide. Matte blued finish. Lowered and flared ejection port. Made from 1995 to 1998.
Model L45 . . . . NiB $469 Ex $398 Gd $306
Model L45C . . . . NiB $487 Ex $366 Gd $305
Model L45T . . . . NiB $487 Ex $366 Gd $305

"PATRIOT SERIES" SA AUTOMATIC PISTOL
Caliber: .45 ACP. Seven-round magazine, 3.25- and 4-inch bbl., weight: 33-37 oz. Wood grips. Fixed rear sights. Made 1996 to 1997.
Model P45 . . . . NiB $627 Ex $469 Gd $301
Model P45C (disc. 1997) . . . . NiB $638 Ex $479 Gd $311
Model P45T (disc. 1997). . . . . NiB $658 Ex $551 Gd $372

"PRO-STOCK AND PRO-COMP" SA PISTOL
Caliber: .45 ACP. Eight-round magazine, 4- or 5-inch bbl., weight: 37 oz. Single action, blued or two-tone finish. Wood grips. Bomar adjustable sights. Made from 1996 to 1997.
Model Pro comp. . . . . NiB $872 Ex $663 Gd $566
Model Pro stock . . . . NiB $714 Ex $551 Gd $475

TAC SERIES
Caliber: .45 ACP. Eight-round magazine, 5-inch bbl., 8.5 inches overall. Weight: 37 oz. Low profile combat or Tritium sights. Beavertail grip safety. Matte blue, chrome or two-tone finish. Checkered wood or contoured black rubber grips. Made from 1997 to 1998.
Model TAC 11 service . . . . NiB $643 Ex $510 Gd $398
Model TAC 11 compact . . . . . . NiB $653 Ex $531 Gd $419
w/Tritium sights, add $100

BANTAM MODEL. . . . . NiB $403 Ex $283 Gd $ 204
Caliber: 9mmPara., .40 S&W. Single or double-action, super compact size, concealed hammer, all steel construction; 3-dot sights; royal blue or matte finish. Manufactured 1999 only.

Browning Model 25 Automatic

BRONCO — Eibar, Spain
Manufactured by Echave y Arizmendi.

MODEL 1918 POCKET
AUTOMATIC PISTOL . . . . NiB $204 Ex $129 Gd $92
Caliber: .32 ACP (7.65mm). Six-round magazine 2.5-inch bbl., 5 inches overall. Weight: 20 oz. Fixed sights. Blued finish. Hard rubber grips. Made circa 1918- to 1925.

VEST POCKET AUTO PISTOL . . NiB $203 Ex $128 Gd $66
Caliber: .25 ACP, 6-round magazine, 2.13-inch bbl., 4.13 inches overall. Weight: 11 oz. Fixed sights. Blued finish. Hard rubber grips. Made from 1919 to 1935.

BROWNING — Morgan, Utah

The following Browning pistols have been manufactured by Fabrique Nationale d'Armes de Guerre (now Fabrique Nationale Herstal) of Herstal, Belgium, by Arms Technology Inc. of Salt Lake City and by J. P. Sauer & Sohn of Eckernforde, W. Germany. See also FN Browning and J.P. Sauer & Sohn listings.

.25 AUTOMATIC PISTOL
Same general specifications as FN Browning Baby (see separate listing). Standard Model, blued finish, hard rubber grips. Light Model, nickel-plated, Nacrolac pearl grips. Renaissance Engraved Model, nickel-plated, Nacrolac pearl grips. Made by FN from 1955 to 1969.
Standard model . . . . NiB $587 Ex $534 Gd $283
Lightweight model . . . . NiB $592 Ex $540 Gd $294
Renaissance model. . . . . NiB $1121 Ex $867 Gd $539

.32 AND .380 AUTOMATIC PISTOL, 1955 TYPE
Same general specifications as FN Browning .32 (7.65mm) and .380 Pocket Auto. Standard Model, Renaissance Engraved Model as furnished in .25 Automatic. Made by FN from 1955 to 1969.
Standard model (.32 ACP). . . . . . NiB $507 Ex $386 Gd $291
Standard model (.380 ACP). . . . . NiB $454 Ex $376 Gd $283
Renaissance model. . . . . NiB $1121 Ex $918 Gd $740

.380 AUTOMATIC PISTOL, 1971 TYPE
Same as .380 Automatic, 1955 Type except has longer slide, 4.44-inch bbl., is 7.06 inches overall, weight: 23 oz. Rear sight adj. for windage and elevation, plastic thumbrest grips. Made 1971 to 1975.
Standard model . . . . NiB $509 Ex $387 Gd $294
Renaissance model. . . . . NiB $1132 Ex $913 Gd $616

**Browning
BDA .380 Nickel Finish**

**Browning
BDM 9mm DA**

**Browning
Buck Mark 22 Field (5.5)**

**Browning
Buck Mark 22 Bullseye**

**Browning
Buck Mark 22 Plus**

BDA .380 DA AUTOMATIC PISTOL
Caliber: .380 Auto. 10- or 13-round magazine, bbl. length: 3.81 inches., 6.75 inches overall. Weight: 23 oz. Fixed blade front sight, square-notch drift-adj. rear sight. Blued or nickel finish. Smooth walnut grips. Made from 1982 to 1997 by Beretta.
Blued finish. . . . . **NiB $602 Ex $454 Gd $284**

BDA DA AUTOMATIC PISTOL
Similar to SIG-Sauer P220. Calibers: 9mm Para., .38 Super Auto, .45 Auto. Nine-round magazine (9mm and .38), 7-round (.45 cal), 4.4-inch bbl., 7.8 inches overall. Weight: 29.3 oz. Fixed sights. Blued finish. Plastic grips. Made from 1977 to 1980 by J. P. Sauer.
BDA model, 9mm, .45 ACP . . . . **NiB $611 Ex $464 Gd $326**
BDA model, .38 Super . . . . **NiB $741 Ex $465 Gd $437**
Nickel finish. . . . . **NiB $692 Ex $524 Gd $377**

BDM SERIES AUTOMATIC PISTOLS
Calibers: 9mm Para., 10-round magazine, 4.73-inch bbl., 7.85 inches overall. Weight: 31 oz., windage adjustable sights w/3-dot system. Low profile removable blade front sights. Matte blued, Bi-Tone or silver chrome finish. Selectable shooting mode and decocking safety lever. Made from 1991 to 1997.
BDM Standard . . . . **NiB $622 Ex $499 Gd $333**
BDM Practical . . . . **NiB $598 Ex $490 Gd $373**
BDM-D Silver Chrome . . . . **NiB $693 Ex $509 Gd $384**

BUCK MARK .22 AUTOMATIC PISTOL
Caliber: .22 LR. 10-round magazine, 5.5-inch bbl., 9.5 inches overall. Weight: 32 oz. Black molded grips. Adj. rear sight. Blued or nickel finish. Made from 1985 to date.
Blued finish . . . . **NiB $342 Ex $221 Gd $143**
Nickel finish. . . . . **NiB $403 Ex $285 Gd $203**

BUCK MARK .22 BULLSEYE PISTOL
Same general specifications as the standard Buck Mark 22 except w/7.25-inch fluted barrel, 11.83 inches overall. Weight: 36 oz. Adjustable target trigger. Undercut post front sight, click-adjustable Pro-Target rear. Laminated, Rosewood, black rubber or composite grips. Made from 1996 to 2006.
Standard model (composite grips)...**NiB $487 Ex $344 Gd $249**
Target model . . . . **NiB $475 Ex $316 Gd $219**

BUCK MARK .22
BULLSEYE TARGET. . . . .**NiB $487 Ex $344 Gd $249**
Caliber: .22 LR. 10-round magazine, 7.25-inch fluted bbl., 11.83 inches overall. Weight: 31 oz. Rosewood wrap-around finger groove grips w/matte blued finish. Made from 1996 to 2005.

BUCK MARK .22 CAMPER . . . . . .**NiB $300 Ex $210 Gd $150**
Similar to Buckmark .22 except w/5.5-inch heavy bbl., matte blued or satin nickel finish. Black polymer grips. Made from 1999 to 2012.
Stainless. . . . . **NiB $320 Ex $230 Gd $17**

Browning
Buck Mark .22 Silhouette

Browning
Buck Mark .22 Target
(5.5)

BUCK MARK .22 CHALLENGER NiB $345   Ex $220   Gd $165
Similar to Buckmark .22 except w/smaller grip. 5.5-inch bbl., matte blued finish. Made from 1999 to 2010.
Micro Challenge (4-in. bbl.) . . . . . NiB $300   Ex $210   Gd $155

BUCK MARK .22 5.5 FIELD . . NiB $487   Ex $344   Gd $249
Similar to Buck Mark 5.5 Traget except w/standard sights. Made from 1991 to 2011.

BUCK MARK .22 LITE SPLASH URXNiB $375   Ex $235   Gd $200
Similar to Buck Mark except w/5.5- or 7.25-in. round aluminum bbl. sleeve. TruGlo fibrtr optic sights. Made from 2006 to 2009.

BUCK MARK .22 MICRO AUTOMATIC PISTOL
Same general specifications as standard Buck Mark .22 except w/4-inch bbl., 8 inches overall. Weight: 32 oz. Molded composite grips. Ramp front sight, Pro Target rear sight. URX grip introduced in 2007. Made from 1992 to 2013.
Blued finish . . . . NiB $367   Ex $271   Gd $181
Nickel finish. . . . . NiB $418   Ex $321   Gd $244
Stainless finish . . . . NiB $367   Ex $271   Gd $181

BUCK MARK .22 MICRO PLUS AUTO PISTOL
Same specifications as the Buck Mark .22 Micro except ambidextrous, laminated wood grips. Made from 1996 to 2001.
Blued finish . . . . NiB $285   Ex $234   Gd $192
Nickel finish. . . . . NiB $382   Ex $321   Gd $204

Browning
Buck Mark .22 Micro Plus

BUCK MARK .22 PLUS AUTO PISTOL
Same general specifications as standard Buck Mark .22 except for black molded, impregnated hardwood grips. Made from 1987 to 2001.
Blued finish . . . . NiB $383   Ex $321   Gd $204
Nickel finish. . . . . NiB $404   Ex $329   Gd $223

BUCK MARK .22 5.5 TARGET AUTO PISTOL
Caliber: .22 LR. 10-round magazine, 5.5-inch bbl., 9.6 inches overall. Weight: 35.5 oz. Pro target sights. Wrap-around walnut or contoured finger groove grips. Made from 1990 to 2009.
Matte blue finish . . . . NiB $455   Ex $374   Gd $223
Nickel finish (1994 to date) . . . . NiB $499   Ex $395   Gd $245
Gold finish (1991-99) . . . . NiB $385   Ex $270   Gd $184

BUCK MARK .22 SILHOUETTE NiB $544   Ex $372   Gd $220
Same general specifications as standard Buck Mark .22 except for 9.88-inch bbl. Weight: 53 oz. Target sights mounted on full-length scope base, and laminated hardwood grips and forend. Made from 1987 to 1999.

Browning Challenger
Standard Model

**BUCK MARK .22
UNLIMITED SILHOUETTE.** . . . . . . NiB $547   Ex $431   Gd $285
Same general specifications as standard Buck Mark .22 Silhouette except w/14-inch bbl., 18.69 inches overall. Weight: 64 oz. Interchangeable post front sight and Pro Target rear. Nickel finish. Made from 1991 to 1999.

**BUCK MARK .22
VARMINT AUTO PISTOL** . . . . NiB $346   Ex $282   Gd $230
Same general specifications as standard Buck Mark .22 except for

Browning Challenger
Renaissance Model

**Browning
Challenger III Sporter .22**

**Browning
Hi-Power Mark
III**

**Browning
9mm Hi-Power w/Molded Grips**

**Browning
9mm Hi-Power AmbidExtrous Safety**

**Browning
Hi-Power Captain**

9.88-inch bbl. Weight: 48 oz. No sights, full-length scope base, and laminated hardwood grips. Made from 1987 to 1999.

CHALLENGER AUTOMATIC PISTOL
Caliber: .22 LR. 10-round magazine, bbl. lengths: 4.5 and 6.75-inches. 11.44 inches overall (with 6.75-inch bbl.). Weight: 38 oz. (6.75-inch bbl.). Removable blade front sight, screw adj. rear. Standard finish, blued, also furnished gold inlaid (Gold model) and engraved and chrome-plated (Renaissance model). Checkered walnut grips. Finely figured and carved grips on Gold and Renaissance models. Standard made by FN 1962-75, higher grades. Intro. 1971. Disc.
Standard model . . . . NiB $590   Ex $427   Gd $285
Gold model . . . . NiB $3172   Ex $2448   Gd $1742
Renaissance model. . . . . NiB $3058   Ex $2445   Gd $1744

CHALLENGER II
AUTOMATIC PISTOL . . . . .NiB $363   Ex $259   Gd $164
Same general specifications as Challenger Standard model w/6.75-inch bbl. except changed grip angle and impregnated hardwood grips. Original Challenger design modified for lower production costs. Made by ATI from 1976 to 1983.

CHALLENGER III
AUTOMATIC PISTOL . . . . .NiB $266   Ex $217   Gd $153
Same general description as Challenger II except has 5.5 inch bull bbl., alloy frame and new sight system. Weight: 35 oz. Made from 1982-84. Sporter Model w/6.75-inch bbl.. Made from 1982-85.

HI-POWER AUTOMATIC PISTOL
Same general specifications as FN Browning Model 1935 except chambered for 9mm Para., .30 Luger or .40 S&W. 10- or 13-round magazine, 4.63-inch bbl., 7.75 inches overall. Weight: 32 oz. (9mm) or 35 oz. (.40 S&W). Fixed sights, also available w/rear sight adj. for windage and elevation, and ramp front sight. AmbidExtrous safety added after 1989. Standard model blued, chrome-plated or Bi-Tone finish. Checkered walnut, contour-molded Polyamide or wraparound rubber grips. Renaissance Engraved model chrome-plated, w/Nacrolac pearl grips. Made by FN from 1954 to 2002.
Standard model,
   fixed sights, 9mm . . . . NiB $895   Ex $689   Gd $510
Standard model, fixed sights,
   .40 S&W (intro. 1995) . . . . . . NiB $784   Ex $683   Gd $582
Standard model,
   .30 Luger (1986-89). . . . . NiB $942   Ex $702   Gd $489
Renaissance model,
   fixed sights . . . . NiB $4098   Ex $3651   Gd $2688
w/adjustable rear sight, add $75
w/ambidextrous safety, add. $110

Browning
Hi-Power Practical

Browning
Hi-Power Silver Chrome

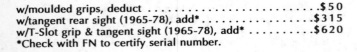

w/moulded grips, deduct $50
w/tangent rear sight (1965-78), add* $315
w/T-Slot grip & tangent sight (1965-78), add* $620
*Check with FN to certify serial number.

HI-POWER CAPTAIN
AUTOMATIC PISTOL . . . . **NiB $804 Ex $605 Gd $429**
Similar to the standard Hi-Power except fitted w/adj. 500-meter tangent
rear sight and rounded serrated hammer. Made from 1993 to 2000.

HI-POWER MARK III
AUTOMATIC PISTOL . . . . **NiB $793 Ex $498 Gd $398**
Calibers: 9mm or .40 S&W. 10-round magazine, 4.75-inch bbl., 7.75
inches overall. Weight: 32 oz. Fixed sights with molded grips. Durable
non-glare matte blue or black epoxy finish. Made from 1985 to 2000;
reintro. 2002.

HI-POWER PRACTICAL AUTOMATIC PISTOL
Similar to the standard Hi-Power except has silver-chromed frame
and blued slide w/Commander-style hammer. Made from 1991 to
2006.
w/fixed sights . . . . **NiB $729 Ex $533 Gd $385**
w/adj. sights, add $75

HI-POWER SILVER CHROME
AUTOMATIC PISTOL . . . . **NiB $792 Ex $650 Gd $407**
Calibers: 9mm or .40 S&W. 10-round magazine, 4.75-inch bbl., 7.75
inches overall. Weight: 36 oz. Adjustable sights with Pachmayer grips.
Silver-chromed finish. Made from 1991 to 2000.

HI-POWER 9MM CLASSIC
Limited Edition 9mm Hi-Power, w/silver-gray finish, high-grade engraving and finely-checkered walnut grips w/double border. Proposed
production of the Classic was 5000 w/less than half that number produced. Gold Classic limited to 500 w/two-thirds proposed production
in circulation. Made from 1985 to 1986.
Gold classic . . . . **NiB $5401 Ex $4999 Gd $3495**
Standard classic . . . . **NiB $895 Ex $657 Gd $542**

INTERNATIONAL MEDALIST EARLY MODEL
TARGET PISTOL . . . . **NiB $1197 Ex $992 Gd $804**
Modification of Medalist to conform w/International Shooting Union
rules. 5.9-inch bbl., Smaller grip with no forearm. Weight: 42 oz. Made
from 1970-73. Subtract 30% for post 1974 models

Browning
Hi-Power 9mm Classic

Browning
Medalist International

Browning
Medalist Automatic Target Pistol

**Browning
Medalist
Renaissance**

**Charter Arms
Bonnie**

**Charter Arms
Clyde**

MEDALIST AUTOMATIC TARGET PISTOL

Caliber: .22 LR. 10-round magazine, 6.75-inch bbl. w/vent rib, 11.94 inches overall. Weight: 46 oz. Removable blade front sight, click-adj. micrometer rear. Standard finish, blued also furnished gold-inlaid (Gold Model) and engraved and chrome-plated (Renaissance Model). Checkered walnut grips w/thumbrest (for right- or left-handed shooter). Finely figured and carved grips on Gold and Renaissance Models. Made by FN from 1962 to 1975. Higher grades. Intro. 1971.

Standard model	NiB $1552	Ex $1333	Gd $1072
Gold model	NiB $3071	Ex $1835	Gd $1032
Renaissance model	NiB $2631	Ex $2183	Gd $1426

NOMAD

AUTOMATIC PISTOL . . . . NiB $486   Ex $328   Gd $227
Caliber: .22 LR. 10-round magazine, bbl. lengths: 4.5 and 6.75-inches, 8.94 inches overall (4.5-inch bbl.). Weight: 34 oz. (with 4.5-inch bbl.). Removable blade front sight, screw adj. rear. Blued finish. Plastic grips. Made by FN from 1962 to 1974.

RENAISSANCE 9MM, .25 AUTO AND .380 AUTO (1955) ENGRAVED

MODELS, CASED SET. . . . NiB $4080   Ex $3565   Gd $3160
One pistol of each of the three models in a special walnut carrying case, all chrome-plated w/Nacrolac pearl grips. Made by FN from 1964 to 1975. Options and engraving varies.

BRYCO ARMS INC. — Irvine, California

Distributed by Jennings Firearms. Inc. Carson City, NV.

MODELS J22, J25 AUTO PISTOL

Calibers: .22 LR, .25 ACP. Six-round magazine, 2.5-inch bbl., about 5 inches overall. Weight: 13 oz. Fixed sights. Chrome, satin nickel or black Teflon finish. Walnut, grooved black Cycolac or resin-impregnated wood grips. Made from 1981 to 1985.

Model J-22 (disc. 1985)	NiB $73	Ex $56	Gd $45
Model J-25 (disc. 1995)	NiB $123	Ex $90	Gd $75

MODELS M25, M32, M38 AUTO PISTOL

Calibers: .25 ACP, .32 ACP, .380 ACP. Six-round magazine, 2.81-inch bbl., 5.31 inches overall. Weight: 11oz. to 15 oz. Fixed sights. Chrome, satin nickel or black Teflon finish. Walnut, grooved, black Cycolac or resin-impregnated wood grips. Made from 1988 to 2000.

Model M25 (disc.)	NiB $119	Ex $92	Gd $74
Model M32	NiB $143	Ex $102	Gd $77
Model M38	NiB $147	Ex $108	Gd $91

MODEL M48

AUTO PISTOL . . . . NiB $128   Ex $102   Gd $81
Calibers: .22 LR, .32 ACP, .380 ACP. Seven-round magazine, 4-inch bbl., 6.69 inches overall. Weight: 20 oz. Fixed sights. Chrome, satin nickel or black Teflon finish. Smooth wood or black Teflon grips. Made from 1989 to 1995.

MODEL M58

Auto Pistol . . . . NiB $132   Ex $108   Gd $90
Caliber: .380 ACP. 10-round magazine, 3.75-inch bbl., 5.5 inches overall. Weight: 30 oz. Fixed sights. Chrome, satin nickel, blued or black Teflon finish. Smooth wood or black Teflon grips. Made 1993 to 1995.

MODEL M59

AUTO PISTOL . . . . NiB $128   Ex $102   Gd $82
Caliber: 9mm Para. 10-round magazine, 4-inch bbl., 6.5 inches overall. Weight: 33 oz. Fixed sights. Chrome, satin nickel, blued or black Teflon finish. Smooth wood or black Teflon grips. Made 1994 to 1996.

MODEL NINE SA

AUTO PISTOL . . . . NiB $171   Ex $136   Gd $112
Similar to Bryco/Jennings Model M59 except w/redesigned slide w/ loaded chamber indicator and frame mounted ejector. Weight: 30 oz. Made from 1997 to 2003.

MODEL 5 AUTO PISTOL . . . . . . NiB $102   Ex $69   Gd $46
Caliber: .380 ACP, 9mm Para.; 10- or 12-shot magazine. Bbl: 3.25 inches. Blue or nickel finish, black synthetic grips. Weight: 36 oz. Disc. 1995.

BUDISCHOWSKY — Mt. Clemens, Michigan

Mfd. by Norton Armament Corporation

TP-70 DA AUTOMATIC PISTOL

Calibers: .22 LR, .25 Auto. Six-round magazine, 2.6-inch bbl., 4.65 inches overall. Weight: 12.3 oz. Fixed sights. Stainless steel. Plastic grips. Made from 1973 to 1977.

.22 LR . . . . NiB $487   Ex $361   Gd $372
.25 ACP . . . . NiB $362   Ex $249   Gd $192

CALICO LIGHT WEAPONS SYSTEM — Hillsboro, Oregon

MODEL 110 AUTO PISTOL . . . . NiB $635   Ex $576   Gd $486
Caliber: .22 LR. 100-round magazine, 6-inch bbl., 17.9 inches over-all. Weight: 3.75 lbs. Adj. post front sight, fixed U-notch rear. Black finish aluminum frame. Molded composition grip. Made from 1986 to 1994.

MODEL M-950 AUTO PISTOL NiB $850   Ex $479   Gd $362
Caliber 9mm Para. 50- or 100-round magazine, 7.5-inch bbl., 14 inches overall. Weight: 2.25 lbs. Adj. post front sight, fixed U-notch rear. Glass-filled polymer grip. Made from 1989 to 1994.

Charter Arms
Bulldog Police

CHARTER ARMS CORPORATION — Shelton, Connecticut

MODEL 40 AUTOMATIC PISTOL. NiB $283   Ex $224   Gd $171
Caliber: .22 LR. Eight-round magazine, 3.3-inch bbl., 6.3 inches overall. Weight: 21.5 oz. Fixed sights. Checkered walnut grips. Stainless steel finish. Made from 1985 to 1986.

MODEL 79K
DA AUTOMATIC PISTOL . . . . . . .NiB $362   Ex $286   Gd $230
Calibers: .380 or .32 Auto. Seven-round magazine, 3.6-inch bbl., 6.5 inches overall. Weight: 24.5 oz. Fixed sights. Checkered walnut grips. Stainless steel finish. Made from 1985 to 1986.

BONNIE AND CLYDE SET . . . NiB $454   Ex $342   Gd $297
Matching pair of shrouded 2.5-inch bbl., revolvers chambered for .32 Magnum (Bonnie) and .38 Special (Clyde). Blued finish w/scrolled name on bbls.. Made 1989 to 1990.

Charter Arms
Bulldog Pug

BULLDOG .44 DA REVOLVER
Caliber: .44 Special. Five-round cylinder, 2.5- or 3-inch bbl., 7 or 7.5 inches overall. Weight: 19 or 19.5 oz. Fixed sights. Blued, nickel-plated or stainless finish. Checkered walnut Bulldog or square buttgrips. Made from 1973 to 1996.
Blued finish/
   Pocket Hammer (2.5-inch) . . . . . NiB $260   Ex $192   Gd $134
Blued finish/
   Bulldog grips (3-inch disc. 1988) NiB $244   Ex $206   Gd $147
Electroless nickel . . . . NiB $274   Ex $223   Gd $146
Stainless steel/
   Bulldog grips (disc. 1992) . . . . . . NiB $220   Ex $193   Gd $132
Neoprene grips/
   Pocket Hammer . . . . NiB $242   Ex $203   Gd $148

BULLDOG .357 DA REVOLVER . NiB $214   Ex $169   Gd $129
Caliber: .357 Magnum. Five-round cylinder, 6-inch bbl., 11 inches overall. Weight: 25 oz. Fixed sights. Blued finish. Square, checkered walnut grips. Made from 1977 to 1996.

BULLDOG NEW POLICE DA REVOLVER
Same general specifications as Bulldog Police except chambered for .44 Special. Five-round cylinder, 2.5- or 3.5-inch bbl. Made from 1990 to 1992.

Charter Arms
Bulldog Target

Charter Arms
Explorer II

Charter
Arms Pathfinder

Charter Arms Explorer II
Silvertone w/optional barrels

Charter Arms Police Undercover
.32 H&R Magnum

Blued finish . . . . NiB $263   Ex $201   Gd $148
Stainless finish (2.5-inch bbl. only) . . NiB $202   Ex $166   Gd $114

BULLDOG POLICE DA REVOLVER
Caliber: .38 Special or .32 H&R Magnum. Six-round cylinder, 4-inch bbl.,
8.5 inches overall. Weight: 20.5 oz. Adj. rear sight, ramp front. Blued or
stainless finish. Square checkered walnut grips. Made from 1976-93. No
shroud on new models.
Blued finish . . . . NiB $272   Ex $204   Gd $158
Stainless finish . . . . NiB $234   Ex $194   Gd $147
.32 H&R Magnum (disc.1992). . . NiB $270   Ex $204   Gd $142

BULLDOG PUG DA REVOLVER
Caliber: .44 Special. Five-round cylinder, 2.5 inch bbl., 7.25 inches overall.
Weight: 20 oz. Blued or stainless finish. Fixed ramp front sight, fixed square-
notch rear. Checkered Neoprene or walnut grips. Made from 1988 to 1993.
Blued finish . . . . NiB $262   Ex $224   Gd $183
Stainless finish . . . . NiB $224   Ex $172   Gd $121

BULLDOG TARGET DA REVOLVER
Calibers: .357 Magnum, .44 Special (latter intro. in 1977). Four-inch bbl.,
8.5 inches overall. Weight: 20.5 oz. in .357. Adj. rear sight, ramp front.
Blued finish. Square checkered walnut grips. Made 1976 to 1992.
Stainless steel . . . . NiB $271   Ex $203   Gd $147

BULLDOG TRACKER
DA REVOLVER . . . . NiB $207   Ex $134   Gd $102
Caliber: .357 Mag. Five-round cylinder, 2.5-, 4- or 6-inch bbl., 11 inches
overall (6-inch bbl.). Weight: 21 oz. (2.5-inch bbl.). Adj. rear sight, ramp
front. Checkered walnut grips. Blued finish. 4- or 6-inch bbl., Disc.1986.
Reintroduced 1989 to 1992.

EXPLORER II SEMIAUTO SURVIVAL PISTOL
Caliber: .22 LR, 8-round magazine, 6-, 8- or 10-inch bbl., 13.5 inches

Charter Arms Undercover
.32 S&W Long

Charter Arms
Undercover Stainless

overall (6-inch bbl.). Weight: 28 oz. finishes: Black, heat cured, semigloss textured enamel or silvertone anticorrosion. Disc. 1987.

Standard model . . . . NiB $158 Ex $100 Gd $66
Silvertone (w/optional
   6- or 10-inch bbl.). . . . . NiB $143 Ex $123 Gd $83

OFF-DUTY DA REVOLVER
Calibers: .22 LR or .38 Special. Six-round (.22 LR) or 5-round (.38 Special) cylinder. Two-inch bbl., 6.25 inches overall. Weight: 16 oz. Fixed rear sight, Partridge-type front sight. Plain walnut grips. Matte black, nickel or stainless steel finish. Made from 1992 to 1996.

Matte black finish . . . . NiB $185 Ex $153 Gd $112
Nickel finish. . . . . NiB $230 Ex $194 Gd $150
Stainless steel. . . . . NiB $260 Ex $194 Gd $128

PATHFINDER DA REVOLVER
Calibers: .22 LR, .22 WMR. Six-round cylinder, bbl. lengths: 2-, 3-, 6-inches, 7.13 inches overall (in 3-inch bbl.), and regular grips. Weight: 18.5 oz. (3-inch bbl.). Adj. rear sight, ramp front. Blued or stainless finish. Plain walnut regular, checkered Bulldog or square buttgrips. Made 1970 to date. Note: Originally designated "Pocket Target," name was changed in 1971 to "Pathfinder." Grips changed in 1984. Disc. 1990.

Blued finish . . . . NiB $203 Ex $148 Gd $112
Stainless finish . . . . NiB $240 Ex $192 Gd $128

PIT BULL DA REVOLVER
Calibers: 9mm, .357 Magnum, .38 Special. Five-round cylinder, 2.5-, 3.5- or 4-inch bbl., 7 inches overall (2.5-inch bbl.). Weight: 21.5 to 25 oz. All stainless steel frame. Fixed ramp front sight, fixed square-notch rear. Checkered Neoprene grips. Blued or stainless finish. Made from 1989 to 1991.

Blued finish . . . . NiB $261 Ex $223 Gd $137
Stainless finish . . . . NiB $270 Ex $ 230 Gd $143

UNDERCOVER DA REVOLVER
Caliber: .38 Special. Five-round cylinder,. bbl., lengths: 2-, 3-, 4-inches, 6.25 inches overall (2-inch bbl.), and regular grips. Weight: 16 oz. (2-inch bbl.). Fixed sights. Plain walnut, checkered Bulldog or square buttgrips. Made from 1965 to 1996.

Blued or nickel-plated finish. . . . NiB $216 Ex $120 Gd $101
Stainless finish . . . . NiB $281 Ex $230 Gd $148

UNDERCOVER DA REVOLVER
Same general specifications as standard Undercover except chambered for .32 H&R Magnum or .32 S&W Long, has 6-round cylinder and 2.5-inch bbl.

.32 H&R Magnum (blued) . . . . . . NiB $316 Ex $253 Gd $170
.32 H&R Magnum nickel . . . . . . NiB $212 Ex $171 Gd $109
.32 H&R Magnum (stainless) . . . . NiB $332 Ex $268 Gd $187
.32 S&W Long (blued) disc. 1989. . . NiB $303 Ex $225 Gd $179

UNDERCOVER POCKET POLICE DA REVOLVER
Same general specifications as standard Undercover except has 6-round cylinder and pocket-type hammer. Blued or stainless steel finish. Made from 1969 to 1981.

Blued finish . . . . NiB $342 Ex $283 Gd $ 214
Stainless steel. . . . . NiB $356 Ex $290 Gd $219

UNDERCOVER POLICE DA REVOLVER
Same general specifications as standard Undercover except has 6-round cylinder. Made from 1984 to 1989. Reintroduced 1993.

Blued, .38 Special . . . . NiB $337 Ex $ 279 Gd $204
Stainless, .38 Special . . . . NiB $270 Ex $204 Gd $158
.32 H&R Magnum. . . . . NiB $250 Ex $200 Gd $143

**Cimarron
El Pistolero**

UNDER-COVERETTE DA REVOLVER NiB $179 Ex $130 Gd $101
Same as Undercover except w/2-in. bbl., caliber .32 S&W Long, 6-round cylinder, blued finish only. Weight: 16.5 oz. Made 1972 to 1983.

CIMARRON F.A. CO. — Fredricksburg, Texas
Currently imports, distrbutes and retails black powder and cartridge firearms manufactured by Armi-Sport, Chiappa, Pedersoli, Pietta, and Uberti.

1872 OPEN-TOP SA REVOLVER NiB $510 Ex $345 Gd $270
Reproduction of Colt Navy and Army open-top conversion revolvers. Calibers: .38 Long Colt, .38 Spl., .44-40, .44 Spl., 44 Russian, .45 Schofield or .45 Long Colt. Six-round cylinder, 4.75- 5.5- or 7.5-inch bbl., brass backstrap and triggerguard, blued finish. Made from 1999 to date.

Silver plated backstrap (2010). . . NiB $550 Ex $385 Gd $310
Engraved, add $1000

BADLAND SA REVOLVER. . . . NiB $280 Ex $210 Gd $180
Calibers: .357 Mag., .45 Colt. 6-round cylinder, 4.75-in. bbl., brass backstrap and triggerguard, wood grip. Made from 2005 to 2007.

BADLAND SA REVOLVER. . . . NiB $400 Ex $315 Gd $200
Calibers: .44 Spl./.44 Mag. 6-round cylinder, 4.75-, 6- or 7.5-in. bbl., brass or steel backstrap and triggerguard, wood grip. Made from 1984 to 1993.

Buntline. . . . . NiB $415 Ex $330 Gd $220

EL PISTOLERO SA REVOLVER. NiB $444 Ex $336 Gd $260
Calibers: .357 Mag., .45 Colt. Six-round cylinder, 4.75- 5.5- or 7.5-inch bbl., polished brass backstrap and triggerguard. Otherwise, same as Colt Single-Action Army revolver w/parts being interchangeable. Made from 1997 to 1998; reitro. 2007 to 2013.

FRONTIER SIX SHOOTER. . . . NiB $730 Ex $580 Gd $450
Calibers: .22 LR, .22 Mag., .38 Spl./.357 Mag., .38-40, .44 Spl., .44-40 or .45 Long Colt. 6-round cylinder, 4.75-, 5.5- or 7.5-in. bbl., steel backstrap. Oringila Colt-like finish. Made from 2008 to 2010.

Sheriff's model (3- or 4-in. bbl.) . NiB $400 Ex $300 Gd $220
Target model (adj. rear sight) . . . NiB $360 Ex $270 Gd $200

COLT'S MANUFACTURING CO., INC. — Hartford, Connecticut

Previously Colt Industries, Firearms Division. Production of some Colt handguns spans the period before World War II to the postwar years. Values shown for these models are for earlier production. Those manufactured c. 1946 and later generally are less desirable to collectors and values are approximately 30 percent lower.

Colt
Model 1902 Military

Colt
1903 Early Hammer

Colt
Model 1903 Pocket
Hammerless

NOTE: *For ease in finding a particular firearm, Colt handguns are grouped into three sections: Automatic Pistols, Single-Shot Pistols & Derringers, and Revolvers. For a complete listing, please refer to the Index.*

- AUTOMATIC PISTOLS -

MODEL 1900 .38 AUTOMATIC PISTOL
Caliber: .38 ACP (modern high-velocity cartridges should not be used in this pistol). Seven-round magazine, 6-inch bbl., 9 inches overall. Weight: 35 oz. Fixed sights. Blued finish. Hard rubber and plain or checkered walnut grips. Sharp-spur hammer. Combination rear sight and safety unique to the Model 1900 (early production). In mid-1901 a solid rear sight was dovetailed into the slide. (S/N range 1-4274) Made 190003. Note: 250 models were sold to the military (50 Navy and 200 Army).
Early commercial model
  (w/sight/safety) . . . . NiB $15,810 Ex $14,586 Gd $11,220
Late commercial model
  (w/dovetailed sight) . . NiB $15,810 Ex $14,586 Gd $11,220
Army Model w/U.S. inspector marks (1st Series - S/N 90-150
  w/inspector mark J.T.T). NiB $32,130 Ex $27,540 Gd $22,185
  (2nd Series - S/N 1600-1750

w/inspector mark R.A.C.) . . NiB $11,577 Ex $9736 Gd $6700
Navy model (Also marked
  w/USN-I.D. number). . . NiB $18,967 Ex $13,107 Gd $10,200

MODEL 1902 MILITARY .38 AUTOMATIC PISTOL
Caliber: .38 ACP (modern high-velocity cartridges should not be used in this pistol). Eight-round magazine, 6-inch bbl., 9 inches over-all. Weight: 37 oz. Fixed sights w/blade front and V-notch rear. Blued finish. Checkered hard rubber grips. Round back hammer, changed to spur type in 1908. No safety but fitted w/standard military swivel. About 18,000 produced with split S/N ranges. The government contract series (15,001-15,200) and the commercial sales series (15,000 receding to 11,000) and (30,200-47,266). Made from 1902 to 1929.
Early military model (w/front
  slide serrations) . . . . .NiB $6,120 Ex $3871 Gd $3528
Late military model (w/rear
  slide serrations) . . . . NiB $6115 Ex $3732 Gd $2525
MARKED "U.S. ARMY"
  (S/N 15,001-15,200). . . NiB $19,635 Ex $17,340 Gd $15,402

MODEL 1902 SPORTING
.38 AUTOMATIC PISTOL . NiB $5008 Ex $3213 Gd $2443
Caliber: .38 ACP (modern high-velocity cartridges should not be used in this pistol). Seven-round magazine, 6-inch bbl., 9 inches overall. Weight: 35 oz. Fixed sights w/blade front and V-notch rear. Blued finish. Checkered hard rubber grips. Round back hammer was standard but some spur hammers were installed during late production. No safety and w/o swivel as found on military model. Total production about 7,500 w/split S/N ranges (4275-10,999) and (30,000-30,190) Made from 1902 to 1908.

MODEL 1903 POCKET .32 AUTOMATIC PISTOL
FIRST ISSUE - COMMERCIAL SERIES
Caliber: .32 Auto. Eight-round magazine, 4-inch bbl., 7 inches overall. Weight: 23 oz. Fixed sights. Blued or nickel finish. Checkered hard rubber grips. Hammerless (concealed hammer). Slide lock and grip safeties. Fitted w/barrel bushing but early models have no magazine safety. Total production of the Model 1903 reached 572,215. The First Issue maded from 1903 to 1908 (S/N range 1-72,000).
Blued finish . . . . NiB $1132 Ex $806 Gd $587
Nickel finish. . . . . NiB $1153 Ex $826 Gd $602

MODEL 1903 POCKET .32 AUTOMATIC PISTOL
SECOND ISSUE - COMMERCIAL SERIES
Same as First Issue but with 3.75-inch bbl. and small Extractor. Made from 1908 to 1910 (S/N range 72,001 -105,050).
Blued finish . . . . NiB $816 Ex $602 Gd $474
Nickel finish. . . . . NiB $842 Ex $689 Gd $498

MODEL 1903 POCKET .32 AUTOMATIC PISTOL,
THIRD ISSUE - COMMERCIAL SERIES
Caliber: .32 Auto. Similar to Second Issue w/3.75-inch bbl. except with integral barrel bushing and locking lug at muzzle end of bbl. Production occurred 1910 to 1926 (S/N range 105,051-468,096).
Blued finish . . . . NiB $1326 Ex $1030 Gd $813
Nickel finish. . . . . NiB $1474 Ex $1234 Gd $918

MODEL 1903 POCKET .32 AUTOMATIC PISTOL
FOURTH ISSUE - COMMERCIAL SERIES
Caliber: .32 Auto. Similar to Third Issue except a slide lock safety change was made when a Tansley-style disconnector was added on all pistols above S/N 468,097, which prevents firing of cartridge in chamber when the magazine is removed. Blued or nickel finish. Checkered walnut grips. These design changes were initiated 1926 to 1945 (S/N range 105,051-554,446).

Blued finish . . . . NiB $1331   Ex $1020   Gd $804
Nickel finish. . . . . NiB $1535   Ex $1132   Gd $945

MODEL 1903 POCKET (HAMMER) .38 AUTOMATIC PISTOL
Caliber: .38 ACP (modern high-velocity cartridges should not be used in this pistol). Similar to Model 1902 Sporting .38 but w/shorter frame, slide and 4.5-inch bbl. Overall dimension reduced to 7.5 inches. Weight: 31 oz. Fixed sights w/blade front and V-notch rear. Blued finish. Checkered hard rubber grips. Round back hammer, changed to spur type in 1908. No safety. (S/N range 16,001-47,226 with some numbers above 30,200 assigned to 1902 Military). Made from 1903 to 1929.
Early model
  (round hammer) . . . . NiB $2030   Ex $1713   Gd $1418
Late model
  (spur hammer) . . . . NiB $2254   Ex $1953   Gd $1641

MODEL 1903 POCKET HAMMERLESS (CONCEALED HAMMER) .32 AUTOMATIC PISTOL - MILITARY
Caliber: .32 ACP. Eight-round magazine, Similar to Model 1903 Pocket .32 except concealed hammer and equipped w/magazine safety. Parkerized or blued finish. (S/N range with "M" prefix M1-M200,000) Made from 1941 to 1945.
Blued service model (marked
  "U.S. Property") . . . . NiB $1333   Ex $1179   Gd $852
Parkerized service model (marked
  "U.S. Property") . . . . NiB $2162   Ex $1821   Gd $1520
Blued documented
  Officer's model . . . . NiB $3182   Ex $2880   Gd $1760
Parkerized documented
  Officer's model . . . . NiB $3182   Ex $2880   Gd $1760

MODEL 1905 .45 AUTOMATIC PISTOL
Caliber: .45 (Rimless) Automatic. Seven-round magazine, 5-inch bbl., 8 inches overall. Weight: 32.5 oz. Fixed sights w/blade front and V-notch rear. Blued finish. Checkered walnut, hard rubber or pearl grips. Predecessor to Model 1911 Auto Pistol and contributory to the development of the .45 ACP cartridge. (S/N range 1-6100) Made from 1905 to 1911.
Commercial model . . . . NiB $7461   Ex $5579   Gd $3784
w/slotted backstrap
  (500 produced) . . . . .NiB $10,761   Ex $8966   Gd $7359
w/shoulder stock/holster, add . . . . $7650 to $10,200

MODEL 1905 .45 (1907)
CONTRACT PISTOL   NiB $22,440   Ex $17,340   Gd $10,200
Variation of the Model 1905 produced to U.S. Military specifications, including loaded chamber indicator, grip safety and lanyard loop. Only 201 were produced, but 200 were delivered and may be identified by the chief inspector's initials "K.M." (S/N range 1-201) Made from 1907 to 1908.

MODEL 1908 POCKET .25 HAMMERLESS AUTO PISTOL
Caliber: .25 Auto. Six-round magazine, 2-inch bbl., 4.5 inches overall. Weight: 13 oz. Flat-top front, square-notch rear sight in groove. Blued, nickel or Parkerized finish. Checkered hard rubber grips on early models, checkered walnut on later type, special pearl grips illustrated. Both a grip safety and slide lock safety are included on all models. The Tansley-style safety disconnector was added in 1916 at pistol No. 141000. (S/N range 1-409,061) Made 1908 to 1941.
Blued finish . . . . NiB $1734   Ex $1415   Gd $1137
Nickel finish, add. $125
Marked "U.S. Property"
  (w/blued finish) . . . . NiB $3213   Ex $2861   Gd $2560

MODEL 1908 POCKET .380 AUTOMATIC PISTOL
Similar to Pocket .32 Auto w/3.75-inch bbl. except chambered for .380 Auto w/seven-round magazine. Weight: 23 oz. Blue, nickel or Parkerized finish. (S/N range 1-138,009) Made from 1908 to 1945.

Colt
Model 1905 Military

Colt
Model 1908 Pocket 25

Colt
Model 1911

Colt
1991 A1

Colt Cadet .22

**Colt All American
Model 2000**

First Issue (made 1908-11, w/bbl., lock and bushing,
w/S/N 1-6,250). . . . . .NiB $1734 Ex $1528 Gd $1312
Second Issue (made 1911-28,w/o bbl., lock and bushing,
w/S/N 6,251-92,893). . . . . NiB $2017 Ex $1693 Gd $1528
Third Issue (made 1928-45, w/safety disconnector,
w/S/N 92,894-138,009) . . . NiB $1734 Ex $1528 Gd $1312
Parkerized service model (Marked "U.S. Property" made
1942-45, w/S/N "M" prefix.). NiB $2649 Ex $1972 Gd $1723
Documented officer's model (service model w/military
assignment papers) . . . . . . NiB $3162 Ex $2557 Gd $1804

NOTE: *During both World Wars, Colt licensed other firms to make
these pistols under government contract, including Ithaca Gun Co.,
North American Arms Co., Ltd. (Canada), Remington-Rand Co.,
Remington-UMC, Singer Sewing Machine Co., and Union Switch &
Signal Co. M1911 also produced at Springfield Armory.*

MODEL 1911 AUTOMATIC PISTOL
Caliber: .45 Auto. Seven-round magazine, 5-inch bbl., 8.5 inches overall.
Weight: 39 oz. Fixed sights. Blued finish on Commercial model. Parkerized
or similar finish on most military pistols. Checkered walnut grips (early
production), plastic grips (later production). Checkered, arched mainspring
housing and longer grip safety spur adopted in 1923 (on M1911A1).
Model 1911
 commercial (C-series) NiB $15,300 Ex $13,255 Gd $11,424
Model 1911A1 commercial
 (Pre-WWII) . . . . NiB $3886 Ex $3172 Gd $2240

U.S. GOVERNMENT MODEL 1911
Colt manufacture . . . . NiB $10,353 Ex $8975 Gd $6849
North American Arms Co.
 manufacture . . . . NiB $36,720 Ex $29,580 Gd $24,990
Remington-UMC manufacture . . .NiB $6120 Ex $4070 Gd $2458
Springfield manufacture . . . . NiB $6120 Ex $4070 Gd $2458
Navy Model M1911 type . . . NiB $8771 Ex $6654 Gd $4995

U.S. GOVERNMENT MODEL 1911A1
Singer manufacture. . . . NiB $45,900 Ex $39,015 Gd $25,455
Colt, Ithaca, Remington-
 Rand manufacture . . . . . . NiB $2647 Ex $2254 Gd $1902
Union Switch &
 Signal manufacture. . . . . . . .NiB $6727 Ex $6847 Gd $6047

M1911 SERIES 70 WWI MODEL 1918
REPRODUCTION . . . . NiB $1500 EX $950 GD $700
Reproduction of Model 1911 (see above) w/black finish, original WWI
rollmarks. Made from 2008 to 2009.

M1911 MODEL O SERIES 70
REPRODUCTION . . . . NiB $1500 EX $950 GD $700
Reproduction of Model 1911 (see above) w/original 1911 U.S. Military
rollmarks, carbonia blue finish. Made from 2003 to 2009.

M1911A1 MODEL O SERIES 70 WWII
REPRODUCTION . . . . NiB $1300 EX $850 GD $680
Reproduction of Model 1911A1 (see above) w/pakerized finish, original
WWII rollmarks. Made from 2001 to 2004.

1991 SERIES GOVERNEMNT MODEL SERIES 70 MODEL O
Reissue of Series 70 action. Caliber: .38 Super, .45 ACP. Seven-round
magazine, 5-inch bbl., 8.5 inches overall. Weight: 39 oz. Fixed blade
front sight, square notch rear. Blued or stainless finish. Made from 2003
to date.
Blued. . . . . .NiB $1080 Ex 900 Gd $600
Stainless. .NiB $1120 Ex $940 Gd $650
.38 Super (stainless) . . . . .NiB $800 Ex $700 Gd $600
.38 Super (bright stainless) . . . . .NiB $1200 Ex $900 Gd $600

1991 SERIES GOVERNMENT MODEL SERIES 80 MODEL O
Similar to Series 80 model except w/9mm or .45 ACP. Seven-round
magazine, 5-inch bbl., 8.5 inches overall. Weight: 39 oz. Fixed sights.
Rollmarked "Colt M1991A1" on slide. Blued, stainless or parkerized fin-
ish. Made from 1991 to date.
Blued. . . . . .NiB $975 Ex $600 Gd $300
Parkerized . . . . .NiB $975 Ex $600 Gd $300
Stainless. .NiB $1040 Ex $750 Gd $380
Commander model. . . . . .NiB $995 Ex $560 Gd $380
Officer's Compact model . . . . .NiB $620 Ex $430 Gd $380

.22 CADET AUTOMATIC PISTOL NiB $479 Ex $343 Gd $270
Caliber: 22 LR. 10-round magazine, 4.5-inch vent rib bbl., 8.63 inches
overall. Weight: 33.5 oz. Blade front sight, dovetailed rear. Stainless
finish. TExtured black polymer grips w/Colt medallion. Made 1993
to 1995. Note: The Cadet Model name was disc. under litigation but
the manufacturer continued to produce this pistol configuration as the
Model "Colt 22". For this reason the "Cadet" model will command slight
premiums.

.22 SPORT AUTOMATIC PISTOL NiB $485 Ex $345 Gd $270
Same specifications as Cadet Model except renamed Colt .22 w/composi-
tion monogrip or wraparound black rubber grip. Made 1994 to 1998.

.22 TARGET PISTOL . . . . NiB $464 Ex $321 Gd $204
Similar to Colt 22 Sport Model except w/6-inch vent rib bbl., 10.12 inches
overall. Weight: 40.5 oz. Partridge style front sight, adjustable white outline rear on full length grooved rib. Made from 1995 to 1999.

ACE AUTOMATIC PISTOL
Caliber: .22 LR (regular or high speed). 10-round magazine. Built on the
same frame as the Government Model .45 Auto w/same safety features,
etc. Hand-honed action, target bbl., adj. rear sight. 4.75-inch bbl., 8.25.
inches overall. Weight: 38 oz. Made 1930 to 1940.

Commercial model . . . . **NiB $4650 Ex $3783 Gd $3264**
Service model (1938-42). . . . **NiB $7710 Ex $5498 Gd $4769**
Post-War model (1978-89) . . . **NiB $1500 Ex $1000 Gd $800**

ALL AMERICAN
MODEL 2000 DA PISTOL . . . . NiB $785 Ex $566 Gd $408
Hammerless semiautomatic w/blued slide and polymer or alloy receiver fitted w/roller-bearing trigger. Caliber: 9mm Para. 15-round magazine, 4.5-inch bbl., 7.5 inches overall. Weight: 29 oz. (Polymer) or 33 oz (Alloy). Fixed blade front sight, square-notch rear w/3-dot system. Matte blued slide w/black polymer or anodized aluminum receiver. Made from 1992 to 1994.

AUTOMATIC .25 PISTOL
As a result of the 1968 Firearms Act restricting the importation of the Colt Pocket Junior that was produced in Spain, Firearms International was contracted by Colt to manufacture a similar blowback action with the same Exposed hammer configuration. Both the U.S. and Spanish-made .25 automatics were recalled to correct an action malfunction. Returned firearms were fitted with a rebounding firing pin to prevent accidental discharges. Caliber: .25 ACP. Six-round magazine, 2.25-inch bbl., 4.5 inches overall. Weight: 12.5 oz. Integral blade front, square-notch rear sight groove. Blued finish. Checkered wood grips w/Colt medallion. Made from 1970 to 1975.
Model as issued . . . . NiB $386 Ex $316 Gd $198
Model recalled
& refitted . . . . NiB $386 Ex $316 Gd $198

CHALLENGER
AUTOMATIC PISTOL . . . . . . NiB $734 Ex $478 Gd $282
Same basic design as Woodsman Target, Third Issue but lacks some of the refinements. Fixed sights. Magazine catch on butt as in old Woodsman. Does not stay open on last shot. Lacks magazine safety. 4.5- or 6-inch bbl., 9 to 10.5 inches overall. Weight: 30 oz. (4.5-inch bbl.) or 31.5 oz. (6-inch bbl.) Blued finish. Checkered plastic grips. Made from 1950 to 1955.

COMMANDER (pre-Series 70) AUTOMATIC PISTOL
Same basic design as Government Model except w/shorter 4.25-inch bbl., and a special lightweight "Coltalloy" receiver and mainspring housing. Calibers: .45 Auto, .38 Super Auto, 9mm Para. Seven-round magazine (.45 cal.), nine-round (.38 Auto and 9mm), 8 inches overall. Weight: 26.5 oz. Fixed sights. Round spur hammer. Improved safety lock. Blued finish. Checkered plastic or walnut grips. Made from 1950 to 1969.
9mm Para. . . . . NiB $1350 Ex $1000 Gd $700
.38 Super, .45 ACP . . . . NiB $1450 Ex $1150 Gd $900

SERIES 70 COMBAT COMMANDER AUTOMATIC PISTOL
Similar to Lightweight Commander except w/steel frame, blued or nickel-plated finish. Made from 1971 to 1980.
9mm Para. . . . . NiB $736 Ex $590 Gd $444
.38 Super, .45 ACP . . . . NiB $852 Ex $691 Gd $486

SERIES 70 LIGHTWEIGHT COMMANDER AUTOMATIC PISTOL
Same as Commander except w/blued or nickel-plated finish. Made from 1970 to 1983.
9mm Para. . . . . NiB $1350 Ex $1000 Gd $700
.38 Super, .45 ACP . . . . NiB $1150 Ex $870 Gd $620

CONVERSION
UNIT—.22-.45 . . . . NiB $306 Ex $255 Gd $179
Converts Service Ace .22 to National Match .45 Auto. Unit consists of match-grade slide assembly and bbl., bushing, recoil spring, recoil

**Colt
National Match**

**Colt MK II/Series 90
Double Eagle**

spring guide and plug, magazine and slide stop. Made from 1938 to 1942.

CONVERSION
UNIT — .45-.22 . . . . NiB $617 Ex $489 Gd $362
Converts Government Model .45 Auto to a .22 LR target pistol. Unit consists of slide assembly, bbl., floating chamber (as in Service Ace), bushing, ejector, recoil spring, recoil spring guide and plug, magazine and slide stop. The component parts differ and are not interchangable between post war, series 70, series 80, ACE I and ACE II units. Made from 1938 to 1984.

DEFENDER . . . . NiB $1100 Ex $700 Gd $480
Caliber: 9mm, .40 S&W or .45 ACP. 3-inch bbl. 7-round magazine, Three-dot, sights. rubber finger-groove wrap around grips. Matte stainless finish. Made from 1998 to date.
Defender Plus (2002-03) . . . . . NiB $880 Ex $660 Gd $5801

DELTA ELITE SEMIAUTO PISTOL
Caliber: 10mm. Five-inch bbl., 8.5 inches overall. Eight-round magazine, Weight: 38 oz. Checkered Neoprene combat grips w/Delta medallion. Three-dot, high-profile front and rear combat sights. Blued or stainless finish. Made from 1987 to 1996.
First Edition
(500 Ltd. edition) . . . . NiB $975 Ex $784 Gd $551

**Colt MK IV/
Series 80 .380**

**Colt Series 70 Combat
Commander**

**Colt MK IV/Series 80
Gold Cup National
Match**

**Colt MK IV/Series 80
Government Model**

Blued finish . . . . NiB $923   Ex $626   Gd $468
Matte stainless finish . . . . NiB $975   Ex $784   Gd $551
Ultra bright stainless finish, add $100

DELTA ELITE (CURRENT MFG.)
SEMIAUTOMATIC PISTOL . . . . . NiB $1115   Ex $830   Gd $520
Updated model similar to earlier Delta Elite except stainless finish only.
Made from 2008 to date.

DELTA GOLD CUP SEMIAUTO PISTOL
Same general specifications as Delta Elite except w/Accro adjustable rear
sight. Made 1989 to 1993; 1995 to 1996.
Blued finish (disc. 1991) . . . . . . NiB $997   Ex $693   Gd $474
Stainless steel finish . . . . NiB $1076   Ex $792   Gd $576

GOLD CUP TROPHY NATIONAL
MATCH .45 AUTO . . . . NiB $1250   Ex $900   Gd $640
Similar to MK IV Series 80 Gold Cup National Match except w/aluminum
trigger, Bo-Mar raer adj. sight, black checkered rubber wrap around grips, 7
or 8-round magazine. Weight: 39 oz. Made 1997 to 2010.

GOLD CUP NATIONAL MATCH . . NiB $1220   Ex $880   Gd $700
Similar to Gold Cup Trophy National Match. Made 2010 to date.
Stainless steel finish . . . . NiB $1240   Ex $750   Gd $530

GOVERNMENT MODEL 1911/1911A1
See Colt Model 1911.

HUNTSMAN . . . . NiB $683   Ex $453   Gd $348
Same specifications as the Challenger. Made from 1955 to 1976.

MK I & II/SERIES 90 DOUBLE EAGLE
COMBAT COMMANDER . . . NiB $2080   Ex $1832   Gd $1433
SA/DA trigger. Calibers: .40 S&W, .45 ACP. Seven-round magazine, 4.25-
inch bbl., 7.75 inches overall. Weight: 36 oz. Fixed blade front sight, square-
notch rear. Checkered Xenoy grips. Stainless finish. Made from 1992 to 1996.

MK II/SERIES 90 DOUBLE EAGLE SEMIAUTO PISTOL
SA/DA trigger. Calibers: .38 Super, 9mm, .40 S&W, 10mm, .45 ACP.
Seven-round magazine. Five-inch bbl., 8.5 inches overall. Weight: 39
oz. Fixed or Accro adj. sights. Matte stainless finish. Checkered Xenoy
grips. Made from 1991 to 1996.
.38 Super, 9mm,
.40 S&W (fixed sights) . . . . NiB $760   Ex $581   Gd $425
.45 ACP (adjustable sights) . . . . . NiB $729   Ex $577   Gd $428
.45 ACP (fixed sights) . . . . NiB $714   Ex $546   Gd $407
10mm (adjustable sights) . . . . . . NiB $729   Ex $576   Gd $434
10mm (fixed sights) . . . . NiB $714   Ex $550   Gd $407

MK II/SERIES 90 DOUBLE EAGLE
OFFICER'S ACP . . . . NiB $2141   Ex $1641   Gd $1448
Same general specifications as Double Eagle Combat Commander
except chambered for .45 ACP only, 3.5-inch bbl., 7.25 inches overall.
Weight: 35 oz. Also available in lightweight (25 oz.) w/blued finish
(same price). Made from 1990 to 1993.

MK II/MK III NATIONAL MATCH
MID-RANGE . . . . NiB $1241   Ex $1020   Gd $704
Similar to Gold Cup National Match .45 Auto except chambered for .38
Special Mid Range. Five-round magazine, Made 1961 to 1974.

MK IV/SERIES 70 COMBAT COMMANDER
Same general specifications as the Lightweight Commander except
made from 1970 to 1983.
Blued finish . . . . NiB $1020   Ex $903   Gd $750
Nickel finish. . . . . NiB $1193   Ex $974   Gd $815

MK IV/SERIES 70 GOLD CUP
NATIONAL MATCH . . . . NiB $1743 Ex $1356 Gd $1153
Match version of MK IV/Series '70 Government Model. Caliber: .45 Auto only. Flat mainspring housing. Accurizor bbl., and bushing. Solid rib, Colt-Elliason adj. rear sight undercut front sight. Adj. trigger, target hammer. 8.75 inches overall. Weight: 38.5 oz. Blued finish. Checkered walnut grips. Made from 1970 to 1984.

MK IV/SERIES 70 GOVERNMENT
AUTO PISTOL . . . . NiB $1120 Ex $815 Gd $570
Calibers: .45 Auto, .38 Super Auto, 9mm Para. Seven-round magazine in .45, 9-round in .38 and 9mm. Five-inch bbl., 8.38 inches overall. Weight: 38 oz., (.45); 39 oz. in .38 and 9mm. Fixed rear sight and ramp front sight. Blued or nickel-plated finish. Checkered walnut grips. Made from 1970 to 1984.

MK IV/SERIES 80 .380 GOVERNMENT AUTOMATIC PISTOL
Caliber: .380 ACP, 3.29-inch bbl., 6.15 inches overall. Weight: 21.8 oz. Composition grips. Fixed sights. Made since 1983 to 1996.
Blued finish (disc.1997) . . . . . . NiB $1132 Ex $918 Gd $712
Bright nickel (disc.1995). . . . . . NiB $1181 Ex $974 Gd $729
Satin nickel Coltguard (disc.1989)NiB $1219 Ex $1016 Gd $751
Stainless finish . . . . NiB $1173 Ex $974 Gd $755

MK IV/SERIES 80 COMBAT COMMANDER
Simialr specifications as MK IV/Series 80 Governemnt except w/ steel frame, 4.25-in. bbl. Made 1983 to 1993.
Blued finish (disc.1996) . . . . . .NiB $950 Ex $620 Gd $470
Satin nickel (disc.1987) . . . . . . NiB $975 Ex $650 Gd $580
Stainless finish (disc.1998) . . . . NiB $860 Ex $570 Gd $450
Two-tone finish (disc.1998). . . . NiB $810 Ex $600 Gd $450
Gold Cup (disc.1993) . . . . NiB $1200 Ex $930 Gd $830

MK IV/SERIES 80 COMBAT
GOVERNMENT . . . . NiB $960 EX $670 GD $480
Same general specifications as MK IV/Series 80 Government except w/ matte black finish. Calibers: .45 ACP. Made from 1983 to 1998.
Combat Elite (.38 Super). . . . . . NiB $980 Ex $700 Gd $600
Combat Target (adj. sights) . . . . . NiB $770 Ex $530 Gd $460

MK IV/SERIES 80 GOLD CUP NATIONAL MATCH
Same general specifications as Match Series 70 except w/additional finishes and "pebbled" wraparound Neoprene grips. Made from 1983 to 1996.
Blued finish . . . . NiB $1071 Ex $714 Gd $490
Bright blued finish . . . . .NiB $1071 Ex $714 Gd $490
Stainless finish . . . . NiB $1148 Ex $867 Gd $638

MK IV/SERIES 80 GOVERNMENT MODEL
Similar specifications as Government Model Series 70 except w/firing pin safety feature. Made 1983 to 1997.
Blued finish . . . . NiB $1117 Ex $755 Gd $520
Nickel finish. . . . . NiB $1150 Ex $800 Gd $570
Stain nickel/blue finish . . . . NiB $1150 Ex $800 Gd $570
Matte stainless finish . . . . NiB $1100 Ex $730 Gd $490
Bright stainless finish . . . . NiB $1410 Ex $1010 Gd $580

MK IV/SERIES 80 LIGHT-
WEIGHT COMMANDER . . . . . . NiB $1071 Ex $714 Gd $490
Updated version of the MK IV/Series 70 w/same general specifications.

MK IV/SERIES 80
MUSTANG .380 AUTOMATIC
Caliber: .380 ACP. Five- or 6-round magazine, 2.75-inch bbl., 5.5 inches overall. Weight: 18.5 oz. Blued, nickel or stainless finish. Black composition grips. Made from 1983 to 1998.

Colt MK IV/Series
80 Mustang Plus II

Colt MK IV/
Series 80 Mustang
Pocketlite

Colt MK IV/Series
80 Officer's ACP

Blued finish . . . . NiB $638 Ex $437 Gd $296
Nickel finish
(disc.1994). . . . . NiB $770 Ex $479 Gd $308
Satin nickel
Coltguard (disc.1988). . . . . NiB $740 Ex $474 Gd $306
Stainless finish . . . . NiB $709 Ex $397 Gd $306

Colt Pocket Junior

Colt Super Match .38

Colt Targetsman

Colt Woodsman Match Target First Issue

MK IV/SERIES 80 MUSTANG POCKETLITE
Same general specifications as the Mustang 30 except weight: 12.5 oz. w/aluminum alloy receiver. Blued, chrome or stainless finish. Optional wood grain grips. Made since 1987.

Blued finish . . . . NiB $683   Ex $405   Gd $305
Lady Elite
  (two-tone) finish . . . . NiB $683   Ex $405   Gd $305
Stainless finish . . . . NiB $683   Ex $405   Gd $305
Teflon/stainless finish . . . . NiB $683   Ex $405   Gd $305

MK IV/SERIES 80 OFFICER'S ACP AUTOMATIC PISTOL
Caliber: .45 ACP, 3.63-inch bbl., 7.25 inches overall. 6-round magazine. Weight: 34 oz. Made from 1984 to 1998.

Blued finish (disc.1996) . . . . NiB $605   Ex $500   Gd $357
Matte finish (disc.1991) . . . . NiB $581   Ex $474   Gd $349
Satin nickel finish (disc.1985) . . . NiB $669   Ex $544   Gd $378
Stainless steel (disc.1997) . . . . . . NiB $630   Ex $514   Gd $367
Lightweight (disc.1997) . . . . NiB $900   Ex $710   Gd $520
Conceal Carry (disc.1998) . . . . . . NiB $900   Ex $710   Gd $520
General's Officer (disc.1996) . NiB $1350   Ex $1040   Gd $680

MK IV/SERIES 80
SA LIGHTWEIGHT CONCEALED
CARRY OFFICER . . . . NiB $741   Ex $581   Gd $415
Caliber: .45 ACP. Seven-round magazine, 4.25-inch bbl., 7.75 inches over-all. Weight: 35 oz. Aluminum alloy receiver w/stainless slide. Dovetailed low-profile sights w/3-dot system. Matte stainless finish w/blued receiver. Wraparound black rubber grip w/finger grooves. Made in 2000.

MK IV/SERIES 80 SPECIAL COMBAT GOVERNMENT AUTOMATIC
PISTOL . . . . NiB $2100   Ex $1450   Gd $800
Calibers: .38 Super or .45 ACP, 5-inch bbl., custom tuned for competition. Blued, hard crome or two-tone finsh. Made from 1992 to date.
Carry (1992-00, reintro. 1996) . . NiB $2095   Ex $1450   Gd $800
CMC Marine Pistol . . . . NiB $2160   Ex $1200   Gd $820

MK IV/SERIES 90 DEFENDER
SA LIGHTWEIGHT . . . . NiB $918   Ex $576   Gd $398
Caliber: .45 ACP. Seven-round magazine, 3-inch bbl., 6.75 inches over-all. Weight: 22.5 oz. Aluminum alloy receiver w/stainless slide. Dovetailed low-profile sights w/3-dot system. Matte stainless finish w/Nickel-Teflon receiver. Wraparound black rubber grip w/finger grooves. Made since 1998.

MK IV/SERIES 90
PONY DAO PISTOL . . . . NiB $772   Ex $567   Gd $396
Caliber: .380 ACP. Six-round magazine, 2.75-inch bbl., 5.5 inches over-all. Weight: 19 oz. Ramp front sight, dovetailed rear. Stainless finish. Checkered black composition grips. Made 1997 to 1998.

MK IV/SERIES 90
PONY POCKETLITE . . . . NiB $794   Ex $577   Gd $396
Similar to standard weight Pony Model except w/aluminum frame. Brushed stainless and Teflon finish. Made from 1997 to 1999.

NATIONAL MATCH (PRE-WWWII)
Identical to the Government Model .45 Auto but w/hand-honed action, match-grade bbl., adj. rear and ramp front sights or fixed sights. Made from 1932 to 1940.
w/adjustable sights . . . . NiB $10,000   Ex $8000   Gd $4300
w/fixed sights . . . . NiB $8500   Ex $7000   Gd $4000

NATIONAL MATCH (WWII & POST-WWII)
AUTOMATIC PISTOL . . . . NiB $2500   Ex $1600   Gd $900
Similar to Pre-WWII National Match except in .45 Auto only. Made from 1957 to 1970.

MK IV/SERIES 80 MUSTANG PLUS II
Caliber: .380 ACP, 7-round magazine, 2.75-inch bbl., 5.5 inches over-all. Weight: 20 oz. Blued or stainless finish w/checkered black composition grips. Made from 1988 to 1996.
Blued finish . . . . NiB $693   Ex $407   Gd $302
Stainless finish . . . . NiB $693   Ex $407   Gd $302

GRADING: **NiB** = New in Box   **Ex** = Excellent or NRA 95%   **Gd** = Good or NRA 68%

NEW AGENT . . . . NIB $1080 EX $800 GD $500
Series 80 system. Similar to Defender except in 9mm or .45 ACP w/ trench style sights, hammerless. Made from 2008 to date.

**NRA CENTENNIAL .45 GOLD CUP
NATIONAL MATCH**   NiB $1321 Ex $1024 Gd $841
Only 2500 produced in 1971.

**POCKET JUNIOR MODEL
AUTOMATIC PISTOL** . . . . .NiB $464 Ex $344 Gd $260
Made in Spain by Unceta y Cia (Astra). Calibers: .22 Short, .25 Auto. Six-round magazine, 2.25 inch bbl., 4.75 inches overall. Weight: 12 oz. Fixed sights. Checkered walnut grips. Note: In 1980, this model was subject to recall to correct an action malfunction. Returned firearms were fitted with a rebounding firing pin to prevent accidental discharges. Made from 1958 to 1968.

SUPER .38 AUTOMATIC PISTOL
Identical to Government Model .45 Auto except for caliber and magazine capacity. Caliber: .38 Automatic. Nine-round magazine, Made from 1928 to 1970.
Pre-war . . . . NiB $6125 Ex $4429 Gd $3010
Post-war. . . . . NiB $2709 Ex $2199 Gd $2008

SUPER MATCH .38 AUTOMATIC PISTOL
Identical to Super .38 Auto but w/hand-honed action, match grade bbl., adjustable rear sight and ramp front sight or fixed sights. Made from 1933 to 1946.
w/adjustable sights . . . . NiB $11,595 Ex $6125 Gd $3162
w/fixed sights . . . . NiB $10,125 Ex $5125 Gd $2125

TARGETSMAN . . . . NiB $831   Ex $668   Gd $357
Similar to Woodsman Target but has "economy" adj. rear sight, lacks automatic slide stop. Made from 1959 to 1976.

USMC M45 CQBP . . . . NIB $1995 EX $1500 GD $1000
Caliber: .45 ACP. Same general specifications as MK IV/Series 80 Rail Gun except w/Cerakote desert tan finish, stainless barrel, G10 grips. Made from 2013 to date.

**WOODSMAN MATCH TARGET AUTOMATIC PISTOL
FIRST ISSUE** . . . . .NiB $3356 Ex $1947 Gd $1039
Same basic design as other Woodsman models. Caliber: .22 LR. 10-round magazine, 6.5-inch bbl., slightly tapered w/flat sides, 11 inches overall. Weight: 36 oz. Adjustable rear sight. Blued finish. Checkered walnut one-piece grip w/Extended sides. Made from 1938 to 1942.

**WOODSMAN MATCH TARGET AUTO PISTOL,
SECOND ISSUE** . . . . NiB $1029 Ex $765 Gd $632
Same basic design as Woodsman Target Third Issue. Caliber: .22 LR (reg. or high speed). 10-round magazine, Six-inch flat-sided heavy bbl., 10.5 inches overall. Weight: 40 oz. Click adj. rear sight, ramp front. Blued finish. Checkered plastic or walnut grips. Made from 1948 to 1976.

**WOODSMAN MATCH TARGET "4 1/2"
AUTOMATIC PISTOL** . . . . .NiB $714 Ex $453 Gd $316
Same as Match Target second issue except w/4.5-inch bbl., 9 inches overall. Weight: 36 oz. Made from 1950 to 1976.

**WOODSMAN SPORT MODEL AUTOMATIC PISTOL,
FIRST ISSUE** . . . . NiB $1066 Ex $893 Gd $621
Caliber: .22 LR (reg. or high speed). Same as Woodsman Target second issue except has 4.5-inch bbl., adjustable rear sight w/fixed or adjustable front sight. Weight: 27 oz., 8.5 inches overall. Made from 1933 to 1948.

**WOODSMAN SPORT MODEL AUTOMATIC
PISTOL, SECOND ISSUE** . . . . . NiB $2064 Ex $1418 Gd $1145
Same as Woodsman Target third Issue but w/4.5-inch bbl., 9 inches overall. Weight: 30 oz. Made from 1948 to 1976.

Colt Woodsman
Sport Model First Issue

Colt Woodsman
Sport Model Second Issue

Colt Woodsman
Target Model First Issue

Colt Woodsman
Target Model Second Issue

Colt Woodsman
Target Model Third Issue

www.skyhorsepublishing.com

Colt World War II
D-Day Invasion
Commemorative

Colt World
War II
50th Anniversary
Commemorative

WOODSMAN TARGET MODEL
AUTOMATIC, FIRST ISSUE . . . NiB $1729 Ex $1097 Gd $785
Caliber: .22 LR (reg. velocity). 10-round magazine, 6.5-inch
bbl., 10.5 inches overall. Weight: 28 oz. Adjustable sights. Blued
finish. Checkered walnut grips. Made 1915 to 1932. Note: The
mainspring housing of this model is not strong enough to permit
safe use of high-speed cartridges. Change to a new heat-treated
mainspring housing was made at pistol No. 83,790. Many of the
old models were converted by installation of new housings. The
new housing may be distinguished from the earlier type by the
checkering in the curve under the breech. The new housing is
grooved straight across, while the old type bears a diagonally-
checkered oval.

WOODSMAN TARGET MODEL
AUTOMATIC, SECOND ISSUE . . .NiB $954 Ex $561 Gd $444
Caliber: .22 LR (reg. or high speed). Same as original model except
has heavier bbl., and high-speed mainspring housing. (See note under
Woodsman, First Issue). Weight: 29 oz. Made from 1932 to 1948.

WOODSMAN TARGET MODEL
AUTOMATIC, THIRD ISSUE . . . . .NiB $836 Ex $515 Gd $326
Same basic design as previous Woodsman pistols but w/longer grip,
magazine catch on left side, larger thumb safety, slide stop, slide stays
open on last shot, magazine disconnector thumbrest grips. Caliber: .22 LR
(reg. or high speed). 10-round magazine, 6-inch bbl., 10.5 inches overall.
Weight: 32 oz. Click adjustable rear sight, ramp front sight. Blued finish.
Checkered plastic or walnut grips. Made 1948 to 1976.

WORLD WAR I 50TH ANNIVERSARY
COMMEMORATIVE SERIES
Limited production replica of Model 1911 .45 Auto engraved w/
battle scenes, commemorating Battles at Chateau Thierry, Belleau

Wood Second Battle of the Marne, Meuse Argonne. In special
presentation display cases. Production: 7,400 Standard model, 75
Deluxe, 25 Special Deluxe grade. Match numbered sets offered.
Made 1967 to 1969. Values indicated are for commemoratives in
new condition.

Standard grade	NiB $1046	Ex $780	Gd $638
Deluxe grade	NiB $2152	Ex $1743	Gd $1220
Special Deluxe grade	NiB $4687	Ex $3890	Gd $2448

WORLD WAR II COMMEMORATIVE
.45 AUTO . . . . NiB $1047 Ex $774 Gd $562
Limited production replica of Model 1911A1 .45 Auto engraved w/
respective names of locations where historic engagements occurred
during WW II, as well as specific issue and theater identification.
European model has oak leaf motif on slide, palm leaf design frames
the Pacific issue. Cased. 11,500 of each model were produced. Made
in 1970. Value listed is for gun in new condition.

Colt
Camp Perry First Issue

Colt
Camp Perry Second Issue

Colt Agent
First Issue

Colt Anaconda

WORLD WAR II 50TH ANNIVERSARY
COMMEMORATIVE . . . . . **NiB $2647   Ex $2064   Gd $1629**
Same general specifications as the Colt World War II Commemorative .45 Auto except slightly different scroll engraving, 24-karat gold-plate trigger, hammer, slide stop, magazine catch, magazine catch lock, safety lock and four grip screws. Made in 1995 only.

WORLD WAR II D-DAY
INVASION COMMEMORATIVE. . . . . **NiB $1550   Ex $1436   Gd $1138**
High-luster and highly decorated version of the Colt Model 1911A1. Caliber: .45 ACP. Same general specifications as the Colt Model 1911 except for 24-karat gold-plated hammer, trigger, slide stop, magazine catch, magazine catch screw, safety lock and four grip screws. Also has scrolls and inscription on slide. Made in 1991 only.

WORLD WAR II GOLDEN ANNIVERSARY V-J DAY
TRIBUTE .45 AUTO . . . . : . . . . **NiB $2662   Ex $2239   Gd $1658**
Basic Colt Model 1911A1 design w/highly-polished bluing and decorated w/specialized tributes to honor V-J Day. Two 24-karat gold scenes highlight the slide. 24-karat gold-plated hammer. Checkered wood grips w/gold medallion on each side. Made 1995.

XSE SERIES MODEL O SEMI-AUTOMATIC PISTOL
Caliber: .45 Auto. 8-round magazine, 4.24- or 5-in. bbl. Novak sights, front/rear slide serrations, extanded ambi. thumb safety. Checkered rosewood grips. Made 2000 to date.

Combat Elite	NiB $1100	Ex $700	Gd $500
Commander	NiB $1200	Ex $730	Gd $530
Government	NiB $1100	Ex $700	Gd $500
Ligthweight Commander.	NiB $1100	Ex $700	Gd $500
Ligthweight Government.	NiB $1100	Ex $700	Gd $500
Rail Gun	NiB $1200	Ex $730	Gd $530

- SINGLE-SHOT PISTOLS & DERRINGERS -

CAMP PERRY MODEL SINGLE-
SHOT PISTOL, FIRST ISSUE . . **NiB $1892   Ex $1540   Gd $1097**
Built on Officers' Model frame. Caliber: .22 LR (embedded head chamber for high-speed cartridges after 1930). 10 inch bbl., 13.75 inches overall. Weight: 34.5 oz. Adj. target sights. Hand-finished action. Blued finish. Checkered walnut grips. Made 1926 to 1934.

CAMP PERRY MODEL
SECOND ISSUE . . . . **NiB $1647   Ex $1392   Gd $998**
Same general specifications as First Issue except has shorter hammer fall and 8-inch bbl., 12 inches overall. Weight: 34 oz. Made from 1934 to 1941 (about 440 produced).

CIVIL WAR CENTENNIAL MODEL PISTOL
Single-shot replica of Colt Model 1860 Army Revolver. Caliber: .22 Short. Six-inch bbl., weight: 22 oz. Blued finish w/gold-plated frame, grip frame, and trigger guard, walnut grips. Cased. 24,114 were produced. Made in 1961.
Single pistol . . . . **NiB $362   Ex $265   Gd $204**
Pair w/consecutive serial numbers . . **NiB $689   Ex $541   Gd $408**

DERRINGER NO. 4
Replica of derringer No. 3 (1872 Thuer Model). Single-shot w/sideswing bbl., Caliber: .22 Short, 2.5-inch bbl., 4.9 inches overall. Weight: 7.75 oz. Fixed sights. Gold-plated frame w/blued bbl., and walnut grips or completely nickel- or gold-plated w/simulated ivory or pearl grips. Made 1959 to 1963. 112,000 total production. (S/N w/D or N suffix)
Single pistol (gun only) . . . . **NiB $128   Ex $88   Gd $61**
Single pistol (cased w/accessories) . . . . . **NiB $408   Ex $281   Gd $189**

DERRINGER NO. 4 COMMEMORATIVE MODELS
Limited production version of .22 derringers issued, w/appropriate inscription, to commemorate historical events. Additionally, non-firing models (w/unnotched bbls.) were furnished in books, picture frames and encased in plExiglass as singles or in cased pairs.
No. 4 Presentation Derringers
   (Non-firing w/accessories) . . . . **NiB $408   Ex $281   Gd $189**
Ltd. Ed. Book Series

Colt Banker's Special

Colt Bisley

Colt Buntline Special .45

Colt Commando Special

LORD AND LADY DERRINGERS (NO. 5)
Same as Derringer No. 4. Lord model with blued bbl., w/gold-plated frame and walnut grips. Lady model is gold-plated w/simulated pearl grips. Sold in cased pairs. Made from 1970 to 1972. (S/N w/Der suffix)

Lord derringer, pair in case . . . . NiB $577 Ex $408 Gd $301
Lady derringer, pair in case . . . . NiB $577 Ex $408 Gd $301
Lord and Lady derringers,
    one each, in case . . . . NiB $577 Ex $408 Gd $301

ROCK ISLAND ARSENAL
CENTENNIAL PISTOL . . . . NiB $520 Ex $489 Gd $332
Limited production (550 pieces) version of Civil War Centennial Model single-shot .22 pistol, made Exclusively for Cherry's Sporting Goods, Geneseo, Illinois, to commemorate the centennial of the Rock Island Arsenal in Illinois. Cased. Made in 1962.

NOTE: *This section of Colt handguns contains only revolvers. For automatic pistols or single-shot pistols and derringers, please see the two sections that precede this. For a complete listing, please refer to the Index.*

- REVOLVERS -

.38 DS II REVOLVER. . . . . NiB $540 Ex $437 Gd $306
Caliber: .38 Special. Six-round cylinder, 2-inch bbl., 7 inches overall. Weight: 21 oz. Ramp front sight, fixed notch rear. Satin stainless finish. Black rubber combat grip w/finger grooves. Made from 1997 to 1998.

AGENT DA REVOLVER,
FIRST ISSUE . . . . NiB $556 Ex $468 Gd $326
Same as Cobra, first issue except has short-grip frame .38 Special only, weight: 14 oz. Made from 1955 to 1972.

AGENT (LW) DA REVOLVER,
SECOND ISSUE . . . . NiB $541 Ex $444 Gd $270
Same as Colt Agent, first issue except has shrouded ejector rod and alloy frame. Made from 1973 to 1986.

ANACONDA DA REVOLVER
Calibers: .44 Mag., .45 Colt., bbl. lengths: 4, 6 or 8 inches; 11.63 inches overall (with 6-inch bbl.). Weight: 53 oz. (6-inch bbl.). Adj. white outline rear sight, red insert ramp-style front. Matte stainless or Realtree gray camo finish. Black Neoprene combat grips w/finger grooves. Made 1990 to 1999 and 2002 to 2006.

Matte stainless . . . . NiB $1100 Ex $714 Gd $487
Realtree gray camo
  finish (disc. 1996) . . . . NiB $1632 Ex $1357 Gd $1151
Custom model
  (.44 Mag. w/ported bbl.) . . . . . NiB $1203 Ex $816 Gd $587
First Edition model
  (Ltd. Edition 1000) . . . . NiB $1100 Ex $714 Gd $487
Hunter model
  (.44 Mag. w/2x scope) . . . . . NiB $1652 Ex $1357 Gd $1151

ANACONDA TITANIUM DA REVOLVER
Same general specifications as the standard Anaconda except chambered .44 Mag. only w/titanium-plated finish, gold-plated trigger, hammer and cylinder release. Limited edition of 1,000 distributed by American Historical Foundation w/personalized inscription. Made in 1996.
One of 1000 . . . . NiB $2744 Ex $2242 Gd $1624
Presentation case, add $255

ARMY SPECIAL DA REVOLVER . NiB $1015 Ex $831 Gd $530
.41-caliber frame. Calibers: .32-20, .38 Special (.41 Colt). Six-round cylinder, right revolution. Bbl., lengths: 4-, 4.5, 5-, and 6-inches, 9.25 inches overall (4-inch bbl.). Weight: 32 oz. (4-inch bbl.). Fixed sights. Blued or nickel-plated finish. Hard rubber grips. Made 1908-27. Note: This model has a somewhat heavier frame than the New Navy, which it replaced. Serial

(w/nickel-plated derringers) . . . . NiB $388 Ex $255 Gd $143
1st Presentation Series
  (Leatherette covered metal case) NiB $408 Ex $281 Gd $189
2nd Presentation Series
  (Single wooden case) . . . . NiB $408 Ex $281 Gd $189
2nd Presentation Series
  (Paired wooden case) . . . . NiB $423 Ex $291 Gd $198
1961 Issue Geneseo, Illinois,
  125th Anniversary (104 produced) NiB $729 Ex $556 Gd $388
1962 Issue Fort McPherson, Nebraska, Centennial
  (300 produced) . . . . NiB $729 Ex $556 Gd $388

**Colt Cobra
Round Butt First Issue**

**Colt
Detective Special First Issue**

numbers begin w/300,000. The heavy .38 Special High velocity loads should not be used in .38 Special arms of this model.

BANKER'S SPECIAL DA REVOLVER
This is the Police Positive w/a 2-inch bbl., otherwise specifications same as that model, rounded butt intro. in 1933. Calibers: .22 LR (embedded head-cylinder for high speed cartridges intro. 1933), .38 New Police. 6.5 inches overall. Weight: 23 oz. (.22 LR), 19 oz. (.38). Made from 1926 to 1940.
.38 caliber . . . . NiB $1566 Ex $1352 Gd $203
.22 caliber . . . . NiB $2651 Ex $2387 Gd $2152

BISLEY MODEL SA REVOLVER
Variation of the Single-Action Army, developed for target shooting w/modified grips, trigger and hammer. Calibers: General specifications same as SA Army. Target Model made w/flat-topped frame and target sights. Made 1894 to 1915.
Standard model . . . . NiB $8578 Ex $6945 Gd $4723
Target model (flat-top) . . .NiB $12,470 Ex $10,277 Gd $7166

BUNTLINE SPECIAL .45 . . . . . NiB $1448 Ex $1137 Gd $816
Same as standard SA Army except has 12-inch bbl., caliber .45 Long Colt. Made from 1957 to 1975.

COBRA DA REVOLVER,
ROUND BUTT, FIRST ISSUE. . . . . NiB $599 Ex $489 Gd $357
Lightweight Detective Special w/same general specifications as that model except w/Colt-alloy frame. Two-inch bbl., calibers: .38 Special, .38 New Police, .32 New Police. Weight: 15 oz., (.38 cal.). Blued finish. Checkered plastic or walnut grips. Made 1951 to 1973.

COBRA DA REVOLVER,
SECOND ISSUE . . . . NiB $643 Ex $577 Gd $388
Lightweight version of Detective Special, Second Issue has aluminum alloy frame. 16.5 oz. Made from 1973-81.

COBRA DA REVOLVER
SQUARE BUTT. . . . . NiB $530 Ex $425 Gd $304
Lightweight Police Positive Special w/same general specifications except has Colt-alloy frame, 4-inch bbl., Calibers: .38 Special, .38 New Police, .32 New Police. Weight: 17 oz. in .38 caliber. Blued finish. Checkered plastic or walnut grips. Made from 1951-73.

COMMANDO SPECIAL
DA REVOLVER. . . . . NiB $546 Ex $423 Gd $329
Caliber: .38 Special. Six-round cylinder, 2-inch bbl., 6.88 inches overall. Weight: 21.5 oz. Fixed sights. Low-luster blued finish. Made from 1982-86.

**Colt
Detective Special Second
Issue**

**Colt
Diamondback**

DETECTIVE SPECIAL DA REVOLVER, FIRST ISSUE
Similar to Police Positive Special w/2-inch bbl., otherwise specifications same as that model, rounded butt intro. 1933. .38 Special only in pre-war issue. Blued or nickel-plated finish. Weight: 17 oz. 6.75 inches overall. Made 1926-46.

Colt Lightning/Thunderer
1877-1912

Colt Idaho Territorial
Centennial 1963 Issue

Colt New Jersey Tercentenary 1964 issue

Colt General Hood
Centennial 1964 issue

Blued finish . . . . NiB $530 Ex $464 Gd $342
Nickel finish . . . . NiB $1030 Ex $811 Gd $610

DETECTIVE SPECIAL DA REVOLVER, SECOND ISSUE
Similar to Detective special first issue except w/2- or 3-inch bbl., and also chambered .32 New Police, .38 New Police. Wood, plastic or oversized grips. Made from 1947 to 1972.
Blued finish . . . . NiB $556 Ex $459 Gd $346
Nickel finish . . . . NiB $648 Ex $509 Gd $362
w/three-inch bbl., add $110

DETECTIVE SPECIAL DA REVOLVER, THIRD ISSUE
"D" frame, shrouded ejector rod. Caliber: .38 Special. Six-round cylinder, 2-inch bbl., 6.88 inches overall. Weight: 21.5 oz. Fixed rear sight, ramp front. Blued or nickel-plated finish. Checkered walnut wraparound grips. Made from 1973 to 1984.
Blued finish . . . . NiB $561 Ex $443 Gd $316

Nickel finish . . . . NiB $571 Ex $464 Gd $342
w/three-inch bbl., add $90

DETECTIVE SPECIAL DA REVOLVER, FOURTH ISSUE
Similar to Detective Special, Third Issue except w/alloy frame. Blued or chrome finish. Wraparound black neoprene grips w/Colt medallion. Made from 1993 to 1995.
Blued finish . . . . NiB $500 Ex $362 Gd $296
Chrome finish. . . . . NiB $525 Ex $377 Gd $306
DAO model (bobbed hammer) . . NiB $658 Ex $497 Gd $347

DIAMONDBACK DA REVOLVER
"D" frame, shrouded ejector rod. Calibers: .22 LR, .22 WRF, .38 Special. Six-round cylinder, 2.5-, 4- or 6-inch bbl., w/vent rib, 9 inches overall (with 4-inch bbl). Weight: 31.75 oz. (.22 cal., 4-inch bbl.), 28.5 oz. (.38 cal.). Ramp front sight, adj. rear. Blued or nickel finish. Checkered walnut grips. Made from 1966 to 1984.
Blued finish . . . . NiB $1336 Ex $1127 Gd $826
Nickel finish. . . . . NiB $1545 Ex $1231 Gd $986
.22 Mag. model . . . . NiB $2118 Ex $1937 Gd $1754
w/2.5-inch bbl., add. $90

DA ARMY (1878) . . . . NiB $6140 Ex $4524 Gd $3177
Also called DA Frontier. Similar in appearance to the smaller Lightning Model but has heavier frame of different shape, round disc on left side of frame, lanyard loop in butt. Calibers: .38-40, .44-40, .45 Colt. Six-round cylinder, bbl. lengths: 3.5- and 4-inches (w/o ejector), 4.75-, 5.5- and 7.5-inches w/ejector. 12.5 inches overall (7.5-inch bbl.). Weight: 39 oz. (.45 cal., 7.5-inch bbl.). Fixed sights. Hard rubber bird's-head grips. Blued or nickel finish. Made from 1878 to 1905.

FRONTIER SCOUT REVOLVER
SA Army replica, scale. Calibers: .22 Short, Long, LR or .22 WMR (interchangeable cylinder available). Six-round cylinder, 4.75-inch bbl., 9.9 inches overall. Weight: 24 oz. Fixed sights. Plastic grips. Originally made w/ bright alloy frame. Since 1959 w/steel frame and blued finish or all-nickel finish w/composition, wood or Staglite grips. Made 1958 to 1971.
Blued finish, plastic grips . . . . . . NiB $464 Ex $395 Gd $272
Nickel finish, wood grips . . . . NiB $499 Ex $407 Gd $286
Buntline model, add. $75
Extra interchangeable
    cylinder, add $100

FRONTIER SCOUT REVOLVER COMMEMORATIVE MODELS
Limited production versions of Frontier Scout issued, w/appropriate inscription, to commemorate historical events. Cased, in new condition.

1961 ISSUES
Kansas Statehood Centennial
    (6201 produced) . . . . NiB $536
Pony Express Centennial
    (1007 produced) . . . . NiB $638

1962 ISSUES
Columbus, Ohio, Sesquicentennial
    (200 produced). . . . . NiB $638
Fort Findlay, Ohio, Sesqui-
    centennial (130 produced) . . . . NiB $913
Fort Findlay Cased Pair, .22 Long
    Rifle and .22 Magnum (20 produced) . . . . NiB $2627
New MExico Golden Anniversary. . . . . NiB $638
West Virginia Statehood
    Centennial (3452 produced) . . . . NiB $6130

1963 ISSUES
Arizona Territorial Centennial
    (5355 produced) . . . . NiB $638
Battle of Gettysburg Centennial
    (1019 produced) . . . . NiB $638

GRADING: NiB = New in Box   Ex = Excellent or NRA 95%   Gd = Good or NRA 68%

Carolina Charter Tercentenary
(300 produced) . . . . NiB $2270
Fort Stephenson, Ohio, Sesquicentennial
(200 produced) . . . . NiB $638
General John Hunt Morgan Indiana Raid . . . . NiB $689
Idaho Territorial Centennial (902 produced). . . . . NiB $638

1964 ISSUES
California Gold Rush
(500 produced) . . . . NiB $638
Chamizal Treaty (450 produced) . . . . NiB $638
General Hood Centennial
(1503 produced) . . . . NiB $638
Montana Territorial Centennial
(2300 produced) . . . . NiB $638
Nevada "Battle Born"
(981 produced) . . . . NiB $597
Nevada Statehood Centennial
(3984 produced). . . . . NiB $2678
New Jersey Tercentenary
(1001 produced) . . . . NiB $577
St. Louis Bicentennial
(802 produced) . . . . NiB $638
Wyoming Diamond Jubilee
(2357 produced) . . . . NiB $638

1965 ISSUES
Appomattox Centennial
(1001 produced). . . . . NiB $577
Forty-Niner Miner
(500 produced) . . . . NiB $638
General Meade Campaign
(1197 produced) . . . . NiB $1647
Kansas Cowtown Series—Wichita
500 produced) . . . . NiB $577
Old Fort Des Moines Reconstruction
(700 produced) . . . . NiB $2280
Oregon Trail (1995 produced) . . . . NiB $638
St. Augustine Quadricentennial
(500 produced) . . . . NiB $638

1966 ISSUES
Colorado Gold Rush
(1350 produced) . . . . .NiB $638
Dakota Territory (1000 produced). . . . . NiB $638
Indiana Sesquicentennial
(1500 produced) . . . . .NiB $638
Kansas Cowtown Series—Abilene
(500 produced) . . . . NiB $577
Kansas Cowtown Series—Dodge City
(500 produced) . . . . NiB $577
Oklahoma
Jubilee (1343 produced) . . . . NiB $638

1967 ISSUES
Alamo (4500 produced) . . . . NiB $577
Kansas Cowtown Series—Coffeyville
(500 produced) . . . . NiB $561
Kansas Trail Series—Chisholm
Trail (500 produced). . . . . NiB $577
Lawman Series—
Bat Masterson (3000 produced) . . . . NiB $570

1968 ISSUES
Kansas Cowtown Series—Santa Fe Trail
(501 produced) . . . . .NiB $577
Kansas Trail Series—Pawnee Trail

Colt Indiana
Sesquicentennial 1966
Issue

Colt Golden Spike
Centennial 1969 Issue

Colt King Cobra

(501 produced) . . . . NiB $577
Lawman Series—Pat Garrett
(3000 produced). . . . . NiB $638
Nebraska Centennial
(7001 produced). . . . . NiB $577

1969 ISSUES
Alabama Sesquicentennial
(3001 produced). . . . . NiB $577
Arkansas Territory Sesquicentennial
(3500 produced). . . . . NiB $561
California Bicentennial (5000 produced). . . . . .NiB $577
General Nathan Bedford Forrest
(3000 produced) . . . . NiB $577
Golden Spike (11,000 produced). . . . . .NiB $577
Kansas Trail Series—Shawnee Trail
(501 produced) . . . . NiB $577
Lawman Series—Wild Bill Hickock
(3000 produced). . . . . NiB $638

1970 ISSUES
Kansas Fort Series—Fort Larned
(500 produced) . . . . NiB $577

56

**Colt Lawman
MK V**

**Colt Model 1877
Lightning**

**Colt New
Navy**

Kansas Fort Series—Fort Hays
(500 produced) ....NiB $577
Kansas Fort Series—Fort Riley
(500 produced) ....NiB $577
Lawman Series—Wyatt Earp
(3000 produced) ....NiB $780
Maine Sesquicentennial
(3000 produced) ....NiB $577
Missouri Sesquicentennial (3000 produced) .... NiB $577

1971 ISSUES
Kansas Fort Series—Fort Scott (500 produced) ...... NiB $577

1972 ISSUES
Florida Territory Sesquicentennial (2001 produced) . NiB $638

1973 ISSUES Arizona ranger
(3001 produced) .... NiB $638

KING COBRA REVOLVER
Caliber: .357 Mag., bbl. lengths: 2.5-, 4-, 6- or 8-inches, 9 inches overall (with 4-inch bbl.). Weight: 42 oz., average. Matte stainless steel finish. Black Neoprene combat grips. Made 1986 to date. 2.5-inch bbl. and "Ultimate" bright or blued finish. Made from 1988 to 1992.
Matte stainless .... NiB $658 Ex $447 Gd $321
Ultimate bright stainless .... NiB $780 Ex $468 Gd $362
Blued..................... NiB $587 Ex $475 Gd $321

LAWMAN MK III DA REVOLVER
Shrouded ejector rod on 2-inch bbl., only. Caliber: .357 Magnum. Six-round cylinder, bbl. lengths: 2-, 4-inch. 9.38 inches overall (w/4-inch bbl.), Weight: (with 4-inch bbl.), 35 oz. Fixed rear sight, ramp front. Service trigger and hammer or target trigger and wide-spur hammer. Blued or nickel-plated finish. Checkered walnut service or target grips. Made from 1969 to 1982.
Blued finish .... NiB $499 Ex $402 Gd $265
Nickel finish .... NiB $546 Ex $412 Gd $274

LAWMAN MK V DA REVOLVER
Similar to Trooper MK V. Caliber: .357 Mag. Six-round cylinder, 2- or 4-inch bbl., 9.38 inches overall (4-inch bbl.). Weight: 35 oz. (4-inch bbl.). Fixed sights. Checkered walnut grips. Made 1984 and 1991.
Blued finish .... NiB $362 Ex $295 Gd $214
Nickel finish. .... NiB $397 Ex $304 Gd $228

MAGNUM CARRY DA REVOLVER ..... NiB $489 Ex $373 Gd $296
Similar to Model DS II except chambered for .357 Magnum. Made from 1998 to date.

MARINE CORPS MODEL (1905) DA REVOLVER
General specifications same as New Navy Second Issue except has round butt, was supplied only in .38 caliber (.38 Short & Long Colt, .38 Special) w/6-inch bbl. (S/N range 10,001-10,926) Made 1905 to 1909.
Marine Corps model... NiB $15,606 Ex $14,050 Gd $13,260
Marked "USMC".......... NiB $7803 Ex $5636 Gd $3886

METROPOLITAN MK III
DA REVOLVER..............NiB $536 Ex $423 Gd $316
Same as Official Police MK III except has 4-inch bbl. w/service or target grips. Weight: 36 oz. Made from 1969 to 1972.

MODEL 1877
LIGHTNING REVOLVER .....NiB $4197 Ex $3264 Gd $2973
Also called Thunderer Model. Calibers: .38 and .41 centerfire. Six-round cylinder, bbl. lengths: 2.5-, 3.5-, 4.5- and 6-inch without ejector, 4.5- and 6-inch w/ejector, 8.5 inches overall (3.5-inch bbl.). Weight: 23 oz. (.38 cal., with 3.5-inch bbl.) Fixed sights. Blued or nickel finish. Hard rubber bird's-head grips. Made 1877 to 1909.

NEW FRONTIER BUNTLINE SPECIAL
Same as New Frontier SA Army except has 12-inch bbl.,
Second generation (1962-75) NiB $2570 Ex $2028 Gd $1392
Third generation (1976-92)... NiB $1352 Ex $1120 Gd $861

NEW FRONTIER SA ARMY REVOLVER
Same as SA Army except has flat-top frame, adj. target rear sight, ramp front sight, smooth walnut grips. 5.5- or 7.5-inch bbl., Calibers: .357 Magnum, .44 Special, .45 Colt. Made 1961 to 1992.
Second generation (1961-75) NiB $2902 Ex $2647 Gd $2458
Third generation (1976-92)... NiB $1362 Ex $1118 Gd $857

NEW FRONTIER SA .22 REVOLVER ....NiB $532 Ex $342 Gd $235
Same as Peacemaker .22 except has flat-top frame, adj. rear sight, ramp front sight. Made from 1971-76; reintro. 1982 to 1986.

NEW NAVY (1889) DA, FIRST ISSUE
Also called New Army. Calibers: .38 Short & Long Colt, .41 Short & Long Colt. Six-round cylinder, left revolution. Bbl. lengths: 3-, 4.5- and 6-inches, 11.25 inches overall (with 6-inch bbl.). Weight: 32 oz. with 6-inch bbl. Fixed sights, knife-blade and V-notch. Blued or nickel-plated finish. Walnut or hard rubber grips. Made 1889 to 1994. Note: This model, which was adopted by both the Army and Navy, was Colt's first revolver of the solid frame, swing-out cylinder type. It lacks the cylinder-locking notches found on later models made on this .41 frame; ratchet on the back of the cylinder is held in place by a double projection on the hand.

First issue . . . . NiB $2018 Ex $1644 Gd $1182
First issue w/3-inch bbl. . . . . . NiB $2539 Ex $2040 Gd $1484
Navy contract, marked
  U.S.N.(S/N 1-1500) . . . . NiB $3682 Ex $2981 Gd $2121

NEW NAVY (1892) DA, SECOND ISSUE
Also called New Army. General specifications same as First Issue except has double cylinder notches and double locking bolt. Calibers: .38 Special added in 1904 and .32-20 in 1905. Made 1892 to 1907. Note: The heavy .38 Special High Velocity loads should not be used in .38 Special arms of this model.
Second issue . . . . NiB $1750 Ex $1446 Gd $1020
Second issue w/3-inch bbl. . . NiB $2746 Ex $2264 Gd $1619
Navy contract, marked "U.S.N" . . . . . NiB $2865 Ex $2344 Gd $1644

NEW POCKET DA REVOLVER . . . NiB $770 Ex $620 Gd $464
Caliber: .32 Short & Long Colt. Six-round cylinder. bbl. lengths: 2.5, 3.5- and 6-inches. 7.5 inches overall w/3.5-inch bbl., Weight: 16 oz., with 3.5-inch bbl. Fixed sights, knife-blade and V-notch. Blued or nickel finish. Rubber grips. Made from 1893 to 1905.

NEW POLICE DA REVOLVER . . . NiB $1020 Ex $638 Gd $445
Built on New Pocket frame but w/larger grip. Calibers: .32 Colt New Police, .32 Short & Long Colt. Bbl. lengths: 2.5-, 4- and 6-inches; 8.5 inches overall (with 4-inch bbl.). Weight: 17 oz., with 4-inch bbl. Fixed knife-blade front sight, V-notch rear. Blued or nickel finish. Rubber grips. Made from 1896 to 1905.

NEW POLICE TARGET DA REVOLVER . . NiB $1258 Ex $1111 Gd $893
Target version of the New Police w/same general specifications. Target sights. Six-inch bbl., blued finish only. Made 1896 to 1905.

NEW SERVICE DA REVOLVER
Calibers: .38 Special, .357 Magnum (intro. 1936), .38-40, .44-40, .44 Russian, .44 Special, .45 Auto, .45 Colt, .450 Eley, .455 Eley, .476 Eley. Six-round cylinder, bbl. lengths: 4-, 5- and 6-inch in .38 Special and .357 Magnum, 4.5-, 5.5- and 7.5 inches in other calibers; 9.75 inches overall (with 4.5-inch bbl.). Weight: 39 oz. (.45 cal. with 4.5-inch bbl.). Fixed sights. Blued or nickel finish. Checkered walnut grips. Made 1898-42. Note: More than 500,000 of this model in caliber .45 Auto (designated "Model 1917 Revolver") were purchased by the U.S. Gov't. during WW I. These arms were later sold as surplus to National Rifle Association members through the Director of Civilian Marksmanship. Price was $16.15 plus packing charge. Supply Exhausted during the early 1930s.
Commercial model . . . . NiB $1851 Ex $1507 Gd $1086
Magnum . . . . NiB $1223 Ex $1018 Gd $729
1917 Army . . . . NiB $1188 Ex $683 Gd $597

NEW SERVICE TARGET . . . . NiB $1336 Ex $1188 Gd $770
Target version of the New Service. Calibers: Originally chambered for .44 Russian, .450 Eley, .455 Eley and .476 Eley, later models in .44 Special, .45 Colt and .45 Auto. Six- or 7.5-inch bbl., 12.75 inches overall (7.5-inch bbl.). Adj. target sights. Hand-finished action. With blued finish. Checkered walnut grips. Made 1900 to 1940.

OFFICERS' MODEL MATCH . . NiB $852 Ex $714 Gd $425
Same general design as Officers' Model revolvers. Has tapered heavy bbl., wide hammer spur, Adjustable rear sight ramp front sight, large target grips of checkered walnut. Calibers: .22 LR, .38 Special. Six-inch bbl., 11.25 inches overall. Weight: 43 oz. (in .22 cal.), 39 oz. (.38 cal.). Blued finish. Made from 1953 to 1970.

OFFICERS' MODEL SPECIAL . . NiB $894 Ex $621 Gd $423
Target version of Officers' Model Second Issue w/similar characters except w/heavier, nontapered bbl. redesigned hammer. Ramp front sight, Colt Officers' Model Special "Coltmaster" rear sight adj. for windage and elevation. Calibers: .22 LR, .38 Special. Six-inch bbl. 11.25

Colt New Service

Colt New Service Target

Colt Officers' Match

Colt
Officers' Target Second Issue

inches overall. Weight: 39 oz. (in .38 cal.), 43 oz., (.22 cal.). Blued finish. Checkered plastic grips. Made from 1949 to 1953.

OFFICERS' MODEL TARGET
DA REVOLVER, FIRST ISSUE . . . NiB $1343 Ex $1099 Gd $791
Caliber: .38 Special. Six-inch bbl., hand-finished action, adj. target sights. Checkered with walnut grips. General specifications same as New Navy, Second Issue. Made from 1904 to 1908.

OFFICERS' MODEL TARGET, SECOND ISSUE
Calibers: .22 LR (intro. 1930, embedded head-cylinder for high-speed cartridges after 1932), .32 Police Positive (made 1932-1942), .38 Special. Six-round cylinder, bbl. lengths: 4-, 4.5-, 5-, 6- and 7.5-inch (in .38 Special) or 6-inch only (.22 LR and .32 PP), 11.25 inches overall (6-inch bbl. in .38 Special). Adj. target sights. Blued finish. Hand-finished action. General features same as Army Special and Official Police of same date. Made from 1908 to 1949 (w/exceptions noted).

**Colt
Official Police**

**Colt
Peacekeeper**

**Colt
Pocket Positive**

**Colt
Police Positive First Issue**

oz. (standard 6-inch bbl.) in .38 Special. Fixed sights. Blued or nickel-plated finish. Checkered walnut grips on all revolvers of this model except some of postwar production had checkered plastic grips. Made 1927-69. Note: This model is a refined version of the Army Special, which it replaced in 1928 at about serial number 520,000. The Commando .38 Special was a wartime adaptation of the Official Police made to government specifications. Commando can be identified by its sandblasted blued finish. Serial numbers start w/number 1-50,000 (Made 1942 to 1945).

Commercial model (pre-war). . . . NiB $638   Ex $510   Gd $388
Commercial model (post-war). . . NiB $557   Ex $476   Gd $362
Commando model . . . . NiB $669   Ex $564   Gd $398

**OFFICIAL POLICE MK III
DA REVOLVER** . . . . NiB $321   Ex $262   Gd $198
"J" frame, without shrouded ejector rod. Caliber: .38 Special. Six-round cylinder. bbl., lengths: 4-, 5-, 6-inches, 9.25 inches overall w/4-inch bbl., weight: 34 oz. (4-inch bbl.). Fixed rear sight, ramp front. Service trigger and hammer or target trigger and wide-spur hammer. Blued or nickel-plated finish. Checkered walnut service grips. Made 1969 to 1975.

PEACEKEEPER DA REVOLVER. NiB $499   Ex $418   Gd $220
Caliber: .357 Mag. Six-round cylinder, 4- or 6-inch bbl., 11.25 inches overall (6-inch bbl.). Weight: 46 oz. (with 6-inch bbl.). Adj. white outline rear sight, red insert ramp-style front. Non-reflective matte blued finish. Made from 1985 to 1989.

**PEACEMAKER .22 SECOND AMENDMENT
COMMEMORATIVE** . . . . NiB $660   Ex $544   Gd $286
Caliber: .22, revolver w/7.5-inch bbl., nickel-plated frame, bbl. ejector rod assembly, hammer and trigger, blued cylinder, backstrap and trigger guard. Black pearlite grips. bbl., inscribed "The Right to Keep and Bear Arms." Presentation case. Limited edition of 3000 issued in 1977. Top value is for revolver in new condition.

PEACEMAKER .22 SA REVOLVER .NiB $423   Ex $332   Gd $275
Calibers: .22 LR and .22 WMR. Furnished w/cylinder for each caliber, 6-round. Bbl.: 4.38-, 6- or 7.5-inches, 11.25 inches overall (with 6-inch bbl.). Weight: 30.5 oz. (with 6-inch bbl.). Fixed sights. Black composite grips. Made from 1971 to 1976.

POCKET POSITIVE DA REVOLVER
General specifications same as New Pocket except this model has positive lock feature (see Police Positive). Calibers: .32 Short & Long Colt (disc. 1914), .32 Colt New Police (.32 S&W Short & Long). Fixed sights, flat top and square notch. Blue or nickel finish. Made from 1905 to 1940.
Blue finish . . . . NiB $635   Ex $577   Gd $388
Nickel finish. . . . . NiB $699   Ex $571   Gd $435

POLICE POSITIVE DA, FIRST ISSUE
Improved version of the New Police w/the "Positive Lock," which prevents the firing pin coming in contact w/the cartridge except when the trigger is pulled. Calibers: .32 Short & Long Colt (disc. 1915), .32 Colt New Police (.32 S&W Short & Long), .38 New Police (.38 S&W). Six-round cylinder, bbl. lengths: 2.5- (.32 cal. only), 4- 5- and 6-inches; 8.5 inches overall (with 4-inch bbl.). Weight 20 oz. (with 4-inch bbl.). Fixed sights. Blued or nickel finish. Rubber or checkered walnut grips. Made from 1905 to 1947.
Blue finish . . . . NiB $529   Ex $439   Gd $351
Nickel finish. . . . . NiB $581   Ex $475   Gd $340

Second issue (.38 caliber). . . . . NiB $1130   Ex $930   Gd $653
Second issue (.32 caliber). . . . NiB $1744   Ex $1426   Gd $984
Second issue (.22 caliber). . . . NiB $1232   Ex $1018   Gd $729
w/shorter bbls. (4-, 4.5- or 5-inches), add 50%

OFFICIAL POLICE DA REVOLVER
Calibers: .22 LR (intro. 1930, embedded head-cylinder for high-speed cartridges after 1932), .32-20 (disc. 1942), .38 Special, .41 Long Colt (disc. 1930). Six-round cylinder, bbl. lengths: 4-, 5-, 6-inch or 2-inch and 6-inch heavy bbl. in .38 Special only; .22 LR w/4- and 6-inch bbls. only; 11.25 inches overall. Weight: 36

POLICE POSITIVE DA, SECOND ISSUE
Same as Detective Special second issue except has 4-inch bbl., 9 inches overall, weight: 26.5 oz. Intro. in 1977. Note: Original Police Positive (First Issue) has a shorter frame, is not chambered for .38 Special.
Blue finish . . . . NiB $524   Ex $437   Gd $351
Nickel finish. . . . . NiB $581   Ex $469   Gd $342

GRADING: **NiB** = New in Box   **Ex** = Excellent or NRA 95%   **Gd** = Good or NRA 68%   **59**

POLICE POSITIVE SPECIAL
DA REVOLVER . . . . **NiB $581 Ex $498 Gd $356**
Based on the Police Positive w/frame lengthened to permit longer cylinder. Calibers: .32-20 (disc. 1942), .38 Special, .32 New Police and .38 New Police (intro. 1946). Six-round cylinder; bbl. lengths: 4-(only length in current production), 5- and 6-inch; 8.75 inches overall (with 4-inch bbl.). Weight: 23 oz. (with 4-inch bbl. in .38 Special). Fixed sights. Checkered grips of hard rubber, plastic or walnut. Made 1907 to 1973.

COLT POLICE POSITIVE TARGET
DA REVOLVER . . . . **NiB $884 Ex $724 Gd $523**
Target version of the Police Positive. Calibers: .22 LR (intro. 1910, embedded-head cylinder for high-speed cartridges after 1932), .22 WRF (1910-35), .32 Short & Long Colt, (1915), .32 New Police (.32 S&W Short & Long). Six-inch bbl., blued finish only, 10.5 inches overall. Weight: 26 oz. in .22 cal. Adj. target sights. Checkered walnut grips. Made from 1905 to 1940.

PYTHON DA REVOLVER
"I" frame, shrouded ejector rod. Calibers: .357 Magnum, .38 Special. Six-round cylinder, 2.5-, 4-, 6- or 8-inch vent rib bbl., 11.25 inches overall (with 6-inch bbl.). Weight: 44 oz. (6-inch bbl.). Adj. rear sight, ramp front. Blued, nickel or stainless finish. Checkered walnut target grips. Made from 1955 to 1996. Ultimate stainless finish made in 1985.

Blued finish . . . . **NiB $1316 Ex $924 Gd $437**
Royal blued
finish . . . . **NiB $1316 Ex $924 Gd $437**
Nickel finish . . . . **NiB $1316 Ex $924 Gd $437**
Stainless finish . . . . **NiB $1357 Ex $975 Gd $479**
Ultimate stainless
finish . . . . **NiB $1357 Ex $975 Gd $479**
Hunter model
(w/2x scope) . . . . **NiB $1907 Ex $1510 Gd $926**
Silhouette model
(w/2x scope) . . . . **NiB $2152 Ex $1803 Gd $1039**

Colt SA Army

Colt
Police Positive Target

Colt Python

SHOOTING MASTER DA REVOLVER
Deluxe target arm based on the New Service model. Calibers: Originally made only in .38 Special, .44 Special, .45 Auto and .45 Colt added in 1933, .357 Magnum in 1936. Six-inch bbl., 11.25 inches overall. Weight: 44 oz., in (.38 cal.), adj. target sights. Hand-finished action. Blued finish. Checkered walnut grips. Rounded butt. Made from 1932 to 1941.
Shooting Master
.38 Special . . . . **NiB $1507 Ex $1344 Gd $915**
Shooting Master
.357 Mag. . . . . **NiB $1533 Ex $1269 Gd $908**
Shooting Master
.44 Special, .45 ACP, .45LC . **NiB $4092 Ex $3773 Gd $2285**

SINGLE ACTION ARMY (SAA) REVOLVER
Also called Frontier Six-Shooter and Peacemaker. Available in more than 30 calibers including: .22 Rimfire (Short, Long, LR), .22 WRF, .32 Rimfire, .32 Colt, .32 S&W, .32-20, .38 Colt, .38 S&W, .38 Special, .357 Magnum, .38-40, .41 Colt, .44 Rimfire, .44 Russian, .44 Special, .44-40, .45 Colt, .45 Auto, .450 Boxer, 450 Eley, .455 Eley, .476 Eley. Six-round cylinder. Bbl. lengths: 4.75, 5 .5 and 7.5 inches w/ejector or 3 and 4 inches w/o ejector. 10.25 inches overall (with 4.75-inch bbl.). Weight: 36 oz. (.45 cal. w/4.75-inch bbl.). Fixed sights. Also made in Target Model w/flat top-strap and target sights. Blued finish w/casehardened frame or nickel-plated. One-piece smooth walnut or checkered black rubber grips. Note: S.A. Army Revolvers w/serial numbers above 165,000 (circa 1896) are adapted to smokeless powder and cylinder pin screw was changed to spring catch at about the same time. The "First Generation" of SA Colts included both blackpowder and smokeless configurations and were manufactured from 1873 to 1940. Production resumed in 1955 w/serial number 1001SA and continued through 1975 to complete the second series, which is referred to as the "Second Generation." In 1976, the "Third Generation" of production began and continues to to date. However, several serial number rollovers occurred at 99,999. For Example, in 1978 the "SA" suffix became an "SA" prefix and again in 1993, when the serial number SA99,999 was reached, the serialization format was changed again to include both an "S" prefix and an "A" suffix. Although the term "Fourth Generation" is frequently associated with this rollover, no series change actually occurred, therefore, the current production is still a "Third Generation" series. Current calibers: .357 Magnum, .44 Special, .45 Long Colt.

Pinched frame
(1873 only) . . . . **NiB $84,558 Ex $68,034 Gd $46,138**
Early commercial
(1873-77) . . . . **NiB $43,631 Ex $34,945 Gd $23,792**
Early military
(1873-77) . . . . **NiB $50,184 Ex $39,984 Gd $27,335**
Large bore rimfire
(1875-80) . . . . **NiB $40,565 Ex $33,558 Gd $22,313**
Small bore
rimfire (1875-80) . . . . . **NiB $31,391 Ex $25,169 Gd $17,151**
Frontier six-shooter, .44-40
(1878-82) . . . . **NiB $47,323 Ex $37,964 Gd $25,875**
Storekeeper's model, no ejector
(1883-98) . . . . **NiB $49,980 Ex $40,025 Gd $27,311**
Sheriff's model
(1883-98) . . . . **NiB $47,226 Ex $37,954 Gd $25,760**
Target model, flat top strap,
target sights . . . . **NiB $26,204 Ex $20,808 Gd $14,229**
U.S. Cavalry model, .45
(1873-92) . . . . **NiB $45,890 Ex $36,705 Gd $25,194**

Colt SA Army — 125th Anniversary

Colt 150th Anniversary Deluxe

Colt 150th Anniversary Engraving Sampler

In the previous section the GTG deviates from the observed practice of listing only the value of firearms produced after 1900. This deliberate departure from the standard format is intended to provide a general reference and establish proper orientation for the reader, because the Colt SSA had its origins in the last quarter of the 19th century. Consequently, antique firearms produced prior to 1898 have been listed as a preface and introduction to the first series of production (what is now recognized as "1st Generation") in order to systematically demonstrate the progressive and sequential development of the multi-generation Colt SAA. Therefore, the previous general values have been provided to establish a point of reference to allow a more comprehensive Examination of the evolution of the Colt SAA. However, please note that the following values apply only to original models, not to similar S.A.A. revolvers of more recent manufacture.

Standard model, pre-war
 (1st generation) . . . . $13,770 to $66,810
Standard model (1955-75)
 (2nd generation) . . . . NiB $2509 Ex $2050 Gd $1499
Standard model (1976 to date) NiB $1275 Ex $1122 Gd $824

SA ARMY — 125TH ANNIVERSARY . NiB $1668 Ex $1438 Gd $1239
Limited production deluxe version of SA Army issued in commemoration of Colt's 125th Anniversary. Caliber: .45 Long Colt., 7.5-inch bbl., cold-plated frame trigger, hammer, cylinder pin, ejector rod tip, and grip medallion. Presentation case w/anniversary medallion. Serial numbers "50AM." 7368 were made in 1961.

GRADING: **NiB** = New in Box   **Ex** = Excellent or NRA 95%   **Gd** = Good or NRA 68%   **61**

SA ARMY COMMEMORATIVE MODELS

Limited production versions of SA Army .45 issued, w/appropriate inscription to commemorate historical events. Cased. Note: Values indicated are for commemorative revolvers in new condition.

1963 ISSUES
Arizona Territorial Centennial
(1280 produced)........................NiB $1663
West Virginia Statehood
Centennial (600 produced)..................NiB $1663

1964 ISSUES
Chamizal Treaty (50 produced)..........NiB $1867
Colonel Sam Colt Sesquicentennial
Presentation (4750 produced)...............NiB $1663
Deluxe Presentation
(200 produced).....................NiB $3621
Special Deluxe Presentation
(50 produced)......................NiB $5687
Montana Territorial Centennial
(851 produced).....................NiB $1724
Nevada "Battle Born"
(100 produced).....................NiB $2672
Nevada Statehood Centennial
(1877 produced)....................NiB $2275
New Jersey Tercentenary
(250 produced).....................NiB $1663
Pony Express Presentation
(1004 produced)....................NiB $1836
St. Louis Bicentennial
(450 produced).....................NiB $1663
Wyatt Earp Buntline
(150 produced).....................NiB $2809

1965 ISSUES
Appomattox Centennial
(500 produced) ....NiB $1454
Old Fort Des Moines Recon-
struction (200 produced) ....NiB $1454

1966 ISSUES
Abercrombie & Fitch Trailblazer
—Chicago (100 produced) ....NiB $1423
Abercrombie & Fitch Trailblazer
—New York (200 produced) ....NiB $1423
Abercrombie & Fitch Trailblazer
—San Francisco (100 produced) ....NiB $1423
California Gold Rush
(130 produced) ....NiB $1423
General Meade (200 produced) ....NiB $1663
Pony Express Four Square (4 guns) ....NiB $7268

1967 ISSUES
Alamo (1000 produced) ....NiB $1663
Lawman Series—Bat Masterson
(500 produced).....................NiB $1760

1968 ISSUES
Lawman Series—Pat Garrett (500 produced) ....NiB $1663
1969 ISSUES
Lawman Series—Wild Bill Hickok
(500 produced) ....NiB $1663

1970 ISSUES
Lawman Series—Wyatt Earp
(501 produced).....................NiB $2907

Colt New Frontier

Missouri Sesquicentennial
(501 produced) ....NiB $1627
Texas Ranger
(1000 produced)....................NiB $2351

1971 ISSUES
NRA Centennial, .357 or .45
(5001 produced)....................NiB $1525

1975 ISSUES
Peacemaker Centennial .45
(1501 produced) ....NiB $1872
Peacemaker Centennial .44-40
(1501 produced)....................NiB $1872
Peacemaker Centennial Cased
Pair (501 produced) ....NiB $1872

1979 ISSUES
Ned Buntline .45
(3000 produced) ....NiB $1367

1986 ISSUES
Colt 150th Anniversary (standard) ....NiB $2064
Colt 150th Anniversay (engraved)................NiB $3647

COLT COWBOY REVOLVER.....NiB $632 Ex $468 Gd $363
SA variant designed for "Cowboy Action Shooting" w/ safety transfer bar system. Caliber: .45 Colt. Six-round cylinder, 5.5-inch bbl., 11 inches overall. Weight: 42 oz. Blade front sight, fixed V-notch rear. Blued finish w/color casehardened frame. Smooth walnut grips. Made from 1999 to 2003.

SA SHERIFF'S MODEL .45
Limited edition replica of Storekeeper's Model in caliber .45 Colt, made Exclusively for Centennial Arms Corp. Chicago, Illinois. Numbered "1SM." Blued finish w/casehardened frame or nickel-plated. Walnut grips. Made in 1961.
Blued finish (478 produced) . NiB $2152 Ex $1780 Gd $1454
Nickel finish (25 produced) . NiB $8155 Ex $5763 Gd $4024

THREE-FIFTY-SEVEN DA REVOLVER
Heavy frame. Caliber: .357 Magnum. Six-shot cylinder, 4 or 6-inch bbl. Quickdraw ramp front sight, Accro rear sight. Blued finish. Checkered walnut grips. 9.25 or 11.25 inches overall. Weight: 36 oz. (4-inch bbl.), 39 oz. (6 inch bbl.). Made from 1953 to 1961.
w/standard hammer and service grips ...NiB $711 Ex $601 Gd $431
w/wide-spur hammer and target grips ...NiB $733 Ex $612 Gd $444

TROOPER DA REVOLVER
Same specifications as Officers' Model Match except has 4-inch bbl. w/ quick-draw ramp front sight, weight: 34 oz. in .38 caliber. Made from 1953 to 1969.
w/standard hammer and service grips .. NiB $536 Ex $ 464 Gd $357
w/wide-spur hammer and target grips ...NiB $632 Ex $525 Gd $408

Colt Trooper

Colt Trooper MK V

Colt U.S. Bicentennial Commemorative Set

CZ (CESKA ZBROJOVKA), INC. – 37th Edition

TROOPER MK III DA REVOLVER
"J"frame, shrouded ejector rod. Calibers: .22 LR, .22 Magnum, .38 Special, .357 Magnum. Six-round cylinder. bbl. lengths: 4-, 6-inches. 9.5 inches overall (with 4-inch bbl.). Weight: 39 oz. (4-inch bbl.). Adj. rear sight, ramp front. Target trigger and hammer. Blued or nickel-plated finish. Checkered walnut target grips. Made 1969 to 1978.

Blued finish	NiB $587	Ex $418	Gd $224
Nickel finish.	NiB $643	Ex $452	Gd $224

TROOPER MK V REVOLVER
Re-engineered Mark III for smoother, faster action. Caliber: .357 Magnum. Six-round cylinder, bbl. lengths: 4-, 6-, 8-inch w/vent rib. Adj. rear sight, ramp front, red insert. Checkered walnut grips. Made from 1982 to 1986.

Blued finish	NiB $562	Ex $437	Gd $321
Nickel finish.	NiB $577	Ex $499	Gd $316

VIPER DA REVOLVER . . . . . . NiB $760   Ex $602   Gd $356
Same as Cobra, Second Issue except has 4-inch bbl., 9 inches overall, weight: 20 oz. Made from 1977 to 1984.

U.S. BICENTENNIAL
COMMEMORATIVE SET . . . . .NiB $3290
Replica Colt 3rd Model Dragoon revolver w/accessories, Colt SA Army revolver, and Colt Python revolver. Matching roll-engraved unfluted cylinders, blued finish and rosewood grips w/Great Seal of the United States silver medallion. Dragoon revolver has silver grip frame. Serial numbers 0001 to 1776. All revolvers in set have same number. Deluxe drawer-style presentation case of walnut w/book compartment containing a reproduction of "Armsmear." Issued in 1976. Value is for revolvers in new condition.

COONAN ARMS, INC. — Blaine, MN
Formerly Maplewood, Minnesota and St. Paul, Minnesota.

MODEL .357 MAGNUM AUTO PISTOL
Caliber: .357 Mag. Seven-round magazine, 5- or 6-inch bbl., 8.3 inches overall (with 5-inch bbl.). Weight: 42 oz. Front ramp interchangeable sight, fixed rear sight, adj. for windage. Black walnut grips. Made from 1983 to 1999; reintro. 2010.

Model A Std. grade w/o grip
safety (disc. 1991)	NiB $1221	Ex $1056	Gd $869
Model B Std. grade w/5-inch bbl.,.	NiB $944	Ex $703	Gd $500
Model B Std. grade w/6-inch bbl.,.	NiB $714	Ex $601	Gd $437

Model B w/5-inch
compensated bbl., (Classic). . .	NiB $1336	Ex $1122	Gd $923

Model B w/6-inch
compensated bbl	NiB $1016	Ex $789	Gd $561

.357 MAGNUM CADET COMPACT
Similar to the standard .357 Magnum model except w/3.9-inch bbl., on compact frame. Six-round (Cadet), 7- or 8-round magazine (Cadet II). Weight: 39 oz., 7.8 inches overall. Made 1993 to 1999; reintro. 2010.

Cadet model.	NiB $897	Ex $653	Gd $497
Cadet II model	NiB $897	Ex $653	Gd $497

CZ (CESKA ZBROJOVKA), INC. — Uhersky Brod Czechoslovakia
Formerly Strakonice, Czechoslovakia. Mfd. by Ceska Zbrojovka-Nardoni Podnik formerly Bohmische Waffenfabrik A. G. Currently imported by CZ-USA (cz-usa.com), Kansas City, KS. Previously by Magnum Research and Action Arms. Vintage importation is by Century International Arms. Also, see Dan Wesson Firearms listings.

CZ P-01 . . . . NiB $658   Ex $406   Gd $305
Caliber: 9mm Para. Based on CZ-75 design but with improved metals, aluminum alloy frame, hammer forged bbl. (3.8 inches), checkered rubber grips, matte black polycoat finish. Imported 2003.

CZ P-07 DUTY . . . . NiB $440   Ex $330   Gd $270
Caliber: 9mm Para. or .40 S&W. Polymer frame in black or OD green, 3.8-in. bbl. Made from 2009 to 2013.

CZ 2075 RAMI P . . . . NiB $440   Ex $330   Gd $270
Caliber: 9mm Para. or .40 S&W. Polymer frame in black, 3-in. bbl. Made from 2006 to 2011.

CZ 40 . . . . NiB $530   Ex $372   Gd $321
Caliber: .40 S&W. M1911-style frame, CZ-75B operating mechanism; single or double-action; black polycoat finish. Fixed sights; 10-round mag.

MODEL 27 AUTO PISTOL . . . . . . NiB $653   Ex $555   Gd $385
Caliber: .32 Automatic (7.65mm). Eight-round magazine, 4-inch bbl., 6 inches overall. Weight: 23.5 oz. Fixed sights. Blued finish. Plastic grips. Made from 1927 to 1951. Note: After the German occupation (March 1939), Models 27 and 38 were marked w/manufacturer code "fnh." Designation of Model 38 was changed to "Pistole 39(t)."

MODEL 38 AUTO PISTOL (VZ SERIES)
Caliber: .380 Automatic (9mm). Nine-round magazine, 3.75-inch bbl., 7 inches overall. Weight: 26 oz. Fixed sights. Blued finish. Plastic grips. After 1939 designated as T39. Made 1938 to 1945.
CZ DAO model . . . . NiB $518   Ex $442   Gd $358
CZ SA/DA model . . . . NiB $1451   Ex $1144   Gd $825

MODEL 50 DA AUTO PISTOL NiB $265   Ex $191   Gd $153
Similar to Walther Model PP except w/frame-mounted safety and trigger guard not hinged. Caliber: .32 ACP (7.65mm), 8-round magazine, 3.13-inch bbl., 6.5 inches overall. Weight: 24.5 oz. Fixed sights. Blued finished. Intro. in 1950. disc. Note: "VZ50" is the official designation of this pistol used by the Czech National Police ("New Model .006" was the Export designation but very few were released).

MODEL 52 SA AUTO PISTOL . NiB $248   Ex $202   Gd $137
Roller-locking breech system. Calibers: 7.62mm or 9mm Para. Eight-round magazine, 4.7-inch bbl., 8.1 inches overall. Weight: 31 oz. Fixed sights. Blued finish. Grooved composition grips. Made 1952 to 1956.

MODEL 70 DA AUTO PISTOL NiB $530   Ex $420   Gd $296
Similar to Model 50 but redesigned to improve function and dependability. Made from 1962 to 1983.

MODEL 75 DA/DAO AUTOMATIC PISTOL
Calibers: 9mm Para. or .40 S&W w/selective action mode. 10-, 13- or 15-round magazine, 3.9-inch bbl., (Compact) or 4.75-inch bbl., (Standard), 8 inches overall (Standard). Weight: 35 oz. Fixed sights. Blued, nickel, Two-Tone or black polymer finish. Checkered wood or high-impact plastic grips. Made from 1994 to date.
Black polymer finish . . . . NiB $459   Ex $385   Gd $284
High-polish blued finish . . . . NiB $526   Ex $453   Gd $347
Matte blued finish . . . . NiB $499   Ex $398   Gd $295
Nickel finish. . . . . NiB $541   Ex $442   Gd $330
Two-tone finish . . . . NiB $530   Ex $431   Gd $325
w/.22 Kadet conversion, add. $281
Compact model, add $65
Champion (1999-04, 2006-09)..NiB $1430   Ex $1055   Gd $610

CZ Shadow

CZ Model 75 Compact

CZ Model 75 Kadet

CZ Model 83

MODEL 75 SHADOW AUTOMATIC PISTOL
Competition variant of the Model 75 except w/DA/SA or SAO trigger and Model 85 style trigger. Caliber: 9mm Para. Made from 2011 to 2013.
DA/SA . . . . NiB $920   Ex $730   Gd $580
SAO. . . . . NiB $850   Ex $660   Gd $460
CTS LS-P (long slide) . . . . NiB $1300   Ex $1030   Gd $780

MODEL 75 SP-01 PHANTOM . NiB $530   Ex $380   Gd $280
Caliber: 9mm Para. Polymer black frame. Made from 2009 to 2013.

MODEL 75 B DA/DAO AUTOMATIC PISTOL
Similar to Model 75 except w/firing pin safety block. Made from 1998 to date.
Military (2000-02) . . . . NiB $370   Ex $275   Gd $230
Target SA (2010) . . . . NiB $1055   Ex $800   Gd $530

MODEL 82 DA AUTO PISTOL NiB $407   Ex $306   Gd $221
Similar to the standard CZ 83 model except chambered in 9x18 Makarov. This model currently is the Czech military sidearm since 1983.

MODEL 83 DA AUTOMATIC PISTOL
Calibers: .32 ACP, .380 ACP. 15-round (.32 ACP) or 13-round (.380 ACP) magazine, 3.75-inch bbl., 6.75 inches overall. Weight: 26.5 oz.

85

CZ Model 85 Combat

CZ Model 97B

CZ Model 100

Daewoo DH40

CZ 2075 Rami P shown w/ extended magazine

CZ VZ 61 Skorpion

Fixed sights. Blued (standard); chrome and nickel (optional special edition) w/brushed, matte or polished finish. Checkered black plastic grips. Made from 1985 to 2012.

Standard finish	NiB $434	Ex $357	Gd $221
Special edition	NiB $580	Ex $453	Gd $322
Engraved	NiB $1234	Ex $1017	Gd $718

MODEL 85 AUTOMATIC DA PISTOL
Same as CZ 75 except w/ambidExtrous slide release and safety. Calibers: 9mm Para., 7.65mm. Made 1986 to date.

Black polymer finish	NiB $478	Ex $388	Gd $274
High-polish blued finish	NiB $576	Ex $477	Gd $319
Matte blued finish	NiB $529	Ex $372	Gd $267

MODEL 85 COMBAT DA AUTOMATIC PISTOL
Similar to the standard CZ 85 model except w/13-round magazine, combat-style hammer, fully adj. rear sight and walnut grips. Made from 1986 to date.

Black polymer finish	NiB $569	Ex $489	Gd $306
High-polished blued finish	NiB $610	Ex $498	Gd $373
Matte blued finish	NiB $614	Ex $486	Gd $366

MODEL 97B DA
AUTOLOADING PISTOL . . . . NiB $629 Ex $540 Gd $344
Similar to the CZ Model 75 except chambered for the .45 ACP cartridge. 10-round magazine, Frame-mounted thumb safety that allows single-action, cocked-and-locked carry. Made from 1998 to date.

MODEL 100 DA
AUTOMATIC PISTOL . . . . NiB $488 Ex $398 Gd $265
Caliber: 9mm, .40 S&W. 10-round magazine, 3.8-inch bbl., Weight: 25 oz. Polymer grips w/fixed low-profile sights. Made from 1996 to 2007. Reintroduced 2009.

MODEL 1945 DA
POCKET AUTO PISTOL . . . . NiB $328 Ex $241 Gd $183
Caliber: .25 Auto (6.35mm). Eight-round magazine, 2.5-inch bbl., 5 inches overall. Weight: 15 oz. Fixed sights. Blued finish. Plastic grips. Intro. 1945. disc.

CZ VZ 61 SKORPION . . . . NiB $599 Ex $340 Gd $300
Semi-automatic version of VZ 61 Skorpion submachine gun. Caliber: .32 ACP. 20-round magazine, 4.5-in. bbl. Made from 2009 to 2010.

DUO POCKET AUTO PISTOL . . . NiB $328 Ex $252 Gd $174
Caliber: .25 Automatic (6.35mm). Six-round magazine, 2.13 inch bbl., 4.5 inches overall. Weight: 14-.5 oz. Fixed sights. Blued or nickel finish. Plastic grips. Made circa 1926 to 1960.

DAEWOO — Seoul, Korea

Mfd. by Daewoo Precision Industries Ltd. Imported by Daewoo Precision Industries, Southhampton, PA, Previously by Nationwide Sports Distributors and KBI, Inc.

DH40 AUTO PISTOL . . . . NiB $357 Ex $255 Gd $172
Caliber: .40 S&W. 12-round magazine, 4.25-inch bbl., 7 inches overall. Weight: 28 oz. Blade front sight, dovetailed rear w/3-dot system. Blued finish. Checkered composition grips. DH/DP series feature a patented "fastfire" action w/5-6 lb. trigger pull. Made from 1994 to 1996.

DH45 AUTO PISTOL . . . . NiB $346 Ex $248 Gd $189
Caliber: .45 ACP. 13-round magazine, 5-inch bbl., 8.1 inches over all. Weight: 35 oz. Blade front sight, dovetailed rear w/3-dot system. Blued finish. Checkered composition grips. Announced 1994, but not imported.

DP51 AUTO PISTOL. . . . . NiB $330 Ex $221 Gd $148
Caliber: 9mm Para. 13-round magazine, 4.1-inch bbl., 7.5 inches overall. Weight: 28 oz. Blade front and square-notch rear sights. Matte black finish. Checkered composition grips. Made from 1991 to 1996.

DP52 AUTO PISTOL. . . . . NiB $358 Ex $255 Gd $172
Caliber: .22 LR. 10-round magazine, 3.8-inch bbl., 6.7 inches overall. Weight: 23 oz. Blade front sight, dovetailed rear w/3-dot system. Blued finish. Checkered wood grips. Made from 1994 to 1996.

DAKOTA/E.M.F. CO. — Santa Ana, California

MODEL 1873 SA REVOLVER
Calibers: .22 LR, .22 Mag., .357 Mag., .45 Long Colt, .30 M1 carbine, .38-40, .32-20, .44-40. Bbl. lengths: 3.5, 4.75, 5.5, 7.5 inches. Blued or nickel finish. Engraved models avail.
Standard model . . . . NiB $347 Ex $305 Gd $229
Nickel finish, add. 40%

MODEL 1875 OUTLAW
SA REVOLVER . . . . NiB $525 Ex $420 Gd $293
Calibers: .45 Long Colt, .357 Mag., .44-40. 7.5-inch bbl. Casehardened frame, blued finish. Walnut grips. This is an Exact replica of the Remington Number 3 revolver produced 1875 to 1889.

MODEL 1890 REMINGTON POLICE
Calibers: .357 Mag., .44-40, .45 Long Colt, 5.75-inch bbl., blued or nickel finish. Similar to Outlaw w/lanyard ring and no bbl. web .
Standard model . . . . NiB $560 Ex $441 Gd $332
Nickel model . . . . NiB $637 Ex $523 Gd $371
Engraved model . . . . NiB $780 Ex $603 Gd $444

BISLEY SA REVOLVER
Calibers: .44-40, .45 Long Colt, .357 Mag, 5.5- or 7.5-inch bbl., disc. 1992. Reintroduced 1994.
Standard model . . . . NiB $459 Ex $378 Gd $272
Engraved model . . . . NiB $638 Ex $509 Gd $283

HARTFORD SA REVOLVER
Calibers: .22 LR, .32-20, .357 Mag., .38-40, .44-40, .44 Special, .45 Long Colt. These are Exact replicas of the original Colts w/steel backstraps, trigger guards and forged frames. Blued or nickel finish. Imported from 1990 to 2008.
Standard model . . . . NiB $444 Ex $367 Gd $274
Engraved model . . . . NiB $734 Ex $546 Gd $499
Hartford Artillery,
   U.S. Cavalry models. . . . . NiB $484 Ex $401 Gd $267

Dakota
Hartford
Engraved
Model

SHERIFF'S MODEL
SA REVOLVER . . . . NiB $437 Ex $377 Gd $271
Calibers: .32-20, .357 Mag., .38-40, .44 Special, .44-40, .45 LC. 3.5-inch bbl. Reintroduced 1994.

TARGET SA REVOLVER . . . . . NiB $478 Ex $351 Gd $279
Calibers: .45 Long Colt, .357 Mag., .22 LR; 5.5- or 7.5-inch bbl. Polished, blued finish, casehardened frame. Walnut grips. Ramp front, blade target sight, adj. rear sight.

CHARLES DALY — Currently imported by K.B.I., Harrisburg, Pennsylvania

MODEL M1911-A1 FIELD FS AUTOMATIC PISTOL
Caliber: .45 ACP. Eight- or 10-round magazine (Hi-Cap), 5-inch bbl., 8.75 inches overall. Weight: 38 oz. Blade front sight, drift adjustable rear w/3-dot system. Skeletonized tactical hammer and trigger. Extended slide release and beavertail grip safety. Matte blue, stainless or Duo finish. Checkered composition or wood stocks. Imported from 1999 to 2000.
Matte blue (Field FS) . . . . NiB $525 Ex $479 Gd $326
Stainless (Empire EFS) . . . . NiB $560 Ex $459 Gd $361
Duo (Superior FS) . . . . NiB $653 Ex $497 Gd $363
w/.22 conversion kit, add $204

DAN WESSON — Kansas City, KS

Currently owned by CZ-USA. Also see Wesson Arms.

COMMANDER CLASSIC BOBTAIL NiB $1050 Ex $780 Gd $610
1911 platform. Caliber: 10mm or .45 Auto. 4.25-in. bbl., bobbed frame. Series 70. Made 2005 to 2009.

GLOBAL . . . . NiB $1000 Ex $790 Gd $610
1911 platform. Caliber: 10mm or .45 Auto. 5- or 6-in. bbl., accessory rail or full length dust cover frame. Series 70. Made 2005.

PATRIOT . . . . NiB $830 Ex $660 Gd $480
1911 platform. Caliber: 10mm or .45 Auto. 4.25- or 5-in. bbl., blued or stainless. Series 70. Made 2001 to 2005.

POINTMAN SEVEN . . . . NiB $1050 Ex $780 Gd $610
1911 platform. Caliber: .40 S&W, 10mm or .45 Auto. 5-in. bbl., blued or stainless, adj. target sights. Series 70. Made 2005 to 2009.

DAVIS INDUSTRIES, INC. — Chino, California

MODEL D DERRINGER
Single-action double derringer. Calibers: .22 LR, .22 Mag., .25 ACP, .32 Auto, .32 H&R Mag., 9mm, .38 Special. Two-round capacity, 2.4-inch or 2.75-inch bbl., 4 inches overall (2.4-inch bbl.). Weight: 9 to 11.5 oz.

Detonics Combatmaster

Detonics Scoremaster

Dreyse Model 1907

Laminated wood grips. Black Teflon or chrome finish. Made from 1987 to 2001.

.22 LR or .25 ACP. . . . . .NiB $192   Ex $109   Gd $88
.22 Mag., .32 H&R Mag., .38 Spec. . NiB $204   Ex $128   Gd $91
.32 Auto. NiB $214   Ex $115   Gd $91
9mm Para. . . . . NiB $170   Ex $122   Gd $96

LONG BORE DERRINGER. . . . . NiB $219   Ex $122   Gd $97
Similar to Model D except in calibers .22 Mag., .32 H&R Mag., .38 Special, 9mm Para. 3.75-inch bbl., weight: 16 oz. Made from 1995 to 2001.

MODEL P-.32. . . . . .NiB $152   Ex $101   Gd $78
Caliber: .32 Auto. Six-round magazine, 2.8-inch bbl., 5.4 inches overall. Weight: 22 oz. Black Teflon or chrome finish. Laminated wood grips. Made from 1987 to 2001.

MODEL P-.380. . . . . NiB $192   Ex $115   Gd $89
Caliber: .380 Auto. Five-round magazine, 2.8-inch bbl., 5.4 inches overall. Weight: 22 oz. Black Teflon or chrome finish. Made from 1990 to 2001.

DESERT INDUSTRIES, INC. — Las Vegas, Nevada
Previously Steel City Arms, Inc.

DOUBLE DEUCE DA PISTOL . NiB $386   Ex $286   Gd $225
Caliber: .22 LR. Six-round magazine, 2.5-inch bbl., 5.5 inches overall. Weight: 15 oz. Matte-finish stainless steel. Rosewood grips.

TWO-BIT SPECIAL PISTOL . . . NiB $431   Ex $326   Gd $237
Similar to the Double Deuce model except chambered in .25 ACP w/5-shot magazine.

DETONICS FIREARMS IND. — Phoenix, Arizona
Previously Detonics Firearms Industries, Bellevue, WA.

COMBATMASTER
Calibers: .45 ACP, .451 Detonics Mag. Six-round magazine, 3.5-inch bbl., 6.75 inches overall. Combat-type w/fixed or adjustable sights. Checkered walnut grip. Stainless steel construction. Disc. 1992.
MK I, matte stainless,
   fixed sights (disc. 1981) . . . . . .NiB $1097   Ex $963   Gd $893
MK II polished finish, (disc. 1979) . NiB $1494   Ex $1370   Gd $1133
MK III chrome,
   (disc. 1980) . . . . .NiB $551   Ex $443   Gd $328
MK IV polished blued,
   adj. sights, (disc. 1981). . . . . . .NiB $612   Ex $500   Gd $373
MK V matte stainless,
   fixed sights, (disc. 1985). . . . . . .NiB $762   Ex $621   Gd $499
MK VI polished stainless, fixed
   sights, (disc. 1985) . . . . .NiB $831   Ex $666   Gd $509
MK VI in .451 Magnum,
   (disc. 1986) . . . . .NiB $1199   Ex $979   Gd $695
MK VII matte stainless steel,
   no sights, (disc. 1985) . . . . . . .NiB $1037   Ex $845   Gd $591
MK VII in .451 Magnum,
   (disc. 1980) . . . . .NiB $1380   Ex $1131   Gd $806

POCKET 9 . . . . NiB $668   Ex $541   Gd $426
Calibers: 9mm Para., .380. Six-round magazine, three-inch bbl., 5.88 inches overall. Fixed sights. Double- and single-action trigger mechanism. Disc. 1986.

SCOREMASTER . . . . NiB $1550   Ex $1257   Gd $1120
Calibers: .45 ACP, .451 Detonics Mag. Seven-round magazine. Five- or 6-inch heavyweight match bbl., 8.75 inches overall. Weight: 47 oz. Stainless steel construction, self-centering bbl., system. Disc. 1992.

SERVICEMASTER . . . . NiB $1117   Ex $780   Gd $530
Caliber: .45 ACP. Seven-round magazine, 4.25-inch bbl., weight: 39 oz. Interchangeable front sight, Millett rear sight. Disc. 1986.

SERVICEMASTER II . . . . NiB $1117   Ex $780   Gd $530
Same general specifications as standard Service Master except comes in polished stainless steel w/self-centering bbl., system. Disc. 1992.

DOWNSIZER CORPORATION — Santee, California

MODEL WSP DAO PISTOL . . . . . .NiB $499   Ex $381   Gd $264
Single-round, tip-up pistol. Calibers: .22 Mag., .32 Mag., .380 ACP. 9mm Parabellum, .357 Mag., .40 S&W, .45 ACP. Six-round cylinder, 2.10-inch bbl. w/o Extractor, 3.25 inches overall. Weight: 11 oz. No sights. Stainless finish. Synthetic grips. Made from 1994 to 2007.

DREYSE — Sommerda, Germany
Mfd. by Rheinische Metallwaren und Maschinenfabrik ("Rheinmetall").

MODEL 1907 AUTOMATIC PISTOL NiB $273   Ex $224   Gd $179
Caliber: .32 Auto (7.65mm). Eight-round magazine, 3.5-inch bbl., 6.25 inches overall. Weight: About 24 oz. Fixed sights. Blued finish. Hard rubber grips. Made circa 1907 to 1914.

VEST POCKET
AUTOMATIC PISTOL . . . . . . NiB $357 Ex $293 Gd $204
Conventional Browning type. Caliber: .25 Auto (6.35mm). Six-round magazine, 2-inch bbl., 4.5 inches overall. Weight: About 14 oz. Fixed sights. Blued finish. Hard rubber grips. Made 1909 to 1914.

DWM — Berlin, Germany
Mfd. by Deutsche Waffen-und-Munitionsfabriken.

POCKET AUTOMATIC PISTOLNiB $1050 Ex $918 Gd $713
Similar to the FN Browning Model 1910. Caliber: .32 Automatic (7.65mm). 3.5-inch bbl., 6 inches overall. Weight: About 21 oz. Blued finish. Hard rubber grips. Made circa 1921 to 1931.

ED BROWN — Perry, Montana

CLASS A LTD SA
AUTOMATIC PISTOL . . . . . . NiB $2312 Ex $2152 Gd $1041
Caliber: .38 Super, 9mm, 9x23, .45 ACP. Seven-round magazine, 4.25- or 5-inch bbl., weight: 34-39 oz. Rubber checkered or optional Hogue Exotic wood grip. M1911 style single action pistol. Fixed front and rear Novak Lo-mount or fully adjustable sights.

CLASSIC CUSTOM SA
AUTOMATIC PISTOL . . . . . . NiB $3231 Ex $2553 Gd $1527
Caliber: .45 ACP. Seven-round magazine, 4.25- or 5-inch bbl., weight: 39 oz. Exotic Hogue wood grip w/modified ramp or post front and rear adjustable sights.

SPECIAL FORCES SA
AUTOMATIC PISTOL . . . . . . NiB $2240 Ex $1918 Gd $1437
Caliber: .45 ACP. Seven-round magazine, 4.25- or 5-inch bbl., weight: 34-39 oz. Rubber checkered, optional exotic wood grips. Single action M1911 style pistol.

E.M.F. Co., In. — Santa Anna, California
Importer, distrributor and retailer of numerous reproduction and new deisgn pistols and revolvers. See Davide Pedersoli & Co., F.A.P F.LLI. Pietta, and Uberti.

ENFIELD — Enfield Lock, Middlesex, England
Mfd. by Rheinische Metallwaren und Manufactured by Royal Small Arms Factory.

(BRITISH SERVICE) NO. 2 MK 1
DA REVOLVER . . . . NiB $362 Ex $271 Gd $221
Webley pattern. Hinged frame. Double action. Caliber: .380 British Service (.38 S&W w/200-grain bullet). Six-round cylinder, 5-inch bbl., 10.5 inches overall. Weight: About 27.5 oz. Fixed sights. Blued finish. Vulcanite grips. First issued in 1932, this was the standard revolver of the British Army in WW II. Now obsolete. Note: This model also produced w/spurless hammer as No. 2 Mk 1* and Mk 1**.

ENTREPRISE ARMS — Irwindale, California

ELITE SERIES SA
AUTO PISTOL . . . . NiB $661 Ex $498 Gd $401
Single action M1911 style pistol. Caliber: .45 ACP. 10-round magazine, 3.25-, 4.25-, 5-inch bbl., (models P325, P425, P500). Weight: 36-40 oz. Ultraslim checkered grips, Tactical 2 high profile sights w/3-dot system.

Enfield
(British Service) No. 2 MK 1
Revolver

Erma
Model ER-772 Match Revolver

Lightweight adjustable trigger. Blued or matte black oxide finish. Made from 1997 to date.

MEDALIST SA AUTOMATIC PISTOL
Similar to Elite model except machined to match tolerances and target configuration. Caliber: .45 ACP, .40 S&W. 10-round magazine, 5-inch compensated bbl. w/dovetail front and fully adjustable rear Bo-Mar sights. Weight: 40 oz. Made from 1997 to date.
.40 S&W model . . . . NiB $1015 Ex $862 Gd $689
.45 ACP model. . . . . NiB $893 Ex $740 Gd $577

TACTICAL SA AUTOMATIC PISTOL
Similar to Elite model except in combat carry configuration. De-horned frame and slide w/ambidExtrous safety. Caliber: .45 ACP. 10-round magazine, 3.25-, 4.25-, 5-inch bbl., weight: 36-40 oz. Tactical 2 Ghost Ring or Novak Lo-mount sights.
Tactical 2 ghost
  ring sights . . . . NiB $917 Ex $724 Gd $571
Novak Lo-Mount . . . . NiB $917 Ex $724 Gd $571
Tactical plus model . . . . NiB $917 Ex $724 Gd $571

BOXER SA
AUTOMATIC PISTOL . . . . . NiB $1243 Ex $1122 Gd $831
Similar to Medalist model except w/profiled slide configuration and fully adjustable target sights. weight: 42 oz. Made from 1997 to date.

TOURNAMENT SHOOTER MODEL SA AUTOMATIC PISTOL
Similar to Elite model except in IPSC configuration. Caliber: .45 ACP, .40 S&W. 10-round magazine, 5-inch compensated bbl., w/dovetail front and fully adjustable rear Bo-Mar sights. Weight: 40 oz. Made from 1997 to date.
TSM I model . . . . NiB $2145 Ex $1986 Gd $1637
TSM II model . . . . NiB $1834 Ex $1687 Gd $1331
TSM III model . . . . NiB $2575 Ex $1403 Gd $1661

ERMA-WERKE — Dachau, Germany

MODEL ER-772
MATCH REVOLVER . . . . . . NiB $1132 Ex $1071 Gd $655

European American Armory
Big Bore Bounty Hunter shown
w/optional scope

Erma-Werke
Model KGP69

Model ESP-85A
Competition Pistol

adj. rear sight. Checkered walnut sporter or match-style grip (interchangeable). Made from 1991 to 1995.

MODEL ESP-85A COMPETITION PISTOL
Calibers: .22 LR and .32 S&W Wadcutter. Eight- or 5-round magazine, 6-inch bbl., 10 inches overall. Weight: 40 oz. Adj. rear sight, blade front sight. Checkered walnut grip w/thumbrest. Made from 1991 to 1997.

Match model	NiB $1280	Ex $1128	Gd $716
Chrome match	NiB $1540	Ex $1330	Gd $998
Sporting model	NiB $1251	Ex $1049	Gd $735
Conversion unit .22 LR	NiB $1566	Ex $1212	Gd $1030
Conversion unit .32 S&W	NiB $1566	Ex $1212	Gd $1030

MODEL KGP68
AUTOMATIC PISTOL . . . . NiB $484 Ex $306 Gd $239
Luger type. Calibers: .32 Auto (7.65mm), .380 Auto (9mm Short). Six-round magazine (.32 Auto), 5-round (.380 Auto), 4-inch bbl., 7.38 inches overall. Weight: 22.5 oz. Fixed sights. Blued finish. Checkered walnut grips. Made from 1968 to 1993.

MODEL KGP69
AUTOMATIC PISTOL . . . . NiB $357 Ex $291 Gd $214
Luger type. Caliber: .22 LR. Eight-round magazine, 4-inch bbl., 7.75 inches overall. Weight: 29 oz. fixed sights. Blued finish. Checkered walnut grips. Imported from 1969 to 1993.

EUROPEAN AMERICAN ARMORY —
Rockledge, Florida
See also listings under Astra Pistols.

EUROPEAN MODEL AUTO PISTOL
Calibers: .32 ACP (SA only), .380 ACP (SA or DA), 3.85-inch bbl., 7.38 overall, 7-round magazine, Weight: 26 oz. Blade front sight, drift-adj. rear. Blued, chrome, blue/chrome, blue/gold, Duo-Tone or Wonder finish. Imported 1991 to date.

Blued .32 ACP (disc. 1995)	NiB $140	Ex $101	Gd $81
Blue/chrome .32 caliber (disc. 1995)	NiB $204	Ex $117	Gd $81
Chrome .32 caliber (Disc. 1995)	NiB $137	Ex $101	Gd $81
Blued .380 caliber	NiB $158	Ex $116	Gd $88
Blue/chrome .380 caliber (disc. 1993)	NiB $204	Ex $136	Gd $91
DA .380 caliber (disc. 1994)	NiB $398	Ex $267	Gd $167
Lady .380 caliber (disc. 1995)	NiB $270	Ex $203	Gd $143
Wonder finish .380 caliber	NiB $275	Ex $186	Gd $131

MODEL KGP68
Caliber: .22 LR. Six-round cylinder, 6-inch bbl., 12 inches overall. Weight: 47.25 oz. Adjustable micrometer rear sight and front sight blade. Adjustable trigger. Interchangeable walnut sporter or match grips. Polished blued finish. Made from 1991 to 1994.

MODEL ER-773
MATCH REVOLVER . . . . NiB $957 Ex $831 Gd $587
Same general specifications as Model 772 except chambered for .32 S&W. Made from 1991 to 1995.

MODEL ER-777
MATCH REVOLVER . . . . NiB $923 Ex $785 Gd $623
Caliber: .357 Magnum. Six-round cylinder. 4- or 5.5-inch bbl., 9.7 to 11.3 inches overall. Weight: 43.7 oz. (with 5.5-inch bbl.). Micrometer

BIG BORE BOUNTY HUNTER SA REVOLVER
Calibers: .357 Mag., .41 Mag., .44-40, .44 Mag., .45 Colt. Bbl., lengths: 4.63, 5.5, 7.5 inches. Blade front and grooved topstrap rear sights. Blued or chrome finish w/color casehardened or gold-plated frame. Smooth walnut grips. Imported 1992.

Blued finish	NiB $377	Ex $255	Gd $189
Blued w/color- casehardened frame	NiB $388	Ex $265	Gd $190
Blued w/gold-plated frame	NiB $403	Ex $281	Gd $214
Chrome finish.	NiB $408	Ex $286	Gd $219
Gold-plated frame, add. $110			

BOUNTY HUNTER SA REVOLVER
Calibers: .22 LR, .22 Mag. Bbl. lengths: 4.75, 6 or 9 inches. Blade front and dovetailed rear sights. Blued finish or blued w/gold-plated frame. European hardwood grips. Imported from 1997 to date.

Blued finish (4.75-inch bbl.)	NiB $281	Ex $191	Gd $128
Blued .22 LR/.22 WRF combo (4.75-inch bbl.)	NiB $281	Ex $191	Gd $128
Blued .22 LR/.22 WRF combo (6-inch bbl.).	NiB $281	Ex $191	Gd $128
Blued .22 LR/.22 WRF combo (9-inch bbl.).	NiB $281	Ex $191	Gd $128

EA22 TARGET . . . . **NiB $398   Ex $281   Gd $214**
Caliber: .22 LR. 12-round magazine, 6-inch bbl., 9.10 inches overall. Weight: 40 oz. Ramp front sight, fully adj. rear. Blued finish. Checkered walnut grips w/thumbrest. Made from 1991 to 1994.

FAB 92 AUTO PISTOL
Similar to the Witness model except chambered in 9mm only w/slide-mounted safety and no cock-and-lock provision. Imported 1992 to 1995.

FAB 92 standard.	NiB $437	Ex $342	Gd $223
FAB 92 compact.	NiB $437	Ex $342	Gd $223

STANDARD GRADE REVOLVER
Calibers: .22 LR, .22 WRF, .32 H&R Mag., .38 Special. Two-, 4- or 6-inch bbl., blade front sight, fixed or adj. rear. Blued finish. European hardwood grips w/finger grooves. Imported 1991 to date.

.22 LR (4-inch bbl.)	NiB $215	Ex $171	Gd $128
.22 LR (6-inch bbl.)	NiB $228	Ex $181	Gd $133
.22 LR combo (4-inch bbl.).	NiB $301	Ex $237	Gd $171
.22 LR combo (6-inch bbl.).	NiB $337	Ex $265	Gd $187
.32 H&R, .38 Special (2-inch bbl.)	NiB $231	Ex $174	Gd $128
.38 Special (4-inch bbl.)	NiB $235	Ex $187	Gd $132
.357 Mag	NiB $242	Ex $206	Gd $144

TACTICAL GRADE REVOLVER
Similar to the Standard model except chambered in .38 Special only. Two- or 4-inch bbl., fixed sights. Available w/compensator. Imported from 1991-93.

Tactical revolver	NiB $229	Ex $185	Gd $109
Tactical revolver w/compensator. . . .	NiB $316	Ex $270	Gd $192

WINDICATOR TARGET REVOLVER. . **NiB $444   Ex $381   Gd $255**
Calibers: .22 LR, .38 Special, .357 Magnum. Eight-round cylinder in .22 LR, 6-round in .38 Special and .357 Magnum. Six-inch bbl. w/bbl. weights. 11.8 inches overall. Weight: 50.2 oz. Interchangeable blade front sight, fully adj. rear. Walnut competition-style grips. Imported from 1991-93.

WITNESS DA AUTO PISTOL
Similar to the Brno CZ-75 w/a cocked-and-locked system. Double or single action. Calibers: 9mm Para. .38 Super, .40 S&W, 10mm; .41 AE and .45 ACP. 16-round magazine (9mm), 12 shot (.38 Super/.40 S&W), or 10-round (10mm/.45 ACP), 4.75-inch bbl., 8.10 inches overall. Weight: 35.33 oz. Blade front sight, rear sight adj. for windage w/3-dot sighting system. Steel or

European American Armory
Windicator Target

European American Armory
Witness

polymer frame. Blued, satin chrome, blue/chrome, stainless or Wonder finish. Checkered rubber grips. EA Series imported 1991 to date.

9mm blue	NiB $475	Ex $337	Gd $249
9mm chrome or blue/chrome	NiB $475	Ex $337	Gd $249
9mm stainless.	NiB $469	Ex $337	Gd $283
9mm Wonder finish	NiB $500	Ex $356	Gd $265
.38 Super and .40 S&W blued.	NiB $475	Ex $337	Gd $237
.38 Super and .40 S&W chrome or blue/chrome	NiB $469	Ex $388	Gd $273
.38 Super and .40 S&W stainless.	NiB $546	Ex $425	Gd $292
.38 Super and .40 S&W Wonder finish . .	NiB $577	Ex $340	Gd $296
10mm, .41 AE and .45 ACP blued.	NiB $474	Ex $346	Gd $235
10mm, .41 AE and .45 ACP chrome or blue/chrome	NiB $546	Ex $437	Gd $316
10mm, .41 AE and .45 ACP stainless. . .	NiB $577	Ex $464	Gd $337
10mm, .41 AE and .45 ACP Wonder finish	NiB $562	Ex $439	Gd $321

WITNESS COMPACT DA AUTO PISTOL (L SERIES)
Similar to the standard Witness series except more compact w/ 3.625-inch bbl., and polymer or steel frame. Weight: 30 oz. Matte blued or Wonder finish. EA Compact series imported 1999 to date.

9mm blue	NiB $468	Ex $330	Gd $235
9mm Wonder finish	NiB $468	Ex $330	Gd $235
.38 Super and .40 S&W blued.	NiB $468	Ex $330	Gd $235
.38 Super and .40 S&W Wonder finish . .	NiB $468	Ex $330	Gd $235
10mm, .41 AE and .45 ACP blued.	NiB $549	Ex $369	Gd $273
10mm, .41 AE and .45 ACP Wonder fin.	NiB $549	Ex $369	Gd $273
w/ported bbl., add $50			

Feather Guardian Angel Derringer

FEG Mark II AP-.22

WITNESS CARRY COMP

Double/Single action. Calibers: .38 Super, 9mm Parabellum, .40 S&W, 10mm, .45 ACP. 10-, 12- or 16-round magazine, 4.25-inch bbl., w/1-inch compensator. Weight: 33 oz., 8.10 inches overall. Black rubber grips. Post front sight, drift adjustable rear w/3-dot system. Matte blue, Duo-Tone or Wonder finish. Imported 1992 to 2004.

9mm, .40 S&W	. . . . NiB $453	Ex $359	Gd $273
.38 Super, 10mm, .45 ACP	. . . . . NiB $453	Ex $359	Gd $273
w/Duo-Tone finish (disc.), add	. . . .	.	$40
w/Wonder finish, add	. . . .	.	$20

WITNESS LIMITED

CLASS AUTO PISTOL . . . . **NiB $909   Ex $734   Gd $559**
Single action. Calibers: .38 Super, 9mm Parabellum, .40 S&W, .45 ACP. 10-round magazine, 4.75-inch bbl., Weight: 37 oz. Checkered competition-style walnut grips. Long slide w/post front sight, fully adj. rear. Matte blue finish. Imported 1994 to 1998.

WITNESS SUBCOMPACT DA AUTO PISTOL

Calibers: 9mm Para., .40 S&W, 41 AK, .45 ACP. 13-round magazine in 9mm, 9-round in .40 S&W, 3.66-inch bbl., 7.25 inches overall. Weight: 30 oz. Blade front sight, rear sight adj. for windage. Blued, satin chrome or blue/chrome finish. Imported from 1995 to 1997.

9mm blue	. . . . NiB $408	Ex $281	Gd $204
9mm chrome or blue/chrome	. . . NiB $453	Ex $306	Gd $225
.40 S&W blue	. . . . NiB $453	Ex $306	Gd $225
.40 S&W chrome or blue/chrome	NiB $497	Ex $366	Gd $229
.41 AE blue	. . . . NiB $525	Ex $429	Gd $308
.41 AE chrome or blue/chrome	. . NiB $577	Ex $448	Gd $319
.45 ACP blued	. . . . NiB $525	Ex $336	Gd $308
.45 ACP chrome or blue/chrome	. NiB $500	Ex $439	Gd $321

WITNESS TARGET PISTOLS

Similar to standard Witness model except fitted w/2- or 3-port compensator, competition frame and S/A target trigger. Calibers: 9mm Para., 9x21, .40 S&W, 10mm and .45 ACP, 5.25-inch match bbl., 10.5 inches overall. Weight: 38 oz. Square post front sight, fully adj. rear or drilled and tapped for scope. Blued or hard chrome finish. Low-profile competition grips. Imported 1992 to date.

**Silver Team (blued w/2-port
compensator)** . . . . **NiB $895   Ex $785   Gd $561**
**Gold Team (chrome
w/3-port compensator)** . . . . . . **NiB $1810   Ex $1632   Gd $1331**

FAS — Malino, Italy

Currently imported by Nygord Precision Products. Previously by Beeman Precision Arms and Osborne's, Cheboygan, MI.

OP601 SEMIAUTOMATIC MATCH TARGET PISTOL

Caliber: .22 Short. Five-round top-loading magazine, 5.6-inch ported and ventilated bbl., 11 inches overall. Weight: 41.5 oz. Removable, adj. trigger group. Blade front sight, open-notch fully adj. rear. Stippled walnut wraparound or adj. target grips.

Right-hand model	. . . . NiB $1076	Ex $930	Gd $714
Left-hand model	. . . . NiB $1153	Ex $985	Gd $755

602 SEMIAUTOMATIC MATCH TARGET PISTOL

Similar to Model FAS 601 except chambered for .22 LR. Weight: 37 oz.

Right-hand model	. . . . NiB $960	Ex $705	Gd $581
Left-hand model	. . . . NiB $1030	Ex $830	Gd $691

CF603 SEMIAUTOMATIC

MATCH TARGET PISTOL . . . . . . **NiB $1030   Ex $816   Gd $647**
Similar to Model FAS 601 except chambered for .32 S&W (wadcutter).

SP607 SEMIAUTOMATIC

MATCH TARGET PISTOL . . . . . . **NiB $1030   Ex $804   Gd $658**
Similar to Model FAS 601 except chambered for .22 LR, w/removable bbl. weights. Imported 1995 to date.

FEATHER INDUSTRIES — Boulder, Colorado

GUARDIAN ANGEL DERRINGER

Double-action over/under derringer w/interchangeable drop-in loading blocks. Calibers: .22 LR, .22 WMR, 9mm, .38 Spec. Two-round capacity, 2-inch bbl., 5 inches overall. weight: 12 oz. Stainless steel. Checkered black grip. Made from 1988 to 1995.

.22 LR, .22 WMR	. . . . NiB 165	Ex $101	Gd $81
9mm, .38 Special (disc. 1989)	. . . NiB $233	Ex $189	Gd $150

FEG (FEGYVERGYAN) — Budapest, Soroksariut, Hungary

Currently imported by KBI, Inc. and Century International Arms. Previously by Interarms.

MARK II AP-.22 DA AUTOMATIC PISTOL . . **NiB $271   Ex $219   Gd $179**
Caliber: .22 LR. 8-round magazine, 3.4-inch bbl., Weight: 23 oz. Drift-adj. sights. Double action, all-steel pistol. Imported 1997 to 1998.

MARK II AP-.380 DA AUTOMATIC PISTOL. **NiB $271   Ex $219   Gd $179**
Caliber: .380. 7-round magazine, 3.9-inch bbl., weight 27 oz. Drift-adj. sights. Double action, all-steel pistol. Imported 1997 to 1998.

**MARK II APK-.380 DA
AUTOMATIC PISTOL.** . . . . **NiB $271   Ex $219   Gd $179**
Caliber: .380. 7-round magazine, 3.4-inch bbl., weight: 25 oz. Drift-adj. sights. Double action, all-steel pistol. Imported 1997 to 1998.

MODEL GKK-9 (92C) AUTO PISTOL ...... NiB $321 Ex $240 Gd $204
Improved version of the double-action FEG Model MBK. Caliber: 9mm Para. 14-round magazine, 4-inch bbl., 7.4 inches overall. Weight: 34 oz. Blade front sight, rear sight adj. for windage. Checkered wood grips. Blued finish. Imported from 1992 to 1993.

MODEL GKK-.45 AUTO PISTOL
Improved version of the double-action FEG Model MBK. Caliber: .45 ACP. Eight-round magazine, 4.1-inch bbl., 7.75 inches overall. Weight: 36 oz. Blade front sight, adj. rear sight w/3-dot system. Checkered walnut grips. Blued or chrome finish. Imported 1993 to 1996.
Blued model (disc. 1994) .... NiB $325 Ex $265 Gd $204
Chrome model .... NiB $362 Ex $281 Gd $220

MODEL MBK-9HP AUTO PISTOL NiB $469 Ex $306 Gd $281
Similar to the double-action Browning Hi-Power. Caliber: 9mm Para. 14-round magazine, 4.6-inch bbl., 8 inches overall. Weight: 36 oz. Blade front sight, rear sight adj. for windage. Checkered wood grips. Blued finish. Imported from 1992 to 1993.

MODEL PA-63
AUTO PISTOL .... NiB n/a Ex $175 Gd $95
Hungary's military pistol. Similar to the Walther PP. Caliber: 9x18mm Makarov. 7-round magazine, 3.95-inch bbl., 6.9 inches overall. Weight: 21 oz. Fixed sights. Two-tone finish; blued slide natutal aluminum frame. Checkered plasic grips. Military surplus.

MODEL PJK-9HP AUTO PISTOL
Similar to the single-action Browning Hi-Power. Caliber: 9mm Para. 13-round magazine, 4.75-inch bbl., 8 inches overall. Weight: 21 oz. Blade front sight, rear sight adj. for windage w/3-dot system. Checkered walnut or rubber grips. Blued or chrome finish. Imported 1992 to 2003.
Blued model. .... NiB $469 Ex $388 Gd $265
Chrome model .... NiB $500 Ex $408 Gd $316

MODEL PSP-.25 AUTO PISTOL
Similar to the Browning .25. Caliber: .25 ACP. Six-round magazine, 2.1-inch bbl., 4.1 inches overall. Weight: 9.5 oz. Fixed sights. Checkered composition grips. Blued or chrome finish.
Blued model. .... NiB $316 Ex $204 Gd $150
Chrome model .... NiB $316 Ex $204 Gd $150

MODEL SMC-.22 AUTO PISTOL NiB $222 Ex $130 Gd $79
Same general specifications as FEG Model SMC-.380 except in .22 LR. Eight-round magazine, 3.5-inch bbl., 6.1 inches overall. Weight: 18.5 oz. Blade front sight, rear sight adj. for windage. Checkered composition grips w/thumbrest. Blued finish.

MODEL SMC-.380 AUTO PISTOL NiB $222 Ex $130 Gd $79
Similar to the Walther DA PPK w/alloy frame. Caliber: .380 ACP. Six-round magazine, 3.5-inch bbl., 6.1 inches overall. Weight: 18.5 oz. Blade front sight, rear sight adj. for windage. Checkered composition grips w/ thumbrest. Blued finish. Imported 1993 to 1997.

MODEL SMC-918 AUTO PISTOL NiB $203 Ex $120 Gd $90
Same general specifications as FEG Model SMC-.380 except chambered in 9x18mm Makarov. Imported from 1994 to 1997.

FIALA OUTFITTERS, INC. — New York

REPEATING PISTOL .... NiB $689 Ex $479 Gd $365
Hand-operated, not semi-auto. Caliber: .22 LR. 10-round magazine, bbl. lengths: 3-, 7.5- and 20-inch. 11.25 inches overall (with 7.5-inch bbl.). Weight: 31 oz. (with 7.5-inch bbl.). Target sights. Blued finish. Plain wood grips. Shoulder stock was originally supplied for use w/20-inch

FEG Model PJK-9HP

**F.I.E. Model
A27BW**

F.I.E. Arminius

bbl. Made from 1920 to 1923. Value shown is for pistol w/one bbl., no shoulder stock. Three bbl. cased sets start at $3,030.

F.I.E. CORPORATION — Hialeah, Florida
The F.I.E. Corporation became QFI (Quality Firearms Corp.) of Opa Locka, Fl., about 1990, when most of F.I.E.'s models were discontinued.

MODEL A27 "THE BEST"
SEMIAUTO .... NiB $140 Ex $95 Gd $55
Caliber: .25 ACP. Six-round magazine, 2.5-inch bbl., 6.75 inches overall. Weight: 13 oz. Fixed sights. Checkered walnut grip. Discontinued in 1990.

ARMINIUS DA STANDARD REVOLVER
Calibers: .22 LR, .22 combo w/interchangeable cylinder, .32 S&W, .38 Special, .357 Magnum. Six, 7 or 8 rounds depending on caliber. Swing-out cylinder. bbl., lengths: 2-, 3-, 4, 6-inch. Vent rib on calibers other than .22, 11 inches overall (with 6-inch bbl.). Weight: 26 to 30 oz. Fixed or micro-adj. sights. Checkered plastic or walnut grips. Blued finish. Made in Germany. Disc.

F.I.E. Titan Tiger

F.I.E. Titan II

F.I.E. Model TZ75

Calibers: .357 Magnum, .44 Magnum, .45 Colt. Six-round cylinder. bbl. lengths: 6 or 7.5 inches, 11 inches overall (with -inch bbl.). Weight: 45 oz. (6-inch bbl.). Fixed sights. Blued bbl. w/color-casehardened receiver. Smooth walnut grips. Made from 1979 to 1990.

SUPER TITAN II
Caliber: .32 ACP or .380 ACP, 3.25-inch bbl., weight: 28 oz. Blued or chrome finish. Disc. 1990.
.32 ACP blue;	NiB $138	Ex $95	Gd $70
.32 ACP chrome.	NiB $138	Ex $95	Gd $70
.380 ACP blue;	NiB $138	Ex $95	Gd $70
.380 ACP chrome.	NiB $138	Ex $95	Gd $70

TEXAS RANGER SINGLE-ACTION REVOLVER
Calibers: .22 LR, .22 WRF, .22 combo w/interchangeable cylinder. bbl., lengths: 4.75-, 6.5-, 9-inch. 10 inches overall (with 4.75-inch bbl.). Weight: 32 oz. (with 4.75-inch bbl.). Fixed sights. Blued finish. Smooth walnut grips. Made from 1983 to 1990.
Standard	NiB $97	Ex $75	Gd $55
Convertible	NiB $97	Ex $75	Gd $55

LITTLE RANGER SA REVOLVER
Same as the TExas Ranger except w/3.25-inch bbl. and bird's-head grips. Made from 1986 to 1990.
Standard.	NiB $97	Ex $75	Gd $55
Convertible	NiB $109	Ex $81	Gd $61

TITAN TIGER DOUBLE-ACTION REVOLVER . . . . NiB $78 Ex $47 Gd $35
Caliber: .38 Special. Six-round cylinder, 2- or 4-inch bbl., 8.25 inches overall (with 4-inch bbl.). Weight: 30 oz. (4-inch bbl.). Fixed sights. Blued finish. Checkered plastic or walnut grips. Made in the U.S. Disc. 1990.

TITAN II SEMIAUTOMATIC
Caiibers: .22 LR, .32 ACP, .380 ACP. 10-round magazine, integral tapered post front sight, windage-adjustable rear sight. European walnut grips. Blued or chrome finish. Disc. 1990.
.22 LR in blue	NiB $140	Ex $108	Gd $88
.32 ACP in blued	NiB $211	Ex $170	Gd $128
.32 ACP in chrome.	NiB $221	Ex $176	Gd $141
.380 ACP in blue	NiB $221	Ex $176	Gd $141
.380 ACP in chrome	NiB $235	Ex $181	Gd $158

MODEL TZ75 DA SEMIAUTOMATIC
Double action. Caliber: 9mm. 15-round magazine, 4.5-inch bbl., 8.25 inches overall. Weight: 35 oz. Ramp front sight, windage-adjustable rear sight. European walnut or black rubber grips. Imported from 1988 to 1990.
Blued finish	NiB $387	Ex $302	Gd $214
Satin chrome	NiB $425	Ex $321	Gd $255

YELLOW ROSE SA REVOLVER
Same general specifications as the Buffalo Scout except in .22 combo w/interchangeable cylinder and plated in 24-karat gold. Limited Edition w/scrimshawed ivory polymer grips and American walnut presentation case. Made from 1987 to 1990.
Yellow Rose .22 combo	NiB $140	Ex $93	Gd $59
Yellow Rose Limited Edition . . .	NiB $292	Ex $229	Gd $188

.22 LR	NiB $130	Ex $89	Gd $67
.22 Combo.	NiB $198	Ex $148	Gd $101
.32 S&W.	NiB $207	Ex $149	Gd $101
.38 Special.	NiB $161	Ex $95	Gd $70
.357 Magnum.	NiB $240	Ex $179	Gd $135

BUFFALO SCOUT SA REVOLVER
Calibers: .22 LR, .22 WRF, .22 combo w/interchangeable cylinder. 4.75-inch bbl., 10 inches overall. Weight: 32 oz. Adjustable sights. Blued or chrome finish. Smooth walnut or black checkered nylon grips. Made in Italy. Disc.
Blued standard	NiB $84	Ex $62	Gd $40
Blued convertible	NiB $91	Ex $62	Gd $40
Chrome standard	NiB $91	Ex $62	Gd $40
Chrome convertible	NiB $91	Ex $62	Gd $40

HOMBRE SA REVOLVER . . . . . . NiB $230 Ex $179 Gd $105

FIREARMS INTERNATIONAL CORP. — Washington, D.C.

MODEL D
AUTOMATIC PISTOL . . . . NiB $219 Ex $179 Gd $95
Caliber: .380 Automatic. Six-round magazine, 3.3-inch bbl., 6.13 inches overall. Weight: 19.5 oz. Blade front sight, windage-adjustable rear sight. Blued, chromed, or military finish. Checkered walnut grips. Made from 1974 to 1977.

REGENT
DA REVOLVER . . . . **NiB $189 Ex $130 Gd $101**
Calibers: .22 LR, .32 S&W Long. Eight-round cylinder (.22 LR), or 7-round (.32 S&W). Bbl. lengths: 3-, 4-, 6-inches (.22 LR) or 2.5-, 4-inches (.32 S&W). Weight: 28 oz.(with 4-inch bbl.). Fixed sights. Blued finish. Plastic grips. Made from 1966 to 1972.

FN BROWNING — Liege, Belgium.
Mfd. by Fabrique Nationale Herstal

See also Browning handguns

6.35MM POCKET AUTO PISTOL
See FN Browning Baby Auto Pistol.

MODEL 1900 POCKET
AUTO PISTOL . . . . **NiB $842 Ex $702 Gd $485**
Caliber: .32 Automatic (7.65mm). Seven-round magazine, 4-inch bbl., 6.75 inches overall. Weight: 22 oz. Fixed sights. Blued finish. Hard rubber grips. Made from 1899 to 1910.

MODEL 1903 MILITARY AUTO PISTOL
Caliber: 9mm Browning Long. Seven-round magazine, 5-inch bbl., 8 inches overall. Weight: 32 oz. Fixed sights. Blued finish. Hard rubber grips. Note: Aside from size, this pistol is of the same basic design as the Colt Pocket .32 and .380 Automatic pistols. Made from 1903 to 1939.
Model 1903
  Standard . . . . **NiB $1285 Ex $1152 Gd $880**
Model 1903
  (w/slotted backstrap) . . . . **NiB $1285 Ex $1152 Gd $880**
**Model 1903 (w/slotted backstrap, shoulder stock
  and Extended magazine)** . . . . **NiB $2525 Ex $2270 Gd $1790**

MODEL 1910
POCKET AUTO PISTOL . . . . **NiB $577 Ex $431 Gd $286**
Calibers: .32 Auto (7.65mm), .380 Auto (9mm). Seven-round magazine (.32 cal.), or 6-round (.380 cal.), 3.5-inch bbl., 6 inches overall. Weight: 20.5 oz. Fixed sights. Blued finish. Hard rubber grips. Made from 1910 to 1954.

MODEL 1922 (10/.22) POLICE/MILITARY AUTO
Calibers: .32 Auto (7.65mm), .380 Auto (9mm). Nine-round magazine (.32 cal.), or 8-round (.380 cal.), 4.5-inch bbl., 7 inches overall. Weight: 25 oz. Fixed sights. Blued finish. Hard rubber grips. Made from 1922 to 1959.
Model 1922
  commercial . . . . **NiB $459 Ex $326 Gd $265**
Model 1922
  Military contract. . . . . **NiB $414 Ex $301 Gd $204**
Model 1922 (w/Nazi proofs) . . . . **NiB $414 Ex $326 Gd $265**

MODEL 1935 MILITARY HI-POWER PISTOL
Variation of the Browning-Colt .45 Auto design. Caliber: 9mm Para.13-round magazine, 4.63-inch bbl., 7.75 inches overall. Weight: About 35 oz. Adjustable rear sight and fixed front, or both fixed. Blued finish (Canadian manufacture Parkerized). Checkered walnut or plastic grips. Note: Above specifications in general apply to both the original FN production and the pistols made by John Inglis Company of Canada for the Chinese government. A smaller version, w/shorter bbl. and slide and 10-round magazine, was made by FN for the Belgian and Rumanian Governments about 1937 to 191940. Both types were made at the FN plant during the German occupation of Belgium.

**Firearms International
Model D**

**Firearms
International Regent**

**FN Browning
6.35mm Pocket**

**FN Browning
1900 Pocket**

Pre-war commercial (w/fixed sights) . . .NiB $1152 Ex $918 Gd $729
Pre-war commercial
(w/tangent sight only) . . . . .NiB $2040 Ex $1347 Gd $712
Pre-war commercial
(w/tangent sight, slotted backstrap) . .NiB $3014 Ex $2652 Gd $1448
Pre-war Belgian military contract . . . .NiB $1234 Ex $1020 Gd $704
Pre-war Foreign military contract . . .NiB $2212 Ex $1785 Gd $1225
War production (w/fixed sights). . . . . . .NiB $861 Ex $674 Gd $485
War production (w/tangent sight only) . NiB $1405 Ex $1133 Gd $783
War production (w/tangent sight and slotted
   backstrap). . . . . NiB $3488 Ex $2770 Gd $1913
Post-war/pre-BAC (w/fixed sights) . . . . . .NiB $842 Ex $577 Gd $392
Post-war/pre-BAC (w/tangent sight only) .NiB $893 Ex $577 Gd $392
Post-war/pre-BAC (w/tangent sight,
   slotted backstrap) . . . . NiB $663 Ex $784 Gd $756
Inglis manufacture
   Canadian military (w/fixed sights)NiB $1015 Ex $743 Gd $571
Canadian military
   (w/fixed sight, slotted) . . . . . NiB $1871 Ex $1494 Gd $1021
Canadian military
   (w/tangent sight, slotted). . . . . NiB $1533 Ex $1235 Gd $884
Canadian military
   (marked w/Inglis logo) . . . . . NiB $2654 Ex $2149 Gd $1462
Chinese military contract
   (w/tangent sight, slotted). . . . NiB $3421 Ex $2754 Gd $1876
Canadian military
   (w/fixed sight, slotted backstrap)NiB $1879 Ex $1503 Gd $1029
Canadian military
   (marked w/Inglis logo) . . . . . NiB $2642 Ex $2147 Gd $1460
   w/issue wooden holster, add. $408

BABY AUTO PISTOL . . . . NiB $638 Ex $530 Gd $377
Caliber: .25 Automatic (6.35mm). Six-round magazine, 2.13-inch bbl., 4 inches overall. Weight: 10 oz. Fixed sights. Blued finish. Hard rubber grips. Made from 1931 to 1983.

FOREHAND & WADSWORTH — Worcester, Massachusetts

See listings of comparable Harrington & Richardson and Iver Johnson revolvers for values.

FORT WORTH FIREARMS — Fort Worth, Texas

MATCH MASTER STANDARD. . . . . NiB $499 Ex $283 Gd $225
Semi-automatic. Caliber: .22LR. Equipped with 3 7/8-, 4 1/2-, 5 1/2-, 7 1/2- or 10-inch bull bbl., double Extractors, includes upper push button and standard magazine release, angled grip, low profile frame. Made from 1995 to 2000.

**MATCH MASTER
DOVETAIL** . . . . .NiB $500 Ex $408 Gd $321
Similar to Match Master except has 3 7/8-, 4 1/2-, or 5 1/2-inch bbl. with dovetail rib.

MATCH MASTER DELUXE . . . . NiB $581 Ex $464 Gd $367
Similar to Match master Standard except has Weaver rib on bbl.
w/10-in. bbl., add. $128

FN Browning 1910 Pocket

FN Browning 1922 Police/Military

FN Browning 1935 Military Hi-Power

FN Browning Baby

SPORT KING . . . . NiB $601 Ex $321 Gd $270
Semi-automatic. Caliber: .22 LR. Equipped with 4 1/2- or 5 1/2-inch bbl., blued finish, military grips, drift sights, 10 round magazine. Made from 1995 to 2000.

CITATION . . . . NiB $439 Ex $319 Gd $265
Semi-automatic. Caliber: .22 LR. Equipped with 5 1/2-inch bull bbl. or 7 1/2-inch fluted bbl., military grips, 10-round magazine.

TROPHY . . . . NiB $433 Ex $332 Gd $270
Semi-automatic. Caliber: .22 LR. Equipped with 5 1/2- or 7 1/2- inch bull bbl. blued finish, military grips, 10-round magazine.
w/LH action (5 1/2-inch bbl. only), add $65

VICTOR . . . . NiB $499 Ex $398 Gd $301
Semi-automatic. Caliber: .22LR. Equipped with 3 7/8-, 4 1/2- (VR or Weaver rib), 8- (Weaver rib) or 10-inch (Weaver rib) bbls.; blued finish, military grips, 10-round magazine.
w/4 1/2- or 4 1/2-inch Weaver rib bbls, add $100
w/8- or 10-inch Weaver rib bbls, add $190

OLYMPIC. . . . . NiB $668 Ex $525 Gd $410
Semi-automatic. Caliber: .22 LR or Short. Equipped with 6 1/2-inch fluted bbl., blued finish, military grips, 10-round magazine.

SHARPSHOOTER . . . . NiB $499 Ex $365 Gd $259
Semi-automatic. Caliber: .22 LR. Equipped with 5 1/2-inch bull bbl.,blued finish, military grips, 10-round magazine.

LE FRANCAIS — St. Etienne, France
Produced by Manufacture Francaise d'Armes et Cycles.

ARMY MODEL
AUTOMATIC PISTOL . . . . NiB $1749 Ex $1305 Gd $842
Similar in operation to the Le Francais .25 Automatics. Caliber: 9mm Browning Long. Eight-round magazine, 5-inch bbl., 7.75 inches overall. Weight: About 34 oz. Fixed sights. Blued finish. Checkered walnut grips. Made from 1928 to 1938.

POLICEMAN MODEL
AUTOMATIC PISTOL . . . . NiB $1020 Ex $917 Gd $416
DA. Hinged bbl., Caliber: .25 Automatic (6.35mm). Seven-round magazine, 3.5-inch bbl., 6 inches overall. Weight: About 12 oz. Fixed sights. Blued finish. Hard rubber grips. Introduced in 1914. disc.

STAFF OFFICER MODEL
AUTOMATIC PISTOL . . . . NiB $388 Ex $301 Gd $205
Caliber: .25 Automatic. Similar to the "Policeman" model except does not have cocking-piece head, barrel, is about an inch shorter and weight is an ounce less. Introduced in 1914. disc.

FREEDOM ARMS — Freedom, Wyoming

MODEL 97 PREMIER GRADE SA REVOLVER
Calibers: .17 HMR, .22 LR, .224-32 F.A., .327 Fed., .32 H&R Mag., .357 Mag., .41 Mag. or .45 LC. Five- or 6-round cylinder, 4.25, 5, 5.5, 6 or 7.5-inch bbl., removable front blade with adjustable or fixed rear sight. Hardwood or black Micarta grips. Satin stainless finish. Made from 1997 to date.
Premier grade 97 . . . . NiB $2178 Ex $1775 Gd $890
w/extra cylinder, add $225
w/fixed sights, deduct. $150

MODEL 83 FIELD GRADE
SA REVOLVER. . . . . .NiB $2283 Ex $1825 Gd $870
Calibers: .22LR, .357 Mag., .41 Mag., .44 Mag., .454 Casull, .475 Linebaugh , .50 AE or .500 Wyoming Express. Five-round cylinder, bbl. lengths: 4.75-, 6-, 7.5-, 9- or 10-in. Adj. sight or fixed. Impregnated hardwood grips. Brushed matte stainless steel finish. Made from 1988 to date.

MODEL 83 FIELD GRADE HUNTER PACK
SA REVOLVER. . . . . NiB $1160 Ex $900 Gd $710
Similar to Model 83 Field Grade except calibers: .357 Mag., .44 Mag., .454 Casull only. 7.5-in. bbl., sling studs. Made from 1990 to 1993.

MODEL 83 PREMIER GRADE
SA REVOLVER. . . . . .NiB $2686 Ex $2175 Gd $1000
Calibers: .357 Mag., .41 Mag., .44 Mag., .454 Casull, .475 Linebaugh, .50 AE or .500 Wyoming Express.Adjustable sight or fixed. Impregnated hardwood grips. Brushed bright stainless steel finish. Made from 1983 to date.

MODEL 83 PREMIER GRADE HUNTER PACK
SA REVOLVER. . . . . NiB $1400 Ex $930 Gd $760
Similar to Model 83 Field Grade except calibers: .357 Mag., .44 Mag., or .454 Casull only. 7.5-in. bbl., sling studs. Made from 1990 to 1993.

MODEL 83 RIMFIRE GRADE
SA REVOLVER. . . . . .NiB $2484 Ex $1525 Gd $800
Calibers: .22 LR. Bbl. length: 10-in. Adjustable sights. Brushed matte stainless finish. Rosewood grips. Made from 1991 to date.

MODEL 83 SILHOUETTE GRADE (RIMFIRE)
SA REVOLVER. . . . . .NiB $2603 Ex $1875 Gd $830
Calibers: .22 LR. Bbl. lengths: 5.13 or 10 inches. Adjustable competition silhouette sights. Brushed or matte stainless finish. Black Micarta grips. Made from 1991 to date.

MODEL 83 SILHOUETTE GRADE (CENTERFIRE)
SA REVOLVER. . . . . .NiB $2318 Ex $1975 Gd $1000
Calibers: .357 Mag., .41 Mag., or .44 Mag. Bbl. lengths: 9- or 10-in. Removable blade front sight w/hood, adjustable rear. Brushed matte stainless finish. Wood grips.
.454 Casull. . . . . NiB $1600 Ex $1080 Gd $850

MODEL U.S. DEPUTY MARSHAL
SA REVOLVER. . . . . NiB $1330 Ex $780 Gd $540
Bbl. lengths: 3-in. Adj. or fixed sights. No ejector rod. Brushed matte stainless. Made from 1990 to 1993.

Freedom Arms
Model 83 Varmint

Frommer Stop

MODEL FA-L-22LR MINI-REVOLVER NiB $204 Ex $159 Gd $103
Caliber: .22 LR, 1.75-inch contoured bbl., partial high-gloss stainless
steel finish. Bird's-head-type grips. Disc. 1987.

MODEL FA-S-22LR MINI-REVOLVER NiB $214 Ex $189 Gd $105
Caliber: .22 LR. One-inch contoured bbl., partial high-gloss stainless
steel finish. Disc. 1988.
w/1.75-in. bbl . . . . NiB $204 Ex $159 Gd $103
w/3-in. bbl . . . . NiB $237 Ex $165 Gd $128

MODEL FA-S-22M MINI-REVOLVER . NiB $189 Ex $135 Gd $101
Same general specifications as Model FA-S-22LR except in caliber .22
WMR. Disc. 1988.

FRENCH MILITARY PISTOLS — Cholet, France
*Manufactured originally by Société Alsacienne de Constructions
Mécaniques (S.A.C.M.). Currently made by Manufacture d'Armes
Automatiques, Lotissement Industriel des Pontots, Bayonne.*

MODEL 1935A AUTOMATIC PISTOL . NiB $377 Ex $274 Gd $143
Caliber: 7.65mm Long. Eight-round magazine, 4.3-inch bbl., 7.6 inches
overall. Weight: 26 oz. Two-lug locking system similar to the Colt U.S.
M1911A1. Fixed sights. Blued finish. Checkered grips. Made 1935-45.
Note: This pistol was used by French troops during WW II and in Indo-China
1945 to 1954.

MODEL 1935S AUTOMATIC PISTOL . . NiB $342 Ex $281 Gd $135
Similar to Model 1935A except shorter (4.1-inch bbl., and 7.4 inches overall) and
heavier (28 oz.). Single-step lug locking system.

MODEL 1950 AUTOMATIC PISTOL . . . NiB $485 Ex $397 Gd $270
Caliber: 9mm Para. Nine-round magazine, 4.4-inch bbl., 7.6 inches overall.
Weight: 30 oz. Fixed sights, tapered post front and U-notched rear. Similar
in design and function to the U.S. .45 service automatic except no bbl.
bushing.

MODEL MAB F1 AUTOMATIC PISTOL NiB $653 Ex $587 Gd $270
Similar to Model MAB P-15 except w/6-inch bbl. and 9.6 inches overall.
Adjustable target-style sights. Parkerized finish.

MODEL MAB P-8 AUTOMATIC PISTOL NiB $576 Ex $464 Gd $342
Similar to Model MAB P-15 except w/8-round magazine,

MODEL MAB P-15 AUTOMATIC PISTOL . . NiB $632 Ex $474 Gd $385
Caliber: 9mm Para. 15-round magazine, 4.5-inch bbl., 7.9 inches overall. Weight:
38 oz. Fixed sights, tapered post front and U-notched rear.

FROMMER — Budapest, Hungary
Manufactured by Fémáru-Fegyver-és Gépgyár R.T.

**LILIPUT POCKET
AUTOMATIC PISTOL** . . . . NiB $437 Ex $362 Gd $240
Caliber: .25 Automatic (6.35mm). Six-round magazine, 2.14-inch
bbl., 4.33 inches overall. Weight: 10.13 oz. Fixed sights. Blued finish.
Hard rubber grips. Made during early 1920s. Note: Although similar in
appearance to the Stop and Baby, this pistol is designed for blowback
operation.

STOP POCKET AUTOMATIC PISTOL . NiB $414 Ex $321 Gd $165
Locked-breech action, outside hammer. Calibers: .32 Automatic
(7.65mm), .380 Auto (9mm short). Seven-round (.32 cal.) or 6-round
(.380 cal.) magazine, 3.88-inch bbl., 6.5 inches overall. Weight: About
21 oz. Fixed sights. Blued finish. Hard rubber grips. Made 1912 to
1920.

BABY POCKET AUTOMATIC PISTOL NiB $321 Ex $262 Gd $143
Similar to Stop model except has 2-inch bbl., 4.75 inches overall.
Weight 17.5 oz. Magazine capacity is one round less than Stop Model.
Intro. shortly after WW I.

GALENA INDUSTRIES INC. — Sturgis, South Dakota
*Galena Industries purchased the rights to use the AMT trademark in
1998. Many, but not all, original AMT designs were included in the
transaction.*

AMT BACKUP . . . . NiB $474 Ex $291 Gd $219
Caliber: .380 (small frame, 2.5-inch bbl. only), .38 Super, .357 Sig, .40
S&W, .400 CorBon, .45 ACP, 9mm; magazine capacity: 5 or 6 rounds.
Double action, 3-inch bbl., weight: 18 oz. (in .380), or 23 oz.
.38 Super, .357 Sig, .400 CorBon, add $75

AUTOMAG II SEMI AUTO . . . . . . NiB $831 Ex $587 Gd $321
Caliber: .22 WMR, 9-round magazine (except 7-round in 3.38-inch
bbl.); 3.38- 4.5- or 6-inch bbls.; weight: About 32 oz.

HANDGUNS

AUTOMAG III . . . . .NiB $561 Ex $500 Gd $377
Similar to Automag II except chambered for the .30 Carbine cartridge, 6.38-inch bbl., stainless steel finish, weight: About 43 oz.

AUTOMAG IV . . . . .NiB $561 Ex $500 Gd $377
Caliber: .45 Winchester Magnum; 7-round magazine, 6.5-inch bbl., weight: 46 oz.

AUTOMAG .440 CORBON . . . . .NiB $816 Ex $689 Gd $571
Semiautomatic, 7.5-inch bbl., 5-round magazine, checkered walnut grips, matte black finish, weight: 46 oz. Intro. in 2000.

HARDBALLER II . . . . .NiB $505 Ex $347 Gd $235
Based on the Colt Model 1911 frame. Caliber: .45 ACP, .40 S&W, .400 CorBon, 7-round magazine capacity, 5-inch bbl., weight: About 38 oz.

HARDBALLER II LONGSLIDE . . . .NiB $530 Ex $431 Gd $342
Similar to Hardballer model except caliber: .45 ACP, 7-inch bbl., 7-round magazine capacity, stainless steel finish, weight: About 46 ounces.

HARDBALLER ACCELERATOR . . .NiB $587 Ex $437 Gd $332
Similar to Hardballer model except caliber: .400 CorBon, 7-inch bbl., 7-round magazine capacity, stainless steel finish, weight: About 46 ounces.

COMMANDO . . . . .NiB $474 Ex $326 Gd $220
Similar to Hardballer model except caliber: .40 S&W, 4-inch bbl., 8-round magazine capacity, stainless steel finish, weight: About 38 ounces.

GALESI — Collebeato (Brescia), Italy
Manufactured by Industria Armi Galesi.

MODEL 6
POCKET AUTOMATIC PISTOL . . .NiB $227 Ex $179 Gd $128
Calibers: .22 Long, .25 Automatic (6.35mm). Six-round magazine, 2.25-inch bbl., 4.38 inches overall. Weight: About 11 oz. Fixed sights. Blued finish. Plastic grips. Made from 1930 to date.

MODEL 9 POCKET AUTOMATIC PISTOL
Calibers: .22 LR, .32 Auto (7.65mm), .380 Auto (9mm Short). Eight-round magazine, 3.25-inch bbl., 5.88 inches overall. Weight: About 21 oz. Fixed sights. Blued finish. Plastic grips. Made from 1930 to date.

AUTOMATIC PISTOL
Note: Specifications vary, but those shown for .32 Automatic are common.
.22 LR or
.380 Auto. . . . . .NiB $273 Ex $191 Gd $135
.32 Auto. . . . . .NiB $265 Ex $180 Gd $110

GLISENTI — Carcina (Brescia), Italy
Mfd. by Societa Siderurgica Glisenti.

MODEL 1910 ITALIAN
SERVICE AUTOMATIC . . . . . .NiB $1397 Ex $1214 Gd $1015
Caliber: 9mm Glisenti. Seven-round magazine, 4-inch bbl., 8.5 inches overall. Weight: About 32 oz. Fixed sights. Blued finish. Hard rubber or plastic grips. Adopted 1910 and used through WWII.

BRIXIA MODEL . . . . .NiB $1627 Ex $1122 Gd $943
Similar to Glisenti Model 1910 except mass produced using simplified mfg. techniques for the civilian market.

Galesi
Model 6 Pocket

SOSSO MODEL . . . . .EXTREMELY RARE
Experimental semi-auto. Cal.: 9 mm Para. Double action (marked "Sosso"), later single action. Mag.: 19 or 21 rounds. Made by FNA. Fewer than 10 made.

GLOCK, INC. — Austria
Manufactured in Austria and since 2005 in Smyrna, Georgia. NOTE: From 1986 to 1988 Generation 1 models were produced with a pepple texture grip; from 1988 to 1997 Generation 2 models were produced with a checkered grenade type grip texture with horizontal serrations on the front and back grips straps; from 1995 to 2014 Generation 3 models were first produced w/finger grooves in the front grip strap and thumbrests, they then transitioned into finger grooves with thumbrests and checkered finished frame with a front accessory rail. Generation 4 production began from 2010 to date and have interchangable backstraps. The "C" suffix added to model numbers indicated a compensated model. All use a striker-fired system and generally differ in barrel length, overal size, caliber and magazine capacity.

MODEL 17 . . . . NiB $505 Ex $385 Gd $301
Striker-fire action. Caliber: 9mm Parabellum. 10-, 17- or 19-round magazine, 4.5-inch bbl., 7.2 inches overall. Weight: 22 oz. w/o magazine, Polymer frame, steel bbl., slide and springs. Fixed or adj. rear sights. Matte, nonglare finish. Made of only 35 components, including three internal safety devices. Imported from 1985 to date.
Model 17C (compensated bbl.) . . NiB $672 Ex $562 Gd $398
w/adjustable sights, add $75
w/Meprolight sights, add. $100
w/Trijicon sights, add $120
Gen4 variant, add $50

MODEL 17L . . . . NiB $714 Ex $577 Gd $396
Same general specifications as Model 17 except w/long slide and with 6-in. bbl., 8.85 inches overall., weight: 23.35 oz. Imported 1988 to 1999, Gen 3 1998 to date.
w/ported bbl., (early production), add. $75
w/adjustable sights, add $50

Glock Model 19
Gen 1

Glock
Model 30
Gen 3

MODEL 19 COMPACT. . . . . NiB $499 Ex $395 Gd $255
Same general specifications as Model 17 except smaller compact version with 4-inch bbl., 6.85 inches overall and weight: 21 oz. Imported
from 1988 to date.
Model 20C (compensated bbl.) . . . . .NiB $602 Ex $498 Gd $362
w/adjustable sights, add $75
w/Meprolight sights, add. $95
w/Trijicon sights, add $120
Gen4 variant, add $50

MODEL 20 . . . . NiB $530 Ex $377 Gd $270
Caliber: 10mm. 15-round, hammerless, 4.6-inch bbl., 7.59 inches
overall. Weight: 26.3 oz. Fixed sights. Matte, non-glare finish. Made
from 1990 to date.
Model 19C (compensated bbl.) . . NiB $632 Ex $485 Gd $377
w/adjustable sights, add $75
w/Meprolight sights, add. $95
w/Trijicon sights, add $120
Gen4 variant, add $50

MODEL 21 . . . . .NIB $530 EX $377 GD $270
Caliber: .45 ACP. 13-round magazine, 7.59 inches overall. Weight:
25.2 oz. Imported from 1990 to date.
Model 21C (compensated bbl.) . . NiB $632 Ex $485 Gd $377
w/adjustable sights, add $75
w/Meprolight sights, add. $95
w/Trijicon sights, add $120
Gen4 variant, add $50

MODEL 22 . . . . NiB $505 Ex $348 Gd $270
Similar to Model 17 except chambered for .40 S&W. 15-round magazine,
7.4 inches overall. Imported from 1990 to date.
Model 22C (compensated bbl.) . . NiB $612 Ex $362 Gd $281
w/adjustable sights, add $75
w/Meprolight sights, add. $95
w/Trijicon sights, add $120
Gen4 variant, add $50

MODEL 23 COMPACT. . . . . NiB $505 Ex $348 Gd $270
Same general specifications as Model 19 except chambered for .40
S&W. 13-round magazine, 6.97 inches overall, fixed sights. Imported
from 1990 to date.
Model 23C (compensated bbl.) . . NiB $586 Ex $434 Gd $357
w/adjustable sights, add $50
w/Meprolight sights, add. $80
w/Trijicon sights, add $105
Gen4 variant, add $50

MODEL 24 COMPETITION . . . . . NiB $617 Ex $530 Gd $431
Caliber: .40 S&W, 10- and 15-round magazine, 6.02-in. bbl., 8.85
inches overall. Weight: 26.5 oz., fixed sights. Made from 1994-99.
Model 24C (compensated bbl.) . . NiB $816 Ex $648 Gd $500
w/adjustable sights, add $75

MODEL 26 SUB-COMPACT. . . . . NiB $505 Ex $357 Gd $306
Caliber: 9mm, 10-round magazine, 3.47-inch bbl., 6.3 inches overall.
Weight: 19.77 oz., fixed sights. Imported from 1995 to date.
w/adjustable sights, add $75
Gen4 variant, add $50

MODEL 27 SUB-COMPACT. . . . . NiB $505 Ex $389 Gd $290
Similar to the Model 22 except subcompact. Caliber: .40 S&W,
10-round magazine, 3.5-inch bbl., Weight: 21.7 oz. Polymer stocks,
fixed sights. Imported from 1995 to date.
w/adjustable sights, add $75
w/Meprolight sights, add. $95
w/Trijicon sights, add $120

MODEL 29 SUB-COMPACT. . . . NiB $546 Ex $365 Gd $270
Similar to the Model 20 except subcompact. Caliber: 10mm. 10-round
magazine, 3.8-inch bbl., weight: 27.1 oz. Polymer stocks, fixed sights.
Imported from 1997 to date.
w/adjustable sights, add $75
w/Meprolight sights, add. $95
w/Trijicon sights, add $120
Gen4 variant, add $50

MODEL 30 SUB-COMPACT. . . . . NiB $546 Ex $365 Gd $270
Similar to the Model 21 except subcompact. Caliber: .45 ACP. 10-round
magazine, 3.8-inch bbl., weight: 26.5 oz. Polymer stocks, fixed sights.
Imported from 1997 to date.
w/adjustable sights, add $75
w/Meprolight sights, add. $90
w/Trijicon sights, add $120
Gen4 variant, add $50

MODEL 31 . . . . NiB $546 Ex $357 Gd $270
Caliber: .357 Sig. 10- 15- or 17-round magazine, 4.49-inch bbl.,
weight: 23.28 oz., fixed sights. Imported from 1998 to date.
Model 31C (compensated bbl.) . . .NiB $612 Ex $464 Gd $270
w/adjustable sights, add $75
w/Meprolight sights, add. $95
w/Trijicon sights, add $120
Gen4 variant, add $50

MODEL 32 COMPACT. . NiB $546 Ex $357 Gd $270
Caliber: .357 Sig., safe action system. 10- 13- or 15-round magazine,
4.02-inch bbl., weight: 21.52 oz. Imported from 1998 to date.

Model 32C. . . . . NiB $648   Ex $485   Gd $395
w/adjustable sights, add $75
w/Meprolight sights, add $95
w/Trijicon Sights, add $120
Gen4 variant, add $50

MODEL 33 SUB-COMPACT. . . . . NIB $530   EX $357   GD $286
Caliber: .357 Sig., safe action system. Nine- or 11-round magazine,
3.46-inch bbl. Weight: 19.75 oz. Imported from 1998 to date.
w/adjustable sights, add $75
w/Meprolight sights, add $95
w/Trijicon sights, add $120
Gen4 variant, add $50

MODEL 34 COMPETITION. . . NiB $577   Ex $485   Gd $377
Similar to Model 17 except w/longer slide and extended slide-stop lever
and magazine release. 10-, 17- or 19-round magazine, 5.31-in. bbl.
Weight: 22.9 oz., adj. sights. Imported from 1998 to date.
Gen4 variant, add $50

MODEL 35 COMPETITION. . . NiB $581   Ex $469   Gd $362
Similar to Model 34 except .40 S&W. Imported from 1998 to date.
Gen4 variant, add $50

MODEL 36 SUB-COMPACT. . . . . NiB $536   Ex $444   Gd $342
Similar to Model 30 sub-compact except w/6-round single stackmaga-
zine. Weight: 20.11 oz. Imported from 1999 to date.
w/adjustable sights, add $75
w/Meprolight sights, add $95
w/Trijicon sights, add $120

MODEL 37 . . . . NIB $614   EX $450   GD $290
Similar to Model 21 except chambered in .45 G.A.P. Made from 2003
to date.
Gen4 variant, add $50

MODEL 38 COMPACT. . . . . NIB $614   EX $450   GD $290
Similar to Model 37 except more compact w/4-in. bbl. Made from
2005 to date.
Gen4 variant, add $50

MODEL 39 SUB-COMPACT. . . . NIB $614   EX $450   GD $290
Similar to Model 37 except more sub-compact w/3.4-in. bbl. Made
from 2005 to date.
Gen4 variant, add $50

MODEL 41 . . . . NIB $599   EX $395   GD $340
Similar to Model 21 except w/long slide and 5.3-in. bbl. Made 2014 to date.

MODEL 42 SUB-COMPACT. . . . NIB $599   EX $395   GD $340
Caliber: .380 ACP; 3.25-inch bbl. Weight: 13.7 ozs. Made 2014 to date.

**DESERT STORM
COMMEMORATIVE** . . . . . NiB $1525   Ex $1375   Gd $1225
Same specifications as Model 17 except "Operation Desert Storm,
January 16-February 27, 1991" engraved on side of slide w/list of coali-
tion forces. Limited issue of 1,000 guns. Made in 1991.

GREAT WESTERN ARMS CO. — North Hollywood, California

NOTE: *Values shown are for improved late model revolvers early Great
Westerns are variable in quality and should be evaluated accordingly.
It should also be noted that, beginning about July 1956, these revolvers
were offered in kit form. Values of guns assembled from these kits will,
in general, be of less value than factory-completed weapons.*

Grendel Model P-12

DOUBLE BARREL DERRINGER NiB $884   Ex $780   Gd $536
Replica of Remington Double Derringer. Caliber: .38 S&W, .38 S&W
Spl. . Double bbls. (superposed), 3-inch bbl. Overall length: 5 inches.
Fixed sights. Blued finish. Checkered black plastic grips. Made 1953 to
1962 in various configurations.

SA FRONTIER REVOLVER. . . . . . NiB $793   Ex $530   Gd $388
Replica of the Colt Single Action Army Revolver. Calibers: .22 LR, .22
WMR, .357 Magnum, .38 Special, .44 Special, .44 Magnum .45 Colt. Six-
round cylinder, bbl. lengths: 4.75-, 5.5 and 7.5-inches. Weight: 40 oz.
in .22 cal. w/5.5-inch bbl. Overall length: 11.13 inches w/5.5-inch bbl.
Fixed sights. Blued finish. Imitation stag grips. Made from 1951 to 1962.

SHERIFF'S MODEL . . . . NiB $791   Ex $638   Gd $500
Reportedly made from old Colt parts inventory. Cal.: .45 Long Colt.
Blue, nickel, or case-colored finish. Plastic staghorn grips.

FAST DRAW MODEL . . . . NiB $714   Ex $601   Gd $439
Similar to Frontier Six Shooter. Bbl.: 4.75 inches. Brass backstrap and
trigger guard; blue finish; plastic staghorn grips. Longer, turned-up
hammer spur.

TARGET MODEL . . . . NiB $740   Ex $616   Gd $474
Similar to Frontier Six Shooter. Cal.: .22 LR. Adj. rear sights, Micro front
blade. Blue or case colored frame. Bbl.: Various lengths.

DEPUTY MODEL . . . . NiB $831   Ex $709   Gd $500
Cal.: .22 LR, .38 Spl., .357 Mag. Bbl.: 4 inches. Deluxe blue finish, walnut grips. Adj. rear sight. Fewer than 100 made.

GRENDEL, INC. — Rockledge, Florida

MODEL P-10 AUTOMATIC PISTOL
Hammerless, blow-back action. DAO with no external safety. Caliber:
.380 ACP. 10-round box magazine integrated in grip. Three-inch bbl.,
5.3 inches overall. Weight: 15 oz. Matte blue, nickel or green Teflon
finish. Made from 1988 to 1991.
Blued finish . . . . NiB $219   Ex $160   Gd $105
Nickel finish. . . . . NiB $227   Ex $179   Gd $120
Green finish . . . . NiB $227   Ex $179   Gd $105
w/compensated bbl., add $65

MODEL P-12 DA AUTOMATIC PISTOL
Caliber: .380 ACP. 11-round Zytel magazine, 3-inch bbl., 5.3 inches
overall. Weight: 13 oz. Fixed sights. Polymer DuPont ST-800 grip.
Made from 1991 to 1995.
Standard model . . . . NiB $214   Ex $135   Gd $105
Electroless nickel . . . . NiB $219   Ex $135   Gd $105

Hämmerli Model
33MP Free Pistol

Hämmerli Model
101

Hämmerli
Model 102 Deluxe

Hämmerli Model
105

MODEL P-30 AUTOMATIC PISTOL
Caliber: .22 WMR. 30-round magazine, 5-or 8-inch bbl., 8.5 inches overall w/5-inch bbl., weight: 21 oz. Blade front sight, fixed rear sight. Made from 1991 to 1995.
w/5-inch bbl., ... NiB $337   Ex $255   Gd $214
w/8-inch bbl., ... NiB $337   Ex $255   Gd $214

MODEL P-31
AUTOMATIC PISTOL . . . . NiB $474   Ex $352   Gd $281
Caliber: .22 WMR. 30-round Zytel magazine, 11-inch bbl., 17.3 inches overall. Weight: 48 oz. Adjustable blade front sight, fixed rear. Checkered black polymer DuPont ST-800 grip and forend. Made from 1991 to 1995.

GUNSITE — Paulden, Arizona

"ADVANCED TACTICAL" SA AUTO PISTOL
Manufactured w/Colt 1911 or Springfield 1911 parts. Caliber: .45 ACP. Eight-round magazine, 3.5-, 4.25-, 5-inch bbl. Weight: 32-38 oz. Checkered or laser-engraved walnut grips. Fixed or Novak Lo-mount sights.
Stainless finish . . . . NiB $1193   Ex $974   Gd $704
Blued finish . . . . NiB $1030   Ex $836   Gd $621

"CUSTOM CARRY" SA AUTO PISTOL
Caliber: .45 ACP. Eight-round magazine, 3.5-, 4.25-, 5-inch bbl., Weight: 32-38 oz. Checkered or laser-engraved walnut grips. Fixed

Novak Lo-mount sights. Single action, manufactured based on enhanced colt models.
Stainless finish . . . . NiB $1219   Ex $990   Gd $740
Blued finish . . . . NiB $1151   Ex $927   Gd $709

H&R 1871, INC. — Gardner, Massachusetts

NOTE: *In 1991, H&R 1871, Inc. was formed from the residual of the parent company, Harrington & Richardson, and then took over the New England Firearms facility. H&R 1871 produced firearms under both their logo and the NEF brand name until 1999, when the Marlin Firearms Company acquired the assets of H&R 1871. See listings under Harrington & Richardson, Inc.*

HÄMMERLI — Lenzburg, Switzerland.
Currently imported by Sigarms, Inc., Exeter, NH. Previously by Hämmerli, USA; Beeman Precision Arms & Mandall Shooting Supplies.

MODEL 33MP FREE PISTOL . . . . . NiB $964   Ex $863   Gd $577
System Martini single-shot action, set trigger. Caliber: .22 LR. 11.5-inch octagon bbl., 16.5 inches overall. Weight: 46 oz. Micrometer rear sight, interchangeable front sights. Blued finish. Walnut grips, forearm. Imported from 1933 to 1949.

MODEL 100 FREE PISTOL
Same general specifications as Model 33MP. Improved action and sights, redesigned stock. Standard model has plain grips and forearm, deluxe model has carved grips and forearm. Imported 1950 to 1956.
Standard model . . . . NiB $938   Ex $775   Gd $556
Deluxe model. . . . . NiB $1020   Ex $893   Gd $612

MODEL 101 . . . . NiB $913   Ex $791   Gd $612
Similar to Model 100 except has heavy round bbl. w/matte finish, improved action and sights, adj. grips. Weight: About 49 oz. Imported from 1956 to 1960.

MODEL 102
Same as Model 101 except bbl., has highly polished blued finish. Deluxe model (illustrated) has carved grips and forearm. Made from 1956 to 1960.
Standard model . . . . NiB $928   Ex $760   Gd $561
Deluxe model. . . . . NiB $1035   Ex $791   Gd $602

MODEL 103 . . . . NiB $969   Ex $826   Gd $536
Same as Model 101 except has lighter octagon bbl. (as in Model 100) w/highly polished blued finish, grips and forearm of select French walnut. Weight: About 46 oz. Imported 1956 to 1960.

MODEL 104 . . . . NiB $804   Ex $673   Gd $439
Similar to Model 102 except has lighter round bbl., improved action redesigned grips and forearm. Weight: 46 oz. Imported 1961 to 1965.

MODEL 105 . . . . NiB $960   Ex $779   Gd $500
Similar to Model 103 except has improved action, redesigned grips and forearm. Imported from 1961 to 1965.

MODEL 106 . . . . NiB $933   Ex $796   Gd $464
Similar to Model 104 except has improved trigger and grips. Made from 1966 to 1971.

MODEL 107
Similar to Model 105 except has improved trigger and stock. Deluxe model (illustrated) has engraved receiver and bbl., carved grips and forearm. Imported from 1966 to 1971.
Standard model . . . . NiB $1034   Ex $831   Gd $462
Deluxe model. . . . . NiB $1025   Ex $826   Gd $474

GRADING: **NiB** = New in Box   **Ex** = Excellent or NRA 95%   **Gd** = Good or NRA 68%

Hämmerli
Model 106

Hämmerli
Model 107 Deluxe

MODEL 120 HEAVY BARREL

Same as Models 120-1 and 120-2 except has 5.7-inch heavy bbl., weight: 41 oz. Avail. w/standard or adj. grips. 1,000 made. Imported from 1972.
w/standard grips . . . . NiB $627 Ex $459 Gd $388
w/adj. grips . . . . NiB $761 Ex $588 Gd $377

MODEL 120-1 SINGLE-

SHOT FREE PISTOL . . . . NiB $658 Ex $536 Gd $385
Side lever-operated bolt action. Adj. single-stage or two-stage trigger. Caliber: .22 LR, 9.9-inch bbl., 14.75 inches overall. Weight: 44 oz. Micrometer rear sight, front sight on high ramp. Blued finish bbl., and receiver, lever and grip frame anodized aluminum. Checkered walnut thumbrest grips. Imported from 1972 to date.

MODEL 120-2 . . . . NiB $734 Ex $648 Gd $377

Same as Model 120-1 except has hand-contoured grips w/adj. palm rest (available for right or left hand). Imported from 1972 to date.

Hämmerli
Model 120 Heavy
Barrel

MODELS 150/151 FREE PISTOLS

Improved Martini-type action w/lateral-action cocking lever. Set trigger adj. for weight, length and angle of pull. Caliber: .22 LR, 11.3-inch round free-floating bbl., 15.4 inches overall. Weight: 43 oz. (w/Extra weights, 49.5 oz.). Micrometer rear sight, front sight on high ramp. Blued finish. Select walnut forearm and grips w/adj. palm shelf. Imported from 1972 to 1993.
Model 150 (disc. 1989) . . . . . NiB $1938 Ex $1709 Gd $1020
Model 151 (disc. 1993) . . . . . NiB $1938 Ex $1709 Gd $1020

MODEL 152 ELECTRONIC PISTOL

Same general specifications as Model 150 except w/electronic trigger. Made from 1990 to 1992
Right hand . . . . NiB $1812 Ex $1700 Gd $1036
w/adj. grips, add $306

Hämmerli
Model 120-1

MODELS 160/162 FREE PISTOLS

Caliber: .22 LR. Single-shot. 11.31-inch bbl., 17.5 inches overall. Weight: 46.9 oz. Interchangeable front sight blades, fully adj. match rear. Match-style stippled walnut grips w/adj. palm shelf and poly-carbon fiber forend. Imported from 1993 to 2002.
Model 160 w/mechanical
  set trigger (disc. 2000) . . . . NiB $1812 Ex $1681 Gd $1005
Model 162 w/electronic trigger NiB $1982 Ex $1622 Gd $1132

MODEL 208 STANDARD

AUTO PISTOL . . . . NiB $1802 Ex $1488 Gd $959
Caliber: .22 LR. Eight-round magazine, 5.9-inch bbl., 10 inches overall. Weight: 35 oz. (bbl. weight adds 3 oz.). Micrometer rear sight, ramp front. Blued finish. Checkered walnut grips w/adj. heel plate. Imported from 1966 to 1988.

MODEL 208S TARGET PISTOL . . .NiB $2540 Ex $2232 Gd $2066

Caliber: .22 LR. Eight-round magazine, 6-inch bbl., 10.2 inches overall. Weight: 37.3 oz. Micrometer rear sight, ramp front sight. Blued finish. Stippled walnut grips w/adj. heel plate. Imported from 1988 to 2000.

MODEL 211 . . . . NiB $1601 Ex $1458 Gd $847

Same as Model 208 except has standard. Thumbrest grips. Imported from 1966 to 1990.

Hämmerli
Model 150

Hämmerli
Model 160

Hämmerli
Model 208

Hämmerli
Model 215

Hämmerli
International Model 206

Hämmerli
International Model
207

Hämmerli
International Model
210

Hämmerli
Model 232 Rapid Fire

MODEL 212
HUNTER'S PISTOL . . . . NiB $2146 Ex $1816 Gd $1436
Caliber: .22 LR, 4.88-inch bbl., 8.5 inches overall. Weight: 31 oz. Blade front sight, square-notched fully adj. rear. Blued finish. Checkered walnut grips. Imported from 1984 to 1993.

MODEL 215 . . . . NiB $2368 Ex $2035 Gd $1734
Similar to the Model 208 except w/heavier bbl. and fewer deluxe features. Imported from 1990 to 1993.

MODEL 230-1 RAPID FIRE
AUTO PISTOL . . . . NiB $755 Ex $576 Gd $478
Caliber: .22 Short. Five-round magazine, 6.3-inch bbl., 11.6 inches overall. Weight: 44 oz. Micrometer rear sight, post front. Blued finish. Smooth walnut thumbrest grips. Imported from 1970 to 1983.

MODEL 230-2 RAPID FIRE
AUTO PISTOL . . . . NiB $785 Ex $601 Gd $444
Same as Model 230-1 except has checkered walnut grips w/adj. heel plate. Imported from 1970 to 1983.

MODEL 232 RAPID FIRE
AUTO PISTOL . . . . NiB $1454 Ex $1256 Gd $780
Caliber: .22 Short. Six-round magazine, 5.1-inch ported bbl., 10.5 inches overall. Weight: 44 oz. Fully adj. target sights. Blued finish. Stippled walnut wraparound target grips. Imported 1984 to 1993.

INTERNATIONAL MODEL 206
AUTO PISTOL . . . . NiB $709 Ex $469 Gd $306
Calibers: .22 Short, .22 LR. Six-round (.22 Short) or 8-round (.22 LR) magazine, 7.1-inch bbl. w/muzzle brake, 12.5 inches overall. Weight: 33 oz. (.22 Short), 39 oz. (.22 LR) (supplementary weights add 5 and 8 oz.). Micrometer rear sight, ramp front. Blued finish. Standard thumbrest grips. Imported from 1962 to 1969.

INTERNATIONAL MODEL 207
AUTO PISTOL . . . . NiB $760 Ex $621 Gd $469
Same as Model 206 except has grips w/adj. heel plate, weight: 2 oz. more. Made from 1962 to 1969.

INTERNATIONAL MODEL 209
AUTO PISTOL . . . . NiB $825 Ex $672 Gd $562
Caliber: .22 Short. Five-round mag., 4.75-inch bbl., w/muzzle brake and gas-escape holes, 11 inches overall. Weight: 39 oz. (interchangeable front weight adds 4 oz.). Micrometer rear sight, post front. Blued finish. Standard thumbrest grips of checkered walnut. Imported from 1966 to 1970.

INTERNATIONAL MODEL 210 . . . NiB $827 Ex $676 Gd $530
Same as Model 209 except has grips w/adj. heel plate, is 0.8-inch longer and weighs 1 ounce more. Made from 1966 to 1970.

MODEL 280 TARGET PISTOL
Carbon-reinforced synthetic frame and bbl., housing. Calibers: .22 LR, .32 S&W Long WC. Six-round (.22 LR) or 5-round (.32 S&W) magazine, 4.5-inch bbl. w/interchangeable metal or carbon fiber counterweights. 11.88 inches overall. Weight: 39 oz. Micro-adj. match sights w/interchangeable elements. Imported from 1988 to 2000.

.22 LR . . . . NiB $1550 Ex $1295 Gd $627
.32 S&W Long WC . . . . NiB $1729 Ex $1550 Gd $842
.22/.32 Conversion kit, add. $816

VIRGINIAN SA REVOLVER . . . . . NiB $780 Ex $602 Gd $ 440
Similar to Colt Single-Action Army except has base pin safety system (SWISSAFE). Calibers: .357 Magnum, .45 Colt. Six-round cylinder. 4.63-, 5.5- or 7.5-inch bbl., 11 inches overall (with 5.5-inch bbl.). Weight: 40 oz. (with 5.5-inch bbl.). Fixed sights. Blued bbl. and cylinder, casehardened frame, chrome-plated grip frame and trigger guard. One-piece smooth walnut stock. Imported from 1973 to 1976 by Interarms, AlExandria, Va.

WALTHER OLYMPIA MODEL 200
AUTOMATIC PISTOL, 1952-TYPE . . NiB $704 Ex $598 Gd $479
Similar to 1936 Walther Olympia Funfkampf model. Calibers: .22 Short, .22 LR. Six-round (.22 Short) or 10-round (.22 LR) magazine, 7.5-inch bbl., 10.7 inches overall. Weight: 27.7 oz. (.22 Short, light alloy breech-block), 30.3 oz. (.22 LR). Supplementary weights provided. Adj. target sights. Blued finish. Checkered walnut thumbrest grips. Imported 1952 to 1958.

WALTHER
OLYMPIA MODEL 200,1958-TYPE. . NiB $780 Ex $632 Gd $530
Same as Model 200 1952 type except has muzzle brake, 8-round magazine (.22 LR). 11.6 inches overall. Weight: 30 oz. (.22 Short), 33 oz. (.22 LR). Imported 1958 to 1963.

WALTHER
OLYMPIA MODEL 201 . . . . NiB $704 Ex $546 Gd $437
Same as Model 200,1952-Type except has 9.5-inch bbl. Imported from 1955 to 1957.

WALTHER
OLYMPIA MODEL 202 . . . . NiB $780 Ex $632 Gd $530
Same as Model 201 except has grips w/adjustable heel plate. Imported from 1955 to 1957.

WALTHER OLYMPIA MODEL 203
Same as corresponding Model 200 (1955 type lacks muzzle brake) except has grips w/adjustable heel plate. Imported 1955 to 1963.
1955 type. . . . . NiB $794 Ex $638 Gd $479
1958 type. . . . . NiB $842 Ex $709 Gd $475

WALTHER OLYMPIA MODEL 204
American model. Same as corresponding Model 200 (1956-Type lacks muzzle brake) except in .22 LR only, has slide stop and micrometer rear sight. Imported from 1956 to 1963.
1956-type . . . . NiB $760 Ex $606 Gd $464
1958-type . . . . NiB $816 Ex $680 Gd $556

WALTHER OLYMPIA MODEL 205
American model. Same as Model 204 except has grips w/adjustable heel plate. Imported from 1956 to 1963.
1956-type . . . . NiB $842 Ex $714 Gd $610
1958-type . . . . NiB $893 Ex $727 Gd $556

Hämmerli-Walther
Olympia Model 203 1958-Type

Hämmerli-Walther
Olympia Model 205

SIG-Hämmerli
Model P240 Target

MODEL P240 TARGET AUTO PISTOL
Calibers: .32 S&W Long (wadcutter), .38 Special (wadcutter). Five-round magazine, 5.9-inch bbl., 10 inches overall. Weight: 41 oz. Micrometer rear sight, post front. Blued finish/smooth walnut thumbrest grips. Accessory .22 LR conversion unit available. Imported from 1975 to 1986.
.32 S&W Long . . . . NiB $1540 Ex $1329 Gd $755
.38 Special. . . . . NiB $2545 Ex $2353 Gd $2025
.22 LR conversion unit, add $561

Harrington & Richardson SL .32

Harrington & Richardson USRA
Model Single-Shot Target Pistol

Harrington & Richardson Model 4

Harrington & Richardson Model 5

HARRINGTON & RICHARDSON, INC. —
Gardner, Massachusetts

Formerly Harrington & Richardson Arms Co. of Worcester, Mass. One of the oldest and most distinguished manufacturers of handguns, rifles and shotguns, H&R suspended operations on January 24, 1986. In 1987, New England Firearms was established as an independent company producing selected H&R models under the NEF logo. In 1991, H&R 1871, Inc., was formed from the residual of the parent company and then took over the New England Firearms facility. H&R 1871 produced firearms under both its logo and the NEF brand name until 1999, when the Marlin Firearms Company acquired the assets of H&R 1871.

NOTE: *For ease in finding a particular firearm, H&R handguns are grouped into Automatic/Single-Shot Pistols, followed by Revolvers. For a complete listing, please refer to the index.*

- AUTOMATIC/SINGLE-SHOT PISTOLS -

SL .25 PISTOL . . . . .NiB $587 Ex $405 Gd $290
Modified Webley & Scott design. Caliber: .25 Auto. Six-round magazine, 2-inch bbl., 4.5 inches overall. Weight: 12 oz. Fixed sights. Blued finish. Black hard rubber grips. Made from 1912 to 1916.

SL .32 PISTOL . . . . .NiB $562 Ex $321 Gd $205
Modified Webley & Scott design. Caliber: .32 Auto. Eight-round magazine, 3.5-inch bbl., 6.5 inches overall. Weight: About 20 oz. Fixed sights. Blued finish. Black hard rubber grips. Made from 1916 to 1924.

**USRA MODEL SINGLE-
SHOT TARGET PISTOL** . . . . .NiB $548 Ex $500 Gd $288
Hinged frame. Caliber: .22 LR, bbl. lengths: 7-, 8- and 10-inch. Weight: 31 oz. w/10-inch bbl., Adj. target sights. Blued finish. Checkered walnut grips. Made from 1928 to 1941.

- REVOLVERS -

MODEL 4 (1904) DA . . . . NiB $255 EX $180 GD $90
Solid frame. Calibers: .32 S&W Long, .38 S&W. Six-round cylinder (.32 cal.), or 5-round (.38 cal.), bbl. Lengths: 2.5-, 4.5- and 6-inch. Weight: About 16 oz. (in .32 cal.) Fixed sights. Blued or nickel finish. Hard rubber grips. Disc. prior to 1942.

MODEL 5 (1905) DA . . . . .NiB $237 Ex $159 Gd $77
Solid frame. Caliber: .32 S&W. Five-round cylinder, bbl., lengths: 2.5-,4.5- and 6-inch. Weight: About 11 oz. Fixed sights. Blued or nickel finish. Hard rubber grips. Disc. prior to 1942.

MODEL 6 (1906) DA . . . . .NiB $198 Ex $115 Gd $75
Solid frame. Caliber: .22 LR. Seven-round cylinder, bbl. lengths: 2.5, 4.5- and 6-inches. Weight: About 10 oz. Fixed sights. Blued or nickel finish. Hard rubber grips. Disc. prior to 1942.

.22 SPECIAL DA . . . . .NiB $351 Ex $197 Gd $101
Heavy hinged frame. Calibers: .22 LR, .22 Mag. Nine-round cylinder, 6-inch bbl., weight: 23 oz. Fixed sights, front gold-plated. Blued finish. Checkered walnut grips. Recessed safety cylinder on later models for high-speed ammunition. Disc. prior to 1942.

**MODEL 199 SPORTSMAN
SA REVOLVER** . . . . **NiB $347 Ex $291 Gd $158**
Hinged frame. Caliber: .22 LR. Nine-round cylinder, 6-inch bbl., 11 inches overall. Weight: 30 oz. Adj. target sights. Blued finish. Checkered walnut grips. Disc. 1951.

MODEL 504 DA . . . . **NiB $255 Ex $189 Gd $143**
Caliber: .32 H&R Magnum. Five-round cylinder, 4- or 6-inch bbl., (square butt), 3- or 4-inch bbl., round butt. Made 1984 to 1986.

MODEL 532 DA . . . . **NiB $179 Ex $129 Gd $88**
Caliber: .32 H&R Magnum. Five-round cylinder, 2.5- or 4-inch bbl., weight: Approx. 20 and 25 oz. respectively. Fixed sights. American walnut grips. Lustre blued finish. Made 1984 to 1986.

MODEL 586 DA . . . . **NiB $290 Ex $188 Gd $130**
Caliber: .32 H&R Magnum. Five-round cylinder. bbl. lengths: 4.5, 5.5, 7.5, 10 inches. Weight: 30 oz. average. Adj. rear sight, blade front. Walnut finished hardwood grips. Made from 1984 to 1986.

MODEL 603 TARGET . . . . **NiB $219 Ex $158 Gd $115**
Similar to Model 903 except in .22 WMR. Six-round capacity w/ unfluted cylinder. Made from 1980 to 1983.

MODEL 604 TARGET . . . . **NiB $219 Ex $158 Gd $115**
Similar to Model 603 except w/6-inch bull bbl., weight: 38 oz. Made from 1980 to 1983.

MODEL 622/623 DA . . . . **NiB $170 Ex $128 Gd $79**
Solid frame. Caliber: .22 Short, Long, LR, 6-round cylinder. bbl., lengths: 2.5-, 4-, 6-inches. Weight: 26 oz. (with 4-inch bbl.). Fixed sights. Blued finish. Plastic grips. Made from 1957 to 1986. Note: Model 623 is same except chrome or nickel finish.

**MODEL 632/633
GUARDSMAN DA REVOLVER** . . . **NiB $171 Ex $128 Gd $79**
Solid Frame. Caliber: .32 S&W Long. Six-round cylinder, bbl., lengths: 2.5- or 4-inch. Weight: 19 oz. (with 2.5-inch bbl.). Fixed sights. Blued or chrome finish. Checkered Tenite grips (round butt on 2.5-inch, square butt on 4-inch). Made from 1953 to 1986. Note: Model 633 is the same except for chrome or nickel finish.

MODEL 649/650 DA . . . . **NiB $265 Ex $158 Gd $95**
Solid frame. Side loading and ejection. Convertible model w/two 6-round cylinders. Calibers: .22 LR, .22 WMR. 5.5-inch bbl., Weight: 32 oz. Adj. rear sight, blade front. Blued finish. One-piece, Western-style walnut grip. Made from 1976 to 1986. Note: Model 650 is same except nickel finish.

MODEL 666 DA . . . . **NiB $151 Ex $104 Gd $64**
Solid frame. Convertible model w/two 6-round cylinders. Calibers: .22 LR, .22 WMR. Six-inch bbl., weight: 28 oz. Fixed sights. Blued finish. Plastic grips. Made from 1976 to 1978.

MODEL 676 DA . . . . **NiB $283 Ex $200 Gd $104**
Solid frame. Side loading and ejection. Convertible model w/two 6-round cylinders. Calibers: .22 LR, .22 WMR, bbl. lengths: 4.5, 5.5, 7.5, 12-inches. Weight: 32 oz. (with 5.5-inch bbl.). Adj. rear sight, blade front. Blued finish, color-casehardened frame. One-piece, Western-style walnut grip. Made from 1976 to 1980.

MODEL 686 DA . . . . **NiB $306 Ex $205 Gd $128**
Caliber: .22 LR and .22 WMR. Six-round magazine, 4.5, 5.5, 7.5, 10 or 12-inch bbl. Adj. rear sight, ramp and blade front. Blued, color-casehardened frame. Weight: 31 oz. (with 4.5-inch bbl.). Made from 1980 to 1986.

Harrington &
Richardson Model 6

Harrington &
Richardson .22 Special

Harrington & Richardson
Model 199 Sportsman

Harrington & Richardson
Model 622

Harrington & Richardson
Model 649

Harrington & Richardson
Model 686

Harrington & Richardson
Model 650

Harrington & Richardson
Model 733

Harrington & Richardson
Model 666

MODEL 732/733 DA . . . . **NiB $198   Ex $129   Gd $83**
Solid frame, swing-out 6-round cylinder. Calibers: .32 S&W, .32 S&W
Long. bbl., lengths: 2.5 and 4-inch. Weight: 26 oz. (with 4-inch bbl.).
Fixed sights (windage adj. rear on 4-inch bbl. model). Blued finish. Plastic
grips. Made from 1958 to 1986. Note: Model 733 is the same except
with nickel finish.

MODEL 826 DA . . . . **NiB $200   Ex $135   Gd $88**
Caliber: .22 WMR. Six-round magazine, 3-inch bull bbl., ramp and
blade front sight, adj. rear. American walnut grips. Weight: 28 oz. Made
from 1981 to 1983.

MODEL 829/830 DA
Same as Model 826 except in .22 LR caliber. Nine round capacity.
Made from 1981 to 1983.
Model 829, blued . . . . NiB $189 Ex $143 Gd $94
Model 830, nickel . . . . NiB $181 Ex $135 Gd $90

MODEL 832/833 DA
Same as Model 826 except in .32 SW Long. Blued or nickel finish.
Made from 1981 to 1983.
Model 832, blued . . . . NiB $199 Ex $112 Gd $77
Model 833, nickel . . . . NiB $199 Ex $112 Gd $77

Harrington & Richardson
Model 676

MODEL 900/901 DA . . . . **NiB $179   Ex $105   Gd $70**
Solid frame, snap-out cylinder. Calibers: .22 Short, Long, LR. Nine-
round cylinder, bbl. lengths: 2.5, 4, and 6-inches. Weight: 26 oz.
(with 6-inch bbl.). Fixed sights. Blued finish. Cycolac grips. Made from
1962 to 1973. Note: Model 901 (disc. in 1963) is the same except has
chrome finish and white Tenite grips.

MODEL 903 TARGET . . . . **NiB $240   Ex $177   Gd $112**
Caliber: .22 LR. Nine round capacity. SA/DA, 6-inch target-weight flat-
side bbl., swing-out cylinder. Weight: 35 oz. Blade front sight, adj. rear.
American walnut grips. Made from 1980 to 1983.

MODEL 904 TARGET . . . . **NiB $265   Ex $177   Gd $116**
Similar to Model 903 except 4 or 6-inch bull bbl. Weight: 32 oz. with
4-inch bbl. Made from 1980 to 1986.

Harrington & Richardson
Model 830

GRADING: **NiB** = New in Box   **Ex** = Excellent or NRA 95%   **Gd** = Good or NRA 68%

Harrington & Richardson
Model 900

Harrington & Richardson
Model 925

Harrington & Richardson
Model 903

Harrington & Richardson
Model 905

Harrington & Richardson
Model 922, First Issue

Harrington & Richardson
Model 922, Second Issue

Harrington & Richardson
Model 926

MODEL 905 TARGET . . . . **NiB $270 Ex $183 Gd $137**
Same as Model 904 except w/4-inch bbl. only. Nickel finish. Made
from 1981 to 1983.

MODEL 922 DA REVOLVER
FIRST ISSUE . . . . **NiB $232 Ex $189 Gd $148**
Solid frame. Caliber: .22 LR. Nine-round cylinder, 10-inch octagon bbl.,
(early model) or 6-inches, round bbl. (later production). Weight: 26 oz.
(with 6-inch bbl.). Fixed sights. Blued finish. Checkered walnut grips.
Safety cylinder on later models. Disc. prior to 1942.

MODEL 922/923 DA REVOLVER,
SECOND ISSUE . . . . **NiB $220 Ex $112 Gd $88**
Solid frame. Caliber: .22 LR. Nine-round cylinder, bbl. lengths: 2.5,
4, and 6-inches. Weight: 24 oz. (with 4-inch bbl.). Fixed sights. Blued
finish. Plastic grips. Made 1950 to 1986. Note: Second Issue Model
922 has a different frame from that of the First Issue. Model 923 is
same as Model 922, Second Issue except for nickel finish.

MODEL 925
DEFENDER . . . . **NiB $255 Ex $148 Gd $110**
DA. Hinged frame. Caliber: .38 S&W. Five-round cylinder, 2.5-inch
bbl., weight: 22 oz. Adj. rear sight, fixed front. Blued finish. One-piece
wraparound grip. Made from 1964 to 1978.

MODEL 926 DA . . . . **NiB $255 Ex $158 Gd $110**
Hinged frame. Calibers: .22 LR, .38 S&W. Nine-round (.22 LR) or
5-round (.38) cylinder, 4-in. bbl., weight: 31 oz. Adj. rear sight, fixed
front. Blued finish. Checkered walnut grips. Made 1968 to 1978.

Harrington & Richardson
Model 939

Harrington & Richardson
Model 949

Harrington & Richardson
Model 950

Harrington & Richardson
Model 999, First Issue

Harrington & Richardson
Model 999, Second Issue

Harrington &
Richardson Model 929

MODEL 929/930
SIDEKICK DA REVOLVER . . . . **NiB $219 Ex $130 Gd $95**
Caliber: .22 LR. Solid frame, swing-out 9-round cylinder, bbl. lengths: 2.5-, 4-, 6-inches. Weight: 24 oz. (with 4-inch bbl.). Fixed sights. Blued finish. Checkered plastic grips. Made from 1956 to 1986. Note: Model 930 is same except with nickel finish.

MODEL 939/940 ULTRA SIDEKICK
DA REVOLVER . . . . **NiB $290 Ex $187 Gd $112**
Solid frame, swing-out 9-round cylinder. Safety lock. Calibers: .22 Short, Long, LR. Flat-side 6-inch bbl. w/vent rib. Weight: 33 oz. Adj. rear sight, ramp front. Blued finish. Checkered walnut grips. Made 1958 to 1986, reintroduced by H&R 1871 in 1992. Note: Model 940 is same except has round bbl.

MODEL 949/950 FORTY-NINER
DA REVOLVER . . . . **NiB $270 Ex $190 Gd $110**
Solid frame. Side loading and ejection. Calibers: .22 Short, Long, LR. Nine-round cylinder, 5.5- or 7.5 inch bbl., weight: 31 to 38 oz. Adj. rear sight, blade front. Blued or nickel finish. One-piece, Western-style walnut grip. Made 1960 to 1986, reintroduced by H&R 1871 in 1992 to 1999. Note: Model 950 is same except has nickel finish.

MODEL 976 DA . . . . **NiB $310 Ex $197 Gd $109**
Same as Model 949 except has color-casehardened frame, 7.5-inch bbl. Weight: 36 oz. Intro. 1977. Disc.

MODEL 999 SPORTSMAN DA REVOLVER,
FIRST ISSUE . . . . **NiB $499 Ex $316 Gd $200**
Hinged frame. Calibers: .22 LR, .22 Mag. Same specifications as Model 199 Sportsman Single Action. Disc. before 1942.

MODEL 999 SPORTSMAN DA REVOLVER
SECOND ISSUE . . . . **NiB $464 Ex $309 Gd $197**
Hinged frame. Caliber: .22 LR. Nine-round cylinder, 6-inch bbl. w/vent rib. Weight: 30 oz. Adj. sights. Blued finish. Checkered walnut grips. Made from 1950 to 1986.

(NEW) MODEL 999 SPORTSMAN
DA REVOLVER . . . . **NiB $499 Ex $316 Gd $197**
Hinged frame. Caliber: .22 Short, Long, LR. Nine-round cylinder. Six-inch bbl. w/vent rib. Weight: 30 oz. Blade front sight adj. for elevation, square-notched rear adj. for windage. Blued finish. Checkered hardwood grips. Reintroduced by H&R 1871 in 1992.

AMERICAN DA . . . . **NiB $245 Ex $115 Gd $79**
Solid frame. Calibers: .32 S&W Long, .38 S&W. Six-round (.32 cal.) or
5-round (.38 cal.) cylinder, bbl. lengths: 2.5-,4.5- and 6-inches. Weight:
About 16 oz. Fixed sights. Blued or nickel finish. Hard rubber grips.
Disc. prior to 1942.

AUTOMATIC EJECTING DA REVOLVER . . . **NiB $231 Ex $174 Gd $120**
Hinged frame. Calibers: .32 S&W Long, .38 S&W. Six-round (.32 cal.)
or 5-round (.38 cal.) cylinder, bbl. lengths: 3.25-, 4-, 5- and 6-inches.
Weight: 16 oz. (.32 cal.), 15 oz. (.38 cal.). Fixed sights. Blued or nickel
finish. Black hard rubber grips. Disc. prior to 1942.

**Harrington & Richardson
Automatic Ejecting**

BOBBY DA . . . . **NiB $316 Ex $219 Gd $160**
Hinged frame. Calibers: .32 S&W, .38 S&W. Six-round cylinder (.32 cal.)
or 5-round (.38 cal.). Four-inch bbl., 9 inches overall. Weight: 23 oz.
Fixed sights. Blued finish. Checkered walnut grips. Disc. 1946. Note:
Originally designed and produced for use by London's bobbies.

DEFENDER .38 DA . . . . **NiB $346 Ex $219 Gd $110**
Hinged frame. Based on the Sportsman design. Caliber: .38 S&W. Bbl.
lengths: 4- and 6-inches, 9 inches overall (with 4-inch bbl.). Weight: 25
oz. with 4-inch bbl. Fixed sights. Blued finish. Black plastic grips. Disc.
1946. Note: This model was manufactured during WW II as an arm for
plant guards, auxiliary police, etc.

Harrington & Richardson Bobby

EXPERT MODEL DA . . . . **NiB $499 Ex $283 Gd $110**
Same specifications as .22 Special except has 10-inch bbl., weight: 28
oz. Disc. prior to 1942.

HAMMERLESS DA, LARGE FRAME . . . . . **NiB $206 Ex $137 Gd $115**
Hinged frame. Calibers: .32 S&W Long 38 S&W. Six-round (.32 cal.), or
5-round (.38 cal.) cylinder, bbl. lengths: 3.25, 4, and 6-inches. Weight:
About 17 oz. Fixed sights. Blued or nickel finish. Hard rubber grips.
Disc. prior to 1942.

HAMMERLESS DA, SMALL FRAME . . . . . **NiB $189 Ex $130 Gd $101**
Hinged frame. Calibers: .22 LR, .32 S&W. Seven-round (.22 cal.) or
5-round (.32 cal.) cylinder, bbl. lengths: 2, 3, 4, 5 and 6-inches. Weight:
About 13 oz. Fixed sights. Blued or nickel finish. Hard rubber grips.
Disc. prior to 1942.

**Harrington & Richardson
Defender .38**

HUNTER MODEL DA . . . . **NiB $601 Ex $410 Gd $309**
Solid frame. Caliber: .22 LR. Nine-round cylinder, 10-inch octagon bbl.,
weight: 26 oz. Fixed sights. Blued finish. Checkered walnut grips. Safety
cylinder on later models. Note: An earlier Hunter Model was built on
the smaller 7-round frame. Disc. prior to 1942.

NEW DEFENDER DA . . . . **NiB $346 Ex $244 Gd $189**
Hinged frame. Caliber: .22 LR. Nine-round cylinder, 2-inch bbl., 6.25
inches overall. Weight: 23 oz. Adj. sights. Blued finish. Checkered walnut grips, round butt. Note: Basically, this is the Sportsman DA w/a short
bbl., Disc. prior to 1942.

PREMIER DA . . . . **NiB $306 Ex $198 Gd $109**
Small hinged frame. Calibers: .22 LR, .32 S&W. Seven-round (.22 LR) or
5-round (.32) cylinder. Bbl. Lengths: 2, 3, 4, 5, and 6-inches. Weight: 13 oz.
(in .22 LR), 12 oz. (in .32 S&W). Fixed sights. Blued or nickel finish. Black
hard rubber grips. Disc. prior to 1942.

MODEL STR 022 BLANK REVOLVER . . . **NiB $143 Ex $90 Gd $70**
Caliber: .22 RF blanks. Nine-round cylinder, 2.5-inch bbl. Weight: 19
oz. Satin blued finish.

MODEL STR 032 BLANK REVOLVER . . . **NiB $148 Ex $95 Gd $75**
Same general specifications as STR 022 except chambered for .32 S&W
blank cartridges.

**Harrington & Richardson
Hammerless, Small Frame**

Harrington &
Richardson Premier

Harrington & Richardson
Vest Pocket

Harrington &
Richardson Target

Harrington & Richardson
Young American

Harrington & Richardson
Trapper

Harrington &
Richardson Ultra
Sportsmen

TARGET MODEL DA . . . . **NiB $237 Ex $166 Gd $120**
Small hinged frame. Calibers: .22 LR, .22 W.R.F. Seven-round cylinder,
6-inch bbl., weight: 16 oz. Fixed sights. Blued finish. Checkered walnut
grips. Disc. prior to 1942.

TRAPPER MODEL DA . . . . **NiB $388 Ex $219 Gd $130**
Solid frame. Caliber: .22 LR. Seven-round cylinder, 6-inch octagon bbl.,
weight: 12.5 oz. Fixed sights. Blued finish. Checkered walnut grips.
Safety cylinder on later models. Disc. prior to 1942.

ULTRA SPORTSMAN . . . . **NiB $321 Ex $219 Gd $165**
SA. Hinged frame. Caliber: .22 LR. Nine-round cylinder, 6-inch bbl.,
weight: 30 oz. Adj. target sights. Blued finish. Checkered walnut grips.
This model has short action, wide hammer spur, cylinder is length of a
.22 LR cartridge. Disc. prior to 1942.

VEST POCKET DA . . . . **NiB $138 Ex $95 Gd $70**
Solid frame. Spurless hammer. Calibers: .22 Rimfire, .32 S&W. Seven-
round (.22 cal.) or 5-round (.32 cal.) cylinder, 1.13-inch bbl., weight:
About 9 oz. Blued or nickel finish. Hard rubber grips. Disc. prior to
1942.

YOUNG AMERICA DA . . . . **NiB $241 Ex $109 Gd $81**
Solid frame. Calibers: .22 Long, .32 S&W. Seven-round (.22 cal.) or
5-round (.32 cal.) cylinder. Bbl. lengths: 2-, 4.5- and 6-inches. Weight:
About 9 oz. Fixed sights. Blued or nickel finish. Hard rubber grips. Disc.
prior to 1942.

HARTFORD ARMS & EQUIPMENT CO. — Hartford, Connecticut

Hartford pistols were the forebearer of the original High Standard line. High Standard Mfg. Corp. acquired Hartford Arms & Equipment Co. in 1932. The High Standard Model B is essentially the same as the Hartford Automatic.

AUTOMATIC TARGET PISTOL NiB $648   Ex $534   Gd $431
Caliber: .22 LR. 10-round magazine, 6.75-inch bbl., 10.75 inches overall. Weight: 31 oz. Target sights. Blued finish. Black rubber grips. This gun closely resembles the early Colt Woodsman and High Standard pistols. Made 1929 to 1930.

REPEATING PISTOL . . . . NiB $785   Ex $576   Gd $342
Check for authenticity. This model is a hand-operated repeating pistol similar to the Fiala and Schall pistols Made from 1929 to 1930.

SINGLE-SHOT TARGET PISTOLNiB $785   Ex $577   Gd $342
Similar in appearance to the Hartford Automatic. Caliber: .22 LR, 6.75-inch bbl., 10.75 inches overall. Weight: 38 oz. Target sights. Mottled frame and slide, blued bbl., Black rubber or walnut grips. Made from 1929 to 1930.

HASKELL MANUFACTURING — Lima, Ohio

See listings under Hi-Point.

HAWES FIREARMS — Van Nuys, California

DEPUTY MARSHAL SA REVOLVER
Calibers: .22 LR, also .22 WMR in two-cylinder combination. Six-round cylinder, 5.5-inch bbl., 11 inches overall. Weight: 34 oz. Adj. rear sight, blade front. Blued finish. Plastic or walnut grips. Imported 1973 to 1981.
.22 LR (plastic grips). . . . . NiB $219   Ex $120   Gd $88
Combination, .22 LR/.22 WMR (plastic). .NiB $293   Ex $219   Gd $130
Walnut grips, add $20

DEPUTY DENVER MARSHAL
Same as Deputy Marshal SA except has brass frame. Imported 1973 to 1981.
.22 LR (plastic grips). . . . . .NiB $265   Ex $212   Gd $110
Combination, .22 LR/.22 WMR (plastic). .NiB $293   Ex $219   Gd $130
Walnut grips add $10

DEPUTY MONTANA MARSHAL
Same as Deputy Marshal except has brass grip frame. Walnut grips only. Imported from 1973 to 1981.
.22 LR . . . . NiB $283   Ex $198   Gd $118
Combination, .22 LR/.22 WMR . . NiB $321   Ex $235   Gd $128

DEPUTY SILVER CITY MARSHAL
Same as Deputy Marshal except has chrome-plated frame, brass grip frame, blued cylinder and bbl., Imported from 1973 to 1981.
.22 LR (plastic grips). . . . . .NiB $281   Ex $209   Gd $158
Combination, .22 LR/.22 WMR (plastic). .NiB $306   Ex $205   Gd $115
Walnut grips, add $15

DEPUTY TEXAS MARSHAL
Same as Deputy Marshal except has chrome finish. Imported 1973 to 1981.
.22 LR (plastic grips). . . . . .NiB $293   Ex $205   Gd $110
Combination, .22 LR/.22 WMR (plastic). .NiB $306   Ex $190   Gd $110
Walnut grips, add. $15

FAVORITE SINGLE-SHOT TARGET PISTOLNiB $219   Ex $128   Gd $90
Replica of Stevens No. 35. Tip-up action. Caliber: .22 LR. Eight-inch bbl., 12 inches overall. Weight: 24 oz. Target sights. Chrome-plated frame. Blued bbl., Plastic or rosewood grips (add $5). Imported 1972- to 1976.

Hawes
Deputy Marshal

Hawes
Deputy Montana Marshal

Hawes
Deputy Silver City

Hawes
Deputy Texas Marshal

www.skyhorsepublishing.com

Hawes Sauer
Chief Marshal

Hawes Sauer
Federal Marshal

Hawes Sauer
Montana Marshal

Hawes Sauer
Montana Marshal .22

Hawes Sauer
Silver City Marshal

Hawes Sauer
Texas Marshal

SAUER CHIEF MARSHAL SA TARGET REVOLVER
Same as Western Marshal except has adjustable rear sight and front sight, oversized rosewood grips. Not made in .22 caliber. Imported from 1973 to 1981.

.357 Magnum or .45 Colt . . . . .NiB $326 Ex $254 Gd $189
.44 Magnum. .NiB $362 Ex $282 Gd $214
Combination .357 Magnum and 9mm Para.
  .45 Colt and .45 Auto. . . . . .NiB $362 Ex $282 Gd $214
Combination
  .44 Magnum and .44-40 . . . . . . .NiB $369 Ex $290 Gd $225

SAUER FEDERAL MARSHAL
Same as Western Marshal except has color-casehardened frame, brass grip frame, one-piece walnut grip. Not made in .22 caliber. Imported from 1973 to 1981.

.357 Magnum or .45 Colt . . . . .NiB $321 Ex $235 Gd $198
.44 Magnum. .NiB $362 Ex $235 Gd $198
Combination .357 Magnum and 9mm Para.,
  .45 Colt and .45 Auto. . . . . .NiB $362 Ex $290 Gd $198
Combination .44 Magnum and .44-40 . . .NiB $369 Ex $305 Gd $189

SAUER MONTANA MARSHAL
Same as Western Marshal except has brass grip frame. Imported from 1973 to 1981.

.357 Magnum or .45 Colt . . . . .NiB $326 Ex $270 Gd $190
.44 Magnum. .NiB $357 Ex $281 Gd $214
Combination .357 Magnum and 9mm Para.,
  .45 Colt and .45 Auto. . . . . .NiB $377 Ex $301 Gd $219
Combination .44 Magnum and .44-40 . . .NiB $385 Ex $309 Gd $220
.22 LR . . . . .NiB $306 Ex $240 Gd $180
Combination .22 LR and .22 WMR . . . . .NiB $332 Ex $281 Gd $190

SAUER SILVER CITY MARSHAL
Same as Western Marshal except has nickel plated frame, brass grip frame, blued cylinder and barrel, pearlite grips. Imported from 1973 to 1981.

.44 Magnum. .NiB $377 Ex $289 Gd $219
Combination .357 Magnum and 9mm Para.
  .45 Colt and .45 Auto. . . . . .NiB $362 Ex $270 Gd $180
Combination .44 Magnum and .44-40 . . .NiB $365 Ex $270 Gd $214

SAUER TEXAS MARSHAL
Same as Western Marshal except nickel plated, has pearlite grips. Imported from 1973 to 1981.

.357 Magnum or .45 Colt . . . . .NiB $362 Ex $270 Gd $204
.44 Magnum. .NiB $365 Ex $303 Gd $214
Combination .357 Magnum and 9mm Para.,
  .45 Colt and .45 Auto. . . . . .NiB $388 Ex $321 Gd $225
Combination .44 Magnum and .44-40 . . .NiB $395 Ex $332 Gd $239
.22 LR . . . . .NiB $321 Ex $244 Gd $189
Combination .22 LR and .22 WMR . . . . .NiB $336 Ex $265 Gd $189

SAUER WESTERN MARSHAL SA REVOLVER

Calibers: .22 LR (disc.), .357 Magnum, .44 Magnum, .45 Auto. Also in two-cylinder combinations: .22 WMR (disc.), 9mm Para., .44-40, .45 Auto. Six-round cylinder, bbl. lengths: 5.5-inch (disc.), 6-inch, 11.75 inches overall (with 6-inch bbl.). Weight: 46 oz. Fixed sights. Blued finish. Originally furnished w/simulated stag plastic grips. Recent production has smooth rosewood grips. Made from 1968 by J. P. Sauer & Sohn, Eckernforde, Germany. Imported from 1973 to 1981.

.357 Magnum or .45 LC . . . . NiB $357 Ex $265 Gd $200
.44 Magnum. . . . . NiB $377 Ex $290 Gd $219
Combination .357 Magnum and 9mm Para.,
 .45 Colt and .45 Auto. . . . . NiB $385 Ex $270 Gd $214
Combination .44 Magnum
 and .44-40. . . . . NiB $385 Ex $270 Gd $214
.22 LR . . . . NiB $281 Ex $198 Gd $160
Combination .22 LR
 and .22 WMR . . . . NiB $281 Ex $198 Gd $160

Hawes Sauer
Western
Marshal

HECKLER & KOCH — Oberndorf am Neckar, Germany, and Chantilly, Virginia

MODEL HK4 DA AUTO PISTOL

Calibers: .380 Automatic (9mm Short), .22 LR, .25 Automatic (6.35mm), .32 Automatic (7.65mm) w/conversion kits. Seven-round magazine (.380 Auto), 8-round in other calibers, 3.4-inch bbl., 6.19 inches overall. Weight: 18 oz. Fixed sights. Blued finish. Plastic grip. Disc. 1984.

.22 LR or .380 units to kit. . . . . NiB $536 Ex $388 Gd $265
.25 ACP or .32 ACP units to kit. . NiB $536 Ex $377 Gd $255
.380 units to kit w/.22
 conversion unit . . . . NiB $530 Ex $357 Gd $225
.380 units to kit w/.22, .25, .32
 conversion units. . . . . NiB $530 Ex $357 Gd $225

Heckler & Koch
Model HK4

MARK 23 DA AUTO PISTOL NiB $2356 Ex $1831 Gd $1290

Short-recoil semiautomatic pistol w/polymer frame and steel slide. Caliber: .45 ACP. 10-round magazine, 5.87-inch bbl., 9.65 inches overall. Weight: 43 oz. Seven interchangeable rear sight adjustment units w/3-dot system. Developed primarily in response to specifications by the Special Operations Command (SOCOM) for a Special Operations Forces Offensive Handgun Weapon System. Imported from 1996 to date.

Heckler &
Koch Mark 23

MODEL P7 K3 DA AUTO PISTOL

Caliber: .380 ACP. Eight-round magazine, 3.8 inch-bbl., 6.3 inches overall. Weight: About 26 oz. Adj. rear sight. Imported 1988 to 1994.

.380 Cal. . . . . NiB $954 Ex $785 Gd $546
.22 LR conversion kit . . . . NiB $713 Ex $611 Gd $434
.32 ACP conversion kit . . . . NiB $388 Ex $328 Gd $228

MODEL P7 M8 . . . . NiB $1295 Ex $804 Gd $577

Squeeze-cock SA semiautomatic pistol. Caliber: 9mm Para. Eight-round magazine, 4.13-inch bbl., 6.73 inches overall. Weight: 29.9 oz. Matte black or nickel finish. Adjustable rear sight. Imported from 1985 to 2005.

MODEL P7 M10

Caliber: .40 S&W. Nine-round magazine, 4.2-inch bbl., 6.9 inches overall. Weight: 43 oz. Fixed front sight blade, adj. rear w/3-dot system. Imported from 1992 to 1994.

Blued finish . . . . NiB $1163 Ex $879 Gd $643
Nickel finish. . . . . NiB $1163 Ex $879 Gd $643

Heckler & Koch
Model P7K3

Heckler & Koch
Model P7M13

Heckler & Koch USP45

Heckler & Koch
Model P7 (PSP)

Heckler & Koch
Model P9S DA

MODEL P7 M13 . . . . NiB $2219   Ex $1848   Gd $1632
Caliber: 9mm. 13-round magazine, 4.13-inch bbl., 6.65 inches overall. Weight: 34.42 oz. Matte black finish. Adj. rear sight. Imported 1985 to 1994.

MODEL P7 (PSP) AUTO PISTOL . . . NiB $917   Ex $701   Gd $510
Caliber: 9mm Para. Eight-round magazine, 4.13-inch bbl., 6.54 inches overall. DA. Weight: About 33.5 oz. Blued finish. Imported 1983 to 1985 and again in 1990 with limited availability.

MODEL P9S DA AUTOMATIC PISTOL
Calibers: 9mm Para., .45 Automatic. Nine-round (9mm) or 7-round (.45 Auto) magazine. Four-inch bbl., 7.63 inches overall. Weight: 32 ounces. Fixed sights. Blued finish. Contoured plastic grips. This model disc. 1986.
9mm . . . . NiB $893   Ex $663   Gd $486
.45 Automatic . . . . NiB $918   Ex $713   Gd $500

MODEL P9S TARGET COMPETITION KIT
Same as Model P9S Target except comes w/Extra 5.5-inch bbl. and bbl. weights. Also available w/walnut competition grip.
w/standard grip . . . . NiB $1061   Ex $973   Gd $745
w/competition grip . . . . NiB $1199   Ex $1121   Gd $891

MODEL SP89 . . . . NiB $4023   Ex $3224   Gd $2227
Semiautomatic, recoil-operated, delayed roller-locked bolt system. Caliber: 9mm Para. 15-round magazine, 4.5-inch bbl., 13 inches overall. Weight: 68 oz. Hooded front sight, adj. rotary-aperture rear. Imported 1989 to 1993.

MODEL USP . . . . NiB $928   Ex $627   Gd $468
Polymer integral grip/frame design w/recoil reduction system. Calibers: 9mm Para., .40 S&W or .45 ACP. 15-round (9mm) or 13-round (.40 S&W and .45ACP) magazine, 4.13- or 4.25-inch bbl., 6.88 to 7.87 inches overall. Weight: 26.5-30.4 oz. Blade front sight, adj. rear w/3-dot system. Matte black finish. Stippled black polymer grip. Available in SA/DA or DAO. Imported 1993 to date.
Stainless finish . . . . NiB $816   Ex $510   Gd 332
w/Tritium sights, add $100
w/ambidextrous decocking lever, add $30

Heckler & Koch Model USP45
Compact 50th Anniversary

Heckler & Koch
Model USP9 Compact (Stainless)

Heckler & Koch
Model USP357 Compact

Heckler & Koch
Model USP Expert

Heckler & Koch
Model USP Tactical

MODEL USP9 COMPACT . . . .NiB $1301 Ex $1193 Gd $1029
Caliber: 9mm. 10-round magazine, 4.25-inch bbl., 7.64 inches overall.
Weight: 25.5 oz. Short recoil w/modified Browning action. 3-dot sighting system. Polymer frame w/integral grips, blued slide finish. Imported from 1993 to date.
Stainless slide finish . . . . NiB $1301 Ex $1193 Gd $1029
w/ambidextrous decocking lever, add $75

MODEL USP40 COMPACT
Caliber: .40 S&W. 10-round magazine, 3.58- inch bbl., 6.81 inches overall. Weight: 27 oz. Short recoil w/modified Browning action. 3-dot sighting system. Polymer frame w/integral grips, blued slide finish. Imported from 1993 to date.
Blued finish . . . . NiB $857 Ex $615 Gd $437
Stainless finish . . . . NiB $774 Ex $627 Gd $431
w/ambidextrous decocking lever, add $50

MODEL USP45 COMPACT . . . . . NiB $918 EX $615 GD $410
Caliber: .45 ACP. Eight-round magazine, 3.8- inch bbl., 7.09 inches overall. Weight: 28 oz. Short recoil w/modified Browning action. 3-dot sighting system. Polymer frame w/integral grips. Imported from 1998 to date.
Stainless slide finish . . . . NiB $816 Ex $639 Gd $431
w/ambidextrous decocking lever, add $50
50th Anniversary (1 of 1,000) . . NiB $1199 Ex $947 Gd $709

MODEL USP EXPERT . . . . NiB $1301 Ex $1142 Gd $842
Caliber: .45 ACP. 10-round magazine, 6.2- inch bbl., 9.65 inches overall. Weight: 30 oz. Adjustable 3-dot target sights. Short recoil modified Browning action w/recoil reduction system. Reinforced polymer frame w/integral grips and match-grade slide. Imported from 1999 to 2009.

MODEL USP TACTICAL . . . . NiB $1178 Ex $933 Gd $638
SOCOM Enhanced version of the USP Standard Model, w/4.92-inch threaded bbl. Chambered for .45 ACP only. Imported from 1998 to date.

MODEL VP 70Z AUTO PISTOL NiB $791 Ex $536 Gd $377
Caliber: 9mm Para. 18-round magazine, 4.5-inch bbl., 8 inches overall. Weight: 32.5 oz. DA Fixed sights. Blued slide, polymer receiver and grip. Disc. 1986.

Heckler & Koch Model VP 7OZ

Heritage Rough Rider shown w/ birds head grip

Heritage Sentry

HELWAN
See listings under Interarms.

HERITAGE MANUFACTURING — Opa Locka, Florida
Acquired by Taurus Int'l. in 2012

MODEL H-25 AUTO PISTOL
Caliber: .25 ACP. Six-round magazine, 2.5-inch bbl., 4.63 inches overall. Weight: 12 oz. Fixed sights. Blued or chrome finish. Made 1995 to 1999.
Blued . . . . NiB **$136** Ex **$95** Gd **$75**
Nickel, add $20

ROUGH RIDER SA REVOLVER
Calibers: .22 LR, .22 Mag. Six-round cylinder. bbl. lengths: 2.75, 3.75, 4.75, 6.5 or 9 inches. Weight: 31-38 oz. Blade front sight, fixed rear. High-polished blued finish w/gold accents. Smooth walnut grips. Made from 1993 to date.
.22 LR . . . . NiB **$247** Ex **$115** Gd **$95**
.22 LR/.22 Mag. combo . . . . NiB **$291** Ex **$179** Gd **$110**

SENTRY DA REVOLVER
Calibers: .22 LR, .22 Mag., .32 Mag., 9mm or .38 Special. Six- or 8-round (rimfire) cylinder, 2- or 4-inch bbl., 6.25 inches overall (2-inch bbl.). Ramp front sight, fixed rear. Blued or nickel finish. Checkered polymer grips. Made from 1993 to 1997.
Blued . . . . NiB **$131** Ex **$95** Gd **$75**
Nickel, add $15

STEALTH DA AUTO PISTOL . . . . . NiB **$241** Ex **$179** Gd **$101**
Calibers: 9mm, .40 S&W. 10-round magazine, 3.9-inch bbl., weight: 20.2 oz. Gas-delayed blowback, double action only. AmbidExtrous trigger safety. Blade front sight, drift-adj. rear. Black chrome or stainless slide. Black polymer grip frame. Made from 1996 to 2000.

HI-POINT FIREARMS — Mansfield, Ohio

MODEL JS-9MM
AUTO PISTOL . . . . NiB **$158** Ex **$101** Gd **$75**
Caliber: 9mm Para. Eight-round magazine, 4.5-inch bbl., 7.75 inches overall. Weight: 39 oz. Fixed low-profile sights w/3-dot system. Matte blue, matte black or chrome finish. Checkered synthetic grips. Made from 1990 to 2000.

MODEL JS-9MM COMPETITION PISTOL
(STALLARD) . . . . NiB **$151** Ex **$90** Gd **$69**
Similar to standard JS-9 except w/4-inch compensated bbl. w/ shortened slide and adj. sights. 10-round magazine, 7.25 inches overall. Weight: 30 oz. Made from 1998 to 2006.

MODEL JS-9MM/C-9MM COMPACT PISTOL
(BEEMILLER) . . . . NiB **$148** Ex **$90** Gd **$75**
Similar to standard JS-9 except w/3.5-inch bbl. and shortened slide w/ alloy or polymer frame. 6.72 inches overall. Weight: 29 oz. or 32 oz. Three-dot-style sights. Made from 1993 to date.

MODEL CF-.380
POLYMER . . . . NiB **$158** Ex **$88** Gd **$61**
Caliber: .380 ACP. Eight-round magazine, 3.5-inch bbl., 6.72 inches overall. Weight: 32 oz. Three-dot sights. Made from 1994 to date.

MODEL JS-.40/JC-.40 AUTO PISTOL
(IBERIA) . . . . NiB **$171** Ex **$110** Gd **$75**
Similar to Model JS-9mm except in caliber .40 S&W.

MODEL JS-.45/JH-.45 AUTO PISTOL
(HASKELL) . . . . NiB **$150** Ex **$101** Gd **$70**
Similar to Model JS-9mm except in caliber .45 ACP w/7-round magazine and two-tone Polymer finish.

J. C. HIGGINS

See Sears, Roebuck & Company.

HIGH STANDARD SPORTING FIREARMS —
East Hartford, Connecticut

Formerly High Standard Mfg. Co., Hamden, ConnecticutA long-standing producer of sporting arms, High Standard disc. its operations in 1984. See new High Standard models under separate entry, HIGH STANDARD MFG. CO., INC.

NOTE: *For ease in finding a particular firearm, High Standard handguns are grouped into three sections: Automatic pistols, derringers and revolvers. For a complete listing, please refer to the Index.*

- AUTOMATIC PISTOLS -

MODEL A HAMMERLESS . . . . NiB $847 Ex $748 Gd $497
Caliber: .22 LR. 10-round magazine, bbl. lengths: 4.5-, 6.75-inch. 11.5 inches overall (6.75-inch bbl.). Weight: 36 oz. (in 6.75-inch bbl.). Adj. target sights. Blued finish. Checkered walnut grips. Made from 1938 to 1942.

MODEL B AUTOMATIC PISTOL . . NiB $668 Ex $444 Gd $367
Original Standard pistol. Hammerless. Caliber: .22 LR. 10-round magazine, bbl. lengths: 4.5-, 6.75-inch, 10.75 inches overall (with 6.75-inch bbl.). Weight: 33 oz. (6.75-inch bbl.). Fixed sights. Blued finish. Hard rubber grips. Made from 1932 to 1942.

MODEL C AUTOMATIC PISTOL . . NiB $979 Ex $826 Gd $549
Same as Model B except in .22 Short. Made from 1935 to 1942.

MODEL D AUTOMATIC PISTOL NiB $1020 Ex $774 Gd $544
Same general specifications as Model A but heavier bbl., weight: 40 oz. (6.75-inch bbl.). Made from 1937 to 1942.

DURA-MATIC. . . . . NiB $362 Ex $301 Gd $204
Takedown. Caliber: .22 LR. 10-round magazine, 4.5 or 6.5 inch interchangeable bbl., 10.88 inches overall (6.5-inch bbl.). Weight: 35 oz. (in 6.5-inch bbl.). Fixed sights. Blued finish. Checkered grips. Made from 1952 to 1970.

MODEL E AUTOMATIC PISTOL NiB $1275 Ex $1051 Gd $929
Same general specifications as Model A but w/Extra heavy bbl. and thumbrest grips. Weight: 42 oz. (6.75-inch bbl.). Made 1937 to 1942.

FIELD-KING AUTOMATIC PISTOL FIRST MODEL
Same general specifications as Sport-King but w/heavier bbl. and target sights. Late model 6.75-inch bbls. have recoil stabilizer and lever take-down feature. Weight: 43 oz. (6.75-inch bbl.). Made from 1951 to 1958.
w/one bbl. . . . . NiB $683 Ex $529 Gd $408
w/both bbls., add $204

FIELD-KING AUTOMATIC PISTOL SECOND MODEL
Same general specifications as First Model Field-King but w/button take-down and marked FK 100 or FK 101.
w/one bbl. . . . . NiB $852 Ex $588 Gd $324
w/both bbls., add $204

High Standard
Model A

High Standard
Model B

High Standard
Model D

High Standard
Dura-Matic

High Standard
Model E

**High Standard
G-380**

**High Standard
Model G-B**

**High Standard
Model G-E**

**High Standard
Model H-A**

**High Standard
Model H-B**

FLITE-KING AUTOMATIC PISTOL — FIRST MODEL

Same general specifications as Sport-King except in .22. Short w/aluminum alloy frame and slide and marked FK 100 or FK 101. Weight: 26 oz. (6.5-inch bbl.). Made from 1953 to 1958.

w/one bbl. . . . . NiB $668 Ex $469 Gd $342
w/both bbls. . . . . NiB $872 Ex $660 Gd $546

FLITE-KING AUTOMATIC PISTOL — SECOND MODEL

Same as Flite-King—First Model except w/steel frame and marked in the 102 or 103 series. Made from 1958 to 1966.

Model 102 . . . . NiB $556 Ex $398 Gd $265
Model 103 . . . . NiB $536 Ex $388 Gd $219

MODEL G-380 AUTOMATIC PISTOL NiB $668 Ex $571 Gd $408

Lever takedown. Visible hammer. Thumb safety. Caliber: .380 Automatic. Six-round magazine, 5-inch bbl., weight: 40 oz. Fixed sights. Blued finish. Checkered plastic grips. Made 1943 to 1950.

MODEL G-B AUTOMATIC PISTOL

Lever takedown. Hammerless. Interchangeable bbls. Caliber: .22 LR. 10-round magazine, bbl. lengths: 4.5, 6.75 inches, 10.75 inches overall (with 6.75-inch bbl.). Weight: 36 oz. (with 6.75-inch bbl.). Fixed sights. Blued finish. Checkered plastic grips. Made 1948 to 1951.

w/one bbl. . . . . NiB $689 Ex $500 Gd $365
w/both bbls. . . . . NiB $893 Ex $704 Gd $576

MODEL G-D AUTOMATIC PISTOL

Lever takedown. Hammerless. Interchangeable bbls. Caliber: .22 LR. 10-round magazine, bbl. lengths: 4.5, 6.75 inches. 11.5 inches overall (with 6.75-inch bbl.). Weight: 41 oz. (6.75-inch bbl.). Target sights. Blued finish. Checkered walnut grips. Made 1948 to 1951.

w/one bbl. . . . . NiB $1076 Ex $917 Gd $709
w/both bbls. . . . . NiB $1275 Ex $1048 Gd $898

MODEL G-E AUTOMATIC PISTOL

Same general specifications as Model G-D but w/Extra heavy bbl. and thumbrest grips. Weight: 44 oz. (with 6.75-inch bbl.). Made from 1949 to 1951.

w/one bbl. . . . . NiB $1488 Ex $1266 Gd $1015
w/both bbls. . . . . NiB $1692 Ex $1470 Gd $1200

MODEL H-A

AUTOMATIC PISTOL . . . . NiB $2230 Ex $1355 Gd $859
Same as Model A but w/visible hammer, no thumb safety. Made from 1939 to 1942.

MODEL H-B

AUTOMATIC PISTOL . . . . NiB $816 Ex $590 Gd $433
Same as Model B but w/visible hammer, no thumb safety. Made from 1940 to 1942.

MODEL H-D

AUTOMATIC PISTOL . . . . NiB $1282 Ex $1122 Gd $806
Same as Model D but w/visible hammer, no thumb safety. Made from 1939 to 1942.

MODEL H-DM

AUTOMATIC PISTOL . . . . NiB $663 Ex $524 Gd $429
Also called H-D Military. Same as Model H-D but w/thumb safety. Made from 1941 to 1951.

MODEL H-E

AUTOMATIC PISTOL . . . . NiB $2275 Ex $2142 Gd $1197
Same as Model E but w/visible hammer, no thumb safety. Made from 1939 to 1942.

GRADING: **NiB** = New in Box   **Ex** = Excellent or NRA 95%   **Gd** = Good or NRA 68%

High Standard
Olympic
Military

High Standard
Model H-E

High Standard Olympic
Automatic – First Model

High Standard Olympic
Automatic – Second
Model

High Standard
Olympic I.S.U.

High Standard Olympic
I.S.U. Military

OLYMPIC AUTOMATIC PISTOL FIRST MODEL (G-O)
Same general specifications as Model G-E but in .22 Short w/light alloy slide. Made from 1950 to 1951.
w/one bbl. . . . . NiB $1785 Ex $1153 Gd $629
w/both bbls, add. $408

OLYMPIC AUTOMATIC SECOND MODEL
Same general specifications as Supermatic but in .22 Short w/light alloy slide. Weight: 39 oz. (6.75-inch bbl.). Made 1951 to 1958.
w/one bbl.. . . . . NiB $1325 Ex $1076 Gd $730
w/both bbls, add. $306

OLYMPIC AUTOMATIC PISTOL,
THIRD MODEL. . . . . .NiB $1213 Ex $984 Gd $734
Same as Supermatic Trophy w/bull bbl. except in .22 Short. Made from 1963 to 1966.

OLYMPIC COMMEMORATIVE
Limited edition of Supermatic Trophy Military issued to commemorate the only American-made rimfire target pistol ever to win an Olympic gold medal. Highly engraved w/Olympic rings inlaid in gold. Deluxe presentation case. Two versions issued: In 1972 (.22 LR) and 1980 (.22 Short).
1972 issue . . . . NiB $6523 Ex $5416 Gd $3550
1980 issue . . . . NiB $2243 Ex $1877 Gd $1215

OLYMPIC I.S.U . . . . NiB $1316   Ex $1020   Gd $798
Same as Supermatic Citation except caliber .22 Short, 6.75- or 8-inch tapered bbl. w/stabilizer, detachable weights. Made from 1958 to 1977. Eight-inch bbl. disc. in 1966.

OLYMPIC I.S.U. MILITARY . . NiB $1120   Ex $940   Gd $702
Same as Olympic I.S.U. except has military grip and bracket rear sight. Intro. in 1965. Disc.

OLYMPIC MILITARY. . . . . . . NiB $1142   Ex $932   Gd $755
Same as Olympic — Third Model except has military grip and bracket rear sight. Made in 1965.

SHARPSHOOTER
AUTOMATIC PISTOL . . . . NiB $385 Ex $267 Gd $197
Takedown. Hammerless. Caliber: .22 LR. 10-round magazine, 5.5-inch bull bbl., 9 inches overall. Weight: 42 oz. Micrometer rear sight, blade front sight. Blued finish. Plastic grips. Made from 1971 to 1983.

SPORT-KING AUTOMATIC PISTOL FIRST MODEL
Takedown. Hammerless. Interchangeable barrels. Caliber: .22 LR. 10-round magazine, barrel lengths: 4.5-, 6.75-inches. 11.5 inches overall (with 6.75-inch barrel). Weight: 39 oz. (with 6.75-inch barrel). Fixed sights. Blued finish. Checkered plastic thumbrest grips. Made from 1951 to 1958. Note: 1951 to 1954 production has lever takedown as in "G" series. Later version (illustrated at left) has push-button takedown.

**High Standard Sport-King
Automatic — First Model**

**High Standard Sport-King
Automatic — Second
Model**

**High Standard Sport-King
Automatic — Third Model**

**High Standard
Supermatic**

w/one bbl. . . . . NiB $388 Ex $306 Gd $220
w/both bbls. . . . . NiB $590 Ex $500 Gd $408

SPORT-KING AUTOMATIC PISTOL
SECOND MODEL . . . . NiB $357 Ex $279 Gd $204
Caliber: .22 LR. 10-round magazine, 4.5- or 6.75 inch interchangeable bbl. 11.25 inches overall (with 6.75-inch barrel). Weight: 42 oz. (with 6.75-inch barrel). Fixed sights. Blued finish. Checkered grips. Made from 1958 to 1970.

SPORT-KING AUTOMATIC PISTOL
THIRD MODEL. . . . . NiB $305 Ex $204 Gd $135
Similar to Sport-King — Second Model with same general specifications for weight and length. Blued or nickel finish. Introduced in 1974. Disc.

SPORT-KING LIGHTWEIGHT
Same as standard Sport-King except lightweight has forged aluminum alloy frame. Weight: 30 oz. with 6.75-inch barrel Made from 1954 to 1965.
w/one bbl. . . . . NiB $590 Ex $380 Gd $255
w/both bbls. . . . . NiB $791 Ex $602 Gd $453

SUPERMATIC AUTOMATIC PISTOL
Takedown. Hammerless. Interchangeable bbls. Caliber: .22 LR. 10-round magazine, barrel lengths: 4.5-, 6.75-inches. Late model 6.75-inch barrel have recoil stabilizer feature. Weight: 43 oz. (with 6.75-inch barrel) 11.5 inches overall (with 6.75-inch barrel). Target sights. Elevated serrated rib between sights. Adjustable barrel weights add 2 or 3 oz. Blued finish. Checkered plastic thumb-rest grips. Made from 1951 to 1958.
w/one bbl. . . . . NiB $872 Ex $683 Gd $509
w/both bbls. . . . . NiB $1070 Ex $893 Gd $714

SUPERMATIC CITATION
Same as Supermatic Tournament except 6.75-, 8- or 10-inch tapered bbl. with stabilizer and two removable weights. Also furnished with Tournament's 5.5-inch bull barrel, adjustable trigger pull, recoil-proof click-adjustable rear sight (barrel-mounted on 8- and 10-inch barrels), checkered walnut thumbrest grips on bull barrel model. Currently manufactured with only bull barrel. Made from 1958 to 1966.
w/5.5-inch bull bbl. . . . . NiB $893 Ex $612 Gd $377
w/6.75-inch tapered bbl. . . . . NiB $893 Ex $612 Gd $377
w/8-inch tapered bbl. . . . . . . NiB $1066 Ex $760 Gd $536
w/10-inch tapered bbl. . . . . . NiB $1099 Ex $811 Gd $571

**High Standard Mfg.
Co. 10-X Supermatic
Citation (current mfg.)**

**High Standard Victor
Solid Rib Barrel**

**High Standard
Supermatic Citation Bull Barrel**

**High Standard
Supermatic Citation Military Fluted Barrel**

**High Standard
Supermatic Tournament Bull Barrel**

**High Standard
Supermatic Tournament Military Tapered
Barrel**

**High Standard
Supermatic Trophy Bull Barrel**

SUPERMATIC CITATION MILITARY
Same as Supermatic Citation except has military grip and bracket
rear sight as in Supermatic Trophy. Made from 1965 to 1973.
w/bull bbl. . . . . NiB $897 Ex $581 Gd $499
w/fluted bbl.. . . . . NiB $964 Ex $806 Gd $602

SUPERMATIC
TOURNAMENT . . . . NiB $734 Ex $587 Gd $362
Takedown. Caliber: .22 LR. 10-round magazine, interchangeable 5.5-inch bull or 6.75-inch heavy tapered bbl., notched and
drilled for stabilizer and weights. 10 inches overall (with 5.5-
inch bbl.). Weight: 44 oz. (5.5-inch bbl.). Click adj. rear sight,
undercut ramp front. Blued finish. Checkered grips. Made from
1958 to 1966.

SUPERMATIC TOURNAMENT
MILITARY. . . . . NiB $1305 Ex $997 Gd $836
Same as Supermatic Tournament except has military grip. Made
from 1965 to 1971.

SUPERMATIC TROPHY
Same as Supermatic Citation except with 5.5-inch bull bbl., or
7.25-inch fluted bbl., w/detachable stabilizer and weights, Extra
magazine, High-luster blued finish, checkered walnut thumbrest
grips. Made from 1963 to 1966.
w/bull bbl. . . . . NiB $1305 Ex $1090 Gd $638
w/fluted bbl.. . . . . NiB $1305 Ex $1090 Gd $638

SUPERMATIC TROPHY MILITARY
Same as Supermatic Trophy except has military grip and bracket
rear sight. Made from 1965 to 1984.
w/bull bbl. . . . . NiB $1357 Ex $1060 Gd $760
w/fluted bbl.. . . . . NiB $1408 Ex $1120 Gd $813

THE VICTOR AUTOMATIC NiB $3299 Ex $2798 Gd $2550
Takedown. Caliber: .22 LR. 10-round magazine, 4.5-inch solid
or vent rib and 5.5-inch vent rib, interchangeable bbl., 9.75
inches overall (with 5.5-inch bbl.). Weight: 52 oz. (with 5.5-
inch bbl.). Rib mounted target sights. Blued finish. Checkered
walnut thumbrest grips. Standard or military grip configuration.
Made from 1972 to 1984 (standard-grip model made from1974
to 1975).

**High Standard
Derringer**

**High Standard
Double-Nine — Steel
Frame**

**High Standard
Durango**

**High Standard
Sierra**

- DERRINGERS -

DERRINGER
Hammerless, double action, two-round, double bbl. (over/under). Calibers: .22 Short, Long, LR or .22 Magnum Rimfire, 3.5-inch bbls., 5 inches overall. Weight: 11 oz. Standard model has blued or nickel finish w/plastic grips. Presentation model is goldplated in walnut case. Standard model made from

1963 (.22 S-L-LR) and 1964 (.22 MRF) to 1984. Gold model, made from 1965 to 1983.

Standard model (blue)	NiB $332	Ex $225	Gd $204
Standard model (nickel)	NiB $332	Ex $225	Gd $204
Standard model (Electroless nickel)	NiB $337	Ex $291	Gd $230
Gold Presentation One Derringer	NiB $541	Ex $362	Gd $286
Silver Presentation One Derringer	NiB $592	Ex $431	Gd $342
Presentation Set, Matched pair, consecutive numbers (1965 only)	NiB $1392	Ex $1180	Gd $836

- REVOLVERS -

CAMP GUN . . . . NiB $270 Ex $220 Gd $189
Same as Sentinel Mark I/Mark IV except has 6-inch bbl., adj. rear sight, target-style checkered walnut grips. Caliber: .22 LR or .22 WMR. Made from 1976 to 1983.

DOUBLE-NINE DA REVOLVER —ALUMINUM FRAME
Western-style version of Sentinel. Blued or nickel finish w/simulated ivory, ebony or stag grips, 5.5-inch bbl., 11 inches overall. Weight: 27.25 oz. Made from 1959 to 1971.
Blue model . . . . NiB $255 Ex $190 Gd $150

DOUBLE-NINE—STEEL FRAME
Similar to Double-Nine—Aluminum Frame, w/same general specifications except w/steel frame and has Extra cylinder for .22 WMR, walnut grips. Intro. in 1971. Disc.
Blue model . . . . NiB $291 Ex $225 Gd $179
Nickel model . . . . NiB $306 Ex $225 Gd $190

DOUBLE-NINE DELUXE . . . . . NiB $326 Ex $240 Gd $198
Same as Double-Nine Steel Frame except has adj. target rear sight. Intro. in 1971. Disc.

DURANGO
Similar to Double-Nine—Steel Frame except .22 LR only, available w/4.5- or 5.5-inch bbl. Made from 1971 to 1973.
Blue model . . . . NiB $275 Ex $189 Gd $150
Nickel model . . . . NiB $301 Ex $219 Gd $170

HIGH SIERRA DA REVOLVER
Similar to Double-Nine—Steel Frame except has 7-inch octagon bbl., w/gold-plated grip frame, fixed or adj. sights. Made 1973 to 1983.
w/fixed sights . . . . NiB $352 Ex $286 Gd $214
w/adj. sights . . . . NiB $362 Ex $306 Gd $230

HOMBRE
Similar to Double-Nine—Steel Frame except .22 LR only, lacks single-action type ejector rod and tube, has 4.5-inch bbl. Made from 1971 to 1973.
Blue model . . . . NiB $281 Ex $204 Gd $143
Nickel model . . . . NiB $306 Ex $220 Gd $165

KIT GUN DA REVOLVER . . . . NiB $275 Ex $214 Gd $150
Solid frame, swing-out cylinder. Caliber: .22 LR. Nine-round cylinder, 4-inch bbl., 9 inches overall. Weight: 19 oz. Adj. rear sight, ramp front. Blued finish. Checkered walnut grips. Made from 1970 to 1973.

**High Standard
Longhorn Steel Frame**

**High Standard
Sentinel**

**High Standard
Kit Gun**

**High Standard
Longhorn Aluminum Frame**

**High Standard
Natchez**

**High Standard
Posse**

LONGHORN ALUMINUM FRAME

Similar to Double-Nine—Aluminum Frame except has Longhorn hammer spur, 4.5-, 5.5- or 9.5-inch bbl., Walnut, simulated pearl or simulated stag grips. Blued finish. Made from 1960 to 1971.

w/4.5- or 5.5-inch bbl. . . . . NiB $357 Ex $254 Gd $190
w/9.5-inch bbl . . . . NiB $357 Ex $254 Gd $190

LONGHORN STEEL FRAME

Similar to Double-Nine — Steel Frame except has 9.5-inch bbl. w/fixed or adj. sights. Made from 1971 to1983

w/fixed sights . . . . NiB $362 Ex $270 Gd $204
w/adj. sights . . . . NiB $377 Ex $316 Gd $229

NATCHEZ . . . . NiB $418 Ex $270 Gd $209

Similar to Double-Nine — Aluminum Frame except 4.5-inch bbl., 10 inches overall, weight: 25.25 oz., blued finish, simulated ivory bird's-head grips. Made 1961-66.

POSSE . . . . NiB $281 Ex $180 Gd $148

Similar to Double-Nine — Aluminum Frame except 3.5-inch bbl., 9 inches overall, weight: 23.25 oz. Blued finish, brass-grip frame and trigger guard, walnut grips. Made from 1961 to 1966.

SENTINEL DA REVOLVER

Solid frame, swing-out cylinder. Caliber: .22 LR. Nine-round cylinder, 3- 4- or 6-inch bbl. Nine inches overall (with 4-inch-bbl.). Weight: 19 oz. (with 4-inch bbl.). Fixed sights. Aluminum frame. Blued or nickel finish. Checkered grips. Made from 1955 to 1956.

Blue model . . . . NiB $302 Ex $156 Gd $120
Blue/green model . . . . NiB $577 Ex $439 Gd $319
Gold model . . . . NiB $555 Ex $397 Gd $317
Nickel model . . . . NiB $270 Ex $214 Gd $158
Pink model. . . . . NiB $536 Ex $306 Gd $180

SENTINEL DELUXE

Same as Sentinel except w/4- or 6-inch bbl., wide trigger, drift-adj. rear sight, two-piece square-butt grips. Made from 1957 to 1974. Note: Designated Sentinel after 1971.

Blue model . . . . NiB $270 Ex $170 Gd $128
Nickel model . . . . NiB $296 Ex $189 Gd $160

High Standard
Sentinel I

High Standard
Sentinel Mark II

High Standard
Sentinel Mark III

High Standard
Sentinel Snub

SENTINEL IMPERIAL

Same as Sentinel except has onyx-black or nickel finish, two-piece checkered walnut grips, ramp front sight. Made from 1962 to 1965.

Blue model . . . . NiB $270 Ex $179 Gd $130
Nickel model . . . . NiB $281 Ex $189 Gd $143

SENTINEL MARK 1 DA REVOLVER

Steel frame. Caliber: .22 LR. Nine-round cylinder, bbl. lengths: 2-, 3-, 4-inch, 6.88 inches overall (with 2-inch bbl.). Weight: 21.5 oz. (2-inch bbl.). Ramp front sight, fixed or adj. rear. Blued or nickel finish. Smooth walnut grips. Made from 1974 to 1983.

Blue model . . . . NiB $265 Ex $219 Gd $179
Nickel model . . . . NiB $296 Ex $255 Gd $190
w/adj. sights. . . . . NiB $337 Ex $270 Gd $225

SENTINEL MARK II

DA REVOLVER . . . . .NiB $326 Ex $255 Gd $179
Caliber: .357 Magnum. Six-round cylinder, bbl. lengths: 2.5-, 4-, 6-inch, 9 inches overall w/4-inch bbl., weight: 38 oz. (with 4-inch bbl.). Fixed sights. Blued finish. Walnut service or combat-style grips. Made from 1974 to 1976.

SENTINEL MARK III

. . . . .NiB $326 Ex $255 Gd $175
Same as Sentinel Mark II except has ramp front and adj. rear sights. Weight: 40 oz. (with 4-inch bbl.). Blued finish. Made 1974 to 1976.

SENTINEL MARK IV

Same as Sentinel Mark I except in .22 WMR. Made 1974 to 1983.

Blue model . . . . NiB $301 Ex $230 Gd $175
Nickel model . . . . NiB $326 Ex $265 Gd $198
w/adj. sights. . . . . NiB $352 Ex $255 Gd $220

SENTINEL SNUB

Same as Sentinel Deluxe except w/2.75-inch bbl., (7.25 inches overall, weight: 15 oz.), checkered bird's head-type grips. Made 1957 to 1974.

Blued finish . . . . NiB $255 Ex $190 Gd $148
Nickel finish. . . . . NiB $274 Ex $160 Gd $109

HIGH STANDARD MFG. CO., INC. —
Houston, Texas

In 1993, High Standard acquired original assets and moved to Houston, Texas. The first Texas-manufactured firearms began shipping in March 1994 to date.

VICTOR 10X AUTO PISTOL . . . .NiB $1120 Ex $840 Gd $540

Caliber: .22 LR. 10-round magazine, 5.5-inch bbl., 9.5 inches overall. Weight: 45 oz. Checkered walnut grips. Blued finish. Made from 1994 to date.

OLYMPIC I.S.U. AUTOMATIC PISTOL

Same specifications as the 1958 I.S.U. issue. See listing under previous High Standard Section.

Olympic I.S.U. model. . . . . NiB $592 Ex $345 Gd $270
Olympic I.S.U. military model . . NiB $816 Ex $577 Gd $336

SPORT KING AUTO PISTOL . . . . .NiB $694 Ex $434 Gd $305

Caliber: .22 LR. 10-round magazine, 4.5- or 6.75-inch bbl., 8.5 or 10.75 inches overall. Weight: 44 oz. (with 4.5-inch bbl.), 46 oz. (with 6.75-inch bbl.). Fixed sights, slide mounted. Checkered walnut grips. Parkerized finish. Manufactured in limited quantities.

SUPERMATIC CITATION AUTO PISTOL NiB $536 Ex $399 Gd $254

Caliber: .22 LR. 10-round magazine, 5.5- or 7.75-inch bbl., 9.5 or 11.75 inches overall. Weight: 44 oz. (with 5.5-inch bbl.), 46 oz. (with 7.75-inch bbl.). Frame-mounted, micro-adj. rear sight, undercut ramp front sight. Blued or Parkerized finish. Made from 1994 to 2003.
.22 Short conversion. . . . . NiB $408 Ex $337 Gd $255

CITATION MS AUTO PISTOL . NiB $821   Ex $638   Gd $474
Similar to the Supermatic Citation except has 10-inch bbl., 14 inches overall. Weight: 49 oz. Made from 1994 to date.

SUPERMATIC TOURNAMENT. NiB $745   Ex $377   Gd $274
Caliber: .22 LR. 10-round magazine, bbl. lengths: 4.5, 5.5, or 6.75 inches, overall length: 8.5, 9.5 or 10.75 inches. Weight: 43, 44 or 45 oz. depending on bbl. length. Micro-adj. rear sight, undercut ramp front sight. Checkered walnut grips. Parkerized finish. Made from 1995 to 1997.

SUPERMATIC TROPHY. . . . . . NiB $719   Ex $356   Gd $220
Caliber: .22 LR. 10-round magazine, 5.5 or 7.25-inch bbl., 9.5 or 11.25 inches overall. Weight: 44 oz. (with 5.5-inch bbl.). Micro-adj. rear sight, undercut ramp front sight. Checkered walnut grips w/thumbrest. Blued or Parkerized finish. Made from 1994 to date.
.22 Short Conversion . . . . NiB $1301   Ex $890   Gd $779

VICTOR AUTOMATIC . . . . . NiB $723   Ex $475   Gd $270
Caliber: .22 LR.10-round magazine, 4.5- or 5.5-inch ribbed bbl., 8.5 or 9.5 inches overall. Weight: 45 oz. (with 4.5-inch bbl.), 46 oz. (with 5.5-inch bbl.). Micro-adj. rear sight, post front. Checkered walnut grips. Blued or Parkerized finish. Made from 1994 to date.
.22 Short conversion. . . . . NiB $1193   Ex $925   Gd $780

HOPKINS & ALLEN ARMS CO. — Norwich, Connecticut

See listings of comparable Harrington & Richardson and Iver Johnson models for values.

INGRAM — Mfd. by Military Armament Corp.

See listings under M.A.C. (Military Armament Corp.

Note: *Military Armament Corp. ceased production of the select-fire automatic, M10 (9mm & .45 ACP) and M11 (.380 ACP) in 1977. Commercial production resumed on semiautomatic versions under the M.A.C. banner until 1982.*

INTERARMS — Alexandria, Virginia

Also see Bersa.

HELWAN BRIGADIER
AUTO PISTOL . . . . NiB $265   Ex $203   Gd $143
Caliber: 9mm Para. Eight-round magazine, 4.25-inch bbl., 8 inches overall. Weight: 32 oz. Blade front sight, dovetailed rear. Blued finish. Grooved plastic grips. Imported from 1987 to 1995.

VIRGINIAN DRAGOON SA REVOLVER
Calibers: .357 Magnum, .44 Magnum, .45 Colt. Six-round cylinder. Bbls.: 5- (not available in .44 Magnum), 6-, 7.5-, 8.38-inch (latter only in .44 Magnum w/adj. sights), 11.88 inches overall with (6-inch bbl.). Weight: 48 oz. (with 6-inch bbl.). Fixed sights or micrometer rear and ramp front sights. Blued finish w/color-casetreated frame. Smooth walnut grips. SWISSAFE base pin safety system. Mfg. by Interarms Industries Inc., Midland, VA. from 1977 to 1984.
Standard Dragoon. . . . . NiB $388   Ex $281   Gd $214
Engraved Dragoon . . . . NiB $785   Ex $530   Gd $362

Interarms/Helwan
Brigadier

Interarms
Virginian SA
Revolver

Deputy model . . . . NiB $377   Ex $274   Gd $179
Stainless. . . . . NiB $398   Ex $265   Gd $165

VIRGINIAN REVOLVER
SILHOUETTE MODEL. . . . . NiB $385   Ex $274   Gd $244
Same general specifications as regular model except designed in stainless steel w/untapered bull bbl., lengths of 7.5, 8.38 and 10.5 inches. Made from 1985 to 1986.

VIRGINIAN SA REVOLVER . . . NiB $388   Ex $270   Gd $265
Similar to Colt Single Action Army except has base pin safety system. Imported from 1973-76. (See also listing under Hämmerli.)

INTRATEC U.S.A., INC. — Miami, Florida

CATEGORY 9 DAO
SEMIAUTOMATIC   NiB $270   Ex $177   Gd $120
Blowback action w/polymer frame. Caliber: 9mm Par Eight-round magazine, 3-inch bbl., 7.7 inches overall. Weight: 18 oz. TExtured black polymer grips. Matte black finish. Made from 1993 to 2000.

CATEGORY 40
DAO SEMIAUTOMATIC . . . . NiB $270   Ex $177   Gd $120
Locking-breech action w/polymer frame. Caliber: .40 S&W. Seven-round magazine, 3.25-inch bbl., 8 inches overall. Weight: 21 oz. TExtured black polymer grips. Matte black finish. Made from 1994 to 2000.

CATEGORY 45
DAO SEMIAUTOMATIC . . . . NiB $295   Ex $184   Gd $133
Locking-breech action w/polymer frame. Caliber: .45 ACP. Six-round magazine, 3.25-inch bbl., 8 inches overall. Weight: 21 oz. TExtured black polymer grips. Matte black finish. Made from 1994 to 2000.

Japanese
Model 14 (1925)

Japanese
Model 26 DAO Revolver

MODEL PROTEC .25 ACP DA SEMIAUTOMATIC
Caliber: .25 ACP. 10-round magazine, 2.5-inch bbl., 5 inches overall.
Weight: 14 oz. Wraparound composition grips. Black Teflon, satin grey
or Tec-Kote finish. Disc. 2000..
ProTec .25 standard....................NiB $128 Ex $88 Gd $61
ProTec .25 w/satin or Tec-Kote ....NiB $130 Ex $90 Gd $65

MODEL TEC-DC9 SEMIAUTOMATIC
Caliber: 9mm Para. 20- or 36-round magazine, 5-inch bbl., weight:
50-51 oz. Open fixed front sight, adj. rear. Military nonglare blued or
stainless finish.
Tec-9 w/blued finish......... NiB $510 Ex $332 Gd $270
Tec-9 w/Tec Kote finish .... NiB $546 Ex $342 Gd $301
Tec 9S w/stainless finish....... NiB $576 Ex $398 Gd $301

MODEL TEC-DC9M SEMIAUTOMATIC
Same specifications as Model Tec-9 except has 3-inch bbl. without
shroud and 20-round magazine, blued or stainless finish.
Tec-9M w/blued finish .... NiB $546 Ex $337 Gd $281
Tec-9MS w/stainless finish ..... NiB $622 Ex $398 Gd $255

MODEL TEC-22T SEMIAUTOMATIC
Caliber: .22 LR. 10/.22-type 30-round magazine, 4-inch bbl., 11.19
inches overall. Weight: 30 oz. Protected post front sight, adj. rear sight.
Matte black or Tec-Kote finish. Made from 1991 to 1994.
Tec-22T standard .... NiB $434 Ex $220 Gd $189
Tec-22TK Tec-Kote, add $50

TEC-38
DERRINGER..................NiB $183 Ex $129 Gd $101
Calibers: .22 Mag., .32 H&R Mag., .357 Mag., .38 Special. Two-round
capacity, 3-inch blued bbl., 4.63 inches overall. Weight: 13 oz. Fixed
sights. Synth. black frame. Double-action. Made from 1986 to 1988.

ISRAEL ARMS — Kfar Sabs, Israel
Imported by Israel Arms International, Houston, TX.

BUL-M5 LOCKED
BREECH (2000) AUTO PISTOL ... NiB $398 Ex $235 Gd $148
Similar to the M1911 U.S. Government model. Caliber: .45 ACP. Seven-
round magazine, 5-inch bbl., 8.5 inches overall. Weight: 38 oz. Blade
front and fixed, low-profile rear sights.

KAREEN MK II (1500) AUTO PISTOL
Single-action only. Caliber: 9mm Para. 10-round magazine, 4.75-inch
bbl., 8 inches overall. Weight: 33.6 oz. Blade front sight, rear adjustable
for windage. TExtured black composition or rubberized grips. Blued, two-
tone, matte black finish. Imported from 1997 to 1998.
Blued or matte black finish..... NiB $386 Ex $301 Gd $219
Two-tone finish .... NiB $556 Ex $386 Gd $304
Meprolite sights, add $50

KAREEN MK II COMPACT
(1501) AUTO PISTOL ....NiB $386 Ex $290 Gd $204
Similar to standard Kareen MKII except w/3.85-inch bbl., 7.1 inches
overall. Weight: 32 oz. Imported 1999 to 2000.

GOLAN MODEL (2500) AUTO PISTOL
Single or double action. Caliber: 9mm Para., .40 S&W. 10-round magazine, 3.85-inch bbl., 7.1 inches overall. Weight: 34 oz. Steel slide and
alloy frame w/ambidExtrous safety and decocking lever. Matte black
finish. Imported 1999.
9mm Para................... NiB $954 Ex $755 Gd $536
.40 S&W .... NiB $954 Ex $755 Gd $536

GAL MODEL
(5000) AUTO PISTOL ....NiB $437 Ex $289 Gd $220
Caliber: .45 ACP. Eight-round magazine, 4.25-inch bbl., 7.25 inches
overall. Weight: 42 oz. Low profile 3-dot sights. Combat-style black
rubber grips. Imported from 1999 to 2001.

JAPANESE MILITARY PISTOLS — Tokyo, Japan
Manufactured by Government Plant.

MODEL 14 (1925)
AUTOMATIC PISTOL .... NiB $1423 Ex $1009 Gd $658
Modification of the Nambu Model 1914, changes chiefly intended to
simplify mass production. Standard round trigger guard or oversized
guard for use w/gloves. Caliber: 8mm Nambu. Eight-round magazine,
4.75-inch bbl., 9 inches overall. Weight: About 29 oz. Fixed sights.
Blued finish. Grooved wood grips. Intro. 1925 and mfd. through WW II.

MODEL 26 DAO REVOLVER. . . NiB $1586 Ex $1120 Gd $779
Top-break frame. Caliber: 9mm. Six-round cylinder w/automatic
Extractor/ejector, 4.7-inch bbl., adopted by the Japanese Army from
1893 to 1914, replaced by the Model 14 Automatic Pistol but remained
in service through World War II.

MODEL 94 (1934)

AUTOMATIC PISTOL . . . . NiB $780 Ex $464 Gd $342
Poorly designed and constructed, this pistol is unsafe and can be
fired merely by applying pressure on the sear, which is Exposed
on the left side. Caliber: 8mm Nambu. Six-round magazine, 3.13-
inch bbl., 7.13 inches overall. Weight: About 27 oz. Fixed sights.
Blued finish. Hard rubber or wood grips. Intro. in 1934, principally
for Export to Latin American countries, production continued thru
WW II.

NAMBU MODEL

1914 AUTOMATIC PISTOL . . . . . NiB $1389 Ex $989 Gd $785
Original Japanese service pistol, resembles Luger in appearance and
Glisenti in operation. Caliber: 8mm Nambu. Seven-round magazine,
4.5-inch bbl., 9 inches overall. Weight: About 30 oz. Fixed front sight,
adj. rear sight. Blued finish. Checkered wood grips. Made from 1914
to 1925.

**Japanese Model 94
(1934)**

JENNINGS FIREARMS INC. — Irvine, California
*Currently Manufactured by Bryco Arms, Irvine, California. Previously
by Calwestco, Inc. & B.L. Jennings. See additional listings under Bryco
Arms.*

MODEL J-22 AUTO PISTOL
Calibers: .22 LR, .25 ACP. Six-round magazine, 2.5-inch bbl., about
5 inches overall. Weight: 13 oz. Fixed sights. Chrome, satin nickel or
black Teflon finish. Walnut, grooved black Cycolac or resin-impregnated wood grips. Made from 1981-85 under Jennings and Calwestco
logos; disc. 1985 by Bryco Arms.
Model J-22 . . . . NiB $81   Ex $50 Gd $40
Model J-25 . . . . NiB $91   Ex $61 Gd $50

**Jennings Model J Auto
Pistol**

IVER JOHNSON ARMS, INC. — Jacksonville, Arkansas

*Operation of this company dates back to 1871, when Iver Johnson
and Martin Bye partnered to manufacture metallic cartridge revolvers. Johnson became the sole owner and changed the name to Iver
Johnson's Arms & Cycle Works, which it was known as for almost
100 years. Modern management shortened the name, and after
several owner changes the firm was moved from Massachusetts,
its original base, to Jacksonville, Arkansas. In 1987, the American
Military Arms Corporation (AMAC) acquired the operation, which
subsequently ceased in 1993.*

NOTE: *For ease in finding a particular firearm, Iver Johnson handguns
are divided into two sections: Automatic Pistols (below) and Revolvers,
which follow. For the complete handgun listing, please refer to the Index.*

- AUTOMATIC PISTOLS -

9MM DA AUTOMATIC . . . . NiB $474   Ex $357 Gd $265
Caliber: 9mm. Six-round magazine, 3-inch bbl., 6.5 inches overall.
Weight: 26 oz. Blade front sight, adj. rear. Smooth hardwood grip.
Blued or matte blued finish. Intro. 1986.

COMPACT .25 ACP . . . . NiB $273   Ex $190 Gd $148
Bernardelli V/P design. Caliber: .25 ACP. Five-round magazine, 2.13-
inch bbl., 4.13 inches overall. Weight: 9.3 oz. Fixed sights. Checkered
composition grips. Blued slide, matte blued frame and color-casehardened trigger. Made from 1991 to 1993.

ENFORCER . . . . NiB $893   Ex $643 Gd $431

Iver Johnson Enforcer

Caliber: .30 U.S. Carbine. Five-, 15-, or 30-round magazine, 9.5- inch
bbl., weight: 5.5 lbs. Adj. sights. Walnut stock. Made 1986.

I.J. SUPER

ENFORCER AUTOMATIC . . . . NiB $893   Ex $643 Gd $431
Caliber: .30 U.S. Carbine. Fifteen- or 30-round magazine, 9.5-inch bbl.,
17 inches overall. Weight: 4 pounds. Adj. peep rear sight, blade front.
American walnut stock. Made from 1978 to 1993.

PONY AUTOMATIC PISTOL
Caliber: .380 Auto. Six-round magazine, 3.1-inch bbl., 6.1 inches over-
all. Blue, matte blue, nickel finish or stainless. Weight: 20 oz. Wooden
grips. Smallest of the locked breech automatics. Made from 1982-88.
Reintroduced from 1989 to 1991.
Blue or matte blue finish. . . . . . . .NiB $434 Ex $342 Gd $270
Nickel finish. . . . . NiB $464 Ex $345 Gd $290
Deluxe finish . . . . NiB $464 Ex $377 Gd $281

Iver Johnson
Model 57A Target

Iver Johnson
Model TP

Iver Johnson
Model 55 Target

Iver Johnson
Model 55-S

Iver Johnson
Model 56 Blank Revolver

MODEL TP-22 DA
AUTOMATIC . . . . NiB $316 Ex $219 Gd $160
Calibers: .22 LR, Seven-round magazine, 2.85-inch bbl., 5.39 inches overall. Blued finish. Weight: 14.46 oz. Made from 1982 to 1989.

MODEL TP25 DA
POCKET PISTOL. . . . . NiB $271 Ex $190 Gd $143
Double-action automatic. Caliber: .25 ACP. Seven-round magazine, 3-inch bbl., 5.5 inches overall. Weight: 12 oz. Black plastic grips and blued finish. Made from 1981 to 1982.

TRAILSMAN AUTOMATIC PISTOL
Caliber: .22 LR. 10-round magazine, 4.5 or 6-inch bbl., 8.75 inches overall (with 4.5-inch bbl.). Weight: 46 oz. Fixed target-type sights. Checkered composition grips. Made from 1985 to 1991.
Standard model . . . . NiB $306 Ex $220 Gd $160
Deluxe model. . . . . NiB $321 Ex $230 Gd $170

- REVOLVERS -

MODEL 55 TARGET DA REVOLVER . NiB $237 Ex $160 Gd $115
Solid frame. Caliber: .22 LR. Eight-round cylinder, bbl. lengths: 4.5-, 6-inches. 10.75 inches overall (with 6-inch bbl.). Weight: 30.5 oz. (with 6-inch bbl.). Fixed sights. Blued finish. Walnut grips. Note: Original model designation was 55; changed to 55A when loading gate was added in 1961. Made from 1955 to 1960.

MODEL 55-S REVOLVER . . . . NiB $265 Ex $165 Gd $110
Same general specifications as the Model 55 except for 2.5-inch bbl. and small, molded pocket-size grip.

MODEL 56
BLANK REVOLVER. . . . . NiB $128 Ex $81 Gd $55
Solid frame. Caliber: .22 blanks only. Eight-round cylinder, 2.5-inch solid bbl., 6.75 inches overall. Weight: 10 oz.

MODEL 57A
TARGET DA REVOLVER . . . . . NiB $255 Ex $143 Gd $101
Solid frame. Caliber: .22 LR. Eight-round cylinder, bbl. lengths: 4.5, and 6-inches. 10.75 inches overall. Weight: 30.5 oz. with 6-inch bbl. Adj. sights. Blued finish. Walnut grips. Note: Original model designation was 57, changed to 57A when loading gate was added in 1961. Made from 1961 to 1978.

TRAILSMAN
DA REVOLVER. . . . . NiB $306 Ex $209 Gd $160
Hinged frame. Rebounding hammer. Caliber: .22 LR. Eight-round cylinder, 6-inch bbl., 11 inches overall. Weight: 34 oz. Adj. sights. Blued finish. Walnut grips. Made from 1985 to 1991.

Iver Johnson
Model 66 Trailsman

Iver Johnson
Model 67 Viking

MODEL 67 VIKING DA REVOLVER. . . . . NiB $273 Ex $165 Gd $110
Hinged frame. Caliber: .22 LR. Eight-round cylinder, bbl. lengths: 4.5- and
6-inches, 11 inches overall (with 6-inch bbl.). Weight: 34 oz. (with 6-inch
bbl.). Adj. sights. Walnut grips w/thumbrest. Made 1964 to 1978.

**MODEL 67S VIKING
SNUB REVOLVER. . . . . NiB $286 Ex $189 Gd $179**
DA. Hinged frame. Calibers: .22 LR, .32 S&W Short and Long, .38 S&W.
Eight-round cylinder in .22, 5-round in .32 and .38 calibers; 2.75-inch bbl.
Weight: 25 oz. Adj. sights. Tenite grips. Made from 1964 to 1978.

MODEL 1900 DA REVOLVER . . . . . . NiB $158 Ex $90 Gd $65
Solid frame. Calibers: .22 LR, .32 S&W, .32 S&W Long, .38 S&W.
Seven-round cylinder in .22 cal. , 6-round (.32 S&W), 5-round (.32
S&W Long, .38 S&W); bbl. lengths: 2.5-, 4.5- and 6-inches. Weight: 12
oz. (in .32 S&W w/2.5-inch bbl.). Fixed sights. Blued or nickel finish.
Hard rubber grips. Made from 1900 to 1941.

Iver Johnson
Model 67S Viking Snub

**MODEL 1900
TARGET DA REVOLVER . . . . NiB $222 Ex $175 Gd $135**
Solid frame. Caliber: .22 LR. Seven-round cylinder, bbl. lengths: 6- and
9.5-inches. Fixed sights. Blued finish. Checkered walnut grips. (This
earlier model does not have counterbored chambers as in the Target
Sealed 8. Made from 1925 to 1942.)

AMERICAN BULLDOG DA REVOLVER
Solid frame. Calibers: .22 LR, .22 WMR, .38 Special. Six-round cylinder in .22, 5-round in .38. Bbl. lengths: 2.5-, 4-inch. 9 inches overall
(with 4-inch bbl.). Weight: 30 oz. (with 4-inch bbl.). Adj. sights. Blued
or nickel finish. Plastic grips. Made from 1974 to 1976.
.38 Special. . . . . NiB $464 Ex $286 Gd $204
Other calibers . . . . NiB $464 Ex $286 Gd $204

Iver Johnson
Model 1900 Target

ARMSWORTH MODEL 855 SA . . . NiB $464 Ex $290 Gd $198
Hinged frame. Caliber: .22 LR. Eight-round cylinder, 6-inch bbl., 10.75
inches overall. Weight: 30 oz. Adj. sights. Blued finish. Checkered walnut
one-piece grip. Adj. finger rest. Made from 1955 to 1957.

CADET DA REVOLVER . . . . . . NiB $255 Ex $165 Gd $101
Solid frame. Calibers: .22 LR, .22 WMR, .32 S&W Long, .38 S&W, .38
Special. Six- or 8-round cylinder in .22, 5-round in other calibers, 2.5-inch
bbl., 7 inches overall. Weight: 22 oz. Fixed sights. Blued finish or nickel finish. Plastic grips. Note: Loading gate added in 1961, .22 cylinder capacity
changed from 8 to 6 rounds in 1975. Made 1955 to 1977.

Iver Johnson
Cadet

CATTLEMAN SA REVOLVER . . NiB $369 Ex $301 Gd $170
Patterned after the Colt Army SA revolver. Calibers: .357 Magnum, .44
Magnum, .45 Colt. Six-round cylinder. Bbl. lengths: 4.75-, 5.5- (not available
in .44), 6- (.44 only), 7.25-inch. Weight: About 41 oz. Fixed sights. Blued bbl.,
and cylinder color-casehardened frame, brass grip frame. One-piece walnut
grip. Made by Aldo Uberti, Brescia, Italy, from 1973 to 1978.
.44 Magnum, add. $50

Iver Johnson
Cattleman

Iver Johnson
Champion .22
Target

Iver Johnson
Protector
Sealed 8

Iver Johnson
Rookie

Iver Johnson
Safety Hammer

CATTLEMAN BUCKHORN SA REVOLVER
Same as standard Cattleman except has adj. rear and ramp front sights. Bbl. lengths: 4.75- (.44 only), 5.75- (not available in .44), 6- (.44 only), 7.5- or 12-inches bbl., weight: About 44 oz. Made from 1973 to 1978.
.357 Magnum or .45
  Colt w/12-inch bbl. . . . . .NiB $439 Ex $326 Gd $219
.357 Magnum or .45
  Colt w/5.75- or 7.5-inch bbl. . . .NiB $342 Ex $255 Gd $158
.44 Magnum, w/12-inch bbl.. . . . NiB $459 Ex $367 Gd $279
.44 Magnum, other bbls.. . . . . . . NiB $439 Ex $326 Gd $219

CATTLEMAN BUNTLINE SA REVOLVER
Same as Cattleman Buckhorn except has 18-inch bbl., walnut shoulder stock w/brass fittings. Weight: About 56 oz. Made from 1973 to 1978.
.44 Magnum. . . . . NiB $443 Ex $332 Gd $225
Other calibers . . . . NiB $443 Ex $332 Gd $225

CATTLEMAN
TRAIL BLAZER . . . . NiB $377 Ex $274 Gd $189
Similar to Cattleman Buckhorn except .22 caliber has interchangeable .22 LR and .22 WMR cylinders, 5.5- or 6.5-inch bbl., weight: About 40 oz. Made from 1973 to 1978.

CHAMPION 822
.22 TARGET SA . . . . .NiB $499 Ex $326 Gd $175
Hinged frame. Caliber: .22 LR. Eight-round cylinder. Single action. Counterbored chambers as in Sealed 8 model, 6-inch bbl., 10.75 inches overall. Weight: 28 oz. Adj. target sights. Blued finish. Checkered walnut grips, adj. finger rest. Made from 1938 to 1948.

DELUXE TARGET . . . . NiB $305 Ex $225 Gd $175
Same as Sportsman except has adj. sights. Made from 1975 to 1976.

PROTECTOR SEALED 8
DA REVOLVER. . . . . .NiB $453 Ex $337 Gd $204
Hinged frame. Caliber: .22 LR. Eight-round cylinder, 2.5-inch bbl., 7.25 inches overall. Weight: 20 oz. Fixed sights. Blued finish. Checkered walnut grips. Made from 1933 to 1949.

ROOKIE DA REVOLVER . . . . . . NiB $270 Ex $204 Gd $90
Solid frame. Caliber: .38 Special. Five-round cylinder, 4-inch bbl., 9-inches overall. Weight: 30 oz. Fixed sights. Blued or nickel finish. Plastic grips. Made from 1975 to 1977.

SAFETY HAMMER
DA REVOLVER. . . . . .NiB $342 Ex $170 Gd $105
Hinged frame. Calibers: .22 LR, .32 S&W, .32 S&W Long, .38 S&W. Seven-round cylinder in .22 cal.,or 6-round (.32 S&W Long), 5-round (.32 S&W, .38 S&W). bbl. lengths: 2, 3, 3.25, 4, 5 or 6 inches. Weight w/4-inch bbl.: 15 oz. (.22, .32 S&W), 19.5 oz. (.32 S&W Long) or 19 oz. (.38 S&W). Fixed sights. Blued or nickel finish. Hard rubber, round butt grips or square butt, rubber or walnut grips available. Note: .32 S&W Long and .38 S&W models built on heavy frame. Made from 1892 to 1950.

SAFETY HAMMERLESS
DA REVOLVER. . . . . .NiB $337 Ex $219 Gd $129
Similar to the Safety Hammer Model except w/shrouded hammerless frame. Made from 1895 to 1950.

SIDEWINDER
DA REVOLVER . . . . .NiB $281 Ex $179 Gd $110
Solid frame. Caliber: .22 LR. Six- or 8-round cylinder, bbl. lengths: 4.75, 6 inches; 11.25 inches overall (with 6-inch bbl.). Weight: 31 oz. (with 6-inch bbl.). Fixed sights. Blued or nickel finish w/ plastic staghorn grips or color-casehardened frame w/walnut grips. Note: Cylinder capacity changed from 8 to 6 rounds in 1975. Made from 1961 to 1978

SIDEWINDER "S" . . . . NiB $281 Ex $179 Gd $110
Same as Sidewinder except has interchangeable cylinders in .22 LR and .22 WMR, adj. sights. Intro. 1974. Disc.

SPORTSMAN
DA REVOLVER . . . . .NiB $222 Ex $165 Gd $109
Solid frame. Caliber: .22 LR. Six-round cylinder. Bbl. lengths: 4.75-, 6-inches, 10.75 inches overall (with 6-inch bbl.). Weight: 30.5 oz. (with 6-inch bbl.). Fixed sights. Blued finish. Plastic grips. Made 1974 to 1976.

SUPERSHOT .22 DA REVOLVER . .NiB $273 Ex $175 Gd $119
Hinged frame. Caliber: .22 LR. Seven-round cylinder, 6-inch bbl. Fixed sights. Blued finish. Checkered walnut grips. This earlier model does not have counterbored chambers as in the Supershot Sealed 8. Made from 1929 to 1949.

SUPERSHOT 9
DA REVOLVER . . . . .NiB $273 Ex $175 Gd $119
Same as Supershot Sealed 8 except has nine non-counterbored chambers. Made from 1929 to 1949.

SUPERSHOT MODEL 844 DA . . . .NiB $336 Ex $204 Gd $129
Hinged frame. Caliber: .22 LR. Eight-round cylinder, bbl. lengths: 4.5- or 6-inch, 9.25 inches overall (with 4.5-inch bbl.). Weight: 27 oz. (4.5-inch bbl.). Adj. sights. Blued finish. Checkered walnut one-piece grip. Made from 1955 to 1956.

SUPERSHOT SEALED
8 DA REVOLVER . . . . .NiB $316 Ex $180 Gd $140
Hinged frame. Caliber: .22 LR. Eight-round cylinder, 6-inch bbl., 10.75 inches overall. Weight: 24 oz. Adj. target sights. Blued finish. Checkered walnut grips. Postwar model does not have adj. finger rest as earlier version. Made from 1931 to 1957.

SWING-OUT DA REVOLVER
Calibers: .22 LR, .22 WMR, .32 S&W Long, .38 Special. Six-round cylinder in .22, 5-round in .32 and .38. Two, 3-, 4-inch plain bbl., or 4- 6-inch vent rib bbl., 8.75 inches overall (with 4-inch bbl.). Fixed or adj. sights. Blue or nickel finish. Walnut grips. Made in 1977.
w/plain barrel, fixed sights . . . . . NiB $220 Ex $158 Gd $115
w/vent rib, adj. sights . . . . NiB $204 Ex $148 Gd $110

TARGET 9 DA REVOLVER . . . . NiB $265 Ex $180 Gd $135
Same as Target Sealed 8 except has nine non-counterbored chambers. Made from 1929 to 1946.

TARGET SEALED 8 DA REVOLVER . . . . . NiB $273 Ex $166 Gd $135
Solid frame. Caliber: .22 LR. Eight-round cylinder, bbl. lengths: 6- and 10-inches. 10.75 inches overall (with 6-inch bbl.). Weight: 24 oz. (with 6-inch bbl.). Fixed sights. Blued finish. Checkered walnut grips. Made from 1931 to 1957.

TRIGGER-COCKING SA TARGET . . . . . . NiB $321 Ex $239 Gd $187
Hinged frame. First pull on trigger cocks hammer, second pull releases hammer. Caliber: .22 LR. Eight-round cylinder, counterbored chambers, 6-inch bbl., 10.75 inches overall. Weight: 24 oz. Adj. target sights. Blued finish. Checkered walnut grips. Made from 1940 to 1947.

Iver Johnson Sidewinder

Iver Johnson Supershot Sealed 8

Iver Johnson Target Sealed 8

Kahr Model K9

KAHR ARMS — Worcester, Massachusetts
Formerly Pearl River, New York.

MODEL K9 DAO AUTO PISTOL
Caliber: 9mm Para. Seven-round magazine, 3.5-inch bbl., 6 inches overall. Weight: 24 oz. Fixed sights. Matte black, electroless nickel, Birdsong Black-T or matte stainless finish. Wraparound textured polymer or hardwood grips. Made from 1994 to 2003.

Duo-Tone finish	NiB $587	Ex $464	Gd $321
Electroless nickel finish	NiB $657	Ex $577	Gd $395
Black-T finish	NiB $740	Ex $602	Gd $464
Matte stainless finish	NiB $785	Ex $631	Gd $453
Kahr Lady K9 model	NiB $530	Ex $345	Gd $270
Elite model.	NiB $836	Ex $610	Gd $399
Tritium Night Sights, add			$100

MODEL K40 DAO AUTO PISTOL
Similar to Model K9 except chambered .40 S&W w/5- or 6-round magazine, Weight: 26 oz. Made from 1997 to 2003.

Matte black finish.	NiB $590	Ex $433	Gd $321
Electroless nickel finish	NiB $668	Ex $595	Gd $395
Black-T finish	NiB $740	Ex $562	Gd $362
Matte black stainless finish	NiB $653	Ex $485	Gd $345
Covert model (shorter grip-frame).	NiB $536	Ex $395	Gd $306
Elite model.	NiB $826	Ex $602	Gd $437
Tritium Night Sights, add			$100

MODEL K9 DAO AUTO PISTOL
Similar to Model K9 except w/Micro-Compact frame. Six- or 7- round magazine, 3- inch bbl., 5.5 inches overall. Weight: 22 oz. Stainless or Duo-Tone finish. Made from 1993 to 2003.

Duo-Tone finish	NiB $665	Ex $530	Gd $398
Matte stainless finish.	NiB $437	Ex $347	Gd $301
Elite model.	NiB $830	Ex $544	Gd $429
Tritium Night Sights, add			$100

Kel-Tec Model P-11

Kimber Model Classic .45

CW series DAO Auto Pistol. . . . . . NiB **$425** Ex **$325** Gd **$250**
Caliber: 9mm Para., .40 S&W, .45 ACP. Seven-round magazine (9mm Para), 3.6-inch bbl., 6 inches overall. Weight: 15.8 oz. Fixed sights. Textured black polymer frame, matte stainless steel slide. Made from 2005 (9mm para), 2008 (.40 S&W, .45 ACP).

CM series DAO Auto Pistol. . . . . . NiB **$450** Ex **$350** Gd **$250**
Caliber: 9mm Para., .40 S&W, .45 ACP. Six-round magazine (9mm Para), 3-inch bbl., 6 inches overall. Weight: 15.8 oz. Fixed sights. Textured black polymer frame, matte stainless steel slide. Made from 2011 (9mm para), 2012 (.40 S&W), 2013 (.45 ACP).

E9 DAO Auto Pistol . . . . NiB **$425** Ex **$340** Gd **$250**
Caliber: 9mm Para. Seven-round magazine, 3.5-inch bbl., 6 inches overall. Weight: 15.8 oz. Fixed sights. Textured black polymer frame. Made from 1997, reintro. 2003.

MK Micro series DAO Auto Pistol. . NiB **$450** Ex **$350** Gd **$250**
Caliber: 9mm Para., .40 S&W. Six-round magazine (9mm para), 3-inch bbl., 5.5 inches overall. Weight: 15.8 oz. Fixed sights., Matte stainless steel slide and frame. Made from 1998-99 (9mm para), intro. 1999 (.40 S&W).

T series DAO Auto Pistol . . . . NiB **$600** Ex **$450** Gd **$290**
Caliber: 9mm Para., .40 S&W. 8-round magazine (9mm para), 4-inch bbl., 6.5 inches overall. Weight: 26 oz. Fixed sights., Matte stainless steel slide and frame, wood grips. Made from 2002 (9mm para), 2004 (.40 S&W).

TP series DAO Auto Pistol . . . . . . NiB **$500** Ex **$430** Gd **$285**
Similar to T series except polymer frame and matte stainless steel slide. Made from 2004.

KBI, INC — Harrisburg, Pennsylvania

MODEL PSP-.25 AUTO PISTOL. . . NiB **$308** Ex **$244** Gd **$157**
Caliber: .25 ACP. Six-round magazine, 2.13-inch bbl., 4.13 inches overall. Weight: 9.5 oz. All-steel construction w/dual safety system. Made 1994.

KEL-TEC CNC INDUSTRIES, INC. — Cocoa, Florida

MODEL P-11 DAO PISTOL
Caliber: 9mm Parabellum or .40 S&W. 10-round magazine, 3.1- inch bbl., 5.6 inches overall. Weight: 14 oz. Blade front sight, drift adjustable rear. Aluminum frame w/steel slide. Checkered black, gray, or green polymer grips. Matte blue, nickel, stainless steel or Parkerized finish. Made from 1995 to date.
9mm . . . . NiB **$305** Ex **$214** Gd **$156**
.40 S&W . . . . NiB **$590** Ex **$399** Gd **$243**

KIMBER MANUFACTURING, INC. – 37th Edition

Parkerized finish, add $75
Nickel finish (disc. 1995) add $75
Stainless finish, (1996 to date) add $75
Tritium Night Sights, add $90
.40 S&W conversion kit, add $204

P-32. . . . . NiB **$291** Ex **$170** Gd **$90**
Semi-auto, double-action. Cal.: .32 ACP. Internal block safety. 7-round mag. Bbl.: 2.68 inches; Parkerized, blue, or chrome finish. Choice of ivory or colored grips. Weight: 6.6 oz.

P-3AT . . . . NiB **$301** Ex **$180** Gd **$95**
Similar to P-32. Cal.: .380 ACP. Bbl.: 2.76 inches. 6-round mag. Black composite frame with Parkerized steel slide. Weight: 8.3 oz.

P-40. . . . . NiB **$290** Ex **$175** Gd **$88**
Semi-auto, double-action. 9- or 10-round mag. Composite frame with steel slide. Bbl.: 3.3 inches. Parkerized, blue, or chrome finish. Made from 1999 to 2001.
Parkerized finish, add $50
Hard chrome finish, add $70

PLR-16. . . . . NiB **$638** Ex **$495** Gd **$281**
M-16-type gas operated. Cal.: .223 Rem., 10-round mag. Bbl.: 9.2 inches. Upper w/Picatinny accessory rail. Black composite frame. Weight: 3.2 lbs.

PLR-22 . . . . NiB **$357** Ex **$265** Gd **$170**
Similar to PLR-16 except in .22 LR; 26-round mag. Weight: 2.8 lbs.

PF-9. . . . . NiB **$306** Ex **$198** Gd **$143**
Similar to P-11, cal.: 9 mm Para. Bbl.: 3.1 inches. 7-round mag., lower accessory rail. Black finish. Weight: 12.7 oz. Limited production in 2006, reintro. 2008.
Parkerized finish, add $50
Hard chrome finish, add $65

PMR-30 . . . . NiB **$408** Ex **$301** Gd **$189**
Cal.: .22 Mag. Bbl.: 4.3 inches. 30-round mag, blowback action, manual safety. Lower Picatinny accessory rail. Steel slide and bbl., fiber optic sights. Weight: 19.5 oz. Made 2010 to date.

KIMBER MANUFACTURING, INC. — Yonkers, New York

Formerly Kimber of America, Inc.

MODEL CLASSIC .45
Similar to Government 1911 built on steel, polymer or alloy full-size or compact frame. Caliber: .45 ACP. Seven-, 8-, 10- or 14-round magazine, 4- or 5-inch bbl., 7.7 or 8.75 inches overall. Weight: 28 oz. (Compact LW), 34 oz. (Compact or Polymer) or .38 oz. (Custom FS). McCormick low-profile combat or Kimber adj. target sights. Blued, matte black oxide or stainless finish. Checkered custom wood or black synthetic grips. Made from 1994 to date.
Custom (matte black) . . . . NiB **$882** Ex **$599** Gd **$431**
Custom Royal (polished blue) . NiB **$774** Ex **$612** Gd **$443**
Custom stainless (satin stainless)NiB **$737** Ex **$577** Gd **$439**
Custom Target (matte black) . . NiB **$755** Ex **$581** Gd **$453**
Target Gold Match
  (polished blue) . . . . NiB **$1020** Ex **$755** Gd **$587**
Target stainless Match
  (polished stainless) . . . . NiB **$852** Ex **$669** Gd **$474**
Polymer (matte black) . . . . NiB **$852** Ex **$669** Gd **$474**
Polymer Stainless
  (satin stainless slide) . . . . NiB **$967** Ex **$784** Gd **$577**
Polymer Target
  (matte black slide) . . . . NiB **$918** Ex **$744** Gd **$536**
Compact (matte black) . . . . NiB **$644** Ex **$541** Gd **$377**
Compact stainless (satin stainless) . . . NiB **$714** Ex **$559** Gd **$437**

GRADING: NiB = New in Box   Ex = Excellent or NRA 95%   Gd = Good or NRA 68%   **113**

**Compact LW (matte
black w/alloy frame)** . . . . NiB $733 Ex $577 Gd $408

SERIES II MODELS

Similar to Classic 1911 models except includes firing pin block safety
and denoted with "II" following all model names. Size configurations
vary per model and include from smallest to largest: Micro (2.75-in.
bbl., micro frame), Ultra (3-in. bbl., short frame), Ultra+ (3-in. bbl., full
size frame), Compact (4-in. bbl., short frame), Pro (4-in. bbl., full size
frame), Custom (5-in. bbl., full size frame). Made from 2001 to date.

	NiB	Ex	Gd
Aegis II (intro. 2006)	$1200	$1140	$840
CDP II (intro. 2000)	$1150	$1095	$805
Compact II	$960	$912	$500
Covert II (intro. 2007)	$1450	$1100	$650
Crimson Cary II (laser grip)	$1050	$900	$735
Custom II	$730	$525	$330
Custom II Stainless	$855	$655	$365
Custom Royal II	$1900	$1000	$580
Eclipse II (intro. 2002)	$1100	$1045	$570
Gold Match II	$1300	$1000	$580
Master Carry II (intro. 2013)	$1330	$1265	$931
Micro Carry (intro. 2013, .380 ACP)	$580	$475	$375
Raptor II (intro. 2004)	$1300	$1235	$910
Super Carry II (intro. 2010)	$1350	$1285	$945
Tactical II (intro. 2003)	$1130	$1075	$795
Ultra Carry II (intro. 1999)	$800	$760	$560
Custom Royal II	$1900	$1000	$580

KORTH — Lollar, Germany

*Previously Ratzeburg, Germany. Currently imported by Korth USA
(Earl's Repair Service, Tewkberry, MA). Previously by Keng's Firearms
Specialty, Inc., Beeman Precision Arms; Osborn Beeman Precision
Arms; Osborne's and Mandall Shooting Supply.*

REVOLVERS COMBAT, SPORT, TARGET

Calibers: .357 Mag. and .22 LR w/interchangeable combination cylinders
of .357 Mag./9mm Para. or .22 LR/.22 WMR also .22 Jet, .32 S&W and
.32 H&R Mag. Bbls: 2.5-, 3-, 4-inch (combat) and 5.25- or 6-inch (target).
Weight: 33 to 42 oz. Blued, stainless, matte silver or polished silver finish.
Checkered walnut grips. Imported 1967 to date.

	NiB	Ex	Gd
Standard rimfire model	$4590	$2735	$1895
Standard centerfire model	$6899	$5100	$4029
ISU Match Target model	$7429	$5433	$3329
Custom stainless finish, add			$485
Matte silver finish, add			$689
Polished silver finish, add			$950

SEMIAUTOMATIC PISTOL

Calibers: 30 Luger, 9mm Para., .357 SIG, .40 S&W, 9x21mm. 10- or
14-round magazine, 4- or 5-inch bbl., all-steel construction, recoil-operated.
Ramp front sight, adj. rear. Blued, stainless, matte silver or polished silver
finish. Checkered walnut grips. Limited import from 1988 .

	NiB	Ex	Gd
Standard model	$6495	$5040	$3934
Matte silver finish, add			$332
Polished silver finish, add			$791

LAHTI — Sweden & Finland

*Mfd. by Husqvarna Vapenfabriks A. B. Huskvarna, Sweden, and Valtion
Kivaar Tedhas ("VKT") Jyväskyla, Finland.*

AUTOMATIC PISTOL

Caliber: 9mm Para. Eight-round magazine, 4.75-inch bbl., weight: About
46 oz. Fixed sights. Blued finish. Plastic grips. Specifications given are those
of the Swedish Model 40 but also apply in general to the Finnish Model
L-35, which differs only slightly. A considerable number of Swedish Lahti
pistols were imported and sold in the U.S. The Finnish model, somewhat
better made, is rare. Finnish Model L-35 adopted 1935. Swedish Model 40

Lahti Automatic Pistol

L.A.R. Mark I Grizzly

Laseraim
Series I

Laseraim
Series II

adopted 1940, mfd. through 1944.

	NiB	Ex	Gd
Finnish L-35 model			
(1st Variation)	$4120	$3020	$2455
Swedish 40 model	$648	$449	$332

L.A.R. MANUFACTURING, INC. — West Jordan, Utah

MARK I GRIZZLY WIN. MAG. AUTOMATIC PISTOL

Calibers: .357 Mag., .45 ACP, .45 Win. Mag. Seven-round magazine,
6.5-inch bbl., 10.5 inches overall. Weight: 48 oz. Fully adj. sights.
Checkered rubber combat-style grips. Blued finish. Made from 1983 to
date. 8- or 10-inch bbl., Made from 1987 to 1999.

	NiB	Ex	Gd
.357 Mag. (6.5 inch barrel)	$918	$643	$434
.45 Win. Mag.(6.5 inch barrel)	$918	$740	$444
8-inch barrel	$1237	$1040	$943
10-inch barrel	$1320	$1118	$1029

MARK 4 GRIZZLY

AUTOMATIC PISTOL . . . . NiB $918 Ex $740 Gd $629
Same general specifications as the L.A.R. Mark I except chambered
for .44 Magnum, has 5.5- or 6.5-inch bbl., beavertail grip safety, matte
blued finish. Made from 1991 to 1999.

MARK 5 AUTO PISTOL . . . . NiB $918 Ex $734 Gd $631
Similar to the Mark I except chambered in 50 Action Express. Six-round
magazine, 5.4- or 6.5-inch bbl., 10.6 inches overall (with 5.4-inch bbl.).
Weight: 56 oz. Checkered walnut grips. Made 1993 to 1999.

LASERAIM TECHNOLOGIES, INC. — Little Rock, Arkansas

SERIES I SA AUTO PISTOL
Calibers: .40 S&W, .45 ACP, 10mm. Seven or 8- round magazine, 3.875- or 5.5-inch dual-port compensated bbl., 8.75 or 10.5 inches overall. Weight: 46 or 52 oz. Fixed sights w/Laseraim or adjustable Millet sights. TExtured black composition grips. Extended slide release, ambidExtrous safety and beveled magazine well. Stainless or matte black Teflon finish. Made from 1993 to 1999.
Series I w/adjustable sights . . . . . . NiB $362 Ex $255 Gd $188
Series I w/fixed sights . . . . NiB $362 Ex $255 Gd $188
Series I w/fixed sights (HotDot) . . . NiB $479 Ex $270 Gd $203
Series I Dream Team (RedDot) . . NiB $479 Ex $ 270 Gd $203
Series I Illusion (Laseraim) . . . . . . NiB $479 Ex $270 Gd $203

SERIES II SA AUTO PISTOL
Similar to Series I except w/stainless finish and no bbl., compensator. Made from 1993 to 1996.
Series II w/adjustable sights . . . . . NiB $530 Ex $365 Gd $265
Series II w/fixed sights . . . . NiB $530 Ex $365 Gd $265
Series II Dream Team . . . . NiB $602 Ex $437 Gd $279
Series II Illusion . . . . NiB $540 Ex $439 Gd $321

SERIES III SA AUTO PISTOL
Similar to Series II except w/serrated slide and 5-inch compensated bbl., only. Made 1994. Disc.
Series III w/adjustable sights . . . . . NiB $632 Ex $536 Gd $398
Series III w/fixed sights . . . . NiB $632 Ex $599 Gd $362

VELOCITY SERIES SA AUTO PISTOL
Similar to Series I except chambered for .357 Sig. or .400 Cor-Bon, 3.875-inch unported bbl., (compact) or 5.5-inch dual-port compensated bbl. Made from 1993 to 1999. See illustration previous page.
Compact model (unported) . . . . . . NiB $362 Ex $290 Gd $204
Government model (ported) . . . . . NiB $362 Ex $290 Gd $204
w/wireless laser (HotDot), add $175

LIGNOSE — Suhl, Germany
Aktien-Gesellschaft "Lignose" Abteilung

The following Lignose pistols were manufactured from 1920 to the mid-1930s. They were also marketed under the Bergmann name.

EINHAND MODEL 2A
POCKET AUTO PISTOL . . . . NiB $434 Ex $305 Gd $209
As the name implies, this pistol is designed for one-hand operation, pressure on a "trigger" at the front of the guard retracts the slide. Caliber: .25 Auto. (6.35 mm). Six-round magazine, 2-inch bbl., 4.75 inches overall. Weight: About 14 oz. Blued finish. Hard rubber grips.

MODEL 2 POCKET
AUTO PISTOL . . . . NiB $362 Ex $237 Gd $175
Conventional Browning type. Same general specifications as Einhand Model 2A but lacks the one-hand operation.

EINHAND MODEL
3A POCKET AUTO PISTOL . . . . . . NiB $479 Ex $369 Gd $270
Same as the Model 2A except has longer grip, 9-round magazine, weight: About 16 oz.

LLAMA — Vitoria, Spain
Manufactured by Gabilondo y Cia, Vitoria, Spain, imported by S.G.S., Wanamassa, New Jersey.

NOTE: *For ease in finding a particular Llama handgun, the listings are divided into two groupings: Automatic Pistols (below) and Revolvers, which follow. For a complete listing of Llama handguns, please refer to the index.*

Laseraim Series III
w/LA93 Illusion III scope

Llama Model IIIA
Deluxe Chrome Engraved First
Issue

Llama Model IIIA
Deluxe Blue Engraved Second
Issue

GRADING: **NiB** = New in Box   **Ex** = Excellent or NRA 95%   **Gd** = Good or NRA 68%

- AUTOMATIC PISTOLS -

MODEL IIIA
AUTOMATIC PISTOL . . . . NiB $337 Ex $170 Gd $109
Caliber: .380 Auto. Seven-round magazine, 3.69-inch bbl., 6.5 inches overall. Weight: 23 oz. Adj. target sights. Blued finish. Plastic grips. Intro. 1951. Disc.

MODELS IIIA, XA, XV DELUXE
Same as standard Model IIIA, XA and XV except engraved w/blued or chrome finish and simulated pearl grips.
Chrome-engraved finish . . . . NiB $365 Ex $306 Gd $219
Blue-engraved finish. . . . . NiB $356 Ex $290 Gd $204

MODEL VIII
AUTOMATIC PISTOL . . . . NiB $377 Ex $306 Gd $255
Caliber: .38 Super. Nine-round magazine, 5-inch bbl., 8.5 inches overall. Weight: 40 oz. Fixed sights. Blued finish. Wood grips. Intro. in 1952. Disc.

MODELS VIII, IXA, XI DELUXE
Same as standard Models VIII, IXA and XI except finish (chrome engraved or blued engraved) and simulated pearl grips. Disc. 1984.
Chrome-engraved finish . . . . NiB $377 Ex $290 Gd $190
Blue-engraved finish. . . . . NiB $377 Ex $290 Gd $190

MODEL IXA AUTOMATIC PISTOL . . NiB $377 Ex $290 Gd $190
Same as model VIII except .45 Auto, 7-round magazine,

MODEL XA AUTOMATIC PISTOL . . NiB $377 Ex $290 Gd $190
Same as model IIIA except .32 Auto, 8-round magazine,

MODEL XI AUTOMATIC PISTOL . . NiB $377 Ex $290 Gd $190
Same as model VIII except 9mm Para.

MODEL XV AUTOMATIC PISTOL . . NiB $321 Ex $255 Gd $170
Same as model XA except .22 LR.

MODELS BE-IIIA, BE-XA, BE-XV . . . NiB $530 Ex $332 Gd $235
Same as models IIIA, XA and XV except w/blued-engraved finish. Made from 1977-84.

MODELS BE-VIII,
BE-IXA, BE-XI DELUXE . . . . NiB $530 Ex $398 Gd $281
Same as models VIII, IXA and XI except w/blued-engraved finish. Made from 1977 to 1984.

MODELS C-IIIA, C-XA, C-XV. . NiB $408 Ex $365 Gd $259
Same as models IIIA, XA and XV except in satin chrome.

MODELS C-VIII, C-IXA, C-XI. . . . . NiB $475 Ex $357 Gd $244
Same as models VIII, IXA and XI except in satin chrome.

MODELS CE-IIIA,
CE-XA, CE-XV. . . . . NiB $398 Ex $347 Gd $230
Same as models IIIA, XA and XV except w/chrome engraved finish. Made from 1977 to 1984.

MODELS CE-VIII,
CE-IXA, CE-XI. . . . . NiB $475 Ex $357 Gd $244
Same as models VIII, IXA and XI, w/except chrome engraved finish. Made from 1977 to 1984.

COMPACT FRAME
AUTO PISTOL . . . . NiB $345 Ex $270 Gd $204
Calibers: 9mm Para., .38 Super, .45 Auto. Seven-, 8- or 9-round magazine, 5-inch bbl., 7.88 inches overall. Weight: 34 oz. Blued, satin-chrome or Duo-Tone finishes. Made from 1986 to 1997. Duo-Tone disc. 1993.

Llama Model XA First Issue

Llama Model C-XI

Llama Model CE-IIIA

Llama Model Compact

www.skyhorsepublishing.com

**Llama Duo-Tone
Large Frame**

**Llama M-82
DA Auto**

Llama MINI-MAX II

Llama MAX-I

DUO-TONE LARGE
FRAME AUTO PISTOL . . . . **NiB $449 Ex $368 Gd $305**
Caliber: .45 ACP. Seven-round magazine, 5-inch bbl., 8.5 inches overall. Weight: 36 oz. Adj. rear sight. Blued finished w/satin chrome. Polymer black grips. Made from 1991 to 1993.

DUO-TONE SMALL
FRAME AUTO PISTOL . . . . **NiB $306 Ex $209 Gd $150**
Calibers: .22 LR, .32 and .380 Auto. Seven- or 8-round magazine, 3.69 inch bbl., 6.5 inches overall. Weight: 23 oz. Square-notch rear sight, Partridge-type front. Blued finish w/chrome. Made from 1990 to 1993.

MODEL G-IIIA DELUXE . . **NiB $2520 Ex $1944 Gd $1659**
Same as Model IIIA except gold damascened w/simulated pearl grips. Disc. 1982.

LARGE-FRAME AUTOMATIC PISTOL (IXA)
Caliber: .45 Auto. Seven-round magazine, 5-inch bbl., weight: 2 lbs., 8 oz. Adj. rear sight, Partridge-type front. Walnut grips or teakwood on satin chrome model. Later models w/polymer grips.
Blued finish . . . . **NiB $369 Ex $258 Gd $198**
Satin chrome finish. . . . . **NiB $538 Ex $444 Gd $290**

M-82 DA AUTOMATIC PISTOL. . . . . . . **NiB $587 Ex $398 Gd $270**
Caliber: 9mm Para. 15-round magazine, 4.25-inch bbl., 8 inches overall. Weight: 39 oz. Drift-adj. rear sight. Matte blued finish. Matte black polymer grips. Made from 1988 to 1993.

M-87 COMPETITION PISTOL NiB $1029 Ex $816 Gd $634
Caliber: 9mm Para. 15-round magazine, 5.5-inch bbl., 9.5 inches overall. Weight: 40 oz. Low-profile combat sights. Satin nickel finish. Matte black grip panels. Built-in ported compensator to minimize recoil and muzzle rise. Made from 1989 to 1993.

MICRO-MAX SA AUTOMATIC PISTOL
Caliber: .380 ACP. Seven-round magazine, 3.125-inch bbl., weight: 23 oz. Blade front sight, drift adjustable rear w/3-dot system. Matte blue or satin chrome finish. Checkered polymer grips. Imported from 1997 to 2005.
Matte blue finish . . . . **NiB $281 Ex $204 Gd $165**
Satin chrome finish. . . . . **NiB $288 Ex $230 Gd $219**

MINI-MAX SA AUTOMATIC PISTOL
Calibers: 9mm, .40 S&W or .45 ACP. Six- or 8-round magazine, 3.5-inch bbl., 8.3 inches overall. Weight: 35 oz. Blade front sight, drift adjustable rear w/3-dot system. Matte blue, Duo-Tone or satin chrome finish. Checkered polymer grips. Imported 1996 to 2005.
Duo-Tone finish . . . . **NiB $290 Ex $204 Gd $158**
Matte blue finish . . . . **NiB $306 Ex $220 Gd $170**
Satin chrome finish. . . . . **NiB $326 Ex $240 Gd $190**
Stainless (disc.). . . . . **NiB $359 Ex $301 Gd $235**

MINI-MAX II SA AUTOMATIC PISTOL
Cal. .45 ACP only. 10-round mag., 3.625 inch bbl., 7.375 inch overall. Wt: 37 oz. Blade front sight, drift adj. rear w/3-dot system. Shortened barrel and grip. Matte and Satin Chrome finish. Imp. 2005.
Matte blue finish . . . . **NiB $290 Ex $225 Gd $170**
Satin chrome finish. . . . . **NiB $316 Ex $255 Gd $189**

MAX-I SA AUTOMATIC PISTOL
Calibers: 9mm or .45 ACP. 7- or 9-round magazine, 4.25- to 5.125 inch bbl., weight: 34 or 36 oz. Blade front sight, drift adj. rear w/3-dot system. Matte blue, Duo-Tone or satin chrome finish. Checkered black rubber grips. Imported from 1995 to 1999.
Duo-Tone finish . . . . **NiB $306 Ex $265 Gd $198**
Matte blue finish . . . . **NiB $301 Ex $240 Gd $189**
Satin chrome finish. . . . . **NiB $316 Ex $270 Gd $219**

MAX-II SA AUTOMATIC PISTOL
Same as the MAX-I with 4.25 bbl. except w/10-round mag. Weight 40 oz., made 2005.
Matte blue finish . . . . NiB $306 Ex $265 Gd $198
Satin chrome finish. . . . . NiB $332 Ex $270 Gd $219

OMNI 45 DOUBLE-ACTION
AUTOMATIC PISTOL . . . . NiB $437 Ex $291 Gd $220
Caliber: .45 Auto. Seven-round magazine, 4.25-inch bbl., 7.75 inches overall. Weight: 40 oz. Adj. rear sight, ramp front. Highly polished deep blued finish. Made from 1984-86.

OMNI 9MM DOUBLE-ACTION
AUTOMATIC . . . . NiB $469 Ex $347 Gd $290
Same general specifications as .45 Omni except chambered for 9mm w/13-round magazine. Made from 1983-86.

SINGLE-ACTION
AUTOMATIC PISTOL . . . . NiB $485 Ex $386 Gd $270
Calibers: .38 Super, 9mm, .45 Auto. Nine-round magazine (7-round for .45 Auto), 5-inch bbl., 8.5 inches overall. Weight: 2 lbs., 8 oz. Intro. in 1981.

SMALL-FRAME AUTOMATIC PISTOL
Calibers: .380 Auto (7-round magazine), .22 RF (8-round magazine), 3.69-inch bbl., weight: 23 oz. Partridge-blade front sight, adj. rear. Blued or satin-chrome finish. Disc. 1997.
Blued finish . . . . NiB $255 Ex $204 Gd $165
Satin-chrome finish. . . . . NiB $270 Ex $220 Gd $175

- REVOLVERS -

MARTIAL DOUBLE-
ACTION REVOLVER. . . . . NiB $255 Ex $170 Gd $120
Calibers: .22 LR, .38 Special. Six-round cylinder, bbl. lengths: 4-inch (.38 Special only) or 6-inch; 11.25 inches overall (w/6-inch bbl.). Weight: About 36 oz. w/6-inch bbl. Target sights. Blued finish. Checkered walnut grips. Made from 1969 to 1976.

MARTIAL DOUBLE-ACTION DELUXE
Same as standard Martial except w/satin chrome, chrome-engraved, blued engraved or gold damascened finish. Simulated pearl grips. Made from 1969 to 1976.
Satin-chrome finish. . . . . NiB $306 Ex $225 Gd $165
Chrome-engraved finish . . . . NiB $581 Ex $431 Gd $286
Blue-engraved finish. . . . . NiB $638 Ex $453 Gd $332
Gold-damascened finish . . . . NiB $2810 Ex $2647 Gd $2299

COMANCHE I DOUBLE-ACTION
REVOLVER. . . . . NiB $270 Ex $204 Gd $160
Same general specifications as Martial .22. Made 1977 to 1982.

COMANCHE II . . . . NiB $265 Ex $189 Gd $150
Same general specifications as Martial .38. Made 1977 to 1982.

COMANCHE III DOUBLE-ACTION
REVOLVER. . . . . NiB $306 Ex $219 Gd $144
Caliber: .357 Magnum. Six-round cylinder, 4-inch bbl., 9.25 inches overall. Weight: 36 oz. Adj. rear sight, ramp front. Blued finish. Checkered walnut grips. Made from 1975 to 1995. Note: Prior to 1977, this model was designated "Comanche."

COMANCHE III
CHROME. . . . . NiB $362 Ex $270 Gd $204
Same gen. specifications as Comanche III except has satin chrome finish, 4- or 6-inch bbl. Made from 1975 to 1995.

Llama
Comanche I

Llama
Comanche III Chrome

Llama
Martial Double-Action Revolver

Llama
Martial Deluxe Gold-
Damascened

Llama
Super Comanche IV

**Luger 1900
American
Eagle**

SUPER COMANCHE IV DA REVOLVER NiB $388 Ex $301 Gd $204
Caliber: .44 Magnum. Six-round cylinder, 6-inch bbl., 11.75 inches overall. Weight: 50 oz. Adj. rear sight, ramp front. Polished deep blued finish. Checkered walnut grips. Disc. 1998.

SUPER COMANCHE V DA REVOLVER NiB $362 Ex $270 Gd $214
Caliber: .357 Mag. Six-round cylinder, 4-, 6- or 8.5-inch bbl., weight: 48 ozs. Ramped front blade sight, click-adj. Rear. Made from 1980 to 1988.

LORCIN ENGINEERING CO., INC. — Mira Loma, California

MODEL L-22 SEMIAUTOMATIC PISTOL NiB $120 Ex $90 Gd $70
Caliber: 22 LR. Nine-round magazine, 2.5-inch bbl., 5.25 inches overall. Weight: 16 oz. Blade front sight, fixed notch rear w/3-dot system. Black Teflon or chrome finish. Black, pink or pearl composition grips. Made from 1990 to 1998.

MODEL L-25, LT-.25 SEMIAUTOMATIC PISTOL
Caliber: 25 ACP. Seven-round magazine, 2.4-inch bbl., 4.8 inches overall. Weight: 12 oz. (LT-25) or 14.5 oz. (L-25). Blade front sight, fixed rear. Black Teflon or chrome finish. Black, pink or pearl composition grips. Made from 1989-98.
Model L-25 . . . . NiB $89 Ex $61 Gd $40
Model LT-25 . . . . NiB $79 Ex $50 Gd $35
Model Lady Lorcin . . . . NiB $81 Ex $55 Gd $35

MODEL L-32 SEMIAUTOMATIC PISTOL NiB $90 Ex $65 Gd $50
Caliber: 32 ACP. Seven-round magazine, 3.5-inch bbl., 6.6 inches overall. Weight: 27 oz. Blade front sight, fixed notch rear. Black Teflon or chrome finish. Black composition grips. Made from 1992 to 1998.

MODEL L-380 SEMIAUTOMATIC PISTOL
Caliber: .380 ACP. Seven- or 10-round magazine, 3.5-inch bbl., 6.6 inches overall. Weight: 23 oz. Blade front sight, fixed notch rear. Matte Black finish. Grooved black composition grips. Made 1994 to 1998.
Model L-380 (10-round) . . . . NiB $158 Ex $95 Gd $65
Model L-380 (13-round) . . . . NiB $128 Ex $90 Gd $61

MODEL L9MM SEMIAUTOMATIC PISTOL
Caliber: 9mm Parabellum. 10- or 13-round magazine, 4.5-inch bbl., 7.5 inches overall. Weight: 31 oz. Blade front sight, fixed notch rear w/3-dot system. Black Teflon or chrome finish. Black composition grips. Made from 1992 to 1998.
Model L-9mm (7-round) . . . . NiB $158 Ex $95 Gd $65
Model L-9mm (10-round) . . . . NiB $158 Ex $95 Gd $65

O/U DERRINGER . . . . NiB $198 Ex $105 Gd $70
Caliber: .38 Special/.357 Mag., .45LC. Two-round derringer. 3.5-inch

bbls. 6.5 inches overall. Weight: 12 oz. Blade front sight, fixed notch rear. Stainless finish. Black composition grips. Made from 1996-98.

LUGER — Manufactured by Deutsche Waffen und Munitionsfabriken (DWM), Berlin, Germany

1900 AMERICAN EAGLE . . . . . NiB $6900 Ex $6555 Gd $4830
Caliber: 7.65 mm. Eight-round magazine; thin, 4.75-inch; tapered bbl.; 9.5 inches overall. Weight: 32 oz. Fixed rear sight, dovetailed front sight. Grip safety. Checkered walnut grips. Early-style toggle, narrow trigger, wide guard, no stock lug. American Eagle over chamber. Estimated 8,000 production.

1900 COMMERCIAL . . . . NiB $6910 Ex $6565 Gd $4837
Same specifications as Luger 1900 American Eagle except DWM on early-style toggle, no chamber markings. Estimated 8000 production.

1900 SWISS . . . . NiB $6700 Ex $6365 Gd $4700
Same specifications as Luger 1900 American Eagle except Swiss cross in sunburst over chamber. Estimated 9,000 production.

1902 AMERICAN EAGLE NiB $16,650 Ex $14,000 Gd $12,990
Caliber: 9mm Para. Eight-round magazine, 4-inch heavy tapered bbl., 8.5 inches overall. Weight: 30 oz. Fixed rear sight, dovetailed front sight. Grip safety. Checkered walnut grips. American Eagle over chamber, DWM on early-style toggle, narrow trigger, wide guard, no stock lug. Estimated 700 production.

1902 CARBINE
Caliber: 7.65mm. Eight-round magazine, 11.75-inch tapered bbl., 16.5 inches overall. Weight: 46 oz. Adj. 4-position rear sight, long ramp front sight. Grip safety. Checkered walnut grips and forearm. DWM on early-style toggle, narrow trigger, wide guard, no chamber markings, stock lug. Estimated 3,200 production.
Model 1902 carbine (gun only) . . . .NiB $12,245 Ex $11,353 Gd $7015
Model 1902 carbine
(gun only, American Eagle), add .45%
w/issued stock and matching numbers, add 20%
w/original stock and non-matching numbers, deduct 20%

1902 CARTRIDGE COUNTER . . . . NiB $45,200 Ex $38,990 Gd $29,900
Caliber: 9mm Para. Eight-round magazine, Heavy, tapered 4-inch bbl., 8.75 inches overall. Weight: 30 oz. Fixed rear sight, dovetailed front sight. Grip safety. Checkered walnut grips. DWM on dished toggle w/lock, American Eagle over chamber when marked. No stock lug. Estimated production unknown.

1902 COMMERCIAL . . . . . NiB $13,600 Ex $10,895 Gd $5,500
Same basic specifications as Luger 1902 Cartridge Counter except DWM on early-style toggle, narrow trigger, wide guard, no chamber markings, no stock lug. Estimated 400 production.

1902 AMERICAN EAGLE. .NiB $16,600 Ex $13,995 Gd $7,900
Same basic specifications as Luger 1902 Commercial except American Eagle over chamber, DWM on early-style toggle, narrow guard, no stock lug. Estimated 700 production.

**1902 AMERICAN EAGLE
CARTRIDGE COUNTER** . . . . . .NiB $45,200 Ex $38,650 Gd $15,088
Same basic specifications as Luger 1902 Cartridge Counter except American Eagle over chamber, DWM on early-style toggle, narrow trigger, wide guard, no stock lug. Estimated 700 production.

GRADING: **NiB** = New in Box **Ex** = Excellent or NRA 95% **Gd** = Good or NRA 68%

1904 GL "BABY" NiB $197,500   Ex $166,000   Gd $110,000
Caliber: 9mm Para. Seven-round magazine, 3.25-inch bbl., 7.75 inches overall. Weight: Approx. 20 oz. Serial number 10077B. "GL" marked on rear of toggle. Georg Luger's personal sidearm. Only one made in 1904.

1904 NAVAL (REWORKED) .... NiB $14,000   Ex $11,000   Gd $8,250
Caliber: 9mm Para. Eight-round magazine, bbl., length altered to 4 inches., 8.75 inches overall. Weight: 30 oz. Adj. two-position rear sight, dovetailed front sight. Thumb lever safety. Checkered walnut grips. Heavy tapered bbl., DWM on new-style toggle w/lock, 1902 over chamber. w/or without grip safety and stock lug. Estimated 800 production. Untouched original (rare) worth $50,000.

1906 (11.35MM) .....NiB $119,000   Ex $95,900   Gd $66,500
Caliber: .45 ACP. Six-round magazine, 5-inch bbl., 9.75 inches overall. Weight: 36 oz. Fixed rear sight, dovetailed front sight. Grip safety. Checkered walnut grips. GL monogram on rear toggle link, larger frame w/altered trigger guard and trigger, no proofs, no markings over chamber. No stock lug. Only two were known to be made. Note: This version of the Luger pistol is the most valuable nExt to the "GL" Baby Luger.

1906 AMERICAN EAGLE
(7.65MM)............... NiB $4235   Ex $3300   Gd $2200
Caliber: 7.65mm. Eight-round magazine, thin 4.75-inch tapered bbl., 9.5 inches overall. Weight: 32 oz. Fixed rear sight, dovetailed front sight. Grip safety. Checkered walnut grips. DWM on new-style toggle, American Eagle over chamber. No stock lug. Estimated 8,000 production.

1906 AMERICAN EAGLE (9MM) .... NiB $4600   Ex $4370   Gd $2000
Same basic specifications as the 7.65mm 1906 except in 9mm Para. w/4-inch barrel, 8.75 inches overall, weight: 30 oz. Estimated 3,500 production.

1906 BERN (7.65MM)....... NiB $4430   Ex $2520   Gd $1996
Same basic specifications as the 7.65mm 1906 American Eagle except checkered walnut grips w/.38-inch borders, Swiss Cross on new-style toggle, Swiss proofs, no markings over chamber, no stock lug. Estimated 17,874 production.

1906 BRAZILIAN (7.65MM) .... NiB $3550   Ex $3375   Gd $1910
Same general specifications as the 7.65mm 1906 American Eagle except w/Brazilian proofs, no markings over chamber, no stock lug. Estimated 4,500 produced.

1906 BRAZILIAN (9MM)..... NiB $1691   Ex $1390   Gd $1039
Same basic specifications as the 9mm 1906 American Eagle except w/Brazilian proofs, no markings over chamber, no stock lug. Production fewer than 4,000 estimated.

1906 COMMERCIAL........ NiB $4000   Ex $3400   Gd $1500
Calibers: 7.65mm or 9mm. Same specifications as the 1906 American Eagle versions (above) except no chamber markings and no stock lug. Estimated production: 6,000 (7.65mm) and 3,500 (9mm).

1906 DUTCH............. NiB $4200   Ex $3699   Gd $2809
Caliber: 9mm Para. Same specifications as the 9mm 1906 American Eagle except tapered bbl., w/proofs, no markings over chamber, no stock lug. Arsenal rework. Estimated 3,000 production.
Original finish, add 100%

1906 LOEWE AND COMPANY.... NiB $4823   Ex $3899   Gd $2744
Caliber: 7.65mm. Eight-round magazine, 6-inch tapered bbl., 10.75 inches overall. Weight: 35 oz. Adj. two-position rear sight, dovetailed front sight. Grip safety. Checkered walnut grips. Loewe & Company over chamber, Naval proofs, DWM on new-style toggle, no stock lug. Estimated production unknown.

1906 NAVY
Caliber: 9mm Para. Eight-round magazine, 6-inch tapered bbl., 10.75 inches overall. Weight: 35 oz. Adj. two-position rear sight, dovetailed front sight. Grip safety and thumb safety w/lower marking (1st issue), higher marking (2nd issue). Checkered walnut grips. No chamber markings, DWM on new-style toggle w/o lock, but w/stock lug. Est. production: 9,000 (lst issue); 2,000 (2nd issue).
First issue............. NiB $7020   Ex $5630   Gd $4490

1906 NAVY COMMERCIAL... NiB $5600   Ex $5320   Gd $2350
Same as the 1906 Navy except lower marking on thumb safety, no chamber markings.   DWM on new-style toggle, w/stock lug and commercial proofs. Estimated 3,000 production.

1906 PORTUGUESE ARMY... NiB $3400   Ex $3230   Gd $1720
Same specifications as the 7.65mm 1906 American Eagle except w/Portuguese proofs, crown and crest over chamber. No stock lug. Estimated 3,500 production.

1906 PORTUGUESE NAVAL...... NiB $11,560   Ex $9260   Gd $7300
Same as the 9mm 1906 American Eagle except w/Portuguese proofs, crown and anchor over chamber, no stock lug.

1906 RUSSIAN........NiB $18,650   Ex $15,767   Gd $12,890
Same general specifications as the 9mm 1906 American Eagle except thumb safety has markings concealed in up position, DWM on new-style toggle, DWM bbl., proofs, crossed rifles over chamber. Estimated production unknown.

1906 SWISS........... NiB $3900   Ex $2709   Gd $2100
Same general specifications as the 7.65mm 1906 American Eagle Luger except Swiss Cross in sunburst over chamber, no stock lug. Estimated 10,300 production.

1906 SWISS (REWORK) ..... NiB $3750   Ex $3250   Gd $2000
Same basic specifications as the 7.65mm 1906 Swiss except in bbl. lengths of 3.63, 4 and 4.75 inches, overall length 8.38 inches (with 4-inch bbl.). Weight 32 oz. (with 4-inch bbl.). DWM on new-style toggle, bbl., w/serial number and proof marks, Swiss Cross in sunburst or shield over chamber, no stock lug. Estimated production unknown.

1906 SWISS POLICE........ NiB $3189   Ex $2910   Gd $2397
Same general specifications as the 7.65mm 1906 Swiss except DWM on new-style toggle, Swiss Cross in matted field over chamber, no stock lug. Estimated 10,300 production.

1908 BULGARIAN .... NiB $3860   Ex $2450   Gd $2600
Caliber: 9mm Para. Eight-round magazine, 4-inch tapered bbl., 8.75 inches overall. Weight: 30 oz. Fixed rear sight dovetailed front sight. Thumb safety w/lower marking concealed. Checkered walnut grips. DWM chamber marking, no proofs, crown over shield on new-style toggle lanyard loop, no stock lug. Estimated production unknown.

1908 COMMERCIAL........ NiB $2560   Ex $2010   Gd $1713
Same basic specifications as the 1908 Bulgarian except higher marking on thumb safety. No chamber markings, commercial proofs, DWM on new-style toggle, no stock lug. Estimated 4,000 production.

1908 ERFURT MILITARY..... NiB $2555   Ex $2055   Gd $1824
Caliber: 9mm Para. Eight-round magazine, 4-inch tapered bbl., 8.75 inches overall. Weight: 30 oz. Fixed rear sight dovetailed front sight. Thumb safety w/higher marking concealed. Checkered walnut grips. Serial number and proof marks on barrel, crown and Erfurt on new-style toggle, dated chamber, but no stock lug. Estimated production unknown.

Luger 1923 Stoeger

1908 MILITARY

Same general specifications as the 9mm 1908 Erfurt Military Luger except first and second issue have thumb safety w/higher marking concealed, serial number on bbl., no chamber markings, proofs on frame, DWM on new-style toggle but no stock lug. Estimated production: 10,000 (first issue) and 5000 (second issue). Third issue has serial number and proof marks on barrel, dates over chamber, DWM on new-style toggle but no stock lug. Estimated 3,000 production.

First issue. . . . . NiB $2460   Ex $2160   Gd $1645
Second issue . . . . NiB $2010   Ex $1605   Gd $1320
Third issue . . . . NiB $2299   Ex $1897   Gd $1645

1908 NAVY . . . . NiB $8405   Ex $79849   Gd $3475

Same basic specifications as the 9mm 1908 military Lugers except w/6-inch bbl, adj. two-position rear sight, no chamber markings, DWM on new-style toggle, w/stock lug. Estimated 26,000 production.

1908 NAVY (COMMERCIAL)NiB $6600   Ex $6270   Gd $4620

Same specifications as the 1908 Naval Luger except no chamber markings or date. Commercial proofs, DWM on new-style toggle, w/stock lug. Estimated 1,900 produced.

1914 ERFURT ARTILLERY . NiB $4670   Ex $4435   Gd $3040

Caliber: 9mm Para. Eight-shot magazine, 8-inch tapered bbl., 12.75 inches overall. Weight: 40 oz. Artillery rear sight, Dovetailed front sight. Thumb safety w/higher marking concealed. Checkered walnut grips. Serial number and proof marks on barrel, crown and Erfurt on new-style toggle, dated chamber, w/stock lug. Estimated production unknown.

1914 ERFURT MILITARY. . NiB $2170   Ex $2061   Gd $1190

Same specifications as the 1914 Erfurt Artillery except w/4-inch bbl., and corresponding length, weight, etc.; fixed rear sight. Estimated 3,000 production.

1914 NAVY . . . . NiB $6000   Ex $5700   Gd $3000

Same specifications as 9mm 1914 Lugers except has 6-inch bbl. w/corresponding length and weight, adj. two-position rear sight. Dated chamber, DWM on new-style toggle, w/stock lug. Estimated 40,000 produced.

1914 1918 DWM ARTILLERY .NiB $3600   Ex $3090   Gd $1997

Caliber: 9mm Para. Eight-shot magazine, 8-inch tapered bbl., 12.75 inches overall. Weight: 40 oz. Artillery rear sight, dovetailed front sight. Thumb safety w/higher marking concealed. Checkered walnut grips.

Serial number and proof marks on barrel, DWM on new-style toggle, dated chamber, w/stock lug. Estimated 3,000 production.

1914–1918 DWM MILITARY. . .NiB $2200   Ex $1899   Gd $1100

Same specifications as the 9mm 1914-1918 DWM Artillery except w/4-inch tapered bbl., and corresponding length, weight, etc., and fixed rear sight. Production unknown.

1920 CARBINE

Caliber: 7.65mm. Eight-round magazine, 11.75-inch tapered bbl., 15.75 inches overall. Weight: 44 oz. Four-position rear sight, long ramp front sight. Grip (or thumb) safety. Checkered walnut grips and forearm. Serial numbers and proof marks on barrel, no chamber markings, various proofs, DWM on new-style toggle, w/stock lug. Estimated production unknown.

gun only . . . . NiB $7430   Ex $7058   Gd $3000
w/shoulder stock, add. . . . . .35 %

1920 NAVY CARBINE. . . . NiB $4800   Ex $4560   Gd $3360

Caliber: 7.65mm. Eight-round magazine, 11.75-inch tapered bbl., 15.75 inches overall. Two-position sliding rear sight. Naval military proofs and no forearm. Production unknown.

1920 COMMERCIAL . . . . NiB $1450   Ex $1250   Gd $1018

Calibers: 7.65mm, 9mm Para. Eight-round magazine, 3.63-, 3.75-, 4-, 4.75-, 6-, 8-, 10-, 12-, 16-, 18- or 20-inch tapered bbl., overall length: 8.375 to 24.75 inches. Weight: 30 oz. (with 3.63-inch bbl.). Varying rear sight configurations, dovetailed front sight. Thumb safety. Checkered walnut grips. Serial numbers and proof marks on barrel, no chamber markings, various proofs, DWM or crown over Erfurt on new-style toggle, w/stock lug. Production not documented.

1920 POLICE . . . . .NiB $1410   Ex $1200   Gd $931

Same specifications as 9mm 1920 DWM w/some dated chambers, various proofs, DWM or crown over Erfurt on new-style toggle, identifying marks on grip frame, w/stock lug. Estimated 3,000 production.

1923 COMMERICAL . . . . NiB $1600   Ex $1520   Gd $1120

Calibers: 7.65mm and 9mm Para. Eight-round magazine, 3.63, 3.75, 4, 6, 8, 12 or 16-inch tapered bbl., overall length: 8.38 inches (with 3.63-inch bbl.). Weight: 30 oz. (with 3.63-inch bbl.). Various rear sight configurations, dovetailed front sight. Thumb lever safety. Checkered walnut grips. DWM on new-style toggle, serial number and proofs on barrel, no chamber markings, w/stock lug. Estimated 15,000 production.

1923 DUTCH COMMERICAL . . . NiB $2320   Ex $2088   Gd $1872

Same basic specifications as 1923 Commercial Luger w/same caliber offerings, but only 3.63 or 4-inch bbl. Fixed rear sight, thumb lever safety w/arrow markings. Production unknown.

1923 KRIEGHOFF COMMERCIAL . . . NiB $2340   Ex $2223   Gd $1638

Same specifications as 1923 Commercial Luger, w/same caliber offerings but bbl., lengths of 3.63, 4, 6, and 8 inches. "K" marked on new-style toggle. Serial number, proofs and Germany on barrel. No chamber markings, but w/ stock lug. Production unknown.

1923 SAFE AND LOADED . . . NiB $2460   Ex $2337   Gd $1722

Same caliber offerings, bbl., lengths and specifications as the 1923 Commercial except thumb lever safety, "safe" and "loaded" markings, w/stock lug. Estimated 10,000 production.

1923 STOEGER

Same general specifications as the 1923 Commercial Luger with the same caliber offerings and bbl., lengths of 3.75, 4, 6, 8 and up to 24 inches. Thumb lever safety. DWM on new-style toggle, serial number and/or proof marks on barrel. American Eagle over chamber but no stock lug. Estimated production less than 1000 (also see Stoeger listings). Note: Qualified appraisals should be obtained on all Stoeger Lugers with bbl. lengths over 8 inches to ensure accurate values.

3.75-, 4-, or 6-inch bbl. . . . . NiB $5660   Ex $5377   Gd $2730
8-inch bbl. . . . . NiB $6350   Ex $6035   Gd $2255

1926 "BABY" PROTOTYPE NiB $112,750   Ex $90,295   Gd $62,355

Calibers: 7.65mm Browning and 9mm Browning (short). Five-round magazine, 2.31-inch bbl., about 6.25 inches overall. Small-sizedframe and toggle assembly. Prototype for a Luger "pocket pistol," but never manufactured commercially. Checkered walnut grips, slotted for safety. Only four known to Exist, but as many as a dozen could have been made.

1929 SWISS . . . . NiB $2017   Ex $1486   Gd $989

Caliber: 7.65mm. Eight-round magazine, 4.75-inch tapered bbl., 9.5 inches overall. Weight: 32 oz. Fixed rear sight, dovetailed front sight. Long grip safety and thumb lever w/S markings. Stepped receiver and straight grip frame. Checkered plastic grips. Swiss Cross in shield on new-style toggle. Serial numbers and proofs on barrel, no markings over chamber and no stock lug. Estimated 1,900 production.

1934 KRIEGHOFF

COMMERCIAL (SIDE FRAME) . . . . . . NiB $ 7100   Ex $6350   Gd $2895
Caliber: 7.65mm or 9mm Para. Eight-round magazine, bbl. lengths: 4, 6, and 8 inches, overall length: 8.75 (with 4-inch bbl.). Weight: 30 oz. (with 4-inch bbl.). Various rear sight configurations w/dovetailed front sight. Thumb lever safety. Checkered brown plastic grips. Anchor w/H K Krieghoff Suhl on new-style toggle, but no chamber markings. Tapered bbl., w/serial number and proofs; w/stock lug. Estimated 1,700 production.

1934 KRIEGHOFF S CODE MODELS

Caliber: 9mm Para. Eight-round magazine, 4-inch tapered bbl., 8.75 inches overall. Weight: 30 oz. Fixed rear sight, dovetailed front sight. Thumb lever safety. Anchor w/H K Krieghoff Suhl on new-style toggle, S dated chamber, bbl., proofs and stock lug. Early model: Checkered walnut or plastic grips. Estimated 2,500 production. Late model: Checkered brown plastic grips. Estimated 1,200 production.

Early model . . . . NiB $4660   Ex $4077   Gd $2976
Late model . . . . NiB $4460   Ex $3900   Gd $1464

1934 BYF . . . . NiB $2170   Ex $1950   Gd $1000

Caliber: 9mm Para. Eight-round magazine, 4-inch tapered bbl., 8.75 inches overall. Weight: 30 oz. Fixed rear sight, dovetailed front sight. Thumb lever safety. Checkered walnut or plastic grips. "byf" on new-style toggle, serial number and proofs on bbl., 41-42 dated chamber and w/stock lug. Estimated 3,000 productlon.

1934 MAUSER S/42 K. . . . NiB $7950   Ex $6800   Gd $3500

Caliber: 9mm Para. Eight-round magazine, 4-inch tapered bbl., 8.75 inches overall. Weight: 30 oz. Fixed rear sight dovetailed front sight. Thumb lever safety. Checkered walnut or plastic grips. "42" on new-style toggle, serial number and proofs on barrel, 1939-40 dated chamber markings and w/stock lug. Estimated 10,000 production.

1934 MAUSER S/42 (DATED)NiB $2244   Ex $2117   Gd $1599

Same specifications as Luger 1934 Mauser 42 except 41 dated chamber markings and w/stock lug. Production unknown.

Luger S42

1934 MAUSER BANNER (MILITARY) . . . NiB $4190   Ex $3455   Gd $3097

Same specifications as Luger 1934 Mauser 42 except Mauser in banner on new-style toggle, tapered bbl., w/serial number and proofs usually, dated chamber markings and w/stock lug. Production unknown.

1934 MAUSER BANNER COMMERCIAL . . NiB $4400   Ex $3760   Gd $3156

Same specifications as Luger 1934 Mauser 42 except checkered walnut grips. Mauser in banner on new-style toggle, tapered bbl., usually w/ serial number and proofs, no chamber markings, but w/ stock lug. Production unknown.

1934 MAUSER BANNER DUTCH . . . NiB $3787   Ex $3375   Gd $3099

Same specifications as Luger 1934 Mauser 42 except checkered walnut grips. Mauser in banner on new-style toggle, tapered bbl., w/caliber, 1940 dated chamber markings and w/stock lug. Production unknown.

1934 MAUSER LATVIAN. . . . . NiB $3260   Ex $2355   Gd $1989

Caliber: 7.65mm. Eight-round magazine, 4-inch tapered bbl., 8.75 inches overall. Weight: 30 oz. Fixed square-notched rear sight, dovetailed Partridge front sight. Thumb lever safety. Checkered walnut stocks. Mauser in banner on new-style toggle, 1937 dated chamber markings and w/stock lug. Production unknown.

1934 MAUSER (OBERNDORF) . . . . . NiB $3155   Ex $2535   Gd $1733

Same as 1934 Mauser 42 except checkered walnut grips. Oberndorf 1934 on new-style toggle, tapered bbl., w/proofs and caliber, Mauser banner over chamber and w/stock lug (also see Mauser).

1934 SIMSON-S TOGGLE. . . . NiB $4459   Ex $4188   Gd $3799

Same as 1934 Mauser 42 except checkered walnut grips, "S" on new-style toggle, tapered bbl., w/serial number and proofs, no chamber markings; w/stock lug. Estimated 10,000 production.

42 MAUSER BANNER (BYF)NiB $3877   Ex $3078   Gd $2689

Same specifications as Luger 1934 Mauser 42 except weight: 32 oz. Mauser in banner on new-style toggle, tapered bbl., w/serial number and proofs usually, dated chamber markings and w/stock lug. Estimated 3,500 production.

ABERCROMBIE AND FITCH . . . . NiB $5465   Ex $4876   Gd $2879

Calibers: 7.65mm and 9mm Para. Eight-round magazine, 4.75-inch tapered bbl., 9.5 inches overall. Weight: 32 oz. Fixed rear sight, dovetailed front sight. Grip safety. Checkered walnut grips. DWM on new-style toggle Abercrombie & Fitch markings on barrel, Swiss Cross in sunburst over chamber, no stock lug. Est. 100 production.

Luna Model 200 Free Pistol

DUTCH ROYAL AIR FORCE NiB $3324   Ex $2190   Gd $998
Caliber: 9mm Para. Eight-round magazine, 4-inch tapered bbl., 8.75 inches overall. Weight: 30 oz. Fixed rear sight dovetailed front sight. Grip safety and thumb safety w/markings and arrow. Checkered walnut grips. DWM on new-style toggle, bbl., dated w/serial number and proofs, no markings over chamber, no stock lug. Estimated 4,000 production.

DWM (G DATE) . . . . NiB $2189   Ex $1953   Gd $1645
Caliber: 9mm Para. Eight-round magazine, 4-inch tapered bbl., 8.75 inches overall. Weight: 30 oz. Fixed rear sight, dovetailed front sight. Thumb lever safety. Checkered walnut grips. DWM on new-style toggle, serial number and proofs on barrel, G (1935 date) over chamber and w/ stock lug. Production unknown.

DWM AND ERFURT . . . . . . NiB $1357   Ex $1134   Gd $876
Caliber: 9mm Para. Eight-round magazine, 4- or 6-inch tapered bbl., overall length: 8.75 or 10.75 inches. Weight: 30 or 38 oz. Fixed rear sight, dovetailed front sight. Thumb safety. Checkered walnut grips. Serial numbers and proof marks on barrel, double dated chamber, various proofs, DWM or crown over Erfurt on new-style toggle and w/stock lug. Production unknown.

KRIEGHOFF 36 . . . . NiB $4550   Ex $3799   Gd $1899
Caliber: 9mm Para. Eight-round magazine, 4-inch tapered bbl., 8.75 inches overall. Weight: 30 oz. Fixed rear sight, dovetailed front sight. Thumb lever safety. Checkered brown plastic grips. Anchor w/H K Krieghoff Suhl on new-style toggle, 36 dated chamber, serial number and proofs on barrel and w/stock lug. Estimated 700 production.

KRIEGHOFF DATED (1936 - 1945)
Same specifications as Luger Krieghoff 36 except 1936-45 dated chamber, bbl. proofs. Est. 8,600 production.
1936, 1937 and 1940 . . . . . . NiB $5500   Ex $4779   Gd $2735
1938 and 1941 . . . . NiB $6500   Ex $5779   Gd $2735
1942 thru 1943, add 60%
1945, add 110%

KRIEGHOFF (GRIP SAFETY)NiB $4977   Ex $3965   Gd $2790
Same specifications as Luger Krieghoff 36 except grip safety and thumb lever safety. No chamber markings, tapered bbl., w/serial number, proofs and caliber, no stock lug. Production unknown.

MAUSER BANNER (GRIP SAFETY)NiB $2874 Ex $2050 Gd $1465
Caliber: 7.65mm. Eight-round magazine, 4.75-inch tapered bbl., 9.5 inches overall. Weight: 30 oz. Fixed rear sight, dovetailed front sight. Grip safety and thumb lever safety. Checkered walnut grips. Mauser in banner on new-style toggle, serial number and proofs on barrel, 1939 dated chamber markings, but no stock lug. Production unknown.

MAUSER BANNER 42 (DATED) . . . NiB 2170 Ex $1196 Gd $100
Caliber: 9mm Para. Eight-round magazine, 4-inch tapered bbl., 8.75 inches overall. Weight: 30 oz. Fixed rear sight, dovetailed front sight. Thumb lever safety. Checkered walnut or plastic grips. Mauser in banner on new-style toggle serial number and proofs on bbl., (usually) 1942 dated chamber markings and stock lug. Production unknown.

MAUSER BANNER (SWISS PROOF)NiB $3460 Ex $2830 Gd $1540
Same specifications as Luger Mauser Banner 42 except checkered walnut grips and 1939 dated chamber.

MAUSER FREISE . . . . NiB $4960   Ex $4090   Gd $2866
Same specifications as Mauser Banner 42 except checkered walnut grips, tapered bbl. w/proofs on sight block and Freise above chamber. Production unknown.

S/42
Caliber: 9mm Para. Eight-round magazine, 4-inch tapered barrel. 8.75 inches overall. Weight: 30 oz. Fixed rear sight, dovetailed front sight. Thumb lever safety. Checkered walnut grips. S/42 on new-style toggle, serial number and proofs on barrel and w/stock lug. Dated Model: Has dated chamber; estimated 3000 production. G Date: Has G (1935 date) over chamber; estimated 3000 production. K Date: Has K (1934 date) over chamber; production unknown.
Dated model . . . . NiB $6780   Ex $5977   Gd $4538
G date model. . . . . NiB $2669   Ex $2380   Gd $2010
K date model . . . . NiB $6876   Ex $5986   Gd $4610

RUSSIAN COMMERCIAL. . NiB $3146   Ex $2548   Gd $1713
Caliber: 7.65mm. Eight-round magazine, 3.63-inch tapered bbl., 8.38 inches overall. Weight: 30 oz. Fixed rear sight, dovetailed front sight. Thumb lever safety. Checkered walnut grips. DWM on new-style toggle, Russian proofs on barrel, no chamber markings but w/stock lug. Production unknown.

SIMSON AND COMPANY
Calibers: 7.65mm and 9mm Para. Eight-round magazine, Weight: 32 oz. Fixed rear sight, dovetailed front sight. Thumb lever safety. Checkered walnut grips. Simson & Company Suhl on new-style toggle, serial number and proofs on barrel, date over chamber and w/stock lug. Estimated 10,000 production.
Simson and Company
 (9mm w/1925 date) . . . . NiB $6300   Ex $5300   Gd $300
Simson and Company
 (undated) . . . . NiB $4300   Ex $3650   Gd $200
Simson and Company
 (S code) . . . . NiB $5600   Ex $4800   Gd $2389

VICKERS-DUTCH . . . . NiB $4375   Ex $3968   Gd $3316
Caliber: 9mm Para. Eight-round magazine, 4-inch tapered bbl., 8.75 inches overall. Weight: 30 oz. Fixed rear sight, dovetailed front sight. Grip safety and thumb lever w/arrow markings. Checkered walnut grips (coarse). Vickers LTD on new-style toggle, no chamber markings, dated barrel but no stock lug. Estimated 10,000 production.

LUNA FREE PISTOL — Zella-Mehlis, Germany
Originally mfd. by Ernst Friedr. Buchel and later by Udo Anschutz.

MODEL 200 FREE PISTOL. . NiB $1198   Ex $1027   Gd $784
Single-shot. System Aydt action. Set trigger. Caliber: .22 LR. Eleven-inch bbl., weight: 40 oz. Target sights. Blued finish. Checkered and carved walnut grip and forearm; improved design w/adj. hand base on later models of Udo Anschutz manufacture. Made prior to WWII.

M.A.C. (Military Armament Corp.) — Ducktown, Tennessee

Ingram Model 10 Auto Pistol Select fire (NFA-Title II-Class III) SMG based on Ingram M10 blowback system using an open bolt design with or without telescoping stock. Calibers: 9mm or .45 ACP. Cyclic rate: 750 RPM (9mm) or 900 RPM (.45 ACP). 32- or 30-round magazine, 5.75-inch threaded bbl. (to accept muzzle brake) bbl. Extension or suppressor, 10.5 inches overall w/o stock or 10.6 (w/telescoped stock) and 21.5 (w/Extended stock). Weight: 6.25 pounds. Front protected post sight, fixed aperture rear sight.

9mm model	NiB $1113	Ex $920	Gd $669
ACP model	NiB $998	Ex $877	Gd $668
w/bbl. extension, add			$255
w/suppressor, add			$587

INGRAM MODEL 10A1S SEMIAUTOMATIC
Similar to the Model 10 except (Class I) semiautomatic w/closed bolt design to implement an interchangable component system to easily convert to fire 9mm and .45 ACP.

9mm model	NiB $408	Ex $332	Gd $225
.45 ACP model	NiB $431	Ex $342	Gd $235
w/bbl. extension, add			$204
w/fake suppressor, add			$225

INGRAM MODEL 11 SEMIAUTOMATIC
Similar to the Model 10A1 except (Class I) semiautomatic chambered .380 ACP.

.380 ACP model	NiB $862	Ex $714	Gd $536
w/bbl. extension, add			$204
w/fake suppressor, add			$225

MAGNUM RESEARCH, INC. (MRI) —
Minneapolis, Minnesota
Originally mfd. by IMI (Isreal Military Industries). MRI purchased by Kahr Arms in 2010.

BABY EAGLE SEMI-AUTOMATIC . . . . . . NiB $577 Ex $479 Gd $365
DA. Calibers: 9mm, .40 S&W, .41 AE. 15-shot magazine (9mm), 9-round magazine (.40 S&W), 10-round magazine (.41 AE), 4.75-inch bbl., 8.15 inches overall. Weight: 35.4 oz. Combat sights. Matte blued finish. Imported from 1991-96 and 1999 to 2007.

BABY EAGLE II SEMI-AUTOMATIC . . . . . NiB $656 Ex $430 Gd $335
Similar to Baby Eagle except w/accessory rail. Imported from 2008 to date.

BFR LONG CYLINDER REVOVER . . NiB $1050 EX $780 GD $550
SA. Calibers: .30-30 Win., .444 Marlin, .45 LC/.410, .450 Marlin, .45-70 Gov't., .460 S&W Mag., and .50 S&W Mag. 5-round cylinder, bbl. lengths: 7.5- or 10-in. Stainless finish. Weight: 4-4.4 lbs. Rubber grips. Made from 1999 to date.

BFR SHORT CYLINDER REVOVER . NiB $1050 EX $780 GD $550
SA. Calibers: .44 Mag., .454 Casull, .475 Linebaugh, and .480 Ruger, 5-round cylinder, bbl. lengths: 5-, or 7.5-in. Stainless finish. Rubber grips. Weight: 3.2-4.4 lbs. Made from 1999 to date.

DESERT EAGLE MK VII SEMIAUTOMATIC
Gas-operated. Calibers: .357 Mag., .41 Mag., .44 Mag., .50 Action Express (AE). Eight- or 9-round magazine, 6-inch w/standard bbl., or 10- and 14-inch w/polygonal bbl., 10.6 inches overall (with 6-inch bbl.). Weight: 52 oz. (w/alum. alloy frame) to 67 oz. (w/steel frame). Fixed or adj. combat sights. Combat-type trigger guard. finish: Military black oxide, nickel, chrome, stainless or blued. Wraparound rubber grips. Made from 1983 to 1995 and 1998 to 2001.
.357 standard (steel) or alloy (6-inch bbl.) . NiB $903 Ex $658 Gd $562

Magnum Research Model Desert Eagle Mark XIX shown w/optional Leupold scope

Magnum Research Model One Pro .45

.357 stainless steel (6-inch bbl.) . . .	NiB $940	Ex $704	Gd $536
.41 Mag. standard (steel) or alloy (6-inch bbl.)	NiB $1099	Ex $831	Gd $638
.41 Mag. stainless steel (6-inch bbl.)	NiB $1145	Ex $984	Gd $780
.44 Mag. standard (steel) or alloy (6-inch bbl.)	NiB $1015	Ex $798	Gd $567
.44 Mag. stainless steel (6-inch bbl.)	NiB $991	Ex $806	Gd $559
.50 AE Magnum standard	NiB $1135	Ex $968	Gd $689
For 10-inch bbl., add	NiB $204	Ex $148	Gd $110
For 14-inch bbl., add	NiB $225	Ex $175	Gd $128

DESERT EAGLE MARK XIX SEMI-AUTOMATIC PISTOL
Interchangeable component system based on .50-caliber frame. Calibers: .357 Mag., .44 Mag., .50 AE. Nine-, 8-, 7-round magazine, 6- or 10-inch bbl. w/dovetail design and cross slots to accept scope rings. Weight: 70.5 oz. (6-inch bbl.) or 79 oz. 10.75 or 14.75 inches overall. Sights: Post front and adjustable rear. Blue, chrome or nickel finish; available brushed, matte or polished. Hogue soft rubber grips. Made from 1995 to 1998..

.357 Mag. and .44 Mag. (w/6-inch bbl.) .	NiB $1400	Ex $1150	Gd $900
.50 AE (w/6-inch bbl.)	NiB $1435	Ex $1164	Gd $989
w/10-inch bbl., add			$100
Two caliber conversion (bbl., bolt & mag.), add			$444
XIX Platform System (three-caliber conversion kit w/six bbls.)	NiB $4335	Ex $3799	Gd $3260
XIX6 System (two-caliber conversion kit w/two 6-inch bbls.)	NiB $2675	Ex $2254	Gd $1969
XIX10 System (two-caliber conversion kit w/two 10-inch bbls.)	NiB $2150	Ex $1720	Gd $1196
Custom shop finish, add			$20%
24K gold finish, add			$40%

MICRO DESERT EAGLE. . . . . NiB $647 Ex $380 Gd $265
DAO. Calibers: .380 ACP. 6-shot magazine, 2-2-inch bbl. Weight: 14 oz. Imported from 2009 to 2013.

(ASAI) MODEL ONE PRO .45 PISTOL
Calibers: .45 ACP or .400 COR-BON, 3.75- inch bbl., 7.04 or 7.83 (IPSC Model) inches overall. Weight: 23.5 (alloy frame) or 31.1 oz. 10-round magazine. Short recoil action. SA or DA mode w/de-cocking lever. Steel or alloy grip-frame. Textured black polymer grips. Imported from 1998.
Model 1P45 . . . . .NiB $740 Ex $567 Gd $399
Model 1C45/400 (compensator kit), add $204
Model 1C400NC (400 conversion kit), add $150

Magnum Research SSP-91 Lone Eagle Pistol shown w/Optional Leupold Scope

Mauser Model 80-SA

Mauser Model 90-DA

MOUNTAIN EAGLE SEMIAUTOMATIC
Caliber: .22 LR. 15-round polycarbonate resin magazine, 6.5-inch injection-molded polymer and steel bbl., 10.6 inches overall. Weight: 21 oz. Ramp blade front sight, adj. rear. Injection-molded, checkered and textured grip. Matte black finish. Made 1992 to 1996.
Standard, w/6-inch bb. . . . . .NiB $214 Ex $160 Gd $143
Compact, w/4.5-inch bbl. . . . . .NiB $190 Ex $143 Gd $110
Target, w/8-inch bbl. . . . . .NiB $240 Ex $150 Gd $120

SSP-91 LONE EAGLE PISTOL
Single-shot action w/interchangeable rotating breech bbl., assembly. Calibers: .22 LR, .22 Mag., .22 Hornet, .22-250, .223 Rem., .243 Win., 6mm BR, 7mm-08, 7mm BR, .30-06, .30-30, .308 Win., .35 Rem., .357 Mag., .44 Mag., .444 Marlin. 14-inch interchangeable bbl. assembly, 15 inches overall. Weight: 4.5 lbs. Black or chrome finish. Made from 1991 to 2001.
Black finish . . . . .NiB $434 Ex $321 Gd $165
Chrome finish . . . . .NiB $464 Ex $342 Gd $186
Extra 14-inch bbl., black finish $150
Extra 14-inch bbl., chrome finish, ... $175
Ambidextrous stock assembly (only) $220
w/muzzle brake, add $408
w/open sights, add $45

MAUSER — Oberndorf, Germany, Waffenfabrik Mauser of Mauser-Werke A.G.

MODEL 80-SA AUTOMATIC. . NiB $577 Ex $395 Gd $255
Caliber: 9mm Para. 13-round magazine, 4.66-inch bbl., 8 inches overall. Weight: 31.5 oz. Blued finish. Hardwood grips. Made 1992 to 1996.

MODEL 90 DA AUTOMATIC . NiB $530 Ex $354 Gd $234
Caliber: 9mm Para. 14-round magazine, 4.66-inch bbl., 8 inches overall. Weight: 35 oz. Blued finish. Hardwood grips. Made 1992 to 1996.

MODEL 90 DAC COMPACT . . NiB $571 Ex $405 Gd $270
Caliber: 9mm Para. 14-round magazine, 4.13-inch bbl., 7.4 inches overall. Weight: 33.25 oz. Blued finish. Hardwood grips. Made 1992 to 1996.

MODEL 1898 (1896) "BROOMHANDLE" MILITARY AUTO PISTOL
Caliber: 7.63mm Mauser, but also chambered for 9mm Mauser and 9mm Para. w/the latter being identified by a large red "9" in the grips. 10-round box magazine, 5.25-inch bbl., 12 inches overall. Weight: 45 oz. Adj. rear sight. Blued finish. Walnut grips. Made from 1897 to 1939. Note: Specialist collectors recognize a number of variations at significantly higher values. Price here is for more common commercial and military types with original finish.
Commercial model (pre-war) . . . . .NiB $3520 Ex $2735 Gd $1096
Commercial model (wartime). . . . . .NiB $3015 Ex $2512 Gd $1040
Red 9 Commercial model (fixed sight) . .NiB $3265 Ex $2979 Gd $1049
Red 9 WWI Contract (tangent sight) . . .NiB $3300 Ex $2670 Gd $1300
w/stock sssembly (matching S/N), add $1300

MODEL HSC DA AUTO PISTOL
Calibers: .32 Auto (7.65mm), .380 Auto (9mm Short). Eight-round (.32) or 7-round (.380) magazine, 3.4-inch bbl., 6.4 inches overall. Weight: 23.6 oz. Fixed sights. Blued or nickel finish. Checkered walnut grips. Made from 1938 to 1945 and from 1968 to 1996.
Military model (low grip screw) . . . . . . .NiB $6200 Ex $5110 Gd $2820
Commercial model (wartime). . . . . .NiB $536 Ex $398 Gd $249
Nazi military model (pre-war) . . . . .NiB $1148 Ex $974 Gd $632
Nazi military model (wartime) . . . . .NiB $600 Ex $499 Gd $270

**Mauser Model 1898
(1896) Military**

**Mauser Parabellum Luger
shown w/6-in. barrel**

French production (postwar) . . . . .NiB $474 Ex $398 Gd $239
Mauser production (postwar) . . . . .NiB $497 Ex $377 Gd $235
Recent importation (Armes De Chasse) . . . .NiB $478 Ex $398 Gd $270
Recent importation (Interarms) . . . . .NiB $388 Ex $289 Gd $230
Recent importation (European Amer. Arms) .NiB $328 Ex $196 Gd $115
Recent importation (Gamba, USA) . . . . .NiB $431 Ex $316 Gd $194
American Eagle model (1 of 5000) . . . . . . .NiB $562 Ex $433 Gd $319

LUGER LANGE PISTOL 08
Caliber: 9mm Para. Eight-inch bbl., Checkered grips. Blued finish. Accessorized w/walnut shoulder stock, front sight tool, spare magazine, leather case. Currently in production. Commemorative version made in limited quantities w/ivory grips and 14-carat gold monogram plate.
Commemorative model (100 produced) . NiB $2855 Ex $2330 Gd $1875
Commemorative matched pair . . . . .NiB $5423 Ex $4412 Gd $3099
Cartridge counter model . . . . .NiB $4010 Ex $2907 Gd $2017
Carbine model (w/matching buttstock) . .NiB $8025 Ex $6309 Gd $3718

PARABELLUM LUGER AUTO PISTOL
Current commercial model. Swiss pattern with grip safety. Calibers: 7.65mm Luger, 9mm Para. Eight-round magazine, bbl. lengths: 4-, 6-inch, 8.75 inches overall (with 4-inch bbl.). Weight: 30 oz. (with 4-inch bbl.). Fixed sights. Blued finish. Checkered walnut grips. Made from 1970 to date. Note: Pistols of this model sold in the U.S. have the American Eagle stamped on the receiver.
Standard model (blue). . . . . . . NiB $1603 Ex $1230 Gd $704

POCKET MODEL 1910 AUTO PISTOL
Caliber: .25 Auto (6.35mm). Nine-round magazine, 3.1-inch bbl., 5.4 inches overall. Weight: 15 oz. Fixed sights. Blued finish. Checkered walnut or hard rubber grips. Made from 1910 to 1934.
Model 1910 (standard) . . . . NiB $691 Ex $461 Gd $306
Model 1910 (w/side latch) . . . . . NiB $546 Ex $431 Gd $309

POCKET MODEL 1914 AUTOMATIC. . .NiB $691 Ex $485 Gd $314
Similar to Pocket Model 1910. Caliber: .32 Auto (7.65mm). Eight-round magazine, 3.4-inch bbl., 6 inches overall. Weight: 21 oz. Fixed sights. Blued finish. Checkered walnut or hard rubber grips. Made 1914 to 1934

POCKET MODEL 1934 . . . . . . NiB $816 Ex $595 Gd $410
Similar to Pocket Models 1910 and 1914 in the respective calibers. Chief difference is in the more streamlined, one-piece grips. Made from 1934 to 1939.

WTP MODEL I AUTO PISTOL. NiB $779 Ex $610 Gd $413
"Westentaschen-Pistole" (Vest Pocket Pistol). Caliber: .25 Automatic (6.35mm). Six-round magazine, 2.5-inch bbl., 4 inches overall. Weight: 11.5 oz. Blued finish. Hard rubber grips. Made from 1922 to 1937.

WTP MODEL II AUTO PISTOLNiB $1398 Ex $1137 Gd $895
Similar to Model I but smaller and lighter. Caliber: .25 Automatic (6.35mm). Six-round magazine, 2-inch bbl., 4 inches overall. Weight: 9.5 oz. Blued finish. Hard rubber grips. Made from 1938 to 1940.

MERWIN HULBERT & CO. — New York

FIRST MODEL
FRONTIER ARMY . . . . NiB $9679 Ex $8023 Gd $6029
Single action, .44 caliber, 7.5-inch bbl. Square butt, open top, scoop flutes on cylinder, two screws above trigger guard

SECOND MODEL
FRONTIER ARMY . . . . NiB $8617 Ex $7608 Gd $6138
Similar to First Model except has only one screw above trigger guard

SECOND MODEL
POCKET ARMY . . . . .NiB $7740 Ex $ 6487 Gd $5009
Similar to Second Model except has bird's-head butt instead of square butt, 3.5- or 7-inch (scarce) bbl. Some models may be marked "Pocket Army."

THIRD MODEL
FRONTIER ARMY . . . . NiB $6995 Ex $3429 Gd $2152
Caliber: .44, 7-inch round bbl. with no rib, single action. Square butt, top strap, usually has conventional fluting on cylinder but some have scoop flutes.

THIRD MODEL DA
FRONTIER ARMY . . . . NiB $6775 Ex $5254 Gd $4890
Similar to Third Model Frontier Army SA except is double action.

THIRD MODEL POCKET ARMY . . .NiB $7610 Ex $5366 Gd $4997
Caliber: .44, 3.5- or 7.5-inch bbl. with no rib. Single action, bird's-head butt, top strap.

THIRD MODEL POCKET ARMY DA . . .NiB $6648 Ex $5096 Gd $3930
Similar to Third Model Pocket Army SA except is double action.

FOURTH MODEL
FRONTIER ARMY . . . . NiB $9010 Ex $8188 Gd $4992
Caliber: .44, 3.5- 5- or 7-inch unique ribbed bbl. Single action, square butt, top strap, conventional flutes on cylinder.

FOURTH MODEL FRONTIER
ARMY DA . . . . NiB $8189 Ex $5883 Gd $5409
Similar to Fourth Model Frontier Army SA except is double action.

NOTE: *The following handguns are foreign copies of Merwin Hulbert Co. guns and may be marked as such, or as "Sistema Merwin Hulbert," but rarely with the original Hopkins & Allen markings. These guns will usually bring half or less of a comparable genuine Merwin Hulbert product.*

FIRST POCKET MODEL. . . . . . NiB $2270 Ex $1996 Gd $1416
Caliber: .38 Special, 5-round cylinder (w/cylinder pin Exposed at front of frame), single action. Spur trigger; round loading hole in recoil shield, no loading gate.

Mitchell Arms
Citation II

Mitchell Arms
Sharpshooter II

SECOND POCKET MODEL . . . NiB $1815 Ex $1595 Gd $1416
Similar to First Pocket Model except has sliding loading gate.

THIRD POCKET MODEL . . . . . NiB $1633 Ex $1270 Gd $1111
Similar to First Pocket Model except has enclosed cylinder pin.

**THIRD POCKET
MODEL W/TRIGGER GUARD . . NiB $1517 Ex $1319 Gd $1133**
Similar to First Pocket Model except w/conventional trigger guard.

**SMALL FRAME
POCKET MODEL . . . . NiB $1360 Ex $1120 Gd $601**
Caliber: .38 Spec., 5-round cylinder, DA, may have hammer spur.

**SMALL FRAME
POCKET MODEL 32 . . . . NiB $1377 Ex $1190 Gd $979**
Similar to Medium Frame Pocket Model except .32 caliber, 7-round cylinder, double action.

TIP-UP MODEL 22 . . . . NiB $1579 Ex $1367 Gd $1056
Similar to S&W Model One except .22 caliber, 7-round cylinder, spur trigger. Scarce.

MITCHELL ARMS, INC. — Santa Ana, California

MODEL 1911 GOLD SIGNATURE
Caliber: .45 ACP. Eight-round mag, 5-inch bbl., 8.75 inches overall. Weight: 39 oz. Interchangeable blade front sight, drift-adj. combat or fully adj. rear. Smooth or checkered walnut grips. Made 1994 to 1996.
Blued model w/fixed sights . . . . . NiB $512 Ex $393 Gd $301
Blued model w/adj. sights. . . . . . NiB $554 Ex $456 Gd $412
Stainless model w/fixed sights . . . NiB $709 Ex $549 Gd $464
Stainless model w/adj. sights. . . . NiB $755 Ex $601 Gd $530

ALPHA MODEL AUTO PISTOL
Dual action w/interchangeable trigger modules. Caliber: .45 ACP. Eight-round magazine, 5-inch bbl., 8.75 inches overall. Weight: 39 oz. Interchangeable blade front sight, drift-adj. rear. Smooth or checkered walnut grips. Blued or stainless finish. Made in 1994 . Advertised in 1995 but not manufactured.

AMERICAN EAGLE LUGER PISTOLNiB $900 Ex $678 Gd $369
Stainless-steel re-creation of the American Eagle Parabellum auto pistol. Caliber: 9mm Para. Seven-round magazine, 4-inch bbl., 9.6 inches

overall. Weight: 26.6 oz. Blade front sight, fixed rear. Stainless finish. Checkered walnut grips. Made from 1993 to 1994.

CITATION II AUTO PISTOL . . NiB $433 Ex $309 Gd $228
Re-creation of the High Standard Supermatic Citation Military. Caliber: .22 LR. 10-round magazine, 5.5-inch bull bbl. or 7.25 fluted bbl., 9.75 inches overall (5.5-inch bbl.). Weight: 44.5 oz. Ramp front sight, slide-mounted micro-adj. rear. Satin blued or stainless finish. Checkered walnut grips w/thumbrest. Made 1992 to 1996.

**OLYMPIC I.S.U.
AUTO PISTOL . . . . NiB $659 Ex $556 Gd $434**
Similar to the Citation II model except chambered in .22 Short, 6.75-inch round tapered bbl. w/stabilizer and removable counterweights. Made from 1992 to 1996.

**SHARPSHOOTER I
AUTO PISTOL . . . . NiB $362 Ex $288 Gd $212**
Re-creation of the High Standard Sharpshooter. Caliber: .22 LR. 10-round magazine, 5-inch bull bbl., 10.25 inches overall. Weight: 42 oz. Ramp front sight, slide-mounted micro-adj. rear. Satin blued or stainless finish. Checkered walnut grips w/thumbrest. Made 1992 to 1996.

MODEL SA SPORT KING II . . . NiB $304 Ex $226 Gd $170
Caliber: .22 LR. 10-round magazine, 4.5- or 6.75-inch bbl., 9 or 11.25 inches overall. Weight: 39 or 42 oz. Checkered walnut or black plastic grips. Blade front sight and drift adjustable rear. Made 1993 to 1994.

SA ARMY REVOLVER
Calibers: .357 Mag., .44 Mag., .45 Colt/.45 ACP. Six-round cylinder. bbl., lengths: 4.75, 5.5, 7.5 inches, weight: 40-43 oz. Blade front sight, grooved top strap or adj. rear. Blued or nickel finish w/color-casehardened frame. Brass or steel backstrap/trigger guard. Smooth one-piece walnut grips. Imported from 1987-94 and 1997. Disc.
Standard model w/blued finish . . . . NiB $431 Ex $319 Gd $235
Standard model w/nickel finish. . . . . NiB $464 Ex $398 Gd $303
Standard model w/steel backstrap . . . . . . NiB $541 Ex $422 Gd $317
.45 Combo w/blued finish. . . . . NiB $544 Ex $429 Gd $346
.45 Combo w/nickel finish . . . . NiB $601 Ex $562 Gd $433

**TROPHY II
AUTO PISTOL . . . . NiB $464 Ex $337 Gd $270**
Similar to the Citation II model except w/gold-plated trigger and gold-filled markings. Made from 1992 to 1996.

VICTOR II AUTO PISTOL . . . . **NiB $544 Ex $419 Gd $342**
Re-creation of the High Standard Victor w/full-length vent rib. Caliber:
.22 LR. 10-round magazine, 4.5- or 5.5-inch bbl., 9.75 inches overall
(with 5.5-inch bbl.). Weight: 52 oz. (with 5.5-inch bbl.). Rib-mounted
target sights. Satin blued or stainless finish. Checkered walnut grips w/
thumbrest. Made from 1992 to 1996.

GUARDIAN ANGEL
DERRINGER . . . . **NiB $158 Ex $120 Gd $101**
Hammerless, double-action O/U derringer w/interchangeable drop-in
breech block. Calibers: .22 LR, .22 WRM. Two-round capacity. Two-
inch bbl., 5 inches overall. Weight: 12 oz. Blue, nickel or gold finish.
Blade front and fixed rear sights. Checkered black grips. Made from
1996 to 1997.

GUARDIAN II. . . . . **NiB $327 Ex $235 Gd $169**
Caliber: .38 Special, Six-round cylinder, 2-, 4- or 6-inch bbl., 8.5 inches
overall (with 4-inch bbl.). Weight: 32 oz (with 4-inch bbl.). Blade ramp
front and fixed rear sights. Checkered combat or target grips. Blued
finish. Made in 1995.

GUARDIAN III . . . . **NiB $369 Ex $272 Gd $181**
Same specifications as Guardian II model except w/adjustable rear
sights. Made in 1995.

TITAN II DA. . . . . **NiB $295 Ex $259 Gd $175**
Caliber: .357 Mag. Six-round cylinder. 2-, 4- or 6-inch bbl., 7.75 inches
overall (with 4-inch bbl.). Weight: 38 oz (with 4-inch bbl.). Blade front
and fixed rear sights. Crane mounted cylinder release. Blued or stainless finish. Made in 1995.

TITAN III DA . . . . **NiB $345 Ex $204 Gd $119**
Same specification as the Titan II except w/adjustable rear sight. Made
in 1995.

MKE — Ankara, Turkey
Manufactured by Makina ve Kimya Endüstrisi Kurumu.

KIRIKKALE DA
AUTOMATIC PISTOL . . . . **NiB $399 Ex $283 Gd $212**
Similar to Walther PP. Calibers: .32 Auto (7.65mm), .380 Auto (9mm Short).
Seven-round magazine, 3.9-inch bbl., 6.7 inches overall. Weight: 24 oz.
Fixed sights. Blued finish. Checkered plastic grips. Made from 1948 to 1988.
Note: This is a Turkish Army standard service pistol.

MOA CORPORATION — Dayton, Ohio

MAXIMUM SINGLE-SHOT PISTOL
Calibers: .22 Hornet to .454 Casull Mag. Armoloy, Chromoloy or stain-
less falling block action fitted w/blued or stainless 8.75-, 10- or 14-inch
Douglas bbl., weight: 60-68 oz. Smooth walnut grips. Made from 1986.
Chromoloy receiver
(blued bbl.) . . . . **NiB $806 Ex $588 Gd $475**
Armoloy receiver (blued bbl.) . . . **NiB $933 Ex $836 Gd $497**
Stainless receiver (blued bbl.) . . **NiB $1028 Ex $916 Gd $689**
w/stainless bbl., add **$306**
w/Extra bbl., add **$388**

MAXIMUM CARBINE PISTOL
Similar to Maximum Pistol except w/18-inch bbl. Made intermittently
from 1986-88 and from 1994 to date.
MOA Maximum (blued bbl.) . . . . **NiB $984 Ex $780 Gd $601**
MOA Maximum (stainless bbl.) . **NiB $1100 Ex $890 Gd $597**

Mitchell Arms SA
Army Revolver

Mitchell Arms
Victor II

MKE Kirikkale

MOA Maximum
Carbine Pistol

**Mossberg Brownie
"Pepperbox" Pistol**

**Navy Arms
Model 1875 Schofield**

**Navy Arms
Model 1875 SA
Revolver**

**Navy Arms
Frontier Standard**

**Navy Arms
Frontier Target Model**

O.F. MOSSBERG & SONS, INC. — North Haven, Connecticut

BROWNIE "PEPPERBOX" PISTOL . . . NiB $816   Ex $562   Gd $375
Hammerless, top-break, double-action, four bbls. w/revolving firing pin. Caliber: .22 LR, 2.5-inch bbls., weight: 14 oz. Blued finish. Serrated grips. Approximately 37,000 made from 1919-32.

NAMBU

See Listings under Japanese Military Pistols.

NAVY ARMS COMPANY — Martinsburg, West Virginia

MODEL 1873 SA REVOLVER
Calibers: .44-40, .45 Colt. Six-round cylinder, bbl. lengths: 3, 4.75, 5.5, 7.5 inches, 10.75 inches overall (with 5.5-inch bbl.). Weight: 36 oz. Blade front sight, grooved topstrap rear. Blued w/color-casehardened frame or nickel finish. Smooth walnut grips. Made from 1991 to 2009.
Blued finish w/brass backstrap . . NiB $468   Ex $357   Gd $235
U.S. Artillery model w/5-inch bbl. . NiB $544   Ex $386   Gd $270
U.S. Cavalry model w/7-inch bbl   NiB $544   Ex $386   Gd $270
Bisley model . . . . NiB $536   Ex $359   Gd $225
Sheriff's model (disc. 1998). . . . . NiB $434   Ex $356   Gd $220

MODEL 1875 SCHOFIELD REVOLVER
Replica of S&W Model 3, top-break single-action w/auto ejector. Calibers: .44-40 or .45 LC. Six-round cylinder, 5- or 7-inch bbl., 10.75 or 12.75 inches overall. Weight: 39 oz. Blade front sight, square-notched rear. Polished blued finish. Smooth walnut grips. Made from 1999 to 2009.
Cavalry model (7-inch bbl.) . . . . NiB $668   Ex $544   Gd $336
**Deluxe Cavalry model
  (engraved) . . . . NiB $1720   Ex $1398   Gd $1176**
Wells Fargo model (5-inch bbl.) . NiB $840   Ex $636   Gd $447
**Deluxe Wells Fargo
  model (engraved) . . . . NiB $1479   Ex $1266   Gd $1122**
Hideout model (3.5-inch bbl.). . . NiB $748   Ex $590   Gd $398

1875 REMINGTON SA REVOLVER NiB $398   Ex $283   Gd $194
Replica of Remington Model 1875. Calibers: .357 Magnum, .44-40, .45 Colt. Six-round cylinder, 7.5-inch bbl., 13.5 inches overall. Weight: About 48 oz. Fixed sights. Blued or nickel finish. Smooth walnut grips. Made in Italy c.1955-1980 and 1994 to 2000. Originally marketed in the U.S. as Replica Arms Model 1875 (that firm was acquired by Navy Arms Co).

FRONTIER SA REVOLVER. . . . NiB $397   Ex $290   Gd $224
Calibers: .22 LR, .22 WMR, .357 Mag., .45 Colt. Six-round cylinder, bbl. lengths: 4.5-, 5.5-, 7.5-inches, 10.25 inches overall (with 4.5-inch bbl.). Weight: About 36 oz. (with 4.5-inch bbl.). Fixed sights. Blued bbl., and cylinder, color-casehardened frame, brass grip frame. One-piece smooth walnut grip. Imported from 1975 to 1979.

FRONTIER TARGET MODEL . . NiB $416   Ex $312   Gd $225
Same as standard Frontier except has adj. rear sight and ramp front sight. Imported from 1975 to 1979.

BUNTLINE FRONTIER . . . . . . NiB $569   Ex $467   Gd $342
Same as Target Frontier except has detachable shoulder stock and 16.5-inch bbl. Calibers: .357 Magnum and .45 Colt only. Made from 1975 to 1979.

LUGER AUTOMATIC . . . . **NiB $166 Ex $112 Gd $88**
Caliber: .22 LR, standard or high velocity. 10-round magazine, bbl. length: 4.5 inches, 8.9 inches overall. Weight: 1 lb., 13.5 oz. Square blade front sight w/square notch, stationary rear sight. Walnut checkered grips. Non-reflecting black finish. Made 1986 to 1988.

ROLLING BLOCK
SINGLE-SHOT PISTOL . . . . **NiB $418 Ex $345 Gd $231**
Calibers: .22 LR, .22 Hornet, .357 Magnum. Eight-inch bbl., 12 inches overall. Weight: About 40 oz. Adjustable sights. Blued bbl., color-case-hardened frame, brass trigger guard. Smooth walnut grip and forearm. Imported from 1965 to 1980.

TT-OLYMPIA PISTOL . . . . **NiB $283 Ex $214 Gd $170**
Reproduction of the Walther Olympia Target Pistol. Caliber: .22 LR. Eight inches overall 4.6-inch bbl., weight: 28 oz. Blade front sight, adj. rear. Blued finish. Checkered hardwood grips. Imported 1992 to 1994.

NEW ENGLAND FIREARMS — Gardner, Massachusetts

In 1987, New England Firearms was established as an independent company producing select H&R models under the NEF logo. In 1991, H&R 1871, Inc. was formed from the residual of the parent company and took over the New England Firearms facility. H&R 1871 produced firearms under both their logo and the NEF brand name until 1999, when the Marlin Firearms Company acquired the assets of H&R 1871. Purchased by Freedom Group in 2008.

MODEL R73 REVOLVER . . . . **NiB $158 Ex $98 Gd $67**
Caliber: .32 H&R Mag. Five-round cylinder, 2.5- or 4-inch bbl., 8.5 inches overall (with 4-inch bbl.). Weight: 26 oz. (with 4 inch bbl.). Fixed or adjustable sights. Blued or nickel finish. Walnut-finish hardwood grips. Made from 1988 to 1999.

MODEL R92 REVOLVER . . . . **NiB $137 Ex $90 Gd $64**
Same general specifications as Model R73 except chambered for .22 LR. Nine-round cylinder. Weight: 28 oz. w/4 inch bbl., Made 1988 to 1999.

MODEL 832 STARTER PISTOL . . . . **NiB $148 Ex $101 Gd $75**
Calibers: .22 Blank, .32 Blank. Nine- and 5-round cylinders, respectively. Push-pin swing-out cylinder. Solid wood grips w/NEF medallion insert.

ULTRA REVOLVER . . . . **NiB $170 Ex $109 Gd $70**
Calibers: .22 LR, .22 Mag. Nine-round cylinder in .22 LR, 6-round cylinder in .22 Mag., 4- or 6-inch ribbed bull bbl., 10.75 inches overall (with 6-inch bbl.). Weight: 36 oz. (with 6-inch bbl.). Blade front sight, adj. square-notched rear. Blued or nickel finish. Walnut-finish hardwood grips. Made from 1989 to 1999.

LADY ULTRA REVOLVER . . . . **NiB $169 Ex $144 Gd $106**
Same basic specifications as the Ultra except in .32 H&R Mag. w/5-round cylinder and 3-inch ribbed bull bbl., 7.5 inches overall. Weight: 31 oz. Made from 1992 to 1999.

NORTH AMERICAN ARMS — Provo, Utah

MODEL NAA .22LR . . . . **NiB $175 Ex $149 Gd $70**
Same as Model 22S except chambered for .22 LR., is 3.88-inches overall, weight: 4.5 oz. Made from 1975 to date.

MODEL NAA 22S MINI REVOLVER NiB $170 Ex $150 Gd $70
Single-Action. Caliber: .22 Short. Five-round cylinder, 1.13-inch bbl., 3.5-inches overall. Weight: 4 oz. Fixed sights. Stainless steel. Plastic grips. Made from 1975 to date.

Navy Arms
Rolling Block Single-Shot

Navy Arms
TT-Olympia Pistol

New England Firearms
Model R73 Revolver

New England Firearms
Model 832 Starter Pistol

MODEL 450 MAGNUM EXPRESS
Single-Action. Calibers: .450 Magnum Express, .45 Win. Mag. Five-round cylinder, 7.5- or 10.5-inch bbl., matte or polished stainless steel finish. Walnut grips. Presentation case. Disc. 1984.
Matte stainless model . . . . **NiB $1259 Ex $1066 Gd $808**
Polished stainless model . . . . . **NiB $1528 Ex $1234 Gd $856**
w/10-inch bbl., add $281
w/combo cylinder, add $255

Ortgies
Pocket Automatic Pistol

Olympic Arms OA-93

OLYMPIC ARMS, INC. — Olympia, Washington

OA-93 AR SEMIAUTOMATIC PISTOL

AR-15 style receiver with no buffer tube or charging handle. Caliber: .223 Rem. or 7.62x39mm. Five-, 20- or 30-round detachable magazine, 6-, 9- or 14-inch stainless steel bbl., 15.75 inches overall w/6-inch bbl., weight: 4 lbs., 3 oz. Flattop upper with no open sights. VortEx flash suppressor. A2 stowaway pistol grip and forward pistol grip. Made 1993-94. Note: All post-ban versions of OA-93 style weapons are classified by BATF as "Any Other Weapon" and must be transferred by a Class III dealer. Values listed here are for limited-production, pre-ban guns.

(.223 Rem.) . . . . NiB $1134 Ex $871 Gd $687
(7.62x39mm) . . . . NiB $2234 Ex $1669 Gd $1378

OA-96 AR SEMI-

AUTOMATIC PISTOL . . . . NiB $904 Ex $804 Gd $637
Similar to Model OA-93 AR except w/6.5-inch bbl. only chambered for .223 Rem. Additional compliance modifications include a fixed (nonremovable) well-style magazine and no forward pistol grip. Made from 1996 to 2000.

ORTGIES PISTOLS — Erfurt, Germany
Manufactured by Deutsche Werke A.G.

POCKET-

AUTOMATIC PISTOL . . . . NiB $399 Ex $305 Gd $225
Calibers: .32 Auto (7.65mm), .380 Auto (9mm). Seven-round magazine (.380 cal.), 8-round (.32 cal.), 3.25-inch bbl., 6.5-inches overall. Weight: 22 oz. Fixed sights. Blued finish. Plain walnut grips. Made in 1920's.

VEST POCKET

AUTOMATIC PISTOL . . . . NiB $365 Ex $289 Gd $203
Caliber: .25 Auto (6.35mm). Six-round magazine, 2.75-inch bbl., 5.19 inches overall. Weight: 13.5 oz. Fixed sights. Blued finish. Plain walnut grips. Made in 1920's.

PARA USA, INC. — Pineville, North Carolina
Purchased by Freedom Group in 2012.

LIMITED EDITION SERIES
Custom-tuned and fully accessorized "Limited Edition" versions of standard "P" Models. Enhanced-grip frame and serrated slide fitted w/match-grade bbl., and full-length recoil spring guide system. Beavertail grip safety and skeletonized hammer. Ambidextrous safety and trigger-stop adjustment. Fully adjustable or contoured low-mount sights. For pricing see individual models.

MODEL P-10 SA AUTO PISTOL
Super compact. Calibers: .40 S&W, .45 ACP. 10-round magazine, 3-inch bbl., weight: 24 oz. (alloy frame) or 31 oz. (steel frame). Ramp front sight and drift adjustable rear w/3-dot system. Steel or alloy frame. Matte black, Duo-Tone or stainless finish. Made from 1997 to 2002.

Alloy model . . . . NiB $637 Ex $540 Gd $413
Duo-Tone model . . . . NiB $688 Ex $581 Gd $464
Stainless steel model. . . . . NiB $693 Ex $577 Gd $447
Steel model . . . . NiB $648 Ex $536 Gd $410
Limited model (tuned & accessorized), add $150

P-12 COMPACT AUTO PISTOL
Calibers: .45 ACP. 11-round magazine, 3.5-inch bbl., 7-inches overall. Weight: 24 oz. (alloy frame). Blade front sight, adj. rear w/3-dot system. Textured composition grips. Matte black alloy or steel finish. Made from 1990 to 2003.

BLACK WIDOW REVOLVER
SA. Calibers: .22 LR., .22 WMR. Five-round cylinder, 2-inch heavy vent bbl., 5.88-inches overall. Weight: 8.8 oz. Fixed or adj. sights. Full-size black rubber grips. Stainless steel brush finish. Made from 1990 to date.

Adj. sight model. . . . . NiB $257 Ex $188 Gd $135
Adj. sight combo model, add $45
Fixed sight model. . . . . NiB $257 Ex $188 Gd $135
Fixed sight combo model, add $40

GUARDIAN DAO PISTOL. . . . NiB $377 Ex $286 Gd $198
Caliber: .25 ACP, .32 ACP or .380. Six-round magazine (.32 ACP), 2-inch bbl., 4.4 inches overall. Weight: 13.5 oz. Fixed sights. Black synthetic grips. Stainless steel. Made from 1997 to date.

MINI-MASTER TARGET REVOLVER
SA. Calibers: .22 LR., .22 WMR. Five-round cylinder, 4-inch heavy vent rib bbl., 7.75-inches overall. Weight: 10.75 oz. Fixed or adj. sights. Black rubber grips. Stainless steel brush finish. Made from 1990 to date.

Adj. sight model. . . . . NiB $270 Ex $214 Gd $165
Adj. sight combo model, add $35
Fixed sight model. . . . . NiB $270 Ex $214 Gd $165
Fixed sight combo model, add $35

NORWEGIAN MILITARY PISTOLS — Manufactured by Kongsberg Vaapenfabrikk, Government Arsenal at Kongsberg, Norway

MODEL 1914
AUTOMATIC PISTOL . . . . NiB $511 Ex $378 Gd $283
Similar to Colt Model 1911 .45 Automatic w/same general specifications except has lengthened slide stop. Made 1919-46.

MODEL 1912. . . . . NiB $2885 Ex $2289 Gd $1588
Same as the model 1914 except has conventional slide stop. Only 500 were made.

Model P1245 (alloy) . . . . NiB $779 Ex $606 Gd $530
Model P1245C (steel) . . . . NiB $857 Ex $686 Gd $541
Limited model (tuned & accessorized), add $150

P-13 AUTO PISTOL
Same general specifications as Model P-12 except w/12-round magazine, 4.5-inch bbl., 8-inches overall. Weight: 25 oz. (alloy frame). Blade front sight, adj. rear w/3-dot system. TExtured composition grips. Matte black alloy or steel finish. Made from 1993 to 2003.
Model P1345 (alloy) . . . . NiB $779 Ex $606 Gd $530
Model P1345C (steel) . . . . NiB $772 Ex $586 Gd $337
Limited model
  (tuned & accessorized), add $150

P-14 AUTO PISTOL
Caliber: .45 ACP. 13-round magazine, 5-inch bbl., 8.5 inches overall. Weight: 28 oz. Alloy frame. Blade front sight, adj. rear w/3-dot system. TExtured composition grips. Matte black alloy or steel finish. Made from 1990 to 2003.
Model P1445 (alloy) . . . . NiB $685 Ex $474 Gd $332
Model P1445C (stainless) . . . . . . NiB $755 Ex $546 Gd $395
Limited model (tuned & accessorized), add $128

MODEL P-15 AUTO PISTOL
Caliber: .40 S&W. 10-round magazine, 4.25-inch bbl., 7.75 inches overall. Weight: 28 to 36 oz. Steel, alloy or stainless receiver. Matte black, Duotone or stainless finish. Made 1996 to 1999.
Model P1540 (alloy) . . . . NiB $740 Ex $495 Gd $362
Model P1540C (steel) . . . . NiB $665 Ex $544 Gd $468
Duotone stainless model . . . . . NiB $740 Ex $495 Gd $362
Stainless model. . . . . NiB $700 Ex $602 Gd $536

MODEL P-16 SA AUTO PISTOL
Caliber: .40 S&W. 10- or 16-round magazine, 5-inch bbl., 8.5 inches overall. Weight: 40 oz. Ramp front sight and drift adjustable rear w/3-dot system. Carbon steel or stainless frame. Matte black, Duotone or stainless finish. Made from 1995 to 2002.
Blue steel model. . . . . .NiB $683 Ex $536 Gd $437
Duotone model. . . . . .NiB $709 Ex $572 Gd $362
Stainless model. . . . . .NiB $740 Ex $576 Gd $485
Limited model (tuned & accessorized), add $175

MODEL P-18 SA AUTO PISTOL
Caliber: 9mm Parabellum. 10- or 18-round magazine, 5-inch bbl., 8.5 inches overall. Weight: 40 oz. Dovetailed front sight and fully adjustable rear. Bright stainless finish. Made from 1998 to 2003.
Stainless model. . . . . NiB $816 Ex $652 Gd $523
Limited model (tuned & accessorized), add $150

PXT SINGLE STACK SERIES AUTO PISTOL
Caliber: 9mm Para. , .38 Super or .45 ACP. Eight- or 9-round (9mm Para) magazine, 3-, 3.5-, 4.25-, 5- or 6-inch bbl., 8.5 inches overall (5-in. bbl.). Weight: 30 oz. (5-in. bbl.). Steel or stainless frame. Blade front sight, adj. rear w/3-dot system. Textured composition grips. Matte black alloy or steel finish. Made from 2004 to date.
1911 OPS (disc. 2008) . . . . NiB $980 Ex $931 Gd $450
1911 LTC (intro. 2009). . . . . . . NiB $780 Ex $741 Gd $330
1911 Wild Bunch (intro. 2011) . . NiB $660 Ex $550 Gd $340
GI Expert (intro. 2009) . . . . . . NiB $580 Ex $440 Gd $355
Slim Hawg (.45 ACP, 3-in. bbl.) NiB $860 Ex $670 Gd $400

PXT HIGH CAPACITY SERIES AUTO PISTOL
Similar to PXT Single Stack series except 10-, 14-, or 18-round magazine.Made from 2004 to date.
P14.45 (.45 ACP, 14-rnd.
  magazine). . . . . NiB $880 Ex $650 Gd $410

Para-Ordnance
P-12 Compact

Para-Ordnance
P-14 Auto Pistol

P18.9 (9mm Para, 18-rnd.
  magazine) . . . . .NiB $1030 Ex $840 Gd $470
Warthog (.45 ACP, 10-rnd. magazine)NiB $900 Ex $700 Gd $400

PHOENIX ARMS — Ontario, California

MODEL HP22/HP25 SA
AUTO PISTOLS . . . . NiB $170 Ex $95 Gd $66
Caliber: .22 LR, .25 ACP. 10-round magazine, 3-inch bbl., 5.5 inches overall. Weight: 20 oz. Checkered synthetic grips. Blade front sight, adj. rear. Blue, chrome or nickel finish. Made from 1994 to date.

MODEL HP RANGE-MASTER TARGET SA
AUTO PISTOL . . . . NiB $170 Ex $95 Gd $66
Similar to Model HP .22 except w/5.5-inch target bbl. and Extended magazine, Ramp front sight, adj. notch rear on vent rib. Checkered synthetic grips. Blue or satin nickel finish. Made from 1998 to date.

MODEL HP RANGE-MASTER DELUXE TARGET
SA AUTO PISTOL. . . . . NiB $204 Ex $165 Gd $110
Similar to Model HP Rangemaster Target model except w/dual-2000 laser sight and custom wood grips. Made from 1998 to date.

RAVEN SA AUTO PISTOL . . . . . NiB $88 Ex $61 Gd $45
Caliber: .25 ACP. Six-round magazine, 2.5 inch bbl., 4.75 inches overall. Weight: 15 oz. Ivory, pink pearl, or black slotted stocks. Fixed sights. Blue, chrome or nickel finish. Made from 1993 to 1998.

www.skyhorsepublishing.com

Plainfield Model 71

Plainfield Model 72

Radom P-35

P-83 Wanad

PLAINFIELD MACHINE COMPANY—Dunellen, New Jersey

This firm disc. operation about 1982.

MODEL 71 AUTOMATIC PISTOL
Calibers: .22 LR, .25 Automatic w/conversion kit available. 10-round magazine (.22 LR) or 8-round (.25 Auto), 2.5-inch bbl., 5.13 inches overall. Weight: 25 oz. Fixed sights. Stainless steel frame/slide. Checkered walnut grips. Made from 1970-82.
.22 LR or .25 Auto . . . . NiB $200 Ex $177 Gd $128
w/conversion kit. . . . . NiB $222 Ex $188 Gd $119

MODEL 72 AUTOMATIC PISTOL
Same as Model 71 except has aluminum slide, 3.5-inch bbl., 6 inches overall. Made from 1970 to 1982
.22 LR or .25 Auto only . . . . NiB $220 Ex $177 Gd $101
w/conversion kit. . . . . NiB $235 Ex $166 Gd $128

POLISH MILITARY PISTOLS — Radom, Poland
Manufactured at Łucznik Arms Factory.

MODEL P-64 . . . . NiB n/a Ex $250 Gd $125
SA/DA. Similar to Walther PPK. Caliber: 9x18mm Makarov. 3.3-in. bbl., 22 ozs. Military surplus. Made 1965 to date.

MODEL P-83 WANAD . . . . NiB n/a Ex $350 Gd $220
SA/DA. Caliber: 9x18mm Makarov. 8-round magazine. 3.5-in. bbl., 26 ozs. Military surplus. Made 1983 to date.

PROFESSIONAL ORDNANCE, INC. — Lake Havasu City, Arizona

MODEL CARBON-15 TYPE 20
SEMIAUTOMATIC PISTOL . . . . . . NiB $944 Ex $819 Gd $581
Similar to Carbon-15 Type 97 except w/unfluted barrel. Weight: 40 oz. Matte black finish. Made from 1999 to 2000.

MODEL CARBON-15 TYPE 97
SEMIAUTOMATIC PISTOL . . . . . NiB $1030 Ex $927 Gd $588
AR-15 operating system w/recoil reduction system. Caliber: .223 Rem. 10-round magazine, 7.25-inch fluted bbl., 20 inches overall. Weight: 46 oz. Ghost ring sights. Carbon-fiber upper and lower receivers w/ Chromoly bolt carrier. Matte black finish. Checkered composition grip. Made from 1996 to 2003.

RADOM — Radom, Poland
Manufactured by the Polish Arsenal.

P-35 AUTOMATIC PISTOL
Variation of the Colt Government Model .45 Auto. Caliber: 9mm Para. Eight-round magazine, 4.75-inch bbl., 7.75 inches overall. Weight: 29 oz. Fixed sights. Blued finish. Plastic grips. Made from 1935 thru WWII.
Commercial model
  (Polish Eagle) . . . . NiB $4599 Ex $4370 Gd $2555
Nazi military model
  (w/slotted backstrap). . . . . . . NiB $1629 Ex $1199 Gd $877
Nazi military model
  (w/takedown lever). . . . . NiB $1300 Ex $1000 Gd $431
Nazi military model
  (No takedown lever or slot) . . . NiB $459 Ex $356 Gd $232
Nazi military model (Parkerized), add $357

RANDALL FIREARMS COMPANY —
Sun Valley, California

The short-lived Randall firearms Company (1982 to 1984) was a leader in the production of stainless steel semi-autimatic handguns, particularly in left-handed configurations. Prices shown are for production models. Add 50% for prototype models (t-prefix on serial numbers) and $125 for guns with serial numbers below 2000. Scare models (C311, C332, etc., made in lots of four pieces or less) valued substantially higher to avid collectors.

MODEL A111 . . . . NiB $791 Ex $479 Gd $316
Caliber: .45 Auto. Barrel: 5 inches. Round-slide top; right-hand model. Sights: Fixed. Total production: 3,431 pieces.

MODEL A112 . . . . NiB $920 Ex $689 Gd $581
Calibers: 9mm. Barrel: 5 inches. Round-slide top; right-hand model. Sights: Fixed.

MODEL A121 . . . . NiB $734 Ex $643 Gd $377
Caliber: .45 Auto. Barrel: 5 inches. Flat-slide top; right-hand model. Sights: Fixed.

MODEL A211 . . . . NiB $785 Ex $571 Gd $479
Caliber: .45 Auto. Barrel: 4.25 inches. Round-slide top; right-hand model. Sights: Fixed.

MODEL A232 . . . . NiB $1560 Ex $1357 Gd $1100
Caliber: 9mm. Barrel: 4.25 inches. Flat-slide top; right-hand model. Sights: Fixed.

MODEL A331 . . . . NiB $1808 Ex $1566 Gd $1234
Caliber: .45 Auto. Barrel: 4.25 inches. Flat-slide top; right-hand model. Sights: Fixed.

MODEL B111 . . . . NiB $1270 Ex $1124 Gd $890
Caliber: .45 Auto. Barrel: 5 inches. Round-slide top; left-hand model. Sights: Fixed. Toatal production: 297 pieces

MODEL B131 . . . . NiB $1470 Ex $1326 Gd $1152
Caliber: .45 Auto. Barrel: 5 inches. Flat-slide top; left-hand model. Sights: Millet. Total production: 225 pieces.

MODEL B311 . . . . NiB $1632 Ex $1418 Gd $1206
Caliber: .45 Auto. Barrel: 4.25 inches. Round-slide top; left-hand model. Sights: Fixed. Total production: 52 pieces.

MODEL B312 LEMAY . . . . NiB $5170 Ex $1669 Gd $3090
Caliber: 9mm. Barrel: 4.25 inches. Round-slide top; left-hand model. Sights: Fixed. Total production: 9 pieces.

MODEL B331 . . . . NiB $1800 Ex $1589 Gd $1356
Caliber: .45 Auto. Barrel: 4.25 inches. Flat-slide top; left-hand model. Sights: Millet. Total production: 45 pieces.

RECORD-MATCH PISTOLS — Zella-Mehlis, Germany. Manufactured by Udo Anschütz

MODEL 200 FREE PISTOL . . . . NiB $1039 Ex $760 Gd $616
Basically the same as Model 210 except w/different stock design and conventional set trigger, spur trigger guard. Made prior to WW II.

MODEL 210 FREE PISTOL . . NiB $1355 Ex $1206 Gd $919
System Martini action, set trigger w/button release. Caliber: .22 LR. Single-shot, 11-inch bbl., weight: 46 oz. Target sights micrometer rear.

Remington
95 Double Derringer

Record-Match
Model 200 Free Pistol

Blued finish. Carved and checkered walnut forearm and stock w/adj. hand base. Also made w/dual action (Model 210A); weight 35 oz. Made prior to WWII.

REISING ARMS CO. — Hartford, Connecticut

TARGET AUTOMATIC PISTOL NiB $1132 Ex $862 Gd $587
Hinged frame. Outside hammer. Caliber: .22 LR. 12-round magazine, 6.5-inch bbl., fixed sights. Blued finish. Hard rubber grips. Made 1921 to 1924.

REMINGTON ARMS COMPANY — Madison, NC
Manufacturing in Ilion, New York; Lonoke, AR; and Mayfield, KY. Owned by the Freedom Group.

MODEL 51 AUTOMATIC PISTOL
Calibers: .32 Auto, .380 Auto. Seven-round magazine, 3.5-inch bbl., 6.63 inches overall. Weight: 21 oz. Fixed sights. Blued finish. Hard rubber grips. Made from 1918 to 1926.
.32 ACP . . . . NiB $887 Ex $780 Gd $453
.380 ACP . . . . NiB $899 Ex $790 Gd $495

MODEL 95 DOUBLE DERRINGER
SA. Caliber: 41 Short Rimfire. Three-inch double bbls. (superposed), 4.88 inches overall. Early models have long hammer spur and two-armed Extractor, but later guns have short hammer spur and sliding Extractor (a few have no Extractor). Fixed blade front sight and grooved rear. finish: Blued, blued w/nickel-plated frame or fully nickel-plated; also w/factory engraving. Grips: Walnut, checkered hard rubber, pearl, ivory. Weight: 11 oz. Made 1866-1935. Approximately 150,000 were manufactured. Note: During

the 70 years of its production, serial numbering of this model was repeated two or three times. Therefore, aside from hammer and Extractor differences between the earlier and later models, the best clue to the age of a Double Derringer is the stamping of the company's name on the top of the bbl., or side rib. Prior to 1888, derringers were stamped "E. Remington & Sons, Ilion, N.Y." on one side rib and "Elliot's Patent Dec. 12, 1865" on the other (Type I-early & mid-production) and on the top rib (Type I-late production). In 1888-1911, "Remington Arms Co., Ilion, N.Y." and patent date were stamped on the top rib (Type II) and from 1912-35 "Remington Arms - U.M.C. Co., Ilion, N.Y." and patent date were stamped on the top rib.

Model 95 (Early Type I, w/o Extractor) . . . . NiB $6600 Ex $5000 Gd $3800

Model 95 (Mid Type I, w/Extractor) . . . . .NiB $11,000 Ex $8000 Gd $4000

Model 95 (Late Type I, w/Extractor) . . . . NiB $5000 Ex $4219 Gd $1000

M95 (TYPE II produced 1888-1911) . . . . . . NiB $3700 Ex $2588 Gd $909

Model 95 (Type III, produced 1912-35) . . . . NiB $3600 Ex $3000 Gd $1099

Factory-engraved model w/ivory or pearl grips, add 40%

NEW MODEL SINGLE-SHOT TARGET PISTOL
Also called Model 1901 Target. Rolling-block action. Calibers: .22 Short & Long, .25 Stevens, .32 S&W, .44 S&W Russian. 10-inch half-octagon bbl., 14 inches overall. Weight: 45 oz. (.22 cal.). Target sights. Blued finish. Checkered walnut grips and forearm. Made from 1901 to 1909.

Model 1901 (.22 caliber) . . . NiB $3750 Ex $2550 Gd $1203

Model 1901 (.25 Stevens, .32 S&W) . . . . . NiB $3449 Ex $2988 Gd $1380

Model 1901 (.44 Russian) . . . NiB $3969 Ex $2709 Gd $1190

MODEL XP-100
SINGLE-SHOT PISTOL . . . . .NiB $984 Ex $622 Gd $464
Bolt action. Caliber: 221 Rem. Fireball. 10.5-inch vent rib bbl., 16.75 inches overall. Weight: 3.75 lbs. Adj. rear sight, blade front, receiver drilled and tapped for scope mounts. Blued finish. One-piece brown nylon stock. Made from 1963 to 1988.

MODEL XP-100 CUSTOM PISTOL . . NiB $1096 Ex $755 Gd $596
Bolt-action, single-shot, long-range pistol. Calibers: .223 Rem., 7mm-08 or .35 Rem. 14.5-inch bbl., standard contour or heavy. Weight: About 4.25 lbs. Currently in production.

MODEL XP-100 SILHOUETTE . NiB $984 Ex $622 Gd $464
Same general specifications as Model XP-100 except chambered for 7mm BR Rem. and 35 Rem. 14.75-inch bbl., weight: 4.13 lbs. Made from 1987 to 1992.

MODEL XP-100
VARMINT SPECIAL . . . . NiB $984 Ex $622 Gd $464
Bolt-action, single-shot, long-range pistol. Calibers: .223 Rem., 7mm BR. 14.5-inch bbl., 21.25 inches overall. Weight: About 4.25 lbs. One-piece Du Pont nylon stock w/universal grips. Made from 1986 to 1992.

MODEL XP-100R
CUSTOM REPEATER
Same general specifications as Model XP-100 Custom except 4- or 5-round repeater chambered for .22-250, .223 Rem., .250 Savage, 7mm-08 Rem., .308 Win., .35 Rem. and .350 Rem. Mag. Kevlar-reinforced synthetic or fiberglass stock w/blind magazine and sling swivel studs. Made from 1992-94 and from 1998 to 1999.

Model XP-100R (fiberglass stock) . . . . . .NiB $984 Ex $622 Gd $464
Model XP-100R KS (kevlar stock) . . . . . .NiB $984 Ex $622 Gd $464

NOTE: *The following Remington derringers were produced from the mid-1860s through the mid-1930s. The Zig-Zag model is reputed to be the first cartridge handgun ever produced at the Remington plant. Few if any Remington derringers Exiswt in "new" or "in box" condition, therefore, guns in 90-percent condition command top price.*

ZIG-ZAG DERRINGER . . . . . . NiB $6155 Ex $5875 Gd $4145
Caliber: .22S, L, LR. Six shot, six-barrel (rotating) cluster. 3-inch bbl., blued, ring trigger. Two-piece rubber grips. Fewer than 1,000 pieces produced from 1861 to 1863.

ELIOT'S FIVE-SHOT
DERRINGER . . . . .NiB $1897 Ex $1268 Gd $1091
Caliber: .22S, L, LR. Five shot, five-barrel fixed cluster. 3-inch bbl., ring trigger, blue and/or nickel finish. Two-piece rubber, walnut, ivory or pearl grips.

ELIOT'S FOUR-SHOT
DERRINGER . . . . NiB $5000 Ex $4275 $3795
Caliber: .32. Four shot, four-barrel fixed cluster. 3-3/8 inch bbl., ring trigger, blue and/or nickel finish. Two-piece rubber, walnut, ivory or pearl grips. Approx. 25,000 pieces (.22 and .32) produced.

VEST POCKET DERRINGER . . .NiB $3255 Ex $2920 Gd $2635
Caliber: .22, .30, .32, .41 rimfire . Two shot, various bbl. lengths, blue or nickel finish. Two-piece walnut grips. Spur trigger. Made from 1865 to 1888.

OVER AND UNDER DERRINGER. .NiB $6270 Ex $4720 Gd $3955
Caliber: .41 rimfire. Two shot, 3-inch super imposed bbl., spur trigger, blue and/or nickel finish. Two-piece rubber, walnut, ivory or pearl grips. Oscillating firing pin. Produced 1866-1934. Also known as Double Derringer or Model 95. Type 1 and variatitons bear maker's name, patent data stamped between the barrels, with or without Extractor. Types Two and Three marked "Remington Arms Company, Ilion, NY. Type Four marked on top of barrel, "Remington Arms-U.M.C. Co. Ilion, NY."

MODEL 1866
ROLLING BLOCK PISTOL . . . .NiB $6210 Ex $4329 Gd $3144
Caliber: .50 rimfire. Single-shot, 8-1/2 inch round, blue finish. Walnut grip and forearm. Spur trigger. Made from 1866-67. Mistakenly designated as Model 1865 Navy. Top values are for military-marked, pristine pieces. Very few of these guns remain in original condition.

MODEL 1870 NAVY
ROLLING BLOCK PISTOL . . . .NiB $4225 Ex $3199 Gd $1905
Caliber: .50 centerfire. Single shot, 7-inch round bbl. Standard trigger with trigger guard, walnut grip and forearm. Approx. 6,400 pieces made from 1870-75. Modified for the Navy from Model 1866. Higher values are for 8--inch commercial version without proof marks.

RIDER'S
MAGAZINE PISTOL . . . . .NiB $3577 Ex $2885 Gd $2389
Caliber: .32. Five shot, 3-inch octagon bbl. blued (add 50 percent for case-hardened receiver). Walnut, rosewood, ivory or pearl grips. Spur trigger. Made from 1871 to 1888.

ELIOT'S VEST POCKET
SINGLE-SHOT DERRINGER . . . NiB $3387 Ex $1109 Gd $879
Caliber: .41 rimfire. Single-shot, 2-1/2-inch round bbl., blue and/or nickel finish. Also known as "Mississippi Derringer." Two-piece walnut grips. Spur trigger. Approx. 10,000 made from 1867 to 1888.

MODEL 1890 SINGLE-ACTION
REVOLVER . . . . **NiB $15,210 Ex $14,070 Gd $7680**
Caliber: .41 centerfire . Six shot, 5-3/4 or 7-1/2-inch round bbl., blue
or nickel finish. Standard trigger with trigger guard. Two-piece ivory or
pearl grips with Remington monogram. nickel finish valued about 15
percent less.

MODEL 1911
REMINGTON UMC . . . . **NiB $7000 Ex $5550 Gd $1650**
Caliber: .45 ACP. WWII military contract production. Blued finish.
Made from 1918 to 1919, with serial numbers 1 to 21,676.

MODEL 1911A1
REMINGTON RAND . . . . **NiB $2500 Ex $2079 Gd $1086**
Caliber: .45 ACP. Parkerized finish. Two-piece walnut grips. Made from
1943-45 by Remington Rand Co., not Remington Arms Co.

RG — Manufactured by Rohm Gmbh, Germany (imported by R.G. Industries, Miami, FL)

MODEL 23 . . . . **NiB $115 Ex $88 Gd $70**
SA/DA. 6-round magazine, swing-out cylinder. Caliber: .22 LR. 1.75- or
3.38-inch bbl., Overall length: 5.13 and 7.5 inches. Weight: 16-17 oz.
Fixed sights. Blued or nickel finish. Disc. 1986.

MODEL 385
SA/DA. Caliber: .38 Special. Six-round magazine, swing-out cylinder.
Three- or 4-inch bbl., overall length: 8.25 and 9.25 inches. Weight:
32-34 oz. Windage-adj. rear sight. Blued finish. Disc. 1986.
w/plastic grips . . . . **NiB $177 Ex $140 Gd $101**
w/wood grips . . . . **NiB $212 Ex $130 Gd $95**

ROSSI — Sáo Leopoldo, Brazil
*Manufactured by Amadeo Rossi S.A., imported by BrazTech, Int'l., in
Miami, Florida; previously by Interarms, Alexandria, VA.*

MODEL 31 DA REVOLVER . . . . . **NiB $144 Ex $78 Gd $62**
Caliber: .38 Special. Five-round cylinder, 4-inch bbl., weight: 20 oz.
Blued or nickel finish. Disc. 1985.

MODEL 51 DA REVOLVER . . . . . **NiB $147 Ex $82 Gd $61**
Caliber: .22 LR. Six-round cylinder, 6-inch bbl., weight: 28 oz. Blued
finish. Disc. 1985.

MODEL 68 . . . . **NiB $177 Ex $147 Gd $101**
Caliber: .38 Special. Five-round magazine, 2- or 3-inch bbl., overall
length: 6.5 and 7.5 inches. Weight: 21-23 oz. Blued finish. Nickel finish
available w/3-inch bbl. Disc. 1998.

MODEL 84 DA REVOLVER . . . **NiB $209 Ex $160 Gd $110**
Caliber: .38 Special. Six-round cylinder, 3-inch bbl., 8 inches overall.
Weight: 27.5 oz. Stainless steel finish. Imported 1984 to 1986.

MODEL 85 DA REVOLVER . . . **NiB $209 Ex $160 Gd $110**
Same as Model 84 except has vent rib. Imported from 1985 to 1986.

MODEL 88 DA REVOLVER
Caliber: .38 Special. Five-round cylinder, 2- or 3-inch bbl., weight: 21
oz. Stainless steel finish. Imported from 1988 to 1998.
Model 88 (disc.) . . . . **NiB $219 Ex $180 Gd $148**
Model 88 Lady Rossi
(round butt) . . . . **NiB $225 Ex $189 Gd $152**

MODEL 88/2 DA REVOLVER . **NiB $219 Ex $180 Gd $140**
Caliber: .38 Special. Five-round cylinder, 2- or 3-inch bbl., 6.5 inches overall. Weight: 21 oz. Stainless steel finish. Imported 1985 to 1987.

MODEL 89 DA REVOLVER . . . . **NiB $184 Ex $110 Gd $75**
Caliber: .32 S&W. Six-round cylinder, 3-inch bbl., 7.5 inches overall.
Weight: 17 oz. Stainless steel finish. Imported 1989 to 1990.

MODEL 94 DA REVOLVER . . . . . **NiB $175 Ex $109 Gd $88**
Caliber: .38 Special. Six-round cylinder, 3-inch bbl., 8 inches overall.
Weight: 29 oz. Imported from 1985 to 1988.

MODEL 95 (951) REVOLVER . **NiB $219 Ex $175 Gd $141**
Caliber: .38 Special. Six-round magazine, 3-inch bbl., 8 inches overall.
Weight: 27.5 oz. Vent rib. Blued finish. Imported 1985 to 1990.

MODEL 351/352 REVOLVERS
Caliber: .38 Special. Five-round cylinder, 2-inch bbl., 6.87 inches
overall. Weight: 22 oz. Ramp front and rear adjustable sights. Stainless
or matte blued finish. Imported from 1999 to date.
Model 351 (matte blue finish) . . . . **NiB $362 Ex $255 Gd $186**
Model 352 (stainless finish) . . . . . . **NiB $437 Ex $326 Gd $265**

MODEL 461/462 REVOLVERS
Caliber: .357 Magnum. Six-round cylinder, 2-inch heavy bbl., 6.87
inches overall. Weight: 26 oz. Rubber grips w/ serrated ramp front sight.
Stainless or matte blued finish. Imported 1999 to date.
Model 461 (matte blue finish) . . . . **NiB $365 Ex $265 Gd $188**
Model 462 (stainless finish) . . . . . . **NiB $439 Ex $290 Gd $219**

MODEL 511 DA REVOLVER . . . . . **NiB $195 Ex $170 Gd $75**
Similar to the Model 51 except in stainless steel. Imported 1986 to 1990.

MODEL 515 DA REVOLVER . . . . . **NiB $214 Ex $105 Gd $70**
Calibers: .22 LR, .22 Mag. Six-round cylinder, 4-inch bbl., 9 inches
overall. Weight: 30 oz. Red ramp front sight, adj. square-notched rear.
Stainless finish. Checkered hardwood grips. Imported from 1994 to 1998.

MODEL 518 DA REVOLVER . . . **NiB $214 Ex $105 Gd $70**
Similar to the Model 515 except in caliber .22 LR. Imported from 1993
to 1998.

MODEL 677 DA REVOLVER . . **NiB $225 Ex $180 Gd $128**
Caliber: .357 Mag. Six-round cylinder, 2-inch bbl., 6.87 inches overall.
Weight: 26 oz. Serrated front ramp sight, channel rear. Matte blue finish.
Contoured rubber grips. Imported from 1997 to 1998.

MODEL 720 DA REVOLVER . . **NiB $235 Ex $170 Gd $141**
Caliber: .44 Special. Five-round cylinder, 3-inch bbl., 8 inches overall. Weight: 27.5 oz. Red ramp front sight, adj. square-notched rear.
Stainless finish. Checkered Neoprene combat-style grips. Imported from
1992 to 1998.

MODEL 841 DA REVOLVER . . . . . **NiB $319 Ex $225 Gd $160**
Same general specifications as Model 84 except has 4-inch bbl., (9
inches overall), weight: 30 oz. Imported from 1985 to 1986.

MODEL 851 DA REVOLVER . . . . . **NiB $336 Ex $259 Gd $158**
Same general specifications as Model 85 except w/3-or 4-inch bbl.,
8 inches overall (with 3-inch bbl.). Weight: 27.5 oz. (with 3-inch
bbl.). Red ramp front sight, adj. square-notched rear. Stainless finish.
Checkered hardwood grips. Imported from 2001 to 2009 to date.

MODEL 877 DA REVOLVER . . . . . **NiB $230 Ex $160 Gd $110**
Same general specifications as Model 677 except stainless steel. Made
from 1996 to date.

Ruger Mark I Target w/5.5-inch Untapered Bull Barrel

Ruger Mark II

Ruger Mark II 22/45

Blade front sight, adj. square-notched rear. Blued or stainless finish. Checkered hardwood grips. Imported from 1988 to 1998.

Blued finish . . . . NiB $219 Ex $166 Gd $129
Stainless finish . . . . NiB $240 Ex $175 Gd $101
w/compensated bbl., add $25

MODEL 971 VRC
DA REVOLVER . . . . NiB $321 Ex $270 Gd $175
Same general specifications as Model 971 stainless except w/ventilated rib and compensated bbl. Made 1988 to 1998.

CYCLOPS DA REVOLVER . . . . . . NiB $425 Ex $362 Gd $274
Caliber: .357 Mag. Six-round cylinder, 6- or 8-inch compensated slab-sided bbl., 11.75 or 13.75 inches overall. Weight: 44 oz. or 51 oz. Undercut blade front sight, fully adjustable rear. B-Square scope mount and rings. Stainless steel finish. Checkered rubber grips. Made from 1997 to 1998.

DA REVOLVER . . . . NiB $220 Ex $170 Gd $124
Calibers: .22 LR, .32 S&W Long, .38 Special. Five-round (.38) or 6-round cylinder (other calibers), bbl. lengths: 3-, 6-inches. Weight: 22 oz. (3-inch bbl.). Adj. Rear sight, ramp front. Blued or nickel finish. Wood or plastic grips. Imported from 1965-91.

SPORTSMAN'S .22 . . . . NiB $279 Ex $219 Gd $170
Caliber: .22 LR. Six-round magazine, 4-inch bbl., 9 inches overall. Weight: 30 oz. Stainless steel finish. Disc. 1991.

RUBY — Manufactured by Gabilondo y Urresti, Eibar, Spain, and others

**7.65MM
AUTOMATIC PISTOL** . . . . NiB $342 Ex $255 Gd $129
Secondary standard service pistol of the French Army in world wars I and II. Essentially the same as the Alkartasuna (see separate listing). Other manufacturers: Armenia Elgoibarresa y Cia., Eceolaza y Vicinai y Cia., Hijos de Angel Echeverria y Cia., Bruno Salaverria y Cia., Zulaika y Cia., all of Eibar, Spain-Gabilondo y Cia., Elgoibar Spain; Ruby Arms Company, Guernica, Spain. Made from 1914 to 1922.

RUGER — Southport, Connecticut
Manufactured by Sturm, Ruger & Co. Rugers made in 1976 are designated "Liberty" in honor of the U.S. Bicentennial and bring a premium of approximately 25% in value over regular models.

NOTE: *For ease in finding a particular Ruger handgun, the listings are divided into two groups: Automatic/Single-Shot Pistols (below) and Revolvers, which follow. For a complete listing, please refer to the index.*

- *AUTOMATIC/SINGLE-SHOT PISTOLS -*

22 CHARGER AUTOMATIC . . . . NiB $330 EX $230 GD $180
Uses Ruger 10/22 action. Caliber: .22 LR, 10-in. bbl., black/grey laminated pistol grip and forend, bipod, matte black finish. Made from 2008 to 2012.

HAWKEYE SINGLE-SHOT PISTOL . . NiB $2555 Ex $2427 Gd $1000
Built on a SA revolver frame w/cylinder replaced by a swing-out breechblock and fitted w/a bbl., w/integral chamber. Caliber: .256 Magnum. 8.5-inch bbl., 14.5 inches overall. Weight: 45 oz. Blued finish. Ramp front sight, click adj. rear. Smooth walnut grips. Made from 1963 to 1965 (3,300 produced).

MODEL 941 DA REVOLVER . . . . . . NiB $214 Ex $109 Gd $82
Caliber: .38 Special. Six-round cylinder, 4-inch bbl., 9 inches overall. Weight: 30 oz. Blued finish. Imported from 1985-86.

MODEL 951 DA REVOLVER . . . . . . NiB $214 Ex $109 Gd $82
Previous designation M95 w/same general specifications.

MODEL 971 DA REVOLVER
Caliber: .357 Magnum. Six-round cylinder, 2.5-, 4- or 6-inch bbl., 9 inches overall (with 4-inch bbl.). Weight: 36 oz. (with 4-inch bbl.).

MARK I TARGET MODEL AUTOMATIC PISTOL
Caliber: .22 LR. 10-round magazine, 5.25- and 6.88-inch heavy tapered or 5.5-inch untapered bull bbl., 10.88 inches overall (with 6.88-inch bbl.). Weight: 42 oz. (in 5.5- or 6.88-inch bbl.). Undercut target front sight, adj. rear. Blued finish. Hard rubber grips or checkered walnut thumbrest grips. Made from 1952 to 1982.
Standard model . . . . NiB $877 Ex $791 Gd $612
w/red medallion . . . . NiB $975 Ex $859 Gd $712
Walnut grips, add $434

MARK II AUTOMATIC PISTOL
Caliber: .22 LR, standard or high velocity 10-round magazine, 4.75- or 6-inch tapered bbl., 8.31 inches overall (with 4.75-inch bbl.). Weight: 36 oz. Fixed front sight, square notch rear. Blued or stainless finish. Made from 1982 to 2004.
Blued . . . . .NiB $265 Ex $305 Gd $158
Stainless . . . . .NiB $321 Ex $265 Gd $204
Bright stainless (ltd.
 prod. 5,000 in 1982) . . . . .NiB $590 Ex $479 Gd $346

MARK II 22/45 AUTOMATIC PISTOL
Same general specifications as Ruger Mark II .22 LR except w/blued or stainless receiver and bbl., in four lengths: 4-inch tapered w/adj. sights (P4), 4.75-inch tapered w/fixed sights (KP4), 5.25-inch tapered w/adj. sights (KP 514) and 5.5-inch bull (KP 512). Fitted w/Zytel grip frame of the same design as the Model 1911 45 ACP. Made from 1993 to 2004.
Model KP4 (4.75-inch bbl.). . . . . .NiB $255 Ex $177 Gd $140
Model KP512, KP514
 (w/5.5- or 5.25-inch bbl.) . . . . . . NiB $365 Ex $229 Gd $126
Model P4, P512
 (Blued w/4- or 5.5-inch bbl.) . . . NiB $270 Ex $216 Gd $160

MARK II BULL BARREL MODEL
Same as standard Mark II except for bull bbl. (5.5- or 10-inch). Weight: About 2.75 lbs.
Blued finish . . . . NiB $319 Ex $237 Gd $175
Stainless finish (intro. 1985) . . . . NiB $430 Ex $379 Gd $128

MARK II GOVERNMENT MODEL AUTO PISTOL
Civilian version of the Mark II used by U.S. Armed Forces. Caliber: .22LR. 10-round magazine, 6.88-inch bull bbl., 11.13 inches overall. Weight: 44 oz. Blued or stainless finish. Made from 1986 to 1999.
Blued model (MK687G commercial) . . . .NiB $388 Ex $286 Gd $198
Stainless steel model
 (KMK678G commercial) . . . . . . NiB $444 Ex $337 Gd $270
w/U.S. markings (military model) . . . . .NiB $1148 Ex $910 Gd $629

MARK II TARGET MODEL
Caliber: .22 LR. 10-round magazine, 4-, 5.5- and 10-inch bull bbl. or 5.25- and 6.88-inch heavy tappered bbl., weight: 38 oz. to 52 oz. 11.13 inches overall (with 6.88-inch bbl.). Made 1982 to 2004.
Blued . . . . NiB $375 Ex $303 Gd $128
Stainless steel . . . . NiB $444 Ex $377 Gd $290

MARK III AUTOMATIC PISTOL
Similar to Mark II pistol except w/magazine button on left side grip, tapered bolt ears, and improved ejection port. Made from 2005 to date.
Blued . . . . .NiB $389 Ex $190 Gd $120

MARK III TARGET AUTOMATIC PISTOL
Same as Mark III pistol except w/tapered barrel, adj. rear sight, laminated grips. Made from 2005 to date.
Blued . . . . .NiB $460 Ex $240 Gd $180
Stainless steel . . . . NiB $569 Ex $290 Gd $190
Government Competition . . . . . . NiB $659 Ex $350 Gd $250

Ruger P-89
DAC/DAO

Ruger P-90

Ruger P-93
Compact

MARK III 22/45 AUTOMATIC PISTOL

Similar to Mark II 22/45 pistol except w/Mark III improvements. Made from 2005 to 2012.

Blued.	NiB $265	Ex $180	Gd $140
Stainless steel.	NiB $335	Ex $200	Gd $150
Hunter (fluted bbl.).	NiB $435	Ex $250	Gd $170
Lite (2012 to date)	NiB $499	Ex $330	Gd $270
Target (4- or 5.5-in. bull bbl.)	NiB $359	Ex $255	Gd $175
Threaded Barrel (2011 to date)	NiB $449	Ex $230	Gd $175

MODEL LCP AUTOMATIC PISTOL . . NiB $379 Ex $230 Gd $150

DOA. Caliber: .380 ACP, 6- or 7-round magazine, 2.75 in. bbl. Weight: 9.4 oz. Fixed sights. Made from 2008 to date.

w/Crimsontrace sight, add.	$150
w/LaserMax sight, add	$75
Stainless steel slide finish	NiB $429 Ex $225 Gd $175

MODEL LC9 PISTOL . . . . .NiB $379 Ex $230 Gd $150

DAO. Caliber: 9mm. 7- or 9-round magazine, 3.12 inch bbl. Weight: 17.1 oz. Fixed 3-dot sights. Blued finish. Made from 2011 to date.

w/Crimsontrace sight, add.	$150
w/LaserMax sight, add	$75

MODEL LC380 PISTOL . . . . .NiB $379 Ex $230 Gd $150

Similar to LC9 pistol except chambered in .380 ACP. Blued finish. Made from 2013 to date.

w/Crimsontrace sight, add.	$150
w/LaserMax sight, add	$75

MODEL P-85 AUTOMATIC PISTOL

Caliber: 9mm. DA, recoil-operated. 15-round capacity, 4.5 inch bbl., 7.84 inches overall. Weight: 32 oz. Fixed rear sight, square-post front. Available w/decocking levers, ambidExtrous safety or in DA only. Blued or stainless finish. Made from 1987 to 1992.

Blued finish	NiB $332	Ex $214	Gd $110
Stainless steel finish	NiB $439	Ex $365	Gd $291

MODEL P-89 AUTOMATIC PISTOL

Caliber: 9mm. DA w/slide-mounted safety levers. 15-round magazine, 4.5-inch bbl., 7.84 inches overall. Weight: 32 oz. Square-post front sight, adj. rear w/3-dot system. Blued or stainless steel finish. Grooved black Xenoy grips. Made from 1992 to 2007.

P-89 blued	NiB $434	Ex $321	Gd $225
P-89 stainless	NiB $546	Ex $453	Gd $388

MODEL P-89 DAC/DAO AUTO PISTOLS

Similar to the standard Model P-89 except the P-89 DAC has ambidExtrous decocking levers. The P-89 DAO operates in double-action-only mode. Made from 1991 to 2009.

P-89 DAC blued	NiB $431	Ex $316	Gd $225
P-89 DAC/DAO stainless	NiB $530	Ex $431	Gd $316

MODEL P-90, KP90 DA AUTOMATIC PISTOL

Caliber: .45 ACP. Seven-round magazine, 4.5-inch bbl., 7.88 inches overall. Weight: 33.5 oz. Square-post front sight adj. square-notched rear w/3-dot system. Grooved black Xenoy composition grips. Blued or stainless finish. DAC model has ambidExtrous decocking levers. Made from 1991 to 2010.

Model P-90 blued.	NiB $530	Ex $342	Gd $240
Model P-90 DAC (decocker)	NiB $530	Ex $342	Gd $240
Model KP-90 DAC stainless	NiB $536	Ex $367	Gd $270
Model KP-90 DAC (decocker)	NiB $536	Ex $367	Gd $270

MODEL P-91 DA AUTOMATIC PISTOL

Same general specifications as the Model P-90 except chambered for .40 S&W w/12-round double-column magazine, Made 1992 to 1994.

Model P-91 DAC (decockers)	NiB $444	Ex $289	Gd $225
Model P-91 DAO (DA only)	NiB $444	Ex $289	Gd $225

Ruger Bearcat SA
(Old Model)

Ruger Bisley
Colt .45 Long (New Model)

Ruger Bisley
Single-Six Small Frame

Ruger Blackhawk

Ruger Super Blackhawk

GRADING: NiB = New in Box   Ex = Excellent or NRA 95%   Gd = Good or NRA 68%

Ruger P-97

MODEL P-93D AUTO PISTOL

Similar to the standard Model P-89 except w/3.9-inch bbl., (7.3 inches overall). Weight: 31 oz. Stainless steel finish. Made from 1993 to 2004.

Model P-93 DAC (decocker) (disc. 1994)...NiB $444 Ex $289 Gd $225
Model P-93 Stainless ....NiB $485 Ex $357 Gd $283

MODEL P-94 AUTOMATIC PISTOL

Similar to the Model P-91 except w/4.25-inch bbl., Calibers: 9mm or .40 S&W. Blued or stainless steel finish. Made 1994 to 2004.

Model KP-94 DAC (S/S decocker) ....NiB $444 Ex $289 Gd $225
Model KP-94 DAO (S/S dble. action only) ..NiB $444 Ex $289 Gd $225
Model P-94 DAC (Blued decocker) ....NiB $444 Ex $289 Gd $225
Model P-94 DAO (blued dble. action only) . NiB $395 Ex $290 Gd $198

MODEL P-95PR AUTO PISTOL

Caliber: 9mm Parabellum. 10-round magazine, 3.9-inch bbl., 7.3 inches overall. Weight: 27 oz. Square-post front sight, drift adjustable rear w/3-dot system. Molded polymer grip-frame fitted w/stainless or chrome-moly slide. AmbidExtrous decocking levers (P-95D) or double action only (DAO). Matte black or stainless finish. Made 1997 to date.

P-95 blued .... NiB $444 Ex $289 Gd $225
KP-95PR stainless .... NiB $398 Ex $270 Gd $190

MODEL P-97D AUTOMATIC PISTOL

Caliber: .45 ACP. Eight-round magazine, 4.5- inch bbl., 7.25 inches overall. Weight: 30.5 oz. Square-post front sight adj. square-notched rear w/3-dot system. Grooved black Xenoy composition grips. Blued or stainless finish. DAC model has ambidExtrous decocking levers. Made from 2002 to 2004.

Model KP-97 DAO stainless .... NiB $444 Ex $289 Gd $225
Model P-97D DAC (decockers) .. NiB $377 Ex $306 Gd $219

MODEL P-345 AUTOMATIC PISTOL

SA/DA. Caliber: .45 ACP. 8-round magazine, 4.25-in. bbl. Black polymer frame w/rail, blued steel slide. Weight: 29 oz. Fixed sights. Ambidextrous safety or decocking levers. Made from 2005 to 2012.

P345 .... NiB $490 Ex $340 Gd $225
KP345 (decocker)........... NiB $520 Ex $350 Gd $230

MODEL P-944................... NIB $450 EX $300 GD $220

Similar to Model P-94 except in .40 S&W, ambidextrous safety and blued finish. Many variations of safety type, decocker or DAO. Made from 1999 to 2010.

Stainless finish, add $50

MODEL SR22 .... NIB $399 EX $265 GD $230

SA/DA. Caliber: .22 LR. 10-round magazine, 3.25-in. bbl. Polymer frame, steel slide w/front/rear serrations. Weight: 17.5 oz. 3-dot adj. sights. Blued finish. Two backstrap inserts. Made 2012 to date.

Threaded barrel, add $50
Two-tone finish, add................................$30

MODEL SR9 .... NIB $399 EX $265 GD $230

Striker fired system. Caliber: 9mm. 10- or 17-round magazine, 4.1-in. bbl. Polymer frame w/reversible backstrap. Weight: 26.5 oz. 3-dot low profile sights. Black stainless, brushed stainless, or OD green finish. Made 2007 to date.

Black stainless finish.......... NiB $529 Ex $400 Gd $280
Matte stainless finish .... NiB $529 Ex $400 Gd $280
OD green finish (2009-10) ..... NiB $529 Ex $400 Gd $280

MODEL SR9C................... NIB $529 EX $360 GD $280

Similar to SR9 except compcat version w/3.5-in. bbl. Made 2010 to date.

MODEL SR40 .... NIB $529 EX $360 GD $280

Similar to SR9 except chambered in .40 S&W. Made 2011 to date.

MODEL SR40C................... NIB $529 EX $360 GD $280

Similar to SR40 except compcat version w/3.5-in. bbl. Made 2011 to date.

MODEL SR45 .... NIB $529 EX $360 GD $280

Similar to SR9 except chambered in .45 ACP. Made 2013 to date.

MODEL SR1911 .... NIB $829 EX $470 GD $330

1911 platform. Caliber: .45 ACP. 5-in. bbl., 7- and 8-round magazine. Stainless steel, checkered cocobola grips. Navak 3-dot sights. Made 2011 to date.

Commander model (4.25-in. bbl.) ...NiB $829 Ex $470 Gd $330

STANDARD MODEL AUTOMATIC PISTOL

Caliber: .22 LR. Nine-round magazine, 4.75- or 6-in. bbl., 8.75 inches overall (with 4.75-inch bbl.). Weight: 36 oz. (with 4.75 inch bbl.). Fixed sights. Blued finish. Hard rubber or checkered walnut grips. Made from 1949 to 1952. Known as the "Red Eagle Automatic," this early type is now a collector's item. Note: After the death of Alexander Sturm in 1951, the color of the eagle on the grip medallion was changed from red to black as a memorial. Made from 1952 to 1981.

w/red eagle medallion .... NiB $689 Ex $536 Gd $431
w/black eagle medallion........ NiB $430 Ex $379 Gd $170
Walnut grips, add..............................$40

- REVOLVERS -

BEARCAT, SUPER (OLD MODEL) ... NiB $602 Ex $365 Gd $291

Same general specifications as Bearcat except has steel frame. Weight: 25 oz. Made from 1971 to 1974.

NEW MODEL BEARCAT REVOLVER

Same general specifications as Super Bearcat except all steel frame and trigger guard. Interlocked mechanism and transfer bar. Calibers: .22 LR and .22WMR. Interchangeable 6-round cylinders (disc. 1996). Smooth walnut stocks w/Ruger medallion. Made from 1994 to date.

Convertible model (disc.
1996 after factory recall) ....NiB $469 Ex $362 Gd $291
Standard model (.22 LR only)........NiB $485 Ex $326 Gd $225

BISLEY SA REVOLVER, LARGE FRAME
Calibers: .357 Mag., .41 Mag. .44 Mag., .45 Long Colt. 7.5-inch bbl., 13 inches overall. Weight: 48 oz. Non-fluted or fluted cylinder, no engraving. Ramp front sight, adj. rear. Satin blued or stainless. Made from 1986 to date.
Blued finish . . . . NiB $485 Ex $365 Gd $270
Vaquero/Bisley (blued w/case colored fr.) . .NiB $612 Ex $474 Gd $398
Vaquero/Bisley (stainless steel) . NiB $587 Ex $434 Gd $357
w/ivory grips, add. $5 0

BISLEY SINGLE-SIX REVOLVER, SMALL FRAME
Calibers: .22 LR and .32 Mag. Six-round cylinder, 6.5-inch bbl., 11.5 inches overall. Weight: 41 oz. Fixed rear sight, blade front. Blue finish. Goncalo Alves grips. Made from 1986 to date.
.22 caliber . . . . NiB $485 Ex $365 Gd $270
.32 H&R Mag. . . . . NiB $693 Ex $601 Gd $479

BLACKHAWK SA CONVERTIBLE (OLD MODEL)
Same as Blackhawk except has Extra cylinder. Caliber combinations: .357 Magnum and 9mm Para., .45 Colt and .45 Automatic. Made 1967 to 1972.
.357/9mm combo (early w/o prefix S/N) .NiB $556 Ex $437 Gd $290
.357/9mm combo (late w/prefix S/N). . . .NiB $556 Ex $437 Gd $290
.45 LC/.45 ACP combo
  (1967-85 & 1999 to date) . . . . . . NiB $556 Ex $437 Gd $290

BLACKHAWK SA REVOLVER (OLD MODEL)
Calibers: .30 Carbine, .357 Mag., .41 Mag., .45 Colt. Six-round cylinder, bbl. lengths: 4.63-inch (.357, .41, .45 caliber), 6.5-inch (.357, .41 caliber), 7.5-inch (.30, .45 caliber). 10.13 inches overall (.357 Mag. w/4.63-inch bbl.). Weight: 38 oz. (.357 w/4.63-inch bbl.). Ramp front sight, adj. rear. Blued finish. Checkered hard rubber or smooth walnut grips. Made from 1955 to 1962.
.30 Carbine, .357 Mag. . . . . NiB $510 Ex $432 Gd $325
.41 Mag. . . . . NiB $760 Ex $660 Gd $265
.45 Colt . . . . NiB $875 Ex $532 Gd $255

BLACKHAWK SA "FLAT-TOP" REVOLVER (OLD MODEL)
Similar to standard Blackhawk except w/"Flat Top" cylinder strap. Calibers: .357 Mag. or .44 Mag. Six-round fluted cylinder, 4.625-, 6.5-, 7.5- or 10-inch bbl., adj. rear sight, ramp front. Blued finish. Black rubber or smooth walnut grips. Made from 1955 to 1962.
.357 Mag. (w/4.625-inch bbl.) . . . . . .NiB $1235 Ex $1148 Gd $975
.357 Mag. (w/6.5-inch bbl.) . . . . .NiB $479 Ex $342 Gd $198
.357 Mag. (w/10-inch bbl.) . . . . .NiB $2540 Ex $1650 Gd $1030
.44 Mag. (w/fluted cylinder/ 4.625-inch bbl.) NiB $1336 Ex $1270 Gd $1030
.44 Mag. (w/fluted cylinder/ 6.5-inch bbl.) NiB $1020 Ex $666 Gd $408
.44 Mag. (w/fluted cylinder/ 10-inch bbl.) NiB $2540 Ex $1945 Gd $1779

GP-100 DA REVOLVER
Caliber: .357 Magnum. Three- to 4-inch heavy bbl., or 6-inch standard or heavy bbl., Overall length: 9.38 or 11.38 inches. Cushioned grip panels. Made from 1986 to date.
Blued finish . . . . NiB $590 Ex $434 Gd $274
Stainless steel finish . . . . NiB $570 Ex $410 Gd $290

GP-100 MATCH CHAMPION . . . . . . NiB $899 EX $580 GD $430
Similar to GP-100 except yuned for competiotion w/slab side, half under lug 4.25-in. bbl. Matte stainless finish. Hogue stippled hardwood grip. Made from 2014 to date.

LCR DAO REVOLVER. . . . . NiB $545 EX $670 GD $300
DAO. Caliber: .22 LR, .22 WMR, .38 Spl.+P, or .357 Mag. Hammless design, polymer fire control housing, monolithic aluminum frame, stainless cylinder, 1.87-in. bbl., fixed sights, Hogue rubber grip. Made from 2010 to date.
.357 Mag., add $80
Crimson Trace laser grips, add. $280

**Ruger GP-100
DA Revolver**

Ruger New Model Blackhawk Convertible

**Ruger Blackhawk High-Gloss Stainless
(New Model) .357 Magnum**

LCRX model (external hammer), add $50
LCRX model (3-in. bbl.), add $20

NEW MODEL BLACKHAWK SA REVOLVER
Safety transfer bar mechanism. SA. Calibers: .30 Carbine, .357 Magnum, .357 Maximum, .41 Magnum, .44 Magnum, .44 Special, .45 Colt. Six-round cylinder, bbl. lengths: 4.63-inch (.357, .41, .45 Colt); 5.5 inch (.44 Mag., .44 Spec.); 6.5-inch (.357, .41, .45 Long Colt); 7.5-inch (.30, .45, .44 Special, .44 Mag.); 10.5-inch in .44 Mag; 10.38 inches overall (.357 Mag. w/4.63-inch bbl.). Weight: 40 oz. (.357 w/4.63-inch bbl.). Adj. rear sight, ramp front. Blued finish or stainless steel; latter only in .357 or .45 LC. Smooth walnut grips. Made from 1973.
Blued finish . . . . NiB $464 Ex $326 Gd $203
High-gloss stainless (.357 Mag., .45 LC) NiB $459 Ex $316 Gd $190
Satin stainless (.357 Mag., .45 LC) . . . . NiB $418 Ex $332 Gd $265
.357 Maximum SRM (1984-85) . . . . . . NiB $452 Ex $357 Gd $226

NEW MODEL BLACKHAWK BISLEY
Similar to New Model Blackhawk except w/Bisley shaped grip and hammer, fluted or unfluted cylinder. Made from 1986 to date.
Blued finish . . . . .NiB $799 Ex $430 Gd $320
Unfluted cylinder, add $120

Ruger Single-Six SSM
(New Model)

Ruger Super
Blackhawk (New
Model)

Ruger Super Single-
Six Convertible (New
Model)

Ruger Police Service-
Six Stainless Steel

Ruger Redhawk

Ruger Super Redhawk
Stainless shown w/optional
scope

NEW MODEL BLACKHAWK CONVERTIBLE

Same as New Model Blackhawk except has Extra cylinder. Blued finish only. Caliber combinations: .357 Magnum/9mm Para., .44 Magnum/.44-40, .45 Colt/.45 ACP. (Limited Edition Buckeye Special .32-20/.32 H&R Mag. or .38-40/10mm). Made from 1973 to 1985. Reintro. 1999.

.32-20/.32 H&R Mag. (1989-90) . . . . . . .NiB $556 Ex $386 Gd $259
.38-40/10mm (1990-91) . . . . .NiB $556 Ex $386 Gd $259
.357/9mm combo. . . . . .NiB $556 Ex $386 Gd $259
.44/.44-40 combo (disc.1982). . . . . . . .NiB $834 Ex $579 Gd $389
.45 LC/.45 ACP combo (disc. 1985) . . . .NiB $556 Ex $386 Gd $259

NEW MODEL SUPER SINGLE-SIX SSM

SA REVOLVER . . . . .NiB $555 Ex $480 Gd $209
Same general specifications as standard Single-Six except chambered for .32 H&R Magnum cartridge. Bbl. lengths: 4.63, 5.5, 6.5 or 9.5 inches.

NEW MODEL SUPER BLACKHAWK SA REVOLVER

Safety transfer bar mechanism. SA. Caliber: .44 Magnum. Six-round cylinder, 5.5-inch, 7.5-inch and 10.5-inch bull bbl. 13.38 inches overall. Weight: 48 oz. Adj. rear sight, ramp front. Blued and stainless steel finish. Smooth walnut grips. Made 1973 to date, 5.5-inch bbl. made from 1973 to date.

Blued finish . . . . .NiB $570 Ex $477 Gd $281
High-gloss stainless
  (1994-96). . . . . .NiB $580 Ex $486 Gd $290
Satin stainless steel . . . . .NiB $570 Ex $480 Gd $295
Stainless steel Hunter (intro. 2002)NiB $780 Ex $490 Gd $295

NEW MODEL SUPER BLACKHAWK BISLEY

Similar to New Model Super Blackhawk except w/Bisley shaped grip and hammer, fluted or unfluted cylinder. Made from 1986 to date.
Blued finish .NiB $729 Ex $330 Gd $260
Stainless Hunter model . . . . .NiB $859 Ex $480 Gd $340

NEW MODEL SUPER SINGLE-SIX CONVERTIBLE REVOLVER

Safety transfer bar mechanism. SA. Calibers: .22 LR and .22 WMR. Interchangeable 6-round cylinders. Bbl. lengths: 4.63, 5.5, 6.5, 9.5 inches. 10.81 inches overall (with 4.63 inch bbl.). Weight: 33 oz. (with 4.63-inch bbl.). Adj. rear sight, ramp front. Blued finish or stainless steel; latter only w/5.5- or 6.5-inch bbl., smooth walnut grips. Made from 1994 to 2004.

Blued finish . . . . NiB $500 Ex $306 Gd $190
Stainless steel . . . . NiB $530 Ex $316 Gd $219
Stainless steel Hunter
   (intro. 2002) . . . . NiB $660 Ex $560 Gd $295
Stainless steel Hunter 17 HMR/.17 Mach 2
   (2005-06) . . . . NiB $760 Ex $560 Gd $295

NEW MODEL VAQUERO. . . . . . . NiB $590 Ex $431 Gd $316
Similar to Vaquero except w/smaller pre-1962 XR-3 style grip frame,
reverse indexing cylinder, recontoured hammer, beveled cylinder, cre-
sent shaped ejector rod. Blued w/case-color or bright stainless finish.
Checkered rubber or smooth rosewood grips. Made 2005 to date.

NEW MODEL VAQUERO BISLEY . NiB $810 Ex $440 Gd $315
Similar to New Model Vaquero except w/Bisley shaped grip and hammer,
fluted cylinder. Made from 2009 to date.

POLICE SERVICE-SIX
Same general specifications as Speed-Six except has square butt.
Stainless steel models and 9mm Para. caliber available w/only 4-inch
bbl., Made from 1971 to 1988.
.38 Special, blued finish . . . . NiB $434 Ex $306 Gd $230
.38 Special, stainless steel . . . . . NiB $345 Ex $290 Gd $270
.357 Magnum or 9mm Para.,
   blued finish . . . . NiB $444 Ex $309 Gd $235
.357 Magnum, stainless steel . . . NiB $439 Ex $306 Gd $225

REDHAWK DA REVOLVER
Calibers: .357 Mag., .41 Mag., .45 LC, .44 Mag. Six-round cylinder, 5.5-
and 7.5-inch bbl., 11 and 13 inches overall, respectively. Weight: About
52 oz. Adj. rear sight, interchangeable front sights. Stainless finish. Made
from 1979 to 2009; .357 Mag. disc. 1986. Alloy steel model w/blued finish
intro. in 1986 in .41 Mag. and .44 Mag. calibers.
Blued finish . . . . NiB $620 Ex $450 Gd $270
Stainless steel . . . . NiB $789 Ex $499 Gd $300

SUPER REDHAWK DA REVOLVER
Calibers: .44 Mag., .454 Casull and .480 Ruger. Six-round cylinder,
7.5- to 9.5- inch bbl., 13 to 15 inches overall. Weight: 53 to 58 oz.
Integral scope mounting system w/stainless rings. Adjustable rear sight.
Cushioned grip panels. Made from 1987 to date.
Model .44 Mag. 7.5- inch
   bbl., stainless . . . . NiB $795 Ex $546 Gd $434
Model .44 Mag. 9.5- inch
   bbl., stainless . . . . NiB $830 Ex $577 Gd $444
Model .454 Casull & .480 Ruger
   Stainless/target gray stainless . . . NiB $862 Ex $590 Gd $474
Alaskan (intro. 2005) . . . . NiB $880 Ex $590 Gd $480

SECURITY-SIX DA REVOLVER
Caliber: .357 Magnum, handles .38 Special. Six-round cylinder, bbl. lengths:
2.25-, 4-, 6-inch, 9.25 inches overall (with 4-inch bbl.). Weight: 33.5 oz.
(with 4-inch bbl.). Adj. rear sight, ramp front. Blued finish or stainless steel.
Square butt. Checkered walnut grips. Made 1971 to 1985.
Blued finish . . . . NiB $410 Ex $280 Gd $214
Stainless steel . . . . NiB $420 Ex $300 Gd $265

SINGLE-SIX REVOLVER (OLD MODEL)
Calibers: .22 LR, .22 WMR. Six-round cylinder. bbl., lengths: 4.63, 5.5,
6.5, 9.5 inches, 10.88 inches overall (with 5.5-inch bbl.). Weight: About
35 oz. Fixed sights. Blued finish. Checkered hard rubber or smooth walnut grips. Made 1953-73. Note: Pre-1956 model w/flat loading gate is
worth about twice as much as later version.
Standard. . . . . NiB $879 Ex $602 Gd $439
Convertible (w/two cylinders,
   .22 LR/.22 WMR) . . . . NiB $561 Ex $398 Gd $272

**Ruger
Super Redhawk Stainless**

**Ruger
Single-Six**

**Ruger
Single-Six Lightweight**

**Ruger
Super Single-Six
Convertible**

**Ruger Single-Six Fixed
Sight**

Ruger Vaquero Stainless Steel

Tokarev TT30

Ruger Vaquero Blued

Ruger Speed-Six Stainless Steel

SINGLE-SIX - LIGHTWEIGHT NiB $1086 Ex $816 Gd $530
Same general specifications as Single-Six except has 4.75-inch bbl., lightweight alloy cylinder and frame, 10 inches overall length, weight: 23 oz. Made in 1956.

SINGLE-NINE . . . . NiB $639 Ex $380 Gd $280
Same general specifications as New Model Single-Six except chambered in .22 WMR, 9-round cylinder, 6.5-in. bbl. Stainless steel. Made in 2013 to date.

SINGLE-TEN . . . . NiB $639 Ex $370 Gd $270
Same general specifications as New Model Single-Six except w/10-round cylinder, 5.5-in. bbl. Stainless steel. Made in 2012 to date.

SP101 DA REVOLVER
Calibers: .22 LR, .32 Mag., 9mm, .38 Special+P, .357 Mag. Five- or 6-round cylinder, 2.25-, 3.06- or 4-inch bbl., weight: 25-34 oz. Stainless steel finish. Cushioned grips. Made from 1989 to date.
Standard model . . . . NiB $530 Ex $321 Gd $204
DAO model (DA only, spurless hammer) NiB $530 Ex $321 Gd $204

SPEED-SIX DA REVOLVER
Calibers: .38 Special, .357 Magnum, 9mm Para. Six-round cylinder, 2.75-, 4-inch bbl., (9mm available only w/2.75-inch bbl.). 7.75 inches overall (2.75-inch bbl.). Weight: 31 oz. (with 2.75-inch bbl.).
Fixed sights. Blued or stainless steel finish; latter available in .38 Special (with 2.75 inch bbl.), .357 Magnum and 9mm w/either bbl., Round butt. Checkered walnut grips. Made from 1973 to 1987.
blued finish . . . . NiB $439 Ex $272 Gd $190
stainless steel . . . . NiB $449 Ex $303 Gd $214
9mm Para., blued finish . . . . . NiB $689 Ex $522 Gd $440
9mm Para., stainless steel . . . . . . NiB $690 Ex $540 Gd $442

SUPER BLACKHAWK (OLD MODEL)
SA w/heavy frame and unfluted cylinder. Caliber: .44 Magnum. Six-round cylinder. 6.5- or 7.5-inch bbl., Adj. rear sight, ramp front. Steel or brass grip frame w/square-back trigger guard. Smooth walnut grips.

Blued finish. Made from 1956 to 1973.
w/6.5-inch bbl., ... NiB $1316 Ex $1148 Gd $918
w/7.5-inch bbl., ... NiB $806 Ex $385 Gd $281
w/brass gripframe . . . . NiB $1599 Ex $1316 Gd $1153

VAQUERO . . . . NiB $590 EX $431 GD $316
SA. Calibers: .357 Mag., .44-40, .44 Magnum, .45 Colt. Six-round cylinder. Bbl. lengths: 4.625, 5.5, 7.5 inches, 13.63 inches overall (with 7.5-inch bbl.). Weight: 41 oz. (with 7.5-inch bbl.). Blade front sight, grooved topstrap rear. Blued w/color casehardened frame or polished stainless finish. Smooth rosewood grips w/Ruger medallion. Made from 1993 to 2004.

VAQUERO BISLEY . . . . NiB $575 Ex $460 Gd $230
Similar to Vaquero except w/Bisley shaped grip and hammer, fluted cylinder. Blued or bright stainless finish. Made from 1999 to 2004.

RUSSIAN SERVICE PISTOLS — Manufactured by Government plants at Tula and elsewhere

Tokarev-type pistols have also been made in Hungary, Poland, Yugoslavia, People's Republic of China, N. Korea.

MODEL TT30 TOKAREV SERVICE AUTOMATIC
Modified Colt-Browning type. Caliber: 7.62mm Russian Auto (also uses 7.63mm Mauser Auto cartridge). Eight-round magazine, 4.5-inch bbl., 7.75 inches overall. Weight: About 29 oz. Fixed sights. Made from 1930 to mid-1950s. Note: A slightly modified version w/improved locking system and different disconnector was adopted in 1933.
Standard Service Model TT30 . . NiB $1239 Ex $1127 Gd $918
Standard Service Model TT33 . NiB $2490 Ex $2285 Gd $1879
Recent imports (distinguished
    by importer marks) . . . . NiB $209 Ex $158 Gd $109

MODEL PM
MAKAROV AUTO PISTOL . . . NiB $3000 Ex $2445 Gd $2000
Double-action, blowback design. Caliber: 9x18mm Makarov. Eight-round magazine, 3.8-inch bbl., 6.4 inches overall. Weight: 26 oz. Blade front sight, square-notched rear. Checkered composition grips.
Standard Service Model PM
(Pistole Makarov) . . . . NiB $3595 Ex $3125 Gd $2890
Recent imports (distinguished
by importer marks) . . . . NiB $434 Ex $306 Gd $170

SAKO — Riihimaki, Finland
Manufactured by Oy Sako Ab.

.22-.32 OLYMPIC PISTOL (TRIACE)
Calibers: .22 LR, .22 Short, .32 S&W Long. Five-round magazine, 6- or 8.85- (.22 Short) inch bbl., weight: About 46 oz. (.22 LR); 44 oz. (.22 Short); 48 oz. (.32). Steel frame. ABS plastic, anatomically designed grip. Non-reflecting matte black upper surface and chromium-plated slide. Equipped w/carrying case and tool set. Limited importation from 1983 to 1989.
Sako .22 or .32
Single pistol . . . . NiB $1355 Ex $1240 Gd $1090
Sako Triace, triple-barrel set
w/wooden grip . . . . NiB $2647 Ex $2279 Gd $2045

SAUER — Germany
Manufactured through WW II by J. P. Sauer & Sohn, Suhl, Germany. Now manufactured by J. P. Sauer & Sohn, GmbH, Ecmernförde, West Germany

See also listings under Sig Sauer for automatic pistols, see listings under Hawes for single action revolvers.

MODEL 1913 POCKET
AUTOMATIC PISTOL . . . . NiB $342 Ex $240 Gd $179
Caliber: .32 Automatic (7.65mm). Seven-round magazine, 3-inch bbl., 5.88 inches overall. Weight: 22 oz. Fixed sights. Blued finish. Black hard rubber grips. Made from 1913 to 1930.

MODEL 1930 POCKET AUTOMATIC PISTOL
Authority Model (Behorden Model). Successor to Model 1913, has improved grip and safety. Caliber: .32 Auto (7.65mm). Seven-round magazine, 3-inch bbl., 5.75 inches overall. Weight: 22 oz. Fixed sights. Blued finish. Black hard rubber grips. Made from 1930-38. Note: Some pistols made w/indicator pin showing when cocked. Also mfd. w/dual slide and receiver; this type weight: about 7 oz. less than the standard model.
Steel model . . . . NiB $405 Ex $290 Gd $203
Dural (alloy) model . . . . . . NiB $1454 Ex $1367 Gd $1209

MODEL 38H DA AUTOMATIC PISTOL
Calibers: .25 Auto (6.35mm), .32 Auto (7.65mm), .380 Auto (9mm). Specifications shown are for .32 Auto model. Seven-round magazine, 3.25-inch bbl., 6.25 inches overall. Weight: 20 oz. Fixed sights. Blued finish. Black plastic grips. Also made in dual model weighing about 6 oz. less. Made 1938-1945. Note: This pistol, designated Model .38, was mfd. during WW II for military use. Wartime models are inferior in design to earlier production, as some lack safety lever.
.22 caliber . . . . NiB $5625 Ex $3410 Gd $2200
.32 ACP . . . . NiB $643 Ex $410 Gd $281
.32 ACP (w/Nazi proofs) . . . . NiB $709 Ex $453 Gd $326
.380 ACP . . . . NiB $4500 Ex $4255 Gd $3975

POCKET .25 (1913)
AUTOMATIC PISTOL . . . . NiB $398 Ex $286 Gd $214
Smaller version of Model 1913, issued about same time as .32 caliber model. Caliber: .25 Auto (6.35mm). Seven-round magazine, 2.5-inch bbl., 4.25 inches overall. Weight: 14.5 oz. Fixed sights. Blued finish. Black hard rubber grips. Made 1913 to 1930.

Sako Model .22-.32 Olympic

Sauer 1930 Pocket

Savage Model 101

SAVAGE ARMS — Utica, New York

MODEL 101 SA
SINGLE-SHOT PISTOL . . . . NiB $255 Ex $170 Gd $105
Barrel integral w/swing-out cylinder. Calibers: .22 Short, Long, LR. 5.5-inch bbl. Weight: 20 oz. Blade front sight, slotted rear, adj. for windage. Blued finish. Grips of compressed, impregnated wood. Made 1960 to 1968.

MODEL 501/502F "STRIKER" SERIES PISTOLS
Calibers: .22 LR., and .22 WMR. 5- or 10- round magazine, 10-inch bbl., 19 inches overall. Weight: 4 lbs. Drilled and tapped sights for scope mount (installed). AmbidExtrous rear grip. Made from 2000 to 2005.
Model 501F, .22 LR . . . . NiB $359 Ex $206 Gd $165
Model 502F, .22 WMR . . . . NiB $301 Ex $190 Gd $158

MODEL 510/516 "STRIKER" SERIES PISTOLS
Calibers: .223 Rem., .22-250 Rem., .243 Win., 7mm-08 Rem., .260 Rem., and .308 Win. Three-round magazine, 14-inch bbl., 22.5 inches overall. Drilled and tapped for scope mounts. Left hand bolt with right hand ejection. Stainless steel finish. Made from 1998 to 2005.

Model 510F	NiB $495	Ex $395	Gd $235
Model 516FSAK	NiB $546	Ex $474	Gd $230
Model 516FSS	NiB $546	Ex $474	Gd $230
Model 516FSAK	NiB $704	Ex $468	Gd $408
Model 516BSS	NiB $755	Ex $500	Gd $437

MODEL 1907 AUTOMATIC PISTOL
Caliber: .32 ACP, 10-round magazine, 3.25-inch bbl., 6.5 inches overall. Weight: 19 oz. Checkered hard rubber or steel grips marked "Savage Quality," circling an Indian-head logo. Optional pearl grips. Blue, nickel, silver or gold finish. Made from 1910 to 1917.

Blued model (.32 ACP)	NiB $610	Ex $430	Gd $175
Blued model (.380 ACP)	NiB $709	Ex $495	Gd $326

MODEL 1907 AUTOMATIC PISTOL
Calibers: .32 Auto, .380 Auto. 10-round magazine (.32 cal.), 9-round (.380 cal.). 3.75-inch bbl., (.32 cal.), 4.25-inch (.380 cal.). 6.5 inches overall (.32 cal.), 7 inches (.380 cal.). Weight: About 23 oz. Fixed sights. Blued finish. Hard rubber grips. Made in hammerless type w/grip safety or w/Exposed hammer spur. Made from 1910 to 1917.

.32 ACP	NiB $601	Ex $457	Gd $270
.380 ACP	NiB $700	Ex $560	Gd $499

MODEL 1915 AUTOMATIC PISTOL
Same general specifications as the Savage Model 1907 except the Model 1915 is hammerless and has a grip safety. It is also chambered for both the .32 and .380 ACP. Made froim 1915 to 1917.

.32 ACP	NiB $930	Ex $729	Gd $500
.380 ACP	NiB $1400	Ex $857	Gd $643

U.S. ARMY TEST MODEL ... NiB $12,650 Ex $8990 Gd $653
Caliber: .45 ACP, Seven-round magazine w/Exposed hammer. An enlarged version of the Model 1910 manufactured for military trials between 1907 and 1911. Note: Most "Trial Pistols" were refurbished and resold as commercial models. Values are for original Government Test Issue models.

MODEL 1917 AUTOMATIC PISTOL
Same specifications as 1910 Model except has spur-type hammer and redesigned, heavier grip. Made from 1917 to 1928.

.32 ACP	NiB $564	Ex $445	Gd $279
.380 ACP	NiB $646	Ex $486	Gd $336

SEARS, ROEBUCK & COMPANY — Chicago, Illinois

J.C. HIGGINS MODEL 80
AUTO PISTOL .... NiB $281 Ex $165 Gd $109
Caliber: .22 LR. 10-round magazine, 4.5- or 6.5-inch interchangeable bbl., 10.88 inches overall (with 6.5-inch bbl.). Weight: 41 oz. (with 6.5-inch bbl.). Fixed Partridge sights. Blued finish. Checkered grips w/thumbrest.

J.C. HIGGINS MODEL 88
DA REVOLVER .... NiB $209 Ex $105 Gd $75
Caliber: .22 LR. Nine-round cylinder, 4- or 6-inch bbl., 9.5 inches (with 4-inch bbl.). Weight: 23 oz. (with 4-inch bbl.). Fixed sights. Blued or nickel finish. Checkered plastic grips.

Sears/J.C. Higgins
Model 88 DA
Revolver

Security Industries of
America Model PM 357

Security Industries of
America Model PPM 357

Security Industries of
America Model PSS38

J.C. HIGGINS RANGER
DA REVOLVER . . . . NiB $219   Ex $137   Gd $88
Caliber: .22 LR. Nine-round cylinder, 5.5-inch bbl., 10.75 inches overall. Weight: 28 oz. Fixed sights. Blued or chrome finish. Checkered plastic grips.

SECURITY INDUSTRIES OF AMERICA — Little Ferry, New Jersey

MODEL PM 357 DA REVOLVER . .NiB $255   Ex $198   Gd $160
Caliber: .357 Magnum. Five-round cylinder, 2.5-inch bbl., 7.5 inches overall. Weight: 21 oz. Fixed sights. Stainless steel. Walnut grips. Made 1975. Disc..

MODEL PPM357 DA REVOLVER. .NiB $255   Ex $198   Gd $160
Caliber: .357 Magnum. Five-round cylinder, 2-inch bbl., 6.13 inches overall. Weight: 18 oz. Fixed sights. Stainless steel. Walnut grips. Made in 1975. Note: Spurless hammer (illustrated) was disc. in 1975; this model has the same conventional hammer as other Security revolvers.

MODEL PSS 38 DA REVOLVER . . . NIB $197   EX $112   GD $90
Caliber: .38 Special. Five-round cylinder, 2-inch bbl., 6.5 inches overall. Weight: 18 oz. Fixed sights. Stainless steel. Walnut grips. Intro. 1973. disc.

R. F. SEDGLEY. INC. — Philadelphia, Pennsylvania

BABY HAMMERLESS
EJECTOR REVOLVER . . . . NiB $704   Ex $556   Gd $290
DA. Solid frame. Folding trigger. Caliber: .22 Long. Six-round cylinder, 4 inches overall. Weight: 6 oz. Fixed sights. Blued or nickel finish. Rubber grips. Made 1930 to 1939.

L. W. SEECAMP, INC. — Milford, Connecticut

MODEL LWS .25 DAO PISTOL . . . NiB $439   Ex $398   Gd $281
Caliber: .25 ACP. Seven-round magazine, 2-inch bbl., 4.125 inches overall. Weight: 12 oz. Checkered black polycarbonate grips. Matte stainless finish. No sights. Made from 1981 to 1985.

MODEL LWS 32 DAO PISTOL
Caliber: .32 ACP. Six-round magazine, 2-inch bbl., 4.25 inches overall. Weight: 12.9 oz. Ribbed sighting plane with no sights. Checkered black LExon grips. Stainless steel. Made from 1985 to date. Limited production results in inflated resale values.
Matte stainless finish . . . . NiB $464   Ex $398   Gd $272
Polished stainless finish, add. $128

MODEL LWS-380 DAO PISTOL NiB $795   Ex $650   Gd $470
Similar to LWS 32 except chambered in .380 ACP. Made from 2000 to date.

SHERIDAN PRODUCTS, INC. — Racine, Wisconsin

KNOCKABOUT
SINGLE-SHOT PISTOL . . . . NiB $305   Ex $189   Gd $108
Tip-up type. Caliber: .22 LR, Long, Short; 5-inch bbl., 6.75 inches overall. Weight: 24 oz. Fixed sights. Checkered plastic grips. Blued finish. Made from 1953 to 1960.

SIG
Model P210-1

SIG
Model P210-6 Target Pistol

SIG — Neuhausen am Rheinfall, Switzerland

See also listings under SIG-Sauer.

MODEL P210-1
AUTOMATIC PISTOL . . . . NiB $2878   Ex $2662   Gd $2288
Calibers: .22 LR, 7.65mm Luger, 9mm Para. Eight-round magazine, 4.75-inch bbl., 8.5 inches overall. Weight: 33 oz. (.22 cal.) or 35 oz. (7.65mm, 9mm). Fixed sights. Polished blued finish. Checkered wood grips. Made from 1949 to 1986.

MODEL P210-2 . . . . NiB $1835   Ex $1590   Gd $1409
Same as Model P210-1 except has sandblasted finish, plastic grips. Not avail. in .22 LR. Disc. 2002.

MODEL P210-5
TARGET PISTOL . . . . NiB $2330   Ex $2190   Gd $1902
Same as Model P210-2 except has 6-inch bbl., micrometer adj. rear sight, target front sight, adj. trigger stop, 9.7 inches overall. Weight: About 38.3 oz. Disc. 2007.

MODEL P210-6 TARGET PISTOL . . . NiB $1910   Ex $1720   Gd $1525
Same as Model P210-2 except has micrometer adj. rear sight, target front sight, adj. trigger stop. Weight: About 37 oz. Disc. 1987.

P210 .22 CONVERSION UNIT, add $1525
Converts P210 pistol to .22 LR. Consists of bbl., w/recoil spring, slide and magazine,

SIG SAUER — Neuhausen, Switzerland and Exeter, New Hampshire
Manufactured by J. P. Sauer & Sohn of Germany, SIG of Switzerland, and other manufacturers.

MODEL P220 DA/DAO AUTOMATIC PISTOL

Calibers: 22LR, 7.65mm, 9mm Para., .38 Super, .45 ACP. Seven-round in .45 ACP, 9-round in other calibers, 4.4-inch bbl., 8 inches overall. Weight: 26.5 oz. (9mm). Fixed sights. Blue, electroless nickel, K-Kote, Duo/nickel or Ilaflon finish. Alloy frame. Checkered plastic grips. Imported from 1976 to date. Note: Also sold in U.S. as Browning BDA.

Blue finish . . . . NiB $918 Ex $734 Gd $499
Duo/nickel finish . . . . NiB $1030 Ex $712 Gd $523

SIG Sauer
P220

SIG Sauer
P225

SIG Sauer
P230

Nickel finish. . . . . NiB $988 Ex $784 Gd $546
K-Kote finish . . . . NiB $974 Ex $693 Gd $474
Ilaflon finish. . . . . NiB $969 Ex $689 Gd $507
.22 LR conversion kit, add $434
w/Siglite sights, add $100

MODEL P220 SPORT AUTOMATIC. . NiB $1415 Ex $1119 Gd $1016
Similar to Model P220 except .45 ACP only w/4.5-inch compensated bbl., 10-round magazine, adj. target sights. Weight: 46.1 oz. Stainless finish. Made from 1999 to date.

MODEL P225 DA AUTOMATIC
Caliber: 9mm Para. Eight-round magazine, 3.85-inch bbl., 7 inches overall. Weight: 26.1 oz. Blue, nickel, K-Kote, Duo/nickel or Ilaflon finish.
Blued finish . . . . NiB $628 Ex $556 Gd $431
Duo/nickel finish . . . . NiB $669 Ex $588 Gd $500
Nickel finish. . . . . NiB $700 Ex $612 Gd $478
K-Kote finish . . . . NiB $700 Ex $612 Gd $478
w/Siglite sights, add $128

MODEL P226 DA/DAO AUTOMATIC
Caliber: .357 SIG, 9mm Para., .40 S&W, 10- or 15-round magazine, 4.4-inch bbl., 7.75 inches overall. Weight: 29.5 oz. Alloy frame. Blue, electroless nickel, K-Kote, Duo/nickel or Nitron finish. Imported from 1983 to date.
Blued finish . . . . NiB $882 Ex $724 Gd $444
Duo/nickel finish . . . . NiB $898 Ex $809 Gd $496
Nickel finish. . . . . NiB $804 Ex $659 Gd $478
K-Kote finish . . . . NiB $804 Ex $639 Gd $485
Nitron finish
(blackened stainless). . . . . NiB $826 Ex $658 Gd $479
w/Siglite sights, add $100

MODEL P228 DA AUTOMATIC
Same general specifications as Model P226 except w/3.86-inch bbl., 7.13 inches overall. 10- or 13-round magazine, Imported 1990 to 1997.
Blued finish . . . . NiB $831 Ex $709 Gd $455
Duo/nickel finish . . . . NiB $860 Ex $755 Gd $499
Electroless nickel finish . . . . NiB $895 Ex $780 Gd $530
K-Kote finish . . . . NiB $882 Ex $743 Gd $541
w/Siglite night sights, add $130

MODEL P229 DA/DAO AUTOMATIC
Same general specifications as Model P228 except w/3.86-inch bbl., 10- or 12-round magazine, weight: 32.5 oz. Nitron or Satin Nickel finish. Imported from 1991 to date.
Nitron finish
(Blackened stainless). . . . . NiB $860 Ex $755 Gd $464
Satin nickel finish. . . . . NiB $890 Ex $791 Gd $500
For Siglite nite sights, add. $128

MODEL P229
SPORT AUTOMATIC . . . . NiB $1292 Ex $1035 Gd $871
Similar to Model P229 except .357 SIG only w/4.5-inch compensated bbl., adj. target sights. Weight: 43.6 oz. Stainless finish. Made from 1998 to 2003. Reintroduced 2003 to 2005.

MODEL P230 DA AUTOMATIC PISTOL
Calibers: .22 LR, .32 Auto (7.65mm), .380 Auto (9mm Short), 9mm Ultra. 10-round magazine in .22, 8-round in .32, 7-round in 9mm; 3.6-inch bbl., 6.6 inches overall. Weight: 18.2 oz. or 22.4 oz. (steel frame). Fixed sights. Blued or stainless finish. Plastic grips. Imported 1976 to 1996.
Blued finish . . . . NiB $530 Ex $408 Gd $308
Stainless finish (P230SL) . . . . NiB $602 Ex $500 Gd $367

MODEL P232 DA/DAO AUTOMATIC PISTOL

Caliber: .380 ACP. Seven-round magazine, 3.6-inch bbl., 6.6 inches overall. Weight: 16.2 oz. or 22.4 oz. (steel frame). Double/single action or double action only. Blade front and notch rear drift adjustable sights. Alloy or steel frame. Automatic firing pin lock and heelmounted magazine release. Blue, Duo or stainless finish. Stippled black composite stocks. Imported 1997 to date.

Blued finish	NiB $576	Ex $467 Gd $316
Duo finish	NiB $601	Ex $498 Gd $321
Stainless finish	NiB $588	Ex $523 Gd $433
w/Siglite night sights, add $65		

MODEL P239 DA/DAO AUTOMATIC PISTOL

Caliber: .357 SIG, 9mm Parabellum or .40 S&W. Seven- or 8-round magazine, 3.6-inch bbl., 6.6 inches overall. Weight: 28.2 oz. Double/single action or double action only. Blade front and notch rear adjustable sights. Alloy frame w/stainless slide. AmbidExtrous frame- mounted magazine release. Matte black or Duo finish. Stippled black composite stocks. Made from 1996 to date.

Matte black finish.	NiB $590	Ex $524 Gd $301
DAO finish.	NiB $638	Ex $530 Gd $365
w/Siglite night sights, add $128		

SMITH & WESSON — Springfield, Massachusetts

NOTE: *For ease in locating a particular S&W handgun, the listings are divided into two groupings: Automatic/Single-Shot Pistols (below) and Revolvers (page 156). For a complete handgun listing, please refer to the index.*

In 1957 S&W started to use a number system for each model. Models with a dash followed by a one, two or three digit number indicate a model that has had a design and/or production change, i.e.: Model 29-2 indicates this Model 29 was produced during the second design and/or production change. To determine the model number of a revolver, swing out the cylinder and where the yoke meets the frame the model name is stamped.

Since 1990 S&W's Performance Center has been building or modifying existing guns. Many handguns have come out of the shop and it is difficult to keep an accurate accounting of all models and variants. Note that guns from the Performance Center in the past decade are marked with the Performance Center logo on the frame. Champion and Pros Series handguns are designed in collaboration with professional competition shooters. Since 2007, S&W began the Classics Series reissuing revolvers with aestetics of orginal revolver models.

- AUTOMATIC/SINGLE-SHOT PISTOLS -

MODEL 35 (1913) AUTOMATIC PISTOL . NiB $979 Ex $780 Gd $469
Caliber: 35 S&W Auto. Seven-round magazine, 3.5-inch bbl., (hinged to frame). 6.5 inches overall. Weight: 25 oz. Fixed sights. Blued or nickel finish. Plain walnut grips. Made from 1913 to 1921.

MODEL .32 AUTOMATIC PISTOL. . NiB $3097 Ex $2315 Gd $1699
Caliber: .32 Automatic. Same general specifications as .35 caliber model, but barrel is fastened to the receiver instead of hinged. Made from 1924 to 1937.

MODEL .22A SPORT SERIES

Caliber: .22 LR. 10-round magazine, 4-, 5.5- or 7-inch standard (A-series) or bull bbl., (S-series). Single action. Eight, 9.5 or 11 inches overall. Weight: 28 oz. to 33 oz. Partridge front sight, fully adjustable rear. Alloy frame w/stainless slide. Blued finish. Black polymer or Dymondwood grips. Made from 1997 to date.

Model 22A (w/4-inch bbl.)	NiB $255	Ex $190 Gd $105
Model 22A (w/5.5-inch bbl.). . . .	NiB $265	Ex $204 Gd $120

Smith & Wesson
Model 22A Sport Series

Smith & Wesson
Model 22S Sport Series
w/Dymondwood Grips

Smith & Wesson
Model 41 .22 w/muzzle brake

Model 22A (w/7-inch bbl.)	NiB $265	Ex $204 Gd $120
Model 22S (w/5.5-inch bbl.)	NiB $362	Ex $290 Gd $214
Model 22S (w/7-inch bbl.)	NiB $395	Ex $337 Gd $265
w/bull bbl., add $65		
w/Dymondwood grips, add $100		

MODEL 39 9MM DA AUTO PISTOL

Calibers: 9mm Para. Eight-round magazine, 4-inch barrel. Overall length: 7.44-inches. Steel or alloy frames. Weight: 26.5 oz. (w/alloy frame). Click adjustable rear sight, ramp front. Blued or nickel finish. Checkered walnut grips. Made 1954-82. Note: Between 1954 and 1966, 927 pistols were produced w/steel instead of alloy. In 1970, Model 39-1 w/alloy frame and steel slide. In 1971, Model 39-2 was introduced as an improved version of the original Model 39 w/modified Extractor.

Model 39 (early production) 1954-70
First series (S/N 1000-2600) .... NiB $1566 Ex $1418 Gd $1299
9mm blue (w/steel frame & slide,
  produced 1966) .... NiB $1866 Ex $1618 Gd $1299
9mm blue (w/alloy frame) .... NiB $622 Ex $437 Gd $225
Nickel finish, add $45
Models 39-1, 39-2 (late production, 1970-82),
  9mm blue (w/alloy frame)...... NiB $534 Ex $331 Gd $220
Nickel finish, add $50

MODEL 41 .22 AUTOMATIC PISTOL
Caliber: .22 LR, .22 Short (not interchangeably). 10-round magazine, bbl. lengths: 5-, 5.5-, 7.75-inches; latter has detachable muzzle brake, 12 inches overall (with 7.75-inch bbl.). Weight: 43.5 oz. (with 7.75-inch bbl.). Click adj. rear sight, undercut Partridge front. Blued finish. Checkered walnut grips w/thumbrest. 1957 to date.
.22 LR model .... NiB $1200 Ex $870 Gd $529
.22 Short model (w/counter-
  weights & muzzle brake) ... NiB $2700 Ex $1299 Gd $1120
w/Extended sight, add $128
w/muzzle brake, add $50

MODEL 46 .22 AUTO PISTOL .. NiB $1225 Ex $765 Gd $448
Caliber: .22 LR. 10-round magazine, bbl. lengths: 5-, 5.5-, 7-inches. 10.56 inches overall (with 7-inch bbl.). Weight: 42 oz. (with 7-inch bbl.). Click adj. rear sight, undercut Partridge front. Blued finish. Molded nylon grips w/thumbrest. Only 4,000 produced. Made from 1957 to 1966.

MODEL 52 .38 MASTER AUTO
Caliber: .38 Special (midrange wadcutter only). Five-round magazine, 5-inch bbl., overall length: 8.63 inches. Weight: 41 oz. Micrometer click rear sight, Partridge front on ramp base. Blued finish. Checkered walnut grips. Made from 1961 to 1963.

Smith & Wesson
Model 59

Smith & Wesson
Model 422

Smith & Wesson
Model 41

Smith & Wesson
Model 52

Smith & Wesson
Model 439

Model 52 (1961-63) .... NiB $1109 Ex $915 Gd $546
Model 52-1 (1963-71) .... NiB $1029 Ex $915 Gd $546
Model 52-2 (1971-93) .... NiB $1029 Ex $915 Gd $546
Model 52-A USA Marksman
(fewer than 100 mfg.) ...... NiB $3820 Ex $3470 Gd $3139

MODEL 59 9MM DA AUTO
Similar specifications as Model 39 except has 14-round staggered column magazine, checkered nylon grips. Made 1971 to 1981.
Model 59, blue. . . . . NiB $549 Ex $431 Gd $290
Model 59, nickel . . . . NiB $600 Ex $444 Gd $326
Model 59 (early production
  w/smooth grip frame) . . . . . . NiB $1647 Ex $1508 Gd $1015

MODEL 61 ESCORT POCKET AUTOMATIC PISTOL
Caliber: .22 LR. Five-round magazine, 2.13-inch bbl., 4.69 inches overall. Weight: 14 oz. Fixed sights. Blued or nickel finish. Checkered plastic grips. Made from 1970 to 1974.
Model 61, blue. . . . . NiB $380 Ex $270 Gd $165
Model 61, nickel . . . . NiB $431 Ex $316 Gd $220

MODEL 410
AUTO PISTOL . . . . NiB $561 Ex $444 Gd $244
Caliber: .40 S&W. Double action. 10-round magazine, 4-inch bbl., 7.5 inches overall. Weight: 28.5 oz. Alloy frame w/steel slide. Post front sight, fixed rear w/3-dot system. Matte blue finish. Checkered synthetic grips w/straight backstrap. Made from 1996 to 2007.

MODEL 411
AUTO PISTOL . . . . NiB $530 Ex $433 Gd $386
Similar to S&W Model 915 except in caliber .40 S&W. 11-round magazine, made from 1994 to 1996.

MODEL 422 SA AUTO PISTOL
Caliber: .22 LR. 10-round magazine, 4.5- or 6-inch bbl., 7.5 inches overall (with 4.5-inch bbl.). Weight: 22-23.5 oz. Fixed or adjustable sights. Checkered plastic or walnut grips. Blued finish. Made from 1987 to 1996.
Standard model . . . . NiB $220 Ex $175 Gd $150
Target model . . . . NiB $274 Ex $198 Gd $170

MODEL 439 9MM AUTOMATIC
DA. Caliber: 9mm Para. Two 8-round magazines, 4-inch bbl., 7.44 inches overall. Alloy frame. Weight: 30 oz. Serrated ramp square front sight, square notch rear. Checkered walnut grips. Blued or nickel finish. Made from 1979 to 1988.
Model 439, blue . . . . NiB $530 Ex $368 Gd $306
Model 439, nickel . . . . NiB $529 Ex $386 Gd $316
w/adjustable sights, add $40

MODEL 457
COMPACT AUTO PISTOL. . . . . . NiB $571 Ex $434 Gd $265
Caliber: .45 ACP. Double action. Seven-round magazine, 3.75-inch bbl., 7.25 inches overall. Weight: 29 oz. Alloy frame w/steel slide. Post front sight, fixed rear w/3-dot system. Bobbed hammer. Matte blue finish. Wraparound synthetic grip w/straight backstrap. Made from 1996 to 2006.

MODEL 459 DA AUTOMATIC
Caliber: 9mm Para. Two 14-round magazines, 4-inch bbl., 7.44 inches overall. Alloy frame. Weight: 28 oz. Blued or nickel finish. Made from 1979 to 1987.
Model 459, blue. . . . . NiB $485 Ex $431 Gd $319
Model 459, nickel . . . . NiB $527 Ex $475 Gd $377
FBI Model (brushed finish) . . . . . NiB $733 Ex $599 Gd $437

MODEL 469
(MINI) AUTOMATIC. . . . . NiB $485 Ex $388 Gd $270
DA. Caliber: 9mm Para. Two 12-round magazines, 3.5-inch bbl., 6.88 inches overall. Weight: 26 oz. Yellow ramp front sight, dovetail mounted square-notch rear. Sandblasted blued finish. Optional ambidExtrous safety. Made from 1982 to 1988.

MODEL 539 DA AUTOMATIC
Similar to Model 439 except w/steel frame. Caliber: 9mm Para. Two 8-round magazines, 4-inch bbl., 7.44 inches overall. Weight: 36 oz. Blued or nickel finish. Made from 1980 to 1983.
Model 539, blue. . . . . NiB $590 Ex $486 Gd $368
Model 539, nickel . . . . NiB $601 Ex $530 Gd $408
w/adjustable sights, add $50

MODEL 559 DA AUTOMATIC
Similar to Model 459 except w/steel frame. Caliber: 9mm Para. Two 14-round magazines, 4-inch bbl., 7.44 inches overall. Weight: 39.5 oz. Blued or nickel finish. (3750 produced) Made 1980 to 1983.
Model 559, blue. . . . . NiB $612 Ex $536 Gd $408
Model 559, nickel . . . . NiB $648 Ex $561 Gd $444
w/adjustable sights, add $50

MODEL 622 SA AUTO PISTOL
Same general specifications as Model 422 except w/stainless finish. Made from 1989 to 1996.
Standard model . . . . NiB $265 Ex $197 Gd $120
Target model . . . . NiB $309 Ex $212 Gd $146

MODEL 639 AUTOMATIC . . . . . . NiB $530 Ex $377 Gd $304
Caliber: 9mm Para. Stainless. Two 12-round magazines, 3.5-inch bbl., 6.9 inches overall. Weight: 36 oz. Made from 1986 to 1988.

Smith & Wesson
Model 645

Smith &
Wesson Model
459

Smith & Wesson
Model 745

Smith & Wesson
Model 1026

Smith & Wesson
Model 469

Smith & Wesson
Model 639

Smith & Wesson
Model 659

MODEL 645 DA AUTOMATIC
Caliber: .45 ACP. Eight-round. 5-inch bbl., overall length: 8.5 inches. Weight: Approx. 38 oz. Red ramp front, fixed rear sights. Stainless. Made from 1986-88.
Model 645 (w/fixed sights) . . . . . NiB $601   Ex $433   Gd $346
Model 645 (w/adjustable sights) . NiB $638   Ex $464   Gd $366

MODEL 659 9MM AUTOMATIC
DA. Similar to S&W Model 459 except weight: 39.5 oz. and finish is satin stainless steel finish. Made from 1983-88.
Model 659 (w/fixed sights) . . . . . NiB $517   Ex $419   Gd $326
Model 659 (w/adjustable sights) . NiB $528   Ex $444   Gd $356

MODEL 669 AUTOMATIC . . . . . . NiB $559   Ex $345   Gd $274
Caliber: 9mm. 12-round magazine, 3.5 inch bbl., 6.9 inches overall. Weight: 26 oz. Serrated ramp front sight w/red bar, fixed rear. Non-glare stainless steel finish. Made from 1986-88.

MODEL 745 AUTOMATIC PISTOL
Caliber: .45 ACP. Eight-round magazine, 5-inch bbl., 8.63 inches overall. Weight: 38.75 oz. Fixed sights. Blued slide, stainless frame. Checkered walnut grips. Similar to the model 645, but w/o DA capability. Made from 1987-90.
w/standard competition features . . . . . . .NiB $760   Ex $549   Gd $433
IPSC Commemorative (first 5,000). . . . . .NiB $798   Ex $638   Gd $429

MODEL 908/910 AUTO PISTOLS
Caliber: 9mm Parabellum. Double action. Eight-round (Model 908), 9-round (Model 909) or 10-round (Model 910) magazine; 3.5- or 4-inch bbl.; 6.83 or 7.38 inches overall. Weight: 26 oz. to 28.5 oz. Post front sight, fixed rear w/3-dot system. Matte blue steel slide w/alloy frame. Delrin synthetic wrap-around grip w/straight backstrap. Made from 1994 to date.

Model 908 . . . . NiB $541 Ex $397 Gd $272
Model 909 (disc 1996) . . . . NiB $479 Ex $347 Gd $239
Model 910 . . . . NiB $497 Ex $348 Gd $255

MODEL 915 AUTO PISTOL . . . . . NiB $434 Ex $306 Gd $220
DA. Caliber: 9mm Para. 15-round magazine, 4-inch bbl., 7.5 inches
overall. Weight: 28.5 oz. Post front sight, fixed square-notched rear w/3-
dot system. Xenoy wraparound grip. Blued steel slide and alloy frame.
Made from 1992-94.

MODEL 1000 SERIES DA AUTO
Caliber: 10mm. Nine-round magazine, 4.25- or 5-inch bbl., 7.88 or
8.63 inches overall. Weight: About 38 oz. Post front sight, adj. or fixed
square-notched rear w/3-dot system. One-piece Xenoy wraparound
grips. Stainless slide and frame. Made from 1990-94.
Model 1006 (fixed sights, 5-inch bbl.) . . NiB $724 Ex $530 Gd $433
Model 1006 (adj. sights, 5-inch bbl.) . . . . NiB $740 Ex $544 Gd $479
Model 1026 (fixed sights, 5-inch bbl.,
   decocking lever) . . . . NiB $724 Ex $530 Gd $433
Model 1066 (fixed
   sights, 4.25 inch bbl.) . . . . NiB $678 Ex $530 Gd $362
Model 1076 (fixed sights, 4.25 inch bbl.,
   frame-mounted decocking lever, NiB $730 Ex $536 Gd $439
Model 1076 (same as above
   w/Tritium night sight) . . . . NiB $730 Ex $536 Gd $439
Model 1086 (same as model
   1076 in DA only) . . . . NiB $760 Ex $544 Gd $429

MODEL 2206 SA AUTOMATIC PISTOL
Similar to Model 422 except w/stainless-steel slide and frame, weight:
35-39 oz. Partridge front sight on adj. sight model; post w/white dot on
fixed sight model. Plastic grips. Made from 1990-96.
Standard model . . . . NiB $342 Ex $227 Gd $130
Target model . . . . NiB $377 Ex $239 Gd $178

MODEL 2213
SPORTSMAN AUTO . . . . NiB $279 Ex $180 Gd $119
Caliber: .22 LR. Eight-round magazine, 3-inch bbl., 6.13 inches overall.
Weight: 18 oz. Partridge front sight, fixed square-notched rear w/3-
dot system. Black synthetic molded grips. Stainless steel slide w/alloy
frame. Made from 1992-99.

MODEL 2214
SPORTSMAN AUTO . . . . NiB $362 Ex $190 Gd $126
Same general specifications as Model 2214 except w/blued slide and
matte black alloy frame. Made from 1990-99.

MODEL 3904/3906 DA AUTO PISTOL
Caliber: 9mm. Eight-round magazine, 4-inch bbl., 7.5 inches overall.
Weight: 25.5 oz. (Model 3904) or 34 oz. (Model 3906). Fixed or adj.
sights. Delrin one-piece wraparound checkered grips. Alloy frame w/
blued carbon steel slide (Model 3904) or satin stainless (Model 3906).
Made from 1989 to 1991.
Model 3904 w/adjustable sights . . . . NiB $536 Ex $362 Gd $287
Model 3904 w/fixed sights . . . . NiB $497 Ex $328 Gd $249
Model 3904 w/Novak LC sight . . . . NiB $536 Ex $362 Gd $287
Model 3906 w/adjustable sights . . . . NiB $576 Ex $497 Gd $431
Model 3906 w/Novak LC sight . . . . NiB $546 Ex $499 Gd $366

MODEL 3913/3914 DA AUTOMATIC
Caliber: 9mm Parabellum (Luger). Eight-round magazine, 3.5-inch bbl.,
6.88 inches overall. Weight: 25 oz. Post front sight, fixed or adj. square-
notched rear. One-piece Xenoy wraparound grips w/straight backstrap.
Alloy frame w/stainless or blued slide. Made from 1990 to 1999.

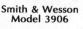

Smith & Wesson
Model 3906

Smith & Wesson
Model 3953

Smith & Wesson
Model 4013

Smith & Wesson
Model 4046

Model 3913 stainless . . . . .NiB $577 Ex $449 Gd $346
Model 3913LS Lady Smith stainless
   w/contoured trigger guard . . . . . NiB $755 Ex $588 Gd $479
Model 3913TSW (intro. 1998). . . . . . . .NiB $739 Ex $596 Gd $479
Model 3914 blued compact
   (disc 1995). . . . . NiB $559 Ex $467 Gd $386

MODEL 3953/3954 DA AUTO PISTOL
Same general specifications as Model 3913/3914 except double action
only. Made from 1990 to 2002.
Model 3953 stainless,
   double action only . . . . NiB $590 Ex $444 Gd $396
Model 3954 blued, double
   action only (disc. 1992) . . . . NiB $530 Ex $431 Gd $340

MODEL 4000 SERIES DA AUTO
Caliber: .40 S&W. 11-round magazine, 4-inch bbl., 7.88 inches overall.
Weight: 28-30 oz. w/alloy frame or 36 oz. w/stainless frame. Post front
sight, adj. or fixed square-notched rear w/2 white dots. Straight back-
strap. One-piece Xenoy wraparound grips. Blued or stainless finish.
Made between 1991 to 1993.
Model 4003 stainless w/alloy frame . . . .NiB $658 Ex $498 Gd $388
Model 4003 TSW w/
   S&W Tactical options. . . . . NiB $870 Ex $779 Gd $608
Model 4004 blued w/alloy frame . . . . . .NiB $601 Ex $449 Gd $397
Model 4006 stainless
   frame, fixed sights . . . . NiB $711 Ex $562 Gd $431
Model 4006 stainless
   frame, Adj. sights . . . . NiB $744 Ex $634 Gd $498
Model 4006 TSW w/
   S&W Tactical options. . . . . NiB $855 Ex $760 Gd $475
Model 4013 stainless frame,
   fixed sights. . . . . NiB $622 Ex $419 Gd $377
Model 4013 TSW w/
   S&W Tactical options. . . . . NiB $855 Ex $760 Gd $475
Model 4014 blued, fixed sights
   (disc. 1993) . . . . NiB $581 Ex $419 Gd $398
Model 4026 w/decocking
   Lever (disc. 1994) . . . . NiB $659 Ex $562 Gd $449
Model 4043 DA only, stainless
   w/alloy frame. . . . . NiB $693 Ex $580 Gd $497
Model 4044 DA only,
   blued w/alloy frame . . . . NiB $569 Ex $448 Gd $346
Model 4046 DA only, stainless
   frame, fixed sights . . . . NiB $739 Ex $668 Gd $499
Model 4046 TSW w/
   S&W Tactical options. . . . . NiB $700 Ex $632 Gd $485
Model 4046 DA only, stainless
   frame, Tritium night sight . . . . . . NiB $724 Ex $634 Gd $475

Smith & Wesson
Model 4053

Smith & Wesson
Model 4586

Smith & Wesson Model 5904
w/Adjustable Sights

MODEL 4013/4014 DA AUTOMATIC
Caliber: .40 S&W. Eight-round capacity, 3.5-inch bbl., 7 inches overall.
Weight: 26 oz. Post front sight, fixed Novak LC rear w/3-dot system.
One-piece Xenoy wraparound grips. Stainless or blued slide w/alloy
frame. Made from 1991 to 1996.
Model 4013 w/stainless slide (disc. 1996) . .NiB $643 Ex $536 Gd $327
Model 4013 Tactical w/stainless slide . . . . .NiB $860 Ex $693 Gd $588
Model 4014 w/blued slide (disc. 1993). . . .NiB $587 Ex $464 Gd $328

MODEL 4053/4054 DA AUTO PISTOL
Same general specifications as Model 4013/4014 except double action
only. Alloy frame fitted w/blued steel slide. Made from 1991 to 1997.
Model 4053 DA only w/stainless slide . . . . .NiB $668 Ex $530 Gd $458
Model 4053 TSW w/ S&W Tactical options NiB $760 Ex $648 Gd $541
Model 4054 DA only w/blued slide
   (disc. 1992) . . . . NiB $709 Ex $464 Gd $378

MODEL 4500 SERIES DA AUTOMATIC
Caliber: .45 ACP. Six-, 7- or 8-round magazine, bbl. lengths: 3.75, 4.25 or 5
inches; 7.13 to 8.63 inches overall. Weight: 34.5 to 38.5 oz. Post front sight,
fixed Novak LC rear w/3-dot system or adj. One-piece Xenoy wraparound
grips. Satin stainless finish. Made from 1991 to 1997.
Model 4505 w/fixed sights, 5-inch bbl. . . . .NiB $693 Ex $597 Gd $386
Model 4505 w/Novak LC sight, 5-inch bbl. .NiB $653 Ex $578 Gd $431
Model 4506 w/fixed sights, 5-inch bbl. . . . .NiB $744 Ex $581 Gd $523
Model 4506 w/Novak LC sight, 5-inch bbl. .NiB $755 Ex $590 Gd $500
Model 4513T (TSW) w/3.75-inch bbl.
   Tactical Combat . . . . .NiB $781 Ex $633 Gd $499

Model 4516 w/3.75-inch bbl . . . . NiB $724 Ex $622 Gd $479
Model 4526 w/5-inch bbl., alloy frame,
  decocking lever, fixed sights. . . . NiB $734 Ex $590 Gd $500
Model 4536, decocking lever . . . . NiB $734 Ex $590 Gd $500
Model 4546, w/3.75-inch bbl., DA only . . . NiB $734 Ex $590 Gd $500
Model 4553T (TSW) w/3.75-inch bbl.
  Tactical Combat. . . . . NiB $780 Ex $665 Gd $459
Model 4556, w/3.75-inch bbl., DA only . . . NiB $700 Ex $601 Gd $397
Model 4563 TSW w/4.25-inch bbl.
  Tactical Combat . . . . NiB $779 Ex $658 Gd $499
Model 4566 w/4.25-inch bbl.,
  ambidextrous safety, fixed sights NiB $693 Ex $536 Gd $453
Model 4566 TSW w/4.25-inch bbl.
  Tactical Combat. . . . . NiB $693 Ex $536 Gd $453
Model 4576 w/4.25-inch bbl.,
  decocking lever . . . . NiB $691 Ex $607 Gd $449
Model 4583T TSW w/4.25-inch bbl.
  Tactical Combat. . . . . NiB $780 Ex $665 Gd $459
Model 4586 w/4.25-inch bbl., DA only . . . . NiB $780 Ex $610 Gd $500
Model 4586 TSW w/4.25-inch bbl.
  Tactical Combat. . . . . NiB $734 Ex $590 Gd $500

MODEL 5900 SERIES DA AUTOMATIC
Caliber: 9mm. 15-round magazine, 4-inch bbl., 7.5 inches overall.
Weight: 26-38 oz. Fixed or adj. sights. One-piece Xenoy wraparound
grips. Alloy frame w/stainless-steel slide (Model 5903) or blued slide
(Model 5904) stainless-steel frame and slide (Model 5906). Made from
1990 to 1997.
Model 5903 w/adjustable sights . . . . NiB $693 Ex $556 Gd $386
Model 5903 w/Novak LC rear sight . . . . . . NiB $780 Ex $691 Gd $386
Model 5903 TSW w/4-inch bbl.,
  Tactical Combat. . . . . NiB $767 Ex $658 Gd $497
Model 5904 w/adjustable sights . . . . NiB $581 Ex $468 Gd $376
Model 5904 w/Novak LC rear sight . . . . . . NiB $599 Ex $474 Gd $398
Model 5905 L/C Adjustable Sights . . . . . . NiB $693 Ex $549 Gd $398
Model 5905 w/Novak LC rear sight . . . . . . NiB $733 Ex $634 Gd $464
Model 5906 w/adjustable sights . . . . NiB $658 Ex $544 Gd $439
Model 5906 w/Novak LC rear sight . . . . . . NiB $658 Ex $544 Gd $439
Model 5906 w/Tritium night sight . . . . NiB $755 Ex $650 Gd $562
Model 5906 TSW w/4-inch bbl.,
  Tactical Combat. . . . . NiB $862 Ex $733 Gd $544
Model 5924 w/anodized frame, blued slide NiB $659 Ex $508 Gd $337
Model 5926 w/stainless frame, decocking lever NiB $644 Ex $543 Gd $444
Model 5943 w/alloy frame/
  stainless slide, DA only . . . . NiB $601 Ex $444 Gd $351
Model 5943 TSW w/4-inch bbl., DA only . . NiB $650 Ex $546 Gd $429
Model 5944 w/alloy frame/
  blued slide, DA only . . . . NiB $689 Ex $556 Gd $456
Model 5946 w/stainless frame/slide, DA only NiB $658 Ex $534 Gd $376
Model 5946 TSW w/4-inch bbl., DA only . . NiB $774 Ex $632 Gd $337

MODEL 6900 COMPACT SERIES
Double action. Caliber: 9mm. 12-round magazine, 3.5-inch bbl., 6.88 inches
overall. Weight: 26.5 oz. AmbidExtrous safety. Post front sight, fixed Novak LC
rear w/3-dot system. Alloy frame w/blued carbon steel slide (Model 6904) or
stainless steel slide (Model 6906). Made 1989 to 1997.
Model 6904 . . . . NiB $601 Ex $499 Gd $377
Model 6906 w/fixed sights . . . . NiB $621 Ex $546 Gd $499
Model 6906 w/Tritium night sight . . . . . . NiB $843 Ex $621 Gd $500
Model 6926
  w/decocking lever . . . . NiB $691 Ex $587 Gd $374
Model 6944
  in DA only . . . . NiB $612 Ex $546 Gd $342

Model 6946
in DA only ,fixed sights . . . . NiB $709 Ex $577 Gd $395
Model 6946 w/Tritium night sight . . . . . . NiB $709 Ex $544 Gd $433

M&P9 AUTOMATIC PISTOL . . . . NiB $569 Ex $320 Gd $270
Striker fired action. Caliber: 9mm. 10- or 17-round magazine. 4.25-in.
bbl., polymer frame w/three interchangeable grip inserts and accessory
rail, low profile fixed sights, w/ or w/o thumb safety. Weight: 24 oz.
Black Melonite finish. Made from 2006 to date.
M&P9L (5-in. bbl., discont. 2010) . . . . . NiB $575 Ex $400 Gd $330
M&P9 Compact (3.5-in. bbl.) . . . . NiB $569 Ex $320 Gd $270
M&P9 JG (Julie Goloski-Golob design collaboration,
discont. 2012). . . . . NiB $465 Ex $330 Gd $280
M&P9 VTAC (Viking Tactics design collaboration,
  4.5-in. bbl. w/full size frame, FDE finish)NiB $799 Ex $430 Gd $330

M&P9 C.O.R.E. AUTOMATIC PISTOL . . . NiB $729 Ex $480 Gd $350
Similar to M&P9 or M&P40 except set up for competition w/optic
mount, fixed 3-dot sights. Made from 2013 to date.

M&P9 PRO SERIES AUTOMATIC PISTOL NiB $699 Ex $410 Gd $310
Similar to M&P9 except w/5-in. bbl., fiber optic Novak sights, optic
ready. Made from 2012 to date.

M&P40 AUTOMATIC PISTOL . . . . NiB $569 Ex $320 Gd $270
Similar to M&P9 except in .40 S&W w/10- or 15-round magazine.
Made from 2006 to date.
M&P40 Compact (3.5-in. bbl.) . . . . NiB $569 Ex $320 Gd $270
M&P40 VTAC (Viking Tactics design collaboration,
  4.5-in. bbl. w/full size frame, FDE finish)NiB $799 Ex $430 Gd $330

M&P40 PRO SERIES AUTOMATIC PISTOL NiB $699 Ex $410 Gd $310
Similar to M&P40 except w/5-in. bbl., fiber optic Novak sights, optic
ready. Made from 2012 to date.

M&P45 AUTOMATIC PISTOL . . . . NiB $599 Ex $330 Gd $270
Similar to M&P9 except in .45 ACP w/10-round magazine. Made from
2006 to date.
M&P45 Compact (4-in. bbl.) . . . . NiB $599 Ex $330 Gd $270

M&P357 AUTOMATIC PISTOL . . . . NiB $585 Ex $380 Gd $280
Similar to M&P9 except in .357 SIG w/10- or 15-round magazine.
Made from 2006 to 2010.
M&P357 Compact (3.5-in. bbl.) . . . . NiB $585 Ex $380 Gd $280

M&P BODYGUARD AUTOMATIC PISTOL NiB $380 Ex $240 Gd $185
DAO. Caliber: .380 ACP. 6-round magazine, 2.75-in. bbl., polymer
frame. Weight: 11.9 oz. Black Melonite finish. Made from 2014 to
date.

Smith & Wesson
Model 1

SIGMA SW380 AUTOMATIC PISTOL . . . **NiB $536 Ex $357 Gd $290**
Caliber: .380 ACP. Double-action only. Six-round magazine, 3-inch bbl., weight: 14 oz. Black integral polymer gripframe w/checkered back and front straps. Fixed channel sights. Polymer frame w/hammerless steel slide. Made from 1994 to 1996.

SIGMA SW9 SERIES AUTOMATIC PISTOL
Caliber: 9mm Parabellum. Double action only. 10-round magazine, 3.25-, 4- or 4.5-inch bbl., weight: 17.9 oz. to 24.7 oz. Polymer frame w/ hammerless steel slide. Post front sight and drift adjustable rear w/3-dot system. Gray or black integral polymer gripframe w/checkered back and front straps. Made from 1994 to 1996.
Model SW9C (compact w/3.25-inch bbl.) . .NiB $500 Ex $425 Gd $326
Model SW9F (blue slide w/4.5-inch bbl.). . .NiB $500 Ex $425 Gd $326
Model SW9M (compact w/3.25-inch bbl.) . .NiB $342 Ex $255 Gd $165
Model SW9V (stainless slide w/4-inch bbl.) .NiB $408 Ex $304 Gd $229
Tritium night sight, add $25

M&P SHIELD AUTOMATIC PISTOL. . . . . **NiB $449 Ex $280 Gd $210**
Similar to M&P9 and M&P40 except sub-compact variant w/3.1-in. bbl., 6-, 7- or 8-round magazine. Weight: 19 oz. Black Melonite finish. Made from 2012 to date.

SW40 SERIES AUTOMATIC PISTOL
Same general specifications as SW9 series except chambered for .40 S&W w/4- or 4.5-inch bbl., weight: 24.4 to 26 oz. Made 1994 to 1998.
Model SW40C (compact w/4-inch bbl.) . . . .NiB $497 Ex $346 Gd $249
Model SW40F (blue slide w/4.5-inch bbl.) . .NiB $497 Ex $346 Gd $249
Model SW40V (stainless slide
   w/4-inch bbl.) . . . . NiB $497 Ex $346 Gd $249
w/Tritium night sight, add $25

MODEL 1891 SINGLE-SHOT TARGET PISTOL, FIRST MODEL
Hinged frame. Calibers: .22 LR, .32 S&W, .38 S&W. Bbl. lengths: 6-, 8- and 10-inches, approx. 13.5 inches overall (with 10-inch bbl.). Weight: About 25 oz. Target sights, barrel catch rear adj. for windage and elevation. Blued finish. Square butt, hard rubber grips. Made 1893-1905. Note: This model was available also as a combination arm w/accessory .38 revolver bbl. and cylinder enabling conversion to a pocket revolver. It has the frame of the .38 SA revolver Model 1891 w/side flanges, hand and cylinder stop slots.
Single-shot pistol, .22 LR . . . . .NiB $2890 Ex $2643 Gd $2425
Single-shot pistol, .32 S&W or .38 S&W NiB $2320 Ex $1996 Gd $1748
Combination set, revolver
   and single-shot barrel. . . . . . NiB $3635 Ex $3145 Gd $2869

MODEL 1891 SINGLE-SHOT TARGET PISTOL,
SECOND MODEL. . . . . NiB $2797 Ex $2466 Gd $1580
Similar to the First Model except side flanges, hand and stop slots eliminated, cannot be converted to revolver, redesigned rear sight. Caliber: .22 LR only, 10-inch bbl. only. Made from 1905 to 1909.

PERFECTED SINGLE-SHOT TARGET PISTOL
Similar to Second Model except has double-action lockwork. Caliber: .22 LR only, 10-inch bbl. Checkered walnut grips, Extended square-butt target type. Made 1909-23. Note: In 1920 and thereafter, this model was made w/barrels having bore diameter of .223 instead of .226 and tight, short chambering. The first group of these pistols was produced for the U.S. Olympic Team of 1920, thus the designation Olympic Model.
Pre-1920 type. . . . . NiB $2314 Ex $1945 Gd $1566
Olympic model . . . . NiB $2665 Ex $2380 Gd $2235

STRAIGHT LINE SINGLE-SHOT
TARGET PISTOL. . . . . NiB $3345 Ex $3267 Gd $3095
Frame shaped like that of an automatic pistol, barrel swings to the left on pivot for Extracting and loading, straight-line trigger and hammer movement. Caliber: .22 LR. 10-inch bbl., 11.25 inches overall. Weight: 34 oz. Target sights. Blued finish. Smooth walnut grips. Supplied in metal case w/ screwdriver and cleaning rod. Made from 1925 to 1936.

- REVOLVERS -

MODEL 1 HAND EJECTOR
DA REVOLVER. . . . . NiB $2670   Ex $2000   Gd $1289
First Model. Forerunner of the .32 Hand Ejector and Regulation Police models, this was the first S&W revolver of the solid-frame, swing-out cylinder type. Top strap of this model is longer than those of later models, and it lacks the usual S&W cylinder latch. Caliber: .22 Long. Bbl., lengths: 3.25-, 4.25-, and 6-inches. Fixed sights. Blued or nickel finish. Round butt, hard rubber stocks. Made from 1896 to 1903.

NO. 3 SA FRONTIER . . . . NiB $5170 Ex $4350 Gd $3095
Caliber: .44-40 WCF. Bbl., lengths: 4-, 5- and 6.5-inch. Fixed or target sights. Blued or nickel finish. Round, hard rubber or checkered walnut grips. Made from 1885 to 1908.

NO. 3 SA (NEW MODEL) . NiB $7245 Ex $6095 Gd $4270
Hinged frame. Six-round cylinder. Caliber: .44 S&W Russian. Bbl., lengths: 4-, 5-, 6-, 6.5-, 7.5- and 8-inches. Fixed or target sights. Blued or nickel finish. Round, hard rubber or checkered walnut grips. Made from 1878 to 1908. Note: Value shown is for standard model. Specialist collectors recognize numerous variations w/a range of higher values.
Performance Center Schofield Model of 2000
   (modern repro) . . . . NiB $1800

NO. 3 SA TARGET . . . . . NiB $6996 Ex $3890 Gd $3175
Hinged frame. Six-round cylinder. Calibers: .32/.44 S&W, .38/.44 S&W Gallery & Target. 6.5-inch bbl. only. Fixed or target sights. Blued or nickel finish. Round, hard rubber or checkered walnut grips. Made from 1887 to 1910.

Smith & Wesson
Model 10 (Two-inch Barrel)

Smith & Wesson
Model 12 (Two-inch Barrel)

Smith & Wesson Model 13
(Heavy Barrel)

Smith & Wesson
Model 14

MODEL 10 .38 MILITARY & POLICE DA

Also called Hand Ejector Model of 1902, Hand Ejector Model of 1905, Model K. Manufactured substantially in its present form since 1902, this model has undergone numerous changes, most of them minor. Round- or square-butt models, the latter intro. in 1904. Caliber: .38 Special. Six-round cylinder, bbl. lengths: 2-(intro. 1933), 4-, 5-, 6- and 6.5-inch (latter disc. 1915) also 4-inch heavy bbl., (intro. 1957); 11.13 inches overall (square-butt model). Round-butt model is 1/4-inch shorter, weight: About 1/2 oz. less. Fixed sights. Blued or nickel finish. Checkered walnut grips, hard rubber available in round-butt style. Current Model 10 has short action. Made 1902 to date. Note: S&W Victory Model, wartime version of the M & P .38, was produced for the U.S. Government from 1940 to the end of the war. A similar revolver, designated .38/200 British Service Revolver, was produced for the British Government during the same period. These arms have either brush-polish or sandblast blued finish, and most of them have plain, smooth walnut grips, lanyard swivels.

Model of 1902 (1902-05)	NiB $639	Ex $536	Gd $362
Model of 1905 (1905-40)	NiB $1165	Ex $910	Gd $602
.38/200 British Service (1940-45)	NiB $1165	Ex $910	Gd $602
Victory Model (1942-45)	NiB $643	Ex $529	Gd $425
Model of 1944 (1945-48)	NiB $785	Ex $431	Gd $319
Model 10 (1948-date)	NiB $530	Ex $437	Gd $319

MODEL 10 .38 MILITARY
& POLICE HEAVY BARREL . . . . . . NiB $632 Ex $499 Gd $337
Same as standard Model 10 except has heavy 4-inch bbl., weight: 34 oz. Made from 1957 to 1986.

MODEL 10 CLASSICS SERIES . . . . NiB $632 Ex $499 Gd $337
Recent manufacture of Model 10 except chambered in .38 Spl.+P and w/heavy 4-in. bbl., fixed sights, blued finish, checkered wood grips. Made from 2010 to date.

MODEL 12 .38 M&P
AIRWEIGHT . . . . NiB $544 Ex $388 Gd $290
Same as standard Military & Police except has light alloy frame, f8rnished w/2- or 4-inch bbl. only, weight: 18 oz. (w/2-inch bbl.). Made from 1952 to 1986.

MODEL 12/13 (AIR FORCE MODEL)
DA REVOLVER . . . . NiB $536 Ex $439 Gd $265
Special "Air Force" Model designed with alloy cylinder and frame to be used as a "Survival Weapon" for air crews. Athough this weapon was actually a first-series Model 12, the Air Force stamped "M13" on the top strap. Issued 1953 but recalled for function problems in 1954.

MODEL 13 .357
MILITARY/POLICE . . . . NiB $487 Ex $318 Gd $204
Same as Model 10 .38 Military & Police Heavy Barrel except chambered for .357 Magnum and .38 Special w/3- or 4-inch bbl. Round or square butt configuration. Made from1974 to 1998.

MODELS 14 (K-38) AND 16 (K-32) MASTERPIECE REVOLVERS
Calibers: .22 LR, .22 Magnum Rimfire, .32 S&W Long, .38 Special. Six-round cylinder. DA/SA. Bbl. lengths: 4- (.22 WMR only), 6-, 8.38-inch (latter not available in K32), 11.13 inches overall (with 6-inch bbl.). Weight: 38.5 oz. (with 6-inch bbl.). Click adj. rear sight, Partridge front. Blued finish. Checkered walnut grips. Made from 1947 to date. (Model 16 disc. 1974; 3,630 produced; reissued 1990 to 1993.)

Model 14 (K-38 DA)	NiB $577	Ex $318	Gd $209
Model 14 (K-38 SA, 6-in. bbl.)	NiB $693	Ex $366	Gd $220
Model 14 (K-38 SA, 8.38-in. bbl.)	NiB $474	Ex $351	Gd $259
Model 16 (K-32 DA) 1st Issue	NiB $3500	Ex $3316	Gd $889
Model 16 (K-32 DA)	NiB $2579	Ex $1138	Gd $974

MODEL 14 CLASSICS SERIES . . . . NiB $695 EX $375 GD $340
Recent manufacture of Model 14 except chambered in .38 Spl.+P and 6-in. bbl., adj. sights, blued or nickel finish, checkered wood grips. Made from 2009 to 2011.

MODELS 15 (.38) AND 18 (.22) COMBAT MASTERPIECE DA REVOLVERS
Same as K-22 and K-38 Masterpiece but w/2- (.38) or 4-inch bbl., and Baughman quick-draw front sight. 9.13 inches overall w/4-inch bbl., Weight: 34 oz. (.38 cal.). Made from 1950 to 1999.

Model 15	NiB $805	Ex $602	Gd $456
Model 18 (disc. 1985)	NiB $691	Ex $523	Gd $487
w/target options TH & TT, add			$50

MODEL 15 CLASSICS SERIES . . . . NiB $780 EX $300 GD $270
Recent manufacture of Model 15 except chambered in .38 Spl.+P and 4-in. bbl., adj. sights, blued finish, checkered wood grips. Made from 2010 to 2011.

MODEL 17 K-22 MASTERPIECE DA REVOLVER
Caliber: 22 LR. Six-round cylinder, Bbl lengths: 4, 6 or 8.38 inches. 11.13 inches overall (with 6-inch bbl.). Weight: 38 oz. (with 6-inch bbl.). Partridge-type front sight, S&W micrometer click rear. Checkered walnut Service grips with S&W momogram. S&W blued finish. Made from 1947-93 and from 1996-98.

Model 17 (4-inch bbl.)	NiB $632	Ex $453	Gd $347
Model 17 (6-inch bbl.)	NiB $632	Ex $453	Gd $347
Model 17 (8.38-inch bbl.)	NiB $823	Ex $546	Gd $479
w/target options TH & TT, add			$50

MODEL 17 CLASSICS SERIES . . . . NiB $989 EX $480 GD $430
Recent manufacture of Model 17 except w/6-in. bbl., adj. sights, blued finish, checkered wood grips. Made from 2009 to date.

MODEL 18 . . . . NiB $750 EX $480 GD $420
Similar to Model 17 except w/4-in. bbl., adj. sights, blued finish, checkered wood grips. Made from 1949 to 1986.

MODEL 18 CLASSICS SERIES . . . . NiB $695 EX $400 GD $360
Recent manufacture of Model 18. Made from 2009 to 2011.

MODEL 19 .357 COMBAT MAGNUM DA REVOLVER

Caliber: .357 Magnum. Six-round cylinder, bbl. lengths: 2.5 (round butt), 4, or 6 inches, 9.5 inches overall (with 4-inch bbl.). Weight: 35 oz. (with 4-inch bbl.). Click adj. rear sight, ramp front. Blued or nickel finish. Target grips of checkered Goncalo Alves. Made from 1956 to date (2.5- and 6-inch bbls. were disc. in 1991).

Model 19 (2.5-inch bbl.). . . . . . . NiB $601 Ex $431 Gd $319
Model 19 (4-inch bbl.) . . . . NiB $601 Ex $431 Gd $319
Model 19 (6-inch bbl.) . . . . NiB $601 Ex $431 Gd $319
Model 19 (8.38-inch bbl.). . . . . . NiB $601 Ex $431 Gd $319
w/target options TH & TT, add $75

MODEL 20 .38/44 HEAVY DUTY DA

Caliber: .38 Special. Six-round cylinder, bbl. lengths: 4, 5 and 6.5 inches;10.38 inches overall (with 5-inch bbl.). Weight: 40 oz. (with 5-inch bbl.). Fixed sights. Blued or nickel finish. Checkered walnut grips. Short action after 1948. Made from 1930-56 and from 1957 to 67.

Pre-World War II . . . . NiB $1970 Ex $1770 Gd $525
Post-war. . . . . NiB $2270 Ex $1620 Gd $910

MODEL 21 .44 MILITARY DA REVOLVER

Postwar version of the 1926 Model 44 Military. Caliber: .44 Special, 6-round cylinder. Bbl. lengths: 4-, 5- and 6.5-inches. 11.75 inches overall (w/6.5-inch bbl.) Weight: 39.5 oz. (w/6.5-inch bbl.). Fixed front sight w/ square-notch rear sight; target model has micrometer click rear sight adj. for windage and elevation. Checkered walnut grips w/S&W monogram. Blued or nickel finish. Made 1950 to 1967.

Model 21 (4- or 5-inch bbl.). . . . . . .NiB $2979 Ex $2035 Gd $809
Model 21 (6.5-inch bbl.), add. 50%

MODEL 22 1950 ARMY DA . . . . . NiB $2025 Ex $1735 Gd $816
Postwar version of the 1917 Army w/same general specifications except redesigned hammer. Made from 1950 to 1967.

MODEL 22 CLASSICS SERIES . . . . . . NiB $850 Ex $470 Gd $420
Recent manufacture of Model 22 except in .45 ACP, 4- or 5.5-in. bbl., blued finish, Altamont wood grip. Made from 2007 to 2010.

MODEL 22 CLASSICS SERIES

MODEL OF 1917. . . . . NiB $999 Ex $470 Gd $420
Recent manufacture of Model 1917 except in .45 ACP, 5.5-in. bbl., N-Frame, lanyard loop, blued finish, Altamont wood grip. Made from 2008 to 2012.

.22/.32 TARGET DA REVOLVER

Also known as the "Bekeart Model." Design based upon ".32 Hand Ejector." Caliber: .22 LR (recessed head cylinder for high-speed cartridges intro. 1935). Six-round cylinder, 6-inch bbl., 10.5 inches overall. Weight: 23 oz. Adj. target sights. Blued finish. Checkered walnut grips. Made from 1911-53. Note: In 1911, San Francisco gun dealer Phil Bekeart, who suggested this model, received 292 pieces.

Smith & Wesson Model 17 K-22

Smith & Wesson Model 18 (See Model 15 for description)

Smith & Wesson Model 19 (Round Butt)

Smith & Wesson Model 15

These are the true "Bekeart Model" revolvers and are marked with separate identification numbers on the base of the wooden grip.
.22/.32 TARGET DA REVOLVER . . . . .NiB $1160 Ex $760 Gd $498
.22/.32 (early prod. 1-3000), add. 20%
.22/.32 Bekeart model . . . . .NiB $1565 Ex $1329 Gd $752

.22/.32 KIT GUN . . . . NiB $850 Ex $580 Gd $319
Same as .22/.32 Target except has 2- or 4-inch bbl., round grips, 6 or 8 inches overall, weight: 19-21oz. Made from 1935 to 1953.

Smith & Wesson
Model 19 (Square Butt)

Smith & Wesson
Model 22/32 Kit Gun

Smith & Wesson
Model 20

Smith & Wesson
Model 22/32 Target
Revolver

Smith & Wesson
Model 21

Smith & Wesson
Model 23

Smith & Wesson
Model 22

MODEL 24 1950 .44 TARGET DA REVOLVER

Postwar version of the 1921 Model .44 Hand Ejector. .44 Special with 4-, 5- or 6.5-inch ribbed bbl., redesigned hammer, micrometer click rear sight. Matte or polished blue finish. Made from 1950-67. Model 24 reintroduced in 1983 only.

Model 24 (1950 w/6.5-inch bbl. . . . . . .NiB $2770 Ex $1696 Gd $897
Model 24 (1950) w/4-inch bbl., add. 20%
Model 24 (1950) w/5-inch bbl., add 100%
Model 24 (1950) w/polished
  blue finish, add 25%
Model 24 (1950)
  w/nickel finish, add 65%
Model 24
.44 Target reintroduced (7,500 produced in 1983-84)
  (w/4-inch bbl.) . . . . .NiB $760 Ex $560 Gd $402
Model 24 (w/6.5-inch bbl.). . . . . .NiB $730 Ex $553 Gd $365
Model 24-3 .44
Lew Horton Special
w/3-inch bbl. (produced in 1983) . . . . . .NiB $860 Ex $654 Gd $380
Classics w/6.5-inch bbl. (2008-2012) . . .NiB $770 Ex $554 Gd $370
Classics w/ nickel finish, add 8%

MODEL 23 .38-44 OUTDOORSMAN DA REVOLVER

Target version of the .38/44 Heavy Duty. 6.5- or 8.75-inch bbl., weight: 41.75 oz. Target sights, micrometer-click rear on postwar models. Blued or nickel finish. 1950 transition model has ribbed barrel, redesigned hammer. Made from 1930 to 1967.

Pre-war model (plain bbl.) . . NiB $2555 Ex $1958 Gd $1278
Post-war (ribbed bbl.). . . . . . . NiB $1724 Ex $1398 Gd $780

MODEL 24-6 CLASSICS SERIES . . . . . NiB $770 Ex $470 Gd $420
Recent manufacture of Model 24 except in .45 ACP, 3- or 6.5-in. bbl., blued or nickel finish, square butt wood grip. Made from 2006 to 2012.

MODEL 25 1955 .45 TARGET DA REVOLVER
Same as 1950 Model .44 Target, but chambered for .45 ACP, .45 Auto Rim or .45 LC w/4-, 6- or 6.5-inch bbl. Made from 1955 to 1991 in several variations. Note: In 1961, the .45 ACP was designated Model 25-2, and in 1978 the .45 LC was designated Model 25-5.

Model 25 1955 .45 Target
.45 ACP w/4- or 6-inch bbl. . . . . NiB $780 Ex $587 Gd $434
.45 ACP w/6.5-inch pinned bbl. . . . . NiB $767 Ex $660 Gd $449
.45 LC early production . . . . NiB $4245 Ex $4040 Gd $3779
Model 25-2 .45 ACP
  Lew Horton Specialw/3-inch bbl. NiB $541 Ex $453 Gd $346
Model 25-2 (w/4-inch bbl.) . . . . NiB $601 Ex $485 Gd $402
Model 25-3 (w/6.5-inch bbl.) . . . . NiB $734 Ex $544 Gd $429
Model 25-5 .45 LC w/4-inch bbl. . . . . NiB $601 Ex $484 Gd $377
Model 25-3 (w/6.5-inch bbl.) . . . . NiB $648 Ex $530 Gd $362
Model 25 Classics (reintro. 2008) . . . . NiB $980 Ex $530 Gd $362

MODEL 25 CLASSICS SERIES . . . . . NiB $1010 Ex $470 Gd $420
Recent manufacture of Model 25 except w/3- or 6.5-in. bbl., blued or nickel finish, square butt, wood grip. Made from 2007 to date.

MODEL 26 1950 .45 LIGHT TARGET DA REVOLVER
Similar to 1950 Model Target except w/lighter bbl. Note: Lighter profile was not well received. (Only 2,768 produced)
Model 26 (.45 ACP or .45 Auto Rim
w/6.5-inch bbl.) . . . . NiB $4590 Ex $4295 Gd $3988
Model 26 .45 LC, (200 produced) . . . . . NiB $4590 Ex $4295 Gd $3988
w/4- or 5-inch bbl., ... $50

MODEL 27 .357 MAGNUM DA
Caliber: .357 Magnum. Six-round cylinder, bbl. lengths: 3.5-, 4-, 5-, 6-, 6.5-and 8.38-inches, 11.38 inches overall (with 6-inch bbl.). Weight: 44 oz. (with 6-inch bbl.). Adj. target sights, Baughman quick-draw ramp front sight on 3.5-inch bbl., Blued or nickel finish. Checkered walnut grips. Made from 1935-94. Note: Until 1938, the .357 Magnum was custom made in any barrel length from 3.5-inch to 8.75-inch. Each of these revolvers was accompanied by a registration certificate and has its registration number stamped on the inside of the yoke. Postwar magnums have a redesigned hammer w/shortened fall and the new S&W micrometer click rear sight.
Pre-war model
(Reg number on yoke) . . . . NiB $893 Ex $730 Gd $615
Pre-war model w/out reg number . . . . NiB $862 Ex $653 Gd $612
Early model w/pinned bbl., recessed cyl. . . . NiB $895 Ex $755 Gd $624
Late model w/8. 38-inch bbl. . . . . NiB $895 Ex $755 Gd $624
Late model w/3.5 to 5-inch bbl. . . . . NiB $895 Ex $755 Gd $624
Late model, other bbl. lengths . . . . NiB $915 Ex $785 Gd $612

MODEL 27 CLASSICS SERIES . . NiB $1020 Ex $470 Gd $420
Recent manufacture of Model 25 except w/4- or 6.5-in. bbl., blued or nickel finish, wood grip. Made from 2008 to date.

MODEL 28 HIGHWAY PATROLMAN
Caliber: .357 Magnum. Six-round cylinder, bbl. lengths: 4- or 6-inches, 11.25 inches overall (with 6-inch bbl.). Weight: 44 oz. (with 6-inch bbl.). Adj. rear sight, ramp front. Blued finish. Checkered walnut grips, Magna or target type. Made from 1954 to 1986.
Pre-war registered model
(reg number on yoke) . . . . NiB $893 Ex $780 Gd $610
Pre-war model without registration numberNiB $1190 Ex $975 Gd $700
Early model w/pinned bbl.,
  recessed cylinder, 5-screws . . . . NiB $895 Ex $734 Gd $632
Late model, all bbl. lengths . . . . NiB $536 Ex $362 Gd $255

Smith & Wesson
Model 24 Target

Smith & Wesson
Model 25 Target

Smith & Wesson
Model 27

Smith & Wesson
Model 28

MODEL 29 .44 MAGNUM DA REVOLVER
Caliber: .44 Magnum. Six-round cylinder. bbl., lengths: 4-, 5-, 6.5-, 8.38-inches. 11.88 inches overall (with 6.5-inch bbl.). Weight: 47 oz. (with 6.5-inch bbl.). Click adj. rear sight, ramp front. Blued or nickel finish. Checkered Goncalo Alves target grips. Made from 1956 to 1998. Early Production Standard Series (disc. 1983)
3-Screw model (1962-83) . . . . NiB $970 Ex $843 Gd $686
4-Screw model (1957-61) . . . . NiB $2200 Ex $1693 Gd $880
5-Screw model (1956-57) . . . . NiB $3497 Ex $2895 Gd $2630
w/5-inch bbl., 3- or 4-screw models, add 100%

Smith & Wesson
Model 29

Smith & Wesson
Model 31

Smith & Wesson
Model 32

Smith & Wesson
Model 34

Late Production standard series (disc. 1998)
Model 29 (w/4- or 6.5-inch bbl.) . . . . .NiB $870   Ex $669   Gd $432
Model 29 (w/3-inch bbl.,
  Lew Horton Special) . . . . .NiB $920   Ex $689   Gd $432
Model 29 (w/8.38-inch bbl.) . . . . .NiB $895   Ex $679   Gd $432
Model 29 Classic (w/5- or 6.5-inch bbl.) . . .NiB $610   Ex $539   Gd $332
Model 29 Classic (w/8.38-inch bbl.) . . . . . .NiB $630   Ex $540   Gd $345
Model 29 Classic DX (w/6.5-in. and
  8.38-in. bbl.) . . . . .NiB $1260   Ex $648   Gd $556
Model 29 Classic DX (w/5-inch bbl.) . . . .NiB $1410   Ex $798   Gd $656
Model 29 Magna Classic (w/7.5-inch
  ported bbl.) . . . . .NiB $1170   Ex $859   Gd $537
Model 29 Silhouette (w/10.63-inch bbl.) . . .NiB $860   Ex $656   Gd $437

MODEL 29 CLASSICS SERIES . . . . . . NiB $999   Ex $480   Gd $420
Recent manufacture of Model 29 except w/3-, 4- or 6.5-in. bbl., blued or nickel finish, wood grip. Made from 2008 to date.

MODEL 30 .32 HAND EJECTOR
DA REVOLVER . . . . .NiB $554   Ex $469   Gd $356
Caliber: .32 S&W Long. Six-round cylinder, bbl. lengths: 2-(intro. 1949), 3-, 4- and 6-inches, 8 inches overall (with 4-inch bbl.). Weight: 18 oz. (with 4-inch bbl.). Fixed sights. Blued or nickel finish. Round, checkered walnut or hard rubber grips. Made from 1903-76.

MODELS 31 & 33 REGULATION POLICE DA REVOLVER
Same basic type as .32 Hand Ejector except has square buttgrips. Calibers: .32 S&W Long (Model 31) .38 S&W (Model 33). Six-round cylinder in .32 cal., 5-round in .38 caliber. Bbl., lengths: 2- (intro. 1949), 3-, 4- and 6-inches in .32 cal., 4-inch only in .38 cal., 8.5 inches overall (with 4-inch bbl.). Weight: 18 oz. (.38 cal. w/4-inch bbl.), 18.75 oz. (.32 cal. w/4-inch bbl.). Fixed sights. Blued or nickel finish. Checkered walnut grips. Made from 1917. Model 33 disc. in 1974; Model 31 disc. in 1992.
Model 31 . . . . NiB $546   Ex $306   Gd $255
Model 33 . . . . NiB $448   Ex $283   Gd $198

MODEL 32 DA REVOLVER . . . . .NiB $546   Ex $467   Gd $219
Hinged frame. Caliber: .32 S&W. Five-round cylinder, bbl. lengths: 3-, 3.5- and 6-inches. Fixed sights. Blued or nickel finish. Hard rubber grips. Made from 1880-1919. Note: Value shown applies generally to the several varieties. exception is the rare first issue of 1880 (identified by squared sideplate and serial no. 1 to 30) valued up to $2,500.

MODEL 32 TERRIER DA . . . . .NiB $479   Ex $342   Gd $255
Caliber: .38 S&W. Five-round cylinder, 2-inch bbl., 6.25 inches overall. Weight: 17 oz. Fixed sights. Blued or nickel finish. Checkered walnut or hard rubber grips. Built on .32 Hand Ejector frame. Made from 1936-74.

MODEL 33 .32-20 MILITARY & POLICE
DA REVOLVER . . . . .NiB $2845   Ex $2719   Gd $2530
Same as M&P 38 except chambered for .32-20 Winchester cartridge. First intro. in the 1899 model, M&P revolvers were produced in this caliber until about 1940. Values same as M&P .38 models.

MODEL 34
DA REVOLVER . . . . .NiB $756   Ex $408   Gd $305
Caliber: .22 LR. Six-shot cylinder, 2-inch or 4-inch bbl. and round or square grips, blued or nickel finish. Made from 1936-91.

MODEL 35 1953
.22/.32 TARGET . . . . .NiB $772   Ex $590   Gd $362
Same general specifications as previous model .22/.32 Target except has micrometer-click rear sight. Magna type target grips. Weight: 25 oz. Made from 1953-74.

GRADING: **NiB** = New in Box   **Ex** = Excellent or NRA 95%   **Gd** = Good or NRA 68%

MODEL 36 CHIEFS SPECIAL DA
Based on .32 Hand Ejector w/frame lengthened to permit longer cylinder for .38 Special cartridge. Caliber: .38 Special. Five-round cylinder, bbl. lengths: 2- or 3-inches, 6.5 inches overall (with 2-inch bbl.). Weight: 19 oz. Fixed sights. Blued or nickel finish. Checkered walnut grips, round or square butt. Made from 1952 to date.

Blued model . . . . NiB $638 Ex $425 Gd $255
Nickel model . . . . NiB $648 Ex $437 Gd $265
Early model (5-screw, small trigger
  guard, S/N 1-2500) . . . . NiB $668 Ex $541 Gd $386
Model 36 Ladysmith (1990-2008) NiB $480 Ex $290 Gd $186

MODEL 37 AIRWEIGHT
CHIEFS SPECIAL . . . . NiB $500 Ex $366 Gd $225
Same general specifications as standard Chiefs Special except has light alloy frame, weight: 12.5 oz. w/2-inch bbl., blued finish only. Made from 1954 to 1995

MODEL 38 BODYGUARD AIRWEIGHT DA REVOLVER
Shrouded hammer. Light alloy frame. Caliber: .38 Special. Five-round cylinder, 2- or 3-inch bbl., 6.38 inches overall (w/2-inch bbl). Weight: 14.5 oz. Fixed sights. Blued or nickel finish. Checkered walnut grips. Made from 1955 to 1998.

Blued model. . . . . NiB $479 Ex $347 Gd $235
Nickel model . . . . NiB $500 Ex $362 Gd $274
Early model (pinned bbl. &
  recessed cyl., pre-1981) . . . . . . NiB $485 Ex $342 Gd $243

MODEL .38 DA REVOLVER . . NiB $945 Ex $734 Gd $544
Hinged frame. Caliber: .38 S&W. Five-round cylinder, bbl. lengths: 4-, 4.25-, 5-, 6-, 8- and 10-inch. Fixed sights. Blued or nickel finish. Hard rubber grips. Made from 1880-1911. Note: Value shown applies generally to the several varieties. exceptions are the first issue of 1880 (identified by squared sideplate and serial no. 1 to 4,000) and the 8- and 10-inch bbl. models of the third issue (1884 to 1995).

MODEL .38 HAND EJECTOR DA
Military & Police — First Model. Resembles Colt New Navy in general appearance, lacks bbl., lug and locking bolt common to all later S&W hand ejector models. Caliber: .38 Long Colt. Six-round cylinder, bbl. lengths: 4-, 5-, 6- and 6.5-inch, 11.5 inches overall (with 6.5-inch bbl.). Fixed sights. Blued or nickel finish. Round, checkered walnut or hard rubber grips. Made from 1899 to 1902.

Standard model
  (civilian issue) . . . . NiB $1870 Ex $1322 Gd $1132
Army Model (marked U.S.
  Army Model, 1000 issued) . . NiB $3725 Ex $3397 Gd $2935
Navy Model (marked USN,
  1000 issued) . . . . NiB $4495 Ex $3800 Gd $3412

.38 MILITARY & POLICE
TARGET DA . . . . NiB $3725 Ex $3397 Gd $2740
Target version of the Military & Police w/standard features of that model. Caliber: .38 Special, six-inch bbl. Weight: 32.25 oz. Adj. target sights. Blued finish. Checkered walnut grips. Made from 1899 to1940. For values, add $175 for corresponding M&P 38 models.

MODEL .38 PERFECTED DA . . NiB $1465 Ex $1336 Gd $1145
Hinged frame. Similar to earlier .38 DA Model but heavier frame, side latch as in solid-frame models, improved lockwork. Caliber: .38 S&W. Five-round cylinder, bbl. lengths: 3.25, 4, 5 and 6 inches. Fixed sights. Blued or nickel finish. Hard rubber grips. Made 1909 to 1920.

MODEL 40 CENTENNIAL
DA HAMMERLESS REVOLVER
Similar to Chiefs Special but has Safety Hammerless-type mechanism w/

**Smith & Wesson
Model 36**

**Smith & Wesson
Model 37**

**Smith & Wesson
Model 38 Bodyguard Airweight**

grip safety. Two-inch bbl. Weight: 19 oz. Made from 1953 to 1974.
Blued model. . . . . NiB $633 Ex $437 Gd $398
Nickel model . . . . NiB $1319 Ex $1109 Gd $895

MODEL 42 CENTENNIAL AIRWEIGHT
Same as standard Centennial model except has light alloy frame, weight: 13 oz. Made from 1954 to 1974.
Blued model . . . . NiB $648 Ex $429 Gd $351
Nickel model . . . . NiB $1250 Ex $1062 Gd $884

MODEL 42 CLASSICS SERIES . . . . . . NiB $999 Ex $480 Gd $420
Recent manufacture of Model 42 except in .38 Spl.+P w/1.87-in. bbl., aluminum frame, grip safety, blued finish, checkered wood grip. Made from 2009 to 2010.

MODEL 43 1955 .22/.32
KIT GUN AIRWEIGHT . . . . NiB $760 Ex $543 Gd $274
Same as Model 34 Kit Gun except has light alloy frame, square grip. Furnished w/3.5-inch bbl., weight: 14.25 oz. Made 1954 to 1974.

Smith & Wesson
Model 48

Smith & Wesson
Model 63

Smith & Wesson
Model 49
Bodyguard

Smith & Wesson
Model 64

Smith & Wesson
Model 57

Smith & Wesson
Model 60

MODEL 44 1926 MILITARY DA REVOLVER

Same as the early New Century model with Extractor rod casing but lacking the "Triple Lock" feature. Caliber: .44 S&W Special. Six-round cylinder, bbl. lengths: 4, 5 and 6.5 inches, 11.75 inches overall (with 6.5-inch bbl.). Weight: 39.5 oz. (with 6.5-inch bbl.). Fixed sights. Blued or nickel finish. Checkered walnut grips. Made 1926 to 1941.

Standard model . . . . NiB $3715 Ex $3409 Gd $3135
Target model w/6.5-inch bbl.,
  target sights, blued . . . . NiB $3715 Ex $3409 Gd $3095

.38 AND .44 DA REVOLVERS

Also called Wesson Favorite (lightweight model), Frontier (caliber .44-40). Hinged frame. Six-round cylinder. Calibers: .44 S&W Russian, .38-40, .44-40. Bbl. lengths: 4-, 5-, 6- and 6.5-inch. Weight: 37.5 oz. (with 6.5-inch bbl.). Fixed sights. Blued or nickel finish. Hard rubber grips. Made from 1881 to 1913, Frontier disc. 1910.

Standard model, .44 Russian NiB $10,930 Ex $9795 Gd $6579
Standard model, .38-40 . . . . NiB $6030 Ex $5095 Gd $1479
Frontier model . . . . NiB $5089 Ex $3240 Gd $1939
Favorite model . . . . NiB $10,600 Ex $8499 Gd $2977

.44 HAND EJECTOR MODEL DA REVOLVER

First Model, New Century, also called "Triple Lock" because of its third cylinder lock at the crane. Six-round cylinder. Calibers: .44 S&W Special, .450 Eley, .455 Mark II. Bbl. lengths: 4-, 5-, 6.5- and 7.5-inch. Weight: 39 oz. (with 6.5-inch bbl.). Fixed sights. Blued or nickel finish. Checkered walnut grips. Made 1907 to 1966.
Second Model is basically the same as New Century except crane lock ("Triple Lock" feature) and Extractor rod casing eliminated. Calibers: .44 S&W Special .44-40 Win. .45 Colt. Bbl. lengths: 4-, 5-, 6.5- and 7.5-inch; 11.75 inches overall (with 6.5-inch bbl.). Weight: 38 oz. (with 6.5-inch bbl.). Fixed sights. Blued or nickel finish. Checkered walnut grips. Made from 1915 to 1937.

First Model w/triple lock (1907-15)
Standard model,
.44 S&W Special . . . . NiB $4735 Ex $4380 Gd $4335
Standard model
other calibers. . . . . NiB $2865 Ex $2555 Gd $2339
British .455
Target model . . . . NiB $3520 Ex $3299 Gd $1135
Second Model
w/o triple lock (1915-37) . . . NiB $3520 Ex $3266 Gd $1117
.44 S&W Special . . . . NiB $2420 Ex $2119 Gd $1972
Second model,
other calibers. . . . . NiB $5200 Ex $4190 Gd $3977

**.44 HAND EJECTOR, SECOND MODEL
DA REVOLVER. . . . . NiB $2425 Ex $2174 Gd $1981**
Basically the same as New Century except crane lock ("Triple Lock" feature) and Extractor rod casing eliminated. Calibers: .44 S&W Special .44-40 Win. .45 Colt. Bbl. lengths: 4-, 5-, 6.5- and 7.5-inches, 11.75 inches overall (with 6.5-inch bbl.). Weight: .38 oz. (with 6.5-inch bbl.). Fixed sights. Blued or nickel finish. Checkered walnut grips. Made from 1915 to 1937.

MODEL 48 (K-22) MASTERPIECE M.R.F. DA REVOLVER
Caliber: .22 Mag. and .22 LR. Six-round cylinder, bbl. lengths: 4, 6 and 8.38 inches, 11.13 inches overall (w/ 6-inch bbl.). Weight: 39 oz. Adj. rear sight, ramp front. Made from 1959 to 1986.
Model 48 (4- or 6-inch bbl.). . . . NiB $862 Ex $668 Gd $495
Model 48 (8.38-inch bbl.). . . . . NiB $826 Ex $612 Gd $439
w/target options TH & TT, add $75

MODEL 48 CLASSICS SERIES . . . . . . NiB $999 Ex $480 Gd $420
Recent manufacture of Model 48 except w/4- or 6-in. bbl., blued finish, checkered wood grip. Made from 2010 to date.

MODEL 49 BODYGUARD
Same as Model 38 Bodyguard Airweight except has steel frame, weight: 20.5 oz. Made from 1959 to 1996.
Blued model . . . . NiB $478 Ex $337 Gd $244
Nickel model . . . . NiB $530 Ex $377 Gd $270

MODEL 51 1960 .22/.32 KIT GUN . . . . NiB $755 Ex $549 Gd $319
Same as Model 34 Kit Gun except chambered for .22 WMR 3.5-inch bbl., weight: 24 oz. Made from 1960 to 1974.

MODEL 53 .22 REM. JET DA
Caliber: .22 Rem. Jet C.F. Magnum. Six-round cylinder (inserts permit use of .22 Short, Long, or LR cartridges). Bbl. lengths: 4, 6, 8.38 inches, 11.25 inches overall (with 6-inch bbl.). Weight: 40 oz. (with 6-inch bbl.). Micrometer-click rear sight ramp front. Checkered walnut grips. Made from 1960 to 1974.
Model 53 (4- or 6-inch bbl.). . . . NiB $933 Ex $749 Gd $633
Model 53 (8.38-inch bbl.). . . . . NiB $1040 Ex $844 Gd $704
w/target options TH & TT, add $75

MODEL 57 .41 MAGNUM DA REVOLVER
Caliber: 41 Magnum. Six-round cylinder, bbl. lengths: 4-, 6-, 8.38-inch. Weight: 40 oz. (with 6-inch bbl.). Micrometer click rear sight, ramp front. Target grips of checkered Goncalo Alves. Made from 1964 to 1993.
Model 57 (w/4- or 6-inch bbl.) . . . . . . .NiB $812 Ex $627 Gd $429
Model 57 (w/8.63-inch bbl.). . . . . .NiB $852 Ex $677 Gd $449
Model 57 (w/pinned bbl., recessed cylinder), add 10%

MODEL 57 CLASSICS SERIES . . . . . NiB $1010 Ex $470 Gd $420
Recent manufacture of Model 57 except w/4- or 6-in. bbl., blued finish, checkered wood grip. Made from 2009 to date.

**Smith & Wesson
Model 66 Combat Magnum**

**Smith & Wesson
Model 67 Combat Masterpiece**

**MODEL 58 .41 MILITARY& POLICE
DA REVOLVER. . . . . NiB $855 Ex $709 Gd $576**
Caliber: 41 Magnum. Six-round cylinder, 4-inch bbl. 9.25 inches overall. Weight: 41 oz. Fixed sights. Checkered walnut grips. Made from 1964 to 1982.

MODEL 58 CLASSICS SERIES . . . . . NiB $780 Ex $470 Gd $420
Recent manufacture of Model 58 except w/blued or nickel finish, checkered wood grip. Made from 2009 to 2011.

MODEL 60 STAINLESS DA
Caliber: .38 Special or .357 Magnum. Five-round cylinder, bbl. lengths: 2, 2.1 or 3 inches, 6.5 or 7.5 inches overall. Weight: 19 to 23 oz. Square-notch rear sight, ramp front. Satin finish stainless steel. Made from 1965-96 (.38 Special) and from 1996 to date (.357/.38).
.38 Special (disc. 1996) . . . . NiB $474 Ex $346 Gd $270
.357 Mag. . . . . NiB $498 Ex $366 Gd $283
Lady Smith (w/smaller grip). . . . . . NiB $544 Ex $377 Gd 280

MODEL 63 (1977) KIT GUN DA. . . . . . NiB $474 Ex $319 Gd $265
Caliber: .22 LR. Six-round cylinder, 2- or 4-inch bbl., 6.5 or 8.5 inches overall. Weight: 19 to 24.5 oz. Adj. rear sight, ramp front. Stainless steel. Checkered walnut or synthetic grips.

MODEL 64 .38 M&P STAINLESS . . . . . . NiB $498 Ex $362 Gd $287
Same as standard Model 10 except satin-finished stainless steel, square butt w/4-inch heavy bbl., or round butt w/2-inch bbl. Made from 1970 to date.

**MODEL 65 .357 MILITARY/
POLICE STAINLESS. . . . . NiB $499 Ex $357 Gd $290**
Same as Model 13 except satin-finished stainless steel. Made 1974 to 2004.
Lady Smith (w/smaller grip) . . . . .NiB $540 Ex $377 Gd $302

MODEL 66 .357 COMBAT MAGNUM STAINLESS
Same as Model 19 except satin-finished stainless steel. Made from 1971 to date.
Model 66 (2.5-inch bbl.). . . . . . NiB $536 Ex $439 Gd $328
Model 66 (3-inch bbl.) . . . . NiB $536 Ex $431 Gd $303
Model 66 (4-inch bbl.) . . . . NiB $536 Ex $431 Gd $303
Model 66 (6-inch bbl.) . . . . NiB $562 Ex $456 Gd $346
w/target options TH & TT, add . . . .$ 6 5

MODEL 67 .38 COMBAT
MASTERPIECE STAINLESS. . . . . . NiB $597 Ex $440 Gd $337
Same as Model 15 except satin-finished stainless steel available only
w/4-inch bbl. Made from 1972-1988 and from 1991-1998.

MODEL 68 .38 COMBAT
MASTERPIECE STAINLESS. . . . . . NiB $831 Ex $668 Gd $601
Same as Model 66 except w/4- or 6-inch bbl., chambered for .38 Special.
Made to accommodate CA Highway Patrol because they were not authorized
to carry .357 magnums. Made from 1976 yo 1983. (7,500 produced)

125th Anniversary Commemorative
Issued to celebrate the 125th anniversary of the 1852 partnership of
Horace Smith and Daniel Baird Wesson. Standard Edition is a Model
25 revolver in .45 Colt w/6.5-inch bbl., bright blued finish, gold-filled
bbl., roll mark "Smith & Wesson 125th Anniversary," sideplate marked
w/gold-filled Anniversary seal, smooth Goncalo Alves grips, in presenta-
tion case w/nickel silver Anniversary medallion and book, "125 Years w/
Smith & Wesson," by Roy Jinks. Deluxe Edition is same except revolver is
Class A engraved w/gold-filled seal on sideplate, ivory grips, Anniversary
medallion is sterling silver and book is leather bound. Limited to 50 units.
Total issue is 10,000 units, of which 50 are Deluxe Edition and two are a
Custom Deluxe Edition and not for sale. Made in 1977.
Standard edition. . . . . NiB $648 Ex $377 Gd $305
Deluxe edition . . . . NiB $2579 Ex $2365 Gd $2094

MODEL 242 AIRLITE TI
CENTENNIAL . . . . NiB $500 Ex $300 Gd $220
DAO. Caliber: .38 Spl.+P. 7-round titanium cylinder, 2.5-in. bbl., alloy
L-frame. Uncle Mike's boot grip. Made 1990 only.

MODEL 296 AIRLITE TI
CENTENNIAL . . . . NiB $650 Ex $400 Gd $260
DAO. Caliber: .44 Spl. 5-round titanium cylinder, 2.5-in. bbl., alloy
L-frame. Uncle Mike's boot grip. Made 1990 only.

MODEL 310 NIGHTGUARD . . . . NiB $895 Ex $540 Gd $360
SA/DA. Caliber: .40 S&W or 10mm. 6-round stainless cylinder, 2.5-in.
bbl., scandium alloy N-frame. Fixed sights. Pachmayr grip. Made 2009
to 2010.

MODEL 315 NIGHTGUARD . . . . NiB $895 EX $540 GD $360
SA/DA. Caliber: .40 S&W or 10mm. 6-round stainless cylinder, 2.5-in.
bbl., scandium alloy N-frame. Fixed sights. Pachmayr grip. Made 2009
to 2010.

MODEL 317 AIRLITE DA REVOLVER
Caliber: .22 LR. Eight-round cylinder, 1.88- or 3-in. bbl., 6.3 or 7.2 inches
overall. Weight: 9.9 oz. or 11 oz. Ramp front sight, notched frame rear.
Aluminum, carbon fiber, stainless and titanium construction. Brushed aluminum finish. Synthetic or Dymondwood grips. Made from 1997 to date.
w/1.88-in. bbl. . . . . NiB $590 Ex $380 Gd $306
w/3-in. bbl. . . . . NiB $683 Ex $453 Gd $356
w/Dymondwood grips, add. $100

MODEL 325 NIGHTGUARD . . . . NiB $830 Ex $430 Gd $350
SA/DA. Caliber: .45 ACP. 6-round stainless cylinder, 2.5-in. bbl., alloy
N-frame. Fixed sights. Weight: 26.5 oz. Pachmayr rubber grip. Made
2008 to 2012.

Smith & Wesson
Model 629 Classic

Smith & Wesson
Model 586 Distinguished Combat
Magnum

Smith & Wesson
Model 625

Smith & Wesson
Model 629

GRADING: **NiB** = New in Box **Ex** = Excellent or NRA 95% **Gd** = Good or NRA 68%

MODEL 325 PD-AIRLITE SC. . . . . NIB $800 EX $490 GD $340
SA/DA. Caliber: .45 ACP. 6-round titanium cylinder, 2.5- or 4-in. bbl.,
scandium alloy N-frame. Weight: 21.5-25 oz. Hogue rubber grip.
Made 2004 to 2007.

MODEL 327 NIGHTGUARD . . . . NIB $830 EX $430 GD $350
SA/DA. Caliber: .357 Mag. 8-round stainless cylinder, 2.5-in. bbl.,
alloy N-frame. Fixed sights. Weight: 28 oz. Pachmayr rubber grip.
Made 2008 to 2012.

MODEL 327 PD-AIRLITE SC. . . . . NIB $960 EX $460 GD $320
SA/DA. Caliber: .357 Mag. 8-round titanium cylinder, 4-in. bbl., scandium alloy N-frame. Fixed sights. Weight: 28 oz. Wood grip. Made
2008 to 2009.

MODEL 329 NIGHTGUARD . . . . NIB $830 EX $430 GD $350
SA/DA. Caliber: .44 Mag. 6-round stainless cylinder, 2.5-in. bbl., alloy
N-frame. Fixed sights. Weight: 28 oz. Pachmayr rubber grip. Made
2008 to 2012.

MODEL 329 PD-AIRLITE SC. . . . NIB $1160 EX $530 GD $350
SA/DA. Caliber: .44 Mag. 6-round titanium cylinder, 4-in. bbl., scandium alloy N-frame. Fixed sights. Weight: 28 oz. Wood grip. Made
2003 to date.

MODEL 331 AIRLITE TI
CHIEFS SPECIAL . . . . NIB $675 EX $465 GD $310
SA/DA. Caliber: .32 H&R Mag. 6-round titanium cylinder, 1.87-in.
bbl., alloy J-frame. Fixed sights. Weight: 28 oz. Wood or Uncle Mike's
grip. Made 1999 to 2003.

MODEL 332 AIRLITE TI
CENTENNIAL . . . . NIB $575 EX $455 GD $310
DAO. Caliber: .32 H&R Mag. 6-round titanium cylinder, 1.87-in. bbl.,
alloy J-frame. Fixed sights. Weight: 28 oz. Uncle Mike's grip. Made
1999 to 2003.

MODEL 337 AIRLITE TI
CHIEFS SPECIAL . . . . NIB $675 EX $465 GD $310
SA/DA. Caliber: .38 Spl.+P. 5-round titanium cylinder, 1.87-in. bbl.,
alloy J-frame. Fixed sights. Weight: 12 oz. Made 1999 to 2003.

MODEL 337 AIRLITE TI
KIT GUN. . . . . NIB $600 EX $350 GD $290
SA/DA. Caliber: .38 Spl.+P. 5-round cylinder, 3.12-in. bbl., J-frame.
Fixed sights. Weight: 12 oz. Made 2000 to 2003.

MODEL 337 PD AIRLITE TI . . . . NIB $585 EX $345 GD $315
SA/DA. Caliber: .38 Spl.+P. 5-round titanium cylinder, 1.87-in. bbl.,
alloy J-frame. Fixed sights. Weight: 10.7 oz. Made 2000 to 2003.

MODEL 340 AIRLITE SC
CENTENNIAL . . . . NIB $775 EX $410 GD $350
DAO. Caliber: .357 Mag. 5-round titanium cylinder, 1.87-in. bbl.,
alloy J-frame. Fixed sights. Weight: 10.7 oz. Made 2001 to 2008.

MODEL 340 PD-AIRLITE SC
CENTENNIAL . . . . NIB $775 EX $410 GD $350
DAO. Caliber: .357 Mag. 5-round titanium cylinder, 1.87-in. bbl.,
alloy J-frame. HiViz fixed sights. Weight: 10.7 oz. Made 2000 to date.

MODEL 340 M&P
CENTENNIAL . . . . NIB $869 EX $500 GD $280
DAO. Caliber: .357 Mag. 5-round cylinder, 1.87-in. bbl.,
alloy J-frame. HiViz fixed sights. Weight: 10.7 oz. Made 2007 to date.

MODEL 342 AIRLITE TI
CENTINNIAL. . . . . NIB $575 EX $355 GD $310
DAO. Caliber: .38 Spl.+P. 5-round titanium cylinder, 1.87-in. bbl.,
alloy J-frame. Fixed sights. Weight: 12 oz. Made 1999 to 2003.

MODEL 342 PD AIRLITE TI
CENTINNIAL. . . . . NIB $575 EX $355 GD $310
DAO. Caliber: .38 Spl.+P. 5-round titanium cylinder, 1.87-in. bbl.,
alloy J-frame. Fixed sights. Weight: 10.8 oz. Made 1999 to 2003.

MODEL 351 PD AIRLITE SC
CHEIFS SPECIAL . . . . NIB $759 EX $400 GD $310
SA/DA. Caliber: .22 WMR. 7-round cylinder, 1.87-in. bbl., alloy
J-frame. Fixed sights. Weight: 10.6 oz. Made 2004 to date.

MODEL 351 PD AIRLITE
CENTINNIAL. . . . . NIB $689 EX $375 GD $300
DAO. Caliber: .22 WMR. 7-round cylinder, 1.87-in. bbl., alloy J-frame.
Fixed sights. Weight: 11 oz. Made 2010 to date.

MODEL 357 PD . . . . NIB $815 EX $405 GD $345
SA/DA. Caliber: .41 Mag. 6-round titanium cylinder, 4-in. bbl., scan-
dium alloy N-frame. HiViz front, adj. rear sights. Weight: 27.5 oz.
Ahrends wood grip. Made 2005 to 2007.

MODEL 357 NIGHTGUARD . . . . NIB $895 EX $430 GD $355
SA/DA. Caliber: .41 Mag. 6-round stainless cylinder, 2.5-in. bbl.,
alloy N-frame. Fixed sights. Weight: 29.7 oz. Rubber grip. Made
2010 only.

MODEL 360 AIRLITE SC
CHEIFS SPECIAL . . . . NIB $780 EX $410 GD $345
SA/DA. Caliber: .357 Mag. 5-round titanium cylinder, 1.87-in. bbl.,
alloy J-frame. Fixed sights. Weight: 12 oz. Hogue rubber grip. Made
2001 to 2007.
Kit Gun model (3.1-in. bbl.). . . . . NiB $775 Ex $440 Gd $330

MODEL 360 PD AIRLITE SC
CHEIFS SPECIAL . . . . NIB $1020 EX $400 GD $345
SA/DA. Caliber: .357 Mag. 5-round titanium cylinder, 1.87-in. bbl.,
alloy J-frame. Fixed sights. Weight: 12 oz. Hogue rubber grip. Matte
grey finish. Made 2002 to date.

MODEL 360 M&P
CHEIFS SPECIAL . . . . NIB $1020 EX $400 GD $345
SA/DA. Caliber: .357 Mag. 5-round stainless cylinder, 1.87-in. bbl.,
scandium alloy J-frame. Fixed sights. Weight: 13.3 oz. Rubber grip.
Matte black finish. Made 2007 to 2010.

MODEL 386 AIRLITE SC
MOUNTAIN LITE . . . . NIB $660 EX $3700 GD $325
SA/DA. Caliber: .357 Mag. 7-round titanium cylinder, 2.5- or
3.1-in. bbl., scandium alloy L-frame. HiViz front, adj. rear sights.
Weight: 18.5 oz. Rubber grip. Matte black finish. Made 2001 to
2007.

MODEL 386 PD-AIRLITE SC. . . . NIB $1020 EX $400 GD $345
SA/DA. Caliber: .357 Mag. 7-round titanium cylinder, 2.5-in. bbl.,
scandium alloy L-frame. Adj. sights. Weight: 17.5 oz. Hogue rubber
grip. Matte grey finish. Made 2001 to 2005.

MODEL 386 SC/S . . . . NIB $780 EX $390 GD $340
SA/DA. Caliber: .357 Mag. 7-round stainless cylinder, 2.5-in. bbl.,
scandium alloy L-frame. Adj. sights. Weight: 21.2 oz. Made 2007 to
2008.

MODEL 386 NIGHTGUARD . . . . NIB $750 EX $460 GD $410
SA/DA. Caliber: .357 Mag. 7-round stainless cylinder, 2.5-in. bbl., alloy L-frame. Fixed sights. Weight: 24.5 oz. Made 2008 to 2012.

MODEL 386 XL HUNTER
AIRLITE SC . . . . NIB $795 EX $430 GD $380
SA/DA. Caliber: .357 Mag. 7-round stainless cylinder, 6-in. bbl., alloy L-frame. Fixed sights. Weight: 30 oz. Matte black finish. Made 2010 to 2012.

MODEL 396 AIRLITE TI
MOUNTAIN LITE . . . . NIB $625 EX $360 GD $320
SA/DA. Caliber: .44 Spl. 5-round titanium cylinder, 3.1-in. bbl., alloy L-frame. Adj. sights. Weight: 18 oz. Matte grey finish. Made 2001 to 2004.

MODEL 396 NIGHTGUARD . . . . NIB $825 EX $480 GD $430
SA/DA. Caliber: .44 Spl. 5-round stainless cylinder, 2.5-in. bbl., alloy L-frame. Fixed sights. Weight: 24.2 oz. Made 2008 to 2009.

MODEL 431 AIRWEIGHT . . . . . . NIB $525 EX $355 GD $300
SA/DA. Caliber: .32 H&R Mag. 6-round cylinder, 2-in. bbl., J-frame. Fixed sights. Blued finish. Made 2004 to 2005.

MODEL 431 CENTENNIAL
AIRWEIGHT . . . . NIB $5505 EX $380 GD $310
DAO. Caliber: .32 H&R Mag. 6-round cylinder, 2-in. bbl., J-frame. Fixed sights. Blued finish. Made 2004 to 2005.

MODEL 438 AIRWEIGHT . . . . . . NIB $525 EX $355 GD $300
SA/DA. Caliber: .38 Spl.+P. 5-round cylinder, 1.87-in. bbl., J-frame. Fixed sights. Weight: 15 oz. Matte black finish. Made 2004 to 2005.

MODEL 442 AIRWEIGHT
CENTINNIAL . . . . NIB $470 EX $220 GD $180
DAO. Caliber: .38 Spl.+P. 5-round cylinder, 1.87-in. bbl., J-frame. Fixed sights. Weight: 15 oz. Matte black, blued, or nickel finish. Made 1993 to date.
442 Pro Series (moon clips) . . . . . NiB $499 Ex $230 Gd $190

MODEL 469 V/XVR . . . . NIB $1370 EX $700 GD $600
SA/DA. Caliber: .460 S&W Mag. 5-round cylinder, 5- or 8.5-in. bbl., X-frame. HiViz adj. sights. Matte stainless finish. Made 2005 to date.

MODEL 500
Caliber: .500 S&W Magnum. Uses S&W's largest revolver frame: X-frame. 5-round cylinder, bbl. lengths: 4, 6.5 and 8.38 inches, ported barrel, overall length: 15 inches (8.38-inch bbl.). Weight: 71.9 oz. (8.38-inch bbl.). Interchangeable front sight, micrometer-click adj. rear. Synthetic grip. Satin stainless finish. Made from 2003 to date.
w/6- or 8.38-inch bbl. . . . . NiB $1299 Ex $740 Gd $459
w/4-inch bbl. , add $70
w/ factory HI-VIZ sights (8.38-in. bbl.), add $70

MODEL 520
DA REVOLVER . . . . NiB $556 Ex $410 Gd $321
Caliber: .357 Mag. Six-round cylinder. N-Frame w/4-inch bbl. Weight: 40 oz. Fixed sights. In 1980, 3000 pieces were made for the N.Y. State Police but that agency did not purchase those firearms, so they were sold commercially.

MODEL 547
DA REVOLVER . . . . NiB $816 Ex $709 Gd $499
Caliber: 9mm. Six-round cylinder, bbl. length: 3 or 4 inches, 7.31 inches overall. Weight: 32 oz. Square-notch rear sight, ramp front. Disc. 1986.

MODEL 586 DISTINGUISHED COMBAT MAGNUM
Caliber: .357 Magnum. Six-round cylinder, bbl. lengths: 4, 6 and 8.38 inches, overall length: 9.75 inches (with 4-inch bbl.). Weight: 42, 46, 53 oz., respectively. Red ramp front sight, micrometer-click adj. rear. Checkered grip. Blued or nickel finish. Made 1980 to 1999.
Model 586 (w/4- or 6-inch bbl.) . NiB $691 Ex $479 Gd $345
Model 586 (w/8.63-inch bbl.) . . . NiB $709 Ex $499 Gd $359
Model 586 (w/adjustable front sight), add $50
Model 586 (w/nickel finish), add $65

MODEL 581 DISTINGUISHED
SERVICE MAGNUM . . . . NiB $7 50 Ex $520 Gd $420
SA/DA. Caliber: .357 Mag. 6-round cylinder, 4-in. full lug bbl., L-frame, fixed sights, blued or nickel finish. Made from 1981 to 1992.
Nickel finish, add $25

MODEL 586 DISTINGUISHED
COMBAT MAGNUM . . . . NiB $650 Ex $380 Gd $300
SA/DA. Caliber: .357 Mag. 6-round cylinder. 4-, 6- or 8.37-in. full lug bbl. L-frame, Adj. sights, blued or nickel finish. Made from 1980 to 1999.

MODEL 610 DA REVOLVER . . . . . NiB $755 Ex $612 Gd $500
Similar to Model 625 except in caliber .40 S&W/10mm. Magna classic grips. Made from 1990 to 1991 and from 1998 to 2004.

MODEL 610 CLASSIC . . . . NiB $860 Ex $580 Gd $480
SA/DA. Caliber: .40 S&W/10mm. 6-round fluted or unfluted cylinder. 4-, 5- or 6.5-in. full lug bbl. N-frame, Adj. sights, stainless finish. Made from 1990; 1998 to 2005; 2009.
10-round cylinder, add $80

MODEL 617 K-22 MASTERPIECE. . NiB $830 Ex $480 Gd $360
SA/DA. Caliber: .22 LR. 6- or 10-round cylinder. 4-, 6- or 8.37-in. full lug bbl. K-frame, Adj. sights, matte stainless finish, Hogue rubber grips. Made from 1990 to date.
Semi-target model w/4- or 6-inch bbl. . . . . . NiB $648 Ex $530 Gd $362
Target model w/6-inch bbl. . . . . NiB $648 Ex $530 Gd $362
Target model w/8.38-inch bbl. . . . . NiB $615 Ex $485 Gd $332
w/10-round cylinder, add $128

Smith & Wesson Model 500

Smith & Wesson
Model 642 Centennial
Airweight

Smith & Wesson
Model 640

MODEL 619 . . . . NiB $450 Ex $230 Gd $190
SA/DA. Caliber: .357 Mag. 7-round cylinder. 5-in. bbl. L-frame, fixed sights, matte stainless finish, rubber grips. Made from 2005 to 2006.

MODEL 620 . . . . NiB $450 Ex $230 Gd $190
SA/DA. Caliber: .357 Mag. 7-round cylinder. 4-in. bbl., L-frame, adj. sights, matte stainless finish, rubber grips. Made from 2005 to 2009.

MODEL 624 . . . . NiB $750 Ex $530 Gd $460
SA/DA. Caliber: .44 Spl. 6-round cylinder. 4- or 6.5-in. bbl., N-frame, adj. sights, matte stainless finish. Made from 1986 to 1987.

MODEL 625 DA REVOLVER . . . . NiB $866 Ex $733 Gd $569
Same general specifications as Model 25 except 3-, 4- or 5-inch bbl., round-butt Pachmayr grips and satin stainless steel finish. Made 1989 to 2007.

MODEL 625 JM . . . . NiB $979 Ex $480 Gd $430
SA/DA. Caliber: .45 ACP. 6-round cylinder. 3-, 4- or 5-in. full lug bbl., N-frame, adj. sights, matte stainless finish, made in colaboration with competitive shooter Jerry Miculek. Made from 1988 to date.

MODEL 627 DA REVOLVER . . NiB $730 Ex $427 Gd $337
SA/DA. Caliber: .357 Mag. unfluted cylinder, 5.5-in. full lug bbl., N-frame, adj. sights, satin stainless steel finish. Made from 1989 to 2008.

MODEL 627 . . . . NiB $730 Ex $427 Gd $337
SA/DA. Caliber: .357 Mag. 8-round cylinder. 4-in. bbl., N-frame, adj. sights, satin stainless steel finish. Made from 2008 to 2009.

MODEL 629 DA REVOLVER
Same as Model 29 in .44 Magnum except in stainless steel. Classic made from 1990 to date.
w/ 3-inch bbl.(Backpacker model) . . . . . NiB $774 Ex $567 Gd $408
w/4- or 6-inch bbls. . . . . NiB $774 Ex $567 Gd $408
w/8.38-inch bbl. . . . . NiB $774 Ex $567 Gd $408
Classic model (w/5- or 6.5-inch bbl.) . . . NiB $829 Ex $581 Gd $444
Classic model (w/8.38-inch bbl.) . . . . . . NiB $685 Ex $576 Gd $469
Classix DX model (w/6.5-inch bbl.) . . . . NiB $685 Ex $576 Gd $469
Classic DX model (w/8.38-inch bbl.) . . . NiB $685 Ex $576 Gd $469
Magna Classic model . . . . NiB $979 Ex $680 Gd $530
MODEL 631 DA REVOLVER

Similar to Model 31 except chambered for .32 H&R Mag. Goncalo Alves combat grips. Made in 1991 to 1992.
Fixed sights, 2-inch bbl. . . . . NiB $800 Ex $659 Gd $246
Adjustable sights, 4-inch bbl., add 10%
Lady Smith, 2-inch bbl. . . . . NiB $410 Ex $329 Gd $246
Lady Smith, 2-inch bbl. (black stainless). NiB $420 Ex $329 Gd $246

MODEL 632 CENTENNIAL DA REVOLVER
Same general specifications as Model 640 except chambered for .32 H&R Mag. 2- or 3-inch bbl., weight: 15.5 oz. Stainless slide w/alloy frame. Fixed sights. Santoprene combat grips. Made 1991 to 1992.
w/2-inch bbl. . . . . NiB $693 Ex $408 Gd $321
w/3-inch bbl. . . . . NiB $789 Ex $485 Gd $930

MODEL 637 CHIEFS SPECIAL AIRWEIGHT
DA REVOLVER . . . . NiB $485 Ex $357 Gd $289
Same general specifications as Model 37 except w/clear anodized fuse alloy frame and stainless cylinder. 560 made in 1991 and reintroduced in 1996.

MODEL 638 BODYGUARD
AIRWEIGHT DA . . . . NiB $468 Ex $367 Gd $326
Same general specifications as Model .38 except w/clear anodized fuse alloy frame and stainless cylinder. 1,200 made in 1990 and reintroduced in 1998.

MODEL 640 CENTENNIAL DA . . . NiB $648 Ex $398 Gd $326
Caliber: .38 Special. Five-round cylinder, 2, 2.1 or 3-inch bbl., 6.31 inches overall. Weight: 20-22 oz. Fixed sights. Stainless finish. Smooth hardwood service grips. Made from 1990 to date.

MODEL 642 CENTENNIAL AIRWEIGHT
DA Revolver . . . . NiB $479 Ex $365 Gd $290
Same general specifications as Model 640 except w/stainless steel/aluminum alloy frame and finish. Weight 15.8 oz. Santoprene combat grips. Made from 1990-93 and reintroduced 1996.

Smith & Wesson
Model 696

Smith & Wesson
Model K-22 Outdoorsman

Smith & Wesson
Lady Smith First Model

Smith & Wesson
Lady Smith Second Model

Lady Smith model
(w/smaller grip) . . . . NiB $648 Ex $478 Gd $377
2.125-in. bbl. w/ PowerPort (2009-2010), add $150
Pro Series w/ full moon clips (intro. 2010), add $30

MODEL 648
DA REVOLVER . . . . NiB $695 Ex $506 Gd $450
Same general specifications as Models 17/617 except in stainless and
chambered for .22 Mag. Made from 1990 to 1993.
Model 648-2 (2003-2005) . . . . . . NiB $660   Ex $500   Gd $390

MODEL 649 BODYGUARD
DA REVOLVER . . . . NiB $644 Ex $369 Gd $290
Caliber: .38 Special. Five-round cylinder, bbl. length: 2 inches, 6.25
inches overall. Weight: 20 oz. Square-notch rear sight ramp front.
Stainless frame and finish. Made from 1986 to date.

MODEL 650
REVOLVER . . . . NiB $856 Ex $680 Gd $525
Caliber: .22 Mag. Six-round cylinder, 3-inch bbl., 7 inches overall.
Weight: 23.5 oz. Serrated ramp front sight, fixed square-notch rear.
Round butt, checkered walnut monogrammed grips. Stainless steel fin-
ish. Made from 1983 to 1986.

MODEL 651 STAINLESS DA
Caliber: .22 Mag. Rimfire. Six-round cylinder, bbl. length: 3 and 4
inches, 7 and 8.63 inches, respectively, overall. Weight: 24.5 oz. Adj.
rear sight, ramp front. Made from 1983 to 1987 and from 1990 to 1998.
Note: .22 LR cylinder available during early production.
w/3- or 4-inch bbl. . . . . NiB $561 Ex $366 Gd $345
w/extra cylinder . . . . NiB $862 Ex $386 Gd $365

MODEL 657 REVOLVER
Caliber: 41 Mag. Six-round cylinder. Bbl. lengths: 4, 6 or 8.4 inches; 9.6,
11.4, and 13.9 inches overall. Weight: 44.2, 48 and 52.5 oz. Serrated black
ramp front sight on ramp base click rear, adj. for windage and elevation.
Satin finished stainless steel. Made from 1986 to 2008.
w/4- or 6-inch bbl. . . . . NiB $601 Ex $433 Gd $398
w/8.4-inch bbl. . . . . NiB $882 Ex $464 Gd $377

MODEL 681 DSM. . . . . NiB $464   Ex $329   Gd $255
Same as S&W Model 581 except in stainless finish only. Made 1991 to 1993.

MODEL 686
Same as S&W Model 586 Distinguished Combat Magnum except in
stainless finish w/additional 2.5-inch bbl. Made from 1991 to date.
w/2.5-inch bbl. . . . . NiB $639 Ex $434 Gd $332
w/4- or 6-inch bbl. . . . . NiB $639 Ex $434 Gd $332
w/8.63-inch bbl. . . . . NiB $639 Ex $434 Gd $332
Model 686 (w/adjustable
front sight), add $50

MODEL 686 PLUS
Same as standard Model 686 Magnum except w/7-round cylinder and
2.5-, 4- or 6-inch bbl. Made from 1996 to date.
w/2.5-inch bbl. . . . . NiB $689 Ex $617 Gd $499
w/4-inch bbl. . . . . NiB $704 Ex $595 Gd $408
w/6-inch bbl. . . . . NiB $700 Ex $631 Gd $429

MODEL 696 . . . . NiB $546   Ex $386   Gd $337
Caliber: .44 S&W Special. L-Frame w/five-round cylinder, 3-inch
shrouded bbl., 8.38 inches overall. Weight: 48 oz. Red ramp front
sight, micrometer-click adj. rear. Checkered synthetic grip. Satin stainless steel. Made from 1997 to 2002.

MODEL 940 CENTENNIAL DA NiB $479 Ex $367 Gd $290
Same general specifications as Model 640 except chambered for 9mm. Two- or 3-inch bbl., Weight: 23-25 oz. Santoprene combat grips. Made from 1991 to 1998.

MODEL 1891 SA REVOLVERNiB $2779 Ex $2465 Gd $2190
Hinged frame. Caliber: .38 S&W. Five-round cylinder, bbl. lengths: 3.25, 4, 5 and 6-inches. Fixed sights. Blued or nickel finish. Hard rubber grips. Made 1891-1911. Note: Until 1906, an accessory single-shot target bbl. (see Model 1891 Single-Shot Target Pistol) was available for this revolver.
w/extra .22 single-shot bbl.. . NiB $5300 Ex $4220 Gd $3690

MODEL 1917 ARMY DA REVOLVER
Caliber: .45 Automatic, using 3-cartridge half-moon clip or .45 Auto Rim, without clip. Six-round cylinder, 5.5-inch bbl., 10.75 inches overall. Weight: 36.25 oz. Fixed sights. Blued finish (blue-black finish on commercial model, brush polish on military). Checkered walnut grips (commercial model, smooth on military). Made under U.S. Government contract 1917-19 and produced commercially 1919-1941. Note: About 175,000 of these revolvers were produced during WW I. The DCM sold these to NRA members during the 1930s at $16.15 each.
Commercial model . . . . NiB $2500 Ex $2168 Gd $1870
Military model . . . . NiB $1860 Ex $1640 Gd $1389

K-22 MASTERPIECE DA . . NiB $5100 Ex $4390 Gd $2724
Improved version of K-22 Outdoorsman w/same specifications but w/ micrometer-click rear sight, short action and antibacklash trigger. Fewer than 1,100 manufactured in 1940.

K-22 OUTDOORSMAN DANiB $2552 Ex $1906 Gd $1392
Design based on the .38 Military & Police Target. Caliber: .22 LR. Six-round cylinder, 11.13 inches overall. Weight: 35 oz. Adj. target sights. Blued finish. Checkered walnut grip. Made 1931 to 1940.

K-32 AND K-38 HEAVY MASTERPIECES
Same as K32 and K38 Masterpiece but w/heavy bbl. Weight: 38.5 oz. Made 1950-53. Note: All K32 and K38 revolvers made after September 1953 have heavy bbls. and the "Heavy Masterpiece" designation was disc. Values for Heavy Masterpiece models are the same as shown for Models 14 and 16. (See separate listing).

K-32 TARGET DA REVOLVER NiB $18,600 Ex $15,400 Gd $9900
Same as .38 Military & Police Target except chambered for .32 S&W Long cartridge, slightly heavier bbl., weight: 34 oz. Only 98 produced. Made from 1938 to 1940.

LADY SMITH (MODEL M HAND EJECTOR) DA REVOLVER
Caliber: .22 LR. Seven-round cylinder, bbl. length: 2.25-, 3-, 3.5- and 6-inch (Third Model only), approximately 7 inches overall w/3.5-inch bbl., weight: About 9.5 oz. Fixed sights, adj. target sights available on Third Model. Blued or nickel finish. Round butt, hard rubber grips on First and Second models; checkered walnut or hard rubber square buttgrips on Third Model. First Model —1902-06: Cylinder locking bolt operated by button on left side of frame, no bbl., lug and front locking bolt. Second Model —1906-11: Rear cylinder latch eliminated, has bbl. lug, forward cylinder lock w/draw-bolt fastening. Third Model —1911-21: Same as Second Model except has square grips, target sights and 6-inch bbl. available. Note: Legend has it that a straight-laced D.B. Wesson ordered discontinuance of the Lady Smith when he learned of the little revolver's reputed popularity w/ladies of the evening. The story, which undoubtedly has enhanced the appeal of this model to collectors, is not true: The Lady Smith was disc. because of difficulty of manufacture and high frequency of repairs.
First model . . . . NiB $3140 Ex $2130 Gd $1696
Second model . . . . NiB $2315 Ex $1779 Gd $1015

**Smith & Wesson
Regulation Police
Target**

**Smith & Wesson
Safety Hammerless**

**Third model, w/fixed sights,
2.25- or 3.5-inch bbl. . . . . . NiB $2315 Ex $1779 Gd $1015**
**Third model, w/fixed sights,
6-inch bbl. . . . . NiB $2315 Ex $1779 Gd $1015**
**Third model, w/adj. sights,
6-inch bbl. . . . . NiB $2215 Ex $1888 Gd $934**

REGULATION POLICE
DA (I Frame) . . . . NiB $811 Ex $602 Gd $434
Calibers: .32 S&W (6-round) or .38 S&W (5-round) built on .32 Hand Ejector frames. Two-, 3-, 3.25-, 4-, 4.25- or 6-inch bbl., weight: 20-24 oz. Fixed sights. Blue or nickel finish. Checkered walnut grips. Made 1917-57. Note: After 1957 "J" Frames replaced the older "I" Frames and designations changed to Model 31 and 33 respectively.
Regulation Police, .32 S&W . . . NiB $1097 Ex $920 Gd $599
Regulation Police, .38 S&W . . . NiB $1097 Ex $920 Gd $599

REGULATION POLICE TARGET DA
Target version of the Regulation Police w/standard features of that model. Calibers: .32 S&W Long or .38 S&W. 6-inch bbl., 10.25 inches overall. Weight: 20 oz. Adjustable target sights. Blue or nickel finish. Checkered walnut grips. Made from about 1917 to 1957.
Regulation Police Target, .32 S&W . . .NiB $2600 Ex $2470 Gd $780
Regulation Police Target, .38 S&W (pre-war)NiB $3000 Ex$2855 Gd$900

SAFETY HAMMERLESS
REVOLVER. . . . . NiB $1396 Ex $1178 Gd $1024
Also called New Departure Double Action. Hinged frame. Calibers: .32 S&W, .38 S&W. Five-round cylinder, bbl. lengths: 2, 3- and 3.5-inch (.32 cal.) or 2-, 3.25-, 4-, 5- and 6-inch (.38 cal.); 6.75 inches overall (.32 cal. w/3-inch bbl.) or 7.5 inches (.38 cal. w/3.25-inch bbl.). Weight: 14.25 oz. (.32 cal. w/3-inch bbl.) or 18.25 oz. (.38 cal. 2.5-inch bbl.). Fixed sights. Blued or nickel finish. Hard rubber grips. Made from 1888 to 1937 (.32 cal.); 1887 to 1941 (.38 cal. w/various minor changes.)

Springfield Armory
1911-A1 Post '90 Series Trophy
Model

Springfield Armory
1911-A1 PDP Series Defender

Springfield Armory
1911-A1 Champion

Springfield Armory
1911-A1 Compact

Sphinx
Model AT2000S w/optional
scope

**TEXAS RANGER
COMMEMORATIVE** . . . . NiB $658 Ex $359 Gd $270
Issued to honor the 150th anniversary of the TExas Rangers. Model
19 .357 Combat Magnum w/4-inch bbl., sideplate stamped w/TExas
Ranger Commemorative Seal, smooth Goncalo Alves grips. Special
Bowie knife in presentation case. 8,000 sets made in 1973. Top value
is for set in new condition.

SPHINX ENGINEERING S.A. — Matten b. Interlaken, Switzerland

MODEL AT-380 DA PISTOL
Caliber: .380 ACP. 10-round magazine, 3.27- inch bbl., 6.03 inches
overall. Weight: 25 oz. Stainless steel frame w/blued slide or Palladium
finish. Slide latch w/ambidExtrous magazine release. Imported from
1993 to 1996.
Two-tone (w/blued slide) . . . . NiB $474 Ex $336 Gd $240
w/Palladium finish . . . . NiB $561 Ex $431 Gd $336

NOTE: *The AT-88 pistol series was previously manufactured by ITM
in Switzerland and imported by Action Arms before Sphinx-Muller
resumed production of these firearms, now designated as the AT-2000
series.*

MODEL 2000S DA AUTOMATIC PISTOL
Calibers: 9mm Parabellum, .40 S&W. 15- or 11-round magazine
respectively, 4.53-inch bbl., (S-standard), 3.66-inch bbl., (P-compact),
3.34-inch bbl., (H-subcompact), 8.25 inches overall. Weight: 36.5 oz.
Fixed sights w/3-dot system. Stainless frame w/blued slide or Palladium
finish. AmbidExtrous safety. Checkered walnut or neoprene grips.
Imported 1993 to 1996.
Standard model . . . . NiB $990 Ex $903 Gd $581
Compact model . . . . NiB $890 Ex $755 Gd $536
Sub-compact model . . . . NiB $890 Ex $755 Gd $536
.40 S&W, add. $50
Palladium finish, add $100

MODEL AT2000C/2000CS COMPETITOR
Similar to the Model AT2000S except also chambered for 9x21mm. 10-round
magazine, 5.31-inch compensated bbl., 9.84 inches overall. Weight: 40.56 oz.
Fully adjustable BoMar or ProPoint sights. Made 1993 to 1996.
w/Bomar sight . . . . NiB $1844 Ex $1599 Gd $1418
w/ProPoint sight . . . . NiB $2254 Ex $1923 Gd $1690

MODEL AT2000GM/GMS GRAND MASTER
Similar to the AT2000C except single action only w/square trigger guard and Extended beavertail grip. Imported 1993 to 1996.
w/BoMar sight . . . . .NiB $1872 Ex $1624 Gd $1375
w/ProPoint sight . . . . .NiB $2179 Ex $1919 Gd $1699

SPRINGFIELD ARMORY — Geneseo, Illinois

Formerly U.S. Government run Springfield Armory in Springfield, Massachusetts. Springfield Armory name purchased in 1974 for commercial/civilian manufacturing.

MODEL M1911 SERIES AUTO PISTOL
Springfield builds the "PDP" (Personal Defense Pistol) Series based on the self-loading M 1911-A1 pistol (military specifications model) as adopted for a standard service weapon by the U.S. Army. With enhancements and modifications they produce a full line of firearms including Ultra-Compacts, Lightweights, Match Grade and Competition Models. For values see specific models.

MODEL 1911-A1 GOVERNMENT
Calibers: 9mm Para., .38 Super, .40 S&W, 10mm or .45 ACP., 7-, 8-, 9- or 10-round magazine, 4- or 5-inch bbl., 8.5 inches overall. Weight: 36 oz. Fixed combat sights. Blued, Parkerized or Duo-Tone finish. Checkered walnut grips. Note: This is an Exact duplicate of the Colt M1911-A1 that was used by the U.S. Armed Forces as a service weapon.
Blued finish . . . . NiB $453 Ex $347 Gd $265
Parkerized finish. . . . . NiB $453 Ex $347 Gd $265

MODEL 1911-A1 (PRE '90 SERIES)
Calibers: 9mm Parabellum, .38 Super, 10mm, .45 ACP. Seven-, 8-, 9- or 10-round magazine, bbl. length: 3.63, 4, 4.25 or 5 inches, 8.5 inches overall. Weight: 36 oz. Fixed combat sights. Blued, Duo-Tone or Parkerized finish. Checkered walnut stocks. Made 1985 to 1990.
Government model (blued) . . . . . NiB $453 Ex $347 Gd $265
Government model (Parkerized) . NiB $621 Ex $436 Gd $362
Bullseye model (wadcutter). . . NiB $1474 Ex $1345 Gd $866
Combat Commander model (blued). . NiB $474 Ex $386 Gd $321
Combat Commander model
  (Parkerized) . . . . .NiB $650 Ex $475 Gd $353
Commander model (blued) . . . . . NiB $479 Ex $306 Gd $219
Commander model (Duo-Tone). . NiB $567 Ex $473 Gd $397
Commander model (Parkerized) . NiB $650 Ex $536 Gd $386
Compact model (blued) . . . . . . .NiB $ 470 Ex $347 Gd $265
Compact model (Duo-Tone) . . . . NiB $559 Ex $500 Gd $434
Compact model (Parkerized) . . . NiB $668 Ex $500 Gd $342
Defender model (blued) . . . . NiB $546 Ex $434 Gd $290
Defender model (Parkerized). . . NiB $704 Ex $556 Gd $377
Defender model (Custom Carry) . NiB $540 Ex $429 Gd $326
National Match model (Hardball) NiB $829 Ex $709 Gd $546
Trophy Master (Competition). . NiB $1355 Ex $1265 Gd $918
Trophy Master (Distinguished) NiB $2152 Ex $2030 Gd $1234
Trophy Master (Expert) . . . . . NiB $1723 Ex $1528 Gd $1322

MODEL 1911-A1 (CUSTOM LOADED SERIES)
1911 style operating system w/steel or alloy frame. Calibers: 9mm Parabellum, .38 Super, .40 S&W, 10mm, .45 ACP. Seven-, 8-, 9- or 10-round magazine, bbl. length: 3.63, 4, 4.25 or 5 inches; 8.5 inches overall. Weight: 28 oz. to 36 oz. Fixed combat sights. Blued, Duo-Tone, Parkerized or stainless finish. Checkered composition or walnut stocks. Made from 1990 to 1998.
Mil-Spec model (blued) . . . . NiB $595 Ex $419 Gd $340
Mil-Spec model (Parkerized). . . . NiB $809 Ex $644 Gd $444
Standard model (blued). . . . . NiB $879 Ex $689 Gd $499
Standard model (Parkerized) . . . NiB $1068 Ex $998 Gd $826
Standard model (stainless). . . . . . NiB $806 Ex $699 Gd $497
Trophy model (blued) . . . . NiB $1440 Ex $1240 Gd $989

Springfield Armory
M1911-A1 Ultra
Compact Parkerized

Trophy model (Hi-Tone) . . . . NiB $1437 Ex $1245 Gd $1029
Trophy model (stainless) . . . . NiB $709 Ex $577 Gd $429

MODEL 1911-A1 PDP SERIES
PDP Series (Personal Defense Pistol). Calibers: .38 Super, .40 S&W, .45 ACP. Seven-, 8-, 9-, 10-, 13- or 17-round magazine, bbl. length: 4, 5, 5.5 or 5.63 inches, 9 to 11 inches overall w/compensated bbl. Weight: 34.5 oz. to 42.8 oz. Post front sight, adjustable rear w/3-dot system. Blued, Duo-Tone, Parkerized or stainless finish. Checkered composition or walnut stocks. Made from 1991 to 1998.
Defender model (blued) . . . . . NiB $910 Ex $780 Gd $586
Defender model (Duo-Tone) . . . . NiB $910 Ex $780 Gd $586
Defender model (Parkerized). . . . NiB $910 Ex $780 Gd $586
.45 ACP Champion Comp (blued) . . . . NiB $780 Ex $562 Gd $431
.45 ACP Compact Comp HC (blued)NiB $602 Ex $453 Gd $398
.380 Sup Factory Comp (blued). . . . . . . .NiB $740 Ex $546 Gd $431
.45 ACP Factory Comp (blued). . . . . . . NiB $866 Ex $780 Gd $544
.380 Sup Factory Comp HC (blued)NiB $740 Ex $546 Gd $398
.45 ACP Factory Comp HC (blued). . . . . NiB $733 Ex $789 Gd $556

MODEL M1911-A1 CHAMPION
Calibers: .380 ACP, 9mm Para., .45 ACP. Six- or 7-round magazine, 4-inch bbl. Weight: 26.5 to 33.4 oz. Low profile post front sight and drift adjustable rear w/3-dot sighting system. Commander-style hammer and slide. Checkered walnut grips. Blue, Bi-Tone, Parkerized or stainless finish. Made from 1992 to 2002.
.380 ACP standard
  (disc. 1995) . . . . .NiB $850 Ex $807 Gd $479
.45 ACP (parkerized or blued) . . NiB $700 Ex $665 Gd $480
.45 ACP (Bi-Tone) (B/H Model). . NiB $912 Ex $790 Gd $386
.45 ACP (stainless) . . . . NiB $742 Ex $707 Gd $522
.45 ACP Super Tuned (1997-1999) . . .NiB $850 Ex $807 Gd $479

MODEL M1911-A1 COMPACT
Similar to the standard M1911 w/champion length slide on a steel or alloy frame w/a shortened grip. Caliber: .45 ACP. Six- or 7-round magazine (10+ law enforcement only), 4-inch bbl. weight: 26.5 to 32 oz. Low profile sights w/3-dot system. Checkered walnut grips. Matte blue, Duo-Tone or Parkerized finish. Made 1991 to 1996.
Compact (Parkerized) . . . . NiB $464 Ex $380 Gd $290
Compact (blued). . . . . NiB $464 Ex $380 Gd $290
Compact (Duo-Tone) . . . . NiB $577 Ex $500 Gd $434
Compact (stainless). . . . . NiB $556 Ex $376 Gd $270
Compact Comp (ported) . . . . . . NiB $882 Ex $792 Gd $587
High capacity (blued) . . . . NiB $595 Ex $369 Gd $321
High capacity (stainless) . . . . NiB $831 Ex $638 Gd $499

MODEL M1911-A1 ULTRA COMPACT
Similar to M1911 Compact except chambered for .380 ACP or .45 ACP. 6- or 7-round magazine, 3.5-inch bbl., weight: 22 oz. to 30 oz. Matte Blue, Bi-Tone, Parkerized (military specs) or stainless finish. Made from 1995 to 2003.

www.skyhorsepublishing.com

Springfield Armory
M1911-A1 Ultra Compact Bi-Tone

Springfield Armory
P9 Combat

Springfield Armory
M1911-A1 Ultra Compact Stainless

Springfield Armory
Panther

.380 ACP Ultra (disc. 1996) .... NiB $740 Ex $585 Gd $388
.45 ACP Ultra (Parkerized or blued)NiB $740 Ex $585 Gd $388
.45 ACP Ultra (Bi-Tone) .... NiB $844 Ex $709 Gd $500
.45 ACP (stainless) .... NiB $740 Ex $585 Gd $388
.45 ACP ultra high capacity (Parkerized) .... NiB $740 Ex $585 Gd $388
.45 ACP ultra high capacity (blued)NiB $780 Ex $615 Gd $499
.45 ACP ultra high capacity (stainless) ... NiB $780 Ex $615 Gd $499
.45 ACP V10 ultra comp (Parkerized) NiB $979 Ex $806 Gd $495
.45 ACP V10 ultra comp (blued) NiB $979 Ex $806 Gd $495
.45 ACP V10 ultra comp (stainless) NiB $979 Ex $806 Gd $495
.45 ACP V10 ultra (super tuned) NiB $1090 Ex $974 Gd $577

MODEL 1911-A1 TRP (TACITCAL RESPONSE PISTOL) OPERATOR
SA AUTO PISTOL .... NiB $1620 EX $1460 GD $780
1911 style operating system w/steel frame. Caliber: .45 ACP. Seven-round magazine, bbl. length: 5 inches; 8.5 inches overall. Weight: 36 oz. Fixed combat sights. Black Armory Kote or stainless finish. Checkered front strap, composition stocks. Made from 2008 to date.

MODEL 1911-A1 LONG SLIDE CUSTOM LOADED
SA AUTO PISTOL .... NiB $1100 EX $960 GD $480
1911 style operating system w/steel frame. Caliber: .45 ACP or .45 Super. Seven-round magazine, bbl. length: 6 inches; 8.5 inches overall. Weight: 36 oz. Fixed combat sights. Black Armory Kote or stainless finish. Checkered wood stocks. Made from 2001 to 2012.

FIRECAT AUTOMATIC PISTOL
Calibers: 9mm, .40 S&W. Eight-round magazine (9mm) or 7-round magazine (.40 S&W), 3.5-inch bbl., 6.5 inches overall. Weight: 25.75 oz. Fixed sights w/3-dot system. Checkered walnut grip. Matte blued finish. Made from 1991 to 1993.
9mm . . . . NiB $556 Ex $408 Gd $289
.40 S&W . . . . NiB $556 Ex $408 Gd $289

PANTHER
AUTO PISTOL . . . . NiB $606 Ex $453 Gd $346
Calibers: 9mm, .40 S&W. 15-round magazine (9mm) or 11-round magazine (.40 S&W), 3.8-inch bbl., 7.5 inches overall. Weight: 28.95 oz. Blade front sight, rear adj. for windage w/3-dot system. Checkered walnut grip. Matte blued finish. Made from 1991 to 1993.

MODEL P9 DA COMBAT SERIES
Calibers: 9mm, .40 S&W, .45 ACP. Magazine capacity: 15-round (9mm), 11-round (.40 S&W) or 10-round (.45 ACP), 3.66-inch bbl., (Compact and Sub-Compact), or 4.75-inch bbl., (Standard), 7.25 or 8.1 inches overall. Weight: 32 to 35 oz. Fixed sights w/3-dot system. Checkered walnut grip. Matte blued, Parkerized, stainless or Duo-Tone finish. Made from 1990 to 1994.

Compact model (9mm, Parkerized)NiB $464 Ex $342 Gd $279
Sub-Compact model (9mm,
  Parkerized). . . . . .NiB $433 Ex $309 Gd $235
Standard model (9mm,
  Parkerized). . . . . NiB $498 Ex $377 Gd $304
w/blued finish, add. $50
w/Duo-Tone finish, add $100
w/stainless finish, add. $128
.40 S&W, add. $35
.45 ACP add $50

MODEL P9 COMPETITION SERIES
Same general specifications as Model P9 except in target configuration w/5-inch bbl., (LSP Ultra) or 5.25-inch bbl. Factory Comp model w/dual port compensator system, Extended safety and magazine release.
Factory Comp model
  (9mm Bi-Tone). . . . . NiB $648 Ex $444 Gd $337
Factory Comp model
  (9mm stainless) . . . . NiB $733 Ex $431 Gd $281
IPSC Ultra model
  (9mm Bi-Tone). . . . . NiB $689 Ex $431 Gd $270
LSP Ultra model
  (9mm stainless) . . . . NiB $785 Ex $580 Gd $425
.40 S&W, .45 ACP: add $128

XD SERIES
Based on HS 2000 pistol manufactured in Croatia. Striker fired. Calibers: 9mm, .357 SIG, .40 S&W, .45 ACP or .45 G.A.P. Polymer frame. 9-, 10-, 12- or 15-rnd. magazine depending on caliber. Matte black or bi-tone finish. Imported 2002 to date.
5-in. bbl. NiB $599 Ex $400 Gd $270
4-in. bbl. NiB $580 Ex $370 Gd $240
3-in. bbl. NiB $550 Ex $370 Gd $240

XD(M) Series . . . . NiB $697 Ex $470 Gd $320
Similar to XD series except w/modular backstraps, diagonal slide serrations. Striker fired. Calibers: 9mm, .40 S&W, or .45 ACP. Bbl. lengths: 3.8- or 4.5-in. Made 2008 to date.
Compact . . . . NiB $700 Ex $470 Gd $320
Competition . . . . NiB $780 Ex $550 Gd $350

STALLARD ARMS — Mansfield, Ohio
See listings under Hi-Point.

STAR — Eibar, Spain
Manufactured by Star, Bonifacio Echeverria, S.A.

MODEL 30M DA AUTO PISTOL NiB $431 Ex $288 Gd $189
Caliber: 9mm Para. 15-round magazine, 4.38-inch bbl., 8 inches overall. Weight: 40 oz. Steel frame w/combat features. Adj. sights. Checkered composition grips. Blued finish. Made from 1984 to 1991.

MODEL 30PK DA AUTO PISTOL . . . NiB $431 Ex $288 Gd $189
Same gen. specifications as Star Model 30M except 3.8-inch bbl., weight: 30 oz. Alloy frame. Made from 1984 to 1989.

Star Model 30M

Star Model 30PK

Star Model AS

Star Model BKS

Star Model F

Star Model F
Olympic Rapid-
Fire

Star Model FS

MODEL 31P DA AUTO PISTOL
Same general specifications as Model 30M except removable backstrap houses complete firing mechanism. Weight: 39.4 oz. Made from 1990 to 1994.
Blued finish . . . . NiB $431 Ex $288 Gd $189
Starvel finish, add. $50

MODEL 31 PK DA AUTO PISTOL . . . . . .NiB $431 Ex $288 Gd $189
Same general specifications as Model 31P except w/alloy frame. Weight: 30 oz. Made from 1990 to 1997.

MODEL A AUTOMATIC PISTOL NiB $365 Ex $259 Gd $169
Modification of the Colt Government Model .45 Auto, which it closely resembles, but lacks grip safety. Caliber: .38 Super. Eight-round magazine, 5-inch bbl., 8 inches overall. Weight: 35 oz. Fixed sights. Blued finish. Checkered grips. Made from 1934-97. (No longer imported.)

MODELS AS, BS, PS . . . . .NiB $500 Ex $380 Gd $279
Same as Models A, B and P except have magazine safety. Made in 1975.

MODEL B. . . . . .NiB $498 Ex $365 Gd $259
Same as Model A except in 9mm Para. Made from 1934 to 1975.

MODEL BKM . . . . .NiB $398 Ex $306 Gd $225
Similar to Model BM except has aluminum frame weight: 25.6 oz. Made from 1976 to 1992.

MODEL BKS STARLIGHT
AUTOMATIC PISTOL . . . . .NiB $431 Ex $279 Gd $209
Light alloy frame. Caliber: 9mm Para. Eight-round magazine, 4.25-inch bbl., 7 inches overall. Weight: 25 oz. Fixed sights. Blued or chrome finish. Plastic grips. Made from 1970 to 1981.

MODEL BM AUTOMATIC PISTOL
Caliber: 9mm. Eight-round magazine, 3.9-inch bbl., 6.95 inches overall. Weight: 34.5 oz. Fixed sights. Checkered walnut grips. Blued or Starvel finish. Made from 1976 to 1992.
Blued finish . . . . NiB $367 Ex $279 Gd $220
Starvel finish . . . . NiB $380 Ex $304 Gd $240

MODEL CO POCKET
AUTOMATIC PISTOL . . . . .NiB $316 Ex $217 Gd $126
Caliber: .25 Automatic (6.35mm), 2.75-inch bbl., 4.5 inches overall. Weight: 13 oz. Fixed sights. Blued finish. Plastic grips. Made from 1941 to 197.

MODEL CU STARLET
POCKET PISTOL. . . . . .NiB $291 Ex $198 Gd $124
Light alloy frame. Caliber: .25 Auto (6.35mm). Eight-round magazine, 2.38-inch bbl., 4.75 inches overall. Weight: 10.5 oz. Fixed sights. Blued or chrome-plated slide w/frame anodized in black, blue, green, gray or gold. Plastic grips. Made from 1957 to 1997. (U.S. importation disc. 1968.)

MODEL F
AUTOMATIC PISTOL . . . . .NiB $362 Ex $268 Gd $130
Caliber: .22 LR. 10-round magazine, 4.5-inch bbl., 7.5 inches overall. Weight: 25 oz. Fixed sights. Blued finish. Plastic grips. Made from 1942 to 1967.

MODEL F
OLYMPIC RAPID-FIRE . . . . .NiB $556 Ex $408 Gd $230
Caliber: .22 Short. Nine-round magazine, 7-inch bbl., 11.06 inches overall. Weight: 52 oz. w/weights. Adj. target sight. Adj. 3-piece bbl. weight. Aluminum alloy slide. Muzzle brake. Plastic grips. Made from 1942 to 1967.

MODEL FM . . . . .NiB $362 Ex $279 Gd $171
Similar to Model FR except has heavier frame w/web in front of trigger guard, 4.25-inch heavy bbl., Weight: 32 oz. Made from 1972 to 1991.

MODEL FR. . . . . .NiB $362 Ex $279 Gd $171
Similar to Model F w/same general specifications but restyled, has slide stop and adj. rear sight. Made from 1967 to 1972.

MODEL FR SPORT . . . . .NiB $398 Ex $306 Gd $229
Same as Model FR except has 6-inch bbl., weight: 28 oz. Also avail. in chrome finish. Made from 1967 to 1991.

MODEL FS . . . . .NiB $362 Ex $309 Gd $165
Same as regular Model F but w/6-inch bbl. and adj. sights. Weight: 27 oz. Made from 1942 to 1967.

MODEL HK LANCER
AUTOMATIC PISTOL . . . . **NiB $319 Ex $225 Gd $249**
Similar to Starfire w/same general specifications except .22 LR. Made from 1955 to 1968.

MODEL HN
AUTOMATIC PISTOL . . . . **NiB $431 Ex $279 Gd $220**
Caliber: .380 Auto (9mm Short). Six-round magazine, 2.75-inch bbl., 5.56 inches overall. Weight: 20 oz. Fixed sights. Blued finish. Plastic grips. Made from 1934 to 1941.

MODEL H
. . . . **NiB $357 Ex $281 Gd $165**
Same as Model HN except .32 Auto (7.65mm), 7-round magazine, weight: 20 oz. Made from 1934 to 1941.

MODEL I
AUTOMATIC PISTOL . . . . **NiB $398 Ex $302 Gd $177**
Caliber: .32 Auto (7.65mm). Nine-round magazine, 4.81-inch bbl., 7.5 inches overall. Weight: 24 oz. Fixed sights. Blued finish. Plastic grips. Made from 1934 to 1936.

MODEL IN
. . . . **NiB $434 Ex $290 Gd $175**
Same as Model I except caliber .380 Auto (9mm Short), 8-round magazine, weight: 24.5 oz. Made from 1934-36.

MODEL M MILITARY
AUTOMATIC PISTOL . . . . **NiB $398 Ex $337 Gd $219**
Modification of the Model M without grip safety. Calibers: 9mm Bergmann (Largo), .45 ACP, 9mm Para. Eight-round magazine except 7-shot in .45 caliber, 5-inch bbl., 8.5 inches overall. Weight: 36 oz. Fixed sights. Blued finish. Checkered grips. Made from 1934 to 1939.

MODELS M40, M43, M45 FIRESTAR AUTO PISTOLS
Calibers: 9mm, .40 S&W, .45 ACP. Seven-round magazine (9mm) or 6-round (other calibers). 3.4-inch bbl., 6.5 inches overall. Weight: 30.35 oz. Blade front sight, adj. rear w/3-dot system. Checkered rubber grips. Blued or Starvel finish. Made 1990 to 1997.

M40 blued (.40 S&W)	NiB $367	Ex $289	Gd $232
M40 Starvel (.40 S&W)	NiB $398	Ex $304	Gd $239
M43 blued (9mm)	NiB $365	Ex $294	Gd $237
M43 Starvel (9mm)	NiB $398	Ex $304	Gd $239
M45 blued (.45 ACP)	NiB $357	Ex $270	Gd $120
M45 Starvel (.45 ACP)	NiB $377	Ex $290	Gd $143

MEGASTAR AUTOMATIC PISTOL
Calibers: 10mm, .45 ACP. 12-round magazine, 4.6-inch bbl., 8.44 inches overall. Weight: 47.6 oz. Blade front sight, adj. rear. Checkered composition grip. finishes: Blued or Starvel. Made from 1992 to 1997.

Blued finish, 10mm or .45 ACP	NiB $500	Ex $397	Gd $274
Starvel finish, 10mm or .45 ACP	NiB $544	Ex $416	Gd $305

MODEL P
. . . . **NiB $464 Ex $345 Gd $283**
Same as Model A except caliber .45 Auto, has 7-round magazine. Made from 1934 to 1975.

MODEL PD AUTOMATIC PISTOL
Caliber: .45 Auto. Six-round magazine, 3.75-inch bbl., 7 inches overall. Weight: 25 oz. Adj. rear sight, ramp front. Blued or Starvel finish. Checkered walnut grips. Made from 1975 to 1992.

Blued finish	NiB $398	Ex $304	Gd $224
Starvel finish	NiB $422	Ex $342	Gd $270

MODEL S
. . . . **NiB $319 Ex $220 Gd $159**
Same as Model SI except caliber .380 Auto (9mm), 7-round magazine, weight: 19 oz. Made from 1941 to 1965.

Star
Model M Military

Star
Model PD

MODEL SI AUTOMATIC PISTOL
. . . . . . **NiB $316 Ex $225 Gd $130**
Reduced-size modification of the Colt Government Model .45 Auto, lacks grip safety. Caliber: .32 Auto (7.65mm). Eight-round magazine, 4-inch bbl., 6.5 inches overall. Weight: 20 oz. Fixed sights. Blued finish. Plastic grips. Made from 1941 to 1965.

STARFIRE DK AUTOMATIC PISTOL
. . . . **NiB $453 Ex $337 Gd $255**
Light alloy frame. Caliber: .380 Automatic (9mm Short). Seven-round magazine, 3.13-inch bbl.. 5.5 inches overall. Weight: 14.5 oz. Fixed sights. Blued or chrome-plated slide w/frame anodized in black, blue, green, gray or gold. Plastic grips. Made 1957-97. U.S. importation disc. 1968.

MODEL SUPER A AUTOMATIC PISTOL
. **NiB $499 Ex $431 Gd $220**
Caliber: .38 Super. Improved version of Model A but has disarming bolt permitting easier takedown, cartridge indicator, magazine safety, take-down magazine, improved sights w/luminous spots for aiming in darkness. This is the standard service pistol of the Spanish Armed Forces, adopted 1946.

MODEL SUPER B AUTOMATIC PISTOL
Caliber: 9mm Para. Similar to Model B except w/improvements described under Model Super A. Made 1946 to 1990.

Super blued finish	NiB $453	Ex $342	Gd $225
Starvel finish	NiB $456	Ex $366	Gd $249

MODELS SUPER M, SUPER P
. . . . **NiB $852 Ex $685 Gd $478**
Calibers: .45 ACP, 9mm Parabellum or 9mm Largo, (Super M) and 9mm Parabellum (Super P). Improved versions of the Models M & P w/ same general specifications, but has disarming bolt permitting easier takedown, cartridge indicator, magazine safety, take-down magazine, improved sights w/luminous spots for aiming in darkness.

Sterling
Model 283 Target 300

Sterling
Model 284 Target 300L

Sterling
Model 285 Husky

Sterling
Model 286 Trapper

Sterling
Model 300

Sterling
Model 400

ULTRASTAR DA AUTOMATIC PISTOL NiB $365   Ex $290   Gd $200
Calibers: 9mm Parabellum or .40 S&W. Nine-round magazine, 3.57-inch bbl., 7 inches overall. Weight: 26 oz. Blade front, adjustable rear w/3-dot system. Polymer frame. Blue metal finish. Checkered black polymer grips. Imported from 1994 to 1997.

STENDA-WERKE — Suhl, Germany

POCKET AUTOMATIC PISTOL NiB $337   Ex $279   Gd $160
Essentially the same as the Beholla (see listing of that pistol for specifications). Made circa 1920-.25. Note: This pistol may be marked "Beholla" along w/the Stenda name and address.

STERLING ARMS CORPORATION — Gasport, New York

MODEL 283 TARGET 300
AUTO PISTOL . . . . NiB $189   Ex $109   Gd $90
Caliber: .22 LR. 10-round magazine, bbl. lengths: 4.5-, 6- 8-inch. 9 inches overall w/4.5-inch bbl., Weight: 36 oz. w/4.52-inch bbl. Adj. sights. Blued finish. Plastic grips. Made from 1970 to 1971.

MODEL 284 TARGET 300L . . . . NiB $179   Ex $115   Gd $90
Same as Model 283 except has 4.5- or 6-inch Luger-type bbl. Made from 1970 to 1971.

MODELS SUPER SI, SUPER S . . . . NiB $332   Ex $239   Gd $274
Same general specifications as the regular Model SI and S except w/ improvements described under Super Star. Made 1946 to 1972.

MODEL SUPER SM. . . . . NiB $398   Ex $386   Gd $204
Similar to Model Super S except has adj. rear sight, wood grips. Made from 1973 to 1981.

SUPER TARGET MODEL . . . . . NiB $1595   Ex $1396   Gd $1309
Same as Super Star model except w/adj. target rear sight. (Disc.)

GRADING: **NiB** = New in Box   **Ex** = Excellent or NRA 95%   **Gd** = Good or NRA 68%

MODEL 285 HUSKY . . . . NiB $179 Ex $115 Gd $90
Same as Model 283 except has fixed sights, 4.5-inch bbl only. Made from 1970 to 1971.

MODEL 286 TRAPPER . . . . NiB $129 Ex $115 Gd $90
Same as Model 284 except w/fixed sights. Made from 1970 to 1971.

MODEL 287 PPL-.380
AUTOMATIC PISTOL . . . . NiB $179 Ex $115 Gd $90
Caliber: .380 Auto. Six-round magazine, 1-inch bbl., 5.38 inches overall. Weight: 22.5 oz. Fixed sights. Blued finish. Plastic grips. Made from 1971 to 1972.

MODEL 300
AUTOMATIC PISTOL . . . . NiB $150 Ex $90 Gd $75
Caliber: .25 Auto. Six-round magazine, 2.33-inch bbl., 4.5 inches overall. Weight: 13 oz. Fixed sights. Blued or nickel finish. Plastic grips. Made from 1972 to 1983.

MODEL 300S . . . . NiB $179 Ex $115 Gd $90
Same as Model 300 except in stainless steel. Made 1976 to 1983.

MODEL 302 . . . . NiB $179 Ex $115 Gd $90
Same as Model 300 except in .22 LR. Made from 1973 to 1983.

MODEL 302S . . . . NiB $179 Ex $115 Gd $90
Same as Model 302 except in stainless steel. Made 1976 to 1983.

MODEL 400 DA
AUTOMATIC PISTOL . . . . NiB $309 Ex $214 Gd $129
Caliber: .380 Auto. Seven-round magazine, 3.5-inch bbl., 6.5 inches overall. Weight: 24 oz. Adj. rear sight. Blued or nickel finish. Checkered walnut grips. Made from 1975 to 1983.

MODEL 400S . . . . NiB $309 Ex $214 Gd $129
Same as Model 400 except stainless steel. Made from 1977 to 1983.

MODEL 450 DA
AUTO PISTOL . . . . NiB $309 Ex $214 Gd $129
Caliber: .45 Auto. Eight-round magazine, 4-inch bbl., 7.5 inches overall. Weight: 36 oz. Adj. rear sight. Blued finish. Smooth walnut grips. Made from 1977 to 1983.

MODEL PPL-22
AUTOMATIC PISTOL . . . . NiB $309 Ex $214 Gd $129
Caliber: .22 LR. 10-round magazine, 1-inch bbl., 5.5 inches overall. Weight: About 24 oz. Fixed sights. Blued finish. Wood grips. Only 382 made in 1970 to 1971.

J. STEVENS ARMS & TOOL CO. — Chicopee Falls, Massachusetts

This firm was established in Civil War era by Joshua Stevens, for whom the company was named. In 1999 Savage Arms began manufacture of Stevens designs.

NO. 10 SINGLE-SHOT
TARGET PISTOL . . . . NiB $249 Ex $207 Gd $160
Caliber: .22 LR. 8-inch bbl., 11.5 inches overall. Weight: 37 oz. Target sights. Blued finish. Hard rubber grips. In External appearance this arm resembles an automatic pistol but it has a tip-up action. Made from 1919 to 1939.

Stevens No. 10

Stevens No. 35

Stevens No. 38

NO. 35 OFFHAND MODEL SINGLE-SHOT
TARGET PISTOL . . . . NiB $377 Ex $301 Gd $255
Tip-up action. Caliber: .22 LR. Bbl. lengths: 6, 8, 10, 12.25 inches. Weight: 24 oz. w/6-inch bbl. Target sights. Blued finish. Walnut grips. Note: This pistol is similar to the earlier "Gould" model. Made from 1907 to 1939.

OFFHAND NO. 35 SINGLE-SHOT
PISTOL/SHOTGUN . . . . NiB $377 Ex $301 Gd $255
Same general specifications as the standard No. 35 pistol except chambered for the .410 shotshell. Six-, 8-, 10-, or 12-inch half-ocatagonal bbl., iron frame either blued, nickel plated, or case-hardened. BATF Class 3 license required to purchase. Made from 1923 to 1942.

NO. 36
SINGLE-SHOT PISTOL . . . . NiB $842 Ex $577 Gd $439
Tip-up action. Calibers: .22 Short and LR, .22 WRF, .25 Stevens, .32 Short Colt, .38 Long Colt, .44 Russian. 10- or 12-inch half-octagonal bbl., iron or brass frame w/nickel plated finish. Blued bbl. Checkered walnut grips. Made from 1880 to 1911.

NO. 37
SINGLE-SHOT PISTOL . . . . NiB $1020 Ex $836 Gd $544
Similar specifications to the No. 38 except the finger spur on the trigger guard has been omitted. Made from 1889 to 1919.

**Stoeger
American Eagle Luger P08 Stainless**

**Stoeger
American Eagle Luger Navy Model**

**Stoeger
Standard Luger .22**

**Targa
Model GT380XE**

NO. 38
SINGLE-SHOT PISTOL . . . . . . NiB $536 Ex $437 Gd $247
Tip-up action. Calibers: .22 Short and LR, .22 WRF, .25 Stevens, .32 Stevens, .32 Short Colt. Iron or brass frame. Checkered grips. Made from 1884 to 1903.

NO. 41 TIP-UP
SINGLE-SHOT PISTOL . . . . . . NiB $342 Ex $281 Gd $204
Tip-up action. Caliber: .22 Short, 3.5-inch half-octagonal bbl. Blued metal parts w/optional nickel frame. Made from 1896 to1915.

STEYR — Steyr, Austria

GB SEMIAUTOMATIC PISTOL
Caliber: 9mm Para. 18-round magazine, 5.4-inch bbl., 8.9 inches overall. Weight: 2.9 lbs. Post front sight, fixed, notched rear. Double, gas-delayed, blow-back action. Made from 1981 to 1988.
Commercial model . . . . NiB $680 Ex $530 Gd $337
**Military model
 (Less than 1000 imported)** . . . . . NiB $800 Ex $652 Gd $377

STEYR-HAHN (M12) AUTOMATIC PISTOL
Caliber: 9mm Steyr. Eight-round fixed magazine, charger loaded; 5.1-inch bbl., 8.5 inches overall. Weight: 35 oz. Fixed sights. Blued finish. Checkered wood grips. Made from 1911-19. Adopted by the Austro-Hungarian Army in 1912. Note: Confiscated by the Germans in 1938, an estimated 250,000 of these pistols were converted to 9mm Para. and stamped w/an identifying "08" on the left side of the slide. Mfd. by Osterreichische Waffenfabrik-Gesellschaft.
Commercial model (9mm Steyr) . NiB $544 Ex $468 Gd $377
**Military model (9mm Steyr-
 Austro-Hungarian Army)** . . . . . . NiB $568 Ex $479 Gd $229
**Military model (9mm Parabellum
 Conversion marked "08")** . . . . . NiB $1033 Ex $879 Gd $498

STOEGER LUGERS — South Hackensack, NJ
Formerly manufactured by Stoeger Industries, So. Hackensack, New Jersey; later by Classic Arms, Union City, New Jersey.

AMERICAN EAGLE LUGER
Caliber: 9mm Para. Seven-round magazine, 4- or 6-inch bbl., 8.25 inches overall (with 4-inch bbl.). or 10.25 inches (with 6-inch bbl.). Weight: 30 or 32 oz. Checkered walnut grips. Stainless steel w/brushed or matte black finish. Intro. 1994. Disc.
Model P-08 stainless (4-inch bbl.) NiB $774 Ex $499 Gd $366
Navy model (6-inch bbl.) . . . . NiB $854 Ex $811 Gd $400
w/matte black finish, add $85

STANDARD LUGER .22
AUTOMATIC PISTOL . . . . NiB $299 Ex $137 Gd $101
Caliber: .22 LR. 10-round magazine, 4.5- or 5.5-inch bbl., 8.88 inches overall (with 4.5-inch bbl.). Weight: 29.5 oz. (with 4.5-inch bbl.). Fixed sights. Black finish. Smooth wood grips. Made 1969 to 1986.

STEEL FRAME LUGER
.22 AUTO PISTOL . . . . NiB $290 Ex $133 Gd $95
Caliber: .22 LR. 10-round magazine, 4.5-inch bbl., 8.88 inches overall. Blued finish. Checkered wood grips. Features one piece forged and machined steel frame. Made from 1980 to 1986.

Taurus Model .44

Taurus Model 66

TARGET LUGER
.22 AUTO PISTOL . . . . **NiB $227 Ex $160 Gd $110**
Same as Standard Luger .22 except has target sights 9.38 inches overall
w/4.5-inch bbl., Checkered wood grips. Made from 1975 to 1986.

TARGA PISTOLS — Italy
Manufactured by Armi Tanfoglio Guiseppe.

MODEL GT26S
AUTO PISTOL . . . . **NiB $166 Ex $98 Gd $79**
Caliber: .25 ACP. Six-round magazine, 2.5-inch bbl., 4.63 inches overall. Weight: 15 oz. fixed sights. Checkered composition grips. Blued or
chrome finish. Disc. 1990.

MODEL GT32 AUTO PISTOL
Caliber: .32 ACP. Six-round magazine, 4.88-inch bbl., 7.38 inches over-
all. Weight: 26 oz. fixed sights. Checkered composition or walnut grips.
Blued or chrome finish.
Blued finished . . . . **NiB $166 Ex $109 Gd $88**
Chrome finish. . . . . **NiB $179 Ex $118 Gd $89**

MODEL GT380 AUTOMATIC PISTOL
Same as the Targa GT32 except chambered for .380 ACP.
Blued finish . . . . **NiB $179 Ex $118 Gd $89**
Chrome finish. . . . . **NiB $197 Ex $137 Gd $101**

MODEL GT380XE
AUTOMATIC PISTOL . . . . **NiB $220 Ex $165 Gd $101**
Caliber: .380 ACP. 11-round magazine, 3.75-inch bbl., 7.38 inches
overall. Weight: 28 oz. Fixed sights. Blued or satin nickel finish. Smooth
wooden grips. Made from 1980 to 1990.

Taurus
Model 74 Target Grade

Taurus Model 80

TAURUS INT'L. MFG. — Porto Alegre, Brazil
*Manufactured by FORJAS TAURUS S.A. Porto Alegre, Brazil; imported
Miami, FL.*

NOTE: *For ease in locating a particular Taurus handgun, the listings
are divided into two groupings: Automatic Pistols (page 184) and
Revolvers (below). For a complete handgun listing, please refer to
the index.*

- REVOLVERS -

MODEL GAUCHO. . . . . **NIB $425 EX $285 GD $245**
SA. Colt SAA reproduction. Caliber: .357 Mag., .44-40, or .45 LC. Six-
round cylinder, 4.75-, 5.5-, 7.5- or 12-in. bbl. Blued, case color, matte
or bright stainless finish. Made from 2005 to 2007.

MODEL 17C . . . . **NIB $300 EX $190 GD $170**
SA/DA. Caliber: .17 HMR or .17 Mach 2. 8-round cylinder, 2-, 4-, 5-in.
bbl. Adj. sights, rubber grips. Blued finish. Made from 2003 to 2007.

Taurus Model 82

www.skyhorsepublishing.com

Ultra-Lite (2-in. bbl.) . . . . NiB $340 Ex $200 Gd $180
Polished stainless finish . . . . NiB $330 Ex $195 Gd $175

MODEL 17IB . . . . NIB $295 EX $185 GD $170
SA/DA. Caliber: .17 HMR or .17 Mach 2. 8- or 9-round cylinder, 1.75-in. bbl. Adj. sights, rubber grips. Blued finish. Made from 2005 to 2007.
Matte stainless finish . . . . NiB $330 Ex $195 Gd $175

MODEL 17 TRACKER . . . . NiB $481 Ex $265 Gd $225
SA/DA. Caliber: .17 HMR. 7-round cylinder, 4-, 6.5-, 8.6-in. vent rib bbl. Adj. sights, rubber grips. Made from 2003 to date.
Matte stainless, add $50
Two-tone finish, add. $50
Silhoutte model (12-in. bbl., optic mount,
discont. 2004) . . . . NiB $320 Ex $205 Gd $185

MODEL 21T TRACKER . . . . NiB $330 Ex $205 Gd $185
SA/DA. Caliber: .218 Bee. 7-round cylinder, 6.5-in. vent rib bbl. Adj. sights, rubber grips. Made from 2003 to 2005.

MODEL 22H RAGING HORNET . NiB $800 Ex $530 Gd $455
SA/DA. Caliber: .22 Hornet. 8-round cylinder, 10-in. vent rib bbl. Adj. sights, optic mount, rubber grips. Made from 1999 to 2004.

MODEL 30C RAGING THIRTY
HUNTER . . . . NiB $800 Ex $530 Gd $455
SA/DA. Caliber: .30 Carbine. 8-round cylinder, 12-in. vent rib full lug bbl. Adj. sights, optic mount, adj. trigger, rubber grips. Made from 2003 to 2004.
Silhoutte model (12-in. half lug bbl., optic mount,
discont. 2004) . . . . NiB $795 Ex $525 Gd $450

MODEL 44 DA REVOLVER
Caliber: .44 Mag. Six-round cylinder, 4-, 6.5-, or 8.38-inch bbl. Weight: 44.75 oz., 52.5 or 57.25 oz. Brazilian hardwood grips. Blued or stainless steel finish. Made from 1994 to 2004.
Blued finish . . . . NiB $433 Ex $327 Gd $220
Model 44SS Stainless finish (intro. 1994)NiB $600 Ex $487 Gd $274

MODEL 44C TRACKER . . . . NiB $646 EX $430 GD $380
SA/DA. Caliber: .44 Mag. 5-round cylinder, 4-in. ported bbl. Blued or matte stainless finish. Made from 2005 to date.

MODEL 45-410 "THE JUDGE" . . . NiB $610 EX $355 GD $300
SA/DA. Caliber: .45 LC/.410 3-in. chamber. 5-round cylinder, 2.5-, 3-, 6.5-in. bbl. Blued or matte stainless finish. Made from 2006 to date.
Ultra-Lite . . . . NiB $580 Ex $400 Gd $355

MODEL 45-410 "THE JUDGE"
PUBLIC DEFENDER . . . . NiB $610 EX $355 GD $300
SA/DA. Caliber: .45 LC/.410 2.5-in. chamber. 5-round stainless or titanium cylinder, 2-in. bbl. smaller hammer. Blued or matte stainless finish. Made from 2009 to date.
Ultra-Lite . . . . NiB $580 Ex $400 Gd $355
Polymer frame . . . . NiB $550 Ex $400 Gd $355

MODEL 65 DA REVOLVER
Caliber: .357 Magnum. 6-round cylinder, 3- or 4-inch bbl., weight: 32 oz. Front ramp sight, square notch rear. Checkered walnut target grip. Royal blued or satin nickel finish. Imported 1992 to 1997 and from 1999 to date.
Blue finish . . . . NiB $398 Ex $289 Gd $171
Stainless finish . . . . NiB $427 Ex $351 Gd $212

MODEL 66 DA REVOLVER
Calibers: .357 Magnum, .38 Special. Six-round cylinder, 3-, 4- and 6-inch bbl., weight: 35 oz. Serrated ramp front sight, rear click adj. Checkered walnut grips. Royal blued or nickel finish. Imported 1992-1997 and from 1999 to date.

Blue finish . . . . NiB $500 Ex $351 Gd $212
Model 66SS Stainless finish. . . . . NiB $550 Ex $398 Gd $229

MODEL 73 DA REVOLVER . . . NiB $211 Ex $121 Gd $101
Caliber: .32 Long. Six-round cylinder, 3-inch heavy bbl., weight: 20 oz. Checkered grips. Blued or satin nickel finish. Disc. 1993.

MODEL 76 TARGET
GRADE DA REVOLVER. . . . . . NiB $244 Ex $279 Gd $118
Caliber: .32 S&W Long. Six-round cylinder, 3-inch bbl., 8.25 inches overall. Weight: 20 oz. Adj. rear sight, ramp front. Blued or nickel finish. Checkered walnut grips. Made from 1971 to 1990.

MODEL 80 DA REVOLVER
Caliber: .38 Special. Six-round cylinder, bbl. lengths: 3, 4 inches, 9.25 inches overall (with 4-inch bbl.). Weight: 30 oz. (with 4-inch bbl.) Fixed sights. Blued or nickel finish. Checkered walnut grips. Made 1996 to 1997.
Blued finish . . . . NiB $214 Ex $140 Gd $98
Model 80SS Stainless finish. . . . . NiB $431 Ex $337 Gd $258

MODEL 82 HEAVY BARREL
Same as Model 80 except has heavy bbl., weight: 33 oz. w/4-inch bbl., Made from 1971 to date.
Blued finish . . . . NiB $366 Ex $290 Gd $212
Model 82SS Stainless finish (intro. 1993). . . . NiB $437 Ex $327 Gd $259

MODEL 83 HEAVY BARREL TARGET GRADE
Same as Model 84 except has heavy bbl., weight: 34.5 oz. Made from 1977 to date.
Blued finish . . . . NiB $255 Ex $160 Gd $105
Model 83SS Stainless finish. . . . . NiB $281 Ex $198 Gd $128

Taurus Model 83

Taurus Model 84

**Taurus
Model 85 Concealed Hammer**

Taurus Model 86

**Taurus
Model 85 w/Spur Hammer**

MODEL 84 TARGET
GRADE REVOLVER . . . . **NiB $312 Ex $235 Gd $170**
Caliber: .38 Special. Six-round cylinder, 4-inch bbl., 9.25 inches over-all. Weight: 31 oz. Adj. rear sight, ramp front. Blued or nickel finish. Checkered walnut grips. Made from 1971 to 1989.

MODEL 85 DA REVOLVER
Caliber: .38 Special. Five-round cylinder, 2- or 3-inch. bbl., weight: 21 oz. Fixed sights. Checkered walnut grips. Blued, satin nickel or stainless-steel finish. Model 85CH is the same as the standard version except for concealed hammer. Made from 1997 to 2012.

Blued or satin nickel finish . . . . . **NiB $377   Ex $302   Gd $143**
Stainless steel finish . . . . **NiB $437   Ex $362   Gd $189**
Titanium Ultra-Lightweight . . . . . **NiB $540   Ex $370   Gd $320**

MODEL 85PLYB2
"PROTECTOR PLY" . . . . **NiB $355   EX $230   GD $210**
SA/DA. Caliber: .38 Spl.+P. Five-round blued or matte stainless cylinder, 1.25- or 1.75-in. vent rib bbl., polymer frame. Weight: 16.5 oz. Fixed fiber optic sights. Made from 2011 to 2012.

MODEL 86 CUSTOM TARGET
DA REVOLVER . . . . **NiB $301   Ex $208   Gd $110**
Caliber: .38 Special. Six-round cylinder, 6-inch bbl., 11.25 inches overall. Weight: 34 oz. Adj. rear sight, Partridge-type front. Blued finish. Checkered walnut grips. Made from 1971 to 1994.

MODEL 94 DA REVOLVER
Same as Model 74 except .22 LR. w/9-round cylinder, 3- or 4-inch bbl., weight: 25 oz. Blued or stainless finish. Made from 1971 to date.
Blued finish . . . . **NiB $362   Ex $306   Gd $219**
Model 94SS Stainless finish . . . . . **NiB $386   Ex $348   Gd $255**

MODEL 96 TARGET SCOUT . . . . . **NiB $301   Ex $209   Gd $112**
Same as Model 86 except in .22 LR. Made from 1971 to 1998.

MODEL 431 DA REVOLVER
Caliber: .44 Spec. Five-round cylinder, 3- or 4-inch solid-rib bbl. w/ejector shroud. Weight: 35 oz. w/4-inch bbl., Serrated ramp front sight, notched topstrap rear. Blued or stainless finish. Made 1992 to 1997.
Blued finish . . . . **NiB $239   Ex $198   Gd $144**
Stainless finish . . . . **NiB $434   Ex $306   Gd $265**

MODEL 441 DA REVOLVER
Similar to the Model 431 except w/6-inch bbl. and fully adj. target sights. Weight: 40 oz. Made from 1991 to 1997.
Blued finish . . . . **NiB $306   Ex $237   Gd $144**
Stainless finish . . . . **NiB $434   Ex $306   Gd $225**

MODEL 445 DA REVOLVER
Caliber: .44 Special. Five-round cylinder, 2-inch bbl., 6.75 inches over-all. Weight: 28.25 oz. Serrated ramp front sight, notched frame rear. Standard or concealed hammer. Santoprene I grips. Blue or stainless finish. Imported from 1997 to 2003.
Blued finish . . . . **NiB $306   Ex $239   Gd $190**
Stainless finish . . . . **NiB $342   Ex $265   Gd $204**

MODEL 454 DA RAGING BULL REVOLVER
Caliber: .454 Casull. Five-round cylinder, ported 6.5- or 8.4-inch vent rib bbl., 12 inches overall (w/6.5-inch bbl.). Weight: 53 or 63 oz. Partridge front sight, micrometer adj. rear. Santoprene I or walnut grips. Blue or stainless finish. Imported from 1997 to date.
Blued finish . . . . **NiB $862   Ex $730   Gd $587**
Stainless finish . . . . **NiB $877   Ex $791   Gd $648**

MODEL 669/669VR DA REVOLVER
Caliber: .357 Mag. Six-round cylinder, 4- or 6-inch solid-rib bbl. w/ ejector shroud Model 669VR has vent rib bbl., weight: 37 oz. w/4-inch bbl., Serrated ramp front sight, micro-adj. rear. Royal blued or stainless finish. Checkered Brazilian hardwood grips. Made from 1989 to 1998.
Blued finish . . . . **NiB $283   Ex $214   Gd $165**
Stainless finish . . . . **NiB $362   Ex $286   Gd $240**
Model 669VR, blued finish . . . . . **NiB $301   Ex $225   Gd $175**
Model 669VR, stainless finish . . . **NiB $362   Ex $286   Gd $255**

MODEL 741/761 DA REVOLVER
Caliber: .32 H&R Mag. Six-round cylinder, 3- or 4-inch solid-rib bbl. w/ejector shroud. Weight: 20 oz. w/3-inch bbl., Serrated ramp front sight, micro-adj. rear. Blued or stainless finish. Checkered Brazilian hardwood grips. Made from 1991 to 1997.
Blued finish . . . . NiB $225 Ex $129 Gd $90
Stainless finish . . . . NiB $291 Ex $204 Gd $150
MODEL 761(6-inch bbl.,
   34 oz., blued finish) . . . . NiB $281 Ex $204 Gd $143

MODEL 941 TARGET REVOLVER
Caliber: .22 Magnum. Eight-round cylinder. Solid-rib bbl. w/ejector shroud. Micro-adj. rear sight. Brazilian hardwood grips. Blued or stainless finish.
Blued finish . . . . NiB $357 Ex $306 Gd $204
Stainless finish . . . . NiB $408 Ex $365 Gd $274

- AUTOMATIC PISTOLS -

MODEL 22 PLY . . . . NiB $285 Ex $177 Gd $101
DAO. Caliber: .22 LR. 8-round magazine, tip-up 2.3-in. bbl., polymer frame. Weight: 10.8 oz. Fixed sights. Made from 2012 to date.

MODEL 25 PLY . . . . NiB $285 Ex $177 Gd $101
Similar to Model 22 PLY model except chambered in .25 ACP. Made from 2012 to date.

MODEL PT-22 . . . . NiB $285 Ex $177 Gd $101
SA/DA. Caliber: .22 LR. Nine-round magazine, 2.75-inch bbl., weight: 12.3 oz. Fixed open sights. Brazilian hardwood grips. Blued finish. Made from 1991 to date.

MODEL PT-24/7 . . . . NIB $455 EX $300 GD $260
DAO. Caliber: 9mm, .40 S&W or .45 ACP. 10-, 12-, 15, or 17-round magazine, 4-in. bbl. Polymer frame w/blued or stainless slide. 3-dot sights. Acessory rail. Made from 2004 to 2005.

**MODEL PT-24/7
PRO FULL SIZE** . . . . NIB $420 EX $290 GD $240
SA with DA second strike trigger. Caliber: 9mm, .40 S&W or .45 ACP. 10-, 12-, 15, or17-round magazine, 4-in. bbl. Polymer frame w/blued or stainless slide. 3-dot sights. Acessory rail. Made from 2006 to 2010.
Pro Compact (3.1-in. bbl.) . . . . . NiB $420 Ex $280 Gd $250
Pro Long Slide (5.2-in. bbl.) . . . . NiB $450 Ex $295 Gd $255

MODEL PT-24/7 G2 . . . . NIB $530 EX $300 GD $260
SA with DA second strike trigger. Caliber: 9mm, .40 S&W or .45 ACP. 10-, 12-, 15, or17-round magazine, 4-in. bbl. Polymer frame w/interchangeable backstraps, ambidextrous controls, blued or stainless slide. 3-dot sights. Acessory rail. Made from 2011 to date.
Compact (3.1-in. bbl.) . . . . NIB $530 EX $300 GD $260

MODEL PT-24/7 OSS . . . . NIB $480 EX $330 GD $290
Similar to PT-24/7 Pro Full Size except w/5.25-in. bbl. and tan or black polymer frame. Made from 2007 to 2010.

MODEL PT-25 . . . . NiB $285 Ex $170 Gd $92
Same general specifications as Model PT 22 except in .25 ACP w/eight-round magazine. Made from 1992 to date.

MODEL PT-58 . . . . NiB $408 Ex $332 Gd $240
Caliber: .380 ACP. Twelve-round magazine, 4-inch bbl., 7.2 inches overall. Weight: 30 oz. Blade front sight, rear adj. for windage w/3-dot sighting system. Blued, satin nickel or stainless finish. Made from 1988 to 1996.

**Taurus
Model 669**

**Taurus
Model PT-22**

**Taurus
Model PT-58**

**Taurus
Model PT-92AF**

MODEL PT-92AF
SA/DA. Similar to Beretta M92 SB-F. Caliber: 9mm Para. 15-round magazine, 5-inch bbl., 8.5 inches overall. Weight: 24 oz. Blade front sight, notched bar rear. Smooth Brazilian walnut grips. Blued, satin nickel or stainless finish. Made from 1991 to date.

Blued finish . . . . NiB $670 Ex $377 Gd $286
Satin nickel finish. . . . . NiB $720 Ex $418 Gd $319
Stainless finish . . . . NiB $679 Ex $398 Gd $306
Deluxe (blue/gold or stainless/gold)NiB $520 Ex $390 Gd $300

Taurus
Model PT-99AF

Taurus
Model PT-908

MODEL PT-92AFC COMPACT PISTOL
Same general specs as Model PT-92AF except w/13-round magazine, 4.25-inch bbl., 7.5 inches overall. Weight: 31 oz. Made 1991 to 1996

Blued finish . . . . NiB $362 Ex $283 Gd $214
Satin nickel finish. . . . . NiB $408 Ex $328 Gd $266
Stainless finish . . . . NiB $434 Ex $346 Gd $220

MODEL PT-99AF
SEMI-AUTOMATIC PISTOL . . . . . NiB $530 Ex $437 Gd $301
Same general specifications as Model PT-92AF except rear sight is adj. for elevation and windage, and finish is blued or satin nickel.

MODEL PT-100 DA AUTOMATIC PISTOL
Caliber: .40 S&W. Eleven-round magazine, 5-inch bbl., weight: 34 oz. Fixed front sight, adj. rear w/3-dot system. Smooth hardwood grip. Blued, satin nickel or stainless finish. Made from 1991 to 1997.

Blued finish . . . . NiB $500 Ex $444 Gd $362

Satin finish. . . . . NiB $546 Ex $469 Gd $377
Stainless finish . . . . NiB $536 Ex $444 Gd $367

MODEL PT-101 DA AUTOMATIC PISTOL
Same general specifications as Model 100 except w/micrometer click adj. sights. Made from 1992 to 1996.

Blued finish . . . . NiB $536 Ex $444 Gd $367
Satin nickel finish. . . . . NiB $576 Ex $453 Gd $367
Stainless finish . . . . NiB $536 Ex $444 Gd $367

MODEL PT-111 MILLENNIUM DAO PISTOL
Caliber: 9mm Parabellum. 10-round magazine, 3.12-inch bbl., 6 inches overall. Weight: 19.1 oz. Fixed low-profile sights w/3-dot system. Black polymer grip/frame. Blue or stainless slide. Imported from 1998 to 2004.

Blue finish . . . . NiB $362 Ex $265 Gd $130
Stainless finish . . . . NiB $380 Ex $286 Gd $185

MODEL PT-908 SEMIAUTOMATIC PISTOL
Caliber: 9mm Para. Eight-round magazine, 3.8-inch bbl., 7 inches overall. Weight: 30 oz. Post front sight, drift-adj. combat rear w/3-dot system. Blued, satin nickel or stainless finish. Made 1993 to 1997.

Blued finish . . . . NiB $357 Ex $286 Gd $204
Satin nickel finish. . . . . NiB $388 Ex $316 Gd $205
Stainless finish . . . . NiB $431 Ex $321 Gd $265

MODEL PT-911 COMPACT SEMIAUTOMATIC PISTOL
Caliber: 9mm Parabellum. 10-round magazine, 3.75-inch bbl., 7.05 inches overall. Weight: 28.2 oz. Fixed low-profile sights w/3-dot system. Santoprene II grips. Blue or stainless finish. Imported from 1997 to date.

Blued finish . . . . NiB $546 Ex $408 Gd $270
Stainless finish . . . . NiB $546 Ex $408 Gd $270

MODEL PT-938 COMPACT SEMIAUTOMATIC PISTOL
Caliber: 380 ACP. 10-round magazine, 3.72-inch bbl., 6.75 inches overall. Weight: 27 oz. Fixed low-profile sights w/3-dot system. Santoprene II grips. Blue or stainless finish. Imported 1997 to 2005.

Blue finish . . . . NiB $499 Ex $357 Gd $265
Stainless finish . . . . NiB $469 Ex $377 Gd $286

MODEL PT-940 COMPACT SEMIAUTOMATIC PISTOL
Caliber: .40 S&W. 10-round magazine, 3.75-inch bbl., 7.05 inches overall. Weight: 28.2 oz. Fixed low-profile sights w/3-dot system. Santoprene II grips. Blue or stainless finish. Imported from 1997 to date.

Blue finish . . . . NiB $546 Ex $437 Gd $290
Stainless finish . . . . NiB $571 Ex $499 Gd $316

MODEL PT-945 COMPACT SEMIAUTOMATIC PISTOL
Caliber: .45 ACP. Eight-round magazine, 4.25-inch bbl., 7.48 inches overall. Weight: 29.5 oz. Fixed low-profile sights w/3-dot system. Santoprene II grips. Blue or stainless finish. Imported from 1995 to date.

Blue finish . . . . NiB $601 Ex $530 Gd $377
Stainless finish . . . . NiB $587 Ex $437 Gd $316

TEXAS ARMS — Waco, Texas

DEFENDER DERRINGER . . . . . NiB $306 Ex $218 Gd $120
Calibers: 9mm, .357 Mag., .44 Mag., .45 ACP, .45 Colt/.410. Three-inch bbl., 5 inches overall. Weight: 21 oz. Blade front sight, fixed rear. Matte gun-metal gray finish. Smooth grips. Made from 1993 to 1999.

TEXAS LONGHORN ARMS — Richmond, Texas

"THE JEZEBEL" PISTOL . . . . . . NiB $337   Ex $265   Gd $200
Top-break, single-shot. Caliber: .22 Short, Long or LR. Six-inch half-round bbl., 8 inches overall. Weight: 15 oz. Bead front sight, adj. rear. One-piece walnut grip. Stainless finish. Intro. in 1987.

SA REVOLVER CASED SET
Set contains one each of the Texas Longhorn Single Actions. Each chambered in the same caliber and w/the same serial number. Intro. in 1984.
Standard set . . . . NiB $1620   Ex $1400   Gd $1000
Engraved set . . . . NiB $1820   Ex $1615   Gd $1219

SOUTH TEXAS ARMY LIMITED
EDITION SA REVOLVER . . . . . NiB $1840   Ex $1418   Gd $1120
Calibers: All popular centerfire pistol calibers. Six-round cylinder, 4.75-inch bbl.,10.25 inches overall. Weight: 40 oz. Fixed sights. Color casehardened frame. One-piece deluxe walnut grips. Blued bbl., Intro. in 1984.

SESQUICENTENNIAL SA REVOLVER . . . NiB $2613   Ex $2114   Gd $1489
Same as South Texas Army Limited Edition except engraved and nickel-plated w/one-piece ivory grip. Intro. in 1986.

TEXAS BORDER SPECIAL
SA REVOLVER . . . . NiB $1744   Ex $1316   Gd $954
Same as South Texas Army Limited Edition except w/3.5-inch bbl. and bird's-head grips. Intro. in 1984.

WEST TEXAS FLAT TOP
TARGET SA REVOLVER . . . . . . NiB $1633   Ex $1316   Gd $896
Same as South TExas Army Limited Edition except w/choice of bbl. lengths from 7 .5 to 15 inches. Same special features w/flat-top style frame and adj. rear sight. Intro. in 1984.

THOMPSON — West Hurley, New York
Manufactured by Auto-Ordnance Corporation; owned by Kahr Arms.
Also see Auto-Ordnance handgun section.

MODEL 1927A-5 . . . . NiB $1071   Ex $855   Gd $668
Similar to Thompson Model 1928A submachine gun except has no provision for automatic firing, does not have detachable buttstock. Caliber: .45 Auto, 20-round detachable box magazine (5-, 15- and 30-round box magazines, 39-round drum also available), 13-inch finned bbl., overall length: 26 inches. Weight: About 6.75 lbs. Adj. rear sight, blade front. Blued finish. Walnut grips. Intro. in 1977.

THOMPSON/CENTER ARMS — Rochester, New Hampshire
Acquired by Smith & Wesson in 2006.

CONTENDER SINGLE-SHOT PISTOL
Break frame, underlever action. Calibers: (rimfire) .22 LR. .22 WMR, 5mm RRM; (standard centerfire), .218 Bee, .22 Hornet, .22 Rem. Jet, .221 Fireball, .222 Rem., .25-35, .256 Win. Mag., .30 M1 Carbine, .30-30, .38 Auto, .38 Special .357 Mag./Hot Shot, 9mm Para., .45 Auto, .45 Colt, .44 Magnum/Hot Shot; (wildcat centerfire) .17 Ackley Bee, .17 Bumblebee, .17 Hornet, .17 K Hornet, .17 Mach IV, .17-.222, .17-.223, .22 K Hornet, .30 Herrett, .357 Herrett, .357-4 B&D. Interchangeable

Thompson/Center
Vent Rib Barrel

TThompson/Center
Contender Bull Barrel

bbls.: 8.75- or 10-inch standard octagon (.357 Mag., .44 Mag. and .45 Colt available w/detachable choke for use w/Hot Shot cartridges); 10-inch w/vent rib and detachable internal choke tube for Hot Shots, .357 and .44 Magnum only; 10-inch bull bbl., .30 or .357 Herrett only. 13.5 inches overall w/10-inch bbl., Weight: 43 oz. (w/standard 10-inch bbl.). Adj. rear sight, ramp front; vent rib model has folding rear sight, adj. front; bull bbl., available w/or w/o sights. Lobo 1.5/ scope and mount (add $40 to value). Blued finish. Receiver photoengraved. Checkered walnut thumbrest grip and forearm (pre-1972 model has different grip w/silver grip cap). Made from 1967 to date, w/the following revisions and variations.
Standard model . . . . NiB $419   Ex $321   Gd $204
Vent rib model . . . . NiB $439   Ex $342   Gd $230
Bull bbl. model, w/sights . . . . NiB $434   Ex $326   Gd $214
Bull bbl. model, without sights . . . . NiB $431   Ex $316   Gd $204
Extra standard bbl., add $255
Extra vent rib or bull bbl., add $306

CONTENDER BULL BARREL . . NiB $408   Ex $321   Gd $204
Caliber offerings of the bull bbl. version Expanded in 1973 and 1978, making it the Contender model w/the widest range of caliber options: .22 LR, .22 Win. Mag., .22 Hornet, .223 Rem., 7mm T.C.U., 7x30 Waters, .30 M1 Carbine, .30-30 Win., .32 H&R Mag., .32-20 Win., .357 Rem. Max., .357 Mag., 10mm Auto, .44 Magnum, .445 Super Magnum. 10-inch heavy bbl., Partridge-style iron sights. Contoured Competitor grip. Blued finish.

CONTENDER INTERNAL
CHOKE MODEL . . . . NiB $434   Ex $347   Gd $225
Originally made in 1968-69 w/octagonal bbl., this Internal Choke version in .45 Colt/.410 caliber only was reintroduced in 1986 w/10-inch bull bbl. Vent rib also was available. Fixed iron rear sight, bead front. Detachable choke screws into muzzle. Blued finish. Contoured American black walnut Competitor grip, also since 1986, has nonslip rubber insert permanently bonded to back of grip.
w/bull bbl, add $50
w/vent rib, add $61

**Uberti
Rolling Block Target**

**Uberti
Model 1873 Cattleman**

**Uberti
Cattleman Buntline Target**

CONTENDER OCTAGON BARREL . . NiB $388 Ex $290 Gd $204
The original Contender design, this octagonal bbl., version began to see the discontinuance of caliber offerings in 1980. Now it is available in .22 LR only, 10-inch octagonal bbl., Partridge-style iron sights. Contoured Competitor grip. Blued finish.

CONTENDER STAINLESS
Similar to the standard Contender models except stainless steel w/blued sights. Black Rynite forearm and ambidExtrous finger-groove grip. Made from 2006 to date.
Standard SS model (10-inch bbl.) . . . . . .NiB $469 Ex $386 Gd $306
SS Super 14 . . . . .NiB $377 Ex $291 Gd $143
SS Super 16 . . . . .NiB $377 Ex $291 Gd $143

CONTENDER SUPER (14 IN./16 IN.)
Calibers: .22 LR, .222 Rem., .223 Rem., 6mm T.C.U., 6.5mm T.C.U., 7mm T.C.U., 7x30 Waters, .30 Herrett, .30-30 Win., .357 Herrett, .357 Rem. Max., .35 Rem., 10mm Auto, .44 Mag., .445 Super Mag. 14- or 16.25-inch bull bbl., 18 or 20.25 inches overall. Weight: 43-65 oz. Partridge-style ramp front sight, adj. target rear. Blued finish. Made from 1978 to 1997.
Super 14 . . . . NiB $380 Ex $306 Gd $204
Super 16 . . . . NiB $380 Ex $306 Gd $204

CONTENDER TC ALLOY II
Calibers: .22 LR, .223 Rem., .357 Magnum, .357 Rem. Max., .44 Magnum, 7mm T.C.U., .30-30 Win., .45 Colt/.410 (w/internal choke), .35 Rem. and 7-30 Waters (14-inch bbl.). 10- or 14-inch bull bbl. or 10-inch vent rib bbl. (w/internal choke). All metal parts permanently electroplated w/T/C Alloy II, which is harder than stainless steel, ensur-

ing smoother action, 30 percent longer bbl. life. Other design specifications the same as late model Contenders. Made from 1986 to 1989.
w/10-inch bull bbl. . . . . .NiB $377 Ex $306 Gd $214
w/vent rib bbl. and choke. . . . . .NiB $464 Ex $377 Gd $286
Super 14 . . . . .NiB $388 Ex $306 Gd $219

ENCORE SINGLE-SHOT PISTOL
Similar to the standard Contender models except w/10-, 12- or 15-inch bbl., Calibers: .22-250 Rem., .223 Rem., .243 Win., .260 Rem., .270 Win., 7mm BR Rem., 7mm-08 Rem., 7.62x39mm, .308 Win., .30-06 Spfd., .44 Rem. Mag., .444 Marlin, .45-70 Govt., .45 LC/410. Blue or stainless finish. Walnut or composition, ambidExtrous finger-groove grip. Hunter Model w/2.5-7x pistol scope. Note: Encore bbls. are not interchangeable with Contenter models. Made from 1998 to date.
w/10-inch bbl. (blue, disc.). . . . . .NiB $561 Ex $499 Gd $270
w/12-inch bbl., blued . . . . .NiB $561 Ex $499 Gd $270
w/15-inch bbl., blued . . . . .NiB $576 Ex $464 Gd $286
Hunter model w/2,5-7x scope . . . . .NiB $755 Ex $546 Gd $365
Encore model (stainless finish), add. $25

G2 CONTENDER SINGLE-SHOT PISTOL
Similar to the Contender model except w/12- or 14-in. bbl., various rimfire and centerfire calibers. Walnut grip. Note: older Contender bbls. are compatiable with G2 Contenter models. Made from 2002 to 2012.
Blued finish . . . . .NiB $650 Ex $400 Gd $350
Stainless finish . . . . .NiB $695 Ex $425 Gd $370

PRO-HUNTER SINGLE-SHOT PISTOL . NiB $655 Ex $430 Gd $360
Similar to the Contender model except w/15-in. fluted stainless steel bbl., various calibers. Walnut or composite grip. Made from 2006 to 2012.

UBERTI — Ponte Zanano, Italy
Manufactured by Aldo Uberti, imported by Uberti USA, Inc.
Manufactures many reproduction revolvers for a variety of companies including EMF, Taylor's & Co., and Cimarron Firearms.

**MODEL 1871 ROLLING BLOCK
TARGET PISTOL** . . . . NiB $418 Ex $321 Gd $230
Single shot. Calibers: .22 LR, .22 Magnum, .22 Hornet and .357 Magnum; 9.5-inch bbl., 14 inches overall. Weight: 44 oz. Ramp front sight, fully adjustable rear. Smooth walnut grip and forearm. Color casehardened frame w/brass trigger guard. Blued half-octagon or full round barrel. Made 2002 to 2006.

MODEL 1873 CATTLEMAN SA REVOLVER
Calibers: .357 Magnum, .38-40, .44-40, .44 Special, .45 Long Colt, .45 ACP. Six-round cylinder, Bbl length: 3.5, 4.5, 4.75, 5.5, 7.5 or 18 inches; 10.75 inches overall (5.5-inch bbl.). Weight: 38 oz. (5.5-inch bbl.). Color casehardened steel frame w/steel or brass back strap and trigger guard. Nickel-plated or blued barrel and cylinder. Imported from 1997 to 2010.
First issue . . . . .NiB $459 Ex $386 Gd $235
Bisley . . . . .NiB $459 Ex $386 Gd $235
Bisley (flattop) . . . . .NiB $459 Ex $386 Gd $235
Buntline (reintroduced 1992) . . . . .NiB $500 Ex $395 Gd $244
Quick Draw . . . . .NiB $459 Ex $386 Gd $235
Sabre (bird head) . . . . .NiB $459 Ex $386 Gd $235
Sheriff's model . . . . .NiB $459 Ex $386 Gd $235
Convertible cylinder, add $75
Stainless steel, add $150
Steel backstrap and trigger guard, add $75
Target sights, add $75

MODEL 1875 REMINGTON OUTLAW
Replica of Model 1875 Remington. Calibers: .357 Mag., .44-40, .45 ACP, .45 Long Colt. Six-round cylinder, 5.5- to 7.5-inch bbl., 11.75 to

13.75 inches overall. Weight: 44 oz. (with 7.5 inch bbl). Color case-hardened steel frame w/steel or brass back strap and trigger guard. Blue or nickel finish.

Blue finish .NiB $479   Ex $366   Gd $219
Nickel finish (disc. 1995) . . . . .NiB $541   Ex $473   Gd $321
Convertible cylinder
(.45 LC/.45 ACP), add. $50

MODEL 1890 REMINGTON POLICE
Similar to Model 1875 Remington except without the web under the ejector housing.
Blue Model .NiB $464   Ex $346   Gd $198
Nickel finish (disc. 1995) . . . . .NiB $862   Ex $704   Gd $345
Convertible Cylinder (.45 LC/.45 ACP), add $50

ULTRA LIGHT ARMS, INC — Granville, West Virginia

MODEL 20 SERIES PISTOLS
Calibers: .22-250 thru .308 Win. Five-round magazine, 14-inch bbl., weight: 4 lbs. Composite Kevlar, graphite reinforced stock. Benchrest grade action available in right- or left-hand models. Timney adjustable trigger w/three function safety. Bright or matte finish. Made 1987 to 1999.
Model 20 Hunter's Pistol (disc. 1989) NiB $1295 Ex $1057 Gd $974
Model 20 Reb Pistol (disc. 1999) . . .NiB $1508 Ex $1345 Gd $1199

UNIQUE — Hendaye, France
Manufactured by Manufacture d'Armes des Pyrénées. Currently import-ed by Nygord Precision Products, previously by Beeman Precision Arms.

MODEL B/CF AUTOMATIC PISTOL. . . NiB $220   Ex $115   Gd $70
Calibers: .32 ACP, .380 ACP. Nine-round (.32) or 8-round (.38) maga-zine, 4-inch bbl., 6.6 inches overall. Weight: 24.3 oz. Blued finish. Plain or thumbrest plastic grips. Intro. in 1954. Disc.

MODEL D2 . . . . NiB $326   Ex $219   Gd $177
Same as Model D6 except has 4.5-inch bbl., 7.5 inches overall, weight: 24.5 oz. Made from 1954. Disc.

MODEL D6 AUTOMATIC PISTOL. . . NiB $332   Ex $239   Gd $118
Caliber: .22 LR. 10-round magazine, 6-inch bbl., 9.25 inches overall. Weight: About 26 oz. Adj. sights. Blued finish. Plain or thumbrest plas-tic grips. Intro. in 1954. Disc.

MODEL DES/32U RAPID FIRE PISTOL
Caliber: .32 S&W Long (wadcutter). Five- or 6-round magazine, 5.9-inch bbl., weight: .40.2 oz. Blade front sight, micro-adj. rear. Trigger adj. for weight and position. Blued finish. Stippled handrest grips. Imported from 1990 to date.
Right-hand model . . . . NiB $1418   Ex $1316   Gd $1155
Left-hand model . . . . NiB $1486   Ex $1366   Gd $1220

MODEL DES/69-U STANDARD MATCH PISTOL
Caliber: .22 LR. Five-round magazine, 5.9-inch bbl., w/250 gm counter-weight. 10.6 inches overall. Trigger adjusts for position and pull. Weight: 35.3 oz. Blade front sight, micro-adj. rear. Checkered walnut thumbrest grips w/adj. handrest. Blued finish. Imported from 1969 to 1999.
Right-hand model . . . . NiB $1234   Ex $1138   Gd $909
Left-hand model . . . . NiB $1240   Ex $1144   Gd $941

MODEL DES 823U RAPID FIRE
MATCH AUTOMATIC PISTOL. . . . . . . NiB $1122   Ex $950   Gd $836
Caliber: .22 Short. Five-round magazine, 5.9-inch bbl., 10.4 inches overall. Weight: 43 oz. Click adj. rear sight blade front. Checkered walnut thumbrest grips w/adj. handrest. Trigger adj. for length of pull. Made from 1974 to 1998.

Unique D6

Unique
DES/69 Standard Match

Unique
Model DES/VO Rapid Fire
Match

KRIEGSMODELL L AUTOMATIC PISTOL. . . NiB $362   Ex $255   Gd $180
Caliber: .32 Auto (7.65mm). Nine-round magazine, 3.2-inch bbl., 5.8 inches overall. Weight: 26.5 oz. Fixed sights. Blued finish. Plastic grips. Mfd. during German occupation of France 1940 to 194545. Note: Bears the German military acceptance marks and may have grips marked "7.65m/m 9 SCHUSS."

MODEL L AUTOMATIC PISTOL . . . . NiB $283   Ex $204   Gd $149
Calibers: .22 LR, .32 Auto (7.65mm), .380 Auto (9mm Short). 10-round magazine in .22, 7 in .32, 6 in .380; 3.3-inch bbl.; 5.8 inches overall. Weight: 16.5 oz. (.380 Auto w/light alloy frame), 23 oz. (w/steel frame). Fixed sights. Blued finish. Plastic grips. Intro. in 1955. Disc.

MODEL MIKROS POCKET
Automatic Pistol . . . . .NiB $225   Ex $150   Gd $97
Calibers: .22 Short, .25 Auto (6.35mm). Six-round magazine, 2.25-inch bbl., 4.44 inches overall. Weight: 9.5 oz. (light alloy frame), 12.5 oz. (steel frame.). Fixed sights. Blued finish. Plastic grips. Intro. in 1957. Disc.

GRADING: **NiB** = New in Box   **Ex** = Excellent or NRA 95%   **Gd** = Good or NRA 68%

Unique Mikros Pocket

U.S. Arms Abilene

Universal Enforcer (3000)

Uzi Semi-automatic Pistol

MODEL RR AUTOMATIC PISTOL . NiB $218 Ex $109 Gd $68
Postwar commercial version of WWII Kriegsmodell w/same general specifications. Intro. in 1951. Disc.

MODEL 2000-U MATCH PISTOL
Caliber: .22 Short. Designed for U.I.T. rapid fire competition. Five-round top-inserted magazine, 5.5-inch bbl., w/five vents for recoil reduction. 11.4 inches overall. Weight: 43.4 oz. Special light alloy frame, solid steel slide and shock absorber. Stippled French walnut w/ adj. handrest. Imported from 1990 to 1996.
Right-hand model . . . . NiB $1367 Ex $1199 Gd $1122
Left-hand model . . . . NiB $1398 Ex $1250 Gd $1196

UNITED STATES ARMS CORPORATION — Riverhead, New York

ABILENE SA REVOLVER
Safety Bar action. Calibers: .357 Mag., .41 Mag., .44 Mag., .45 Colt and .357/9mm convertible model w/two cylinders. Six-round cylinder, bbl. lengths: 4.63-, 5.5-, 6.5-inch, 7.5- and 8.5-inches in .44

Mag. only. Weight: About 48 oz. Adj. rear sight, ramp front. Blued finish or stainless steel. Smooth walnut grips. Made 1976 to 1983.
.44 Magnum, blued finish . . . . . . NiB $365 Ex $306 Gd $225
Magnum, stainless steel . . . . NiB $437 Ex $336 Gd $265
Other calibers, blued finish . . . . . NiB $327 Ex $209 Gd $200
.357 Magnum, stainless steel . . . NiB $433 Ex $342 Gd $266
Convertible, .357 Mag./9mm
Para., blued finish . . . . NiB $362 Ex $224 Gd $207

UNITED STATES FIRE ARMS MFG CO., INC. — Hartford, CT
Manufacturer of high quality reproduction Colt SAA revolver and Colt 1911 pistols from 1995 to 2012. The facility was once located in the old Colt factory building.

1910 COMMERCIAL MODEL
AUTOMATIC PISTOL . . . . NiB $1650 Ex $1300 Gd $800
Full size 1911-style pistol. Caliber: .45 ACP, 7-round magazine, 5-inch bbl., 8.3 inches overall. High polish Armory Blue finish, checkered walnut grips. Made from 2006 to 2009.
1911 Military Model (similar
Colt 1911 rollmarks) . . . . . . NiB $1650 Ex $1300 Gd $800
1911 Super 38 (.38 Super) . . . NiB $1650 Ex $1300 Gd $800

SINGLE ACTION ARMY
REVOLVER PREMIUM GRADE . . NIB $910 EX $660 GD $400
Calibers: .22 LR, .22 WMR, .32-20, .357 Mag., .38 Special, .38-40, .41 Colt, .44-40, .44 Special, .45 Long Colt, .45 ACP. Six-round cylinder, Bbl length: 3, 4, 4.75, 5.5, 7.5 or 10 inches. Dome Blue, Old Armory, Bone Case or nickel finish.
Flat Top (adj. sights) . . . . . . NiB $1509 Ex $1186 Gd $710
U.S. Pre-War . . . . NiB $1400 Ex $1000 Gd $610
New Buntline Special (16-in. bbl.,
skeleton stock) . . . . NiB $1900 Ex $1550 Gd $990
Bisley . . . . NiB $1560 Ex $1210 Gd $710
Sheriff's Model . . . . NiB $1060 Ex $900 Gd $500
Rodeo (matte finish) . . . . NiB $700 Ex $500 Gd $350
Cowboy (Dome Blue finish,
brown rubber grips) . . . . NiB $775 Ex $600 Gd $400
Omni-Potent (Bisley style grip) NiB $1500 Ex $1060 Gd $675

UNIVERSAL FIREARMS CORPORATION — Hialeah, Florida

This company was purchased by Iver Johnson Arms in the mid-1980s, when the Enforcer listed below was disc. An improved version was issued under the Iver Johnson name (see separate listing).

ENFORCER (3000)
SEMIAUTOMATIC PISTOL . . . . . . NiB $479 Ex $337 Gd $265
M-1 Carbine-type action. Caliber: 30 Carbine. Five-, 15- or 30-round clip magazine, 10.25-inch bbl., 17.75 inches overall. Weight: 4.5 lbs. (with 30-round magazine). Adj. rear sight, blade front. Blued finish. Walnut stock w/pistol grip and handguard. Made from 1964 to 1983.

UZI — Israel
Manufactured by Israel Military Industries, Israel currently imported by UZI America.

SEMIAUTOMATIC PISTOL . . NiB $1044 Ex $855 Gd $658
Caliber: 9mm Para. 20-round magazine, 4.5-inch bbl., about 9.5 inches overall. Weight: 3.8 lbs. Front post-type sight, rear open-type, both adj. Disc. in 1993.

"EAGLE" SERIES SEMIAUTOMATIC DA PISTOL
Caliber: 9mm Parabellum, .40 S&W, .45 ACP (Short Slide). 10-round magazine, 3.5-, 3.7- and 4.4-inch bbl., weight: 32 oz. to 35 oz. Blade front sight, drift adjustable tritium rear. Matte blue finish. Black synthetic grips. Imported from 1997 to 1998.

Compact model
  (DA or DAO) . . . . NiB $540 Ex $406 Gd $317
Polymer compact model . . . . . . NiB $540 Ex $496 Gd $317
Full-size model . . . . NiB $540 Ex $496 Gd $317
Short slide model . . . . NiB $540 Ex $496 Gd $317

WALTHER — Manufactured by German, French, Swiss and U.S. firms

The following Walther pistols were made before and during World War II by Waffenfabrik Walther, Zella-Mehlis (Thür.), Germany.

MODEL 1
AUTOMATIC PISTOL . . . . NiB $900 Ex $581 Gd $316
Caliber: .25 Auto (6.35mm). Six-round. 2.1-inch bbl., 4.4 inches overall. Weight: 12.8 oz. Fixed sights. Blued finish. Checkered hard rubber grips. Intro. in 1908.

MODEL 2 AUTOMATIC PISTOL
Caliber: .25 Auto (6.35mm). Six-round magazine, 2.1-inch bbl., 4.2 inches overall. Weight: 9.8 oz. Fixed sights. Blued finish. Checkered hard rubber grips. Intro. in 1909.
Standard model . . . . NiB $663 Ex $468 Gd $227
Pop-up sight model . . . . NiB $1950 Ex $1345 Gd $1188

MODEL 3 AUTOMATIC PISTOL . . . . NiB $4010 Ex $3286 Gd $1005
Caliber: .32 Auto (7.65mm). Six-round magazine, 2.6-inch bbl., 5 inches overall. Weight: 16.6 oz. Fixed sights. Blued finish. Checkered hard rubber grips. Intro. in 1910.

MODEL 4 AUTOMATIC PISTOL . . . . NiB $556 Ex $425 Gd $235
Caliber: .32 Auto (7.65mm). Eight-round magazine, 3.5-inch bbl., 5.9 inches overall. Weight: 18.6 oz. Fixed sights. Blued finish. Checkered hard rubber grips. Made from 1910 to 1918.

MODEL 5 AUTOMATIC PISTOL . . . . NiB $660 Ex $541 Gd $204
Improved version of Model 2 w/same general specifications, distinguished chiefly by better workmanship and appearance. Intro. in 1913.

MODEL 6 AUTOMATIC PISTOL . . . . NiB $9570 Ex $7933 Gd $5420
Caliber: 9mm Para. Eight-round magazine, 4.75-inch bbl., 8.25 inches overall. Weight: 34 oz. Fixed sights. Blued finish. Checkered hard rubber grips. Made from 1915-17. Note: The 9mm Para. cartridge is too powerful for the simple blow-back system of this pistol, so firing is not recommended.

MODEL 7 AUTOMATIC PISTOL . . . . NiB $759 Ex $553 Gd $301
Caliber: .25 Auto. (6.35mm). Eight-round magazine, 3-inch bbl., 5.3 inches overall. Weight: 11.8 oz. Fixed sights. Blued finish. Checkered hard rubber grips. Made from 1917 to 1918.

MODEL 8 AUTOMATIC PISTOL . . . . NiB $770 Ex $639 Gd $240
Caliber: .25 Auto. (6.35mm). Eight-round magazine, 2.88-inch bbl., 5.13 inches overall. Weight: 12.38 oz. Fixed sights. Blued finish. Checkered plastic grips. Made from 1920 to 1945.

MODEL 8 LIGHTWEIGHT
AUTOMATIC PISTOL . . . . NiB $733 Ex $530 Gd $422
Same as standard Model Eight except about 25 percent lighter due to use of aluminum alloys.

MODEL 9 VEST POCKET
AUTOMATIC PISTOL . . . . NiB $779 Ex $577 Gd $396
Caliber: .25 Auto (6.35mm). Six-round magazine, 2-inch bbl., 3.94 inches overall. Weight: 9 oz. Fixed sights. Blued finish. Checkered plastic grips. Made from 1921 to 1945.

Walther Model 5

Walther Model 8

Walther Model 9

MODEL HP DOUBLE-ACTION AUTOMATIC
Prewar commercial version of the P38 marked with an "N" proof over an "Eagle" or "Crown." The "HP" is an abbreviation of "Heeres Pistole" (Army Pistol). Caliber: 9mm Para. 8-round magazine, 5-inch bbl., 8.38 inches overall. Weight: About 34.5 oz. Fixed sights. Blued finish. Checkered wood or plastic grips. The Model HP is distinguished by its notably fine material and workmanship. Made from 1937 to 1944. (S/N range 1000-25900)
First production (Swedish Trials
  model H1000-H2000) . . . . NiB $3595 Ex $2765 Gd $2064

Walther PP
(Prewar)

Standard commercial production
(2000-24,000) . . . . NiB $2152 Ex $1825 Gd $1743
War production - marked "P38"
(24,000-26,000) . . . . NiB $1722 Ex $1550 Gd $1289
w/Nazi proof "Eagle/359," add $270

OLYMPIA FUNFKAMPF
MODEL AUTOMATIC. . . . . . . NiB $3266 Ex $2430 Gd $2220
Caliber: .22 LR. 10-round magazine, 9.6-inch bbl., 13 inches overall.
Weight: 33 oz., less weight. Set of 4 detachable weights. Adj. target
sights. Blued finish. Checkered grips. Intro. in 1936.

OLYMPIA HUNTING
MODEL AUTOMATIC. . . . . . . NiB $2762 Ex $2430 Gd $2220
Same general specifications as Olympia Sport Model but w/4-inch bbl.,
Weight: 28.5 oz.

OLYMPIA RAPID FIRE AUTO . NiB $2550 Ex $1620 Gd $1244
Caliber: .22 Short. Six-round magazine, 7.4-inch bbl., 10.7 inches overall.
Weight: (without 12.38 oz. detachable muzzle weight,) 27.5 oz. Adj. target
sights. Blued finish. Checkered grips. Made 1936 to 1940.

OLYMPIA SPORT
MODEL AUTOMATIC. . . . . . . NiB $2090 Ex $1398 Gd $1269
Caliber: .22 LR. 10-round magazine, 7.4-inch bbl., 10.7 inches over-
all. Weight: 30.5 oz., less weight. Adj. target sights. Blued finish.
Checkered grips. Set of four detachable weights was supplied at Extra
cost. Made about 1936 to 1940.

P38 MILITARY DA AUTOMATIC
Modification of the Model HP adopted as an official German Service
arm in 1938 and produced throughout WW II by Walther (code "ac"),
Mauser (code "byf") and a few other manufacturers. General specifica-
tions and appearance same as Model HP, but w/a vast difference in
quality, the P38 being a mass-produced military pistol. Some of the
late wartime models were very roughly finished and tolerances were
quite loose.
War Production w/Walther banner (1940)
Zero S/N 1st issue (S/N01-01,000) . . . . . . NiB $8130 Ex $6160 Gd $2445
Zero S/N. 2nd issue (S/N 01,000-03,500). . NiB $6515 Ex $5125 Gd $2309
Zero S/N. 3rd issue (S/N 03,500-013,000) . NiB $3130 Ex $2112 Gd $1021

WALTHER CONTRACT PISTOLS (LATE 1940-44)
"480" code Series (S/N 1-7,600) . . . . NiB $5745 Ex $3937 Gd $1590
"ac" code Ser. w/no date (S/N 7,350-9,700) NiB $6079 Ex $4390 Gd $2244
"ac" code Ser. w/.40 below
code (S/N 9,700-9,900A) . . . NiB $4435 Ex $3866 Gd $1879
"ac40" code inline Ser. (S/N 1-9,900B) . . . . NiB $2360 Ex $1966 Gd $909
"ac" code Ser. w/41 below code (S/N 1-4,5001) . .NiB $1897 Ex $1633 Gd $974
"ac" code Ser. w/42 below code
(S/N 4,5001-9,300K) . . . . NiB $1610 Ex $1364 Gd $869
"ac" code Ser. w/43 date (inline or below). . . . NiB $831 Ex $633 Gd $478
"ac" code Ser. w/45 (inline or below) . . . . NiB $780 Ex $599 Gd $439

MAUSER CONTRACT PISTOLS (LATE 1942-44)
"byf" code Ser. w/42 date (19,000 prod.). . . NiB $1418 Ex $1023 Gd $816
"bcf" code Ser. w/43, 44 or 45 date
(inline or below) . . . . NiB $984 Ex $744 Gd $612
"svw" code Ser. (French prod. w/Nazi proofs)NiB $1316 Ex $1066 Gd $693
"svw" code Ser. (French prod. w/star proof). . . NiB $576 Ex $500 Gd $376

SPREEWERKE CONTRACT PISTOLS (LATE 1942-45)
"cyq" code 1st Ser. w/Eagle over
359 (500 prod.) . . . . NiB $1866 Ex $1598 Gd $1135
"cyq" code Standard Ser. (300,000 prod.) . . . . NiB $989 Ex $590 Gd $478
"cyq" code "0" Ser. (5,000 prod.) . . . . NiB $1132 Ex $741 Gd $562

MODEL PP DA AUTOMATIC PISTOL
Polizeipistole (Police Pistol). Calibers: .22 LR (5.6mm), .25 Auto
(6.35mm), .32 Auto (7.65mm), .380 Auto (9mm). Eight-round magazine, (7-round in .380), 3.88-inch bbl., 6.94 inches overall. Weight: 23
oz. Fixed sights. Blued finish. Checkered plastic grips. 1929-45. Post-
War production and importation 1963 to 2000.

NOTE: *Wartime models are inferior in quality to prewar commercial
pistols.*

COMMERICAL MODEL WITH CROWN "N" PROOF
.22 cal. . . . . .NiB $1599 Ex $1033 Gd $713
.25 cal. . . . . .NiB $8554 Ex $3390 Gd $1729
.32 cal. . . . . .NiB $890 Ex $568 Gd $376
.32 cal. (w/Dural alloy frame) . . . . .NiB $1025 Ex $979 Gd $377
.32 cal. (w/Verchromt Fin., pre-war) . . . . . .NiB $3560 Ex $2533 Gd $907
.32 cal. (A.F.Stoeger Contract, pre-war) . . .NiB $2550 Ex $1656 Gd $691
.32 cal. (Allemagne French contract,
pre-war). . . . . NiB $1489 Ex $1189 Gd $712
.380 cal. (w/Comm. Crown "N" proof). . . . .NiB $1578 Ex $1266 Gd $831
.380 cal. (w/Verchromt Fin., pre-war) . . . .NiB $2779 Ex $2465 Gd $1109

WARTIME MODEL WITH EAGLE "N" PROOF
.32 cal. (w/Waffenampt proofs) . . . . .NiB $980 Ex $544 Gd $475
.32 cal. (w/Eagle "C" Nazi Police markings). .NiB $1056 Ex $744 Gd $496
.32 cal. (w/Eagle "F" Nazi Police markings) . .NiB $1060 Ex $748 Gd $500
.32 cal. (w/NSKK markings) . . . . .NiB $3277 Ex $3417 Gd $1100
.32 cal. (w/NSDAP Gruppe markings) . . . .NiB $2660 Ex $2245 Gd $1033
.380 cal. (w/Waffenampt proofs). . . . . . .NiB $1440 Ex $1187 Gd $899

COMMERCIAL MODEL (POST-WAR)
.22 cal. (German manufacture) . . . . .NiB $1203 Ex $1032 Gd $601
.32 cal. (German manufacture) . . . . .NiB $1044 Ex $806 Gd $577
.380 cal. (German manufacture). . . . . .NiB $1181 Ex $1099 Gd $444
.22 cal. (French manufacture) . . . . .NiB $601 Ex $498 Gd $290
.32 cal. (French manufacture) . . . . .NiB $601 Ex $498 Gd $290
.380 cal. (French manufacture) . . . . .NiB $610 Ex $567 Gd $289
.22, .32 or .380 Cal. (other foreign manuf.) . . .NiB $449 Ex $346 Gd $240

MODEL PP SPORT DA AUTOMATIC PISTOL
Target version of the Model PP. Caliber: .22 LR. Eight-round maga-
zine, 5.75- to 7.75 inch bbl. w/adjustable sights. Blue or nickel finish.
Checkered plastic grips w/thumbrest. Made from 1953 to 1970.
Walther manufacture. . . . . .NiB $1233 Ex $730 Gd $464
Manurhin manufacture. . . . . .NiB $990 Ex $834 Gd $561
C Model (comp./SA). . . . . .NiB $1294 Ex $920 Gd $668
w/nickel finish, add $204
w/matched bbl., weights, add $100

MODEL PP DELUXE ENGRAVED
These elaborately engraved models are available in blued finish, silver-
or gold-plated.

Blued finish . . . . NiB $ 1667 Ex $1462 Gd $1230
Silver-plated. . . . . NiB $1922 Ex $1530 Gd $1306
Gold-plated . . . . NiB $2130 Ex $1830 Gd $1488
w/ivory grips, add. $281
w/presentation case, add $4750
.22 caliber, add $75
.380 caliber, add 100%

MODEL PP LIGHTWEIGHT
Same as standard Model PP except about 25 percent lighter due to use of aluminum alloys (Dural). Values 40 percent higher. (See individual listings).

MODEL PP SUPER
DA PISTOL. . . . . NiB $1066 Ex $831 Gd $623
Caliber: 9x18mm. Seven-round magazine, 3.6-inch bbl., 6.9 inches overall. Weight: 30 oz. Fixed sights. Blued finish. Checkered plastic grips. Made from 1973 to 1979.

MODEL PP 7.65MM
PRESENTATION . . . . NiB $2100 Ex $1596 Gd $1214
Made of soft aluminum alloy in green-gold color, these pistols were not intended to be fired.

MODEL PPK DOUBLE-ACTION AUTOMATIC PISTOL
Polizeipistole Kriminal (Detective Pistol). Calibers: .22 LR (5.6mm), .25 Auto (6.35mm), .32 Auto (7.65mm), .380 Auto (9mm). Seven-round magazine, (6-round in .380), 3.25-inch bbl., 5.88 inches overall. Weight: 19 oz. Fixed sights. Blued finish. Checkered plastic grips. **Note**: *Wartime models are inferior in workmanship to prewar commercial pistols. Made 1931 to 1945.*

NOTE: *After both World Wars, the Walther manufacturing facility was required to cease the production of "restricted" firearms as part of the armistice agreements. Following WW II, Walther moved its manufacturing facility from the original location in Zella/ Mehilis, Germany to Ulm/Donau. In 1950, the firm Manufacture de Machines du Haut Rhine at Mulhouse, France was licensed by Walther and started production of PP and PPK models at the Manurhin facility in 1952. The MK II Walthers as produced at Manurhin were imported into the U.S. until 1968 when CGA importation requirements restricted the PPK firearm configuration from further importation. As a result, Walther developed the PPK/S to conform to the new regulations and licensed Interarms to produce the firearm in the U.S. from 1986-99. From 1984- 86, Manurhin imported PP and PPK/S type firearms under the Manurhin logo. Additional manufacturing facilities (both licensed & unlicensed) that produced PP and PPK type firearms were established after WW II in various locations and other countries including: China, France, Hungary, Korea, Romania and Turkey. In 1996, Walther was sold to UmarEx Sportwaffen GmbH and manufacturing facilities were relocated in Arnsberg, Germany. In 1999, Walther formed a partnership with Smith and Wesson and selected Walther firearms were licensed for production in the U.S.*

COMMERCIAL MODEL W/EAGLE PROOF (PREWAR)
.22 cal. . . . . .NiB $2560 Ex $1735 Gd $1509
.25 cal. . . . . NiB $10,620 Ex $6387 Gd $4960
.32 cal. . . . . .NiB $1533 Ex $831 Gd $567
.380 cal. . . . . .NiB $4530 Ex $3789 Gd $3320

WARTIME MODEL W/EAGLE "N" PROOF
.22 cal. . . . . .NiB $2522 Ex $1733 Gd $1458
.22 cal. (w/Dural frame). . . . . .NiB $1920 Ex $1779 Gd $1357
.32 cal. . . . . .NiB $1599 Ex $1022 Gd $879
.32 cal. (w/Dural frame). . . . . .NiB $1199 Ex $ 1022 Gd $879

Walther PPK
(WW II)

Walther PPK
Silver-Plated

.32 cal. (w/Verchromt Fin., Pre-War) . . . .NiB $1199 Ex $1022 Gd $879
.380 cal. . . . . .NiB $3885 Ex $2345 Gd $2097
.380 cal. (w/Dural frame). . . . . .NiB $3885 Ex $2345 Gd $2097
.380 cal. (w/Verchromt Fin., Pre-War) . .NiB $3885 Ex $2345 Gd $2097
.32 cal. (w/Waffenampt proofs) . . . . .NiB $2132 Ex $882 Gd $453
.32 cal. (w/Eagle "C" Nazi Police markings)NiB $2132 Ex $882 Gd $453
.32 cal. (w/Eagle "F" Nazi Police markings) . .NiB $2566 Ex $1145 Gd $650
.32 cal. (w/NSKK markings) . . . . .NiB $2366 Ex $1918 Gd $1333
.32 cal. (w/NSDAP Gruppe markings) . .NiB $8560 Ex $5788 Gd $1225
.380 cal. (w/Waffenampt proofs) . . . . . .NiB $1474 Ex $1198 Gd $1029

COMMERCIAL MODEL (POST-WAR)
.22 cal. (German manufacture). . . . . .NiB $1076 Ex $945 Gd $411
.32 cal. (German manufacture). . . . . NiB $850 Ex $601 Gd $383
.380 cal. (German manufacture). . . . . . . .NiB $1091 Ex $591 Gd $498
.22 cal. (French manufacture) . . . . .NiB $2212 Ex $924 Gd $538
.32 cal. (French manufacture) . . . . NiB $857 Ex $651 Gd $437
.380 cal. (French manufacture). . . . . .NiB $1173 Ex $839 Gd $452
.22, .32 or .380 cal. (other foreign manuf.) NiB $332 Ex $281 Gd $201

COMMERCIAL MODEL (U.S. PRODUCTION 1986-2001)
.380 cal. (w/blue finish). . . . . .NiB $658 Ex $499 Gd $403
.380 cal. (w/nickel finish). . . . . .NiB $658 Ex $499 Gd $403
.32 or .380 Cal. (stainless steel) . . . . .NiB $658 Ex $499 Gd $403

MODEL PPK DELUXE ENGRAVED
These elaborately engraved models are available in blued finish, chrome-, silver- or gold-plated.
Blued finish . . . . NiB $1932 Ex $1543 Gd $1199
Chrome-plated . . . . NiB $3087 Ex $2156 Gd $1779
Silver-plated. . . . . NiB $2234 Ex $1789 Gd $1418

Gold-plated . . . . .NiB $2567 Ex $1979 Gd $1598
w/ivory grips, add. $306
w/Presentation case, add $791
.22 cal, add $75
.25 cal, add $128
.380 cal, add $110

Walther
Free Pistol

MODEL PPK LIGHTWEIGHT
Same as standard Model PPK except about 25 percent lighter due to aluminum alloys. Values 50 percent higher.

MODEL PPK 7.65MM
PRESENTATION . . . . NiB $1856 Ex $1418 Gd $966
Made of soft aluminum alloy in green-gold color, these pistols were not intended to be fired.

MODEL PPK/S DA AUTOMATIC PISTOL
Designed to meet the requirements of the U.S. Gun Control Act of 1968, this model has the frame of the PP and the shorter slide and bbl., of the PPK. Overall length: 6.1 inches. Weight: 23 oz. Other specifications are the same as those of standard PPK except steel frame only. German, French and U.S. production 1971 to date. U.S. version made by Interarms 1978-1999, Smith & Wesson production from 2002-2009.

Walther GSP

.22 cal. (German manufacture) NiB $1336 Ex $1016 Gd $660
.32 cal. (German manufacture) . . NiB $997 Ex $789 Gd $497
.380 cal. (German manufacture) NiB $1321 Ex $997 Gd $577
.22 cal. (French manufacture) . . . NiB $968 Ex $760 Gd $561
.32 cal. (French manufacture) . . . NiB $973 Ex $781 Gd $577
.380 cal. (French manufacture) . . NiB $944 Ex $632 Gd $500
.22, .32 or .380 cal., blue
  (U.S. manufacture) . . . . .NiB $638 Ex $508 Gd $398
.22, .32 or .380 cal., stainless
  (U.S. manufacture) . . . . .NiB $638 Ex $508 Gd $398

NOTE: *Interarms (Interarmco) acquired a license from Walther in 1978 to manufacturer PP and PPK models at the Ranger Manufacturing Co., Inc. in Gadsden, Alabama. In 1988 the Ranger facility was licensed as EMCO and continued to produce Walther firearms for Interarms until 1996. From 1996-99, Black Creek in Gadsden, Alabama, produced Walther pistols for Interarms. In 1999, Smith & Wesson acquired manufacturing rights for Walther firearms at the Black Creek facility.*

MODELS PPK/S DELUXE ENGRAVED
These elaborately engraved models are available in blued finish, chrome-, silver- or gold-plated.
Blued finish . . . . NiB $1634 Ex $1216 Gd $1094
Chrome-plated . . . . NiB $1552 Ex $1268 Gd $976
Silver-plated. . . . . NiB $1755 Ex $1296 Gd $966
Gold-plated . . . . NiB $1889 Ex $1566 Gd $1034

NOTE: *The following Walther pistols are now manufactured by Carl Walther, Waffenfabrik, Ulm/Donau, Germany.*

SELF-LOADING
SPORT PISTOL. . . . . NiB $866 Ex $856 Gd $546
Caliber: .22 LR. 10-round magazine, bbl. lengths: 6- and 9-inch, 9.88 inches overall w/6-inch bbl. Target sights. Blued finish. One-piece, wood or plastic grips, checkered. Intro. in 1932.

MODEL FREE PISTOL . . . . NiB $1533 Ex $1367 Gd $1159
Single-Shot. Caliber: .22 LR. 11.7-inch heavy bbl., Weight: 48 oz. Adj. grips and target sights w/electronic trigger. Importation disc. 1991.

MODEL GSP TARGET AUTOMATIC PISTOL
Calibers: .22 LR, .32 S&W Long Wadcutter. Five-round magazine, 4.5-

Walther P5

inch bbl., 11.8 inches overall. Weights: 44.8 oz. (.22 cal.) or 49.4 oz. (.32 cal.). Adj. target sights. Black finish. Walnut thumbrest grips w/adj. handrest. Made from 1969 to 1994.
.22 LR . . . . NiB $1598 Ex $1432 Gd $889
.32 S&W Long Wadcutter . . . NiB $2773 Ex $2513 Gd $2122
Conversion unit. .22 Short or .22 LR, add $1071

MODEL OSP RAPID
FIRE TARGET PISTOL . . . . NiB $1744 Ex $1509 Gd $1345
Caliber: .22 Short. Five-round magazine, 4.5-inch bbl., 11.8 inches overall. Weight: 42.3 oz. Adj. target sights. Black finish. Walnut thumbrest grips w/adj. handrest. .22 LR conversion unit available (add $281.) Made from 1968 to 1994.

MODEL P4 (P38-LV)
DA PISTOL. . . . . **NiB $844 Ex $712 Gd $448**
Similar to P38 except has an uncocking device instead of a manual safety. Caliber: 9mm Para. 4.3-inch bbl., 7.9 inches overall. Other general specifications same as for current model P38. Made from 1974 to 1982.

MODEL P5 DA PISTOL
. . . . **NiB $1654 Ex $804 Gd $543**
Alloy frame w/frame-mounted decocking levers. Caliber: 9mm Para. Eight-round magazine, 3.5-inch bbl., 7 inches overall. Weight: 28 oz. blued finish. Checkered walnut or synthetic grips. Made from 1997 to date.

MODEL P5 COMPACT
DA PISTOL. . . . . **NiB $1693 Ex $988 Gd $497**
Similar to model P5 except w/3.1-inch bbl. and weight: 26 oz. Imported from 1987.

MODEL P1 DA AUTOMATIC
Postwar commercial version of the P38, has light alloy frame. Calibers: .22 LR, 7.65mm Luger, 9mm Para. Eight-round magazine, bbl., lengths: 5.1-inch in .22 caliber, 4.9- inch in 7.65mm and 9mm, 8.5 inches overall. Weight: 28.2 oz. Fixed sights. Nonreflective black finish. Checkered plastic grips. Made from 1957 to 1989. Note: The "P1" was W. German Armed Forces official pistol.
.22 LR . . . . **NiB $805 Ex $644 Gd $433**
Other calibers . . . . **NiB $806 Ex $610 Gd $398**

MODEL P38 DELUXE ENGRAVED PISTOL
Elaborately engraved, available in blued or chrome-, silver- or gold-plated finish.
Blued finish . . . . **NiB $2077 Ex $1566 Gd $1028**
Chrome-plated . . . . **NiB $1776 Ex $1432 Gd $998**
Silver-plated . . . . **NiB $1712 Ex $1429 Gd $1043**
Gold-plated . . . . **NiB $1987 Ex $1603 Gd $1163**

MODEL P38K
. . . . **NiB $886 Ex $781 Gd $468**
Short-barreled version of current P38, the "K" standing for "kurz" (meaning short). Same general specifications as standard model except 2.8-inch bbl., 6.3 inches overall, weight: 27.2 oz. Front sight is slide mounted. Caliber: 9mm Para. Made from 1974 to 1980.

MODEL P88 DA AUTOMATIC
PISTOL. . . . . **NiB $1132 Ex $988 Gd $774**
Caliber: 9mm Para. 15-round magazine, 4-inch bbl., 7.38 inches overall. Weight: 31.5 oz. Blade front sight, adj. rear. Checkered black synthetic grips. External hammer w/ambidExtrous decocking levers. Alloy frame w/matte blued steel slide. Made 1987 to 1993.

MODEL P88 DA COMPACT
Similar to the standard P88 Model except w/10- or 13-round magazine, 3.8-inch bbl., 7.1 inches overall. Weight: 29 oz. Imported from 1993 to 2003.
Model P88
(early importation) . . . . **NiB $1088 Ex $975 Gd $648**
Model P88
(post 1994 importation) . . . . . . **NiB $1088 Ex $975 Gd $648**

MODEL P99 DA
AUTOMATIC PISTOL . . . . **NiB $756 Ex $576 Gd $486**
Calibers: 9mm Para., .40 S&W or 9x21mm. 10-round magazine, 4-inch bbl., 7.2 inches overall. Weight: 22-25 oz. AmbidExtrous magazine release, decocking lever and 3-function safety. Interchangeable front post sight, micro-adj. rear. Polymer gripframe w/blued slide. Imported from 1995 to date.

Walther P38

Walther P38K

Walther P88

Walther TPH

Webley 9MM
Military Police Automatic

Webley Mark III
38 Military & Police Revolver

MODEL TPH DA POCKET PISTOL
Light alloy frame. Calibers: .22 LR, .25 ACP (6.35mm). Six-round magazine, 2.25-inch bbl., 5.38 inches overall. Weight: 14 oz. Fixed sights. Blued finish. Checkered plastic grips. Made 1968 to date. Note: Few Walther-made models reached the U.S. because of import restrictions. A U.S.-made version was mfd. by Interarms from 1986 to 1999.
German model . . . . NiB $1100   Ex $756   Gd $602
U.S. model . . . . NiB $900   Ex $743   Gd $436

NOTE: *The Walther Olympia Model pistols were manufactured 1952-1963 by Hämmerli AG Jagd-und Sportwaffenfabrik, Lenzburg, Switzerland, and marketed as "Hämmerli-Walther." See Hämmerli listings for specific data.*

OLYMPIA MODEL 200 AUTO PISTOL,
1952 TYPE . . . . NiB $729   Ex $612   Gd $453
Similar to 1936 Walther Olympia Funfkampf Model.

For the following Hämmerli-Walther Models—200, 201, 202, 203, 204, and 205—see listings under Hämmerli Section.

WARNER — Norwich, Connecticut
Warner Arms Corp. or Davis-Warner Arms Co.

INFALLIBLE POCKET
AUTOMATIC PISTOL . . . . NiB $507   Ex $356   Gd $253
Caliber: .32 Auto. Seven-round magazine, 3-inch bbl., 6.5 inches overall. Weight: About 24 oz. Fixed sights. Blued finish. Hard rubber grips. Made from 1917 to 1919.

WEBLEY & SCOTT LTD. — London and Birmingham, England

MODEL 1909 9MM MILITARY
& POLICE AUTOMATIC . . . . . . .NiB $2090 Ex $1465 Gd $1288
Caliber: 9mm Browning Long. Eight-round magazine, 8 inches overall. Weight: 32 oz. Fixed sights. Blued finish. Checkered Vulcanite grips. Made from 1909 to 1930.

MODEL 1907 HAMMER
AUTOMATIC . . . . NiB $1006   Ex $866   Gd $207
Caliber: .25 Automatic. Six-round magazine, overall length: 4.75 inches. Weight: 11.75 oz. No sights. Blued finish. Checkered Vulcanite grips. Made from 1906 to 1940.

MODEL 1912 HAMMERLESS
AUTOMATIC . . . . NiB $1500 Ex $1306 Gd $1233
Caliber: .25 Automatic. Six-round magazine, overall length: 4.25 inches, weight: 9.75 oz. Fixed sights. Blued finish. Checkered Vulcanite grips. Made from 1909 to 1940.

MARK I 455
AUTOMATIC PISTOL . . . . NiB $2505 Ex $1988 Gd $1600
Caliber: .455 Webley Auto. Seven-round magazine, 5-inch bbl., 8.5 inches overall. Weight: About 39 oz. Fixed sights. Blued finish. Checkered Vulcanite grips. Made 1913-31. Reissued during WWII. Total production about 9,300. Note: Mark I No. 2 is same pistol w/adj. rear sight and modified manual safety.

MARK III 38 MILITARY & POLICE
DA REVOLVER . . . . NiB $974   Ex $789   Gd $633
Hinged frame. DA. Caliber: .38 S&W. Six-round cylinder, bbl. lengths: 3- and 4-inches. 9.5 inches overall (with 4-inch bbl.). Weight: 21 oz. (with 4-inch bbl.). Fixed sights. Blued finish. Checkered walnut or Vulcanite grips. Made from 1897 to 1945.

MARK IV 22 CALIBER
TARGET REVOLVER . . . . NiB $806   Ex $691   Gd $386
Same frame and general appearance as Mark IV .38. Caliber: .22 LR. Six-round cylinder, 6-inch bbl., 10.13 inches overall. Weight: 34 oz. Target sights. Blued finish. Checkered grips. Disc. in 1945.

MARK IV 38 MILITARY & POLICE
DA REVOLVER . . . . NiB $806   Ex $691   Gd $386
Identical in appearance to the double-action Mark IV .22 w/hinged frame except chambered for .38 S&W. Six-round cylinder, bbl. length: 3-, 4- and 5-inches; 9.13 inches overall (with 5-inch bbl.). Weight: 27 oz. (with 5-inch bbl.). Fixed sights. Blued finish. Checkered grips. Made from 1929 to 1957.

MARK VI NO. 1 BRITISH SERVICE
DA REVOLVER . . . . NiB $691   Ex $567   Gd $478
Hinged frame. Caliber: 455 Webley. Six-round cylinder, bbl. lengths: 4-, 6- and 7.5-inches; 11.25 inches overall (with 6-inch bbl.). Weight: 38 oz. (with 6-inch bbl.). Fixed sights. Blued finish. Checkered walnut or Vulcanite grips. Made from 1915 to 1947.

MARK VI 22
TARGET REVOLVER . . . . NiB $1266 Ex $1096   Gd $909
Same frame and general appearance as the Mark VI 455. Caliber: .22 LR. Six-round cylinder, 6-inch bbl., 11.25 inches overall. Weight: 40 oz. Target sights. Blued finish. Checkered walnut or Vulcanite grips. Disc. in 1945.

METROPOLITAN POLICE
AUTOMATIC PISTOL . . . . **NiB $1629 Ex $1528 Gd $1266**
Calibers: .32 Auto, .380 Auto. Eight-round (.32) or 7-round (.380) magazine, 3.5-inch bbl., 6.25 inches overall. weight: 20 oz. Fixed sights. Blued finish. Checkered Vulcanite grips. Made from 1906-40 (.32) and 1908 to 1920 (.380).

R.I.C. MODELS DA REVOLVER . . . **NiB $950 Ex $700 Gd $500**
Royal Irish Constabulary or Bulldog Model. Solid frame. Caliber: .455 Webley. Five-round cylinder, 2.25-inch bbl., weight: 21 oz. Fixed sights. Blued finish. Checkered walnut or vulcanite grips. Made from 1897-1939.

SEMIAUTOMATIC
SINGLE-SHOT PISTOL . . . . **NiB $1090 Ex $ 916 Gd $617**
Similar in appearance to the Webley Metropolitan Police Automatic, this pistol is "semiautomatic" in the sense that the fired case is Extracted and ejected and the hammer cocked as in a blow-back automatic pistol; it is loaded singly and the slide manually operated in loading. Caliber: .22 Long, 4.5- or 9-inch bbl., 10.75 inches overall (with 9-inch bbl.). Weight: 24 oz. (with 9-inch bbl.). Adj. sights. Blued finish. Checkered Vulcanite grips. Made from 1911 to 1927.

SINGLE-SHOT TARGET PISTOL . . **NiB $1588 Ex $1469 Gd $1190**
Hinge frame. Caliber: .22 LR. 10-inch bbl., 15 inches overall. Weight: 37 oz. Fixed sights on earlier models, current production has adj. rear sight. Blued finish. Checkered walnut or Vulcanite grips. Made from 1909.

WEBLEY-FOSBERY AUTOMATIC REVOLVER
Hinged frame. Recoil action revolves cylinder and cocks hammer. Caliber: 455 Webley. Six-round cylinder, 6-inch bbl., 12 inches overall. Weight: 42 oz. Fixed or adjustable sights. Blued finish. Checkered walnut grips. Made 1901-1939. Note: A few were produced in caliber .38 Colt Auto w/an 8-shot cylinder (very rare).

1901 model . . . . **NiB $12,600 Ex $8600 Gd $5500**		
1902 model .38 Colt (8-round), add, add **300%**		
1903 model . . . . **NiB $10,000 Ex $7600 Gd $4600**		
Target model w/adjustable sights, add. **20%**		

WESSON FIREARMS CO., INC. — Palmer, Massachusetts
Formerly Dan Wesson Firearms, Inc. Acquired by CZ-USA in 2005.

MODEL 8 SERVICE
Same general specifications as Model 14 except caliber .38 Special. Made from 1971 to 1975. Values same as for Model 14.

MODEL 8-2 SERVICE
Same general specifications as Model 14-2 except caliber .38 Special. Made from 1975 to date. Values same as for Model 14-2.

MODEL 9 TARGET
Same as Model 15 except caliber .38 Special. Made from 1971 to 1975. Values same as for Model 15.

MODEL 9-2 TARGET
Same as Model 15-2 except caliber .38 Special. Made from 1975 to date. Values same as for Model 15-2.

MODEL 9-2H HEAVY BARREL
Same general specifications as Model 15-2H except caliber .38 Special. Made from 1975 to date. Values same as for Model 15-2H. Disc. 1983.

Dan Wesson
Model 14-2
Service

Dan Wesson
Model 15-2H Interchangeable Heavy

MODEL 9-2HV VENT RIB HEAVY BARREL
Same as Model 15-2HV except caliber .38 Special. Made from 1975 to date. Values same as for Model 15-2HV.

MODEL 9-2V VENT RIB
Same as Model 15-2V except caliber .38 Special. Made from 1975 to date. Values same as for Model 15-2H.

MODEL 11 SERVICE DA REVOLVER
Caliber: .357 Magnum. Six-round cylinder. bbl. lengths: 2.5-, 4-, 6-inches interchangeable bbl. assemblies, 9 inches overall (with 4-inch bbl.). Weight: 38 oz. (with 4-inch bbl.). Fixed sights. Blued finish. Interchangeable grips. Made from 1970-71. Note: The Model 11 has an External bbl. nut.

w/one bbl. assembly and grip . . . **NiB $274 Ex $180 Gd $101**		
Extra bbl. assembly, add. **$75**		
Extra grip, add **$50**		

MODEL 12 TARGET
Same general specifications as Model 11 except has adj. sights. Made from 1970-71.

w/one-bbl. assembly and grip . . . **NiB $290 Ex $204 Gd $135**		
Extra bbl. assembly, add. **$75**		
Extra grip, add **$50**		

MODEL 14 SERVICE DA REVOLVER
Caliber: .357 Magnum. Six-round cylinder, bbl. length: 2.25-, 3.75, 5.75-inches; interchangeable bbl. assemblies, 9 inches overall (with 3.75-inch bbl.). Weight: 36 oz. (with 3.75-inch bbl.). Fixed sights. Blued or nickel finish. Interchangeable grips. Made from 1971 to 1975. Note: Model 14 has recessed bbl. nut.

w/one-bbl. assembly and grip . . . . **NiB $225 Ex $158 Gd $101**		
Extra bbl. assembly, add. **$61**		
Extra grip, add **$25**		

MODEL 14-2 SERVICE DA REVOLVER
Caliber: .357 Magnum. Six-round cylinder, bbl. lengths: 2.5-, 4-, 6-, 8-inch; interchangeable bbl. assemblies, 9.25 inches overall (with

4-inch bbl.) Weight: 34 oz. (with 4-inch bbl.). Fixed sights. Blued finish. Interchangeable grips. Made from 1975 to 1995. Note: Model 14-2 has recessed bbl. nut.

w/one bbl. assembly
(8 inch) and grip. . . . . NiB $270 Ex $204 Gd $158
w/one bbl. assembly
(other lengths) and grip . . . . NiB $270 Ex $204 Gd $158
Extra bbl. assembly, 8 inch, add $75
Extra bbl. assembly,
other lengths, add $75
Extra grip, add $50

MODEL 15 TARGET
Same general specifications as Model 14 except has adj. sights. Made from 1971 to 1975.

w/one bbl. assembly
and grip. . . . . NiB $306 Ex $230 Gd $190
Extra bbl. assembly, add. $75
Extra grip, add $50

MODEL 15-2 TARGET
Same general specifications as Model 14-2 except has adj. rear sight and interchangeable blade front; also avail. w/10-, 12- or 15-inch bbl., Made from 1975 to 1995.

w/one bbl. assembly (8 inch) and grip NiB $362 Ex $289 Gd $187
w/one bbl. assembly (10 inch) and grip NiB $362 Ex $289 Gd $187
w/one bbl. assembly
(12 inch)/grip. Disc. . . . . NiB $362 Ex $289 Gd $187
w/one bbl. assembly
(15 inch)/grip. Disc. . . . . NiB $362 Ex $289 Gd $187
w/one-bbl. assembly
(other lengths)/grip . . . . NiB $244 Ex $159 Gd $133
Extra bbl. assembly, add. $75
Extra grip, add $50

MODEL 15-2H HEAVY BARREL
Same as Model 15-2 except has heavy bbl., assembly weight: with 4-inch bbl., 38 oz. Made from 1975 to 1983.

w/one bbl. assembly . . . . .NiB $500 Ex $345 Gd $235
Extra bbl. assembly, add $75
Extra grip, add. $50

MODEL 15-2HV VENT RIB HEAVY BARREL
Same as Model 15-2 except has vent rib heavy bbl. assembly; weight: (w/4-inch bbl.) 37 oz. Made from 1975 to 1995.

w/one bbl. assembly (8 inch) and grip NiB $303 Ex $240 Gd $162
w/one bbl. assembly (10 inch) and grip NiB $303 Ex $240 Gd $162
w/one bbl. assembly (12 inch) and grip NiB $303 Ex $240 Gd $162
w/one bbl. assembly (15 inch) and gripNiB $321 Ex $273 Gd $192
w/one bbl. assembly
(other lengths) and grip . . . . NiB $198 Ex $241 Gd $163
Extra bbl. assembly (8 inch), add $75
Extra bbl. assembly (10 inch), add. $75
Extra bbl. assembly (12 inch), add. $75
Extra bbl. assembly (15 inch), add. $75
Extra bbl. assembly (other lengths), add $75
Extra grip, add $50

MODEL 15-2V VENT RIB
Same as Model 15-2 except has vent rib bbl. assembly, weight: 35 oz. (with 4-inch bbl.). Made from 1975 to date. Values same as for 15-2H.

HUNTER PACS
Dan Wesson Hunter Pacs are offered in all Magnum calibers and include heavy vent rib 8-inch shrouded bbl., Burris scope mounts, bbl. changing tool in a case.

HP22M-V	NiB $893	Ex $660	Gd $473
HP22M-2	NiB $733	Ex $612	Gd $447
HP722M-V	NiB $843	Ex $632	Gd $439
HP722M-2	NiB $806	Ex $612	Gd $408
HP32-V	NiB $785	Ex $571	Gd $395
HP32-2	NiB $691	Ex $530	Gd $425
HP732-V	NiB $816	Ex $597	Gd $434
HP732-2.	NiB $755	Ex $608	Gd $449
HP15-V	NiB $755	Ex $608	Gd $449
HP15-2	NiB $780	Ex $601	Gd $437
HP715-V	NiB $831	Ex $654	Gd $479
HP715-2.	NiB $755	Ex $657	Gd $478
HP41-V	NiB $688	Ex $556	Gd $425
HP741-V	NiB $841	Ex $689	Gd $495
HP741-2	NiB $739	Ex $607	Gd $439
HP44-V	NiB $884	Ex $700	Gd $536
HP44-2	NiB $739	Ex $607	Gd $439
HP744-V	NiB $933	Ex $781	Gd $576
HP744-2	NiB $897	Ex $738	Gd $546
HP40-V	NiB $616	Ex $497	Gd $366
HP40-2	NiB $827	Ex $691	Gd $496
HP740-V	NiB $988	Ex $816	Gd $590
HP740-2.	NiB $918	Ex $729	Gd $526
HP375-V	NiB $595	Ex $500	Gd $356
HP375-2	NiB $944	Ex $786	Gd $590
HP45-V	NiB $734	Ex $626	Gd $439

WHITNEY FIREARMS COMPANY —
Hartford, Connecticut
NOTE: *Since 2004 the Whitney Wolverine design is currently manufactured by Olympic Arms, Olympia, WA.*

WOLVERINE AUTOMATIC PISTOL
Dural frame/shell contains all operating components. Caliber: .22 LR. 10-round magazine, 4.63-inch bbl., 9 inches overall. Weight: 23 oz. Partridge-type sights. Blued or nickel finish. Plastic grips. Made from 1955 to 1962.

Blue finish . . . . .NiB $680 Ex $575 Gd $383
Nickel finish. . . . . .NiB $1330 Ex $1080 Gd $610

Whitney Firearms Company Wolverine
w/nickel finish

WICHITA ARMS — Wichita, Kansas

CLASSIC PISTOL
Caliber: Chambered to order. Bolt-action, single-shot. 11.25-inch octagonal bbl., 18 inches overall. Weight: 78 oz. Open micro sights. Custom-grade checkered walnut stock. Blued finish. Made from 1980 to 1997.

Standard. . . . . .NiB $3310 Ex $2546 Gd $2245
**Presentation grade
  (engraved)** . . . . NiB $5379 Ex $3916 Gd $2166

HIUNTER PISTOL . . . . . . .NiB $1433 Ex $1096 Gd $872
Bolt-action, single-shot. Calibers: .22 LR, .22 WRF, 7mm Super Mag., 7-30 Waters, .30-30 Win., .32 H&R Mag., .357 Mag., .357 Super Mag. 10.5-inch bbl., 16.5 inches overall, weight: 60 oz. No sights (scope mount only). Stainless steel finish. Walnut stock. Made from 1983 to 1994.

INTERNATIONAL PISTOL . . NiB $733   Ex $567   Gd $453
Top-break, single-shot. SA. Calibers: 7-30 Waters, 7mm Super Mag., 7R (.30-30 Win. necked to 7mm), .30-30 Win. .357 Mag., .357 Super Mag., .32 H&R Mag., .22 Mag., .22 LR. 10- and 14-inch bbl. (10.5 inch for centerfire calibers). Weight: 50-71 oz. Partridge front sight, adj. rear. Walnut forend and grips.

MK-40 SILHOUETTE PISTOL NiB $1613   Ex $1407   Gd $1206
Calibers: .22-250, 7mm IHMSA, .308 Win. Bolt-action, single-shot. 13-inch bbl., 19.5 inches overall. Weight: 72 oz. Wichita Multi-Range sight system. Aluminum receiver w/blued bbl., gray Fiberthane glass stock. Made from 1981 to 1994.

**SILHOUETTE
PISTOL (WSP)**. . . . . .NiB $1587 Ex . $1453 Gd $1356
Calibers: .22-250, 7mm IHMSA 308 Win. Bolt-action, single-shot. 14.94-inch bbl., 21.38 inches overall. Weight: 72 oz. Wichita Multi-Range sight system. Blued finish. Walnut or gray Fiberthane glass stock. Walnut center or rear grip. Made from 1979 to 1994.

WILKINSON ARMS — Parma, Idaho

**LINDA SEMI-AUTOMATIC
PISTOL**. . . . . NiB $680 Ex $557 Gd $360
Caliber: 9mm Para. 31-round magazine, 8.25-in. bbl., 12.25 inches overall. Weight: 77 oz. Rear peep sight w/blade front. Blued finish. Checkered composition grips. Made from 2000 to 2005.

**SHERRY SEMI-AUTOMATIC
PISTOL**. . . . . NiB $274 Ex $188 Gd $126
Caliber: .22 LR. Eight-round magazine, 2.13-in. bbl., 4.38 inches overall. Weight: 9.25 oz. Crossbolt safety. Fixed sights. Blued or blue-gold finish. Checkered composition grips. Made from 2000 to 2005.

DIANE SEMI-AUTOMATIC PISTOL NiB $160 Ex $97 Gd $55
Caliber: .25 ACP, 6-round magazine, 2.125-in. bbl., matte blue. nches overall. Weight: 77 oz. Rear peep sight w/blade front. Blued finish. Checkered composition grips. Made from 2000 to 2005.

Wilkinson Arms Linda

Rifles

Man-Eating Tiger Rifle

Jim Corbett (July 25, 1875 – April 19, 1955) was a legendary British hunter who hunted man-eating tigers and leopards between 1907 and 1938. In total, Corbett killed thirty-three big cats. The first tiger he killed, called the Champawat Tiger, was documented to have killed 436 persons. Corbett wrote about his hunting exploits in his book, *Man Eaters of Kumaon*. To hunt these killer cats Corbett took great personal risks. Elmer Keith was a lifelong hunter having hunted extensively in the western United States as well as trips to Africa. Keith acquired the late Jim Corbett's W. J. Jeffery & Co. Best Quality boxlock side-by-side rifles chambered in .450/400. At auction the rifle sold for $264,500.

Corbett's rifle is S/N 20176 chambered in .450/400 3" Jeffery Cordite. The Best Quality cased boxlock ejector double rifle was made by W. J. Jeffery and Co. London, circa 1909.

The Jeffery features 24-inch Krupp Gussstahl chopper-lump barrels, with dolls head extension, proved Cordite 55-400 Max. Barrels use a concave engine turned quarter rib, sunken concave engine turned mid-rib, and engine turned caterpillar ramp, with a gold bead sight. The rear sight has one standing and four folding leaves from 100–500 yards with shallow Vs and platinum center lines.

For such a well-used hunting rifle, the Jeffery has a patina of use but was hardly abused. Note the elaborate receiver engraving.

The rifle was cased in its original Best Quality beveled edge brass-cornered oak and leather case with a red baise lined interior.

A top view of the flowing scrollback top lever action. Note the dolls head extension.

From the muzzle the front sight is described as an engine turned caterpillar ramp, with gold bead sight.

Jim Corbett shot the man-eating Bachelor of Powalgarh in the winter of 1930 in Powalgarh, Kumaon, India. Locals feared the tiger, calling it *shaitan*, the Hindi word for devil. The tiger measured ten feet, seven inches.

Photos courtesy of James D. Julia Auctioneers, Fairfield, Maine USA www.jamesdjulia.com

The Jeffery, like most double rifles, uses double triggers.

Action Arms Timber Wolfe

Alpha Arms Custom

Alpha Arms Alaskan

Alpha Arms Jaguar

A.A. ARMS — Monroe, North Carolina

AR-9 SEMIAUTOMATIC CARBINE . . NiB $805 Ex $641 Gd $439
Semiautomatic recoil-operated rifle w/side-folding metal stock design. Fires from a closed bolt. Caliber: 9mm Parabellum. 20-round magazine. 16.25-inch bbl., 33 inches overall. Weight: 6.5 lbs. Fixed blade, protected postfront sight adjustable for elevation, winged square notched rear. Matte phosphate/blue or nickel finish. Checkered polymer grip/frame. Made 1991 to 1994 (banned)

ACTION ARMS — Philadelphia, Pennsylvania

MODEL B SPORTER
SEMI-AUTOMATIC CARBINE. . . . . NiB $650 Ex $572 Gd $380
Similar to Uzi Carbine (see separate listing) except w/thumbhole stock. Caliber: 9mm Parabellum, 10-round magazine. 16-inch bbl. Weight: 8.75 lbs. Post front sight; adj. rear. Imported 1994.

TIMBERWOLF REPEATING RIFLE
Calibers: .357 Mag./.38 Special and .44 Mag. slide-action. Tubular magazine holds 10 and 8 rounds, respectively. 18.5-inch bbl. 36.5 inches overall. Weight: 5.5 lbs. Fixed blade front sight; adj. rear. Receiver w/integral scope mounts. Checkered walnut stock. Imported from 1989 to 1993, later by I.M.I. Israel.

Blued model. . . . . NiB $338 Ex $271 Gd $190
Chrome model, add $75
.44 Mag., add. $126

ALPHA ARMS, INC. — Dallas, Texas

CUSTOM BOLT-ACTION RIFLE NiB $1707 Ex $1335 Gd $876
Calibers: .17 Rem. thru .338 Win. Mag. Right or left-hand action in three action lengths w/three-lug locking system and 60-degree bolt rotation. 20- to 24-inch round or octagonal bbl. Weight: 6 to 7 lbs. No sights. Presentation-grade California Claro walnut stock w/hand-rubbed oil finish, custom inletted sling swivels and ebony forend tip. Made from 1984 to 1987.

ALASKAN BOLT-ACTION RIFLE . NiB $1706 Ex $1337 Gd $869
Similar to Custom model but w/stainless-steel bbl. and receiver w/all other parts coated w/Nitex. Weight: 6.75 to 7.25 lbs. Open sights w/bbl-band sling swivel. Classic-style Alpha wood stock w/Niedner-style steel grip cap and solid recoil pad. Made from 1985 to 1987.

GRAND SLAM
BOLT-ACTION RIFLE . . . . NiB $1322 Ex $1065 Gd $795
Same as Custom model but has Alphawood (fiberglass and wood) classic-style stock featuring Niedner-style grip cap. Wt: 6.5 lbs. Left-hand models same value. Made 1985 to 1987.

CUSTOM BOLT-ACTION RIFLE

Same as Custom Rifle except designed on Mauser-style action w/claw extractor drilled and tapped for scope. Originally designated Alpha Model 1. Calibers: .243, 7mm-08, .308 original chambering (1984 to 1985) up to .338 Win. Mag. in standard model; .338 thru .458 Win. Mag. in Big Five model (1987). Teflon-coated trigger guard/floorplate assembly. Made from1984 to 1987.

Jaguar Grade I	NiB $1035	Ex $855	Gd $624
Jaguar Grade II	NiB $1268	Ex $684	Gd $707
Jaguar Grade III	NiB $1319	Ex $1046	Gd $756
Jaguar Grade IV	NiB $1424	Ex $1056	Gd $755
Big Five model	NiB $1717	Ex $1198	Gd $977

AMERICAN ARMS — N. Kansas City, Missouri

1860 HENRY . . . . NiB $926 Ex $698 Gd $530
Replica of 1860 Henry rifle. Calibers: .44-40 or .45 LC. 24.25-inch half-octagonal bbl. 43.75 inches overall. Weight: 9.25 lbs. Brass frame and appointments. Straight-grip walnut buttstock.

1866 WINCHESTER
Replica of 1866 Winchester. Calibers: .44-40 or .45 LC. 19-inch round tapered bbl. (carbine) or 24.25-inch tapered octagonal bbl. (rifle). 38 to 43.25 inches overall. Weight: 7.75 or 8.15 lbs. Brass frame, elevator and buttplate. Walnut buttstock and forend.

Carbine	NiB $743	Ex $625	Gd $409
Rifle	NiB $743	Ex $625	Gd $409

1873 WINCHESTER
Replica of 1873 Winchester rifle. Calibers: .44-40 or .45 LC. 24.25-inch tapered octagonal bbl. w/tubular magazine. Color casehardened steel frame w/brass elevator and ejection port cover. Walnut buttstock w/ steel buttplate.

Standard model	NiB $876	Ex $710	Gd $419
Deluxe model	NiB $1141	Ex $924	Gd $640

AMERICAN SPIRIT ARMS CORP. — Scottsdale, Arizona

ASA BULL BARREL FLATTOP RIFLE . . .NiB $1043 Ex $709 Gd $533
Semi-automatic. Caliber: ..223 Rem. Patterned after AR-15. Forged steel lower receiver, aluminum flattop upper receiver, 24-inch stainless bull barrel, free-floating aluminum hand guard, includes Harris bipod.

ASA BULL BARREL A2 RIFLE . . . . . . .NiB $989 Ex $733 Gd $535
Similar to Flattop Rifle except has A2 upper receiver with carrying handle and sights. Introduced 1999.

OPEN MATCH RIFLE . . . . .NiB $1471 Ex $1097 Gd $745
Caliber: .223 Rem. Bbl.: 16-inch fluted and ported stainless steel match with round shroud. Flattop without sights, forged upper and lower receiver, match trigger. Introduced 2001.

LIMITED MATCH RIFLE . . . . . . .NiB $1411 Ex $909 Gd $579
Caliber: .223 Rem. Bbl.: 16-inch fluted stainless steel match with round shroud. National Match front and rear sights; match trigger.

DCM SERVICE RIFLE . . . . .NiB $1412 Ex $915 Gd $618
Caliber: .223 Rem. Bbl.: 20-inch stainless steel match type with free-floating shroud. National Match front and rear sights; match trigger; pistol grip.

ASA M4 RIFLE . . . . .NiB $944 Ex $679 Gd $482
Caliber: .223 Rem. Non-collapsible stock, M4 hand guard, 16-inch bbl. w/muzzle brake; aluminum flattop upper receiver.

ASA A2 RIFLE . . . . .NiB $926 Ex $633 Gd $509
Caliber: .223 Rem. A2 receiver; 20-inch National Match barrel. Intro. 1999.

ASA CARBINE . . . . NiB $1077 Ex $707 Gd $589
Caliber: .223 Rem. or Short. Side-charging, flattop receiver; M4 hand guard; 16-inch National Match bbl. w/slotted muzzle brake.

POST-BAN CARBINE . . . . .NiB $909 Ex $690 Gd $482
Caliber: .223 Rem. Wilson 16-inch National Match bbl.; non-collapsible stock. Introduced 1999.

BULL BARREL A2 INVADER . . . .NiB $1032 Ex $710 Gd $544
Caliber: .223 Rem. Similar to ASA 24-inch bull bbl. rifle except has 16-inch stainless steel bbl.. Introduced 1999.

A2 CAR CARBINE . . . . .NiB $1041 Ex $703 Gd $544
Caliber: 9mm Parabellum. Forged receiver, non-collapsible stock. Bbl.: 16-inch Wilson w/o muzzle brake, bird cage flash hider (pre-ban) or muzzle brake (post-ban).

FLATTOP CAR RIFLE . . . . .NiB $1041 Ex $703 Gd $544
Caliber: 9mm Parabellum. Similar to A2 CAR Rifle except flattop design w/o sights. Introduced 2002.

ASA TACTICAL RIFLE . . . . .NiB $1788 Ex $1096 Gd $780
Caliber: .308 Win. Bbl.: 16-inch stainless steel regular or match; side-charging handle; pistol grip.
Match model (w/fluted bbl. match trigger, chrome finish) Add $525

ASA 24-INCH MATCH RIFLE . . . . .NiB $1806 Ex $1106 Gd $789
Caliber: .308 Win. Bbl.: 24-inch stainless steel match with or w/o fluting/porting. Side-charging handle; pistol grip. Introduced 2002.

AMT (ARCADIA MACHINE & TOOL) — Irwindale, California (1998)

BOLT-ACTION REPEATING RIFLE

Winchester-type push-feed or Mauser-type controlled-feed short-, medium- or long-action. Calibers: .223 Remington, .22-250 Remington, .243 A, .243 Winchester, 6mm PPC, .25-06 Remington, 6.5x08, .270 Winchester, 7x57 Mauser, 7mm-08 Remington, 7mm Remington Mag., 7.62x39mm, .308 Winchester, .30-06, .300 Winchester Mag., .338 Winchester Mag., .375 H&H, .416 Remington, .416 Rigby, .458 Winchester Mag. 22- to 28-inch number 3 contour bbl. Weight: 7.75 to 8.5 lbs. Sights: None furnished; drilled and tapped for scope mounts. Classic composite or Kevlar stock. Made from 1996 to 1997.

Standard model	NiB $899	Ex $720	Gd $531
Deluxe model	NiB $1087	Ex $830	Gd $529

BOLT-ACTION SINGLE-SHOT RIFLE

Winchester-type cone breech push-feed or Mauser-type controlled-feed action. Calibers: .22 Hornet, .22 PPC, .222 Remington, .223 Remington, .22-250 Remington, .243 A, .243 Winchester, 6mm PPC, 6.5x08, .270 Win., 7mm-08 Remington, .308 Winchester 22- to 28-inch #3 bbl. Weight: 7.75 to 8.5 lbs. Sights: None furnished; drilled and tapped for scope mounts. Classic composite or Kevlar stock. Made from1996.

Standard model	NiB $865	Ex $733	Gd $520
Deluxe model	NiB $1077	Ex $744	Gd $500

**Anschutz Model
54.18MS-REP**

CHALLENGER AUTOLOADING TARGET RIFLE SERIES I, II & III
Similar to Small Game Hunter except w/McMillan target fiberglass stock. Caliber: .22 LR. 10-round magazine. 16.5-, 18-, 20- or 22-inch bull bbl. Drilled and tapped for scope mount; no sights. Stainless steel finish. Made from 1994 to 1998.
Challenger I Standard . . . . NiB $822 Ex $577 Gd $409
Challenger II w/muzzle brake . . . . NiB $926 Ex $755 Gd $554
Challenger III w/bbl extension. . . . NiB $976 Ex $588 Gd $452
w/jeweled trigger, add $227

LIGHTNING 25/22
AUTOLOADING RIFLE . . . . NiB $316 Ex $237 Gd $170
Caliber: .22 LR. 25-round magazine. 18-inch tapered or bull bbl. Weight: 6 lbs. 37 inches overall. Sights: Adj. rear; ramp front. Folding stainless-steel stock w/matte finish. Made 1986 to 1993.

SMALL GAME HUNTER SERIES
Similar to AMT 25/22 except w/conventional matte black fiberglass/nylon stock. 10-round rotary magazine. 22-inch bbl. 40.5 inches overall. Weight: 6 lbs. Grooved for scope; no sights. Made from 1986 to 1994 (Series I), and 1993 (Series II).
Hunter I . . . . NiB $333 Ex $218 Gd $155
Hunter II (w/22-inch
  heavy target bbl.) . . . . NiB $269 Ex $223 Gd $159

MAGNUM HUNTER AUTO RIFLE . . . . . NiB $495 Ex $455 Gd $240
Similar to Lightning Small Game Hunter II model except chambered in .22 WRF w/22-inch match-grade bbl. Made from 1995 to 1998.

ANSCHUTZ — Ulm, Germany

Currently imported by Merkel USA. Anschutz models 1407 ISU, 1408-ED, 1411, 1413, 1418, 1432, 1433, 1518 and 1533 were marketed in the U.S. by Savage Arms. Further, Anschutz models 1403, 1416, 1422D, 1441, 1516 and 1522D were sold as Savage/Anschutz with Savage model designations (see also listings under Savage Arms).

MODEL 54.18MS . . . . NiB $1300 Ex $899 Gd $469
Bolt-action, single-shot, Caliber: .22 LR. 22-inch bbl. European hardwood stock w/cheekpiece. Stipple-checkered forend and Wundhammer swell pistol-grip. Receiver grooved, drilled and tapped for scope blocks. Weight: 8.4 lbs. Imported 1982 to 1997.

MODEL 54.18MS-REP REPEATING RIFLE
Same as model 54.18MS except w/repeating action and 5-round magazine. 22- to 30-inch bbl. 41-49 inches overall. Avg. weight: 7 lbs., 12 oz. Hardwood or synthetic gray thumbhole stock. Imported from 1989 to 1997.
Standard MS-REP model . . . . . . NiB $2050 Ex $1569 Gd $880
Left-hand model . . . . NiB $2070 Ex $1579 Gd $790

MODEL 64S BOLT-ACTION SINGLE-SHOT RIFLE
Bolt-action, single-shot. Caliber: .22 LR. 26-inch bbl. Checkered European hardwood stock w/Wundhammer swell pistol-grip and adj. buttplate. Single-stage trigger. Aperture sights. Weight: 8.25 lbs. Imported from 1963 to 1981.
Standard . . . . NiB $480 Ex $370 Gd $250
Left-hand model . . . . NiB $480 Ex $370 Gd $250

MODEL 64MS BOLT-ACTION SINGLE-SHOT RIFLE
Bolt-action, single-shot. Caliber: .22 LR. 21.25-inch bbl. European hardwood silhouette-style stock w/cheekpiece. Forend base and Wundhammer swell pistol-grip, stipple-checkered. Adj. two-stage trigger. Receiver grooved, drilled and tapped for scope blocks. Weight: 8 lbs. Imported from 1982 to 1996.
Standard or Featherweight
  (disc. 1988) . . . . NiB $1133 Ex $780 Gd $620
Left-hand model . . . . NiB $1133 Ex $780 Gd $620

MODEL 64MSR BOLT-ACTION REPEATER
Similar to Anschutz Model 64MS except repeater w/5-round magazine. Imported from 1996.
Standard model . . . . NiB $1045 Ex $789 Gd $603
Left-hand model . . . . NiB $1045 Ex $789 Gd $603

MODEL 520/61 SEMIAUTOMATIC . . . . . NiB $331 Ex $270 Gd $167
Caliber: .22 LR. 10-round magazine. 24-inch bbl. Sights: Folding leaf rear, hooded ramp front. Receiver grooved for scope mounting. Rotary-style safety. Monte Carlo stock and beavertail forend, checkered. Weight: 6.5 lbs. Imported from 1982 to 1983.

MODEL 525 AUTOLOADER
Caliber: .22 LR. 10-round magazine. 20- or 24-inch bbl. 39 to 43 inches overall. Weight: 6.1 to 6.5 lbs. Adj. folding rear sight; hooded ramp front. Checkered European hardwood Monte Carlo style buttstock and beavertail forend. Sling swivel studs. Imported 1984 to 1995.
Carbine model
  (disc. 1986) . . . . NiB $430 Ex $324 Gd $227
Rifle model (24-inch bbl.) . . . . . . NiB $500 Ex $443 Gd $319

MODEL 1403B . . . . NiB $904 Ex $745 Gd $440
A lighter-weight model designed for Biathlon competition. Caliber: .22 LR. 21.5-inch bbl. Adj. two-stage trigger. Adj. grooved wood buttplate, stipple-checkered deep thumb-rest flute and straight pistol-grip. Weight: 9 lbs. w/sights. Imported from 1990 to 1992.

MODEL 1403D MATCH SINGLE-SHOT TARGET RIFLE
Caliber: .22 LR. 25-inch bbl. 43 inches overall. Weight: 8.6 lbs. No sights, receiver grooved for Anschutz target sights. Walnut-finished hardwood target stock w/adj. buttplate. Importation disc. 1992.
Standard model . . . . NiB $707 Ex $567 Gd $417
W/match sights. . . . . NiB $988 Ex $779 Gd $555

Anschutz Model 1416D

Anschutz Model 1418

Anschutz Model 1422D

MODEL 1407 I.S.U. MATCH 54 RIFLE
Bolt-action, single-shot, caliber: .22 LR. 26.88-inch bbl. Scope bases. Receiver grooved for Anschutz sights. Single-stage adj. trigger. Select walnut target stock w/deep forearm for position shooting, adj. buttplate, hand stop and swivel. Weight: 10 lbs. Imported 1970 to 1981.

Standard model	NiB $653	Ex $535	Gd $291
Left-hand model	NiB $653	Ex $535	Gd $291
w/international sights, add			$75

MODEL 1408 . . . . NiB $466 Ex $408 Gd $370
Bolt-action, single-shot, caliber: .22 LR. 23.5-inch bbl. w/sliding weights. No metallic sights. Receiver drilled and tapped for scope-sight bases. Single-stage adj. trigger. Oversize bolt knob. Select walnut stock w/thumbhole, adj. comb and buttplate. Weight: 9.5 lbs. Intro. 1976. Disc. Add $175 for ED model.

MODEL 1411 MATCH 54 RIFLE
Bolt-action, single-shot. Caliber: .22 LR. 27.5-inch extra heavy bbl. w/ mounted scope bases. Receiver grooved for Anschutz sights. Single-stage adj. trigger. Select walnut target stock w/cheekpiece (adj. in 1973 and later production), full pistol-grip, beavertail forearm, adj. buttplate, hand stop and swivel. Model 1411-L has left-hand stock. Weight: 11 lbs. Disc.

w/Non-adj. cheekpiece	NiB $678	Ex $423	Gd $269
w/adj. cheekpiece	NiB $703	Ex $532	Gd $402
w/Anschutz International Sight set, add			$300

MODEL 1413 SUPER MATCH 54 RIFLE
Freestyle international target rifle w/specifications similar to those of Model 1411, except w/special stock w/thumbhole, adj. pistol grip, adj. cheekpiece in 1973 and later production, adj. hook buttplate, adj. palmrest. Model 1413-L has left-hand stock. Weight: 15.5 lbs. Disc.

w/non-adj. cheekpiece	NiB $830	Ex $733	Gd $400
w/adj. cheekpiece	NiB $704	Ex $572	Gd $399
w/Anschutz International sight set, add			$300

MODEL 1416D . . . . NiB $790 Ex $577 Gd $368
Bolt-action sporter. Caliber: .22 LR. 22.5-inch bbl. Sights: Folding leaf rear; hooded ramp front. Receiver grooved for scope mounting. Select European stock w/cheekpiece, skip-checkered pistol grip and forearm. Weight: 6 lbs. Imported 1982 to 2007.

MODEL 1416D CLASSIC/CUSTOM SPORTERS
Same as Model 1416D except w/American classic-style stock (Classic) or modified European-style stock w/Monte Carlo roll-over cheekpiece and Schnabel forend (Custom). Weight: 5.5 lbs. (Classic); 6 lbs. (Custom). Imported 1986 to 2007.

Model 1416D Classic	NiB $995	Ex $549	Gd $380
Model 1416D Classic, "True" left-hand	NiB $1095	Ex $577	Gd $419
Model 1416D Custom	NiB $980	Ex $750	Gd $380
Model 1416D fiberglass (1991-92)	NiB $760	Ex $623	Gd $445

MODEL 1418 BOLT-ACTION
SPORTER . . . . NiB $452 Ex $352 Gd $200
Caliber: .22 LR. 5- or 10-round magazine. 19.75-inch bbl. Sights: Folding leaf rear; hooded ramp front. Receiver grooved for scope mounting. Select walnut stock, Mannlicher type w/cheekpiece, pistol-grip and forearm skip checkered. Weight: 5.5 lbs. Intro. 1976. Disc.

MODEL 1418D BOLT-ACTION
SPORTER . . . . NiB $1008 Ex $886 Gd $533
Caliber: .22 LR. 5- or 10-round magazine. 19.75-inch bbl. European walnut Monte Carlo stock, Mannlicher type w/cheekpiece, pistolgrip and forend skip-line checkered, buffalo horn Schnabel tip. Weight: 5.5 lbs. Imported from 1982 to 1995 and 1998 to 2003.

MODEL 1422D CLASSIC/CUSTOM RIFLE
Bolt-action sporter. Caliber: .22 LR. Five-round removable straight-feed clip magazine. 24-inch bbl. Sights: Folding leaf rear; hooded ramp front. Select European walnut stock, classic type (Classic); Monte Carlo w/ hand-carved rollover cheekpiece (Custom). Weight: 7.25 lbs. (Classic) 6.5 lbs. (Custom). Imported 1982 to 1989.

Model 1422D Classic	NiB $833	Ex $670	Gd $432
Model 1422D Custom	NiB $896	Ex $833	Gd $479

Anschutz Model 1427B

Anschutz Model 1432

Anschutz Model 1432D

Model 1827B Biathlon Rifle . . . NiB $1943 Ex $1377 Gd $937
Bolt-action clip repeater. Caliber: .22 LR. 21.5-inch bbl. Two-stage trigger w/wing-type safety. Hardwood stock w/deep fluting, pistol grip and deep forestock with adj. hand stop rail. Target sights w/adjustable weights. Advertised in 1981 but imported from 1982 to date as Model 1827B.

MODEL 1430D MATCH . . . . NiB $976 Ex $650 Gd $429
Improved version of Model 64S. Bolt-action, single-shot. Caliber: .22 LR. 26-inch medium-heavy bbl. Walnut Monte Carlo stock w/cheekpiece, adj. buttplate, deep midstock tapered to forend. Pistol-grip and contoured thumb groove w/stipple checkering. Single-stage adj. trigger. Target sights. Weight: 8.38 lbs. Imported from 1982 to 1990.

MODEL 1432 BOLT-ACTION SPORTER
Caliber: .22 Hornet. 5-round box magazine. 24-inch bbl. Sights: Folding leaf rear, hooded ramp front. Receiver grooved for scope mounting. Select walnut stock w/Monte Carlo comb and cheekpiece, pistol-grip and forearm skip-checkered. Weight: 6.75 lbs. Imported from 1974 to 1987. (Reintroduced as 1707/1730 series)
Early model (1974-85) . . . . NiB $1347 Ex $988 Gd $721
Late model (1985-87) . . . . NiB $1145 Ex $933 Gd $631

MODEL 1432D CLASSIC/CUSTOM RIFLE
Bolt-action sporter similar to Model 1422D except chambered for Caliber: .22 Hornet. 4-round magazine. 23.5-inch bbl. Weight: 7.75 lbs. (Classic); 6.5 lbs. (Custom). Classic stock on Classic model; fancy-grade Monte Carlo w/hand-carved rollover cheekpiece (Custom). Imported from 1982 to 1987. (Reintroduced as 1707/1730 series)
Model 1432D Classic . . . . NiB $1347 Ex $982 Gd $733
Model 1432D Custom. . . . . NiB $1175 Ex $923 Gd $634

MODEL 1433 BOLT-ACTION SPORTER NiB $1131 Ex $916 Gd $650
Caliber: .22 Hornet. 5-round box magazine. 19.75-inch bbl. Sights: Folding leaf rear, hooded ramp front. Receiver grooved for scope

mounting. Single-stage or double-set trigger. Select walnut Mannlicher stock; cheekpiece, pistol-grip and forearm skip-checkered. Weight: 6.5 lbs. Imported from 1976 to 1986.

MODEL 1448D. . . . . NiB $421 Ex $324 Gd $236
Similar to Model 1449 except chambered for Caliber: .22 LR. w/22.5-inch smooth bore bbl. and no sights. Walnut-finished hardwood stock. Imported from 1999 to 2001.

MODEL 1449D YOUTH SPORTER NiB $300 Ex $233 Gd $177
Bolt-action sporter version of Model 2000. Caliber: .22 LR. 5-round box magazine. 16.25-inch bbl. Weight: 3.5 lbs. Hooded ramp front sight, addition. Walnut-finished hardwood stock. Imported from 1990 to 1991.

MODEL 1450B TARGET RIFLE . . . NiB $703 Ex $533 Gd $397
Biathlon rifle developed on 2000 Series action. 19.5-inch bbl. Weight: 5.5 lbs. Adj. buttplate. Target sights. Imported 1993 to 1994.

MODEL 1451 E/R SPORTER/TARGET
Bolt-action, single-shot (1451E) or repeater (1451R). Caliber: .22 LR. 22- or 22.75-inch bbl. w/o sights. Select hardwood stock w/stippled pistolgrip and vented forearm. beavertail forend, adj. cheekpiece, and deep thumb flute. Weight: 6.5 lbs. Imported from 1996 to 2001.
Model 1451E (disc. 1997) . . . . . NiB $487 Ex $370 Gd $254
Model 1451R . . . . NiB $479 Ex $455 Gd $310

MODEL 1451D CLASSIC/CUSTOM RIFLE
Same as Model 1451R except w/walnut-finished hardwood stock (Classic) or modified European-style walnut stock w/Monte Carlo rollover cheekpiece and Schnabel forend (Custom). Weight: 5 lbs. Imported from 1998 to 2001.
Model 1451D Classic (Super) . . . . NiB $367 Ex $288 Gd $199
Model 1451D Custom. . . . . NiB $488 Ex $455 Gd $321

Anschutz Model 1707

Anschutz Model 1803D

Anschutz Model 1907

MODEL 1451 ST- R RIFLE. . . . . . NiB $499 Ex $454 Gd $342
Same as Model 1451R except w/two-stage trigger and walnut-finished hardwood uncheckered stock. Imported 1996 to 2001.

MODEL 1516D CLASSIC/CUSTOM RIFLE
Same as Model 1416D except chambered for Caliber: .22 Magnum RF, with American classic-style stock (Classic) or modified European-style stock w/Monte Carlo rollover cheekpiece and Schnabel forend (Custom). Weight: 5.5 lbs. (Classic), 6 lbs. (Custom). Imported from 1986 to 2003.
Model 1516D Classic . . . . NiB $704 Ex $572 Gd $379
Model 1516D Custom. . . . . NiB $639 Ex $600 Gd $423

MODELS 1516D/1518D LUXUS RIFLES
The alpha designation for these models was changed from Custom to Luxus in 1996 to 1998. (See Custom listings for Luxus values.)

MODELS 1518/1518D SPORTING RIFLES
Same as Model 1418 except chambered for .22 Magnum RF, 4-round box magazine. Model 1518 intro. 1976. Disc. Model 1518D has full Mannlicher-type stock. Imported from 1982 to 2001.
Model 1518 . . . . NiB $766 Ex $650 Gd $423
Model 1518D. . . . . NiB $974 Ex $788 Gd $544
w/set trigger, add $150

MODEL 1522D CLASSIC/CUSTOM RIFLE
Same as Model 1422D except chambered for .22 Magnum RF, 4-round magazine. Weight: 6.5 lbs. (Custom). Fancy-grade Classic or Monte Carlo stock w/hand-carved rollover cheekpiece. Imported 1982 to 1989. (Reintroduced as 1707D/1730D series)
Model 1522D Classic . . . . NiB $1197 Ex $869 Gd $633
Model 1522D Custom. . . . . NiB $1197 Ex $869 Gd $633

MODEL 1532D CLASSIC/CUSTOM RIFLE
Same as Model 1432D except chambered for .222 Rem. Three-round mag. Weight: 6.5 lbs. (Custom). Classic stock on Classic Model; fancy-grade Monte Carlo stock w/handcarved rollover cheekpiece (Custom). Imported from 1982 to 1989. (Reintroduced as 1707D/174 D0 series)
Model 1532D Classic . . . . NiB $1019 Ex $795 Gd $448
Model 1532D Custom. . . . . NiB $1297 Ex $996 Gd $698

MODEL 1533 . . . . NiB $1090 Ex $844 Gd $589
Same as Model 1433 except chambered for .222 Rem. Three-shot box magazine. Imported from 1976 to 1994.

MODEL 1707 SERIES BOLT-ACTION REPEATER
Match 54 Sporter. Calibers: .22 LR, .22 Mag., .22 Hornet, .222 Rem. Five-shot removable magazine 24-inch bbl. 43 inches overall. Weight: 7.5 lbs. Folding leaf rear sight, hooded ramp front. Select European walnut stock w/cheekpiece and Schnabel forend tip. Imported from 1989 to 2001.
Standard Model 1707
  Bavarian — rimfire cal. . . . . . . NiB $1018 Ex $933 Gd $580
Standard Model 1707
  Bavarian — centerfire cal. . . . NiB $1342 Ex $1056 Gd $697
Model 1707D Classic (Classic stock, 6.75 lbs.)
  rimfire cal. . . . . NiB $1179 Ex $994 Gd $698
Model 1707D Classic — centerfire cal. . . NiB $1279 Ex $1044 Gd $748
Model 1707D Custom — rimfire cal. . . . . NiB $1094 Ex $893 Gd $633
Model 1707D Custom — centerfire cal. . . NiB $1332 Ex $1088 Gd $775
Model 1707D Graphite Cust. (McMillan graphite reinforced stock,
  22-inch bbl., intro. 1991) . . . . NiB $1156 Ex $985 Gd $641
Select walnut and gold trigger, add $200
Model 1707 FWT (featherweight, 6.5 lbs.) –
  rimfire cal. . . . . NiB $1122 Ex $909 Gd $641
Model 1707 FWT — centerfire cal. . . . . . NiB $1289 Ex $1136 Gd $703

Anschutz Model 2013

MODEL 1733D MANNLICHER . . . . . . NiB $1370 Ex $1168 Gd $860
Same as Model 1707D except w/19-inch bbl. and Mannlicher-style stock. 39 inches overall. Weight: 6.25 lbs. Imported from 1993 to 1995 (Reintroduced in 1998, disc. 2001).

MODEL 1740 MONTE CARLO SPORTER
Caliber: .22 Hornet or .222 Rem. Three and 5-round magazines respectively. 24-inch bbl. 43.25 inches overall. Weight: 6.5 lbs. Hooded ramp front, folding leaf rear. Drilled and tapped for scope mounts. Select European walnut stock w/roll-over cheekpiece, checkered grip and forend. Imported from 1998 to 2006.
Model 1740 Classic
  (Meistergrade) . . . . NiB $1504 Ex $1237 Gd $866
Model 1740 Custom . . . . NiB $1370 Ex $1089 Gd $733

MODEL 1743 MONTE CARLO
SPORTER . . . . NiB $1370 Ex $1132 Gd $769
Similar to Model 1740 except w/Mannlicher full stock. Imported from 1997 to 2001.

MODEL 1903D MATCH SINGLE-SHOT TARGET RIFLE
Caliber: .22 LR. 25.5-inch bbl. 43.75 inches overall. Weight: 8.5 lbs. No sights; receiver grooved, drilled and tapped for scope mounts. Blonde or walnut-finished hardwood stock w/adj. cheekpiece, stippled grip and forend. Left-hand version. Imported 1987 to 1993.
Right-hand model
  (Reintroduced as 1903D) . . . . . NiB $1006 Ex $844 Gd $544
Left-hand model . . . . NiB $1108 Ex $866 Gd $633

MODEL 1807 ISU
STANDARD MATCH. . . . . NiB $1359 Ex $1094 Gd $708
Bolt-action single-shot. Caliber: 22 LR. 26-inch bbl. Improved Super Match 54 action. Two-stage match trigger. Removable cheekpiece, adj. buttplate, thumbpiece and forestock w/stipple-checkered. Weight: 10 lbs. Imported 1982 to 1988. (Reintroduced as 1907 ISU)

MODEL 1808ED SUPER RUNNING TARGET
Bolt-action single-shot. Caliber: .22 LR. 23.5-inch bbl. w/sliding weights. Improved Super Match 54 action. Heavy beavertail forend w/adj.cheekpiece and buttplate. Adj. single-stage trigger. Weight: 9.5 lbs. Imported from 1982 to 1998.
Right-hand model . . . . NiB $1677 Ex $1328 Gd $869
Left-hand model . . . . NiB $1688 Ex $1377 Gd $973

MODEL 1808MS-R
METALLIC SILHOUETTE . . . . . NiB $2021 Ex $1565 Gd $932
Bolt-action repeater. Caliber: .22 LR. 19.2-inch bbl. w/o sights. Thumbhole Monte Carlo stock w/grooved forearm enhanced w/ "Anschutz" logo. Weight: 8.2 lbs. Imported from 1998 to date.

MODEL 1810 SUPER MATCH II NiB $1979 Ex $1440 Gd $937
A less detailed version of the Super Match 1813 model. Tapered forend w/deep receiver area. Select European hardwood stock. Weight: 13.5 lbs. Imported from 1982 to 1988 (reintroduced as 1910 series).

MODEL 1811 PRONE MATCH . NiB $1843 Ex $1623 Gd $877
Bolt-action single-shot. Caliber: .22 LR. 27.5-inch bbl. Improved Super Match 54 action. Select European hardwood stock w/beavertail forend, adj. cheekpiece, and deep thumb flute. Thumb groove and pistol grip w/stipple checkering. Adj. buttplate. Weight: 11.5 lbs. Imported 1982 to 1988. (Reintroduced as 1911 Prone Match)

MODEL 1813 SUPER MATCH. . NiB $2281 Ex $1951 Gd $869
Bolt-action single-shot. Caliber: .22 LR. 27.5-inch bbl. Improved Super Match 54 action w/light firing pin, one-point adj. trigger. European walnut thumbhole stock, adj. palm rest, forend and pistol grip stipple checkered. Adj. cheekpiece and hook buttplate. Weight: 15.5 lbs. Imported from 1979 to 1988. (Reintroduced as 1913 Super Match)

MODEL 1827B BIATHLON RIFLE
Bolt-action clip repeater. Caliber: .22 LR. 21.5-inch bbl. 42.5 inches overall. Weight: 8.5 to 9 lbs. Slide safety. Adj. target sight set w/snow caps. European walnut stock w/cheekpiece, stippled pistol grip and forearm w/adj. weights. Fortner straight pull bolt option offered in 1986. Imported from 1982 to date.
Mdl. 1827B w/Sup. Mat. 54 action . . NiB $2359 Ex $2153 Gd $1020
Model 1827B, left-hand . . . . NiB $2101 Ex $1716 Gd $1224
Model 1827BT w/Fortner
  Option, right-hand . . . . NiB $2467 Ex $2261 Gd $1032
Model 1827BT, left-hand . . . . NiB $2604 Ex $2127 Gd $1513
Model 1827BT w/laminated stock, add $175
w/stainless steel bbl., add $205

MODEL 1907 ISU INTERNATIONAL MATCH RIFLE
Updated version of Model 1807 w/same general specifications as Model 1913 except w/26-inch bbl. 44.5 inches overall. Weight: 11 lbs. Designed for ISU 3-position competition. Fitted w/vented beechwood or walnut, blonde or color-laminated stock. Imported from 1989 to date.
Right-hand model . . . . NiB $1544 Ex $1353 Gd $838
Left-hand model . . . . NiB $1730 Ex $1415 Gd $1012
w/laminated stock, add $135
w/walnut stock, add $100
w/stainless steel bbl., add $130

MODEL 1910 INTERNATIONAL SUPER MATCH RIFLE
Updated version of Model 1810 w/same general specifications Model 1913 except w/less-detailed hardwood stock w/tapered forend. Weight: 13.5 lbs. Imported from 1989 to 1998.
Right-hand model . . . . NiB $2566 Ex $2077 Gd $1103
Left-hand model . . . . NiB $2560 Ex $2097 Gd $1506

MODEL 1911 PRONE MATCH RIFLE
Updated version of Model 1811 w/same general specifications Model 1913 except w/specialized prone match hardwood stock w/beavertail forend. Weight: 11.5 lbs. Imported from 1989 to date.
Right-hand model . . . . NiB $1854 Ex $1764 Gd $849

RIFLES

Anschutz Achiever

MODEL 1912
LADIES' SPORT RIFLE . . . . **NiB $1837 Ex $1932 Gd $865**
Similar to the Model 1907 designed for ISU 3-position competition w/same general U.I.T. specifications except w/shorter dimensions to accomodate smaller competitors. Weight: 11.4 lbs. Imported from 1999 to date.

MODEL 1913 STANDARD RIFLE . . . . . **NiB $1611 Ex $1235 Gd $909**
Similar to 1913 Super Match w/economized appointments. Imported from 1997 to date.

MODEL 1913 SUPER MATCH RIFLE
Bolt-action single-shot Super Match (updated version of Model 1813). Caliber: .22 LR. 27.5-inch bbl. Weight: 14.2 lbs. Adj. two-stage trigger. Vented International thumbhole stock w/adj. cheekpiece, hand and palm rest, fitted w/10-way butthook. Imported from 1989 to date.
Right-hand model . . . . **NiB $3310 Ex $1989 Gd $879**
Left-hand model . . . . **NiB $2370 Ex $1909 Gd $1343**
W/laminated stock, add **$150**
W/stainless steel bbl., add **$175**

MODEL 2007 ISU STANDARD RIFLE
Bolt-action single-shot. Caliber: .22 LR. 19.75-inch bbl. 43.5 to 44.5 inches overall. Weight: 10.8 lbs. Two-stage trigger. Standard ISU stock w/adj. cheekpiece. Imported from 1992 to date.
Right-hand model . . . . **NiB $1997 Ex $1529 Gd $909**
Left-hand model . . . . **NiB $2040 Ex $1719 Gd $1244**
W/stainless steel bbl., add **$175**

MODEL 2013
LADIES' SPORT RIFLE . . . . **NiB $2197 Ex $2021 Gd $933**
Similar to the Model 2007 designed for ISU 3-position competition w/same general U.I.T. specifications except w/shorter dimensions to accomodate smaller competitors. Weight: 11.4 lbs. Imported from 1999 to date.

MODEL 2013
BENCHREST RIFLE (BR-50) . . . . **NiB $1889 Ex $1624 Gd $877**
Bolt-action single-shot. Caliber: .22 LR. 19.6-inch bbl. 43 inches overall. Weight: 10.3 lbs. Adjustable trigger for single or two-stage function. Benchrest-configuration stock. Imported from 1999 to date.

MODEL 2013 SILHOUETTE RIFLE . . . . . . **NiB $2187 Ex $1675 Gd $944**
Bolt-action single-shot. Caliber: .22 LR. 20-inch bbl. 45.5 inches overall. Weight: 11.5 lbs. Two-stage trigger. Thumbhole black synthetic or laminated stock w/adj. cheekpiece, hand and palm rest. Imported from 1994 to date.

MODEL 2013 SUPER MATCH RIFLE
Bolt-action single-shot. Caliber: .22 LR. 19.75- or 27.1-inch bbl. 43 to 50.1 inches overall. Weight: 15.5 lbs. Two-stage trigger. International thumbhole, black synthetic or laminated stock w/adj. cheekpiece, hand and palm rest; fitted w/10-way butthook. Imported from 1992 to date.
Right-hand model . . . . **NiB $3566 Ex $2317 Gd $1149**

Left-hand model . . . . **NiB $2588 Ex $1290 Gd $1482**
W/laminated stock, add **$200**

ACHIEVER BOLT-ACTION RIFLE . . . . . . **NiB $422 Ex $337 Gd $219**
Caliber: .22 LR. 5-round magazine. Mark 2000-type repeating action. 19.5-inch bbl. 36.5 inches overall. Weight: 5 lbs. Adj. open rear sight; hooded ramp front. Plain European hardwood target-style stock w/ vented forend and adj. buttplate. Imported 1987 to 1995.

ACHIEVER ST-SUPER TARGET . . . **NiB $559 Ex $431 Gd $269**
Same as Achiever except single-shot w/22-inch bbl. and adj. stock. 38.75 inches overall. Weight: 6.5 lbs. Target sights. Imported since 1994 to 1995.

BR-50 BENCH REST RIFLE . . . **NiB $2123 Ex $1707 Gd $1026**
Single-shot. Caliber: .22 LR. 19.75-inch bbl. (23 inches w/muzzle weight). 37.75-42.5 inches overall. Weight: 11 lbs. Grooved receiver, no sights. Walnut-finished hardwood or synthetic benchrest stock w/adj. cheekpiece. Imported from 1994 to 1997. (Reintroduced as Model 2013 BR-50)

KADETT BOLT-ACTION
REPEATING RIFLE . . . . **NiB $370 Ex $241 Gd $198**
Caliber: .22 LR. 5-round detachable box magazine. 22-inch bbl. 40 inches overall. Weight: 5.5 lbs. Adj. folding leaf rear sight; hooded ramp front. Checkered European hardwood stock w/walnut-finish. Imported 1987.

MARK 2000 MATCH. . . . . **NiB $448 Ex $355 Gd $221**
Takedown, bolt-action single-shot. Caliber: .22 LR. 26-inch heavy bbl. Walnut stock w/deep-fluted thumb-groove, Wundhammer swell pistol grip, beavertail forend. Adj. buttplate, single-stage adj. trigger. Weight: 8 lbs. Imported from 1982 to 1988.

ARMALITE, INC. — Geneseo, Illinois
Formerly Costa Mesa, California. Armalite was in Costa Mesa, California from 1959-73. Following the acquisition by Eagle Arms in 1995, production resumed under the Armalite, Inc. Logo in Geneseo, Illinois.

Production by ARMALITE

AR-7 EXPLORER SURVIVAL RIFLE . **NiB $469 Ex $345 Gd $290**
Takedown. Semiautomatic. Caliber: .22 LR. Eight-round box magazine. 16-inch cast aluminum bbl. w/steel liner. Sights: Peep rear; blade front. Brown plastic stock, recessed to stow barrel, action, and magazine. Weight: 2.75 lbs. Will float stowed or assembled. Made from 1959-1973 by Armalite; from 1974-90 by Charter Arms; from 1990-97 by Survival Arms, Cocoa, FL.; from 1997 to date by Henry Repeating Arms Co., Brooklyn, NY.

AR-7 EXPLORER CUSTOM RIFLE . . **NiB $325 Ex $270 Gd $199**
Same as AR-7 Survival Rifle except w/deluxe walnut stock w/cheek-piece and pistol grip. Weight: 3.5 lbs. Made from 1964 to 1970.

Armalite AR-10

Armalite AR-10 (T) Target Carbine

Armalite M-15A2 National Match

Armalite M-15A2 HBAR

AR-180 SEMIAUTOMATIC RIFLE
Commercial version of full automatic AR-18 Combat Rifle. Gas-operated semiautomatic. Caliber: .223 Rem. (5.56mm). 5-, 20-, 30-round magazines. 18.25-inch bbl. w/flash hider/muzzle brake. Sights: Flip-up "L" type rear, adj. for windage; post front, adj. for elevation. Accessory: 3x scope and mount (add $60 to value). Folding buttstock of black nylon, rubber buttplate and pistol grip, heat dissipating fiberglass forend (hand guard), swivels, sling. 38 inches overall, 28.75 inches folded. Weight: 6.5 lbs. Note: Made by Armalite Inc. 1969 to 1972, manufactured for Armalite by Howa Machinery Ltd., Nagoya, Japan, from 1972 to 1973; by Sterling Armament Co. Ltd., Dagenham, Essex, England, from 1976 to 1994. Importation disc.

Armalite AR-180 (Mfg. by
Armalite–Costa Mesa) . . . . . . NiB $2189 Ex $1543 Gd $1043
Armalite AR-180 (Mfg. by Howa) . . . . NiB $2109 Ex $1535 Gd $990

Armalite AR-180 (Mfg. by Sterling) . . . NiB $1809 Ex $1404 Gd $933
w/3x scope and mount, add $250

AR-10 SEMIAUTOMATIC SERIES
Gas-operated semiautomatic action. Calibers: .243 Win. or .308 Win. (7.62 x 51mm). 10-round magazine. 16- or 20-inch bbl. 35.5 or 39.5 inches overall. Weight: 9 to 9.75 lbs. Post front sight, adj. aperature rear. Black or green composition stock. Made from 1995 to date.

AR-10 A2 (Std. carbine) . . . . . . NiB $1190 Ex $1088 Gd $707
AR-10 A2 (Std. rifle) . . . . NiB $1190 Ex $1088 Gd $707
AR-10 A4 (S.P. carbine) . . . . NiB $1080 Ex $905 Gd $600
AR-10 A4 (S.P. rifle) . . . . NiB $1080 Ex $905 Gd $600
w/stainless steel bbl., add $150

Armi Jager AP-74 Wood Stock

AR-10 T (TARGET)
Similar to AR-10A except in National Match configuration w/three-slot short Picatinny rail system and case deflector. Additional calibers: .260 Rem., .300 RUM, 7mm-08 Rem., .338 Fed. 16- or 24-inch bbl. Weight: 8.25 to 10.4 lbs. Composite stock and handguard. No sights. Optional National Match carry handle and detachable front sight. Made from 1995 to date.
AR-10 T (Rifle) . . . . NiB $1579 Ex $1289 Gd $1043
AR-10 T (Carbine). . . . . NiB $1479 Ex $1289 Gd $1043

MODEL AR-50 SS BOLT-ACTION
RIFLE . . . . NiB $3198 Ex $2645 Gd $1370
Caliber: .50 BMG. 31-inch bbl. w/muzzle brake. 59 inches overall. Weight: 41 lbs. Modified octagonal-form receiver, drilled and slotted for scope rail. Single-stage trigger. Triple front-locking bolt lug w/spring-loaded plunger for automatic ejection. Magnesium phosphate steel, hard-anodized aluminum finish. Made from 1999 to date.

M15 SERIES
Gas-operated semiautomatic w/A2-style forward-assist mechanism and push-type pivot pin for easy takedown. Caliber: .223 Rem., 5.56 NATO or 6.8 SPC. 7-round magazine. 16-, 20- or 24-inch bbl. Weight: 7-9.2 lbs. Composite or retractable stock. Fully adj. sights. Black anodized finish. Made from 1995 to date.
M-15A2 (Carbine) . . . . NiB $927 Ex $800 Gd $647
M-15A2 (Service Rifle) . . . . NiB $989 Ex $845 Gd $655
M-15A2 (National Match) . . . . .NiB $1350 Ex $1123 Gd $770
M-15A2
   (Golden Eagle heavy bbl.). . . . NiB $1332 Ex $1086 Gd $730
M-15A2 M4C
   (retractable stock, disc. 1997). NiB $1299 Ex $1021 Gd $698
M-15A4 (Action Master, disc. 1997) . . . NiB $1139 Ex $934 Gd $670
M-15A4 (Predator) . . . . NiB $977 Ex $855 Gd $654
M-15A4 S.P. R. (Special Purpose Rifle) . . NiB $956 Ex $799 Gd $535
M-15A4 (S.P. Carbine) . . . . NiB $875 Ex $720 Gd $463
M-15A4T (Eagle Eye Carbine) . . . . .NiB $1326 Ex $1090 Gd $775
M-15A4T (Eagle Eye Rifle) . . . . .NiB $1377 Ex $1030 Gd $755

ARMI JAGER — Turin, Italy

AP-74 COMMANDO . . . . NiB $322 Ex $248 Gd $166
Similar to standard AP-74 but styled to resemble original version of Uzi 9mm submachine gun w/wood buttstock. Lacks carrying handle and flash suppressor. Has different type front sight mount and guards, wood stock, pistol grip and forearm. Intro. 1976. Disc.

AP-74 SEMIAUTOMATIC RIFLE
Styled after U.S. M16 military rifle. Caliber: .22 LR, .32 Auto (pistol cartridge). Detachable clip magazine; capacity: 14 rounds caliber .22 LR, 9 rounds .32 ACP. 20-inch bbl. w/flash suppressor. Weight: 6.5 lbs. M16 type sights. Stock, pistol-grip and forearm of black plastic, swivels and sling. Intro. 1974. Disc.

.22 LR. . . . . NiB $359 Ex $290 Gd $200
.32 Auto. . . . . NiB $379 Ex $322 Gd $209
AP-74 WOOD STOCK MODEL
Same as standard AP-74 except w/wood stock, pistol-grip and forearm weight: 7 lbs. Disc.
.22 LR . . . . NiB $448 Ex $380 Gd $250
.32 Auto. . . . . NiB $448 Ex $380 Gd $250

ARMSCOR (Arms Corp.) — Manila, Philippines
Imported by Armscor Precision Int'l.

MODEL 20 AUTO RIFLE
Caliber: .22 LR. 15-round magazine. 21-inch bbl. 39.75 inches overall. Weight: 6.5 lbs. Sights: Hooded front; adj. rear. Checkered or plain walnut finished mahogany stock. Blued finish. Imported 1990 to 1991. (Reinstated by Ruko in the M series.)
Model 20 (checkered stock) . . . . . . NiB $167 Ex $130 Gd $97
Model 20C (carbine-style stock) . . . NiB $144 Ex $122 Gd $98
Model 20P (plain stock) . . . . NiB $126 Ex $100 Gd $78

MODEL 1600 AUTO RIFLE
Caliber: .22 LR. 15-round magazine. 19.5-inch bbl. 38 inches overall. Weight: 6 lbs. Sights: Post front; aperture rear. Plain mahogany stock. Matte black finish. Imported 1987 to 1991. (Reinstated by Ruko in the M series.)
Standard model . . . . NiB $180 Ex $155 Gd $100
Retractable stock model . . . . NiB $190 Ex $167 Gd $110

MODEL AK22 AUTO RIFLE
Caliber: .22 LR. 15- or 30-round magazine. 18.5-inch bbl. 36 inches overall. Weight: 7 lbs. Sights: Post front; adj. rear. Plain mahogany stock. Matte black finish. Imported 1987 to 1991.
Standard model . . . . NiB $179 Ex $150 Gd $110
Folding stock model . . . . NiB $269 Ex $220 Gd $166

MODEL M14 SERIES BOLT-ACTION RIFLE
Caliber: .22 LR. 10-round magazine. 23-inch bbl. Weight: 6.25 lbs. Open sights. Walnut or mahogany stock. Imported 1991 to 1997.
M14P Standard model . . . . NiB $129 Ex $98 Gd $70
M14D Deluxe model
   (checkered stock, disc. 1995) . . . . NiB $149 Ex $110 Gd $90

MODEL M20 SERIES SEMIAUTOMATIC RIFLE
Caliber: .22 LR. 10- or 15-round magazine. 18.25- or 20.75-inch bbl. Weight:5.5 to 6.5 lbs. 38 to 40.5 inches overall. Hooded front sight w/ windage adj. rear. Walnut finished mahogany stock. Imported 1990 to 1997.
M20C (carbine model) . . . . NiB $144 Ex $109 Gd $80
M20P (standard model). . . . . NiB $128 Ex $100 Gd $78
M20S Sporter Deluxe (w/checkered
   mahogany stock) . . . . NiB $167 Ex $150 Gd $97
M20SC Super Classic (w/checkered
   walnut stock) . . . . NiB $281 Ex $227 Gd $108

A-Square Hannibal

MODEL M1400 BOLT-ACTION RIFLE
Similar to Model 14P except w/checkered stock w/Schnabel forend. Weight: 6 lbs. Imported from 1990 to 1997.
M1400LW (Lightweight, disc. 1992) .... NiB $239 Ex $199 Gd $137
M1400S (Sporter) .... NiB $177 Ex $150 Gd $100
M1400SC (Super Classic) .... NiB $300 Ex $255 Gd $179

MODEL M1500 BOLT-ACTION RIFLE
Caliber: .22 Mag. 5-round magazine. 21.5-inch bbl. Weight: 6.5 lbs. Open sights. Checkered mahogany stock. Imported 1991 to 1997.
M1500 (standard) .... NiB $198 Ex $137 Gd $105
M1500LW (Euro-style walnut
  stock, disc. 1992) .... NiB $219 Ex $188 Gd $135
M1500SC (Monte Carlo stock)........ NiB $224 Ex $190 Gd $140

MODEL M1600 AUTO RIFLE
Rimfire replica of Armalite Model AR 180 (M16) except chambered for Caliber .22 LR. 15-round magazine. 18-inch bbl. Weight: 5.25 lbs. Composite or retractable buttstock w/composite handguard and pistol grip. Carrying handle w/adj. aperture rear sight and protected post front. Black anodized finish. Imported from 1991 to 1997.
M-1600 (standard w/fixed stock) ....NiB $190 Ex $149 Gd $110
M-1600R (retractable stock) ....NiB $200 Ex $161 Gd $120

MODEL M1800 BOLT-ACTION RIFLE
Caliber: .22 Hornet. 5-round magazine. 22-inch bbl. Weight: 6.6 lbs. Checkered hardwood or walnut stock. Sights: Post front; adj. rear. Imported from 1996 to 1997.
M-1800 (standard) .... NiB $310 Ex $233 Gd $175
M-1800SC (checkered walnut stock) .... NiB $400 Ex $327 Gd $255

MODEL M2000 BOLT-ACTION RIFLE
Similar to Model 20P except w/checkered mahogany stock and adj. sights. Imported from 1991 to 1997.
M2000S (standard) .... NiB $177 Ex $139 Gd $100
M2000SC (w/checkered walnut stock)... NiB $279 Ex $220 Gd $167

ARNOLD ARMS — Arlington, Washington

AFRICAN SAFARI
Calibers: .243 to .458 Win. Mag. and proprietary cartridges. 22- to 26-inch bbl. Weight: 7-9 lbs. Scope mount standard or w/optional M70 Express sights. Chrome-moly in four finishes. "A" and "AA" Fancy Grade English walnut stock with number 5 standard wraparound checkering pattern. Ebony forend tip. Made from 1994 to 2001.
w/ "A" Grade English
  walnut stock, blue finish.... NiB $4732 Ex $3841 Gd $2690
Std. polish .... NiB $4969 Ex $4000 Gd $2821
Hi-Luster .... NiB $5189 Ex $4290 Gd $2950
Stainless steel matte .... NiB $4733 Ex $3847 Gd $2993
w/ "AA" Grade English
  walnut stock, C-M matte blue finish NiB $4707 Ex $3810 Gd $2688
Std. polish .... NiB $4988 Ex $4037 Gd $2835
Hi-Luster .... NiB $5188 Ex $4200 Gd $2969
Stainless steel matte finish .... NiB $4707 Ex $3875 Gd $2710

ALASKAN TROPHY
Calibers: .300 Magnum to .458 Win. Magnum. 24- to 26-inch bbl. Weight: 7-9 lbs. Scope mount w/Express sights standard. Stainless steel or chrome-moly Apollo action w/fibergrain or black synthetic stock. Barrel band on 357 H&H and larger magnums. Made from 1996 to 2000.
Matte finish .... NiB $3330 Ex $2689 Gd $1900
Std. polish .... NiB $3559 Ex $2900 Gd $2044
Stainless steel............. NiB $3386 Ex $2744 Gd $1935

A-SQUARE COMPANY INC. — Glenrock, Wyoming

CAESAR BOLT-ACTION RIFLE
Custom rifle built on Remington's 707 receiver. Calibers: Same as Hannibal, Groups I, II and III. 20- to 26-inch bbl. Weight: 8.5 to 11 lbs. Express 3-leaf rear sight, ramp front. Synthetic or classic Claro oil-finished walnut stock w/flush detachable swivels and Coil-Chek recoil system. Three-way adj. target trigger; 3-position safety. Right- or left-hand. Made from 1986 to 2012.
Synthetic stock model ....NiB $3512 Ex $2790 Gd $1947
Walnut stock model........NiB $4044 Ex $2379 Gd $1756

GENGHIS KHAN BOLT-ACTION RIFLE
Custom varmint rifle developed on Winchester's M70 receiver; fitted w/ heavy tapered bbl. and Coil-Chek stock. Calibers: .22-250 Rem., .243 Win., .25-06 Rem., 6mm Rem. Weight: 8-8.5 lbs. Made from 1995 to 2012.
Synthetic stock model....... NiB $3566 Ex $2312 Gd $2044
Walnut stock model .... NiB $3482 Ex $2854 Gd $2023

HAMILCAR BOLT-ACTION RIFLE
Similar to Hannibal Model except lighter. Calibers: .25-06, .257 Wby., 6.5x55 Swedish, .270 Wby., 7x57, 7mm Rem., 7mm STW, 7mm Wby., .280 Rem., .30-06, .300 Win., .300 Wby., .338-06, 9.3x62. Weight: 8-8.5 lbs. Made from 1994 to 2012.
Synthetic stock model....... NiB $3554 Ex $2909 Gd $2011
Walnut stock model .... NiB $3508 Ex $2866 Gd $2009

HANNIBAL BOLT-ACTION RIFLE
Custom rifle built on reinforced P-17 Enfield receiver. Calibers: Group I: 30-06; Group II: 7mm Rem. Mag., .300 Win. Mag., .416 Taylor, .425 Express, .458 Win. Mag.; Group III: .300 H&H, .300 Wby. Mag., 8mm Rem. Mag., .340 Wby. Mag., .375 H&H, .375 Wby. Mag., .404 Jeffery, .416 Hoffman, .416 Rem Mag., .450 Ackley, .458 Lott; Group IV: .338 A-Square Mag., .375 A-Square Mag., .378 Wby. Mag., .416 Rigby, .416 Wby. Mag., .460 Short Square Mag., .500 A-Square Mag. 20- to 26-inch bbl. Weight: 9 to 11.75 lbs. Express 3-leaf rear sight, ramp front. Classic Claro oil-finished walnut stock or synthetic stock w/flush detachable swivels and Coil-Chek recoil system. Adj. trigger w/2-position safety. Made from 1986 to 2012.
Synthetic stock model....... NiB $3614 Ex $2870 Gd $1921
Walnut stock model .... NiB $3707 Ex $2795 Gd $2021

Auto-Ordnance
Thompson Model 27A-1
Deluxe

Auto-Ordnance
Thompson Model 27A-1
Standard Carbine

Auto-Ordnance
Thompson M1 Carbine

AUSTRIAN MILITARY RIFLES — Steyr, Austria

Manufactured at Steyr Armory.

MODEL 90
STEYR-MANNLICHER RIFLE . . . . . NiB $337 Ex $189 Gd $139
Straight-pull bolt action. Caliber: 8mm. 5-round magazine. Open sights. 10-inch bayonet. Cartridge clip forms part of the magazine mechanism. Some of these rifles were provided with a laced canvas hand guard, others were of wood.

MODEL 90
STEYR-MANNLICHER CARBINE . . NiB $339 Ex $228 Gd $139
Same general specifications as Model 90 rifle except w/19.5-inch bbl., weight 7 lbs. No bayonet stud or supplemental forend grip.

MODEL 95
STEYR-MANNLICHER CARBINE . . NiB $329 Ex $250 Gd $141
Same general specifications as Model 95 rifle except w/19.5-inch bbl., weight 7 lbs. Post front sight; adj. rear carbine sight.

MODEL 95 STEYR-MANNLICHER
SERVICE RIFLE . . . . NiB $299 Ex $190 Gd $137
Straight-pull bolt action. Caliber: 8x50R Mannlicher (many of these rifles were altered during World War II to use the 7.9mm German service ammunition). 5-round Mannlicher-type box magazine. 30-inch bbl. Weight: 8.5 lbs. Sights: Blade front; rear adj. for elevation. Military-type full stock.

AUTO-ORDNANCE CORPORATION — Worcester, Massachusetts

A division of Kahr Arms.

THOMPSON
MODEL 22-27A-3. . . . . NiB $997 Ex $754 Gd $498
Similar as Deluxe Model 27A-1 except 22 LR w/lightweight alloy receiver, weight 6.5 lbs. Magazines include 5-, 20-, 30- and 50-round box types, 80-round drum. Made from 1977 to 1994.

THOMPSON
MODEL 27A-1 DELUXE. . . . . NiB $1100 Ex $879 Gd $530
Same as Standard Model 27A-1 except w/finned bbl. w/compensator, adj. rear sight, pistol-grip forestock. Caliber: .22 LR, l0mm (1991 to 1993) or 45 ACP. Weight: 11.5 lbs. Made from 1976 to 1999.
.22 LR (Limited production) . . . NiB $1190 Ex $1000 Gd $770
10-round stick magazine, add. $70
20- or 30-round stick magazine, add. $80
10-round drum magazine, add $200
50-round drum magazine, add $300
100-round drum magazine, add $600
Violin carrying case, add $227
Hard carrying case, add $200
Detacable stock/horizontal grip (2007), add $440

THOMPSON MODEL 27A-1 STANDARD
SEMIAUTO CARBINE . . . . **NiB $689 Ex $641 Gd $440**
Similar to Thompson submachine gun ("Tommy Gun") except has no provision for automatic firing. Caliber: .45 ACP. 20-round detachable box magazine (5-,15- and 30-round box magazines, 39-round drum also available). 16-inch plain bbl. Weight: 14 lbs. Sights: Aperture rear; blade front. Walnut buttstock, pistol grip and grooved forearm, sling swivels. Made from 1976-86.

THOMPSON
27A-1C LIGHTWEIGHT . . . . . . **NiB $1090 Ex $900 Gd $707**
Similar to Model 27A-1 except w/lightweight alloy receiver. Weight: 9.25 lbs. Made 1984 to date.

THOMPSON M1 . . . . **NiB $1070 Ex $660 Gd $479**
Similar to Model 27A-1 except in M-1 configuration w/side cocking lever and horizontal forearm. Weight: 11.5 lbs. Made from 1986 to date.
M1-C (lightweight) . . . . **NiB $1080 Ex $860 Gd $570**

THOMPSON
27A-1 COMMANDO . . . . **NiB $1098 Ex $860 Gd $579**
Similar to Model 27A-1 except parkerized finish and black stock. 13 lbs. Made from 1997 to date.

BAIKAL — Izhevsk, Russia
Imported by RWC, Tullytown, PA. Formerly imported by EAA, Corp., Rockledge, Florida.

MP221 Side By Side . . . . **NiB $910 Ex $700 Gd $300**
Double barrel, boxlock, break action. Caliber: .223 Rem., .270 Win., .30-06, .308 Win., or .45-70. 23.5-inch bbl., 40 inches overall. Matte blue finish, checkered walnut stock. Imported from 2003 to 2009, reintro. 2011 to date.

MP161K Semi Automatic . . . . **NiB $330 Ex $250 Gd $170**
Caliber: .17 HMR, .22 LR or .22 WMR. 10-round magazine. 19.5-inch bbl., 39 inches overall. Matte blue finish, polymer thumbhole stock. Imported from 2009 to date.
.17 HMR or .22 WMR, add **20%**

IZH-18MN Single Shot . . . . **NiB $250 Ex $190 Gd $110**
Boxlock, break action. Caliber: .222 Rem., .223 Rem., .243 Win., .270 Win., 7.62x39mm, .308 Win., .30-06, or .45-70. 23.5-inch bbl., 40 inches overall. Matte blue finish, checkered walnut stock. Imported from 2003 to 2009.

BALLARD ARMS, INC. — Onsted, MI
Formerly Ballard Rifle LLC, Cody WY. Firearms manufactured since 1996.

1-1/2 HUNTER'S RIFLE . . . . . . **NiB $3200 Ex $2440 Gd $1833**
Calibers: Seven calibers from .22 LR to .50-70. Single trigger, S-style lever action; uncheckered stock. Weight: 10.5 lbs.

1-3/4 FAR WEST RIFLE . . . . . . **NiB $2902 Ex $2045 Gd $1471**
Calibers: Eight calibers from .32-40 WCF to .50-90 SS. Patterned after original Ballard Far West model. 30 or 32-inch bbl., standard or heavyweight octagon; double set triggers; ring-style lever. Weight: 9.75 to 10.5 lbs.

NO. 5 PACIFIC . . . . **NiB $3208 Ex $2460 Gd $1996**
Calibers: Nine calibers between .32-40 WCF and .50-90 SS. Similar to No. 1-3/4 Far West model but with under-barrel wiping rod.

NO. 4-1/2
MID-RANGE RIFLE . . . . **NiB $2900 Ex $2080 Gd $1765**
Calibers: Five calibers between .32-40 WCF and .45-110. Designed for black powder silhouette shooting. 30 or 32-inch bbl., half-octagonal heavyweight; single or double set triggers; pistol grip stock; full loop lever; hard rubber Ballard buttplate; Vernier tang sight. Weight: 10.75 to 11.5 lbs.

NO. 7
LONG-RANGE RIFLE . . . . **NiB $3369 Ex $2390 Gd $1479**
Caliber: Five calibers between .40-65 Win. and .45-110. Similar to No. 4-1/2 Mid-Range Rifle; designed for long-range shooting. 32 or 34-inch half-octagon standard or heavyweight bbl.

MODEL 1885
HIGH WALL RIFLE . . . . **NiB $3190 Ex $2444 Gd $1954**
Calibers: Various. Exact replica of Winchester Model 1885 (parts are interchangeable). 30 or 32-inch bbl., octagon; case-colored receiver, uncheckered straight-grip stock and forearm. Weight: Approx. 9 lbs. Introduced 2001.
Deluxe model, add **$1717**
Sporting model, add **$250**
Shuetzen model, add **$400**

BANSNER'S ULTIMATE RIFLES, LLC — Adamstown, Pennsylvania
Established in 1981 in Adamstown, Pennsylvania, as Basner's Gunsmithing Specialties. Company name changed in 2000.

ULTIMATE
ONE RIFLE . . . . **NiB $5540 Ex $3766 Gd $3060**
Calibers: Various. Bolt-action, modeled on Winchester M70 and Remington 707 actions. Various metal finishes; muzzle brake; custom trigger; custom stock; Pachmayer decelerator pad; custom scope mounts and bases.
Three-position safety, add **$250**

HIGH TECH
SERIES RIFLE . . . . **NiB $1032 Ex $790 Gd $641**
Calibers: Various. Steel or stainless steel action with factory bbl. Bansner's synthetic stock and Pachmayer decelerator pad.
Stainless steel model, add **$300**

SAFARI
HUNTER RIFLE . . . . **NiB $6200 Ex $4396 Gd $2398**
Calibers: Various dangerous game calibers. Based on Model 70 Classic action; muzzle brake; Lilja Precision stainless steel barrel; synthetic stock; matte black Teflon metal finish. Introduced 2003.

WORLD SLAM LIMITED EDITION
RIFLE . . . . **NiB $5345 Ex $3850 Gd $2300**
Calibers: Various. Customized Model 707 action; fluted bold body. jeweled trigger. three-position safety; synthetic stock. Only 25-50 of limited edition models were made beginning in 2003.

BARRETT FIREARMS MFG., INC. — Murfreesboro, Tennessee

MODEL 82A1
SEMI-AUTOMATIC RIFLE .... **NiB $8900 Ex $7760 Gd $5100**
Caliber: .50 BMG. 10-round detachable box magazine. 29-inch recoiling bbl. w/muzzle brake. 57 inches overall. Weight: 28.5 lbs. Open iron sights and 10x scope. Composit stock w/Sorbothance recoil pad and self-leveling bipod. Blued finish. Made in various configurations from 1985 to date.

MODEL 90 BOLT-ACTION RIFLE. . **NiB $3530 Ex $3099 Gd $2020**
Caliber: .50 BMG. Five round magazine. 29-inch match bbl. 45 inches overall. Weight: 22 lbs. Composite stock w/retractable bipod. Made from 1990 to 1995.

MODEL 95 BOLT-ACTION . . . **NiB $6635 Ex $4890 Gd $3530**
Similar to Model 90 bullpup design chambered for .50 BMG except w/ improved muzzle brake and extendable bipod. Made from 1995 to date.

MODEL 98B BOLT-ACTION . . **NiB $4699 Ex $4400 Gd $2530**
Caliber: .338 Lapua Mag. 20-, 26-, or 27-inch bbl. Weight: 13.5 lbs. 10-round magazine. Muzzle brake, adj. stock. Made from 2009 to date.

MODEL M4468 SEMI-AUTOMATIC . **NiB $2100 Ex $1707 Gd $1000**
AR-style rifle. Caliber: 6.8 SPC. 16-inch bbl. Weight: 8 lbs. 5-, 10-, 30-round magazine. Made from 2005 to 2008.

BEEMAN PRECISION ARMS INC. — Santa Rosa, California
Since 1993 all European firearms imported by Beeman have been distributed by Beeman Outdoor Sports, Div., Roberts Precision Arms, Inc., Santa Rosa, CA.

WEIHRAUCH HW MODELS 60J AND
60J-ST BOLT-ACTION RIFLES
Calibers: .22 LR (60J-ST), .222 Rem. (60J). 22.8-inch bbl. 41.7 inches overall. Weight: 6.5 lbs. Sights: Hooded blade front; open adj. rear. Blued finish. Checkered walnut stock w/cheekpiece. Made from 1988 to 1994.
Model 60J . . . . **NiB $835 Ex $746 Gd $615**
Model 60J-ST . . . . **NiB $655 Ex $539 Gd $398**

WEIHRAUCH HW MODEL 60M
Small Bore Rifle . . . . **NiB $690 Ex $579 Gd $389**
Caliber: .22 LR. Single-shot. 26.8-inch bbl. 45.7 inches overall. Weight: 10.8 lbs. Adj. trigger w/push-button safety. Sights: Hooded blade front on ramp, precision aperture rear. Target-style stock w/stippled forearm and pistol grip. Blued finish. Made from 1988 to 1994.

WEIHRAUCH HW
MODEL 660 MATCH RIFLE . . . . . **NiB $1023 Ex $855 Gd $445**
Caliber: .22 LR. 26-inch bbl. 45.3 inches overall. Weight: 10.7 lbs. Adj. match trigger. Sights: globe front, precision aperture rear. Match-style walnut stock w/adj. cheekpiece and buttplate. Made from 1988 to 1994.

FEINWERKBAU MODEL 2600 SERIES TARGET RIFLE
Caliber: .22 LR. Single-shot. 26.3-inch bbl. 43.7 inches overall. Weight: 10.6 lbs. Match trigger w/fingertip weight adjustment dial. Sights: Globe front; micrometer match aperture rear. Laminated hardwood stock w/adj. cheekpiece. Made from 1988 to 1994.
Standard Model 2600 (left-hand) . . . **NiB $1733 Ex $1360 Gd $944**
Standard Model 2600
(right-hand) . . . . **NiB $1560 Ex $1239 Gd $816**

Free Rifle Model 2602
(left-hand) . . . . **NiB $2196 Ex $1755 Gd $1024**
Free Rifle Model 2602
(right-hand) . . . . **NiB $2196 Ex $1755 Gd $1024**

BELGIAN MILITARY RIFLES — Belgium
Mfd. by Fabrique Nationale D'Armes de Guerre, Herstal, Belgium; Fabrique D'Armes de L'Etat, Lunich, Belgium. Hopkins & Allen Arms Co. of Norwich, Conn., as well as contractors in Birmingham, England, also produced these guns during World War I.

MODEL 1889 MAUSER
MILITARY RIFLE . . . . **NiB $279 Ex $230 Gd $156**
Caliber: 7.65mm Belgian Service (7.65mm Mauser). 5-round projecting box magazine. 30.75-inch bbl. w/jacket. Weight: 8.5 lbs. Adj. rear sight, blade front. Straight-grip military stock. This, and the carbine version, was the principal weapon of the Belgian Army at the start of WWII. Made from 1889 to c.1935.

MODEL 1916
MAUSER CARBINE . . . . **NiB $300 Ex $240 Gd $190**
Same as Model 1889 Rifle except w/20.75-inch bbl. Weighs 8 lbs. and has minor differences in the rear sight graduations, lower band closer to the muzzle and swivel plate on side of buttstock.

MODEL 1935 MAUSER
MILITARY RIFLE . . . . **NiB $370 Ex $292 Gd $169**
Same general specifications as F.N. Model 1924; minor differences. Caliber: 7.65mm Belgian Service. Mfd. by Fabrique Nationale D'Armes de Guerre.

MODEL 1936 MAUSER
MILITARY RIFLE . . . . **NiB $378 Ex $290 Gd $166**
An adaptation of Model 1889 w/German M/98-type bolt, Belgian M/89 protruding box magazine. Caliber: 7.65mm Belgian Service. Mfd. by Fabrique Nationale D'Armes de Guerre.

BENELLI — Urbino, Itay
Imported by Benelli USA, Accokeek, MD.

R1 Semi-Automatic. . . . . **NiB $910 Ex $700 Gd $500**
Caliber: .270 WSM, .308 Win., .30-06, .300 WSM, .300 Win. Mag. or .338 Win. Mag. 20-, 22- or 24-inch bbl. Matte black finish, checkered walnut or polymer stock. Designated Argo in Europe. Imported from 2002 to date.
ComforTech stock, add. **$125**

BENTON & BROWN FIREARMS, INC. — Fort Worth, Texas
MODEL 93 BOLT-ACTION RIFLE
Similar to Blaser Model R84 (the B&B rifle is built on the Blaser action, see separate listing) with an interchangeable bbl. system. Calibers: .243 Win., 6mm Rem., .25-06, .257 Wby., .264 Win., .270 Win., .280 Rem., 7mm Rem Mag., .30-06, .308, .300 Wby., .300 Win. Mag., .338 Win., .375 H&H. 22- or 24-inch bbl. 41 or 43 inches overall. Bbl.-mounted scope rings and one-piece base; no sights. Two-piece walnut or fiberglass stock. Made from 1993 to 1996.
Walnut stock model . . . . **NiB $1896 Ex $1744 Gd $1012**
Fiberglass stock model add **$227**
Extra bbl. assembly, add **$525**
Extra bolt assembly, add **$450**

Beretta 501
Bolt-Action Sporter

Beretta AR-70

BERETTA U.S.A. CORP. — Accokeek, Maryland

Manufactured by Fabbrica D'Armi Pietro Beretta, S.P.A., Gardone Val Trompia (Brescia), Italy.

455 SIDE BY SIDE EXPRESS DOUBLE RIFLE
Sidelock action w/removable sideplates. Calibers: .375 H&H, .458 Win. Mag., .470 NE, .500 NE (3 inches), .416 Rigby. Bbls.: 23.5 or 25.5-inch. Weight: 11 lbs. Double triggers. Sights: Blade front; V-notch folding leaf rear. Checkered European walnut forearm and buttstock w/recoil pad. Color casehardened receiver w/blued bbls. Various grades of engraving. Custom built. Made from 1990 to date.
Model 455 . . . . .NiB $100,000
Model 455EELL . . . . .NiB $150,000

500 BOLT-ACTION SPORTER
Centerfire bolt-action rifle w/Sako A I short action. Calibers: .222 Rem., .223 Rem. Five round magazine. 23.63-inch bbl. Weight: 6.5 lbs. Available w/ or w/o iron sights. Tapered dovetailed receiver. European walnut stock. Disc. 1998.
Standard . . . . NiB $707 Ex $590 Gd $475
DL Model. . . . . NiB $1590 Ex $1288 Gd $909
500 EELLEngraved . . . . NiB $1670 Ex $1465 Gd $990
w/iron sights, add. 10%

501 BOLT-ACTION SPORTER
Same as Model 500 except w/Sako A II medium action. Calibers: .243 Win., .308 Win. Weight: 7.5 lbs. Disc. 1986.
Standard. . . . . NiB $625 Ex $466 Gd $420
Standard w/iron sights . . . . NiB $707 Ex $650 Gd $430
DL model. . . . . NiB $1386 Ex $1097 Gd $944
501 EELL (engraved). . . . . NiB $1607 Ex $1329 Gd $989
w/iron sights, add 10%

502 BOLT-ACTION SPORTER
Same as Model 500 except w/Sako A III long action. Calibers: .270 Win., 7mm Rem. Mag., .30/06, 375 H&H. Weight: 8.5 lbs. Disc. 1986.

Standard model . . . . NiB $675 Ex $534 Gd $460
DL model. . . . . NiB $1565 Ex $1299 Gd $980
502 EELL (engraved). . . . . NiB $1607 Ex $1347 Gd $1088
w/iron sights, add. 10%

AR-70 SEMIAUTOMATIC RIFLE. . . . . NiB $2020 Ex $1788 Gd $1077
Caliber: .223 Rem. (5.56mm). 30-round magazine. 17.75-inch bbl. Weight: 8.25 lbs. Sights: Rear peep adj. for windage and elevation; blade front. High-impact synthetic buttstock. Imported 1984 to 1989.

EXPRESS S686/S689 SILVER SABLE O/U RIFLE
Calibers: .30-06 Spfld., 9.3x74R, and .444 Marlin. 24-inch bbl. Weight: 7.7 lbs. Drilled and tapped for scope mount. European-style cheek rest and ventilated rubber recoil pad. Imported 1995.
Model S686/S689 Silver Sable II . . . . .NiB $4720 Ex $3800 Gd $2244
Model S689 Gold Sable . . . . .NiB $6347 Ex $5329 Gd $3144
Model S686/S689 EELL
 Diamond Sable . . . . .NiB $13,325 Ex $9765 Gd $6479
w/extra bbl. set, add $350
w/detachable claw mounts, add $645

EXPRESS SSO O/U EXPRESS DOUBLE RIFLE
Sidelock. Calibers: .375 H&H Mag., .458 Win. Mag., 9.3 x 74R. 23-24- or 25.5-inch blued bbls. Weight: 11 lbs. Double triggers. Express sights w/blade front and V-notch folding leaf rear. Optional Zeiss scope w/ claw mounts. Color casehardened receiver w/scroll engraving, game scenes and gold inlays on higher grades. Checkered European walnut forearm and buttstock w/cheekpiece and recoil pad. Imported 1985 to 1989.
Model SS0 (disc. 1989). . . . . . . .NiB $15,800 Ex $10,600 Gd $6545
Model SS05 (disc. 1990). . . . . . . NiB $18600 Ex $14,300 Gd $7600
Model SS06 Custom . . . . NiB $75,000
Model SS06 EELL Gold Custom . . . . NiB $125,000
Extra bbl. assembly, add. $7070
Claw mounts, add $800

Blaser Model R84

MATO . . . . **NIB $1015   EX $733   GD $533**
Calibers: .270 Win., .280 Rem., 7mm Rem. Mag., .300 Win. Mag., .338 Win. Mag., .375 H&H. 23.6-inch bbl. Weight: 8 lbs. Adjustable trigger. Drop-out box magazine. Drilled and tapped for scope w/ or w/o adj. sights. Walnut or synthetic stock. Manufactured based on Mauser 98 action. Made from 1997 to 2002.
Deluxe model . . . . **NiB $2015   Ex $1723   Gd $976**
.375 H&H w/iron sights, add **$350**

SMALL BORE SPORTING CARBINE/TARGET RIFLE
Semiautomatic w/bolt handle in raised or conventional single-shot bolt-action w/handle in lowered position. Caliber: .22 LR. Four, 5-, 8-, 10- or 20-round magazines. 20.5-inch standard or heavy bbl. Sights: 3-leaf folding rear, partridge front. Target or sporting stock w/checkered pistol grip and forend and sling swivels. Weight: 5.5 to 6 lbs.
Sporter model (Super Sport X) . . . . **NiB $460   Ex $355   Gd $256**
Target model (Olympia X) . . . . . . **NiB $340   Ex $520   Gd $345**

VINCENZO BERNARDELLI — Brescia, Italy

Currently headquartered in Brescia, Italy, Bernardelli arms were manufactured from 1721 to 1997 in Gardone, Italy. Imported and distributed by Armsport, Inc., Miami, Florida. Also handled by Magnum Research, Inc., Quality Arms, Inc., Armes De Chasse, Stoeger and Action Arms.

EXPRESS VB . . . . **NiB $5768   Ex $4755   Gd $3690**
Double barrel. Calibers: Various. Side-by-side sidelock action. Ejectors, double triggers. Imported from 1990 to1997.
Deluxe model (w/double triggers), add **$1125**

EXPRESS 2000 . . . . **NiB $2707   Ex $2025   Gd $1580**
Calibers: .30-06, 7x65R, 8x57JRS, 9.3x74R. Over/under boxlock design. Single or double triggers, extractors. Checkered walnut stock and forearm. Imported from 1994 to 1997.
Single trigger, add **$200**

MINERVA EXPRESS . . . . **NiB $5200   Ex $3890   Gd $4098**
Caliber: Various. Exposed hammers. Extractors, double triggers. Moderate engraving. Imported from 1995 to 1997.

CARBINA .22 . . . . **NiB $580   Ex $300   Gd $170**
Semi-auto. Caliber: .22 rimfire. Blow-back action. Imported from 1990 to 1997.

MODEL 120 . . . . **NiB $2120   Ex $1587   Gd $1100**
Combination gun; over-under boxlock; 12 gauge over .22 Hornet, .222 Rem., 5.6x50R Mag., .243 Win., 6.5x57R, .270 Win., 7x57R, .308 Win., .30-06, 6.5x55, 7x65R, 8x57JRS, 9.3x74R. Iron sights. Checkered walnut stock and forearm. Double triggers, automatic ejectors or extractors. Ventilated recoil pad. Engraved action. Made in Italy. Discontinued.

MODEL 190 . . . . **NiB $1489   Ex $1129   Gd $1069**
Combination gun; over-under boxlock. Calibers: 12, 16 or 20 ga. Over .222 Rem., .243 Win., .30-06, .308 Win., 5.6x50R Mag., .5.6x57R,

6.5x55, 6.5x57R, 7x57R, 7x65R, 8x57JRS, 9.3x74R. Iron sights. Checkered walnut stock. Double triggers; extractors. Made in Italy. Introduced in 1969, discontinued 1989.

MODEL 2000 . . . . **NiB $2713   Ex $1866   Gd $1390**
Combination gun; over-under boxlock action. Calibers: 12, 16 or 20 ga. Over .222 Rem., .22 Hornet, 5.6x50R Mag., .243 Win., 6.5x55, 6.5x57R, .270 Win., 7x57R, .308 Win., .30-06, 8x57JRS, 9.3x74R. Bbl: 23 inches. Sights: Blade front, open rear. Hand checkered, oil-finished select European walnut stock, double-set triggers, auto ejectors. Silvered, engraved action. Made in Italy. Introduced in 1990, disconti nued 1991.
Extra bbl. assembly, add **$595**

BLASER U.S.A., INC. — Fort Worth, Texas
Manufactured by Blaser Jagdwaffen GmbH, Germany, imported by Sigarms, Exeter, NH; Autumn Sales, Inc., Fort Worth, Texas.

MODEL R-84 BOLT-ACTION RIFLE
Calibers: .22-250, .243, 6mm Rem., .25-06, .270, .280 Rem., .30-06- .257 Wby. Mag., .264 Win. Mag., 7mm Rem Mag., .300 Win. Mag., .300 Wby. Mag., .338 Win. Mag., .375 H&H. Interchangeable bbls. w/standard or Magnum bolt assemblies. Bbl. length: 23 inches (standard); 24 inches (Magnum). 41 to 42 inches overall. Weight: 7 to 7.25 lbs. No sights. Bbl.-mounted scope system. Two-piece Turkish walnut stock w/solid black recoil pad. Imported from 1989 to 1994.
Model R84 Standard . . . . **NiB $2245   Ex $1725   Gd $1190**
Model R84 Deluxe
  (engraved game scene) . . . . . **NiB $2400   Ex $2021   Gd $1200**
Model R84 Super Deluxe
  (Gold and silver inlays) . . . . **NiB $2449   Ex $1990   Gd $1590**
Left-hand model, add **$150**
Extra bbl. assembly, add **$600**

MODEL R-93 SAFARI SERIES BOLT-ACTION REPEATER
Similar to Model R-84 except restyled action w/straight-pull bolt, unique safety and searless trigger mechanism. Additional chamberings: 6.5x55, 7x57, .308, .416 Rem. Optional open sights. Imported 1994 to 1998.
Model R93 Safari . . . . **NiB $3598   Ex $2277   Gd $1844**
Model R93 Safari Deluxe . . . . **NiB $3943   Ex $4134   Gd $3297**
Model R84 Safari
  Super Deluxe . . . . **NiB $4854   Ex $4326   Gd $3458**
Extra bbl. assembly, add **$600**

MODEL R-93 CLASSIC SERIES BOLT-ACTION REPEATER
Similar to Model R-93 Safari except w/expanded model variations. Imported from 1998 to 2002.
Model R93 Attache
  (Premium wood, fluted bbl.) . **NiB $3566   Ex $3887   Gd $3110**
Model R93 Classic
  (.22-250 to .375 H&H) . . . . . **NiB $3525   Ex $2889   Gd $2009**
Model R93 Classic Safari (.416 Rem.) . . **NiB $3535   Ex $3279   Gd $2270**
Model R93 LX (.22-250 to .416 Rem.) . . . **NiB $1799   Ex $1445   Gd $996**
Model R93 Synthetic (.22-250
  to .375 H&H) . . . . **NiB $1908   Ex $1235   Gd $855**
Extra bbl. assembly, add **$600**

Brno Model II

Brno Model 21H
Bolt-Action Sporting Rifle

Brno Model 22F

Brno Hornet
Bolt-Action Sporting Rifle

RIFLES

BRITISH MILITARY RIFLES — England
Manufactured at Royal Small Arms Factory, Enfield Lock, Middlesex, England, private contractors.

RIFLE NO. 1 MARK III . . . . .NiB $338 Ex $209 Gd $144
Short magazine Lee-Enfield (S.M.L.E.). Bolt action. Caliber: .303 British. 10-round box magazine. 25.25-inch bbl. Weight: 8.75 lbs. Sights: Adj. rear; blade front w/guards. Two-piece, full-length military stock. Note: The earlier Mark III (approved 1907) is virtually the same as Mark III (adopted 1918) except for sights and different magazine cut-off that was eliminated on the latter.

RIFLE NO. 3 MARK I (PATTERN 14) . . . . NiB $347 Ex $255 Gd $160
Modified Mauser-type bolt action. Except for caliber .303 British and long-range sight, this rifle is the same as U.S. Model 1917 Enfield. See listing of the latter for general specifications.

RIFLE NO. 4 MARK I . . . . .NiB $278 Ex $230 Gd $155
Post-World War I modification of the S.M.L.E. intended to simplify mass production. General specifications same as Rifle No. 1 Mark III except w/aperture rear sight and minor differences in construction and weighs 9.25 lbs.

LIGHT RIFLE NO. 4 MARK I . . . . .NiB $227 Ex $170 Gd $133
Modification of the S.M.L.E. Caliber: .303 British. 10-round box magazine. 23-inch bbl. Weight: 6.75 lbs. Sights: Micrometer click rear peep; blade front. One-piece military-type stock w/recoil pad. Made during WWII.

RIFLE NO. 5 MARK I . . . . .NiB $369 Ex $244 Gd $175
Jungle Carbine. Modification of the S.M.L.E. similar to Light Rifle No. 4 Mark I except w/20.5-inch bbl. w/flash hider, carbine-type stock. Made during WWII, originally designed for use in the Pacific Theater.

BRNO SPORTING RIFLES — Brno, Czech Republic
Manufactured by Ceska Zbrojovka; Imported by Euro-Imports, El Cajon, California, previously by Bohemia Arms & Magnum Research. See also CZ rifles.

**MODEL I BOLT-ACTION
SPORTING RIFLE** . . . . .NiB $689 Ex $615 Gd $437
Caliber: .22 LR. Five round detachable magazine. 22.75-inch bbl. Weight: 6 lbs. Sights: three-leaf open rear; hooded ramp front. Sporting stock w/checkered pistol grip, swivels. Made 1946 to 1973.

**MODEL II BOLT-ACTION
SPORTING RIFLE** . . . . .NiB $641 Ex $543 Gd $444
Same as Model I except w/deluxe grade stock. Made 1949 to 1957.

**MODEL III BOLT-ACTION
TARGET RIFLE** . . . . .NiB $707 Ex $567 Gd $495
Same as Model I except w/heavy bbl. and target stock. Made from 1948-56.

**MODEL IV BOLT-ACTION
TARGET RIFLE** . . . . .NiB $755 Ex $587 Gd $488
Same as Model III except w/improved target trigger mechanism. Made 1956 to 1962.

**MODEL V BOLT-ACTION
SPORTING RIFLE** . . . . .NiB $789 Ex $633 Gd $456
Same as Model I except w/improved trigger mechanism. Made from 1956 to 1973.

Brno Model-ZKM 611

Brown Precision High Country Youth Rifle

MODEL 21H BOLT-ACTION
SPORTING RIFLE . . . . .NiB $1590 Ex $1325 Gd $1009
Mauser-type action. Calibers: 6.5x57mm, 7x57mm 8x57mm. Five round box magazine. 20.5-inch bbl. Double set trigger. Weight: 6.75 lbs. Sights: Two-leaf open rear-hooded ramp front. Half-length sporting stock w/cheekpiece, checkered pistol-grip and forearm, swivels. Made from 1946 to 1955.

MODEL 22F . . . . .NiB $1408 Ex $1010 Gd $679
Same as Model 21H except w/full-length Mannlicher-type stock, weight: 6 lbs., 14 oz. Disc.

MODEL 98 STANDARD
Calibers: .243 Win., .270 Win., .30-06, .308 Win., .300 Win. Mag., 7x57mm, 7x64mm, or 9.3x62mm. 23.8-inch bbl. Overall 34.5 inches. Weight: 7.25 lbs. Checkered walnut stock w/Bavarian cheekpiece. Imported from 1998. Disc.
Standard calibers	NiB $560	Ex $439	Gd $300
Calibers .300 Win., Mag., 9.3x62mm . . .	NiB $580	Ex $469	Gd $386
w/single set trigger, add $150			

MODEL 98 MANNLICHER
Similar to Model 98 Standard except full length stock and set triggers. Imported from 1998. Disc.
Standard calibers	NiB $724	Ex $545	Gd $390
Calibers .300 Win. Mag., 9.3x62mm. . . .	NiB $755	Ex $600	Gd $445

ZKB-110 SINGLE-SHOT
Calibers: .22 Hornet, .222 Rem., 5.6x52R, 5.6x50 Mag., 6.5x57R, 7x57R, and 8x57JRS. 23.8-inch bbl. Weight: 6.1 lbs. Walnut checkered buttstock and forearm w/Bavarian cheekpiece. Imported from 1998 to 2003.
Standard model	NiB $279	Ex $218	Gd $177
Lux model	NiB $448	Ex $333	Gd $266
Calibers 7x57R and 8x57 JRS, add $50			
w/interchangeable 12 ga.			
shotgun bbl., add $150			

HORNET BOLT-ACTION
SPORTING RIFLE . . . . .NiB $1278 Ex $1043 Gd $689
Miniature Mauser action. Caliber: .22 Hornet. Five-round detachable box magazine. 23-inch bbl. Double set trigger. Weight: 6.25 lbs. Sights: Three-leaf open rear hooded ramp front. Sporting stock w/

checkered pistol grip and forearm, swivels. Made 1949-74. Note: This rifle was also marketed in U.S. as "Z-B Mauser Varmint Rifle." (Reintroduced as Model ZKB 689)

MODEL ZKB 689
BOLT-ACTION RIFLE . . . . .NiB $482 Ex $345 Gd $296
Calibers: .22 Hornet, .222 Rem. Five-round detachable box magazine. 23.5-inch bbl. Weight: 5.75 lbs. Double-set triggers. Adj. open rear sight, hooded ramp front. Walnut stock. Imported from 1985 to 1992.

MODEL ZKM 611 SEMIAUTOMATIC RIFLE
Caliber: .22 WMR. Six-round magazine. 20-inch bbl. 37 inches overall. Weight: 6.2 lbs. Hooded front sight; mid-mounted rear sight. Checkered walnut or beechwood stock. Single thumbscrew take-down. Grooved receiver for scope mounting. Imported from 2006 to date.
Standard beechwood model	NiB $508	Ex $412	Gd $389
Deluxe walnut model	NiB $600	Ex $482	Gd $328

BROWN PRECISION COMPANY — Los Molinos, California

MODEL 7 SUPER LIGHT SPORTER . . NiB $1128 Ex $1086 Gd $775
Lightweight sporter built on a Remington Model 7 barreled action w/18-inch factory bbl. Weight: 5.25 lbs. Kevlar stock. Made from 1984 to 1992.

HIGH COUNTRY BOLT-ACTION SPORTER
Custom sporting rifles built on Blaser, Remington 707, Ruger 77 and Winchester 70 actions. Calibers: .243 Win., .25-06, .270 Win., 7mm Rem. Mag., .308 Win., .30-06. Five-round magazine (4-round in 7mm Mag.). 22- or 24-inch bbl. Weight: 6.5 lbs. Fiberglass stock w/recoil pad, sling swivels. No sights. Made from 1975 to 1992.
Standard High Country	NiB $1624	Ex $1043	Gd $855
Custom High Country	NiB $4490	Ex $3124	Gd $1876
Left-hand action, add $250			
Stainless bbl., add $250			
70, 77 or Blaser actions, add $150			
70 SG action, add $400			

Brown Precision Pro-
Hunter

Brown Precision Tactical
Elite

HIGH COUNTRY YOUTH RIFLE . . . . . NiB $1336 Ex $1023 Gd $688
Similar to standard Model 7 Super Light except w/Kevlar or graphite
stock, scaled-down to youth dimensions. Calibers: .223, .243, 6mm,
7mm-08, .308. Made from 1993 to 2000.

PRO-HUNTER BOLT-ACTION RIFLE
Custom sporting rifle built on a Remington 707 or Winchester 70 SG
action fitted w/match-grade Shilen bbl. chambered in customer's
choice of caliber. Matte blued, nickel or Teflon finish. Express-style
rear sight hooded ramp front. Synthetic stock. Made from 1989 to
date
Standard Pro-Hunter. . . . . NiB $4597 Ex $3150 Gd $2370
Pro-Hunter Elite (1993 to date) . . . . NiB $6066 Ex $3886 Gd $2125
Pro-Hunter w/Rem 40X action add $650

PRO-VARMINTER BOLT-ACTION RIFLE
Custom varminter built on a Remington 707 or 40X action fitted w/
Shilen stainless steel benchrest bbl. Varmint or benchrest-style stock.
Made from 1993 to date.
Standard Pro-Varminter. . . . . NiB $3735 Ex $2966 Gd $969

SELECTIVE TARGET MODEL . . . . NiB $1044 Ex $835 Gd $590
Tactical law-enforcement rifle built on a Remington 707V action.
Caliber: .308 Win. 20-, 22- or 24-inch bbl. Synthetic stock. Made from
1989 to 1992.

TACTICAL ELITE RIFLE . . . . . NiB $4566 Ex $3290 Gd $1977
Similar to Selective Target Model except fitted w/select match-grade
Shilen benchrest heavy stainless bbl. Calibers: .223, .308, .300 Win.
Mag. Black or camo Kevlar/graphite composite fiberglass stock w/adj.
buttplate. Non-reflective black Teflon metal finish. Made from 1997 to
date.

BROWNING — Morgan, Utah
*Manufactured for Browning by Fabrique Nationale d'Armes de Guerre
(now Fabrique Nationale Herstal), Herstal, Belgium; Miroku Firearms
Mfg. Co., Tokyo, Japan; A.T.I., Salt Lake City, UT; Oy Sako Ab,
Riihimaki, Finland.*

.22 AUTOMATIC RIFLE, GRADE I
Similar to discontinued Remington Model 241A. Autoloading. Take-down.
Calibers: .22 LR. .22 Short (not interchangeably). Tubular magazine in buttstock

holds 11 LR. 16 Short. Bbl. lengths: 19.25 inches (.22 LR), 22.25 inches (.22
Short). Weight: 4.75 lbs. (.22 LR); 5 lbs. (.22 Short). Receiver scroll engraved.
Open rear sight, bead front. Checkered pistol-grip buttstock, semibeavertail
forearm. Made from 1956 to 1972 by FN; from 1972 to date by Miroku. Note:
Illustrations are of rifles manufactured by FN.
FN manufacture . . . . NiB $899 Ex $500 Gd $265
Miroku manufacture . . . . NiB $650 Ex $398 Gd $327

.22 AUTOMATIC RIFLE, GRADE II
Same as Grade I except satin chrome-plated receiver engraved w/small
game animal scenes, gold-plated trigger select walnut stock and fore-
arm. .22 LR only. Made from 1972 to 1984.
FN manufacture . . . . NiB $1200 Ex $909 Gd $369
Miroku manufacture . . . . NiB $554 Ex $439 Gd $300

.22 AUTOMATIC RIFLE, GRADE III
Same as Grade I except satin chrome-plated receiver elaborately
hand-carved and engraved w/dog and game-bird scenes, scrolls
and leaf clusters: gold-plated trigger, extra-fancy walnut stock
and forearm, skip-checkered. .22 LR only. Made from 1972 to
1984.
FN manufacture . . . . NiB $1500 Ex $1125 Gd $880
Miroku manufacture . . . . NiB $822 Ex $590 Gd $480

.22 AUTOMATIC, GRADE VI . . . NiB $1190 Ex $798 Gd $600
Same general specifications as standard .22 Automatic except for
engraving, high-grade stock w/checkering and glossy finish. Made by
Miroku from 1986 to date.

MODEL 52 BOLT-ACTION RIFLE . . . . . . NiB $800 Ex $655 Gd $443
Limited edition of Winchester Model 52C Sporter. Caliber: .22 LR.
Five-round magazine. 24-inch bbl. Weight: 7 lbs. Micro-Motion
trigger. No sights. Checkered select walnut stock w/rosewood
forend and metal grip cap. Blued finish. 5000 made from 1991
to 1992.

MODEL 53 LEVER-ACTION RIFLE . . . . . . NiB $833 Ex $724 Gd $480
Limited edition of Winchester Model 53. Caliber: .32-20. Seven-
round tubular half-magazine. 22-inch bbl. Weight: 6.5 lbs. Adj.
rear sight, bead front. Select walnut checkered pistol-grip stock w/
high-gloss finish. Classic-style forearm. Blued finish. 5000 made
in 1990.

Browning Model 53
Lever-Action Limited Edition

Browning Model 71
Grade I Lever-Action

Browning Model 71
High-Grade Carbine

Browning Model 71
High-Grade

Browning Model 78
Single-Shot .45-70

**MODEL 65 GRADE I
LEVER-ACTION RIFLE** . . . . .NiB $730 Ex $445 Gd $370
Caliber: .218 Bee. 7-round tubular half-magazine. 24-inch bbl. Weight: 6.75 lbs. Sights: Adj. buckhorn-style rear, hooded bead front. Select walnut pistol-grip stock w/high-gloss finish. Semibeavertail forearm. Limited edition of 3500 made in 1989.

MODEL 65 HIGH GRADE RIFLE . . . . . . NiB $1009 Ex $733 Gd $528
Same general specifications as Model 65 Grade I except w/engraving and gold-plated animals on grayed receiver. Cut checkering on pistol grip and forearm. Limited edition of 1500 made in 1989.

MODEL 71 GRADE I CARBINE . . . . NiB $880 Ex $640 Gd $455
Same general specifications as Model 71 Grade I Rifle except carbine w/20-inch round bbl. and weighs 8 lbs. Limited edition of 4000 made in 1986 to 1987.

**MODEL 71 GRADE I
LEVER-ACTION RIFLE** . . . . .NiB $916 Ex $710 Gd $497
Caliber: .348 Win. 4-round magazine. 24-inch round bbl. Weight: 8 lbs., 2 oz. Open buckhorn sights. Select walnut straight grip stock w/ satin finish. Classic-style forearm, flat metal buttplate. Limited edition of 3000 made in 1986 to 1987.

MODEL 71 HIGH-GRADE CARBINE . . . . NiB $1332 Ex $1123 Gd $765
Same general specifications as Model 71 High Grade Rifle, except carbine w/20-inch round bbl. Limited edition of 3000 made 1986 to 1988.

MODEL 71 HIGH-GRADE RIFLE . . . . . NiB $1440 Ex $1110 Gd $823
Caliber: .348 Win. Four round magazine. 24-inch round bbl. Weight: 8 lbs., 2 oz. Engraved receiver. Open buckhorn sights. Select walnut checkered pistol-grip stock w/high-gloss finish. Classic-style forearm, flat metal buttplate. Limited edition of 3000 made in 1987.

M-78 BICENTENNIAL SET. . . . . NiB $3866 Ex $3121 Gd $2140
Special Model 78 .45-70 w/same specifications as standard type, except sides of receiver engraved w/bison and eagle, scroll engraving on top of receiver, lever, both ends of bbl. and buttplate; high-grade walnut stock and forearm. Accompanied by an engraved hunting knife and stainless steel commemorative medallion, all in an alder wood presentation case. Each item in set has matching serial number beginning with "1776" and ending with numbers 1 to 1,000. Edition limited to 1,000 sets. Made in 1976.

MODEL 78 SINGLE-SHOT RIFLE
Falling-block lever-action similar to Winchester 1885 High Wall single-shot rifle. Calibers: .22-250, 6mm Rem., .243 Win., .25-06, 7mm Rem. Mag., .30-06, .45-70 Govt. 26-inch octagon or heavy round bbl.; 24-inch octagon bull bbl. on .45-70 model. Weight: 7.75 lbs. w/octagon bbl.; w/round bbl., 8.5 lbs.; .45-70, 8.75 lbs. Furnished w/o sights except .45-70 model w/open rear sight, blade front. Checkered fancy walnut stock and forearm. .45-70 model w/straight-grip stock and curved buttplate; others have Monte Carlo comb and cheekpiece, pistol-grip w/cap, recoil pad. Made from 1973 to 1983 by Miroku. Reintroduced in 1985 as Model 1885.
All calibers except .45-70. . . . . NiB $1500 Ex $1274 Gd $1010
.45-70 . . . . NiB $970 Ex $766 Gd $523

Browning Model 1885
High-Wall Single-Shot

Browning Model 1885
High-Wall Traditional Hunter

Browning Model 1885
Low-Wall Single-Shot

Browning Model 1885
BPCR Single-Shot

MODEL 1885 SINGLE-SHOT RIFLE
Calibers: .22 Hornet, .223, .243, (Low Wall); .357 Mag., .44 Mag., .45 LC (L/W Traditional Hunter); .22-250, .223 Rem., .270 Win., 7mm Rem. Mag., .30-06, .454 Casull Mag., .45.70 (High Wall); .30.30 Win., .38-55 WCF, .45 Govt. (H/W Traditional Hunter); .40-65, .45 Govt. and .45.90 (BPCR). 24-, 28-, 30 or 34-inch round, octagonal or octagonal and round bbl. 39.5, 43.5, 44.25 or 46.125 inches overall. Weight: 6.25, 8.75, 9, 11, or 11.75 lbs. respectively. Blued or color casehardened receiver. Gold-colored adj. trigger. Drilled and tapped for scope mounts w/no sights or vernier tang rear sight w/globe front and open sights on .45-70 Govt. Walnut straight-grip stock and Schnabel forearm w/cut checkering and high-gloss or oil finish. Made from 1985 to 2001.
Low Wall model w/o sights (Intro. 1995) . . **NiB $1400 Ex $976 Gd $540**
Traditional Hunter model (Intro. 1998) . **NiB $1450 Ex $990 Gd $575**
High Wall model w/o sights (Intro. 1985) . **NiB $1390 Ex $1020 Gd $770**
Traditional Hunter model (Intro. 1997) . .**NiB $1390 Ex $1020 Gd $770**
BPCR model w/o
ejector (Intro. 1996) . . . . **NiB $1933 Ex $1442 Gd $1041**
BPCR Creedmoor Model .45-90
(Intro. 1998) . . . . **NiB $1933 Ex $1442 Gd $1041**

MODEL 1886 MONTANA
CENTENNIAL RIFLE . . . .**NiB $2120 Ex $1670 Gd $1097**
Same general specifications as Model 1886 High Grade lever-action except w/specially engraved receiver designating Montana Centennial; also different stock design. Made in 1986 in limited issue by Miroku.

MODEL 1886 GRADE I
LEVER-ACTION RIFLE . . . .**NiB $1255 Ex $712 Gd $495**
Caliber: .45-70 Govt., 8-round magazine. 26-inch octagonal bbl. 45 inches overall. Weight: 9 lbs., 5 oz. Deep blued finish on receiver. Open buckhorn sights. Straight-grip walnut stock. Classic-style forearm. Metal buttplate. Satin finish. Made in 1986 in limited issue 7070 by Miroku.

MODEL 1886 HIGH-
GRADE LA RIFLE . . . . **NiB $2055 Ex $1359 Gd $933**
Same general specifications as the Model 1886 Grade I except receiver is grayed, steel embellished w/scroll; elk and American bison engraving. High-gloss stock. Made in 1986 in limited issue of 3000 by Miroku.

MODEL 1895 GRADE I LA RIFLE . . . . . .**NiB $979 Ex $911 Gd $765**
Caliber: .30-06, .30-40 Krag. Four round magazine. 24-inch round bbl. 42 inches overall. Weight: 8 lbs. French walnut stock and Schnabel forend. Sights: Rear buckhorn; gold bead on elevated ramp front. Made in 1984 in limited issue of 8,000 (2,000 chambered for .30-40 Krag and 6,000 chambered for .30-06). Mfd. by Miroku.

MODEL 1895 HIGH-
GRADE LA RIFLE . . . .**NiB $1630 Ex $1379 Gd $996**
Same general specifications as Model 1895 Grade I except engraved receiver and Grade III French walnut stock and forend w/fine checkering. Made in 1985 in limited issue of 1000 in each caliber by Miroku.

Browning Model 1886
Grade I

Browning Model 1886
High-Grade

Browning Model 1895
Grade I

Browning
A-Bolt Eclipse

MODEL A-BOLT .22 RIFLE

Calibers: .22 LR, .22 Magnum. Five- and 15-round magazines. 22-inch round bbl. 40.25 inches overall. Weight: 5 lbs., 9 oz. Gold-colored adj. trigger. Laminated walnut stock w/checkering. Rosewood forend grip cap; pistol grip. With or w/o sights. Ramp front and adj. folding leaf rear on open sight model. 22 LR made 1985 to 1996; 22 Magnum, 1990 to 1996.

Grade I .22 LR . . . . NiB $575 Ex $340 Gd $255
Grade I .22 Magnum . . . . NiB $600 Ex $423 Gd $269
Deluxe Grade
  Gold Medallion . . . . NiB $620 Ex $479 Gd $354

MODEL A-BOLT ECLIPSE BOLT RIFLE

Same general specifications as Hunter Grade except fitted w/gray and black laminated thumbhole stock. Available in both short and long action w/two bbl. configurations w/BOSS. Mfd. by Miroku 1996 to 2006.

Eclipse w/standard bbl. . . . . NiB $955 Ex $821 Gd $677
Eclipse Varmint w/heavy bbl. . . . . NiB $1123 Ex $978 Gd $720
Eclipse M-1000
  Target (.300 Win. Mag.) . . . . . NiB $1304 Ex $1038 Gd $796

MODEL A-BOLT EURO-BOLT RIFLE

Same general specifications as Hunter Grade except w/checkered satin-finished walnut stock. W/continental-style cheekpiece, palm-swell grip and Schnabel forend. Mannlicher-style spoon bolt handle and contoured bolt shroud. 22- or 26-inch bbl. w/satin blued finish. Weight: 6.8 to 7.4 lbs. Calibers: .22-250 Rem., .243 Win., .270 Win., .30.06, .308 Win., 7mm Rem. Mag. Mfd. by Miroku 1993 to 1994; 1994 to 1996 (Euro-Bolt II).

Euro-Bolt . . . . NiB $679 Ex $536 Gd $369
Euro-Bolt II . . . . NiB $755 Ex $640 Gd $470
BOSS option, add $100

MODEL A-BOLT HUNTER GRADE RIFLE

Calibers: .22 Hornet, .223 Rem., .22-250 Rem., .243 Win., .257 Roberts, 7mm-08 Rem., .308 Win., (short action) .25-06 Rem., .270 Win., .280 Rem., .284 Win., .30-06, 7mm Rem. Mag., .300 Win. Mag., .338 Win. Mag. Four-round magazine (standard), 3-round (magnum). 22-inch bbl. (standard), 24-inch (magnum). Weight: 7.5 lbs. (standard), 8.5 lbs. (magnum). With or w/o sights. Classic-style walnut stock. Produced in two action lengths w/nine locking lugs, fluted bolt w/60 degree rotation. Mfd. by Miroku from 1985 to 1993; from 1994 to 2007 (Hunter II).

Hunter . . . . NiB $489 Ex $333 Gd $269
Hunter II . . . . NiB $590 Ex $389 Gd $310
Hunter Micro . . . . NiB $596 Ex $395 Gd $317
BOSS option, add $100
Open sights, add $75

MODEL A-BOLT MEDALLION GRADE RIFLE

Same as Hunter Grade except w/high-gloss deluxe stock rosewood grip cap and forend; high-luster blued finish. Also in .375 H&H w/open sights. Left-hand models available in long action only. Mfd. by Miroku from 1988 to 1993; from 1994 to 2009 (Medallion II). Bighorn Sheep Ltd. Ed.

.270 Win. (600 made 1986) . . . . NiB $1412 Ex $1096 Gd $790
Gold Medallion Deluxe Grade . . . . NiB $679 Ex $500 Gd $346
Gold Medallion II Deluxe Grade . . . . . . NiB $670 Ex $525 Gd $380
Medallion, Standard Grade . . . . NiB $633 Ex $488 Gd $354
Medallion II, Standard Grade . . . . NiB $655 Ex $500 Gd $397
Medallion, .375 H&H . . . . NiB $999 Ex $770 Gd $488
Medallion II, .375 H&H . . . . NiB $1012 Ex $790 Gd $497
Micro Medallion. . . . . NiB $690 Ex $557 Gd $367
Micro Medallion II . . . . NiB $707 Ex $569 Gd $415
Pronghorn Antelope Ltd. Ed. 243 Win.
  (500 made 1987) . . . . NiB $1266 Ex $1139 Gd $923
w/BOSS option, add $100
w/Open sights, add $75

Browning A-Bolt .22

Browning A-Bolt
Euro-Bolt

Browning A-Bolt
Hunter

Browning A-Bolt
Hunter with BOSS

Browning A-Bolt
Medallion Custom Trophy

Browning A-Bolt
Medallion White Gold

Browning A-Bolt
Medallion

Browning A-Bolt
Medallion (Left-Handed)

Browning A-Bolt
Composite Stalker

Browning A-Bolt
Stainless Stalker

Browning BAR, Grade IV

Browning BAR, Grade V

MODEL A-BOLT STALKER RIFLE

Same general specifications as Model A-Bolt Hunter Rifle except w/ checkered graphite-fiberglass composite stock and matte blued or stainless metal. Non-glare matte finish of all exposed metal surfaces. 3 models: Camo Stalker orig. w/multi-colored laminated wood stock, matte blued metal; Composite Stalker w/graphite-fiberglass stock, matte blued metal; w/composite stock, stainless metal. Made by Miroku from 1987 to 1993; 1994 to date. (Stalker II).

Camo Stalker (orig. laminated stock)	NiB $960	Ex $709	Gd $350
Composite Stalker	NiB $990	Ex $656	Gd $433
Composite Stalker II	NiB $990	Ex $656	Gd $433
Stainless Stalker	NiB $1045	Ex $745	Gd $500
Stainless Stalker II.	NiB $876	Ex $655	Gd $571
Stainless Stalker, .375 H&H	NiB $909	Ex $808	Gd $667
W/BOSS option, add. $100			
Left-hand model, add $100			

MODEL A-BOLT
VARMINT II RIFLE . . . . NiB $805 Ex $723 Gd $577
Same general specifications as Stalker model except w/22-inch heavy bbl. w/BOSS system and varmint-style black laminated wood stock. Calibers: .22-250, .223 or .308. No sights. Bright blue or satin finish. Made by Miroku from 2002 to 2008.

MODEL B-92 LEVER-ACTION RIFLE . . . . NiB $534 Ex $467 Gd $288
Calibers: .357 Mag. and .44 Rem. Mag. 11-round magazine. 20-inch round bbl. 37.5 inches overall. Weight: 5.5 to 6.4 lbs. Seasoned French walnut stock w/high gloss finish. Cloverleaf rear sight; steel post front. Made from1979 to 1989 by Miroku.

BAR AUTOMATIC RIFLE,
GRADE I, STANDARD CALIBERS. . .NiB $805 Ex $ 623 Gd $455
Gas-operated semiautomatic. Calibers: .243 Win., .270 Win., .280 Rem., .308 Win., .30-06. Four-round box magazine. 22-inch bbl. Weight: 7.5 lbs. Folding leaf rear sight, hooded ramp front. French walnut stock and forearm checkered, QD swivels. Made from 1967 to 1992 by FN.

BAR, GRADE I, MAGNUM CALIBERS . . . . . NiB $809 Ex $733 Gd $590
Same as BAR in standard calibers, except w/24-inch bbl. 7mm Rem. Mag. or .300 Win. Mag. .338 Win. Mag. w/3-round box magazine and recoil pad. Weight: 8.5 lbs. Made 1969 to 1992 by FN.

BAR, GRADE II
Same as Grade I except receiver engraved w/big-game heads (deer and antelope on standard-caliber rifles, ram and grizzly on Magnum-caliber) and scrollwork, higher grade wood. Made 1967 to 1974 by FN.

Standard calibers	NiB $1229	Ex $976	Gd $657
Magnum calibers	NiB $1338	Ex $875	Gd $617

BAR, GRADE III
Same as Grade I except receiver of grayed steel engraved w/big-game heads (deer and antelope on standard-caliber rifles, moose and elk on Magnum-caliber) framed in fine-line scrollwork, gold-plated trigger, stock and forearm of highly figured French walnut, hand-checkered and carved. Made from 1971 to 1974 by FN.

Standard calibers	NiB $1554	Ex $993	Gd $591
Magnum calibers	NiB $1617	Ex $1230	Gd $725

BAR, GRADE IV
Same as Grade I except receiver of grayed steel engraved w/full detailed rendition of running deer and antelope on standard-caliber rifles, moose and elk on Magnum-caliber gold-plated trigger, stock and forearm of highly figured French walnut, hand checkered and carved. Made frm 1971 to 1986 by FN.

Standard calibers	NiB $2490	Ex $1546	Gd $1110
Magnum calibers	NiB $2669	Ex $1721	Gd $1300

BAR, GRADE V
Same as Grade I except receiver w/complete big-game scenes executed by a master engraver and inlaid w/18K gold (deer and antelope on standard-caliber rifles, moose and elk on Magnum caliber), gold-plated trigger, stock and forearm of finest French walnut, intricately hand-checkered and carved. Made from 1971 to 1974 by FN.

Standard calibers	NiB $6457	Ex $4707	Gd $2897
Magnum calibers	NiB $6844	Ex $5110	Gd $3194

Browning BAR
Mark II Safari

Browning BAR
Mark II Safari

Browning BAR 22

Browning BAR 22
('82 Model)

BAR MARK II SAFARI AUTOMATIC RIFLE
Same general specifications as standard BAR semiautomatic rifle, except w/redesigned gas and buffer systems, new bolt release lever, and engraved receiver. Made from 1993 to date.

Standard calibers . . . . NiB $1019 Ex $707 Gd $505
Magnum calibers . . . . NiB $1040 Ex $808 Gd $617
Lightweight (alloy receiver
  w/20-inch bbl.) . . . . NiB $765 Ex $588 Gd $380
BAR Mk II Grade III (intro. 1996) . . . NiB $3520 Ex $2377 Gd $1290
BAR Mk II Grade IV (intro. 1996) . . . NiB $3609 Ex $2303 Gd $1829
W/BOSS option, add $75
W/open sights, add $25

BAR 22 AUTOMATIC RIFLE
Semiautomatic. Caliber: .22 LR. Tubular magazine holds 15 rounds. 20.25-inch bbl. Weight: 6.25 lbs. Sights: Folding-leaf rear, gold bead front on ramp. Receiver grooved for scope mounting. French walnut pistol-grip stock and forearm checkered. Made from 1977 to 1985.

Grade I . . . . NiB $641 Ex $369 Gd $322
Grade II . . . . NiB $1011 Ex $555 Gd $375

BBR LIGHTNING BOLT-ACTION RIFLE . . NiB $606 Ex $495 Gd $400
Bolt-action rifle w/short bolt throw of 60 degrees. Calibers: .25-06 Rem., .270 Win., .30-06, 7mm Rem. Mag., .300 Win. Mag. 24-inch bbl. Weight: 8 lbs. Made from 1979 to 1984.

BL-22 LEVER-ACTION REPEATING RIFLE
Short-throw lever-action. Caliber: .22 LR, Long, Short. Tubular magazine holds 15 LR, 17 Long 22 Short rounds. 20-inch bbl. Weight: 5 lbs. Sights: Folding leaf rear; bead front. Receiver grooved for scope mounting.

Walnut straight-grip stock and forearm, bbl. band. Made from 1970 to date by Miroku.

Grade I . . . . NiB $445 Ex $379 Gd $290
Grade II (w/scroll engraving) . . . . . NiB $498 Ex $390 Gd $300

BLR LEVER-ACTION REPEATING RIFLE
Calibers: (short action only) .243 Win., .308 Win., .358 Win. Four round detachable box magazine. 20-inch bbl. Weight: 7 lbs. Sights: Windage and elevation adj. open rear; hooded ramp front. Walnut straight-grip stock and forearm, checkered, bbl. band, recoil pad. Made in 1966 by BAC/USA; from 1969 to 1973 by FN; from 1974 to 1980 by Miroku. Note: USA manufacture of this model was limited to prototypes and pre-production guns only and may be identified by the "MADE IN USA" roll stamp on the bbl.

FN model . . . . NiB $1000 Ex $699 Gd $554
Miroku model . . . . NiB $690 Ex $500 Gd $398
USA model . . . . NiB $1245 Ex $1097 Gd $686

BLR LIGHTNING MODEL
Lightweight version of the Browning BLR '81 w/forged alloy receiver and redesigned trigger group. Calibers: Short Action— .22-250 Rem., .223 Rem., .243 Win., 7mm-08 Rem., .308 Win.; Long Action— .270 Win., 7mm Rem. Mag., .30-06, .300 Win. Mag. Three or 4-round detachable box magazine. 20-, 22- or 24-inch bbl. Weight: 6.5 to 7.75 lbs. Pistol-grip style walnut stock and forearm, cut checkering and recoil pad. Made by Miroku from 1995 to 2002.

Short action model . . . . NiB $690 Ex $586 Gd $390
Long action model . . . . NiB $707 Ex $596 Gd $400

Browning BBR Lightning

Browning BL-22, Grade I

Browning BPR Pump Rifle

BLR MODEL '81

Redesigned version of the Browning BLR. Calibers: .222-50 Rem., .243 Win., .308 Win., .358 Win; Long Action— .270 Win., 7mm Rem. Mag., .30-06. Fourround detachable box magazine. 20-inch bbl. Weight: 7 lbs. Walnut straight-grip stock and forearm, cut checkering, recoil pad. Made by Miroku from 1981 to 1995; Long Action intro. 1991.

Short action model . . . . NiB $780 Ex $592 Gd $396
Long action model . . . . NiB $850 Ex $505 Gd $390

BPR-22 PUMP RIFLE

Hammerless slide-action repeater. Specifications same as for BAR-.22, except also available chambered for .22 Magnum RF; magazine capacity, 11 rounds. Made from 1977 to 1982 by Miroku.

Model I . . . . NiB $355 Ex $274 Gd $200
Model II . . . . NiB $425 Ex $437 Gd $262

BPR PUMP RIFLE

Slide-action repeater based on proven BAR designs w/forged alloy receiver and slide that cams down to clear bbl. and receiver. Calibers: .243 Win., .308 Win., .270 Win., .30-06, 7mm Rem. Mag. .300 Win. Mag. Three or 4-round detachable box magazine. 22- or 24-inch bbl. w/ramped front sight and open adj. rear. Weight: 7.2 to 7.4 lbs. Made from 1997 to 2001 by Miroku.

BPR Model standard calibers. . . . . NiB $743 Ex $533 Gd $390
BPR Model magnum calibers add $75

HIGH-POWER BOLT-ACTION
RIFLE, MEDALLION GRADE . . . . NiB $3877 Ex $3488 Gd $1967
Same as Safari Grade except receiver and bbl. scroll engraved, ram's head engraved on floorplate; select walnut stock w/rosewood forearm tip, grip cap. Made from 1961 to 1974.

HIGH-POWER BOLT-ACTION
RIFLE, OLYMPIAN GRADE . . . . NiB $3831 Ex $3435 Gd $1925
Same as Safari Grade except bbl. engraved; receiver, trigger guard and floorplate satin chrome-plated and engraved w/game scenes appropriate to caliber; finest figured walnut stock w/rosewood forearm tip and grip cap, latter w/18K-gold medallion. Made from 1961 to 1974.

HIGH-POWER BOLT-ACTION RIFLE,
SAFARI GRADE, MEDIUM ACTION . . . NiB $1443 Ex $988 Gd $733
Same as Standard except medium action. Calibers: .22-250, .243 Win., .264 Win. Mag., .284 Win. Mag., .308 Win. Bbl.: 22-inch lightweight bbl.; .22-250 and .243 also available w/24-inch heavy bbl. Weight: 6 lbs., 12 oz. w/lightweight bbl.; 7 lbs. 13 oz. w/heavy bbl. Made 1963 to 1974 by Sako.

HIGH-POWER BOLT-ACTION RIFLE,
SAFARI GRADE, SHORT ACTION . . . . . NiB $1722 Ex $933 Gd $747
Same as Standard except short action. Calibers: .222 Rem., .222 Rem. Mag. 22-inch lightweight or 24-inch heavy bbl. No sights. Weight: 6 lbs., 2 oz. w/lightweight bbl.; 7.5 lbs. w/heavy bbl. Made from 1963 to 1974 by Sako.

HIGH-POWER BOLT-ACTION RIFLE,
SAFARI GRADE, STANDARD ACTION NiB $1523 Ex $1133 Gd $944
Mauser-type action. Calibers: .270 Win., .30-06, 7mm Rem. Mag., .300 H&H Mag., .300 Win. Mag., .308 Norma Mag. .338 Win. Mag., .375 H&H Mag., .458 Win. Mag. Cartridge capacity: 6 rounds in .270, .30-06; 4 in Magnum calibers. Bbl. length: 22 in., in .270, .30-06; 24 in., in Magnum calibers. Weight: 7 lbs., 2 oz., in .270, .30-06; 8.25 lbs. in Mag. calibers. Folding leaf rear sight, hooded ramp front. Checkered stock w/ pistol grip, Monte Carlo cheekpiece, QD swivels; recoil pad on Magnum models. Made from 1959 to 1974 by FN.

T-BOLT T-1 .22 REPEATING RIFLE

Straight-pull bolt action. Caliber: .22 LR. Five round clip magazine. 24-inch bbl. Peep rear sight w/ramped blade front. Plain walnut stock w/pistol grip and laquered finish. Weight: 6 lbs. Also left-hand model. Made from 1965 to 1974 by FN.

Right-hand model . . . . NiB $650 Ex $469 Gd $300
Left-hand model . . . . NiB $675 Ex $512 Gd $409

T-BOLT T-2

Same as T-1 Model except w/checkered fancy figured walnut stock. Made from 1966-74 by FN. (Reintroduced briefly during the late 1980's with oil-finished stock)

Original model . . . . NiB $909 Ex $579 Gd $289
Reintroduced model . . . . NiB $589 Ex $433 Gd $266

Browning
BL-22 II

Browning
BLR Model '81

Browning High-Power
Bolt-Action Rifle, Medallion Grade

Browning High-Power
Safari Grade Medium Action, Heavy Barrel

Browning High-Power
Safari Grade Short Action, Heavy Barrel

Browning High-Power
Safari Grade Standard Action

F.N. BROWNING FAL SEMIAUTOMATIC RIFLE
Same as F.N. FAL Semiautomatic Rifle. See F.N. listing for specifications.
Sold by Browning for a brief period c. 1960.
F.N. FAL standard
  model (G-series). . . . . NiB $4977 Ex $3677 Gd $2928
F.N. FAL lightweight
  model (G-series). . . . . NiB $5310 Ex $4400 Gd $3090
F.N. FAL heavy bbl..
  model (G-series). . . . . NiB $7175 Ex $6230 Gd $4956
BAC FAL model . . . . NiB $5320 Ex $4952 Gd $4915

BSA GUNS LTD. — Birmingham, England
*Previously imported by Samco Global Arms, BSA Guns Ltd and
Precision Sports.*

NO. 12 MARTINI SINGLE-SHOT
TARGET RIFLE . . . . .NiB $766 Ex $567 Gd $433
Caliber .22 LR. 29-inch bbl. Weight: 8.75 lbs. Parker-Hale Model 7 rear sight and
Model 2 front sight. Straight-grip stock, checkered forearm. Note: This model was
also available w/open sights or w/BSA No. 20 and 30 sights. Made before WWII.

BSA
Model 12/15 Martini

BSA
Model 15 Martini

MODEL 12/15 MARTINI HEAVY . . . . NiB $765 Ex $544 Gd $379
Same as Standard Model 12/15 except w/extra heavy bbl., weighs 11 lbs.

**MODEL 12/15 MARTINI
SINGLE-SHOT TARGET RIFLE . . . . NiB $650 Ex $479 Gd $355**
Caliber: .22 LR. 29-inch bbl. Weight: 9 lbs. Parker-Hale No. PH-7A rear
sight and No. FS-22 front sight. Target stock w/high comb and cheekpiece,
beavertail forearm. Note: This is a post-WWII model; however, a similar
rifle, the BSA-Parker Model 12/15, was produced c. 1938.

**NO. 13 MARTINI SINGLE-SHOT
TARGET RIFLE . . . . NiB $756 Ex $579 Gd $443**
Caliber: .22 LR. Lighter version of the No.12 w/same general specifica-
tions except w/25-inch bbl., weighs 6.5lbs. Made before WWII.

NO. 13 SPORTING RIFLE
Same as No. 13 Target except fitted w/Parker-Hale "Sportarget" rear sight and
bead front sight. Also available in .22 Hornet. Made before WWII.
.22 Long Rifle. . . . . NiB $756 Ex $579 Gd $443
.22 Hornet . . . . NiB $976 Ex $800 Gd $579

**MODEL 15 MARTINI
SINGLE-SHOT TARGET RIFLE. . . . . NiB $765 Ex $577 Gd $338**
Caliber: .22 LR. 29-inch bbl. Weight: 9.5 lbs. BSA No. 30 rear sight
and No. 20 front sight. Target stock w/cheekpiece and pistol-grip, long,
semi-beavertail forearm. Made before WWII.

**CENTURION MODEL
MATCH RIFLE . . . . NiB $522 Ex $423 Gd $320**
Same general specifications as Model 15 except w/Centurion match
bbl. Made before WWII.

**CF-2 BOLT-ACTION
HUNTING RIFLE . . . . NiB $543 Ex $399 Gd $265**
Mauser-type action. Calibers: 7mm Rem. Mag., .300 Win. Mag. Three-round
magazine. 23.6-inch bbl. Weight: 8 lbs. Sights: Adj. rear; hooded ramp front.
Checkered walnut stock w/Monte Carlo comb, rollover cheekpiece, rosewood
forend tip, recoil pad, sling swivels. Made 1975 to 1987.

CF-2 STUTZEN RIFLE . . . . NiB $577 Ex $437 Gd $333
Calibers: .222 Rem., .22-250, .243 Win., .270 Win., .308 Win. .30-06. Four
round capacity (5 in 222 Rem.). 20.6-inch bbl. 41.5 inches (approx.) overall
length. Weight: 7.5 to 8 lbs. Williams front and rear sights. Hand-finished
European walnut stock. Monte Carlo cheekpiece and Wundhammer palm
swell. Double-set triggers. Importation disc. 1987.

CFT TARGET RIFLE. . . . . NiB $926 Ex $735 Gd $533
Single-shot bolt action. Caliber: 7.62mm. 26.5-inch bbl. About 47.5
inches overall. Weight: 11 lbs., incl. accessories. Bbl. and action
weight: 6 lbs., 12 oz. Importation disc. 1987.

MAJESTIC DELUXE FEATHERWEIGHT BOLT-ACTION HUNTING RIFLE
Mauser-type action. Calibers: .243 Win., .270 Win., .308 Win., .30-
06, .458 Win. Mag. Four round magazine. 22-inch bbl. w/BESA recoil
reducer. Weight: 6.25 lbs.; 8.75 lbs. in 458. Folding leaf rear sight,
hooded ramp front. Checkered European-style walnut stock w/cheek-
piece, pistol-grip, Schnabel forend, swivels, recoil pad. Made from
1959 to 1965.
.458 Win. Mag. caliber. . . . . NiB $650 Ex $508 Gd $380
Other calibers . . . . NiB $506 Ex $433 Gd $298

**BSA MAJESTIC DELUXE
STANDARD WEIGHT . . . . NiB $508 Ex $332 Gd $255**
Same as Featherweight model except heavier bbl. w/o recoil reducer.
Calibers: .22 Hornet, .222 Rem., .243 Win., 7x57mm, .308 Win., .30-
06. Weight: 7.25 to 7.75 lbs. Disc.

**MARTINI-INTERNATIONAL
ISU MATCH RIFLE . . . . NiB $944 Ex $708 Gd $577**
Similar to MK III, but modified to meet International Shooting Union
"Standard Rifle" specifications. 28-inch standard weight bbl. Weight:
10.75 lbs. Redesigned stock and forearm, latter attached to bbl. w/"V"
section alloy strut. Intro. 1968. Disc.

**MARTINI-INTERNATIONAL
MARK V MATCH RIFLE. . . . . NiB $1077 Ex $897 Gd $623**
Same as ISU model except w/heavier bbl. Weight: 12.25 lbs. Intro. 1976. Disc.

**MARTINI-INTERNATIONAL MATCH
RIFLE SINGLE-SHOT HEAVY PATTERN . . NiB $866 Ex $630 Gd $443**
Caliber: .22 LR. 29-inch heavy bbl. Weight: 14 lbs. Parker-Hale
"International" front and rear sights. Target stock w/full cheekpiece and
pistol-grip, broad beavertail forearm, handstop, swivels. Right- or left-
hand models. Made from 1950 to 1953.

**MARTINI-INTERNATIONAL
MATCH RIFLE — LIGHT PATTERN . . . . . . NiB $775 Ex $584 Gd $455**
Same general specifications as Heavy Pattern except w/26-inch lighter
weight bbl. Weight: 11 lbs. Disc.

**MARTINI-INTERNATIONAL
MK II MATCH RIFLE. . . . . NiB $1043 Ex $720 Gd $630**
Same general specifications as original model. Heavy and Light Pattern.
Improved trigger mechanism and ejection system. Redesigned stock
and forearm. Made from 1953 to 1959.

**MARTINI-INTERNATIONAL
MK III MATCH RIFLE . . . . NiB $1044 Ex $812 Gd $613**
Same general specifications as MK II Heavy Pattern. Longer
action frame w/I-section alloy strut to which forearm is attached;
bbl. is fully floating. Redesigned stock and forearm. Made 1959
to 1967.

BSA CFT Target

BSA
Martini-International ISU Match

BSA
Martini-International Mark V
Match

BSA
Martini-International MK III Match

BSA
Monarch Deluxe Varmint

**MONARCH DELUXE BOLT-ACTION
HUNTING RIFLE** . . . . **NiB $714 Ex $349 Gd $260**
Same as Majestic Deluxe Standard Weight model except w/rede-
signed stock of U.S. style w/contrasting hardwood forend tip and grip
cap. Calibers: .222 Rem., .243 Win., .270 Win., 7mm Rem. Mag.,
.308 Win., .30-06. 22-inch bbl. Weight: 7 to 7.25 lbs. Made 1965
to 1974.

**MONARCH DELUXE
VARMINT RIFLE** . . . . **NiB $710 Ex $420 Gd $290**
Same as Monarch Deluxe except w/24-inch heavy bbl. and weighs 9
lbs. Calibers: .222 Rem., .243 Win.

BUSHMASTER FIREARMS — Ilion, NY
*Quality Parts Company. Currently Ilion, NY, formerly Windham,
Maine. Purchased by Freedom Group Inc. 2011.*

M17S BULLPUP . . . . **NiB $735 Ex $600 Gd $466**
Caliber: .223. 21.5-inch bbl. Weight: 8.2 lbs. Polymer stocks. Handle
w/fixed open sights w/Weaver-type rail for any optics. Semi-auto,
self-compensating short stroke gas piston. Forward trigger/grip w/rear
chamber. Bullpup style. Alloy receiver. Synthetic lower receiver is
hinged to upper w/hinged takedown system. Accepts M-16 type magazines. Made from 1992 to 2005.

MODEL XM15 E2S SERIES
Caliber: .223. 16-, 20-, 24- or 26-inch bbl. Weight: 7 to 8.6 lbs.
Polymer stocks. Adjustable sights w/dual flip-up aperture; optional flat-
top rail accepts scope. Direct gas-operated w/rotating bolt. Forged alloy
receiver. All steel-coated w/manganese phosphate. Accepts M-16 type
magazines. Made from 1989 to date.
XM15 E2S Carbine . . . . **NiB $1210 Ex $989 Gd $750**
XM15 E2S Target Rifle . . . . **NiB $1244 Ex $1018 Gd $707**

CABELA'S, INC. — Sidney, Nebraska

Cabela's is a sporting goods dealer and catalog company headquartered in Sidney, Nebraska. Cabela's imports black powder cartridge Sharps replicas, revolvers and other reproductions and replicas manufactured in Italy by A. Uberti, Pedersoli, Pietta and others.

1858 HENRY REPLICA . . . . **NiB $707 Ex $599 Gd $524**
Lever-action. Modeled after the original Henry rifle. Caliber: .44-40. Thirteen-round magazine; Bbl: 24 inches. Overall length: 43 inches. Weight: 9 pounds. European walnut stock. Sights: Bead front, open adjustable rear. Brass receiver and buttplate. Introduced 1994.

1866 WINCHESTER REPLICA . . . . **NiB $599 Ex $425 Gd $347**
Lever-action modeled after the original Model 1866 rifle. Caliber: .44-40. Thirteen-round magazine. Bbl: 24 inches, octagonal; overall length: 43 inches. Weight: 9 pounds. European walnut stock, brass receiver, butt plate and forend cap. Sights: Bead front, open adjustable rear.

1873 WINCHESTER REPLICA . . . . **NiB $525 Ex $455 Gd $390**
Lever-action modeled after the original Model 1873 rifle. Caliber: .44-40, .45 Colt. Thirteen-round magazine. Bbl: 30 inches. Overall length: 43 inches. Weight: 8 pounds. European walnut stock. Sights: Bead front, open adjustable rear or globe front and tang rear. Color case-hardened steel receiver. Introduced 1994.
w/tang rear sight, globe front, add **$175**

1873 SPORTING MODEL REPLICA . . . **NiB $655 Ex $577 Gd $500**
Same as 1873 Winchester except with 30-inch bbl.
w/half-round, half-octagonal bbl., half magazine, add **$126**

CATTLEMAN CARBINE . . . . **NiB $355 Ex $290 Gd $227**
Revolver with shoulder stock. Caliber: .44-40; six-round cylinder. Bbl: 18 inches. Overall length: 34 inches. Weight: 4 pounds. European walnut stock. Sights: Blade front, notch rear. Color case-hardened frame, remainder blued. Introduced 1994.

SHARPS SPORTING RIFLE . . . . . . **NiB $879 Ex $779 Gd $576**
Single-shot. Caliber: .45-70. Bbl: Tapered octagon, 32 inches. Overall length: 47 inches. Weight: 9 pounds. Checkered walnut stock. Sights: Blade front, open adjustable rear. Color case-hardened receiver and hammer; remainder blued. Introduced 1995.

CALICO LIGHT WEAPONS SYSTEMS — Cornelius, OR

Formerly Bakersville, California.

LIBERTY 50/100 SEMIAUTOMATIC RIFLE
Retarded blowback action. Caliber: 9mm. 50- or 100-round helical-feed magazine. 16.1-inch bbl. 34.5 inches overall. Weight: 7 lbs. Adjustable post front sight and aperture rear. Ambidextrous rotating safety. Glass-filled polymer or thumbhole-style wood stock. Made 1995 to 2001; reintro. 2007.
Model Liberty 50 . . . . **NiB $800 Ex $668 Gd $410**
Model Liberty 100 . . . . **NiB $909 Ex $869 Gd $495**

MODEL M-100 SEMIAUTOMATIC SERIES
Similar to the Liberty 100 Model except chambered for .22 LR. Weight: 5 lbs. 34.5 inches overall. Folding or glass-filled polymer stock and forearm. Made from 1986 to 1994; reintro. 2007.
Model M-100 w/folding
   stock (disc. 1994) . . . . **NiB $600 Ex $355 Gd $300**
Model M-100 FS w/fixed
   stock disc. 1996 . . . . **NiB $400 Ex $379 Gd $320**

MODEL M-105 SEMI-AUTOMATIC
SPORTER . . . . **NiB $688 Ex $492 Gd $333**
Similar to the Liberty 100 Model except fitted w/walnut buttstock and forearm. Made from 1989 to 1994.

MODEL M-900 SEMIAUTOMATIC CARBINE
Caliber: 9mm Parabellum. 50- or 100-round magazine. 16.1-inch bbl. 28.5 inches overall. Weight: 3.7 lbs. Post front sight adj. for windage and elevation, fixed notch rear. Collapsible steel buttstock and glass-filled polymer grip. Matte black finish. Made from 1989 to 1990, 1992 to 1993 and 2007.
Model M-100 w/folding
   stock (disc. 1994) . . . . **NiB $808 Ex $497 Gd $338**
Model M-100 FS w/fixed
   stock (intro. 1996) . . . . **NiB $677 Ex $533 Gd $390**

MODEL M-951 TACTICAL CARBINE
Similar to Model 900 except w/long compensator and adj. forward grip. Made from 1990 to 1994.
Model 951 . . . . **NiB $725 Ex $533 Gd $445**
Model 951-S . . . . **NiB $725 Ex $533 Gd $445**

CANADIAN MILITARY RIFLES — Quebec, Canada
Manufactured by Ross Rifle Co.

MODEL 1907 MARK II
ROSS MILITARY RIFLE . . . . **NiB $409 Ex $299 Gd $277**
Straight-pull bolt action. Caliber: .303 British. Five-round box magazine. 28-inch bbl. Weight: 8.5 lbs. Sights: adj. rear; blade front. Military-type full stock. Note: The Ross was originally issued as a Canadian service rifle in 1907. There were several variations; it was the official weapon at the start of WWI, but has been obsolete for many years. For Ross sporting rifle, see listing under Ross Rifle company.

CENTURY INTERNATIONAL ARMS, INC. — Delray Beach, Florida

Importer of military surplus and sporting firearms as well as manufacturer of firearms.

CENTURION M38/M96 BOLT-ACTION SPORTER
Sporterized Swedish M38/96 Mauser action. Caliber: 6.5x55mm. Five-round magazine. 24-inch bbl. 44 inches overall. Adj. rear sight. Blade front. Black synthetic or checkered European hardwood Monte Carlo stock. Holden Ironsighter see-through scope mount. Imported from 1987 to date.
w/hardwood stock . . . . **NiB $277 Ex $190 Gd $133**
w/synthetic stock . . . . **NiB $280 Ex $198 Gd $144**

CENTURION M98 BOLT-ACTION SPORTER
Sporterized VZ24 or 98 Mauser action. Calibers: .270 Win., 7.62x39mm, .308 Win., .30-06. Five round magazine. 22-inch bbl. 44 inches overall. Weight: 7.5 lbs. W/Millet or Weaver scope base(s), rings and no iron sights. Classic or Monte Carlo laminated hardwood, black synthetic or checkered European hardwood stock. Imported from 1992 to date.
M98 Action W/black
   synthetic stock (w/o rings) . . . . . **NiB $300 Ex $220 Gd $167**
M98 Action W/hardwood Stock(w/o rings) . . . **NiB $290 Ex $190 Gd $126**
VZ24 action w/laminated
   hardwood stock (Elite) . . . . **NiB $355 Ex $289 Gd $188**
VZ24 action w/black
   synthetic stock . . . . **NiB $338 Ex $269 Gd $175**
w/Millet base and rings, add **$45**

CENTURION P-14 SPORTER
Sporterized P-14 action. Caliber: 7mm Rem. Mag., .300 Win. Mag. Five-round magazine. 24-inch bbl. 43.4 inches overall. Weight: 8.25 lbs. Weaver-type scope base. Walnut stained hardwood or fiberglass stock. Imported from 1987 to date.

w/hardwood stock . . . . NiB $269 Ex $211 Gd $157
w/fiberglass stock . . . . NiB $299 Ex $223 Gd $167

ENFIELD SPORTER 4 BOLT-ACTION RIFLE
Sporterized Lee-Enfield action. Caliber: .303 British. 10-round magazine. 25.25-inch bbl. 44.5 inches overall. Blade front sight, adj. aperture rear. Sporterized beechwood military stock or checkered walnut
Monte Carlo stock. Blued finish. Imported from 1987 to date.
w/sporterized military stock . . . . . . NiB $169 Ex $128 Gd $90
w/checkered walnut stock . . . . . . NiB $223 Ex $190 Gd $135

L1A1 FAL SPORTER . . . . NiB $944 Ex $749 Gd $588
Sporterized L1A1 FAL semiautomatic. Caliber: .308 Win. 20.75-inch
bbl. 41 inches overall. Weight: 9.75 lbs. Protected front post sight, adj.
aperture rear. Matte blued finish. Black or camo Bell & Carlson thumbhole sporter stock w/rubber buttpad. Imported from 1988-98.

M-14 SPORTER . . . . NiB $460 Ex $338 Gd $255
Sporterized M-14 gas operated semiautomatic action. Caliber: .308 Win.
10-round magazine. 22-inch bbl. 41 inches overall. Weight: 8.25 lbs.
Blade front sight, adj. aperture rear sight. Parkerized finish. Walnut stock w/
rubber recoil pad. Forged receiver. Imported from 1991 to date.

TIGER DRAGUNOV . . . . NiB $1023 Ex $790 Gd $545
Russian SVD semiautomatic sniper rifle. Caliber: 7.62x54R. Five-round
magazine. 21-inch bbl. 43 inches overall. Weight: 8.5 lbs. Blade front
sight, open rear adj. for elevation. Blued finish. European laminated
hardwood thumbhole stock. 4x range-finding scope w/lighted reticle and
sunshade. Quick detachable scope mount. Imported from 1994 to 1995.

GAMESTALKER . . . . NiB $1399 Ex $1088 Gd $946
Cal.: .243 WSSM, .25 WSSM, .300 WSSM. Bbl.: 22 inches, stainless steel,
flattop upper, free-floating aluminum hand guard. ACE skeleton stock
with ERGO Sure Grip. 100% camo. Weight: 7 lbs.

G-3 SPORTER . . . . NiB $866 Ex $633 Gd $425
Semi-auto. Cal.: .308 Win. Made from G3 parts, American-made receiver
with integrated scope rail. Bbl.: 19 inches. 20-round mag. Pistol grip stock,
matte black finish. Weight: 9.3 pounds. Imported 1999 to 2006.

CETME SPORTER . . . . NiB $754 Ex $577 Gd $387
Cal.: .308 Win. Bbl.: 19.5 inches. 20-round mag. Blue or Mossy Oak
Break-Up camo finish, wood or synthetic stock w/pistol grip. Vented
forearm. Weight: 9.7 lbs.

S.A.R. 1 . . . . NiB $835 Ex $600 Gd $380
AK-47-type by Romarm. Cal.: 7.62x39mm. Bbl.: 16 inches. Wood
stock and forearm. Includes one 10 and one 30-round double-stack
magazine. Disc. 2003
S.A.R. 2 (5.45x39mm) . . . . NiB $835 Ex $600 Gd $380
S.A.R. 3 (.223 Rem.) . . . . NiB $835 Ex $600 Gd $380

MODEL B-82 . . . . NiB $835 Ex $600 Gd $380
Limited production Italian police model; serial no. with "D" suffix. Cal.:
.30 Luger, .32 ACP, 9 mm Ultra.

GP WASR-10 . . . . NiB $555 Ex $370 Gd $244
AK-47 type by Romarm. Cal.: 7.62x39mm. Bbl.: 16.25 inches. Wood stock
and forearm, includes one 5- and one 10-round mag. Weight: 7.5 lbs.
High-Cap series . . . . NiB $529 Ex $345 Gd $221

L1A1/R1A1 SPORTER . . . . NiB $1044 Ex $835 Gd $229
Modeled after British L1A1. Cal.: .308 Win. Bbl.: 22.5 inches. Carrying
handle, synthetic furn. 20-round mag. Folding rear sight. Weight: 9.5 lbs.

GOLANI SPORTER . . . . NiB $835 Ex $650 Gd $456
Made in Israel. Cal.: .223 Rem. Bbl.: 21 inches. Folding stock, opt.
bayonet lug., 35-round mag. Weight: 8 lbs.

Century International Arms GP WASR-10

Century International Arms Tantal Sporter

Century International Arms VZ 2008 Sporter

Century International Arms GP 1975

Century International Arms Degtyarev DP28

Century International Arms Sterling SA

TANTAL SPORTER . . . . NiB $735 Ex $555 Gd $455
Cal.: 5.45x39mm. Bbl.: 18 inches, flash hider. Folding wire stock.
Parkerized finish. Includes extra mag. Weight. 8 lbs.

VZ 2008 SPORTER . . . . NiB $865 Ex $645 Gd $465
Copy of the Czech V258. Cal.: 7.62x39mm. Bbl.: 16.25 inches; steel
receiver w/matte finish; wood or plastic stock. Weight: 7 lbs.

GRADING: **NiB** = New in Box **Ex** = Excellent or NRA 95% **Gd** = Good or NRA 68%

M-76 SNIPER . . . . NiB $1956 Ex $1538 Gd $967
Semi-auto version of Yugoslav M76. Cal.: 8mm Mauser. Bbl.: 21.5 inches. U.S.-made receiver. Includes scope, mount and 10-round mag. Weight: 11.3 lbs.

GP 1975 . . . . NiB $650 Ex $440 Gd $300
Cal.: 7.62x39mm. Bbl.: 16.25 inches. Black synthetic furniture, U.S.-made receiver and bbl. Weight: 7.4 lbs.

DEGTYAREV DP28 . . . . NiB $4125 Ex $3155 Gd $2390
Semi-auto, top-mounted magazine. Cal.: 7.62x54R. Gas operated. Full stock. 47- to 50-round mag. Weight: 10 lbs.
DPM 28 (pistol grip) . . . . .NiB $3970 Ex $3289 Gd $2410
DPX Tank Model . . . . .NiB $3970 Ex $3289 Gd $2410

STERLING SA . . . . .NiB $745 Ex $560 Gd $380
Semi-auto version of Sterling sub-machine gun. Cal.: 9mm Para., 34-round mag. Bbl.: 16 inches. U.S.-made receiver and bbl., crinkle finish; folding stock.

PAR 1 . . . . NiB $439 Ex $300 Gd $218
AK-47 receiver, made by PAR. Cal.: 7.62x39mm; 10-round mag. Bbl.: 20.9 inches. Weight: 7.6 lbs. Imported 2002 to 2009.
PAR 3 (.223 Rem.) . . . . .NiB $439 Ex $300 Gd $218

CHARTER ARMS CORPORATION — Shelton, Connecticut

AR-7 EXPLORER
SURVIVAL RIFLE . . . . .NiB $139 Ex $120 Gd $99
Same as Armalite AR-7, except w/black, instead of brown, "wood grain" plastic stock. See listing of that rifle for specifications. Made from 1973 to 1990.

CHIPMUNK RIFLES — Milltown, PA
Formerly Prospect, Oregon. Manufactured by Rogue Rifle Company, formerly Oregon Arms Company and Chipmunk Manufacturing, Inc.

BOLT-ACTION SINGLE-SHOT RIFLE
Calibers: .22 LR. or .22 WMR. 16.13-inch standard or 18.13-inch bull bbl. Weight: 2.5 lbs. (standard) or 4 lbs. (Bull bbl.) Peep sight rear; ramp front. Plain or checkered American walnut, laminated or black hardwood stock. Made from 1982 to 2007.
Standard model
w/plain walnut stock . . . . NiB $235 Ex $156 Gd $103
Standard model
w/black hardwood stock . . . . . . .NiB $195 Ex $155 Gd $99
Standard model
w/camouflage stock . . . . NiB $227 Ex $170 Gd $130
Standard model
w/laminated stock . . . . NiB $200 Ex $160 Gd $126
Deluxe grade
w/checkered walnut stock . . . . NiB $289 Ex $227 Gd $144
.22 WMR, add $40

E.J. CHURCHILL — England
Manufactured in High Wycombe, England, imported by Elliot Brothers, Chapin, SC.

HIGHLANDER BOLT-ACTION RIFLE . . NiB $439 Ex $367 Gd $298
Calibers: .243 Win., .25-06 Rem., .270 Win., .308 Win., .30-06, 7mm Rem. Mag., .300 Win. Mag. Four round magazine (standard); 3-round (magnum). Bbl. length: 22-inch (standard); 24-inch (magnum). 42.5 to 44.5 inches overall. Weight: 7.5 lbs. Adj. rear sight, blade front. Checkered European walnut pistol-grip stock. Imported from 1986 to 1991.

"ONE OF ONE THOUSAND" . . . . NiB $4220 Ex $2535 Gd $1966
Made for Interarms to commemorate that firm's 20th anniversary. Mauser-type action. Calibers: .270, 7mm Rem. Mag., .308, .30-06, .300 Win. Mag., .375 H&H Mag., .458 Win. Mag. Five round magazine (3-round in Magnum calibers). 24-inch bbl. Weight: 8 lbs. Classic-style French walnut stock w/cheekpiece, black forend tip, checkered pistol grip and forearm, swivel-mounted recoil pad w/cartridge trap, pistol-grip cap w/trap for extra front sight, barrel-mounted sling swivel. Limited issue of 1,000 rifles made in 1973. See illustration next page.

REGENT
BOLT-ACTION RIFLE . . . . .NiB $577 Ex $423 Gd $290
Calibers: .243 Win., .25-06 Rem., .270 Win., .308 Win., .30-06, 7mm Rem. Mag., .300 Win. Mag. Four round magazine. 22-inch round bbl. 42.5 inches overall. Weight: 7.5 lbs. Ramp front sight w/gold bead; adj. rear. Hand-checkered Monte Carlo-style stock of select European walnut; recoil pad. Made from 1986 to 1988.

CIMARRON ARMS — Fredericksburg, Texas
Importer of reproductions and replicas manufactured in Italy by A. Uberti, Pedersoli, Pietta and others.

1860 HENRY LEVER-ACTION REPLICA
Replica of 1860 Henry w/original Henry loading system.Calibers: .44-40, .44 Special, .45 Colt. 13-round magazine. 22-inch bbl. (carbine) or 24.25-inch bbl. (rifle). 43 inches overall (rifle). Weight: 9.5 lbs. (rifle). Bead front sight, open adj. rear. Brass receiver and buttplate. Smooth European walnut buttstock. Imported from 1991.
Carbine model . . . . NiB $1460 Ex $1096 Gd $735
Rifle model . . . . NiB $1390 Ex $1087 Gd $675
Civil War model
(U.S. issue martially marked) . NiB $1466 Ex $1100 Gd $709
w/ standard engraving add $2550
w/standard engraving, deluxe wood, add $3150
w/Lincoln hand engraving (disc. 2009), add $4500
w/Lincoln hand engraving,
  deluxe wood (disc. 2009), add $5000

1866 YELLOWBOY LEVER-ACTION
Replica of 1866 Winchester. Calibers: .22 LR, 22WMR, .38 Special, .44-40, .45 Colt. 16-inch round bbl. (Trapper), 19-inch round bbl. (Carbine) or 24.25-inch ocatagonal bbl. (rifle). 43 inches overall (rifle). Weight: 9 lbs. (rifle). Bead front sight, open adj. rear. Brass receiver, buttplate and forend cap. Smooth European walnut stock. Imported 1991 to date.
Carbine . . . . NiB $1075 Ex $787 Gd $581
Rifle . . . . NiB $1050 Ex $612 Gd $406
Indian model (disc.) . . . . NiB $895 Ex $585 Gd $379
Trapper Model (.44-40 WCF only, disc.) . . . NiB $995 Ex $756 Gd $502
w/A-engraving, add $2025
w/B-engraving, add $2500
w/C-engraving, add $3000

1873 LEVER-ACTION
Replica of 1873 Winchester. Calibers: .22 LR. .22WMR, .357 Magnum, .44-40 or .45 Colt. 16-inch round bbl. (Trapper), 19-inch round bbl. (SRC), 20-inch octagonal bbl. (short rifle), 24.25-inch octagonal bbl. (sporting rifle) and 30-inch octagonal bbl. (express rifle). 43 inches overall (sporting rifle). Weight: 8 lbs. Fixed blade front sight, adj. semi-buckhorn rear or tang peep sight. Walnut stock and forend. Color case-hardened receiver. Imported from 1989 to date.

Churchill "One of One Thousand"

Churchill Regent

Express Rifle .... NiB $1235 Ex $960 Gd $677
Short Rifle (disc.) .... NiB $1235 Ex $960 Gd $677
Sporting Rifle .... NiB $1235 Ex $960 Gd $677
SRC Carbine .... NiB $1235 Ex $960 Gd $677
Trapper (disc.) .... NiB $1268 Ex $980 Gd $697
One of 1000 engraved model ...... NiB $2409 Ex $2033 Gd $1354

1874 FALLING BLOCK SPORTING RIFLE
Replica of 1874 Sharps Sporting Rifle. Calibers: .45-65, .45-70, .45-90 or .45-120. 32- or 34-inch round or octagonal bbl. Weight: 9.5 to 10 lbs. Blade or globe front sight w/adj. open rear or sporting tang peep sight. Single or double set triggers. Checkered walnut stock and forend w/nose cap. Color case-hardened receiver. Imported from 1997 to date.
1874 Sporting Rifle - Billy Dixon Model ... NiB $1754 Ex $1289 Gd $1100
1874 Sporting Rifle - Quigley Model.. NiB $1556 Ex $1178 Gd $909
Sharps Sporting No. 1 Silhoette Rifle . NiB $1577 Ex $1133 Gd $926

1883 BURGESS RIFLE....... NiB $1489 Ex $1077 Gd $744
Caliber: .45 Long Colt. Bbl.: 20 or 25   inches. Reproduction. Importation began in 2010.

LIGHTNING RIFLE ...... NiB $1488 Ex $1088 Gd $755
Reproduction of Colt Lightning Rifle. Cal.: .357 Mag., .44-40 WCF or .45 Long Colt. Bbl.: round; 20 or 24 inches; octagon: 20, 24, or 26 inches. Blue or case-colored frame.
W/octagon bbl., add $150
Color case-hardened frame, add $300

MODEL 1871 ROLLING BLOCK
BABY CARBINE .... NiB $379 Ex $290 Gd $195
Remington repro. Caliber: .22 LR, .22 Hornet, .22 Mag. Or .357 Mag. Bbl: 22 inches. Walnut stock and forearm. Brass trigger guard and buttplate. Disc. 1990.
Deluxe model. .... NiB $785 Ex $580 Gd $338

LONG RANGE CREEDMOOR ..... NiB $1279 Ex $899 Gd $655
Cal.: .45-70 Gov't. Barrel: 30-inch octagon. Deluxe checkered walnut stock.

ADOBE WALLS FALLING
BLOCK RIFLE............... NiB $1754 Ex $1310 Gd $976
Cal.: .45-70 Gov't. Bbl.: 30 inches, octagon. Case hardened receiver, hand checkered walnut stock, German silver nose cap. Optional Creedmoor sights.

SHARPS NO. 1 RIFLE .... NiB $1087 Ex $755 Gd $544
Sharps reproduction. Cal.: .40-65 Win. or .45-70 Gov't. Bbl.: 32 inches, octagon; pistol grip stock. Imported 2000 to 2002.
No. 1 Silhouette............ NiB $1588 Ex $1011 Gd $744

MODEL 1874 SPORTING RIFLE . NiB $1377 Ex $986 Gd $650
Armi-Sport Billy Dixon model. Cal.: .38-55 WCF, .45-70 Gov't., .45-90 Win., .45-110, .50-90. Bbl.: 32 inches. Checkered deluxe walnut stock. Double set triggers.
Pedersoli model .... NiB $1809 Ex $1335 Gd $1088
Quigley II model .... NiB $1569 Ex $1104 Gd $854
Pedersoli Quigley....... NiB $2188 Ex $1598 Gd $1077
Big 50 model .... NiB $2769 Ex $1988 Gd $1369
Sharps Pride model...... NiB $2240 Ex $1674 Gd $1290
Pride II model .... NiB $1544 Ex $1068 Gd $909
Professional Hunter ...... NiB $1357 Ex $1068 Gd $909
Texas Ranger .... NiB $1271 Ex $933 Gd $730

SHARPS ROCKY MOUNTAIN II
MODEL 74................NiB $1498 Ex $1043 Gd $677
Repro. Cal.: .45-70 Gov't. Bbl.: 30 inches, octagon. Silver receiver, checkered walnut stock. Optional 6x Malcolm rifle scope.
w/scope, add $650

MODEL 1860 SPENCER RIFLE.. NiB $1560 Ex $1154 Gd $933
By Armi Sport. Cal.: 56-50. Bbl.: 30 inches. Plain walnut stock and forearm. Case hardened receiver, trigger guard and hammer. Three barrel bands.

MODEL 1865 SPENCER
REPEATING RIFLE .... NiB $1490 Ex $1167 Gd $770
By Armi Sport. Cal.: .44-40 WCF, .45 Schofield, .45 Long Colt, .56-50. Bbl.: 20 or 30 inches (in 56-50 only, disc. 2009). Blue finish, color case hardened frame. Straight grip walnut stock.
w/30-inch bbl., add $227

CIVIL WAR HENRY RIFLE..... NiB $1344 Ex $1269 Gd $976
By Uberti. Cal.: .44-40 WCF or .45 Long Colt. Bbl.: 24 inches. Includes military inspector's marks and cartouche; military-type sling swivels.

1866 YELLOWBOY CARBINE .. NiB $1192 Ex $1054 Gd $593
By Uberti. Cal.: .32-20 WCF, .38 SP, .38-55 WCF, .44 SP, .44-40 WCF, .45 Long Colt. Similar to Model 1866 Sporting Rifle except w/19-inch round bbl., two barrel bands, saddle ring, smooth walnut stock, and forearm.
Trapper model .... NiB $1167 Ex $866 Gd $546
Indian Carbine model....... NiB $1056 Ex $679 Gd $496
Red Cloud model .... NiB $1056 Ex $679 Gd $496

1873 SADDLE RING CARBINE . NiB $1355 Ex $1089 Gd $733
Cal.: .22 LR, .22 Mag., .32-20 WCF, .357 Mag./.38 SP, .38-40 WCF, .44 SP., .44-40 WCF, .45 Long Colt. Bbl.: 19 inches, round. Blued receiver, saddle ring.
Trapper Carbine .... NiB $1490 Ex $1100 Gd $977

1876 CENTENNIAL
SPORTING RIFLE . . . . NiB $1525 Ex $1260 Gd $995
Cal.: .40-60 WCF, .45-60 WCF, .45-70 WCF, .50-95 WCF; bbl.: 22 or 28 inches, octagon. Blue finish, case hardened frame. Full-length magazine, iron sights, walnut stock, and forearm.

1876 CARBINE . . . . NiB $1788 Ex $1388 Gd $1100
By Uberti. Cal.: .45-60 WCF, .45-75. Bbl.: 22 inches, round. Full length fore end and barrel band. Canadian NWMP model has blued frame and saddle ring.

1885 HI-WALL RIFLE . . . . NiB $1169 Ex $977 Gd $749
Cal.: .30-40 Krag, .348 Win., .38-55 Win., .405 Win., .40-65 WCF, .45-70 Gov't., .45-90 WCF, .45-120 WCF. Bbl.: 28 or 30 inches, octagon. Case hardened finish frame. Iron sights standard or optional aperture rear and globe front offered.
Pedersoli mode. . . . . NiB $2378 Ex $1956 Gd $1100

1885 LOW-WALL RIFLE . . . . NiB $1077 Ex $800 Gd $654
Cal.: .22 LR, .22 Hornet, .22 Mag., .30-30 Win., .32-20 WCF, .357 Mag., .38-40 WCF, .44 Mag., .38-55, .44-40 WCF, .45-70 Gov't., .45 Long Colt. Bbl.: 30 inches. Hand checkered walnut stock, single- or double-set trigger.
Deluxe model, add $200
Standard custom engraving, add $1750
Double set triggers, add $400

1892 RIFLE. . . . . NiB $1288 Ex $800 Gd $643
Cal.: .357 Mag., .44 Mag., .44-40 WCF, .45 Long Colt. Bbl.: 20 or 24 inches. Solid or take-down frame, smooth walnut stock and forearm, case colored receiver.
w/take-down frame, add $200
.44-40 WCF, .44 Mag., add $50

1892 CARBINE. . . . . NiB $1235 Ex $866 Gd $650
Cal.: .357 Mag., .44 Mag., .44-40 WCF, .45 Long Colt. Bbl.: 16 (Trapper model) or 20 inches. Solid frame, choice of big loop lever (El Dorado) or standard with 20-inch bbl. Saddle ring with 20-inch bbl. only.

CLERKE RECREATION PRODUCTS — Santa Monica, California

DELUXE HI-WALL . . . . NiB $337 Ex $290 Gd $219
Same as standard model, except w/adj. trigger, half-octagon bbl., select wood, stock w/cheekpiece and recoil pad. Made 1972 to 1974.

HI-WALL
SINGLE-SHOT RIFLE. . . . . NiB $310 Ex $234 Gd $177
Falling-block lever-action similar to Winchester 1885 High Wall S.S. Color casehardened investment-cast receiver. Calibers: .222 Rem., .22-250, .243 Rem., 6mm Rem., .25-06, .270 Win., 7mm Rem. Mag., .30-06, .45-70 Govt. 26-inch medium-weight bbl. Weight: 8 lbs. Furnished w/o sights. Checkered walnut pistol-grip stock and Schnabel forearm. Made from 1972 to 1974.

CLIFTON ARMS — Medina, Texas

SCOUT BOLT-ACTION RIFLE
Custom rifle built on the Dakota .76, Ruger .77 or Winchester .70 action. Shilen match-grade barrel cut and chambered to customer's specification. Clifton composite stock fitted and finished to customer's preference. Made from 1992 to 1997.

Cimarron 1883 Burgess Rifle

Cimarron Adobe Walls Falling Block Rifle

Cimarron Sharps Rocky Mountain II Model 74

Cimarron Civil War Henry Rifle

Cimarron 1876 Centennial Sporting Rifle

Cimarron 1892 Carbine

African Scout	NiB $3175	Ex $2690	Gd $2310
Pseudo Scout	NiB $3160	Ex $2211	Gd $1589
Standard Scout	NiB $3122	Ex $2520	Gd $1443
Super Scout	NiB $3145	Ex $2175	Gd $1590

COLT'S MFG. CO., INC. — West Hartford, Connecticut

NOTE: *Add $200 to pre-ban models made prior to 10/13/94.*

AR-15 A2 DELTA
MATCH H-BAR RIFLE . . . . NiB $2300 Ex $1977 Gd $1492
Similar to AR-15A2 Government Model except w/standard stock and heavy refined bbl. Furnished w/3-9x rubber armored scope and removeable cheekpiece. Made from 1986 to 1991.

AR-15 A2 GOVERNMENT
MODEL CARBINE. . . . . NiB $1945 Ex $1044 Gd $813
Caliber: .223 Rem., Five-round magazine. 16-inch bbl. w/flash suppressor. 35 inches overall. Weight: 5.8 lbs. Telescoping aluminum buttstock; sling swivels. Made from 1985 to 1991.

Colt AR-15 A2

Colt AR-15 A2 Delta Match H-BAR

Colt AR-15 A2 Government Model

Colt AR-15 Sporter Competition H-BAR

AR-15 A2 SPORTER II. . . . . . . NiB $1937 Ex $1347 Gd $1136
Same general specifications as standard AR-15 Sporter except heavier bbl., improved pistol-grip. Weight 7.5 lbs.; optional 3x or 4x scope. Made from 1985 to 1989.

AR-15 COMPACT 9MM CARBINE. . . NiB $2255 Ex $1990 Gd $1176
Semiautomatic. Caliber: 9mm NATO. 20-round detachable magazine. Bbl.: 16-inch round. Weight: 6.3 lbs. Adj. rear and front sights. Adj. buttstock. Ribbed round handguard. Made from 1985 to 1986.

Colt Stagecoach

Colteer 1-.22

Colteer .22 Autoloader

Coltsman Deluxe

Coltsman 1957 Standard

AR-15 SEMIAUTOMATIC SPORTER
Commercial version of U.S. M16 rifle. Gas-operated. Takedown. Caliber: .223 Rem. (5.56mm). 20-round magazine w/spacer to reduce capacity to 5 rounds. 20-inch bbl. w/flash suppressor. Sights: Rear peep w/windage adjustment in carrying handle; front adj. for windage. 3x scope and mount optional. Black molded buttstock of high-impact synthetic material, rubber buttplate. Barrel surrounded by handguard of black fiberglass w/heat-reflecting inner shield. Swivels, black web sling strap. Weight: w/o accessories, 6.3 lbs. Made from 1964 to 1994.
Standard Sporter . . . . .NiB $1951 Ex $1447 Gd $1133
w/adj. stock, redesigned
   forearm (disc. 1988), add $227
w/3x scope and mount, add $126

AR-15 SPORTER COMPETITION
H-BAR RIFLE . . . . .NiB $1997 Ex $1126 Gd $766
Similar to AR-15 Sporter Target model except w/integral Weaver-type mounting system on a flat-top receiver. 20-inch bbl. w/counter-bored muzzle and 1:9 rifling twist. Made from 1991 to date.

AR-15 SPORTER
COMPETITION H-BAR (RS) . . . .NiB $2009 Ex $1143 Gd $931
Similar to AR-15 Sporter Competition H-BAR Model except "Range Selected" for accuracy w/3x9 rubber-clad scope w/mount. Carrying handle w/iron sights. Made from 1992 to 1994.

AR-15 SPORTER MATCH TARGET LIGHTWEIGHT
Calibers: .223 Rem., 7.62x39mm, 9mm. Five-round magazine. 16-inch bbl. (non-threaded after 1994). 34.5-35.5 inches overall. Weight: 7.1 lbs. Redesigned stock and shorter handguard. Made from 1991 to 2002.
Standard LW Sporter (except 9mm) . . . . NiB $976 Ex $755 Gd $612
Standard LW Sporter, 9mm . . . . .NiB $1077 Ex $776 Gd $556
.22 LR conversion (disc. 1994), add $200

AR-15 SPORTER TARGET RIFLE
Caliber: .223 Rem. Five-round magazine. 20-inch bbl. w/flash suppressor (non-threaded after 1994). 39 inches overall. Weight: 7.5 lbs. Black composition stock, grip and handguard. Sights: post front; adj. aperture rear. Matte black finish. Made from 1993 to date.
Sporter Target Rifle . . . . .NiB $1244 Ex $1087 Gd $722
.22 LR conversion (disc. 1994), add $227

LIGHTNING MAGAZINE RIFLE – LARGE FRAME
Similar to Medium Frame model except w/large frame to accommodate larger calibers: .38-56, .44-60, .45-60, .45-65, .45-85, or .50-95 Express. Standard 22-inch (carbine & baby carbine) or 28-inch round or octagonal bbl. (rifle). Note: Additional bbl. lengths optional. Weight: 8 to 10.5 lbs. Sights: Open rear; bead or blade front. Walnut stock and checkered forearm. Made 1887 to 1994. (6,496 produced)
Rifle . . . . .NiB $11,765 Ex $7390 Gd $3469
Carbine . . . . .NiB $10,576 Ex $7798 Gd $4479
Baby Carbine . . . . .NiB $14,475 Ex $9077 Gd $5796
.50-95 Express, add 40%

Coltsman 1961 Custom

Coltsman 1961 Standard

Colt-Sauer Grand African

LIGHTNING MAGAZINE RIFLE - MEDIUM FRAME

Slide-action w/12-round tubular magazine Carbine & Baby Carbine) or 15-round tubular magazine (rifle). Calibers: .32-20, .38-40, .44-40. Standard 20-inch (Carbine & Baby Carbine) or 26-inch round or octagonal bbl.(rifle). Note: Additional bbl. lengths optional. Weight: 5.5 lbs. (Baby Carbine), 6.25 lbs. (carbine) or 7 to 9 lbs. (rifle). Sights: Open rear; bead or blade front. Walnut stock and checkered forearm. Blue finish w/color casehardened hammer. Made from 1884 to 1902. (89,777 produced)

Rifle	NiB $6096	Ex $3822	Gd $2274
Carbine	NiB $7778	Ex $4966	Gd $2988
Baby Carbine	NiB $9380	Ex $5246	Gd $4012

Military model w/bayonet
lug & sling swivels . . . . NiB $5250 Ex $3844 Gd $2691

LIGHTNING MAGAZINE RIFLE - SMALL FRAME

Similar to Medium Frame model except w/smaller frame and chambered for .22 caliber only. Standard 24-inch round or octagonal bbl. w/half magazine. Note: Additional bbl. lengths optional. Weight: 6 lbs. Sights: Open rear; bead or blade front. Walnut stock and checkered forearm. Made from 1884 to 1902. (89,912 produced)

Standard Rifle model . . . . NiB $5599 Ex $4125 Gd $2889
W/Deluxe or optional features, add. 25%

STAGECOACH .22 AUTOLOADER . . . . . NiB $395 Ex $298 Gd $200
Same as Colteer .22 Autoloader except w/engraved receiver, saddle ring, 16.5-inch bbl. Weight: 4 lbs., 10 oz. Made from 1965 to 1975.

COLTEER 1-.22 SINGLE-SHOT

BOLT-ACTION RIFLE . . . . NiB $403 Ex $397 Gd $159
Caliber: .22 LR. Long, Short. 20- or 22-inch bbl. Sights: Open rear; ramp front. Pistol-grip stock w/Monte Carlo comb. Weight: 5 lbs. Made from 1957 to 1967.

.22 AUTOLOADER . . . . .NiB $390 Ex $288 Gd $227
Caliber: .22 LR. 15-round tubular magazine. 19.38-inch bbl. Sights: Open rear; hooded ramp front. Straight-grip stock, Western carbine-style forearm w/bbl. band. Weight: 4.75 lbs. Made 1964 to 1975.

CUSTOM BOLT-ACTION

SPORTING RIFLE . . . . .NiB $600 Ex $498 Gd $338
FN Mauser action, side safety, engraved floorplate. Calibers: .30-06, .300 H&H Mag. Five round box magazine. 24-inch bbl., rampfront sight. Fancy walnut stock. Monte Carlo comb, cheekpiece, pistol-grip, checkered, QD swivels. Weight: 7.25 lbs. Made 1957 to 1961.

DELUXE RIFLE . . . . .NiB $977 Ex $798 Gd $569
FN Mauser action. Same as Custom model, except plain floorplate, plainer wood and checkering. Made from 1957-61. Value shown is for rifle as furnished by manufacturer w/o rear sight.

1957 SERIES RIFLES

Sako medium action. Calibers: .243, .308. Weight: 6.75 lbs. Other specifications similar to those of models w/FN actions. Made from 1957 to 1961.

Standard.	NiB $755	Ex $486	Gd $417
Custom	NiB $944	Ex $697	Gd $488
Deluxe.	NiB $944	Ex $697	Gd $488

1961 MODEL

CUSTOM RIFLE . . . . NiB $733 Ex $568 Gd $422
Sako action. Calibers: .222, .222 Mag., .223, .243, .264, .270, .308, .30-06, .300 H&H. 23-, 24-inch bbl. Sights: Folding leaf rear; hooded ramp front. Fancy French walnut stock w/Monte Carlo comb, rosewood forend tip and grip cap skip checkering, recoil pad, sling swivels. Weight: 6.5 - 7.5 lbs. Made from 1963 to 1965.

1961 MODEL,

STANDARD RIFLE . . . . .NiB $744 Ex $578 Gd $432
Same as Custom model except plainer, American walnut stock. Made from 1963 to 1965.

STANDARD RIFLE . . . . .NiB $689 Ex $533 Gd $390
FN Mauser action. Same as Deluxe model except in .243, .30-06, .308, .300 Mag. and stock w/o cheekpiece, bbl. length 22 inches. Made from 1957 to 1961. Value shown is for rifle as furnished by manufacturer w/o rear sight.

COLT-SAUER DRILLINGS *See Colt shotgun listings.*

GRAND AFRICAN . . . . .NiB $2656 Ex $1966 Gd $1049

Colt-Sauer Grand Alaskan

Colt-Sauer Short Action

Cooper Arms Model 22 Pro Varmint

Same specifications as standard model except .458 Win. Mag., weight: 9.5 lbs. Sights: Adj. leaf rear; hooded ramp front. Magnum-style stock of Bubinga. Made from 1973 to 1985.

GRAND ALASKAN . . . . NiB $2606 Ex $1989 Gd $1008
Same specifications as standard model except .375 H&H, weight: 8.5 lbs. Sights: Adj. leaf rear; hooded ramp front. Magnum-style stock of walnut.

MAGNUM . . . . NiB $2506 Ex $1923 Gd $778
Same specifications as standard model except calibers 7mm Rem. Mag., .300 Win. Mag., .300 Weatherby. Weight: 8.5 lbs. Made from 1973 to 1985.

SHORT ACTION. . . . . NiB $2390 Ex $1613 Gd $766
Same specifications as standard model except shorter action chambered for the following calibers: .22-250, .243 Win., .308 Win. and similar length cartridges. Weight: 7.5 lbs.; 8.25 lbs. (.22-250). Drilled and tapped for scope mount. No front or rear open sights. Made from 1973 to 1988.

SPORTING RIFLE,
STANDARD MODEL . . . . NiB $2077 Ex $1405 Gd $766
Sauer 80 non-rotating bolt action. Calibers: .25-06, .270 Win., .30-06. Three-round detachable box magazine. 24-inch bbl. Weight: 7.75 lbs., 8.5 lbs. (.25-06). Furnished w/o sights. American walnut stock w/Monte Carlo cheekpiece, checkered pistol grip and forearm, rosewood forend tip and pistol-grip cap, recoil pad. Made from 1973 to 1988.

COMMANDO ARMS — Knoxville, Tennessee
Formerly Volunteer Enterprises, Inc.
MARK III SEMIAUTOMATIC CARBINE

Blow-back action, fires from closed bolt. Caliber: .45 ACP. 15- or 30-round magazine. 16.5-inch bbl. w/cooling sleeve and muzzle brake. Weight: 8 lbs. Sights: peep rear; blade front. "Tommy Gun" style stock and forearm or grip. Made from 1969 to 1976.
w/horizontal forearm . . . . NiB $510 Ex $399 Gd $277

MARK 9
Same specifications as Mark III and Mark 45 except caliber 9mm Luger. Made from 1976 to 1981.
w/horizontal forearm . . . . NiB $545 Ex $439 Gd $333
w/vertical foregrip . . . . NiB $650 Ex $565 Gd $389

MARK 45
Same specifications as Mark III. Has redesigned trigger housing and magazines. Made from 1976 to 1988.
w/horizontal forearm . . . . NiB $499 Ex $438 Gd $293
w/vertical foregrip . . . . NiB $596 Ex $484 Gd $341

CONTINENTAL ARMS CORP. — New York, NY
Manufactured in Belgium for Continental Arms Corp., New York, New York.

DOUBLE RIFLE
Calibers: .270, .303 Sav., .30-40, .348 Win., .30-06, .375 H&H, .400 Jeffrey, .465, .470, .475 No. 2, .500, .600. Side-by-side. Anson-Deeley reinforced boxlock action w/triple bolting lever work. Two triggers. Non-automatic safety. 24- or 26-inch bbls. Sights: Express rear; bead front. Checkered cheekpiece stock and forend. Weight: From 7 lbs., depending on caliber. Imported from 1956 to 1975.
.270 to .348 Win. . . . . NiB $5077 Ex $3966 Gd $3095
.375 H&H & larger calibers, add. 60%

CZ Model ZKK 600

COOPER FIREARMS OF MONTANA, INC. —
Stevensville, Montana (Previously COOPER ARMS)

MODEL 21
Similar to Model 36C except in calibers .17 Rem., .17 Mach IV, .221 Fireball, .222, .223, 6x45, 6x47. 24-inch stainless or chrome-moly bbl. 43.5 inches overall. Weight: 8.75 lbs. Made from 1994 to date.

21 Benchrest	NiB $1513	Ex $1207	Gd $943
21 Classic	NiB $2223	Ex $1766	Gd $1007
21 Custom Classic	NiB $2178	Ex $1859	Gd $1032
21 Western Classic	NiB $3030	Ex $1956	Gd $1043
21 Varminter	NiB $1408	Ex $976	Gd $800
21 Varmint Extreme	NiB $1944	Ex $1244	Gd $976

MODEL 22
Bolt-action, single-shot. Calibers: .22 BR. .22-250 Rem., .220 Swift, .243 Win., 6mm PPC, 6.5x55mm, 25-06 Rem., 7.62x39mm 26-inch bbl, 45.63 inches overall. Weight: 8 lbs., 12 oz. Single-stage trigger. AAA Claro walnut stock. Made from 1999 to date.

22 Benchrest	NiB $1533	Ex $1377	Gd $1079
22 Classic	NiB $2176	Ex $1312	Gd $755
22 Custom Classic	NiB $1370	Ex $1244	Gd $879
22 Western Classic	NiB $2244	Ex $1359	Gd $954
22 Varminter	NiB $1468	Ex $934	Gd $650
22 Pro-Varmint Extreme	NiB $2011	Ex $1143	Gd $836
22 Black Jack	NiB $1895	Ex $1154	Gd $846

MODEL 36 RF/BR 50
MODEL 36 RF/BR 50 . . . . NiB $1608 Ex $1266 Gd $880
Caliber: .22 LR. Bolt-action. Single-shot. 22-inch bbl. 40.5 inches overall. Weight: 6.8 lbs. No sights. Fully-adj. match-grade trigger. Stainless barrel. McMillan benchrest stock. Three mid-bolt locking lugs. Made from 1993 to 1999.

MODEL 36 CF BOLT-ACTION RIFLE
Calibers: .17 CCM, .22 CCM, .22 Hornet. Four-round mag. 23.75 inch bbl. 42.5 inch overall. Weight: 7 lbs. Walnut or synthetic stock. Made from 1992 to 1994.

Marksman	NiB $1635	Ex $880	Gd $654
Sportsman	NiB $730	Ex $544	Gd $343
Classic Grade	NiB $1863	Ex $1154	Gd $866
Custom Grade	NiB $1744	Ex $937	Gd $665
Custom Classic Grade	NiB $1706	Ex $1266	Gd $876

MODEL 36 RF BOLT-ACTION RIFLE
Similar to Model 36CF except in caliber .22 LR. Five round magazine. Weight: 6.5-7 lbs. Made from 1992 to 1994.

BR-50 (22-inch stainless bbl.)	NiB $1755	Ex $1139	Gd $768
Custom Grade	NiB $1756	Ex $906	Gd $675
Custom Classic Grade	NiB $1670	Ex $951	Gd $688
Featherweight	NiB $1617	Ex $988	Gd $709

MODEL 36 TRP-1 SERIES
Similar to Model 36RF except in target configuration w/ ISU or silhouette-style stock. Made from 1992 to 1993.

TRP-1 (ISU single-shot)	NiB $944	Ex $778	Gd $533
TRP-1S (Silhouette)	NiB $944	Ex $778	Gd $533

MODEL 38 SINGLE SHOT
Similar to Model 36CF except in calibers .17 or .22 CCM w/3-round magazine. Weight: 8 lbs. Walnut or synthetic stock. Made 1992 to 1993.

Standard Sporter	NiB $1544	Ex $1023	Gd $688
Classic Grade	NiB $2239	Ex $1836	Gd $989
Custom Grade	NiB $3035	Ex $1997	Gd $977
Custom Classic Grade	NiB $1570	Ex $1267	Gd $855

MODEL 40 CLASSIC BOLT-ACTION RIFLE
Calibers: .17 CCM, .17 Ackley Hornet, .22 Hornet, .22K Hornet, .22 CCM, 4- or 5-round magazine. 23.75-inch bbl. Checkered oil-finished AAA Claro walnut stock. Made from 1995 to 1996.

Classic	NiB $1644	Ex $1233	Gd $886
Custom Classic	NiB $1844	Ex $1450	Gd $1139
Classic Varminter	NiB $1844	Ex $1450	Gd $1139

CUMBERLAND MOUNTAIN ARMS —
Winchester, Tennessee

PLATEAU RIFLE
Falling block action w/underlever. Calibers: .40-65, and .45-70. 32-inch round bbl. 48 inches overall. Weight: 10.5 lbs. American walnut stock. Bead front sight, adj. buckhorn rear. Blued finish. Lacquer finish walnut stock w/crescent buttplate. Made from 1993 to 1999.

Standard model	NiB $1133	Ex $829	Gd $631
Deluxe model, add			$375

CZ (CESKA ZBROJOVKA), INC. — Uhersk Brod, Moravia, Czech Republic

Formerly Strankonice, Czechoslovakia, currently CZ-USA Kansas City, Kansas, formerly Czechpoint, Inc.

See also listings under Brno Sporting Rifles and Springfield, Inc.

ZKK 600 BOLT-ACTION RIFLE
Calibers: .270 Win., 7x57, 7x64, .30-06. Five round magazine. 23.5-inch bbl. Weight: 7.5 lbs. Adj. folding-leaf rear sight, hooded ramp front. Pistol-grip walnut stock. Imported from 1990 to 1995.

Standard model	NiB $613	Ex $479	Gd $350
Deluxe model	NiB $688	Ex $554	Gd $400

ZKK 601 BOLT-ACTION RIFLE
Similar to Model ZKK 600 except w/short action in calibers .223 Rem., .243 Win., .308 Win. 43 inches overall. Weight: 6 lbs., 13 oz. Checkered walnut pistol-grip stock w/Monte Carlo cheekpiece. Imported from 1990 to 1995.

Standard model	NiB $570	Ex $495	Gd $443
Deluxe model	NiB $641	Ex $567	Gd $423

ZKK 602 BOLT-ACTION RIFLE
Similar to Model ZKK 600 except w/Magnum action in calibers .300 Win. Mag., 8x68S, .375 H&H, .458 Win. Mag. 25-inch bbl. 45.5 inches overall. Weight: 9.25 lbs. Imported from 1990 to 1997.

Standard model	NiB $727	Ex $650	Gd $468
Deluxe model	NiB $896	Ex $744	Gd $505

CA Model ZKM 452 LUX Model

CZ 511

CZ Model ZKM 527

CZ 550 LUX Model

CZ 452 BOLT-ACTION REPEATING RIFLE
Calibers: .22 LR. or .22 WMR. Five, 6- or 10-round magazine. 25-inch bbl. 43.5 inches overall. Weight: 6 lbs. Adj. rear sight, hooded bead front. Oil-finished beechwood or checkered walnut stock w/Schnabel forend. Imported 1995 and 2007.

Standard model (22 LR)	NiB $455	Ex $338	Gd $200
Deluxe model (22 LR)	NiB $455	Ex $338	Gd $200
Varmint model (22 LR)	NiB $458	Ex $370	Gd $215
.22 WMR, add			$50

CZ 527 BOLT-ACTION RIFLE
Calibers: .22 Hornet, .222 Rem., .223 Rem., 7.62x39mm. Five round magazine. 23.5-inch bbl. 42.5 inches overall. Weight: 6.75 lbs. Adj. rear sight, hooded ramp front. Grooved receiver. Adj. double-set triggers. Oil-finished beechwood or checkered walnut stock . Imported 1995.

Standard model	NiB $650	Ex $465	Gd $340
Classic model	NiB $655	Ex $470	Gd $338
Carbine model (shorter configuration)	NiB $600	Ex $466	Gd $345
Deluxe model	NiB $657	Ex $572	Gd $373

CZ 537 SPORTER BOLT-ACTION RIFLE
Calibers: .243 Win., .270 Win., 7x57mm, .308 Win., .30-06. Four or 5-round magazine. 19- or 23.5-inch bbl. 40.25 or 44.75 inches overall. Weight: 7 to 7.5 lbs. Adj. folding leaf rear sight, hooded ramp front. Shrouded bolt. Standard or Mannlicher-style checkered walnut stock. Imported 1995.

Standard model	NiB $529	Ex $460	Gd $345
Mountain Carbine model	NiB $555	Ex $439	Gd $326

CZ-511 SEMI-AUTO RIFLE	NiB $355	Ex $252	Gd $155
Mannlicher model,			add $126

Caliber: .22 LR. 8-round magazine. 22- inch bbl., 38.6 inches

overall. Weight: 5.39 lbs. Receiver top fitted for telescopic sight mounts. Walnut wood-lacquered checkering stock. Imported 1996, 1998 to 2001, 2005 to 2006.

CZ 550 BOLT-ACTION SERIES
Calibers: .243 Win., 6.5x55mm, .270 Win., 7mm Mag., 7x57, 7x64, .30-06, .300 Win Mag., .375 H&H, .416 Rem., .416 Rigby, .458 Win. Mag., 9.3x62. Four or 5-round detachable magazine. 20.5- or 23.6-inch bbl. Weight: 7.25 to 8 lbs. No sights or Express sights on magnum models. Receiver drilled and tapped for scope mount. Standard or Mannlicher-style checkered walnut stock w/buttpad. Imported 1995 to 2000.

Standard	NiB $510	Ex $423	Gd $326
Magnum	NiB $855	Ex $633	Gd $465
Lux	NiB $530	Ex $456	Gd $355
Battue Lux (1998)	NiB $500	Ex $426	Gd $325
Mannlicher	NiB $817	Ex $579	Gd $370
Calibers .416 Rem., .416 Rigby, .458 Win. Mag., add			$100

CZECHOSLOVAKIAN MILITARY RIFLES — Brno, Czechoslovakia

Manufactured by Ceska Zbrojovka.

MODEL 1924 (VZ24)
MAUSER MILITARY RIFLE . . . . NiB $331 Ex $243 Gd $176
Basically same as German Kar., 98k and F.N. (Belgian Model 1924.) Caliber: 7.9mm Mauser. Five round box magazine. 23.25-inch bbl. Weight: 8.5 lbs. Sights: Adj. rear; blade front w/guards. of Belgian-type military stock, full handguard. Made from 1924 thru WWII. Many of these rifles were made for export. As produced during the German occupation, this model was known as Gewehr 24t.

Daisy V/L Collector's Kit

Daisy V/L Standard

MODEL 1933 (VZ33) MAUSER
MILITARY CARBINE . . . . **NiB $380 Ex $300 Gd $227**
Modification of German M/98 action w/smaller receiver ring. Caliber: 7.9mm Mauser. 19.25-inch bbl. Weight: 7.5 lbs. Sights: Adj. rear; blade front w/guards. Military-type full stock. Mfd. 1933 thru WWII. A similar model, produced during the German occupation, was designated Gew. 33/40.

DAEWOO PRECISION INDUSTRIES — Korea
Manufactured in Korea, previously imported by Kimber of America; Daewoo Precision Industries; Nationwide Sports and KBI, Inc.

DR200 SA SEMIAUTOMATIC SPORTER
Caliber: .223 Rem. (5.56mm). Six or 10-round magazine. 18.4-inch bbl. 39.25 inches overall. Weight: 9 lbs. Protected post front sight, fully-adj. aperture rear. Forged aluminum receiver w/rotating locking bolt assembly. Synthetic sporterized thumbhole stock. Imported from 1994 to 1996.
Sporter model. . . . . **NiB $679 Ex $545 Gd $459**
Varmint model . . . . **NiB $650 Ex $579 Gd $356**

DR300 SA SEMIAUTOMATIC
SPORTER . . . . **NiB $670 Ex $602 Gd $421**
Similar to Model Daewoo DR200 except chambered for 7.62x39mm. Imported from 1994 to 1996.

DAISY — Rogers, Arkansas
Daisy V/L rifles carry the first and only commercial caseless cartridge system. These rifles are expected to appreciate considerably in future years. The cartridge, no longer made, is also a collector's item.

Production was discontinued following BATF ruling the V/L model to be a firearm.

COLLECTOR'S KIT . . . . **NiB $590 Ex $427 Gd $304**
Presentation-grade rifle w/gold plate inscribed w/owner's name and gun serial number mounted on the stock. Also includes a special gun case, pair of brass gun cradles for wall-hanging, 300 rounds of 22 V/L ammunition and a certificate signed by Daisy president Cass S. Hough. Approx. 1,000 manufactured from 1968 to 1969.

PRESENTATION
GRADE . . . . **NiB $347 Ex $296 Gd $245**
Same specifications as standard model except w/walnut stock. Approx. 4,000 manufactured from 1968 to 1969.

STANDARD RIFLE . . . . **NiB $269 Ex $224 Gd $175**
Single-shot under-lever action. Caliber: .22 V/L (caseless cartridge, propellant ignited by jet of hot air). 18-inch bbl. Weight: 5 lbs. Sights: Adj. open rear, ramp w/blade front. Wood-grained Lustran stock (foam-filled). About 19,000 manufactured from 1968 to 1969.

DAKOTA ARMS, INC. — Sturgis, South Dakota
Currently owned by Freedom Arms Inc.

MODEL 10 SINGLE-SHOT RIFLE
Chambered for most commercially-loaded calibers. 23-inch bbl. 39.5 inches overall. Weight: 5.5 lbs. Top tang safety. No sights. Checkered pistol-grip buttstock and semi-beavertail forearm, QD swivels, rubber recoil pad. Made from 1992 to date.
Standard calibers . . . . **NiB $4679 Ex $3066 Gd $1977**
Deluxe model, add. **$1,375**

Dakota Model 10 Single-Shot Rifle

Dakota Arms Model 76
African Grade

Dakota Arms Model 76
Classic Grade

Dakota Arms Model 97
Hunter

MODEL 22 BOLT-ACTION
SPORTER RIFLE . . . . NiB $2735 Ex $1217 Gd $823
Calibers: .22 LR. .22 Hornet. Five round magazine. 22-inch bbl.
Weight: 6.5 lbs. Adj. trigger. Checkered classic-style Claro or English
walnut stock w/black recoil pad. Made from 2003 to 2004.

MODEL 76 AFRICAN
BOLT-ACTION RIFLE . . . . NiB $7998 Ex $4056 Gd $2597
Same general specifications as Model 76 Safari. Calibers: .404 Jeffery, .416
Rigby, .416 Dakota, .450 Dakota. 24-inch bbl. Weight: 8 lbs. Checkered
select walnut stock w/two cross bolts. "R" prefix on ser. nos.
Intro. 1989.

MODEL 76 ALPINE
BOLT-ACTION RIFLE . . . . NiB $5634 Ex $2789 Gd $2009
Same general specifications as Model 76 Classic except short action w/
blind magazine. Calibers: .22-250, .243, 6mm Rem., .250-3000, 7mm-08,
.308. 21-inch bbl. Weight: 7.5 lbs. Made from 1989 to 1992.

MODEL 76 CLASSIC
BOLT-ACTION RIFLE . . . . NiB $5629 Ex $3467 Gd $2240
Calibers: .257 Roberts, .270 Win., .280 Rem., .30-06, 7mm Rem. Mag.,
.300 Win. Mag., .338 Win. Mag., .375 H&H Mag., .458 Win. Mag.
21- or 23-inch bbl. Weight: 7.5 lbs. Receiver drilled and tapped for
sights. Adj. trigger. Classic-style checkered walnut stock w/steel grip cap and solid
recoil pad. Right- and left-hand models. Made from 1987 to date.

MODEL 76 LONGBOW TACTICAL
BOLT-ACTION RIFLE . . . . NiB $4466 Ex $3459 Gd $2390
Calibers: .300 Dakota Mag., .330 Dakota Mag., .338 Lapua Mag.
Blind magazine. Ported 28-inch bbl. 50 to 51 inches overall. Weight:
13.7 lbs. Black or oliver green fiberglass stock w/adj. cheekpiece and
buttplate. Receiver drilled and tapped w/one-piece rail mount and no
sights. Made from 1997 to 2009.

MODEL 76 SAFARI
BOLT-ACTION RIFLE . . . . . . NiB $7533 Ex $5416 Gd $2307
Calibers: .300 Win. Mag., .338 Win. Mag., .375 H&H Mag. .458 Win.
Mag. 23-inch bbl. w/bbl. band swivel. Weight: 8.5 lbs. Ramp front
sight, standing leaf rear. Checkered fancy walnut stock w/ebony forend
tip and solid recoil pad. Made from 1987 to date.

MODEL 76 TRAVELER SERIES RIFLES
Threadless take-down action w/interchangeable bbl. capability based on the
Dakota 76 design. Calibers: .257 through .458 Win (Standard-Classic & Safari)
and .416 Dakota, .404 Jeffery, .416 Rigby, .338 Lapua and .450 Dakota Mag. (E/F
Family-African Grade). 23- to 24- inch bbl. Weight: 7.5 to 9.5 lbs. Right or left-
hand action. X grade (Classic) or XXX grade (Safari or African) oil finish English
Bastogne or Claro walnut stock. Made from 1999 to date.

Classic Grade	NiB $6644	Ex $5428	Gd $2380
Safari Grade	NiB $8577	Ex $6502	Gd $2866
African Grade	NiB $9233	Ex $7544	Gd $3209
Interchangeable bbl. assemblies			
Standard calibers, add			$2500
Safari calibers, add			$2700
African calibers, add			$2970

MODEL 76 VARMINT
BOLT-ACTION RIFLE . . . . NiB $2710 Ex $1988 Gd $1165
Similar to Model 76 Classic except single-shot action w/ heavy bbl.
chambered for .17 Rem. to 6mm PPC. Weight: 13.7 lbs. Checkered
walnut or synthetic stock. Receiver drilled and tapped for scope mounts
and no sights. Made from 1994 to 1998.

MODEL 97 HUNTER BOLT-ACTION SERIES
Calibers: .22-250 Rem. to .330 Dakota Mag.(Lightweight), .25-06 to
.375 Dakota Mag. (Long Range). 22-, 24- or 26-inch bbl. 43 to 46
inches overall. Weight: 6.16 lbs. to 7.7 lbs.

Black composite fiberglass stock w/recoil pad. Fully adj. match trigger. Made from 1997 to 2004.

Lightweight . . . . NiB $2744 Ex $1675 Gd $944
Long Range . . . . NiB $3440 Ex $2475 Gd $1755

MODEL 97 VARMINT HUNTER

BOLT-ACTION RIFLE . . . . NiB $3734 Ex $2566 Gd $1896
Similar to Model 97 Hunter except single-shot action w/ heavy bbl. chambered .22-250 Rem. to .308 Win. Checkered walnut stock. Receiver drilled and tapped for scope mounts and no sights. Made from 1998 to 2004.

CHARLES DALY — Harrisburg, Pennsylvania

Imported by K.B.I., Inc., Harrisburg, PA; previously by Outdoor Sports Headquarters, Inc.

EMPIRE GRADE BOLT-ACTION RIFLE (RF)
Similar to Superior Grade except w/checkered California walnut stock w/rosewood grip cap and forearm cap. High polished blued finish and damascened bolt. Made from 1998. Disc.

Empire Grade (.22 LR) . . . . NiB $370 Ex $324 Gd $223
Empire Grade (.22WMR) . . . . NiB $406 Ex $322 Gd $235
Empire Grade (.22 Hornet) . . . . . . NiB $556 Ex $444 Gd $320

FIELD GRADE BOLT-ACTION RIFLE (RF)
Caliber: .22 LR. 16.25-, 17.5- or 22.63-inch bbl. 32 to 41 inches overall. Single-shot (True Youth) and 6- or 10-round magazine. Plain walnut-finished hardwood or checkered polymer stock. Blue or stainless finish. Imported from 1998. Disc.

Field Grade (Standard w/22.63-inch bbl.) . NiB $157 Ex $128 Gd $95
Field Grade (Youth w/17.5-inch bbl.) . . . . NiB $170 Ex $139 Gd $99
Field Grade (True Youth
  w/16.25-inch bbl.) . . . . NiB $188 Ex $155 Gd $131
Field Grade (Polymer w/stainless action) . NiB $158 Ex $130 Gd $100

FIELD GRADE HUNTER BOLT-ACTION RIFLE
Calibers: .22 Hornet, .223 Rem., .243 Win., .270 Win., 7mm Rem. Mag. .308 Win., .30-06, .300 Win. Mag., .300 Rem. Ultra Mag., .338 Win. Mag. Three, 4-, or 5-round magazine. 22- or 24-inch bbl. w/o sights. Weight: 7.2 to 7.4 lbs. Checkered walnut or black polymer stock. Receiver drilled and tapped. Blue or stainless finish. Imported from 1998. Disc.

Field Grade Hunter (walnut stock) . . . . . NiB $572 Ex $457 Gd $339
Field Grade Hunter (polymer stock) . . . . NiB $589 Ex $478 Gd $339
w/Left-hand model, add $35

HAMMERLESS DRILLING
See listing under Charles Daly shotguns.

HORNET RIFLE. . . . . NiB $1299 Ex $1088 Gd $759
Same as Herold Rifle. See listing of that rifle for specifications. imported during the 1930s. Disc.

MAUSER 98
Calibers: .243 Win., .270 Win., 7mm Rem. Mag. .308 Win., .30-06, .300 Win. Mag., .375 H&H, or .458 Win. Mag. Three, 4-, or 5-round magazine. 23-inch bbl. 44.5 inches overall. Weight: 7.5 lbs. Checkered European walnut (Superior) or fiberglass/graphic (Field) stock w/recoil pad. Ramped front sight, adj. rear. Receiver drilled and tapped w/side saftey. Imported from 1998. Disc.

Field Grade (standard calibers) Disc. . . . . NiB $466 Ex $423 Gd $155
Field Grade (375 H&H
  and 458 Win. Mag.) . . . . NiB $669 Ex $572 Gd $354
Superior Grade (standard calibers) Disc. . NiB $669 Ex $572 Gd $454
Superior Grade (magnum calibers) Disc. . NiB $903 Ex $766 Gd $641

MINI-MAUSER 98
Similar to Mauser 98 except w/19.25-inch bbl. chambered for .22 Hornet, .22-250 Rem., .223 Rem., or 7.62x39mm. Five round magazine. Imported from 1998. Disc.

Field Grade . . . . NiB $409 Ex $358 Gd $233
Superior Grade . . . . NiB $533 Ex $447 Gd $259

SUPERIOR GRADE BOLT-ACTION RIFLE
Calibers: .22 LR. .22 WMR, .22 Hornet. 20.25- to 22.63-inch bbl. 40.5 to 41.25 inches overall. Five, 6-, or 10-round magazine. Ramped front sight, adj. rear w/grooved receiver. Checkered walnut stock. Made from 1998. Disc.

Superior Grade (.22 LR) . . . . NiB $179 Ex $150 Gd $100
Superior Grade (.22WMR) . . . . NiB $244 Ex $190 Gd $145
Superior Grade (.22 Hornet) . . . . . NiB $399 Ex $345 Gd $239

SEMIAUTOMATIC RIFLE
Caliber: .22 LR. 20.75-inch bbl. 40.5 inches overall. 10-round magazine. Ramped front sight, adj. rear w/grooved receiver. Plain walnut-finished hardwood stock (Field), checkered walnut (Superior), checkered polymer stock or checkered California walnut stock w/rosewood grip cap and forearm cap (Empire). Blue or stainless finish. Imported from 1998. Disc.

Field Grade . . . . NiB $145 Ex $126 Gd $85
Field Grade (Polymer
  w/stainless action) . . . . NiB $161 Ex $136 Gd $92
Superior Grade . . . . NiB $215 Ex $188 Gd $132
Empire Grade . . . . NiB $355 Ex $290 Gd $200

BOLT ACTION RIFLE . . . . NiB $922 Ex $659 Gd $560
Calibers: .22 Hornet. Bbl.: 24 inches. Five round box magazine, hinged floorplate. Sights: Ramp front, leaf rear. Walnut stock, checkered grip and forearm. Early version rifle, introduced 1931 by Franz Jaeger Co. Discontinued 1939. Imported by Charles Daly but same model was imported by A. F. Stoeger as Herold Rifle.

SUPERIOR
COMBINATION GUN. . . . . . . NiB $1354 Ex $1149 Gd $1013
Calibers: 12-guage shotgun over .22 Hornet, .223 Remington, .22-250, .243 Win., .270 Win., or .30-06. Barrels: 23 1/2 inches. Shotgun choked Imp. Cyl. Weight: About 7.5 pounds. Checkered walnut, pistol grip, semi-beavertail forend. Silvered, engraved receiver. Chrome-moly steel barrels, double triggers, extractors. Gold bead front sight. Introduced 1997, imported by K.B.I.

EMPIRE COMBINATION GUN . . NiB $1743 Ex $1540 Gd $1179
Similar to Superior Combination Gun but with fancy grade wood, European style comb and cheekpiece, slimmer forend. Introduced 1997, imported by K.B.I.

FIELD GRADE AUTO RIFLE. . . . . . . NiB $167 Ex $109 Gd $94
Calibers: .22 LR. Semiautomatic, 10-round magazine, shell deflector. Bbl.: 20 3/4 inches. Weight: 6.5 pounds. Overall length: 40.5 inches. Stock: Hardwood, walnut-finished, Monte Carlo style. Sights: Hooded front, adjustable open rear. Grooved for scope mounting. Blued finish. Introduced 1998. Imported by K. B. I.

EMPIRE GRADE AUTO RIFLE . . . NiB $210 Ex $166 Gd $135
Similar to Field Grade Auto Rifle but with select California walnut stock, hand checkering. Contrasting forend and grip caps. Damascened bolt, high-polish blued finish. Introduced 1998; discontinued.

TRUE YOUTH
BOLT-ACTION RIFLE . . . . NiB $156 Ex $100 Gd $75
Caliber: .22 LR. Single-shot, bolt-action. Bbl.: 16.25 inches. Weight: 3 pounds. Overall length: 32 inches. Walnut-finished hardwood stock. Sights: Blade front, adjustable rear. Blued finish. Introduced 1998. Imported by K. B. I.

RIFLES

EMF AP-74 Semiautomatic

DPMS FIREARMS — St. Cloud, MN

Previously in Becker, MN; previously called DPMS, Inc. (Defense Procurement Manufacturing Facilities); currently owned by The Freedom Group.

PANTHER CARBINE . . . . NIB **$830** EX **$450** GD **$410**
Semi-automatic AR15 platform. Caliber: .223 Rem. 30-round magazine. 16-in. heavy bbl. w/A2 flash hider, A3 flat top upper, A2 pistol grip, Pardus collapsible buttstock. Weight: 7.1 lbs. Made 1993 to date.
6.8mm Carbine (2006-2011) . . . . NiB **$880** Ex **$600** Gd **$520**
6.8mm SPCII Hunter (2011-2012) . NiB **$1050** Ex **$730** Gd **$630**
7.62x39mm Carbine (2000-2011) NiB **$730** Ex **$480** Gd **$430**
A2 "The Agency" (16-in. bbl., Surefire flashlight, EOTech sight,
   2007-2012) . . . . NiB **$1730** Ex **$650** Gd **$580**
A2 Tactical (16-in. heavy bbl., A2 handguard,
   2004-2013) . . . . NiB **$740** Ex **$480** Gd **$430**
AP4 (16-in. M4 contour bbl., fixed M4 buttstock
   2004-2012) . . . . NiB **$630** Ex **$480** Gd **$380**
DCM (20-in. heavy stainless bbl.,
   1998-2003; 2006-2012) . . . . . . NiB **$970** Ex **$600** Gd **$520**
Lo-Pro Classic (16-in. heavy bbl., A2 buttstock,
   flat top upper, 2002-2012) . . . . . NiB **$650** Ex **$450** Gd **$400**
Pardus (16-in. heavy stainless bbl., aluminum free float handguard,
   adj. stock, 2006-2008) . . . . NiB **$1350** Ex **$800** Gd **$680**
Race Gun (24-in. stainless bbl., Hot Rod handguard,
   IronStone stock, 2001-2008) . . . NiB **$1450** Ex **$950** Gd **$840**
SDM-R (20-in. heavy bbl., aluminum free float handguard,
   Harris bipod, 2007-2008) . . . . . NiB **$1180** Ex **$830** Gd **$730**
Tuber (16-in. heavy bbl., aluminum free float handguard,
   flat top upper, 2002-2008) . . . . . NiB **$650** Ex **$450** Gd **$400**

PANTHER .22 . . . . NIB **$780** EX **$550** GD **$480**
Similar to Panther model except chambered in .22 LR w/16-in. heavy bbl. Weight: 7.85 lbs. Made 2003 to 2008.
AP4 (16-in. M4 contour bbl.,
   2004-2008) . . . . NiB **$750** Ex **$500** Gd **$470**
DCM (20-in. fluted bbl.,
   2004-2008) . . . . NiB **$850** Ex **$550** Gd **$480**

PANTHER LR-.308 . . . . NIB **$1200** EX **$650** GD **$580**
Similar to Panther model except chambered in .308 Win. w/24-in. free float heavy bbl. Weight: 11.25 lbs. Made 2003 to date.
LR-.308B (18-in. bbl., 2003-12) . . NiB **$995** Ex **$650** Gd **$580**
LR-.308T (24-in. bbl., 7.62x51mm NATO,
   2004-2012) . . . . NiB **$995** Ex **$650** Gd **$580**
LR-.308 AP4 (20-in. bbl., 7.62x51mm NATO,
   2003-2012) . . . . NiB **$1100** Ex **$730** Gd **$600**
LR-.308C (20-in. bbl., 7.62x51mm NATO, A3 flat top w/handle
   2003-2012) . . . . NiB **$1050** Ex **$730** Gd **$600**

PANTHER LR-30S . . . . NiB **$1050** Ex **$730** Gd **$600**
Similar to Panther LR-.308 model except chambered in .300 RSUM w/20-in. free float heavy bbl. Made 2004 to 2008.

PANTHER LR-243 . . . . NiB **$1280** Ex **$730** Gd **$600**
Similar to Panther LR-.308 model except chambered in .243 Win. w/20-in. free float heavy bbl. Made 2006 to 2013.

PANTHER CSAT TACTICAL . . . NiB **$1500** EX **$830** GD **$730**
Similar to Panther model except chambered in 5.56x45mm NATO. w/16-in. bbl., Magpul buttstock and psitol grip. Weight: 7.8 lbs. Made 2010 to 2012.

PANTHER RAPTR . . . . NiB **$1400** EX **$850** GD **$730**
Similar to Panther model except chambered in 5.56x45mm NATO. w/16-in. bbl., Crimson Trace laser, Ergo Z-Rail, AP4 buttstock Weight: 8.2 lbs. Made 2010 to 2011.

PANTHER REPR . . . . NiB **$2590** Ex **$1400** Gd **$1200**
Similar to Panther LR-.308 model except w/18- or 20-in. free float fluted heavy bbl., Magpul stock, Hogue rubber pistol grip, Gem Tech flash hider. Made 2009 to date.

PRAIRIE PANTHER . . . . NiB **$1240** EX **$750** GD **$580**
Similar to Panther model except w/20-in. heavy fluted free floated bbl. Weight: 8.75 lbs. Made 1993 to 1999; 2010 to date.

EAGLE ARMS INC. — Geneseo, Illinois
Previously Coal Valley, Illinois.
In 1995, Eagle Arms Inc., became a division of ArmaLite and reintroduced that logo. For current ArmaLite production see models under that listing.

MODEL EA-15 CARBINE
Caliber: .223 Rem. (5.56mm). 30-round magazine. 16-inch bbl. and collapsible buttstock. Weight: 5.75 lbs. (E1); 6.25 lbs. (E2 w/heavy bbl. & National Match sights). Made 1990 to 1995; reintro. 2002 to 2005.
E1 Carbine . . . . NiB **$976** Ex **$739** Gd **$510**
E2 Carbine . . . . NiB **$976** Ex **$739** Gd **$510**

MODEL EA-15 GOLDEN
EAGLE MATCH RIFLE . . . . NiB **$1244** Ex **$977** Gd **$657**
Same general specifications as EA-15 Standard, except w/E2-style National Match sights. 20-inch Douglas Heavy Match bbl. NM trigger and bolt-carrier group. Weight: 12.75 lbs. Made 1991 to 1995, reintro. 2002.

MODEL EA-15
SEMIAUTOMATIC RIFLE . . . . NiB **$1221** Ex **$722** Gd **$504**
Same as EA-15 Carbine except 20-inch bbl., 39 inches overall and weighs 7 lbs. Made from 1990 to 1993; reintro. 2002 to 2005.

Erma EG712

Erma EGM1

Erma EM1 22

EMF COMPANY, INC. — Santa Ana, California

MODEL AP-74
SEMI-AUTOMATIC CARBINE ... NiB $397 Ex $300 Gd $221
Calibers: .22 LR or .32 ACP, 15-round magazine. 20-inch bbl. w/flash reducer. 38 inches overall. Weight: 6.75 lbs. Protected pin front sight; protected rear peep sight. Lightweight plastic buttstock; ventilated snap-out forend. Importation disc. 1989.

MODEL AP74-W
SPORTER CARBINE. . . . . NiB $419 Ex $321 Gd $213
Sporterized version of AP-74 w/wood buttstock and forend. Importation disc. 1989.

MODEL AP74 PARATROOPER . . NiB $433 Ex $260 Gd $242
Same general specifications as Model AP74-W except w/folding tubular buttstock. Made in .22 LR. only. Importation disc. 1987.

MODEL 1860 HENRY RIFLE
Calibers: .44-40 and .45 LC. 24.25-inch bbl.; upper-half octagonal w/ magazine tube in one-piece steel. 43.75-inches overall. Weight: 9.25 lbs. Varnished American walnut wood stock. Polished brass frame and brass buttplate. Original rifle was patented by B. Tyler Henry and produced by the New Haven Arms Company, when Oliver Winchester was president. Imported 1987 to 2008.
Deluxe model. . . . . NiB $968 Ex $688 Gd $347
Engraved model . . . . NiB $1123 Ex $832 Gd $560

MODEL 1866
YELLOW BOY RIFLE. . . . . NiB $754 Ex $558 Gd $359
Calibers: .44-40, .45 LC and .38 Special. Lever-action. Bbl: 24 inches, 43 inches overall. Bead front sight. Offered w/blued finish, walnut stock and brass frame 2005 to 2008.

MODEL 1866 YELLOW BOY CARBINE
Same features as 1866 Yellow Boy Rifle except carbine.
Standard carbine . . . . NiB $933 Ex $465 Gd $333

Engraved carbine . . . . NiB $933 Ex $465 Gd $333

MODEL 1873 SPORTING RIFLE
Calibers: .22 LR. .22 WMR, .357 Mag., .44-40 and .45 LC. 24.25-inch octagonal bbl. 43.25 inches overall. Weight: 8.16 lbs. Color casehardened frame w/blued steel magazine tube. Walnut stock and forend.
Standard Rifle. . . . . .NiB $922 Ex $707 Gd $459
Engraved Rifle. . . . . .NiB $1007 Ex $657 Gd $482
Boy's Rifle (Youth Model, .22 LR) . . . . . .NiB $674 Ex $558 Gd $369

MODEL 1873 SPORTING RIFLE CARBINE
Same features as 1873 sporting rifle except w/19-inch bbl. Overall length: 38.25 inches. Weight: 7.38 lbs. Color casehardened or blued frame. Made 1988 to 1989.
Standard carbine . . . . .NiB $904 Ex $689 Gd $466

ERMA-WERKE — Dachau, Germany

Previously imported by Precision Sales International; Nygord Precision Products; Mandall's Shooting Supplies.

MODEL EG72
PUMP-ACTION REPEATER . . . . . . .NiB $158 Ex $110 Gd $98
Visible hammer. Caliber: .22 LR. 15-round magazine. 18.5-inch bbl. Weight: 5.25 lbs. Sights: open rear; hooded ramp front. Receiver grooved for scope mounting. Straight-grip stock, grooved slide handle. Imported from 1970 to 1976.

MODEL EG73. . . . . .NiB $288 Ex $223 Gd $172
Same as Model EG712 except chambered for .22 WMR w/12-round tubular magazine, 19.3-inch bbl. Imported from 1973 to 1997.

MODEL EG712 LEVER-ACTION
REPEATING CARBINE. . . . . NiB $297 Ex $229 Gd $167
Styled after Winchester Model 94. Caliber: .22 LR. Long, Short. Tubul33 magazine holds 15 LR, 17 Long, 21 Short. 18.5-inch bbl. Weight: 5.5 lbs. Sights: Open rear; hooded ramp front. Receiver grooved for scope mounting. Western carbine-style stock and forearm w/bbl. band. Imported 1976

F.N. Model 1949

F.N. Model 1950 Mauser

F.N. Deluxe Mauser

F.N. Supreme Mauser

F.N. FAL Semiautomatic

to 1997. Note: A similar carbine of Erma manufacture is marketed in U.S. as Ithaca Model 72 Saddle Gun.

MODEL EGM1 . . . . **NiB $290 Ex $247 Gd $180**
Same as Model EM1 except w/unslotted buttstock, ramp front sight, 5-round magazine standard. Imported from 1970 to 1995.

MODEL EM1 .22
SEMIAUTOMATIC CARBINE . . . . . **NiB $387 Ex $320 Gd $222**
Styled after U.S. Carbine cal. 30 M1. Caliber: .22 LR. 10- or 15-round magazine. 18-inch bbl. Weight: 5.5 lbs. Carbine-type sights. Receiver grooved for scope mounting. Military stock/handguard. Imported 1966 to 1997.

EUROPEAN AMERICAN ARMORY — Sharpes, Florida

MODEL HW 660 BOLT-ACTION
SINGLE-SHOT RIFLE . . . . **NiB $909 Ex $745 Gd $495**

Caliber: .22 LR. 26.8-inch bbl., 45.7 inches overall. Weight: 10.8 lbs. Match-type aperture rear sight; Hooded ramp front. Stippled walnut stock. Imported from 1992 to 1996.

MODEL HW BOLT-ACTION
SINGLE-SHOT TARGET RIFLE . . . . **NiB $895 Ex $740 Gd $485**
Same general specification as Model HW 660 except equipped w/ target stock. Imported from 1995 to 1996.

MODEL SABITTI SP1822
Caliber: .22 LR. 10-round detachable magazine. 18.5 inch bbl. 37.5 inches overall. Weight: 5.25 to 7.15 lbs. No sights. Hammer-forged heavy non-tapered bbl. Scope-mounted rail. Flush-mounted magazine release. Alloy receiver w/non-glare finish. Manual bolt lock. Wide claw extractor. Blowback action. Cross-trigger safety. Imported 1994 to 1996.
Traditional Sporter model . . . . **NiB $259 Ex $206 Gd $149**
Thumbhole Sporter
  model (synthetic stock) . . . . **NiB $379 Ex $312 Gd $221**

FABRIQUE NATIONALE HERSTAL — Herstal & Liege, Belgium
Formerly Fabrique Nationale d'Armes de Guerre.

MODELS 1924, 1934/30 AND
1930 MAUSER MILITARY RIFLES . **NiB $445 Ex $337 Gd $241**
Similar to German Kar. 98k w/straight bolt handle. Calibers: 7mm, 7.65mm and 7.9mm Mauser. Five round box magazine. 23.5-inch bbl. Weight: 8.5 lbs. Sights: Adj. rear; blade front. Military stock of M/98 pattern w/slight modification. Model differences are minor. Also produced in a short carbine model w/17.25-inch bbl. Note: These rifles were manufactured under contract for Abyssinia, Argentina, Belgium, Bolivia, Brazil, Chile, China, Colombia, Ecuador, Iran, Luxembourg, Mexico, Peru, Turkey, Uruguay and Yugoslavia. Such arms usually bear the coat of arms of the country for which they were made together with the contractor's name and date of manufacture. Also sold commercially and exported to all parts of the world. MODEL 1949 SEMIAUTOMATIC

MILITARY RIFLE . . . . NiB $799 Ex $647 Gd $328
Gas-operated. Calibers: 7mm, 7.65mm, 7.92mm, .30-06. 10-round box magazine, clip fed or loaded singly. 23.2-inch bbl. Weight: 9.5 lbs. Sights: Tangent rear-shielded post front. Pistol-grip stock, handguard. Note: Adopted by Belgium in 1949; also by Belgian Congo, Brazil, Colombia, Luxembourg, Netherlands, East Indies, and Venezuela. Approx. 160,000 were made.

MODEL 1950 MAUSER
MILITARY RIFLE . . . . .NiB $533 Ex $360 Gd $287
Same as previous F.N. models of Kar. 98k type except chambered for .30-06.

DELUXE MAUSER BOLT-ACTION
SPORTING RIFLE . . . . .NiB $799 Ex $689 Gd $443
American calibers: .220 Swift, .243 Win., .244 Rem., .250/3000, .257 Roberts, .270 Win., 7mm, .300 Sav., .308 Win. .30-06. European calibers: 7x57, 8x57JS, 8x60S, 9.3x62, 9.5x57, 10.75x68mm. Five round box magazine. 24-inch bbl. Weight: 7.5-8.25 lbs. American model is standard w/hooded ramp front sight and Tri-Range rear; Continental model w/two-leaf rear. Checkered stock w/cheekpiece, pistol-grip, swivels. Made from 1947 to 1963.

DELUXE MAUSER —
PRESENTATION GRADE . . . . . .NiB $1337 Ex $1096 Gd $752
Same as regular model except w/select grade stock; engraving on receiver, trigger guard, floorplate and bbl. breech. Disc. 1963.

FAL/FNC/LAR SEMIAUTOMATIC
Same as standard FAL military rifle except w/o provision for automatic firing. Gas-operated. Calibers: 7.62mm NATO (.308 Win.) or 5.56mm (.223 Rem.). 10- or 20-round box magazine. 25.5-inch bbl. (including flash hider). Weight: 9 lbs. Sights: Post front; aperture rear. Fixed wood or folding buttstock, pistol-grip, forearm/handguard w/carrying handle and sling swivels. Disc. 1988.
F.N. FAL/LAR model (Light
  Automatic Rifle) . . . . NiB $2594 Ex $2216 Gd $1402
F.N. FAL/HB model (heavy bbl.) . . . . NiB $2955 Ex $2343 Gd $1644
F.N. FAL/PARA (Paratrooper). . . . . . NiB $3566 Ex $2886 Gd $1854
F.N. FNC Carbine
  model (.223 cal.) . . . . NiB $2715 Ex $1954 Gd $1294
F.N. FNC Carbine model w/flash
  suppresser (.223 cal.) . . . . . . NiB $2790 Ex $2033 Gd $1387

SUPREME MAUSER BOLT-ACTION
SPORTING RIFLE . . . . .NiB $808 Ex $865 Gd $443
Calibers: .243, .270, 7mm, .308, .30-06. Four round magazine in .243 and .308; 5-round in other calibers. 22-inch bbl. in .308; 24-inch in other calibers. Sights: Hooded ramp front, Tri-Range peep rear. Checkered stock w/ Monte Carlo cheekpiece, pistol-grip, swivels. Weight: 7.75 lbs. Made from 1957 to 1975.

SUPREME MAGNUM MAUSER . . . . NiB $865 Ex $689 Gd $474
Calibers: .264 Mag., 7mm Mag., .300 Win. Mag. Specifications same as for standard caliber model except 3-round magazine capacity.

FEATHER INDUSTRIES, INC. — Boulder, Colorado

See MITCHELL ARMS for current production.

MODEL AT-9 SEMIAUTOMATIC RIFLE
Caliber: 9mm Parabellum. 10-, 25-, 32-, or 100-round magazine. 17-inch bbl. 35 inches overall (extended). Hooded post front sight, adj. aperture rear. Weight: 5 lbs. Telescoping wire stock w/composition pistol-grip and barrel-shroud handguard. Matte black finish. Made from

1988 to 1995.
Model AT-9 . . . . .NiB $898 Ex $714 Gd $479
w/32-round magazine, add $100
w/100-round drum magazine, add. $300

MODEL AT-22 . . . . .NiB $355 Ex $232 Gd $171
Caliber: .22 LR. 20-round magazine. 17-inch bbl. 35 inches overall (extended). Hooded post front sight; adj. aperture rear. Weight: 3.25 lbs. Telescoping wire stock w/composition pistol-grip and barrel shroud handguard. Matte black finish.

MODEL F2 SA CARBINE . . . . .NiB $331 Ex $258 Gd $149
Similar to AT-22, except w/fixed Polymer stock and pistol-grip. Made from 1992 to 1995.

MODEL F9 SA CARBINE . . . . .NiB $758 Ex $599 Gd $400
Similar to AT-9, except w/fixed Polymer stock and pistol-grip. Made from 1992 to 1995.

FINNISH LION — Jyväkylylä, Finland
Manufactured by Valmet Oy, Tourula Works.

CHAMPION FREE RIFLE . . . . .NiB $688 Ex $545 Gd $390
Bolt-action single-shot target rifle. Double-set trigger. Caliber: .22 LR. 28.75-inch heavy bbl. Weight: 16 lbs. Sights: Extension rear peep; aperture front. Walnut free-rifle stock w/full pistol-grip, thumbhole, beavertail forend, hook buttplate, palm rest, hand stop, swivel. Made from 1965 to 1972.

STANDARD ISU
TARGET RIFLE . . . . .NiB $421 Ex $337 Gd $213
Bolt-action, single-shot. Caliber: .22 LR. 27.5-inch bbl. Weight: 10.5 lbs. Sights: extension rear peep; aperture front. Walnut target stock w/full pistol-grip, checkered beavertail forearm, adj. buttplate, sling swivel. Made from 1966 to 1977.

MATCH RIFLE . . . . .NiB $569 Ex $510 Gd $343
Bolt-action, single-shot. Caliber: .22 LR. 28.75-inch heavy bbl. Weight: 14.5 lbs. Sights: Extension rear peep; aperture front. Walnut free-rifle stock w/full pistol-grip, thumbhole, beavertail forearm, hook buttplate, palm rest, hand stop, swivel. Made from 1937 to 1972.

STANDARD TARGET RIFLE
Bolt-action, single-shot. Caliber: .22 LR. 27.5-inch bbl. 44.5 inches overall. Weight: 10.5 lbs. No sights; micrometer rear and globe front International-style sights available. Select walnut stock in target configuration. Made 1966 to 1997..
Standard model . . . . NiB $808 Ex $679 Gd $448
Thumbhole stock model . . . . NiB $893 Ex $733 Gd $533
Deluxe model. . . . . NiB $439 Ex $350 Gd $259

LUIGI FRANCHI, S.P.A. — Brescia, Italy

CENTENNIAL AUTOMATIC RIFLE
Commemorates Franchi's 100th anniversary (1868-1968). Centennial seal engraved on receiver. Semiautomatic. Take-down. Caliber: .22 LR. 11-round magazine in buttstock. 21-inch bbl. Weight: 5.13 lbs. Sights: Open rear; gold bead front on ramp. Checkered walnut stock and forend. Deluxe model w/ fully engraved receiver, premium grade wood. Made in 1968.
Standard model . . . . NiB $433 Ex $321 Gd $224
Engraved model . . . . NiB $478 Ex $379 Gd $270

Finnish Lion Champion

Finnish Lion Match

FRANCOTTE — Leige, Belgium
Imported by Armes de Chasse, Hertford, NC; previously by Abercrombie & Fitch.

BOLT-ACTION RIFLE
Custom rifle built on Mauser style bolt action. Available in three action lengths. Calibers: .17 Bee to .505 Gibbs. Barrel length: 21- to 24.5-inches. Weight: 8 to 12 lbs. Stock dimensions, wood type and style to customer's specifications. Engraving, appointments and finish to customer's preference. Note: Deduct 25% for models w/o engraving.
Short action . . . . NiB $9770 Ex $7725 Gd $4690
Standard action . . . . NiB $7859 Ex $6233 Gd $3834
Magnum Francotte action . . . . NiB $14,000 Ex $11,770 Gd $7690

BOXLOCK MOUNTAIN RIFLE
Custom single-shot rifle built on Anson & Deeley style boxlock or Holland & Holland style sidelock action. 23- to 26-inch barrels chambered to customer's specification. Stock dimensions, wood type and style to customer's specifications. Engraving, appointments and finish to customer's preference. Note: Deduct 30% for models w/o engraving.
Boxlock . . . . NiB $14,299 Ex $12,200 Gd $7800
Sidelock. . . . . NiB $22,438 Ex $17,950 Gd $12,206

DOUBLE RIFLE
Custom side-by-side rifle. Built on Francotte system boxlock or back-action sidelock. 23.5- to 26-inch barrels chambered to customer's specification. Stock dimensions, wood type and style to customer's specifications. Engraving, appointments and finish to customer's preference. Note: Deduct 30% for models w/o engraving.
Boxlock . . . . NiB $26,750 Ex $16,875 Gd $10,270
Sidelock. . . . . NiB $31,760 Ex $26,900 Gd $16,975

FRENCH MILITARY RIFLE — Saint Etienne, France

MODEL 1936
MAS MILITARY RIFLE . . . . NiB $209 Ex $170 Gd $103

Bolt-action. Caliber: 7.5mm MAS. Five-round box magazine. 22.5-inch bbl. Weight: 8.25 lbs. Sights: Adj. rear; blade front. Two-piece military-type stock. Bayonet carried in forend tube. Made from 1936 to 1940 by Manufacture Francaise d'Armes et de Cycles de St. Etienne (MAS).

GALIL — Israel
Manufactured by Israel Military Industries, Israel. Not currently imported, previously imported by UZI America Inc., North Haven, CT; previously by Action Arms, Springfield Armory and Magnum Research, Inc.

AR SEMIAUTOMATIC RIFLE
Calibers: .308 Win. (7.62 NATO), .223 Rem. (5.56mm). 25-round (.308) or 35-round (.223) magazine. 16-inch (.223) or 18.5-inch (.308) bbl. w/flash suppressor. Weight: 9.5 lbs. Folding aperture rear sight, post front. Folding metal stock w/carrying handle. Imported 1982 to 1994. Currently select fire models available to law enforcement only.
Model .223 AR. . . . . NiB $3233 Ex $1998 Gd $1200
Model .308 AR. . . . . NiB $3233 Ex $1998 Gd $1200
Model .223 ARM . . . . NiB $3227 Ex $2290 Gd $1669
Model .308 ARM . . . . NiB $3227 Ex $2290 Gd $1669

SPORTER SEMIAUTOMATIC RIFLE . . . NiB $1723 Ex $1009 Gd $707
Same general specifications as AR Model except w/hardwood thumbhole stock and 5-round magazine. Weight: 8.5 lbs. Imported 1991 to 1994.

GARCIA CORPORATION — Teaneck, New Jersey

BRONCO 22 SINGLE-SHOT RIFLE . . . . . . NiB $151 Ex $112 Gd $88
Swing-out action. Takedown. Caliber: .22 LR, Long, Short. 16.5-inch bbl. Weight: 3 lbs. Sights: Open rear-blade front. One-piece stock and receiver, crackle finish. Intro. 1967. Discontinued.

Franchi Deluxe Centennial

Francotte Sidelock Double Rifle

Galil .223 AR Semiautomatic Rifle

Francotte Boxlock Mountain Rifle w/
claw mounts and scope

GERMAN MILITARY RIFLES — Germany

Manufactured by Ludwig Loewe & Co., Berlin, other contractors and by German arsenals and various plants under German government control.

MODEL 24T (GEW. 24T) MAUSER RIFLE . . **NiB $598 Ex $443 Gd $300**
Same general specifications as Czech Model 24 (VZ24) Mauser Rifle w/minor modification and laminated wood stock. Weight: 9.25 lbs. Made in Czechoslovakia during German occupation; adopted 1940.

MODEL 29/40 (GEW. 29/40)
MAUSER RIFLE . . . . **NiB $433 Ex $329 Gd $244**
Same general specifications as Kar. 98K w/minor differences. Made in Poland during German occupation; adopted 1940.

MODEL 33/40 (GEW. 33/40)
MAUSER RIFLE . . . . **NiB $1030 Ex $799 Gd $515**
Same general specifications as Czech Model 33 (VZ33) Mauser Carbine w/minor modifications and laminated wood stock as found in war-time Model 98K carbines. Made in Czechoslovakia during German occupation; adopted 1940.

MODELS 41 AND 41-W (GEW. 41, GEW. 41-W)
SEMIAUTOMATIC MILITARY RIFLES
Gas-operated, muzzle cone system. Caliber: 7.9mm Mauser. Ten-round box magazine. 22.5-inch bbl. Weight: 10.25 lbs. Sights: Adj. leaf rear; blade front. Military-type stock w/semi-pistol grip, plastic handguard. Note: Model 41 lacks bolt release found on Model 41-W; otherwise, the models are the same. These early models were mfd. in Walther's

Zella-Mehlis plant. Made c.1941 to 1943.
Model 41 . . . . **NiB $4460 Ex $3588 Gd $2510**
Model 41-W . . . . **NiB $3488 Ex $2789 Gd $1809**

MODEL 43 (GEW. 43, KAR. 43)
SEMIAUTO MILITARY RIFLES . . . . **NiB $1399 Ex $1125 Gd $848**
Gas-operated, bbl. vented as in Russian Tokarev. Caliber: 7.9mm Mauser. 10-round detachable box magazine. 22- or 24-inch bbl. Weight: 9 lbs. Sights: Adj. rear; hooded front. Military-type stock w/ semi-pistol-grip, wooden handguard. Note: These rifles are alike except for minor details, have characteristic late WWII mfg. short cuts: cast receiver and bolt cover, stamped steel parts, etc. Gew. 43 may have either 22- or 24-inch bbl. The former length was standardized in late 1944, when weapon designation was changed to "Kar. 43." Made from 1943 to 1945.

MODEL 1888 (GEW. 88) MAUSER-
MANNLICHER SERVICE RIFLE . . . . **NiB $433 Ex $265 Gd $221**
Bolt-action w/straight bolt handle. Caliber: 7.9mm Mauser (8x57mm). Five round Mannlicher box magazine. 29-inch bbl. w/jacket. Weight: 8.5 lbs. Fixed front sight, adj. rear. Military-type full stock. Mfd. by Ludwig Loewe & Co., Haenel, Schilling and other contractors.

MODEL 1888 (KAR. 88) MAUSER-
MANNLICHER CARBINE . . . . **NiB $337 Ex $249 Gd $245**
Same general specifications as Gew. 88 except w/18-inch bbl., w/o jacket, flat turned-down bolt handle, weight: 6.75 lbs. Mfd. by Ludwig Loewe & Co., Haenel, Schilling and other contractors.

Golden Eagle Model 7000

Carl Gustaf Model 2000

Carl Gustaf Deluxe

Carl Gustaf Grand Prix

Carl Gustaf Sporter

MODEL 1898 (GEW. 98)
MAUSER MILITARY RIFLE.......NiB $572 Ex $434 Gd $270
Bolt action with straight bolt handle. Caliber: 7.9mm Mauser (8x57mm). Five round box magazine. 29-inch stepped bbl. Weight: 9 lbs. Sights: Blade front; adj. rear. Military-type full stock w/rounded bottom pistol grip. Adopted 1898.

MODEL 1898A (KAR. 98A)
MAUSER CARBINE...........NiB $521 Ex $433 Gd $329
Same general specifications as Model 1898 (Gew.98) Rifle except has turned-down bolt handle, smaller receiver ring, light 23.5-inchstraight taper bbl., front sight guards, sling is attached to left side of stock, weight: 8 lbs. Note: Some of these carbines are marked "Kar. 98;" the true Kar. 98 is the earlier original M/98 carbine w/17-inch bbl. and is rarely encountered.

MODEL 1898B (KAR. 98B)
MAUSER CARBINE............NiB $475 Ex $397 Gd $294
Same general specifications as Model 1898 (Gew.98) Rifle except has turned-down bolt handle and sling attached to left side of stock. This is post-WWI model.

MODEL 1898K (KAR. 98K)
MAUSER CARBINE............NiB $515 Ex $423 Gd $320
Same general specifications as Model 1898 (Gew.98) Rifle except has turned-down bolt handle, 23.5-inch bbl., may have hooded front sight, sling attached to left side of stock, weighs about 8.5 lbs. Adopted in 1935, this was the standard German service rifle of WWII. Note: Late-war models had stamped sheet steel trigger guards and many of the Model 98K carbines made during WWII had laminated wood stocks These weigh .5 to .75 pound more than the previous Model 98K. Value shown is for earlier type.

MODEL VK 98
PEOPLE'S RIFLE ("VOLKSGEWEHR") NiB $290 Ex $233 Gd $166
Kar. 98K-type action. Caliber: 7.9mm. Single-shot or repeater (latter w/ rough hole-in-the-stock 5-round "magazine" or fitted w/10-round clip of German Model 43 semiauto rifle). 20.9-inch bbl. Weight: 7 lbs. Fixed V-notch rear sight dovetailed into front receiver ring; front blade welded

Hammerli Model 45

Hammerli-Tanner 300M

to bbl. Crude, unfinished, half-length stock w/o buttplate. Last ditch weapon made in 1945 for issue to German civilians. Note: Of value only as a military arms collector's item, this hastily-made rifle should be regarded as unsafe to shoot.

GÉVARM — Saint Etienne, France
Manufactured by Gevelot.

E-1 AUTOLOADING RIFLE . . . . . . NiB $234 Ex $190 Gd $150
Caliber: .22 LR. Eight-round clip magazine. 19.5-inch bbl. Sights: Open rear; post front. Pistol-grip stock and forearm of French walnut.

GOLDEN EAGLE — Houston, Texas
Manufactured by Nikko Firearms Ltd., Tochigi, Japan.

MODEL 7000 GRADE I AFRICAN . . . . . NiB $743 Ex $578 Gd $468
Same as Grade I Big Game except: Caliber: .375 H&H Mag. and .458 Win. Mag. Two-round magazine in .458, weight: 8.75 lbs. in .375 and 10.5 lbs. in .458, furnished w/sights. Imported 1976 to 1981.

MODEL 7000 BIG GAME SERIES
Bolt action. Calibers: .22-250, .243 Win., .25-06, .270 Win., Weatherby Mag., 7mm Rem. Mag., .30-06, .300 Weatherby Mag., .300 Win. Mag., .338 Win. Mag. Magazine capacity: 4 rounds in .22-250, 3 rounds in other calibers. 24- or 26-inch bbl. (26-inch only in 338). Weight: 7 lbs., .22-250; 8.75, lbs., other calibers. Furnished w/o sights. Fancy American walnut stock, skip checkered, contrasting wood forend tip and grip cap w/gold eagle head, recoil pad. Imported 1976 to 1981.
Grade I . . . . NiB $722 Ex $630 Gd $455
Grade II . . . . NiB $755 Ex $689 Gd $479

GREIFELT & CO. — Suhl, Germany

**SPORT MODEL 22 HORNET
BOLT-ACTION RIFLE . . . . NiB $2388 Ex $1907 Gd $1412**
Caliber: .22 Hornet. Five round box magazine. 22-inch Krupp steel bbl. Weight: 6 lbs. Sights: Two-leaf rear; ramp front. Walnut stock, checkered pistol-grip and forearm. Made before WWII.

CARL GUSTAF — Eskilstuna, Sweden
Manufactured by Carl Gustaf Stads Gevärsfaktori.

MODEL 2000 BOLT-ACTION RIFLE
Calibers: .243, 6.5x55, 7x64, .270, .308 Win., .30-06, 7mm Rem. Mag., .300 Win. Mag. Three round magazine. 24-inch bbl. 44 inches overall. Weight: 7.5 lbs. Receiver drilled and tapped. Hooded ramp front sight, open rear. Adj. trigger. Checkered European walnut stock w/ Monte Carlo cheekpiece and Wundhammer palmswell grip. Imported 1991 to 1995
w/o sights. . . . . NiB $1443 Ex $1235 Gd $879
w/sights . . . . NiB $1790 Ex $1390 Gd $1009
LUXE . . . . NiB $1744 Ex $1689 Gd $1035

DELUXE . . . . NiB $707 Ex $579 Gd $522
Same specifications as Monte Carlo Standard. Calibers: 6.5x55, 308 Win., .30-06, 9.3x62. Four round magazine in 9.3x62. Jeweled bolt. Engraved floorplate and trigger guard. Deluxe French walnut stock w/ rosewood forend tip. Imported 1970 to 1977.

**GRAND PRIX SINGLE-SHOT
TARGET RIFLE . . . . NiB $577 Ex $459 Gd $202**
Special bolt action with "world's shortest lock time." Single-stage trigger adjusts down to 18 oz. Caliber: .22 LR. 26.75-inch heavy bbl. w/adj. trim weight. Weight: 9.75 lbs. Furnished w/o sights. Target-type Monte Carlo stock of French walnut, adj. cork buttplate. Imported from 1970 to 1977.

**MONTE CARLO STANDARD
BOLT-ACTION SPORTING RIFLE . . . . . . NiB $507 Ex $422 Gd $370**
Carl Gustaf 1900 action. Calibers: 6.5x55, 7x64, .270 Win., 7mm Rem. Mag., .308 Win., .30-06, 9.3x62. Five round magazine, except 4-round in 9.3x62 and 3-round in 7mm Rem. Mag. 23.5-inch bbl. Weight: 7 lbs. Sights: Folding leaf rear; hooded ramp front. French walnut Monte Carlo stock w/cheekpiece, checkered forearm and pistol grip, sling swivels. Also available in left-hand model. Imported from 1970 to 1977.

SPECIAL . . . . NiB $575 Ex $401 Gd $376
Also designated "Grade II" in U.S. and "Model 9000" in Canada. Same specifications as Monte Carlo Standard. Calibers: .22-250, .243 Win., .25-06, .270 Win., 7mm Rem. Mag., .308 Win., .30-06, .300 Win. Mag. Three round magazine in magnum calibers. Select wood stock w/rosewood forend tip. Left-hand model avail. Imported from 1970 to 1977.

Harrington & Richardson
Model 60 Reising

Harrington & Richardson
Model 65 Military

Harrington & Richardson
Model 150 Leatherneck

SPORTER . . . . **NiB $512 Ex $355 Gd $291**
Also designated "Varmint-Target" in U.S. Fast bolt action w/large Bakelite bolt knob. Trigger pull adjusts down to 18 oz. Calibers: .222 Rem., .22-250, .243 Win., 6.5x55. Five round magazine except 6-round in .222 Rem. 26.75-inch heavy bbl. Weight: 9.5 lbs. Furnished w/o sights. Target-type Monte Carlo stock of French walnut. Imported from 1970 to 1977.

STANDARD . . . . **NiB $512 Ex $355 Gd $291**
Same specifications as Monte Carlo Standard. Calibers: 6.5x55, 7x64, .270 Win., .308 Win., .30-06, 9.3x62. Classic-style stock w/o Monte Carlo. Imported from 1970 to 1977.

TROFÉ . . . . **NiB $588 Ex $479 Gd $382**
Also designated "Grade III" in U.S. and "Model 8000" in Canada. Same specifications as Monte Carlo Standard. Calibers: .22-250, .25-06, 6.5x55, .270 Win., 7mm Rem. Mag., .308 Win., .30-06, .300 Win. Mag. Three round magazine in magnum calibers. Furnished w/o sights. Fancy wood stock w/rosewood forend tip, high-gloss lacquer finish. Imported from 1970 to 1977.

C.G. HAENEL — Suhl, Germany

'88 MAUSER SPORTER . . . . **NiB $813 Ex $508 Gd $380**
Same general specifications as Haenel Mauser-Mannlicher except w/ Mauser 5-round box magazine.

MAUSER-MANNLICHER
BOLT-ACTION SPORTING RIFLE **NiB $821 Ex $572 Gd $400**
Mauser M/88-type action. Calibers: 7x57, 8x57, 9x57mm. Mannlicher clip-loading box magazine, 5-round. 22- or 24-inch half or full octagon bbl. w/ raised matted rib. Double-set trigger. Weight: 7.5 lbs. Sights: Leaf-type open rear; ramp front. Sporting stock w/cheekpiece, checkered pistol-grip, raised side-panels, Schnabel tip, swivels.

HÄMMERLI AG JAGD-UND-SPORTWAFFENFABRIK — Lenzburg, Switzerland
Imported by Sigarms, Exeter, NH; previously by Hammerli USA; Mandall Shooting Supplies, Inc. & Beeman Precision Arms.

MODEL 45 SMALLBORE BOLT-ACTION
SINGLE-SHOT MATCH RIFLE . . . . **NiB $765 Ex $654 Gd $453**
Calibers: .22 LR. 22 Extra Long. 27.5-inch heavy bbl. Weight: 15.5 lbs. Sights: Micrometer peep rear; globe front. Free-rifle stock w/cheekpiece, full pistol-grip, thumbhole, beavertail forearm, palmrest, Swiss-type buttplate, swivels. Made from 1945 to 1957.

MODEL 54 SMALLBORE
MATCH RIFLE . . . . **NiB $709 Ex $544 Gd $423**
Bolt-action, single-shot. Caliber: .22 LR. 27.5-inch heavy bbl. Weight: 15 lbs. Sights: Micrometer peep rear; globe front. Free-rifle stock w/ cheekpiece, thumbhole, adj. hook buttplate, palm rest, swivel. Made from 1954 to 1957.

MODEL 508 FREE RIFLE . . . . **NiB $707 Ex $546 Gd $413**
Bolt-action, single-shot. Caliber: .22 LR. 27.5-inch heavy bbl. Weight: 15 lbs. Sights: Micrometer peep rear; globe front. Free-rifle stock w/ cheekpiece, thumbhole, adj. hook buttplate, palm rest, swivel. Made from 1957 to 1962.

MODEL 506 SMALLBORE MATCH RIFLE. . . **NiB $769 Ex $650 Gd $439**
Bolt-action, single-shot. Caliber: .22 LR. 26.75-inch heavy bbl. Weight: 16.5 lbs. Sights: Micrometer peep rear; globe front. Free-rifle stock w/ cheekpiece, thumbhole adj. hook buttplate, palmrest, swivel. Made from 1963 to 1966.

MODEL OLYMPIC 300 METER BOLT-ACTION
SINGLE-SHOT FREE RIFLE . . . . **NiB $905 Ex $755 Gd $556**
Calibers: .30-06, .300 H&H Magnum for U.S.A.; ordinarily produced in 7.5mm, other calibers available on special order. 29.5-inch heavy bbl.

Harrington & Richardson
Model 155

Harrington & Richardson
Model 157

Harrington & Richardson
Model 158 Topper Jet

Harrington & Richardson
Model 158C w/extra shotgun barrel

Double-pull or double-set trigger. Sights: Micrometer peep rear, globe front. Free-rifle stock w/cheekpiece, full pistol grip, thumbhole, beavertail forend, palmrest, Swiss-type buttplate, swivels. Made 1945 to 1959.

TANNER 300 METER FREE RIFLE. . . . NiB $937 Ex $740 Gd $534
Bolt-action, single-shot. Caliber: 7.5mm standard, available in most popular centerfire calibers. 29.5-inch heavy bbl. Weight: 16.75 lbs. Sights: Micrometer peep rear; globe front. Free-rifle stock w/cheekpiece, thumbhole, adj. hook buttplate, palmrest, swivel. Intro. 1962. Disc. See Illustration previous page.

HARRINGTON & RICHARDSON, INC. —
Gardner, Massachusetts
Currently H&R 1872, formerly Harrington & Richardson Arms Co. of Worcester, Mass. One of the oldest and most distinguished manufacturers of handguns, rifles and shotguns, H&R suspended operations on January 24, 1986. In 1987, New England Firearms was established as an independent company producing selected H&R models under the NEF logo. In 1991, H&R 1871, Inc. was formed from the residual of the parent company and that took over the New England Firearms facility. H&R 1871 produced firearms under both its logo and the NEF brand name until 1999, when the Marlin Firearms Company acquired the assets of H&R 1871. Marlin was purchased by the Freedom Group Inc. in 2008.

MODEL 60 REISING SEMI-
AUTOMATIC RIFLE . . . . NiB $1266 Ex $899 Gd $598

Caliber: .45 Automatic. 12- and 20-round detachable box magazines. 18.25-inch bbl. Weight: 7.5 lbs. Sights: Open rear; blade front. Plain pistol-grip stock. Made from 1944 to 1946.

MODEL 65 MILITARY
AUTOLOADING RIFLE . . . . . . NiB $496 Ex $322 Gd $208
Also called "General." Caliber: .22 LR. 10-round detachable box magazine. 23-inch heavy bbl. Weight: 9 lbs. Sights: Redfield 70 rear peep, blade front w/protecting "ears." Plain pistol-grip stock, "Garand" dimensions. Made from 1944 to 1946. Note: This model was used as a training rifle by the U.S. Marine Corps.

MODEL 150
LEATHERNECK AUTOLOADER . . . . NiB $338 Ex $234 Gd $110
Caliber: .22 LR. only. Five round detachable box magazine. 22-inch bbl. Weight: 7.25 lbs. Sights: Open rear; blade front, on ramp. Plain pistol-grip stock. Made from 1949 to 1953.

MODEL 151 . . . . NiB $338 Ex $234 Gd $110
Same as Model 150 except w/Redfield 70 rear peep sight.

MODEL 155
SINGLE-SHOT RIFLE. . . . . NiB $279 Ex $178 Gd $126
Model 158 action. Calibers: .44 Rem. Mag., .45-70 Govt. 24- or 28-inch bbl. (latter in .44 only). Weight: 7 or 7.5 lbs. Sights: Folding leaf rear; blade front. Straight-grip stock, forearm w/bbl. band, brass cleaning rod. Made from 1972 to 1982.

Harrington & Richardson
Model 171

Harrington & Richardson
Model 171 Deluxe

Harrington & Richardson
Model 172

Harrington & Richardson
Model 173

Harrington & Richardson
Model 174 Little Big Horn Commemorative

Harrington & Richardson
Model 178

MODEL 157
SINGLE-SHOT RIFLE. . . . . NiB $333 Ex $154 Gd $121
Model 158 action. Calibers: .22 WMR, .22 Hornet, .30-30. 22-inch bbl.
Weight: 6.25 lbs. Sights: Folding leaf rear; blade front. Pistol-grip stock,
full-length forearm, swivels. Made from 1976 to 1986.

MODEL 158 TOPPER JET SINGLE-SHOT COMBINATION RIFLE
Shotgun-type action w/visible hammer, side lever, auto ejector. Caliber:

.22 Rem. Jet. 22-inch bbl. (interchanges with .30-30, .410 ga., 20 ga.
bbls.). Weight: 5 lbs. Sights: Lyman folding adj. open rear; ramp front.
Plain pistol-grip stock and forearm, recoil pad. Made from 1963 to
1967.
Rifle only. . . . . NiB $250 Ex $171 Gd $126
Interchangeable bbl.
    .30-30, shotgun, add $75

Harrington & Richardson
Model 300

Harrington & Richardson
Model 301 Carbine

Harrington & Richardson
Model 317P

Harrington & Richardson
Model 330

Harrington & Richardson
Model 360 Ultra

Harrington & Richardson
Model 370 Ultra Medalist

MODEL 158C . . . .**NiB $250 Ex $171 Gd $126**
Same as Model 158 Topper Jet except calibers .22 Hornet, .30-30, .357
Mag., .357 Mag., .44 Mag. Straight-grip stock. Made 1963 to 1986.

**MODEL 163 MUSTANG
SINGLE-SHOT RIFLE** . . . . **NiB $250 Ex $168 Gd $124**
Same as Model 158 Topper except w/gold-plated hammer and trigger,
straight-grip stock and contoured forearm. Made 1964 to 1967.

**MODEL 165
LEATHERNECK AUTOLOADER** . . . . **NiB $250 Ex $170 Gd $126**
Caliber: .22 LR. 10-round detachable box magazine. 23-inch bbl.
Weight: 7.5 lbs. Sights: Redfield 70 rear peep; blade front, on ramp.

Plain pistol-grip stock, swivels, web sling. Made from 1945 to 1961.

MODEL 171   **NiB $633 Ex $466 Gd $257**
Model 1873 Springfield Cavalry Carbine replica. Caliber: .45-70.
22-inch bbl. Weight: 7 lbs. Sights: Leaf rear; blade front. Plain walnut
stock. Made from 1972 to 1981.

MODEL 171 DELUXE . . . .**NiB $776 Ex $523 Gd $309**
Same as Model 171 except engraved action and different sights. Made
from 1972-86. See illustration next page.

MODEL 172 . . . .**NiB $759 Ex $588 Gd $454**
Same as Model 171 Deluxe except silver-plated, w/fancy walnut stock,

GRADING: **NiB** = New in Box   **Ex** = Excellent or NRA 95%   **Gd** = Good or NRA 68%

253

Harrington & Richardson
Model 700 Deluxe

Harrington & Richardson
Model 750 Pioneer

Harrington & Richardson
"New" Model 750

Harrington & Richardson
Model 755

checkered, w/grip adapter; tang-mounted aperture sight. Made from 1972 to 1986.

MODEL 173 . . . . NiB $1663 Ex $963 Gd $538
Model 1873 Springfield Officer's Model replica, same as 100th Anniversary Commemorative except w/o plaque on stock. Made from 1972 to 1986.

MODEL 174 . . . . NiB $1266 Ex $1009 Gd $633
Little Big Horn Commemorative Carbine. Same as Model 171 Deluxe except w/tang-mounted aperture sight, grip adapter. Made from 1972 to 1984.

MODEL 178 . . . . NiB $735 Ex $422 Gd $328
Model 1873 Springfield Infantry Rifle replica. Caliber: .45-70. 32-inch bbl. Weight: 8 lbs. 10 oz. Sights: Leaf rear; blade front. Full-length stock w/bbl. bands, swivels, ramrod. Made 1973 to 1986.

**MODEL 250 SPORTSTER BOLT-ACTION
REPEATING RIFLE** . . . . NiB $220 Ex $111 Gd $80
Caliber: .22 LR. Five-round detachable box magazine. 23-inch bbl. Weight: 6.5 lbs. Sights: Open rear; blade front, on ramp. Plain pistol-grip stock. Made from 1948 to 1961.

MODEL 251 . . . . NiB $255 Ex $128 Gd $90
Same as Model 250 except w/Lyman No. 55H rear sight.

**MODEL 265 "REG'LAR" BOLT-
ACTION REPEATING RIFLE** . . . . . . NiB $337 Ex $140 Gd $98
Caliber: .22 LR. 10-round detachable box magazine. 22-inch bbl. Weight: 6.5 lbs. Sights: Lyman No. 55 rear peep; blade front, on ramp. Plain pistol-grip stock. Made from 1946 to 1949.

**MODEL 300 ULTRA
BOLT-ACTION RIFLE** . . . . NiB $572 Ex $521 Gd $302
Mauser-type action. Calibers: .22-250, .243 Win., .270 Win., .30-06, .308 Win., 7mm Rem. Mag., .300 Win. Mag. Three round magazine in 7mm and .300 Mag. calibers, 5-round in others. 22- or 24-inch bbl. Sights: Open rear; ramp front. Checkered stock w/rollover cheekpiece and full pistol grip, contrasting wood forearm tip and pistol grip, rubber buttplate, sling swivels. Weight: 7.25 lbs. Made 1965 to 1982.

MODEL 301 CARBINE . . . . NiB $523 Ex $412 Gd $287
Same as Model 300 except w/18-inch bbl., Mannlicher-style stock, weighs 7.25 lbs.; not available in caliber .22-250. Made 1967 to 1982.

Harrington & Richardson
Model 760

Harrington & Richardson
Model 866

Harrington & Richardson
Model 1873 — 100th Anniversary

Harrington & Richardson
Model 5200 Sporter

Harrington & Richardson
Ultra Varmint

MODEL 308 AUTOMATIC RIFLENiB $531 Ex $390 Gd $277
Original designation of the Model 360 Ultra. Made 1965 to 1967.

MODEL 317 ULTRA WILDCAT
BOLT-ACTION RIFLE . . . . NiB $650 Ex $495 Gd $380
Sako short action. Calibers: .17 Rem. 17/.223 (handload), .222 Rem., .223 Rem. Six round magazine. 20-inch bbl. No sights, receiver dovetailed for scope mounts. Checkered stock w/cheekpiece and full pistol grip, contrasting wood forearm tip and pistol-grip cap, rubber buttplate. Weight: 5.25 lbs. Made from 1968 to 1976.

MODEL 317P
PRESENTATION GRADE . . . . . . .NiB $710 Ex $546 Gd $488
Same as Model 317 except w/select grade fancy walnut stock w/basket weave carving on forearm and pistol-grip. Made from 1968 to 1976.

MODEL 330 HUNTER'S RIFLE . . .NiB $439 Ex $326 Gd $244
Similar to Model 300, but w/plainer stock. Calibers: .243 Win., .270 Win., .30-06, .308 Win., 7mm Rem. Mag., .300 Win. Mag. Weight: 7.13 lbs. Made from 1967 to 1972.

MODEL 333 . . . . .NiB $439 Ex $326 Gd $244
Plainer version of Model 300 w/uncheckered walnut-finished hardwood stock. Calibers: 7mm Rem. Mag. and .30-06. 22-inch bbl. Weight: 7.25 lbs. No sights. Made in 1974.

MODEL 340 . . . . .NiB $450 Ex $341 Gd $259
Mauser-type action. Calibers: .243 Win., .308 Win., .270 Win., .30-06, 7x57. 22-inch bbl. Weight: 7.25 lbs. Hand-checkered American walnut stock. Made from 1982 to 1984.

MODEL 360
ULTRA AUTOMATIC RIFLE . . . . . .NiB $534 Ex $380 Gd $300
Gas-operated semiautomatic. Calibers: .243 Win., .308 Win. Three round detachable box magazine. 22-inch bbl. Sights: Open rear; ramp front. Checkered stock w/rollover cheekpiece, full pistol grip, contrasting wood forearm tip and pistol-grip cap, rubber buttplate, sling swivels. Weight: 7.25 lbs. Made from 1967 to 1978.

MODEL 361 . . . . .NiB $556 Ex $439 Gd $333
Same as Model 360 except w/full rollover cheekpiece for right- or left-

hand shooters. Made from 1970 to 1973.

MODEL 369 ACE BOLT-ACTION
SINGLE-SHOT RIFLE . . . .**NiB $178 Ex $140 Gd $96**
Caliber: .22 LR. 22-inch bbl. Weight: 6.5 lbs. Sights: Lyman No. 55 rear peep, blade front, on ramp. Plain pistol-grip stock. Made 1946 to 1947.

MODEL 370 ULTRA MEDALIST . .**NiB $555 Ex $423 Gd $320**
Varmint and target rifle based on Model 300. Calibers: .22-250, .243 Win., 6mm Rem. Three round magazine. 24-inch varmint weight bbl. No sights. Target-style stock w/semibeavertail forearm. Weight: 9.5 lbs. Made from 1968 to 1973.

MODEL 422 SLIDE-ACTION
REPEATER . . . . **NiB $375 Ex $234 Gd $141**
Caliber: .22 LR. Long, Short. Tubular magazine holds 21 Short, 17 Long, 15 LR. 24-inch bbl. Weight: 6 lbs. Sights: Open rear; ramp front. Plain pistol-grip stock grooved slide handle. Made 1956 to 1958.

MODEL 450 . . . .**NiB $403 Ex $221 Gd $130**
Same as Model 451 except w/o front and rear sights.

MODEL 451 MEDALIST
BOLT-ACTION TARGET RIFLE . . .**NiB $433 Ex $222 Gd $130**
Caliber: .22 LR. Five round detachable box magazine. 26-inch bbl. Weight: 10.5 lbs. Sights: Lyman No. 524F extension rear; Lyman No. 77 front, scope bases. Target stock w/full pistol-grip and forearm, swivels and sling. Made from 1948 to 1961.

MODEL 465 TARGETEER SPECIAL
BOLT-ACTION REPEATER. . . . . . .**NiB $423 Ex $233 Gd $144**
Caliber: .22 LR. 10-round detachable box magazine. 25-inch bbl. Weight: 9 lbs. Sights: Lyman No. 57 rear peep; blade front, on ramp. Plain pistol-grip stock, swivels, web sling strap. Made from 1946 to 1947.

MODEL 707
AUTOLOADER. . . . .**NiB $456 Ex $321 Gd $188**
Caliber: .22 WMR. Five-round magazine. 22-inch bbl. Weight: 6.5 lbs. Sights: Folding leaf rear; blade front, on ramp. Monte Carlo-style stock of American walnut. Made from 1977 to 1986.

MODEL 707 DELUXE . . . .**NiB $508 Ex $381 Gd $285**
Same as Model 707 Standard except w/select custom polished and blued finish, select walnut stock, hand checkering, and no iron sights. Fitted w/H&R Model 432 4x scope. Made from 1980 to 1986.

MODEL 750 PIONEER BOLT-ACTION
SINGLE-SHOT RIFLE. . . . .**NiB $145 Ex $104 Gd $80**
Caliber: .22 LR, Long, Short. 22- or 24-inch bbl. Weight: 5 lbs. Sights: Open rear; bead front. Plain pistol-grip stock. Made from 1954 to 1981; redesigned 1982; disc. 1985.

MODEL 751 SINGLE-SHOT RIFLE. . . . . . .**NiB $170 Ex $95 Gd $77**
Same as Model 750 except w/Mannlicher-style stock. Made in 1971.

MODEL 755 SAHARA
SINGLE-SHOT RIFLE. . . . .**NiB $166 Ex $90 Gd $67**
Blow-back action, automatic ejection. Caliber: .22 LR, Long, Short. 18-inch bbl. Weight: 4 lbs. Sights: Open rear; military-type front. Mannlicher-style stock. Made from 1963 to 1971.

MODEL 760 SINGLE-SHOT . . . . . .**NiB $188 Ex $100 Gd $80**
Same as Model 755 except w/conventional sporter stock. Made from

1965 to 1970.

MODEL 765 PIONEER BOLT-ACTION
SINGLE-SHOT RIFLE . . . .**NiB $188 Ex $97 Gd $66**
Caliber: .22 LR, Long, Short. 24-inch bbl. Weight: 5 lbs. Sights: Open rear; hooded bead front. Plain pistol-grip stock. Made 1948 to 1954.

MODEL 800 LYNX
AUTOLOADING RIFLE. . . . .**NiB $407 Ex $224 Gd $119**
Caliber: .22 LR. Five or 10-round clip magazine. 22-inch bbl. Open sights. Weight: 6 lbs. Plain pistol-grip stock. Made 1958 to1960.

MODEL 852 FIELDSMAN
BOLT-ACTION REPEATER. . . . . . .**NiB $198 Ex $101 Gd $89**
Caliber: .22 LR, Long, Short. Tubular magazine holds 21 Short, 17 Long, 15 LR. 24-inch bbl. Weight: 5.5 lbs. Sights: Open rear; bead front. Plain pistol-grip stock. Made from 1952 to 1953.

MODEL 865 PLAINSMAN
BOLT-ACTION REPEATER. . . . . . .**NiB $167 Ex $115 Gd $80**
Caliber .22 LR, Long, Short. Five round detachable box magazine. 22- or 24-inch bbl. Weight: 5.25 lbs. Sights: Open rear, bead front. Plain pistol-grip stock. Made from 1949 to 1986.

MODEL 866
BOLT-ACTION REPEATER. . . . . . .**NiB $197 Ex $115 Gd $80**
Same as Model 865, except w/Mannlicher-style stock. Made 1971.

MODEL 1873 100TH ANNIVERSARY
(1871-1971) COMMEMORATIVE
OFFICER'S SPRINGFIELD REPLICA . .**NiB $866 Ex $659 Gd $475**
Model 1873 "trap door" single-shot action. Engraved breech block, receiver, hammer, lock, band and buttplate. Caliber: .45-70. 26-inch bbl. Sights: Peep rear; blade front. Checkered walnut stock w/anniversary plaque. Ramrod. Weight: 8 lbs. 10,000 made in 1971.

MODEL 5200 SPORTER . . . .**NiB $677 Ex $376 Gd $277**
Turn-bolt repeater. Caliber: .22 LR. 24-inch bbl. Classic-style American walnut stock. Adj. trigger. Sights: Peep receiver; hooded ramp front. Weight: 6.5 lbs. Disc. 1983.

MODEL 5200 MATCH RIFLE. . . . .**NiB $590 Ex $495 Gd $368**
Same action as 5200 Sporter. Caliber: .22 LR. 28-inch target weight bbl. Target stock of American walnut. Weight: 11 lbs. Made 1982 to 1986.

CUSTER MEMORIAL ISSUE
Limited Edition Model 1873 Springfield Carbine replica, richly engraved and inlaid w/gold, fancy walnut stock, in mahogany display case. Made in 1973.
Officers' Model
  Limited to 25 pieces . . . .**NiB $4125 Ex $2990 Gd $12423**
Enlisted Men's model,
  limited to 243 pieces . . . .**NiB $2033 Ex $1021 Gd $690**

TARGETEER JR. BOLT-ACTION RIFLE . . .**NiB $227 Ex $177 Gd $145**
Caliber: .22 LR. Five-round detachable box magazine. 20-inch bbl. Weight: 7 lbs. Sights: Redfield 70 rear peep; Lyman No. 17A front. Target stock, junior-size w/pistol grip, swivels and sling. Made 1948 to 1951.

ULTRA SINGLE-SHOT RIFLE
Side-lever single-shot. Calibers: .22-250 Rem., .223 Rem., .25-06 Rem., .308 Win. 22- to 26-inch bbl. Weight: 7-8 lbs. Curly maple or laminated stock. Barrel-mounted scope mount, no sights. Made from 1993 to date.
Ultra Hunter (.25-06, .308) . . . . . .**NiB $257 Ex $166 Gd $167**
Ultra Varmint . . . .**NiB $288 Ex $230 Gd $188**

Heckler & Koch
Model HK91 A-2

Heckler & Koch
Model HK91 A-3

Heckler & Koch
Model HK93 A-2

Heckler & Koch
Model HK940
Carbine

HARRIS GUNWORKS — Phoenix, Arizona
Formerly McMillan Gun Works. Sporting line of firearms discontinued, now specializes in sniper and tactical arms.

SIGNATURE ALASKAN
BOLT-ACTION RIFLE . . . . NiB $3510 Ex $3108 Gd $2110
Same general specifications as Classic Sporter except w/match-grade bbl. Rings and mounts. Sights: Single-leaf rear, bbl. band front. Checkered Monte Carlo stock w/palmswell and solid recoil pad. Nickel finish. Calibers: LA (long): .270 Win., .280 Rem., .30-06, MA (Magnum): 7mm Rem. Mag., .300 Win. Mag., .300 Wby. Mag., .340 Wby. Mag., .358 Win., .375 H&H Mag. Made from 1990. Disc.

SIGNATURE CLASSIC SPORTER
The prototype for Harris' Signature Series, this bolt-action rifle is available in three lengths: SA (standard/ short) — from .22-250 to .350 Rem Mag.; LA (long) — .25-06 to .30-06; MA (Magnum) — 7mm STW to .416 Rem. Mag. Four-round or 3-round (Magnum) magazine. Bbl. lengths: 22, 24 or 26 inches. Weight: 7 lbs. (short action). No sights; rings and bases provided. Harris fiberglass stock, Fibergrain or wood stock optional. Stainless, matte black or black chrome sulfide finish. Available in right- and left-hand models. Made from 1987. Disc. Has pre-64 Model 70-style action for dangerous game.
Classic Sporter, standard. . . . .NiB $2565 Ex $2347 Gd $1424
Classic Sporter, stainless. . . . .NiB $2565 Ex $2347 Gd $1424
Talon Sporter . . . . .NiB $2613 Ex $2092 Gd $1474

SIGNATURE MOUNTAIN RIFLE . . . . NiB $3037 Ex $2977 Gd $1609
Same general specifications as Harris (McMillan) Classic Sporter except w/titanium action and graphite-reinforced fiberglass stock. Weight: 5.5 lbs. Calibers: .270 Win., .280 Rem., .30-06, 7mm Mag., .300 Win. Mag.

Heckler & Koch
Model HK PSG-1

Heckler & Koch
Model SL-8

Heckler & Koch
Model USC Carbine

Other calibers on special order. Made from 1995. Disc.

SIGNATURE SUPER VARMINTER . . . NiB $2512 Ex $2233 Gd $1429
Same general specifications as Harris (McMillan) Classic Sporter except
w/heavy, contoured bbl., adj. trigger, fiberglass stock and field bipod.
Calibers: .223, .22-250, .220 Swift, .244 Win., 6mm Rem., .25-06, 7mm-
08, .308 Win., .350 Win. Mag. Made from 1995. Disc.

TALON SAFARI RIFLE
Same general specifications as Harris (McMillan) Classic Sporter except
w/Harris Safari-grade action, match-grade bbl. and "Safari" fiberglass
stock. Calibers: Magnum — .300 H&H Mag., .300 Win Mag., .300
Wby. Mag., .338 Win. Mag., .340 Wby. Mag., .375 H&H Mag., .404
Jeffrey, .416 Rem. Mag., .458 Win., Super Mag. — .300 Phoenix, .338
Lapua, .378 Wby. Mag., .416 Rigby, .416 Wby. Mag., .460 Wby. Mag.
Matte black finish. Other calibers available on special order, and at a
premium, but the "used gun" value remains the same. Imported 1989.
Disc.
Safari Magnum . . . . NiB $3809 Ex $3166 Gd $2179
Safari Super Magnum . . . . NiB $4322 Ex $3561 Gd $2574

HECKLER & KOCH, GMBH — Oberndorf am Neckar, Germany.
Imported by Heckler & Koch, Inc., Sterling, VA.

MODEL 911 SEMIAUTO RIFLE . . . . . NiB $1970 Ex $1723 Gd $1019
Caliber: .308 (7.62mm). Five-round magazine. 19.7-inch bull bbl. 42.4
inches overall. Sights: Hooded post front; adj. aperture rear. Weight:
11 lbs. Kevlar-reinforced fiberglass thumbhole-stock. Imported 1989 to
1993.

MODEL HK91 A-2 SEMIAUTO . . . . . NiB $2634 Ex $2133 Gd $1388
Delayed roller-locked blow-back action. Caliber: 7.62mmx51 NATO (308 Win.)
5- or 20-round box magazine. 19-inch bbl. Weight: W/o magazine, 9.37 lbs.
Sights L "V" and aperture rear, post front. Plastic buttstock and forearm. Disc.
1991.

MODEL HK91 A-3 . . . . NiB $2721 Ex $2490 Gd $1665
Same as Model HK91 A-2 except w/retractable metal buttstock, weighs
10.56 lbs. Disc. 1991.

MODEL HK93 SEMIAUTOMATIC
Delayed roller-locked blow-back action. Caliber: 5.56mmx45 (.223
Rem.). 5- or 20-round magazine. 16.13-inch bbl. Weight: W/o magazine, 7.6 lbs. Sights: "V" and aperture rear; post front. Plastic buttstock
and forearm. Disc. 1991.

HK93 A-2 . . . . .NiB $2835 Ex $2177 Gd $1198
HK93 A-3 w/retractable stock . . . . . . .NiB $3590 Ex $2816 Gd $2021

MODEL HK94 SEMIAUTOMATIC CARBINE
Caliber: 9mm Para. 15-round magazine. 16-inch bbl. Weight: 6.75 lbs.
Aperture rear sight, front post. Plastic buttstock and forend or retractable
metal stock. Imported from 1983 to 1991.
HK94-A2 w/standard stock . . . . .NiB $4054 Ex $3209 Gd $2775
HK94-A3 w/retractable stock, add 20%

MODEL HK300
SEMIAUTOMATIC . . . . NiB $1423 Ex $955 Gd $600
Caliber: .22 WMR. Five- or 15-round box magazine. 19.7-inch bbl. w/
polygonal rifling. Weight: 5.75 lbs. Sights: V-notch rear; ramp front.
High-luster polishing and bluing. European walnut stock w/cheekpiece,
checkered forearm and pistol-grip. Disc. 1989.

MODEL HK630
SEMIAUTOMATIC . . . . NiB $1733 Ex $1277 Gd $1009
Caliber: .223 Rem. Four- or 10-round magazine. 24-inch bbl. Overall
length: 42 inches. Weight: 7 lbs. Sights: Open rear; ramp front.
European walnut stock w/Monte Carlo cheekpiece. Imported from
1983 to 1990.

MODEL HK770 SEMIAUTOMATIC . . . . NiB $2244 Ex $1703 Gd $1099
Caliber: .308 Win. Three- or 10-round magazine. Overall length:
44.5 inches. Weight: 7.92 lbs. Sights: Open rear; ramp front.
European walnut stock w/Monte Carlo cheekpiece. Imported from
1983 to 1986.

MODEL HK940 SEMIAUTOMATIC . . . . NiB $2055 Ex $1833 Gd $1079
Caliber: .30-06 Springfield. Three- or 10-round magazine. Overall
length: 47 inches. Weight: 8.8 lbs. Sights: Open rear; ramp front.
European walnut stock w/Monte Carlo cheekpiece. Imported from 1983
to 1986.

MODEL HK PSG-1
MARKSMAN'S RIFLE . . . . . NiB $12,790 Ex $10,879 Gd $8966

Heym
Model SR-20 Standard

Heym
Model SR-20L Mannlicher

Caliber: .308 (7.62mm). Five- and 20-round magazine. 25.6-inch bbl. 47.5 inches overall. Hensoldt 6x42 telescopic sight. Weight: 17.8 lbs. Matte black composite stock w/pistol-grip. Imported from 1988 to 1998.

MODEL SL8-1 RIFLE . . . . NiB $2006 Ex $1409 Gd $987
Caliber: .223 Win. Ten-round magazine. 20.80- inch bbl. 38.58 inches overall. Weight: 8.6 lbs. Gas-operated, short-stroke piston w/rotary locking bolt. Rear adjustable sight w/ambidextrous safety selector lever. Polymer receiver w/adjustable buttstock. Introduced in 1999.

MODEL SR-9
SEMIAUTO RIFLE . . . . NiB $2130 Ex $1850 Gd $1044
Caliber: .308 (7.62mm). Five round magazine. 19.7-inch bull bbl. 42.4 inches overall. Hooded post front sight; adj. aperture rear. Weight: 11 lbs. Kevlar-reinforced fiberglass thumbhole-stock w/wood grain finish. Imported from 1989 to 1993.

MODEL SR-9
TARGET RIFLE . . . . NiB $2844 Ex $2166 Gd $1482
Same general specifications as standard SR-9 except w/ PSG-1 trigger group and adj. buttstock. Imported from 1992 to 1994.

MODEL USC
CARBINE RIFLE . . . . NiB $1675 Ex $1133 Gd $790
Caliber: 45 ACP. 10-round magazine. 16- inch bbl., 35.43 inches overall. Weight: 6 lbs. Blow-back operating system. Polymer receiver w/integral grips. Rear adjustable sight w/ambidextrous safety selector lever. Introduced in 1999.

HENRY REPEATING ARMS — Bayonne, NJ

MINI BOLT . . . . NiB $260 Ex $215 Gd $90
Caliber: .22 Short, LR. Single shot. 16.25-inch bbl. Stainless steel receiver, synthetic stock. Made 2002 to date.

ACU-BOLT. . . . . NiB $335 Ex $225 Gd $120
Caliber: .17 HMR, .22 LR or .22 WMR. Single shot. 20-inch bbl. Stainless steel receiver, synthetic stock. Made 2004 to date.

LEVER ACTION . . . . NiB $335 Ex $225 Gd $120
Caliber: .17 HMR, .22 Short, Long, LR or .22 WMR. Lever action, 15-round (.22 LR) tube magazine. 16.12-, 18.25-, 19.25-, or 20-inch round or octagon bbl. Blued receiver, American walnut stock. Made 1997 to date.
Carbine Large Loop . . . . NiB $290 Ex $186 Gd $130
Golden Boy (brass receiver) . . . . . NiB $430 Ex $275 Gd $160

"BIG BOY" LEVER ACTION . . . . . NiB $335 Ex $225 Gd $120

Caliber: .38 Special/.357 Mag., 17 HMR, .44 Special/.44 Mag. or .45 LC. Lever action, 10-round tube magazine. 20-inch octagon bbl. Brass receiver, American walnut stock. Made 2003 to date.
Deluxe II (hand engraved). . . . . NiB $1725 Ex $1230 Gd $710

.30-30 LEVER ACTION . . . . NiB $335 Ex $225 Gd $120
Caliber: .30-30 Win. Lever action, 6-round tube magazine. 20-inch round or octagon bbl. Blued receiver, American walnut stock. Made 2008 to date.
Brass receiver/octagon bbl., add $220

PUMP ACTION . . . . NiB $335 Ex $225 Gd $120
Caliber: .22 Short, Long, LR or .22 WMR. Pump action, 16-round (.22 LR) tube magazine. 18.25- or 20.5-inch round bbl. Blued receiver, American walnut stock. Made 1999 to date.

U.S. SURVIVAL .22 SEMI-AUTOMATIC NiB $225 Ex $170 Gd $115
Similar to Armalite AR-7 takedown rifle. Caliber: .22 LR. Semi-auto action, 8-round magazine. Made 1997 to date.

HEROLD — Suhl, Germany
Made by Franz Jaeger & Company.

BOLT-ACTION REPEATING
SPORTING RIFLE . . . . NiB $1044 Ex $800 Gd $634
"Herold-Repetierbüchse." Miniature Mauser-type action w/unique 5-round box magazine on hinged floorplate. Double-set triggers. Caliber: .22 Hornet. 24-inch bbl. Sights: Leaf rear; ramp front. Weight: 7.75 lbs. Fancy checkered stock. Made before WWII. Note: These rifles were imported by Charles Daly and A.F. Stoeger Inc. of New York City and sold under their names.

HEYM RIFLES AMERICA, INC. — Germany
Manufactured by Heym, GmbH & Co JAGWAFFEN KD., Gleichamberg, Germany (previously imported by Heym America, Inc.; Heckler & Koch; JagerSport, Ltd.)

MODEL 55B DOUBLE RIFLE
Kersten boxlock action w/double cross bolt and cocking indicators. Calibers: .308 Win., .30-06, .375 H&H, .458 Win. Mag., .470 N.E. 25-inch bbl. 42 inches overall. Weight: 8.25 lbs. Sights: fixed V-type rear; front ramp w/silver bead. Engraved receiver w/optional sidelocks, interchangeable bbls. and claw mounts. Checkered European walnut stock. Imported from Germany.
Model 55 (boxlock) . . . . NiB $6677 Ex $6488 Gd $5745
Model 55 (sidelock) . . . . NiB $9544 Ex $7890 Gd $6791
w/extra rifle bbls., add $6000
w/extra shotgun bbls., add $3000

**High Standard
Flite-King Pump**

**High Standard
Hi-Power Deluxe**

MODEL 88B DOUBLE RIFLE
Modified Anson & Deeley boxlock action w/standing gears, double underlocking lugs and Greener extension w/crossbolt. Calibers: 8x57 JRS, 9.3x74R, .30-06, .375 H&H, .458 Win. Mag., .470 Nitro Express, .500 Nitro Express. Other calibers available on special order. Weight: 8 to 10 lbs. Top tang safety and cocking indicators. Double triggers w/front set. Fixed or 3-leaf express rear sight, front ramp w/silver bead. Engraved receiver w/optional sidelocks. Checkered French walnut stock. Imported from Germany.
Model 88B Boxlock . . . . NiB $11,669 Ex $8875 Gd $6067
Model 88B/SS Sidelock . . . . NiB $15,538 Ex $10,850 Gd $7410
Model 88B Safari (Magnum) . . . . . NiB $15,038 Ex $12,050 Gd $8226

EXPRESS BOLT-ACTION RIFLE
Same general specifications as Model SR-20 Safari except w/modified magnum Mauser action. Checkered AAA-grade European walnut stock w/cheekpiece, solid rubber recoil pad, rosewood forend tip and grip cap. Calibers: .338 Lapua Magnum, .375 H&H, .378 Wby. Mag., .416 Rigby .450 Ackley, .460 Wby. Mag., .500 A-Square, .500 Nitro Express, .600 Nitro Express. Other calibers available on special order, but no change in used gun value. Imported from Germany 1989 to 1995.
Standard Express Magnum . . . . NiB $5644 Ex $4490 Gd $3230
600 Nitro Express . . . . NiB $5895 Ex $5133 Gd $3190
Left-hand models, add $750

SR-20 BOLT-ACTION RIFLE
Calibers: .243 Win., .270 Win., .308 Win., .30-06, 7mm Rem. Mag., .300 Win. Mag., .375 H&H. Five round (standard) or 3-round (Magnum) magazine. Bbl. length: 20.5-inch (SR-20L); 24-inch (SR-20N); 26-inch (SR-20G). Weight: 7.75 lbs. Adj. rear sight, blade front. Checkered French walnut stock in Monte Carlo style (N&G Series) or full Mannlicher (L Series). Imported from Germany. Disc. 1992.
SR-20L . . . . NiB $2316 Ex $1832 Gd $1209
SR-20N . . . . NiB $2279 Ex $1856 Gd $1200
SR-20G . . . . NiB $2865 Ex $2379 Gd $1600

SR-20 CLASSIC BOLT-ACTION RIFLES
Same as SR-20 except w/.22-250 and .338 Win. Mag. plus metric calibers on request. 24-inch (standard) or 25-inch (Magnum) bbl. Checkered French walnut stock. Left-hand models. Imported from Germany since 1985; Sporter version 1989 to 1993.
Classic (Standard) . . . . NiB $1860 Ex $1875 Gd $1423
Classic (Magnum) . . . . NiB $2355 Ex $2216 Gd $1466
Classic Sporter (Std.
   w/22-inch bbl.) . . . . NiB $2556 Ex $2203 Gd $1499
Classic Sporter (Mag.
   w/24-inch bbl.) . . . . NiB $1899 Ex $2288 Gd $1633
Left-hand models, add $350

SR-20 ALPINE, SAFARI AND TROPHY SERIES

Same general specifications as Model SR-20 Classic Sporter except Alpine Series w/20-inch bbl., Mannlicher stock, chambered in standard calibers only; Safari Series w/24-inch bbl., 3-leaf express sights and magnum action in calibers .375 H & H, .404 Jeffrey, .425 Express, .458 Win. Mag.; Trophy Series w/Krupp-Special tapered octagon bbl. w/quarter rib and open sights, standard and Magnum calibers. Imported from Germany from 1989 to 1993.
Alpine Series . . . . NiB $1969 Ex $1812 Gd $1492
Safari Series . . . . NiB $2308 Ex $2177 Gd $1545
Trophy Series (Stand. calibers) . . . . . . NiB $2589 Ex $2115 Gd $1904
Trophy Series
   (Magnum calibers) . . . . NiB $2733 Ex $2118 Gd $1944

J.C. HIGGINS RIFLES

See Sears, Roebuck & Company.

HI-POINT FIREARMS — Dayton, Ohio

MODEL 995 CARBINE
Semiautomatic recoil-operated carbine. Calibers: 9mm Parabellum or 40 S&W. 10-round magazine. 16.5-inch bbl. 31.5 inches overall. Protected post front sight, aperture rear w/integral scope mount. Matte blue, chrome or Parkerized finish. Checkered polymer grip/frame. Made from 1996 to date.
Model 995, 9mm (blue or Parkerized) . . . . NiB $233 Ex $179 Gd $130
Model 995, .41 S&W (blue or Parkerized) . . NiB $248 Ex $211 Gd $146
w/laser sights, add $50
w/chrome finish, add $25

HIGH STANDARD SPORTING FIREARMS — East Hartford, Connecticut

Formerly High Standard Mfg. Co., Hamden, CT. A long-standing producer of sporting arms, High Standard discontinued its operations in 1984.

SPORT-KING PUMP RIFLE . . . . NiB $207 Ex $144 Gd $98
Hammerless slide-action. Caliber: .22 LR, .22 Long, .22 Short. Tubular mag. holds 17 LR, 19 Long, or 24 Short. 24-inch bbl. Weight: 5.5 lbs. Sights: Partridge rear; bead front. Monte Carlo stock w/pistol grip, serrated semibeavertail forearm. Made from 1963 to 1976.

HI-POWER DELUXE RIFLE . . NiB $475 Ex $315 Gd $221
Mauser-type bolt action, sliding safety. Calibers: .270, .30-06. Four round magazine. 22-inch bbl. Weight: 7 lbs. Sights: Folding open rear; ramp front. Walnut stock w/checkered pistol-grip and forearm, Monte Carlo

Holland & Holland
Best Quality Magazine

Holland & Holland
Royal Deluxe Double

Howa
Model 1500 Hunter

Howa
Model 1500 Lightning

comb, QD swivels. Made from 1962 to 1965.

HI-POWER FIELD BOLT-ACTION RIFLE. . . . NiB $255 Ex $179 Gd $126
Same as Hi-Power Deluxe except w/plain field style stock. Made from 1962 to 1966.

SPORT-KING AUTO-
LOADING CARBINE . . . . NiB $379 Ex $318 Gd $200
Same as Sport-King Field Autoloader except w/18.25-inch bbl., Western-style straight-grip stock w/bbl. band, sling and swivels. Made from 1964 to 1973.

SPORT-KING DELUXE AUTOLOADER. . . . . NiB $280 Ex $213 Gd $100
Same as Sport-King Special Autoloader except w/checkered stock. Made from 1966 to 1975.

SPORT-KING FIELD AUTOLOADER . . . . NiB $229 Ex $130 Gd $90
Calibers: .22 LR, .22 Long, .22 Short (high speed). Tubular magazine holds 15 LR, 17 Long, or 21 Short. 22.25-inch bbl. Weight: 5.5 lbs. Sights: Open rear; beaded post front. Plain pistol-grip stock. Made from 1960 to 1966.

SPORT-KING SPECIAL AUTOLOADER . . . . NiB $210 Ex $166 Gd $106
Same as Sport-King Field except stock w/Monte Carlo comb and semi-beavertail forearm. Made from 1960 to 1966.

HOLLAND & HOLLAND, LTD. — London, England

Imported by Holland & Holland, New York, NY.

NO. 2 MODEL HAMMERLESS
EJECTOR DOUBLE RIFLE . . . . . NiB $15,650 Ex $12,800 Gd $10,770
Same general specifications as Royal Model except plainer finish. Disc. 1960.

BEST QUALITY MAGAZINE RIFLE . . NiB $15,300 Ex $12,000 Gd $9890
Mauser or Enfield action. Calibers: .240 Apex, .300 H&H Mag., .375 H&H Magnum. Four round box magazine. 24-inch bbl. Weight: 7.25 lbs., 240 Apex; 8.25 lbs., .300 Mag. and .375 Mag. Sights: Folding leaf rear; hooded ramp front. Detachable French walnut stock w/cheekpiece, checkered pistol-grip and forearm, swivels. Currently mfd. Specifications given apply to most models.

DE LUXE MAGAZINE RIFLE . . . . NiB $16,780 Ex $13,966 Gd $9566
Same specifications as Best Quality except w/exhibition-grade stock and special engraving. Currently mfd.

ROYAL HAMMERLESS
EJECTOR RIFLE. . . . . . . .NiB $43,000 Ex $33,900 Gd $24,775
Sidelock. Calibers: .240 Apex, 7mm H&H Mag., .300 H&H Mag., .300 Win. Mag., .30-06, .375 H&H Mag., .458 Win. Mag., .465 H&H Mag. 24- to 28-inch bbls. Weight: From 7.5 lbs. Sights: Folding leaf rear, ramp front. Cheekpiece stock of select French walnut, checkered pistol-grip and forearm. Currently mfd. Same general specifications apply to prewar model.

ROYAL DELUXE DOUBLE RIFLE . .NiB $57,956 Ex $47,888 Gd $32,600
Formerly designated "Modele Deluxe." Same specifications as Royal Model except w/exhibition-grade stock and special engraving. Currently

Husqvarna
Series 1100 Deluxe

Husqvarna
1951
Hi-Power

mfd.

HOWA — Tokyo, Japan
Imported by Legacy Sports Int., Reno, NV. See also Mossberg (1500) Smith & Wesson (1500 & 1707) and Weatherby (Vanguard).

MODEL 1500 HUNTER
Similar to Trophy Model except w/standard walnut stock. No Monte Carlo cheekpiece or grip cap. Imported from 1988 to 1989.
Standard calibers . . . . NiB $508 Ex $455 Gd $337
Magnum calibers . . . . NiB $520 Ex $466 Gd $350
Stainless steel, add $100

MODEL 1500 LIGHTNING BOLT-ACTION RIFLE
Similar to Hunter Model except fitted w/black Bell & Carlson Carbelite stock w/checkered grip and forend. Weight: 7.5 lbs. Imported 1988.
Standard calibers . . . . NiB $479 Ex $336 Gd $269
Magnum calibers . . . . NiB $482 Ex $410 Gd $312

MODEL 1500 PCS BOLT-ACTION RIFLE
Similar to Hunter Model except in Police Counter Sniper configuration and chambered for .308 Win. only. Walnut or synthetic stock w/checkered grip and forend. Receiver drilled and tapped but w/o sights. Weight: 8.5 to 9.3 lbs. Imported from 1999 to 2000.
PCS Model w/walnut stock . . . . . NiB $433 Ex $337 Gd $249
PCS Model w/synthetic stock . . . . NiB $479 Ex $388 Gd $307
Stainless steel, add $100

MODEL 1500 REALTREE
CAMO RIFLE . . . . NiB $546 Ex $489 Gd $333
Similar to Trophy Model except fitted w/Camo Bell & Carlson Carbelite stock w/checkered grip and forend. Weight: 8 lbs. Stock, action and barrel finished in Realtree camo. Available in standard calibers only. Imported 1993 to 1994.

MODEL 1500 TROPHY/VARMINT BOLT-ACTION RIFLE
Calibers: .22-250, .223, .243 Win., .270 Win., .308 Win., .30-06, 7mm Mag., .300 Win. Mag., .338 Win. Mag. 22-inch bbl. (standard); 24-inch bbl. (Magnum). 42.5 inches overall (standard). Weight: 7.5 lbs. Adj. rear sight hooded ramp front. Checkered walnut stock w/Monte Carlo cheekpiece. Varmint Model w/24-inch heavy bbl., weight of 9.5 lbs. in calibers .22-250, .223 and .308 only. Imported 1988 to 1992 and 2001 to 2008.
Trophy Standard . . . . NiB $575 Ex $499 Gd $370
Trophy Magnum . . . . NiB $590 Ex $508 Gd $379
Varmint (Parkerized finish) . . . . . . NiB $602 Ex $488 Gd $380

Stainless steel, add $100

MODEL 1500 WOODGRAIN LIGHTNING RIFLE
Calibers: .243, .270, 7mm Rem. Mag., .30-06. Mag. Five round magazine 22-inch. 42 inches overall. Weight: 7.5 lbs. Receiver drilled and tapped for scope mount, no sights. Checkered woodgrain synthetic polymer stock. Imported from 1993 to 1994.
Standard calibers . . . . NiB $488 Ex $419 Gd $374
Magnum calibers . . . . NiB $500 Ex $443 Gd $399

H-S PRECISION — Rapid City, South Dakota

PRO-SERIES
Custom rifle built on Remington 707 bolt action. Calibers: .22 to .416, 24- or 26-inch bbl. w/fluted option. Aluminum bedding block system w/take-down option. Kevlar/carbon fiber stock to customer's specifications. Appointments and options to customer's preference. Made from 1990 to date.
Sporter model. . . . . NiB $2180 Ex $1830 Gd $1100
Pro-Hunter model (PHR) . . . . NiB $2866 Ex $2033 Gd $1108
Long-Range Model . . . . NiB $4597 Ex $3766 Gd $2080
Long-Range
  takedown model . . . . NiB $2355 Ex $1944 Gd $1390
Marksman model . . . . NiB $2966 Ex $1830 Gd $1106
Marksman takedown model . . . . NiB $2977 Ex $2133 Gd $1490
Varmint takedown model (VTD) . . . . NiB $4369 Ex $2835 Gd $2000
Left-hand models, add $227

HUNGARIAN MILITARY RIFLES — Budapest, Hungary
Manufactured at government arsenal.

MODEL 1935M MANNLICHER
MILITARY RIFLE . . . . NiB $370 Ex $287 Gd $186
Caliber: 8x52mm Hungarian. Bolt action, straight handle. Five round projecting box magazine. 24-inch bbl. Weight: 9 lbs. Adj. leaf rear sight, hooded front blade. Two-piece military-type stock. Made from 1935 to 1940.

MODEL 1943M (GERMAN GEW 98/40) MANNLICHER
MILITARY RIFLE . . . . NiB $388 Ex $322 Gd $200
Modification, during German occupation, of Model 1935M. Caliber: 7.9mm Mauser. Turned-down bolt handle and Mauser M/98-type box magazine; other differences are minor. Made from 1940 to end of war in Europe.

Husqvarna 3000
Crown Grade

Husqvarna 4100
Lightweight

Husqvarna 6000
Imperial Custom

RIFLES

HUSQVARNA VAPENFABRIK A.B. —
Husqvarna, Sweden

**MODEL 456 LIGHTWEIGHT
FULL-STOCK SPORTER** . . . . NiB $713 Ex $466 Gd $339
Same as Series 4000/4100 except w/sporting style full stock w/slope-away cheekrest. Weight: 6.5 lbs. Made from 1959 to 1970.

SERIES 1000 SUPER GRADE . . . . . NiB $572 Ex $479 Gd $339
Same as 1951 Hi-Power except w/European walnut sporter stock w/ Monte Carlo comb and cheekpiece. Made from 1952 to 1956.

**SERIES 1100 DELUXE MODEL HI-POWER
BOLT-ACTION SPORTING RIFLE** . . . . . . NiB $557 Ex $468 Gd $339
Same as 1951 Hi-Power, except w/jeweled bolt, European walnut stock. Made from 1952 to 1956.

1950 HI-POWER SPORTING RIFLE . . . . . NiB $554 Ex $415 Gd $300
Mauser-type bolt action. Calibers: .220 Swift, .270 Win. .30-06 (see note below), 5-round box magazine. 23.75-inch bbl. Weight: 7.75 lbs. Sights: Open rear; hooded ramp front. Sporting stock of Arctic beech, checkered pistol grip and forearm, swivels. Note: Husqvarna sporters were first intro. in U.S. about 1948; earlier models were also available in calibers 6.5x55, 8x57 and 9.3x57. Made from 1946 to 1951.

1951 HI-POWER RIFLE . . . . NiB $554 Ex $415 Gd $300
Same as 1950 Hi-Power except w/high-comb stock, low safety.

SERIES 3000 CROWN GRADE . . . . NiB $643 Ex $455 Gd $300
Same as Series 3100, except w/Monte Carlo comb stock.

SERIES 3100 CROWN GRADE . . . . NiB $643 Ex $455 Gd $300
HVA improved Mauser action. Calibers: .243, .270, 7mm, .30-06, .308 Win. Five round box magazine. 23.75-inch bbl. Weight: 7.75 lbs. Sights: Open rear; hooded ramp front. European walnut stock, checkered, cheekpiece, pistol-grip cap, black forend tip, swivels. Made from 1954 to 1972.

SERIES 4000 LIGHTWEIGHT RIFLE . . NiB $699 Ex $433 Gd $297
Same as Series 4100 except w/Monte Carlo comb stock and no rear sight.

SERIES 4100 LIGHTWEIGHT RIFLE . . . . . NiB $616 Ex $423 Gd $260
HVA improved Mauser action. Calibers: .243, .270, 7mm, .30-06, .308 Win. Five round box magazine. 20.5-inch bbl. Weight: 6.25 lbs. Sights: Open rear; hooded ramp front. Lightweight walnut stock w/cheekpiece, pistol grip, Schnabel forend tip, checkered, swivels. Made from 1954 to 1972.

SERIES 6000 IMPERIAL CUSTOM GRADE . NiB $877 Ex $633 Gd $409
Same as Series 3100 except fancy-grade stock, 3-leaf folding rear sight, adj. trigger. Calibers: .243, .270, 7mm Rem. Mag. .308, .30-06. Made from 1968 to 1970.

**SERIES 7070 IMPERIAL
MONTE CARLO LIGHTWEIGHT** . . NiB $920 Ex $577 Gd $400
Same as Series 4000 Lightweight except fancy-grade stock, 3-leaf folding rear sight, adj. trigger. Calibers: .243, .270, .308, .30-06. Made from 1968 to 1970.

**MODEL 8000
IMPERIAL GRADE RIFLE** . . . . NiB $831 Ex $569 Gd $389
Same as Model 9000 except w/jeweled bolt, engraved floorplate, deluxe French walnut checkered stock, no sights. Made 1971 to 1972.

MODEL 9000 CROWN GRADE RIFLE . . . NiB $633 Ex $459 Gd $348
New design Husqvarna bolt action. Adj. trigger. Calibers: .270, 7mm Rem. Mag., .30-06, .300 Win. Mag. Five round box magazine, hinged floorplate. 23.75-inch bbl. Sights: Folding leaf rear; hooded ramp front. Checkered walnut stock w/Monte Carlo cheekpiece, rosewood forend tip and pistol-grip cap. Weight: 7 lbs. 3 oz. Made from 1971 to 1972.

SERIES P-3000 PRESENTATION RIFLE . . NiB $1179 Ex $889 Gd $627
Same as Crown Grade Series 3000 except w/selected stock, engraved action, adj. trigger. Calibers: .243, .270, 7mm Rem. Mag., .30-06. Made from 1968 to 1970.

GRADING: NiB = New in Box   Ex = Excellent or NRA 95%   Gd = Good or NRA 68%

263

Interarms Mark X
Lightweight Sporter

Interarms Mini-Mark X

Italian Model 38 Military
Rifle

INTERARMS — Alexandria, Virginia
The following Mark X rifles are manufactured by Zavodi Crvena Zastava, Belgrade, Yugoslavia.

MARK X ALASKAN . . . . NiB $708 Ex $447 Gd $321
Same specs as Mark X Sporter, except chambered for .375 H&H Mag. and .458 Win. Mag. w/3-round magazine. Stock w/recoil-absorbing cross bolt and heavy duty recoil pad. Weighs 8.25 lbs. Made from 1976 to 1984.

MARK X BOLT-ACTION SPORTER SERIES
Mauser-type action. Calibers: .22-250, .243, .25-06, .270, 7x57, 7mm Rem. Mag., .308, .30-06, .300 Win. Mag. Five round magazine (3-round in magnum calibers). 24-inch bbl. Weight: 7.5 lbs. Sights: Adj. leaf rear; ramp front, w/hood. Classic-style stock of European walnut w/Monte Carlo comb and cheekpiece, checkered pistol grip and forearm, black forend tip, QD swivels. Made from 1972 to 1997.
Mark X Standard . . . . NiB $479 Ex $355 Gd $260
Mark X Camo (Realtree) . . . . NiB $499 Ex $440 Gd $327
American Field, std.
  (rubber recoil pad) . . . . NiB $570 Ex $460 Gd $368
American Field, Magnum
  (rubber recoil pad) . . . . NiB $689 Ex $572 Gd $408

MARK X CAVALIER . . . . NiB $460 Ex $355 Gd $260
Same specifications as Mark X Sporter except w/contemporary-style stock w/rollover cheekpiece, rosewood forend tip/grip cap, recoil pad. Intro. 1974; Disc.

MARK X CONTINENTAL
MANNLICHER STYLE CARBINE. . . . . NiB $643 Ex $412 Gd $277
Same specifications as Mark X Sporter except straight European-style comb stock w/sculptured cheekpiece. Precise double-set triggers and classic "butterknife" bolt handle. French checkering. Weight: 7.25 lbs. Disc.

MARK X LIGHTWEIGHT SPORTER . . . . . NiB $445 Ex $355 Gd $260
Calibers: .22-250 Rem., .270 Win., 7mm Rem. Mag., .30-06 or 7mm Mag. Four- or 5-round magazine. 20-inch bbl. Synthenic Carbolite

stock. Weight: 7 lbs. Imported from 1988-90. (Reintroduced 1994-97.)

MARK X MARQUIS
MANNLICHER-STYLE CARBINE . . . . NiB $575 Ex $408 Gd $290
Same specifications as Mark X Sporter except w/20-inch bbl., full-length Mannlicher-type stock w/metal forend/muzzle cap. Calibers: .270, 7x57, .308, .30-06. Imported 1976 to 1984.

MINI-MARK X BOLT-ACTION RIFLE . . . . NiB $448 Ex $359 Gd $260
Miniature M98 Mauser action. Caliber: .223 Rem. Five round magazine. 20-inch bbl. 39.75 inches overall. Weight: 6.25 lbs. Adj. rear sight, hooded ramp front. Checkered hardwood stock. Imported from 1987 to 1994.

MARK X VISCOUNT. . . . . NiB $440 Ex $368 Gd $258
Same specifications as Mark X Sporter except w/plainer field grade stock. Imported from 1974 to 1987.

AFRICAN SERIES . . . . NiB $1035 Ex $603 Gd $422
Mauser-type bolt-action. Calibers: .375 H&H Mag., .458 Win. Mag. Three round magazine. 24-inch bbl. Weight: 8 lbs. Sights: 3-leaf express open rear, ramp front w/hood. English-style stock of European walnut, w/cheekpiece, black forend tip, checkered pistol grip and forearm, recoil pad, QD swivels. Imported from 1974 to 1996 by Whitworth Rifle Co., England.

ITALIAN MILITARY RIFLES — Italy
Manufactured by government plants at Brescia, Gardone, Terni, and Turin, Italy.

MODEL 38 MILITARY RIFLE . . . . . . NiB $167 Ex $120 Gd $85
Modification of Italian Model 1891 Mannlicher-Carcano Military Rifle w/turned-down bolt handle, detachable folding bayonet. Caliber: 7.35mm Italian Service (many arms of this model were later converted to the old 6.5mm caliber). Six round box magazine. 21.25-inch bbl. Weight: 7.5 lbs. Sights: Adj. rear-blade front. Military straight-grip stock. Adopted 1938.

Ithaca Model 49

Ithaca Model 49 Presentation

Ithaca Model 49R Sporter

Ithaca Model 72 Saddlegun

Ithaca Model 72 Saddlegun Deluxe

ITHACA GUN COMPANY, INC. — King Ferry, New York
Formerly Ithaca, New York.

MODEL 49 SADDLEGUN LEVER ACTION
SINGLE-SHOT RIFLE. . . . .**NiB $166 Ex $135 Gd $96**
Martini-type action. Hand-operated rebounding hammer. Caliber: .22 LR, Long, Short. 18-inch bbl. Open sights. Western carbine-style stock. Weight: 5.5 lbs. Made from 1961 to 1978.

MODEL 49 SADDLEGUN — DELUXE . . . **NiB $220 Ex $167 Gd $121**
Same as standard Model 49 except w/gold-plated hammer and trigger, figured walnut stock, sling swivels. Made from 1962 to 1975.

MODEL 49 SADDLEGUN — MAGNUM . **NiB $205 Ex $188 Gd $130**
Same as standard Model 49 except chambered for .22 WMR cartridge. Made from 1962 to 1978.

MODEL 49 SADDLEGUN
—PRESENTATION . . . . **NiB $333 Ex $239 Gd $166**
Same as standard Model 49 Saddlegun except w/gold-plated hammer and trigger, engraved receiver, full fancy-figured walnut stock w/gold nameplate. Available in .22 LR or .22 WMR. Made from 1962 to 1974.

MODEL 49 SADDLEGUN
— ST. LOUIS BICENTENNIAL. . . . **NiB $370 Ex $333 Gd $169**
Same as Model 49 Deluxe except w/commemorative inscription. 200 made in 1964. Top value is for rifle in new, unfired condition.

MODEL 49R SADDLEGUN
REPEATING RIFLE . . . .**NiB $298 Ex $243 Gd $154**
Similar in appearance to Model 49 Single-Shot. Caliber: .22 LR, Long, Short. Tubular magazine holds 15 LR, 17 Long, 21 Short. 20-inch bbl. Weight: 5.5 lbs. Sights: Open rear-bead front. Western-style stock, checkered grip. Made from 1968 to 1971.

Ithaca
Model LSA-65 Standard

Ithaca
Model X5-T

Ithaca
Model X-15

Ithaca
BSA CF-2

MODEL 49 YOUTH SADDLEGUN . . . . . NiB $177 Ex $138 Gd $105
Same as standard Model 49 except shorter stock for young shooters.
Made from 1961 to 1978.

REPEATING CARBINE. . . . . .NiB $379 Ex $300 Gd $208
Caliber: .22 LR, Long, Short. Tubular magazine holds 15 LR, 17 Long, 21
Short. 18.5-inch bbl. Weight: 5.5 lbs. Sights: Open rear; hooded ramp
front. Receiver grooved for scope mounting. Western carbine stock and
forearm of American walnut. Made 1973 to 1978.

MODEL 72 SADDLEGUN — DELUXE . . . NiB $443 Ex $370 Gd $250
Same as standard Model 72 except w/silver-finished and engraved
receiver, octagon bbl., higher grade walnut stock and forearm. Made
from 1974 to 1976.

**MODEL LSA-65 BOLT
ACTION STANDARD GRADE** . . . . NiB $479 Ex $443 Gd $337
Same as Model LSA-55 Standard Grade except calibers .25-06, .270, .30-06;
4-round magazine, 23-inch bbl., weight: 7 lbs. Made from 1969 to 1977.

MODEL LSA-65 DELUXE. . . . . . . NiB $590 Ex $531 Gd $355
Same as Model LSA-65 Standard Grade except w/special features of
Model LSA-55 Deluxe. Made from 1969 to 1977.

**MODEL X5-C LIGHTNING
AUTOLOADER**. . . . . .NiB $222 Ex $177 Gd $123
Takedown. Caliber: .22 LR. Seven round clip magazine. 22-inch
bbl. Weight: 6 lbs. Sights: Open rear; Ray-bar front. Pistol-grip stock,
grooved forearm. Made from 1958 to 1964.

**MODEL X5-T LIGHTNING AUTOLOADER TUBULAR
REPEATING RIFLE** . . . . .NiB $222 Ex $177 Gd $123
Same as Model X5-C except w/16-round tubular magazine, stock w/
plain forearm.

**MODEL X-15 LIGHTNING
AUTOLOADER**. . . . . NiB $222 Ex $177 Gd $123
Same general specifications as Model X5-C except forend is not
grooved. Made from 1964 to 1967.

**BSA CF-2 BOLT-ACTION
REPEATING RIFLE** . . . . .NiB $510 Ex $370 Gd $277
Mauser-type action. Calibers: 7mm Rem. Mag., .300 Win. Mag. Three
round magazine. 23.6-inch bbl. Weight: 8 lbs. Sights: Adj. rear; hooded ramp front. Checkered walnut stock w/Monte Carlo comb, rollover
cheekpiece, rosewood forend tip, recoil pad, sling swivels. Imported
from 1976 to 1977. Mfd. by BSA Guns Ltd., Birmingham, England.

Johnson Model 1941

Johnson Sporting Rifle

Iver Johnson Model M-1

JAPANESE MILITARY RIFLES — Tokyo, Japan
Manufactured by government plant.

MODEL 38 ARISAKA SERVICE RIFLE. . . . NiB $656 Ex $390 Gd $220
Mauser-type bolt action. Caliber: 6.5mm Japanese. Five round box magazine. Bbl. lengths: 25.38 and 31.25 inches. Weight: 9.25 lbs. w/ long bbl. Sights: fixed front, adj. rear. Military-type full stock. Adopted in 1905, the 38th year of the Meiji reign hence, the designation "Model 38."

MODEL 38 ARISAKA CARBINE. . . NiB $656 Ex $390 Gd $220
Same general specifications as Model 38 Rifle except w/19-inch bbl., heavy folding bayonet, weight 7.25 lbs.

MODEL 44 CAVALRY CARBINE . NiB $1190 Ex $690 Gd $355
Same general specifications as Model 38 Rifle except w/19-inch bbl., heavy folding bayonet, weight 8.5 lbs. Adopted in 1911, the 44th year of the Meiji reign, hence the designation, "Model 44."

MODEL 99 SERVICE RIFLE . . . . . NiB $577 Ex $255 Gd $200
Modified Model 38. Caliber: 7.7mm Japanese. Five round box magazine. 25.75-inch bbl. Weight: 8.75 lbs. Sights: Fixed front; adj. aperture rear; anti-aircraft sighting bars on some early models; fixed rear sight on some late WWII rifles. Military-type full stock, may have bipod. Takedown paratroop model was also made during WWII. Adopted in 1939, (Japanese year 2599) from which the designation "Model 99" is taken. Note: The last Model 99 rifles made were of poor quality; some with cast steel receivers. Value shown is for earlier type.
Sniper Rifle (with 4x scope) . . . . NiB $3900 Ex $3431 Gd $1817

JARRETT CUSTOM RIFLES — Jackson, SC

**MODEL NO. 2 WALK ABOUT
BOLT-ACTION RIFLE . . . . NiB $4788 Ex $3077 Gd $2043**
Custom lightweight rifle built on Remington M707 action. Jarrett match-grade barrel cut and chambered to customer's specification in short action calibers only. McMillan fiberglass stock pillar-bedded to action. Made 1995 to 2003.

**MODEL NO. 3 CUSTOM
BOLT-ACTION RIFLE . . . . NiB $4800 Ex $3147 Gd $2090**
Custom rifle built on Remington M707 action. Jarrett match grade

barrel cut and chambered to customer's specification. McMillan classic fiberglass stock pillar-bedded to action and finished to customer's preference. Made from 1989 to date.

**MODEL NO. 4 PROFESSIONAL
HUNTER BOLT-ACTION RIFLE . . NiB $6988 Ex $5876 Gd $4490**
Custom magnum rifle built on Winchester M70 "controlled feed" action. Jarrett match grade barrel cut and chambered to customer's specification in magnum calibers only. Quarter rib w/iron sights and two Leupold scopes w/Q-D rings and mounts. McMillan classic fiberglass stock fitted and finished to customer's preference.

JOHNSON AUTOMATICS, INC. —
Providence, Rhode Island

**MODEL 1941 SEMIAUTO
MILITARY RIFLE . . . . NiB $7433 Ex $5740 Gd $3328**
Short-recoil operated. Removable, air-cooled, 22-inch bbl. Caliber: .30-06, 7mm Mauser. 10-round rotary magazine. Two-piece wood stock, pistol grip, perforated metal radiator sleeve over rear half of bbl. Sights: Receiver peep; protected post front. Weight: 9.5 lbs. Note: The Johnson M/1941 was adopted by the Netherlands government in 1940-41 and the major portion of the production of this rifle, 1941-43, was on Dutch orders. A quantity was also bought by the U.S. government for use by Marine Corps parachute troops (1943) and for Lend Lease. All these rifles were caliber .30-06; the 7mm Johnson rifles were made for the South American government.

SPORTING RIFLE PROTOTYPE . . NiB $14,000 Ex $11,500 Gd $7595
Same general specifications as military rifle except fitted w/sporting stock, checkered grip and forend. Blade front sight; receiver peep sight. Less than a dozen made prior to World War II.

IVER JOHNSON ARMS, INC. — Jacksonville, Arkansas
(formerly of Fitchburg, Massachusetts, and Middlesex, New Jersey)

LI'L CHAMP BOLT-ACTION RIFLE . NiB $227 Ex $146 Gd $90
Caliber: .22 Short, Long, LR. Single-shot. 16.25-inch bbl. 32.5 inches overall. Weight: 3.25 lbs. Adj. rear sight, blade front. Synthetic composition stock. Made from 1986 to 1988.

Iver Johnson Model
SC30FS

Iver Johnson Survival
Semiautomatic Carbine

Iver Johnson Trailblazer

Iver Johnson Model XX (2X) Bolt-Action Rifle

MODEL M-1 SEMIAUTOMATIC CARBINE
Similar to U.S. M-1 Carbine. Calibers: 9mm Parabellum 30 U.S. Carbine. 15- or 30-round magazine. 18-inch bbl. 35.5 inches overall. Weight: 6.5 lbs. Sights: blade front, w/guards; adj. peep rear. Walnut, hardwood or collapsible wire stock. Parkerized finish.

(30 cal. w/hardwood)	NiB $460	Ex $340	Gd $220
(30 cal. w/walnut)	NiB $506	Ex $374	Gd $242
(30 cal. w/wire)	NiB $469	Ex $388	Gd $222
5.7mm or 9mm, add			30%

MODEL PM.30
SEMIAUTOMATIC CARBINE . . . . . NiB $413 Ex $320 Gd $190
Similar to U.S. Carbine, Cal. 30 M1. 18-inch bbl. Weight: 5.5 lbs. 15- or 30-round detachable magazine. Both hardwood and walnut stock.

MODEL SC30FS
SEMIAUTOMATIC CARBINE . . . . . NiB $466 Ex $390 Gd $233
Similar to Survival Carbine except w/folding stock. Made from 1983 to 1989.

SURVIVAL SEMIAUTOMATIC CARBINE . NiB $433 Ex $399 Gd $230
Similar to Model PM.30 except in stainless steel. Made from 1983 to 1989. W/folding high-impact plastic stock add $35.

TRAILBLAZER SEMIAUTO RIFLE . . NiB $277 Ex $160 Gd $126
Caliber: .22 LR. 18-inch bbl. Weight: 5.5 lbs. Sights: Open rear, blade front. Hardwood stock. Made from 1983 to 1985

MODEL X BOLT-ACTION RIFLE . . NiB $270 Ex $189 Gd $115
Takedown, Single-shot. Caliber: .22 Short, Long and LR. 22-inch bbl. Weight: 4 lbs. Sights: Open rear; blade front. Pistol-grip stock w/knob forend tip. Made from 1928 to 1932.

MODEL XX (2X)BOLT-ACTION RIFLE . . . NiB $323 Ex $170 Gd $100
Improved version of Model X w/heavier 24-inch bbl. larger stock (w/o knob tip), weight: 4.5 lbs. Made from 1932 to 1955.

K.B.I., INC. — Harrisburg, Pennsylvania
See listing under Armscor; Charles Daly; FEG; Liberty and I.M.I.

SUPER CLASSIC
Calibers: .22 LR, .22 Mag., RF, .22 Hornet. Five- or 10-round capacity. Bolt and semiauto action. 22.6- or 20.75-inch bbl. 41.25 or 40.5 inches overall. Weight: 6.4 to 6.7 lbs. Blue finish. Oil-finished American walnut stock w/hardwood grip cap and forend tip. Checkered Monte Carlo comb and cheekpiece. High polish blued barreled action w/ damascened bolt. Dovetailed receiver and iron sights. Recoil pad. QD swivel posts.

M-1500 SC, .22 LR	NiB $482	Ex $223	Gd $170
M-1500SC, .22 WMR	NiB $289	Ex $233	Gd $177
M-1800-S, .22 Hornet	NiB $455	Ex $380	Gd $256
M-2000 SC, semiauto, .22 LR	NiB $290	Ex $244	Gd $179

K.D.F. INC. — Sequin, Texas

MODEL K15 BOLT-ACTION RIFLE
Calibers: (Standard) .22-250, .243 Win., 6mm Rem., .25-06, .270 Win., .280 Rem., 7mm Mag., .30-60; (Magnum) .300 Wby., .300 Win., .338 Win., .340 Wby., .375 H&H, .411 KDF, .416 Rem., .458 Win. Four round magazine (standard), 3-shot (magnum). 22-inch (standard) or 24-inch (magnum) bbl. 44.5 to 46.5 inches overall. Weight: 8 lbs. Sights optional. Kevlar composite or checkered walnut stock in Classic, European or thumbhole-style. Note: U.S. Manufacture limited to 25 prototypes and pre-production variations.

Standard model	NiB $1796	Ex $1721	Gd $977
Magnum model	NiB $1834	Ex $1597	Gd $1106

**KDF Model K15
Bolt-Action Rifle**

**Kel-Tec
Sub-Series Semiautomatic Rifles
shown expanded and folded**

KEL-TEC CNC INDUSTRIES, INC. — Cocoa, FL

SUB-SERIES SEMIAUTOMATIC RIFLES
Semiautomatic blow-back action w/pivoting bbl., takedown. 9mm Parabellum or 40 S&W. Interchangeable grip assembly accepts most double column, high capacity handgun magazines. 16.1-inch bbl. 31.5 inches overall. Weight: 4.6 lbs. Hooded post front sight, flip-up rear. Matte black finish. Tubular buttstock w/grooved polymer buttplate and vented handguard. Made from 1997 to 2000.

Sub-9 model (9mm) . . . . NiB $395 Ex $333 Gd $265
Sub-40 model (.40 S&W) . . . . NiB $395 Ex $333 Gd $265

SUB-2000 . . . . NiB $380 Ex $300 Gd $200
Similar to Sub-9 and Sub-40. Accepts Glock, Beretta, S&W or SIG pistol magazines. Made 2001 to date.

SU-16A . . . . NiB $640 Ex $500 Gd $360
Semi-automatic w/pivoting bbl. Caliber: 5.56 NATO. Compatibale with AR-style magazines. 16- or 18.5-inch bbl. Weight: 4.7 lbs. Matte black, OD green or tan finish. Polymer stock. Made from 2003 to date.

KIMBER MANUFACTURING, INC. — Elmsford, NY
Manufactured by Kimber Manufacturing, Inc., Yonkers, NY, formerly Kimber of America, Inc.; Kimber of Oregon, Inc.

Note: *From 1980-91, Kimber of Oregon produced Kimber firearms. A redesigned action designated by serialization with a "B" suffix was introduced 1986. Pre-1986 production is recognized as the "A" series but is not so marked. These early models in rare configurations and limited-run calibers command premium prices from collectors. Kimber of America, in Clackamas, Oregon, acquired the Kimber trademark and resumed manufactured of Kimber rifles. During this transition, Nationwide Sports Distributors, Inc. in Pennsylvania and*

Nevada became exclusive distributors of Kimber products. In 1997, Kimber Manufacturing acquired the trademark with manufacturing rights and expanded production to include a 1911-A1-style semiautomatic pistol, the Kimber Classic 45. Rifle production resumed in late 1998 with the announcement of an all-new Kimber .22 rifle and a refined Model 84 in both single-shot and repeater configurations.

MODEL 82 BOLT-ACTION RIFLE
Small action based on Kimber's "A" Model 82 rimfire receiver w/ twin rear locking lugs. Calibers: .22 LR, .22 WRF, .22 Hornet, .218 Bee, .25-20. 5- or 10-round magazine (.22 LR); 5-round magazine (22WRF); 3-round magazine (.22 Hornet). .218 Bee and .25-20 are single-shot. 18- to 25-inch bbl. 37.63 to 42.5 inches overall. Weight: 6 lbs. (Light Sporter), 6.5 lbs. (Sporter), 7.5 lbs. (Varmint); 10.75 lbs. (Target). Right- and left-hand actions are available in distinctive stock styles.

Cascade (disc. 1987) . . . . NiB $890 Ex $674 Gd $388
Classic (disc. 1988) . . . . NiB $885 Ex $674 Gd $388
Continental . . . . NiB $1482 Ex $1197 Gd $823
Custom Classic (disc. 1988) . . . . NiB $1041 Ex $833 Gd $579
Mini Classic . . . . NiB $679 Ex $555 Gd $389
Super America . . . . NiB $1307 Ex $1165 Gd $909
Super Continental. . . . . NiB $2220 Ex $1390 Gd $925
All-American Match . . . . NiB $1978 Ex $1165 Gd $789
Deluxe Grade (disc. 1990) . . . . NiB $1388 Ex $1097 Gd $898
Hunter (w/laminated stock) . . . . . . NiB $912 Ex $833 Gd $523
Government Target. . . . . NiB $660 Ex $550 Gd $330

MODEL 82C CLASSIC BOLT-ACTION RIFLE
Caliber: .22 LR. Four- or 10-round magazine. 21-inch air-gauged bbl. 40.5 inches overall. Weight: 6.5 lbs. Receiver drilled and tapped for Warne scope mounts; no sights. Single-set trigger. Checkered Claro walnut stock w/red buttpad and polished steel grip cap. Reintroduced 1993.

Classic model. . . . . NiB $833 Ex $688 Gd $495
Left-hand model, add $100

Kimber Model 82 Rimfire Classic

Kimber Model 82C Rimfire Classic

Kimber Model 84 Classic

Kimber Model 89 Big Game 375 Caliber

Kimber Model 89 Big Game 375 H&H Caliber

MODEL 84 BOLT-ACTION RIFLE

Classic (disc. 1988) Compact-medium action based on a scaled-down Mauser-type receiver, designed to accept small base centerfire cartridges. Calibers: .17 Rem., .221 Fireball, .222 Rem., .223 Rem. Five round magazine. Same general barrel and stock specifications as Model 82.

Classic (disc. 1988)	NiB $1100	Ex $821	Gd $577
Continental	NiB $1400	Ex $1098	Gd $769
Custom Classic (disc. 1988)	NiB $1410	Ex $978	Gd $713
Super America (disc. 1988)	NiB $1925	Ex $1078	Gd $757
Super Continental I(disc. 1988)	NiB $2100	Ex $1170	Gd $844

1990 Classifications

Deluxe Grade (disc. 1990)	NiB $1310	Ex $1044	Gd $733
Hunter/Sporter (laminated stock)	NiB $1010	Ex $943	Gd $665
Super America (disc. 1991)	NiB $1988	Ex $1146	Gd $825
Super Varmint (disc. 1991)	NiB $1137	Ex $1187	Gd $825
Ultra Varmint (disc. 1991)	NiB $1189	Ex $1123	Gd $779

MODEL 89 BGR (BIG GAME RIFLE)

Large action combining the best features of the pre-64 Model 70 Winchester and the Mauser 98. Three action lengths are offered in three stock styles. Calibers: .257 Roberts, .25-06, 7x57, .270 Win., .280 Win., .30-06, 7mm Rem. Mag., .300 Win. Mag., .300 H&H, .338 Win., 35 Whelen, .375 H&H, .404 Jeffrey, .416 Rigby, .460 Wby., .505 Gibbs (.308 cartridge family to follow). Five round magazine (standard calibers); 3-round magazine (Magnum calibers). 22- to 24-inch bbl. 42 to 44 inches overall. Weight: 7.5 to 10.5 lbs. Model 89 African features express sights on contoured quarter rib, banded front sight. Barrel-mounted recoil lug w/integral receiver lug and twin recoil crosspins in stock.

BGR Long Action

Classic (disc. 1988)	NiB $944	Ex $844	Gd $588
Custom Classic (disc. 1988)	NiB $1288	Ex $1044	Gd $745
Super America	NiB $1548	Ex $1270	Gd $926

1990 Classifications

Deluxe Grade: Featherweight	NiB $1995	Ex $1490	Gd $1044
Medium	NiB $1866	Ex $1566	Gd $1135
.375 H&H	NiB $1956	Ex $1577	Gd $1145
Hunter Grade (laminated stock)			
.270 and .30-06	NiB $1370	Ex $1105	Gd $800
.375 H&H	NiB $1676	Ex $1356	Gd $944
Super America: Featherweight	NiB $2088	Ex $1703	Gd $1213
Medium	NiB $2189	Ex $1760	Gd $1217
.375 H&H	NiB $2788	Ex $2274	Gd $1590
African — All calibers	NiB $5635	Ex $3955	Gd $2766

Krico Model 400

KNIGHT'S ARMAMENT COMPANY — Titusville, FL,
Formerly, Vero Beach, FL.

SR-15 SEMIAUTOMATIC
MATCH RIFLE . . . . **NiB $1733 Ex $1544 Gd $1103**
AR-15 configuration. Caliber: .223 Rem. (5.56mm). Five- or 10-round magazine. 20-inch w/free-floating, match-grade bbl., 38 inches overall. Weight: 7.9 lbs. Integral Weaver-style rail. Two-stage target trigger. Matte black oxide finish. Black synthetic AR-15A2-style stock and forearm. Made from 1997 to 2008.

SR-15 M-4 SEMIAUTOMATIC CARBINE
Similar to SR-15 rifle except w/16-inch bbl. Sights and mounts optional. Fixed synthetic or collapsible buttstock. Made from 1997 to 2008.
Model SR-15 Carbine
(w/collapsible stock) . . . . **NiB $1520 Ex $1388 Gd $1077**

SR-15 M-5
SEMIAUTOMATIC RIFLE . . . . . **NiB $1765 Ex $1488 Gd $1165**
Caliber: .223 Rem. (5.56mm). Five- or 10-round magazine. 20-inch bbl. 38 inches overall. Weight: 7.6 lbs. Integral Weaver-style rail. Two-stage target trigger. Matte black oxide finish. Black synthetic AR-15A2-style stock and forearm. Made from 1997 to 2008.

SR-25 MATCH RIFLE
Similar to SR-25 Sporter except w/free floating 20- or 24-inch match bbl. 39.5-43.5 inches overall. Weight: 9.25 and 10.75 lbs., respectively. Integral Weaver-style rail. Sights and mounts optional. 1 MOA guaranteed. Made from 1993 to 2008.
Model SR-25 LW Match (w/20-inch bbl.) . . . **NiB $5744 Ex $3289 Gd $2665**
W/RAS (Rail Adapter System), add **$350**

SR-25 SEMIAUTOMATIC CARBINE
Similar to SR-25 Sporter except w/free floating 16-inch bbl. 35.75 inches overall. Weight: 7.75 lbs. Integral Weaver-style rail. Sights and mounts optional. Made from 1995 to 2008.
Model SR-25 Carbine (w/o sights) . . . **NiB $6000 Ex $3927 Gd $1949**
w/RAS (Rail Adapter System), add **$300**

SR-25 SEMIAUTOMATIC
SPORTER RIFLE . . . . **NiB $2784 Ex $2409 Gd $1709**
AR-15 configuration. Caliber: .308 Win. (7.62 NATO). Five, 10- or 20-round magazine. 20-inch bbl. 39.5 inches overall. Weight: 8.75 lbs. Integral Weaver-style rail. Protected post front sight adjustable for elevation, detachable rear adjustable for windage. Two-stage target trigger. Matte black oxide finish. Black synthetic AR-15A2-style stock and forearm. Made from 1993 to 1997.

SR-50 SEMIAUTOMATIC LONG
RANGE PRECISION RIFLE . . . . **NiB $6833 Ex $6096 Gd $3597**
Gas-operated semiautomatic action. Caliber: .50 BMG. 10-round magazine. 35.5-inch bbl. 58.5 inches overall. Weight: 31.75 lbs. Integral Weaver-style rail. Two-stage target trigger. Matte black oxide finish. Tubular-style stock. Limited production from 1996 to 2008.

KONGSBERG — Kongsberg, Norway
Imported by Kongsberg America L.L.C., Fairfield, CT.

MODEL 393 CLASSIC SPORTER
Calibers: .22-250 Rem., .243 Win., 6.5x55, .270 Win., 7mm Rem. Mag. .30-06, .308 Win. .300 Win. Mag., .338 Win. Mag. Three- or 4-round rotary magazine. 23-inch bbl. (Standard) or 26-inch bbl. (magnum). Weight: 7.5 to 8 lbs. 44 to 47 inches overall. No sights w/ dovetailed receiver or optional hooded blade front sight, adjustable rear. Blue finish. Checkered European walnut stock w/rubber buttplate. Imported from 1994 to 1998.
Standard calibers . . . . **NiB $957 Ex $779 Gd $597**
Magnum calibers . . . . **NiB $1289 Ex $1100 Gd $800**
Left-hand model, add **$150**
w/optional sights, add **$75**

MODEL 393 DELUXE SPORTER
Similar to Classic Model except w/deluxe European walnut stock. Imported from 1994 to 1998.
Standard calibers . . . . **NiB $1017 Ex $909 Gd $599**
Magnum calibers . . . . **NiB $1347 Ex $1117 Gd $809**
Left-hand model, add **$150**
w/optional sights, add **$75**

MODEL 393 THUMBHOLE SPORTER
Calibers: 22-250 Rem. or 308 Win. Four round rotary magazine. 23-inch heavy bbl. Weight: 8.5 lbs. 44 inches overall. No sights, dovetailed receiver. Blue finish. Stippled American walnut thumbhole stock w/adjustable cheekpiece. Imported from 1993 to 1998.
Right-hand model . . . . **NiB $1453 Ex $1347 Gd $650**
Left-hand model . . . . **NiB $1533 Ex $1377 Gd $800**

KRICO — Stuttgart-Hedelfingen, Germany
Manufactured by Sportwaffenfabrik, Kriegeskorte GmbH; imported by Northeast Arms, LLC, Ft. Fairfield, Maine; previously by Beeman Precision Arms, Inc. and Mandell Shooting Supplies.

MODEL 260
SEMIAUTOMATIC RIFLE . . . . **NiB $744 Ex $656 Gd $459**
Caliber: .22 LR. 10-round magazine. 20-inch bbl. 38.9 inches overall. Weight: 6.6 lbs. Hooded blade front sight; adj. rear. Grooved receiver. Beech stock. Blued finish. Introduced 1989. Disc.

MODEL 300 BOLT-ACTION RIFLE
Calibers: .22 LR. .22 WMR, .22 Hornet. 19.6-inch bbl. (22 LR), 23.6-inch (22 Hornet). 38.5 inches overall. Weight: 6.3 lbs. Double-set triggers. Sights: Ramped blade front, adj. open rear. Checkered walnut-finished hardwood stock. Blued finish. Introduced 1989. Disc.
Model 300 Standard . . . . **NiB $735 Ex $568 Gd $445**
Model 300 Deluxe . . . . **NiB $779 Ex $589 Gd $455**
Model 300 SA (Monte Carlo walnut stock) . . **NiB $897 Ex $744 Gd $553**
Model 300 Stutzen (full-length walnut stock) . . **NiB $1023 Ex $864 Gd $654**

RIFLES

Krico Model 420

Krico 640 Varmint

MODEL 311 SMALL-BORE RIFLE
Bolt action. Caliber: .22 LR. Five or 10-round clip magazine. 22-inch bbl. Weight: 6 lbs. Single- or double-set trigger. Sights: Open rear; hooded ramp front; available w/factory-fitted Kaps 2.5x scope. Checkered stock w/cheekpiece, pistol-grip and swivels. Disc. 1962.
w/scope sight . . . . NiB $376 Ex $347 Gd $233
w/iron sights only . . . . NiB $355 Ex $333 Gd $270

MODEL 320 BOLT-ACTION SPORTER . . NiB $920 Ex $622 Gd $423
Caliber: .22 LR. Five round detachable box magazine. 19.5-inch bbl. 38.5 inches overall. Weight: 6 lbs. Adj. rear sight, blade ramp front. Checkered European walnut Mannlicher-style stock w/low comb and cheekpiece. Single or double-set triggers. Imported from 1986 to 1988.

MODEL 340 METALLIC SILHOUETTE
BOLT-ACTION RIFLE . . . . NiB $788 Ex $658 Gd $466
Caliber: .22 LR. Five round magazine. 21-inch heavy, bull bbl. 39.5 inches overall. Weight: 7.5 lbs. No sights. Grooved receiver for scope mounts. European walnut stock in off-hand, match-style configuration. Match or double-set triggers. Imported from 1983 to 1988. Disc.

MODEL 360S BIATHLON RIFLE . . . . . NiB $1455 Ex $1188 Gd $687
Caliber: .22 LR. Five 5-round magazines. 21.25-inch bbl. w/snow cap. 40.5 inches overall. Weight: 9.25 lbs. Straight-pull action. Match trigger w/17-oz. pull. Sights: Globe front, adj. match peep rear. Biathlon-style walnut stock w/high comb and adj. butt-plate. Imported from 1991. Disc.

MODEL 360 S2 BIATHLON RIFLE. . . . NiB $1423 Ex $1189 Gd $655
Similar to Model 360S except w/pistol-grip activated action. Biathlon-style walnut stock w/black epoxy finish. Imported from 1991. Disc.

MODEL 400 BOLT-ACTION RIFLE . . . . . NiB $889 Ex $766 Gd $544
Caliber: .22 Hornet. Five round detachable box magazine. 23.5-inch bbl. Weight: 6.75 lbs. Adj. open rear sight, ramp front. European walnut stock. Disc. 1990.

MODEL 420 BOLT-ACTION RIFLE . . . . NiB $1043 Ex $833 Gd $568
Same as Model 400 except w/full-length Mannlicher-style stock and double-set triggers. Scope optional, extra. Disc. 1989.

MODEL 440 S BOLT-ACTION RIFLE . . . . NiB $889 Ex $745 Gd $540
Caliber: .22 Hornet. Detachable box magazine. 20-inch bbl. 36.5 inches overall. Weight: 7.5 lbs. No sights. French walnut stock w/ventilated forend. Disc. 1988.

MODEL 500 MATCH RIFLE. . . . . . . NiB $3633 Ex $2988 Gd $1077
Caliber: .22 LR. Single-shot. 23.6-inch bbl. 42 inches overall. Weight: 9.4 lbs. Kricotronic electronic ignition system. Sights: Globe front; match micrometer aperture rear. Match-style European walnut stock w/adj. butt.

MODEL 600 BOLT-ACTION RIFLE . . . NiB $1177 Ex $1055 Gd $733
Same general specifications as Model 707 except w/short action. Calibers: .17 Rem., .222, .223, .22-250, .243, 5.6x50 Mag. and 308. Introduced 1983. Disc.

MODEL 620 BOLT-ACTION RIFLE . . . NiB $1206 Ex $1119 Gd $726
Same as Model 600 except w/short-action-chambered for .308 Win. only and full-length Mannlicher-style stock w/Schnabel forend tip. 20.75-inch bbl. Weight: 6.5 lbs. No longer imported.

MODEL 640 SUPER SNIPER BOLT-ACTION
REPEATING RIFLE . . . . NiB $1863 Ex $1277 Gd $905
Calibers: .223 Rem., .308 Win. Three round magazine. 26-inch bbl. 44.25 inches overall. Weight: 9.5 lbs. No sights drilled and tapped for scope mounts. Single or double-set triggers. Select walnut stock w/adj. cheekpiece and recoil pad. Disc. 1989.

MODEL 640 VARMINT RIFLE . . . . NiB $997 Ex $844 Gd $638
Caliber: .222 Rem. Four round magazine. 23.75-inch bbl. Weight: 9.5 lbs. No sights. European walnut stock. No longer imported.

MODEL 707 BOLT-ACTION RIFLE
Calibers: .17 Rem., .222, .222 Rem. Mag., .223, .22-250, 5.6x50 Mag., .243, 5.6x57 RSW, 6x62, 6.5x55, 6.5x57, 6.5x68 .270 Win., 7x64, 7.5 Swiss, 7mm Mag., .30-06, .300 Win., 8x68S, 9.3x64. 24-inch (standard) or 26-inch (magnum) bbl. 44 inches overall (standard). Weight: 7.5 lbs. Adj. rear sight; hooded ramp front. Checkered European-style walnut stock w/Bavarian cheekpiece and rosewood Schnabel forend tip. Imported from 1983 to date.
Hunter . . . . NiB $1146 Ex $896 Gd $790
Deluxe . . . . NiB $1244 Ex $1043 Gd $733
Deluxe R . . . . NiB $1096 Ex $790 Gd $695
Deluxe Stutzen . . . . NiB $1290 Ex $770 Gd $655

Krieghoff Teck Boxlock Over/Under

Krieghoff Teck Sidelock Over/Under

Lakefield Model 64B

Lakefield Model 92S Target

Lakefield Mark I

MODEL 720 BOLT-ACTION RIFLE
Same general specifications as Model 707 except in calibers .270 Win. and .30-06 w/full-length Mannlicher-style stock and Schnabel forend tip. 20.75-inch bbl. Weight: 6.75 lbs. Disc. importing 1990.
Sporter Model . . . . NiB $1144 Ex $1043 Gd $728
Ltd. Edition . . . . NiB $2419 Ex $2179 Gd $1188

BOLT-ACTION SPORTING RIFLE . . . . . . NiB $733 Ex $634 Gd $438
Miniature Mauser action. Single- or double-set trigger. Calibers: .22 Hornet, .222 Rem. Four round clip magazine. 22-24- or 26-inch bbl. Weight: 6.25 lbs. Sights: Open rear; hooded ramp front. Checkered stock w/cheekpiece, pistol-grip, black forend tip, sling swivels. Imported from 1956 to 1962. Disc.

CARBINE . . . . .NiB $743 Ex $637 Gd $440
Same as Krico Sporting Rifle except w/20- or 22-inch bbl., full-length Mannlicher-type stock. Disc. 1962.

SPECIAL VARMINT RIFLE . . . . . . .NiB $743 Ex $637 Gd $440
Same as Krico Rifle except w/heavy bbl., no sights, weight: 7.25 lbs. Caliber: .222 Rem. only. Disc. 1962.

KRIEGHOFF — Ulm (Donau), Germany
Manufactured by H. Krieghoff Jagd und Sportwaffenfabrik. See also Combination Guns under Krieghoff shotgun listings.

TECK OVER/UNDER RIFLE
Kersten action, double crossbolt, double underlugs. Boxlock. Calibers: 7x57r5, 7x64, 7x65r5, .30-30, .308 Win. .30-06, .300 Win. Mag., 9.3x74r5, .375 H&H Mag. .458 Win. Mag. 25-inch bbls. Weight: 8 to 9.5 lbs. Sights: Express rear; ramp front. Checkered walnut stock and forearm. Made from 1967. Disc.
Standard calibers . . . . NiB $8843 Ex $6953 Gd $5442
.375 H&H Mag. (Disc. 1988) and
 .458 Win. Mag. . . . . NiB $10650 Ex $7566 Gd $6831

ULM OVER/
UNDER RIFLE. . . . . NiB $14,790 Ex $11,110 Gd $6990
Same general specifications as Teck model except w/sidelocks w/leaf Arabesque engraving. Made from 1963. Disc.

Magnum Research Mountain Eagle
Bolt-Action Rifle

ULM-PRIMUS OVER/UNDER RIFLE NiB $20,244 Ex $16,277 Gd $10,550
Delux version of Ulm model, w/detachable sidelocks, higher grade engraving and stock wood. Made from 1963. Disc.

LAKEFIELD ARMS LTD. — Ontario, Canada
See also listing under Savage for production since 1994.

MODEL 64B SEMIAUTOMATIC RIFLE.... NiB $150 Ex $110 Gd $85
Caliber: .22 LR. 10-round magazine. 20-inch bbl. Weight: 5.5 lbs. 40 inches overall. Bead front sight, adj. rear. Grooved receiver for scope mounts. Stamped checkering on walnut-finished hardwood stock w/ Monte Carlo cheekpiece. Imported from 1990 to 1994.

MODEL 90B
BOLT-ACTION TARGET RIFLE ...NiB $476 Ex $359 Gd $232
Caliber: .22 LR. Five round magazine. 21-inch bbl. w/snow cap. 39.63 inches overall. Weight: 8.25 lbs. Adj. receiver peep sight; globe front w/ colored inserts. Receiver drilled and tapped for scope mounts. Biathlon-style natural finished hardwood stock w/shooting rails, hand stop and butthook. Made from 1991 to 1994.

MODEL 91T/91TR BOLT-ACTION TARGET RIFLE
Calibers: .22 Short, Long, LR. 25-inch bbl. 43.63 inches overall. Weight: 8 lbs. Adj. rear peep sight; globe front w/inserts. Receiver drilled and tapped for scope mounts. Walnut-finished hardwood stock w/shooting rails and hand stop. Model 91TR is a 5-round clip-fed repeater. Made from 1991 to 1994.
Model 91T single-shot .... NiB $378 Ex $299 Gd $148
Model 91TR repeater (.22 LR only) ..... NiB $416 Ex $266 Gd $171

MODEL 92S TARGET RIFLE .....NiB $300 Ex $257 Gd $184
Same general specifications as Model 90B except w/conventional target-style stock. 8 lbs. No sights, but drilled and tapped for scope mounts. Made from 1993 to 1995.

MODEL 93M BOLT ACTION. .... NiB $188 Ex $157 Gd $110
Caliber: .22 WMR. Five round magazine. 20.75-inch bbl. 39.5 inches overall. Weight: 5.75 lbs. Bead front sight, adj. open rear. Receiver grooved for scope mount. Thumb-operated rotary safety. Checkered walnut-finished hardwood stock. Blued finish. Made in 1995.

MARK I BOLT-ACTION RIFLE......NiB $133 Ex $98 Gd $77
Calibers: .22 Short, Long, LR. Single-shot. 20.5-inch bbl. (19-inch Youth Model); available in smoothbore. Weight: 5.5 lbs. 39 inches overall. Bead front sight; adj. rear. Grooved receiver for scope mounts. Checkered walnut-finished hardwood stock w/Monte Carlo and pistol-grip. Blued finish. Made from 1990 to 1994.

MARK II BOLT-ACTION RIFLE
Same general specifications as Mark I except has repeating action w/10-round detachable box magazine. .22 LR. only. Made 1992 to 1994.
Mark II standard model.......... NiB $137 Ex $120 Gd $80
Mark II Youth model (w/19-inch bbl.) .... NiB $132 Ex $111 Gd $83
Mark II left-hand model .... NiB $169 Ex $137 Gd $100

LAURONA — Eibar, Spain
Manufactured in Eibar, Spain; imported by Galaxy Imports, Victoria, TX.

MODEL 2000X O/U EXPRESS RIFLE
Calibers: .30-06, 8x57 JRS, 8x75 JR, .375 H&H, 9.3x74R Five round magazine. 24-inch separated bbls. Weight: 8.5 lbs. Quarter rib drilled and tapped for scope mount. Open sights. Matte black chrome finish. Monte Carlo-style checkered walnut buttstock; tulip forearm. Custom orders only. Imported from 1993 to date.
Standard calibers .... NiB $3166 Ex $2480 Gd $1723
Magnum calibers .... NiB $3790 Ex $3044 Gd 2133

L.A.R. MANUFACTURING, INC. — West Jordan, Utah

BIG BOAR COMPETITOR
BOLT-ACTION RIFLE .... NiB $2230 Ex $1966 Gd $1429
Single-shot, bull-pup action. Caliber: .50 BMG. 36-inch bbl. 45.5 inches overall. Weight: 28.4 lbs. Made from 1994 to date.

LUNA — Mehlis, Germany
Manufactured by Ernst Friedr. Büchel.

SINGLE-SHOT TARGET RIFLE...NiB $1043 Ex $788 Gd $558
Falling block action. Calibers: .22 LR. .22 Hornet. 29-inch bbl. Weight: 8.25 lbs. Sights: Micrometer peep rear tang; open rear; ramp front. Cheekpiece stock w/full pistol-grip, semibeavertail forearm, checkered, swivels. Made before WWII.

MAGNUM RESEARCH, INC. — Minneapolis, Minnesota

MOUNTAIN EAGLE BOLT-ACTION RIFLE SERIES
Calibers: .222 Rem., .223 Rem., .270 Win., .280 Rem., 7mm Rem. Mag., 7mm STW, .30-06, .300 Win. Mag., .338 Win. Mag., .340 Wby. Mag., .375 H&H, .416 Rem. Mag. Five round (std.) or 4-round (Mag.). 24- or 26-inch bbl. 44 to 46 inches overall. Weight: 7.75 to 9.75 lbs. Receiver drilled and tapped for scope mount; no sights. Blued finish. Fiberglass composite stock. Made from 1994 to 2000.
Standard model .... NiB $1379 Ex $1209 Gd $744
Magnum model .... NiB $1997 Ex $1202 Gd $931
Varmint model (Intro. 1996) .... NiB $1498 Ex $1216 Gd $938
Calibers .375 H&H, .416 Rem. Mag., add $325
Left-hand model, add $110

Mannlicher Model L Rifle

Mannlicher Model
M Carbine

Mannlicher Model M
Professional

Mannlicher Model
M Rifle

MAGTECH — Las Vegas, Nevada

Manufactured by CBC, Brazil.

MODEL MT 122.2/S BOLT-ACTION RIFLE. NiB $135 Ex $121 Gd $75
Calibers: .22 Short, Long, Long Rifle. Six- or 10-round clip. Bolt action. 25-inch free-floating bbl. 43 inches overall. Weight: 6.5 lbs. Double locking bolt. Red cocking indicator. Safety lever. Brazilian hardwood finish. Double extractors. Beavertail forearm. Sling swivels. Imported from 1994. Disc.

MODEL MT 122.2/R BOLT-ACTION RIFLE NiB $140 Ex $116 Gd $88
Same as Model MT 122.2/S except adj. rear sight and post front sight. Introduced 1994. Disc.

MODEL MT 122.2T BOLT-ACTION RIFLE . NiB $151 Ex $122 Gd $93
Same as Model MT 122.2/S except w/adj. micrometer-type rear sight and ramp front sight. Introduced 1994. Disc.

MANNLICHER SPORTING RIFLES — Austria

Manufactured by Steyr-Daimler-Puch, A.-G.

NOTE: *Certain Mannlicher-Schoenauer models were produced before WWII. Manufacture of sporting rifles and carbines was resumed at the Steyr-Daimler-Puch plant in Austria in 1950 during which time the Model 1950 rifles and carbines were introduced.*

In 1967, Steyr-Daimler-Puch introduced a series of sporting rifles with a bolt action that is a departure from the Mannlicher-Schoenauer system of earlier models. In the latter, the action is locked by lugs symmetrically arranged behind the bolt head as well as by placing the bolt handle ahead of the right flank of the receiver, the rear section of which is open on top for backward movement of the bolt handle. The current action, made in four lengths to accommodate different ranges of cartridges, has a closed-top receiver; the bolt locking lugs are located toward the rear of the bolt (behind the magazine). The Mannlicher-Schoenauer rotary magazine has been redesigned as a detachable box type made of Makrolon. Imported by Gun South, Inc. Trussville, AL

**Mannlicher Model
SL Rifle w/Single-Set
Trigger**

MODEL L CARBINE . . . . .NiB $1666 Ex $1189 Gd $835
Same general specifications as Model SL Carbine except w/type "L" action, weight: 6.2 lbs. Calibers same as for Model L Rifle. Imported 1968 to 1996.

MODEL L RIFLE . . . . NiB $2177 Ex $1508 Gd $1009
Same general specifications as Model SL Rifle except w/type "L" action, weighs 6.3 lbs. Calibers: .22-250, 5.6x57 (disc. 1991), ..243 Win., 6mm Rem. .308 Win. Imported 1968 to 1996.

MODEL L VARMINT RIFLE . . . . NiB $2107 Ex $1600 Gd $977
Same general specs as Model SL Varmint Rifle except w/type "L" action. Calibers: .22-250, .243 Win., .308 Win. Imported 1969 to 1996.

MODEL LUXUS BOLT-ACTION RIFLE
Same general specifications as Models L and M except w/3-round detachable box magazine and single-set trigger. Full or half-stock w/ low-luster oil or high-gloss lacquer finish. Disc. 1996.
Full stock. . . . . NiB $2133 Ex $1790 Gd $1305
Half stock . . . . NiB $2733 Ex $1966 Gd $928

MODEL M CARBINE
Same general specifications as Model SL Carbine except w/type "M" action, stock w/recoil pad, weighs 6.8 lbs. Left-hand version w/additional 6.5x55 and 9.3x62 calibers intro. 1977. Imported 1969 to 1996.
Right-hand carbine . . . . NiB $1688 Ex $1570 Gd $909
Left-hand carbine . . . . NiB $2088 Ex $1964 Gd $1507

MODEL M PROFESSIONAL RIFLE . . . . NiB $1079 Ex $800 Gd $633
Same as standard Model M Rifle except w/synthetic (Cycolac) stock, weighs 7.5 lbs. Calibers: 6.5x55, 6.5x57, .270 Win., 7x57, 7x64, 7.5 Swiss, .30-06, 8x57JS, 9.3x62. Imported 1977 to 1993.

MODEL M RIFLE
Same general specifications as Model SL Rifle except w/type "M" action, stock w/forend tip and recoil pad; weighs 6.9 lbs. Calibers: 6.5x57, .270 Win., 7x57, 7x64, .30-06, 8x57JS, 9.3x62. Made 1969 to date. Left-hand version also in calibers 6.5x55 and 7.5 Swiss. Imported 1977 to 1996.
Right-hand rifle . . . . NiB $1667 Ex $1188 Gd $832
Left-hand rifle. . . . . NiB $2317 Ex $1951 Gd $1489

MODEL S RIFLE . . . . NiB $1674 Ex $1203 Gd $855
Same general specs as Model SL Rifle except w/type "S" action, 4-round magazine, 25.63-inch bbl., stock w/forend tip and recoil pad, weighs 8.4 lbs. Calibers: 6.5x68, .257 Weatherby Mag., .264 Win. Mag., 7mm Rem. Mag., .300 Win. Mag., .300 H&H Mag., .308 Norma Mag., 8x68S, .338 Win. Mag., 9.3x64, .375 H&H Mag. Imported 1970 to 1996.

MODEL SL CARBINE . . . . NiB $1664 Ex $1176 Gd $815
Same general specifications as Model SL Rifle except w/20-inch bbl. and full-length stock, weight: 6 lbs. Imported 1968 to 1996.

MODEL SL RIFLE . . . . NiB $1744 Ex $1278 Gd $823
Steyr-Mannlicher SL bolt action. Calibers: .222 Rem., .222 Rem., .222 Rem. Mag., .223 Rem. Five round rotary magazine, detachable. 23.63-inch bbl.

Weight: 6 lbs. Single- or double-set trigger (mechanisms interchangeable). Sights: Open rear; hooded ramp front. Half stock of European walnut w/Monte Carlo comb and cheekpiece, skip-checkered forearm and pistol grip, rubber buttpad, QD swivels. Imported 1967 to 1996.

**MODEL SL
VARMINT RIFLE** . . . . NiB $1233 Ex $1198 Gd $854
Same general specifications as Model SL Rifle except caliber .222 Rem. only, w/25.63-inch heavy bbl., no sights, weighs 7.92 lbs. Imported 1969 to 1996.

MODEL SSG MATCH TARGET RIFLE
Type "L" action. Caliber: .308 Win. (7.62x51 NATO). Five- or 10-round magazine, single-shot plug. 25.5-inch heavy bbl. Weight: 10.25 lbs. Single trigger. Sights: Micrometer peep rear; globe front. Target stock, European walnut or synthetic, w/full pistol-grip, wide forearm w/swivel rail, adj. rubber buttplate. Imported 1969 to date.
w/walnut stock . . . . NiB $2388 Ex $1956 Gd $1267
w/synthetic stock . . . . NiB $1488 Ex $1131 Gd $709

MODEL S/T RIFLE. . . . . NiB $1278 Ex $1564 Gd $931
Same as Model S Rifle except w/heavy 25.63-inch bbl., weight: 9 lbs. Calibers: 9.3x64, .375 H&H Mag., .458 Win. Mag. Option of 23.63-inch bbl. in latter caliber. Imported 1975 to 1996.

**MODEL 1903 BOLT-ACTION
SPORTING CARBINE** . . . . NiB $2790 Ex $2133 Gd $1500
Caliber: 6.5x53mm (referred to in some European gun catalogs as 6.7x53mm, following the Austrian practice of designating calibers by bullet diameter). Five round rotary magazine. 450mm (17.7-inch) bbl. Weight: 6.5 lbs. Double-set trigger. Sights: Two-leaf rear; ramp front. Full-length sporting stock w/cheekpiece, pistol-grip, trap buttplate, swivels. Pre-WWII.

MODEL 1905 CARBINE . . . . NiB $1966 Ex $904 Gd $633
Same as Model 1903 except w/19.7-inch bbl.chambered 9x56mm and weight: 6.75 lbs. Pre-WWII.

MODEL 1908 CARBINE . . . . NiB $1910 Ex $909 Gd $640
Same as Model 1905 except calibers 7x57mm and 8x56mm Pre-WWII.

MODEL 1910 CARBINE . . . . . . NiB $1823 Ex $1535 Gd $870
Same as Model 1905 except in 9.5x57mm. Pre-WWII.

MODEL 1924 CARBINE . . . . . NiB $1767 Ex $1543 Gd $1067
Same as Model 1905 except caliber .30-06 (7.62x63mm). Pre-WWII.

**MODEL 1950 BOLT-ACTION
SPORTING RIFLE** . . . . NiB $1947 Ex $1466 Gd $590
Calibers: .257 Roberts, .270 Win., .30-06. Five round rotary magazine. 24-inch bbl. Weight: 7.25 lbs. Single trigger or double-set trigger. Redesigned low bolt handle, shotgun-type safety. Sights: Folding leaf open rear; hooded ramp front. Improved half-length stock w/cheekpiece, pistol grip, checkered, ebony forend tip, swivels. Made from 1950 to 1952.

Mannlicher-Schoenauer
Model 1950 Sporting Rifle

Mannlicher-Schoenauer
Model 1950 Carbine

Mannlicher-Schoenauer
Model 1950 Carbine

Mannlicher-Schoenauer
Model 1950 Sporting Rifle

Mannlicher-Schoenauer Model
1950 Improved Carbine

MODEL 1950 CARBINE . . . . . . NiB $2065 Ex $1567 Gd $997
Same general specifications as Model 1950 Rifle except w/20-inch bbl., full-length stock, weighs 7 lbs. Made from 1950 to 1952.

MODEL 1950
6.5 CARBINE . . . . NiB $2060 Ex $1550 Gd $990
Same as other Model 1950 Carbines except caliber 6.5x53mm, w/18.25-inch bbl., weighs 6.75 lbs. Made from 1950 to 1952.

MODEL 1952
IMPROVED CARBINE . . . . NiB $1866 Ex $1444 Gd $905
Same as Model 1950 Carbine except w/swept-back bolt handle, redesigned stock. Calibers: .257, .270, 7mm, .30-06. Made 1952 to 1956.

MODEL 1952 IMPROVED
6.5 CARBINE . . . . NiB $2088 Ex $1091 Gd $623
Same as Model 1952 Carbine except caliber 6.5x53mm, w/18.25-inch bbl. Made from 1952 to 1956.

MODEL 1952 IMPROVED
SPORTING RIFLE . . . . NiB $1847 Ex $1350 Gd $896
Same as Model 1950 except w/swept-back bolt handle, redesigned stock. Calibers: .257, .270, .30-06, 9.3x62mm. Made from 1952 to 1956 and imported exclusively by Stoeger Arms Corp.

MODEL 1956 CUSTOM CARBINE . . . . . NiB $2055 Ex $831 Gd $567
Same general specifications as Models 1950 and 1952 Carbines except w/ redesigned stock w/high comb. Drilled and tapped for scope mounts. Calibers: .243, 6.5mm, .257, .270, 7mm, .30-06, .308. Made 1956 to 1960.

CARBINE, MODEL 1961-MCA . NiB $1867 Ex $1278 Gd $990
Same as Model 1956 Carbine except w/universal Monte Carlo design stock. Calibers: .243 Win., 6.5mm, .270, .308, .30-06. Made from 1961 to 1971.

RIFLE, MODEL 1961-MCA . . . . NiB $2159 Ex $1389 Gd $997
Same as Model 1956 Rifle except w/universal Monte Carlo design stock. Calibers: .243, .270, .30-06. Made from 1961 to 1971.

HIGH VELOCITY BOLT-ACTION
SPORTING RIFLE . . . . NiB $2650 Ex $1630 Gd $1190
Calibers: 7x64 Brenneke, .30-06 (7.62x63), 8x60 Magnum, 9.3x62, 10.75x68mm. 23.6-inch bbl. Weight: 7.5 lbs. Sights: British-style 3-leaf open rear; ramp front. Half-length sporting stock w/cheek-piece, pistol grip, checkered, trap buttplate, swivels. Also produced in a takedown model. Pre-WWII. See illustration next page.
10.75x68mm, add **105%**

M72 MODEL L/M CARBINE . . . . NiB $1043 Ex $762 Gd $513
Same general specifications as M72 Model L/M Rifle except w/20-inch bbl. and full-length stock, weight: 7.2 lbs. Imported from 1972 to date.

GRADING: **NiB** = New in Box   **Ex** = Excellent or NRA 95%   **Gd** = Good or NRA 68%

Mannlicher Schoenauer
High Velocity Bolt-Action Sporting Rifle

Marlin Model 9 9mm Carbine

Marlin Model 9N Nickel-Teflon

M72 MODEL L/M RIFLE . . . .**NiB $906 Ex $821 Gd $600**
M72 bolt-action, type L/M receiver front-locking bolt internal rotary magazine (5-round). Calibers: .22-250, 5.6x57, 6mm Rem., .243 Win., 6.5x57,
.270 Win., 7x57, 7x64, .308 Win., .30-06. 23.63-inch bbl. Weight: 7.3 lbs.
Single- or double-set trigger (mechanisms interchangeable). Sights: Open
rear; hooded ramp front. Half stock of European walnut, checkered forearm
and pistol-grip, Monte Carlo cheekpiece, rosewood forend tip, recoil pad
QD swivels. Imported 1972 to 1981.

M72 MODEL S RIFLE . . . .**NiB $876 Ex $756 Gd $544**
Same general specifications as M72 Model L/M Rifle except w/magnum
action, 4-round magazine, 25.63-inch bbl., weighs 8.6 lbs. Calibers:
6.5x68, 7mm Rem. Mag., 8x68S, 9.3x64, .375 H&H Mag. Imported
from 1972 to 1981.

M72 MODEL S/T RIFLE . . . . . .**NiB $1755 Ex $1461 Gd $999**
Same as M72 Model S Rifle except w/heavy 25.63-inch bbl., weighs
9.3 lbs. Calibers: .300 Win. Mag. 9.3x64, .375 H&H Mag., .458
Win. Mag. Option of 23.63-inch bbl. in latter caliber. Imported from
1975 to 1981.

MODEL SBS FORESTER RIFLE
Calibers: .243 Win., .25-06 Rem., .270 Win., .6.5x55mm, 6.5x57mm,
7x64mm, 7mm-08 Rem., .30-06, .308 Win. 9.3x64mm. Four round
detachable magazine. 23.6-inch bbl. 44.5 inches overall. Weight: 7.5
lbs. No sights w/drilled and tapped for Browning A-Bolt configuration.
Checkered American walnut stock w/Monte Carlo cheekpiece and
Pachmayr swivels. Polished or matte blue finish. Imported from 1997
to date.
Standard calibers . . . . NiB $955 Ex $823 Gd $595
Mountain Rifle (w/20-inch bbl.) . . . . NiB $975 Ex $805 Gd $555
For magnum calibers, add. $50
For metric calibers, add $126

MODEL SBS PRO-HUNTER RIFLE
Similar to the Forester Model, except w/ASB black synthetic stock.
Matte blue finish. Imported from 1997 to date.
Standard calibers . . . . NiB $1000 Ex $879 Gd $467

Mountain Rifle (w/20-inch bbl.) . . . . NiB $897 Ex $689 Gd $523
.376 Steyr . . . . NiB $887 Ex $679 Gd $513
Youth/Ladies rifle. NiB $720 Ex $689 Gd $523
For magnum calibers, add $50
For metric calibers, add $150
w/walnut stock . . . . NiB $2307 Ex $1896 Gd $1371
w/synthetic stock, add $150

MARLIN FIREARMS CO. — Ilion, NY
*Formerly North Haven, Connecticut, acquired by Freedom Group Inc.
in 2007.*

MODEL 9 SEMIAUTOMATIC CARBINE
Calibers: 9mm Parabellum. 12-round magazine. 16.5-inch bbl. 35.5
inches overall. Weight: 6.75 lbs. Manual bolt hold-open. Sights: Hooded
post front; adj. open rear. Walnut-finished hardwood stock w/rubber
buttpad. Blued or nickel-Teflon finish. Made 1985 to 1999.
Model 9. . . . . NiB $525 Ex $387 Gd $213
Model 9N, nickel-Teflon (disc. 1994). . . . . . NiB $475 Ex $390 Gd $146

MODEL 15Y/15YN
Bolt-action, single-shot "Little Buckaroo" rifle. Caliber: .22 Short, Long or
LR. 16.25-inch bbl. Weight: 4.25 lbs. Thumb safety. Ramp front sight; adj.
open rear. One-piece walnut Monte Carlo stock w/full pistol-grip. Made
1984 to 1988. Reintroduced in 1989 as Model 15YN.
Model 15Y . . . . .NiB $200 Ex $130 Gd $98
Model 15YN. .NiB $215 Ex $140 Gd $110

MODEL 18 BABY SLIDE-ACTION
REPEATER . . . . .NiB $1405 Ex $1105 Gd $610
Exposed hammer. Solid frame. Caliber: .22 Short, Long, LR. Tubular
magazine holds 14 Short cartridges. 20-inch bbl., round or octagon.
Weight: 3.75 lbs. Sights: Open rear; bead front. Plain straight-grip stock
and slide handle. Made from 1906 to 1909.

Marlin Model 15Y "Little Buckaroo"

Marlin Model 15YN

Marlin Model 20

Marlin Model 25M Bolt-Action Rifle

Marlin Model 25MB
Midget Magnum

MODEL 20 SLIDE-ACTION
REPEATING RIFLE . . . . **NiB $1405 Ex $1105 Gd $605**
Exposed hammer. Takedown. Caliber: .22 LR, Long, Short. Tubular magazine: Half-length holds 15 Short, 12 Long, 10 LR; full-length holds 25 Short, 20 Long, 18 LR. 24-inch octagon bbl. Weight: 5 lbs. Sights: Open rear; bead front. Plain straight-grip stock, grooved slide handle. Made from 1907 to 1922. Note: After 1920 was designated "Model 20-S."

MODEL 25MB BOLT-ACTION RIFLE . . . . . **NiB $179 Ex $110 Gd $95**
Caliber: .22 Short, Long or LR; 7-round clip. 22-inch bbl. Weight: 5.5 lbs. Ramp front sight, adj. open rear. One-piece walnut Monte Carlo stock w/full pistol-grip Mar-Shield finish. Made 1984 to 1988.

MODEL 25
SLIDE-ACTION REPEATER . . . . **NiB $879 Ex $540 Gd $431**
Exposed hammer. Takedown. Caliber: .22 Short (also handles 22 CB caps). Tubular magazine holds 15 Short. 23-inch bbl. Weight: 4 lbs. Sights: Open rear; beaded front. Plain straight-grip stock and slide handle. Made from 1909 to 1910.
MODEL 25M BOLT ACTION W/SCOPE . . . **NiB $167 Ex $119 Gd $95**

Caliber: .22 WMR. 7-round clip. 22-inch bbl. Weight: 6 lbs. Ramp front sight w/brass bead, adj. open rear. Walnut-finished stock w/Monte Carlo styling and full pistol-grip. Sling swivels. Made 1986 to 1988.

MODEL 25MB MIDGET MAGNUM . . . . . . **NiB $190 Ex $126 Gd $99**
Bolt action. Caliber: .22 WMR. Seven round capacity.16.25-inch bbl. Weight: 4.75 lbs. Walnut-finished Monte Carlo-style stock w/full pistol grip and abbreviated forend. Sights: Ramp front w/brass bead, adj. open rear. Thumb safety. Made from 1986 to 1988.

MODEL 25MG/25MN/25N/25NC BOLT-ACTION RIFLE
Caliber: .22 WMR (Model 25MN) or .22 LR. (Model 25N). Seven round clip magazine. 22-inch bbl. 41 inches overall. Weight: 5.5 to 6 lbs. Adj. open rear sight, ramp front; receiver grooved for scope mounts. One piece walnut-finished hardwood Monte Carlo stock w/pistol grip. Made from 1989 to 2003.
Model 25MG (Garden Gun) . . . . **NiB $218 Ex $179 Gd $126**
Model 25MN . . . . **NiB $200 Ex $167 Gd $110**
Model 25N . . . . **NiB $177 Ex $155 Gd $109**
Model 25 NC (camo stock), add **$50**

Marlin Model 39
Carbine

Marlin Model 39
Century Ltd.

Marlin Model 39 Carbine
90th Anniversary

Marlin Model 39 Rifle
Original First Issue

Marlin Model 39A
90th Anniversary Rifle

MODEL 27 SLIDE-ACTION
REPEATING RIFLE . . . . NiB $1159 Ex $909 Gd $650
Exposed hammer. Takedown. Calibers: .25-20, .32-20. Magazine (tubular) holds 7 rounds. 24-inch octagon bbl. Weight: 5.75 lbs. Sights: Open rear; bead front. Plain, straight-grip stock, grooved slide handle. Made from 1910 to 1916.

MODEL 27S . . . . NiB $909 Ex $579 Gd $388
Same as Model 27 except w/round bbl., also chambered for .25 Stevens rimfire Made from 1920 to 1932.

MODEL 29 SLIDE-ACTION REPEATER . . . NiB $660 Ex $388 Gd $290
Similar to Model 20 w/23-inch round bbl., half magazine only, weight 5.75 lbs. Made from 1913 to 1916.

MODEL 30/30A AND 30AS LEVER-ACTION
Caliber: .30/30 Win. Six-round tubular magazine. 20-inch bbl. w/Micro-Groove rifling. 38.25 inches overall. Weight: 7 lbs. Brass bead front sight, adj. rear. Solid top receiver, offset hammer spur for scope use. Walnut-finished hardwood stock w/pistol-grip. Mar-Shield finish. Made from 1964 to 2000.
Model 30/30A . . . . NiB $290 Ex $198 Gd $160
Model 30AS . . . . NiB $290 Ex $198 Gd $160
Model 30AS w/4x scope, add $25

MODEL 32 SLIDE-ACTION REPEATER. . NiB $1154 Ex $690 Gd $533
Hammerless. Takedown. Caliber: .22 LR, Long, Short. Tubular magazine holds 15 Short, 12 Long, 10 LR; full magazine, 25 Short, 20 Long, 18 LR. 24-inch octagon bbl. Weight: 5.5 lbs. Sights: Open rear; bead front. Plain pistol-grip stock, grooved slide handle. Made from 1914 to 1915.

MODEL 36 LEVER-ACTION REPEATING CARBINE
Calibers: .30-30, .32 Special. Seven-round tubular magazine. 20-inch bbl. Weight: 6.5 lbs. Sights: Open rear; bead front. Pistol-grip stock, semibeavertail forearm w/carbine bbl. band. Early production w/receiver, lever and hammer color casehardened and the remaining metal blued. Late production w/blued receiver. Made 1936 to 1948. Note: In 1936, this was designated "Model 1936" and was so marked on the upper tang. In 1937, the model designation was shortened to "36". An "RC" serial number suffix identifies a "Regular/Carbine".
Model 1936 CC receiver
  (w/long tang, no SN prefix) . . . . . NiB $909 Ex $744 Gd $500
Model 1936 CC receiver
  (w/short tang, no SN prefix) . . . . NiB $645 Ex $531 Gd $390
Model 1936 CC receiver (w/SN prefix) . . NiB $534 Ex $488 Gd $345
Model 36, CC receiver (w/SN prefix) . . . . NiB $508 Ex $433 Gd $300
Model 36, blued receiver (w/SN prefix) . . NiB $482 Ex $390 Gd $289

Marlin Model 39 — ADL

Marlin Model 39AS

MODEL 36 SPORTING CARBINE
Same as M36 carbine except w/6-round, (2/3 magazine) and weighs 6.25 lbs.
Model 1936, CC receiver
   (w/long tang, no SN prefix). . . . . **NiB $860 Ex $707 Gd $499**
Model 1936, CC receiver
   (w/short tang, no SN prefix) . . . . **NiB $656 Ex $567 Gd $380**
Model 1936, CC receiver (w/SN prefix). . **NiB $588 Ex $497 Gd $355**
Model 36, CC receiver (w/SN prefix). . . . **NiB $555 Ex $457 Gd $339**
Model 36, blued receiver (w/SN prefix). . **NiB $480 Ex $413 Gd $303**

MODEL 36A/36A-DL LEVER-ACTION REPEATING RIFLE
Same as Model 36 Carbine except has 24-inch bbl. w/hooded front sight and 2/3 magazine holding 6 cartridges. Weight: 6.75 lbs. Note: An "A" serial number suffix identifies a Rifle while an "A-DL" suffix designates a Deluxe Model w/checkered stock, semibeavertail forearm, swivels and sling. Made from 1936 to 1948.
Model 1936, CC receiver
   (w/long tang, no SN prefix) . . **NiB $1180 Ex $1077 Gd $790**
Model 1936, CC receiver
   (w/short, tang, no SN prefix). . . . **NiB $795 Ex $556 Gd $378**
Model 1936, CC receiver (w/SN prefix). . **NiB $845 Ex $589 Gd $465**
MODEL 36, CC receiver, (w/SN prefix) . . **NiB $775 Ex $451 Gd $348**
Model 36, blued receiver (w/SN prefix). . **NiB $744 Ex $440 Gd $332**
ADL model, add. **$25%**

MODEL 37 SLIDE-ACTION
REPEATING RIFLE . . . . **NiB $650 Ex $442 Gd $237**
Similar to Model 29 except w/24-inch bbl. and full magazine. Weight: 5.25 lbs. Made from 1913 to 1916.

MODEL 38 SLIDE-ACTION
REPEATING RIFLE . . . . **NiB $744 Ex $418 Gd $339**
Hammerless. Takedown. Caliber: .22 LR, Long, Short. 2/3 magazine (tubular) holds 15 Short, 12 Long, 10 LR. 24-inch octagon or round bbls. Weight: 5.5 lbs. Sights: Open rear; bead front. Plain shotgun-type pistol-grip buttstock w/hard rubber buttplate, grooved slide handle. Ivory bead front sight; adj. rear. About 20,000 Model 38 rifles were made 1920 to 1930.

MODEL 39 CARBINE
. . . . **NiB $556 Ex $355 Gd $298**
Same as 39M except w/lightweight bbl., 3/4 magazine (capacity: 18 Short, 14 Long, 12 LR), slimmer forearm. Weight: 5.25 lbs. Made 1963 to 1967.

MODEL 39 90TH
ANNIVERSARY CARBINE . . . . . . **NiB $1244 Ex $976 Gd $835**
Carbine version of 90th Anniversary Model 39A. 500 made in 1960. Top value is for carbine in new, unfired condition.

MODEL 39 CENTURY LTD.
. . . . . **NiB $670 Ex $370 Gd $259**
Commemorative version of Model 39A. Receiver inlaid w/brass medallion, "Marlin Centennial 1870-1970." Square lever. 20-inch octagon bbl. Fancy walnut straight-grip stock and forearm; brass forend cap, buttplate, nameplate in buttstock. 35,388 made in 1970.

MODEL 39 LEVER-ACTION
REPEATER . . . . **NiB $3145 Ex $1189 Gd $1018**
Takedown. Casehardened receiver. Caliber: .22 LR, Long, Short. Tubular magazine holds 25 Short, 20 Long, 18 LR. 24-inch octagon bbl. Weight: 5.75 lbs. Sights: Open rear; bead front. Plain pistol-grip stock and forearm. Made from 1922 to 1938.

MODEL 39A
General specifications same as Model 39 except w/blued receiver, round bbl., heavier stock w/semibeavertail forearm, weight 6.5 lbs. Made from 1939 to 1960.
Early model (no prefix). . . . . . . **NiB $1500 Ex $1178 Gd $800**
Late model ("B" prefix). . . . . **NiB $1166 Ex $895 Gd $650**

MODEL 39A 90TH
ANNIVERSARY RIFLE . . . . **NiB $1268 Ex $1140 Gd $835**
Commemorates Marlin's 90th anniversary. Same general specifications as Golden 39A except w/chrome-plated bbl. and action, stock and forearm of select walnut-finely checkered, carved figure of a squirrel on right side of buttstock. 500 made in 1960. Top value is for rifle in new, unfired condition.

MODEL 39A
ARTICLE II RIFLE . . . . **NiB $489 Ex $420 Gd $338**
Commemorates National Rifle Association Centennial 1871-1971. "The Right to Bear Arms" medallion inlaid in receiver. Similar to Model 39A. Magazine capacity: 26 Short, 21 Long, 19 LR. 24-inch octagon bbl. Fancy walnut pistol-grip stock and forearm; brass forend cap, buttplate. 6,244 made in 1971.

Marlin Model 56

Marlin Model 57

Marlin Model 60C

Marlin Model 60SS

Marlin Model 62

GOLDEN 39A/39AS RIFLE
Same as Model 39A except w/gold-plated trigger, hooded ramp front sight, sling swivels. Made from 1960-87 (39A); Model 39AS from 1988 to date.
Golden 39A . . . . NiB $479 Ex $300 Gd $190
Golden 39AS (W/hammer block safety) . . NiB $479 Ex $300 Gd $190

MODEL 39A "MOUNTIE" LEVER-
ACTION REPEATING RIFLE . . . . . NiB $479 Ex $300 Gd $190
Same as Model 39A except w/lighter, straight-grip stock, slimmer forearm. Weight: 6.25 lbs. Made from 1953 to 1960.
Carbine . . . . NiB $495 Ex $300 Gd $190

MODEL 39A OCTAGON . . . . NiB $645 Ex $579 Gd $390
Same as Golden 39A except w/oct. bbl., plain bead front sight, slimmer stock and forearm, no pistol-grip cap or swivels. Made in1973. (2551 produced).

MODEL 39D . . . . NiB $440 Ex $280 Gd $200
Same as Model 39M except w/pistol-grip stock, forearm w/bbl. band. Made from 1970 to 1974.

39M ARTICLE II CARBINE . . . . . . NiB $488 Ex $469 Gd $300
Same as 39A Article II Rifle except w/straight-grip buttstock, square lever, 20-inch octagon bbl., reduced magazine capacity. 3,824 units, made in 1971.

GOLDEN 39M
Calibers: .22 Short, Long and LR. Tubular magazine holds 21 Short, 16 Long or 15 LR cartridges. 20-inch bbl. 36 inches overall. Weight: 6 lbs. Gold-plated trigger. Hooded ramp front sight, adj. folding semi-buckhorn rear. Two-piece, straight-grip American black walnut stock. Sling swivels. Mar-Shield finish. Made from 1960 to 1987.
Golden 39M. . . . . NiB $445 Ex $338 Gd $266
octagonal bbl. (1973 only) . . . . . . NiB $495 Ex $469 Gd $390

MODEL 39M "MOUNTIE" CARBINE
Same as Model 39A "Mountie" Rifle except w/20-inch bbl. Weight: 6 lbs. 500 made in 1960. (For values See Marlin 39 90th Anniversary Carbine)

MODEL 39TDS
CARBINE . . . . NiB $545 Ex $369 Gd $290
Same general specifications as Model 39M except takedown style w/16.5-inch bbl. and reduced magazine capacity. 32.63 inches overall. Weight: 5.25 lbs. Made from 1988 to 1995.

Marlin Model 70HC w/7-Shot Clip

Marlin Model 70P

MODEL 45 . . . . NiB $390 Ex $290 Gd $198
Semiautomatic action. Caliber: .45 Auto. Seven round clip.16.5-inch bbl. 35.5 inches overall. Weight: 6.75 lbs. Manual bolt hold-open. Sights: Ramp front sight w/brass bead, adj. folding rear. Receiver drilled and tapped for scope mount. Walnut-finished hardwood stock. Made from 1986 to 1999.

MODEL 49/49DL AUTOLOADING RIFLE
Same as Model 99C except w/two-piece stock, checkered after 1970. Made 1968-71. Model 49DL w/scrollwork on sides of receiver, checkered stock and forearm; made from 1971 to 1978.
Model 49 . . . . NiB $200 Ex $190 Gd $145
Model 49DL . . . . NiB $227 Ex $179 Gd $144

MODEL 50/50E AUTOLOADING RIFLE
Takedown. Cal: .22 LR. Six round detachable box mag. 22 inch bbl. Wt: 6 lbs. Sights: Open rear; bead front; Mdl. 50E w/peep rear sight, hooded front. Plain pistol-grip stock, forearm w/finger grooves. Made from 1931 to 1934.
Model 50 . . . . NiB $227 Ex $190 Gd $124
Model 50E . . . . NiB $235 Ex $200 Gd $130

MODEL 56 LEVERMATIC RIFLE. . . NiB $345 Ex $250 Gd $149
Same as Model 57 except clip-loading. Magazine holds eight rounds. Weight: 5.75 lbs. Made from 1955 to 1964.

MODEL 57 LEVERMATIC RIFLE. . . NiB $375 Ex $227 Gd $132
Lever-action. Cal: .22 LR, 22 Long, 22 Short. Tubular mag. holds 19 LR, 21 Long, 27 Short. 22 inch bbl. Wt: 6.25 lbs. Sights: Open rear, adj. for windage and elevation; hooded ramp front. Monte Carlo-style stock w/pistol-grip. Made from 1959 to 1965.

MODEL 57M LEVERMATIC. . . . . . NiB $415 Ex $255 Gd $148
Same as Model 57 except chambered for 22 WMR cartridge, w/24-inch bbl., 15-round magazine. Made from 1960 to 1969.

MODEL 60 SEMIAUTOMATIC RIFLE . . . . . NiB $227 Ex $145 Gd $90
Caliber: .22 LR. 14-round tubular magazine. 22-inch bbl. 40.5 inches overall. Weight: 5.5 lbs. Grooved receiver. Ramp front sight w/removable hood; adj. open rear. Anodized receiver w/blued bbl. Monte Carlo-style walnut-finished hardwood stock w/Mar-Shield finish. Made 1981 to date. Note: Marketed 1960 to 1980 under Glenfield promotion logo and w/ slightly different stock configuration.

MODEL 60C SELF-LOADING RIFLE. . . . . NiB $198 Ex $130 Gd $107
Caliber: .22 LR. 14- round tubular mag. 22 inch Micro-Groove bbl., 40.5 inch overall. Wt: 5.5 lbs. Screw-adjustable open rear and ramp front sights. Aluminum receiver, grooved for scope mount. Hardwood Monte Carlo stock w/ Mossy Oak "Break-Up" camouflage pattern. Made from 2000 to date.

MODEL 60SS SEMIAUTOMATIC RIFLE
Same general specifications as Model 60 except w/stainless bbl. and magazine tube. Synthetic, uncheckered birch or laminated black/ gray birch stock w/nickel-plated swivel studs. Made from 1993 to date.
w/uncheckered birch stock . . . . NiB $278 Ex $200 Gd $135
w/laminated birch stock . . . . NiB $270 Ex $197 Gd $126
w/fiberglass stock . . . . NiB $260 Ex $188 Gd $126

MODEL 62
LEVERMATIC RIFLE . . . . NiB $555 Ex $440 Gd $190
Lever-action. Calibers: .256 Magnum, .30 Carbine. Four round clip magazine. 23-inch bbl. Weight: 7 lbs. Sights: Open rear; hooded ramp front. Monte Carlo-style stock w/pistol-grip, swivels and sling. Made in .256 Magnum 1963 to 1966; in .30 Carbine 1963 to 1969.

MODEL 65 BOLT-ACTION
SINGLE-SHOT RIFLE. . . . . NiB $139 Ex $93 Gd $70
Takedown. Caliber: .22 LR, Long, Short. 24-inch bbl. Weight: 5 lbs. Sights: Open rear; bead front. Plain pistol-grip stock w/grooved forearm. Made 1932-38. Model 65E is same as Model 65 except w/rear peep sight and hooded front sight.

MODEL 70HC SEMIAUTOMATIC
Caliber: .22 LR. Seven and 15-round magazine. 18-inch bbl. Weight: 5.5 lbs. 36.75 inches overall. Ramp front sight; adj. open rear. Grooved receiver for scope mounts. Walnut-finished hardwood stock w/Monte Carlo and pistol-grip. Made from 1988 to 1996.
Marlin model . . . . NiB $200 Ex $155 Gd $124
Glenfield model . . . . NiB $155 Ex $126 Gd $100

MODEL 70P
SEMIAUTOMATIC . . . . NiB $290 Ex $189 Gd $100
"Papoose" takedown. Caliber: .22 LR. Seven round clip. 16.25-inch bbl. 35.25 inches overall. Weight: 3.75 lbs. Sights: Ramp front, adj. open rear. Side ejection, manual bolt hold-open. Cross-bolt safety. Walnut-finished hard-wood stock w/abbreviated forend, pistol-grip. Made 1984 to 1994.

MODEL 70PSS
SELF-LOADING CARBINE . . . . . . NiB $338 Ex $200 Gd $175
"Papoose" takedown carbine. Caliber: .22 LR. Seven round clip. 16.25- inch bbl., 35.25 inches overall. Weight: 3.25 lbs. Ramp front and adjustable open rear sights. Automatic last-shot hold open (1996). Black fiberglass synthetic stock. Made from 1995 to date.

Marlin Model 75C

Marlin Model 80C

Marlin Model 80DL

Marlin Model 81DL

MODEL 75C
SEMIAUTOMATIC . . . . NiB $233 Ex $158 Gd $109
Caliber: .22 LR. 13-round tubular magazine.18-inch bbl. 36.5 inches overall. Weight: 5 lbs. Side ejection. Cross-bolt safety. Sights: Ramp-mounted blade front; adj. open rear. Monte Carlo-style walnut-finished hardwood stock w/pistol-grip. Made 1975 to 1992.

MODEL 80 BOLT-ACTION REPEATING RIFLE
Takedown. Caliber: .22 LR, Long, Short. Eight round detachable box magazine. 24-inch bbl. Weight: 6 lbs. Sights: Open rear; bead front. Plain pistol-grip stock. Made from 1934 to 1939. Model 80E, w/peep rear sight; hooded front, made from 1934 to 1940.
Model 80 Standard. . . . . NiB $190 Ex $135 Gd $95
Model 80E . . . . NiB $175 Ex $110 Gd $85

MODEL 80C/80DL
BOLT-ACTION REPEATER
Improved version of Model 80. Model 80C w/bead from sight, semibea-vertail forearm; made 1940-70. Model 80DL w/peep rear sight; hooded blade front sight on ramp, swivels; made 1940 to 1965.
Model 80C. . . . . NiB $200 Ex $155 Gd $100
Model 80DL. . . . . NiB $167 Ex $110 Gd $90

MODEL 81/81E BOLT-ACTION REPEATER
Takedown. .22 LR, Long, Short. Tubular magazine holds 24 Short, 20 Long, 18 LR. 24-inch bbl. Weight: 6.25 lbs. Sights: Open rear, bead front. Plain pistol-grip stock. Made from 1937 to 1940. Model 81E w/ peep rear sight; hooded front w/ramp.
Model 81. . . . . NiB $220 Ex $176 Gd $110
Model 81E . . . . NiB $245 Ex $195 Gd $139

MODEL 81C/81DL BOLT-ACTION REPEATER
Improved version of Model 81 w/same general specifications. Model 81C w/bead front sight, semibeavertail forearm; made 1940 to 1970. Model 81 DL w/peep rear sight, hooded front, swivels; disc. 1965.
Model 81C. . . . . NiB $239 Ex $188 Gd $100
Model 81DL. . . . . NiB $220 Ex $199 Gd $110

MODEL 88-C/88-DL TAKEDOWN RIFLE
Takedown. Caliber: .22 LR. Tubular magazine in buttstock holds 14 car-tridges. 24-inch bbl. Weight: 6.75 lbs. Sights: Open rear; hooded front. Plain pistol-grip stock. Made from 1947-56. Model 88-DL w/received peep sight, checkered stock and sling swivels; made 1953 to 1956.
Model 88-C . . . . NiB $200 Ex $145 Gd $100
Model 88-DL . . . . NiB $200 Ex $145 Gd $100

Marlin Model 93 Musket

Marlin Model 93 Lever Action

Marlin Model 94 Sporting Carbine

MODEL 89C/89DL AUTOLOADING RIFLE

Clip magazine version of Model 88-C. Seven round clip (12-round in later models); other specifications same. Made from 1950 to 1961. Model 89-DL w/receiver peep sight, sling swivels.

Model 89-C . . . . NiB $200 Ex $145 Gd $100
Model 89-DL . . . . NiB $210 Ex $150 Gd $105

MODEL 92 LEVER-ACTION REPEATING RIFLE

Calibers: .22 Short, Long, LR. .32 Short, Long (rimfire or center-fire by changing firing pin). Tubular magazines holding 25 Short, 20 Long, 18 LR (.22); or 17 Short, 14 Long (.32); 16-inch bbl. model w/shorter magazine holding 15 Short, 12 Long, 10 LR. Bbl. lengths: 16 (.22 cal. only) 24, 26, 28 inches. Weight: 5.5 lbs. w/24-inch bbl. Sights: open rear; blade front. Plain straight-grip stock and forearm. Made 1892 to 1916. Note: Originally designated "Model 1892."

Model 92 (.22 caliber) . . . . NiB $1598 Ex $1400 Gd $883
Model 92 (.32 caliber) . . . . NiB $1554 Ex $1268 Gd $956

MODEL 93/93SC CARBINE

Same as Standard Model 93 Rifle except in calibers .30-30 and .32 Special only. Model 93 w/7-round magazine. 20-inch round bbl., carbine sights, weight: 6.75 lbs. Model 93SC magazine capacity 5 rounds, weight 6.5 lbs.

Model 93 Carbine (w/saddle ring) . . . NiB $1689 Ex $1423 Gd $1108
Model 93 Carbine "Bull's-Eye
  (w/o saddle ring) . . . . NiB $1449 Ex $1188 Gd $976
Model 93SC Sporting Carbine . . . . . . NiB $1377 Ex $1087 Gd $915

MODEL 93 LEVER-ACTION

REPEATING RIFLE . . . . NiB $2833 Ex $2022 Gd $1370
Solid frame or takedown. Calibers: .25-36 Marlin, .30-30, .32 Special, .32-40, .38-55. Tubular magazine holds 10 cartridges. 26-inch round or octagon bbl. standard; also made w/28-, 30- and 32-inch bbls. Weight: 7.25 lbs. Sights: Open rear; bead front. Plain straight-grip stock and forearm. Made from 1893 to 1936. Note: Before 1915 designated "Model 1893."

MODEL 93 MUSKET . . . . NiB $5610 Ex $3766 Gd $2833
Same as Standard Model 93 except w/30-inch bbl., angular bayonet, ramrod under bbl., musket stock, full-length military-style forearm. Weight: 8 lbs. Made from 1893 to 1915.

MODEL 94 LEVER-ACTION

REPEATING RIFLE . . . . . . .NiB $2655 Ex $1840 Gd $989
Solid frame or takedown. Calibers: .25-20, .32-20, .38-40, .44-40. 10-round tubular magazine. 24-inch round or octagon bbl. Weight: 7 lbs. Sights open rear; bead front. Plain straight-grip stock and forearm (also available w/pistol-grip stock). Made from 1894 to 1934. Note: Before 1906 designated "Model 1894."

MODEL 94 LEVER-ACTION COWBOY SERIES

Calibers: .357 Mag., .44-40, .44 Mag., .45 LC. 10-round magazine. 24-inch tapered octagon bbl. Weight: 7.5 lbs. 41.5 inches overall. Marble carbine front sight, adjustable semi-buckhorn rear. Blue finish. Checkered, straight-grip American black walnut stock w/hard rubber buttplate. Made from 1996 to date. Cowboy II introduced in 1997.

Cowboy model (.45 LC) . . . . NiB $833 Ex $650 Gd $466
Cowboy II model
  (.357 Mag., .44-40, .44 Mag.). . . NiB $854 Ex $659 Gd $572

MODEL 97 LEVER-ACTION

REPEATING RIFLE . . . . NiB $2590 Ex $2066 Gd $1269
Takedown. Caliber: .22 LR, Long, Short. Tubular magazine; full length holds 25 Short, 20 Long, 18 LR; half length holds 16 Short, 12 Long and 10 LR. Bbl. lengths: 16, 24, 26, 28 inches. Weight: 6 lbs. Sights: Open rear; bead front. Plain, straight-grip stock and forearm (also avail. w/pistol-grip stock). Made from 1897 to 1922. Note: Before 1905 designated "Model 1897."

MODEL 98 AUTOLOADING RIFLE . . . . . NiB $255 Ex $138 Gd $100

Solid frame. Caliber: .22 LR. Tubular magazine holds 15 cartridges. 22-inch bbl. Weight: 6.75 lbs. Sights: Open rear; hooded ramp front. Monte Carlo stock w/cheekpiece. Made from 1950 to 1961.

MODEL 99 AUTOLOADING RIFLE . . . . . NiB $255 Ex $138 Gd $100

Caliber: .22 LR. Tubular magazine holds 18 cartridges. 22-inch bbl. Weight: 5.5 lbs. Sights: Open rear; hooded ramp front. Plain pistol-grip stock. Made from 1959 to 1961.

MODEL 99C . . . . .NiB $209 Ex $177 Gd $119

Same as Model 99 except w/gold-plated trigger, receiver grooved for tip-off scope mounts, Monte Carlo stock (checkered in later production). Made from 1962 to 1978.

MODEL 99DL . . . . .NiB $266 Ex $255 Gd $144

Same as Model 99 except w/gold-plated trigger, jeweled breech bolt, Monte Carlo stock w/pistol-grip, swivels and sling. Made 1960 to 1965.

GRADING: NiB = New in Box   Ex = Excellent or NRA 95%   Gd = Good or NRA 68%

Marlin Model 336 Cowboy

Marlin Model 336M

Marlin Model 336 Marauder

Marlin Model 336 Sporting Carbine

Marlin Model 336 Zane Grey Century

Marlin Model 336A

Marlin Model 336A-DL

MODEL 100 BOLT-ACTION
SINGLE-SHOT RIFLE. . . . . .NiB **$200** Ex **$123** Gd **$90**
Takedown. Caliber: .22 LR, Long, Short. 24-inch bbl. Weight: 4.5 lbs. Sights: Open rear; bead front. Plain pistol-grip stock. Made 1936 to 1960.

MODEL 100SB. . . . . .NiB **$120** Ex **$90** Gd **$65**
Same as Model 100 except smoothbore for use w/22 shot cartridges, shotgun sight. Made from 1936 to 1941.

MODEL 99M1 CARBINE. . . . . .NiB **$200** Ex **$99** Gd **$80**
Same as Model 99C except styled after U.S. .30 M1 Carbine; 9-round tubular magazine, 18-inch bbl. Sights: Open rear; military-style ramp front; carbine stock w/handguard and bbl. band, sling swivels. Weight: 4.5 lbs. Made 1966 to 1979.

Marlin Model 336DT Deluxe
Texan

Marlin Model 336T Texan

MODEL 100 TOM MIX SPECIAL . . . . NiB $315 Ex $200 Gd $146
Same as Model 100 except w/peep rear sight; hooded front; sling. Made
from 1936 to 1946.

MODEL 101 . . . . NiB $100 Ex $75 Gd $55
Improved version of Model 100 w/same general specifications, except
w/stock w/beavertail forearm, weighs 5 lbs. Intro. 1951. Disc.

MODEL 101 DL . . . . NiB $119 Ex $85 Gd $70
Same as Model 101 except has peep rear sight; hooded front, swivels.
Disc.

**MODEL 122 SINGLE-SHOT
JUNIOR TARGET RIFLE** . . . . NiB $135 Ex $95 Gd $75
Bolt action. Caliber: .22 LR, .22 Long, .22 Short. 22-inch bbl. Weight: 5
lbs. Sights: Open rear; hooded ramp front. Monte Carlo stock w/pistol-
grip, swivels, sling. Made from 1961 to 1965.

**MODEL 322 BOLT-ACTION
VARMINT RIFLE** . . . . NiB $597 Ex $390 Gd $278
Sako short Mauser action. Caliber: .222 Rem. Three round clip magazine.
24-inch medium weight bbl. Checkered stock. Sights: Two-position peep
rear; hooded ramp front. Weight: 7.5 lbs. Made from 1954-57.

**MODEL 336A
LEVER-ACTION RIFLE** . . . . NiB $570 Ex $400 Gd $338
Improved version of Model 36A Rifle w/same general specifications
except w/improved action w/improved breech bolt. Calibers: .30-30, .32
Special (disc. 1963), .35 Rem. (intro. 1952). Made from 1948-63; rein-
troduced 1973, disc. 1980.

MODEL 336A-DL . . . . NiB $665 Ex $544 Gd $351
Same as Model 336A Rifle except w/deluxe checkered stock and forearm, swivels and sling. Made from 1948-63.

**MODEL 336AS
LEVER-ACTION RIFLE** . . . . NiB $475 Ex $291 Gd $139
Similar to Model 30AS. Caliber: .30-30 Win., Six round tubular magazine.
20- inch Micro-Groove bbl. 38.25 inches overall. Weight: 7 lbs. Maine
birch pistol grip stock w/swivel studs and hard rubber butt plate. Tapped for
scope mount and receiver sight. Screw-adjustable open rear and ramp front
sight. Checkered walnut finish. Made from 1999 to date.

**MODEL 336C
LEVER-ACTION CARBINE** . . . . NiB $559 Ex $398 Gd $290
Improved version of Model 36 Carbine w/same general specifications
except w/improved action w/round breech bolt. Original calibers: .30-
30 and .32 Win. Spec. Made from 1948-83. Note: Caliber .35 Rem.
intro. 1953. Caliber .32 Winchester Special disc. 1963.

**MODEL 336 COWBOY
LEVER-ACTION RIFLE** . . . . NiB $600 Ex $445 Gd $380
Calibers: .30-30 Win., or .38-55 Win., 6- round tubular magazine. 24- inch tapered
octagon bbl. 42.5 inches overall. Weight: 7.5 lbs. American black walnut checkering stock. Marble carbine front sight w/solid top receiver drilled and tapped for
scope mount. Mar-Shield finish. Made from 1998 to date.

**MODEL 336CS
W/SCOPE** . . . . NiB $479 Ex $338 Gd $266
Lever-action w/hammer block safety. Caliber: .30/30 Win. or .35 Rem. Six round
tubular magazine. 20-inch round bbl. w/Micro-Groove rifling. 38.5 inches
overall. Weight: 7 lbs. Ramp front sight w/hood, adj. semi-buckhorn folding rear.
Solid top receiver drilled and tapped for scope mount or receiver sight; offset
hammer spur for scope use. American black walnut stock w/pistol-grip, fluted
comb. Mar-Shield finish. Made from 1984 to date.

**MODEL 336DT
DELUXE TEXAN** . . . . NiB $500 Ex $466 Gd $359
Same as Model 336T except w/select walnut stock and forearm, hand-carved
longhorn steer and map of Texas on buttstock. Made from 1962 to 1964.

**MODEL 336M
LEVER-ACTION RIFLE** . . . . NiB $590 Ex $495 Gd $359
Calibers: .30-30 Win., 6- round tubular magazine. 20- inch stainless
steel Micro Groove bbl., 38.5 inches overall. Weight: 7 lbs. American
black walnut w/checkered pistol-grip stock. Adjustable folding semi-
buckhorn rear and ramp front sight w/brass bead and removable Wide-
Scan hood. Tapped for receiver sight and scope mount. Mar-Shield
finish. Made from 1999 to date.

MODEL 336 MARAUDER . . . . NiB $600 Ex $485 Gd $300
Same as Model 336 Texan Carbine except w/16.25-inch bbl., weight:
6.25 lbs. Made from 1963 to 1964.

MODEL 336-MICRO GROOVE ZIPPER . . NiB $845 Ex $633 Gd $390
General specifications same as Model 336 Sporting Carbine except
caliber .219 Zipper. Made from 1955 to 1961.

MODEL 336 OCTAGON . . . . NiB $570 Ex $498 Gd $300
Same as Model 336T except chambered for .30-30 only w/22-inch
octagon bbl. Made in 1973.

MODEL 336 SPORTING CARBINE . . . . . NiB $845 Ex $589 Gd $445
Same as Model 336A rifle except w/20-inch bbl., weight: 6.25 lbs.
Made from 1948 to 1963.

MODEL 336T TEXAN CARBINE . . . . NiB $369 Ex $277 Gd $228
Same as Model 336 Carbine except w/straight-grip stock and is not available in
caliber .32 Special. Made 1953-83. Caliber .44 Magnum made 1963 to 1967.

Marlin Model 336TS Carbine

Marlin Model 444SS

Marlin Model 455 Sporter

MODEL 336TS . . . . .NiB $400 Ex $333 Gd $190
Lever-action w/hammer-block safety. Caliber: .30-30 Win. Six round tubular magazine. 18.5-inch Micro-Groove bbl. 37 inches overall. Weight: 6.5 lbs. Ramp front sight, adj. semi-buckhorn folding rear. Straight-grip American black walnut stock. Made 1983 to 1987.

**MODEL 336 ZANE
GREY CENTURY** . . . . .NiB $488 Ex $439 Gd $300
Similar to Model 336A except w/22-inch octagonal bbl., caliber .30-30, Zane Grey Centennial 1872-1972 medallion inlaid in receiver; select walnut stock w/classic pistol-grip and forearm; brass buttplate, forend cap. Weight: 7 lbs. 10,000 produced (numbered ZG1 through ZG10,000). Made in 1972.

**MODEL 444 LEVER-ACTION
REPEATING RIFLE** . . . . .NiB $482 Ex $390 Gd $235
Action similar to Model 336. Caliber: .444 Marlin. Four round tubular magazine. 24-inch bbl. Weigh: 7.5 lbs. Sights: Open rear; hooded ramp front. Monte Carlo stock w/straight grip, recoil pad. Carbine-style forearm w/bbl. band. Swivels, sling. Made from 1965 to 1971.

MARLIN MODEL 444 SPORTER . . . . NiB $576 Ex $445 Gd $235
Same as Model 444 Rifle except w/22-inch bbl., pistol-grip stock and forearm as on Model 336A, recoil pad, QD swivels and sling. Made from 1972 to 1983.

**MODEL 444P (OUTFITTER)
LEVER-ACTION RIFLE** . . . . .NiB $559 Ex $447 Gd $255
Caliber: .444 Marlin. Five round tubular magazine. 18.5-inch ported bbl., 37 inches overall. Weight: 6.75 lbs. Ramp front and adjustable folding rear sights. Black walnut straight grip stock w/cut checkering and Mar-Shield finish. Made from 1999 to 2002.

MODEL 444SS . . . . .NiB $570 Ex $449 Gd $240
Same general specifications as Model 444 except w/hammer safety. Made from 1984-2002. (Changed to M444 in 2001.)

MODEL 455 BOLT-ACTION SPORTER
FN Mauser action w/Sako trigger. Calibers: .30-06 or .308. Five round box magazine. 24-inch medium weight stainless-steel bbl. Monte Carlo stock w/cheekpiece, checkered pistol grip and forearm. Lyman No. 48

receiver sight; hooded ramp front. Weight: 8.5 lbs. Made from 1957 to 1959.
.30-06 Spfd., 1079 produced . . . . NiB $707 Ex $535 Gd $325
.308 Win., 59 produced . . . . .NiB $800 Ex $610 Gd $475

MODEL 780 BOLT-ACTION REPEATER SERIES
Caliber: .22 LR, Long, Short. Seven round clip magazine. 22-inch bbl. Weight: 5.5 to 6 lbs. Sights: Open rear; hooded ramp front. Receiver grooved for scope mounting. Monte Carlo stock w/checkered pistol-grip and forearm. Made from 1971 to 1988.
Standard model . . . . NiB $145 Ex $100 Gd $85
w/17-round tubular mag. . . . . NiB $145 Ex $100 Gd $85
.22 WMR w/swivels, sling. . . . . NiB $145 Ex $100 Gd $85
w/12-round tubular mag. . . . . NiB $145 Ex $100 Gd $85

MODEL 795 SELF-LOADING RIFLE . . . . . NiB $167 Ex $130 Gd $115
Caliber: .22 LR. 10- round clip. 18- inch Micro-Groove bbl., 37 inches overall. Weight: 5 lbs. Screw-adjustable open rear and ramp front sight. Monte Carlo synthetic stock with checkering swivel studs. Made from 1999 to date.

MODEL 880/881/882/883 BOLT-ACTION REPEATER SERIES
Caliber: .22 rimfire. Seven round magazine. 22-inch bbl. 41 inches overall. Weight: 5.5 to 6 lbs. Hooded ramp front sight; adj. folding rear. Grooved receiver for scope mounts. Checkered Monte Carlo-style walnut stock w/QD studs and rubber recoil pad. Made from 1989 to 1997.
.22 LR . . . . NiB $220 Ex $177 Gd $115
Stainless .22 LR . . . . NiB $269 Ex $200 Gd $150
Squirrel .22 LR . . . . NiB $269 Ex $223 Gd $160
Model 881
   w/7-round tubular magazine . . NiB $244 Ex $175 Gd $110
Model 882 (.22 WMR) . . . . NiB $235 Ex $189 Gd $115
   w/laminated hardwood stock . . . . NiB $277 Ex $189 Gd 120
Stainless w/Fire sights. . . . . NiB $290 Ex $222 Gd $167
Stainless .22 LR . . . . NiB $195 Ex $227 Gd $170
Model 883
(.22 WMR w/12-round tubular mag.) . . NiB $235 Ex $179 Gd $120
   w/nickel-Teflon finish. . . . . NiB $279 Ex $226 Gd $180
Stainless w/laminated stock . . . . NiB $297 Ex $200 Gd $177

Marlin Model 780

Marlin Model 781

Marlin Model 783

Marlin Model 882L

Marlin Model 883N

MODEL 922 MAGNUM
SELF-LOADING RIFLE.........**NiB $390 Ex $244 Gd $160**
Similar to Model 9 except chambered for .22 WMR. Seven round magazine. 20.5-inch bbl. 39.5 inches overall. Weight: 6.5 lbs. American black walnut stock w/Monte Carlo. Blued finish. Made from 1993 to 2001.

MODEL 980 .22 MAGNUM .....**NiB $290 Ex $167 Gd $135**
Bolt action. Caliber: .22 WMR. Eight round clip magazine. 24-inch bbl. Weight: 6 lbs. Sights: Open rear; hooded ramp front. Monte Carlo stock, swivels, sling. Made from 1962 to 1970.

MODEL 989 AUTOLOADING RIFLE ....**NiB $210 Ex $144 Gd $110**
Caliber: .22 LR. Seven round clip magazine. 22-inch bbl. Weight: 5.5 lbs. Sights: Open rear; hooded ramp front. Monte Carlo walnut stock w/ pistol grip. Made from 1962 to 1966.

MODEL 989M2
CARBINE ....**NiB $250 Ex $145 Gd $100**
Same as Model 99M1 except clip-loading, 7-round magazine. Made from 1966 to 199.

MODEL 990 SEMIAUTOMATIC
Caliber: .22 LR. 17-round tubular magazine. 22-inch bbl. 40.75 inches overall. Weight: 5.5 lbs. Side ejection. Cross-bolt safety. Ramp front sight w/brass bead; adj. semi-buckhorn folding rear. Receiver grooved for scope mount. Monte Carlo-style American black walnut stock w/checkered pistol grip and forend. Made from 1979 to 1987.
Model 990 Semiautomatic .... **NiB $135 Ex $100 Gd $85**
  w/14-round mag, laminated hardwood stock, QD swivels, black recoil pad. Made 1992 to date)NiB $208 Ex $155 Gd $110

Marlin Model 980

Marlin Model 989

Marlin Model 989M2

Marlin Model 990

Marlin Model 990L

Marlin Model 995

MODEL 995 SEMIAUTOMATIC. . .NiB $233 Ex $167 Gd $110
Caliber: .22 LR. Seven round clip magazine.18-inch bbl. 36.75 inches overall. Weight: 5 lbs. Cross-bolt safety. Sights: Ramp front w/brass bead; adj. folding semi-buckhorn rear. Monte Carlo-style American black walnut stock w/checkered pistol grip and forend. Made from 1979 to 1994.

MODEL 1870-1970 CENTENNIAL MATCHED
PAIR, MODELS 336 AND 39. . . . . . . NiB $2230 Ex $1766 Gd $1180
Presentation-grade rifles in luggage-style case. Matching serial numbers. Fancy walnut straight-grip buttstock and forearm brass buttplate and forend cap. Engraved receiver w/inlaid medallion; square lever. 20-inch octagon bbl. Model 336: .30-30, 7-round capacity; weight: 7

lbs. Model 39: .22 Short, Long, LR, tubular magazine holds 21 Short, 16 Long, 15 LR. 1,000 sets produced. Made in 1970. Top value is for rifles in new, unfired condition. See image on page 291.

MODEL 1892 LEVER-ACTION RIFLE
See Marlin Model 92 listed previously under this section.

MODEL 1893 LEVER-ACTION RIFLE
See Marlin Model 93 listed previously under this section.

MODEL 1894 LEVER-ACTION RIFLE
See Marlin Model 94 listed previously under this section.

Marlin 1870-1970 Matched Pair

Marlin Model 1894 Carbine

Marlin Model 1894CL

MODEL 1894 CARBINE . . . . **NiB $415 Ex $300 Gd $245**
Replica of original Model 94. Caliber: .44 Rem. 10-round magazine. 20-inch round bbl. Weight: 6 lbs. Sight: Open rear; ramp front. Straight-grip stock. Made from 1969 to 1984.
Octagon bbl. (made 1973) . . . . **NiB $525 Ex $390 Gd $239**
Sporter model
   (w/22-inch bbl. made 1973) . . . . **NiB $585 Ex $369 Gd $345**

MODEL 1894CL CLASSIC . . . . . . **NiB $743 Ex $545 Gd $355**
Calibers: .218 Bee, .25-20 Win., .32-20 Win. Six round tubular magazine. 22-inch bbl. 38.75 inches overall. Weight: 6.25 lbs. Adj. semibuckhorn folding rear sight, brass bead front. Receiver tapped for scope mounts. Straight-grip American black walnut stock w/Mar-Shield finish. Made from 1988 to 1994.

MODEL 1894CS LEVER-ACTION . . . . . . **NiB $779 Ex $545 Gd $369**
Caliber: .357 Magnum, .38 Special. Nine round tubular magazine. 18.5-inch bbl. 36 inches overall. Weight: 6 lbs. Side

ejection. Hammer block safety. Square finger lever. Bead front sight, adj. semi-buckhorn folding rear. Offset hammer spur for scope use. Two-piece straight grip American black walnut stock w/white buttplate spacer. Mar-Shield finish. Made from 1984 to 2002.

MODEL 1894M LEVER-ACTION . . . . . . **NiB $495 Ex $443 Gd $233**
Caliber: .22 WMR.11-round tubular magazine. 20-inch bbl. Weight: 6.25 lbs. Sights: Ramp front w/brass bead and Wide-Scan hood; adj. semi-buckhorn folding rear. Offset hammer spur for scope use. Straight-grip American black walnut stock w/white buttplate spacer. Squared finger lever. Made from 1986 to 1988.

MODEL 1894S LEVER-ACTION . . . . **NiB $522 Ex $347 Gd $245**
Calibers: .41 Mag., .44 Rem. Mag., .44 S&W Special, .45 Colt.10-shot tubular magazine. 20-inch bbl.37.5 inches overall. Weight: 6 lbs. Sights and stock same as Model 1894M. Made 1984 to 2002.

Marlin Model 1894CS

Marlin Model 1894M

Marlin Model 1894S

Marlin Model 1895 .45-70 (New Model)

MODEL 1895 .45-70 REPEATER . . NiB $445   Ex $390   Gd $235
Model 336-type action. Caliber: .45-70 Government. Four round magazine. 22-inch bbl. Weight: 7 lbs. Sights: Open rear; bead front. Straight-grip stock, forearm w/metal end cap, QD swivels, leather sling. Made 1972 to 1979.

MODEL 1895
LEVER-ACTION REPEATER . . . . . . NiB $447   Ex $393   Gd $236
Solid frame or takedown. Calibers: .33 WCF, .38-56, .40-65, .40-70, .40-82, .45-70. Nine round tubular magazine. 24-inch round or octagongon bbl. standard (other lengths available). Weight: 8 lbs. Sights: Open rear; bead front. Plain stock and forearm (also available w/pistol-grip stock). Made 1895 to 1915.

MODEL 1895G (GUIDE GUN)
LEVER-ACTION RIFLE . . . . NiB $590   Ex $389   Gd $280
Caliber: .45-70 Govt., 4- round magazine. 18.5-inch ported bbl., 37 inches overall. Weight: 6.75 lbs. Ramp front and adjustable folding rear sights. Black walnut straight grip stock w/cut checkering and Mar-Shield finish. 2,500 made starting in 1998.

MODEL 1895M
LEVER-ACTION RIFLE . . . . NiB $448   Ex $290   Gd $144
Caliber: .450 Marlin. Four round tubular magazine., 18.5- inch ported bbl. w/Ballard-type rifling. 37 inches overall. Weight: 6.75 lbs. Genuine American black walnut straight-grip stock w/checkering. Ventilated recoil pad. Adjustable folding semi-buckhorn rear and ramp front sights. Mar-Shield finish. Made 2000 to date.
Model 1895GBL (big loop) . . . . NiB $595   Ex $340   Gd $165

MODEL 1895SS LEVER-ACTION . . . . NiB $609   Ex $448   Gd $356
Caliber: .45-70 Govt. Four round tubular magazine. 22-inch bbl. w/ Micro-Groove rifling. 40.5 inches overall. Weight: 7.5 lbs. Ramp front sight w/brass bead and Wide-Scan hood; adj. semi-buckhorn folding rear. Solid top receiver tapped for scope mount or receiver sight. Off-set hammer spur for scope use. Two-piece American black walnut stock w/fluted comb, pistol-grip, sling swivels. Made 1984 to date. (Changed to M1895 in 2001.)

MODEL 1897 LEVER-ACTION RIFLE
See Marlin Model 97 listed previously under this section.

Marlin Model 1895G

Marlin Model 1895M

Marlin Model 1895SS

Marlin Model 1895 Rifle
(Old Model — 1895-1915)

Marlin Model 1897
Cowboy

MODEL 1897 COWBOY
LEVER-ACTION RIFLE. . . . . .NiB $643 Ex $489 Gd $369
Caliber: .22 LR., capacity: 19 LR, 21 L, or 26 S, tubular magazine. 24-inch tapered octagon bbl., 40 inches overall. Weight: 6.5 lbs. Marble front and adjustable rear sight, tapped for scope mount. Black walnut straight grip stock w/cut checkering and Mar-Shield finish. Made from 1999 to 2001.

MODEL 1936 LEVER-ACTION CARBINE
See Marlin Model 36 listed previously under this section.

MODEL 2000 TARGET RIFLE . . . . NiB $590 Ex $479 Gd $338
Bolt-action single-shot. Caliber: .22 LR. Optional 5-round adapter kit available. 22-inch bbl. 41 inches overall. Weight: 8 lbs. Globe front sight, adj. peep or aperture rear. two-stage target trigger. Textured composite Kevlar or black/gray laminated stock. Made from 1991 to 1995.
w/adj. comb (made 1994 only) . . . . NiB $643 Ex $522 Gd $355
w/laminated stock (intro. 1996). . . . . . . NiB $654 Ex $535 Gd $429

MODEL 7000
Caliber: .22 LR. 10-round magazine. 18-inch bbl. Weight: 5.5 lbs. Synthetic stocks. No sights; receiver grooved for scope. Semi-auto. Side ejection. Manual bolt hold-open. Cross-bolt safety. Matte finish. Made from 1997 to 2001.
Model 7000 . . . . NiB $255 Ex $190 Gd $146
Model 7000T . . . . NiB $390 Ex $290 Gd $220

MODEL A-1
AUTOLOADING RIFLE . . . . NiB $185 Ex $110 Gd $90
Takedown. Caliber: .22 LR. Six round detachable box magazine. 24-inch bbl. Weight: 6 lbs. Open rear sight. Plain pistol-grip stock. Made from 1935 to 1946.

MODEL A-1C
AUTOLOADING RIFLE. . . . . .NiB $185 Ex $110 Gd $90
Improved version of Model A-1 w/same general specifications, stock w/ semibeavertail forend. Made from 1940 to 1946.

MODEL A-1DL . . . . .NiB $185 Ex $110 Gd $90
Same as Model A-1C above, except w/peep rear sight; hooded front, swivels.

Marlin Model 2000

Marlin Model 2000L

Marlin Model 7000

Marlin Model 7000T

MODEL A-1E . . . . .NiB $190 Ex $126 Gd $95
Same as Model A-1 except w/peep rear sight; hooded front.

MODEL MR-7 BOLT-ACTION RIFLE NiB $555 Ex $380 Gd $277
Calibers: .25-06 Rem., .270 Win., .280 Rem., .308 Win. or .30-06.
Four round magazine. 22-inch bbl. w/ or w/o sights. 43.31 inches
overall. Weight: 7.5 lbs. Checkered American walnut or birch stock w/
recoil pad and sling-swivel studs. Jeweled bolt w/cocking indicator and
3-position safety. Made from 1996 to 1999.
w/birch stock, intro. 1998. . . . . NiB $460 Ex $379 Gd $255
w/open sights, add $50

MODEL 10 . . . . .NiB $140 Ex $110 Gd $85
Same as Marlin Model 101 except w/walnut-finished hardwood
stock. Made 1966-79. Note: Later production featuring hot-iron-
stamped wood pistol grip to simulate checkering/carving; plain
forend.

MODEL 20 . . . . .NiB $779 Ex $439 Gd $310
Same as Marlin Model 80/780 except w/bead front sight, walnut-
finished hardwood stock. Made 1966 to 1982. Note: Recent production
has stamped pistol grip; plain forend.

MODEL 30 . . . . .NiB $280 Ex $133 Gd $100
Same as Marlin Model 336C except chambered for .30-30 only, w/4-
round magazine, plainer stock and forearm of walnut-finished hardwood. Made 1966 to 1968.

MODEL 30A . . . . .NiB $279 Ex $190 Gd $139
Same as Marlin Model 336C but chambered for .30-30 only, w/check-
ered walnut-finished hardwood stock. Made 1969 to 1983.

MODEL 36G . . . . .NiB $879 Ex $633 Gd $260
Same as Marlin Model 336C except chambered for .30-30 only, w/5-
round magazine, plainer stock. Made 1960 to 1965.

MODEL 60 . . . . .NiB $200 Ex $124 Gd $79
Same as Marlin Model 99C except w/walnut-finished hardwood stock.
Made 1960 to 1980.

MODEL 70 . . . . .NiB $188 Ex $95 Gd $65
Same as Marlin Model 989M2 except w/walnut-finished hardwood
stock; no handguard. Made 1966 to 1969.

MODEL 80G . . . . .NiB $100 Ex $65 Gd $45
Same as Marlin Model 80C except w/plain stock, bead front sight. Made
1960 to 1965.

Marlin Model A-1 Autoloader

Marlin-Glenfield Model 10

Marlin-Glenfield Model 30A

Marlin-Glenfield Model 60

Marlin-Glenfield Model 70

Marlin-Glenfield Model 80G

RIFLES

MODEL 81G . . . . .NiB $110 Ex $78 Gd $66
Same as Marlin Model 81C except w/plain stock, bead front sight. Made from 1960 to 1965.

MODEL 99G . . . . .NiB $170 Ex $75 Gd $65
Same as Marlin Model 99C except w/plain stock, bead front sight. Made from 1960 to 1965.

MODEL 101G . . . . .NiB $110 Ex $79 Gd $55
Same as Marlin Model 101 except w/plain stock. Made 1960 to 1965.

**MODEL 989G
AUTOLOADING RIFLE**. . . . . NiB $179 Ex $110 Gd $79
Same as Marlin Model 989 except w/plain stock, bead front sight. Made from 1962 to 1964.

MAUSER SPORTING RIFLES — Oberndorf am Neckar, Germany

Manufactured by Mauser-Werke GmbH. Imported by Blaser USA in San Antoinio; previously by Brolin Arms, Pomona, CA; Gun South, Inc.; Gibbs Rifle Co.; Precision Imports, Inc. and KDF, Inc.

Before the end of WWI the name of the Mauser firm was "Waffenfabrik Mauser A.-G." Shortly after WWI it was changed to "Mauser-Werke A.-G." This information may be used to determine the age of genuine original Mauser sporting rifles made before WWII because all bear either of these firm names as well as the Mauser banner trademark.

GRADING: **NiB** = New in Box   **Ex** = Excellent or NRA 95%   **Gd** = Good or NRA 68%   **295**

Mauser Model ES340

Mauser Model ES350

The first four rifles listed were manufactured before WWI. Those that follow were produced between World Wars I and II. The early Mauser models can generally be identified by the pistol grip, which is rounded instead of capped, and the M/98 military-type magazine floorplate and catch. The later models have hinged magazine floorplates with lever or button release.

NOTE: The "B" series of Mauser .22 rifles (Model ES340B, MS350B, etc.) were improved versions of their corresponding models and were introduced about 1935.

- PRE-WORLD WAR I MODELS -

BOLT-ACTION SPORTING CARBINE
Calibers: 6.5x54, 6.5x58, 7x57, 8x57, 957mm. 19.75-inch bbl. Weight: 7 lbs. Full-stocked to muzzle. Other specifications same as for standard rifle.
W/20-inch bbl. (Type M). . . . . .NiB $2489 Ex $2066 Gd $1445
W/20- or 24-inch bbl. (Type S) . . . . . .NiB $2566 Ex $2155 Gd $1486

BOLT-ACTION SPORTING RIFLE
Calibers: 6.5x55, 6.5x58, 7x57, 8x57, 9x57, 9.3x62 10.75x68.Five-round box magazine, 23.5-inch bbl. Weight: 7 to 7.5 lbs. Pear-shaped bolt handle. Double-set or single trigger. Sights: Tangent curve rear; ramp front. Pistol-grip stock, forearm w/Schnabel tip and swivels.
Type A, English export . . . . .NiB $2669 Ex $2276 Gd $1559
Type B. .NiB $1790 Ex $1466 Gd $1080

BOLT-ACTION SPORTING RIFLE,
MILITARY MODEL TYPE C . . . . NiB $3854 Ex $3165 Gd $2189
So called because of stepped M/98-type bbl., military front sight and double-pull trigger. Calibers: 7x57, 8x57, 9x57mm. Other specifications same as for standard rifle.

BOLT-ACTION SPORTING RIFLE
SHORT MODEL TYPE K . . . . NiB $3856 Ex $3169 Gd $2190
Calibers: 6.5x54, 8x51mm. 19.75-inch bbl. Weight: 6.25 lbs. Other specifications same as for standard rifle.

- PRE-WORLD WAR II MODELS -

MODEL DSM34 BOLT-ACTION
SINGLE-SHOT SPORTING RIFLE. . . . . . NiB $670 Ex $445 Gd $338
Also called "Sport-model." Caliber: .22 LR. 26-inch bbl. Weight: 7.75 lbs. Sights: Tangent curve open rear; Barleycorn front. M/98 military-type stock, swivels. Intro. c. 1935.

MODEL EL320 BOLT-ACTION
SINGLE-SHOT SPORTING RIFLE. . . . . . NiB $556 Ex $449 Gd $339
Caliber: .22 LR. 23.5-inch bbl. Weight: 4.25 lbs. Sights: Adj. open rear; bead front. Sporting stock w/checkered pistol grip, swivels.

MODEL EN310 BOLT-ACTION
SINGLE-SHOT SPORTING RIFLE. . . . . . NiB $499 Ex $420 Gd $298
Caliber: .22 LR. ("22 Lang fur Buchsen.") 19.75-inch bbl. Weight: 4 lbs. Sights: Fixed open rear, blade front. Plain pistol-grip stock.

MODEL ES340 BOLT-ACTION
SINGLE-SHOT TARGET RIFLE . . . . NiB $765 Ex $455 Gd $338
Caliber: .22 LR. 25.5-inch bbl. Weight: 6.5 lbs. Sights: Tangent curve rear; ramp front. Sporting stock w/checkered pistol-grip and grooved forearm, swivels.

MODEL ES340B BOLT-ACTION SINGLE-SHOT
TARGET RIFLE . . . . .NiB $765 Ex $445 Gd $356
Caliber: .22 LR. 26.75-inch bbl. Weight: 8 lbs. Sights: Tangent curve open rear; ramp front. Plain pistol-grip stock, swivels.

MODEL ES350 BOLT-ACTION SINGLE-SHOT
TARGET RIFLE . . . . .NiB $977 Ex $775 Gd $558
"Meistershaftsbuchse" (Championship Rifle). Caliber: .22 LR. 27.5-inch bbl. Weight: 7.75 lbs. Sights: Open micrometer rear; ramp front. Target stock w/checkered pistol-grip and forearm, grip cap, swivels.

MODEL ES350B BOLT-ACTION SINGLE-SHOT
TARGET RIFLE . . . . .NiB $970 Ex $668 Gd $495
Same general specifications as Model MS350B except single-shot, weight: 8.25 lbs.

MODEL KKW BOLT-ACTION
SINGLE-SHOT TARGET RIFLE. . . . . NiB $944 Ex $667 Gd $544
Caliber: .22 LR. 26-inch bbl. Weight: 8.75 lbs. Sights: Tangent curve open rear; Barleycorn front. M/98 military-type stock, swivels. Note: This rifle has an improved design Mauser 22 action w/separate nonrotating bolt head. In addition to being produced for commercial sale, this model was used as a training rifle by the German armed forces; it was also made by Walther and Gustoff. Intro. just before WWII.

MODEL MM410 BOLT-ACTION
REPEATING SPORTING RIFLE. . . . . . . NiB $2166 Ex $1590 Gd $955
Caliber: .22 LR. Five round detachable box magazine. 23.5-inch bbl. Weight: 5 lbs. Sights: Tangent curve open rear; ramp front. Sporting stock w/checkered pistol-grip, swivels.

Mauser Type "A" Pattern No. 1
shown with floorplate opened.

Mauser Type "B" Pattern No. 60

Mauser Type "M" Pattern No. 270

RIFLES

MODEL MM410B BOLT-ACTION
REPEATING SPORTING RIFLE....... NiB $2166 Ex $1590 Gd $955
Caliber: .22 LR. Five round detachable box magazine. 23.5-inch bbl. Weight: 6.25 lbs. Sights: Tangent curve open rear; ramp front. Lightweight sporting stock w/checkered pistol-grip, swivels.

MODEL MS350B BOLT-ACTION
REPEATING TARGET RIFLE.......... NiB $1268 Ex $800 Gd $556
Caliber: .22 LR. Five round detachable box magazine. Receiver and bbl. grooved for detachable rear sight or scope. 26.75-inch bbl. Weight: 8.5 lbs. Sights: Micrometer open rear; ramp front. Target stock w/checkered pistol grip and forearm, grip cap, sling swivels.

MODEL MS420 BOLT-ACTION
REPEATING SPORTING RIFLE........ NiB $1145 Ex $879 Gd $606
Caliber: .22 LR. Five round detachable box magazine. 25.5-inch bbl. Weight: 6.5 lbs. Sights: Tangent curve open rear; ramp front. Sporting stock w/checkered pistol grip, grooved forearm swivels.

MODEL MS420B BOLT-ACTION
REPEATING TARGET RIFLE.......... NiB $1156 Ex $922 Gd $633
Caliber: .22 LR. Five round detachable box magazine. 26.75-inch bbl. Weight: 8 lbs. Sights: Tangent curve open rear; ramp front. Target stock w/checkered pistol grip, grooved forearm, swivels.

STANDARD MODEL RIFLE..... NiB $339 Ex $210 Gd $159
Refined version of German Service Kar. 98k. Straight bolt handle. Calibers: 7mm Mauser (7x57mm), 7.9mm Mauser (8x57mm). Five round box magazine. 23.5-inch bbl. Weight: 8.5 lbs. Sights: Blade front; adj. rear. Walnut stock of M/98 military-type. Note: These rifles were made for commercial sale and are of the high quality found in the Oberndorf Mauser sporters. They bear the Mauser trademark on the receiver ring.

TYPE "A" BOLT-ACTION
SPORTING RIFLE.......... NiB $7000 Ex $6200 Gd $3005
Special British Model. 7x57, 30-06 (7.62x63), 8x60, 9x57, 9.3x62mm. Five round box mag. 23.5-inch round bbl. Weight: 7.25 lbs. Mil.-type single trigger. Sights: Express rear; hooded ramp front. Circassian walnut sporting stock w/checkered pistol-grip and forearm, w/ or w/o cheekpiece, buffalo horn forend tip and grip cap, detachable swivels. Variations: Octagon bbl., double-set trigger, shotgun-type safety, folding peep rear sight, tangent curve rear sight, three-leaf rear sight.

TYPE "A" BOLT-ACTION SPORTING RIFLE,
MAGNUM MODEL......... NiB $5598 Ex $3473 Gd $2745
Same general specifications as standard Type "A" except w/Magnum action, weighs 7.5 to 8.5 lbs. Calibers: .280 Ross, .318 Westley Richards Express, 10.75x68mm, .404 Nitro Express.

TYPE "A" BOLT-ACTION SPORTING
RIFLE, SHORT MODEL...... NiB $6149 Ex $4144 Gd $2448
Same as standard Type "A" except w/short action, 21.5-inch round bbl., weight 6 lbs. Calibers: .250-3000, 6.5x54, 8x51mm.

TYPE "B" BOLT-ACTION SPORTING
RIFLE.................... NiB $5005 Ex $4885 Gd $2544
Normal Model. Calibers: 7x57, .30-06 (7.62x63), 8x57, 8x60, 9x57, 9.3x62, 10.7568mm. Five round box magazine. 23.5-inch round bbl. Weight: 7.25 lbs. Double-set trigger. Sights: Three-leaf rear, ramp front. Fine walnut stock w/checkered pistol-grip, Schnabel forend tip, cheekpiece, grip cap, swivels. Variations: Octagon or half-octagon bbl., military-type single trigger, shotgun-type safety, folding peep rear sight, tangent curve rear sight, telescopic sight.

TYPE "K" BOLT-ACTION
SPORTING RIFLE.......... NiB $8177 Ex $6805 Gd $4285
Light Short Model. Same specifications as Normal Type "B" model except w/short action, 21.5-inch round bbl., weight: 6 lbs. Calibers: .250-3000, 6.5x54, 8x51mm.

TYPE "M" BOLT-ACTION
SPORTING CARBINE....... NiB $6000 Ex $5133 Gd $3200
Calibers: 6.5x54, 7x57, .30-06 (7.62x63), 8x51, 8x60, 9x57mm. Five round box magazine. 19.75-inch round bbl. Weight: 6 to 6.75 lbs. Double-set trigger, flat bolt handle. Sights: Three-leaf rear; ramp front. Stocked to muzzle, cheekpiece, checkered pistol-grip and forearm, grip cap, steel forend cap, swivels. Variations: Military-type single trigger, shotgun-type trigger, shotgun-type safety, tangent curve rear sight, telescopic sight.

GRADING: **NiB** = New in Box   **Ex** = Excellent or NRA 95%   **Gd** = Good or NRA 68%

Mauser Model 66S Standard

Mauser Model 66S Deluxe

Mauser Model 66SP
Super Match Target
Rifle

Mauser Model 66ST Carbine

TYPE "S" BOLT-ACTION
SPORTING CARBINE . . . . **NiB $6000 Ex $5009 Gd $3005**
Calibers: 6.5x54 7x57, 8x51, 8x60, 9x57mm. Five-round box maga-zine. 19.75-inch round bbl. Weight: 6 to 6.75 lbs. Double-set trigger. Sights: Three-leaf rear; ramp front. Stocked to muzzle, Schnabel forend tip, cheekpiece, checkered pistol-grip w/cap, swivels. Variations: Same as listed for Normal Model Type "B."

- POST-WORLD WAR II MODELS -

NOTE: *Production of original Mauser sporting rifles (66 series) resumed at the Oberndorf plant in 1965 by Mauser-Jagdwaffen GmbH, now Mauser-Werke Oberndorf GmbH. The Series 2000-3000-4000 rifles, however, were made for Mauser by Friedrich Wilhelm Heym Gewehrfabrik, Muennerstadt, West Germany.*

MODEL 66S BOLT-ACTION STANDARD SPORTING RIFLE
Telescopic short action. Bbls. interchangeable within cal. group. Single- or double-set trigger (interchangeable). Cal: .243 Win., 6.5x57, .270 Win., 7x64, .308 Win., .30-06. Three round mag. 23.6 inch bbl. (25.6inch in 7x64). Wt: 7.3 lbs. (7.5 lbs. in 7x64). Sights: Adj. open rear, hooded ramp front. Select Eur. walnut stock, Monte Carlo w/cheek-piece, rosewood forend tip and pistol-grip cap, skip checkering, recoil

pad, sling swivels. Made from 1974 to 1995, export to U.S. disc. 1974. Note: U.S. designation, 1971 to 1973, was "Model 660."
Model 66S . . . . **NiB $4739 Ex $3054 Gd $2044**
w/extra bbl. assembly, add **$600**

MODEL 66S DELUXE SPORTER
Limited production special order. Model 66S rifles and carbines are available with /elaborate engraving, gold and silver inlays and carved select walnut stocks. Added value is upward of $4500.

MODEL 66S ULTRA
Same general specifications as Model 66S Standard except with 20.9-inch bbl., weight: 6.8 lbs.
Model 66S Ultra . . . . **NiB $1754 Ex $1644 Gd $1097**
w/extra bbl. assembly, add **$600**

MODEL 66SG BIG GAME . . . . **NiB $3077 Ex $2100 Gd $1388**
Same general specifications as Model 66S Standard except w/25.6-inch bbl. Calibers: .375 H&H Mag., .458 Win. Mag. Note: U.S. designation, 1971-73, was "Model 660 Safari."
w/ extra bbl. assembly, add **$600**

Mauser Model 99

Mauser Model 201

Mauser Model 3000

Mauser Model 4000

MODEL 66SH HIGH PERFORMANCE .NiB $1706 Ex $1530 Gd $1109
Same general specifications as Model 66S Standard except w/25.6-inch bbl., weighs 7.5 lbs. (9.3 lbs. in 9.3x64). Calibers: 6.5x68, 7mm Rem. Mag., 7mm S.E.v. Hoffe, .300 Win. Mag., 8x68S, 9.3x64.

MODEL 66SP SUPER MATCH
BOLT-ACTION TARGET RIFLE . . . . . NiB $4198 Ex $3707 Gd $2033
Telescopic short action. Adj. single-stage trigger. Caliber: .308 Win. (chambering for other cartridges available on special order). Three round magazine. 27.6-inch heavy bbl. w/muzzle brake, dovetail rib for special scope mount. Weight: 12 lbs. Target stock w/wide and deep forearm, full pistol-grip, thumbhole adj. cheekpiece, adj. rubber buttplate.

MODEL 66ST CARBINE . . . . . NiB $2635 EX $1710 GD $1277
Same general specifications as Model 66S Standard except w/20.9-inch bbl., full-length stock, weight: 7 lbs.
w/extra bbl. assembly, add **$600**

MODEL 83 BOLT-ACTION RIFLE . . . NiB $2215 Ex $2188 Gd $1360
Centerfire single-shot, bolt-action rifle for 300-meter competition. Caliber: .308 Win. 25.5-inch fluted bbl. Weight: 10.5 lbs. Adj. micrometer rear sight globe front. Fully adj. competition stock. Disc. 1988.

MODEL 96 . . . . NiB $677 Ex $633 Gd $455
Calibers: .25-06, .270 Win., 7x64, .308 Win., .30-06, 7mm Rem. Mag., .300 Win. Mag. 22-inch bbl.; magnums 24-inch. Weight: 6.25 lbs. No sights; drilled and tapped for scope. Walnut stock. Five-round top-loading magazine. 3-position safety.
MODEL 99 CLASSIC BOLT-ACTION RIFLE
Calibers: .243 Win., .25-06, .270 Win., .30-06, .308 Win., .257 Wby.,

.270 Wby., 7mm Rem. Mag., .300 Win., .300 Wby. .375 H&H. Four round magazine (standard), 3-round (Magnum). Bbl.: 24-inch (standard) or 26-inch (Magnum). 44 inches overall (standard). Weight: 8 lbs. No sights. Checkered European walnut stock w/rosewood grip cap available in Classic and Monte Carlo styles w/High-Luster or oil finish. Disc. importing 1994.
Standard Classic or
Monte Carlo (oil finish) . . . . . NiB $1156 Ex $1077 Gd $710
Magnum Classic or
Monte Carlo (oil finish) . . . . . NiB $1266 Ex $1109 Gd $800
Standard Classic or
Monte Carlo (H-L finish). . . . . NiB $1188 Ex $1098 Gd $775
Magnum Classic or
Monte Carlo (H-L finish). . . . . NiB $1347 Ex $1109 Gd $790

MODEL 107 BOLT-ACTION RIFLE . . . . . NiB $369 Ex $277 Gd $210
Caliber: .22 LR. Mag. Five round magazine. 21.5-inch bbl. 40 inches overall. Weight: 5 lbs. Receiver drilled and tapped for rail scope mounts. Hooded front sight, adj. rear. Disc. importing 1994.

MODEL 201/201 LUXUS BOLT-ACTION RIFLE
Calibers: .22 LR. .22 Win. Mag. Five round magazine. 21-inch bbl. 40 inches overall. Weight: 6.5 lbs. Receiver drilled and tapped for scope mounts. Sights optional. Checkered walnut-stained beech stock w/Monte Carlo. Model 201 Luxus w/checkered European walnut stock QD swivels, rosewood forend and rubber recoil pad. Made from 1989 to 1997.
Standard model . . . . NiB $670 Ex $555 Gd $400
Magnum. . . . . NiB $722 Ex $569 Gd $440
Luxus Standard model . . . . NiB $756 Ex $544 Gd $468
Luxus Magnum model. . . . . NiB $844 Ex $633 Gd $560

Midland Model 2707 Bolt-Action Rifle

Merkel Model 220

MODEL 2000 BOLT-ACTION
SPORTING RIFLE . . . . NiB $539 Ex $355 Gd $290
Modified Mauser-type action. Calibers: .270 Win., .308 Win., .30-06.
Five-round magazine. 24-inch bbl. Weight: 7.5 lbs. Sights: Folding leaf
rear; hooded ramp front. Checkered walnut stock w/Monte Carlo comb
and cheekpiece, forend tip, sling swivels. Made from 1969 to 1971.
Note: Model 2000 is similar in appearance to Model 3000.

MODEL 2000 CLASSIC BOLT-ACTION SPORTING RIFLE
Calibers: .22-250 Rem., .234 Win., .270 Win., 7mm Mag., .308 Win.,
.30-06, .300 Win. Mag. Three or 5-round magazine. 24-inch bbl. Weight:
7.5 lbs. Sights: Folding leaf rear; hooded ramp front. Checkered walnut
stock w/Monte Carlo comb and cheekpiece, forend tip, sling swivels.
Imported 1998. Note: The Model 2000 Classic is designed to interchange
bbl. assemblies within a given caliber group.
Classic model . . . . NiB $1696 Ex $ 1377 Gd $1044
Professional model . . . . NiB $3228 Ex $2709 Gd $1995
w/recoil compensator . . . . NiB $3245 Ex $2730 Gd $1100
Sniper model . . . . NiB $2010 Ex $1544 Gd $1120
Varmint model . . . . NiB $1996 Ex $1528 Gd $965
Extra bbl. assembly, add $950

MODEL 3000 BOLT-ACTION
SPORTING RIFLE . . . . NiB $570 Ex $440 Gd $400
Modified Mauser-type action. Calibers: .243 Win., .270 Win., .308
Win., .30-06. Five round magazine. 22-inch bbl. Weight: 7 lbs. No
sights. Select European walnut stock, Monte Carlo style w/cheekpiece,
rosewood forend tip and pistol-grip cap, skip checkering, recoil pad,
sling swivels. Made from 1971 to 1974.

MODEL 3000 MAGNUM . . . . NiB $641 Ex $486 Gd $379
Same general specifications as standard Model 3000, except w/3-round
magazine, 26-inch bbl., weight: 8 lbs. Calibers: 7mm Rem. Mag., .300
Win. Mag., .375 H&H Mag.

MODEL 4000 VARMINT RIFLE . . . NiB $466 Ex $380 Gd $269
Same general specifications as standard Model 3000, except w/smaller
action, folding leaf rear sight; hooded ramp front, rubber buttplate
instead of recoil pad, weight 6.75 lbs. Calibers: .222 Rem., .223 Rem.
22-inch bbl. Select European walnut stock w/rosewood forend tip and
pistol-grip cap. French checkering and sling swivels.

McMILLAN GUN WORKS — Phoenix, Arizona
See Harris Gunworks.

GEBRÜDER MERKEL — Suhl, Germany
*For Merkel combination guns and drillings, see listings under Merkel
shotguns.*

OVER/UNDER RIFLES ("BOCK-DOPPELBÜCHSEN")
Calibers: 5.6x35 Vierling, 6.5x58r5, 7x57r5, 8x57JR, 8x60R Magnum,
9.3x53r5, 9.3x72r5, 9.3x74r5, 10.3x60R as well as most of the British
calibers for African and Indian big game. Various bbl. lengths, weights.
In general, specifications correspond to those of Merkel over/under
shotguns. Values of these over/under rifles (in calibers for which
ammunition is obtainable) are about the same as those of comparable
shotgun models currently manufactured. For more specific data, see
Merkel shotgun models indicated below.
Model 210 . . . . NiB $5766 Ex $4470 Gd $3210
Model 210E . . . . NiB $6630 Ex $4950 Gd $3765
Model 213 . . . . NiB $13,760 Ex $10,550 Gd $7330
Model 240E1 . . . . NiB $7113 Ex $4966 Gd $3412
Model 313E . . . . NiB $19,670 Ex $16,750 Gd $10,355
Model 320E . . . . NiB $15,770 Ex $12,559 Gd $9220
Model 321 . . . . NiB $17,210 Ex $13,880 Gd $9155
Model 321E . . . . NiB $17,998 Ex $14,760 Gd $9970
Model 322 . . . . NiB $12,550 Ex $14,770 Gd $10,049
Model 323E . . . . NiB $23,760 Ex $19,210 Gd $12,960
Model 324 . . . . NiB $27,650 Ex $21,880 Gd $15,330

MEXICAN MILITARY RIFLE — Mexico
Manufactured by Government Arsenal, Mexico, D.F.

MODEL 1936 MAUSER MILITARY RIFLE . . NiB $221 Ex $169 Gd $95
Same as German Kar.98k w/minor variations and U.S. M/1903
Springfield-type knurled cocking piece.

MODEL 1936
MAUSER MILITARY RIFLE . . . . NiB $233 Ex $179 Gd $110

Mossberg Model 25

MIDLAND RIFLES — Martinsburg, West Virginia

Manufactured by Gibbs Rifle Company, Inc., Martinsburg, West Virginia.

MODEL 2100 BOLT-ACTION

RIFLE . . . . **NiB $413 Ex $338 Gd $228**
Calibers: .22-250, .243 Win., 6mm Rem., .270 Win., 6.5x55, 7x57, 7x64, .308 Win., and .30-06. Springfield 1903 action. Four-round magazine. 22-inch bbl. 43 inches overall. Weight: 7 lbs. Flip-up rear sight; hooded ramp front. Finely finished and checkered walnut stock w/pistol-grip cap and sling swivels. Steel recoil bar. Action drilled and tapped for scope mounts. Production disc.1997.

MODEL 2600 BOLT-ACTION RIFLE . . . . **NiB $445 Ex $370 Gd $220**
Same general specifications as Model 2100 except no pistol-grip cap, and stock is walnut-finished hardwood. Made 1992 to 1997.

MODEL 2707 BOLT-ACTION RIFLE . . . . **NiB $443 Ex $284 Gd $220**
Same general specifications as Model 2100 except the weight of this rifle as been reduced by utilizing a tapered bbl., anodized aluminum trigger housing and lightened stock. Weight: 6.5 lbs. Disc.

MODEL 2800 LIGHTWEIGHT RIFLE . . . . **NiB $466 Ex $355 Gd $269**
Same general specifications as Model 2100 except w/laminated birch stock. Made from 1992 to 1994 and from 1996 to 1997.

MITCHELL ARMS. INC. — Fountain Valley, California

Formerly Santa Ana, California.

MODEL 15/22 SEMIAUTOMATIC
High Standard-style action. Caliber: .22 LR. 15-round magazine (10-round after 10/13/94). 20.5-inch bbl. 37.5 inches overall. Weight: 6.25 lbs. Ramp front sight; adj. open rear. Blued finish. Mahogany stock; Monte Carlo-style American walnut stock on Deluxe model. Made from 1994 to 1996.
NiB $300 Ex $233 Gd $179 . . . . **NiB $300 Ex $233 Gd $179**
Carbine . . . . **NiB $300 Ex $233 Gd $179**
Deluxe . . . . **NiB $259 Ex $166 Gd $126**

MODEL 9300 SERIES BOLT-ACTION RIFLE
Calibers: .22 LR. .22 Mag. Five or 10-round magazine. 22.5-inch bbl. 40.75 inches overall. Weight: 6.5 lbs. Beaded ramp front sight; adj. open rear. Blued finish. American walnut stock. Made 1994 to 1995.
Model 9302 (.22 LR
  w/checkered stock, rosewood caps) . **NiB $319 Ex $239 Gd $177**
Model 9302 (.22 Mag.,
  checkered stock, rosewood caps) NiB $317 Ex $237 Gd $175
Model 9303 (.22 LR, plain stock) . . . . . . **NiB $317 Ex $237 Gd $175**
Model 9304
  (.22 Mag., checkered stock) . . . . **NiB $266 Ex $201 Gd $177**
Model 9305 (.22 LR, special stock) . . . . . **NiB $221 Ex $179 Gd $235**

AK-22 SEMIAUTOMATIC RIFLE. . . . . . . **NiB $359 Ex $248 Gd $189**
Replica of AK-47 rifle. .22 LR. .22 WMR, 20-round magazine (.22 LR), 10-round (.22 WMR). 18-inch bbl. 36 inches overall. Weight: 6.5 lbs. Sights: Post front; open adj. rear. European walnut stock and forend. Matte black finish. Made from 1985 to 1994.

CAR-15 . . . . **NiB $525 Ex $355 Gd $283**
Replica of AR-15 CAR rifle. Caliber: .22 LR. 15-round magazine.16.25-inch bbl. 32 inches overall. Sights: Adj. post front; adj. aperture rear. Telescoping buttstock and ventilated forend. Matte black finish. Made 1990 to 1994.

GALIL 22 SEMIAUTOMATIC RIFLE . . . . **NiB $439 Ex $289 Gd $198**
Replica of Israeli Galil rifle. Calibers: .22 LR. .22 WMR., 20-round magazine (.22 LR), 10-round (.22 WMR). 18-inch bbl. 36 inches overall. Weight: 6.5 lbs. Sights: Adj. post front; rear adj. for windage. Folding metal stock w/European walnut grip and forend. Matte black finish. Made 1987 to 1993.

M-16A 22 SEMIAUTOMATIC RIFLE. . . . **NiB $479 Ex $266 Gd $179**
Replica of AR-15 rifle. Caliber: .22 LR. 15-round magazine. 20.5-inch bbl. 38.5 inches overall. Weight: 7 lbs. Sights: Adj. post front, adj. aperture rear. Black composite stock and forend. Matte black finish. Made 1990 to 1994.

MAS 22 SEMIAUTOMATIC RIFLE . . . . . . **NiB $439 Ex $290 Gd $221**
Replica of French MAS bullpup rifle. Caliber: .22 LR. 20-round magazine. 18-inch bbl. 28 inches overall. Weight: 7.5 lbs. Sights: Adj. post front, folding aperture rear. European walnut buttstock and forend. Matte black finish. Made from 1987 to 1993.

PPS SEMIAUTOMATIC RIFLE
Caliber: .22 LR. 20-round magazine, 50-round drum. 16.5-inch bbl. 33.5 inches overall. Weight: 5.5 lbs. Sights: Blade front; adj. rear. European walnut stock w/ventilated bbl. shroud. Matte black finish. Made 1989 to 1994.
Model PPS (20-round magazine) . . **NiB $370 Ex $259 Gd $188**
Model PPS/50 (50-round drum) . . . **NiB $522 Ex $402 Gd $300**

O.F. MOSSBERG & SONS, INC. — North Haven, Connecticut

Formerly New Haven, CT.

MODEL 10 BOLT-ACTION
SINGLE-SHOT RIFLE . . . . **NiB $338 Ex $190 Gd $120**
Takedown. Caliber: .22 LR, Long, Short. 22-inch bbl. Weight: 4 lbs. Sights: Open rear; bead front. Plain pistol-grip stock w/swivels, sling. Made 1933 to 1935.

MODEL 14 BOLT-ACTION
SINGLE-SHOT RIFLE . . . . **NiB $338 Ex $190 Gd $120**
Takedown. Caliber: .22 LR, Long, Short. 24-inch bbl. Weight: 5.25 lbs. Sights: Peep rear; hooded ramp front. Plain pistol-grip stock w/semibeavertail forearm, 1.25-inch swivels. Made 1934 to 1935.

MODEL 20 BOLT-ACTION
SINGLE-SHOT RIFLE . . . . **NiB $338 Ex $190 Gd $120**
Takedown. Caliber: .22 LR, Long, Short. 24-inch bbl. Weight: 4.5 lbs. Sights: Open rear; bead front. Plain pistol-grip stock and forearm w/ finger grooves, sling and swivels. Made from 1933 to 1935.

MODEL 25/25A BOLT-ACTION SINGLE-SHOT RIFLE
Takedown. Caliber: .22 LR, Long, Short. 24-inch bbl. Weight: 5 lbs. Sights: Peep rear; hooded ramp front. Plain pistol-grip stock w/semibeavertail forearm. 1.25-inch swivels. Made from 1935 to 1936.
Model 25 . . . . **NiB $338 Ex $190 Gd $120**
Model 25A (Improved Model 25, 1936-38) . . **NiB $325 Ex $190 Gd $120**

Mossberg Model 35A

Mossberg Model 40

Mossberg Model L42A

Mossberg Model 42B

MODEL 26B/26C BOLT-ACTION SINGLE-SHOT
Takedown. Caliber: .22 LR. Long, Short. 26-inch bbl. Weight: 5.5 lbs. Sights; Rear, micrometer click peep or open; hooded ramp front. Plain pistol-grip stock swivels. Made from 1938 to 1941.
Model 26B . . . . NiB $338 Ex $190 Gd $120
Model 26C
 (No rear sights or sling swivels) . . NiB $250 Ex $132 Gd $91

MODEL 30 BOLT-ACTION
SINGLE-SHOT RIFLE . . . . .NiB $338 Ex $190 Gd $120
Takedown. Caliber: .22 LR. Long, Short. 24-inch bbl. Weight: 4.5 lbs. Sights: Peep rear; bead front, on hooded ramp. Plain pistol-grip stock, forearm w/finger grooves. Made from 1933 to 1935.

MODEL 34 BOLT-ACTION
SINGLE-SHOT RIFLE . . . . .NiB $338 Ex $190 Gd $120
Takedown. Caliber: .22 LR. Long, Short. 24-inch bbl. Weight: 5.5 lbs. Sights: Peep rear; hooded ramp front. Plain pistol-grip stock w/semibeavertail forearm, 1.25-inch swivels. Made 1934 to 1935.

MODEL 35 TARGET GRADE
BOLT-ACTION SINGLE-SHOT RIFLE . . . . NiB $440 Ex $300 Gd $166
Caliber: .22 LR. 26-inch heavy bbl. Weight: 8.25 lbs. Sights: Micrometer click rear peep; hooded ramp front. Large target stock w/full pistol grip, cheekpiece, full beavertail forearm, 1.25-inch swivels. Made from 1935 to 1937.

MODEL 35A BOLT-ACTION
SINGLE-SHOT RIFLE . . . . .NiB $440 Ex $300 Gd $166
Caliber: .22 LR. 26-inch heavy bbl. Weight: 8.25 lbs. Sights: Micrometer click peep rear; hooded front. Target stock w/cheekpiece full pistol grip and forearm, 1.25-inch sling swivels. Made from 1937 to 1938.

MODEL 35A-LS . . . . NiB $440 Ex $300 Gd $166
Caliber .22 LR. Same as Model 35A but w/Lyman No. 57 rear sight, 17A front. Target stock w/checkpiece, full pistol-grip and forearm.

MODEL 35B . . . . .NiB $440 Ex $300 Gd $166
Same specifications as Model 44B except single-shot. Made from 1938 to 1940.

MODEL 40 BOLT-ACTION REPEATER . . . NiB $222 Ex $140 Gd $100
Takedown. Caliber: .22 LR. Long, Short, 16-round tubular magazine. 24-inch bbl. Weight: 5 lbs. Sights: Peep rear; bead front, on hooded ramp. Plain pistol-grip stock, forearm w/finger grooves. Made 1933 to 1935.

MODEL 42 BOLT-ACTION REPEATER . . . NiB $278 Ex $155 Gd $110
Takedown. Caliber: .22 LR. Long, Short. Seven-round detachable box magazine. 24-inch bbl. Weight: 5 lbs. Sights: Receiver peep, open rear; hooded ramp front. Pistol-grip stock. 1.25-inch swivels. Made 1935 to 1937.

MODEL 42A/L42A BOLT-ACTION REPEATERS
Takedown. Caliber: .22 LR. Long, Short. Seven-round detachable box magazine. 24-inch bbl. Weight: 5 lbs. Sights: Receiver peep, open rear; ramp front. Plain pistol-grip stock. Made from 1937-38. Model L42A (left-hand action) made from 1937 to 1941.
Model 42A .NiB $279 Ex $169 Gd $120
Model L42A . . . . .NiB $288 Ex $179 Gd $130

MODEL 42B/42C BOLT-ACTION REPEATERS
Takedown. Caliber: .22 LR. Long, Short. Five-round detachable box magazine. 24-inch bbl. Weight: 6 lbs. Sights: Micrometer click receiver peep, open rear hooded ramp front. Plain pistol-grip stock, swivels. Made from 1938 to 1941.
Model 42B . . . . .NiB $289 Ex $190 Gd $100
Model 42C (No rear peep sight) . . NiB $235 Ex $155 Gd $110

Mossberg Model 42C

Mossberg Model L-43

Mossberg Model 43B

Mossberg Model 44US

Mossberg Model L45A
Left-Hand Model

Mossberg Model 45B

Mossberg Model L46A-LS

Mossberg Model 46B

**MODEL 42M BOLT-ACTION
REPEATER** . . . .**NiB $345 Ex $233 Gd $135**
Caliber: .22 LR, Long, Short. Seven-round detachable box magazine.
23-inch bbl. Weight: 6.75 lbs. Sights: Microclick receiver peep, open
rear; hooded ramp front. Two-piece Mannlicher-type stock w/cheek-
piece and pistol-grip, swivels. Made from 1940 to 1950.

**MODEL 43/L43 BOLT-ACTION
REPEATERS** . . . .**NiB $376 Ex $256 Gd $198**
Speedlock, adj. trigger pull. Caliber: .22 LR. Seven-round detach-
able box magazine. 26-inch heavy bbl. Weight: 8.25 lbs. Sights:

Lyman No. 57 rear; selective aperture front. Target stock w/
cheekpiece, full pistol-grip, beavertail forearm, adj. front swivel.
Made from 1937-38. Model L43 is same as Model 43 except w/
left-hand action.

MODEL 43B . . . .**NiB $390 Ex $300 Gd $170**
Same as Model 44B except w/Lyman No. 57 receiver sight and No.
17A front sight. Made from 1938 to 1939.

Mossberg Model 46M

Mossberg Model 50

Mossberg Model 51

Mossberg Model 51M

MODEL 44 BOLT-ACTION REPEATER... NiB $397 Ex $276 Gd $160
Takedown. Caliber: .22 LR, Long, Short. Tubular magazine holds 16 LR. 24-inch bbl. Weight: 6 lbs. Sights: Peep rear; hooded ramp front. Plain pistol-grip stock w/semi-beavertail forearm, 1.25-inch swivels. Made from 1934 to 1935. Note: Do not confuse this rifle w/later Models 44B and 44US, which are clip repeaters.

MODEL 44B BOLT-ACTION
TARGET RIFLE . . . . .NiB $389 Ex $266 Gd $160
Caliber: .22 LR. Seven-round detachable box magazine. Made from 1938 to 1941.

MODEL 44US BOLT-ACTION REPEATER
Caliber: .22 LR. Seven round detachable box magazine. 26-inch heavy bbl. Weight: 8.5 lbs. Sights: Micrometer click receiver peep, hooded front. Target stock, swivels. Made from 1943-48. Note: This model was used as a training rifle by the U.S. Armed Forces during WWII.
Model 44US. NiB $395 Ex $279 Gd $145
Model 44US (marked U.S. Property) . . . . NiB $395 Ex $279 Gd $145

MODEL 45 BOLT-ACTION REPEATER... NiB $254 Ex $178 Gd $117
Takedown. Caliber: .22 LR, Long, Short. Tubular magazine holds 15 LR, 18 Long, 22 Short. 24-inch bbl. Weight: 6.75 lbs. Sights: Rear peep; hooded ramp front. Plain pistol-grip stock, 1.25-inch swivels. Made 1935 to 1937.

MODEL 45A, L45A, 45AC BOLT-ACTION REPEATERS
Takedown. Caliber: .22 LR, Long, Short. Tubular magazine holds 15 LR, 18 Long, 22 Short. 24-inch bbl. Weight: 6.75 lbs. Sights: Receiver peep, open rear; hooded blade front sight mounted on ramp. Plain pistol-grip stock, 1.25-inch sling swivels. Made 1937 to 1938.

Model 45A. NiB $300 Ex $190 Gd $145
Model L45A (Left-hand action) . . . . NiB $655 Ex $355 Gd $279
Model 45AC (No receiver peep sight) . . . NiB $249 Ex $177 Gd $123

MODEL 45B/45C BOLT-ACTION REPEATERS
Takedown. Caliber: .22 LR, Long, Short. Tubular magazine holds 15 LR, 18 Long, 22 Short. 24-inch bbl. Weight: 6.25 lbs. Open rear sight; hooded blade front sight mounted on ramp. Plain pistol-grip stock w/ sling swivels. Made from 1938 to 1940.
Model 45B. . . . . NiB $338 Ex $233 Gd $138
Model 45C (No sights, made 1935 to 1937) NiB $338 Ex $233 Gd $138

MODEL 46 BOLT-ACTION REPEATER... NiB $338 Ex $233 Gd $138
Takedown. Caliber: .22 LR, Long, Short. Tubular magazine holds 15 LR, 18 Long, 22 Short. 26-inch bbl. Weight: 7.5 lbs. Sights: Micrometer click rear peep; hooded ramp front. Pistol-grip stock w/ cheekpiece, full beavertail forearm, 1.25-inch swivels. Made from 1935 to 1937.

MODEL 46A, 46A-LS, L46A-LS BOLT-ACTION REPEATERS
Takedown. Caliber: .22 LR, Long, Short. Tubular magazine holds 15 LR, 18 Long, 22 Short. 26-inch bbl. Weight: 7.25 lbs. Sights: Micrometer click receiver peep, open rear; hooded ramp front. Pistol-grip stock w/ cheekpiece and beavertail forearm, quick-detachable swivels. Made from 1937 to 1938.
Model 46A. . . . . NiB $338 Ex $233 Gd $138
Mdl. 46A-LS (w/Lyman No. 57 receiver sight). . .NiB $386 Ex $276 Gd $189
Model L46A-LS (Left-hand action) . . . . . . NiB $650 Ex $355 Gd $269

Mossberg Model 140B

Mossberg Model 140K

Mossberg Model 144LS

Mossberg Model 146B

RIFLES

MODEL 46B BOLT-ACTION
REPEATER . . . . **NiB $290 Ex $167 Gd $133**
Takedown. Caliber: .22 LR, Long, Short. Tubular magazine holds 15 LR, 18 Long, 22 Short. 26-inch bbl. Weight: 7 lbs. Sights: Micrometer click receiver peep, open rear, hooded front. Plain pistol-grip stock w/cheekpiece, swivels. Note: Postwar version of this model has full magazine holding 20 LR, 23 Long, 30 Short. Made 1938 to 1950.

MODEL 46BT . . . . .NiB $347 Ex $229 Gd $176
Same as Model 46B except w/heavier bbl. and stock. Weight: 7.75 lbs. Made from 1938 to 1939.

MODEL 46C . . . . .NiB $347 Ex $229 Gd $176
Same as Model 46 except w/a heavier bbl. and stock than that model. Weight: 8.5 lbs. Made from 1936 to 1937.

MODEL 46M
BOLT-ACTION REPEATER . . . . **NiB $347 Ex $229 Gd $176**
Caliber: .22 LR, Long, Short. Tubular magazine holds 22 Short, 18 Long, 15 LR. 23-inch bbl. Weight: 7 lbs. Sights: Microclick receiver peep, open rear; hooded ramp front. Two-piece Mannlicher-type stock w/ cheekpiece and pistol-grip, swivels. Made 1940 to 1952.

MODEL 50
AUTOLOADING RIFLE . . . . **NiB $298 Ex $213 Gd $139**
Same as Model 51 except w/plain stock w/o beavertail cheekpiece, swivels or receiver peep sight. Made from 1939 to 1942.

MODEL 51 AUTOLOADING RIFLE . . . . . **NiB $298 Ex $213 Gd $139**
Takedown. Caliber: .22 LR. Fifteen-round tubular magazine in buttstock. 24-inch bbl. Weight: 7.25 lbs. Sights: Micrometer click receiver peep, open rear; hooded ramp front. Cheekpiece stock w/full pistol grip and beavertail forearm, swivels. Made in 1939 only.

MODEL 51M AUTOLOADING RIFLE . . . . **NiB $278 Ex $154 Gd $123**
Caliber: .22 LR. Fifteen-round tubular magazine. 20-inch bbl. Weight: 7 lbs. Sights: Microclick receiver peep, open rear; hooded ramp front. Two-piece Mannlicher-type stock w/pistol-grip and cheekpiece, hard-rubber buttplate and sling swivels. Made from 1939 to 1946.

MODEL 140B SPORTER-TARGET RIFLE . . **NiB $254 Ex $186 Gd $134**
Same as Model 140K except w/peep rear sight, hooded ramp front sight. Made from 1957 to 1958.

MODEL 140K BOLT-ACTION REPEATER . **NiB $248 Ex $197 Gd $123**
Caliber: .22 LR, .22 Long, .22 Short. Seven-round clip magazine. 24.5-inch bbl. Weight: 5.75 lbs. Sights: Open rear; bead front. Monte Carlo stock w/ cheekpiece and pistol-grip, sling swivels. Made 1955 to 1958.

MODEL 142-A BOLT-ACTION
REPEATING CARBINE . . . .**NiB $277 Ex $233 Gd $166**
Caliber: .22 Short Long, LR. Seven-round detachable box magazine. 18-inch bbl. Weight: 6 lbs. Sights: Peep rear, military-type front. Monte Carlo stock w/pistol-grip, hinged forearm pulls down to form hand grip; sling swivels mounted on left side of stock. Made from 1949 to 1957.

Mossberg Model 151K

Mossberg Model 151M

Mossberg Model 152

MODEL 142K . . . . .NiB $244 Ex $152 Gd $109
Same as Model 142 except w/open rear sight. Made 1953 to 1957.

MODEL 144 BOLT-ACTION
TARGET RIFLE . . . . NiB $390 Ex $288 Gd $215
Caliber: .22 LR. Seven-round detachable box magazine. 26-inch heavy bbl. Weight: 8 lbs. Sights: Microclick receiver peep; hooded front. Pistol-grip target stock w/beavertail forearm, adj. hand stop, swivels. Made from 1949 to 1954. Note: This model designation was resumed c.1973 to replace Model 144LS, and then disc. again in 1985.

MODEL 144LS . . . . .NiB $385 Ex $277 Gd $205
Same as Model 144 except w/Lyman No. 57MS or Mossberg S331 receiver sight and Lyman 17A front sight. Made from 1954 to date. Note: Since 1973, this model has been marketed as Model 144.

MODEL 146B BOLT-ACTION REPEATER. NiB $347 Ex $190 Gd $139
Takedown. Caliber: .22 LR, Long, Short. Tubular magazine holds 30 Short, 23 Long, 20 LR. 26-inch bbl. Weight: 7 lbs. Sights: Micrometer click rear peep, open rear; hooded front. Plain stock w/pistol-grip, Monte Carlo comb and cheekpiece, knob forend tip, swivels. Made from 1949 to 1954.

MODEL 151K . . . . .NiB $290 Ex $193 Gd $130
Same as Model 151M except w/24-inch bbl., weight: 6 lbs., w/o peep sight, plain stock w/Monte Carlo comb and cheekpiece, pistol-grip knob, forend tip, w/o swivels. Made from 1950 to 1951.

MODEL 151M AUTOLOADING RIFLE. . . NiB $370 Ex $199 Gd $138
Improved version of Model 51M w/same general specifications, complete action is instantly removable w/o use of tools. Made 1946 to 1958.

MODEL 152 AUTOLOADING CARBINE . NiB $276 Ex $197 Gd $135
Caliber: .22 LR. Seven-round detachable box magazine. 18-inch bbl. Weight: 5 lbs. Sights: Peep rear; military-type front. Monte Carlo stock w/pistol-grip, hinged forearm pulls down to form hand grip, sling mounted on swivels on left side of stock. Made 1948 to 1957.

MODEL 152K . . . . .NiB $233 Ex $176 Gd $121
Same as Model 152 except w/open instead of peep rear sight. Made from 1950 to 1957.

MODEL 320B BOY SCOUT TARGET RIFLE . . NiB $233 Ex $176 Gd $121
Same as Model 340K except single-shot w/auto. safety. Made 1960 to 1971.

MODEL 320K HAMMERLESS
BOLT-ACTION SINGLE-SHOT. . . . . .NiB $200 Ex $123 Gd $90
Same as Model 346K except single-shot, w/drop-in loading platform, automatic safety. Weight: 5.75 lbs. Made from 1958 to 1960.

MODEL 321B . . . . .NiB $347 Ex $190 Gd $139
Same as Model 321K except w/receiver peep sight. Made 1972 to 1975.

MODEL 321K BOLT-ACTION
SINGLE-SHOT . . . . .NiB $347 Ex $190 Gd $139
Same as Model 341 except single-shot. Made 1972 to 1980.

MODEL 333
AUTOLOADING CARBINE . . . . NiB $266 Ex $180 Gd $145
Caliber: .22 LR. 15-round tubular magazine. 20-inch bbl. Weight: 6.25 lbs. Sights: Open rear; ramp front. Monte Carlo stock w/checkered pistol grip and forearm, bbl. band, swivels. Made 1972 to 1973.

MODEL 340B TARGET SPORTER . . . . . . NiB $231 Ex $188 Gd $133
Same as Model 340K except w/peep rear sight, hooded ramp front sight. Made from 1958 to 1981.

MODEL 340K HAMMERLESS
BOLT-ACTION REPEATER. . . . . . . .NiB $231 Ex $188 Gd $133
Same as Model 346K except clip type, 7-round magazine. Made from 1958 to 1971.

MODEL 340M . . . . .NiB $650 Ex $390 Gd $238
Same as Model 340K except w/18.5-inch bbl., Mannlicher-style stock w/swivels and sling. Weight: 5.25 lbs. Made 1970 to 1971.

Mossberg Model 320B

Mossberg Model 320K

Mossberg Model 333

Mossberg Model 340B

Mossberg Model 340K

Mossberg Model 341

Mossberg Model 342K

Mossberg Model 346B

Mossberg Model 346K

GRADING: **NiB** = New in Box   **Ex** = Excellent or NRA 95%   **Gd** = Good or NRA 68%

Mossberg Model 350K
Autoloading — Clip Type

Mossberg Model 351K
Automatic Sporter

Mossberg Model 352K
Carbine

Mossberg Model 353
Carbine

Mossberg Model 377
Plinkster

MODEL 341 BOLT-ACTION REPEATER . . NiB $290 Ex $144 Gd $110
Caliber: .22 Short. Long, LR. Seven-round clip magazine. 24-inch bbl.
Weight: 6.5 lbs. Sights: Open rear, ramp front. Monte Carlo stock w/check-ered pistol-grip and forearm, sling swivels. Made 1972 to 1985.

MODEL 342K HAMMERLESS
BOLT-ACTION CARBINE . . . . . . .NiB $240 Ex $150 Gd $113
Same as Model 340K except w/18-inch bbl., stock w/no cheekpiece,
extension forend is hinged, pulls down to form hand grip; sling swivels
and web strap on left side of stock. Weight: 5 lbs. Made 1958 to 1974.

MODEL 346B . . . . .NiB $240 Ex $180 Gd $113
Same as Model 346K except w/peep rear sight, hooded ramp front sight.
Made from 1958 to 1967.

MODEL 346K HAMMERLESS
BOLT-ACTION REPEATER. . . . . . .NiB $240 Ex $150 Gd $113
Caliber: .22 Short. Long, LR. Tubular magazine holds 25 Short, 20 Long,
18 LR. 24-inch bbl. Weight: 6.5 lbs. Sights: Open rear; bead front.
Walnut stock w/Monte Carlo comb, cheekpiece, pistol-grip, sling swiv-els. Made from 1958 to 1971.

MODEL 350K AUTOLOADING
RIFLE — CLIP TYPE . . . . .NiB $240 Ex $150 Gd $113
Caliber: .22 Short (High Speed), Long, LR. Seven-round clip magazine.

23.5-inch bbl. Weight: 6 lbs. Sights: Open rear; bead front. Monte Carlo
stock w/pistol-grip. Made from 1958 to 1971.

MODEL 351C
AUTOLOADING CARBINE . . . . .NiB $240 Ex $150 Gd $113
Same as Model 351K except w/18.5-inch bbl., Western carbine-style stock w/
barrel band and sling swivels. Weight: 5.5 lbs. Made from 1965 to 1971.

MODEL 351K AUTOLOADING
SPORTER . . . . .NiB $240 Ex $150 Gd $113
Caliber: .22 LR. Fifteen-round tubular magazine in buttstock. 24-inch
bbl. Weight: 6 lbs. Sights: Open rear; bead front. Monte Carlo stock w/
pistol-grip. Made from 1960 to 1971.

MODEL 352K AUTOLOADING CARBINE . . . NiB $240 Ex $150 Gd $113
Caliber: .22 Short, Long, LR. Seven-round clip magazine. 18-inch bbl.
Weight: 5 lbs. Sights: Open rear; bead front. Monte Carlo stock w/pistol
grip; extension forend of Tenite is hinged, pulls down to form hand grip;
sling swivels, web strap. Made from 1958 to 1971.

MODEL 353 AUTOLOADING CARBINE . . NiB $240 Ex $150 Gd $113
Caliber: .22 LR. Seven round clip magazine. 18-inch bbl. Weight: 5 lbs. Sights:
Open rear; ramp front. Monte Carlo stock w/checkered pistol-grip and forearm;
black Tenite extension forend pulls down to form hand grip. Made 1972 to 1985.

Mossberg Model 400

Mossberg Model 402

Mossberg Model 472
Brush Gun

Mossberg Model 472
Carbine (Pistol Grip)

Mossberg Model 472
Carbine (Straight Grip)

Mossberg Model
472 "One in Five
Thousand"

MODEL 377 PLINKSTER AUTOLOADER . NiB $278 Ex $200 Gd $155
Caliber: .22 LR. Fifteen-round tubular magazine. 20-inch bbl. Weight: 6.25 lbs. 4x scope sight. Thumbhole stock w/rollover cheekpiece, Monte Carlo comb, checkered forearm; molded of modified polystyrene foam in walnut-finish; sling swivel studs. Made 1977 to 1979.

MODEL 380 SEMIAUTOMATIC RIFLE . . . NiB $278 Ex $200 Gd $155
Caliber: .22 LR. Fifteen-round buttstock magazine. 20-inch bbl. Weight: 5.5 lbs. Sights: Open rear; bead front. Made 1980 to 1985.

MODEL 400 PALOMINO LEVER-ACTION . . . NiB $390 Ex $242 Gd $161
Hammerless. Caliber: .22 Short, Long, LR. Tubular magazine holds 20 Short, 17 Long, 15 LR. 24-inch bbl. Weight: 5.5 lbs. Sights: Open rear; bead front. Monte Carlo stock w/checkered pistol-grip; beavertail forearm. Made 1959 to 1964.

MODEL 402 PALOMINO CARBINE. . . . . NiB $390 Ex $242 Gd $161
Same as Model 400 except w/18.5-inch (1961-64) or 20-inch bbl. (1964-71), forearm w/bbl. band, swivels; magazine holds two fewer rounds. Weight: 4.75 lbs. Made from 1961 to 1971.

MODEL 430 AUTOLOADING RIFLE . . . . NiB $340 Ex $180 Gd $135
Caliber: .22 LR. Eighteen-round tubular magazine. 24-inch bbl. Weight: 6.25 lbs. Sights: Open rear; bead front. Monte Carlo stock w/checkered pistol grip; checkered forearm. Made 1970 to 1971.

MODEL 432 WESTERN-STYLE AUTO . . . NiB $340 Ex $180 Gd $135
Same as Model 430 except w/plain straight-grip carbine-type stock and forearm, bbl. band, sling swivels. Magazine capacity: 15 cartridges. Weight: 6 lbs. Made from 1970 to 1971.

GRADING: **NiB** = New in Box   **Ex** = Excellent or NRA 95%   **Gd** = Good or NRA 68%

Mossberg Model 640K Chuckster

Mossberg Model 640KS

Mossberg Model 640M

Mossberg Model 642K shown w/forearm extension pulled down

MODEL 472 BRUSH GUN . . . . . .**NiB $340 Ex $180 Gd $135**
Same as Model 472 Carbine w/straight-grip stock except w/18-inch bbl., weight: 6.5 lbs. Caliber: .30-30. Magazine capacity: 5 rounds. Made from 1974 to 1976.

MODEL 472 LEVER-ACTION CARBINE . . **NiB $340 Ex $180 Gd $135**
Calibers: .30-30, .35 Rem. Six round tubular magazine. Weight: 6.75 to 7 lbs. Sights: Open rear; ramp front. Pistol-grip or straight-grip stock, forearm w/bbl. band; sling swivels on pistol-grip model saddle ring on straight-grip model. Made from 1972 to 1979.

MODEL 472 ONE IN FIVE THOUSAND . **NiB $665 Ex $423 Gd $240**
Same as Model 472 Brush Gun except w/Indian scenes etched on receiver; brass buttplate, saddle ring and bbl. bands, gold-plated trigger, bright blued finish, select walnut stock and forearm. Limited edition of 5,000; serial numbered 1 to 5,000. Made in 1974.

MODEL 472 RIFLE . . . .**NiB $340 Ex $180 Gd $135**
Same as Model 472 Carbine w/pistol-grip stock except w/24-inch bbl., 5-round magazine, weight: 7 lbs. Made from 1974 to 1976.

MODEL 479
Caliber: .30-30. Six-round tubular magazine. 20-inch bbl. Weight: 6.75 to 7 lbs. Sights: Open rear; ramp front. Made 1983 to 1985.
Model 479 Rifle . . . . **NiB $340 Ex $180 Gd $135**
Model 479PCA
   (carbine w/20-inch bbl.) . . . .**NiB $340 Ex $180 Gd $135**
Model 479RR
   (Roy Rogers model, 5000 Ltd. Ed.)**NiB $665 Ex $423 Gd $240**

MODEL 620K HAMMERLESS SINGLE-SHOT
BOLT-ACTION RIFLE . . . .**NiB $290 Ex $179 Gd $133**
Single shot. Caliber: .22 WMR. 24-inch bbl. Weight: 6 lbs. Sights: Open rear; bead front. Monte Carlo stock w/cheekpiece, pistol-grip, sling swivels. Made from 1959 to 1960.

MODEL 620K-A . . . .**NiB $290 Ex $179 Gd $133**
Same as Model 640K except w/sight modification. Made 1960 to 1968.

MODEL 640K CHUCKSTER HAMMERLESS
BOLT-ACTION RIFLE . . . .**NiB $338 Ex $228 Gd $136**
Caliber: .22 WMR. Five-round detachable clip magazine. 24-inch bbl. Weight: 6 lbs. Sights: Open rear; bead front. Monte Carlo stock w/ cheekpiece, pistol grip, sling swivels. Made from 1959 to 1984.

MODEL 640KS . . . . **NiB $338 Ex $ 228 Gd $136**
Deluxe version of Model 640K w/select walnut stock hand checkering; gold-plated front sight, rear sight elevator, and trigger. Made from 1960 to 1964.

MODEL 640M . . . .**NiB $665 Ex $423 Gd $240**
Similar to Model 640K except w/heavy receiver and jeweled bolt. 20-inch bbl., full length Mannlicher-style stock w/Monte Carlo comb and cheekpiece, swivels and leather sling. 40.75 inches overall. Weight: 6 lbs. Made from 1971 to 1973.

MODEL 642K CARBINE . . . .**NiB $396 Ex $277 Gd $194**
Caliber: .22 WMR. Five-round detachable clip magazine. 18-inch bbl. Weight: 5 lbs. 38.25 inches overall. Sights: Open rear; bead front. Monte Carlo walnut stock w/black Tenite forearm extension that pulls down to form hand grip. Made from 1961 to 1968.

Mossberg Model 800

Mossberg Model 800D

Mossberg Model 800M

Mossberg Model 810

Mossberg Model L

Mossberg Model R

RIFLES

MODEL 800 BOLT-ACTION
CENTERFIRE RIFLE . . . . NiB $455 Ex $307 Gd $200
.222 Rem., .22-250, .243 Win., .308 Win. Four-round mag., 3-round in .222. 22-inch bbl. Weight: 7.5 lbs. Sights: Folding leaf rear; ramp front. Monte Carlo stock w/cheekpiece, checkered pistol-grip and forearm, sling swivels. Made from 1967 to 1979.

MODEL 800D SUPER GRADE . . . . NiB $455 Ex $307 Gd $200
Deluxe version of Model 800 except w/stock w/rollover comb and cheekpiece, rosewood forend tip and pistol-grip cap. Weight: 6.75 lbs. Chambered for all calibers listed for the Model 800 except for .222 Rem. Sling swivels. Made from 1970 to 1973.

MODEL 800M . . . . NiB $650 Ex $315 Gd $209
Same as Model 800 except w/flat bolt handle, 20-inch bbl., Mannlicher-style stock. Weight: 6.5 lbs. Calibers: .22-250, .243 Win., .308 Win. Made from 1969 to 1972.

MODEL 800VT VARMINT/TARGET . . . . . NiB $455 Ex $307 Gd $200
Similar to Model 800 except w/24-inch heavy bbl., no sights. Weight: 9.5 lbs. Calibers: .222 Rem., .22-250, .243 Win. Made 1968 to 1979.

MODEL 810 BOLT-ACTION CENTERFIRE RIFLE
Calibers: .270 Win., .30-06, 7mm Rem. Mag., .338 Win. Mag. Detachable box magazine (1970-75) or internal magazine w/ hinged floorplate (1972 to date). Capacity: Four-round in .270 and .30-06, 3-round in Magnums. 22-inch bbl. in .270 and .30-06, 24-inch in Magnums. Weight: 7.5 to 8 lbs. Sights: Leaf rear; ramp front. Stock w/Monte Carlo comb and cheekpiece, checkered pistol-grip and forearm, grip cap, sling swivels. Made from 1970 to 1979.
Standard calibers . . . . NiB $390 Ex $333 Gd $232
Magnum calibers . . . . NiB $370 Ex $316 Gd $226

MODEL 1500 MOUNTAINEER
GRADE I CENTERFIRE RIFLE . . . . . NiB $441 Ex $338 Gd $288
Calibers: .223, .243, .270, .30-06, 7mm Mag. 22-inch or 24-inch (7mm Mag.) bbl. Weight: 7 lbs. 10 oz. Hardwood walnut-finished checkered stock. Sights: Hooded ramp front w/gold bead; fully adj. rear. Drilled and tapped for scope mounts. Sling swivel studs. Imported from 1986 to 1987.

Musgrave Premier NR5

Musgrave RSA NR1

Musgrave Valiant NR6

Musketeer Mauser Sporter

MODEL 1500 VARMINT BOLT-ACTION RIFLE
Same as Model 1500 Grade I except w/22-inch heavy bbl. Chambered in .222, .22-250, .223 only. High-luster blued finish or Parkerized satin finished stock. Imported from Japan 1986 to 1987.
High-luster blue . . . . NiB $440 Ex $328 Gd $288
Parkerized satin finish . . . . NiB $455 Ex $338 Gd $298

MODEL 1707LS CLASSIC
HUNTER BOLT-ACTION RIFLE . . . . NiB $479 Ex $369 Gd $266
Same as Model 1500 Grade I except w/checkered classic-style stock and Schnabel forend. Chambered in 243, 270, 30-06 only. Imported from Japan 1986 to 1987.

MODEL B BOLT-ACTION RIFLE . . NiB $340 Ex $205 Gd $113
Takedown. Caliber: .22 LR, Long, Short. Single-shot. 22-inch bbl. Sights: Open rear; bead front. Plain pistol-grip stock. Made from 1930 to 1932.

MODEL K SLIDE-ACTION REPEATER . . . NiB $545 Ex $390 Gd $233
Hammerless. Takedown. Caliber: .22 LR, Long, Short. Tubular magazine holds 20 Short, 16 Long, 14 LR. 22-inch bbl. Weight: 5 lbs. Sights: Open rear; bead front. Plain, straight-grip stock. Grooved slide handle. Made from 1922 to 1931.

MODELS L42A, L43, L45A, L46A-LS
See Models 42A, 43, 45A and 46A-LS respectively; "L" refers to a left-hand version of those rifles.

MODEL L SINGLE-SHOT RIFLE . . . . NiB $850 Ex $535 Gd $429
Martini-type falling-block lever-action. Takedown. Caliber: .22 LR, Long, Short. 24-inch bbl. Weight: 5 lbs. Sights: Open rear; bead front. Plain pistol-grip stock and forearm. Made from 1929 to 1932.

MODEL M SLIDE-ACTION REPEATER . . . NiB $550 Ex $ 340 Gd $227
Specifications same as for Model K except w/24-inch octagon bbl., pistol-grip stock, weighs 5.5 lbs. Made from 1928 to 1931.

MODEL R BOLT-ACTION REPEATER . . . . NiB $379 Ex $265 Gd $190
Takedown. Caliber: .22 LR, Long, Short. Tubular magazine. 24-inch bbl. Sights: Open rear; bead front. Plain pistol-grip stock. Made from 1930 to 1932.

MUSGRAVE MFRS. & DIST. (PTY) LTD. — Bloemfontein, South Africa

PREMIER NR5 BOLT-
ACTION HUNTING RIFLE . . . . . . NiB $460 Ex $375 Gd $288
Calibers: .243 Win., .270 Win., .30-06, .308 Win., 7mm Rem. Mag. Five-round magazine. 25.5-inch bbl. Weight: 8.25 lbs. Furnished w/o sights, but drilled and tapped for scope mount. Select walnut Monte Carlo stock w/cheekpiece, checkered pistol-grip and forearm, contrasting pistol-grip cap and forend tip, recoil pad, swivel studs. Musgrave or Mauser action. Made from 1971 to 1976.

RSA NR1 BOLT-ACTION
SINGLE-SHOT TARGET RIFLE . . . . **NiB $449 Ex $420 Gd $300**
Caliber: .308 Win. (7.62mm NATO). 26.4-inch heavy bbl. Weight: 10 lbs. Sights: Aperture receiver; tunnel front. Walnut target stock w/beavertail forearm, handguard, bbl. band, rubber buttplate, sling swivels. Made from 1971 to 1976.

VALIANT NR6 HUNTING RIFLE . . **NiB $415 Ex $369 Gd $255**
Similar to Premier except w/24-inch bbl.; stock w/straight comb, skip French-style checkering, no grip cap or forend tip. Sights: Leaf rear; hooded ramp front bead sight. Weight: 7.7 lbs. Made from 1971 to 1976.

MUSKETEER RIFLES — Washington, D.C.
Manufactured by Firearms International Corp.

MAUSER SPORTER
FN Mauser bolt action. .243, .25-06, .270, .264 Mag., .308, .30-06, 7mm Mag., .300 Win. Mag. Magazine holds 5 standard, 3 Magnum cartridges. 24-inch bbl. Weight: 7.25 lbs. No sights. Monte Carlo stock w/checkered pistol-grip and forearm, swivels. Made 1963 to 1972.
Standard Sporter . . . . **NiB $415 Ex $295 Gd $255**
Deluxe Sporter . . . . **NiB $459 Ex $380 Gd $276**
Standard Carbine . . . . **NiB $415 Ex $295 Gd $255**

NAVY ARMS — Martinsburg, WV
Importer of reproduction firearms. A division of Forgett Trading LLC which also owns Gibbs Rifle Company. Previously Union City, NJ and Ridgefield, NJ.

.45-70 MAUSER CARBINE . . . . . **NiB $333 Ex $227 Gd $160**
Same as .45-70 Mauser Rifle except w/18-inch bbl., straight-grip stock w/low comb, weight: 7.5 lbs. Disc.

.45-70 MAUSER RIFLE . . . . **NiB $260 Ex $221 Gd $155**
Siamese Mauser bolt action. Caliber: .45-70 Govt. Three-round magazine. 24- or 26-inch bbl. Weight: 8.5 lbs. w/26-inch bbl. Sights: Open rear; ramp front: Checkered stock w/Monte Carlo comb. Intoduced 1973. Disc.

MODEL 1873 WINCHESTER
BORDER RIFLE . . . . **NiB $1077 Ex $869 Gd $378**
Replica of Winchester Model 1873 Short Rifle. Calibers: .357 Mag., .44-40, and .45 Colt. 20- inch bbl., 39.25 inches overall. Weight: 7.6 lbs. Blued full octagonal barrel, color casehardened receiver w/walnut stocks. Made from 1999 to 2009.

MODEL 1873 CARBINE . . . . **NiB $1043 Ex $756 Gd $399**
Similar to Model 1873 Rifle except w/blued receiver, 10-round magazine, 19-inch round bbl. carbine-style forearm w/bbl. band, weighs 6.75 lbs. Disc. Reissued in 1991 in .44-40 or .45 Colt.

MODEL 1873 LEVER-ACTION RIFLE . . . **NiB $1043 Ex $756 Gd $399**
Replica of Winchester Model 1873. Casehardened receiver. Calibers: .22 LR, .357 Magnum, .44-40. 15-round magazine. 24-inch octagon bbl. Weight: 8 lbs. Sights: Open rear; blade front. Straight-grip stock, forearm w/end cap. Disc. Reissued in 1991 in .44-40 or .45 Colt w/12-round magazine. Disc. 1994.

MODEL 1873 TRAPPER . . . . **NiB $744 Ex $560 Gd $425**
Same as Model 1873 Carbine, except w/16.5-inch bbl., 8-round magazine, weighs 6.25 lbs. Disc.

MODEL 1873 SPORTING CARBINE/RIFLE
Replica of Winchester Model 1873 Sporting Rifle. Calibers: .357 Mag. (24.25- inch bbl. only), .44-40 and .45 Colt. 24.25-inch bbl. (Carbine) or 30-inch bbl. (Rifle). 48.75 to 53 inches overall. Weight: 8.14 to 9.3 lbs. Octagonal barrel, casehardened receiver and checkered walnut pistol-grip. Made from 1999 to 2003.
Carbine model . . . . **NiB $970 Ex $844 Gd $630**
Rifle model . . . . **NiB $1035 Ex $928 Gd $670**

MODEL 1874 SHARPS
CAVALRY CARBINE . . . . **NiB $1010 Ex $733 Gd $580**
Replica of Sharps 1874 Cavalry Carbine. Similar to Sniper Model, except w/22-inch bbl. and carbine stock. Caliber: .45-70. Imported from 1997 to 2009.

MODEL 1874 SHARPS SNIPER RIFLE
Replica of Sharps 1874 Sharpshooter's Rifle. Caliber: .45-70. Falling breech, single-shot. 30-inch bbl. 46.75 inches overall. Weight: 8.5 lbs. Double-set triggers. Color casehardened receiver. Blade front sight; rear sight w/elevation leaf. Polished blued bbl. Military three-band stock w/patch box. Imported from 1994 to 2000.
Infantry model (single trigger) . . . . **NiB $933 Ex $790 Gd $630**
Sniper model (double set trigger) . . . . . **NiB $2013 Ex $1118 Gd $956**

ENGRAVED MODELS
Yellowboy and Model 1873 rifles are available in deluxe models w/select walnut stocks and forearms and engraving in three grades. Grade "A" has delicate scrollwork in limited areas. Grade "B" is more elaborate with 40 percent coverage. Grade "C" has highest grade engraving. Add to value:
Grade "A" . . . . **NiB $1023 Ex $779 Gd $615**
Grade "B" . . . . **NiB $1126 Ex $986 Gd $813**
Grade "C" . . . . **NiB $1568 Ex $995 Gd $723**

HENRY LEVER-ACTION RIFLE
Replica of the Winchester Model 1860 Henry Rifle. Caliber: .44-40. Twelve round magazine. 16.5-, 22- or 24.25-inch octagon bbl. Weight: 7.5 to 9 lbs. 35.4 to 43.25 inches overall. Sights: Blade front, adjustable ladder rear. European walnut straight grip buttstock w/bbl. and side stock swivels. Imported from 1985 to date. Brass or steel receiver. Blued or color casehardened metal.
Carbine w/22-inch bbl. (introduced 1992) NiB $735 Ex $479 Gd $376
Military rifle model (w/brass frame) . . . . . NiB $989 Ex $688 Gd $482
Trapper model (w/brass frame) . . . . NiB $735 Ex $479 Gd $376
Trapper model (w/iron frame) . . . . NiB $1055 Ex $800 Gd $479
w/"A" engraving, add $325
w/"B" engraving, add $550
w/"C" engraving, add $950

MARTINI TARGET RIFLE . . . . **NiB $556 Ex $379 Gd $333**
Martini single-shot action. Calibers: .444 Marlin, .45-70. 26- or 30-inch half-octagon or full-octagon bbl. Weight: 9 lbs. w/26-inch bbl. Sights: Creedmoor tang peep, open middle, blade front. Stock w/cheekpiece and pistol-grip, forearm w/Schnabel tip, both checkered. Intro. 1972. Disc.

REVOLVING CARBINE . . . . **NiB $641 Ex $540 Gd $400**
Action resembles that of Remington Model 1875 Revolver. Casehardened frame. Calibers: .357 Magnum, .44-40, .45 Colt. Six round cylinder. 20-inch bbl. Weight: 5 lbs. Sights: Open rear; blade front. Straight-grip stock brass trigger guard and buttplate. Intro. 1968. Disc.

ROLLING BLOCK BABY CARBINE . . . . . **NiB $255 Ex $190 Gd $155**
Replica of small Remington Rolling Block single-shot action. Casehardened frame, brass trigger guard. Calibers: .22 LR, .22 Hornet, .357 Magnum, .44-40. 20-inch octagon or 22-inch round bbl. Weight: 5 lbs. Sights: Open rear; blade front. Straight-grip stock, plain forearm, brass buttplate. Imported from 1968 to 1981.

ROLLING BLOCK BUFFALO CARBINE . . **NiB $439 Ex $333 Gd $227**
Same as Buffalo Rifle except w/18-inch bbl., weight: 10 lbs

RIFLES

Navy Arms 1873 Carbine

Navy Arms Model 1874
Sharps Carbine

Navy Arms 1874
Sharps Sniper Rifle

Navy Arms Martini
Target Rifle

Navy Arms
Yellowboy
Carbine .22 LR

ROLLING BLOCK BUFFALO RIFLE . . . . . **NiB $720 Ex $572 Gd $338**
Replica Remington Rolling Block single-shot action. Casehardened
frame, brass trigger guard. Calibers: .444 Marlin, .45-70, .50-70.
26- or 30-inch heavy half-octagon or full-octagon bbl. Weight: 11 to
12 lbs. Sights: Open rear; blade front. Straight-grip stock w/brass buttplate, forearm w/brass bbl. band. Made from 1971 to 2003.

ROLLING BLOCK CREEDMOOR RIFLE
Same as Buffalo Rifle except calibers .45-70 and .50-70 only, 28- or 30-inch
heavy half-octagon or full-octagon bbl., Creedmoor tang peep sight.
Target model . . . .**NiB $1530 Ex $1109 Gd $775**

Deluxe target model (disc. 1998) . . . . .**NiB $1677 Ex $1330 Gd $190**

YELLOWBOY CARBINE . . . .**NiB $865 Ex $590 Gd $443**
Similar to Yellowboy Rifle except w/19-inch bbl., 10-round magazine
(14-round in 22 Long Rifle), carbine-style forearm. Weight: 6.75 lbs.
Disc. Reissued 1991 in .44-40 only.

YELLOWBOY LEVER-ACTION REPEATER . . **NiB $1035 Ex $567 Gd $359**
Replica of Winchester Model 1866. Calibers: .38 Special, .44-40.
15-round magazine. 24-inch octagon bbl. Weight: 8 lbs. Sights: Folding
leaf rear; blade front. Straight-grip stock, forearm w/end cap. Intro.

Navy Arms
Revolving Carbine

Navy Arms
Rolling Block Baby Carbine

Navy Arms
Rolling Block Buffalo Rifle

1966. Disc. Reissued 1991 in .44-40 only w/12-round magazine and adj. ladder-style rear sight.

YELLOWBOY TRAPPER'S MODEL..... NiB $723 Ex $500 Gd $379
Same as Yellowboy Carbine except w/16.5-inch bbl., 8-round magazine, weighs 6.25 lbs. Disc.

NEW ENGLAND FIREARMS — Gardner, Massachusetts

In 1987, New England Firearms was established as an independent company producing selected H&R models under the NEF logo. In 1991, H&R 1871, Inc. was formed from the residual of the parent company and that took over the New England Firearms facility. H&R 1871 produced firearms under both its logo and the NEF brand name until 1999, when the Marlin Firearms Company acquired the assets of H&R 1871.

HANDI-RIFLE............... NiB $245 Ex $190 Gd $137
Single-shot, break-open action w/side-lever release. Calibers: .22 Hornet, .22-250, .223, .243, .270, .30-30, .30-06, .45-70. 22-inch bbl. Weight: 7 lbs. Sights: Ramp front; folding rear. Drilled and tapped for scope mounts. Walnut-finished hardwood or synthetic stock. Blued finish. Made from 1989 to 2008.

Synthetic	NiB $290	Ex $200	Gd $128
Synthetic/Stainless	NiB $325	Ex $266	Gd $159
Youth model	NiB $300	Ex $233	Gd $144
10th Anniversary model	NiB $822	Ex $555	Gd $375
Trapper's Edition	NiB $337	Ex $265	Gd $190

SUPER LIGHT HANDI-RIFLE..... NiB $378 Ex $229 Gd $145
Cal.: .22 Hornet, .223 Rem., .243 Win. Same as Handi Rifle but with black synthetic stock and forearm, recoil pad. Bbl.: 20-inch special contour w/rebated muzzle. .223 Rem. model includes scope base and hammer extension. Weight: 5.5 lbs. Made 1997 to 2008.

SPORTSTER................ NiB $218 Ex $144 Gd $90
Cal.: .17 HMR, .17 Mach 2, .22 LR, .22 Mag. Bbl.: 20 or 22 inches, Weaver-style rail, no sights. Adult or youth (.22 LR only) dimensions. Stock and forearm: Black polymer. Made 1999 to 2008.

SURVIVOR................. NiB $297 Ex $195 Gd $115
Cal.: .223 Rem., .308 Win., .357 Mag., .410/.45 Long Colt. Similar to Survivor series shotgun but with removable forearm and thumbhole stock (both with ammo compartments). Bbl.: 20 or 22 inches, blue or nickel finish. Weight: 6 lbs. Made 1996 to 2008.

NEWTON SPORTING RIFLES — Buffalo, NY
Manufactured by Newton Arms Co., Charles Newton Rifles Corp. and Buffalo Newton Rifle Co.

BUFFALO
SPORTING RIFLE.......... NiB $2590 Ex $1800 Gd $970
Same general specifications as Standard Model, Second Type. Made c. 1922 to 1932 by Buffalo Newton Rifle Co.

MAUSER
SPORTING RIFLE.......... NiB $2125 Ex $1633 Gd $1110
Mauser (Oberndorf) action. Caliber: .256 Newton. Five round box magazine, hinged floorplate. Double-set triggers. 24-inch bbl. Open rear sight, ramp front sight. Sporting stock w/checkered pistol-grip. Weight: 7 lbs. Made c. 1914 by Newton Arms Co.

STANDARD MODEL
SPORTING RIFLE, FIRST TYPE ..... NiB $3597 Ex $2044 Gd $1035
Newton bolt action, interrupted screw-type breech-locking mechanism, double-set triggers. Calibers: .22, .256, .280, .30, .33, .35 Newton; .30-06. 24-inch bbl. Sights: Open rear or cocking-piece peep; ramp front. Checkered pistol-grip stock. Weight: 7 to 8 lbs.,depending on caliber. Made c. 1916 to 1918 by Newton Arms Co. Second type was prototype only; never manufactured. NEWTON SPRINGFIELD NiB $1568 Ex $1105 Gd $890
Kit including a Marlin-built sporting stock with .256 Newton barrel. Springfield 1903 action and sights provided by customer. Original has square-cut barrels marked "Newton Arms Co. Buffalo, NY." Mfg. 1914 to 1917.

NIKKO FIREARMS, LTD. — Tochiga, Japan
See listings under Golden Eagle Rifles.

Noble Model 10

Noble Model 33

Noble Model 222

Noble Model 236

Noble Model 275

NOBLE MFG. CO. — Haydenville, MA

MODEL 10 BOLT-ACTION
SINGLE-SHOT RIFLE. . . . . .NiB **$121** Ex **$89** Gd **$73**
Caliber: .22 LR, Long, Short. 24-inch bbl. Plain pistol-grip stock. Sights: Open rear, bead front. Weight: 4 lbs. Made 1955 to 1958.

MODEL 20 BOLT-ACTION
SINGLE-SHOT RIFLE. . . . . .NiB **$126** Ex **$92** Gd **$75**
Manually cocked. Caliber: .22 LR, Long, Short. 22-inch bbl. Weight: 5 lbs. Sights: Open rear; bead front. Walnut stock w/pistol grip. Made from 1958 to 1963.

MODEL 33 SLIDE-ACTION REPEATER. . . . . NiB **$230** Ex **$110** Gd **$80**
Hammerless. Caliber: .22 LR, Long, Short. Tubular magazine holds 21 Short, 17 Long, 15 LR. 24-inch bbl. Weight: 6 lbs. Sights: Open rear; bead front. Tenite stock and slide handle. Made 1949 to 1953.
MODEL 33A. . . . . .NiB **$115** Ex **$89** Gd **$69**
Same general specifications as Model 33 except w/wood stock and slide handle. Made from 1953 to 1955.

MODEL 222 BOLT-ACTION
SINGLE-SHOT RIFLE. . . . . .NiB **$240** Ex **$120** Gd **$80**
Manually cocked. Caliber: .22 LR, Long, Short. Barrel integral w/receiver. Overall length: 38 inches. Weight: 5 lbs. Sights: Interchangeable V-notch and peep rear; ramp front. Scope mounting base. Pistol-grip stock. Made from 1958 to 1971.

MODEL 236 SLIDE-ACTION
REPEATING RIFLE . . . . .NiB **$159** Ex **$140** Gd **$97**
Hammerless. Caliber: .22 Short, Long, LR. Tubular magazine holds 21 Short, 17 Long, 15 LR. 24-inch bbl. Weight: 5.5 lbs. Sights: Open rear; ramp front. Pistol-grip stock, grooved slide handle. Made from 1951 to 1971.

MODEL 278 LEVER-ACTION RIFLE . . . . . NiB **$227** Ex **$139** Gd **$110**
Hammerless. Caliber: .22 Short, Long, LR. Tubular magazine holds 21 Short, 17 Long, 15 LR. 24-inch bbl. Weight: 5.5 lbs. Sights: Open rear; ramp front. Stock w/semipistol-grip. Made from 1958 to 1971.

NORINCO — Beijing, China
Manufactured by Northern China Industries Corp., Beijing, China.
Imported by Century International Arms; Interarms; KBI and others.

Model 81S/AK Semiautomatic Rifle
Semiautomatic Kalashnikov style AK-47 action. Caliber: 7.62x39mm. Five, 30- or 40-round magazine. 17.5-inch bbl. 36.75 inches overall. Weight: 8.5 lbs. Hooded post front sight, 500 meters leaf rear sight. Oil-finished hardwood (military style) buttstock, pistol grip, forearm and handguard or folding metal stock. Black oxide finish. Imported 1988 to 1989.
NIdek 81S (w/wood stock) . . . . NiB **$1244** Ex **$965** Gd **$733**
Model 81S (w/folding metal stock) . . . . . . .NiB **$1266** Ex **$1002** Gd **$753**
Model 81S-5/56S-2
  (w/folding metal stock) . . . . . . NiB **$1339** Ex **$1027** Gd **$755**

MODEL 84S/AK SEMIAUTOMATIC RIFLE
Semiautomatic Kalashnikov style AK-47 action. Caliber: .223 (5.56mm). 30-round magazine. 16.25-inch bbl. 35.5 inches overall. Weight: 8.75 lbs. Hooded post front sight, 800 meters leaf rear sight. Oil-finished hardwood (military style) buttstock, pistol grip, forearm and handguard; sporterized composite fiberglass stock or folding metal stock. Black oxide finish. Imported from 1988 to 1989.

Model 84S (w/wood stock) . . . . NiB $1479 Ex $1032 Gd $678
Model 84S-3 (w/folding metal stock) . . . . . NiB $1688 Ex $954 Gd $669
Model 84S-3 (w/composite stock) . . . . NiB $1337 Ex $1043 Gd $645
Model 84S-5 (w/folding metal stock) . . . . . NiB $1613 Ex $981 Gd $687

MODEL AK-47 THUMBHOLE SPORTER
Semiautomatic AK-47 sporterized variant. Calibers: .223 (5.56mm) or 7.62x39mm. Five round magazine. 16.25-inch bbl. or 23.25-inch bbl. 35.5 or 42.5 inches overall. Weight: 8.5 to 10.3 lbs. Adj. post front sight, open adj. rear. Forged receiver w/black oxide finish. Walnut-finished thumbhole stock w/recoil pad. Imported from 1991 to 1993.

5.56mm . . . . NiB $775 Ex $466 Gd $337
7.62x39mm . . . . NiB $564 Ex $466 Gd $339

MODEL MAK 90/01 SPORT . . . . . NiB $733 Ex $455 Gd $337
Similar to Model AK-47 Thumbhole Sporter except w/minor modifications implemented to meet importation requirements. Imported from 1994 to 1995.

OLYMPIC ARMS — Olympia, Washington

PCR SERIES
Gas-operated semi-auto action. Calibers: .17 Rem., .223, 7.62x39, 6x45, 6PPC or 9mm, .40 S&W, 4.5ACP (in carbine version only). Ten-round magazine. 16-, 20- or 24-inch bbl. Weight: 7 to 10.2 lbs. Black composite stocks. Post front, rear adj. sights; scope ready flattop. Barrel fluting. William set trigger. Made from 1994 to date.

PCR-1 Ultra Match . . . . NiB $981 Ex $760 Gd $583
PCR-2 Mult-iMatch ML-1 . . . . . . NiB $1032 Ex $915 Gd $633
PCR-3 Multi-Match ML-2 . . . . . . NiB $1070 Ex $959 Gd $654
PCR-4 AR-15 Match . . . . NiB $877 Ex $808 Gd $521
MCR-5 CAR-15 (.223 Rem.) . . . . . NiB $977 Ex $803 Gd $522
PCR5 CAR-15
  (9mm, 40 S&W, .45 ACP) . . . . . NiB $903 Ex $794 Gd $538
PCR-5 CAR (.223 Rem.) . . . . NiB $955 Ex $731 Gd $510
PCR-6/A-2 (7.62x39mm) . . . . NiB $895 Ex $692 Gd $486

BOLT-ACTION SAKO . . . . NiB $755 Ex $575 Gd $456
Cal.: Various from .17 Rem. to .416 Rem. Mag. Bbl.: Fluted; various stock options. Value is for base model without custom options.

ULTRA CSR TACTICAL . . . . . . NiB $1877 Ex $1355 Gd $1043
Cal.: .308 Win. Sako action. Bbl.: Heavy, 26 inches, broach cut. Stock: Bell & Carlson black or synthetic with aluminum bedding. Harris bipod included. Made from 1996 to 2000.

COUNTER SNIPER RIFLE . . . . NiB $1490 Ex $1266 Gd $1079
Bolt action. Cal.: .308 Win. Bbl.: Heavy, 26-inches. Stock: Camo fiberglass. Weight: 10.5 lbs. Disc. 1987.

SURVIVOR 1 . . . . NiB $455 Ex $276 Gd $264
Converts M1911 into bolt-action carbine. Cal.: .223 Rem., .45 ACP. Bbl.: 16.25 inches. Collapsible stock. Available for S&W and Browning Hi-Power. Weight: 5 lbs.

CAR 97 . . . . NiB $909 Ex $693 Gd $633
Cal.: .223 Rem., 9mm Para., 10mm, .40 S&W, .45 ACP. Similar to PCR-5 but w/ 16-inch button-rifled barrel. A2 sights, fixed CAR stock, post-ban

Olympic Arms LTF Tactical Rifle

Olympic Arms K4B

Olympic Arms K7 Eliminator

muzzle brake. Weight: 7 lbs. Made from 1997 to 2004.
M-4 version (disc. 2004), add $75

FAR-15. . . . . NiB $1035 Ex $780 Gd $669
Featherweight model. Cal.: .223 Rem. Bbl.: 16 inches, lightweight, button-rifled, collapsible stock. Weight: 9.2 lbs. Made from 2001 to 2004.

GI-16. . . . . NiB $989 Ex $760 Gd $590
Cal.: .223 Rem. Forged aluminum receiver, matte finish. Bbl.: Match grade, 16 inches, button rifled. Collapsible stock. Weight: 7 lbs. Made 2004 and 2006.

GI-20 . . . . NiB $877 Ex $698 Gd $549
Cal. .223 Rem. Similar to GI-16 except w/20-inch heavy bbl., A-2 lower. Weight: 8.4 lbs. Made 2004.

OA-93 Carbine. . . . . NiB $1390 Ex $1133 Gd $976
Based on OA-93 pistol. Cal.: .223 Rem. Bbl.: 16 inches. Flattop receiver. Aluminum side folding stock, round aluminum handguard, Vortex flash supp. Weight: 7.5 lbs. Made 1998 and from 2004 to 2007.

OA-93PT . . . . NiB $1077 Ex $976 Gd $692
Similar to OA-93 carbine but with aluminum receiver, black matte anodized finish. Bbl.: 16 inches, match grade chromemoly steel with removable muzzle brake, push-button removable stock. Weight: 7 lbs. Made from 2006 to 2007.

LTF TACTICAL RIFLE . . . . NiB $1338 Ex $1056 Gd $777
Cal. .223 Rem. Bbl.: 16 inches, fluted or non-fluted w/flash supp. Black matte anodized finish. Firsh-type forearm, Picatinny rails, Parkerized steel parts. Tube-style stock. Weight: 6.4 lbs.
Fluted bbl., add 10%

K3B CARBINE . . . . NiB $1189 Ex $873 Gd $689
Cal. .223 Rem. Bbl.: 16 inches, match grade chromemoly steel w/flash supp. A2 rear sight and buttstock; adj. front post sight.
A3 Flattop receiver, add $75
FAR carbine, add $75
M4 carbine, add $75
A3-TC carbine, add $250

Parker-Hale
Model 81 Classic

Parker-Hale
Model 87

K4B/K4B68 . . . . NiB $1087 Ex $764 Gd $590
Cal.: .223 Rem., 6.8 SPC. Bbl.: 20 inches, match grade, chromemoly steel, button rifled; flash supp. Adj. A2 rear sight and front post; A2 buttstock, upper receiver and hand guard. Weight: 8.5 lbs.
Flattop receiver, add $150

K4B-A4 . . . . NiB $1034 Ex $766 Gd $588
Cal.: .223 Rem. Bbl.: 20 inches w/A2 flash supp.; bayonet lug. Flattop receiver. Adj. post front sight. Firsh handguard, Picatinny rails. Made from 2006 to 2008.

K7 ELIMINATOR . . . . NiB $1087 Ex $800 Gd $633
Cal.: .223 Rem. Bbl.: 16 inches, stainless steel w/flash supp.; adj. A2 rear sight and front post; A2 buttstock. Weight: 7.8 lbs.

K8 TARGET MATCH . . . . NiB $1087 Ex $723 Gd $572
Cal.: .223 Rem. Bbl.: 20-inch bull bbl., stainless, button rifling; Picatinny flattop upper, A2 buttstock. Weight: 8.5 lbs.

K8-MAG. . . . . NiB $1423 Ex $1150 Gd $976
Similar to Target Match model. Cal.: .223 WSSM, .243 WSSM, .25 WSSM, .300 WSM. 24-inch bbl. Weight: 9.4 lbs.

K9/K10/K40/K45 . . . . NiB $1132 Ex $955 Gd $780
Cal.: 9mm Para., 10mm Norma, .40 S&W, .45 ACP. Blow-back action. Bbl.: 16 inches w/flash suppressor and bayonet lug. Adj. A2 rear sight. Collapsible stock. Weight: 6.7 lbs.

K9GL/K40GL . . . . NiB $1188 Ex $992 Gd $694
Similar to K9 series. Cal.: 9mm Para., .40 S&W. Lower designed to accept Glock magazines. Bbl.: 16 inches; flash suppressor. Collapsible stock. No magazine furnished.
A3 upper, add $126

K16 . . . . NiB $962 Ex $710 Gd $577
Cal.: .223 Rem. Bbl.: 16 inches, free-floating, button rifled. Picatinny flattop upper; A2 buttstock. Weight: 7.5 lbs.

K30R . . . . NiB $1077 Ex $879 Gd $683
w/A3 upper, add $126

K-30 (.30 carbine) . . . . NiB $978 Ex $668 Gd $533
Cal.: 7.62x39mm. Bbl.: 16-inch stainless steel, adj. rear sight. Parkerized steel parts. Six-point collapsible stock.

K68 . . . . NiB $1198 Ex $978 Gd $645
Cal.: 6.8 Rem. SPC. Bbl.: 16-inch stainless steel, A2 upper with adj. rear sight and flash suppressor. Matte black anodized receiver, Parkerized steel parts. Six-position collapsible A2 stock w/pistol grip.
w/A3 upper, add $126

K74 . . . . NiB $1027 Ex $903 Gd $645
Cal.: 5.45x39mm. Bbl.: 16-inches, button rifling; flash suppressor and adj. front sight. Six-position collapsible stock. Weight 6.75 lbs.

PARKER-HALE LIMITED — Birmingham, England

MODEL 81 AFRICAN . . . . NiB $909 Ex $789 Gd $533
Same general specifications as Model 81 Classic except in caliber .375 H&H only. Sights: African Express rear; hooded blade front. Barrel-band swivel. All-steel trigger guard. Checkered European walnut stock w/pistol grip and recoil pad. Engraved receiver. Imported from 1986 to 1991.

MODEL 81 CLASSIC
BOLT-ACTION RIFLE . . . . NiB $745 Ex $627 Gd $439
Calibers: .22-250, .243 Win., .270 Win., 6mm Rem., 6.5x55, 7x57, 7x64, .308 Win., .30-06, .300 Win. Mag., 7mm Rem. Mag. Four round magazine. 24-inch bbl. Weight: 7.75 lbs. Sights: Adj. open rear, hooded ramp front. Checkered pistol-grip stock of European walnut. Imported from 1984 to 1991.

MODEL 85 SNIPER RIFLE . NiB $2730 Ex $2161 Gd $1578
Caliber: .308 Win. Ten or 20-round M-14-type magazine. 24.25-inch bbl. 45 inches overall. Weight: 12.5 lbs. Blade front sight, folding aperture rear. McMillan fiberglass stock w/detachable bipod. Imported from 1989 to 1991.

MODEL 87 BOLT-ACTION
REPEATING TARGET RIFLE . . . . NiB $1425 Ex $1233 Gd $757
Calibers: .243 Win., 6.5x55, .308 Win., .30-06 Springfield, .300 Win. Mag. Five-round detachable box magazine. 26-inch bbl. 45 inches overall. Weight: 10 lbs. No sights; grooved for target-style scope

Parker-Hale Model
1100 Lightweight

Parker-Hale Model
1200 Super Clip

mounts. Stippled walnut stock w/adj. buttplate. Sling swivel studs. Parkerized finish. Folding bipod. Imported 1988 to 1991.

MODEL 1000 STANDARD RIFLE. . . . . . NiB $460 Ex $359 Gd $248
Calibers: .22-250, .243 Win., .270 Win., 6mm Rem., .308 Win., .30-06. Four-round magazine. Bolt action. 22-inch or 24-inch (22-250) bbl. 43 inches overall. 7.25 lbs. Checkered walnut Monte Carlo-style stock w/ satin finish. Imported from 1984 to 1988.

MODEL 1100 LIGHTWEIGHT
BOLT-ACTION RIFLE . . . . NiB $535 Ex $443 Gd $337
Same general specifications as Model 1000 Standard except w/22-inch lightweight profile bbl., hollow bolt handle, alloy trigger guard and floorplate, 6.5 lbs., Schnabel forend. Imported 1984 to 1991.

MODEL 1100M AFRICAN
MAGNUM RIFLE . . . . NiB $858 Ex $745 Gd $500
Same as Model 1000 Standard except w/24-inch bbl. in calibers .404 Jeffery, .458 Win. Mag. Weight: 9.5 lbs. Sights: Adj. rear; hooded post front. Imported from 1984 to 1991.

MODEL 1200 SUPER CLIP
BOLT-ACTION RIFLE . . . . NiB $763 Ex $555 Gd $423
Same as Model 1200 Super except w/detachable box magazine in calibers .243 Win., 6mm Rem., .270 Win. .30-06 and .308 Win., .300 Win. Mag., 7mm Rem. Mag. Imported from 1984 to 1991.

MODEL 1200 SUPER BOLT-ACTION
SPORTING RIFLE . . . . NiB $586 Ex $480 Gd $355
Mauser-type bolt action. Calibers: .22-250, .243 Win., 6mm Rem., .25-06, .270 Win., .30-06, .308 Win. Four round magazine. 24-inch bbl. Weight: 7.25 lbs. Sights: Folding open rear, hooded ramp front. European walnut stock w/rollover Monte Carlo cheekpiece, rosewood forend tip and pistol-grip cap, skip checkering, recoil pad, sling swivels. Imported from 1968 to 1991.

MODEL 1200 SUPER MAGNUM. . . . . . NiB $556 Ex $550 Gd $369
Same general specifications as 1200 Super except calibers 7mm Rem. Mag. and .300 Win. Mag., 3-round magazine. Imported 1988 to 1991.

MODEL 1200P PRESENTATION . . . . . . NiB $580 Ex $459 Gd $347
Same general specifications as 1200 Super except w/scroll-engraved action, trigger guard and floorplate, no sights. QD swivels. Calibers: .243 Win. and .30-06. Imported from 1969 to 1975.

MODEL 1200V VARMINT. . . . . . NiB $557 Ex $498 Gd $425
Same general specifications as 1200 Super, except w/24-inch heavy bbl., no sights, weight: 9.5 lbs. Calibers: .22-250, 6mm Rem., .25-06, .243 Win. Imported from 1969-89.

MODEL 1300C SCOUT. . . . . NiB $733 Ex $689 Gd $550

Calibers: .243, .308 Win. 10-round magazine. 20-inch bbl. w/muzzle brake. 41 inches overall. Weight: 8.5 lbs. No sights, drilled and tapped for scope. Checkered laminated birch stock w/QD swivels. Imported in 1991.

MODEL 2100 MIDLAND
BOLT-ACTION RIFLE . . . . NiB $380 Ex $321 Gd $244
Calibers: .22-250, .243 Win., 6mm Rem., .270 Win., 6.5x55, 7x57, 7x64, .308 Win, .30-06. Four-round box magazine. 22-inch or 24-inch (22-250) bbl. 43-inches overall. Weight: 7 lbs. Sights: Adj. folding rear; hooded ramp front. Checkered European walnut Monte Carlo stock w/ pistol-grip. Imported from 1984 to 1991.

MODEL 2707 LIGHTWEIGHT. . . . . NiB $370 Ex $329 Gd $237
Same general specifications as Model 2100 Midland except w/tapered lightweight bbl. and aluminum trigger guard. Weight: 6.5 lbs. Imported in 1991.

MODEL 2800 MIDLAND . . . . NiB $375 Ex $319 Gd $245
Same general specifications as model 2100 except w/laminated birch stock. Imported in 1991.

PEDERSEN CUSTOM GUNS — North Haven, Connecticut
Division of O.F. Mossberg & Sons, Inc.

MODEL 3000 GRADE I
BOLT-ACTION RIFLE . . . . NiB $1034 Ex $809 Gd $544
Richly engraved w/silver inlays, full-fancy American black walnut stock. Mossberg Model 810 action. Calibers: .270 Win., .30-06, 7mm Rem. Mag., .338 Win. Mag. Three-round magazine, hinged floorplate. 22-inch bbl. in .270 and .30-06, 24-inch in Magnums. Weight: 7 to 8 lbs. Sights: Open rear; hooded ramp front. Monte Carlo stock w/ roll-over cheekpiece, wraparound hand checkering on pistol grip and forearm, rosewood pistol-grip cap and forend tip, recoil pad or steel buttplate w/trap, detachable swivels. Imported 1973 to 1975.

MODEL 3000 GRADE II . . . . NiB $733 Ex $480 Gd $380
Same as Model 3000 Grade I except less elaborate engraving, no inlays, fancy grade walnut stock w/recoil pad. Imported 1973 to 1975.

MODEL 3000 GRADE III. . . . . NiB $579 Ex $380 Gd $299
Same as Model 3000 Grade I except no engraving or inlays, select grade walnut stock w/recoil pad. Imported from 1973 to 1974.

MODEL 4700 CUSTOM
DELUXE LEVER-ACTION RIFLE. . . . . . . NiB $279 Ex $238 Gd $175
On Mossberg Model .472 action. Calibers: .30-30, 35 Rem. Five-round tubular magazine. 24-inch bbl. Weight: 7.5 lbs. Sights: Open rear, hooded ramp front. Hand-finished black walnut stock and beavertail

---

**Pedersen Model 3000
Grade I Bolt-Action Rifle**

**Pedersen Model 3000
Grade III**

Plainfield M-1 Carbine

Polish Model 1929 Mauser

forearm, barrel band swivels. Imported in 1975.

J.C. PENNEY CO., INC. — Dallas, Texas
Firearms sold under the J.C. Penney label were mfd. by Marlin, High Standard, Stevens, Savage and Springfield.

MODEL 2025 BOLT-ACTION REPEATER . . . NiB $100 Ex $65 Gd $55
Takedown. Caliber: .22 RF. Eight round detachable box magazine. 24-inch bbl. Weight: 6 lbs. Sights: Open rear; bead front. Plain pistol-grip stock. Manufactured by Marlin.

MODEL 2035 BOLT-ACTION REPEATER . . . NiB $100 Ex $65 Gd $55
Takedown. Caliber: .22 RF. Eight round detachable box magazine. 24-inch bbl. Weight: 6 lbs. Sights: Open rear; bead front. Plain pistol-grip stock. Manufactured by Marlin.

MODEL 2935 LEVER-ACTION RIFLE . . . . NiB $210 Ex $170 Gd $121
Same general specifications as Marlin Model 336.

**MODEL 6400 BOLT-ACTION
CENTERFIRE RIFLE** . . . . NiB $210 Ex $170 Gd $110
Same general specifications as Savage Model 340.

**MODEL 6660
AUTOLOADING RIFLE** . . . . NiB $115 Ex $90 Gd $75
Caliber: .22 RF. Tubular magazine. 22-inch bbl. Weight: 5.5 lbs. Sights: Open rear; hooded ramp front. Plain pistol-grip stock. Manufactured by Marlin.

PLAINFIELD MACHINE COMPANY — Dunellen, New Jersey

M-1 CARBINE . . . . NiB $227 Ex $166 Gd $135
Same as U.S. Carbine, Cal. .30, M-1 except also available in caliber 5.7mm

(.22 caliber w/necked-down .30 Carbine cartridge case). Current production w/ventilated metal handguard and barrel band w/o bayonet lug; earlier models have standard military-type fittings. Made from 1960 to 1977.

**M-1 CARBINE,
COMMANDO MODEL** . . . . NiB $232 Ex $171 Gd $145
Same as M-1 Carbine except w/paratrooper-type stock w/telescoping wire shoulderpiece. Made from 1960 to 1977.

M-1 CARBINE, MILITARY SPORTER . . . . NiB $227 Ex $166 Gd $135
Same as M-1 Carbine except w/unslotted buttstock and wood handguard. Made from 1960 to 1977.

M-1 DELUXE SPORTER. . . . . NiB $232 Ex $171 Gd $145
Same as M-1 Carbine except w/Monte Carlo sporting stock Made from 1960 to 1973.

POLISH MILITARY RIFLES — Poland
Manufactured by Government Arsenals at Radom and Warsaw, Poland.

**MODEL 1898 (KARABIN 98, K98)
MAUSER MILITARY CARBINE** . . . . NiB $331 Ex $210 Gd $166
Same as German Kar. 98A except for minor details. First manufactured during early 1920s.

**MODEL 1898 (KARABIN 98, WZ98A)
MAUSER MILITARY RIFLE** . . . . NiB $289 Ex $180 Gd $145
Same as German Kar. 98 used in WWI except for minor details. Manufacture began c. 1921.

**MODEL 1929 (KARABIN 29, WZ29)
MAUSER MILITARY RIFLE** . . . . NiB $331 Ex $210 Gd $166
Same as Czech Model 24, mfd. 1929 thru WWII except for minor details. A similar model produced during German occupation was designated Gew. 29/40.

Purdey Double Rifle

Purdey Bolt-Action
Rifle

WILLIAM POWELL & SON LTD. —
Birmingham, England

DOUBLE-BARREL RIFLE . . . . . .**NiB $32,278 Ex $26,900 Gd $18,900**
Boxlock. Made to order in any caliber during the time that rifle was
manufactured. Bbls.: Made to order in any legal length, but 26 inches
recommended. Highest grade French walnut buttstock and forearm w/
fine checkering. Metal is elaborately engraved. Imported by Stoeger
from 1938 to 1951.

BOLT-ACTION RIFLE . . . .**NiB $2888 Ex $2367 Gd $1699**
Mauser-type bolt action. Calibers: 6x54 through .375 H&H Magnum.
Three and 4-shot magazine, depending upon chambering. 24-inch bbl.
Weight: 7.5 to 8.75 lbs. Sights: Folding leaf rear; hooded ramp front.
Cheekpiece stock, checkered forearm and pistol grip, swivels. Imported
by Stoeger from 1938 to 1951.

PTR 91, INC. — Aynor, SC
Previously Bristol, CT and Farmington, CT.

MODEL PTR-91F
SEMI-AUTOMATIC . . . .**NiB $1150 Ex $900 Gd $600**
Delayed roller-locked blow-back action similar to H&K G3.
Caliber: .308 Win. 20-round magazine. 18-inch bbl. H&K Navy
type polymer trigger group. Sights: H&K style front post and rear
adj. diopter. Plastic buttstock. Matte black finish. and forearm.
Made from 2005 to date.
PTR-91 AI
   (match grade barrel, 2005-2008) **NiB $1170 Ex $730 Gd $570**
PTR-91 Classic
   (black or wood stock, 2012) . . . .**NiB $880 Ex $650 Gd $460**
PTR-91 KC (16-in. bbl.) . . . .**NiB $1160 Ex $910 Gd $600**
PTR-91T (green furniture) . . . . . .**NiB $900 Ex $850 Gd $550**
PTR-MSG 91 Sniper
   (18-in. fluted target bbl.) . . . .**NiB $1980 Ex $1600 Gd $900**

PUMA — Brescia, Italy
*Manufactured by Armisport Chiappa in Brescia, Italy, and imported
by Legacy Sports Int'l., Reno, NV.*

Model 1886 Lever Action . . . . .**NiB $1260 Ex $880 Gd $625**
Reproduction of Winchester 1886 lever action. Caliber: .45-70. 7- or
8-round tube magazine. 22- or 26-inch round or octagon bbl. Case
colored receiver, Italian walnut stock. Made 2009 to date.

Model 92 Lever Action . . . .**NiB $925 Ex $710 Gd $460**
Caliber: .38 Special/.357 Mag., .44 Special/.44 Mag., .45 LC, .454
Casull or .480 Ruger. Lever action, 9- or 10-round tube magazine.

20-inch round or octagon bbl. Blue, brass or case colored receiver,
walnut stock. Made 2001 to date.

PPS/22 . . . .**NiB $480 Ex $330 Gd $280**
Caliber: .22 LR. Semi-auto action, 16-inch bbl., 10- or 50-round (drum)
magazine. Made 2009 to 2010.

JAMES PURDEY & SONS LTD. —
London, England

DOUBLE RIFLE
Sidelock action, hammerless, ejectors. Almost any caliber is available
but the following are the most popular: .375 Flanged Magnum Nitro
Express, .500/465 Nitro Express .470 Nitro Express, .577 Nitro Express.
25.5-inch bbls. (25-inch in .375). Weight: 9.5 to 12.75 lbs. Sights:
Folding leaf rear; ramp front. Cheekpiece stock, checkered forearm and
pistol-grip, recoil pad, swivels. Currently manufactured to individual
measurements and specifications; same general specifications apply to
pre-WWII model.
H&H calibers . . . .**NiB $72,665 Ex $57,550 Gd $38,750**
NE calibers. . . . .**NiB $85,000 Ex $56,000 Gd $39,000**

BOLT-ACTION RIFLE . . . .
NiB $22,800 Ex $19,970 Gd $12,770
Mauser-type bolt action. Calibers: 7x57, .300 H&H Magnum, .375 H&H
Magnum, 10.75x73. Three round magazine. 24-inch bbl. Weight: 7.5 to
8.75 lbs. Sights: Folding leaf rear; hooded ramp front. Cheekpiece stock,
checkered forearm and pistol-grip, swivels. Currently manufactured; same
general specifications apply to pre-WWII model.

RAPTOR ARMS COMPANY, INC. —
Newport, New Hampshire

BOLT-ACTION RIFLE
Calibers: .243 Win., .270 Win., .30-06 or .308 Win. Four round maga-
zine. 22-inch sporter or heavy bbl. Weight: 7.3 to 8 lbs. 42.5 inches
overall. No sights w/drilled and tapped receiver or optional blade
front, adjustable rear. Blue, stainless or "Taloncote" rust-resistant finish.
Checkered black synthetic stock w/Monte Carlo cheepiece and vented
recoil pad. Imported from 1997 to 1999.
Raptor Sporter model . . . .**NiB $255 Ex $190 Gd $155**
Raptor Deluxe Peregrine model (disc. 1998). . .**NiB $258 Ex $195 Gd $159**
Raptor heavy bbl. model. . . . .**NiB $277 Ex $222 Gd $195**
Raptor stainless bbl. model. . . . .**NiB $299 Ex $257 Gd $213**
w/optional sights, add. **$40**

Remington No. 7
Target and Sporting Rifle

REMINGTON ARMS COMPANY — Madison, NC

Manufacturing locations in Ilion, New York, Lonoke, AR, and Mayfield, Kentucky. Acquired by Freedom Group Inc. in 2007.

To facilitate locating Remington firearms, models are grouped into four categories: Single-shot rifles, bolt-action repeating rifles, slide-action (pump) rifles, and semiautomatic rifles. For a complete listing, please refer to the index.

- SINGLE-SHOT RIFLES -

NO. 1 SPORTING RIFLE . . . . . NiB $6223 Ex $3856 Gd $2210
Single-Shot, rolling-block action. Calibers: .40-50, .40-70, .44-77, .50-45, .50-70 Gov't. centerfire and .44 Long, .44 Extra Long, .45-70, .46 Long, .46 Extra Long, .50-70 rimfire. Bbl. lengths: 28- or 30-inch part octagon. Weight: 5 to 7.5 lbs. Sights: Folding leaf rear sight; sporting front, dovetail bases. Plain walnut straight stock; flanged-top, semicarbine buttplate. Plain walnut forend with thin, rounded front end. Made from 1868 to 1902.

NO. 1 1/2 SPORTING RIFLE . . NiB $4190 Ex $1200 Gd $1888
Single-Shot, rolling-block action. Calibers: .22 Short, Long, or Extra Long. 25 Stevens, .32, and .38 rimfire cartridges. .32-20, .38-40 and .44-40 centerfire. Bbl. lengths: 24-, 26-, 28- or 30-inch part octagon. Remaining features similar to Remington No. 1. Made from 1869 to 1902.

NO. 2 SPORTING RIFLE
Single-shot, rolling-block action. Calibers: .22, .25, .32, .38, .44 rimfire or centerfire. Bbl. lengths: 24, 26, 28 or 30 inches. Weight: 5 to 6 lbs. Sights: Open rear; bead front. Straight-grip sporting stock and knobtip forearm of walnut. Made from 1873 to 1909.
Calibers: .22, .25, .32 . . . . NiB $3575 Ex $2040 Gd $989
Calibers: .38, .44 . . . . NiB $9650 Ex $8129 Gd $5450

NO. 3 CREEDMOOR
AND SCHUETZEN RIFLES. . . . NiB $16,187 Ex $12,750 Gd $10,510
Produced in a variety of styles and calibers, these are collector's items and bring far higher prices than the sporting types. The Schuetzen Special, which has an under-lever action, is especially rare — perhaps fewer than 100 have been made.

NO. 3 HIGH POWER RIFLE
Single-shot, Hepburn falling-block action w/side lever. Calibers: .30-30, .30-40, .32 Special, .32-40, .38-55, .38-72 (high-power cartridges). Bbl. lengths: 26-, 28-, 30-inch. Weight: About 8 lbs. Open sporting sights. Checkered pistol-grip stock and forearm. Made from 1893 to 1907.
Calibers: .30-30, .30-40,
**   .32 Special, .32-40 . . . . NiB $9775 Ex $7956 Gd $5110**
Calibers: .38-55, .38-72 . . . . NiB $9688 Ex $8154 Gd $6422

NO. 3 SPORTING RIFLE . . . . . NiB $9775 Ex $7279 Gd $6788
Single-shot, Hepburn falling-block action w/side lever. Calibers: .22 WCF, .22 Extra Long, .25-20 Stevens, .25-21 Stevens, .25-25 Stevens, .32 WCF, .32-40 Ballard & Marlin, .32-40 Rem., .38 WCF, .38-40 Rem., 38-.38-50 Rem., .38-55 Ballard & Marlin, .40-60 Ballard & Marlin, .40-60 WCF, .40-65 Rem. Straight, .40-82 WCF, .45-70 Gov., .45-90 WCF, also was supplied on special order in bottle-necked .40-50, .40-70, .40-90, .44-77, .44-90, .44-105, .50-70 Gov., .50-90 Sharps Straight. Bbl. lengths: 26-inch (22, 25, 32 cal. only), 28-inch, 30-inch; half-octagon or full-octagon. Weight: 8 to 10 lbs. Sights: Open rear; blade front. Checkered pistol-grip stock and forearm. Made from 1880 to c. 1911.

NO. 4 SINGLE-SHOT RIFLE . . . . NiB $1630 EX $944 Gd $755
Rolling-block action. Solid frame or takedown. Calibers: .22 Short and Long, .22 LR, .25 Stevens R.F., .32 Short and Long R.F. 22.5-inch octagon bbl., 24-inch available in .32 caliber only. Weight: About 4.5 lbs. Sights: Open rear; blade front. Plain walnut stock and forearm. Made from 1890-1933.

NO. 4S MILITARY MODEL 22
SINGLE-SHOT RIFLE . . . . NiB $2650 Ex $2033 Gd $997
Rolling-block action. Calibers: .22 Short, Long LR. 28-inch bbl. Weight: About 5 lbs. Sights: Military-type rear; blade front. Military-type stock w/ handguard, stacking swivel, sling. Has a bayonet stud on the barrel; bayonet and scabbard were regularly supplied. Note: At one time the Military Model was the official rifle of the Boy Scouts of America and was called the Boy Scout Rifle. Made from 1913 to 1933.

NO. 5 SPECIAL SINGLE-SHOT RIFLE
Single-shot, rolling-block action. Calibers: 7mm Mauser, .30-30, .30-40 Krag, .303 British, .32-40, .32 Special, .38-55 (high-power cartridges). Bbl. lengths: 24, 26 and 28 inches. Weight: About 7 lbs. Open sporting sights. Plain straight-grip stock and forearm. Made 1902 to 1918. Note: Models 1897 and 1902 Military Rifles, intended for the export market, are almost identical with the No. 5, except for 30-inch bbl. full military stock and weight (about 8.5 lbs.); a carbine was also supplied. The military rifles were produced in caliber 8mm Lebel for France, 7.62mm Russian for Russia and 7mm Mauser for the Central and South American government trade. Also offered to retail buyers.
Sporting model . . . . NiB $934 Ex $733 Gd $530
Military model . . . . NiB $731 Ex $554 Gd $400

NO. 6 TAKEDOWN RIFLE . . . . . . NiB $675 Ex $535 Gd $459
Single-shot, rolling-block action. Calibers: .22 Short, Long, LR; .32 Short, Long RF. 20-inch bbl. Weight: Avg. 4 lbs. Sights: Open front and rear; tang peep. Plain straight-grip stock, forearm. Made from 1901 to 1933.

NO. 7 TARGET AND SPORTING RIFLE . . . NiB $9707 Ex $7235 Gd $6755
Single-shot. Rolling-block Army Pistol frame. Calibers: .22 Short, .22 LR. 25-10 Stevens R.F. (other calibers available on special order). Half-octagon bbls.: 24-, 26-, 28-inch. Weight: About 6 lbs. Sights: Lyman combination rear; Beach combination front. Fancy walnut stock, Swiss buttplate available. Made from 1903 to 1911.

Remington
Model 40X Standard Rimfire

Remington
Model 40-XB Centerfire

Remington
Model 40-XB Rimfire

MODEL 33 BOLT-ACTION
SINGLE-SHOT RIFLE . . . .**NiB $278 EX $190 Gd $239**
Takedown. Caliber: .22 Short, Long, LR. 24-inch bbl. Weight: About 4.5 lbs. Sights: Open rear, bead front. Plain, pistol-grip stock, forearm with grasping grooves. Made from 1931 to 1936.

MODEL 33 NRA
JUNIOR TARGET RIFLE . . . .**NiB $544 Ex $408 Gd $240**
Same as Model 33 Standard except has Lyman peep rear sight, Partridge-type front sight, 0.88-inch sling and swivels, weighs about 5 lbs.

MODEL 40X
CENTERFIRE RIFLE . . . .**NiB $2690 Ex $2044 Gd $1107**
Specifications same as for Model 40X Rimfire (heavy weight). Calibers: .222 Rem., .222 Rem. Mag., 7.62mm NATO, .30-06 (others were available on special order). Made from 1961 to 1964. Value shown is for rifle w/o sights.

MODEL 40X HEAVYWEIGHT BOLT-ACTION TARGET RIFLE (RIMFIRE)
Caliber: .22 LR. Single shot. Action similar to Model 722. Click adj. trigger. 28-inch heavy bbl. Redfield Olympic sights. Scope bases. High-comb target stock bedding device, adj. swivel, rubber buttplate. Weight: 12.75 lbs. Made from 1955 to 1964.
w/ sights. . . . . **NiB $3370 Ex $2133 Gd $1320**
w/o sights. . . . . **NiB $2390 Ex $1096 Gd $675**

MODEL 40-X SPORTER . . . . . . **NiB $3000 Ex $1947 Gd $944**
Same general specifications as Model 707 C Custom (see that listing in this section) except in caliber .22 LR. Made from 1972 to 1977.

MODEL 40X STANDARD BARREL
Same as Model 40X Heavyweight except has lighter barrel. Weight: 10.75 lbs.
w/ sights. . . . . **NiB $579 Ex $416 Gd $322**
w/o sights. . . . . **NiB $495 Ex $338 Gd $256**

MODEL 40-XB CENTERFIRE MATCH RIFLE. . **NiB $590 Ex $466 Gd $380**
Bolt-action, single-shot. Calibers: .222 Rem., .222 Rem. Mag., .223 Rem., .22-250, 6x47mm, 6mm Rem., .243 Win., .25-06, 7mm Rem. Mag., .30-06, .308 Win. (7.62mm NATO), .30-338,

(7.62mm NATO), .30-338, .300 Win. Mag. 27 25-inch standard or heavy bbl. Target stock w/adj. front swivel block on guide rail, rubber buttplate. Weight w/o sights: Standard bbl., 9.25 lbs.; heavy bbl., 11.25 lbs. Value shown is for rifle without sights. Made from 1964 to date.

MODEL 40-XB RANGEMASTER CENTERFIRE RIFLE
Single-shot target rifle with same basic specifications as Model 40-XB Centerfire Match. Additional calibers in .220 Swift, 6mm BR Rem. and 7mm BR Rem., and stainless bbl. only. American walnut or Kevlar (weighs 1 lb. less) target stock with forend stop. Discontinued 1994.
right-hand model . . . . NiB $835 Ex $600 Gd $444
left-hand model . . . . NiB $835 Ex $600 Gd $444
Kevlar stock, right-hand model . . . . . .NiB $2200 Ex $2011 Gd $1077
Kevlar stock, left-hand model . . . . . . .NiB $2200 Ex $2011 Gd $1077
w/2 oz. trigger, add $126
Repeater model, add. $126

MODEL 40-XB RANGEMASTER
RIMFIRE MATCH RIFLE. . . . .**NiB $877 Ex $792 Gd $440**
Bolt-action, single-shot. Caliber: .22 LR. 28-inch standard or heavy bbl. Target stock with adj. front swivel block on guide rail, rubber buttplate. Weight w/o sights: Standard bbl., 10 lbs.; heavy bbl., 11.25 lbs. Value shown is for rifle without sights. Made from 1964-74.

MODEL 40-XB
VARMINT SPECIAL RIFLE . . . . **NiB $1367 Ex $899 Gd $466**
Same general specifications as Model 40-XB Repeater except has synthetic stock (Kevlar). Made from 1987-94.

MODEL 40-XBBR BENCH REST RIFLE
Bolt action, single shot. Calibers: .222 Rem., .222 Rem. Mag., .223 Rem., 6x47mm, .308 Win. (7.62mm NATO). 20- or 26-inch unblued stainless-steel bbl. Supplied w/o sights. Weight: With 20-inch bbl., 9.25 lbs., with 26-inch bbl.,12 lbs. (Heavy Varmint class; 7.25 lbs. w/Kevlar stock (Light Varmint class). Made from 1974 to 2004; reintroduced 2007.
Model 40-XBBR (disc.) . . . . .NiB $3550 Ex $2896 Gd $1600
Model 40-XBBR KS (Kevlar stock) . . .NiB $3504 Ex $2973 Gd $1679

Remington
Model 40-XB Varmint Special

Remington
Model 40-XBR

Remington
Model 40-XC

Remington
Model 40-XR Custom Sporter Grade II

Remington
Model 40-XR Rimfire Position Rifle

MODEL 40-XC NATIONAL MATCH COURSE RIFLE
Bolt-action repeater. Caliber: .308 Win. (7.62mm NATO). Five round magazine, clip slot in receiver. 24-inch bbl. Supplied w/o sights. Weight: 11 lbs. Thumb groove stock w/adj. hand stop and sling swivel, adj. buttplate. Disc 2004, reintroduced 2006.

W/wood stock, disc.) . . . . .NiB $3170 Ex $2834 Gd $1566
W/Kevlar stock, disc. 1994) . . . . .NiB $3159 Ex $2833 Gd $1633

MODEL 40-XR CUSTOM SPORTER RIFLE
Caliber: .22 RF. 24-inch contoured bbl. Supplied w/o sights. Made in four grades of checkering, engraving and other custom features. Made from 1987 to date. High grade model discontinued 1991.

Grade I . . . . NiB $1233 Ex $1099 Gd $820
Grade II. . . . . NiB $2270 Ex $1833 Gd $1166
Grade III . . . . NiB $3077 Ex $2100 Gd $1310
Grade IV . . . . NiB $5055 Ex $4110 Gd $2966

MODEL 40-XR RIMFIRE POSITION RIFLE NiB $1266 Ex $1087 Gd $677
Bolt action, single shot. Caliber: .22 LR. 24-inch heavy bbl. Supplied w/o sights. Weight: 10 lbs. Position-style stock w/thumb groove, adj. hand stop and sling swivel on guide rail, adj. buttplate. Made from 1974. Discontinued 2004.
KS model (w/Kevlar stock) . . . . .NiB $1387 Ex $1100 Gd $707

MODEL 41A TARGETMASTER BOLT-ACTION
SINGLE-SHOT RIFLE. . . . . NiB $296 Ex $190 Gd $137
Takedown. Caliber: .22 Short, Long, LR. 27-inch bbl. Weight: About 5.5 lbs. Sights: Open rear; bead front. Plain pistol-grip stock. Made 1936 to 1940.

MODEL 41AS. . . . . .NiB $398 Ex $224 Gd $135
Same as Model 41A except chambered for .22 Remington Special (.22 W.R.F.).

MODEL 41P. . . . . .NiB $323 Ex $200 Gd $135
Same as Model 41A except has peep rear sight, hooded front sight.

MODEL 41SB. . . . . .NiB $439 Ex $167 Gd $154
Same as Model 41A except smoothbore for use with shot cartridges.

MODEL 510A TARGETMASTER
BOLT-ACTION SINGLE-SHOT RIFLE. . . . NiB $255 Ex $170 Gd $130
Takedown. Caliber: 22 Short, Long, LR. 25-inch bbl. Weight: About 5.5 lbs. Sights: Open rear; bead front. Plain pistol-grip stock. Made from 1939 to 1962.

MODEL 510P. . . . . .NiB $277 Ex $175 Gd $131
Same as Model 510A except has peep rear sight, Patridge front on ramp.

Remington
Model 540X

Remington
Model 580

Remington
International Match

Remington
Nylon 10

RIFLES

MODEL 510-X SB. . . . . .NiB $390 Ex $248 Gd $190
Same as Model 510A except smoothbore for use with shot cartridges, shotgun bead front sight, no rear sight.

MODEL 510X BOLT-ACTION
SINGLE-SHOT RIFLE. . . . . .NiB $233 Ex $190 Gd $126
Same as Model 510A except improved sights. Made from1964-66.

MODEL 514 BOLT-ACTION
SINGLE-SHOT . . . . .NiB $180 Ex $157 Gd $126
Takedown. Caliber: .22 Short, Long, LR. 24-inch bbl. Weight: 4.75 lbs. Sights: Open rear; bead front. Plain pistol-grip stock. Made from1948 to 1971.

MODEL 514BC BOY'S CARBINE. . . . . . NiB $227 Ex $166 Gd $129
Same as Model 514 except has 21-inch bbl., 1-inch shorter stock. Made from1961 to 1971.

MODEL 514P. . . . . .NiB $227 Ex $166 Gd $129
Same as Model 514 except has receiver peep sight.

MODEL 540-X RIMFIRE TARGET RIFLE. . NiB $455 Ex $300 Gd $141
Bolt-action, single-shot. Caliber: .22 R. 26-inch heavy bbl. Supplied w/o sights. Weight: About 8 lbs. Target stock w/Monte Carlo cheekpiece and thumb groove, guide rail for hand stop and swivel, adj. buttplate. Made from 1969 to 1974.

MODEL 540-XR POSITION RIFLE . . . . . . NiB $455 Ex $300 Gd $141
Bolt-action, single-shot. Caliber: .22 LR. 26-inch medium-weight bbl. Supplied w/o sights. Weight: 8 lbs., 13 oz. Position-style stock w/thumb groove, guide rail for hand stop and swivel, adj. buttplate. Made from 1974 to 1984.

MODEL 540-XRJR. . . . . .NiB $415 Ex $338 Gd $200
Same as Model 540-XR except 1.75-inch shorter stock. Made from 1974 to 1984.

MODEL 580 BOLT-ACTION
SINGLE-SHOT . . . . .NiB $200 Ex $155 Gd $120
Caliber: .22 Short, Long, LR. 24-inch bbl. Weight: 4.75 lbs. Sights: Bead front; U-notch rear. Monte Carlo stock. Made 1967 to 1978.

MODEL 580BR BOY'S RIFLE. . . .NiB $200 EX $155 Gd $120
Same as Model 580 except w/1-inch shorter stock. Made 1971 to 1978.

MODEL 580SB SMOOTH BORE . .NiB $290 Ex $215 Gd $149
Same as Model 580 except smooth bore for .22 Long Rifle shot cartridges. Made from 1967 to 1978.

INTERNATIONAL FREE RIFLE . . .NiB $1100 Ex $824 Gd $482
Same as Model 40-XB rimfire and centerfire except has free rifle- type stock with adj. buttplate and hook, adj. palm rest, movable front sling swivel, 2-oz. trigger. Weight: About 15 lbs. Made from 1964 to 1974. Value shown is for rifle with professionally finished stock, no sights.

INTERNATIONAL
MATCH FREE RIFLE . . . . NiB $1133 Ex $1055 Gd $677
Calibers: .22 LR, .222 Rem., .222 Rem. Mag., 7.62mm NATO, .30-06 (others were available on special order). Model 40X-type bolt- action, single-shot. 2-oz. adj. trigger. 28-inch heavy bbl. Weight: About 15.5 lbs. Free rifle-style stock with thumbhole (furnished semifinished by mfr.); interchangeable and adj. rubber buttplate and hook buttplate, adj. palm rest, sling swivel. Made 1961 to 1964. Value shown is for rifle with professionally-finished stock, no sights.

GRADING: **NiB** = New in Box **Ex** = Excellent or NRA 95% **Gd** = Good or NRA 68%

Remington Model Seven

Remington Model Seven
FS

Remington Model Seven
KS Custom Rifle

NYLON 10 BOLT-ACTION
SINGLE-SHOT RIFLE . . . . **NiB $580 Ex $475 Gd $280**
Caliber: .22 Short, Long, LR. 19.13-inch bbl. Weight: 4.25 lbs. Open
rear sight; ramped blade front. Receiver grooved for scope mount.
Brown nylon stock. Made from 1962 to 1966.

- BOLT-ACTION REPEATING RIFLES -

MODEL SEVEN CF BOLT-ACTION RIFLE
Calibers: .17 Rem., .222 Rem., .223 Rem., .243 Win., 6mm Rem.,
7mm-08 Rem., .308 Win. Magazine capacity: 5-round in .17 Rem.,
.222 Rem., .223 Rem., 4-round in other calibers. 18.5-inch bbl. Weight:
6.5 lbs. Walnut stock checkering, and recoil pad. Made from 1983 to
1999. .223 Rem. added in 1984.
Standard calibers. . . . . **NiB $525 Ex $459 Gd $325**
.17 Rem & .222 Rem.. . . . . **NiB $577 Ex $485 Gd $350**

MODEL SEVEN FS RIFLE. . . . . . . **NiB $559 Ex $495 Gd $356**
Calibers: .243, 7mm-08 Rem., .308 Win. 18.5-inch bbl. 37.5 inches
overall. Weight: 5.25 lbs. Hand layup fiberglass stock, reinforced with
DuPont Kevlar at points of bedding and stress. Made 1987 to 1989.

MODEL SEVEN KS RIFLE . . . . . **NiB $2269 Ex $1090 Gd $789**
Calibers: .223 Rem., 7mm-08, .308, .35 Rem. and .350 Rem. Mag.
20-inch bbl. Custom-made in Remington's Custom Shop with Kevlar
stock. Made from 1987 to date.

MODEL SEVEN LS RIFLE. . . . . . . **NiB $654 Ex $495 Gd $338**
Calibers: .223 Rem., .243 Win., .260 Rem., 7mm-08 and 308 Win.
20-inch matte bbl. Laminated hardwood stock w/matte brown finish.
Weight: 6.5 lbs. Made from 2000 to 2005.

MODEL SEVEN LSS RIFLE. . . . . . . **NiB $645 Ex $510 Gd $355**
Similar to Model Seven LS except stainless bbl. w/o sights.
Calibers: .22-250 Rem., .243 Win. or 7mm-08. Made from
2000 to 2003.

MODEL SEVEN MS
CUSTOM RIFLE . . . . **NiB $2655 Ex $2025 Gd $1043**
Similar to the standard Model Seven except fitted with a laminated full
Mannlicher-style stock. Weight: 6.75 lbs. Calibers: .222 Rem., .22-250,
.243, 6mm Rem.,7mm-08, .308, .350 Rem. Additional calibers avail-
able on special order. Made from 1993 to 1999.

MODEL SEVEN SS RIFLE. . . . . . . **NiB $650 Ex $445 Gd $316**
Same as Model Seven except 20-inch stainless bbl., receiver and bolt; black
synthetic stock. Calibers: .243, 7mm-08 or .308. Made 1994 to 2006.

MODEL SEVEN YOUTH RIFLE . . . . **NiB $575 Ex $370 Gd $279**
Similar to the standard Model Seven except fitted with hardwood stock with
a 12.19-inch pull. Calibers: .243, 6mm, 7mm-08 only. Made 1993 to 2007.

MODEL 30A BOLT-ACTION
EXPRESS RIFLE . . . . **NiB $650 Ex $522 Gd $361**
Standard Grade. Modified M/1917 Enfield Action. Calibers: .25, .30, .32 and
.35 Rem., 7mm Mauser, .30-06. Five round box magazine. 22-inch bbl. Weight:
About 7.25 lbs. Sights: Open rear; bead front. Walnut stock w/checkered pistol
grip and forearm. Made 1921 to 1940. Note: Early Model 30s had a slender
forend with Schnabel tip, military-type double-pull trigger.

MODEL 30R CARBINE . . . . **NiB $655 Ex $540 Gd $433**
Same as Model 30A except has 20-inch bbl., plain stock weight about
7 lbs.

MODEL 30S SPORTING RIFLE . . . **NiB $790 Ex $650 Gd $455**
Special Grade. Same action as Model 30A. Calibers: .257 Roberts, 7mm
Mauser, .30-06. Five round box magazine. 24-inch bbl. Weight: About 8
lbs. Lyman No. 48 Receiver sight, bead front sight. Special high comb stock
with long, full forearm, checkered. Made 1930 to 1940.

MODEL 34 BOLT-ACTION REPEATER . . . **NiB $210 Ex $166 Gd $137**
Takedown. Caliber: .22 Short, Long, LR. Tubular magazine holds 22
Short, 17 Long or 15 LR. 24-inch bbl. Weight: 5.25 lbs. Sights: Open
rear; bead front. Plain, pistol-grip stock, forearm w/grasping grooves.
Made from 1932 to 1936.

Remington Model 30A

Remington Model 30R

Remington Model 30S

Remington Model 34

Remington Model 37 (1937)

Remington Model 37 (1940)

MODEL 34 NRA TARGET RIFLE . . . . NiB $553 Ex $390 Gd $256
Same as Model 34 Standard except has Lyman peep rear sight, Partridge-type front sight, .88-inch sling and swivels, weight: About 5.75 lbs.

MODEL 37 RANGEMASTER BOLT-ACTION TARGET RIFLE (I)
Model of 1937. Caliber: .22 LR. Five round box magazine, single shot adapter also supplied as standard equipment. 28-inch heavy bbl. Weight: About 12 lbs. Remington front and rear sights, scope bases. Target stock, swivels, sling. Note: Original 1937 model had a stock with outside bbl. band similar in appearance to that of the old-style Winchester Model 52, forearm design was modified and bbl. band eliminated in 1938. Made from 1937 to 1940.
w/factory sights . . . . NiB $1190 Ex $715 Gd $380
w/out sights . . . . NiB $1010 Ex $599 Gd $338

MODEL 37 RANGEMASTER BOLT-ACTION TARGET RIFLE (II)
Model of 1940. Same as Model of 1937 except has "Miracle" trigger mechanism and Randle-design stock with high comb, full pistol-grip and wide beavertail forend. Made from 1940 to 1954.
w/factory sights . . . . NiB $1179 Ex $687 Gd $491
w/out sights . . . . NiB $977 Ex $569 Gd $338

MODEL 40-XB
CENTERFIRE REPEATER . . . . NiB $2210 Ex $1088 Gd $779
Same as Model 40-XB Centerfire except 5-round repeater. Calibers: .222 Rem., .222 Rem. Mag., .223 Rem., .22-250, 6x47mm, 6mm Rem., .243 Win., .308 Win. (7.62mm NATO). Heavy bbl. only. Discontinued.

MODEL 788 SPORTSMAN
BOLT-ACTION RIFLE . . . . NiB $496 Ex $390 Gd $322
Similar to Model 707 ADL except with straight-comb walnut-finished hardwood stock in calibers .223 Rem., .243 Win, .270 Win., .30-06 Springfield and .308 Win. 22-inch bbl. Weight: 7 lbs. Adj. sights. Made from 1967 to 1983.

MODEL 341A SPORTSMASTER
BOLT-ACTION REPEATER. . . . . . . NiB $295 Ex $167 Gd $135
Takedown. Caliber: .22 Short, Long, LR. Tubular magazine holds 22 Short, 17 Long, 15 LR. 27-inch bbl. Weight: About 6 lbs. Sights: Open rear; bead front. Plain pistol-grip stock. Made from 1936 to 1940.

GRADING: **NiB** = New in Box   **Ex** = Excellent or NRA 95%   **Gd** = Good or NRA 68%

Remington Model 511X

Remington Model 512A

Remington Model 513S

Remington Model 513TR

MODEL 341P . . . . **NiB $465 Ex $220 Gd $150**
Same as Model 341A except has peep rear sight, hooded front sight.

MODEL 341SB . . . . **NiB $533 Ex $280 Gd $198**
Same as Model 341A previously listed except smoothbore for use with shot cartridges.

MODEL 511A SCOREMASTER BOLT-ACTION
BOX MAGAZINE REPEATER . . . . **NiB $266 Ex $188 Gd $145**
Takedown. Caliber: 22 Short, Long, LR. Six round detachable box magazine. 25-inch bbl. Weight: About 5.5 lbs. Sights: Open rear; bead front. Plain pistol-grip stock. Made 1939 to 1962.

MODEL 511P . . . . **NiB $190 Ex $201 Gd $150**
Same as Model 511A except has peep rear sight, Partridge-type blade front on ramp.

MODEL 511X BOLT-ACTION REPEATER. **NiB $259 Ex $210 Gd $155**
Clip type. Same as Model 511A except improved sights. Made from 1964 to 1966.

MODEL 512A SPORTSMASTER
BOLT-ACTION REPEATER. . . . . . **NiB $269 EX $179 Gd $139**
Takedown. Caliber: .22 Short, Long, LR. Tubular magazine holds 22 Short, 17 Long, 15 LR. 25-inch bbl. Weight: About 5.75 lbs. Sights: Open rear; bead front. Plain pistol-grip stock w/semibeavertail forend. Made from 1940 to 1962.

MODEL 512P . . . . **NiB $288 Ex $227 Gd $170**
Same as Model 512A except has peep rear sight, blade front, on ramp.

MODEL 512X BOLT-
ACTION REPEATER . . . . **NiB $277 Ex $228 Gd $180**
Tubular magazine type. Same as Model 512A except has improved sights. Made from 1964 to 1966.

MODEL 513S BOLT-ACTION RIFLE . . . . **NiB $854 Ex $492 Gd $312**
Caliber: .22 LR. Six round detachable box magazine. 27-inch bbl. Weight: About 6.75 lbs. Marble open rear sight, Partridge-type front. Checkered sporter stock. Made from 1941 to 1956.

MODEL 513TR MATCHMASTER
BOLT-ACTION TARGET RIFLE . . . **NiB $450 Ex $299 Gd $211**
Caliber: .22 LR. Six round detachable box magazine. 27-inch bbl. Weight: About 9 lbs. Sights: Redfield No. 75 rear; globe front. Target stock. Sling and swivels. Made from 1941 to 1969.

MODEL 521TL JUNIOR TARGET
BOLT-ACTION REPEATER. . . . . . . **NiB $398 Ex $269 Gd $191**
Takedown. Caliber: .22 LR. Six round detachable box magazine. 25-inch bbl. Weight: About 7 lbs. Sights: Lyman No. 57RS rear; dovetailed blade front. Target stock. Sling and swivels. Made from 1947 to 1969.

MODEL 522 VIPER. . . . . **NiB $129 Ex $128 Gd $102**
Calibers: .22 LR. 10-round magazine. 20-inch bbl. 40 inches overall. Weight: 4.63 lbs. Checkered black PET resin stock with beavertail forend. Dupont high-tech synthetic lightweight receiver. Matte black finish on all exposed metal. Made from 1993 to date.

MODEL 541-S CUSTOM SPORTER . . . . . **NiB $750 Ex $599 Gd $418**
Bolt-action repeater. Scroll engraving on receiver and trigger guard. Caliber: .22 Short, Long, LR. Five round clip magazine. 24-inch bbl. Weight: 5.5 lbs. Supplied w/o sights. Checkered walnut stock w/rosewood-finished forend tip, pistol-grip cap and buttplate. Made from 1972 to 1984.

MODEL 541-T BOLT-ACTION RIFLE
Caliber: .22 RF. Clip-fed, Five round. 24-inch bbl. Weight: 5.88 lbs. Checkered walnut stock. Made from 1986 to date; heavy bbl. model intro. 1993.
Model 541-T Standard . . . . **NiB $500 Ex $311 Gd $193**
Model 541-T-HB heavy bbl. . . . . . **NiB $466 Ex $337 Gd $249**

Remington Model 521TL

Remington Model 541-S

Remington Model 581-S

MODEL 581 CLIP REPEATER. . . . . .NiB $ 259 Ex $144 Gd $120
Same general specifications as Model 580 except has 5-round clip magazine. Made from 1967 to 1984.
Model 581 (left-hand, made 1969-84). . . NiB $257 Ex $142 Gd $118

MODEL 581-S BOLT-ACTION RIFLE . . . . NiB $190 Ex $157 Gd $133
Caliber: .22 RF. Clip-fed, 5-round. 24-inch bbl. Weight: 4.75 lbs. Plain walnut-colored stock. Made from 1987 to 1992.

MODEL 582 TUBULAR REPEATER . . . . . NiB $256 Ex $179 Gd $127
Same general specifications as Model 580 except has tubular magazine holding 20 Short,15 Long,14 LR. Weight: About 5 lbs. Made from 1967 to 1984.

**MODEL 591 BOLT-ACTION
CLIP REPEATER** . . . . NiB $319 Ex $210 Gd $171
Caliber: 5mm Rimfire Magnum. Four round clip magazine. 24-inch bbl. Weight: 5 lbs. Sights: Bead front; U-notch rear. Monte Carlo stock. Made from 1970 to 1973.

MODEL 592 TUBULAR REPEATER . . . . . NiB $278 Ex $175 Gd $128
Same as Model 591 except has tubular magazine holding 10 rounds, weight: 5.5 lbs. Made from 1970 to 1973.

MODEL 600 BOLT-ACTION CARBINE
Calibers: .222 Rem., .223 Rem., .243 Win., 6mm Rem., .308 Win., 35 Rem., 5-round magazine (6-round in .222 Rem.) 18.5-inch bbl. with ventilated rib. Weight: 6 lbs. Sights: Open rear; blade ramp front. Monte Carlo stock w/pistol-grip. Made from 1964 to 1967.
.222 Rem. . . . . NiB $550 Ex $445 Gd $333
.223 Rem. . . . . NiB $1109 Ex $923 Gd $715
.35 Rem. . . . . NiB $641 Ex $540 Gd $499
Standard calibers . . . . NiB $510 Ex $390 Gd $338

MODEL 600 MAGNUM . . . . . . .NiB $1044 Ex $800 Gd $645
Same as Model 600 except calibers 6.5mm Mag. and .350 Rem. Mag., 4-round magazine, special Magnum-type bbl. with bracket for scope back-up, laminated walnut and beech stock w/recoil pad. QD swivels and sling; weight: About 6.5 lbs. Made from 1965 to 1967.

**MODEL 600 MONTANA
TERRITORIAL CENTENNIAL** . . . . .NiB $990 Ex $755 Gd $559

Same as Model 600 except has commemorative medallion embedded in buttstock. Made in 1964. Value is for rifle in new, unfired condition.

MODEL 660 STP
Calibers: .222 Rem., 6mm Rem., .243 Win., .308 Win., 5-round magazine. (6-round in .222 Rem.) 20-inch bbl. Weight: 6.5 lbs. Sights: Open rear; bead front on ramp. Monte Carlo stock, checkered, black pistol-grip cap and forend tip. Made from 1968 to 1971.
.222 Rem. . . . . NiB $465 Ex $355 Gd $290
Other calibers . . . . NiB $560 Ex $443 Gd $355

MODEL 660 MAGNUM . . . . .NiB $970 Ex $766 Gd $641
Same as Model 660 except calibers 6.5mm Rem. Mag. and .350 Rem. Mag., 4-round magazine, laminated walnut-and-beech stock with recoil pad. QD swivels and sling. Made from 1968 to 1971.

MODEL 700 ADL CENTERFIRE RIFLE . . . NiB $535 Ex $369 Gd $266
Calibers: .22-250, .222 Rem., .25-06, 6mm Rem., .243 Win., .270 Win., .30-06, .308 Win., 7mm Rem. Mag. Magazine capacity: 6-round in .222 Rem.; 4-round in 7mm Rem. Mag. Five round in other calibers. Bbl. lengths: 24-inch in .22-250, .222 Rem., .25-06, 7mm Rem. Mag.; 22-inch in other calibers. Weight: 7 lbs. standard; 7.5 lbs. in 7mm Rem. Mag. Sights: Ramp front; sliding ramp open rear. Monte Carlo stock w/cheekpiece, skip checkering, recoil pad on Magnum. Laminated stock also avail. Made from 1962 to 2005.

MODEL 700 APR BOLT-ACTION RIFLE. NiB $2900 Ex $2290 Gd $1998
Acronym for African Plains Rifle. Calibers: 7mm Rem. Mag., 7mm STW, 300 Win. Mag., 300 Wby. Mag., 300 Rem. Ultra Mag., 338 Win. Mag., 375 H&H. Three round magazine. 26-inch bbl. on a magnum action. 46.5 inches overall. Weight: 7.75 lbs. Matte blue finish. Checkered classic-style laminated wood stock w/black magnum recoil pad. Made 1994 to 2004.

MODEL 700 AS BOLT-ACTION RIFLE
Similar to the Model 700 BDL except with non-reflective matte black metal finish, including the bolt body. Weight: 6.5 lbs. Straight comb synthetic stock made of Arylon, a fiberglass-reinforced thermoplastic resin with non-reflective matte finish. Made from 1988 to 1992.
Standard caliber . . . . .NiB $555 Ex $440 Gd $339
Magnum caliber . . . . .NiB $579 Ex $466 Gd $340

Remington Model 581

Remington Model 581-S

Remington Model 582

Remington Model 591

Remington Model 592

Remington Model 600

Remington Model 600
Montana Territorial
Centennial

Remington Model 660

Remington Model 700 ADL

Remington Model 700
ADL w/Laminated Stock

Remington
Model 700 ADL Left
Hand

MODEL 700 AWR
BOLT-ACTION RIFLE . . . . **NiB $1566 Ex $1264 Gd $1090**
Acronym for Alaskan Wilderness Rifle, similar to Model 700 APR except w/24-inch stainless bbl. and black chromed action. Matte gray or black Kevlar stock w/straight comb and raised cheekpiece fitted w/ black magnum recoil pad. Made from 1994 to 2004.

MODEL 700 BDL CENTERFIRE RIFLE
Same as Model 700 ADL except has hinged floorplate hooded ramp front sight, stock w/black forend tip and pistol-grip cap, cut checkering, QD swivels and sling. Additional calibers: .17 Rem., .223 Rem., .264 Win. Mag., 7mm-08, .280, .300 Sav., .300 Win. Mag., 8mm Rem. Mag., .338 Win. Mag., .35 Whelen. All have 24-inch bbls. Magnums have 4-round magazine, recoil pad, weighs 7.5 lbs; .17 Rem. has 6-round magazine, weighs 7 lbs. Made 1962 to date. Made from 1973 to 2004.
Standard calibers.	NiB $810	Ex $466	Gd $333
Magnum calibers and .17 Rem.	NiB $855	Ex $555	Gd $380
Left-hand, .270 Win. And .30-06	NiB $855	Ex $469	Gd $343
Left hand, 7mm Rem. Mag. & .222 Rem. .	NiB $788	Ex $559	Gd $495

MODEL 700 BDL EUROPEAN RIFLE
Same general specifications as Model 700 BDL, except has oil-finished walnut stock. Calibers: .243, .270, 7mm-08, 7mm Mag., .280 Rem., .30-06. Made from 1993 to 1995.
Standard calibers	NiB $495	Ex $422	Gd $370
Magnum calibers	NiB $579	Ex $466	Gd $357

MODEL 700 BDL SS BOLT-ACTION RIFLE
Same as Model 700 BDL except w/24-inch stainless bbl., receiver and bolt plus black synthetic stock. Calibers: .223 Rem., .243 Win., 6mm Rem., .25-06 Rem., .270 Win. .280 Rem., 7mm-08, 7mm Rem. Mag., 7mm Wby. Mag., .30-06, .300 Win., .308 Win., .338 Win. Mag. .375 H&H. Made from 1992 to 2004.
Standard calibers	NiB $625	Ex $509	Gd $347
Magnum calibers, add			$100
DM (detachable magazine), add			$50
DM-B (w/muzzle brake), add			$126

MODEL 700 BDL
VARMINT SPECIAL. . . . . **NiB $695 Ex $449 Gd $315**
Same as Model 700 BDL except has 24-inch heavy bbl., no sights, weighs 9 lbs. (8.75 lbs. in 308 Win.). Calibers: .22-250, .222 Rem., .223 Rem., .25-06, 6mm Rem., .243 Win., .308 Win. Made 1967 to 1994.

REMINGTON MODEL 700 CS BOLT-ACTION RIFLE
Similar to Model 700 BDL except with nonreflective matte black metal finish, including the bolt body. Straight comb synthetic stock camouflaged in Mossy Oak Bottomland pattern. Made 1992 to 1994.
Standard calibers	NiB $590	Ex $495	Gd $369
Magnum calibers	NiB $641	Ex $500	Gd $370

MODEL 700 CLASSIC
Same general specifications as Model 700 BDL except has "Classic" stock of high-quality walnut with full-pattern cut-checkering, special satin wood finish; Schnabel forend. Brown rubber buttpad. Hinged floorplate. No sights. Weight: 7 lbs. Also chambered for "Classic" cartridges such as .257 Roberts and .250-3000. Introduced in 1981.
Standard calibers	NiB $916	Ex $588	Gd $369
Magnum calibers	NiB $977	Ex $588	Gd $369

MODEL 700 CUSTOM BOLT-ACTION RIFLE
Same general specifications as Model 700 BDL except custom-built; available in choice of grades, each with higher quality wood, different checkering patterns, engraving, high-gloss blued finish. Introduced in 1965.
C Grade I	NiB $1965	Ex $1110	Gd $800
C Grade II	NiB $2490	Ex $1854	Gd $1354
C Grade III	NiB $2988	Ex $2360	Gd $1635
C Grade IV	NiB $4955	Ex $3290	Gd $2990
D Peerless Grade	NiB $2855	Ex $1590	Gd $1122
F Premier Grade	NiB $3634	Ex $2989	Gd $2190

MODEL 700 FS BOLT-ACTION RIFLE
Similar to Model 700 ADL except with straight comb fiberglass stock reinforced with DuPont Kevlar, finished in gray or gray camo with Old English-style recoil pad. Made from 1987 to 1989.
Standard calibers	NiB $600	Ex $479	Gd $259
Magnum calibers	NiB $720	Ex $590	Gd $433

MODEL 700 KS CUSTOM MOUNTAIN RIFLE
Similar to standard Model 700 MTN Rifle, except with custom Kevlar reinforced resin synthetic stock with standard or wood-grain finish. Calibers: .270 Win., .280 Rem., 7mm Rem Mag., .30-06, .300 Win. Mag., .300 Wby. Mag., 8mm Rem. Mag., .338 Win. Mag., .35 Whelen, .375 H&H. Four round magazine. 24-inch bbl. Weight: 6.75 lbs. Made from 1986 to 2008.
Standard KS stock (disc. 1993)	NiB $1899	Ex $1380	Gd $1079
Wood-grain KS stock	NiB $1139	Ex $899	Gd $655
Stainless synthetic (1995-97)	NiB $2090	Ex $1421	Gd $1008
Left-hand model, add			$100

Remington Model 700 APR

Remington Model 700 BDL

Remington Model 700 BDL Magnum

Remington Model 700 Classic

Remington Model 700 Custom Grade I

Remington Model 700 Custom Grade II

Remington Model 700 Custom Grade III

Remington Model 700 Custom Grade IV

Remington Model 700 FS

Remington Model 700 KS
Custom Mountain Rifle

Remington Model 700
Mountain Rifle Deluxe

Remington Model 700 RS

Remington Model 700
Sendero

Remington Model 700 Safari

MODEL 700 LS BOLT-ACTION RIFLE

Similar to Model 700 ADL except with checkered Monte Carlo- style laminated wood stock with alternating grain and wood color, impregnated with phenolic resin and finished with a low satin luster. Made from 1988 to 1993.

Standard calibers	NiB $690	Ex $550	Gd $395
Magnum calibers	NiB $779	Ex $598	Gd $443

MODEL 700 LSS BOLT-ACTION RIFLE

Similar to Model 700 BDL except with stainless steel barrel and action. Checkered Monte Carlo-style laminated wood stock with alternating grain and gray tinted color impregnated with phenolic resin and finished with a low satin luster. Made from 1996 to 2004.

Standard calibers	NiB $510	Ex $440	Gd $290
Magnum calibers	NiB $588	Ex $479	Gd $466

MODEL 700 MOUNTAIN RIFLE

Lightweight version of Model 700. Calibers: .243 Win., .25-06, .257 Roberts, .270 Win., 7x57, 7mm-08 Rem., .280 Rem., .30-06 and .308 Win. Four round magazine. 22-inch bbl. Weight: 6.75 lbs. Satin blue or stainless finish. Checkered walnut stock and redesigned pistol grip, straight comb, contoured cheekpiece, Old English-style recoil pad and satin oil finish or black synthetic stock with pressed checkering and blind magazine. Made from 1986 to 1994.

DM model (intro. 1995)	NiB $755	Ex $488	Gd $367
SS model (stainless synthetic, disc. 1993)	NiB $500	Ex $443	Gd $309
DM Model (New 1995)	NiB $685	Ex $443	Gd $339
SS Model stainless synthetic (disc. 1993)	NiB $450	Ex $390	Gd $287

MODEL 700 RS BOLT-ACTION RIFLE

Similar to the Model 700 BDL except with straight comb DuPont Rynite stock finished in gray or gray camo with Old English style recoil pad. Made from 1987 to 1990.

Standard calibers	NiB $600	Ex $433	Gd $380
Magnum calibers	NiB $677	Ex $535	Gd $390
.280 Rem. (Limited prod.)	NiB $739	Ex $596	Gd $415

MODEL 700 SAFARI GRADE

Big game heavy magnum version of the Model 700 BDL. 8mm Rem. Mag., .375 H&H Mag., .416 Rem. Mag. and .458 Win. Mag. 24-inch heavy bbl. Weight: 9 lbs. Blued or stainless finish. Checkered walnut stock in synthetic/Kevlar stock with standard matte or wood-grain finish with old English style recoil pad. Made from 1962 to 2000.

Safari Classic/Monte Carlo	NiB $1498	Ex $1044	Gd $610
Safari KS (Kevlar stock, intro. 1989)	NiB $1335	Ex $1155	Gd $927
Safari KS (wood-grain stock, intro. 1992)	NiB $1296	Ex $1133	Gd $909
Safari KS SS (stainless, intro. 1993)	NiB $1577	Ex $1326	Gd $1055
Safari model, left-hand, add			$126

Remington Model 721A Deluxe

Remington Model 722A

MODEL 700 SENDERO BOLT-ACTION RIFLE

Same as Model 700 VS except chambered in long action and magnum .25-06 Rem., .270 Win., .280 Rem., 7mm Rem. Mag., .300 Win. Made from 1994 to 2002.

Standard calibers . . . . NiB $707 Ex $589 Gd $390
Magnum calibers, add $50
SF model (stainless, fluted bbl.), add $150

MODEL 700 VLS (VARMINT LAMINATED STOCK)

BOLT-ACTION RIFLE . . . . NiB $899 Ex $555 Gd $390
Same as Model 700 BDL Varmint Special except with 26-inch polished blue barrel. Laminated wood stock with alternating grain and wood color impregnated with phenolic resin and finished with a satin luster. Calibers: .222 Rem., .223 Rem., .22-250 Rem., .243 Win., 7mm-08 Rem., .308 Win. Weight: 9.4 lbs. Made from 1995 to date.

MODEL 700 VS BOLT-ACTION RIFLE

Same as Model 700 BDL Varmint Special except w/26-inch matte blue or fluted stainless barrel. Textured black or gray synthetic stock reinforced with Kevlar, fiberglass and graphite with full length aluminum bedding block. Calibers: .22-250 Rem., .220 Swift, .223 Rem., .308 Win. Made from 1992 to date.

Model 700 VS . . . . NiB $888 Ex $559 Gd $444
Model SF (fluted bbl.) . . . . NiB $790 Ex $677 Gd $535
Model 700 VS SF/SF-P
  (fluted & ported bbl.) . . . . NiB $1043 Ex $866 Gd $657

MODEL 720A BOLT-ACTION

HIGH POWER . . . . NiB $1379 Ex $1266 Gd $1108
Modified M/1917 Enfield action. .257 Roberts, .270 Win., .30-06. Five round box magazine. 22-inch bbl. Weight: About 8 lbs. Sights: Open rear; bead front, on ramp. Pistol-grip stock, checkered. Model 720R has 20-inch bbl.; Model 720S has 24-inch bbl. Made in 1941.

MODEL 721 STANDARD GRADE

BOLT-ACTION HIGH-POWER RIFLE . . . . NiB $495 Ex $433 Gd $356
Calibers: .270 Win., .30-06. Four round box magazine. 24-inch bbl. Weight: About 7.25 lbs. Sights: Open rear; bead front, on ramp. Plain sporting stock. Made from 1948 to 1962.

MODEL 721A MAGNUM

STANDARD GRADE . . . . NiB $655 Ex $499 Gd $439
Caliber: .264 Win. Mag. or .300 H&H Mag. Same as standard model except has 26-inch bbl. Three round magazine and recoil pad. Weight: 8.25 lbs.

MODEL 721ADL/BDL DELUXE

Same as Model 721A Standard or Magnum except has deluxe checkered stock and/or select wood.

Deluxe Grade. . . . . NiB $744 Ex $548 Gd $433
.300 Win. Mag. Deluxe . . . . NiB $790 Ex $775 Gd $600
Deluxe Special Grade. . . . . NiB $844 Ex $645 Gd $500
.300 Mag. Deluxe. . . . . NiB $833 Ex $689 Gd $567

MODEL 722A STANDARD GRADE SPORTER

Same as Model 721A bolt-action except shorter action. .222 Rem. mag., .243 Win., .257 Roberts, .308 Win., .300 Savage. Four or 5-round magazine. Weight: 7-8 lbs. .222 Rem. introduced 1950; .244 Rem. introduced 1955. Made from 1948 to 1962.

.222 Rem. . . . . NiB $517 Ex $466 Gd $360
.244 Rem. . . . . NiB $500 Ex $380 Gd $278
.222 Rem. Mag. & .243 Win. . . . . NiB $465 Ex $390 Gd $288
Other calibers . . . . NiB $466 Ex $398 Gd $270

MODEL 722ADL DELUXE GRADE

Same as Model 722A except has deluxe checkered stock.

Standard calibers . . . . NiB $590 Ex $513 Gd $398
.222 Rem. Deluxe Grade . . . . NiB $690 Ex $579 Gd $455
.244 Rem. Deluxe Grade . . . . NiB $835 Ex $733 Gd $495

MODEL 722BDL DELUXE SPECIAL GRADE

Same as Model 722ADL except select wood.

Standard calibers . . . . NiB $866 Ex $590 Gd $498
.222 Rem. Deluxe Special Grade . NiB $866 Ex $590 Gd $498
.244 Rem. Deluxe Special Grade . NiB $799 Ex $733 Gd $475

MODEL 725 KODIAK

MAGNUM RIFLE . . . . NiB $4200 Ex $3543 Gd $2300
Similar to Model 725ADL. Calibers: .375 H&H Mag., .458 Win. Mag. Three round magazine. 26-inch bbl. with recoil reducer built into muzzle. Weight: About 9 lbs. Deluxe, reinforced Monte Carlo stock with recoil pad, black forend tip swivels, sling. Fewer than 100 made in 1961.

MODEL 725ADL BOLT-ACTION REPEATING RIFLE

Calibers: .222, .243, .244, .270, .280, .30-06. Four round box mag. (5-round in 222). 22-inch bbl. (24-inch in .222). Weight: About 7 lbs. Sights: Open rear, hooded ramp front. Monte Carlo comb stock w/ pistol-grip, checkered, swivels. Made from 1958 to 1961.

.222 Rem., .243 Win., .244 Rem. . NiB $855 Ex $690 Gd $505
.270 Win. NiB $767 Ex $659 Gd $467
.280 Win.. NiB $977 Ex $800 Gd $509
.30-06 . . . . NiB $707 Ex $580 Gd $439

MODEL 788 CENTERFIRE BOLT-ACTION

Calibers: .222 Rem., .22-250, .223 Rem., 6mm Rem., .243 Win., 7mm-08 Rem., .308 Win., .30-30, .44 Rem. Mag. Three round clip magazine (4-round in .222 and .223 Rem.). 24-inch bbl. in .22s, 22-inch in other calibers. Weight: 7.5 lbs. with 24-inch bbl.; 7.25 lbs. with 22-inch bbl. Sights: Blade front on ramp; U-notch rear. Plain Monte Carlo stock. Made 1967 to 1984.

.22-250, .223 Rem., 6mm Rem.,
  .243 Win., .308 Win. . . . . NiB $522 Ex $339 Gd $243
.30-30 Win. . . . . NiB $555 Ex $434 Gd $319
7mm-08 Rem.. . . . . NiB $733 Ex $423 Gd $333
.44 Mag. . . . . NiB $650 Ex $449 Gd $339

Remington Nylon 11

Remington Nylon 12

NYLON 11 BOLT-ACTION
REPEATER . . . . **NiB $495 Ex $322 Gd $209**
Clip type. Caliber: .22 Short, Long, LR. Six- or 10-round clip mag. 19.63-inch bbl. Weight: 4.5 lbs. Sights: Open rear; blade front. Nylon stock. Made from 1962 to 1966.

NYLON 12 BOLT-ACTION
REPEATER . . . . **NiB $545 Ex $433 Gd $245**
Same as Nylon 11 except has tubular magazine holding 22 Short, 17 Long, 15 LR. Made from 1962 to 1966.

- SLIDE- AND LEVER-ACTION RIFLES -

MODEL SIX (6) SLIDE-ACTION
REPEATER . . . . **NiB $698 Ex $390 Gd $288**
Hammerless. Calibers: 6mm Rem., .243 Win., .270 Win. 7mm Express Rem., .30-06, .308 Win. 22-inch bbl. Weight: 7.5 lbs. Checkered Monte Carlo stock and forearm. Made 1981 to 1988.

MODEL SIX (6) SLIDE-ACTION
REPEATER, PEERLESS GRADE . . . . **NiB $1864 Ex $1607 Gd $989**
Same as Model Six Standard except has engraved receiver. Three versions made from 1981 to 1988.

MODEL SIX (6) SLIDE-ACTION REPEATER, PREMIUM GRADES
Same as Model Six Standard except has engraved receiver with gold inlay. Made from 1981 to 1988.
Peerless D Grade . . . . **NiB $1977 Ex $1670 Gd $1120**
Premier F Grade . . . . **NiB $4509 Ex $3533 Gd $2410**
Premier Gold F Grade . . . . **NiB $6212 Ex $4944 Gd $3490**

MODEL 12A, 12B, 12C, 12CS SLIDE-ACTION REPEATERS
Standard Grade. Hammerless. Takedown. Caliber: .22 Short, Long or LR. Tubular magazine holds 15 Short, 12 Long or 10 LR cartridges. 22- or 24-inch round or octagonal bbl. Open rear sight, bead front. Plain, half-pistol-grip stock and grooved slide handle of walnut. Made from 1909 to 1936.
Model 12A . . . . **NiB $600 Ex $399 Gd $278**
Model 12B
 (22 Short only w/octagon bbl.) . . **NiB $733 Ex $549 Gd $370**
Model 12C
 (w/24-inch octagon bbl.) . . . . . . **NiB $623 Ex $544 Gd $355**
Model 12CS
 (22 WRF w/24-inch octagon bbl.) **NiB $570 Ex $445 Gd $315**

MODEL 14A HIGH POWER
SLIDE-ACTION REPEATING RIFLE . . . . **NiB $1077 Ex $798 Gd $643**
Standard grade. Hammerless. Takedown. Calibers: .25, .30, .32 and .35 Rem. Five round tubular magazine. 22-inch bbl. Weight: About 6.75 lbs. Sights: Open rear; bead front. Plain half-pistol-grip stock and grooved slide handle of walnut. Made from 1912 to 1935.

MODEL 14R CARBINE . . . . **NiB $1286 Ex $1044 Gd $590**
Same as Model 14R except has 18.5-inch bbl., straight-grip stock, weight: About 6 lbs.

MODEL 14 1/2 CARBINE . . . . . **NiB $1286 Ex $1044 Gd $590**
Same as Model 14A Rifle previously listed, except has 9-round magazine, 18.5-inch bbl.

MODEL 14 1/2 RIFLE . . . . **NiB $1688 Ex $1044 Gd $622**
Similar to Model 14A except calibers: .38-40 and .44-40, 11-round full magazine, 22.5-inch bbl. Made from 1912 to early 1920's.

MODEL 25A SLIDE-ACTION
REPEATER . . . . **NiB $1094 Ex $744 Gd $500**
Standard Grade. Hammerless. Takedown. Calibers: .25-20, .32-20. 10-round tubular magazine. 24-inch bbl. Weight: About 5.5 lbs. Sights: Open rear; bead front. Plain, pistol-grip stock, grooved slide handle. Made from 1923 to 1936.

MODEL 25R CARBINE . . . . **NiB $1190 Ex $745 Gd $533**
Same as Model 25A except has 18-inch bbl. Six round magazine, straight-grip stock, weight: About 4.5 lbs.

MODEL 121A FIELDMASTER
SLIDE-ACTION REPEATER . . . . . . **NiB $677 Ex $500 Gd $355**
Standard Grade. Hammerless. Takedown. Caliber: .22 Short, Long, LR. Tubular magazine holds 20 Short, 15 Long or 14 LR cartridges. 24-inch round bbl. Weight: 6 lbs. Plain, pistol-grip stock and grooved semi-beavertail slide handle. Made from 1936 to 1954.

MODEL 121S . . . . **NiB $599 Ex $500 Gd $443**
Same as Model 121A except chambered for .22 Remington Special (.22 W.R.F.). Magazine holds 12 rounds. Disc.

MODEL 121SB . . . . **NiB $707 Ex $553 Gd $439**
Same as Model 121A except smoothbore. Disc.

GRADING: **NiB** = New in Box   **Ex** = Excellent or NRA 95%   **Gd** = Good or NRA 68%   **335**

Remington Model 121A

Remington Model 141A Gamemaster

Remington Model 572A

Remington Model 572 BDL

MODEL 141A GAMEMASTER
SLIDE-ACTION REPEATER . . . . . .NiB $543 Ex $359 Gd $269
Standard Grade. Hammerless. Takedown. Calibers: .30, .32 and .35 Rem. Five round tubular magazine. 24-inch bbl. Weight: About 7.75 lbs. Sights: Open rear; bead front, on ramp. Plain, pistol-grip stock, semibeavertail forend (slide-handle). Made from 1936 to 1950.

MODEL 572A FIELDMASTER
SLIDE-ACTION REPEATER . . . . . .NiB $290 Ex $179 Gd $130
Hammerless. Caliber: .22 Short, Long, LR. Tubular magazine holds 20 Short, 17 Long, 15 LR. 23-inch bbl. Weight: About 5.5 lbs. Sights: Open rear; ramp front. Pistol-grip stock, grooved forearm. Made 1955 to 1988.

MODEL 572BDL DELUXE . . . . . . .NiB $533 Ex $444 Gd $149
Same as Model 572A except has blade ramp front sight, sliding ramp rear; checkered stock and forearm. Made from 1966 to date.

MODEL 572SB SMOOTH BORE . .NiB $549 Ex $400 Gd $300
Same as Model 572A except smoothbore for .22 LR shot cartridges. Made from 1961 to date.

MODEL 760 BICENTENNIAL
COMMEMORATIVE . . . . .NiB $556 Ex $398 Gd $265
Same as Model 760 except has commemorative inscription on receiver. Made in 1976.

MODEL 760 CARBINE . . . . .NiB $480 Ex $390 Gd $245
Same as Model 760 Rifle except made in calibers .270 Win., .280 Rem., .30-06 and .308 Win. only, has 18.5-inch bbl., weight: 7.25 lbs. Made 1961 to 1980.

MODEL 760 GAMEMASTER
STANDARD GRADE SLIDE-ACTION REPEATING RIFLE
Hammerless. Calibers: .223 Rem., 6mm Rem., .243 Win., .257 Roberts, .270 Win. .280 Rem., .30-06, .300 Sav., .308 Win., .35 Rem. 22-inch bbl. Weight: About 7.5 lbs. Sights: Open rear; bead front, on ramp. Plain pistol-grip stock, grooved slide handle on early models; current production has checkered stock and slide handle. Made from 1952 to 1980.
.222 Rem. . . . . NiB $1195 Ex $1021 Gd $744
.223 Rem. . . . . NiB $1409 Ex $1135 Gd $739
.257 Roberts. . . . . NiB $933 Ex $779 Gd $489
Other calibers . . . . NiB $460 Ex $407 Gd $375

MODEL 760ADL
DELUXE GRADE . . . . NiB $500 Ex $398 Gd $347
Same as Model 760 except has deluxe checkered stock, standard or high comb, grip cap, sling swivels. Made from 1953 to 1963.

MODEL 760BDL
CUSTOM DELUXE . . . . NiB $655 Ex $449 Gd $325
Same as Model 760 Rifle except made in calibers .270, .30-06 and .308 only, has Monte Carlo cheekpiece stock forearm with black tip, basket-weave checkering. Available also in left-hand model. Made from 1953 to 1980.

MODEL 760D
PEERLESS GRADE. . . . . NiB $2589 Ex $1176 Gd $925
Same as Model 760 except scroll engraved, fancy wood. Made from 1953 to 1980.

Remington Model 760
Bicentennial Commemorative

Remington Model 760
Gamemaster

Remington Model 7600 Carbine

Remington Model 7600 Rifle

Remington Nylon 76 Lever-
Action

Remington Sportsman 76

MODEL 760F PREMIER GRADE
Same as Model 760 except extensively engraved with game scenes and scroll, finest grade wood. Also available with receiver inlaid with gold; adds 50 percent to value. Made from 1953 to 1980.
Premier F Grade . . . . NiB $5200 Ex $3288 Gd $2579
Premier Gold F Grade . . . . NiB $7179 Ex $6088 Gd $4439

MODEL 7600 SLIDE-ACTION
CARBINE . . . . NiB $698 Ex $449 Gd $370
Same general specifications as Model 7600 Rifle except has 18.5-inch bbl. and weighs 7.25 lbs. Made from 1987 to date.

MODEL 7600 SLIDE-ACTION RIFLE . . . . NiB $707 Ex $451 Gd $370
Similar to Model Six except has lower grade finishes. Made from 1981 to date.

MODEL 7600 SPECIAL PURPOSE . . . . . . NiB $470 Ex $444 Gd $289
Same general specification as the Model 7600, except chambered only in .270 or .30-06. Special Purpose matte black finish on all exposed metal. American walnut stock with SP non-glare finish.

NYLON 76 LEVER-ACTION REPEATER . . NiB $899 Ex $677 Gd $468
Short-throw lever action. Caliber: .22 LR. 14-round buttstock tubular magazine. Weight: 4 lbs. Black (add $707) or brown nylon stock and forend. Made 1962-64. Remington's only lever-action rifle.

SPORTSMAN 76 SLIDE-ACTION RIFLE . . NiB $375 Ex $300 Gd $200
Caliber: .30-06, 4-round magazine. 22-inch bbl. Weight: 7.5 lbs. Open rear sight; front blade mounted on ramp. Uncheckered hardwood stock and forend. Made from 1985 to 1987.

- SEMIAUTOMATIC RIFLES -

**Remington Sportsman 742
Canadian Centennial**

MODEL FOUR (4) AUTOLOADING RIFLE
Hammerless. Calibers: 6mm Rem., .243 Win., .270 Win. 7mm Express Rem., .30-06, .308 Win. 22-inch bbl. Weight: 7.5 lbs. Sights: Open rear; bead front, on ramp. Monte Carlo checkered stock and forearm. Made from 1981 to 1988.
Standard model . . . . NiB $722 Ex $465 Gd $369
Peerless Grade (engraved receiver) . . . NiB $2219 Ex $1266 Gd $909
Premier Grade (engraved receiver) . . NiB $4155 Ex $3265 Gd $2200
Premier Grade, (engraved receiver,
  gold inlay) . . . . NiB $6544 Ex $5233 Gd $3588

MODEL FOUR DIAMOND
ANNIVERSARY LTD. EDITION . . . . . . NiB $1377 EX $1088 Gd $976
Same as Model Four Standard except has engraved receiver w/inscription, checkered high-grade walnut stock and forend. Only 1,500 produced. Made in 1981 only. (Value for new condition.)

MODEL 8A AUTOLOADING RIFLE . . . . . NiB $766 Ex $645 Gd $473
Standard Grade. Takedown. Calibers: .25, .30, .32 and .35 Rem. Five-round, clip-loaded magazine. 22-inch bbl. Weight: 7.75 lbs. Sights: Adj. and dovetailed open rear; dovetailed bead front. Half-moon metal buttplate on plain straight-grip walnut stock; plain walnut forearm with thin curved end. Made from 1906 to 1936.

MODEL 16 AUTOLOADING RIFLE . . . . . NiB $755 Ex $523 Gd $390
Takedown. Closely resembles the Winchester Model 03 semiautomatic rifle. Calibers: .22 Short, .22 LR, 22 Rem. Auto. 15-round tubular magazine in buttstock. 22-inch bbl. Weight: 5.75 lbs. Sights: Open rear; dovetailed bead front. Plain straight-grip stock and forearm. Made from 1914 to 1928. Note: In 1918 this model was discontinued in all calibers except .22 Rem. Auto; specifications are for that model.

MODEL 24A AUTOLOADING RIFLE . . . . NiB $498 Ex $343 Gd $244
Standard Grade. Takedown. Calibers: .22 Short only, .22 LR. only. Tubular magazine in buttstock, holds 15 Short or 10 LR. 21-inch bbl. Weight: About 5 lbs. Sights: Dovetailed adj. open rear; dovetailed bead front. Plain walnut straight-grip buttstock; plain walnut forearm. Made 1922 to 1935.

MODEL 81A WOODSMASTER
AUTOLOADER . . . . NiB $590 Ex $498 Gd $300
Standard Grade. Takedown. Calibers: .30, .32 and .35 Rem., .300 Sav. Five round box magazine (not detachable). 22-inch bbl. Weight: 8.25 lbs. Sights: Open rear; bead front. Plain walnut pistol-grip stock, forearm. Made from 1936 to 1950.

MODEL 141A SPEEDMASTER
AUTOLOADER . . . . NiB $500 Ex $326 Gd $249
Standard Grade. Takedown. Calibers: .22 Short only, .22 LR. only. Tubular magazine in buttstock, holds 15 Short or 10 LR. 24-inch bbl. Weight: About 6 lbs. Sights: Open rear, bead front. Plain walnut stock and forearm. Made from 1935 to 1951.

MODEL 550A AUTOLOADER . . . . NiB $370 Ex $222 Gd $129
Has "Power Piston" or floating chamber, which permits interchangeable use of 22 Short, Long or LR cartridges. Tubular magazine holds 22 Short, 17 Long, 15 LR. 24-inch bbl. Weight: About 6.25 lbs. Sights: Open rear; bead front. Plain, one-piece pistol-grip stock. Made from 1941 to 1971.

MODEL 550P . . . . NiB $369 Ex $221 Gd $156
Same as Model 550A except has peep rear sight, blade front, on ramp.

MODEL 550-2G . . . . NiB $388 Ex $279 Gd $200
"Gallery Special." Same as Model 550A except has 22-inch bbl., screw eye for counter chain and fired shell deflector.

MODEL 552A SPEEDMASTER
AUTOLOADER . . . . NiB $339 Ex $229 Gd $133
Caliber: .22 Short, Long, LR. Tubular magazine holds 20 Short, 17 Long, 15 LR. 25-inch bbl. Weight: About 5.5 lbs. Sights: Open rear; bead front. Pistol-grip stock, semi-beavertail forearm. Made from 1957 to 1988.

MODEL 552BDL DELUXE . . . . NiB $533 Ex $367 Gd $290
Same as Model 552A except has checkered walnut stock and forearm. Made from 1966 to date.

MODEL 552C CARBINE . . . . NiB $333 Ex $209 Gd $148
Same as Model 552A except has 21-inch bbl. Made 1961 to 1977.

MODEL 552GS GALLERY SPECIAL . . . . . NiB $387 Ex $265 Gd $190
Same as Model 552A except chambered for .22 Short only. Made from 1957 to 1977.

MODEL 740A WOODSMASTER AUTOLOADER
Standard Grade. Gas-operated. Calibers: .30-06 or .308. Four round detachable box magazine. 22-inch bbl. Weight: About 7.5 lbs. Plain pistol-grip stock, semibeavertail forend with finger grooves. Sights: Open rear; ramp front. Made from 1955 to 1959.
Rifle model . . . . NiB $369 Ex $278 Gd $199
Carbine model . . . . NiB $467 Ex $443 Gd $290

MODEL 740ADL/BDL DELUXE
Same as Model 740A except has deluxe checkered stock, standard or high comb, grip cap, sling swivels. Model 740 BDL also has select wood. Made from 1955 to 1960.
Model 740 ADL Deluxe Grade . . . . NiB $480 Ex $572 Gd $410
Model 740 BDL Deluxe Special Grade . . NiB $480 Ex $572 Gd $410

MODEL 742 BICENTENNIAL
COMMEMORATIVE . . . . NiB $588 Ex $380 Gd $355
Same as Model 742 Woodsmaster rifle except has commemorative inscription on receiver. Made in 1976. (Value for new condition.)

MODEL 742 CARBINE . . . . NiB $522 Ex $355 Gd $260
Same as Model 742 Woodsmaster Rifle except made in calibers .30-06 and .308 only, has 18.5-inch bbl., weight 6.75 lbs. Made from 1961 to 1980.

MODEL 742 WOODSMASTER
AUTOMATIC BIG GAME RIFLE . . . . NiB $707 Ex $533 Gd $290
Gas-operated semiautomatic. Calibers: 6mm Rem., .243 Win., .280 Rem., .30-06, .308 Win. Four round clip magazine. 22-inch bbl. Weight: 7.5 lbs. Sights: Open rear; bead front, on ramp. Checkered pistol-grip stock and forearm. Made from 1960 to 1980.

MODEL 742BDL CUSTOM DELUXE . . . . NiB $523 Ex $433 Gd $300
Same as Model 742 Rifle except made in calibers .30-06 and .308 only, Monte Carlo cheekpiece stock, forearm with black tip, basket-weave checkering. Available in left-hand model. Made from 1966 to 1980.

Remington Model 7400

Remington Model 7400 Carbine

Remington Nylon 66
Bicentennial Commemorative

Remington Nylon 66 Mohawk

Remington Sportsman 74

RIFLES

MODEL 742D PEERLESS GRADE . . . . . NiB $2590 Ex $2020 Gd $1100
Same as Model 742 except scroll engraved, fancy wood. Made from 1961 to 1980.

MODEL 742F PREMIER GRADE
Same as Model 742 except extensively engraved with game scenes and scroll, finest grade wood. Also available with receiver inlaid with gold; adds 50 percent to value. Made from 1961 to 1980.
Premier F Grade . . . . NiB $5233 Ex $3288 Gd $2270
Premier Gold F Grade . . . . NiB $7350 Ex $5093 Gd $3466

MODEL 7400 AUTOLOADER
Similar to Model Four w/lower grade finishes. Made from 1981 to date.
Model 7400 Standard . . . . NiB $559 Ex $433 Gd $310
Model 7400 HG
  (High gloss finish) . . . . NiB $559 Ex $433 Gd $310

MODEL 7400 CARBINE . . . . NiB $559 Ex $433 Gd $310
Caliber: .30-06 only. Similar to the Model 7400 rifle except has 18.5-inch bbl. and weight 7.25 lbs. Made from 1988 to date.

MODEL 7400 SPECIAL PURPOSE . . . . . . NiB $476 Ex $434 Gd $289
Same general specification as the Model 7400 except chambered only in .270 or .30-06. Special Purpose matte black finish on metal. American walnut stock with SP nonglare finish. Made 1993 to 1995.

NYLON 66 APACHE BLACK . . . . . NiB $279 Ex $169 Gd $130
Same as Nylon 66 Mohawk Brown listed below except bbl. and receiver cover chrome-plated, black stock. Made 1962 to 1984.

NYLON 66 BICENTENNIAL
COMMEMORATIVE . . . . NiB $597 Ex $433 Gd $259
Same as Nylon 66 Mohawk Brown listed below except has commemorative inscription on receiver. Made 1976 only.

NYLON 66MB AUTOLOADING RIFLE . . NiB $500 Ex $325 Gd $244
Similar to the early production Nylon 66 Black Apache except with blued bbl. and receiver cover. Made from 1978 to 1987.

NYLON 66 MOHAWK
BROWN AUTOLOADER . . . . NiB $450 Ex $278 Gd $230
Caliber: .22 LR. Tubular magazine in buttstock holds 14 rounds. 19.5-inch bbl. Weight: About 4 lbs. Sights: Open rear; blade front. Brown nylon stock and forearm. Made from 1959 to 1987.

NYLON 77 CLIP REPEATER . . . . . NiB $400 Ex $295 Gd $220
Same as Nylon 66 except w/5-round clip magazine. Made 1970 to 1971.

SPORTSMAN 74 AUTOLOADING RIFLE . . . NiB $379 Ex $294 Gd $200
Caliber: .30-06, 4-round magazine. 22-inch bbl. Unchecked buttstock and forend. Open rear sight; ramped blade front sight. Made 1985 to 1988.

GRADING: NiB = New in Box   Ex = Excellent or NRA 95%   Gd = Good or NRA 68%

Rossi Model 62 Stainless Rifle

Rossi Model 62 Stainless Carbine

Rossi Model 62 WMR Rifle

Rossi Model 62 SAC Carbine

Rossi Model 62 Gallery Rifle

JOHN RIGBY & CO. — Paso Robles, California

MODEL 278 MAGAZINE SPORTING RIFLE NiB $6475 Ex $5144 Gd $3576
Mauser action. Caliber: .278 High Velocity or 7x57mm; 5-round box magazine. 25-inch bbl. Weight: about 7.5 lbs. Sights: Folding leaf rear; bead front. Sporting stock w/half-pistol-grip, checkered. Specifications given are those of current model; however, in general, they apply also to prewar model.

**MODEL 278 LIGHTWEIGHT
MAGAZINE RIFLE. . . . . NiB $5110 Ex $4122 Gd $2833**
Same as standard .278 rifle except has 21-inch bbl. Weight: 6.75 lbs.

**MODEL 350 MAGNUM
MAGAZINE SPORTING RIFLE. . . . . . NiB $4332 Ex $3633 Gd $2490**
Mauser action. Caliber: .350 Magnum. Five round box magazine. 24-inch bbl. Weight: About 7.75 lbs. Sights: Folding leaf rear; bead front. Sporting stock with full pistol-grip, checkered. Currently mfd.

**MODEL 416 BIG GAME
MAGAZINE SPORTING RIFLE. . . . . . NiB $7688 Ex $6133 Gd $4286**
Mauser action. Caliber: .416 Big Game. Four round box magazine. 24-inch bbl. Weight: 9 to 9.25 lbs. Sights: Folding leaf rear; bead front. Sporting stock with full pistol-grip, checkered. Currently mfd.

**BEST QUALITY HAMMERLESS
EJECTOR DOUBLE RIFLE . . . . . NiB $73,675 Ex $62,000 Gd $38,550**
Sidelocks. Calibers: .278 Magnum, .350 Magnum, .470 Nitro Express. 24- to 28-inch bbls. Weight: 7.5 to 10.5 lbs. Sights: Folding leaf rear; bead front. Checkered pistol-grip stock and forearm.

**SECOND QUALITY HAMMERLESS
EJECTOR DOUBLE RIFLE . . . . . NiB $13,600 Ex $11,290 Gd $10,375**
Same general specifications as Best Quality double rifle except boxlock.

**THIRD QUALITY HAMMERLESS
EJECTOR DOUBLE RIFLE . . . . . . NiB $11,689 Ex $10,450 Gd $7,800**
Same as Second Quality double rifle except plainer finish and not of as high quality.

ROSS RIFLE CO. — Quebec, Canada

MODEL 1910 BOLT-ACTION SPORTING RIFLE
Straight-pull bolt-action with interrupted screw-type lugs. Calibers: .280 Ross, .303 British. Four round or 5-round magazine. Bbl. lengths: 22, 24, 26 inches. Sights: Two-leaf open rear; bead front. Checkered sporting stock. Weight: About 7 lbs. Made c. 1910 to end of World War I. Note: Most firearm authorities agree that this and other Ross models with interrupted screw-type lugs are unsafe to fire.
Military model . . . . NiB $2175 Ex $1370 Gd $989
Military Match Target model . . . NiB $10,300 Ex $7227 Gd $3590

ROSSI — Sao Leopoldo, Brazil
Currently imported exclusively by BrazTech Int'l. in Miami, FL since 1998; previously by Interarms in Alexandria. VA.

MODEL 62 GALLERY SAC CARBINE
Same as standard Gallery Model except in .22 LR only with 16.25-inch bbl.; weight 5.5 lbs. Imported 1975 to 1998.
Blued finish . . . . NiB $215 Ex $159 Gd $126
Nickel finish. . . . . NiB $220 Ex $163 Gd $130
Stainless. . . . . NiB $220 Ex $163 Gd $130

MODEL 62 GALLERY MAGNUM. . . . . . NiB $235 Ex $200 Gd $135
Same as standard Gallery Model except chambered for .22 WMR, 10-shot magazine. Imported from 1975 to 1998.

Ruger NO.1 Light Sporter

Ruger NO.1 Medium Sporter

Ruger NO.1 "North Americans"

62 GALLERY MODEL SLIDE-ACTION REPEATER

Similar to Winchester Model 62. Calibers: .22 LR, Long, Short or .22 WMR. Tubular magazine holds 13 LR, 16 Long, 20 Short. 23-inch bbl. 39.25 inches overall. Weight: 5.75 lbs. Sights: Open rear; bead front. Straight-grip stock, grooved slide handle. Blued, nickel or stainless finish. Imported 1970 to 1998. Values same as SAC Model.

MODEL 65/92 LEVER-ACTION CARBINE

Similar to Winchester Model 92. Caliber: .38 Special/.357 Mag., .44 Mag., .44-40, .45 LC. 8- or 10-round magazine. 16-, 20- or 24-inch round or half-octagonal bbl. Weight: 5.5 to 6 lbs. 33.5- to 41.5-inches overall. Satin blue, chrome or stainless finish. Brazilian hardwood buttstock and forearm. Made from 1978 to 1998.

.45 LC	NiB $338	Ex $250	Gd $190
.38/.357, .44 Mag.	NiB $338	Ex $250	Gd $190
W/octagon bbl.	NiB $400	Ex $329	Gd $278
LL Lever model.	NiB $510	Ex $396	Gd $280
Engraved, add			$100
Chrome, add			$50
Stainless, add			$50

RUGER — Southport, CT

Manufacturing facilities in Newport, NH, and Prescott, AZ; previously manufactured in Southport, CT.

To facilitate locating Ruger firearms, models are grouped into four categories: Single-shot/lever-action rifles (below), semi-automatic rifles and bolt-action repeating rifles. For a complete listing, please refer to the index.

- SINGLE-SHOT RIFLES / LEVER-ACTION RIFLES -

NO.1 LIGHT SPORTER . . . . NiB $1010 Ex $615 Gd $445
Same as No.1 Standard except has 22-inch bbl., folding leaf rear sight on quarter-rib and ramp front sight, Henry pattern forearm. Made from 1966 to date.

NO.1 MEDIUM SPORTER . . . . NiB $1010 Ex $615 Gd $445
Same as No. 1 Light Sporter except has 26-inch bbl. 22-inch in 45-70); weight: 8 lbs (7.25 lbs. in .45-70). Calibers: 7mm Rem. Mag., .300 Win. Mag., .45-70. Made from 1966 to date.

Stainless model (matte stainless finish, grey laminated stock, made 2001 to 2010). . . . . NiB $980 Ex $480 Gd $400

NO.1 "NORTH AMERICANS"

PRESENTATION RIFLE . . . . NiB $53,950 Ex $43,550 Gd $38,770
Same general specifications as the Ruger No. 1 Standard except highly customized with elaborate engravings, carvings, fine-line checkering and gold inlays. This was a series of 21 rifles depicting a North American big-game animal, chambered in the caliber appropriate to the game. Stock is of Northern California English walnut. Comes in trunk-style Huey case with Leupold scope and other accessories.

NO.1 RSI INTERNATIONAL . . . . NiB $1010 Ex $615 Gd $445
Similar to the No. 1 Light Sporter except with lightweight 20-inch bbl. and full Mannlicher-style forend, in calibers .243 Win., .270 Win., 7x57mm, .30-06. Weight: 7.25 lbs.

NO.1 SPECIAL VARMINTER . . . . NiB $1010 Ex $615 Gd $445
Same as No. 1 Standard except has heavy 24-inch bbl. with target scope bases, no quarter-rib. Weight: 9 lbs. Calibers: .22-250, .25-06, 7mm Rem. Mag., .300 Win. Mag. Made from 1966 to date.
Stainless model (matte stainless finish, grey laminated stock, made 2001 to 2009). . . . . NiB $930 Ex $430 Gd $360

NO.1 STANDARD RIFLE. . . . . NiB $1010 Ex $615 Gd $445
Falling-block single-shot action with Farquharson-type lever. Calibers: .22-250, .243 Win., 6mm Rem., .25-06, .270 Win., .30-06, 7mm Rem. Mag., .300 Win. Mag. 26-inch bbl. Weight: 8 lbs. No sights, has quarter-rib for scope mounting. Checkered pistol-grip buttstock and semibeavertail forearm, QD swivels, rubber buttplate. Made from 1966 to date.
Stainless model (matte stainless finish, grey laminated stock, made 2001 to 2010). . . . . NiB $980 Ex $480 Gd $400

NO.1 TROPICAL RIFLE. . . . . NiB $1010 Ex $615 Gd $445
Same as No. 1 Light Sporter except has heavy 24-inch bbl.; calibers are .375 H&H .404 Jeffery, .416 Rigby, and .458 Win. Mag. Weight: 8.25 to 9 lbs. Made from 1966 to date.
Stainless model (matte stainless finish, grey laminated stock, made 2001 to 2009). . . . . NiB $930 Ex $430 Gd $360

Ruger Number One "North Americans" Presentation Set

Ruger No. 1
International

Ruger No.
1 Special
Varminter

Ruger No. 1
Standard Rifle

Ruger No. 1 Tropical Rifle

Ruger NO.3 Single-Shot Carbine

Ruger Model 10/22 Standard Rifle

Ruger Model 10/22 Deluxe Rifle

Ruger Model 44 Autoloading Carbine

NO.3 CARBINE . . . . NiB $800 Ex $495 Gd $355
Falling-block action with American-style lever. Calibers: .22 Hornet .223 Rem., .30-40 Krag, .357 Win., .44 Mag., .45-70. 22-inch bbl. Weight: 6 lbs. Sights: Folding leaf rear; gold bead front. Carbine-style stock w/curved buttplate, forearm with bbl. band. Made 1972 to 1987.

MODEL 96
Caliber: .22 LR, .22 Mag., .44 Mag. Detachable 10-, 9- or 4-round magazine. 18.5-inch bbl. Weight: 5.25 lbs. Front gold bead sights. Drilled and tapped for scope. American hardwood stock. Made from 1996 to 2008.
96/22 (.22 LR) . . . . NiB $379 Ex $255 Gd $180
96/22M (.22 WMR) . . . . NiB $390 Ex $278 Gd $195
96/44 (.44 Mag.) . . . . NiB $390 Ex $278 Gd $195

- SEMI-AUTOMATIC RIFLES -

MODEL 10/22 CARBINE
Caliber: .22 LR. Detachable 10-round rotary magazine. 18.5-inch bbl. Weight: 5 lbs. Sights: Folding leaf rear; bead front. Carbine-style stock with bbl. band and curved buttplate (walnut stock discontinued 1980). Blued finish. Made from 1964 to date. International and Sporter versions discontinued 1971.
Standard (hardwood stock) . . . . NiB $279 Ex $120 Gd $100
Standard (synthetic stock) . . . . NiB $279 Ex $120 Gd $100
Standard (synthetic stock, LaserMax sight), add $100
Standard (stainless finish) . . . . NiB $310 Ex $130 Gd $110
Standard Sporter (checkered wood stock) . . . NiB $379 Ex $215 Gd $180
Fingergroove Sporter (monte carlo wood stock, 1966-1971) . . . . NiB $679 Ex $455 Gd $380
Fingergroove Sporter (checkered stock), add 30%
International (Mannlicher-style stock, 1966-69) . . . . NiB $680 Ex $460 Gd $375
K-10/22 RB (birch stock, stainless finish) . . NiB $260 Ex $178 Gd $144
Magnum (.22 WMR, 1999-06) . . . . NiB $260 Ex $178 Gd $144
RB (birch stock, blued finish) . . . . NiB $260 Ex $178 Gd $144
RBI International (blued, Mannlicher-style stock, 1994-2003) . . . . NiB $260 Ex $120 Gd $110

RBI International (stainless, Mannlicher-style stock, 1994-2003) . . . . NiB $330 Ex $130 Gd $120
Rifle (20-in. bbl, 2004-06) . . . . NiB $220 Ex $110 Gd $100
SP Deluxe Sporter (intro. 1966) . . . . NiB $260 Ex $178 Gd $144
Tactical (synthetic stock, flash hider 2010-date) . . . . NiB $339 Ex $150 Gd $120
Tactical Target (16.1-in. heavy bbl. w/spiral design, Hogue stock 2010-date) . . . . NiB $599 Ex $280 Gd $240
Takedown (synthetic stock, backpack 2010-date) . . . . NiB $409 Ex $250 Gd $230
Takedown (w/threaded barrel, 2013-date) . NiB $429 Ex $250 Gd $230
Target (20-in. heavy bbl. w/spiral design, blued finish, brown laminated stock, 1996-date) . . . . . NiB $550 Ex $210 Gd $180
Target (20-in. heavy bbl. w/spiral design, stainless finish, black laminated stock, 1996-date) . . . . . NiB $589 Ex $230 Gd $190
Target (thumbhole stock, 2001-02), add $100

MODEL 44
Gas-operated. Caliber: .44 Magnum. Four round tubular magazine (with magazine release button since 1967). 18.5-inch bbl. Weight: 5.75 lbs. Sights: Folding leaf rear; gold bead front. Carbine-style stock w/bbl. band and curved buttplate. Made from 1961 to 1986. International and Sporter versions discontinued 1971.
Standard . . . . NiB $588 Ex $434 Gd $338
International (Mannlicher-style stock) . . . . NiB $944 Ex $597 Gd $488
Sporter (MC stock w/finger groove) . . . . NiB $707 Ex $569 Gd $495
RS (peep rear sight, disc. 1978) . . . . NiB $695 Ex $487 Gd $388

MODEL 99/44 DEERFIELD . . . . NiB $650 Ex $600 Gd $340
Similar to Model 44 except w/four-round rotary detachable box magazine, rotating bolt w/dual front locking lugs, integral scope mount. Made from 2000 to 2006.

MINI-14
Gas-operated. Caliber: .223 Rem. 5-, 10- or 20-round box magazine. 18.5-inch bbl. Weight: About 6.5 lbs. Sights: Peep rear;

Ruger Model 77 Round Top Receiver

Ruger Model 77 Ultra-Light Carbine

Ruger Model 77 International Carbine

Ruger Model 77 Varmint Rifle

Ruger Model 77 Mark II All-Weather Rifle

blade front mounted on removable barrel band. Pistol-grip stock w/curved buttplate, handguard. Made from 1974 to 2004.
Blued finish . . . . NiB $725 Ex $579 Gd $375
K-Mini-14/S stainless steel. . . . . NiB $815 Ex $580 Gd $444
Mini-14/5F w/blued finish,
  folding stock . . . . NiB $1144 Ex $995 Gd $790
K-Mini-14/SF w/stainless finish,
  folding stock . . . . NiB $855 Ex $690 Gd $545

MINI-14 RANCH RIFLE
Similar to Mini-14 except w/receiver machined for scope mounts. Recent manufacture chambered in 5.56mm NATO. Weight: 7 lbs. Made from 1982 to date.
Blued finish . . . . NiB $939 Ex $630 Gd $550
Blued finish (polymer stock), add. $15
Stainless finish . . . . NiB $979 Ex $680 Gd $580
Stainless finish (folding stock), add $350
Stainless finish (polymer stock) . . . . NiB $979 Ex $680 Gd $580
Stainless finish (6.8SPC, 2007-11) . . . . . NiB $979 Ex $680 Gd $580

MINI-14 TARGET . . . . NiB $1199 Ex $780 Gd $650
Similar to Mini-14 Ranch Rifle except w/22-in. stainless heavy bbl. w/harmonic stabilizer, thumbhole stock. Made from 2007 to date.
w/Hogue synthetic stock . . . . NiB $1199 Ex $780 Gd $650

MINI-14 TACTICAL. . . . . NiB $1019 Ex $680 Gd $550
Similar to Mini-14 Ranch Rifle except w/16.1-in. bbl. w/flash hider, synthetic stock. Weight: 6.75 lbs. Made from 2009 to date.
w/folding stock. . . . . NiB $1019 Ex $680 Gd $550

MINI-THIRTY
Similar to Mini-14 except chambered in 7.62 x 39mm. 5-round detachable magazine. 18.5-inch bbl. 37.25 inches overall. Weight: 7 lbs. 3 oz. Designed for use with telescopic sights. Walnut stained stock. Sights: Peep rear; blade front mounted on bbl. band. Blued or stainless finish. Made from 1987 to 2004.
Blued finish. . . . . NiB $625 Ex $439 Gd $300
Stainless finish. . . . . NiB $815 Ex $545 Gd $360
Stainless finish (polymer stock,
  1990 to date) . . . . NiB $979 Ex $730 Gd $580

PC SERIES SEMIAUTOMATIC CARBINES
Calibers: 9mm Parabellum or .40 S&W. 10-round magazine. 15.25-inch bbl. Weight: 6.25 lbs. Integral Ruger scope mounts with or without sights. Optional blade front sight, adjustable open rear. Matte black oxide finish. Matte black Zytel stock w/checkered pistol-grip and forearm. Made from 1997 to date.
Model PC9 (no sights). . . . . NiB $510 Ex $440 Gd $300
Model PC4 (no sights). . . . . NiB $545 Ex $467 Gd $333
w/adjust. sights, add $50

Ruger Model 77 Mark II

Ruger Model 77/.22 Rimfire

Ruger Model 77/.22
All Weather

Ruger Model 77/.44
All Weather

SR-556/SR-556 CARBINE . . . . . NiB $2049 EX $900 GD $800
Semi-automatic AR15 platform w/gas piston system. Caliber: 5.56mm NATO. 10-, 25- or 30-round magazine. 16.1-in. bbl., adj. gas block, Troy folding sights, fixed or collapsible buttstock. Weight: 7.9 lbs. Made 2009 to date.
6.8mm SPC (2010-2011)NiB $2049 EX $900 GD $800
SR-556VT (20-in. bbl., A2 buttstock, Mappul grip
  2013-date) . . . . NiB $2049 Ex $900 Gd $800

SR-762 CARBINE . . . . .NiB $2269 EX $1280 GD $1050
Semi-automatic AR15 platform w/gas piston system. Caliber: 7.62mm NATO. 20-round magazine. 16.1-in. bbl., adj. gas block, adj. folding sights, collapsible buttstock. Weight: 8.6 lbs. Made 2013 to date.

- BOLT-ACTION RIFLES -

MODEL 77 BOLT-ACTION RIFLE
Receiver with integral scope mount base or with round top. Short stroke or magnum length action (depending on caliber) in the former type receiver, magnum only in the latter. .22-250, .220 Swift, 6mm Rem., .243 Win., .250-3000, .25-06, .257 Roberts, 6.5 Rem. Mag., .270 Win., 7x57mm, 7mm-08 7mm Rem. Mag., .280 Rem., .284 Win., .308 Win., .30-06, .300 Win. Mag. .338 Win. Mag., .350 Rem. Mag., .458 Win. Mag. Five round magazine standard, 4-round in .220 Swift, 3-round in magnum calibers. 22 24- or 26-inch bbl. (depending on caliber). Weight: About 7 lbs.; .458 Mag. model, 8.75 lbs. Round-top model furnished w/folding leaf rear sight and ramp front;

integral base model furnished w/scope rings,with or w/o open sights. Stock w/checkered pistol grip and forearm, pistol-grip cap, rubber recoil pad, QD swivel studs. Made from 1968 to 1992.

	NiB	Ex	Gd
Model 77 w/integral base, no sights	$500	$408	$321
6.5 Rem. Mag., add			$100
.284 Win., add			$50
.338 Win. Mag., add			$75
.350 Rem. Mag., add			$75
Model 77RL Ultra Light, w/no sights	$545	$438	$290
Model 77RL Ultra Light, w/open sights	$569	$454	$331
Model 77RS w/integral base, open sights	$569	$454	$331
.338 Win. Mag., .458 Win. Mag., standard stock, add			$100
Model 77RSC, .458 Win. Mag., w/walnut stock, add			$126
w/fancy grade Circassian walnut stock, add			$707
Model 77RSI International w/Mannlicher stock, short action, 18.5-inch bbl.	$675	$466	$339
Model 77ST w/round top, open sights	$575	$439	$369
.338 Win. Mag., add			$75
Model 77V Varmint w/integral base, no sights	$588	$466	$300
Model 77 NV Varmint w/integral base, no sights, stainless steel bbl., laminated wood stock	$593	$468	$379

MODEL 77 MARK II ALL-WEATHER RIFLE NiB $535 Ex $430 Gd $315
Revised Model 77 action. Same general specifications as Model M-77

Ruger Model 96/22 Lever-Action

Ruger Model 96/44 Lever-Action

Ruger Mini-14 Semiautomatic

Ruger Mini-14 with Folding Stock

Ruger Mini-Thirty Autoloader

Ruger Model PC9 Carbine

Ruger Model PC9 w/Ghost Ring Sights

Mark II except with stainless bbl. and action. Zytel injection-molded stock. Calibers: .223, .243, .270, .308, .30-06, 7mm Mag., .300 Win. Mag., .338 Win. Mag. Made from 1999 to 2008.

MODEL 77 MARK II BOLT-ACTION RIFLE
Revised Model 77 action. Same general specifications as Model M-77 except with new 3-position safety and fixed blade ejector system. Calibers .22 PPC, .223 Rem., 6mm PPC, 6.5x55 Swedish, .375 H&H, .404 Jeffery and .416 Rigby also available. Weight: 6 to 10.25 lbs. Made from 1989 to 2012.

MKIIR w/integral base, no sights . . . . NiB $545 Ex $423 Gd $314
Left-hand model, add $50
MKII RL Ultralight, no sights . . . . . . NiB $545 Ex $423 Gd $314
MKII RLS w/open sights . . . . NiB $545 Ex $423 Gd $314
MKII RS w/integral base, open sights. . . . . . . NiB $545 Ex $423 Gd $314
MKII RS Express w/fancy grade French walnut stock, integral base,
   open sights . . . . NiB $1347 Ex $1116 Gd $835
MKII RSI International Mannlicher . . . . . NiB $799 Ex $479 Gd $368
MKII RSM Magnum w/fancy grade Circassian walnut stock,
   integral base, open sights . . . . NiB $1465 Ex $1143 Gd $870
77VT (VBZ or VTM) MKII
   Varmint/Target w/stainless steel action,
   laminated wood stock . . . . NiB $480 Ex $403 Gd $288

MODEL 77 GUNSITE SCOUT . . . . . NiB $1075 EX $480 GD $400
Similar to Model 77 Mark II except w/16.5-in. bbl. w/flash hider, 10-shot detacable box magazine, .308 Win. only, forward scope mount, blued finish, laminated stock w/spacers. Weight: 7 lbs. Made from 2011 to date.
Blued finish (composite stock). . . . . NiB $1075 Ex $480 Gd $400
Stainless finish . . . . NiB $1139 Ex $640 Gd $520
Stainless finish (composite stock) . . . . . NiB $1139 Ex $640 Gd $520

MODEL 77/22 HORNET . . . . NiB $556 EX $445 Gd $339
Mini-Sporter built on the 77/.22 action in caliber .22 Hornet. Six round rotary magazine. 20- inch bbl. 40 inches overall. Weight: 6 lbs. Receiver machined for Ruger rings (included). Beaded front sight and open adj. rear, or no sights. Blued or stainless finish. Checkered American walnut stock. Made from 1994 to date.
Model 77/22RH (rings, no sights) . . . . . . NiB $625 Ex $470 Gd $369
Model 77/22RSH (rings & sights) . . . . . . NiB $625 Ex $470 Gd $369
Model 77/22VHZ (stainless finish,
   laminated wood stock) . . . . NiB $735 Ex $544 Gd $390

MODEL 77/22 RIMFIRE BOLT-ACTION RIFLE
Calibers: .22 LR or .22 WMR. 10-shot (.22 LR) or 9-shot (.22 WMR) rotary magazine. 20-inch bbl. 39.75 inches overall. Weight: 5.75 lbs. Integral scope bases; with or w/o sights. Checkered American walnut or Zytel injection-molded stock. Stainless or blued finish. Made 1983 to date. (Blued); stainless. Introduced 1989.
77/22R w/scope rings, no sights, walnut stock . .NiB $625 Ex $544 Gd $390
77/22RS w/scope rings, sights, walnut stock . .NiB $625 Ex $544 Gd $390
77/22RP w/scope rings, no sights, synthetic stock . .NiB $625 Ex $544 Gd $390
77/22RSP w/scope rings, sights, synthetic stock . .NiB $625 Ex $544 Gd $390
K77/22RP w/stainless scope rings, no sights,
   synthetic stock . . . . .NiB $625 Ex $544 Gd $390
K77/22RSP w/stainless scope rings, sights,
   synthetic stock . . . . .NiB $625 Ex $544 Gd $390
77/22RM (.22 WMR) w/scope rings,no sights,
   walnut stock .NiB $625 Ex $544 Gd $390
K77/22RSMP (.22 WMR) w/stainless scope rings, sights,
   synthetic stock. . . . . .NiB $735 Ex $579 Gd $437
K77/22RMP (.22 WMR) w/stainless scope rings, sights, synthetic
   stock. . . . . .NiB $625 Ex $544 Gd $390
K77/22 VBZ (.22 WMR) w/no sights, laminated stock
   (intro. 1993) . . . . NiB $735 Ex $579 Gd $437

MODEL 77/44
Short-action, carbine-style M77 similar to the 77/22RH. Chambered .44 Rem. Mag. Four round rotary magazine. 18.5-inch bbl. 38.25 inches overall. Weight: 6 lbs. Gold bead front sight, folding adjustable rear w/integral scope base and Ruger rings. Blue or stainless finish. Synthetic or checkered American walnut stock w/rubber buttpad and swivels. Made from 1997 to 2004.
Blued finish . . . . .NiB $625 Ex $544 Gd $390
Stainless finish . . . . .NiB $555 Ex $350 Gd $245

AMERICAN RIFLE
Three-lug push-feed bolt w/70-degree bolt lift, short or long action, integral scope mount, adj. trigger, black polymer stock, flush-fit rotary magzine, no sights. Calibers: .223 Rem., .22-250, .243 Win., .270 Win., 7mm-08, .308 Win., or .30-06. 22-inch bbl. (depending on caliber). Weight: 6.1 to 6.4 lbs. Made 2012 to date.
Standard (blued finish) . . . . NiB $459 Ex $280 Gd $250
All-Weather (22-in. bbl., stainless finish). NiB $595 Ex $320 Gd $280
All-Weather Compact (18-in. bbl.,
   stainless finish). . . . . .NiB $595 Ex $320 Gd $280
Compact (18-in. bbl., blued finish) . . . . . NiB $459 Ex $280 Gd $250

AMERICAN RIFLE RIMFIRE
Push-feed bolt w/60-degree bolt lift, integral scope mount, adj. trigger, black modular polymer stock w/adj. LOP, 22-in. bbl., 9- or 10-round flush-fit rotary magzine, no sights, blued finish. Calibers: .17 HMR, .22 LR, .22 Mag. Weight: 5.5 to 6 lbs. Made 2013 to date.
Standard. NiB $339 Ex $190 Gd $150
Compact (18-in. bbl.) . . . . NiB $339 Ex $190 Gd $150
w/threaded barrel, add $30

GUIDE GUN
Similar to Model HM77 Hawkeye except w/20-in. stainless bbl. w/muzzle brake, adj. sights, laminated stock, matte stainless finish. Weight: 8.15 lbs. Made from 2013 to date.
Standard (blued finish) . . . . NiB $939 Ex $320 Gd $270

MODEL HM77 HAWKEYE
Revised Model 77 Mark II action w/same general specifications except w/Mauser style controlled feed, LC6 trigger, one-piece stainless bolt, integral scope base. no sights. Weight: 7 to 8.25 lbs. Made from 2007 to date.
Standard (blued finish) . . . . NiB $939 Ex $320 Gd $270
African (adj. sights, wood stock w/ebony tip, blued finish,
   2007-12). NiB $939 Ex $400 Gd $370
African (muzzle brake, adj. sights, wood stock w/ebony tip blued
   finish, 2013-date) . . . . NiB $939 Ex $400 Gd $370
Alaskan (adj. sights, Hogue overmold stock stainless finish, 2007-12)
   NiB $939 Ex $400 Gd $370
All-Weather (synthetic stock stainless finish)NiB $939 Ex $320 Gd $270
All-Weather Ultra Light (6.5 lbs., synthetic stock stainless finish,
   2009 only) . . . . NiB $580 Ex $330 Gd $280
Compact (walnut stock, 16.5-in. bbl., blue finish, 2009-date)NiB $939
   Ex $320 Gd $270
Compact Laminate (laminate stock, 16.5-in. bbl., stainless finish,
   2009-date) . . . . NiB $999 Ex $420 Gd $270
International (adj. sights, Mannlicher checkered stock matet blue finish,
   2009-10) . . . . NiB $755 Ex $430 Gd $350
Laminated (laminated stock, stainless finish,
   2008-10) . . . . NiB $939 Ex $400 Gd $370
Magnum Hunter (Hogue green overmold stock, stainless finish,
   24-in. bbl. w/muzzle brake, .300 Win. Mag. only,
   2013-date) . . . . NiB $1139 Ex $530 Gd $455

RIFLES

Sako Model 73

Sako Model 74 Carbine

Sako Model 74 Super Sporter

Sako Model 74 Super Rimfire

Sako Model 75 Hunter

Sako 75 Stainless Synthetic

Sako Model 75 Varmint Rifle

Sako Classic

Sako Deluxe Lightweight

Sako Fiberglass

Sako Finnfire

Sako Finnfire Heavy Barrel

Sako Finnwolf

Predator (22- or 24-in. heavy bbl., laminated stock, stainless finish,2009-date) . . . . NiB $1069 Ex $430 Gd $370
Sporter (22- or 24-in. bbl., brown or black laminate stock matte stainless finish, 2009-13) . . . . . . NiB $765 Ex $320 Gd $270
Tactical (22-in. heavy bbl., Hogue black overmold stock, Harris bipod,matte blue finish, 2009-13)NiB $1050 Ex $650 Gd $580
Ultra Light (6.5 lbs., 20-in. bbl., no sights, walnut stock blue finish, 2009-10) . . . . NiB $695 Ex $410 Gd $360

RUSSIAN MILITARY RIFLES — Tula, Russia
Principal U.S.S.R. Arms Plant, Tula.

MODEL 1891
MOSIN MILITARY RIFLE . . . . NiB $485 Ex $269 Gd $187
Nagant system bolt action. Caliber: 7.62mm Russian. Five round box magazine. 31.5-inch bbl. Weight: About 9 lbs. Sights: Open rear; blade front. Full stock w/straight grip. Specifications given are for WWII version; earlier types differ slightly. Note: In 1916, Remington Arms Co. and New England Westinghouse Co. produced 250,000 of these rifles on a contract from the Imperial Russian Government. Few were delivered to Russia and the balance bought by the U.S. Government for training in 1918. Eventually, many of these rifles were sold to N.R.A. members for about $3 each by the Director of Civilian Marksmanship.

TOKAREV MODEL 40 SEMIAUTOMATIC
MILITARY RIFLE . . . . NiB $844 Ex $438 Gd $270

Gas-operated. Caliber: 7.62mm Russian. 10-round detachable box magazine. 24.5-inch bbl. Muzzle brake. Weight: About 9 lbs. Sights: Leaf rear, hooded post front. Full stock w/pistol grip. Differences among Models 1938,1940 and 1941 are minor.

SAKO — Riihimaki, Finland
Manufactured by Sako L.T.D. Formerly imported by Stoeger Industries, Wayne NJ (formerly by Garcia Corp.) until 2000. Imported by Beretta USA 2001 to date.

MODEL 72 . . . . NiB $1090 Ex $865 Gd $660
Single model designation replacing Vixen Sporter, Vixen Carbine, Vixen Heavy Barrel, Forester Sporter, Forester Carbine, Forester Heavy Barrel, Finnbear Sporter, and Finnbear Carbine, with same specifications, except all but heavy barrel models fitted with open rear sight. Values same as for corresponding earlier models. Imported from 1972 to 1974.

MODEL 73 LEVER-ACTION RIFLE . . . . . NiB $1670 Ex $988 Gd $690
Same as Finnwolf except has 3-round clip magazine, flush floorplate; stock has no cheekpiece. Imported from 1973 to 1975.

MODEL 74 CARBINE . . . . NiB $1141 Ex $735 Gd $600
Long Mauser-type bolt action. Caliber: .30-06. Five round magazine. 20-inch bbl. Weight: 7.5 lbs. No sights. Checkered Mannlicher-type full stock of European walnut, Monte Carlo cheekpiece. Imported from 1974 to 1978.

GRADING: **NiB** = New in Box   **Ex** = Excellent or NRA 95%   **Gd** = Good or NRA 68%

Sako Forester Sporter

Sako Golden Anniversary

Sako Hunter Lightweight

**MODEL 74 HEAVY BARREL RIFLE,
LONG ACTION** . . . . **NiB $1165 Ex $755 Gd $634**
Same specifications as short action except w/24-inch heavy bbl., weighs 8.75 lbs.; magnum w/4-round magazine. Calibers: .25-06, 7mm Rem. Mag. Imported from 1974 to 1978.

**MODEL 74 HEAVY BARREL RIFLE,
MEDIUM ACTION** . . . . **NiB $1165 Ex $755 Gd $634**
Same specifications as short action except w/23-inch heavy bbl., weighs 8.5 lbs. Calibers: .220 Swift, .22-250, .243 Win., .308 Win. Imported from 1974 to 1978.

**MODEL 74 HEAVY BARREL RIFLE,
SHORT ACTION.** . . . . **NiB $1195 Ex $909 Gd $650**
Mauser-type bolt action. Calibers: .222 Rem., .223 Rem. Five round magazine. 23.5-inch heavy bbl. Weight: 8.25 lbs. No sights. Target-style checkered European walnut stock w/beavertail forearm. Imported from 1974 to 1978.

**MODEL 74 SUPER SPORTER,
LONG ACTION** . . . . **NiB $1165 Ex $755 Gd $634**
Same specifications as short action except w/24-inch bbl., weight: 8 lbs.; magnums have 4-round magazine, recoil pad. Calibers: .25-06, .270 Win. 7mm Rem. Mag., .30-06, .300 Win. Mag., .338 Win. Mag., .375 H&H Mag. Imported from 1974-78.

**MODEL 74 SUPER SPORTER,
MEDIUM ACTION** . . . . **NiB $1175 Ex $910 Gd $659**
Same specifications as short action except weight: 7.25 lbs. Calibers: .220 Swift, .22-250, .243 Win. Imported from 1974-78.

**MODEL 74 SUPER SPORTER,
SHORT ACTION.** . . . . **NiB $1175 Ex $910 Gd $659**
Mauser-type bolt action. Calibers: .222 Rem., .223 Rem. Five round magazine. 23.5-inch bbl. Weight: 6.5 lbs. No sights. Checkered European walnut stock w/Monte Carlo cheekpiece, QD swivel studs. Imported 1974. Disc.

MODEL 75 DELUXE . . . . **NiB $1190 Ex $944 Gd $690**
Same specifications as Sako 75 Hunter Model except w/hinged floor plate, deluxe high gloss checkered walnut stock w/rosewood forend cap and grip cap w/silver inlay. Imported from 1998-2006. Disc.

MODEL 75 HUNTER . . . . **NiB $1260 Ex $833 Gd $665**
New bolt action design available in four action lengths fitted with a new bolt featuring three front locking lugs with an external extractor positioned under the bolt. Calibers: .17 Rem., .222 Rem., .223 Rem., (I); .22-250 Rem., .243 Win., 7mm-08 Rem., .308 Win., (III); .25-06 Rem., .270 Win., .280 Rem., .30-06, (IV); 7mm Rem Mag., .300 Win. Mag., .300 Wby. Mag., .338 Win. Mag. 7mm STW, .300 Wby. Mag., .340 Wby. Mag., .375 H&H Mag. and .416 Rem. Mag.,(V). 4-, 5- or 6-round magazine w/ detachable magazine. 22-, 24-, and 26-inch bbls. 41.75 to 45.6 inches over all. Weight: 6.3 to 9 lbs. Sako dovetail scope base integral with receiver with no sights. Checkered high-grade walnut stock w/recoil pad and sling swivels. Made from 1997 to 2006.

MODEL 75 STAINLESS SYNTHETIC. . . . . **NiB $1279 Ex $877 Gd $685**
Similar to Model 75 Hunter except chambered for .22-250 Rem., .243 Win., .25-06 Rem., .270 Win., 7mm-08 Rem., 7mm STW, .30-06, .308 Win., 7mm Rem Mag., .300 Win. Mag., .338 Win. Mag. or .375 H&H Mag. 22-, 24-, and 26-inch bbls. Black composite stock w/soft rubber grips inserts. Matte stainless steel finish. Made from 1997 to 2006.

MODEL 75 VARMINT RIFLE . . . . **NiB $1471 Ex $835 Gd $656**
Similar to Model 75 Hunter except chambered .17 Rem., .222 Rem., .223 Rem. and .22-250 Rem. 24-inch bbl. Matte lacquered walnut stock w/beavertail forearm. Made from 1998 to 2006.

MODEL 78 SUPER HORNET SPORTER . . **NiB $654 Ex $535 Gd $338**
Same specifications as Model 78 Rimfire except chambered for .22 Hornet, 4-round magazine. Imported from 1977 to 1987.

MODEL 78 SUPER RIMFIRE SPORTER . . . **NiB $587 Ex $466 Gd $338**
Bolt action. Caliber: .22 LR. Five round magazine. 22.5-inch bbl. Weight, 6.75 lbs. No sights. Checkered European walnut stock, Monte Carlo cheekpiece. Imported from 1977 to 1986.

MODEL 85 CLASSIC BOLT-ACTION RIFLE
Calibers: .25-06 Rem., .270 Win., .30-06, .308 Win., .300 Win. Mga., .338 Win. Mag. .370 Sako Mag., .375 H&H Mag.., .270 WSM., .300 WSM., 7mm Mag. detachable mag., single stage trigger, pistol grip, checkered walnut stock. Weight: 7 lbs. New 2009.

Sako Mannlicher-Style Carbine

Sako Sporter Deluxe

Sako TRG-21
Target Rifle

Standard calibers . . . . NiB $1937 Ex $1216 Gd $1019
Magnum caliber, add $126

DELUXE GRADE AI . . . . .NiB $1266 Ex $870 Gd $633
Same specifications as Standard Grade except w/22 lines to the inch
French checkering, rosewood grip cap and forend tip, semibeavertail
forend. Disc.

DELUXE GRADE AII . . . . .NiB $1145 Ex $790 Gd $556
Same specifications as Standard Grade except w/22 lines per inch
French checkering, rosewood grip cap and forend tip, semi beavertail
forend. Disc.

DELUXE GRADE AIII . . . . .NiB $1482 Ex $1188 Gd $766
Same specifications as w/standard except w/French checkering, rosewood grip cap and forend tip, semibeavertail forend. Disc.

**DELUXE LIGHTWEIGHT
BOLT-ACTION RIFLE** . . . . NiB $1190 Ex $1021 Gd $699
Same general specifications as Hunter Lightweight except w/beau-
tifully grained French walnut stock; superb high-gloss finish, fine
hand-cut checkering, rosewood forend tip and grip cap. Imported
from 1985-97.

**FIBERCLASS BOLT-ACTION
RIFLE** . . . . NiB $1137 Ex $1077 Gd $650
All-weather fiberglass stock version of Sako barreled long action.
Calibers: .25-06, .270, .30-06, 7mm Rem. Mag., .300 Win. Mag., .338
Win. Mag., .375 H&H Mag. Bbl. length: 22.5 inches. Overall length:
44.25 inches. Weight: 7.25 lbs. Imported 1984 to 1996.

FINNBEAR CARBINE . . . . .NiB $1190 Ex $926 Gd $572
Same as Finnbear Sporter except w/20-inch bbl., Mannlicher-type full
stock. Imported 1971. Disc.

FINNBEAR SPORTER . . . . .NiB $1190 Ex $926 Gd $572
Long Mauser-type bolt action. Calibers: .25-06, .264 Mag. .270, .30-
06, .300 Win. Mag., .338 Mag., 7mm Mag., .375 H&H Mag. Magazine
holds 5 standard or 4 magnum cartridges. 24-inch bbl. Weight: 7 lbs.
Hooded ramp front sight. Sporter stock w/Monte Carlo cheekpiece,
checkered pistol-grip and forearm, recoil pad, swivels. Imported from
1961 to 1971.

FINNFIRE BOLT-ACTION RIFLE
Mini-Sporter built for rimfires on a scaled-down Sako design. Caliber:
.22 LR. 5- or 10-round magazine. 22-inch bbl. 39.5 inches overall.
Weight: 5.25 lbs. Receiver machined for 11mm dovetail scope rings.
Beaded blade front sight, open adj. rear. Blued finish. Checkered
European walnut stock. Imported from 1994 to 2005.
Hunter model. . . . . NiB $926 Ex $694 Gd $533
Varmint model . . . . NiB $988 Ex $696 Gd $580
Sporter model. . . . . NiB $1027 Ex $866 Gd $613

FINNWOLF LEVER-ACTION RIFLE . . . . . . .NiB $975 Ex $733 Gd $621
Hammerless. Calibers: .243 Win., .308 Win. Four round clip magazine.
23-inch bbl. Weight: 6.75 lbs. Hooded ramp front sight. Sporter stock w/
Monte Carlo cheekpiece, checkered pistol-grip and forearm, swivels (available w/right- or left-hand stock). Imported 1963 to 1972.

GRADING: **NiB** = New in Box   **Ex** = Excellent or NRA 95%   **Gd** = Good or NRA 68%

Sako TRG-S Bolt-Action Rifle

Sako Vixen Heavy Barrel

Sako Vixen Sporter

FINNSPORT 2707. . . . . .NiB $808 Ex $597 Gd $466
Bolt-action centerfire rifle. Calibers: .270, .30-06, 7mm Rem. Mag., .300 Win. Mag. Bbl. length: 24 inches. Weight: 8 lbs. Imported 1984 to 1986.

FORESTER CARBINE. . . . . .NiB $1116 Ex $924 Gd $550
Same as Forester Sporter except w/20-inch bbl., Mannlicher-type full stock. Imported from 1958 to 1971.

FORESTER HEAVY BARREL . . . . .NiB $1423 Ex $988 Gd $713
Same as Forester Sporter except w/24-inch heavy bbl. Weight 7.5 lbs. Imported from 1958 to 1971.

FORESTER SPORTER. . . . . .NiB $1141 Ex $1015 Gd $559
Medium-length Mauser-type bolt action. Calibers: .22-250, .243 Win., .308 Win. Five round magazine. 23-inch bbl. Weight: 6.5 lbs. Hooded ramp front sight. Sporter stock w/Monte Carlo cheekpiece, checkered pistol grip and forearm, swivels. Imported 1957 to 1971.

GOLDEN ANNIVERSARY MODEL . . . NiB $2866 Ex $2210 Gd $1570
Special presentation-grade rifle issued in 1973 to commemorate Sako's 50th anniversary. 1,000 (numbered 1 to 1,000) made. Same specifications as Deluxe Sporter: Long action, 7mm Rem. Mag. receiver, trigger guard and floorplate decorated w/gold oak leaf and acorn motif. Stock of select European walnut, checkering bordered w/hand-carved oak leaf pattern.

HIGH-POWER MAUSER SPORTING RIFLE . . NiB $1154 Ex $1043 Gd $831
FN Mauser action. Calibers: .270, .30-06. Five round magazine. 24-inch bbl. Sights: Open rear leaf; Partridge front; hooded ramp. Checkered stock w/Monte Carlo comb and cheekpiece. Weight: 7.5 lbs. Imported from 1950 to 1957.

HUNTER LIGHTWEIGHT BOLT-ACTION RIFLE
5- or 6-round magazine. Bbl. length: 21.5 inches, AI; 22 inches, AII; 22.5 inches, AIII. Overall length: 42.25-44.5 inches. Weight: 5.75 lbs., AI; 6.75 lbs. AII; 7.25 lbs., AIII. Monte Carlo-style European walnut stock, oil finished. Hand-checkered pistol-grip and forend. Imported from 1985-97. Left-hand version intro. 1987.
AI (Short Action) .17 Rem. . . . . NiB $1466 Ex $1224 Gd $1018
.222 Rem., .223 Rem. . . . . NiB $1088 Ex $831 Gd $589
AII (Medium Action) .22-250 Rem.,
   .243 Win., .308 Win. . . . . NiB $976 Ex $798 Gd $543
AII (Long Action) .25-06 Rem.
   .270 Win., .30-06 . . . . .NiB $978 Ex $792 Gd $553
.338 Win. Mag. . . . . .NiB $1154 Ex $976 Gd $735
.375 H&H Mag. . . . . .NiB $1266 Ex $1044 Gd $766
Left-hand model (standard cal.). . . . . . .NiB $1294 Ex $1088 Gd $773

Magnum calibers . . . . .NiB $1590 Ex $1277 Gd $945

LAMINATED STOCK BOLT-ACTION RIFLES
Similar in style and specifications to Hunter Grade except w/stock of resin-bonded hardwood veneers. Available 18 calibers in AI (Short), AII (Medium) or AV action, left-hand version in 10 calibers, AV only. Imported from 1987 to 1995.
Short or medium action . . . . . . .NiB $1043 Ex $899 Gd $577
Long action/Magnum . . . . .NiB $1108 Ex $902 Gd $645

MAGNUM MAUSER . . . . .NiB $1588 Ex $1244 Gd $909
Similar specifications as Standard Model except w/recoil pad and redesigned longer AIII action to handle longer magnum cartridges. Calibers: .300 H&H Magnum, .375 H&H Magnum, standard at time of introduction. Disc.

MANNLICHER-STYLE CARBINE
Similar to Hunter Model except w/full Mannlicher-style stock and 18.5-inch bbl. Weighs 7.5 lbs. Chambered in .243, .25-06, .270, .308, .30-06, 7mm Rem. Mag., .300 Win. Mag., .338 Win. Mag., .375 H&H. Intro. in 1977. Disc.
Standard calibers . . . . NiB $1287 Ex $1021 Gd $734
Magnum calibers (except .375) . . . . . . NiB $1338 Ex $1055 Gd $733
.375 H&H . . . . NiB $1370 Ex $1094 Gd $790

SAFARI GRADE . . . . .NiB $2576 Ex $1988 Gd $1166
Classic bolt-action. Calibers: .300 Win. Mag., .338 Win. Mag., .375 H&H. Oil-finished European walnut stock w/hand-checkering. Barrel band swivel, express-type sight rib; satin or matte blue finish. Imported from 1980 to 1996.

SPORTER DELUXE . . . . .NiB $1290 Ex $1045 Gd $687
Same as Vixen, Forester, Finnbear and Model 74 except w/fancy French walnut stock w/skip checkering, rosewood forend tip and pistol-grip cap, recoil pad, inlaid trigger guard and floorplate. Disc.

STANDARD GRADE AI . . . . .NiB $1077 Ex $823 Gd $440
Short bolt-action. Calibers: .17 Rem., .222 Rem., .223 Rem. Five round magazine. 23.5-inch bbl. Weight: 6.5 lbs. No sights. Checkered European walnut stock w/ Monte Carlo cheekpiece, QD swivel studs. Imported 1978 to 1985.

STANDARD GRADE AII . . . . . . .NiB $1090 Ex $840 Gd $456
Medium bolt-action. Calibers: .22-250 Rem., .243 Win., .308 Win. 23.5-inch bbl. in .22-250; 23-inch bbl. in other calibers. Five round magazine.

Weight: 7.25 lbs. Checkered European walnut stock w/Monte Carlo cheekpiece, QD swivel studs. Imported from 1978 to 1985.

STANDARD GRADE AIII . . . . NiB $1178 Ex $843 Gd $545
Long bolt action. Calibers: .25-06 Rem., .270 Win., .30-06, 7mm Rem. Mag., .300 Win. Mag., .338 Win. Mag., .375 H&H. 24-inch bbl. 4-round magazine. Weight: 8 lbs. Imported from 1978 to 1984.

SUPER DELUXE RIFLE . . . . NiB $2544 Ex $2210 Gd $1347
Available in AI, AII, AIII calibers. Select European walnut stock, hand-checkered, deep oak leaf hand-engraved design. Disc.

TRG BOLT-ACTION TARGET RIFLE
Caliber: .308 Win., .330 Win. or .338 Lapua Mag. Detachable 10-round magazine. 25.75- or 27.2-inch bbl. Weight: 10.5 to 11 lbs. Blued action w/ stainless barrel. Adjustable two-stage trigger. modular reinforced polyurethane target stock w/adj. cheekpiece and buttplate. Options: Muzzle break; detachable bipod; QD sling swivels and scope mounts w/1-inch or 30mm rings. Imported from 1993 to 2004.
TRG 21 .308 Win. . . . . NiB $2376 Ex $2099 Gd $1545
TRG 22 .308 Win. . . . . NiB $2459 Ex $2288 Gd $1590

TRG 41 .338 Lapua . . . . NiB $2788 Ex $2690 Gd $1877
TRG-42 (.300 Win Mag. or .338 Lapua) NiB $3154 Ex $2651 Gd $1835

TRG-S BOLT-ACTION RIFLE
Calibers: .243, 7mm-08, .270, .30-06, 7mm Rem. Mag., .300 Win. Mag., .338 Win. Mag. Five shot magazine (standard calibers), 4-shot (magnum), 22- or 24-inch bbl. 45.5 inches overall. Weight: 7.75 lbs. No sights. Reinforced polyurethane stock w/Monte Carlo. Introduced in 1993.
Standard calibers . . . . NiB $823 Ex $707 Gd $466
Magnum calibers . . . . NiB $880 Ex $844 Gd $545

VIXEN CARBINE . . . . NiB $1096 Ex $954 Gd $868
Same as Vixen Sporter except w/20-inch bbl., Mannlicher-type full stock. Imported from 1947 to 1971.

VIXEN HEAVY BARREL . . . . NiB $1110 Ex $933 Gd $545
Same as Vixen Sporter except calibers .222 Rem., .222 Rem. Mag., .223 Rem., heavy bbl., target-style stock w/beavertail forearm. Weight: 7.5 lbs. Imported from 1947-71.

VIXEN SPORTER . . . . NiB $1100 Ex $969 Gd $546
Short Mauser-type bolt-action. Cals.: .218 Bee, .22 Hornet, .222 Rem., .222 Rem. Mag., .223 Rem. Five round magazine. 23.5-inch bbl. Weight: 6.5 lbs. Hooded ramp front sight. Sporter stock w/Monte Carlo cheekpiece, checkered pistol-grip and forearm, swivels. Imported from 1946 to 1971.

J. P. SAUER & SOHN — Eckernforde, Germany

Formerly Suhl, Germany. Imported by Sigarms Exeter, NH, previously by Paul Company Inc. and G.U. Inc.

MAUSER BOLT-ACTION
SPORTING RIFLE . . . . NiB $1457 Ex $1089 Gd $777
Calibers: 7x57 and 8x57mm most common, but these rifles were produced in a variety of calibers including most of the popular Continental calibers as well as our .30-06. Five round box magazine. 22- or 24-inch Krupp steel bbl., half-octagon w/raised matted rib. Double-set trigger. Weight: 7.5 lbs. Sights: Three-leaf open rear; ramp front. Sporting stock w/ cheekpiece, checkered pistol grip, raised side-panels, Schnabel tip, swivels. Also made w/20-inch bbl. and full-length stock. Mfd. before WWII.

MODEL S-90 BOLT-ACTION RIFLES
Calibers: .243 Win., .308 Win. (Short action); .25-06, .270 Win., .30-06 (Medium action); 7mm Rem. Mag., .300 Win. Mag., .300 Wby., .338 Win., .375 H&H (Magnum action). Four round (standard) or 3-round magazine (magnum). Bbl. length: 20-inch (Stutzen), 24-inch. Weight: 7.6 to 10.75 lbs. Adjustable (Supreme) checkered Monte Carlo style stock. contrasting forend and pistol grip cap w/high-gloss finish or European (Lux) checkered Classic-style European walnut stock w/satin oil finish. Imported from 1983 to 1989.
S-90 Standard. . . . . NiB $1154 Ex $990 Gd $587
S-90 Lux . . . . NiB $1389 Ex $1100 Gd $654
S-90 Safari . . . . NiB $1411 Ex $1127 Gd $665
S-90 Stutzen. . . . . NiB $1144 Ex $994 Gd $482
S-90 Supreme. . . . . NiB $1490 Ex $1167 Gd $800
Grade I engraving, add $650
Grade II engraving, add . . . . $850Grade III engraving add $1200
Grade IV engraving, add $1717

MODEL 200 BOLT-ACTION RIFLES
Calibers: .243 Win., .25-06, .270 Win., 7mm Rem Mag., .30-06, .308 Win., .300 Win. Mag., Detachable box magazine. 24-inch (American) or 26-inch (European) interchangeable bbl. Standard (steel) or lightweight (alloy) action. Weight: 6.6 to 7.75 lbs. 44 inches overall. Stock options: American Model w/checkered Monte Carlo style 2-piece stock contrasting forend and pistol grip cap w/high gloss finish and no sights. European walnut stock w/Schnabel forend, satin oil finish and iron sights. Contemporary Model w/synthetic carbon fiber stock. Imported from 1986 to 1993.
Standard model . . . . NiB $1266 Ex $1093 Gd $707
Lightweight model . . . . NiB $1278 Ex $1043 Gd $580
Contemporary model . . . . NiB $1260 Ex $1017 Gd $565
American model. . . . . NiB $1260 Ex $1017 Gd $565
European model . . . . NiB $1395 Ex $1070 Gd $532
Left-hand model, add $200
Magnum calibers, add $130
Interchangeable barrel assembly, add $325

MODEL 202 BOLT-ACTION RIFLES
Calibers: .243 Win., 6.5x55, 6.5x57, 6.6x68, .25-06, .270 Win., .280 7x64, .308, .30-06, Springfield, 7mm Rem. Mag., .300 Win. Mag., .300 Wby. Mag. 8x68S, .338 Win. Mag., .375 H&H Mag. Removable 3-round box magazine. 23.6- and 26-inch interchangable bbl. 44.3 and 46 inches overall. Modular receiver drilled and tapped for scope bases. Adjustable two-stage trigger w/dual release safety. Weight: 7.7 to 8.4 lbs. Stock options: Checkered Monte Carlo-style select American walnut two-piece stock; Euro-classic French walnut two-piece stock w/semi Schnabel forend and satin oil finish; Super Grade Claro walnut two-piece stock fitted w/rosewood forend and grip cap w/high-gloss epoxy finish. Imported from 1994 to 2004.
Standard model . . . . NiB $2660 Ex $1848 Gd $983
Euro-Classic model . . . . NiB $1369 Ex $897 Gd $633
Super Grade model. . . . . NiB $1119 Ex $888 Gd $603
Left-hand model, add $150
Magnum calibers, add $126
Interchangeable barrel assembly, add $295

SAVAGE ARMS — Westfield, MA
Formerly Chicopee Falls, MA, and Utica, NY. Acquired by ATK in 2013.

MODEL 3 BOLT-ACTION
SINGLE-SHOT RIFLE. . . . . NiB $100 Ex $61 Gd $59
Takedown. Caliber: .22 Short, Long, LR. 26-inch bbl. on prewar rifles, postwar production w/24-inch bbl. Weight: 5 lbs. Sights: Open rear; bead front. Plain pistol-grip stock. Made 1933 to 1952.

Savage Model 3

Savage Model 4

Savage Model 5

Savage Model 6

Savage Model 19 NRA (1933)

Savage Model 20

MODEL 3S . . . . **NiB $116 Ex $89 Gd $59**
Same as Model 3 except w/peep rear sight, hooded front. Made 1933 to 1942.

MODEL 3ST . . . . **NiB $120 Ex $85 Gd $50**
Same as Model 3S except fitted w/swivels and sling. Made from 1933 to 1942.

MODEL 4 BOLT-ACTION REPEATER . . . . . **NiB $149 Ex $90 Gd $59**
Takedown. Caliber: .22 Short, Long, LR. Five round detachable box magazine. 24-inch bbl. Weight: 5.5 lbs. Sights: Open rear; bead front. Checkered pistol-grip stock on prewar models, early production had grooved forearm; postwar rifles have plain stocks. Made from 1933 to 1965.

MODEL 4M . . . . **NiB $121 Ex $87 Gd $64**
Same as Model 4 except chambered for .22 Rimfire Magnum. Made from 1961 to 1965.

MODEL 4S . . . . **NiB $130 Ex $78 Gd $47**
Same as Model 4 except w/peep rear sight, hooded front. Made from 1933 to 1942.

MODEL 5 BOLT-ACTION
REPEATER . . . . **NiB $126 Ex $78 Gd $57**
Same as Model 4 except w/tubular magazine (holds 21 Short, 17 Long, 15 LR), weight: 6 lbs. Made from 1936 to 1961.

MODEL 5S . . . . **NiB $135 Ex $77 Gd $50**
Same as Model 5 except w/peep rear sight, hooded front. Made 1936 to 1942.

MODEL 6 AUTOLOADING RIFLE . . . . **NiB $169 Ex $94 Gd $57**
Takedown. Caliber: .22 Short, Long, LR. Tubular magazine holds 21 Short, 17 Long, 15 LR. 24-inch bbl. Weight: 6 lbs. Sights: Open rear; bead front. Checkered pistol-grip stock on prewar models, postwar rifles have plain stocks. Made from 1938 to 1968.

MODEL 6S . . . . **NiB $170 Ex $95 Gd $48**
Same as Model 6 except w/peep rear sight, bead front. Made 1938 to 1942.

MODEL 7 AUTOLOADING RIFLE . . . . **NiB $167 Ex $105 Gd $59**
Same general specifications as Model 6 except w/5-round detachable box magazine. Made from 1939 to 1951.

Savage Model 23AA

Savage Model 29

Savage Model 40

Savage Model 45

MODEL 7S. . . . .**NiB $167 Ex $105 Gd $62**
Same as Model 7 except w/peep rear sight, hooded front. Made from 1938 to 1942.

MODEL 19 BOLT-ACTION TARGET RIFLE. . . **NiB $325 Ex $270 Gd $209**
Model of 1933. Speed lock. Caliber: .22 LR. Five round detachable box magazine. 25-inch bbl. Weight: 8 lbs. Adj. rear peep sight, blade front on early models, later production equipped w/extension rear sight, hooded front. Target stock w/ full pistol-grip and beavertail forearm. Made 1933 to 1946.

MODEL 19 NRA BOLT-ACTION
MATCH RIFLE . . . .**NiB $300 Ex $205 Gd $126**
Model of 1919. Caliber: .22 LR. Five round detachable box magazine. 25-inch bbl. Weight: 7 lbs. Sights: Adj. rear peep; blade front. Full military stock w/pistol-grip. Made from 1919 to 1933.

MODEL 19H . . . .**NiB $575 Ex $340 Gd $265**
Same as standard Model 19 (1933) except chambered for .22 Hornet, w/Model 23D-type bolt mechanism, loading port and magazine. Made from 1933 to 1942.

MODEL 19L. . . . .**NiB $348 Ex $290 Gd $185**
Same as standard Model 19 (1933) except equipped w/Lyman No. 48Y receiver sight, 17A front sight. Made from 1933 to 1942.

MODEL 19M . . . .**NiB $356 Ex $465 Gd $227**
Same as standard Model 19 (1933) except w/heavy 28-inch bbl. w/ scope bases, weight: 9.25 lbs. Made from 1933 to 1942.

MODEL 20-1926
HI-POWER. . . . .**NiB $944 Ex $725 Gd $420**
Same as Model 1920, listed on page 354, except w/24-inch medium weight bbl., improved stock, Lyman 54 rear peep sight, weight: 7 lbs. Made from 1926 to 1929.

MODEL 23A BOLT-ACTION
SPORTING RIFLE . . . .**NiB $270 Ex $208 Gd $177**
Caliber: 22 LR. Five round detachable box magazine. 23-inch bbl. Weight: 6 lbs. Sights: Open rear, blade or bead front. Plain pistol-grip stock w/slender forearm and Schnabel tip. Made 1923 to 1933.

MODEL 23AA . . . .**NiB $370 Ex $278 Gd $200**
Model of 1933. Improved version of Model 23A w/same general specifications except w/speed lock, improved stock, weighs 6.5 lbs. Made from 1933-42.
MODEL 23B. . . . .**NiB $333 Ex $235 Gd $179**
Same as Model 23A except caliber .25-20, 25-inch bbl. Model of 1933 w/ improved stock w/full forearm instead of slender forearm w/Schnabel found on earlier production. Weight: 6.5 lbs. Made from 1923 to 1942.

MODEL 23C. . . . .**NiB $389 Ex $290 Gd $175**
Same as Model 23B except caliber .32-20. Made 1923 to 1942.

MODEL 23D . . . .**NiB $415 Ex $300 Gd $220**
Same as Model 23B except caliber .22 Hornet. Made 1933 to 1947.
MODEL 25 SLIDE-ACTION REPEATER. . . **NiB $346 Ex $391 Gd $237**
Takedown. Hammerless. Caliber: .22 Short, Long, LR. Tubular magazine holds 20 Short, 17 Long, 15 LR. 24-inch octagon bbl. Weight: 5.75 lbs. Sights: Open rear; blade front. Plain pistol-grip stock, grooved slide handle. Made from 1925 to 1929.

MODEL 29 SLIDE-ACTION
REPEATER . . . .**NiB $500 Ex $380 Gd $265**
Takedown. Hammerless. Caliber: .22 Short, Long, LR. Tubular magazine holds 20 Short, 17 Long, 15 LR. 24-inch bbl., octagon on prewar, round on postwar production. Weight: 5.5 lbs. Sights: Open rear; bead front. Stock w/ checkered pistol grip and slide handle on prewar, plain stock and grooved forearm on postwar production. Made from 1929 to 1967.

Savage Model 60

Savage Model 63K

Savage Model 71 "Stevens Favorite"

**MODEL 40 BOLT-ACTION
SPORTING RIFLE** . . . .**NiB $379 Ex $280 Gd $227**
Standard Grade. Calibers: .250-3000, .300 Sav., .30-30, .30-06. Four round detachable box magazine. 22-inch bbl. in calibers .250-3000 and .30-30; 24-inch in .300 Sav. and .30-06. Weight: 7.5 lbs. Sights: Open rear; bead front, on ramp. Plain pistol-grip stock w/tapered forearm and Schnabel tip. Made 1928 to 1940.

MODEL 45 SUPER SPORTER. . . . .**NiB $423 Ex $265 Gd $220**
Special Grade. Same as Model 40 except w/checkered pistol-grip and forearm, Lyman No. 40 receiver sight. Made 1928 to 1940.

MODEL 60 AUTOLOADING RIFLE . . . .**NiB $115 Ex $80 Gd $48**
Caliber: .22 LR. 15-round tubular magazine. 20-inch bbl. Weight: 6 lbs. Sights: Open rear, ramp front. Monte Carlo stock of walnut w/checkered pistol-grip and forearm. Made from 1969 to 1972.

**MODEL 63K KEY LOCK BOLT-ACTION
SINGLE-SHOT RIFLE.** . . . .**NiB $120 Ex $90 Gd $60**
Trigger locked w/key. Caliber: .22 Short, Long, LR. 18-inch bbl. Weight: 4 lbs. Sights: Open rear; hooded ramp front. Full-length stock w/pistol grip, swivels. Made from 1970 to 1972.

MODEL 63KM . . . .**NiB $126 Ex $98 Gd $63**
Same as Model 63K except chambered for .22 WMR. Made 1970 to 1972.

MODEL 64F AUTOLOADING RIFLE . . . . .**NiB $173 Ex $128 Gd $99**
Same general specifications as Model 64G except w/black graphite/polymer stock. Weight: 5 lbs. Made from 1997 to date.

MODEL 64G AUTOLOADING RIFLE. NiB $177 Ex $126 Gd $100
Caliber: 22 LR. 10-round magazine. 20-inch bbl. Weight: 5.5 lbs. 40 inches overall. Sights: Adj. open rear; bead front. Grooved receiver for scope mounts. Stamped checkering on walnut-finished hardwood stock w/Monte Carlo cheekpiece. Made from 1996 to date.

**MODEL 71 "STEVENS FAVORITE"
SINGLE-SHOT LEVER-ACTION RIFLE** . . . . **NiB $229 Ex $114 Gd $98**

Replica of original Stevens Favorite issued as a tribute to Joshua Stevens, "Father of .22 Hunting." Caliber: .22 LR. 22-inch full-octagon bbl. Brass-plated hammer and lever. Sights: Open rear; brass blade front. Weight: 4.5 lbs. Plain straight-grip buttstock and Schnabel forend; brass commemorative medallion inlaid in buttstock, brass crescent-shaped buttplate. 10,000 produced. Made in 1971 only. Top value is for new, unfired gun.

**MODEL 90 AUTO-LOADING
CARBINE** . . . .**NiB $194 Ex $161 Gd $126**
Similar to Model 60 except w/16.5-inch bbl. w/folding leaf rear sight, bead front. 10-round tubular magazine. Uncheckered, carbine-style walnut stock w/bbl. Band and sling swivels. Weight: 5.75 lbs. Made from 1969 to 1972.

MODEL 93G BOLT-ACTION RIFLE . . . . .**NiB $227 Ex $166 Gd $126**
Caliber: .22 Win Mag. 5-round magazine. 20.75-inch bbl. 39.5 inches overall. Weight: 5.75 lbs. Sights: Adj. open rear; bead front. Grooved receiver for scope mounts. Stamped checkering on walnut-finished hardwood stock w/Monte Carlo cheekpiece. Made from 1996 to date.

MODEL 93F BOLT-ACTION RIFLE . . . . .**NiB $277 Ex $124 Gd $110**
Same general specifications as Model 93G except w/black graphite/polymer stock. Weight: 5.2 lbs. Made from 1997 to date.

NOTE: MODEL 99 LEVER-ACTION REPEATER
Introduced in 1899, this model has been produced in a variety of styles and calibers. Original designation "Model 1899" was changed to "Model 99" c.1920. Earlier rifles and carbines — similar to Models 99A, 99B and 99H — were supplied in calibers .25-35, .30-30, .303 Sav., .32-40 and .38-55. Post-WWII Models 99A, 99C, 99DE, 99DL, 99F and 99PE have top tang safety other 99s have slide safety on right side of trigger guard. Models 99C and 99CD have detachable box magazine instead of traditional Model 99 rotary magazine.

MODEL 99A (I). . . . .**NiB $1015 Ex $768 Gd $545**
Hammerless. Solid frame. Calibers: .30-30, .300 Sav., .303 Sav. Five-round rotary magazine. 24-inch bbl. Weight: 7.25 lbs. Sights: Open

Savage Model 90

Savage Model 99A 1971 Issue

Savage Model 99C

Savage Model 99CD

Savage Model 99DE

rear; bead front, on ramp. Plain straight-grip stock, tapered forearm. Made from 1920 to 1936.

MODEL 99A (II) . . . . **NiB $915 Ex $668 Gd $445**
Current model. Similar to original Model 99A except w/top tang safety, 22-inch bbl., folding leaf rear sight, no crescent buttplate. Calibers: .243 Win., .250 Sav., .300 Sav., .308 Win. Made from 1971 to 1982.

MODEL 99B. . . . . **NiB $1245 Ex $938 Gd $577**
Takedown. Otherwise same as Model 99A except weight: 7.5 lbs. Made from 1920 to 1936.

MODEL 99C. . . . . **NiB $560 Ex $488 Gd $399**
Current model. Same as Model 99F except w/clip magazine instead of rotary. Calibers: .243 Win., .284 Win., .308 Win. Four round detachable magazine holds one round less in .284. Weight: 6.75 lbs. Made from 1965-98.

MODEL 99CD . . . . **NiB $698 Ex $599 Gd $389**
Deluxe version of Model 99C. Calibers: .243 Win., .250 Sav., .308 Win. Hooded ramp front sight. Weight: 8.25 lbs. Stock w/Monte Carlo comb and cheekpiece, checkered pistol-grip, grooved forearm, swivels and sling. Made from 1975 to 81.

MODEL 99DE CITATION
GRADE . . . . **NiB $955 Ex $679 Gd $495**
Same as Model 99PE except w/less elaborate engraving. Made from 1968-70.

MODEL 99DL DELUXE. . . . . **NiB $745 Ex $576 Gd $359**
Postwar model. Calibers: .243 Win., .308 Win. Same as Model 99F, except w/high comb Monte Carlo stock, sling swivels. Weight: 6.75 lbs.

GRADING: **NiB** = New in Box   **Ex** = Excellent or NRA 95%   **Gd** = Good or NRA 68%

Savage Model 99E 1969 Issue

Savage Model 99EG (Post WWII)

Savage Model 99F

Savage Model 99G

Savage Model 99PE Early Issue

Savage Model 99PE Late Issue

Made from 1960-73.

MODEL 99E CARBINE (I) . . . . . . **NiB $656 Ex $500 Gd $439**
Pre-WWII type. Solid frame. Calibers: .22 Hi-Power, .250/3000, .30/30, .300 Sav., .303 Sav. w/22-inch bbl.; .300 Sav. 24-inch. Weight: 7 lbs. Other specifications same as Model 99A. Made from 1920-36.

MODEL 99E CARBINE (II) . . . . . . **NiB $709 Ex $505 Gd $457**
Current model. Solid frame. Calibers: .250 Sav., .243 Win., .300 Sav., .308 Win. 20- or 22-inch bbl. Checkered pistol-grip stock and forearm. Made from 1960-89.

MODEL 99EG (I) . . . . **NiB $877 Ex $687 Gd $476**
Pre-WWII type. Solid frame. Plain pistol-grip stock and forearm. Otherwise same as Model G. Made from 1936 to 1941.

MODEL 99EG (II) . . . . **NiB $1023 Ex $799 Gd $600**
Post-WWII type. Same as prewar model except w/checkered stock and forearm. Calibers: .250 Sav., .300 Sav., .308 Win. (intro. 1955), .243 Win., and .358 Win. Made from 1946 to 1960.

MODEL 99F
FEATHERWEIGHT (I) . . . . **NiB $813 Ex $707 Gd $514**
Pre-WWII type. Takedown. Specifications same as Model 99E, except weight: 6.5 lbs. Made 1920 to 1942. Some marked 99M.

MODEL 99F
FEATHERWEIGHT (II) . . . . **NiB $945 Ex $735 Gd $567**
Postwar model. Solid frame. Calibers: .243 Win., .300 Sav., .308 Win. 22-inch bbl. Checkered pistol-grip stock and forearm. Weight: 6.5 lbs. Made from 195 to 1973.

MODEL 99G . . . . **NiB $1290 Ex $933 Gd $707**
Takedown. Checkered pistol-grip stock and forearm. Weight: 7.25 lbs. Other specifications same as Model 99E. Made 1920 to 1942.

Savage Model 99R (Pre-WWII)

Savage Model 99R (Post-WWII)

Savage Model 99RS (Pre-WWII)

Savage Model 99T

Savage Model 110

Savage Model 110B

MODEL 99H CARBINE . . . . NiB $926 Ex $577 Gd $4455
Solid frame. Calibers: .250/3000, .30/30, .303 Sav. 20-inch special weight bbl. Walnut carbine stock w/metal buttplate; walnut forearm w/ bbl. band. Weight: 6.5 lbs. Open rear sights; ramped blade front sight. Other specifications same as Model 99A. Made 1931 to 1942.

MODEL 99K . . . . NiB $3854 Ex $2650 Gd $2128
Deluxe version of Model G w/similar specifications except w/fancy stock and engraving on receiver and bbl. Lyman peep rear sight and folding middle. Made from 1931 to 1942.

MODEL 99PE PRESENTATION GRADE . NiB $2055 Ex $1717 Gd $854
Same as Model 99DL except w/engraved receiver (game scenes on sides), tang

and lever, fancy walnut Monte Carlo stock and forearm w/hand checkering, QD swivels. Calibers: .243, .284, .308. Made 1968 to 1970.

MODEL 99R (I). . . . . NiB $735 Ex $588 Gd $499
Pre-WWII type. Solid frame. Calibers: .250-3000 (22-inch bbl.), .300 Sav. (24-inch bbl.). Weight: 7.5 lbs. Special large pistol-grip stock and forearm, checkered. General specifications same as other Model 99 rifles. Made from 1936 to 1942.

MODEL 99R (II) . . . . NiB $689 Ex $498 Gd $356
Post-WWII type. Same as prewar mod except w/24-inch bbl. only, w/ screw eyes for sling swivels. Calibers: .250 Sav., .300 Sav., .308 Win., .243 Win. and .358 Win. Made from 1946 to 1960.

Savage Model 110BL

Savage Model 110C

Savage Model 110E

Savage Model 110 MCL

Savage Model 110P

Savage Model 110PE

Savage Model 111 Chieftain

Savage Model 111F

Savage Model 112V

Savage Model 116FCSAK

MODEL 99RS (I) . . . .**NiB $944 Ex $650 Gd $489**
Pre-WWII type. Same as prewar Model 99R except equipped w/Lyman rear peep sight and folding middle sight, quick detachable swivels and sling. Made from 1932 to 1942.

MODEL 99RS (II) . . . .**NiB $756 Ex $600 Gd $467**
Post-WWII type. Same as postwar Model 99RS except equipped w/Redfield 70LH receiver sight, blank in middle sight slot. Made from 1946 to 1960.

MODEL 99T . . . .**NiB $1707 Ex $1032 Gd $744**
Featherweight. Solid frame. Calibers: .22 Hi-Power, .30/30, .303 Sav. w/20-inch bbl.; .300 Sav. w/22-inch bbl. Checkered pistol-grip stock and beavertail forearm. Weight: 7 lbs. General specifications same as other Model 99 rifles. Made from 1936 to 1942.

MODEL 99-358 . . . .**NiB $1156 Ex $903 Gd $657**
Similar to current Model 99A except caliber .358 Win. has grooved forearm, recoil pad, swivel studs. Made from 1977 to 1980.

**MODEL 110 SPORTER
BOLT-ACTION RIFLE** . . . .**NiB $420 Ex $333 Gd $155**
Calibers: .243, .270, .308, .30-06. Four round box magazine. 22-inch bbl. Weight: About 6.75 lbs. Sights: Open rear; ramp front. Standard sporter stock with checkered pistol-grip. Made from 1958 to 1963.

MODEL 110B BOLT-ACTION RIFLE
Same as Model 110E except with checkered select walnut Monte Carlo-style stock (early models) or brown laminated stock (late models). Calibers: .243 Win., .270 Win. .30-06, 7mm Rem. Mag., .338 Win. Mag. Made from 1976 to 1991.
Early model . . . .**NiB $423 Ex $303 Gd $227**
Laminated stock model . . . .**NiB $367 Ex $299 Gd $211**

MODEL 110BL . . . .**NiB $439 Ex $369 Gd $269**
Same as Model 110B except has left-hand action.

MODEL 110C
Calibers: .22-250, .243, .25-06, .270, .308, .30-06, 7mm Rem. Mag., .300 Win. Mag. Four round detachable clip magazine (3-round in Magnum calibers). 22-inch bbl. (24-inch in .22-250 Magnum calibers). Weight: 6.75 lbs., Magnum, 7.75 to 8 lbs. Sights: Open rear; ramp front. Checkered Monte Carlo-style walnut stock (Magnum has recoil pad). Made from 1966 to 1988.
Standard calibers . . . .**NiB $468 Ex $413 Gd $239**
Magnum calibers . . . .**NiB $639 Ex $455 Gd $279**

MODEL 110CL
Same as Model 110C except has left-hand action. (Available only in .243 Win., .30-06, .270 Win. and 7mm Mag.) Made 1963 to 1966.
Standard calibers . . . .**NiB $488 Ex $369 Gd $262**
Magnum calibers . . . .**NiB $459 Ex $350 Gd $255**

**MODEL 110CY
YOUTH/LADIES RIFLE** . . . .**NiB $466 Ex $379 Gd $228**
Same as Model 110G except with walnut-finished hardwood stock with 12.5-inch pull. Calibers: .243 Win. and .300 Savage. Made from 1991 to 2009.

MODEL 110D
Similar to Model 110C except has internal magazine with hinged floorplate. Calibers: .243 Win., .270 Win., .30-06, 7mm Rem. Mag., .300 Win. Mag. Made from 1972 to 1988.
Standard calibers . . . .**NiB $390 Ex $310 Gd $240**
Magnum calibers . . . .**NiB $453 Ex $390 Gd $259**

MODEL 110DL
Same as Model 110D except has left-hand action. Discontinued.

GRADING: NiB = New in Box   **Ex** = Excellent or NRA 95%   **Gd** = Good or NRA 68%

Savage Model 170C Carbine

Savage Model 219

Savage Model 219L

Standard calibers . . . . .NiB $500 Ex $413 Gd $297
Magnum calibers . . . . .NiB $535 Ex $430 Gd $319
MODEL 110E . . . . .NiB $379 Ex $255 Gd $198
Calibers: .22-250, .223 Rem., .243 Win., .270 Win., .308, 7mm Rem. Mag., .30-06. Four round box magazine (3-round in Magnum). 20- or 22-inch bbl. (24-inch stainless steel in Magnum). Weight: 6.75 lbs.; Magnum, 7.75 lbs. Sights: Open rear; ramp front. Plain Monte Carlo stock on early production; current models have checkered stocks of walnut-finished hardwood (Magnum has recoil pad). Made 1963 to 1989.

MODEL 110EL . . . . .NiB $370 Ex $248 Gd $185
Same as Model 110E except has left-hand action made in .30-06 and 7mm Rem. Mag. only. Made from 1969 to 1973.

MODEL 110F/110K BOLT-ACTION RIFLE
Same as Model 110E except Model 110F has black Rynite synthetic stock, swivel studs; made 1988 to 1993. Model 110K has laminated camouflage stock; made from 1986 to 1988.
adj. sights. . . . . NiB $770 Ex $470 Gd $359
w/out sights . . . . NiB $735 Ex $355 Gd $277
Standard calibers . . . . NiB $355 Ex $320 Gd $256
Magnum calibers . . . . NiB $520 Ex $399 Gd $287

MODEL 110FM SIERRA ULTRA LIGHT . . NiB $376 Ex $336 Gd $244
Calibers: .243 Win., .270 Win., .30-06, .308 Win. Five round magazine. 20-inch bbl. 41.5 inches overall. Weight: 6.25 lbs. No sights w/drilled and tapped receiver. Black graphite/fiberglass composition stock. Non-glare matte blue finish. Made 1996 to date.

MODEL 110FP POLICE RIFLE . . . .NiB $610 Ex $355 Gd $265
Calibers: .223, .308 Win. Four round magazine. 24-inch bbl. 45.5 inches overall. Weight: 9 lbs. Black Rynite composite stock. Matte blue finish. Made 1990 to date.

MODEL 110G BOLT-ACTION RIFLE
Calibers: .223, .22-250, .243 Win., .270, 7mm Rem. Mag., .308 Win., .30-06, .300 Win. Mag. Five round (standard) or 4-round magazine (magnum).

22- or 24-inch bbl. 42.38 overall (standard). Weight: 6.75 to 7.5 lbs. Ramp front sight, adj. rear. Checkered walnut-finished hardwood stock with rubber recoil pad. Made from 1989 to 1993.
Standard calibers . . . . NiB $408 Ex $309 Gd $220
Magnum calibers . . . . NiB $455 Ex $338 Gd $259
Left-hand, no sights . . . . NiB $355 Ex $369 Gd $271

MODEL 110GV VARMINT RIFLE. . . . . . . NiB $369 Ex $338 Gd $268
Similar to the Model 110G except fitted with medium-weight varmint bbl. with no sights. Receiver drilled and tapped for scope mounts. Calibers .22-250 and .223 only. Made from 1989-93.

MAGNUM 110M MAGNUM . . . . .NiB $445 Ex $345 Gd $269
Same as Model 110MC except calibers: 7mm Rem. Mag. .264, .300 and .338 Win. 24-inch bbl. Stock with recoil pad. Weight: 7.75 to 8 lbs. Made from 1963 to 1969.

MODEL 110MC . . . . .NiB $444 Ex $229 Gd $149
Same as Model 110 except has Monte Carlo-style stock. Calibers: .22-250, .243 Win., .270, .308, .30-06. 24-inch bbl. in .22-250. Made from 1959 to 1969.
Model 110MCL . . . . NiB $400 Ex $215 Gd $135

MODEL 110P PREMIER GRADE
Calibers: .243 Win., 7mm Rem. Mag., .30-06. Four round magazine (3-round in Magnum). 22-inch bbl. (24-inch stainless steel in Magnum). Weight: 7 lbs.; Magnum, 7.75 lbs. Sights: Open rear folding leaf; ramp front. French walnut stock w/Monte Carlo comb and cheekpiece, rosewood forend tip and pistol-grip cap, skip checkering, sling swivels (Magnum has recoil pad). Made 1964 to 1970.
Calibers .243 Win. and .30-06 . . .NiB $798 Ex $645 Gd $459
Caliber 7mm Rem. Mag . . . . .NiB $945 Ex $765 Gd $545

MODEL 110PE PRESENTATION GRADE
Same as Model 110P except has engraved receiver, floorplate and trigger guard, stock of choice grade French walnut. Made 1968 to 1970.
Calibers .243 Win. and .30-06 . . .NiB $555 Ex $441 Gd $290

Savage Model 340

Savage Model 340C Carbine

Savage Model 1895 Replica

Caliber 7mm Rem. Mag . . . . NiB $600 Ex $455 Gd $347

MODEL 110PEL PRESENTATION GRADE
Same as Model 110PE except has left-hand action.
Calibers .243 Win. and .30-06 . . . NiB $807 Ex $654 Gd $458
Caliber 7mm Rem. Mag . . . . NiB $879 Ex $710 Gd $496

MODEL 110PL PREMIER GRADE
Same as Model 110P except has left-hand action.
Calibers .243 Win. and .30-06 . . . NiB $528 Ex $401 Gd $271
Caliber 7mm Rem. Mag . . . . NiB $549 Ex $401 Gd $293

MODEL 110S/110V
Same as Model 110E except Model 110S in .308 Win. only; discontinued 1985. Model 110V in .22-250 and .223 Rem. w/heavy 2-inch barrel, 47 inches overall, weight: 9 lbs. Discontinued. 1989.
Model 110S . . . . NiB $397 Ex $315 Gd $240
Model 110V . . . . NiB $416 Ex $322 Gd $248

MODEL 111 CHIEFTAIN BOLT-ACTION RIFLE
Calibers: .243 Win., .270 Win., 7x57mm, 7mm Rem. Mag. .30-06. 4-round clip magazine (3-round in Magnum). 22-inch bbl. (24-inch in Magnum). Weight: 7.5 lbs., 8.25 lbs. Magnum. Sights: Leaf rear; hooded ramp front. Select walnut stock w/Monte Carlo comb and cheekpiece, checkered, pistol-grip cap, QD swivels and sling. Made from 1974 to 1979.
Standard calibers . . . . NiB $444 Ex $389 Gd $259
Magnum calibers . . . . NiB $445 Ex $398 Gd $279

MODEL 111F, 11FC, 111FNS CLASSIC HUNTER RIFLE
Similar to the Model 111G except with graphite/fiberglass composite stock. Weight: 6.25 lbs. Made from 1994 to date.
Model 111F (right- or left-hand w/box mag.) NiB $498 Ex $411 Gd $238
Model 111FC (w/detachable mag.) . . . . . NiB $448 Ex $338 Gd $206

Model 111FNS (right- or left-hand
   w/detachable mag.) . . . . NiB $469 Ex $355 Gd $228

MODEL 111G, 111GC, 111GNS CLASSIC HUNTER RIFLE
Calibers: .22-250 Rem., .223 Rem., .243 Win., .25-06 Rem. .250 Sav., .270 Win., 7mm-08 Rem., 7mm Rem. Mag., .30-06, .300 Sav., .300 Win. Mag., .308 Win., .338 Win. 22- or 24-inch bbl. Weight: 7 lbs. Ramp front sight, adj. open rear. Walnut-finished hardwood stock. Blued finish. Made from 1994 to date.
Model 111G (right- or left-hand w/box mag.). NiB $369 Ex $298 Gd $210
Model 111GC (right- or left-hand w/
   detachable mag.) . . . . NiB $465 Ex $358 Gd $227
Model 111GNS (w box mag., no sights) . NiB $370 Ex $300 Gd $198

MODEL 112BV,112BVSS HEAVY VARMINT RIFLES
Similar to the Model 110G except fitted with 26-inch heavy bbl. Laminated wood stock with high comb. .22-250 and .223 only.
Model 112BV (Made 1993-94) . . . . NiB $520 Ex $378 Gd $266
Model 112BVSS (w/fluted stainless
   bbl., intro. 1994) . . . . NiB $556 Ex $422 Gd $315

MODEL 112FVVS, 112FVSS VARMINT RIFLE
Similar to the Model 110G except fitted with 26-inch heavy bbl. and Dupont Rynite stock. Calibers: .22-250, .223 and .220 Swift (112FVS only). Blued or stainless finish. Made from 1991 to date.
Model 112RV (blued finish) . . . . NiB $420 Ex $355 Gd $261
Model 112FV-S (blued finish,
   single-shot, disc. 1993) . . . . NiB $533 Ex $445 Gd $398
Model 112FVSS (stainless finish) . . . . . . NiB $645 Ex $545 Gd $390
Model 112 FVSS-S (stainless finish, single-shot) NiB $645 Ex $545 Gd $390

MODEL 112V VARMINT RIFLE . . . NiB $389 Ex $289 Gd $200
Bolt action, single shot. Caliber: .220 Swift, .222 Rem., .223 Rem., .22-250, .243 Win., .25-06. 26-inch heavy bbl. with scope bases. Supplied w/o sights. Weight: 9.25 lbs. Select walnut stock in varmint style w/checkered

Savage/Anschutz Mark 10D

Savage-Stevens Model 34

Savage-Stevens Model 35

pistol-grip, high comb, QD sling swivels. Made from 1975 to 1979.

MODEL 114C, 114CE, 114CU RIFLES
Calibers: .270 Win., 7mm Rem. Mag., .30-06, .300 Win. Mag. 22- or 24-inch bbl. Weight: 7 lbs. Detachable 3- or 4-round magazine. Ramp front sight; adjustable, open rear; (114CU has no sights). Checkered select walnut stock w/oil finish, red butt pad. Schnabel forend and skip-line checkering (114CE). High-luster blued finish. Made from 1991 to date.

Model 114C (Classic) . . . . NiB $745 Ex $588 Gd $338
Model 114CE (Classic European) . . . . . . NiB $533 Ex $390 Gd $300
Model 114CU (Classic Ultra) . . . . NiB $540 Ex $400 Gd $310

MODELS 116FSAK, 116FCSAK BOLT-ACTION RIFLES
Similar to the Model 116FSK except in calibers .270 Win., .30-06, 7mm Mag., .300 Win. Mag., .338 Win. Mag. Fluted 22-inch stainless bbl. w/ adj. muzzle brake. Weight: 6.5 lbs. Made from 1994 to date.

Model 116FSAK . . . . NiB $590 Ex $443 Gd $338
Model 116FCSAK (detachable mag.) . . . . NiB $645 Ex $547 Gd $379

MODELS 116FSC, 116FSS BOLT-ACTION RIFLES
Improved Model 110 with satin stainless action and bbl. Calibers: .223, .243, .270, .30-06, 7mm Rem. Mag., .300 Win. Mag., .338 Win. Mag. 22- or 24-inch bbl. Four or 5-round capacity. Weight: About 7.5 lbs. Black Rynite stock w/recoil pad and swivel studs. Receiver drilled and tapped for scope mounts, no sights. Made from 1991 to date.

Model 116FSS . . . . NiB $677 Ex $544 Gd $339
Model 116FSC, detachable magazine . . . NiB $688 Ex $554 Gd $349

MODEL 116FSK KODIAK RIFLE
Model 116FSK KODIAK RIFLE . . . . NiB $535 Ex $380 Gd $278
Similar to the Model 116FSS except with 22-inch bbl. chambered for 338 Win. Mag. only. "Shock Suppressor" recoil reducer. Made from 1994 to 2000.

MODEL 116-SE, 116-US RIFLES
Calibers: .270 Win., 7mm Rem Mag., .30-06, .300 Win. Mag. (116US); .300 Win. Mag., .338 Win. mag., .425 Express, .458 Win. Mag. (116SE). 24-inch stainless barrel (with muzzle brake 116SE only). 45.5 inches overall. Weight: 7.2 to 8.5 lbs. Three round magazine. 3-leaf Express sights 116SE only. Checkered Classic style select walnut stock with ebony forend tip. Stainless finish. Made from 1994 to 2004.

Model 116SE (Safari Express) . . . . NiB $947 Ex $788 Gd $556
Model 116US (Ultra Stainless). . . . NiB $660 Ex $498 Gd $400

MODEL 170 PUMP-ACTION
CENTERFIRE RIFLE . . . . .NiB $249 Ex $190 Gd $106
Calibers: .30-30, .35 Rem. Three round tubular magazine. 22-inch bbl. Weight: 6.75 lbs. Sights: Folding leaf rear; ramp front. Select walnut stock w/checkered pistol-grip Monte Carlo comb, grooved slide handle. Made from 1970 to 1981.

MODEL 170C CARBINE
MODEL 170C CARBINE . . . . .NiB $280 Ex $322 Gd $166
Same as Model 170 Rifle except has 18.5-inch bbl., straight comb stock, weight: 6 lbs.; caliber .30-30 only. Made from 1974 to 1981.

MODEL 219 SINGLE-SHOT RIFLE
MODEL 219 SINGLE-SHOT RIFLE . .NiB $227 Ex $119 Gd $67
Hammerless. Takedown. Shotgun-type action with top lever. Calibers: .22 Hornet, .25-20, .32-20, .30-30. 26-inch bbl. Weight: about 6 lbs. Sights: Open rear; bead front. Plain pistol-grip stock and forearm. Made from 1938 to 1965.

Model 219L (w/side lever, made 1965-67). NiB $155 Ex $100 Gd $70

MODEL 221-229 UTILITY GUNS
Same as Model 219 except in various calibers, supplied in combination with an interchangeable shotgun bbl. All versions discontinued.

Model 221 (.30-30,12-ga. 30-inch bbl.). . . . NiB $155 Ex $80 Gd $55
Model 222 (.30-30,16-ga. 28-inch bbl.). . . . NiB $155 Ex $80 Gd $55
Model 223 (.30-30, 20-ga. 28-inch bbl.) . . . NiB $155 Ex $80 Gd $55
Model 227 (.22 Hornet, 12-ga. 30-inch bbl.) . . .NiB $155 Ex $80 Gd $55
Model 228 (.22 Hornet, 16-ga. 28-inch bbl.). . NiB $155 Ex $80 Gd $55
Model 229 (.22 Hornet, 20-ga. 28-inch bbl.). . NiB $155 Ex $80 Gd $55

MODEL 340 BOLT-ACTION REPEATER

Savage-Stevens Model 46

Savage-Stevens Model 65

Savage-Stevens Model 72 — Crackshot

Savage-Stevens Model 73

Savage-Stevens Model 80

Calibers: .22 Hornet, .222 Rem., .223 Rem., .227 Win., .30-30. Clip magazine; 4-round capacity (3-round in 30-30). Bbl. lengths: Originally 20-inch in .30-30, 22-inch in .22 Hornet; later 22-inch in .30-30, 24-inch in other calibers. Weight: 6.5 to 7.5 lbs. depending on caliber and vintage. Sights: Open rear (folding leaf on recent production); ramp front. Early models had plain pistol-grip stock, checkered since 1965. Made from 1950-85. (Note: Those rifles produced between 1947-1950 were .22 Hornet Stevens Model .322 and .30-30 Model .325. The Savage model, however, was designated Model .340 for all calibers.)

Pre-1965 with plain stock . . . . NiB $266 Ex $190 Gd $105
Savage Model 340C Carbine . . . . . NiB $278 Ex $228 Gd $140

MODEL 340S DELUXE . . . . NiB $345 Ex $298 Gd $218
Same as Model 340 except has checkered stock, screw eyes for sling, peep rear sight, hooded front. Made from 1955 to 1960.

MODEL 342 . . . . NiB $345 Ex $298 Gd $218
Designation, 1950 to 1955, of Model 340 .22 Hornet.

MODEL 342S DELUXE . . . . NiB $355 Ex $325 Gd $227

Designation, 1950 to 1955, of Model 340S .22 Hornet.

ANNIVERSARY MODEL
1895 LEVER-ACTION . . . . . . NiB $6235 Ex $4589 Gd $2240
Replica of Savage Model 1895 Hammerless Lever-Action Rifle issued to commemorate the 75th anniversary (1895-1970) of Savage Arms. Caliber: .308 Win. Five round rotary magazine. 24-inch full-octagon bbl. Engraved receiver. Brass-plated lever. Sights: Open rear; brass blade front. Plain straight-grip buttstock, Schnabel-type forend; brass medallion inlaid in buttstock, brass crescent-shaped buttplate. 9,999 produced. Made in 1970 only. Top value is for new, unfired specimen.

MODEL 1903 SLIDE-ACTION
REPEATER . . . . NiB $733 Ex $549 Gd $370
Hammerless. Takedown. Caliber: .22 Short, Long, LR. Detachable box magazine. 24-inch octagon bbl. Weight: About 5 lbs. Sights: Open rear; bead front. Pistol-grip stock, grooved slide handle. Made 1903 to 1921.

MODEL 1904 BOLT-ACTION
SINGLE-SHOT RIFLE . . . . NiB $228 Ex $140 Gd $90

GRADING: **NiB** = New in Box   **Ex** = Excellent or NRA 95%   **Gd** = Good or NRA 68%

Savage-Stevens Model 89

Savage-Stevens Model 987-T

Takedown. .22 Short, Long, LR. 18-inch bbl. Weight: About 3 lbs. Sights: Open rear; bead front. Plain, straight-grip, one-piece stock. Made from 1904 to 1917.

MODEL 1905 BOLT-ACTION
SINGLE-SHOT RIFLE. . . . . .NiB $220 Ex $138 Gd $85
Takedown. .22 Short, Long, LR. 22-inch bbl. Weight: About 5 lbs. Sights: Open rear; bead front. Plain, straight-grip one-piece stock. Made from 1905 to 1919.

MODEL 1909 SLIDE-ACTION
REPEATER . . . . .NiB $800 Ex $533 Gd $337
Hammerless. Takedown. Similar to Model 1903 except has 20-inch round bbl., plain stock and forearm, weight: Approximately 4.75 lbs. Made from 1909 to 1915.

MODEL 1912
AUTOLOADING RIFLE. . . . . NiB $800 Ex $533 Gd $337
Takedown. Caliber: 22 LR. only. Seven round detachable box magazine. 20-inch bbl., plain stock and forearm. Made 1912 to 1916.

MODEL 1914 SLIDE-ACTION
REPEATER . . . . .NiB $520 Ex $347 Gd $239
Hammerless. Takedown. Caliber: .22 Short, Long, LR, Tubular magazine holds 20 Short, 17 Long, 15 LR. 24-inch octagon bbl. Weight: About 5.75 lbs. Sights: Open rear; bead front. Plain pistol-grip stock, grooved slide handle. Made from 1914 to 1924.

MODEL 1920 HI-POWER BOLT-ACTION RIFLE
Short Mauser-type action. Calibers: .250/3000, .300 Sav. Five round box magazine. 22-inch bbl. in .250 cal.; 24-inch in .300 cal. Weight: About 6 lbs. Sights: Open rear; bead front. Checkered pistol-grip stock w/slender forearm and Schnabel tip. Made from 1920 to 1926.
.250-3000 Savage. . . . . NiB $1029 Ex $833 Gd $690
.300 Savage . . . . NiB $969 Ex $755 Gd $588

NOTE: *In 1965, Savage began the importation of rifles manufactured by J. G. Anschutz GmbH, Ulm, West Germany. Models designated "Savage/Anschutz" are listed in this section, those marketed in the U.S. under the "Anschutz" name are included in that firm's listings. Anschutz rifles are now distributed in the U.S. by Precision Sales Int'l., Westfield, Mass. See "Anschutz" for detailed specifications.*

MARK 10 BOLT-ACTION
TARGET RIFLE . . . . NiB $534 Ex $359 Gd $265
Single shot. Caliber: .22 LR. 26-inch bbl. Weight: 8.5 lbs. Sights: Anschutz micrometer rear; globe front. Target stock w/full pistol-grip

and cheekpiece, adj. hand stop and swivel. Made 1967 to 1972.
MARK 10D. . . . . .NiB $544 Ex $369 Gd $259
Same as Mark 10 except has redesigned stock with Monte Carlo comb, different rear sight. Weight: 7.75 lbs. Made in 1972.

MODEL 54
CUSTOM SPORTER . . . . NiB $766 Ex $639 Gd $400
Same as Anschutz Model 1422D.

MODEL 54M . . . . .NiB $945 Ex $670 Gd $439
Same as Anschutz Model 1522D.

MODEL 64 BOLT-ACTION
TARGET RIFLE . . . . .NiB $655 Ex $512 Gd $338
Same as Anschutz Model 1403.

MODEL 153 BOLT-ACTION
SPORTER . . . . NiB $697 Ex $488 Gd $349
Caliber: .222 Rem. Three round clip magazine. 24-inch bbl. Sights: Folding leaf open rear; hooded ramp front. Weight: 6.75 lbs. French walnut stock w/cheekpiece, skip checkering, rosewood forend tip and grip cap, swivels. Made from 1964 to 1967.

MODEL 153S . . . . .NiB $770 Ex $556 Gd $390
Same as Model 153 except has double-set trigger. Made 1965 to 1967.

MODEL 164 CUSTOM SPORTER . . . . . . NiB $775 Ex $561 Gd $195
Same as Anschutz Model 1416.

MODEL 164M . . . . .NiB $660 Ex $454 Gd $300
Same as Anschutz Model 1516.

MODEL 184 SPORTER . . . . .NiB $638 Ex $484 Gd $288
Same as Anschutz Model 1441.

NOTE: *Since J. Stevens Arms (see also separate listing) is a division of Savage Industries, certain Savage models carry the "Stevens" name.*

MODEL 34 BOLT-ACTION
REPEATER . . . . NiB $190 Ex $126 Gd $88
Caliber: .22 Short, Long, LR. 20-inch bbl. Weight: 4.75 lbs. Sights: Open rear; bead front. Plain pistol-grip stock. Made 1965 to 1980.

MODEL 34M . . . . .NiB $190 Ex $146 Gd $98
Same as Model 34 except chambered for 22 WMR. Made 1969 to 1973.

MODEL 35 . . . . .NiB $190 Ex $146 Gd $98
Bolt-action repeater. Caliber: 22 LR. Six round clip magazine. 22-inch bbl. Weight: About 5 lbs. Sights: Open rear; ramp front. Monte Carlo stock w/ checkered pistol grip and forearm. Made from 1982 to 1985.

MODEL 35M . . . . **NiB $219 Ex $140 Gd $100**
Same as Model 35 except chambered for 22 WMR. Made from 1982 to 1985.

MODEL 46 BOLT-ACTION
RIFLE . . . . .NiB $190 Ex $136 Gd $100
Caliber: .22 Short, Long, LR. Tubular magazine holds 22 Short, 17 Long, 15 LR. 20-inch bbl. Weight: 5 lbs. Plain pistol-grip stock on early production; later models have Monte Carlo stock w/checkering. Made from 1969 to 1073.

MODEL 65
BOLT-ACTION RIFLE . . . . .NiB $219 Ex $138 Gd $99
Caliber: .22 Short, Long, LR. Five round clip magazine. 20-inch bbl. Weight: 5 lbs. Sights: Open rear; ramp front. Monte Carlo stock w/ checkered pistol grip and forearm. Made from 1969 to 1973.

MODEL 65M . . . . .NiB $200 Ex $134 Gd $90
Same as Model 65 except chambered for .22 WMR, has 22-inch bbl., weighs 5.25 lbs. Made from 1969 to 1981.

NOTE: *The Model 72 is a "Favorite"-type single-shot unlike the smaller, original "Crackshot" made by Stevens from 1913 to 1939.*

MODEL 72 CRACKSHOT SINGLE-SHOT
LEVER-ACTION RIFLE . . . . NiB $190 Ex $109 Gd $79
Falling-block action. Casehardened frame. Caliber: .22 Short, Long, LR. 22-inch octagon bbl. Weight: 4.5lbs. Sights: Open rear; bead front. Plain straight-grip stock and forend of walnut. Made 1972 to 1989.

MODEL 73 BOLT-ACTION SINGLE-SHOT. NiB $159 Ex $138 Gd $89
Caliber: .22 Short, Long, LR. 20-inch bbl. Weight: 4.75 lbs. Sights: Open rear; bead front. Plain pistol-grip stock. Made 1965 to 1980.

MODEL 73Y YOUTH MODEL . . . . .NiB $150 Ex $110 Gd $90
Same as Model 73 except has 18-inch bbl., 1.5-inch shorter buttstock, weight: 4.5 lbs. Made from 1965 to 1980.

MODEL 74
LITTLE FAVORITE . . . . .NiB $167 Ex $115 Gd $98
Same as Model 72 Crackshot except has black-finished frame, 22-inch round bbl., walnut-finished hardwood stock. Weight: 4.75 lbs. Made from 1972 to 1974.

MODEL 80
AUTOLOADING RIFLE . . . . NiB $215 Ex $170 Gd $126
Caliber: 22 LR. 15-round tubular magazine. 20-inch bbl. Weight: 6 lbs. Sights: Open rear, bead front. Monte Carlo stock of walnut w/checkered pistol-grip and forearm. Made from 1976 to date. (Note: This rifle is essentially the same as the Model 60 of 1969 to 1972 except for a different style of checkering, side instead of top safety and plain bead instead of ramp front sight.)

MODEL 88
AUTOLOADING RIFLE . . . . NiB $190 Ex $110 Gd $88
Similar to Model 60 except has walnut-finished hardwood stock, plain bead front sight. Weight: 5.75 lbs. Made from 1969 to 1972.

MODEL 89 SINGLE-SHOT
LEVER-ACTION CARBINE . . . . .NiB $121 Ex $90 Gd $66
Martini-type action. Caliber: .22 Short, Long, LR. 18.5-inch bbl. Weight: 5 lbs. Sights: Open rear; bead front. Western-style carbine stock w/

straight grip, forearm with bbl. band. Made 1976 to 1989.

MODEL 987-T
AUTOLOADING RIFLE . . . . .NiB $217 Ex $166 Gd $129
Caliber: .22 LR. 15-round tubular magazine. 20-inch bbl. Weight: 6 lbs. Sights: Open rear; ramp front. Monte Carlo stock w/checkered pistol grip and forearm. Made from 1981 to 1989.

"STEVENS FAVORITE"
See Savage Model 71.

V.C. SCHILLING — Suhl, Germany

MAUSER-MANNLICHER
BOLT ACTION SPORTING RIFLE .NiB $938 Ex $744 Gd $539
Same general specifications as given for the Haenel Mauser-Mannlicher Sporter. See separate listing.

'88 MAUSER SPORTER . . . . .NiB $909 Ex $722 Gd $515
Same general specifications as Haenel '88 Mauser Sporter. See separate listing.

SCHULTZ & LARSEN GEVAERFABRIK —
Otterup, Denmark

MATCH RIFLE NO. 47 . . . . .NiB $690 Ex $555 Gd $360
Caliber: .22 LR. Bolt-action, single-shot, set trigger. 28.5-inch heavy bbl. Weight: 14 lbs. Sights: Micrometer receiver, globe front. Free-rifle stock w/cheekpiece, thumbhole, adj. Schuetzen-type buttplate, swivels, palmrest.

FREE RIFLE MODEL 54 . . . . .NiB $866 Ex $780 Gd $598
Calibers: 6.5x55mm or any standard American centerfire caliber. Schultz & Larsen M54 bolt-action, single-shot, set trigger. 27.5-inch heavy bbl. Weight: 15.5 lbs. Sights: Micrometer receiver; globe front. Free-rifle stock w/cheekpiece, thumbhole, adj. Schuetzen-type buttplate, swivels, palm rest.

MODEL 54J
SPORTING RIFLE . . . . .NiB $684 Ex $528 Gd $430
Calibers: .270 Win., .30-06, 7x61 Sharpe & Hart. Schultz & Larsen bolt action. Three-round magazine. 24-inch bbl. in .270 and .30-06, 26-inch in 7x61 S&H. Checkered stock w/Monte Carlo comb and cheekpiece. Value shown is for rifle less sights.

SEARS, ROEBUCK & COMPANY —
Chicago, Illinois

The most encountered brands or model designations used by Sears are J. C. Higgins and Ted Williams. Firearms sold under these designations have been mfd. by various firms including Winchester, Marlin, Savage, Mossberg, etc.

MODEL 2C
BOLT-ACTION RIFLE . . . . .NiB $159 Ex $119 Gd $95
Caliber: .22RF. Seven round clip mag. 21-inch bbl. Weight: 5 lbs. Sights: Open rear; ramp front. Plain Monte Carlo stock. Mfd. by Win.

MODEL 42
BOLT-ACTION REPEATER . . . . .NiB $159 Ex $119 Gd $95
Takedown. Caliber: .22RF. Eight round detachable box magazine. 24-inch bbl. Weight: 6 lbs. Sights: Open rear; bead front. Plain pistol-grip stock. Mfd. by Marlin.

RIFLES

Sedgley Springfield Sporter

Sedgley Springfield — Left Hand

Sedgley Springfield Mannlicher

MODEL 42DL
BOLT-ACTION REPEATER . . . . NiB $159 Ex $119 Gd $95
Same general specifications as Model 42 except fancier grade w/peep sight, hooded front sight and swivels.

MODEL 44DL
LEVER-ACTION RIFLE . . . . NiB $239 Ex $179 Gd $130
Caliber: .22RF. Tubular magazine holds 19 LR cartridges. 22-inch bbl. Weight: 6.25 lbs. Sights: Open rear; hooded ramp front. Monte Carlo-style stock w/pistol grip. Mfd. by Marlin.

MODEL 53
BOLT-ACTION RIFLE . . . . NiB $289 Ex $198 Gd $155
Calibers: .243, .270, .308, .30-06. Four-round magazine. 22-inch bbl. Weight: 6.75 lbs. Sights: Open rear; ramp front. Standard sporter stock w/pistol-grip, checkered. Mfd. by Savage.

MODEL 54 LEVER-ACTION
RIFLE . . . . NiB $222 Ex $188 Gd $135
Similar general specifications as Winchester Model 94 carbine. Made in .30-30 caliber only. Mfd. by Winchester.

MODEL 103 SERIES
BOLT-ACTION REPEATER . . . . NiB $229 EX $121 Gd $98
Same general specifications as Model 103.2 w/minor changes. Mfd. by Marlin.

MODEL 103.2 BOLT-ACTION
REPEATER . . . . NiB $145 Ex $100 Gd $90
Takedown. Caliber: .22RF. Eight-round detachable box magazine. 24-inch bbl. Weight: 6 lbs. Sights: Open rear; bead front. Plain pistol-grip stock. Mfd. by Marlin.

R. F. SEDGLEY, INC. — Philadelphia, Pennsylvania

SPRINGFIELD SPORTER . . . . . NiB $1290 Ex $1189 Gd $633
Springfield '03 bolt action. Calibers: .220 Swift, .218 Bee, .22-3000, R, .22-4000, .22 Hornet, .25-35, .250-3000, .257 Roberts, .270 Win., 7mm, .30-06. 24-inch bbl. Weight: 7.5 lbs. Sights: Lyman No. 48 receiver; bead front on matted ramp. Checkered walnut stock, grip cap, sling swivels. Disc. 1941.

SPRINGFIELD LEFT-HAND SPORTER . NiB $1674 Ex $1412 Gd $954
Bolt-action reversed for left-handed shooter; otherwise the same as standard Sedgley Springfield Sporter. Disc. 1941.

SEDGLEY SPRINGFIELD
MANNLICHER-TYPE SPORTER . . . . . NiB $1515 Ex $1479 Gd $1088
Same as standard Sedgley Springfield Sporter except w/20-inch bbl., Mannlicher-type full stock w/cheekpiece, weight: 7.75 lbs. Disc. 1941.

SHILEN RIFLES, INC. — Enis, Texas

DGA BENCHREST RIFLE . . . . . . NiB $1529 Ex $1244 Gd $977
DGA single-shot bolt-action. Calibers as listed for Sporter. 26-inch medium-heavy or heavy bbl. Weight: From 10.5 lbs. No sights. Fiberglass or walnut stock, classic or thumbhole pattern. Currently manufactured.

DGA SPORTER . . . . NiB $1567 Ex $1189 Gd $843
DGA bolt action. Calibers: .17 Rem., .222 Rem., .223 Rem. .22-250, .220 Swift, 6mm Rem., .243 Win., .250 Sav., .257 Roberts, .284 Win., .308 Win., .358 Win. Three round blind magazine. 24-inch bbl. Average weight: 7.5 lbs. No sights. Select Claro walnut stock w/cheekpiece, pistol grip, sling swivel studs. Currently manufactured.

Shilen DGA
Benchrest Rifle

Shilen DGA Sporter

Shilen DGA Varminter

DGA VARMINTER . . . . NiB $1455 Ex $1209 Gd $1155
Same as Sporter except w/25-inch medium-heavy bbl. Weight: 9 lbs.

SHILOH RIFLE MFG. CO. — Big Timber, MT

SHARPS MODEL 1874 BUSINESS RIFLENiB $1149 Ex $1072 Gd $698
Replica of 1874 Sharps similar to No. 3 Sporting Rifle. .32-40, .38-55, .40-50 BN, .40-70 BN, .40-90 BN, .45-70 ST, .45-90 ST, .50-70 ST, .50-100 ST. 28-inch round heavy bbl. Blade front sight, buckhorn rear. Double-set triggers. Straight-grip walnut stock w/steel crescent butt-plate. Made from 1986 to date.

SHARPS MODEL 1874 LONG
RANGE EXPRESS RIFLE. . . . . NiB $1798 Ex $1703 Gd $1166
Replica of 1874 Sharps w/single-shot falling breech action. .32-40, .38-55, .40-50 BN, .40-70 BN, .40-90 BN, .45-70 ST, .45-90 ST, .45-110 ST, .50-70 ST, .50-90 ST, .50-110 ST. 34-inch tapered octagon bbl. 51

inches overall. Weight: 10.75 lbs. Globe front sight, sporting tang peep rear. Walnut buttstock w/pistol-grip and Schnabel-style forend. Color casehardened action w/double-set triggers Made from 1986 to date.

SHARPS MODEL 1874
SADDLE RIFLE . . . . NiB $1267 Ex $1133 Gd $723
Similar to 1874 Express Rifle except w/30-inch bbl., blade front sight and buckhorn rear. Made from 1986 to date.

SHARPS MODEL 1874
SPORTING RIFLE NO. 1 . . . . . . NiB $1355 Ex $1187 Gd $745
Similar to 1874 Express Rifle except w/30-inch bbl., blade front sight and buckhorn rear. Made from 1986 to date.

SHARPS MODEL 1874
SPORTING RIFLE NO. 3 . . . . . . NiB $1150 Ex $1007 Gd $688
Similar to 1874 Sporting Rifle No. 1 except w/straight-grip stock w/steel crescent buttplate. Made from 1986 to date.

SHARPS MODEL 1874 MONTANA ROUGHRIDER

Similar to 1874 Sporting Rifle No. 1 except w/24- to 34-inch half-octagon or full-octagon bbl. Standard or deluxe walnut stock w/pistol-grip or military-style buttstock. Made from 1989 to date.

Standard model . . . . NiB $1154 Ex $715 Gd $646
Deluxe model. . . . . NiB $1300 Ex $990 Gd $615

SIG SWISS INDUSTRIAL COMPANY __
Neuhausen-Rhine Falls, Switzerland

AMT SEMIAUTOMATIC RIFLE. . . . . . NiB $4798 Ex $3270 Gd $2775
.308 Win.(7.62 NATO). Five, 10, or 20-round magazine. 18.5-inch bbl. w/flash suppressor. Weight: 9.5 lbs. Sights: Adj. aperture rear, post front. Walnut buttstock and forend w/synthetic pistol grip. Imported 1980 to 1988.

AMT SPORTING RIFLE . . . . . NiB $4876 Ex $3129 Gd $2210
Semiautomatic version of SG510-4 automatic assault rifle based on Swiss Army SIGW57. Roller-delayed blowback action. Caliber: 7.62x51mm NATO (.308 Win.). Five, 10- and 20-round magazines. 19-inch bbl. Weight: 10 lbs. Sights, aperture rear, post front. Wood buttstock and forearm, folding bipod. Imported from 1960 to 1988.

PE-57 SEMIAUTOMATIC RIFLE . . . . NiB $6596 Ex $4348 Gd $3100
Caliber: 7.5 Swiss. 24-round magazine. 23.75-inch bbl. Weight: 12.5 lbs. Sights: Adj. aperture rear; post front. High-impact synthetic stock. Imported from Switzerland during the 1980s.

SIG SAUER — Neuhausen, Switzerland
Manufactured and imported by SIG Sauer USA in Exeter, NH.

To facilitate locating SIG Sauer rifles, models are grouped into two categories: bolt-action rifles (below) and semi-automatic rifles. For a complete listing, please refer to the index.

- BOLT-ACTION RIFLES -

TACTICAL 2 . . . . NiB $4171 Ex $2400 Gd $1900
Push-feed, straight pull action. Calibers: .223 Rem., .308 Win., .300 Win. Mag. or .338 Lapua. 4- or 5-round detachable box magazine. 24.7-, 25.6-, or 27-in. fluted bbl. w/muzzle brake. Aluminum chassis, adj. trigger, ambidextrous Blaser stock w/adj. LOP and cheekpiece. Made from 2007 to 2015.

SIG50 . . . . NiB $9825 Ex $5100 Gd $4900
Push-feed action. .50 BMG only. 5-round detachable box magazine. 29-in. fluted bbl. w/muzzle brake. McMillan stock. Made 2011-12; 2014-15.

SIG SSG 3000 Patrol

SIG Tactical 2

SSG 3000. . . . . NiB $2400 Ex $1500 Gd $1250
Push-feed action, .308 Win. only, 5-round detachable box magazine, 23.4-in. heavy bbl. w/muzzle brake, adj. McMillan stock. Made from 2000 to 2012.
Patrol (18-in. bbl.) . . . . NiB $1499 Ex $830 Gd $700

- SEMI-AUTOMATIC RIFLES -

SIG M400 . . . . NiB $1313 EX $874 GD $750
Semi-automatic AR15 platform w/gas impingment system. Caliber: 5.56mm NATO. 30-round magazine. 16-in. bbl., removable adj. sights. Weight: 6.5 lbs. Overall: 39.5 in. Made 2012 to date.
Hunting (20-in. bbl., 2012 only) . . . . . NiB $975 Ex $680 Gd $600
Varminter (22-in. bbl., 2013-15) . . . . NiB $1395 Ex $820 Gd $650

SIG551-A1 . . . . NiB $1599 EX $930 GD $800
Semi-automatic w/gas piston system. Caliber: 5.56mm NATO. 20- or 30-round Swiss 550-style clear magazine. 16-in. bbl., adj. sights, folding polymer stock. Weight: 7 lbs. Overall: 34.6 in. Made 2012 to 2015.

SIG556 CLASSIC . . . . NiB $1299 EX $850 GD $700
Similar to gas piston system SG550 military rifle except semi-automatic. Caliber: 5.56mm NATO. 30-round AR51-style magazine. 16-in. bbl., adj. sights, folding polymer stock. Weight: 8.2 lbs. Overall: 35.8 in. Made 2007 to 2013.
DMR (Magpul PRS stock,18-in. heavy bbl., optic ready
   2008-13) . . . . NiB $1732 Ex $930 Gd $800
Holo (M4-style stock, red dot
   holographic sight) . . . . NiB $1832 Ex $1030 Gd $900
Patrol (polymer handguard, 2010-13) NiB $1266 Ex $850 Gd $700
Patrol SWAT (aluminum handguard,
   2010-13) . . . . NiB $1266 Ex $850 Gd $700
SWAT (quad-rail handguard), add $140

SIG556R. . . . . NiB $1332 EX $900 GD $760
Similar to SG556 except chambered in 7.62x39mm. 30-round AK-style magazine, red dot optic. Weight: 7 lbs. Made 2011 to 2013.

SMITH & WESSON — Springfield, MA
Manufactured by Husqvarna, Vapenfabrik A.B., Huskvarna, Sweden, & Howa Machinery LTD., Shinkawa-Chonear, Nagota 452, Japan.

MODEL 1500 . . . . NiB $410 Ex $339 Gd $269
Bolt-action. .243 Win., .270 Win., .30-06, 7mm Rem. Mag. 22-inch bbl. (24-inch in 7mm Rem. Mag.). Weight: 7.5 lbs. American walnut stock w/Monte Carlo comb and cheekpiece, cut checkering. Sights: Open rear, hooded ramp, gold beadfront. This model was also imported by Mossberg (see separate listings); Imported from 1979 to 1984.

MODEL 1500DL DELUXE . . . . NiB $410 Ex $339 Gd $269
Same as standard model, except w/o sights; w/engine-turned bolt, decorative scroll on floorplate, French checkering. Imported from 1983 to 1984.

MODEL 1707 LS "CLASSIC HUNTER" . . . NiB $460 Ex $388 Gd $318
Bolt action. Calibers: .243 Win., .270 Win., .30-06, 5-round magazine. 22-inch bbl. Weight: 7.5 lbs. Solid recoil pad, no sights, Schnabel forend, checkered walnut stock. Imported 1983 to 1984.

MODEL A BOLT-ACTION RIFLE . . . . NiB $443 Ex $329 Gd $290
Similar to Husqvarna Model 9000 Crown Grade. Mauser-type bolt action. Calibers: .22-250, .243 Win., .270 Win., .308 Win., .30-06, 7mm Rem. Mag., .300 Win. Mag. Five round magazine except 3-round capacity in latter two calibers. 23.75-inch bbl. Weight: 7 lbs. Sights:

Smith & Wesson
Model 1500DL

Smith & Wesson
Model 1707 LS Classic Hunter

Springfield Armory
BM-59

Folding leaf rear; hooded ramp front. Checkered walnut stock w/Monte Carlo cheekpiece, rosewood forend tip and pistol-grip cap, swivels. Made from 1969 to 1972.

MODEL B. . . . . .NiB $460 Ex $367 Gd $238
Same as Model A except w/20.25-inch extra-light bbl., Monte Carlo cheekpiece w/Schnabel-style forearm, weight: 6 lbs., 10 oz. Calibers: .243 Win., .30-06.

MODEL C . . . . .NiB $460 Ex $367 Gd $238
Same as Model B except w/cheekpiece stock w/straight comb.

MODEL D . . . . .NiB $588 Ex $469 Gd $240
Same as Model C except w/full-length Mannlicher-style forearm.

MODEL E. . . . . .NiB $588 Ex $469 Gd $240
Same as Model B except w/full-length Mannlicher-style forearm.

SPRINGFIELD ARMORY INC. — Colona, Illinois

Formerly of Geneseo, IL. This is a private firm not to be confused with the former U.S. Government facility in Springfield, Mass.

BM-59 SEMIAUTOMATIC RIFLE
Gas-operated. Caliber: .308 Win. (7.62mm NATO). 20-round detachable box magazine. 19.3-inch bbl. w/flash suppressor. About 43 inches overall. Weight: 9.25 lbs. Adj. military aperture rear sight, square post front; direct and indirect grenade launcher sights. European walnut stock w/handguard or folding buttstock (Alpine Paratrooper). Made from 1981 to 1990.

Standard model . . . . .NiB $1844 Ex $1329 Gd $911
Paratrooper model . . . . NiB $2136 Ex $1779 Gd $1533

M-1 GARAND SEMIAUTOMATIC RIFLE
Gas-operated. Calibers: .308 Win. (7.62 NATO), .30-06. Eight round stripper clip. 24-inch bbl. 43.5 inches overall. Weight: 9.5 lbs. Adj. aperture rear sight, military square blade front. Standard "Issue-grade" walnut stock or folding buttstock. Made from 1979 to 1990.
Standard model . . . . NiB $779 Ex $588 Gd $353
National Match model . . . . NiB $909 Ex $799 Gd $489
Ultra Match model . . . . NiB $1000 Ex $808 Gd $589
Sniper model . . . . NiB $1264 Ex $876 Gd $665
Tanker model. . . . . NiB $954 Ex $677 Gd $498

MATCH M1A
Same as Standard M1A except w/National Match-grade bbl. w/modified flash suppressor, National Match sights, turned trigger pull, gas system assembly in one unit, modified mainspring guide glass-bedded walnut stock. Super Match M1A w/premium-grade heavy bbl. (weight: 10 lbs).
Match M1A. . . . . .NiB $1277 Ex $1879 Gd $1271
Super Match M1A. . . . . NiB $2695 Ex $1899 Gd $1721

STANDARD M1A SEMIAUTOMATIC
Gas-operated. Similar to U.S. M14 service rifle except w/o provision for automatic firing. Caliber: 7.65mm NATO (.308 Win.). Five, 10- or 20-round detachable box magazine. 25.13-inch bbl w/flash suppressor. Weight: 9 lbs. Sights: Adj. aperture rear; blade front. Fiberglass, birch or walnut stock, fiberglass handguard, sling swivels. Made from 1996 to 2000.
w/fiberglass or birch stock . . . . . NiB $1198 Ex $694 Gd $645
w/walnut stock. . . . . NiB $1412 Ex $1100 Gd $833

**Springfield Armory
SAR-8 Sporter Rifle**

M-6 SCOUT RIFLE/SHOTGUN COMBO
Similar to (14-inch) short-barrel Survival Gun provided as backup weapon to U.S. combat pilots. Calibers: .22 LR/.410 and .22 Hornet/.410. 18.5-inch bbl. 32 inches overall. Weight: 4 lbs. Parkerized or stainless steel finish. Folding detachable stock w/storage for fifteen .22 LR cartridges and four .410 shells. Drilled and tapped for scope mounts. Intro. 1982 and imported from Czech Republic 1995 to 2004.
First Issue (no trigger guard) . . NiB $1709 Ex $1443 Gd $1067
Second Issue (w/trigger guard) . NiB $1797 Ex $1449 Gd $1088

SAR-8 SPORTER RIFLE
Similar to H&K 911 semiautomatic rifle. Calibers: .308 Win., (7.62x51) NATO. Detachable 5- 10- or 20-round magazine. 18- or 20-inch bbl. 38.25 or 45.3 inches overall. Weight: 8.7 to 9.5 lbs. Protected front post and rotary adj. rear sight. Delayed roller-locked blow-back action w/fluted chamber. Kevlar-reinforced fiberglass thumb-hole style wood stock. Imported from 1990 to 1998.
w/wood stock (disc. 1994) . . . . NiB $1077 Ex $877 Gd $658
w/thumb-hole stock . . . . NiB $1127 Ex $976 Gd $679

SAR-48, SAR-4800
Similar to Browning FN FAL/LAR semiautomatic rifle. Calibers: .233 Rem. (5.56x45) and 3.08 Win. (7.62x51) NATO. Detachable 5- 10- or 20-round magazine. 18- or 21-inch chrome-lined bbl. 38.25 or 45.3 inches overall. Weight: 9.5 to 13.25 lbs. Protected post front and adj. rear sight. Forged receiver and bolt w/adj. gas system. Pistol-grip or thumb-hole style; synthetic or wood stock. Imported 1985; reintroduced 1995.
w/pistol-grip stock, disc. 1989 . . . . . . NiB $1788 Ex $1289 Gd $990
w/wood stock, disc. 1989. . . . . .NiB $2577 Ex $2066 Gd $1500
w/folding stock, disc. 1989. . . . . . . .NiB $2854 Ex $2310 Gd $1669
w/thumb-hole stock . . . . .NiB $1329 Ex $1100 Gd $796

SQUIRES BINGHAM CO., INC. — Makati, Rizal, Philippines

MODEL 14D DELUXE BOLT-ACTION
REPEATING RIFLE . . . . .NiB $159 Ex $123 Gd $88
Caliber: .22 LR. Five round box magazine. 24-inch bbl. Sights: V-notch rear; hooded ramp front. Receiver grooved for scope mounting. Pulong Dalaga stock w/contrasting forend tip and grip cap, checkered forearm and pistol-grip. Weight: 6 lbs. Disc.

MODEL 15. . . . . .NiB $189 Ex $127 Gd $115
Same as Model 14D except chambered for .22 WMR. Importation. Disc.

MODEL M16 SEMIAUTOMATIC RIFLE . . NiB $190 Ex $166 Gd $126
Styled after U.S. M16 military rifle. Caliber: .22 LR. 15-round box magazine. 19.5-inch bbl. w/muzzle brake/flash hider. Rear sight in carrying handle, post front on high ramp. Black-painted mahogany buttstock and forearm. Weight: 6.5 lbs. Importation disc.

MODEL M20D DELUXE . . . . .NiB $277 Ex $227 Gd $131
Caliber: .22 LR. 15-round box magazine. 19.5-inch bbl. w/muzzle brake/flash hider. Sights: V-notch rear; blade front. Receiver grooved for scope mounting. Pulong Dalaga stock w/contrasting forend tip and grip cap, checkered forearm/pistol-grip. Weight: 6 lbs. Importation disc.

STAG ARMS, LLC — New Britain, CT

MODEL 1 . . . . NIB $949 EX $600 GD $500
Semi-automatic AR15 platform w/gas impingment system. Caliber: 5.56mm NATO. 30-round magazine. 16-in. bbl., mil-spec collapsible buttstock, A2 flashhider, sights and pistol grip. Removeable carry handle. Weight: 7 lbs. Made 2003 to date.
Model 1L (left-hand variant), add $40

MODEL 2 . . . . NIB $940 EX $590 GD $490
Similar to Model 1 except w/folding rear sight. Weight: 6.5 lbs. Made 2003 to date.
Model 2L (left-hand variant), add $40
Model 2T (quad rail handguard), add $190
Model 2TL (left-hand variant), add $215

MODEL 3 . . . . NIB $895 EX $550 GD $480
Similar to Model 1 except optic ready, Diamondhead VRS handguard. Weight: 6.1 lbs. Made 2011 to date.
Model 3L (left-hand variant), add $25
Model 3G (18-in. bbl. w/3G compensator, Magpul stock and
 pistols grip, Samson Evolution handguard, 6.1 lbs.,
 2011-date) . . . . NiB $1459 Ex $900 Gd $780
Model 3GL (left-hand variant), add $20
Model 3T (Diamondhead folding sights and handguard, 7.4 lbs.,
 2014-date) . . . . NiB $999 Ex $600 Gd $530
Model 3TL (left-hand variant), add $20
Model 3T-M (Diamondhead folding sights and handguard,
 Magpul stock and pistol grip, 7.4 lbs.,
 2014-date) . . . . NiB $1160 Ex $700 Gd $580
Model 3TL-M (left-hand variant), add $20

**Star
Rolling Block Carbine**

MODEL 4 . . . . **NIB $1015 EX $630 GD $560**
Similar to Model 1 except w/20-in. bbl., A2 buttstock, 5-round magazine. Weight: 8.5 lbs. Made 2003 to date.
Model 4L (left-hand variant), add **$50**

MODEL 5 . . . . **NIB $895 EX $550 GD $480**
Similar to Model 1 except w/o rear sight, chambered in 6.8SPC II. Weight: 6.4 lbs. Made 2011 to date.
Model 5L (left-hand variant), add **$50**

MODEL 6 . . . . **NIB $1055 EX $650 GD $530**
Similar to Model 1 except w/o sights, 24.1-in. heavy bbl., Hogue aluminum handguard. Weight: 10 lbs. Made 2011 to date.
Model 6L (left-hand variant), add **$40**

MODEL 7 . . . . **NIB $1055 EX $650 GD $530**
Similar to Model 6 except w/20.8-in. heavy bbl., chambered in 6.8SPC II. Weight: 10 lbs. Made 2003 to date.
Model 7L (left-hand variant), add **$40**

MODEL 8 . . . . **NIB $1055 EX $650 GD $530**
Similar to Model 1 except w/gas piston system, Diamondhead flip-up sights. Weight: 6.9 lbs. Made 2011 to date.
Model 8L (left-hand variant), add **$30**
Model 8T (Diamondhead folding sights and handguard, 7.2 lbs., 2013-date) . . . . **NiB $1275 Ex $730 Gd 600**
Model 8TL (left-hand variant), add **$20**

MODEL 9 . . . . **NIB $990 EX $580 GD $500**
Semi-automatic AR15 platform w/blowback system. Caliber: 9mm. 32-round magazine. 16-in. bbl., mil-spec collapsible buttstock, A2 flashhider and pistol grip, optic ready. Weight: 6.8 lbs. Made 2015 to date.
Model 9L (left-hand variant), add **$35**
Model 9T (Diamondhead folding sights and free float handguard, 7.9 lbs., 2015-date) . **NiB $1275 Ex $730 Gd 600**
Model 9TL (left-hand variant), add **$20**

STANDARD ARMS COMPANY — Wilmington, Delaware

MODEL G AUTOMATIC RIFLE . . . **NiB $815 Ex $569 Gd $355**
Gas-operated. Autoloading. Hammerless. Takedown. .25-35, .30-30, .25 Rem., .30 Rem., .35 Rem. Magazine capacity: 4 rounds in .35 Rem., 5 rounds in other calibers. 22.38-inch bbl. Weight: 7.75 lbs. Sights: Open sporting rear; ivory bead front. Shotgun-type stock. Made c. 1910. Note: This was the first gas-operated rifle manufactured in the U.S. While essentially an autoloader, the gas port can be closed and the rifle may be operated as a slide-action repeater.

MODEL M HAND-OPERATED RIFLE . . . . **NiB $737 Ex $543 Gd $431**
Slide-action repeater w/same general specifications as Model G except

lacks autoloading feature. Weight: 7 lbs.

STAR — Eibar, Spain
Manufactured by Bonifacio Echeverria, S.A.

ROLLING BLOCK CARBINE . . . . . **NiB $500 Ex $337 Gd $178**
Single-shot, similar to Remington Rolling Block. .30-30, .357 Mag., .44 Mag. 20-inch bbl. Weight: 6 lbs. Sights: Folding leaf rear; ramp front. Walnut straight-grip stock w/crescent buttplate, forearm w/bbl. band. Imported 1934 to 1975.

STERLING ARMAMENT, LTD. — Essex, England
Imported by Lanchester U.S.A., Inc., Dallas, Texas.

MARK 6 SEMIAUTOMATIC CARBINE . **NiB $1822 Ex $1177 Gd $987**
Caliber: 9mm Para 34-round magazine. Bbl.: 16.1 inches. Weight: 7.5 lbs. Flip-type rear peep sight, ramp front. Folding metal skeleton stock. Made from 1983 to 1994.

J. STEVENS ARMS CO. — Chicopee Falls, MA
A division of Savage Industries, Westfield, Massachusetts, owned by ATK since 2013. J. Stevens Arms eventually became a division of Savage Industries. Consequently, the "Stevens" brand name is used for some rifles by Savage; see separate Savage-Stevens listings under Savage.

NO. 12 MARKSMAN
SINGLE-SHOT RIFLE . . . . **NiB $456 Ex $324 Gd $189**
Lever-action, tip-up. Takedown. Calibers: .22 LR, .25 R.F., .32 R.F. 22-inch bbl. Plain straight-grip stock, small tapered forearm.

NO. 14 LITTLE SCOUT
SINGLE-SHOT RIFLE . . . . **NiB $455 Ex $310 Gd $180**
Caliber: .22 RF. 18-inch bbl. One-piece slab stock readily distinguishes it from the No. 14X that follows. Made from 1906 to 1910.

NO. 14 1/2 LITTLE SCOUT
SINGLE-SHOT RIFLE . . . . **NiB $455 Ex $309 Gd $200**
Rolling block. Takedown. Caliber: .22 LR. 18- or 20-inch bbl. Weight: 2.75 lbs. Sights: open rear; blade front. Plain straight-grip stock, small tapered forearm.

MODEL 15 . . . . **NiB $227 Ex $150 Gd $144**
Same as Stevens-Springfield Model 15 except w/24-inch bbl., weight: 5 lbs., w/redesigned stock. Made from 1948 to 1965.

MODEL 15Y YOUTH'S RIFLE . . . . **NiB $221 Ex $155 Gd $127**
Same as Model 15 except w/21-inch bbl., short buttstock, weight: 4.75 lbs. Made from 1958 to 1965.

NO. 44 IDEAL
SINGLE-SHOT RIFLE . . . . **NiB $689 Ex $466 Gd $380**
Rolling block. Lever-action. Takedown. Calibers: .22 LR, .25 R.F., .32

RIFLES

Stevens No. 14 Little Scout

Stevens No. 14.5 Little Scout

Stevens No. 44 Ideal

Stevens Ideal Schuetzen Rifle

Stevens Model 87

R.F., .25-20 S.S., .32-20, .32-40, .38-40, .38-55, .44-40. Bbl. lengths: 24-inch, 26-inch (round, half-octagon, full-octagon). Weight: 7 lbs w/26-inch round bbl. Sights: Open rear; Rocky Mountain front. Plain straight-grip stock and forearm. Made from 1894 to 1932.

NO. 44 1/2 IDEAL SINGLE-SHOT RIFLE . NiB $990 Ex $848 Gd $578
Falling-block. Lever-action rifle. Aside from the new design action intro. 1903, specifications of this model are the same as those of Model 44. Model 44X disc. 1916.

NOS. 45-54 IDEAL SINGLE-SHOT RIFLES
These are higher-grade models, differing from the standard No. 44 and 44.5 chiefly in finish, engraving, set triggers, levers, bbls., stock, etc. The Schuetzen types (including the Stevens-Pope models) are in this series. Model Nos. 45 to 54 were intro. 1896 and originally had the No. 44-type rolling-block action, which was superseded in 1903 by the No. 44.5-type falling-block action. These models were all disc. about 1916. Generally speaking, the 45-54 series rifles, particularly the Stevens Pope and higher grade Schuetzen models are collector's items, bringing much higher prices

than the ordinary No. 44 and 44.5.

MODEL 66 BOLT-ACTION
REPEATING RIFLE . . . . .NiB $255 Ex $140 Gd $121
Takedown. Caliber: .22 Short, Long, LR. Tubular magazine holds 13 LR, 15 Long, 19 Short. 24-inch bbl. Weight: 5 lbs. Sights: Open rear, bead front. Plain pistol-grip stock w/grooved forearm. Made from 1931 to 1935.

NO. 70 VISIBLE LOADING
SLIDE-ACTION. . . . . .NiB $579 Ex $398 Gd $255
Exposed hammer. Caliber: .22 LR, Long, Short. Tubular magazine holds 11 LR., 13 Long, 15 Short. 22-inch bbl. Weight: 4.5 lbs. Sights: Open rear; bead front. Plain straight-grip stock, grooved slide handle. Made 1907-34. Note: Nos. 702, 71, 712, 72, 722 essentially the same as No. 70, differing chiefly in bbl. length or sight tooling.

MODEL 87 AUTOLOADING RIFLE . . . . . .NiB $167 Ex $121 Gd $90
Takedown. Caliber: .22 LR. 15-round tubular magazine. 24-inch bbl.

Stevens No. 414 Armory

Stevens Model 416

Stevens Buckhorn Model 53

Stevens Buckhorn Model 055

Stevens Buckhorn Model 56

RIFLES

(20-inch on current model). Weight: 6 lbs. Sights: Open rear, bead front. Pistol-grip stock. Made 1938 to date. Note: This model originally bore the "Springfield" brand name, disc. in 1948.

MODEL 322 HI-POWER
BOLT-ACTION CARBINE . . . . NiB $487 Ex $333 Gd $202
Caliber: .22 Hornet. 4-round detachable magazine. 21-inch bbl. Weight: 6.75 lbs. Sights: Open rear; ramp front. Pistol-grip stock. Made 1947 to 1950 (See Savage models 340, 342.)MODEL 322-SNiB $479 Ex $338 Gd $200
Same as Model 325 except w/peep rear sight. (See Savage models 340S, 342S.)

MODEL 325 HI-POWER
BOLT-ACTION CARBINE . . . . . . NiB $479 Ex $338 Gd $200
Caliber: .30-30. Three round detachable box magazine. 21-inch bbl. Weight: 6.75 lbs. Sights: Open rear; bead front. Plain pistol-grip stock. Made from 1947 to 1950. (See Savage Model 340.)

MODEL 325-S . . . . NiB $479 Ex $338 Gd $200
Same as Model 325 except w/peep rear sight. (See Savage Model 340S.)

NO. 414 ARMORY MODEL
SINGLE-SHOT RIFLE. . . . . .NiB $488 Ex $398 Gd $316
No. 44-type lever-action. Calibers: .22 LR only, .22 Short only. 26-inch bbl. Weight: 8 lbs. Sights: Lyman receiver peep; blade front. Plain straight-grip stock, military-type forearm, swivels. Made from 1912 to 1932.

MODEL 416 BOLT-ACTION
TARGET RIFLE . . . . NiB $159 Ex $100 Gd $77
Caliber: .22 LR. Five round detachable box magazine. 26-inch heavy bbl. Weight: 9.5 lbs. Sights: Receiver peep; hooded front. Target stock, swivels, sling. Made from 1937 to 1949.

NO. 419 JUNIOR TARGET MODEL
BOLT-ACTION SINGLE-SHOT RIFLE. . . . NiB $433 Ex $325 Gd $255
Takedown. Caliber: .22 LR. 26-inch bbl. Weight: 5.5 lbs. Sights: Lyman No. 55 rear peep; blade front. Plain junior target stock w/pistol grip and grooved forearm, swivels, sling. Made 1932 to 1936.

BUCKHORN MODEL 053 BOLT-ACTION
SINGLE-SHOT RIFLE. . . . . .NiB $200 Ex $148 Gd $110
Takedown. Calibers: .22 Short, Long, LR., .22 WRF. .25 Stevens R.F. 24-inch bbl. Weight: 5.5 lbs. Sights: Receiver peep; open middle; hooded front. Sporting stock w/pistol-grip and black forend tip. Made 1935 to 1948.

Stevens Buckhorn Model 066

Stevens Buckhorn Model 66

Stevens Buckhorn Model 76

Stevens Crackshot No. 26

BUCKHORN MODEL 53 . . . . NiB $220 Ex $179 Gd $122
Same as Buckhorn Model 053 except w/open rear sight and plain bead front sight.

BUCKHORN 055 . . . . .NiB $233 Ex $188 Gd $126
Takedown. Same as Model 056 except in single-shot configuration. Weight: 5.5 lbs. Caliber: .22 LR, Long, Short. 24-inch bbl. Weight: 6 lbs. Sights: Receiver peep, open middle, hooded front. Made from 1935 to 1948.

BUCKHORN MODEL 056 . . . . NiB $230 Ex $190 Gd $131
Takedown. Bolt action. Caliber: .22 LR, Long, Short. Five round detachable box magazine. 24-inch bbl. Weight: 6 lbs. Sights: Receiver peep, open middle, hooded front. Sporting stock w/pistol grip and black forend tip. Made from 1935 to 1948.

BUCKHORN MODEL 56 . . . . NiB $230 Ex $190 Gd $131
Same as Buckhorn Model 056 except w/open rear sight and plain bead front sight.

BUCKHORN NO. 057 . . . . NiB $233 Ex $155 Gd $120
Same as Buckhorn Model 076 except w/5-round detachable box magazine. Made from 1939 to 1948.

BUCKHORN NO. 57 . . . . NiB $230 Ex $155 Gd $120
Same as Buckhorn Model 76 except w/5-round detachable box magazine. Made from 1939 to 1948.

BUCKHORN MODEL 066 . . . . NiB $290 Ex $227 Gd $130
Takedown. Bolt action. Caliber: .22 LR, Long, Short. Tubular magazine

holds 21 Short, 17 Long, 15 LR. 24-inch bbl. Weight: 6 lbs. Sights: Receiver peep; open middle; hooded front. Sporting stock w/pistol grip and black forend tip. Made from 1935 to 1948.

BUCKHORN MODEL 66 . . . . .NiB $219 Ex $133 Gd $210
Same as Buckhorn Model 066 except w/open rear sight, plain bead front sight.

BUCKHORN NO. 076
AUTOLOADING RIFLE . . . . .NiB $227 Ex $188 Gd $135
Takedown. Caliber: .22 LR. 15-round tubular magazine. 24-inch bbl. Weight: 6 lbs. Sights: Receiver peep; open middle; hooded front. Sporting stock w/pistol grip, black forend tip. Made 1938 to 1948.

BUCKHORN NO. 76 . . . . .NiB $227 Ex $188 Gd $135
Same as Buckhorn No. 076 except w/open rear sight, plain bead front sight.

CRACKSHOT NO. 26
SINGLE-SHOT RIFLE. . . . . .NiB $338 Ex $229 Gd $170
Lever-action. Takedown. Calibers: .22 LR, .32 R.F. 18-inch or 22-inch bbl. Weight: 3.25 lbs. Sights: Open rear; blade front. Plain straight-grip stock, small tapered forearm. Made from 1913 to 1939.

CRACKSHOT NO. 26.5 . . . . . NiB $325 Ex $220 Gd $195

Same as Crackshot No. 26 on previous page except w/smoothbore bbl. for shot cartridges.

FAVORITE NO. 17
SINGLE-SHOT RIFLE. . . . . .NiB $333 Ex $227 Gd $200

Stevens Walnut
Hill No. 417-1

Stevens Walnut
Hill No. 417.5

Stevens Walnut
Hill No. 418

RIFLES

Lever-action. Takedown. Calibers: .22 LR, .25 R.F., .32 R.F. 24-inch round bbl; other lengths were available. Weight: 4.5 lbs. Sights: Open rear; Rocky Mountain front. Plain straight-grip stock, small tapered forearm. Made from 1894 to 1935.

FAVORITE NO. 18 . . . . **NiB $422 Ex $300 Gd $179**
Same as Favorite No. 17 except w/Vernier peep rear sight, leaf middle sight, Beach combination front sight.

FAVORITE NO. 19 . . . . **NiB $439 Ex $333 Gd $220**
Same as Favorite No. 17 except w/Lyman combination rear sight, leaf middle sight, Lyman front sight.

FAVORITE NO. 20 . . . . **NiB $420 Ex $325 Gd $215**
Same as Favorite No. 17 except w/smoothbore barrel.

FAVORITE NO. 27 . . . . **NiB $439 Ex $333 Gd $220**
Same as Favorite No. 17 except w/octagon bbl.

FAVORITE NO. 28 . . . . **NiB $439 Ex $333 Gd $220**
Same as Favorite No. 18 except w/octagon bbl.

FAVORITE NO. 29 . . . . **NiB $439 Ex $333 Gd $220**
Same as Favorite No. 19 except w/octagon bbl.

WALNUT HILL NO. 417-0
SINGLE-SHOT TARGET RIFLE . . . . **NiB $909 Ex $777 Gd $530**
Lever-action. Calibers: .22 LR only, .22 Short only, .22 Hornet. 28-inch heavy bbl. (extra heavy 29-inch bbl. also available). Weight: 10.5 lbs. Sights: Lyman No. 52L extension rear; 17A front, scope bases mounted on bbl. Target stock w/full pistol-grip, beavertail forearm, bbl. band, swivels, sling. Made from 1932 to 1947.

WALNUT HILL NO. 417-1 . . . . . . **NiB $909 Ex $750 Gd $521**
Same as No. 417-0 except w/Lyman No. 48L receiver sight.

WALNUT HILL NO. 417-2 . . . . . . **NiB $909 Ex $750 Gd $521**
Same as No. 417-0 except w/Lyman No. 144 tang sight.

WALNUT HILL NO. 417-3 . . . . . . **NiB $909 Ex $750 Gd $521**
Same as No. 417-0 except w/o sights.

WALNUT HILL NO. 417.5
SINGLE-SHOT RIFLE . . . . **NiB $909 Ex $750 Gd $521**
Lever-action. Calibers: .22 LR, .22 WMR, .25 R.F., .22 Hornet. 28-inch bbl. Weight: 8.5 lbs. Sights: Lyman No. 144 tang peep, folding middle; bead front. Sporting stock w/pistol-grip, semi-beavertail forearm, swivels, sling. Made from 1932 to 1940.

WALNUT HILL NO. 418
SINGLE-SHOT RIFLE . . . . **NiB $988 Ex $768 Gd $589**
Lever-action. Takedown. Calibers: .22 LR only, .22 Short only. 26-inch bbl. Weight: 6.5 lbs. Sights: Lyman No. 144 tang peep; blade front. Pistol-grip stock, semi-beavertail forearm, swivels, sling. Made from 1932 to 1940.

WALNUT HILL NO. 418-5 . . . . . . **NiB $988 Ex $768 Gd $589**
Same as No. 418 except also available in calibers .22 WRF and .25 Stevens R.F., w/Lyman No. 2A tang peep sight, bead front sight.

STEVENS-SPRINGFIELD

MODEL 82 BOLT-ACTION
SINGLE-SHOT RIFLE . . . . **NiB $178 Ex $144 Gd $115**
Takedown. Caliber: .22 LR, Long, Short. 22-inch bbl. Weight: 4 lbs. Sights: Open rear; gold bead front. Plain pistol-grip stock w/grooved forearm. Made from 1935 to 1939.

Stevens-Springfield
Model 15

Stevens-
Springfield Model
82

Stevens-Springfield
Model 83

Stevens-Springfield
Model 84

Stevens-
Springfield Model
85

Stevens-Springfield
Model 86-S

MODEL 83 BOLT-ACTION
SINGLE-SHOT RIFLE . . . . .NiB $200 Ex $155 Gd $110
Takedown. Calibers: .22 LR, Long, Short; .22 WRF, .25 Stevens R.F.
24-inch bbl. Weight: 4.5 lbs. Sights: Peep rear; open middle; hooded
front. Plain pistol-grip stock w/grooved forearm. Made 1935 to 1939.

MODEL 84 . . . . .NiB $220 Ex $190 Gd $128
Same as Model 86 except w/5-round detachable box magazine. Pre-
1948 rifles of this model were designated Springfield Model 84, later
known as Stevens Model 84. Made from 1940 to 1965.

MODEL 84-S (084) . . . . .NiB $220 Ex $190 Gd $128
Same as Model 84 except w/peep rear sight and hooded front sight. Pre-
1948 rifles of this model were designated Springfield Model 084, later
known as Stevens Model 84-S. Disc.

MODEL 85 . . . . .NiB $244 Ex $199 Gd $139
Same as Stevens Model 87 except w/5-round detachable box magazine. Made 1939
to date. Pre-1948 rifles of this model were designated Springfield Model 85, currently
known as Stevens Model 85. Earlier models command slight premiums.

MODEL 85-S (085) . . . . .NiB $224 Ex $167 Gd $126
Same as Model 85 except w/peep rear sight and hooded front sight.

Pre-1948 models were designated Springfield Model 085; also known
as Stevens Model 85-S.

MODEL 86
BOLT-ACTION . . . . .NiB $224 Ex $167 Gd $126
Takedown. Caliber: .22 LR, Long, Short. Tubular magazine holds 15 LR,
17 Long, 21 Short. 24-inch bbl. Weight: 6 lbs. Sights: Open rear, gold
bead front. Pistol-grip stock, black forend tip on later production. Made
1935 to 1965. Note: The Springfield brand name was disc. in 1948.

MODEL 86-S (086) . . . . .NiB $230 Ex $172 Gd $128
Same as Model 86 except w/peep rear sight and hooded front sight.
Pre-1948 rifles of this model were designated as Springfield Model 086,
later known as Stevens Model 86-S. Disc.

MODEL 87-S (087) . . . . .NiB $233 Ex $215 Gd $156
Same as Stevens Model 87 except w/peep rear sight and hooded
front sight. Pre-1948 rifles of this model were designated as
Springfield Model 087, later known as Stevens Model 87-S. Disc.

STEYR DAIMLER PUCH A.G. — Steyr, Austria
See also listings under Mannlicher.

Thompson/Center
Contender Carbine

Thompson/Center TCR
'83 Aristocrat

Thompson/Center TCR
'87 Hunter

AUG-SA
SEMIAUTOMATIC RIFLE . . . . NiB $4220 Ex $3370 Gd $2340
Gas-operated. Caliber: .223 Rem. (5.56mm). Thirty or 40-round magazine. 20-inch bbl. standard; optional 16-inch or 24-inch heavy bbl. w/
folding bipod. 31 inches overall. Weight: 8.5 lbs. Sights: Integral 1.5x
scope and mount. Green high-impact synthetic stock w/folding vertical
grip.

SMALL BORE CARBINE . . . . . . .NiB $440 Ex $300 Gd $166
Bolt-action repeater. Caliber: .22 LR. Five round detachable box magazine. 19.5-inch bbl. Sights: Leaf rear; hooded bead front. Mannlicher-
type stock, checkered, swivels. Made 1953 to 1967.

STOEGER — New York, NY
*Manufactured by Franz Jaeger & Co., Suhl, Germany; dist. in the U.S.
by A. F. Stoeger, Inc., New York, NY.*

HORNET RIFLE . . . . .NiB $1388 Ex $1008 Gd $659
Same specifications as Herold Rifle, designed and built on a Miniature
Mauser-type action. See listing under Herold Bolt-Action Repeating
Sporting Rifle for additional specifications. Imported during the 1930s.

SURVIVAL ARMS — Orange, Connecticut

AR-7 EXPLORER . . . . .NiB $180 Ex $155 Gd $98
Caliber: .22 LR. Eight round magazine. Weight: 3 lbs. Polymer
stocks. Drift adj. sights. Disassembles into five separate elements,
allowing barrel, action and magazine to fit into buttstock; assembles

quickly w/o tools. Choice of camo, silvertone or black matte finishes.
Made from 1992 to 1995.

THOMPSON/CENTER ARMS — Springfield, MA
Acquired by Smith & Wesson in 2007; formerly in Rochester, NH.

*To facilitate locating Thompson/Center rifles, models are grouped into
three categories: single-shot rifles (below), semi-automatic and bolt-
action rifles. For a complete listing, please refer to the index.*

- SINGLE-SHOT RIFLES -

CONTENDER CARBINE
Calibers: .22 LR, .22 Hornet, .222 Rem., .223 Rem., 7mm T.C.U., 7x30
Waters, .30-30 Win., .35 Rem., .44 Mag., .357 Rem. Max. and .410
bore. 21-inch interchangeable bbls. 35 inches overall. Adj. iron sights.
Checkered American walnut or Rynite stock and forend. Made from
1986 to 2000.
Standard model (rifle calibers) . . .NiB $466 Ex $287 Gd $198
Standard model (.410 bore). . . . . .NiB $459 Ex $280 Gd $210
Rynite stock model
  (rifle calibers). . . . . .NiB $390 Ex $290 Gd $245
Rynite stock model (.410 bore) . . .NiB $390 Ex $300 Gd $244
Youth model (all calibers). . . . . . .NiB $495 Ex $320 Gd $235
Extra bbl. (rifle calibers), add $25
Extra bbl. (.410 bore), add $35

CONTENDER CARBINE
SURVIVAL SYSTEM. . . . . NiB $655 Ex $488 Gd $370
Similar to standard Contender Carbine w/Rynite stock and forend.

Thompson/Center Icon Warlord

Thompson/Center Model R-55 Classic

Thompson/Center Dimension RH Scoped

Thompson/Center Encore Katahdin

Comes w/two 16.25-inch bbls. chambered in .223 and .45/.410 bore. Camo Cordura case.

STAINLESS CONTENDER CARBINE
Same as standard Contender Carbine Model, except stainless steel w/ blued sights. Calibers: .22 LR, .22 Hornet, .223 Rem., 7-30 Waters, .30-30 Win., .410. Walnut or Rynite stock and forend. Made from 1993 to 2000.
Walnut stock model . . . . NiB $445 Ex $390 Gd $325
Rynite stock model . . . . NiB $495 Ex $425 Gd $300
Youth stock model . . . . NiB $467 Ex $388 Gd $287
Extra bbls. (rifle calibers), add. $25

ENCORE RIFLE . . . . NiB $788 Ex $521 Gd $379
Single-shot, break-action. Cal.: Rimfire and centerfire from .17 Mach 2 to .45-70 Gov't. Bbl.: 24 to 16 inches, interchangeable. Hammer block safety, trigger guard opening lever. Stock: Synthetic black, Realtree camo or American walnut; smooth forearm, Monte Carlo stock w/pistol grip; adj. rear sight.
w/extra blued bbls., add $245
Camo models, add $150
w/thumbhole stock, add $227
.17 Mach 2, add $75
w/stainless bbl., add $400
Hunter pkg. (scope, bases, case), add $300

ENCORE KATAHDIN . . . . NiB $633 Ex $467 Gd $379
Same as Encore but with 18-inch blued bbl. Cal.: .444 Marlin, .450 Marlin or .45-70 Gov't. Stock: Black composite. Fiber optic sights, drilled and tapped for scope. Weight: 6.6 lbs. Made from 2002 to 2005.

PRO HUNTER RIFLE . . . . NiB $944 Ex $670 Gd $433
Cal.: Various. Bbl.: 28 inches, stainless steel. Recoil reducing Flex-Tech stock (thumbhole option) in black or camo.
w/camo stock, add $100
w/ extra bbl., add $400

HOTSHOT (CAMO STOCK) . . . . . NiB $395 Ex $299 Gd $214
Youth model. Cal.: 22 LR. Bbl.: 19 inches. Stock: Black synthetic, Realtree AP camo or AP pink camo. Auto safety; drilled and tapped for scope. Weight: 3 lbs.
w/pink camo stock, add $25

TCR '83/ARISTOCRAT MODEL . . NiB $497 Ex $445 Gd $277
Break frame, overlever action. Calibers: .223 Rem., .22/250 Rem., .243 Win., 7mm Rem. Mag., .30-06 Springfield. Interchangeable bbls.: 23 inches in length. Weight: 6 lbs., 14 oz. American walnut stock and forearm, checkered, black rubber recoil pad, cheekpiece. Made from 1983 to 1987.
Aristocrat model. . . . . NiB $569 Ex $439 Gd $280
Extra bbl. (rifle calibers), add $278

TCR '87 HUNTER RIFLE . . . . NiB $544 Ex $345 Gd $200
Similar to TCR '83 except in calibers .22 Hornet, ..222 Rem., 223 Rem., .22-250 Rem., .243 Win., .270 Win., 7mm-08, .308 Win., .30-06, .32-40 Win. Also 12-ga. slug and 10- and 12-ga. field bbls. 23-inch standard or 25.88-inch heavy bbl. interchangeable. 39.5 to 43.38 inches overall. Weight: 6 lbs., 14 oz. to 7.5 lbs. Iron sights optional. Checkered American black walnut buttstock w/fluted end. Disc. 1992.
Extra bbl. (rifle calibers, 10- & 12-ga. field), add $250
Extra bbl. (12-ga. slug), add $300
- BOLT-ACTION RIFLES -

DIMENSION. . . . . NiB $689 Ex $380 Gd $300
Push-feed, short or long action, interchangeable barrels. Calibers.: .204 Ruger, .22-250 Rem., .223 Rem., .243 Win., .270 Win., .308 Win., .30-06, .300 Win. Mag., 7mm-08, 7mm Rem. Mag. Bbl.: 22 or 24 in., 3-round detachable box magazine, black synthetic stock w/ adj. LOP, Weaver style mounts. Made 2012 to date.

ICON. . . . . NiB $1167 Ex $855 Gd $766
Bolt action. Cal.: .22-250 Rem., .270 Win., .30-06, .300 Win. Mag., .308 Win., .30 TC, 6.5 Creedmoor, 7mm Mag. Bbl.: 24 inches. Medium or long action, hinged floor plate (on long action). Stock: Black synthetic or RealTree camo, checkered American walnut, classic walnut or Ultra Wood; pistol grip and forearm. Adj. trigger, cocking indicator, three-shot magazine (on medium action). Jeweled bolt handle. Weaver-style bases. Weight: 7.5 pounds. Made 2007-12.
Walnut stock models, add. $75

ICON PRECISION HUNTER . NiB $1355 Ex $988 Gd $778
Bolt action. Cal.: .204 Ruger, .223 Rem., .22-250 Rem., .243 Win., 6.5 Creedmoor, .308 Win. Bbl.: 22 inches, fluted; 5R button rifling. Tactical-style bolt handle. Stock: Brown synthetic with cheekpiece and beavertail fore end. Detachable 3-round magazine with single-shot adapter. Picatinny rail, adj. trigger, sling studs. Made 2009-12.

Tikka Model 412S
Double Rifle

Tikka Model LSA55
Deluxe

Tikka Model
LSA65 Deluxe

ICON WARLORD . . . . **NiB $1370 Ex $1127 Gd $888**
Bolt action. Cal.: .308 Win. or .338 Lapua; 5- or 10-round magazine. Bbl.: Fluted, stainless steel, hand lapped. Stock: Carbon fiber tactical style with adj. cheek piece available in OD, flat black or desert sand. Adj. trigger, Picatinny rail. Weight: 12.75 to 13.75 lbs. Made 2010-11.

VENTURE . . . . **NiB $632 Ex $495 Gd $375**
Bolt action. Cal.: 270 Win., .30-06, 7 mm Rem. Mag., .300 Win. Mag. Bbl.: 24 inches, tapered match grade with 5R button rifling. Stock: Black synthetic, sporter design, textured grip. Adj. trigger, two-position safety. Made 2009 to date.

VENTURE PREDATOR . . . . . . **NiB $690 Ex $559 Gd $433**
Bolt action. Cal.: .204 Ruger, .223 Rem., .22-250 Rem. or .308 Win. Bbl.: 22 inches, fluted, 3-round magazine. Stock: Composite with 100% Realtree Max-1 camo coating; Hogue panels, Weather Shield bolt handle. Weight. 6.75 lbs. Made 2010 to date.

- SEMI-AUTOMATIC RIFLES -

SILVER LYNX . . . . **NiB $488 Ex $390 Gd $300**
Semi-auto. Cal.: .22 LR. Bbl.: 20 inches, match grade; 5-round magazine, stainless steel action and bbl. Stock: Black composite with Monte Carlo cheek piece. Weight: 5.5 lbs. Made 2004-05.

MODEL R-55 CLASSIC . . . . . . **NiB $629 Ex $428 Gd $326**
Semi-auto. Cal.: .17 Mach 2, .22 LR. Bbl.: 22 inches, match grade; adj. rear sight; blue finish. Blow-back action. Smooth Monte Carlo walnut stock. Weight: 5.5 lbs. Made 2000-09.
R-55 Target . . . . **NiB $677 Ex $466 Gd $389**
R-55 Sporter . . . . **NiB $519 Ex $405 Gd $310**

TIKKA — Riihimaki, Finland
Manufactured by Sako, Ltd. of Riihimaki, Finland and Armi Marocchi

in Italy. Acquired by Beretta Holdings in 2000.

NOTE: *Tikka New Generation, Battue and Continental series bolt action rifles are being manufactured by Sako, Ltd., in Finland. Tikka O/U rifles (previously Valmet) are being manufactured in Italy by Armi Marocchi. For earlier importation see additional listings under Ithaca LSA and Valmet 412S models.*

T3 HUNTER . . . . **NiB $655 Ex $535 Gd $390**
Calibers:..223, .22-250, .243Win., .308 Win., .25-06, .270 Win., 6.5x55, 270 WSM, 7mm Rem. Mag., .30-06, 300 WSM, .300 Win. Mag., .338 Win. Mag., Bbl: 22 7/16 inches (24.37 in magnum calibers). Weight: 6.75 pounds. No sights. Walnut stock with rubber butt pad. Introduced 2003.

T3 LAMINATED
STAINLESS . . . . **NiB $765 Ex $689 Gd $590**
Same as T3 Hunter but with stainless barrel and action; laminated stock.

T3 LITE . . . . **NiB $555 Ex $489 Gd $410**
Similar to T3 Hunter but with synthetic stock; weight: 6 pounds, 3 ounces. Introduced 2003.**T3 LITE STAINLESS** . **NiB $589 Ex $469 Gd $370**

Same as T3 Lite but with stainless barrel and action.

T3 TACTICAL . . . . **NiB $1469 Ex $1210 Gd $1077**
Calibers: .223, .308 Win. Similar to T3 Hunter but designed for law enforcement. Bbl.: 20 inches. Black phosphate finish, synthetic stock with adjustable comb. Five round detachable magazine. Picatinny rail on action, fitted for muzzle brake and bipod use.

T3 VARMINT . . . . **NiB $844 Ex $707 Gd $567**
Calibers: .223, .22-250, .308 Win. Similar to T3 Hunter but with heavy bull barrel, synthetic stock, adjustable trigger. Five round detachable magazine.

Tikka
Model M65
Sporter

Tikka
Model M65 Wild
Boar

T3 VARMINT

STAINLESS . . . . **NiB $844   Ex $707   Gd $567**
Similar to T3 Varmint but with stainless barrel and action.

MODEL 412S DOUBLE RIFLE

Calibers: .308 Win., .30-06, 9.3x74R. 24-inch bbl. w/quarter rib
machined for scope mounts; automatic ejectors (9.3x74R only). 40
inches overall. Weight: 8.5 lbs. Ramp front and folding adj. rear sight.
Barrel selector on trigger. European walnut buttstock and forearm.
Model 412S was replaced by the 512S version in 1994. Imported from
1989 to 1993.

Model 412S
   (disc. 1993) . . . . **NiB $1135   Ex $944   Gd $725**
Extra bbl. assembly
   (O/U shotgun), add **$707**
Extra bbl. assembly
   (O/U Combo), add **$800**
Extra bbl. assembly
   (OU/rifle), add **$1050**

MODEL 512S DOUBLE RIFLE

Formerly Valmet 412S. In 1994, following the joint venture of 1989,
the model designation was changed to 512S. Imported from 1994 to
1997.

Model 512S . . . . **NiB $1559   Ex $1440   Gd $1100**
w/extra bbl. assembly (O/U rifle), add **$800**

LSA55 DELUXE. . . . . **NiB $590   Ex $534   Gd $450**
Same as LSA55 Standard except w/rollover cheekpiece, rosewood grip
cap and forend tip, skip checkering, high-luster blue. Imported from
1965 to 1988.

LSA55 SPORTER . . . . **NiB $580   Ex $482   Gd $369**
Same as LSA55 except has 22.8-inch heavy bbl. w/o sights, special
stock w/beavertail forearm, not available in 6mm Rem. Weighs 9 lbs.
Imported from 1965 to 1988.

LSA55 STANDARD

BOLT-ACTION REPEATER. . . . . . . **NiB $555   Ex $389   Gd $244**
Mauser-type action. Calibers: .222 Rem., .22-250, 6mm Rem. Mag., .243
Win., .308 Win. Three round clip magazine. 22.8-inch bbl. Weight: 6.8
lbs. Sights: Folding leaf rear; hooded ramp front. Checkered walnut stock
w/Monte Carlo cheekpiece, swivels. Made from 1965-88.

LSA65 DELUXE. . . . . **NiB $598   Ex $522   Gd $369**
Same as LSA65 Standard except w/special features of LSA55 Deluxe.
Imported from 1970 to 1988.

LSA65 STANDARD . . . . **NiB $495   Ex $398   Gd $277**
Same as LSA55 Standard except calibers: .25-06, 6.5x55 .270 Win.,
.30-06. Five round magazine, 22-inch bbl., weight: 7.5 lbs. Imported
1970 to 1988.

MODEL M 55

Bolt action. Calibers: .222 Rem., .22-250 Rem., .223 Rem. .243 Win.,
.308 Win. (6mm Rem. and 17 Rem. available in Standard and Deluxe
models only). 23.2-inch bbl. (24.8-inch in Sporter and Heavy Barrel
models). 42.8 inches overall (44 inches in Sporter and Heavy Barrel
models). Weight: 7.25 to 9 lbs. Monte Carlo-style stock w/pistol-grip.
Sling swivels. Imported 1965 to 1988.

Continental	NiB $745	Ex $560	Gd $420
Deluxe model.	NiB $808	Ex $579	Gd $443
Sporter	NiB $733	Ex $577	Gd $400
Sporter w/sights	NiB $755	Ex $572	Gd $390
Standard.	NiB $669	Ex $544	Gd $367
Super Sporter	NiB $833	Ex $466	Gd $398
Super Sporter w/sights	NiB $909	Ex $478	Gd $514
Trapper	NiB $755	Ex $556	Gd $443

Model M65

Bolt action. Calibers: .25-06, .270 Win., .308 Win., .30-06, 7mm Rem.
Mag., .300 Win. Mag. (Sporter and Heavy Bbl. models in .270 Win.,
.308 Win. and .30-06 only). 22.4-inch bbl. (24.8-inch in Sporter and
Heavy Bbl. models). 43.2 inches overall (44 inches in Sporter, 44.8
inches in Heavy Bbl.). Weight: 7.5 to 9.9 lbs. Monte Carlo-style stock
w/pistol-grip. Disc. 1989.

Continental	NiB $755	Ex $572	Gd $439
Deluxe Magnum.	NiB $800	Ex $677	Gd $495
Deluxe model.	NiB $770	Ex $587	Gd $467
Magnum.	NiB $709	Ex $540	Gd $440
Sporter.	NiB $579	Ex $555	Gd $398
Sporter w/sights	NiB $789	Ex $645	Gd $445
Standard.	NiB $670	Ex $690	Gd $479
Super Sporter	NiB $898	Ex $690	Gd $489

Tikka Continental/
Varmint

Tikka
New Generation

Tikka
Premium Grade

Tikka Whitetail/
Battue

Tikka
Whitetail Hunter Deluxe

Tikka
Whitetail Hunter Synthetic

Tikka
Whitetail Hunter Stainless Synthetic

Super Sporter w/sights . . . . NiB $909 Ex $695 Gd $494
Super Sporter Master . . . . NiB $1143 Ex $944 Gd $643

MODEL M65 WILD BOAR . . . . . . NiB $790 Ex $650 Gd $469
Same general specifications as Model M 65 except 20.8-inch bbl., overall length of 41.6 inches, weight: of 7.5 lbs. Disc. 1989.

NEW GENERATION RIFLES
Short-throw bolt available in three action lengths. Calibers: .22-250

Rem., .223 Rem., .243 Win., .308 Win., (medium action) .25-06 Rem.,
.270 Win., .30.06, (Long Action) 7mm Rem. Mag., .300 Win. Mag.,
.338 Win. Mag., (Magnum Action). 22- to 26-inch bbl. 42.25 to 46
inches overall. Weight: 7.2 to 8.5 lbs. Available w/o sights or w/hooded
front and open rear sight on quarter rib. Quick-release 3- or 5-round
detachable magazine w/recessed side release. Barrel selector on trigger
and cocking indicators in tang. European walnut buttstock and forearm
matte lacquer finish. Imported 1989 to 1994.
Standard calibers . . . . NiB $769 Ex $688 Gd $487

GRADING: **NiB** = New in Box   **Ex** = Excellent or NRA 95%   **Gd** = Good or NRA 68%

**Uberti Model
1873 Carbine**

Magnum calibers, add $50

PREMIUM GRADE RIFLE
Similar to New Generation rifles except w/hand-checkered deluxe
wood stock w/roll-over check-piece and rosewood grip cap and forend
tip. High polished blued finish. Imported from 1989 to 1994.
Standard calibers . . . . NiB $923 Ex $755 Gd $488
Magnum calibers, add $50

WHITETAIL BOLT-ACTION RIFLE SERIES
New Generation design in multiple model configurations and three
action lengths chambered .22-250 to .338 Win. Mag.

BATTUE MODEL
Similar to Hunter Model except designed for snapshooting w/hooded
front and open rear sights on quarter rib. Blued finish. Checkered select
walnut stock w/matt lacquered finish. Imported 1991 to 1997.
Battue model (standard w/sights). . NiB $568 Ex $466 Gd $388
Magnum calibers, add $50

CONTINENTAL MODEL
Similar to Hunter Model except w/prone-style stock w/wider forearm
and 26-inch heavy bbl. chambered for 17 Rem., .22-250 Rem., .223
Rem., .308 Win. (Varmint); .25-06 Rem., .270 Win., 7mm Rem. Mag.,
.300 Win. Mag. (Long Range). Weight: 8.6 lbs. Imported from 1991 to
2003.
Continental Long-Range model . . . NiB $690 Ex $558 Gd $390
Continental Varmint model . . . . . NiB $640 Ex $500 Gd $355
Magnum calibers, add 40%

SPORTER MODEL . . . . NiB $909 Ex $779 Gd $633
Similar to Hunter Model except 23.5-inch bbl. Five round detachable
mazigine. Chambered .22-250 Rem., .223 Rem., .308 Win. Weight:
8.6 lbs. Adjustable buttplate and cheekpiece w/stippled pistol grip and
forend. Imported from 1998 to 2003.

WHITETAIL HUNTER MODEL
Calibers: .22-250 Rem., .223 Rem., .243 Win., .25-06 Rem., .270 Win.,
7mm Rem. Mag., .308 Win .30.06, .300 Win. Mag., .338 Win. Mag.
Three or 5-round detachable box magazine. 20.5- to 24.5-inch bbl.
with no sights. 42 to 44.5 inches overall. Weight: 7 to 7.5 lbs. Adj.
single-stage or single-set trigger. Blued or stainless finish. All-Weather
synthetic or checkered select walnut stock w/matt lacquered finish.
Imported from 1991 to 2002.
Standard model . . . . NiB $633 Ex $523 Gd $389
Deluxe model. . . . . NiB $689 Ex $534 Gd $445
Synthetic model . . . . NiB $689 Ex $534 Gd $445

Stainless model . . . . NiB $689 Ex $534 Gd $445
Magnum calibers, add $50
Left-hand model, add $100

UBERTI — Accokeek, Maryland
*Formerly in Lakeville, Connecticut. Manufactured By Aldo Uberti,
Ponte Zanano, Italy. Imported by Stoeger Industries, Accokeek, MD.
Division of Beretta Holdings.*

MODEL 1866 SPORTING RIFLE
Replica of Winchester Model 1866 lever-action repeater. Calibers: .22
LR, .22 WMR, .38 Spec., .44-40, .45 LC. 24.25-inch octagonal bbl.
43.25 inches overall. Weight: 8.25 lbs. Blade front sight,rear elevation
leaf. Brass frame and buttplate. Bbl., magazine tube, other metal parts
blued. Walnut buttstock and forearm.
Rifle. . . . . NiB $976 Ex $667 Gd $390
Carbine (19-inch round bbl.). . . . . NiB $944 Ex $600 Gd $409
Trapper (16-inch bbl.,
  Disc. 1989. . . . . NiB $1145 Ex $855 Gd $600
Rimfire (Indian Rifle) . . . . NiB $744 Ex $523 Gd $379
Rimfire (Indian Carbine) . . . . NiB $744 Ex $523 Gd $379

MODEL 1873 SPORTING RIFLE
Replica of Winchester Model 1873 lever-action repeater. Calibers:
.22 LR, .22 WMR, .38 Spl., .357 Mag., .44-40, .45 LC. 24.25- or
30-inch octagonal bbl. 43.25 inches overall. Weight: 8 lbs. Blade
front sight; adj. open rear. Color case-hardened frame. Bbl., magazine tube, hammer, lever and buttplate blued. Walnut buttstock and
forearm.
Rifle. . . . . NiB $1095 Ex $809 Gd $572
Carbine (19-inch round bbl.). . . . . NiB $790 Ex $666 Gd $445
Trapper (16-inch bbl.,
  disc. 1990) . . . . NiB $1095 Ex $809 Gd $572

HENRY RIFLE
Replica of Henry lever-action repeating rifle. Calibers: .44-40, .45 LC.
24.5-inch half-octagon bbl. 43.75 inches overall. Weight: 9.25 lbs.
Blade front sight; rear sight adj. for elevation. Brass frame, buttplate and
magazine follower. Bbl., magazine tube and remaining parts blued.
Walnut buttstock.
Rifle. . . . . NiB $1177 Ex $808 Gd $590
Carbine (22.5-inch bbl.) . . . . NiB $1177 Ex $808 Gd $590
Trapper (16- or 18-inch bbl.) . . . NiB $1177 Ex $808 Gd $590
Steel frame, add $100

U.S. Model 1903-A1
Springfield

U.S. Model 1903-A3
Springfield

U.S. Model 1917
Enfield

MODEL 1875 ARMY TARGET . . . . NiB $455 Ex $360 Gd $300
Calibers: .357 Mag., .44-40 Colt. Six-round cylinder. Bbl.: 18
inches. Overall length: 37 inches. Weight: 4 1/2 pounds. Carbine
version of Model 1875 single-action revolver. Sights: Adjustable
rear, ramp front. Plain walnut stock, polished brass butt plate and
trigger guard. Case-hardened frame. Blued or nickel-plated cylinder and barrel. Made in Italy. Introduced in 1987, discontinued
1989.
Nickel finish, add $50

ROLLING BLOCK BABY CARBINE NiB $450 Ex $380 Gd $319
Calibers: .22 LR, .22WMR, .22 Hornet, .357 Mag. Bbl.: 22 inches.
Overall length: 35 1/2 inches. Weight: 4 3/4 pounds. Copy of
Remington New Model No. 4 carbine featuring brass butt plate and
trigger guard; blued barrel; color case-hardened frame. Introduced
in 1986.

ULTRA-HI PRODUCTS COMPANY — Hawthorne, New Jersey

**MODEL 2200 SINGLE-SHOT
BOLT-ACTION RIFLE . . . . NiB $235 Ex $166 Gd $120**
Caliber: .22 LR, Long, Short. .23-inch bbl. Weight: 5 lbs. Sights: Open
rear; blade front. Monte Carlo stock w/pistol grip. Made in Japan. Intro.
1977; Disc.

ULTRA LIGHT ARMS COMPANY — Granville, West Virginia

MODEL 20 BOLT-ACTION RIFLE
Calibers: .22-250 Rem., .243 Win., 6mm Rem., .250-3000
Savage, .257 Roberts, .257 Ack., 7mm Mauser, 7mm Ack., 7mm-
08 Rem., .284 Win., .300 Savage, .308 Win., .358 Win. Box
magazine. 22-inch ultra light bbl. Weight: 4.75 lbs. No sights.
Synthetic stock of Kevlar or graphite finished, seven different
colors. Nonglare matte or bright metal finish. Medium-length
action available L.H. models. Made from 1985 to 1999.

Standard model . . . . NiB $2270 Ex $2056 Gd $1190
Left-hand model, add $150

MODEL 20S BOLT-ACTION RIFLE
Same general specifications as Model 20 except w/short action in cali-
bers 17 Rem., .222 Rem., .223 Rem., .22 Hornet only.
Standard model . . . . NiB $2467 Ex $2144 Gd $1180
Left-hand model, add $126

MODEL 24 BOLT-ACTION RIFLE
Same general specifications as Model 20 except w/long action in cali-
bers .25-06, .270 Win., .30-06 and 7mm Express only.
Standard model . . . . NiB $2350 Ex $2123 Gd $1179
Left-hand model, add $126

MODEL 28 BOLT-ACTION RIFLE . . . NiB $2709 Ex $2033 Gd $1190
Same as Model 20 except w/long magnum action in calibers .264
Win. Mag., 7mm Rem. Mag., .300 Win. Mag., .338 Win. Mag. only.
Offered w/recoil arrester. Left-hand model available.

MODEL 40 BOLT-ACTION RIFLE
Similar to Model 28 except in calibers .300 Wby. and .416 Rigby.
Weight: 5.5 lbs. Made from 1994 to 1999.
Standard model . . . . NiB $2770 Ex $2055 Gd $1290
Left-hand, model, add. . . . . . $126UNIQUE — Hendaye, France
Manufactured by Manufacture d'Armes des Pyrénées Francaises.

T66 MATCH RIFLE . . . . NiB $469 Ex $388 Gd $289
Single-shot bolt-action rifle. Caliber: .22 LR. 25.5-inch bbl. Weight:
10.5 lbs. Sights: Micrometer aperture rear; globe front. French walnut
target stock w/Monte Carlo comb, bull pistol-grip, wide and deep forearm, stippled grip surfaces, adj. swivel on accessory track, adj. rubber
buttplate. Made in 1966. Disc.

U.S. MILITARY RIFLES — Springfield, Massachusetts
*Manufactured by Springfield Armory, Remington Arms Co.,
Winchester Repeating Arms Co., Inland Mfg. Div. of G.M.C., and
other contractors. Unless otherwise indicated, the following U.S. military rifles were mfg. at Springfield Armory, Springfield, Mass.*

U.S. Rifle Caliber .30,
M1 (Garand)

U.S. Carbine
Caliber .30, M1

MODEL 1898
KRAG-JORGENSEN CARBINE . NiB $2100 Ex $1879 Gd $1100
Same general specifications as Model 1898 Rifle except w/22-inch bbl.,
weight: 8 lbs., carbine-type stock. Note: The foregoing specifications
apply, in general, to Carbine models 1896 and 1899, which differed
from Model 1898 only in minor details.

MODEL 1898
KRAG-JORGENSEN MILITARY RIFLE . NiB $2100 Ex $1879 Gd $1100
Bolt action. Caliber: .30-40 Krag. Five round hinged box magazine.
30-inch bbl. Weight: 9 lbs. Sights: Adj. rear; blade front. Military-
type stock, straight grip. Note: The foregoing specifications apply, in
general, to Rifle models 1892 and 1896, which differed from Model
1898.

MODEL 1903 MARK I SPRINGFIELD. . NiB $2144 Ex $1844 Gd $945
Same as Standard Model 1903 except altered to permit use of the Pedersen
Device. This device, officially designated "U.S. Automatic Pistol Model
1918," converted the M/1903 to a semiautomatic weapon firing a .30
caliber cartridge similar to .32 automatic pistol ammunition. Mark I rifles
have a slot milled in the left side of the receiver to serve as an ejection port
when the Pedersen Device was in use; these rifles were also fitted w/a
special sear and cut-off. Some 65,000 of these devices were manufactured and, presumably, a like number of M/1903 rifles were converted
to handle them. During the early 1930s, all Pedersen Devices were
ordered destroyed and the Mark I rifles were reconverted by replacement of the special sear and cut-off w/standard components. Some
20-odd specimens are known to have escaped destruction and are
in government museums and private collections. Probably more are
extant. Rarely is a Pedersen Device offered for sale, so a current value
cannot be assigned. However, many of the altered rifles were bought
by members of the National Rifle Association through the Director of
Civilian Marksmanship. Value shown is for the Mark I rifle w/o the
Pedersen Device.

MODEL 1903 NATIONAL
MATCH SPRINGFIELD . . . . . . NiB $1755 Ex $1577 Gd $1109
Same general specifications as Standard Model 1903 except spe-
cially selected w/star-gauged bbl., Type C pistol-grip U.S. Model 1903
National Match Springfield (Con't) stock, polished bolt assembly;
early types have headless firing pin assembly and reversed safety lock.
Produced especially for target shooting.

MODEL 1903 SPRINGFIELD MILITARY RIFLE
Modified Mauser-type bolt action. Caliber: .30-06. Five round
box magazine. 23.79-inch bbl. Weight: 8.75 lbs. Sights: Adj. rear;
blade front. Military-type stock straight grip. Note: M/1903 rifles of
Springfield manufacture w/serial numbers under 800,000 (1903 to
1918) have casehardened receivers; those between 800,000 and
1,278,767 (1918 to 1927) were double heat-treated; rifles numbered
over 1,278,767 have nickle steel bolts and receivers. Rock Island
production from No. 1 to 285,507 have case-hardened receivers.
Improved heat treatment was adopted in May 1918 with No. 285,207;
about three months later, with No. 319,921, the use of nickel steel
was begun, but the production of some double-heat-treated carbon-
steel receivers and bolts continued. Made 1903 to 1930 at Springfield
Armory during WWI, M/1903 rifles were also made at Rock Island
Arsenal, Rock Island, Ill.
w/case-hardened receiver . . . . NiB $5566 Ex $4769 Gd $2270
w/double heat-treated receiver . . .NiB $4410 Ex $3636 Gd $1645
w/nickel steel receiver . . . . NiB $1707 Ex $1530 Gd $977

MODEL 1903 SPRINGFIELD SPORTER NiB $1449 Ex $1978 Gd $899
Same general specifications as National Match except w/sporting
design stock, Lyman No. 48 receiver sight.

MODEL 1903 STYLE T
SPRINGFIELD MATCH RIFLE. . . . . . . NiB $1633 Ex $1290 Gd $934
Similar to Springfield Sporter except w/heavy bbl. (26-, 28- or 30-inch),
scope bases, globe front sight, weight: 12.5 lbs. w/26-inch bbl.

MODEL 1903 TYPE A
SPRINGFIELD FREE RIFLE . . . . NiB $1900 Ex $1544 Gd $1150
Same as Style T except made w/28-inch bbl. only, w/Swiss buttplate,
weight: 13.25 lbs.

MODEL 1903 TYPE B
SPRINGFIELD FREE RIFLE . . . . NiB $3510 Ex $2065 Gd $1400
Same as Type A, except w/cheekpiece stock, palm rest, Woodie double-
set triggers, Garand fast firing pin, weight: 14.75 lbs.

MODEL 1903-A1 SPRINGFIELD
Same general specifications as Model 1903 except may have Type C
pistol-grip stock adopted in 1930. The last Springfields produced at the
Springfield Armory were of this type; final serial number was 1,532,878,
made in 1939. Note: Late in 1941, Remington Arms Co., Ilion, N.Y.,
began production, under government contract, of Springfield rifles
of this type w/a few minor modifications. These rifles are numbered
3,000,001-3,348,085 and were manufactured before the adoption of
Model 1903-A3.
Springfield manufacture . . . . . . NiB $1444 Ex $1266 Gd $845
Remington manufacture . . . . NiB $955 Ex $855 Gd $577

**Uzi Semiautomatic
Model B Carbine**

MODEL 1903-A3 SPRINGFIELD . . . . . NiB $1698 Ex $1492 Gd $978
Same general specifications as Model 1903-A1, except modified to permit increased production and lower cost; may have either straight-grip or pistol-grip stock, bolt is not interchangeable w/ earlier types, w/receiver peep sight, many parts are stamped sheet steel, including the trigger guard and magazine assembly. Quality of these rifles, lower than that of other 1903 Springfields, reflects the emergency conditions under which they were produced. Mfd. during WWII by Remington Arms Co. and L. C. Smith Corona Typewriters, Inc.

**MODEL 1922-M1 22
SPRINGFIELD TARGET RIFLE** . . NiB $1277 Ex $1068 Gd $788
Modified Model 1903. Caliber: .22 LR. Five round detachable box magazine. 24.5-inch bbl. Weight: 9 lbs. Sights: Lyman No. 48C receiver, blade front. Sporting-type stock similar to that of Model 1903 Springfield Sporter. Issued 1927. Note: The earlier Model 1922, which is seldom encountered, differs from the foregoing chiefly in the bolt mechanism and magazine.

M2 22 SPRINGFIELD TARGET RIFLE . . NiB $1370 Ex $1123 Gd $580
Same general specifications as Model 1922-M1 except w/speedlock, improved bolt assembly adj. for headspace. Note: These improvements were later incorporated in many rifles of the preceding models (M1922, M1922MI) and arms so converted were marked "M1922M2" or "M1922MII."

NOTE: *The WWII-vintage .30-caliber U.S. Carbine was mfd. by Inland Mfg. Div. of G.M.C., Dayton, OH; Winchester Repeating Arms Co., New Haven, CT, and other contractors: International Business Machines Corp., Poughkeepsie, NY; National Postal Meter Co., Rochester, NY; Quality Hardware & Machine Co., and Rock-Ola Co., Chicago, IL; Saginaw Steering Gear Div. of G.M.C., Saginaw, M1; Standard Products Co., Port Clinton, OH; Underwood-Elliott-Fisher Co., Hartford, CT.*

**CALIBER .30, M1
(GARAND) MIL. RIFLE** . . . . . . NiB $1441 Ex $1206 Gd $1166
Clip-fed, gas-operated, air-cooled semiautomatic. Uses a clip containing 8 rounds. 24-inch bbl. Weight: W/o bayonet, 9.5 lbs. Sights: Adj. peep rear; blade front w/guards. Pistol-grip stock, handguards. Made 1937-57. Note: Garand rifles have also been produced by Winchester Repeating Arms Co., Harrington & Richardson Arms Co. and International Harvester Co. Deduct 25% for arsenal-assembled mismatches.

**CALIBER .30, M1,
NATIONAL MATCH** . . . . NiB $2389 Ex $1775 Gd $730
Accurized target version of the Garand. Glass-bedded stock; match grade bbl., sights, gas cylinder. "NM" stamped on bbl. forward of handguard.

MODEL 1917 ENFIELD MILITARY RIFLE . NiB $977 Ex $800 Gd $370
Modified Mauser-type bolt action. Caliber: .30-06. Five round box magazine. 26-inch bbl. Weight: 9.25 lbs. Sights: Adj. rear; blade front w/guards. Military-type stock w/semi-pistol-grip. This design originated in Great Britain as the, "Pattern 14" and was mfd. in caliber .303 for the British Government in three U.S. plants. In 1917, the U.S. Government contracted w/these firms to produce the same rifle in caliber .30-06; over two million of these Model 1917 Enfields were mfd. While no more were produced after WWI, the U.S. supplied over a million of them to Great Britain during WWII.

NOTE: *The U.S. Model 1917 Enfield was mfd. 1917 to 1918 by Remington Arms Co. of Delaware (later Midvale Steel & Ordnance Co., Eddystone, PA); Remington Arms Co., Ilion, NY; Winchester Repeating Arms Co., New Haven, CT.*

CARBINE, CALIBER .30, M1 . . . . . NiB $844 Ex $677 Gd $497
Gas-operated (short-stroke piston), semiautomatic. 15- or 30-round detachable box magazine. 18-inch bbl. Weight: 5.5 lbs. Sights: adj. rear; blade front sight w/guards. Pistol-grip stock w/handguard, side-mounted web sling. Made 1942 to 1945. In 1963, 150,000 surplus M1 Carbines were sold at $20 each to members of the National Rifle Assn. by the Dept. of the Army. Note: For Winchester and Rock-Ola, add 30%; for Irwin Pedersen, add 80%. Quality Hardware did not complete its production run. Guns produced by other manufacturers were marked "Unquality" & command premium prices.

U.S. REPEATING ARMS CO.

See Winchester rifle listings.

UNIVERSAL FIREARMS, INC. — Miami, Florida

DELUXE CARBINE . . . . NiB $466 Ex $348 Gd $210
Same as standard model except also available in caliber .256, w/deluxe walnut Monte Carlo stock and handguard. Made fro 1965 to 1987.

Valmet M-62S

Valmet Hunter

Vickers Jubilee
Single-Shot Target Rifle

STANDARD M-1 CARBINE . . . NiB $375 Ex $246 Gd $175
Same as U.S. Carbine, Cal. .30, M1 except may have either wood or
metal handguard, bbl. band w/ or w/o bayonet lug; 5-round magazine
standard. Made from 1964 to 1987.

UZI — Ramat HaSharon, Israel
Manufactured by Israel Military Industries.

SEMIAUTOMATIC MODEL B CARBINE
Calibers: 9mm Parabellum, .41 Action Express, .45 ACP. 20- to
50-round magazine. 16.1-inch bbl. Weight: 8.4 lbs. Metal folding stock.
Front post-type sight, open rear, both adj. Imported by Action Arms
1983 to 1989. NFA (Selective Fire) models imported by UZI America,
INC., 1983 to 1994.
Model B Carbine (9mm or .45 ACP) . . .NiB $1500 Ex $1149 Gd $963
Model B Carbine (.41 AE). . . . . .NiB $1500 Ex $1149 Gd $963
Centerfire conversion unit, add. $215
Rimfire conversion unit, add. $150

SEMIAUTOMATIC
MINI CARBINE. . . . . .NiB $2375 Ex $2153 Gd $1535
Similar to Uzi Model B except with 19.75-inch bbl.and chambered 9mm
Parabellum only. 20-round magazine. Weight: 7.2 lbs. Imported in 1989.

VALMET — Jyväskylä, Finland

M-62S SEMIAUTOMATIC RIFLE . . . . NiB $2590 Ex $2088 Gd $1675
Semiautomatic version of Finnish M-62 automatic assault rifle based on
Russian AK-47. Gas-operated rotating bolt action. Caliber: 7.62mmX39

Russian. 15- and 30-round magazines. 16.63-inch bbl. Weight: 8 lbs.
w/metal stock. Sights: Tangent aperture rear; hooded blade front w/
luminous flip-up post for low-light use. Tubular steel or wood stock.
Intro. 1962. Disc.

M-71S . . . . .NiB $1988 Ex $1766 Gd $1064
Same specifications as M-62S except caliber 5.56mmx45 (.223 Rem.),
w/open rear sight, reinforced resin or wood stock, weight: 7.75 lbs. w/
former. Made from 1971 to 1989.

M-76 SEMIAUTOMATIC RIFLE
Semiautomatic assault rifle. Gas-operated, rotating bolt action. Caliber:
223 Rem. 15- and 30-round magazines. Made 1984 to 1989.
Wood stock . . . . NiB $1788 Ex $1373 Gd $1055
Folding stock . . . . NiB $1947 Ex $1522 Gd $1140

M-78 SEMIAUTOMATIC RIFLE . . . . . NiB $1865 Ex $1492 Gd $1170
Caliber: 7.62x51 (NATO). 24.13-inch bbl. Overall length: 43.25 inches.
Weight: 10.5 lbs.

M-82 SEMIAUTOMATIC CARBINE . . NiB $1748 Ex $1399 Gd $1180
Caliber: .223 Rem. 15- or 30-round magazine. 17-inch bbl. 27 inches
overall. Weight: 7.75 lbs.

MODEL 412 S DOUBLE RIFLE . . . . . . NiB $1095 Ex $1077 Gd $933
Boxlock. Manual or automatic extraction. Calibers: .243, .308, .30-
06, .375 Win., 9.3x74R. Bbls.: 24-inch over/under. Weight: 8.63 lbs.
American walnut checkered stock and forend.

HUNTER SEMIAUTOMATIC RIFLE . . . . . NiB $955 Ex $755 Gd $639
Similar to M-78 except in calibers .223 Rem. (5.56mm), .243 Win., .308

Win. (7.62 NATO) and .30-06. Five , 9- or 15-round magazine. 20.5-inch plain bbl. 42 inches overall. Weight: 8 lbs. Sights: Adj. combination scope mount/rear; blade front, mounted on gas tube. Checkered European walnut buttstock and extended checkered forend and handguard. Imported from 1986 to 1989.

VICKERS LTD. — Crayford, Kent, England

JUBILEE MODEL SINGLE-SHOT-
TARGET RIFLE . . . . .NiB $545 Ex $390 Gd $265
Round-receiver Martini-type action. Caliber: .22 LR. 28-inch heavy bbl. Weight: 9.5 lbs. Sights: Parker-Hale No. 2 front; Perfection rear peep. One-piece target stock w/full forearm and pistol-grip. Made before WWII.

EMPIRE MODEL . . . . .NiB $569 Ex $439 Gd $287
Similar to Jubilee Model except w/27- or 30-inch bbl., straight-grip stock, weight: 9.25 lbs. w/30-inch bbl. Made before WWII.

VOERE — Vohrenvach, Germany

VEC-91 LIGHTNING
BOLT-ACTION RIFLE . . . . . . .NiB $2765 Ex $2165 Gd $1540
Features unique electronic ignition system to activate or fire caseless ammunition. Calibers: 5.56 UCC (.222 Cal.), 6mm UCC caseless. Five round magazine. 20-inch bbl. 39 inches overall. Weight: 6 lbs. Open adj. rear sight. Drilled and tapped for scope mounts. European walnut stock w/cheekpiece. Twin forward locking lugs. Imported from 1992 to date.

VOERE, VOELTER & COMPANY — Vaehrenbach, Germany
Mauser-Werke acquired Voere in 1987 and all models are now marketed under new designations.

MODEL 1007 BIATHLON REPEATER. . . . NiB $466 Ex $350 Gd $254
Caliber: 22 LR. Five round magazine. 19.5-inch bbl. 39 inches overall. Weight: 5.5 lb. Sights: Adj. rear, blade front. Plain beechwood stock. Imported from 1984 to 1986.

MODEL 1013 BOLT-ACTION REPEATER . . . NiB $766 Ex $544 Gd $389
Same as Model 1007 except w/military-style stock in 22 WMR caliber. Double-set triggers optional. Imported 1984 to 1986 by KDF, Inc.

MODEL 2107 BOLT-ACTION REPEATER
Caliber: 22 LR. Five or 8-round magazine. 19.5-inch bbl. 41 inches overall. Weight: 6 lbs. Sights: Adj. rear sight, hooded front. European hardwood Monte Carlo-style stock. Imported 1986 by KDF, Inc.
Standard model . . . . NiB $439 Ex $278 Gd $255
Deluxe model. . . . . NiB $469 Ex $347 Gd $266

WALTHER — Ulm and Arnsberg, Germany
Manufactured by the German firms of Waffenfabrik Walther and Carl Walther Sportwaffenfabrik.

The following Walther rifles were mfd. before WWII by Waffenfabrik Walther, Zella-Mehlis (Thür.), Germany.

MODEL 1 AUTOLOADING
RIFLE (LIGHT) . . . . .NiB $976 Ex $723 Gd $500
Similar to Standard Model 2 but w/20-inch bbl., lighter stock, weight: 4.5 lbs.

MODEL 2 AUTOLOADING RIFLE . . . . . NiB $1045 Ex $690 Gd $533
Bolt-action, may be used as autoloader, manually operated repeater or single-shot. Caliber: .22 LR. Five or 9-round detachable box magazine. 24.5-inch bbl. Weight: 7 lbs. Sights: Tangent-curve rear; ramp front. Sporting stock w/checkered pistol grip, grooved forearm, swivels. Disc.

OLYMPIC BOLT-ACTION
MATCH RIFLE . . . . .NiB $1354 Ex $1095 Gd $800
Single-shot. Caliber: .22 LR. 26-inch heavy bbl. Weight: 13 lbs. Sights: Micrometer extension rear; interchangeable front. Target stock w/checkered pistol-grip, thumbhole, full beavertail forearm covered w/corrugated rubber, palm rest, adj. Swiss-type buttplate, swivels. Disc.

MODEL V BOLT-ACTION
SINGLE-SHOT RIFLE . . . . .NiB $645 Ex $544 Gd $368
Caliber: .22 LR. 26-inch bbl. Weight: 7 lbs. Sights: Open rear; ramp front. Plain pistol-grip stock w/grooved forearm. Disc.

MODEL V MEISTERBÜCHSE
(CHAMPION) . . . . .NiB $675 Ex $494 Gd $338
Same as standard Model V except w/micrometer open rear sight and checkered pistol-grip. Disc.

POST WWII MODELS
The Walther rifles listed below have been manufactured since WWII by Carl Walther Sportwaffenfabrik, Ulm (Donau), Germany.

MODEL GX-1 FREE RIFLE . . . . . NiB $1985 Ex $1544 Gd $933
Bolt-action, single-shot. Caliber: .22 LR. 25.5-inch heavy bbl. Weight: 15.9 lbs. Sights: Micrometer aperture rear; globe front. Thumbhole stock w/adj. cheekpiece and buttplate w/removable hook, accessory rail. Left-hand stock available. Accessories furnished include hand stop and sling swivel, palm rest, counterweight assembly.

MODEL KKJ SPORTER . . . . . . .NiB $1355 Ex $1108 Gd $650
Bolt action. Caliber: .22 LR. Five round box magazine. 22.5-inch bbl. Weight: 5.5 lbs. Sights: Open rear; hooded ramp front. Stock w/cheekpiece, checkered pistol-grip and forearm, sling swivels. Disc.

MODEL KKJ-HO . . . . .NiB $1543 Ex $1337 Gd $1110
Same as Model KKJ except chambered for .22 Hornet. Disc.

MODEL KKJ-MA . . . . .NiB $1321 Ex $1231 Gd $650
Same as Model KKJ except chambered for .22 WMR. Disc.

MODEL KKM INTERNATIONAL
MATCH RIFLE . . . . .NiB $944 Ex $669 Gd $609
Bolt-action, single-shot. Caliber: .22 LR. 28-inch heavy bbl. Weight: 15.5 lbs. Sights: Micrometer aperture rear; globe front. Thumbhole stock w/high comb, adj. hook buttplate, accessory rail. Left-hand stock available. Disc.

MODEL KKM-S. . . . . .NiB $1000 Ex $877 Gd $641
Same specifications as Model KKM, except w/adj. cheekpiece. Disc.

MOVING TARGET MATCH RIFLE . . . . . NiB $1067 Ex $833 Gd $554

Walther Model 1

Walther Model 2

Walther Model GX-1

Walther Model KKM-S

Walther Model U.I.T.
Super Match

Bolt-action, single-shot. Caliber: .22 LR. 23.6-inch bbl. w/weight. Weight: 8.6 lbs. Supplied w/o sights. Thumbhole stock w/adj. cheekpiece and buttplate. Left-hand stock available.

PRONE 400 TARGET RIFLE. . . . . . NiB $833 Ex $715 Gd $500
Bolt-action, single-shot. Caliber: .22 LR. 25.5-inch heavy bbl. Weight: 10.25 lbs. Supplied w/o sights. Prone stock w/adj. cheekpiece and buttplate, accessory rail. Left-hand stock available. Disc.

MODEL SSV VARMINT RIFLE . . . . NiB $770 Ex $697 Gd $488
Bolt-action, single-shot. Calibers: .22 LR, .22 Hornet. 25.5-inch bbl. Weight: 6.75 lbs. Supplied w/o sights. Monte Carlo stock w/high cheekpiece, full pistol grip and forearm. Disc.

MODEL U.I.T. SPECIAL MATCH RIFLE . . NiB $1187 Ex $1070 Gd $833
Bolt-action, single-shot. Caliber: .22 LR. 25.5-inch bbl. Weight: 10.2 lbs. Sights: Micrometer aperture rear; globe front. Target stock w/high comb, adj. buttplate, accessory rail. Left-hand stock avail. Disc. 1993.

MODEL U.I.T. SUPER MATCH RIFLE . . . . NiB $1169 Ex $1966 Gd $788
Bolt-action, single-shot. Caliber: .22 LR. 25.5-inch heavy bbl. Weight: 10.2 lbs. Micrometer aperture rear; globe front. Target stock w/support for off-hand shooting, high comb, adj. buttplate and swivel. Left-hand stock available. Disc. 1993.

Weatherby Mark V Classicmark
I

Weatherby Crown Custom

Weatherby Fiberguard

Weatherby Fibermark

MONTGOMERY WARD — Chicago, Illinois

Firearms under the "private label" names of Western Field and Hercules are manufactured by such firms as Mossberg, Stevens, Marlin, and Savage for distribution and sale by Montgomery Ward.

MODEL 14M-497B WESTERN FIELD
BOLT-ACTION RIFLE . . . . .NiB $160 Ex $121 Gd $90
Caliber: .22 RF. Seven round detachable box magazine. 24-inch bbl. Weight: 5 lbs. Sights: Receiver peep; open rear; hooded ramp front. Pistol-grip stock. Mfg. by Mossberg.

MODEL M771 WESTERN FIELD
LEVER-ACTION RIFLE . . . . .NiB $221 Ex $177 Gd $135
Calibers: .30-30, .35 Rem. Six round tubular magazine. 20-inch bbl. Weight: 6.75 lbs. Sights: Open rear; ramp front. Pistol-grip or straight stock, forearm w/barrel band. Mfg. by Mossberg.

MODEL M772 WESTERN FIELD
LEVER-ACTION RIFLE . . . . .NiB $235 Ex $190 Gd $131
Calibers: .30-30, .35 Rem. Six round tubular magazine. 20-inch bbl. Weight: 6.75 lbs. Sights: Open rear; ramp front. Pistol-grip or straight stock, forearm w/bbl. band. Mfg. by Mossberg.

MODEL M775
BOLT-ACTION RIFLE . . . . .NiB $158 Ex $139 Gd $99
Calibers: .222 Rem., .22-250, .243 Win., .308 Win. Four round magazine. Weight: 7.5 lbs. Sights: Folding leaf rear; ramp front. Monte Carlo stock w/cheekpiece, pistol-grip. Mfg by Mossberg.

MODEL M776
BOLT-ACTION RIFLE . . . . .NiB $260 Ex $227 Gd $159
Calibers: .222 Rem., .22-250, .243 Win., .308 Win. Four round magazine. Weight: 7.5 lbs. Sights: Folding leaf rear; ramp front. Monte Carlo stock w/cheekpiece, pistol-grip. Mfg. by Mossberg.

MODEL M778
LEVER-ACTION . . . . .NiB $255 Ex $188 Gd $138
Calibers: .30-30, .35 Rem. Six round tubular magazine. 20-inch bbl. Weight: 6.75 lbs. Sights: Open rear; ramp front. Pistol-grip or straight stock, forearm w/bbl. band. Mfg. by Mossberg.

MODEL M780
BOLT-ACTION RIFLE . . . . .NiB $265 Ex $237 Gd $168
Calibers: .222 Rem., .22-250, .243 Win., .308 Win. Four round magazine. Weight: 7.5 lbs. Sights: Folding leaf rear; ramp front. Monte Carlo stock w/cheekpiece, pistol grip. Mfg. by Mossberg.

MODEL M782
BOLT-ACTION RIFLE . . . . .NiB $259 Ex $233 Gd $177
Same general specifications as Model M780.

MODEL M808 . . . . .NiB $155 Ex $133 Gd $90
Takedown. Caliber: .22RF. Fifteen round tubular magazine. Bbls.: 20- and 24-inch. Weight: 6 lbs. Sights: Open rear; bead front. Pistol-grip stock. Mfg. by Stevens.

MODEL M832 BOLT-ACTION RIFLE . . . . . NiB $166 Ex $144 Gd $90
Caliber: .22 RF. Seven round clip magazine. 24-inch bbl. Weight: 6.5 lbs. Sights: Open rear; ramp front. Mfg. by Mossberg.

GRADING: **NiB** = New in Box   **Ex** = Excellent or NRA 95%   **Gd** = Good or NRA 68%

Weatherby Mark V Deluxe

Weatherby Mark V Euromark

Weatherby Mark V Lazermark

Weatherby Mark V Safari Grade

MODEL M836 . . . . .NiB $169 Ex $122 Gd $95
Takedown. Caliber: .22RF. Fifteen round tubular magazine. Bbls.: 20-
and 24-inch. Weight: 6 lbs. Sights: Open rear; bead front. Pistol-grip
stock. Mfg. by Stevens.

MODEL M865 LEVER-ACTION CARBINE. NiB $188 Ex $146 Gd $144
Hammerless. Caliber: .22RF. Tubular magazine. Made w/both 18.5-inch
and 20-inch bbls., forearm w/bbl. band, swivels. Weight: 5 lbs. Mfg. by
Mossberg.

**MODEL M894
AUTO-LOADING CARBINE** . . . . .NiB $198 Ex $137 Gd $105
Caliber: .22 RF. Fifteen round tubular magazine. 20-inch bbl. Weight:
6 lbs. Sights: Open rear; ramp front. Monte Carlo stock w/pistol-grip.
Mfg. by Mossberg.

MODEL M-SD57 . . . . .NiB $178 Ex $133 Gd $95
Takedown. Caliber: .22RF. 15-round tubular magazine. Bbls.: 20- and
24-inch. Weight: 6 lbs. Sights: Open rear; bead front. Pistol-grip stock.
Mfg. by Stevens.

WEATHERBY, INC. — Atascadero, California
Formerly South Gate, CA.

CROWN CUSTOM RIFLE . . . .NiB $8656 Ex $6298 Gd $4470
Calibers: .240, .30-06, .257, .270, 7mm, .300, and .340. Bbl.: Made
to order. Super fancy walnut stock. Also available w/engraved barreled
action including gold animal overlay.

DELUXE .378 MAGNUM RIFLE. . . . .NiB $2233 Ex $2148 Gd $1490
Same general specifications as Deluxe Magnum in other calibers
except caliber .378 W. M. Schultz & Larsen action; 26-inch bbl. Disc.
1958.

DELUXE MAGNUM RIFLE. . . . .NiB $1844 Ex $1623 Gd $1189
Calibers: .220 Rocket, .257 Weatherby Mag., .270 Wby. Mag,
7mm Wby. Mag., .300 Wby. Mag., .375 Wby. Mag. Specially pro-
cessed FN Mauser action. 24-inch bbl. (26-inch in .375 cal.). Monte
Carlo-style stock w/cheekpiece, black forend tip, grip cap, checkered
pistol-grip and forearm, quick-detachable sling swivels. Value shown
is for rifle w/o sights. Disc. 1958.

DELUXE RIFLE . . . . .NiB $1844 Ex $1623 Gd $1189
Same general specifications as Deluxe Magnum except chambered for
standard calibers such as .270, .30-06, etc. Disc. 1958.

FIBERGUARD RIFLE . . . . .NiB $810 Ex $679 Gd $485
Same general specifications as Vanguard except for fiberglass stock and
matte metal finish. Disc, 1988.

FIBERMARK RIFLE . . . . .NiB $1377 Ex $1043 Gd $707
Same general specifications as Mark V except w/molded fiberglass
stock, finished in a nonglare black wrinkle finish. The metal is finished
in a non-glare matte finish. Disc. 1993.

MARK V ACCUMARK BOLT-ACTION REPEATING RIFLE
Weatherby Mark V magnum action. Calibers: .257 Wby., .270 Wby.,
7mm Rem. Mag., 7mm Wby., 7mm STW, .300 Win. Mag., .300 Wby.
Mag., .30-338 Wby., .30-378 Wby. and .340 Wby. 26- or 28-inch
stainless bbl. w/black oxide flutes. 46.5 or 48.5 inches overall.
Weight: 8 to 8.5 lbs. No sights, drilled and tapped for scope. Stainless
finish w/blued receiver. H-S Precision black synthetic stock w/alumi-
num bedding plate, recoil pad and sling swivels. Imported from 1996
to date.
.30-338 & .30-378 Wby. Mag. . . . . . .NiB $1674 Ex $1198 Gd $865
All other calibers . . . . .NiB $1589 Ex $1020 Gd $722
Left-hand model, add $100

Weatherby Mark XXII
Deluxe .22 Automatic
Sporter

Weatherby Vanguard (I) VGL
Bolt-Action Sporting Rifle

Weatherby Varmintmaster

MARK V ACCUMARK
LIGHT WEIGHT RIFLE . . . . . . NiB $1357 Ex $1154 Gd $744
Similar to the Mark V Accumark except w/LightWeight Mark V action designed for standard calibers w/sixlocking lugs rather than nine. 24-inch stainless bbl. Weight: 5.75 lbs. Gray or black Monte Carlo-style composite Kevlar/fiberglass stock w/Pachmayr "Decelerator" pad. No sights. Imported from 1997 to 2004.

MARK V CLASSICMARK I RIFLE
Same general specifications as Mark V except w/checkered select American Claro walnut stock w/oil finish and presentation recoil pad. Satin metal finish. Imported from 1992 to 1993.

Calibers .240 to .300 Wby.	NiB $1135	Ex $884	Gd $572
Caliber .340 Wby.	NiB $1135	Ex $884	Gd $572
Caliber .378 Wby.	NiB $1177	Ex $944	Gd $577
Caliber .416 Wby.	NiB $1150	Ex $922	Gd $535
Caliber .460 Wby.	NiB $1313	Ex $1044	Gd $590

MARK V CLASSICMARK LL RIFLE
Same general specifications as Classicmark I except w/checkered select American walnut stock w/oil finish steel grip cap and Old English recoil pad. Satin metal finish. Right-hand only. Imported from 1992 to 1993.

.240 to .340 Wby. (26-inch bbl.)	NiB $1589	Ex $1043	Gd $844
.378 Wby.	NiB $1188	Ex $1044	Gd $909
.426 Wby.	NiB $1207	Ex $1044	Gd $1032
.460 Wby.	NiB $1290	Ex $1170	Gd $1056

MARK V DELUXE RIFLE . . . . . NiB $2633 Ex $1845 Gd $1579
Similar to Mark V Sporter except w/Lightweight Mark V action designed for standard calibers w/sixlocking lugs rather than nine, 4- or 5-round magazine. 24-inch bbl. 44 inches overall. Weight: 6.75 lbs. Checkered Monte Carlo American walnut stock w/rosewood forend and pistol grip and diamond inlay. Imported from 1957 to date.

MARK V DELUXE BOLT-ACTION SPORTING RIFLE
Mark V action, right or left hand. Calibers: .22-250, .30-06- .224 Weatherby Varmintmaster; .240, .257, .270, 7mm, .300, .340, .375,

.378, .416, .460 Weatherby Magnums. Box magazine holds 2 to 5 cartridges depending on caliber. 24- or 26-inch bbl. Weight: 6.5 to 10.5 lbs. Monte Carlo-style stock w/cheekpiece, skip checkering, forend tip, pistol-grip cap, recoil pad, QD swivels. Values shown are for rifles w/o sights. Made in Germany 1958 to 1969; in Japan 1970 to 1994. Values shown for Japanese production.

.22-250, .224 Wby.	NiB $1790	Ex $1408	Gd $956
.375 H&H Magnum	NiB $1835	Ex $1079	Gd $766
.378 Wby. Mag.	NiB $2239	Ex $1177	Gd $897
.416 Wby. Mag..	NiB $2210	Ex $1443	Gd $833
.460 Wby. Mag..	NiB $2633	Ex $1399	Gd $1069

MARK V EUROMARK BOLT-ACTION RIFLE
Same general specifications as other Mark V rifles except w/hand-rubbed, satin oil finish Claro walnut stock and nonglare special process blue matte barreled action. Left-hand models available. Imported from 1986 to 1993. Reintroduced in 1995.

.378 Wby. Mag.	NiB $1855	Ex $1190	Gd $943
.416 Wby. Mag.	NiB $1855	Ex $1190	Gd $943
.460 Wby. Mag.	NiB $1896	Ex $1497	Gd $1108
Other calibers	NiB $1590	Ex $800	Gd $555

MARK V LAZERMARK RIFLE
Same general specifications as Mark V except w/laser-carved stock.

.378 Wby. Mag.	NiB $2022	Ex $1598	Gd $938
.416 Wby. Mag.	NiB $2022	Ex $1598	Gd $938
.460 Wby. Mag.	NiB $1489	Ex $1134	Gd $822
Other calibers	NiB $1489	Ex $1134	Gd $822

MARK V SAFARI GRADE RIFLE . . . . . NiB $2300 Ex $1841 Gd $1283
Same general specifications as Mark V except extra capacity magazine, bbl. sling swivel, and express rear sight typical "Safari" style.

MARK V SPORTER RIFLE
Sporter version of Mark V Magnum w/low-luster metal finish. Checkered Carlo walnut stock w/o grip cap or forend tip. No sights. Imported from 1993 to date.

Calibers .257 to .300 Wby	NiB $1488	Ex $920	Gd $723
.340 Wby. Mag.	NiB $1644	Ex $923	Gd $555

Westley Richards
Best Quality Double

Westley Richards
Best Quality Magazine
Rifle

.375 H&H . . . . NiB $1588 Ex $923 Gd $555

MARK V LIGHTWEIGHT SPORTER RIFLE NiB $1041 Ex $843 Gd $498
Similar to Mark V Sporter except w/Lightweight Mark V action designed
for standard calibers w/six locking lugs rather than nine. Imported from
1998 to date.Mark V Stainless Rifle
Similar to the Mark V Magnum except in 400-series stainless
steel w/bead-blasted matte finish. Weight: 8 lbs. Monte Carlo
synthetic stock w/aluminum bedding block. Imported from 1997
to 2002.
.30-378 Wby Mag. . . . . NiB $1488 Ex $967 Gd $641
.375 H&H . . . . NiB $1455 Ex $975 Gd $643
All other calibers . . . . NiB $1135 Ex $800 Gd $600
w/fluted bbl., add. $150

MARK V (LW) STAINLESS RIFLE . . . . . NiB $1146 Ex $833 Gd $500
Similar to the Mark V (standard calibers) except in 400-series stainless
steel w/bead-blasted matte finish. Five round magazine. 24-inch bbl. 44
inches overall. Weight: 6.5 lbs. Monte Carlo synthetic stock w/alumi-
num bedding block. Imported from 1997 to 2002.

MARK V SLS RIFLE
Acronym for Stainless Laminated Sporter. Similar to the Mark V
Magnum Sporter, except w/stainless 400-series action and 24- or
26-inch stainless bbl. Laminated wood stock. Weight: 8.5 lbs. Black
oxide bead-blasted matte blue finish. Imported from 1997 to date.
.340 Wby. Mag. . . . . NiB $1267 Ex $1088 Gd $777
All other calibers . . . . NiB $1200 Ex $955 Gd $724

MARK V SYNTHETIC RIFLE
Similar to the Mark V Magnum except w/Monte Carlo synthetic stock w/
aluminum bedding block. 24- or 26-inch standard tapper or fluted bbl.
Weight: 7.75 to 8 lbs. Matte blue finish. Imported from 1995 to date.
.340 Wby. Mag. . . . . NiB $1096 Ex $790 Gd $533
.30-378 Wby. Mag. . . . . NiB $1135 Ex $823 Gd $567
All other calibers . . . . NiB $835 Ex $633 Gd $450
W/fluted bbl., add $126

MARK V ULTRA LIGHT WEIGHT RIFLE
Similar to the Mark V Magnum except w/skeletonized bolt handle.
24- or 26-inch fluted stainless bbl. chambered .257 Wby., .270 Wby.,
7mm Rem. Mag., 7mm Wby., .300 Win. Mag., .300 Wby. Monte Carlo
synthetic stock w/aluminum bedding block. Weight: 6.75 lbs. Imported
from 1998 to date.
Standard calibers . . . . NiB $1648 Ex $1396 Gd $879
Weatherby calibers. . . . . NiB $1866 Ex $1545 Gd $1077
Left-hand action, add $200

MARK XXII DELUXE .22 AUTOMATIC

SPORTER, CLIP-FED MODEL . . . . NiB $846 Ex $547 Gd $397
Semiautomatic w/single-shot selector. Caliber: .22 LR. Five and
10-round clip magazines. 24-inch bbl. Weight: 6 lbs. Sights: Folding
leaf open rear; ramp front. Monte Carlo-type stock w/cheekpiece, pistol-grip, forend tip, grip cap, skip checkering, QD swivels. Intro. 1964.
Made in Italy from 1964 to 1969; in Japan, from 1970 to 191981; in
the U.S., from 1982 to 1990.

MARK XXII, TUBULAR
MAGAZINE MODEL . . . . .NiB $844 Ex $546 Gd $397
Same as Mark XXII, clip-fed model except w/15-round tubular maga-
zine. Made in Japan from 1973-81; in the U.S., from 1982-90.

VANGUARD (I) BOLT-ACTION SPORTING RIFLE
Mauser-type action. Calibers: .243 Win., .25-06, .270 Win., 7mm Rem.
Mag., .30-06, .300 Win. Mag. Five round magazine; (3-round in Magnum
calibers). 24-inch bbl. Weight: 7 lbs. 14 oz. No sights. Monte Carlo-type
stock w/cheekpiece, rosewood forend tip and pistol-grip cap, checkering,
rubber buttpad, QD swivels. Imported from 1970 to 1984.
Standard model . . . . NiB $495 Ex $439 Gd $298
VGL model (w/20-inch bbl., plain checkered
  stock, matte finish) . . . . NiB $650 Ex $533 Gd $400
VGS model (w/24-inch bbl.) . . . . NiB $440 Ex $388 Gd $338
VGX model (w/higher grade finish) . . . . . NiB $655 Ex $493 Gd $339

VANGUARD CLASSIC I RIFLE . . . . NiB $555 Ex $439 Gd $321
Same general specifications as Vanguard VGX Deluxe except w/hand-checkered
classic-style stock, black buttpad and satin finish. Calibers .223 Rem., .243 Win.
.270 Win., 7mm-08, 7mm Rem. Mag., .30-06 and .308 Win. Imported 1989 to
1994.

VANGUARD CLASSIC II RIFLE . . . NiB $720 Ex $587 Gd $444
Same general specifications as Vanguard VGX Deluxe except custom checkered classic-style American walnut stock w/black forend
tip, grip cap and solid black recoil pad, satin finish. Imported
1989 to 1994.

VANGUARD VGX DELUXE . . . . . .NiB $650 Ex $456 Gd $398
Calibers: .22-250 Rem., .243 Rem., .270 Wby. Mag., .270 Win., 7mm
Rem. Mag., .30-06, .300 Win. Mag., .300 Wby. Mag., .338 Win. Mag.
Three or 5-round capacity. 24-inch bbl. About 44 inches overall.
Weight: 7 to 8.5 lbs. Custom checkered American walnut stock w/
Monte Carlo and recoil pad. Rosewood forend tip and pistol-grip cap.
High-luster finish. Disc. 1994.

VARMINT SPECIAL BOLT-ACTION RIFLE . .NiB $654 Ex $447 Gd $368
Calibers: .224 Wby., .22-250, 4-round magazine. 26-inch bbl. 45
inches overall. Weight: 7.75 lbs. Checkered walnut stock. No sights.
Disc.

Wickliffe '76 Standard
Single-Shot Rifle

Winchester Model 1873
Lever-Action Rifle

WEATHERMARK RIFLE

Same gen. specs. as Classicmark except w/checkered blk. Weathermark composite stock. Mark V bolt act. Cal: .240, .257, .270, .300, .340, .378, .416 and .460 Weatherby Mag.; plus .270 Win., 7mm Rem. Mag., .30-06 and .375 H&H Mag. Wt: 8 to 10 lbs. Right-hand only. Imp. 1992 to 1994.

Calibers .257 to .300 Wby. Mag. . NiB $798 Ex $616 Gd $452
.340 Wby. Mag.. . . . . NiB $835 Ex $647 Gd $445
.375 H&H . . . . NiB $1079 Ex $835 Gd $450
Non-Wby. calibers . . . . NiB $800 Ex $577 Gd $465

WEATHERMARK ALASKAN RIFLE . . . . . NiB $707 Ex $544 Gd $433
Same general specifications as Weathermark except w/nonglare electroless nickel finish. Right-hand only. Imported from 1992 to 1994.

WEIHRAUCH — Melrichstadt, Germany
Imported by European American Armory, Sharpes, FL.

MODEL HW 60 TARGET RIFLE . . . NiB $677 Ex $559 Gd $445
Single-shot. Caliber: .22 LR. 26.75-inch bbl. Walnut stock. Adj. buttplate and trigger. Hooded ramp front sight. Push button safety. Imported 1995 to 1997.

MODEL HW 66 BOLT-ACTION RIFLE . . . NiB $645 Ex $482 Gd $338
Caliber: .22 Hornet. 22.75-inch bbl. 41.75 inches overall. Weight: 6.5 lbs. Walnut stock w/cheekpiece. Hooded blade ramp front sight. Checkered pistol grip and forend. Imported from 1989 to 1990.

MODEL HW 660 MATCH
BOLT-ACTION RIFLE . . . . NiB $942 Ex $745 Gd $500
Caliber: .22 LR. 26-inch bbl. 45.33 inches overall. Weight: 10.75 lbs. Walnut or laminated stock w/adj. cheekpiece and buttplate. Checkered pistol grip and forend. Adj. trigger. Imported 1991 to 2005.

WESTERN FIELD RIFLES

See listings under "W" for Montgomery Ward.

WESTLEY RICHARDS & CO., LTD. — London, England

BEST QUALITY
DOUBLE RIFLE . . . . NiB $35,000 Ex $28,900 Gd $19,670
Boxlock, hammerless, ejector. Hand-detachable locks. Calibers: .30-06, .318 Accelerated Express, .375 Mag., .425 Mag. Express, .465 Nitro Express, .470 Nitro Express. 25-inch bbls. Weight: 8.5 to 11 lbs. Sights: leaf rear; hooded front. French walnut stock w/cheekpiece, checkered pistol grip and forend.

BEST QUALITY MAGAZINE RIFLE
Mauser or Magnum Mauser action. Calibers: 7mm High Velocity, .30-06, .318 Accelerated Express, .375 Mag., .404 Nitro Express, .425 Mag. Bbl. lengths: 24-inch; 7mm, 22-inch; .425 caliber, 25-inch. Weight 7.25 to 9.25 lbs. Sights: Leaf rear; hooded front.
Standard action . . . . NiB $11,970 Ex $7295 Gd $5790
Magnum action . . . . NiB $13,888 Ex $11,679 Gd $8957

WICHITA ARMS — Wichita, Kansas

MODEL WCR CLASSIC BOLT-ACTION RIFLE
Single-shot. Calibers: .17 Rem through .308 Win. 21-inch octagon bbl. Hand-checkered walnut stock. Drilled and tapped for scope w/no sights. Right or left-hand action w/Canjar trigger. Non-glare blued finish. Made from 1978 to date.
Right-hand model . . . . NiB $2578 Ex $2044 Gd $1760
Left-hand model . . . . NiB $3544 Ex $2967 Gd $2178

MODEL WSR SILHOUETTE BOLT-ACTION RIFLE
Single-shot, bolt action, chambered in most standard calibers. Right or left-hand action w/fluted bolt. Drilled and tapped for scope mount with no sights. 24-inch bbl. Canjar trigger. Metallic gray Fiberthane stock w/vented rubber recoil pad. Made 1983 to 1995.
Right-hand model . . . . NiB $2588 Ex $2066 Gd $1449
Left-hand model . . NiB $2744 Ex $2190 Gd $1633 **MODEL WMR STAINLESS**
MAGNUM BOLT-ACTION RIFLE . . . . . . NiB $2275 Ex $1938 Gd $1179
Single-shot or w/blind magazine action chambered .270 Win. through .458 Win. Mag. Drilled and tapped for scope with no sights. Fully adj. trigger. 22- or 24-inch bbl. Hand-checkered select walnut stock. Made from 1980 to 1984.

Winchester Model 1886 Rifle
w/Case-colored Receiver

Winchester Model 1886 Rifle
w/Blued Receiver

Winchester Model 1886 Saddle-Ring Carbine

Close-up barrel engraving on Winchester
Model 1873 One of One Thousand.

MODEL WVR VARMINT RIFLE
Calibers: .17 Rem through .308 Win. Three round magazine. Right or left-hand action w/jeweled bolt. 21-inch bbl. w/o sights. Drilled and tapped for scope. Hand-checkered American walnut pistol-grip stock. Made from 1978 to 1997.
Right-hand model . . . . NiB $2577 Ex $2038 Gd $1289
Left-hand model . . . . NiB $2798 Ex $2260 Gd $1678

WICKLIFFE RIFLES — Wickliffe, Ohio
Manufactured by Triple S Development Co., Inc.

'76 COMMEMORATIVE
MODEL . . . . NiB $1169 Ex $1044 Gd $939
Limited edition of 100. Same as Deluxe Model except w/filled etching on receiver sidewalls, U.S. silver dollar inlaid in stock, 26-inch bbl. only, comes in presentation case. Made in 1976 only.

'76 DELUXE MODEL . . . . NiB $522 Ex $415 Gd $331
Same as Standard Model except w/22-inch bbl. in .30-06 only; high-luster blued finish, fancy-grade figured American walnut stock w/nickel silver grip cap.

'76 STANDARD MODEL
SINGLE-SHOT RIFLE . . . . NiB $443 Ex $300 Gd $217
Falling-block action. Calibers: .22 Hornet, .223 Rem., .22-250, .243 Win., .25-06, .308 Win., .30-06, .45-70. 22-inch lightweight bbl. (.243 and .308 only) or 26-inch heavy sporter bbl. Weight: 6.75 or 8.5 lbs., depending on bbl. No sights. Select American walnut Monte Carlo stock w/right or left cheekpiece and pistol-grip, semi-beavertail forearm. Intro. 1976. Disc.

STINGER MODEL . . . . NiB $433 Ex $300 Gd $217
Falling block, single-shot. Calibers: .22 Hornet and .223 Rem. .22-inch bbl. w/no sights. American walnut Monte Carlo stock w/continental-type forend. Made from 1979-80.

TRADITIONALIST MODEL . . . . . . NiB $441 Ex $339 Gd $200
Falling block single-shot. Calibers: .30-06, .45-70. 24-inch bbl. w/open sights. Hand-checkered. American walnut classic-style buttstock and forearm. Made from 1979 to 1980.

WILKINSON ARMS CO. — Covina, California

TERRY CARBINE . . . . NiB $551 Ex $408 Gd $354
Caliber: 9mm Para. Semiautomatic. Thirty round magazine. 16-inch bbl. 30 inches overall. Weight: 6 lbs. Dovetailed receiver for scope mounting. Bolt-type safety. Ejection port w/automatic trap door. Blowback action. Fires from closed bolt. Made from 1975. Disc.

TED WILLIAMS RIFLES

See Sears, Roebuck and Company.

WINCHESTER — Columbia, SC
U.S. Reapeating Arms Winchester Repeating Arms Company, formerly in New Haven, Connecticut. In 1987 Fabrique Nationale d'Armes de Guerre (FN) acquired U.S. Repeating Arms Company, including the license to manufacture Winchester-brand firearms.

Formerly Winchester Repeating Arms Co., and then mfd. by Winchester-Western Div., Olin Corp., later by U.S. Repeating Arms Company. In 1999, production rights were acquired by Browning Arms Company. FN acquired Browning in 1977.

EARLY MODELS 1873 – 1918

Winchester Model 1890

Winchester Model 1892

NOTE: *Most Winchester rifles manufactured prior to 1918 used the date of approximate manufacture as the model number. For example, the Model 1894 repeating rifle was manufactured from 1894 to 1937. When Winchester started using two-digit model numbers after 1918, the "18" was dropped and the rifle was then called the Model 94. The Model 1892 was called the Model 92, etc. In light of the recent shut-down, Winchester is no longer made at New Haven.*

MODEL 1873 LEVER-ACTION
CARBINE . . . . NiB $4820 Ex $3933 Gd $2577
Same as Standard Model 1873 Rifle except w/20-inch bbl., 12-round magazine, weight: 7.25 lbs.

MODEL 1873 LEVER-ACTION
RIFLE . . . . NiB $5088 Ex $3482 Gd $2100
Calibers: .32-20, .38-40, .44-40; a few were chambered for .22 rimfire. Fifteen round magazine, also made w/6-round half magazine. 24-inch bbl. (round, half-octagon, octagon). Weight: 8.5 lbs. Sights: Open rear; bead or blade front. Plain straight-grip stock and forearm. Made 1873 to 1924. 720,610 rifles of this model were mfd.

MODEL 1873 —
ONE OF ONE THOUSAND. NiB $196,000+ Ex $150,000 Gd $90,000
During the late 1870s, Winchester offered Model 1873 rifles of superior accuracy and extra finish, designated "One of One Thousand" grade, at $100. These rifles are marked "1 of 1000" or "One of One Thousand." Only 136 of this model are known to have been manufactured. This is one of the rarest of shoulder arms and, because so few have been sold in recent years, it is extremely difficult to assign a value, however, an "excellent" specimen would probably bring a price upward of $200,000.

MODEL 1873 SPECIAL
SPORTING RIFLE . . . . . . NiB $11,375 Ex $10,450 Gd $7,707
Same as Standard Model 1873 Rifle except this type has receiver casehardened in colors, pistol-grip stock of select walnut, octagon bbl. only.

MODEL 1885 SINGLE-SHOT RIFLE
Designed by John M. Browning, this falling-block, lever-action rifle was manufactured from 1885 to 1920 in a variety of models and chambered for most of the popular cartridges of the period — both rimfire and centerfire — from .22 to .50 caliber. There are two basic styles of frames, low-wall and high-wall. The low-wall was chambered only for the lower-powered cartridges, while the high-wall was supplied in all calibers and made in three basic types. The standard model for No. 3 and heavier barrels is the type commonly encountered; the thin-walled version was supplied with No. 1 and No. 2 light barrels and the thick-walled action in the heavier calibers. Made in both solid frame and takedown versions. Barrels were available in five weights ranging from the lightweight No. 1 to the extra-heavy No. 5 in round, half-octagon and full-octagon styles. Many other variations were also

offered.

MODEL 1885 HIGH-WALL
SPORTING RIFLE . . . . NiB $5335 Ex $3100 Gd $2066
Solid frame or takedown. No. 3, 30-inch bbl., standard. Weight: 9.5 lbs. Standard trigger and lever. Open rear sights; blade front sight. Plain stock and forend.

MODEL 1885 LOW-WALL
SPORTING RIFLE . . . . NiB $1550 Ex $1466 Gd $1000
Solid frame. No. 1, 28-inch round or octagon bbl. Weight: 7 lbs. Open rear sight; blade front sight. Plain stock and forend.

MODEL 1885
SCHUETZEN RIFLE . . . . . . NiB $10,000 Ex $7860 Gd $5779
Solid frame or takedown. High-wall action. Schuetzen double-set trigger. Spur finger lever. No. 3, 30-inch octagon bbl. Weight: 12 lbs. Vernier rear peep sight; wind-gauge front sight. Fancy walnut Schuetzen stock with checkered pistol-grip and forend. Schuetzen buttplate; adj. palm rest.

MODEL 1885
SPECIAL SPORTING RIFLE . . . . . NiB $7335 Ex $5550 Gd $5090
Same general specifications as the standard high-wall model except with checkered fancy walnut stock and forend.

MODEL 1885
SINGLE-SHOT MUSKET . . . . . . NiB $1590 Ex $1171 Gd $878
Solid frame. Low-wall. .22 Short and Long Rifle. 28-inch round bbl. Weight: 8.6 lbs. Lyman rear peep sight; blade front sight. Military-type stock and forend. Note: The U.S. Government purchased a large quantity of these muskets during World War I for training purposes.

MODEL 1885 SINGLE-SHOT
"WINDER" MUSKET . . . . NiB $1488 Ex $1203 Gd $1037
Solid frame or takedown. High-wall. Plain trigger. 28-inch round bbl. Weight: 8.5 lbs. Musket rear sight; blade front sight. Military-type stock and forend w/bbl. band and sling stud/rings.

MODEL 1886 LEVER-ACTION RIFLE
Solid frame or takedown. .33 Win., .38-56, .38-70, .40-65, .40-70, .40-82, .45-70, .45-90, .50-100, .50-110. The .33 Win. and .45-70 were the last calibers in which this model was supplied. Eight round tubular magaine; also 4-round half-magazine. 26-inch bbl. (round, half-octagon, octagon). Weight: 7.5 lbs. Sights: Open rear; bead or blade front. Plain straight-grip stock and forend or standard models. Made from 1886 to 1935.
Standard model . . . . NiB $7288 Ex $4399 Gd $3100
Takedown model . . . . NiB $10,270 Ex $7668 Gd $5790
Deluxe model (W/pistol grip and high-quality
  walnut stock) . . . . NiB $17,689 Ex $13,790 Gd $10,777

GRADING: **NiB** = New in Box   **Ex** = Excellent or NRA 95%   **Gd** = Good or NRA 68%

Winchester Model 1894

Winchester Model 1894
Fancy-Grade Takedown

Winchester Model 1894
Saddle-Ring Carbine

Winchester Model 1895
Carbine

Winchester Model 1895
Rifle

Winchester Model 1897
Lee Sporting Rifle

**MODEL 1886 SADDLE-RING
CARBINE** . . . . .NiB $18,690 Ex $15,660 Gd $12,750
Same as standard rifle except with 22-inch bbl., carbine buttstock and
forend. Carbine rear sight. Saddle ring on left side of receiver.

MODEL 1890 SLIDE-ACTION RIFLE
Visible hammer. Calibers: .22 Short, Long, LR; .22 WRF (not interchangeable). Tubular magazine holds 15 Short, 12 Long, 11 LR; 12 WRF. 24-inch
octagon bbl. Weight: 5.75 lbs. Sights: Open rear; bead front. Plain straight-
grip stock, grooved slide handle. Originally solid frame; after No. 15,499, all
rifles of this model were takedown-type. Fancy checkered pistol-grip stock,
nickel-steel bbl. supplied at extra cost, which can also increase the value by
100% or more. Made from 1890 to 1932.
.22 WRF, blued model . . . . .NiB $2079 Ex $1754 Gd $1166
.22 LR, blued model . . . . .NiB $2148 Ex $2066 Gd $1180
Color casehardened receiver . . . . . . .NiB $6689 Ex $5349 Gd $3730

MODEL 1892 LEVER-ACTION

RIFLE . . . . .NiB $3482 Ex $2210 Gd $1588
Solid frame or takedown. Calibers: .25-20, .32-20, .38-40, .44-40.
Thirteen round tubular magazine; also 7-round half-magazine. 24-inch
bbl. (round, octagon, half-octagon). Weight: from 6.75 lbs. up. Sights:
Open rear; bead front. Plain straight-grip stock and forend. Pistol-grip
fancy walnut stocks were available at extra cost and also doubles the
value of the current value for standard models.

**MODEL 1892 SADDLE-RING
CARBINE** . . . . .NiB $5321 Ex $2549 Gd $1266
Same general specifications as the Model 1892 rifle except carbine buttstock,
forend and sights. 20-inch bbl. Saddle ring on left side of receiver.

MODEL 1894 LEVER-ACTION
RIFLE . . . . .NiB $6530 Ex $4739 Gd $3220
Solid frame or takedown. .25-35, .30-30, .32-40, .32 Special, .38-55.
Seven round tubular magazine or 4-round half-magazine. 26-inch bbl.
(round, octagon, half-octagon). Weight: about 7.35 lbs. Sights: Open
rear; bead front. Plain straight-grip stock and forearm on standard model;

Winchester Model 1902

Winchester Model 1903

Winchester Model 1904

Winchester Model 1905

Winchester Model 1906

Winchester Model 1907

Winchester Model 1910

GRADING: **NiB** = New in Box   **Ex** = Excellent or NRA 95%   **Gd** = Good or NRA 68%

**Winchester Model 43
Special Grade**

crescent-shaped or shotgun-style buttplate. Made from 1894-1937. See also Winchester Model 94 for later variations of this model.

MODEL 1894 LA DELUXE . . . . . . NiB $12,890 Ex $10,669 Gd $8777
Same general specifications as the standard rifle except checkered pistol-grip buttstock and forend using high-grade walnut. Engraved versions are considerably higher in value.

**MODEL 1894 SADDLE-RING
CARBINE** . . . . NiB $2866 Ex $1806 Gd $1100
Same general specifications as the Model 1894 standard rifle except 20-inch bbl., carbine buttstock, forend, and sights. Saddle ring on left side of receiver. Weight: about 6.5 lbs.

MODEL 1894 STANDARD CARBINE. NiB $6798 Ex $4890 Gd $3855
Same general specifications as Saddle-Ringle Carbine except shotgun type buttstock and plate, no saddle ring, standard open rear sight. Sometimes called "Eastern Carbine." See also Winchester Model 94 carbine.

**1895 LEVER-ACTION
CARBINE** . . . . NiB $4297 Ex $3037 Gd $1971
Same as Model 95 Standard Rifle except has 22-inch bbl., carbine-style buttstock and forend, weight: About 8 lbs., calibers .30-40 Krag, .30-03, .30-06 and .303, solid frame only.

**MODEL1895 LEVER-
ACTION RIFLE** . . . . NiB $3364 Ex $2130 Gd $1266
Calibers: .30-40 Krag, .30-03, .30-60, .303 British, 7.62mm Russian, .35 Win., .38-72, .40-72, .405 Win. Four round box magazine except .30-40 and .303, which have 5-round magazines. Bbl. lengths: 24-, 26-, 28-inches (round, half-octagon, octagon). Weight: About 8.5 lbs. Sights: Open rear; bead or blade front. Plain straight-grip stock and forend (standard). Both solid frame and takedown models were made from1897 to 1931.

MODEL (1897) LEE BOLT-ACTION RIFLE
Straight-pull bolt-action. .236 U.S. Navy, 5-round box magazine, clip loaded. 24- and 28-inch bbl. Weight: 7.5 to 8.5 lbs. Sights: Folding leaf rear sight on musket; open sporting sight on sporting rifle.Musket model . . . . NiB $1939 Ex $1777 Gd $1129
Sporting rifle . . . . NiB $2000 Ex $1808 Gd $1110

**MODEL 1900 BOLT-ACTION
SINGLE-SHOT RIFLE** . . . . . . NiB $628 Ex $499 Gd $356
Takedown. Caliber: .22 Short and Long. 18-inch bbl. Weight: 2.75 lbs. Open rear sight; blade front sight. One-piece, straight-grip stock. Made from 1899 to 1902.

**MODEL 1902 BOLT-ACTION
SINGLE-SHOT RIFLE** . . . . . . NiB $495 Ex $369 Gd $269

Takedown. Basically the same as Model 1900 with minor improvements. Calibers: .22 Short and Long, .22 Extra Long, .22 LR. Weight: 3 lbs. Made from 1902 to 1931.

**MODEL 1903
SELF-LOADING RIFLE.** . . . . . NiB $1133 Ex $909 Gd $577
Takedown. Caliber: .22 Win. Auto. Ten round tubular magazine in buttstock. 20-inch bbl. Weight: 5.75 lbs. Sights: Open rear; bead front. Plain straight-grip stock and forearm (fancy grade illustrated). Made from 1903 to 1936.

**MODEL (1904) 99 THUMB-TRIGGER BOLT-ACTION
SINGLE-SHOT RIFLE.** . . . . . . NiB $833 Ex $707 Gd $510
Takedown. Same as Model 1902 except fired by pressing a button behind the cocking piece. Made from 1904 to 1923.

**MODEL 1904 BOLT-ACTION
SINGLE-SHOT RIFLE.** . . . . . . NiB $469 Ex $388 Gd $269
Similar to Model 1902. Takedown. Caliber: 22 Short, Long Extra Long, LR. 21-inch bbl. Weight: 4 lbs. Made from 1904 to 1931.

**MODEL 1905
SELF-LOADING RIFLE.** . . . . NiB $768 Ex $580 Gd $500
Takedown. Calibers: .32 Win. SL or .35 Win. SL. Five or 10-round detachable box magazine. 22-inch bbl. Weight: 7.5 lbs. Sights: Open rear; bead front. Plain pistol-grip stock and forearm. Made from 1905 to 1920.

**MODEL 1906
SLIDE-ACTION REPEATER** . . NiB $1590 Ex $1077 Gd $733
Takedown. Visible hammer. Caliber: .22 Short, Long, LR. Tubular magazine holds 20 Short, 16 Long or 14 LR. 20-inch bbl. Weight: 5 lbs. Sights: Open rear; bead front. Straight-grip stock and grooved forearm. Made from 1906 to 1932.

MODEL 1907 SELF-LOADING RIFLE . . . . NiB $733 Ex $589 Gd $421
Takedown. Caliber: .351 Win. SL. Five or 10-round detachable box magazine. 20-inch bbl. Weight: 7.75 lbs. Sights: Open rear; bead front. Plain pistol-grip stock and forearm. Made 1907 to 1957.

MODEL 1910 SELF-LOADING RIFLE . . . . NiB $910 Ex $707 Gd $533
Takedown. Caliber: .401 Win. SL. Four round detachable box magazine. 20-inch bbl. Weight: 8.5 lbs. Sights: Open rear; bead front. Plain pistol-grip stock and forearm. Made from 1910 to 1936.

**MODEL 43
BOLT-ACTION SPORTING RIFLE** .NiB $855 Ex $679 Gd $480
Standard Grade. Calibers: .218 Bee, .22 Hornet, .25-20, .32-20 (latter two discontinued 1950). Three round detachable box magazine. 24-inch bbl. Weight: 6 lbs. Sights: Open rear, bead front on hooded ramp. Plain pistol-grip stock with swivels. Made from 1949 to 1957.

Winchester Model 47

Winchester Model 52 Standard Barrel

Winchester Model 52 International Match

Winchester Model 52 International Prone Target

MODEL 43 SPECIAL GRADE . . . . . NiB $855 Ex $679 Gd $480
Same as Standard Model 43 except has checkered pistol-grip and forearm, grip cap.

MODEL 47 BOLT-ACTION
SINGLE-SHOT RIFLE . . . . NiB $466 Ex $370 Gd $245
Caliber: .22 Short, Long, LR. 25-inch bbl. Weight: 5.5 lbs. Sights: Peep or open rear; bead front. Plain pistol-grip stock. Made from 1949 to 1954.

MODEL 52 BOLT-ACTION TARGET RIFLE
Standard bbl. First type. .22 LR. Five round box magazine. 28-inch bbl. Weight: 8.75 lbs. Sights: Folding leaf peep rear; blade front sight; standard sights various other combinations available. Scope bases. Semi-military-type target stock w/pistol grip; original model has grasping grooves in forearm; higher comb and semi-beavertail forearm on later models. Numerous changes were made in this model; the most important was the adoption of the speed lock in 1929. Model 52 rifles produced before this change are generally referred to as "slow lock" models. Last arms of this type bore serial numbers followed by the letter "A." Made 1919 to 1937.
Slow Lock model . . . . NiB $909 Ex $622 Gd $370
Speed Lock model . . . . NiB $733 Ex $466 Gd $379

MODEL 52 HEAVY BARREL . . . NiB $1379 Ex $1008 Gd $798
First type speed lock. Same general specifications as Standard Model 52 of this type except has heavier bbl., Lyman No. 17G front sight, weight: 10 lbs.

MODEL 52 INTERNATIONAL MATCH RIFLE
Similar to Model 52-D Heavy Barrel except has special lead-lapped bbl., laminated "free rifle"-style stock with high comb, thumbhole, hook buttplate, accessory rail, handstop/swivel assembly, palm rest. Weight: 13.5 lbs. Made from 1969 to 1978.
With standard trigger . . . . NiB $1577 Ex $1103 Gd $922

With Kenyon or I.S.U. trigger, add $350

MODEL 52 INTERNATIONAL PRONE NiB $1470 Ex $1133 Gd $909
Similar to Model 52-D Heavy Barrel except has special lead-lapped bbl., prone stock with full pistol-grip, rollover cheekpiece removable for bore-cleaning. Weight 11.5 lbs. Made from 1975 to 1980.

MODEL 52 SPORTING RIFLE
First type. Same as Standard Model 52 of this type except has lightweight 24-inch bbl., Lyman No. 48 receiver sight and gold bead front sight on hooded ramp, deluxe checkered sporting stock with cheekpiece, black forend tip, etc. Weight: 7.75 lbs. Made 1934 to 1958. Reintroduced 1993.
Model 52 Sporter . . . . NiB $4677 Ex $3200 Gd $1590
Model 52A Sporter . . . . NiB $3290 Ex $2733 Gd $1266
Model 52B Sporter . . . . NiB $4633 Ex $2479 Gd $1790
Model 52C Sporter . . . . NiB $5125 Ex $4120 Gd $2798
Model 52 C Sporter
(1993 BAC re-issue) . . . . NiB $650 Ex $500 Gd $433

MODEL 52-B BOLT-ACTION RIFLE
Standard bbl. Extensively redesigned action. Supplied with choice of "Target" stock, an improved version of the previous Model 52 stock, or "Marksman" stock with high comb, full pistol grip and beavertail forearm. Weight: 9 lbs. Offered with a wide choice of target sight combinations (Lyman, Marble-Goss, Redfield, Vaver, Winchester), value shown is for rifle less sight equipment. Other specifications as shown for first type. Made from 1935 to 1947. Reintroduced 1997.
Target model . . . . NiB $1270 Ex $968 Gd $755
BAC model
(1997 BAC re-issue) . . . . NiB $1270 Ex $968 Gd $755
USRAC Sporting model . . . . NiB $768 Ex $600 Gd $455

MODEL 52-B BULL GUN

Winchester Model 52-B
Standard Barrel

Winchester Model 52-B
Sporter

Winchester Model 52-C
Heavy Barrel

Winchester Model 53

Winchester Model 54
Super Grade

HEAVY BARREL . . . . **NiB $1880 Ex $1144 Gd $600**
Same specifications as Standard Model 52-B except Bull Gun has extra
heavy bbl., Marksman stock only, weight: 12 lbs. Heavy Bbl. model
weight: 11 lbs. Made 1940 to 1947.

MODEL 52-C BOLT-ACTION RIFLE
Improved action with "Micro-Motion" trigger mechanism and new-type
"Marksman" stock. General specifications same as shown for previous
models. Made from 1947 to 1961, Bull Gun from 1952. Value shown
is for rifle less sights.
Bull Gun (w/extra heavy bbl.,
  wt. 12 lbs.) . . . . **NiB $1877 Ex $976 Gd $694**
w/standard bbl.
  (wt. 9.75 lbs.). . . . . **NiB $1466 Ex $800 Gd $659**
Target model
  (w/heavy bbl.) . . . . **NiB $1455 Ex $909 Gd $689**

NOTE: *Following WWI, Winchester had financial difficulties and,
like many other firearm firms of the day, failed. However, Winchester
continued to operate in the hands of receivers. Then, in 1931, The
Western Cartridge Co.—under the leadership of John Olin—purchased
all assets of the firm. After that, Winchester leaped ahead of all other
firms of the day in firearm and ammunition development.*
*The first sporting firearm to come out of the Winchester plant
after WWI was the Model 20 shotgun, but this was quickly*

*followed by the famous Model 52 bolt-action rifle. This was also
a time when Winchester dropped the four-digit model numbers
and began using two-digit numbers instead. This model-
numbering procedure, with one exception (Model 677),
continued for the next several years.*

MODEL 52-D BOLT-ACTION
TARGET RIFLE . . . . **NiB $1377 Ex $976 Gd $488**
Redesigned Model 52 action, Single-Shot. Caliber: .22 LR. 28-inch standard
or heavy bbl., free-floating, with blocks for standard target scopes. Weight:
With standard bbl., 9.75 lbs., with heavy barrel, 11 lbs. Restyled Marksman
stock with accessory channel and forend stop, rubber buttplate. Made 1961
to 1978. Value shown is for rifle without sights.

MODEL 53 LEVER-ACTION
REPEATER . . . . **NiB $2343 Ex $1869 Gd $1333**
Modification of Model 92. Solid frame or takedown. Calibers: .25-20,
.32-20, .44-40. Six round tubular half-magazine in solid frame model.
Seven round in takedown. 22-inch nickel steel bbl. Weight: 5.5 to 6.5
lbs. Sights: Open rear; bead front. Redesigned straight-grip stock and
forearm. Made from 1924 to 1932.

MODEL 54 BOLT-ACTION
HIGH POWER SPORTING RIFLE (I). . . . **NiB $1570 Ex $933 Gd $667**
First type. Calibers: .270 Win., 7x57mm, .30-30, .30-06, 7.65x53mm,

Winchester Model 55 "Automatic" Single-Shot

Winchester Model 55 Lever-Action

Winchester Model 56

Winchester Model 57 Target

9x57mm. Five round box magazine. 24-inch bbl. Weight: 7.75 lbs. Sights: Open rear; bead front. Checkered stock w/pistol grip, tapered forearm w/Schnabel tip. This type has two-piece firing pin. Made from 1925 to 1930.

MODEL 54 BOLT-ACTION
HIGH POWER SPORTING RIFLE (II) . . . **NiB $1180 Ex $922 Gd $744**
Standard Grade. Improved type with speed lock and one-piece firing pin. Calibers: .22 Hornet, .220 Swift, .250/3000, .257 Roberts, .270 Win., 7x57mm, .30-06. Five round box magazine. 24-inch bbl., 26-inch in cal. .220 Swift. Weight: About 8 lbs. Sights: Open rear, bead front on ramp. NRA-type stock w/checkered pistol-grip and forearm. Made 1930 to 1936. Add $200 for .22 Hornet caliber.

MODEL 54 CARBINE (I) . . . . . . **NiB $1495 Ex $884 Gd $601**
First type. Same as Model 54 rifle except has 20-inch bbl., plain lightweight stock with grasping grooves in forearm. Weight: 7.25 lbs.

MODEL 54 CARBINE (II) . . . . . . **NiB $1566 Ex $912 Gd $648**
Improved type. Same as Model 54 Standard Grade Sporting Rifle of this type except has 20-inch bbl. Weight: About 7.5 lbs. This model may have either NRA-type stock or the lightweight stock found on the first-type Model 54 Carbine.

MODEL 54 NATIONAL
MATCH RIFLE . . . . **NiB $1722 Ex $967 Gd $679**
Same as Standard Model 54 except has Lyman sights, scope bases, Marksman-type target stock, weighs 9.5 lbs. Same calibers as Standard Model.

MODEL 54 SNIPER'S
MATCH RIFLE . . . . **NiB $2489 Ex $1388 Gd $633**
Similar to the earlier Model 54 Sniper's Rifle except has Marksman-type target stock, scope bases, weight: 12.5 lbs. Available in same calibers as Model 54 Standard Grade.

MODEL 54 SNIPER'S RIFLE . . . **NiB $2566 Ex $ 1534 Gd $770**
Same as Standard Model 54 except has heavy 26-inch bbl., Lyman No. 48 rear peep sight and blade front sight semi-military stock, weight: 11.75 pounds, cal. .30-06 only.

MODEL 54 SUPER GRADE . . . **NiB $3144 Ex $2057 Gd $1166**
Same as Standard Model 54 Sporter except has deluxe stock with cheekpiece, black forend tip, pistol-grip cap, quick detachable swivels, 1-inch sling strap.

MODEL 54 TARGET RIFLE . . . . . . **NiB $888 Ex $572 Gd $390**
Same as Standard Model 54 except has 24-inch medium-weight bbl. (26-inch in cal. .220 Swift), Lyman sights, scope bases, Marksman-type target stock, weight: 10.5 lbs., same calibers as Standard Model.

MODEL 55 "AUTOMATIC"
SINGLE-SHOT . . . . **NiB $379 Ex $290 Gd $210**
Caliber: .22 Short, Long, LR. 22-inch bbl. Sights: Open rear, bead front. One-piece walnut stock. Weight: About 5.5 lbs. Made from 1958 to 1960.

MODEL 55 LEVER-ACTION REPEATER
Modification of Model 94. Solid frame or takedown. Calibers: .25-35, .30-30, .32 Win. Special. Three round tubular half magazine. 24-inch nickel steel bbl. Weight: About 7 lbs. Sights: Open rear; bead front. Made from 1924 to 1932.
Standard model (straight grip) . . . . . . **NiB $2133 Ex $1670 Gd $1006**
Deluxe model (pistol grip) . . . . **NiB $2287 Ex $1744 Gd $1140**

MODEL 56 BOLT-ACTION
SPORTING RIFLE . . . . **NiB $1179 Ex $1143 Gd $707**

Winchester Model 58

Winchester Model 59

Winchester Model 60A

Winchester Model 61

Winchester Model 62

Winchester Model 63

Solid frame. Caliber: .22 LR., .22 Short. Five or 10-round detachable box magazine. 22-inch bbl. Weight: 4.75 lbs. Sights: Open rear; bead front. Plain pistol-grip with Schnabel forend. Made 1926 to 1929.

MODEL 57 BOLT-ACTION RIFLE
Solid frame. Same as Model 56 except available (until 1929) in .22 Short as well as LR with 5- or 10-round magazine. Has semi-military style target stock, bbl. band on forend, swivels and web sling, Lyman peep rear sight, weight: 5 lbs. Made from 1926 to 1936.
Sporter model. . . . . **NiB $888 Ex $654 Gd $500**
Target model . . . . **NiB $733 Ex $679 Gd $500**

MODEL 58 BOLT-ACTION
SINGLE-SHOT . . . . **NiB $1056 Ex $800 Gd $598**
Similar to Model 52. Takedown. Caliber. .22 Short, Long LR. 18-inch bbl. Weight: 3 lbs. Sights, Open rear; blade front. Plain, flat, straight-grip hardwood stock. Not serial numbered. Made 1928 to 1931.

MODEL 59 BOLT-ACTION
SINGLE-SHOT . . . . **NiB $1268 Ex $1009 Gd $756**
Improved version of Model 58, has 23-inch bbl., redesigned stock w/ pistol grip, weight: 4.5 lbs. Made in 1930.

MODEL 60, 60A BOLT-ACTION SINGLE-SHOT
Redesign of Model 59. Caliber: .22 Short, Long, LR. 23-inch bbl. (27-inch

after 1933). Weight: 4.25 lbs. Sights: Open rear, blade front. Plain pistol-grip stock. Made 1930 to 1934 (60), 1932 to 1939 (60A).
Model 60 . . . . **NiB $445 Ex $276 Gd $200**
Model 60A . . . . **NiB $556 Ex $380 Gd $338**

MODEL 60A TARGET RIFLE . . . . . NiB $670 Ex $448 Gd $338
Essentially the same as Model 60 except has Lyman peep rear sight and square top front sight, semi-military target stock and web sling, weight: 5.5 lbs. Made from 1932 to 1939.

MODEL 61 HAMMERLESS SLIDE-ACTION REPEATER
Takedown. Caliber: .22 Short, Long, LR. Tubular magazine holds 20 Short, 16 Long, 14 LR. 24-inch round bbl. Weight: 5.5 lbs. Sights: Open rear; bead front. Plain pistol-grip stock, grooved semi-beavertail slide handle. Also available with 24-inch full-octagon bbl. and only calibers .22 Short, .22 LR or .22 WRF. Note: Octagon barrel model discontinued 1943 to 1944; assembled 1948.
w/round bbl. . . . . .NiB $1330 Ex $987 Gd $478
w/grooved receiver. . . . . **NiB $1268 Ex $1160 Gd $800**
w/octagon bbl. . . . . **NiB $1766 Ex $1447 Gd $1006**

MODEL 61 MAGNUM . . . . . .NiB $2650 Ex $1854 Gd $1000
Same as Standard Model 61 except chambered for .22 WMR; magazine holds 12 rounds. Made from 1960 to 1963.

Winchester Model 64
Deer Rifle

Winchester Model 64
Standard

Winchester Model 64
1972-74 Type

Winchester Model 65

Winchester Model 67

Winchester Model 68

Winchester Model 69

Winchester Model 69 Match

RIFLES

GRADING: **NiB** = New in Box   **Ex** = Excellent or NRA 95%   **Gd** = Good or NRA 68%

Winchester Model
70 Basic Post-WWII
Model

Winchester Model 70
Standard

Winchester Model 70
African (1964)

Winchester Model 70
Deluxe (1964)]

MODEL 62
VISIBLE HAMMER . . . . **NiB $1560 Ex $1288 Gd $1043**
Modernized version of Model 1890. Caliber: .22 Short, Long, LR. 23-inch bbl. Weight: 5.5 lbs. Plain straight-grip stock, grooved semi-beavertail slide handle. Also available in Gallery Model chambered for .22 Short only. Made from 1932 to 1959. Note: Pre-WWII model (small forearm) commands 25% higher price.

MODEL 63 SELF-LOADING RIFLE
Takedown. Caliber: .22 LR High Speed only. Ten round tubular magazine in buttstock. 23-inch bbl. Weight: 5.5 lbs. Sights: Open rear, bead front. Plain pistol-grip stock and forearm. Originally available with 20-inch bbl. as well as 23-inch. Made from 1933 to 1959. Reintroduced in 1997.
w/23-inch bbl. . . . . NiB $1144 Ex $996 Gd $573
w/20-inch bbl. . . . . NiB $2690 Ex $1877 Gd $1133
w/grooved receiver . . . . NiB $2711 Ex $1912 Gd $995
Grade I (1997 BAC re-issue) . . . . NiB $707 Ex $576 Gd $488
High Grade (1997 BAC re-issue) . . . . NiB $705 Ex $579 Gd $495

MODEL 64 DELUXE
DEER RIFLE . . . . **NiB $1370 Ex $1109 Gd $777**
Same as Standard Model 64 calibers .30-30 and .32 Win. Special, except has checkered pistol-grip and semi-beavertail forearm, swivels and sling, weighs 7.75 lbs. Made from 1933 to 1956.

MODEL 64 LEVER-ACTION REPEATER
Standard Grade. Improved version of Models 94 and 55. Solid frame. Calibers: .25-35, .30-30, .32 Win. Special. Five round tubular two-thirds magazine. 20- or 24-inch bbl. Weight: About 7 lbs. Sights: Open rear; bead front on ramp w/sight cover. Plain pistol-grip stock and forearm. Made from 1933 to 1956. Production resumed in 1972 (caliber .30-30, 24-inch bbl.). Discontinued in 1974.
Original model. . . . . NiB $1079 Ex $883 Gd $620
1972-74 model. . . . . NiB $495 Ex $339 Gd $216

MODEL 64 .219 ZIPPER . . . . . NiB $4107 Ex $3054 Gd $1978
Same as Standard Grade Model 64 except has 26-inch bbl., peep rear sight. Made from 1937 to 1947.

MODEL 65 LEVER-ACTION
REPEATER . . . . **NiB $5044 Ex $3200 Gd $2555**
Improved version of Model 53. Solid frame. Calibers: .25-20 and .32-20. Six round tubular half-magazine. 22-inch bbl. Weight: 6.5 lbs. Sights: Open rear, bead front on ramp base. Plain pistol-grip stock and forearm. Made from 1933 to 1947.

MODEL 65 .218 BEE . . . . NiB $5051 Ex $2979 Gd $2000
Same as Standard Model 65 except has 24-inch bbl., peep rear sight. Made from 1938 ti 1947.

MODEL 67 BOLT-ACTION
SINGLE-SHOT RIFLE   **NiB $345 Ex $259 Gd $200**
Takedown. Calibers: .22 Short, Long, LR, .22 LR round (smoothbore), .22 WRF. 27-inch bbl. Weight: 5 lbs. Sights: Open rear, bead front. Plain pistol-grip stock (original model had grasping grooves in forearm). Made from 1934 to 1963.

MODEL 67 BOY'S RIFLE. . . . . . . NiB $345 Ex $259 Gd $200
Same as Standard Model 67 except has shorter stock, 20-inch bbl., weighs 4.25 lbs.

MODEL 68 BOLT-ACTION
SINGLE-SHOT . . . . **NiB $345 Ex $259 Gd $200**
Same as Model 67 except has rear peep sight. Made 1934 to 1946.

MODEL 69 BOLT-
ACTION RIFLE'S. . . . . **NiB $450 Ex $370 Gd $200**
Takedown. Caliber: .22 Short, Long, LR. Five or 10-round box magazine. 25-inch bbl. Weight: 5.5 lbs. Peep or open rear sight. Plain pistol-grip stock. Rifle cocks on closing motion of the bolt. Made from 1935 to 1937.

Winchester Model 70
Standard Weight Target
Rifle

Winchester Model 70
Heavy Weight Target
Rifle

Winchester Model
70 Bull Gun

Winchester Model 70
(Pre-1964) Standard
Model

MODEL 69A BOLT-ACTION RIFLE

Same as the Model 69 except cocking mechanism was changed to cock the rifle by the opening motion of the bolt. Made from 1937 to 1963. Note: Models with grooved receivers command 20% higher prices.

Model 69A standard . . . . NiB $489 Ex $397 Gd $290
Match model w/Lyman No. 57E
  receiver sight . . . . NiB $546 Ex $444 Gd $314
Target model w/Winchester
  peep rear sight, swivels, sling . . . NiB $690 Ex $567 Gd $389

MODEL 70

Introduced in 1937, the Model 70 Bolt-Action Repeating Rifle was offered in several styles and calibers. Only minor design changes were made over a period of 27 years and more than 500,000 of these rifles were sold. The original model was dubbed "The Rifleman's Rifle." In 1964, the original Model 70 was superseded by a revised version with redesigned action, improved bolt, swaged (free-floating) barrel, restyled stock. This model again underwent major changes in 1972. Most visible: New stock with contrasting forend tip and grip cap, cut checkering (instead of impressed as

in predecessor) knurled bolt handle. The action was machined from a solid block of steel with barrels made from chrome molybdenum steel. Other changes in the design and style of the Model 70 continued. The XTR models were added in 1978 along with the Model 70A, the latter omitting the white liners, forend caps and floor plates. In 1981, an XTR Featherweight Model was added to the line, beginning with serial number G1,440,000. This version featured lighter barrels, fancy-checkered stocks with Schnabel forend. After U.S. Repeating Arms took over the Winchester plant, the Model 70 went through even more changes as described under that section of Winchester rifles.

PRE-1964 MODEL 70

MODEL 70

AFRICAN RIFLE . . . . NiB $8000 Ex $5600 Gd $3809
Same general specifications as Super Grade Model 70 except w/25-inch bbl., 3-round magazine, Monte Carlo stock w/recoil pad. Weight: 9.5 lbs. Caliber: .458 Winchester Magnum. Made from 1956 to 1963.

Winchester Model 70
International Army Match (1964)

Winchester Model 70
Mannlicher (1964)

Winchester Model 70
Standard (1964)

Winchester Model 70
Target (1964)

MODEL 70 ALASKAN
Same as Standard Model 70 except calibers .338 Win. Mag., .375 H&H Mag.; 3-round magazine in .338, 4-round in .375 caliber; 25-inch bbl.; stock w/recoil pad. Weight: 8 lbs. in .338; 8.75 lbs. in .375 caliber. Made from 1960 to 1963.

.338 Win. Mag. . . . . NiB $4135 Ex $2170 Gd $1166
.375 H&H Mag. . . . . NiB $4395 Ex $2100 Gd $1189

MODEL 70 BULL GUN . . . . . . NiB $4467 Ex $3889 Gd $2356
Same as Standard Model 70 except w/heavy 28-inch bbl., scope bases, Marksman stock, weighs 13.25 lbs., caliber .300 H&H Magnum and .30-06 only. Disc. in 1963.

MODEL 70 FEATHERWEIGHT SPORTER
Same as Standard Model 70 except w/redesigned stock and 22-inch bbl., aluminum trigger guard, floorplate and buttplate. Calibers: .243 Win., .264 Win. Mag., .270 Win., .30-06, .358 Win. Weight: 6.5 lbs. Made from 1952 to 1963.

.243 Win. . . . . NiB $1790 Ex $1019 Gd $707
.264 Win. Mag. . . . . NiB $2164 Ex $1443 Gd $998
.270 Win. . . . . NiB $1869 Ex $1233 Gd $854
.30-06 Springfield. . . . . NiB $1043 Ex $888 Gd $596
.308 Win. . . . . NiB $1278 Ex $866 Gd $658
.358 Win. . . . . NiB $4566 Ex $3000 Gd $2043

MODEL 70 NATIONAL
MATCH RIFLE . . . . NiB $3376 Ex $1943 Gd $1723

Same as Standard Model 70 except w/scope bases, Marksman-type target stock, weight: 9.5 lbs. caliber .30-06 only. Disc. 1960.

MODEL 70 STANDARD GRADE
Calibers: .22 Hornet, .220 Swift, .243 Win., .250-3000, .257 Roberts, .270 Win., 7x57mm, .30-06, .308 Win., .300 H&H Mag., .375 H&H Mag. Five round box magazine (4-round in Magnum calibers). 24-inch bbl. standard; 26-inch in .220 Swift and .300 Mag.; 25-inch in .375 Mag.; at one time a 20-inch bbl. was available. Sights: Open rear; hooded ramp front. Checkered walnut stock; Monte Carlo comb standard on later production. Weight: From 7.75 lbs. depending on caliber and bbl. length. Made from 1937 to 1963.

.22 Hornet (1937-58) . . . . NiB $3466 Ex $2033 Gd $1266
.220 Swift (1937-63). . . . . NiB $1497 Ex $1266 Gd $879
.243 Win. (1955-63). . . . . NiB $2145 Ex $1077 Gd $910
.250-3000 Sav. (1937-49) . . . . NiB $5433 Ex $3810 Gd $2244
.257 Roberts (1937-59). . . . . NiB $3809 Ex $2088 Gd $1110
.264 Win. Mag. (1959-63, limited prod.) .NiB $1988 Ex $1154 Gd $877
.270 Win. (1937-63). . . . . NiB $2588 Ex $2000 Gd $1165
7x57mm Mauser (1937-49) . . . . NiB $6970 Ex $4650 Gd $4077
7.65 Argentine (1937, limited prod.) Very Rare
.30-06 Springfield (1937-63). . . . . NiB $3466 Ex $1880 Gd $1299
.308 Win. (1952-63, special order) Very Rare
.300 H&H (1937-63) . . . . NiB $3598 Ex $2079 Gd $1599
.300 Sav. (1944-50, limited prod.) Rare
.300 Win. Mag. (1962-63) . . . . NiB $2244 Ex $1867 Gd $1265
.338 Win. Mag. (1959-63, special order only) NiB $2144 Ex $1675 Gd $1197
.35 Rem. (1941-47, limited prod.) Very Rare

.358 Win. (1955-58) Very Rare
.375 H&H (1937-63) . . . . NiB $4676 Ex $4054 Gd $2354
.458 Win. Mag. (1956-63) Super Grade
  only . . . . NiB $4000 Ex $2978 Gd $2369
9x57 Mauser (1937 only, limited prod.) Very Rare

MODEL 70 SUPER GRADE
Same as Standard Grade Model 70 except w/deluxe stock w/cheek-piece, black forend tip, pistol-grip cap, quick detachable swivels, sling. Disc. 1960. Prices for Super Grade models also reflect rarity in both production and caliber. Values are generally twice that of standard models of similar configuration.

MODEL 70 SUPER GRADE FEATHERWEIGHT
Same as Standard Grade Featherweight except w/deluxe stock w/ cheekpiece, black forend tip, pistol-grip cap, quick detachable swivels, sling. Disc. 1960. Note: SG-FWs are very rare, but unless properly documented will not command premium prices. Prices for authenticated Super Grades Featherweight models are generally 4 to 5 times that of a standard production Featherweight model w/similar chambering.

MODEL 70 TARGET RIFLE
Same as Standard Model 70 except w/24-inch medium-weight bbl., scope bases, Marksman stock, weight 10.5 lbs. Originally offered in all of the Model 70 calibers, this rifle was available later in calibers .243 Win. and .30-06. Disc. 1963. Values are generally twice that of standard models of similar configuration.

MODEL 70 TARGET
HEAVY WEIGHT . . . . NiB $3160 Ex $2244 Gd $1590
Same general specifications as Standard Model 70 except w/either 24- or 26-inch heavy weight bbl. weight: 10.5 lbs. No checkering. .243 and .30-06 calibers.

MODEL 70 TARGET
BULL BARREL . . . . NiB $4466 Ex $2587 Gd $1964
Same general specifications as Standard Model 70 except 28-inch heavy weight bbl. and chambered for either .30-06 or .300 H&H Mag. Drilled and tapped for front sight base. Receiver slotted for clip loading. Weight: 13.25 lbs.MODEL 70

VARMINT RIFLE . . . . NiB $2388 Ex $1454 Gd $1145
Same general specifications as Standard Model 70 except w/26-inch heavy bbl., scope bases, special varminter stock. Calibers: .220 Swift, .243 Win. Made from 1956 to 1963.

MODEL 70
WESTERNER . . . . NiB $707 Ex $569 Gd $355
Same as Standard Model 70 except calibers .264 Win. Mag., .300 Win. Mag.; 3-round magazine; 26-inch bbl. in former caliber, 24-inch in latter. Weight: 8.25 lbs. Made from 1960 to 1963.

1964-TYPE MODEL 70

MODEL 70 AFRICAN . . . . NiB $595 Ex $397 Gd $338
Caliber: .458 Win. Mag. Three round magazine. 22-inch bbl. Weight: 8.5 lbs. Special "African" sights. Monte Carlo stock w/ebony forend tip, hand-checkering, twin stock-reinforcing bolts, recoil pad, QD swivels. Made from 1964 to 1971.

MODEL 70 DELUXE . . . . NiB $790 Ex $588 Gd $445
Calibers: .243, .270 Win., .30-06, .300 Win. Mag. Five round box magazine (3-round in Magnum). 22-inch bbl. (24-inch in Magnum). Weight: 7.5 lbs. Sights: Open rear; hooded ramp front. Monte Carlo stock w/ebony forend tip, hand-checkering, QD swivels, recoil pad on Magnum. Made from 1964 to 1971.

MODEL 70 INTERNATIONAL
ARMY MATCH RIFLE . . . . NiB $1198 Ex $955 Gd $744
Caliber: .308 Win. (7.62 NATO). Five round box magazine. 24-inch heavy barrel. Externally adj. trigger. Weight: 11 lbs. ISU stock w/military oil finish, forearm rail for standard accessories, vertically adj. buttplate. Made in 1971. Value shown is for rifle w/o sights.

MODEL 70 MAGNUM
Calibers: 7mm Rem. Mag.; .264, .300, .338 Win. Mag.; .375 H&H Mag. Three round magazine. 24-inch bbl. Weight: 7.75 to 8.5 lbs. Sights: Open rear; hooded ramp front. Monte Carlo stock w/cheekpiece, checkering, twin stock-reinforcing bolts, recoil pad, swivels. Made from 1964 to 1971.
375 H&H Mag. . . . . NiB $1043 Ex $787 Gd $678
Other calibers . . . . NiB $800 Ex $687 Gd $473

MODEL 70 MANNLICHER . . . . NiB $1266 Ex $1090 Gd $789
Calibers: .243, .270, .308 Win., .30-06. Five round box magazine. 19-inch bbl. Sights: open rear; hooded ramp front. Weight: 7.5 lbs. Mannlicher-style stock w/Monte Carlo comb and cheekpiece, checkering, steel forend cap, QD sling swivels. Made from 1969 to 1971.

MODEL 70 STANDARD . . . . NiB $788 Ex $577 Gd $400
Calibers: .22-250, .222 Rem., .227, .243, .270, .308 Win., .30-06. Five round box magazine. 22-inch bbl. Weight: 7.5 lbs. Sights: Open rear; hooded ramp front. Monte Carlo stock w/cheekpiece, checkering, swivels. Made from 1964 to 1971.

MODEL 70 TARGET . . . . NiB $4200 Ex $2765 Gd $1489
Calibers: .308 Win. (7.62 NATO) and .30-06. Five round box magazine. 24-inch heavy bbl. Blocks for target scope. No factory sights installed, but drilled and tapped for front and rear sights. Weight: 10.25 lbs. High-comb Marksman-style stock, aluminum hand stop, swivels. Straight-grain, one-piece stock w/sling swivels, but no checkering. Made from 1964 to 1971.

MODEL 70 VARMINT . . . . NiB $2160 Ex $1576 Gd $1009
Same as Model 70 Standard except w/24-inch target weight bbl., blocks for target scope. No factory sights installed, but drilled and tapped for

Winchester Model 70
Featherweight

Winchester Model 70
Golden 50th Anniversary

Winchester Model 70
Featherweight Classic

Winchester Model 70
Lightweight

Winchester Model 70
Magnum

Winchester Model 70
Carbine

front and rear sights. Available in calibers .22-250, .222 Rem., and .243 Win. only. Weight: 9.75 lbs. Made 1964 to 1971.

1972-TYPE MODEL 70

MODEL 70 AFRICAN . . . . **NiB $909 Ex $733 Gd $523**
Similar to Model 70 Magnum except w/22-inch bbl. caliber .458 Win. Mag. w/special African open rear sight, reinforced stock w/ebony forend tip, detachable swivels and sling; front sling swivel stud attached to bbl. Weight: 8.5 lbs. Made from 1972 to 1992.

MODEL 70 CLASSIC SM
Similar to Model 70 Classic Sporter except w/checkered black composite stock and matte metal finish. Made from 1994 to 1996.
MODEL 70 CLASSIC SM . . . . **NiB $765 Ex $595 Gd $355**
.375 H&H . . . . **NiB $944 Ex $765 Gd $535**
w/BOSS, add $150

w/open sights, add $50

MODEL 70 CLASSIC SPORTER
Similar to Model 70 Sporter except w/pre-64-style action w/controlled round feeding, classic-style stock. Optional open sights.   Made from 1994 to 2006.
Standard model . . . . **NiB $835 Ex $599 Gd $456**
w/BOSS, add $150
w/open sights, add $50

MODEL 70 CLASSIC SPORTER STAINLESS
Similar to Model 70 Classic Sporter except w/matte stainless steel finish. Weight: 7.5 lbs. No sights. Made from 1994 to 2006.
Standard model . . . . **NiB $875 Ex $679 Gd $369**
Magnum model . . . . **NiB $845 Ex $743 Gd $498**
w/BOSS, add $126

Winchester Model 70
XTR Sporter

Winchester Model 70A

MODEL 70 CUSTOM SHARPSHOOTER
Calibers: .22-250, .223, .308 Win., .300 Win. Mag. 24- or 26-inch bbl. 44.5 inches overall (24-inch bbl.). Weight: 11 lbs. Custom-fitted, hand-honed action. McMillan A-2 target-style stock. Matte blue or stainless finish. Made from 1992 to 1996.
Blued model. . . . . NiB $2145 Ex $1598 Gd $1195
NiB $2145 Ex $1598 Gd $1195 . . . NiB $2167 Ex $1620 Gd $2125

MODEL 70 CUSTOM SPORTING SHARPSHOOTER
Similar to Custom Sharpshooter Model except w/sporter-style gray composite stock. Stainless 24- or 26-inch bbl. w/blued receiver. Calibers: .270, 7mm STW, .300 Win. Mag. Made 1993 to 2006.
Blued model (disc. 1995) . . . . NiB $2155 Ex $1635 Gd $1266
Stainless model . . . . NiB $2260 Ex $1723 Gd $1319

MODEL 70 GOLDEN 50TH ANNIVERSARY EDITION
BOLT-ACTION RIFLE . . . . NiB $1693 Ex $1279 Gd $1039
Caliber: .300 Win. Three round magazine. 24-inch bbl. 44.5 inches overall. Weight: 7.75 lbs. Checkered American walnut stock. Hand-engraved American scroll pattern on bbl., receiver, magazine cover, trigger guard and pistol-grip cap. Sights: Adj. rear; hooded front ramp. Inscription on bbl. reads "The Rifleman's Rifle 1937 to 1987." Only 500 made 1986 to 1987. (Value for guns in new condition.)
MODEL 70 FEATHERWEIGHT CLASSIC. . . . NiB $735 Ex $520 Gd $449
Similar to Model 70 XTR Featherweight except w/controlled-round feeding system. Calibers: .270, .280 and .30-06. Made 1992 to 2006.

MODEL 70 INTERNATIONAL
ARMY MATCH. . . . . NiB $1095 Ex $944 Gd $654
Caliber: .308 Win. (7.62mm NATO). Five round magazine, clip slot in receiver bridge. 24-inch heavy barrel. Weight: 11 lbs. No sights, but drilled and tapped for front and rear iron sights, and/or scope mounts. ISU target stock. Intro. 1973; disc.

MODEL 70 LIGHTWEIGHT. . . . . . NiB $679 Ex $449 Gd $227
Calibers: .22-250 and .223 Rem.; .243, .270 and .308 Win.; .30-06 Springfield. Five round mag. capacity (6-round .223 Rem.). 22-inch barrel. 42 to 42.5 inches overall. Weight: 6 to 6.25 lbs. Checkered classic straight stock. Sling swivel studs. Made from 1986 to 1995.

MODEL 70 MAGNUM
Same as Model 70 except w/3-round magazine, 24-inch bbl., reinforced stock w/recoil pad. Weight: 7.75 lbs. (except 8.5 lbs.

in .375 H&H Mag.). Calibers: .264 Win. Mag., 7mm Rem. Mag., .300 Win. Mag., .338 Win. Mag., .375 H&H Mag. Made from 197 to 1980.
.375 H&H Magnum . . . . NiB $655 Ex $533 Gd $400
Other magnum calibers . . . . NiB $554 Ex $495 Gd $388

MODEL 70 STANDARD . . . . .NiB $677 Ex $439 Gd $331
Same as Model 70A except w/5-round magazine, Monte Carlo stock w/cheekpiece, black forend tip and pistol-grip cap w/white spacers, checkered pistol grip and forearm, detachable sling swivels. Same calibers plus .227 Win. Made from 1972 to 1980.

MODEL 70 STANDARD CARBINE. . . . . NiB $596 Ex $437 Gd $369
Same general specifications as Standard Model 70 except 19-inch bbl. and weight: 7.25 lbs. Shallow recoil pad. Walnut stock and forend w/ traditional Model 70 checkering. Swivel studs. No sights, but drilled and tapped for scope mount.

MODEL 70 SPORTER DBM . . . . NiB $755 Ex $585 Gd $359
Same general specifications as Model 70 Sporter SSM except w/detachable box magazine. Calibers: .22-250 (disc. 1994), .223 (disc. 1994), .243 (disc. 1994), .270, 7mm Rem. Mag., .308 (disc. 1994), .30-06, .300 Win. Mag. Made from 1992 to 1994.
S-model (w/iron sights) . . . . NiB $589 Ex $496 Gd $369

MODEL 70 STAINLESS
SPORTER SSM . . . . .NiB $688 Ex $495 Gd $390
Same general specifications as Model 70 XTR Sporter except w/check-ered black composite stock and matte finished receiver, bbl. and other metal parts. Calibers: .270, 7mm Rem. Mag., .30-06, .300 Win. Mag., .338 Win. Mag. Weight: 7.75 lbs. Made 1992 to 1994.

MODEL 70 CLASSIC SUPER GRADE . . . . NiB $977 Ex $857 Gd $590
Calibers: .270, 7mm Rem. Mag., .30-06, .300 Win. Mag., .338 Win. Mag. Five round magazine (standard), 3-round (magnum). 24-inch bbl. 44.5 inches overall. Weight: 7.75 lbs. Checkered walnut stock w/ sculptured cheekpiece and tapered forend. Scope bases and rings, no sights. Controlled-round feeding system. Made from 1990 to 1995. Improved in 1999. Disc. 2006.

MODEL 70 TARGET . . . . .NiB $976 Ex $945 Gd $588
Calibers: .30-06 and .308 Win. (7.62mm NATO). Five round maga-zine. 26-inch heavy bbl. Weight: 10.5 lbs. No sights, but drilled and tapped for scope mount and open sights. High-comb Marksman-style target stock, aluminum hand stop and swivels. Intro. 1972. Disc.

MODEL 70 ULTRA MATCH . . . . NiB $1099 Ex $976 Gd $569
Similar to Model 70 Target but custom grade w/26-inch heavy bbl. w/ deep counterbore, glass bedding, externally adj. trigger. Intro. 1972. Disc.

MODEL 70 VARMINT (HEAVY BARREL)
Same as Model 70 Standard except w/medium-heavy, counter-bored 26-inch bbl., no sights, stock w/less drop. Weight: 9 lbs. Calibers: .22-250 Rem., .223 Rem., .243 Win., .308 Win. Made 1972-93. Model 70 SHB, in .308 Win. only w/black synthetic stock and matte blue receiver/bbl. Made from 1992 to 1993.
Model 70 Varmint . . . . NiB $699 Ex $633 Gd $390
Model 70 SHB (synthetic stock, heavy bbl.) NiB $745 Ex $641 Gd $440

MODEL 70 WIN-CAM RIFLE . . . . . NiB $576 Ex $488 Gd $338
Caliber: .270 Win. and .30-06 Springfield. 24-inch barrel. Camouflage one-piece laminated stock. Recoil pad. Drilled and tapped for scope. Made from 1986 to 1987.

MODEL 70 WINLITE BOLT-ACTION RIFLE . . . NiB $855 Ex $570 Gd $448
Calibers: .270 Win., .280 Rem., .30-06 Springfield, 7mm Rem., .300 Win. Mag., and .338 Win. Mag. Five round magazine; 3-round for Magnum calibers. 22-inch bbl.; 24-inch for Magnum calibers. 42.5 inches overall; 44.5, Magnum calibers. Weight: 6.25 to 7 lbs. Fiberglass stock w/rubber recoil pad, sling swivel studs. Made from 1986 to 1990.

MODEL 70 WIN-TUFF BOLT-ACTION RIFLE
Calibers: .22-250, .223, .243, .270, .308 and .30-06 Springfield. 22-inch bbl. Weight: 6.25–7 lbs. Laminated dye-shaded brown wood stock w/recoil pad. Barrel drilled and tapped for scope. Swivel studs. FWT Model made from 1986 to 1994. LW Model intro. 1992.
Featherweight model . . . . NiB $590 Ex $470 Gd $388
Lightweight model (Made 1992–93) . . . . NiB $590 Ex $470 Gd $388

MODEL 70 XTR FEATHERWEIGHT . . . . . NiB $590 Ex $470 Gd $388
Similar to Standard Win. Model 70 except lightweight American walnut stock w/classic Schnabel forend, checkered. 22-inch bbl., hooded blade front sight, folding leaf rear sight. Stainless-steel magazine follower. Weight: 6.75 lbs. Made from 1984 to 1994.

MODEL 70 XTR SPORTER RIFLE . . . . NiB $744 Ex $545 Gd $376
Calibers: .264 Win. Mag., 7mm Rem. Mag., .300 Win. Mag., .200 Weatherby Mag., and .338 Win. Mag. Three round magazine. 24-inch barrel. 44.5 inches overall. Weight: 7.75 lbs. Walnut Monte Carlo stock. Rubber buttpad. Receiver tapped and drilled for scope mounting. Made from 1986 to 1994.

MODEL 70 XTR SPORTER MAGNUM . . . NiB $598 Ex $482 Gd $369
Calibers: .264 Win. Mag., 7mm Rem. Mag., .300 Win. Mag., .338 Win. Mag.

Three round magazine. 24-inch bbl. 44.5 inches overall. Weight: 7.75 lbs. No sights furnished, optional adj. folding leaf rear; hooded ramp. Receiver drilled and tapped for scope. Checkered American walnut Monte Carlo-style stock w/satin finish. Made from 1986 to 1994.

MODEL 70 XTR
SPORTER VARMINT . . . . NiB $707 Ex $420 Gd $268
Same general specifications as Model 70 XTR Sporter, except in calibers .223, .22-250, .243 only. Checkered American walnut Monte Carlo-style stock w/cheekpiece. Made from 1986 to 1994.

MODEL 70A . . . . NiB $450 Ex $316 Gd $231
Calibers: .222 Rem., .22-250, .243 Win., .25-06, .270 Win., .30-06, .308 Win. Four round magazine. 22-inch bbl. (except 24- or 26-inch in 25-06). Weight: 7.5 lbs. Sights: Open rear; hooded ramp front. Monte Carlo stock w/checkered pistol grip and forearm, sling swivels. Made from 1972 to 1978.

MODEL 70A MAGNUM . . . . NiB $476 Ex $316 Gd $236
Same as Model 70A except w/3-round magazine, 24-inch bbl., recoil pad. Weight: 7.75 lbs. Calibers: .264 Win. Mag., 7mm Rem. Mag., .300 Win. Mag. Made from 1972 to 1978

MODEL 70 ULTIMATE CLASSIC BOLT-ACTION RIFLE
Calibers: .25-06 Rem., .264 Win., .270 Win., .270 Wby. Mag., .280 Rem., 7mm Rem. Mag., 7mm STW, .30-06, Mag., .300 Win. Mag., .300 Wby. Mag., .300 H&H Mag., .338 Win. Mag., .340 Wby. Mag., .35 Whelen, .375 H&H Mag., .416 Rem. Mag. and .458 Win. Mag. Three, 4- or 5-round magazine. 22- 24- 26-inch stainless bbl. in various configurations including: full-fluted tapered round, half round and half octagonal or tapered full octagonal. Weight: 7.75 to 9.25 lbs. Checkered fancy walnut stock. Made in 1995.
Model 70
Ultimate Classic . . . . NiB $2153 Ex $1999 Gd $1098
Magnum calibers (.375 H&H,
.416 and .458), add $250

MODEL 70 LAMINATED STAINLESS
BOLT-ACTION RIFLE . . . . NiB $2150 Ex $1792 Gd $952
Calibers: .270 Win., .30-06 Spfld., 7mm Rem. Mag., .300 Win. Mag., and .338 Win. Mag. Five round magazine. 24-inch bbl. 44.75 inches overall. Weight: 8 to 8.525 lbs. Gray/Black laminated stock. Made from 1998 to 1999.

MODEL 70 CHARACTERISTICS

MODEL 70 FIRST MODEL (SERIAL NUMBERS 1 – 80,000)
First manufactured in 1936; first sold in 1937. Receiver drilled for Lyman No. 57W or No. 48WJS receiver peep sights. Also drilled and tapped for Lyman or Fecker scope sight block. Weight w/24-inch bbl. in all calibers except .375 H&H Mag.: 8.25 lbs. 9 lbs. in H&H Mag. Early type safety located on bolt top. Production of this model ended in 1942 near serial number 80,000 due to World War II. *Cross-sectional view of the pre-1964 Winchester Model 70's speed lock action. This action cocks on the opening movement of the bolt with polished, smooth-functioning cams and guide lug, ensuring fast and smooth operation.*

MODEL 70 SECOND MODEL (SERIAL NUMBERS 80,000 – 350,000)
All civilian production of Winchester Model 70 rifles halted during World War II. Production resumed in 1947 w/improved safety and integral front-sight ramp. Serial numbers started at around 80,000. This model type was produced until 1954, ending around serial number 350,000.

Winchester Model 70
Black Shadow

Winchester Model
70 Classic Camo

MODEL 70 THIRD MODEL (SERIAL NUMBERS 350,000 – 400,000)

This variety was manufactured from 1954 to 1960 and retained many features of the Second Model except that a folding rear sight replaced the earlier type and front-sight ramps were brazed onto the bbl. rather than being an integral part of the bbl. The Model 70 Featherweight Rifle was intro. in 1954 in .308 WCF caliber. It was fitted w/light 22-inch bbl. and was also available w/either a Monte Carlo or Standard stock. The .243 Win. cartridge was added in 1955 in all grades of the Winchester Model 70 except the National Match and Bull Gun models. The .358 Win. cartridge was also intro. in 1955, along w/new Varmint Model chambered in .243 caliber only.

MODEL 70 FOURTH MODEL (SERIAL NUMBERS 400,000 – 500,000)

Different markings were inscribed on the barrels of these models and new magnum calibers were added; that is, .264 Win Mag., .338 Win. Mag, and .458 Win. Mag. All bbls. of this variation were about 0.13 inch shorter than previous ones. The .22 Hornet and .257 Roberts were disc. in 1962; the .358 Win. caliber in 1963.

MODEL 70 FIFTH MODEL (SERIAL NUMBERS 500,000 TO ABOUT 570,000)

These rifles may be recognized by slightly smaller checkering patterns and slightly smaller lightweight stocks. Featherweight bbls. were marked "Featherweight." Webbed recoil pads were furnished on magnum calibers.

POST-1964 MODEL 70 RIFLES

In 1964, the Winchester-Western Division of Olin Industries claimed that they were losing money on every Model 70 they produced. Both labor and material costs had increased to a level that could no longer be ignored. Other models followed suit. Consequently, sweeping changes were made to the entire Winchester line. Many of the older, less popular models were discontinued. Models that were to remain in production were modified for lower production costs.

1964 WINCHESTER MODEL 70 RIFLES
SERIAL NUMBERS 570,000 TO ABOUT 707,000)

The first version of the "New Model 70s" utilized a free-floating barrel, swaged rifle bore, new stock and sights, new type of bolt and receiver, and a different finish throughout on both the wood and metal parts. The featherweight grade was dropped, but six other grades were available in this new line:

Standard
Deluxe (Replaced Previous Super Grade)
Magnum
Varmint
Target
African

1966 MODEL 70 RIFLES
(SERIAL NUMBERS 707,000-G TO ABOUT 1,005,000)

In general, this group of Model 70s had fancier wood checkering, cross-bolt stock reinforcement, improved wood finish and improved action. One cross-bolt reinforcement was used on standard guns. Magnum calibers, however, used an additional forward cross-bolt and red recoil pad. The free-floating barrel clearance forward of the breech taper was reduced in thickness. Impressed checkering was used on the Deluxe models until 1968. Hand checkering was once again used on Deluxe and Carbine models in 1969; the big, red "W" was removed from all grip caps. A new, red safety-indicator and undercut cheekpiece was introduced in 1971.

1972 MODEL 70 RIFLES
(SERIAL NUMBERS G1,005,000 TO ABOUT G1,360,000)

Both the barrels and receivers for this variety of Model 70s were made from chrome molybdenum (C-M) steel. The barrels were tapered w/spiral rifling, ranging in length from 22 to 24 inches. Calibers .222 Rem., .227 Win. .22-250, .243 Win., .25-06, .270, .308 Win., .30-06 and .458 WM used the 22-inch length, while the following calibers used the 24-inch length: .222 Rem., .22-250, .243 Win., .264 Win. Mag., 7mm Mag., .300 and .375 H&H Mag. The .227 Win caliber was dropped in 1973; Mannlicher stocks were also disc. in 1973. The receiver for this variety of Model 70s was machined from a block of C-M steel. A new improved anti-bind bolt was introduced along with a new type of ejector. Other improvements included hand-cut checkering, pistol-grip stocks with pistol-grip and dark forend caps. An improved satin wood finish was also utilized.

1978 MODEL 70 RIFLES
(SERIAL NUMBERS BEGAN AROUND G1,360,000)

This variety of Model 70 was similar to the 1972 version except that a new XTR style was added which featured high-luster wood and metal finishes, fine-cut checkering, and similar embellishments. All Model 70 rifles made during this period used the XTR style; no standard models were available.

Winchester Model 72

Winchester Model 74

Winchester Model 75
Sporting

Winchester Model 88
Pre-1965

In 1981, beginning with serial number G1,440,000 (approximately), a Featherweight version of the Model 70 XTR was introduced. The receiver was identical to the 1978 XTR, but lighter barrels were fitted. Stocks were changed to a lighter design with larger scroll checkering patterns and a Schnabel forend with no Monte Carlo comb. A satin sheen stock finish on the featherweight version replaced the high-luster finish used on the other XTR models. A new-style red buttplate with thick, black rubber liner was used on the Featherweight models. The grip cap was also redesigned for this model. 2006 – U.S. Repeating Arms Model 70 RIFLES
In the early 1980s, negotiations began between Olin Industries and an employee-based corporation. The result of these negotiations ended with Olin selling all tools, machinery, supplies, etc. at the New Haven plant to the newly-formed corporation which was eventually named U.S. Repeating Arms Company. Furthermore, U.S. Repeating Arms Company purchased the right to use the Winchester name and logo. Winchester Model 70s went through very few changes the first two years after the transition. However, in 1984, the Featherweight Model 70 XTR rifles were offered in a new short action for .22-250 Rem., .223 Rem., .243 Win. and .308 Win. calibers, in addition to their standard action which was used for the longer cartridges. A new Model 70 lightweight carbine was also introduced this same year. Two additional models were introduced in 1985 — the Model 70 Lightweight Mini-Carbine Short Action and the Model 70 XTR Sporter Varmint. The Model 70 Winlite appeared in the 1986 "Winchester" catalog, along with two economy versions of the Model 70 — the Winchester Ranger and the Ranger Youth Carbine. Five or six different versions of the Winchester Model 70 had been sufficient for 28 years (1937 to 1964). Now, changes in design and the addition of new models each year seemed to be necessary to keep the rifle alive. New models were added, old models dropped, changed in design, etc., on a regular basis. Still, the Winchester Model 70 Bolt-Action Repeating Rifle — in any of its variations — is the most popular bolt-action rifle

ever built.

MODEL 70 BLACK SHADOW . . . . **NiB $556 Ex $379 Gd $300**
Calibers: .243 Win., .270 Win., .300 Win. Mag., .308 Win., .338 Win. Mag., .30-06 Spfld., 7mm STW, 7mm Rem. Mag. and 7mm-08 Rem. Three, 4- or 5-round magazine. 20- 24- 25- or 26-inch bbls. 39.5 to 46.75 inches overall. Weight: 6.5 to 8.25 lbs. Composite, Walnut or Gray/Black laminated stocks. Made from 1998 to 2006.

MODEL 70 CLASSIC
CAMO BOLT-ACTION RIFLE. . . . . **NiB $990 Ex $887 Gd $554**
Calibers: .270 Win., 30-06 Spfld., 7mm Rem. Mag., .300 Win. Mag. Three or 5-round magazine. 24- or 26-inch bbl. 44.75 to 46.75 inches overall. Weight; 7.25 to 7.5 lbs. Mossy Oak finish and composite stock. Made from 1998 to 2006.

MODEL 70 CLASSIC COMPACT
BOLT-ACTION RIFLE . . . . **NiB $3329 Ex $2221 Gd $2069**
Calibers: .243 Win., .308 Win., and 7mm-08 Rem. Three round magazine. 20-inch bbl., 39.5 inches overall. Weight: 6.5 lbs. Walnut stock. Made from 1998 to 2006.

MODEL 70 CLASSIC LAREDO RANGE HUNTER BOLT-ACTION RIFLE
Calibers: 7mm STW, 7mm Rem. mag., .300 Win. Mag. Three round magazine. 26-inch bbl. 46.75 inches overall. Weight: 9.5 lbs. Composite stock. Made from 1996 to 1999.
Classic Laredo . . . . NiB $788 Ex $675 Gd $500
w/fluted bbl. (intro. 1998). . . . . NiB $833 Ex $733 Gd $513
Bossa Classic model . . . . NiB $800 Ex $689 Gd $466

MODEL 70 COYOTE . . . . **NiB $875 Ex $612 Gd $432**
Calibers: .22-250 Rem., .223 Rem., and .243 Win. Five or 6-round magazine. 24- inch bbl., 44 inches overall. Weight: 9 lbs. Medium-heavy stainless steel barrel w/laminated stock. Reverse taper forend.

Winchester Model
70 Coyote

Winchester Model 70
Ranger Compact

Winchester Model
70 Stealth

Winchester Model
94 Traditional

Made from 1999. Disc.

MODEL 70 RANGER
COMPACT RIFLE . . . . **NiB $555 Ex $369 Gd $257**
Calibers: .22-250 Rem., .223 Rem., .243 Win., 7mm-08 Rem., Mag., and .308 Win. Five or 6-round magazine. 20- or 22-inch bbl. 41 inches overall. Weight: 6.5 lbs. Adjustable TRUGLO front and rear fiber optic sights. Push-feed action. Made from 1999 to 2000.

MODEL 70
STEALTH RIFLE . . . . **NiB $920 Ex $707 Gd $449**
Varminter style bolt-action rifle. Calibers: .22-250 Rem., .223 Rem., and .308 Win. Five or 6-round magazine. 26- inch bbl. 46 inches overall. Weight: 10.75 lbs. Black synthetic stock w/Pillar Plus Accu Block and full-length aluminum bedding block. Matte blue finish. Made from 1999. Disc.

MODEL 71 LEVER-ACTION REPEATER
Solid frame. Caliber: .348 Win. Four round tubular magazine. 20- or 24-inch bbl. Weight: 8 lbs. Sights: Open or peep rear; bead front on ramp w/hood. Walnut stock. Made from 1935 to 1957.
**Standard Grade (no checkering, grip cap,
sling or swivels)** . . . . **NiB $1370 Ex $1167 Gd $789**
**Special Grade (checkered pistol grip and forearm, grip cap,
  QD swivels and sling)** . . . . .**NiB $2144 Ex $1798 Gd $1129**

**Special Grade carbine (w/20-inch bbl.,
   disc. 1940)**. . . . .**NiB $2695 Ex $2155 Gd $1769**
**Standard Grade carbine
   (20-inch bbl., disc. 1940)** . . . **NiB $2266 Ex $1880 Gd $1249**

MODEL 72 BOLT-ACTION REPEATER . . . NiB $525 Ex $266 Gd $189
Tubular magazine. Takedown. Caliber: .22 Short, Long, LR. Magazine holds 20 Short, 16 Long or 15 LR. 25-inch bbl. Weight: 5.75 lbs. Sights: Peep or open rear; bead front. Plain pistol-grip stock. Made from 1938 to 1959.

MODEL 73 LEVER-ACTION REPEATER
See Model 1873 rifles, carbines, "One of One Thousand" and other variations of this model at the beginning of Winchester Rifle Section. Note: The Winchester Model 1873 was the first lever-action repeating rifle bearing the Winchester name.

MODEL 74 SELF-LOADING RIFLE . . . . . NiB $389 Ex $290 Gd $198
Takedown. Calibers: .22 Short only, .22 LR only. Tubular magazine in buttstock holds 20 Short, 14 LR. 24-inch bbl. Weight: 6.25 lbs. Sights: Open rear; bead front. Plain pistol-grip stock, one-piece. Made from 1939 to 1955.

MODEL 75 SPORTING RIFLE . . . . NiB $600 Ex $299 Gd $210
Same as Model 75 Target except has 24-inch bbl., checkered sporter stock, open rear sight; bead front on hooded ramp, weight: 5.5 lbs.

Winchester Model 94
Long Barrel

Winchester Model 94
Win-Tuff

Winchester Model
94 Wrangler II Angle
Eject

Winchester Model 94
XTR Big Bore

Winchester Model 94
XTR 7-30 Waters

MODEL 75 TARGET RIFLE . . . . . .NiB $600 Ex $299 Gd $210
Caliber: .22 LR. 5- or 10-round box magazine. 28-inch bbl. Weight: 8.75 lbs. Target sights (Lyman, Redfield or Winchester). Target stock w/ pistol grip and semi-beavertail forearm, swivels and sling. Made from 1938 to 1959.

MODEL 77 SEMIAUTOMATIC RIFLE,
CLIP TYPE . . . . .NiB $322 Ex $190 Gd $133
Solid frame. Caliber: .22 LR. Eight round clip magazine. 22-inch bbl. Weight: About 5.5 lbs. Sights: Open rear; bead front. Plain, one-piece pistol-grip stock. Made from 1955 to 1963.

MODEL 77,
TUBULAR MAGAZINE . . . . .NiB $379 Ex $269 Gd $200
Same as Model 77. Clip type except has tubular magazine holding 15 rounds. Made from 1955 to 1963.

MODEL 86 CARBINE AND RIFLE
See Model 1886 at beginning of Winchester Rifle section.

MODEL 88 CARBINE
Same as Model 88 Rifle except has 19-inch bbl., plain carbine-style stock and forearm with bbl. band. Weight: 7 lbs. Made 1968 to 1973.
Standard calibers . . . . NiB $1335 Ex $1098 Gd $866
.284 Win. . . . . NiB $2095 Ex $1788 Gd $1077

MODEL 88 LEVER-ACTION RIFLE
Hammerless. Calibers: .243 Win., .284 Win., .308 Win., .358 Win. Four round box magazine. Three round in pre-1963 models and in .284. 22-inch bbl. Weight: About 7.25 lbs. One-piece walnut stock with pistol-grip, swivels (1965 and later models have basket-weave ornamentation instead of checkering). Made from 1955 to 1973. Note: .243 and .358 introduced 1956, later discontinued 1964; .284 introduced 1963.
Model 88 (checkered stock) . . . . NiB $1045 Ex $744 Gd $469
w/basketweave checkering . . . . NiB $1045 Ex $744 Gd $469
.243 Win.. . . . . NiB $1269 Ex $1088 Gd $899
.284 Win.. . . . . NiB $2300 Ex $1969 Gd $1675

MODEL 1892 GRADE 1 LEVER-ACTION RIFLE
Similar to the original Model 1892. Calibers: .357 Mag., .44-40, .44 Mag., .45 LC. Ten round magazine. 24-inch round bbl. Weight: 6.25 lbs. 41.25 inches overall. Bead front sight, adjustable buckhorn rear. Etched receiver and gold trigger. Blue finish. Smooth straight-grip walnut stock and fore-

Winchester Model 66
Commemorative

Winchester Model 94
Chief Crazy Horse Commemorative

warn w/ metal grip cap. Made from 1997 to 1999.

Standard Rifle . . . . NiB $677 Ex $558 Gd $425
Short Rifle (w/20-inch bbl., .44 Mag. only) . . . NiB $669 Ex $500 Gd $488

MODEL 94 ANTIQUE CARBINE . . NiB $588 Ex $448 Gd $290
Same as standard Post-64 Model 94 Carbine except has decorative
scrollwork and casehardened receiver, brass-plated loading gate, saddle
ring; caliber .30-30 only. Made from 1964 to 1984.

MODEL 94 CARBINE
Same as Model 1894 Rifle except 20-inch round bbl., 6-round full-
length magazine. Weight: About 6.5 lbs. Originally made in calibers
.25-35, .30-30, .32 Special and .38-55. Original version discontinued
1964.
Pre WWII (under No. 1,300,000) . . . . NiB $7250 Ex $5988 Gd $3866
Postwar, pre-1964
  (under No. 2,707,000) . . . . NiB $865 Ex $707 Gd $530

MODEL 94
CLASSIC CARBINE . . . . NiB $655 Ex $443 Gd $400
Same as Canadian Centennial '67 Commemorative Carbine except
without commemorative details; has scroll-engraved receiver, gold-
plated loading gate. Made from 1967 to 1970.

MODEL 94
CLASSIC RIFLE . . . . NiB $6744 Ex $5467 Gd $4388
Same as Model 67 Rifle except without commemorative details;
has scroll-engraved receiver, gold-plated loading gate. Made from
1968 to 1970.

MODEL 94
DELUXE CARBINE . . . . NiB $845 Ex $600 Gd $400
Caliber: .30-30 Win. Six round magazine. 20-inch bbl. 37.75 inches
overall. Weight: 6.5 lbs. Semi-fancy American walnut stock with rub-
ber buttpad, long forearm and specially cut checkering. Engraved with
"Deluxe" script. Made from 1987 to 2006.

MODEL 94 LONG BARREL RIFLE . . . . . . NiB $707 Ex $449 Gd $370
Caliber: .30-30 Win. Seven round magazine. 24-inch bbl. 41.75 inches
overall. Weight: 7 lbs. American walnut stock. Blade front sight. Made
from 1987 to 2006.

MODEL 94 TRAPPER . . . . NiB $779 Ex $588 Gd $430
Same as Winchester Model 94 Carbine except 16-inch bbl. and weight:

6 lbs., 2 oz. Made from 1980 to 2006.

MODEL 94 WIN-TUFF RIFLE . . . . NiB $556 Ex $400 Gd $297
Caliber: .30-30 Win. Six round magazine. 20-inch bbl. 37.75 inches overall.
Weight: 6.5 lbs. Brown laminated wood stock. Made from 198 to -2006.

MODEL 94 WRANGLER CARBINE
Same as standard Model 94 Carbine except has 16-inch bbl., engraved
receiver and chambered for .32 Special & .38-55 Win.
Top-eject model (disc. 1984) . . . . NiB $623 Ex $414 Gd $331
Wranger II, angle-eject model
  (disc. 1985) . . . . NiB $544 Ex $387 Gd $244

MODEL 94 XTR BIG BORE
Modified Model 94 action for added strength. Calibers: .307 Win., .356 Win.,
.375 Win. or .444 Marlin. 20-inch bbl. Six round magazine. Rubber buttpad.
Checkered stock and forearm. Weight: 6.5 lbs. Made from 1978 to 2006.
Top eject (disc. 1984) . . . . NiB $755 Ex $577 Gd $488
Angle eject (intro. 1985) . . . . NiB $441 Ex $379 Gd $255
.356 Win. or .375 Win., add $200

MODEL 94 XTR LEVER-ACTION RIFLE
Same general specifications as standard M94 and Angle Eject M94 except
chambered for .30-30 Win. and 7-30 Waters and has 20- or 24-inch bbl.
Weight: 6.5 to 7 lbs. Made from 1978 to 1988 by U.S. Repeating Arms.
Top eject (disc. 1984) . . . . NiB $744 Ex $ 533 Gd $445
Angle eject (.30-30) . . . . NiB $744 Ex $533 Gd $445
Deluxe angle eject (.30-30) . . . . NiB $744 Ex $533 Gd $445
7-30 Waters, add $100

MODEL 94 COMMEMORATIVES

MODEL 94 ANTLERED GAME. . . . NiB $775 Ex $639 Gd $482
Standard Model 94 action. Gold-colored medallion inlaid in stock.
Antique gold-plated receiver, lever tang and bbl. bands. Medallion
and receiver engraved with elk, moose, deer and caribou. 20.5-inch
bbl. Curved steel buttplate. In .30-30 caliber. 19,999 made in 1978.

MODEL 94 BICENTENNIAL
'76 CARBINE . . . . NiB $944 Ex $812 Gd $654
Same as Standard Model 94 Carbine except caliber .30-30 Win. only;
antique silver-finished, engraved receiver; stock and forearm of fancy
walnut, checkered, Bicentennial medallion embedded in buttstock,
curved buttplate. 20,000 made in 1976.

Winchester Colt
Commemorative
Set

Winchester Model 94
NRA Centennial

MODEL 94 BUFFALO BILL COMMEMORATIVE

Same as Centennial '66 Rifle except receiver is black-chromed, scroll-engraved and bears name "Buffalo Bill"; hammer, trigger, loading gate, saddle ring, forearm cap, and buttplate are nickel-plated; Buffalo Bill Memorial Assn. commemorative medallion embedded in buttstock; "Buffalo Bill Commemorative" inscribed on bbl., facsimile signature "W.F. Cody, Chief of Scouts" on tang. Carbine has 20-inch bbl., 6-round magazine, 7-lb. weight. 112,923 made in 1968.

Carbine	NiB $733	Ex $597	Gd $433
Rifle	NiB $778	Ex $650	Gd $469
Matched carbine/rifle set	NiB $1590	Ex $1370	Gd $1007

CANADIAN CENTENNIAL '67 COMMEMORATIVE

Same as Centennial '66 Rifle except receiver engraved with maple leaves and forearm cap is black-chromed, buttplate is blued, commemorative inscription in gold on barrel and top tang: "Canadian Centennial 1867–1967." Carbine has 20-inch bbl., 6-round magazine, weight: 7 lb., 90,398 made in 1967.

Carbine	NiB $667	Ex $498	Gd $300
Rifle	NiB $667	Ex $498	Gd $300
Matched carbine/rifle set	NiB $725	Ex $535	Gd $350

CENTENNIAL '66 COMMEMORATIVE

Commemorates Winchester's 100th anniversary. Standard Model 94 action. Caliber: .30-30. Full-length magazine holds 8 rounds. 26-inch octagon bbl. Weight: 8 lbs. Gold-plated receiver and forearm cap. Sights: Open rear; post front. Saddle ring. Walnut buttstock and forearm with high-gloss finish, solid brass buttplate. Commemorative inscription on bbl. and top tang of receiver. 100,478 made in 1966.

Carbine	NiB $727	Ex $537	Gd $353

Rifle	NiB $727	Ex $537	Gd $353
Matched carbine/ rifle set	NiB $1579	Ex $1355	Gd $954

MODEL 94 CHEYENNE

COMMEMORATIVE	NiB $976	Ex $755	Gd $642

Available in Canada only. Same as Standard Model 94 Carbine except chambered for .44-40. 11,227 made in 1977.

MODEL 94 CHIEF CRAZY HORSE

COMMEMORATIVE	NiB $888	Ex $733	Gd $521

Cailber: .38-55, 7-round tubular magazine. 24-inch bbl., 41.75 inches overall. Walnut stock with medallion of the United Sioux Tribes; buttstock and forend also decorated with brass tacks. Engraved receiver. Open rear sights; bead front sight. 19,999 made in 1983.

MODEL 94 COLT COMMEMORATIVE

CARBINE SET	NiB $2689	Ex $2077	Gd $1370

Standard Model 94 action. Caliber: .44-40 Win. 20-inch bbl. Weight: 6.25 lbs. Features the horse-and-rider trademark and distinctive WC monogram in gold etching on left side of receiver. Sold in set with Colt Single Action Revolver chambered for same caliber.

MODEL 94 COWBOY COMMEMORATIVE CARBINE

Same as Standard Model 94 Carbine except caliber .30-30 only; nickel-plated receiver, tangs, lever, bbl. bands; engraved receiver, "Cowboy Commemorative" on bbl., commemorative medallion embedded in buttstock; curved buttplate. 20,915 made in 1970. Nickel-silver medallion inlaid in stock. Antique silver-plated receiver engraved with scenes of the old frontier. Checkered walnut stock and forearm. 19,999 made in 1970.

Winchester Model 100

Cowboy carbine . . . . NiB $744 Ex $588 Gd $414
1 of 300 model . . . . NiB $3278 Ex $2966 Gd $2288

MODEL 94 GOLDEN SPIKE COMMEMORATIVE
CARBINE . . . . NiB $855 Ex $670 Gd $495
Same as Standard Model 94 Carbine except caliber .30-30 only; gold-plated receiver, tangs and bbl. bands; engraved receiver, commemorative medallion embedded in stock. 64,758 made in 1969.

MODEL 94 ILLINOIS SESQUICENTENNIAL
COMMEMORATIVE CARBINE . . . . NiB $622 Ex $398 Gd $287
Same as Standard Model 94 Carbine except caliber .30-30 only; gold-plated buttplate, trigger, loading gate, and saddle ring; receiver engraved with profile of Lincoln, commemorative inscription on receiver, bbl.; souvenir medallion embedded in stock. 31,124 made in 1968.

MODEL 94 LEGENDARY FRONTIERSMEN
COMMEMORATIVE . . . . NiB $769 Ex $655 Gd $488
Standard Model 94 action. Caliber: .39-55. 24-inch round bbl. Nickel-silver medallion inlaid in stock. Antique silver-plated receiver engraved with scenes of the old frontier. Checkered walnut stock and forearm. 19,999 made in 1979.

MODEL 94 LEGENDARY LAWMEN
COMMEMORATIVE . . . . NiB $769 Ex $655 Gd $488
Same as Standard Model 94 Carbine except .30-30 Win. only; antique silver-plated receiver engraved with action law-enforcement scenes. 16-inch Trapper bbl., antique silver-plated bbl. bands. 19,999 made in 1978.

MODEL 94 LONE STAR COMMEMORATIVE
Same as Theodore Roosevelt Rifle except yellow-gold plating; "Lone Star" engraving on receiver and bbl., commemorative medallion embedded in buttstock. 30,669 made in 1970.
Rifle or carbine . . . . NiB $754 Ex $598 Gd $449
Matched carbine/rifle set . . . . . NiB $1499 Ex $1288 Gd $955

MODEL 94 NRA
CENTENNIAL MUSKET . . . . NiB $707 Ex $597 Gd $479
Commemorates 100th anniversary of National Rifle Association of America. Standard Model 94 action. Caliber: .30-30. Seven round magazine. 26-inch bbl. Sights: Military folding rear; blade front. Black chrome-finished receiver engraved "NRA 1871–1971" plus scrollwork. Barrel inscribed "NRA Centennial Musket." Musket-style buttstock and full-length forearm; commemorative medallion embedded in buttstock. Weight: 7.13 lbs. Made in 1971.

MODEL 94 NRA
CENTENNIAL RIFLE . . . . NiB $715 Ex $609 Gd $520
Same as Model 94 Rifle except has commemorative details as in NRA Centennial Musket (barrel inscribed "NRA Centennial Rifle"); caliber

.30-30, 24-inch bbl., QD sling swivels. Made in 1971.

MODEL 94 NRA
CENTENNIAL MATCHED SET NiB $1400 Ex $1266 Gd $1077
Rifle and musket were offered in sets with consecutive serial numbers. Note: Production figures not available. These rifles offered in Winchester's 1972 catalog.

MODEL 94 NEBRASKA CENTENNIAL
COMMEMORATIVE CARBINE . . . . NiB $1133 Ex $933 Gd $633
Same as Standard Model 94 Carbine except caliber .30-30 only; gold-plated hammer, loading gate, bbl. band, and buttplate; souvenir medallion embedded in stock, commemorative inscription on bbl. 2,500 made in 1966.

MODEL 94 THEODORE ROOSEVELT
COMMEMORATIVE RIFLE/CARBINE
Standard Model 94 action. Caliber: .30-30. Rifle has 6-round half-magazine, 26-inch octagon bbl., weight: 7.5-lb. Carbine has 6-round full magazine, 20-inch bbl., weight: 7-lb. White gold-plated receiver, upper tang, and forend cap; receiver engraved with American Eagle, "26th President 1901–1909," and Roosevelt's signature. Commemorative medallion embedded in buttstock. Saddle ring. Half pistol-grip, contoured lever. 49,505 made in 1969.
Carbine . . . . NiB $733 Ex $560 Gd $398
Rifle . . . . NiB $733 Ex $560 Gd $398
Matched set . . . . NiB $1415 Ex $1153 Gd $805

MODEL 94 TEXAS RANGER
ASSOCIATION CARBINE . . . . NiB $769 Ex $654 Gd $498
Same as Texas Ranger Commemorative Model 94 except special edition of 150 carbines, numbered 1 through 150, with hand-checkered full-fancy walnut stock and forearm. Sold only through Texas Ranger Association. Made in 1973.

MODEL 94 TEXAS RANGER
COMMEMORATIVE CARBINE . . . . NiB $655 Ex $496 Gd $400
Same as Standard Model 94 Carbine except caliber .30-30 Win. only, stock and forearm of semi-fancy walnut, replica of Texas Ranger star embedded in buttstock, curved buttplate. 5,000 made in 1973.

MODEL 94 TRAPPER
Same as Winchester Model 94 Carbine except w/16-inch bbl. and weighs 6 lbs. 2 oz. Angle Eject introduced in 1985 also chambered for .357 Mag., .44 Mag. and .45 LC. Made from 1980 to 2006.
Top eject (disc. 1984) . . . . NiB $755 Ex $573 Gd $388
Angle eject (.30-30) . . . . NiB $445 Ex $306 Gd $200
.357 Mag., .44 mag., .45 LC, add $50

Winchester Model 250
Deluxe

Winchester Model 270
Deluxe

MODEL 94 JOHN WAYNE
COMMEMORATIVE CARBINE. . . . NiB $1597 Ex $1166 Gd $769
Standard Model 94 action. Caliber: .32-40. 18.5-inch bbl. Receiver is pewter-plated with engraving of Indian attack and cattle drive scenes. Oversized bow on lever. Nickel-silver medallion in buttstock bears a bas-relief portrait of Wayne. Selected American walnut stock with deep-cut checkering. Introduced by U.S. Repeating Arms in 1981.

MODEL 94 WELLS FARGO & CO.
COMMEMORATIVE CARBINE . . . . . NiB $770 Ex $544 Gd $339
Same as Standard Model 94 Carbine except .30-30 Win. only; antique silver-finished, engraved receiver; stock and forearm of fancy walnut, checkered, curved buttplate. Nickel-silver stagecoach medallion (inscribed "Wells Fargo & Co. —1852–1977—125 Years") embedded in buttstock. 20,000 made in 1977.

MODEL 94 O. F. WINCHESTER
COMMEMORATIVE RIFLE. . . . . . . NiB $854 Ex $650 Gd $599
Standard Model 94 action. Caliber: .38-55. 24-inch octagonal bbl. Receiver is satin gold-plated with distinctive engravings. Stock and forearm semi-fancy American walnut with high grade checkering.

MODEL 94 WRANGLER CARBINE
Same as standard Model 94 Carbine except w/16-inch bbl., engraved receiver and chambered for .32 Special and .38-55 Win. Angle Eject introduced in 1985 as Wrangler II, also chambered for .30-30 Win., .44 Mag. and .45 LC. Made 1980 to 1986. Re-introduced in 1992.
Top eject (disc. 1984) . . . . .NiB $398 Ex $290 Gd $200
Wrangler II, angle eject (.30-30). . . . . .NiB $390 Ex $285 Gd $195
.44 Mag or .45 LC, add $50

MODEL 94 WYOMING DIAMOND JUBILEE
COMMEMORATIVE CARBINE . . . . NiB $2166 Ex $1812 Gd $1347
Same as Standard Model 94 Carbine except caliber .30-30 Win. only, receiver engraved and casehardened in colors, brass saddle ring and loading gate, souvenir medallion embedded in buttstock, commemorative inscription on bbl. 1,500 made in 1964.

MODEL 94 ALASKAN PURCHASE CENTENNIAL
COMMEMORATIVE CARBINE . . . . NiB $2379 Ex $2006 Gd $1339
Same as Wyoming issue except different medallion and inscription. 1,501 made in 1967.

MODEL 100 AUTOLOADING RIFLE . . . . . NiB $675 Ex $559 Gd $466
Gas-operated semiautomatic. Calibers: .243, .284, .308 Win. Four round clip magazine (3-round in .284). 22-inch bbl. Weight: 7.25 lbs. Sights: Open rear; hooded ramp front. One-piece stock w/pistol grip, basket-weave checkering, grip cap, sling swivels. Made from 1961 to 1973.

MODEL 100 CARBINE . . . . NiB $800 Ex $622 Gd $482
Same as Model 100 Rifle except has 19-inch bbl., plain carbine-style stock and forearm with bbl. band. Weight: 7 lbs. Made 1967 to 1973.

MODEL 121 DELUXE. . . . . NiB $200 Ex $126 Gd $90
Same as Model 121 Standard except has ramp front sight, stock with fluted comb and sling swivels. Made from 1967 to 1973.

MODEL 121 STANDARD
BOLT-ACTION SINGLE SHOT . . . . . NiB $167 Ex $100 Gd $80
Caliber: .22 Short, Long, LR. 20.75-inch bbl. Weight: 5 lbs. Sights: Open rear; bead front. Monte Carlo-style stock. Made 1967 to 1973.

MODEL 121 YOUTH. . . . . NiB $200 Ex $126 Gd $90
Same as Model 121 Standard except has 1.25-inch shorter stock. Made from 1967 to 1973.

MODEL 131 BOLT-ACTION REPEATER . . . NiB $269 Ex $227 Gd $178
Caliber: .22 Short, Long or LR. Seven round clip magazine. 20.75-inch bbl. Weight: 5 lbs. Sights: Open rear; ramp front. Plain Monte Carlo stock. Made from 1967 to 1973.

MODEL 135. . . . . .NiB $244 Ex $169 Gd $155
Same as Model 131 except chambered for .22 WMR cartridge. Magazine holds 5 rounds. Made in 1967.

MODEL 141 BOLT-ACTION
TUBULAR REPEATER. . . . . NiB $279 Ex $216 Gd $155
Same as Model 131 except has tubular magazine in buttstock; holds 19 Short, 15 Long, 13 LR. Made from 1967 to 1973.MODEL 145NiB $256 Ex $200 Gd $145
Same as Model 141 except chambered for .22 WMR; magazine holds 9 rounds. Made in 1967.

MODEL 150 LEVER-ACTION CARBINE . . . . NiB $244 Ex $180 Gd $126
Same as Model 250 except has straight loop lever, plain carbine-style straight-grip stock and forearm with bbl. band. Made from 1967 to 1973.

MODEL 190 CARBINE . . . . NiB $255 Ex $195 Gd $135
Same as Model 190 rifle except has carbine-style forearm with bbl. band. Made from 1967 to 1973.
MODEL 190 SEMIAUTOMATIC RIFLE . . . . . NiB $265 Ex $210 Gd $145

Winchester Model 310

Winchester Model 320

Winchester Model 490 Rifle

Winchester Model 670 Bolt-Action Rifle

Winchester Model 670 Magnum

Same as current Model 290 except has plain stock and forearm. Made from 1966 to 1978.

MODEL 250 DELUXE RIFLE . . . . . NiB $300 Ex $233 Gd $150
Same as Model 250 Standard Rifle except has fancy walnut Monte Carlo stock and forearm, sling swivels. Made from 1965 to 1971.

MODEL 250 STANDARD
LEVER-ACTION RIFLE. . . . . NiB $249 Ex $175 Gd $126
Hammerless. Caliber: .22 Short, Long or LR. Tubular magazine holds 21 Short, 17 Long, 15 LR. 20.5-inch bbl. Sights: Open rear; ramp front. Weight: About 5 lbs. Plain stock and forearm on early production; later model has checkering. Made from 1963 to 1973.

MODEL 255 DELUXE RIFLE . . . . . NiB $338 Ex $265 Gd $175
Same as Model 250 Deluxe Rifle except chambered for .22 WMR cartridge. Magazine holds 11 rounds. Made 1965 to 1973.

MODEL 255 STANDARD RIFLE. . . NiB $265 Ex $198 Gd $144
Same as Model 250 Standard Rifle except chambered for .22 WMR cartridge. Magazine holds 11 rounds. Made from 1964 to 1970.

MODEL 270 DELUXE RIFLE . . . . . NiB $288 Ex $149 Gd $145
Same as Model 270 Standard Rifle except has fancy walnut Monte Carlo stock and forearm. Made from 1965 to 1973.

MODEL 270 STANDARD
SLIDE-ACTION RIFLE . . . . . . NiB $200 Ex $137 Gd $110
Hammerless. Caliber: .22 Short, Long or LR. Tubular magazine holds 21 Short, 17 Long, 15 LR. 20.5-inch bbl. Sights: Open rear; ramp front. Weight: About 5 lbs. Early production had plain walnut stock and forearm (slide handle); latter also furnished in plastic (Cycolac); last model has checkering. Made from 1963 to 1973.

MODEL 278 DELUXE RIFLE . . . . . NiB $322 Ex $268 Gd $144

Same as Model 270 Deluxe Rifle except chambered for .22 WMR cartridge. Tubular magazine holds 11 rounds. Made 1965–70.

MODEL 278
STANDARD RIFLE . . . . NiB $266 Ex $190 Gd $133
Same as Model 270 Standard Rifle except chambered for .22 WMR cartridge. Magazine holds 11 rounds. Made from 1964–70.

MODEL 290 DELUXE RIFLE . . . . . NiB $325 Ex $278 Gd $175
Same as Model 290 Standard Rifle except has fancy walnut Monte Carlo stock and forearm. Made from 1965 to 1973.

MODEL 290 STANDARD SEMIAUTOMATIC RIFLE
Caliber: .22 Long or LR. Tubular magazine holds 17 Long, 15 LR. 20.5-inch bbl. Sights: Open rear; ramp front. Weight: About 5 lbs. Plain stock and forearm on early production; current model has checkering. Made from 1963 to 1977.
w/plain stock/forearm . . . . NiB $286 Ex $227 Gd $133
w/checkered
   stock/forearm . . . . NiB $300 Ex $255 Gd $156

MODEL 310 BOLT-ACTION
SINGLE SHOT . . . . NiB $370 Ex $300 Gd $210
Caliber: .22 Short, Long, LR. 22-inch bbl. Weight: 5.63 lbs. Sights: Open rear; ramp front. Monte Carlo stock w/checkered pistol-grip and forearm, sling swivels. Made from 1972 to 1975.

MODEL 320 BOLT-ACTION
REPEATER . . . . NiB $370 Ex $300 Gd $210
Same as Model 310 except has 5-round clip magazine. Made from 1972 to 1974.

MODEL 490
SEMIAUTOMATIC RIFLE. . . . . . . NiB $388 Ex $298 Gd $234
Caliber: .22 LR. Five round clip magazine. 22-inch bbl. Weight: 6 lbs. Sights: Folding leaf rear; hooded ramp front. One-piece walnut stock w/

**Winchester Model 9422
Boy Scouts of America Commemorative**

**Winchester Model 9422
Eagle Scout Limited Edtion**

**Winchester Model 9422
WinCam**

**Winchester Model 9422
XTR Classic**

checkered pistol grip and forearm. Made 1975 to 1977.

MODEL 670 BOLT-ACTION
SPORTING RIFLE . . . . .NiB $386 Ex $308 Gd $231
Calibers: .227 Win., .243 Win., .270 Win., .30-06, .308 Win. Four
round magazine. 22-inch bbl. Weight: 7 lbs. Sights: Open rear; ramp
front. Monte Carlo stock w/checkered pistol-grip and forearm. Made
from 1967 to 1973.

MODEL 670 CARBINE . . . . .NiB $356 Ex $338 Gd $244
Same as Model 670 Rifle except has 19-inch bbl. Weight:
6.75 lbs. Calibers: .243 Win., .270 Win., .30-06. Made from 1967
to 1970.

MODEL 670 MAGNUM . . . . .NiB $410 Ex $356 Gd $281
Same as Model 670 Rifle except has 24-inch bbl., reinforced stock
with recoil pad with slightly different checkering pattern. Weight:
7.25 lbs. Calibers: .264 Win. Mag., 7mm Rem. Mag., .300 Win.
Mag. Open rear sight; ramp front sight with hood. Made from 1967
to 1970.

MODEL 770 BOLT-ACTION
SPORTING RIFLE . . . . .NiB $443 Ex $321 Gd $277
Model 70-type action. Calibers: .22-250, .222 Rem., .243, .270 Win.,
.30-06. Four round box magazine. 22-inch bbl. Sights: Open rear; hooded ramp front. Weight: 7.13 lbs. Monte Carlo stock, checkered pistol-grip
and forend; sling swivels. Made from 1969 to 1971.

MODEL 770 MAGNUM . . . . .NiB $443 Ex $318 Gd $233
Same as Standard Model 770 except 24-inch bbl., weight: 7.25 lbs.,
recoil pad. Calibers: 7mm Rem. Mag., .264 and .300 Win. Mag. Made

from 1969 to 1971.

MODEL 9422 LEVER-ACTION RIMFIRE RIFLES
Similar to the standard Model 94 except chambered for .22 Rimfire.
Calibers: .22 Short, Long, LR. (9422) or .22 WMR (9422M). Tubular
magazine holds 21 or 15 Short.17 or 12 Long, 15 or 11 LR (9422 or
Trapper) or 11 or 8 WRM (9422M or Trapper M). 16.5- or 20.5 inch
bbl. 33.125- to 37.125 inches overall. Weight: 5.75 to 6.25 lbs. Open
rear sight; hooded ramp front. Carbine-style stock and barrel-band
forearm. Stock options: Walnut (Standard), laminated brown (WinTuff),
laminated green (WinCam). Made from 1972. Disc.

Standard model	NiB $655	Ex $368	Gd $265
WinCam model	NiB $690	Ex $376	Gd $254
WinTuff model	NiB $533	Ex $337	Gd $233
Legacy model	NiB $844	Ex $577	Gd $300
Trapper model (16.5-inch bbl.)	NiB $765	Ex $456	Gd $268
XTR Classic model	NiB $800	Ex $587	Gd $370
High Grade Series I	NiB $1389	Ex $1085	Gd $770
High Grade Series II	NiB $1389	Ex $1985	Gd $770
25th Anniversary Edition			
Grade (1 of 2,500)	NiB $860	Ex $569	Gd $447
25th Anniversary Edition			
High Grade (1 of 250)	NiB $1688	Ex $1233	Gd $1044
25th Anniversary Edition			
High Grade (1 of 250)	NiB $843	Ex $667	Gd $495
Eagle Scout			
Commemorative (1 of 1,000) .	NiB $1448	Ex $1177	Gd $988
.22 WRM, add 10%			

DOUBLE XPRESS RIFLE . . . . .NiB $3889 Ex $2866 Gd $1744

Winslow Commander Grade

Winslow Crown Grade

Winslow Regent
Grade Bushmaster
Stock

Over/under double rifle. Caliber: .30-06. 23.5-inch bbl. Weight: 8.5 lbs. Made for Olin Corp. by Olin-Kodensha in Japan. Introduced 1982.

RANGER YOUTH
BOLT-ACTION CARBINE . . . . . . NiB $499 Ex $338 Gd $270
Calibers: .223 (discontinued 1989), .243 Win., and .308 Win. Four and 5-round magazine. Bbl.: 20-inch. Weight: 5.75 lbs. American hardwood stock. Open rear sight. Made 1985 to 2006 by U.S. Repeating Arms.

RANGER LEVER-ACTION CARBINE . . . . NiB $655 Ex $398 Gd $290
Caliber: .30-30. Five round tubular magazine. Bbl.: 20-inch round. Weight: 6.5 lbs. American hardwood stock. Economy version of Model 94. Made from 1985 to 2006 by U.S. Repeating Arms.

RANGER BOLT-ACTION CARBINE . . . . NiB $470 Ex $388 Gd $243
Calibers: .223 Rem., .243 Win., .270, .30-06, 7mm Rem. (discontinued 1985), Mag. Three and 4-round magazine. Bbl.: 24-inch in 7mm; 22-inch in .270 and .30-06. Open sights. American hardwood stock. Made from 1985 to 1999 by U.S. Repeating Arms.

Super X (SXR)
Semiautomatic. Caliber: .270 WSM, .30-06, .300 WSM, .300 Win. Mag., 3- or 4-round magazine, 22- or 24-in. bbl., no sights, checkered walnut stock. Blued finish. Made from 2006-09.
Grade I . . . . NiB $790 Ex $600 Gd $450

Wildcat
Bolt action. Caliber: .22 LR, 5- or 10-round magazine, 21-in. regular or heavy bbl., fixed sights, checkered hardwood stock. Blued finish. 4.5 to 5.5 lbs. Imported from Russia 2007-09.
Standard bbl. . . . . NiB $215 Ex $150 Gd $115
Heavy bbl. . . . . NiB $255 Ex $200 Gd $165

MODEL 1892 GRADE I LEVER-ACTION RIFLE
Similar to the original Model 1892. Calibers: .357 Mag., .44-40, .44 Mag., .45 LC. 10-round magazine. 24-inch round bbl. Weight: 6.25 lbs. 41.25 inches overall. Bead front sight, adjustable buckhorn rear. Etched receiver and gold trigger. Blue finish. Smooth straight-grip walnut stock and forearm w/ metal grip cap. Made from 1997. Disc.
Standard Rifle. . . . . NiB $800 Ex $713 Gd $482
Short Rifle (w/20-inch bbl.,
 .44 Mag. only) . . . . NiB $750 Ex $495 Gd $352

MODEL 1892 GRADE
II LEVER-ACTION RIFLE . . . . . . NiB $1388 Ex $1167 Gd $828
Similar to the Grade I Model 1892 except w/gold appointments and receiver game

scene. Chambered .45 LC only. Limited production of 1,000 in 1997.

WINSLOW ARMS COMPANY — Camden, South Carolina

BOLT-ACTION SPORTING RIFLE
Action: FN Supreme Mauser, Mark X Mauser, Remington 707 and 788, Sako, Winchester 70. Standard calibers: .17-222, .17-223, .222 Rem., .22-250, .243 Win., 6mm Rem., .25-06, .257 Roberts, .270 Win., 7x57, .280 Rem., .284 Win., .308 Win., .30-06, .358 Win. Magnum calibers: .17-222 Mag., .257 Wby., .264 Win., .270 Wby., 7mm Rem., 7mm Wby., .300 H&H, .300 Wby., .300 Win., .308 Norma, 8mm Rem., .338 Win., .358 Norma, .375 H&H, .375 Wby., .458 Win. Three-round magazine in standard calibers, 2-round in magnum. 24-inch barrel in standard calibers, 26-inch in magnum. Weight: With 24-inch bbl., 7 to 7.5 lbs.; with 26-inch bbl., 8 to 9 lbs. No sights. Stocks: "Bushmaster" with slender pistol-grip and beavertail forearm, "Plainsmaster" with full curl pistol-grip and flat forearm; both styles have Monte Carlo cheekpiece. Values shown are for basic rifle in each grade; extras such as special fancy wood, more elaborate carving, inlays and engraving can increase these figures considerably. Made from 1962 to 1989.
Commander Grade . . . . NiB $1897 Ex $1565 Gd $1177
Regal Grade . . . . NiB $2066 Ex $1590 Gd $1322
Regent Grade . . . . NiB $2175 Ex $1698 Gd $1443
Regimental Grade . . . . NiB $2966 Ex $2490 Gd $1788
Crown Grade . . . . NiB $3228 Ex $2579 Gd $2188
Royal Grade . . . . NiB $3590 Ex $2666 Gd $2077
Imperial Grade . . . . NiB $4100 Ex $3695 Gd $3000
Emperor Grade . . . . NiB $7070 Ex $5266 Gd $4590

ZEPHYR — U.S.
Manufactured by Victor Sarasqueta Company, Eibar, Spain; imported by Stoeger.

DOUBLE RIFLE . . . . NiB $22,656 Ex $18,622 Gd $12,799
Boxlock. Double barrels. Calibers: Available in practically every caliber from .22 Hornet to .505 Gibbs. Bbls.: 22 to 28 inches standard, but any lengths were available on special order. Weight: 7 lbs. for the smaller calibers up to 12 or more lbs. for the larger calibers. Imported by Stoeger from about 1938 to 1951.

Shotguns

Two gun writers, one Ithaca 10 gauge

Charles Askin Jr. (October 28, 1907 – March 2, 1999) was known as Col. Charles Askins to his gun enthusiast readers. Askins was a US Army officer, border patrol officer, hunter, competitive pistol shooter, and noted gun writer. The Ithaca NID Grade 4E 10 gauge was the very first shotgun designed around the 3-1/2-inch 10 gauge load and is literally the first shotgun made in this gauge and chambering, and was shipped to Charles Askins on March 24, 1932. Keith acquired the shotgun and had it restocked circa 1962 and the bores were also reworked. According to accounts, the Ithaca under Keith's tutelage patterned about 60 percent in a 30-inch circle at 80 yards with 2 ounces of No. 2 shot. Keith hunted goose with the gun and wrote about it in a 1963 story in *Guns & Ammo* magazine titled "Deuces are for Gooses." At auction it was sold for $29,000.

According to factory records, only 887 10-gauge magnum shotguns were produced; 56 in Grade 4.

The engraving is of typical Grade 4E style with large scrolling acanthus in stippled backgrounds, and the game scenes on each side under "Ithaca Gun Co" are typical except that the game birds, a ring-necked duck on left side and pheasant on right side are gold inlaid, which is typically found on Grade 5 guns.

The iconic first Ithaca NID Grade 4E 10 gauge with 3-1/2-inch chambers, S/N 500000, was delivered to Charles Askins in 1932. It features 32-inch barrels with a raised, matted, ventilated rib mounted with two white beads.

Photos courtesy of James D. Julia Auctioneers, Fairfield, Maine USA www.jamesdjulia.com

American Arms
Bristol (Sterling) Over/Under

American Arms
Derby Hammerless Double

American Arms
Gentry/York Hammerless Double

American Arms
Silver Over/Under

SHOTGUNS

ADAMY, GEBR. JAGDWAFFEN — Suhl, Germany

Custom gunmaker established 1820; currently from 1921. Previously imported by New England Custom Gun service, Claremont, NH. Specializes in custom break-action shotguns (S/S, O/U) drillings, vierlings, single-shot rifles. Models and grades are numerous, contact factory for specific information .

ALDENS — Chicago, Illinois

MODEL 670 CHIEFTAIN SLIDE ACTION . NiB $331 Ex $239 Gd $190
Hammerless. Gauges: 12, 20 and others. Three round tubular magazine. Bbl.: 26- to 30-inch; various chokes. Weight: 6.25 to 7.5 lbs. depending on bbl. length and ga. Walnut-finished hardwood stock.

AMERICAN ARMS — N. Kansas City, Missouri

See also Franchi Shotguns.

BRISTOL (STERLING) O/U . . . . NiB $853 Ex $621 Gd $500
Boxlock w/Greener crossbolt and engraved sideplates. Single selective trigger. Selective automatic ejectors. Gauges: 12, 20; 3-inch chambers. 26-, 28-, 30-, or 32-inch vent-rib bbls. w/screw-in choke tubes (Improved

Cylinder/Modified/Full). Weight: 7 lbs. Antique-silver receiver w/game scene or scroll engraving. Checkered full pistol-grip-style buttstock and forearm w/high-gloss finish. Imported 1986-88 designated Bristol; redesignated Sterling 1989 to 1990.

BRITTANY HAMMERLESS DOUBLE. . . . . NiB $863 Ex $744 Gd $508
Boxlock w/engraved case-colored receiver. Single selective trigger. Selective automatic ejectors. Gauges: 12, 20. 3-inch chambers. Bbls.: 25- or 27-inch w/screw-in choke tubes (IC/M/F). Weight: 6.5 lbs. (20 ga.). Checkered English-style walnut stock w/semi-beavertail forearm or pistol-grip stock w/high-gloss finish. Imported 1989 to 2000.

CAMPER SPECIAL. . . . . .NiB $217 Ex $166 Gd $90
Similar to the Single Barrel except takedown model w/21-inch bbl., M choke and pistol-grip stock. Made in 1989.

COMBO. . . . . .NiB $292 Ex $200 Gd $156
Similar to the Single-Barrel model except available w/interchangeable rifle and shotgun bbls. .22 LR/20-ga. shotgun or .22 Hornet/12-ga. shotgun. Rifle bbl. has adj. rear sights; blade-type front sight. Made in 1989.

DERBY HAMMERLESS DOUBLE
Sidelock w/engraved sideplates. Single non-selective or double triggers. Selective automatic ejectors. Gauges: 12, 20, 28 and .410.

**American Arms
WS/SS Hammerless Double**

3 inch chambers. Bbls.: 26-inch (IC/M) or 28-inch (M/F). Weight: 6 lbs. (20 ga.). Checkered English-style walnut stock and splinter forearm w/ hand-rubbed oil finish. Engraved frame/sideplates w/antique silver finish. Imported 1986 to 1994.

12 or 20 ga. . . . . NiB $1254 Ex $907 Gd $677
28 ga. or .410 (disc. 1991) . . . . . NiB $1377 Ex $979 Gd $855

F.S. SERIES O/U
Greener crossbolt in Trap and Skeet configuration. Single selective trigger. Selective automatic ejectors. 12 gauge only. 26-, 28-, 30-, or 32-inch separated bbls. Weight: 6.5 to 7.25 lbs. Black or chrome receiver. Checkered walnut buttstock and forearm. Imported 1986 to 1987.

Model F.S. 200 Boxlock . . . . NiB $867 Ex $677 Gd $490
Model F.S. 300 Boxlock . . . . NiB $1099 Ex $827 Gd $568
Model F.S. 400 Sidelock . . . . . NiB $1386 Ex $1197 Gd $871
Model F.S. 500 Sidelock . . . . . NiB $1386 Ex $1197 Gd $871

GENTRY/YORK HAMMERLESS DOUBLE
Chrome, coin-silver or color casehardened boxlock receiver w/scroll engraving. Double triggers. Extractors. Gauges: 12, 16, 20, 28, .410. 3-inch chambers (16 and 28 have 2.75-inch). Bbls.: 26-inch (IC/M) or 28-inch (M/F, 12, 16 and 20). Weight: 6.75 lbs. (12 ga.). Checkered walnut buttstock w/pistol-grip and beavertail forearm; both w/semi-gloss oil finish. Imported as York from 1986 to 1988, redesignated Gentry 1989 to 2000.

Gentry 12, or 16 or 20 ga. . . . . NiB $733 Ex $577 Gd $428
Gentry 28 ga. or .410. . . . . NiB $755 Ex $590 Gd $488
York 12, 16 or 20 ga. (disc. 1988). NiB $690 Ex $577 Gd $433
York 20 ga. or .410 . . . . NiB $690 Ex $577 Gd $433

GRULLA #2 HAMMERLESS DOUBLE
True sidelock w/engraved detachable sideplates. Double triggers. Extractors and cocking indicators. Gauges: 12, 20, .410 w/3-inch chambers; 28 w/2.75-inch. 26-inch bbl. Imported 1989 to 2000.

Standard model . . . . NiB $3798 Ex $2886 Gd $2166
Two-bbl. set (disc. 1995) . . . . NiB $3876 Ex $3688 Gd $2544

SILVER I O/U
Boxlock. Single selective trigger. Extractors. Gauges: 12, 20 and .410 w/3-inch chambers; 28 w/2.75 inch. Bbls.: 26-inch (IC/M), 28-inch (M/F, 12 and 20 ga. only). Weight: 6.75 lbs. (12 ga.). Checkered walnut stock and forearm. Antique-silver receiver w/scroll engraving. Imported 1987 to 2000.

12 or 20 ga. . . . . NiB $622 Ex $535 Gd $368
28 ga. or .410. . . . . NiB $663 Ex $590 Gd $477

SILVER II O/U
Similar to Model Silver I except w/selective automatic ejectors and 26-inch bbls. w/screw-in tubes (12 and 20 ga.). Fixed chokes (28 and .410). Made 1987 to 2000.

12 or 20 ga . . . . NiB $735 Ex $600 Gd $489
28 ga or .410. . . . . NiB $730 Ex $652 Gd $464

Upland Lite II. . . . . NiB $1254 Ex $1066 Gd $855
Two-bbl. set. . . . . NiB $1293 Ex $1088 Gd $867

SILVER LITE O/U
Similar to Model Silver II except w/blued, engraved alloy receiver. Available in 12 and 20 ga. only. Imported from 1990 to 1992.

Standard Model . . . . NiB $922 Ex $655 Gd $477
Two-bbl. Set . . . . NiB $1169 Ex $908 Gd $733

SILVER SKEET/TRAP . . . . NiB $855 Ex $640 Gd $569
Similar to the Silver II Model except has 28-inch (Skeet) or 30-inch (Trap) ported bbls. w/target-style rib and mid-bead sight. Imported 1992 to 1994.

SILVER SPORTING O/U . . . . NiB $966 Ex $768 Gd $633
Boxlock. Single selective trigger. Selective automatic ejectors. Gauges: 12, 2.75-inch chambers. 28-inch bbls.w/Franchoke tubes (SK, IC, M and F). Weight: 7.5 lbs. Checkered walnut stock and forearm. Special broadway rib and vented side ribs. Engraved receiver w/chrome-nickel finish. Imported from 1990 to 2000.

SINGLE-SHOT SHOTGUN
Break-open action. Gauges: 10 (3.5), 12, 20, .410, 3-inch chamber. Weight: about 6.5 lbs. Bead front sight. Walnut-finished hardwood stock w/checkered grip and forend. Made from 1988 to 1990.

10 ga. (3.5-inch). . . . . NiB $198 Ex $117 Gd $75
12 & 20 ga., .410 . . . . NiB $200 Ex $99 Gd $66
Multi-choke bbl., add $50

SLUGGER SINGLE-SHOT SHOTGUN . . . . NiB $190 Ex $100 Gd $79
Similar to the Single-Shot model except in 12 and 20 ga. only w/24-inch slug bbl. Rifle-type sights and recoil pad. Made 1989 to 1990.

TS/OU 12 SHOTGUN. . . . . .NiB $744 Ex $555 Gd $490
Turkey Special. Boxlock. Single selective trigger. Selective automatic ejectors. Gauge: 12, 3.5-inch chambers. Bbls.: 24-inch O/U w/screw-in tubes (IC, M, F). Weight: 6 lbs. 15 oz. Checkered European walnut stock and beavertail forearm. Matte blue finish. Imported 1987 to 2000.

TS/SS 10 HAMMERLESS DOUBLE . . . . . . NiB $700 Ex $533 Gd $400
Turkey Special. Same general specifications as Model WS/ SS 10, except w/26-inch side-by-side bbls., screw-in choke tubes (F/F) and chambered for 10-ga. 3.5-inch shells. Weight: 10 lbs., 13 oz. Imported 1987 to 1993.

TS/SS 12 HAMMERLESS DOUBLE . . . . . . NiB $766 Ex $533 Gd $421
Same general specifications as Model WS/SS 10 except in 12 ga. w/26-inch side-by-side bbls. and 3 screw-in choke tubes (IC/M/F). Weight: 7 lbs., 6 oz. Imported 1987 to 2000.

WS O/U 12 SHOTGUN . . . . .NiB $644 Ex $538 Gd $377
Waterfowl Special. Boxlock. Single selective trigger. Selective automatic ejectors. Gauge: 12; 3.5-inch chambers. Bbls.: 28-inch O/U w/screw-in tubes (IC/M/F). Weight: 7 lbs. Checkered European walnut stock and beavertail forearm. Matte blue metal finish. Imported 1987-2000.

Armalite AR-17
Golden Gun

Armsport 1050

Armsport 1125

WS/SS 10 HAMMERLESS DOUBLE . . . . . **NiB $883 Ex $671 Gd $428**
Waterfowl Special. Boxlock. Double triggers. Extractors. Gauge: 10; 3.5-inch chambers. Bbls.: 32-inch side/side choked F/F. Weight: About 11 lbs. Checkered walnut stock and beavertail forearm w/satin finish. Parkerized metal finish. Imported from 1987 to 1995.

WT O/U SHOTGUN . . . . **NiB $844 Ex $657 Gd $533**
Same general specifications as Model WS/OU 12 except chambered for 10-ga. 3.5-inch shells. Extractors. Satin wood finish and matte blue metal. Imported 1987 to 2000.

ARMALITE, INC. — Costa Mesa, California

AR-17 GOLDEN GUN . . . . **NiB $863 Ex $643 Gd $559**
Recoil-operated semiautomatic. High-test aluminum bbl. and receiver housing. 12 ga. only. Two round capacity. 24-inch bbl. w/interchangeable choke tubes: IC/M/F. Weight: 5.6 lbs. Polycarbonate stock and forearm recoil pad. Gold-anodized finish standard, also made w/black finish. Made 1964 to 1965. Fewer than 2,000 produced.

ARMSCOR (Arms Corp.) — Manila, Philippines

Imported until 1991 by Armscor Precision, San Mateo, CA; 1991–95 by Ruko Products, Inc., Buffalo NY.

MODEL M-30 FIELD PUMP SHOTGUN
Double slide-action bars w/damascened bolt. Gauge: 12 only w/3-inch chamber. Bbl.: 28-inch w/fixed chokes or choke tubes. Weight: 7.6 lbs. Walnut or walnut finished hardwood stock.
Model M-30F (w/hard
  wood stock, fixed choke) . . . . . .NiB $288 Ex $212 Gd $149
Model M-30F (w/hard-
  wood stock and choke tubes) . . .NiB $288 Ex $212 Gd $149
Model M-30F/IC (w/walnut
  stock and choke tubes). . . . . . . .NiB $366 Ex $247 Gd $169

MODEL M-30 RIOT PUMP
Double-action slide bar w/damascened bolt. Gauge: 12 only w/3-inch chamber. Bbls: 18.5 and 20-inch w/IC bore. Five- or 7-round magazine. Weight: 7 lbs, 2 ozs. Walnut finished hardwood stock.
Model M-30R6 (W/5-round magazine). . . . NiB $190 Ex $121 Gd $90
Model M-30R8 (W/7-round magazine). . . NiB $219 Ex $135 Gd $100

MODEL M-30 SPECIAL COMBO
Simlar to Special Purpose Model except has detachable synthetic stock that removes to convert to pistol-grip configuration.
Model M-30C (disc. 1995) . . . . . . NiB $249 Ex $200 Gd $155
Model M-30RP (disc. 1995) . . . . . NiB $249 Ex $200 Gd $155

MODEL M-30 SPECIAL PURPOSE
Double-action slide bar w/damascened bolt. Seven round magazine. Gauge: 12 only w/3-inch chamber. 20-inch bbl. w/cylinder choke. Iron sights (DG Model) or venter handguard (SAS Model). Weight: 7.5 lbs. Walnut finished hardwood stock.
Model M-30DG (Deer Gun). . . . . NiB $266 Ex $198 Gd $137
Model M-30SAS (Special Air Services) . . . . . NiB $277 Ex $218 Gd $125

ARMSPORT, INC. — Miami, Florida

1000 SERIES HAMMERLESS DOUBLES
Side-by-side w/engraved receiver, double triggers and extractors. Gauges: 10 (3.5), 12, 20, .410- 3-inch chambers. Model 1033: 10 ga., 32-inch bbl. Model 1050/51: 12 ga., 28-inch bbl., M/F choke. Model 1052/53: 20 ga., 26-inch bbl., I/M choke. Model 1054/57: .410 ga., 26-inch bbl., I/M. Model 1055: 28 ga., Weight: 5.75 to 7.25 lbs. European walnut buttstock and forend. Made in Italy. Importation disc. 1993.
Model 1033 (10 ga., disc. 1989) . . . . NiB $844 Ex $690 Gd $497
Model 1050 (12 ga., disc. 1993) . . . . NiB $766 Ex $692 Gd $477
Model 1051 (12 ga., disc. 1985) . . . . NiB $503 Ex $412 Gd $326
Model 1052 (20 ga., disc. 1985) . . . . NiB $477 Ex $390 Gd $288
Model 1053 (20 ga., disc. 1993) . . . . NiB $790 Ex $666 Gd $459
Model 1054 (.410, disc. 1992) . . . . . NiB $888 Ex $739 Gd $522
Model 1055 (28 ga., disc. 1992) . . . . NiB $554 Ex $448 Gd $336
Model 1057 (.410, disc. 1985) . . . . . NiB $569 Ex $481 Gd $357

SHOTGUNS

Armsport 2700

Armsport 2741

MODEL 1125 SINGLE-SHOT SHOTGUN. . . . NiB $196 Ex $139 Gd $98
Bottom-opening lever. Gauges: 12, 20. 3-inch chambers. Bead front
sight. Plain stock and forend. Imported 1987-89.

MODEL 2700 GOOSE GUN
Similar to the 2700 Standard Model except 10 ga. w/3.5-inch cham-
bers. Double triggers w/28-inch bbl. choked IC/M or 32-inch bbl.,
F/F. 12mm wide vent rib. Weight: 9.5 lbs. Canada geese engraved on
receiver. Antiqued silver-finished action. Checkered European walnut
stock w/rubber recoil pad. Imported from Italy 1986 to 1993.
W/fixed choke . . . . NiB $1167 Ex $933 Gd $676
W/choke tubes . . . . NiB $1433 Ex $979 Gd $724

MODEL 2700 OVER/UNDER SERIES
Hammerless, takedown shotgun w/engraved receiver. Selective single or
double triggers. Gauges: 10, 12, 20, 28 and .410. Bbl.: 26-or 28-inch w/
fixed chokes or choke tubes. Weight: 8 lbs. Checkered European walnut
buttstock and forend. Made in Italy. Importation disc. 1993.
Model 2701 12 ga. (disc. 1985) . . . . NiB $613 Ex $500 Gd $357
Model 2702 12 ga.. . . . . NiB $635 Ex $525 Gd $378
Model 2703 20 ga. (disc. 1985) . . . . NiB $668 Ex $544 Gd $365
Model 2704 20 ga.. . . . . NiB $655 Ex $548 Gd $400
Model 2705 (.410, DT, fixed chokes) . . . NiB $775 Ex $638 Gd $454
Model 2730/31 (BOSS-style action,
  SST Choke tubes) . . . . .NiB $868 Ex $733 Gd $538
Model 2733/35 (Boss-style
  action, extractors) . . . . .NiB $790 Ex $644 Gd $466
Model 2741 (Boss-style
  action, ejectors) . . . . .NiB $678 Ex $566 Gd $412
Model 2742 Sporting Clays
  (12 ga./choke tubes) . . . . .NiB $835 Ex $679 Gd $555
Model 2744 Sporting Clays
  (20 ga./choke tubes). . . . . .NiB $855 Ex $677 Gd $499
Model 2750 Sporting Clays
  (12 ga./sideplates) . . . . .NiB $955 Ex $723 Gd $528
Model 2751 Sporting Clays
  (20 ga./sideplates) . . . . .NiB $943 Ex $759 Gd $544

MODEL 2755 SLIDE-ACTION SHOTGUN
Gauge: 12 w/3-inch chamber. Tubular magazine. Bbls.: 28- or 30-inch
w/fixed choke or choke tubes. Weight: 7 lbs. European walnut stock.
Made in Italy 1986 to 1987.
Standard model, fixed choke. . . . . NiB $444 Ex $366 Gd $270
Standard model, choke tubes . . . . NiB $579 Ex $489 Gd $355
Police model, 20-inch bbl. . . . . . . NiB $390 Ex $333 Gd $244

MODEL 2900 TRI-BARREL (TRILLING) SHOTGUN
Boxlock. Double triggers w/top-tang bbl. selector. Extractors. Gauge:
12; 3-inch chambers. Bbls.: 28-inch (IC, M and F). Weight: 7.75 lbs.

Checkered European walnut stock and forearm. Engraved silver receiver.
Imported 1986 to 1987 and 1990 to 1993.
Model 2900 (W/fixed chokes). . NiB $2288 Ex $1844 Gd $1307
Model 2900 (choke tubes) . . . NiB $2945 Ex $2385 Gd $1669
Deluxe grades, add. $600

ARRIETA, S.L. — Elgoibar, Spain.
*Imported by New England Arms Corp., Wingshooting Adventures
Quality Arms, Griffin & Howe and Orvis.*

*Custom double-barreled shotguns with frames scaled to individual gauges.
Standard gauges are 12 and 16. Add: 5% for small gauges (20, 24, 28, 32 and
.410 bore) on currently manufactured models; $900 for single trigger (most
actions); 5% for matched pairs; 10% for rounded action on standard models;
extra bbls., add $1375 to $2000 per set.*

MODEL 557 STANDARD . . . . . . .NiB $4428 Ex $3966 Gd $2044
Gauges: 12, 16 or 20. Demi-Bloc steel barrels, detachable engraved sidelocks, double triggers, ejectors.

MODEL 570 LIEJA . . . . NiB $4949 Ex $4210 Gd $2588
Gauges: 12, 16 or 20. Non-detachable sidelocks.

MODEL 578 VICTORIA . . . . NiB $6280 Ex $4366 Gd $2290
Gauges: 12, 16 or 20. Similar to Model 570 but with fine English
scrollwork.

LIGERA MODEL . . . . NiB $5634 Ex $4247 Gd $3270
Available in all gauges. Lightweight 12 ga. has 2-inch chambers, lightweight or standard action. Includes unique frame engraving and Turkish
wood upgrade. Wt. appox. 6 pounds.

MODEL 590 REGINA . . . . NiB $3589 Ex $3177 Gd $2229
Gauges: 12, 16 or 20. Similar to Model 570 but has more elaborate
engraving.

MODEL 595 PRINCIPE . . . . NiB $5579 Ex $4367 Gd $3410
Available in all gauges, sidelock, engraved hunting scenes,
ejectors,double triggers.

MODEL 600 IMPERIAL . . . . NiB $9115 Ex $5910 Gd $3588
Gauges: 12, 16 or 20. Self-opening action, very ornate engraving
throughout.

AyA Model 53E

AyA Model 76

AyA Model 117

MODEL 601 IMPERIAL TYRO . . . NiB $9350 Ex $6005 Gd $4337
Available in all gauges, sidelock, nickel plating, ejectors, single selective trigger, border engraving.

MODEL 801 . . . . NiB $12,870 Ex $11,665 Gd $10,644
All gauges, detachable sidelocks, ejectors, coin-wash finish, Churchill-style engraving.

MODEL 802 . . . . NiB $13,669 Ex $11,544 Gd $8534
Gauges: 12, 16 or 20. Similar to Model 801 except with non-detach-able sidelocks, finest Holland-style engraving.

BOSS ROUND BODY . . . . . . NiB $8799 Ex $7733 Gd $6477
Available in all gauges, Boss pattern best quality engraving, wood upgrade.

MODEL 803 . . . . .NiB $11,333 Ex $9121 Gd $6344
Available in all gauges. Similar to Model 801 except finest Purdey-style engraving.

MODEL 871 . . . . NiB $7333 Ex $4144 Gd $2608
Available in all gauges. Rounded frame sidelock action with Demi-Bloc barrels, scroll engraving, ejectors, double trigger.

MODEL 871 EXTRA FINISH . . . . .NiB $7555 Ex $4759 Gd $3977
Similar to Model 871 except with standard game scene engraving with woodcock and ruffed grouse.

MODEL 872 . . . . NiB $16,788 Ex $13,690 Gd $11,550
Available in all gauges, rounded frame sidelock action, Demi-Bloc bar-rels, elaborate scroll engraving with third lever fastener.

MODEL 873 . . . . NiB $17,228 Ex $14,788 Gd $11,766
Available in all gauges. Sidelock, gold line engraved action, ejectors, single selective trigger.

MODEL 874 . . . . NiB $12,980 Ex $11,887 Gd $6,777
Available in all gauges. Sidelock, gold line engraved action, Demi-Bloc barrels.

MODEL 875 . . . . NiB $18,960 Ex $14,449 Gd $11,733
Available in all gauges. Custom model built to individual specifications only, elaborate engraving, gold inlays

MODEL 931 . . . . NiB $26,877 Ex $19,785 Gd $15,860
Available in all gauges. Self-opening action, elaborate engraving, H&H selective ejectors.

ASTRA — Guernica, Spain.
Manufactured by Unceta y Compania.

MODEL 650 O/U SHOTGUN
Hammerless, takedown w/double triggers. 12 ga. w/.75-inch cham-bers. Bbls.: 28-inch (M/F or SK/SK); 30-inch (M/F). Weight: 6.75 lbs. Checkered European walnut buttstock and forend. Disc. 1987.
W/extractors . . . . .NiB $733 Ex $579 Gd $454
W/ejectors . . . . .NiB $844 Ex $685 Gd $477

MODEL 750 O/U SHOTGUN
Similar to the Model 650 except w/selective single trigger and ejectors. Made in field, skeet and trap configurations from 1980. Disc. 1987.
Field model w/extractors . . . . .NiB $779 Ex $637 Gd $500
Field model w/ejectors . . . . .NiB $888 Ex $755 Gd $566
Trap or Skeet model . . . . .NiB $1099 Ex $867 Gd $559

AYA (Aguirre Y Aranzabal) — Eibar, Spain
Previously manufactured by Diarm. Imported by Armes De Chasse, Hertford, NC.

MODEL 1 HAMMERLESS DOUBLE
A Holland & Holland sidelock similar to the Model 2 except in 12 and 20 ga. only, w/special engraving and exhibition-grade wood. Weight: 5-8 lbs., depending on ga. Imported by Diarm until 1987, since 1992 by Armes de Chasse.
Model 1 Standard . . . . .NiB $9177 Ex $5448 Gd $3229
Model 1 Deluxe . . . . NiB $13,110 Ex $10,077 Gd $7470
W/Extra set of bbls., add $750

SHOTGUNS

AyA Matador II

AyA Model XXV Boxlock

MODEL 2 HAMMERLESS DOUBLE
Sidelock action w/selective single or double triggers automatic ejectors and safety. Gauges: 12, 20, 28, (2.75-inch chambers); .410 (3-inch chambers). Bbls.: 26- or 28-inch w/various fixed choke combinations. Weight: 7 lbs. (12 ga.). English-style straight walnut buttstock and splinter forend. Imported by Diarm until 1987, since 1992 by Armes de Chasse.
12 or 20 ga. w/double triggers . NiB $4777 Ex $3178 Gd $2090
12 or 20 ga. w/single trigger . . NiB $4777 Ex $3178 Gd $2090
28 ga. or .410 w/double triggers . NiB $4777 Ex $3178 Gd $2090
28 ga. or .410 w/single trigger . . NiB $3533 Ex $2970 Gd $2135
W/Extra set of bbls., add $1450

MODEL 4 HAMMERLESS DOUBLE
Lightweight Anson & Deely boxlock, scalloped frame. Gauges: 12, 16, 20, 28, and .410. Bbls.: 25- to 28-inch w/concave rib. Importation disc. 1987 and resumed in 1992 by Armes de Chasse.
12 ga. . . . . NiB $2098 Ex $1376 Gd $1099
16 ga. (early importation) . . . . NiB $2098 Ex $1376 Gd $1099
20 ga. . . . . NiB $2098 Ex $1376 Gd $1099
28 ga. . . . . NiB $2098 Ex $1376 Gd $1099
.410 ga. . . . . NiB $2098 Ex $1376 Gd $1099
Deluxe grades, add. $700

MODEL 37 SUPER
O/U SHOTGUN . . . . NiB $3266 Ex $2279 Gd $2099
Sidelock. automatic ejectors. Selective single trigger. Made in all gauges, bbl. lengths and chokes. Vent rib bbls. Elaborately engraved. Checkered stock (w/straight or pistol grip) and forend. Disc. 1995.

MODEL 37 SUPER A
O/U SHOTGUN . . . . NiB $14,879 Ex $12,776 Gd $11,340
Similar to the Standard Model 37 Super except has nickel steel frame and is fitted w/detachable sidelocks engraved w/game scenes. Importation disc. 1987 and resumed 1992 by Armes de Chasse. Disc.

MODEL 53E . . . . NiB $6860 Ex $4950 Gd $2910
Same general specifications as Model 117 except more elaborate engraving and select figured wood. Importation disc. 1987 and resumed in 1992 by Armes de Chasse.

MODEL 56 HAMMERLESS DOUBLE
Pigeon weight Holland & Holland sidelock w/Purdey-style third lug and sideclips. Gauges: 12, 16, 20. Receiver has fine-line scroll and rosette engraving; gold-plated locks. Importation disc. 1987 and resumed 1992 by Armes de Chasse.
12 ga. . . . . NiB $10,477 Ex $7880 Gd $4610
16 ga. (early importation), add 20%

20 ga. (early importation), add. 20%

MODEL 76 HAMMERLESS
DOUBLE . . . . NiB $955 Ex $838 Gd $529
Anson & Deeley boxlock. Auto ejectors. Selective single trigger. Gauges: 12, 20 (3-inch). Bbls.: 26-, 28-, 30-inch (latter in 12 ga. only), any standard choke combination. Checkered pistol-grip stock/beavertail forend. Disc.

MODEL 76 .410. . . . . NiB $1099 Ex $877 Gd $669
Same general specifications as 12 and 20 ga. Model 76 except chambered for 3-inch shells in .410, has extractors, double triggers, 26-inch bbls. only, English-style stock w/straight grip and small forend. Disc.

MODEL 117 HAMMERLESS
DOUBLE . . . . NiB $1887 Ex $1077 Gd $868
Holland & Holland-type sidelocks, hand-detachable. Engraved action. Automatic ejectors. Selective single trigger. Gauges: 12, 20 (3-inch). Bbls.: 26-, 27-, 28-, 30-inch; 27- and 30-inch in 12 ga. only; any standard choke combination. Checkered pistol-grip stock and beavertail forend of select walnut. Manufactured in 1985.

BOLERO . . . . NiB $556 Ex $479 Gd $357
Same general specifications as Matador except non-selective single trigger and extractors. Gauges: 12 16, 20, 20 Magnum (3-inch), .410 (3-inch). Note: This model, prior to 1956, was designated F. I. Model 400 by the importer. Made from 1955 to 63.

CONTENTO OVER/UNDER SHOTGUN
Boxlock w/Woodward side lugs and double internal bolts. Gauge: 12 (2.75-inch chambers). Bbls.: 26-, 28-inch field; 30-, 32-inch trap; fixed chokes as required or screw-in choke tubes. Hand-checkered European walnut stock and forend. Single selective trigger and automatic ejectors.
M.K.2. . . . . NiB $1155 Ex $897 Gd $655
M.K.3. . . . . NiB $1887 Ex $1533 Gd $1095
W/extra bbl., add $500

MATADOR HAMMERLESS
DOUBLE. . . . . NiB $619 Ex $490 Gd $339
Anson & Deeley boxlock. Selective automatic ejectors. Selective single trigger. Gauges: 12, 16, 20, 20 Magnum (3-inch). Bbls: 26-, 28-, 30-inches; any standard choke combination. Weight: 6.5 to 7.5 lbs., depending on ga. and bbl. length. Checkered pistol-grip stock and beavertail forend. Note: This model, prior to 1956, was designated F. I. Model 400E by the U.S. importer, Firearms Int'l. Corp. of Washington, D.C. Made from 1955 to 1963.

MATADOR II . . . . .NiB $754 Ex $567 Gd $421
Improved version of Matador w/same general specifications except has vent-rib bbls. Made 1964 to 1969.

MATADOR III. . . . . .NiB $859 Ex $744 Gd $590
Same general specifications as AyA Matador II. Made 1970 to 1985.

MODEL XXV BOXLOCK
Anson & Deeley boxlock w/double locking lugs. Gauges: 12 and 20. 25-inch chopper lump, satin blued bbls. w/Churchill rib. Weight: 5 to 7 lbs. Double triggers. Automatic safety and ejectors. Color-casehardened receiver w/Continental-style scroll and floral engraving. European walnut stock. Imported 1979 to 1986 and 1991.
12 or 20 ga. . . . . NiB $3190 Ex $2688 Gd $2100
W/extra set of bbls., add. $1250

MODEL XXV SIDELOCK
Holland & Holland-type sidelock. Gauges: 12, 20, 28 and .410; 25-, 26-, 27- 28-, 29-, and 32-inch bbls. Chopper lump, satin blued bbls. w/Churchill rib. Weight: 5 to 7 lbs. Double triggers standard or selective or non-selective single trigger optional. Automatic safety and ejectors. Cocking indicators. Color-casehardened or coin-silver-finished receiver w/Continental-style scroll and floral engraving. Select European walnut stock w/hand-cut checkering and oil finish. Imported 1979 to 1986 and 1991.
12 or 20 ga. . . . . .NiB $5975 Ex $4220 Gd $3188
28 ga. (disc. 1997) . . . . .NiB $6177 Ex $5063 Gd $3580
.410 bore (disc. 1997) . . . . . .NiB $6177 Ex $5063 Gd $3580
W/single trigger, add $100
W/single-selective trigger, add $200
W/extra set of bbls., add. $2250

BAIKAL — Izhevsk and Tula, Russia

MODEL IZH-18M SINGLE SHOT. . . . . . NiB $110 Ex $80 Gd $65
Hammerless w/cocking indicator. Automatic ejector. Manual safety. Gauges: 12 , 20, 16 w/2.75-inch chamber or .410 w/3-inch chamber. Bbls.: 26-, 28-inch w/fixed chokes (IC, M, F). Weight: 5.5 to 6 lbs. Made in Russia.

MODEL IZH-27 FIELD O/U. . . . . .NiB $400 Ex $341 Gd $244
Boxlock. Double triggers w/extractors. 12 ga.; 2.75-inch chambers. Bbls.: 26-inch, IC/M; 28-inch, M/F w/fixed chokes. Weight: 6.75 lbs. Made in Russia.

MODEL IZH-43 FIELD SIDE-BY-SIDE
Side-by-side; boxlock. Double triggers; extractors. 12 or 20 ga. w/2.75-inch chambers. Bbls: 20-inch cylinder bbl and 26-or 28-inch modified full bbl. Weight: 6.75 to 7 lbs. Checkered walnut stock, forend. Blued, engraved receiver. Imported 1994 to 1996.
Field model w/20-inch bbl. . . . . NiB $425 Ex $275 Gd $200
Model IJ-43 Field
  Field model w/26- or 28-inch bbls. NiB $425 Ex $275 Gd $200

IZH-43 SERIES SIDE-BY-SIDE
Boxlock. Gauges: 12, 16, 20 or .410 w/2.75- or 3-inch chambers. Bbls.: 20-, 24-, 26- or 28-inch w/fixed chokes or choke tubes. Single selective or double triggers. Weight: 6.75 lbs. Checkered hardwood (standard on Hunter II Model) or walnut stock and forend (standard on Hunter Model). Blued, engraved receiver. Imported 1994 to 1996.
Model IZH-43 Hunter model

w/12 ga. w/walnut stock. . . . . . .NiB $544 Ex $335 Gd $260
Model IZH-43 Hunter
  Hunter model (20 & 16 ga., .410)NiB $457 Ex $366 Gd $255
Model IZH-43 Hunter II
Hunter II model (12 ga.
  w/enternal hammers) . . . . .NiB $477 Ex $366 Gd $257
Model IZH-43 Hunter II
  Hunter II model (12 ga. hammerless) NiB $477 Ex $366 Gd $257
Hunter II model (12, 16
  or 20 ga.) . . . . NiB $477 Ex $366 Gd $257
Hunter II model w/walnut stock, add. $60
Hunter II model w/single-selective trigger, add $75

MODEL IZH-27 O/U
Boxlock. Single selective trigger w/automatic ejectors or double triggers w/extractors. Gauges: 12 or 20 w/2.75-inch chambers. Bbls.: 26-inch or 28-inch w/fixed chokes. Weight: 7 lbs. Checkered European hardwood stock and forearm. Made in Russia.
**Model IJ-27 (w/double
  triggers and extractors.)** . . . . . . NiB $400 Ex $334 Gd $171
**Model IJ-27 (single selective
  trigger and ejectors)** . . . . .NiB $400 Ex $334 Gd $171

MODEL MP94 (IZH-94). . . . . NiB $560 Ex $350 Gd $220
O/U combination shotgun over rifle. Boxlock. Gauges/calibers: 12 or 20 ga./.223 Rem., .30-06, .308 Win. or 7.62x39mm. Double triggers w/extractors. Bbls.: 19.5- or 23.5-in. w/ choke tubes or fixed choke. Weight: 8.5 lbs. Blued. Checkered walnut stock and forearm. Made in Russia. Made 2009 to date. Also sold as Model SPR94.
.410/.22 LR or .22 Mag. . . . . NiB $562 Ex $300 Gd $170

THE BAKER GUN & FORGING CO. — Batavia, New York. Made 1903–1933 by Baker Gun Company

BATAVIA LEADER HAMMERLESS DOUBLE
Sidelock. Plain extractors or automatic ejectors. Double triggers. Gauges: 12, 16, 20. Bbls.: 26- to 32-inch; any standard boring. Weight: About 7.75 lbs. (12 ga. w/30-inch bbls.). Checkered pistol-grip stock and forearm.
w/extractors . . . . NiB $1465 Ex $944 Gd $500
w/ejectors . . . . NiB $1600 Ex $1100 Gd $400

BATAVIA EJECTOR. . . . . .NiB $1258 Ex $1178 Gd $798
Same general specifications as the Batavia Leader except higher quality and finer finish throughout; has Damascus or homotensile steel bbls., checkered pistol-grip stock and forearm of select walnut; automatic ejectors standard; 12 and 16 ga. only. Deduct 60% for Damascus bbls.

BATAVIA SPECIAL . . . . .NiB $2000 Ex $1230 Gd $500
Same general specifications as the Batavia Leader except 12 and 16 ga. only; extractors, Homotensile steel bbls.

BLACK BEAUTY
Same general specifications as the Batavia Leader except higher quality and finer finish throughout; has line engraving, special steel bbls., select walnut stock w/straight, full or half-pistol-grip.
w/extractors . . . . NiB $2000 Ex $1200 Gd $444
Black Beauty Special w/extractors . . NiB $2166 Ex $1790 Gd $577
Black Beauty Special w/ejectors . . NiB $2208 Ex $1834 Gd $544

GRADE R . . . . .NiB $4000 Ex $2833 Gd $1106
High-grade gun w/same general specifications as the Batavia Leader except has fine Damascus or Krupp fluid steel bbls., engraving in line, scroll and game scene designs, checkered stock and forearm of fancy European walnut; 12 and 16 ga. only. Deduct 60% for Damascus bbls.

SHOTGUNS

Benelli Executive Grade I

Benelli Executive Grade II

Benelli Executive Grade III

GRADE S
Same general specifications as the Batavia Leader except higher quality and finer finish throughout; has Flui-tempered steel bbls., line and scroll engraving, checkered stock w/half-pistol-grip and forearm of semi-fancy imported walnut; 10, 12 and 16 ga.

Non-ejector	NiB $3886	Ex $2013	Gd $1077
W/ejectors	NiB $4100	Ex $2315	Gd $1366

PARAGON, EXPERT AND DELUXE GRADES
Made to order only, these are the higher grades of Baker hammerless sidelock double-bbl. shotguns. After 1909, the Paragon Grade, as well as the Expert and Deluxe intro. that year, had a crossbolt in addition to the regular Baker system taper wedge fastening. There are early Paragon guns w/Damascus bbls. and some are non-ejector, but this grade was also produced w/automatic ejectors and w/the finest fluid steel bbls., in lengths to 34 inches, standard on Expert and Deluxe guns. Differences among the three models are in overall quality, finish, engraving and grade of fancy figured walnut in the stock and forearm; Expert and Deluxe wood may be carved as well as checkered. Choice of straight, full or half-pistol grip was offered. A single trigger was available in the two higher grades. The Paragon was available in 10 ga (Damascus bbls. only), and the other two models were regularly produced in 12, 16 and 20 ga.

Paragon grade, no ejector	NiB $4277	Ex $2660	Gd $2033
Paragon grade w/auto ejector	NiB $4455	Ex $2978	Gd $2270
Expert grade	NiB $6177	Ex $4588	Gd $2844
Deluxe grade	NiB $11,477	Ex $9968	Gd $7133
W/ejectors, add			$350

BELKNAP SHOTGUNS — Louisville, Kentucky

MODEL B-68 SINGLE-SHOT . . . . NiB $199 Ex $144 Gd $100
Takedown. Visible hammer. Automatic ejector. Gauges: 12, 16, 20 and .410. Bbls.: 26-inch to 36-inch; F choke. Weight: 6 lbs. Plain pistol-grip stock and forearm.

MODEL B-63 SINGLE-SHOT . . . . NiB $229 Ex $135 Gd $105
Takedown. Visible hammer. Automatic ejector. Gauges: 12, 20 and .410. Bbls.: 26- to 36-inch, F choke. Weight: Average 6 lbs. Plain pistol-grip stock and forearm.

MODEL B-63E SINGLE-SHOT . . . . NiB $209 Ex $133 Gd $95
Same general specifications as Model B-68 except has side lever opening instead of top lever.

MODEL B-64
SLIDE-ACTION SHOTGUN . . . . NiB $339 Ex $244 Gd $225
Hammerless. Gauges: 12, 16, 20 and .410. Three round tubular magazine. Various bbl. lengths and chokes from 26-inch to 30-inch. Weight: 6.25 to 7.5 lbs. Walnut-finished hardwood stock.

MODEL B-65C
AUTOLOADING SHOTGUN . . . . . NiB $533 Ex $400 Gd $290
Browning-type lightweight alloy receiver. 12 ga. only. Four round tubular magazine. Bbl.: plain, 28-inch. Weight: About 8.25 lbs. Disc. 1949.

BENELLI — Urbino, Italy.

Imported by Benelli USA, Accokeek, MD.

MODEL 121 M1 MILITARY/POLICE . . . . . . NiB $656 Ex $432 Gd $335
Semi-automatic. Gauge: 12. Seven round magazine. 19.75-inch bbl. 39.75 inches overall. Cylinder choke, 2.75-inch chamber. Weight: 7.4 lbs. Matte black finish and European hardwood stock. Post front sight, fixed buckhorn rear sight. Imported in 1985. Disc.

BLACK EAGLE
Semi-automatic. Two-piece aluminum and steel receiver. Ga: 12; 3-inch chamber. Four round magazine. Screw-in choke tubes (SK, IC, M, IM, F). Bbls.: Ventilated rib; 21, 24, 26 or 28 inches w/bead front sight; 24-inch rifled slug. 42.5 to 49.5 inches overall. Weight: 7.25 lbs.

Benelli Legacy
Limited Edition (Only 250 Made)

Benelli M1 – Super 90 w/Pistol Grip

(28-inch bbl.). Matte black lower receiver w/blued upper receiver and bbl. Checkered walnut stock w/high-gloss finish and drop adjustment. Imported from 1989 to 1990 and 1997 to 1998.

Limited edition	NiB $1587	Ex $1090	Gd $965
Competition model	NiB $953	Ex $755	Gd $523
Slug model (disc. 1992)	NiB $815	Ex $608	Gd $466
Standard model (disc. 1990)	NiB $879	Ex $770	Gd $505

BLACK EAGLE EXECUTIVE
Semi-automatic. Custom Black Eagle Series. Montefeltro-style rotating bolt w/three locking lugs. All-steel lower receiver engraved, gold inlay by Bottega Incisione di Cesare Giovanelli. 12 ga. only. 21-, 24-, 26-, or 28-inch vent-rib bbl. w/5 screw-in choke tubes (Type I) or fixed chokes. Custom deluxe walnut stock and forend. Built to customer specifications on special order.

Grade I	NiB $4190	Ex $3295	Gd $2293
Grade II	NiB $4378	Ex $3566	Gd $2500
Grade III	NiB $5690	Ex $4177	Gd $2960

LEGACY
Semi-automatic. Gauges: 12 and 20 ga. w/3-inch chambers. 24- 26- or 28-inch bbl. 47.63 to 49.62 inches overall. Weight: 5.8 to 7.5 lbs. Four round magazine. Five screw-in choke tubes. Lower alloy receiver and upper steel reciever cover. Features Benelli's inertia recoil operating system. Imported 1998 to date.

Legacy model	NiB $1292	Ex $977	Gd $877
Limited Edition	NiB $1944	Ex $1620	Gd $1010

M1 FIELD . . . . NiB $867 Ex $767 Gd $671
Interia-operated semi-automatic. Gauge: 20. Chambers: 2.75 or 3 inches. Bbl. 24 or 26 inches, stepped ventilated rib and red bar sights. Stock: Synthetic, black or camo. Weight: 5.7 to 5.8 lbs. Includes set of five choke tubes. Imported from Italy.

M1 SUPER 90 . . . . .NiB $955 Ex $836 Gd $554
Interia-operated semi-automatic. Gauge: 12. Seven round magazine. Cylinder choke. 19.75-inch bbl. 39.75 inches overall. Weight: 7 lbs., 4 oz. to 7 lbs., 10 oz. Matte black finish. Stock and forend made of fiberglass-reinforced polymer. Sights: Post front, fixed buckhorn rear, drift adj. Introduced 1985; when the model line expanded in 1989, this configuration was discontinued.

M1 SUPER 90 DEFENSE . . . . . . .NiB $1093 Ex $966 Gd $509
Same general specifications as Model Super 90 except w/pistol-grip stock. Available w/Ghost-Ring sight option. Imported 1986 to 1998.

M1 SUPER 90 FIELD
Inertia-recoil semiautomatic shotgun. Gauge: 12; 3-inch chamber. Three round magazine. Bbl.: 21, 24, 26 or 28 inches. 42.5 to 49.5 inches overall. Choke: SK, IC, M, IM, F. Matte receiver. Standard polymer stock or satin walnut (26- or 28-inch bbl. only). Bead front sight. Imported from 1990 to 2006.

w/Realtree camo stock	NiB $1066	Ex $743	Gd $488
w/polymer stock	NiB $766	Ex $563	Gd $447
w/walnut stock	NiB $1031	Ex $660	Gd $458

M1 SUPER 90 SLUG
Same general specifications as M1 Super 90 Field except w/5-round magazine. 18.5-inch bbl. Cylinder bore. 39.75 inches overall. Weight: 6.5 lbs. Polymer standard stock. Rifle or Ghost-Ring sights. Imported 1986 to 1998.

w/rifle sights	NiB $988	Ex $677	Gd $549
w/ghost-ring sights	NiB $1096	Ex $786	Gd $659
w/Realtree camo finish, add			$150

M1 SUPER 90 SPECIAL
SPORTING AUTOLOADER . . . . . .NiB $877 Ex $655 Gd $589
Same general specifications as M1 Super 90 Field except w/18.5-inch bbl. 39.75 inches overall. Weight: 6.5 lbs. Ghost-ring sights. Polymer stock. Imported from 1994 to 1998.

M2
Redesign of M1 w/ new receiver, trigger guard, safety. Interia-operated semi-automatic. Imported 2004 to date.

Three Gun	NiB $2350	Ex $1800	Gd $1000
Practical	NiB $1196	Ex $970	Gd $480
Tacical	NiB $1230	Ex $900	Gd $510

M3 SUPER 90 PUMP/AUTOLOADER
Inertia-recoil semiautomatic and/or pump action. Gauge: 12. Seven round magazine. Cylinder choke. 19.75-inch bbl. 41 inches overall (31 inches folded). Weight: 7 to 7.5 lbs. Matte black finish. Stock: standard synthetic, pistol-grip or folding tubular steel. Standard rifle or Ghost-Ring sights. Imported 1989 to date. Caution: Increasing the magazine capacity to more than 5 rounds in M3 shotguns w/pistol-grip stocks violates provisions of the 1994 Crime Bill. This model may be used legally only by the military and law-enforcement agencies.

Standard model	NiB $1477	Ex $1067	Gd $799
Pistol-grip model	NiB $1644	Ex $1133	Gd $990

SHOTGUNS

Benelli Montefeltro
Super 90 Left-Handed
Model

Benelli Montefeltro Realtree Camo

w/folding stock . . . . NiB $1190 Ex $955 Gd $944
w/laser sight . . . . NiB $1766 Ex $1388 Gd $1100
w/ghost-ring sights, add $100

M4 TACTICAL . . . . NiB $1680 Ex $1230 Gd $870
Gas-operated semi-automatic. Civilian version of U.S. military M4, gas
regulating system. Gauge: 12; 3-inch chamber. Four round magazine. Bbl.:
18.5 inches. 40 inches overall. Choke: M. Matte receiver. Standard and
pistol grip sythetic stock. Ghost ring rear, post front sights. Imported from
2003 to date.
M1040 Limited Edition . . . . . . NiB $1380 Ex $960 Gd $660

MONTEFELTRO/SUPER 90
Semi-automatic. Gauges: 12 or 20 gauge w/3-inch chamber. 21- 24-
26- or 28-inch bbl. 43.7 to 49.5 inches overall. Weight: 5.3 to 7.5 lbs.
Four round magazine. Five screw-in choke tubes (C, IC, M, IM, F).
High gloss or satin walnut or Realtree Camo stock. Blued metal finish.
Imported 1987 to 1992.
Standard Hunter model . . . . . . NiB $1155 Ex $865 Gd $490
Slug model (disc. 1992) . . . . NiB $744 Ex $639 Gd $440
Turkey model . . . . NiB $744 Ex $639 Gd $440
Uplander model . . . . NiB $744 Ex $639 Gd $440
Limited Edition (1995-96) . . . . NiB $2077 Ex $1688 Gd $1176
20 ga. w/Realtree camo . . . . . . NiB $1269 Ex $988 Gd $775
20 ga. Youth Model w/short stock, add $75
Left-hand model, add $50

NOVA . . . . NiB $466 Ex $368 Gd $256
Pump-action. Gauge: 12 or 20. Chambers: 2.75 or 3 in.; 3.5 in. 12
gauge only. Four-round magazine. Bbl. 24, 26 or 28 inches; red bar
sights. Stock: Synthetic,(Xtra Brown in 12 gauge or Timber HD in 20
gauge). Montefeltro rotating bolt, magazine cutoff, synthetic trigger
assembly. Introduced 1999. Imported from Italy.

SL 121V (SL-80 SERIES) . . . . Nib $466 Ex $359 Gd $270
Recoil-operated semiautomatic w/split receiver design. Gauge: 12. Five
round capacity. 26-, 28- or 30-inch ventilated rib bbl. (26-inch choked
M, IM, IC, 28-inch, F, M, IM; 30-inch, F choke - Mag.). Straight walnut
stock w/hand-checkered pistol grip and forend. Importation disc. in
1985.

SL 121V SLUG (SL-80 SERIES) . . . . Nib $578 Ex $376 Gd $305
Same general specifications as Benelli SL 121V except designed for
rifled slugs and equipped w/rifle sights. Disc. in 1985.

SL 123V (SL-80 SERIES) . . . . NiB $500 Ex $378 Gd $297
Semi-automatic. Gauge: 12. 26- and 28-inch bbls. 26-inch choked IM,
M, IC; 28-inch choked F, IM, M. Disc. in 1985.

SL 201 (SL-80 SERIES) . . . . NiB $459 Ex $365 Gd $300
Semi-automatic. Gauge: 20. 26-inch bbl. Mod. choke. Weight: 5 lbs., 10
oz. Ventilated rib. Disc. in 1985.

SPORT . . . . NiB $1266 Ex $999 Gd $654
Similar to the Black Eagle Competition model except has one-piece
matte- finished alloy receiver w/inscribed red Benelli logo. 26 or 28 inches bbl. w/2 inchangable carbon fiber vent ribs. Oil-finished checkered
walnut stock w/adjustable buttpad and buttstock. Imported 1997 to 2002.

SUPER BLACK EAGLE
Interia-operated semi-automatic. Same general specifications as Black
Eagle except w/3.5-inch chamber that accepts 2.75-, 3- and 3.5-inch
shells. Two round magazine (3.5-inch), 3-round magazine (2.75- or
3-inch). High-gloss, satin finish or camo stock. Realtree camo, matte
black or blued metal finish. Imported 1991 to 2005.
Standard model . . . . NiB $1096 Ex $933 Gd $766
Realtree camo model . . . . NiB $1221 Ex $1099 Gd $866
Custom slug model . . . . NiB $1254 Ex $958 Gd $744
Limited edition . . . . NiB $1979 Ex $1654 Gd $1177
w/wood stock, add $40
Left-hand model, add $100

ULTRA LIGHT . . . . NiB $1480 Ex $1010 Gd $610
Interia-operated semi-automatic. Gauges: 12, 20 or 28 gauge w/3-inch
chamber. 24- or 26-inch bbl. 45.5 to 47.5 inches overall. Weight: 5.0
to 6.1 lbs. Two round magazine. Five screw-in choke tubes (C, IC, M,
IM, F). High gloss WeatherCoat stock. Blued metal finish. Imported
2006 to date.

CORDOBA . . . . NiB $1800 Ex $1230 Gd $760
Interia-operated semi-automatic. Gauges: 12 or 20 gauge w/3-inch
chamber. 28- or 30-inch bbl. 49.7 to 51.7 inches overall. Weight: 6.3
to 7.3 lbs. Four round magazine. Five screw-in choke tubes (C, IC,
M, IM, F). ComfortTech stock. Matte black finish. Imported 2005 to
date.

VINCI . . . . NiB $1300 Ex $930 Gd $560
Interia-operated semi-automatic. Modular construction. Gauges: 12
gauge w/3-inch chamber. 26- or 28-inch bbl. 45.7 to 49.7 inches overall. Weight: 6.7 to 6.9 lbs. Three round magazine. Five screw-in choke
tubes (C, IC, M, IM, F). ComfortTech stock. Matte black finish. Imported
2009 to date.

BERETTA USA CORP. — Accokeek, Maryland.

*Manufactured by Fabbrica D'Armi Pietro Beretta S.P.A. in Gardone Val
Trompia (Brescia), Italy. Imported by Beretta USA. Previously by Garcia
Corp.*

MODEL 409PB
HAMMERLESS DOUBLE . . . . NiB $966 Ex $733 Gd $545
Boxlock. Double triggers. Plain extractors. Gauges: 12, 16, 20, 28.
Bbls.: 27.5-, 28.5- and 30-inch, IC/M choke or M/F choke. Weight:
from 5.5 to 7.75 lbs., depending on ga. and bbl. length. Straight or
pistol-grip stock and beavertail forearm, checkered. Imported 1934
to 1964.

MODEL 410E
Same general specifications as Model 409PB except has automatic ejectors and is of higher quality throughout. Imported 1934 to 1964.
12 ga. NiB $1367 Ex $1144 Gd $922
20 ga. NiB $2882 Ex $2096 Gd $1377
28 ga. NiB $3881 Ex $3036 Gd $2456

Beretta Model 682 Over/Under Sporting

Beretta Model 682 Over/Under Trap

MODEL 410 10-GA. MAGNUM......NiB $1269 Ex $945 Gd $700
Same as Model 410E except heavier construction. Plain extractors. Double triggers. 10-ga. Magnum, 3.5-inch chambers. 32-inch bbls., both F choke. Weight: about 10 lbs. Checkered pistol-grip stock and forearm, recoil pad. Imported 1934 to 1984.

MODEL 411E
Same general specifications as Model 409PB except has sideplates, automatic ejectors and is of higher quality throughout. Imported 1934 to 1964.
12 ga. . . . . NiB $2077 Ex $1700 Gd $1179
20 ga. . . . . NiB $2866 Ex $2234 Gd $1590
28 ga. . . . . NiB $4339 Ex $3977 Gd $2766

**MODEL 424 HAMMERLESS
DOUBLE** . . . . NiB $1288 Ex $1292 Gd $957
Boxlock. Light border engraving. Plain extractors. Gauges: 12, 20; chambers 2.75-inch in former, 3-inch in latter. Bbls.: 28-inch M/F choke, 26-inch IC/M choke. Weight: 5 lbs. 14 oz. to 6 lbs. 10 oz., depending on ga. and bbl. length. English-style straight-grip stock and forearm, checkered. Imported 1977 to 1984.

MODEL 426E . . . . NiB $1588 Ex $1233 Gd $1067
Same as Model 424 except action body is finely engraved, silver pigeon inlaid in top lever; has selective automatic ejectors and selective single trigger, stock and forearm of select European walnut. Imported 1977-84.

MODEL 450 SERIES HAMMERLESS DOUBLES
Custom English-style sidelock. Single, non-selective trigger or double triggers. Manual safety. Selective automatic ejectors. Gauge: 12; 2.75- or 3-inch chambers. Bbls.: 26, 28 or 30 inches choked to customers' specifications. Weight: 6.75 lbs. Checkered high-grade walnut stock. Receiver w/coin-silver finish. Imported 1948. Disc.
Model 450 EL (disc. 1982). . . . . .NiB $8334 Ex $6688 Gd $4731
Model 450 EELL (disc. 1982). . . . . NiB $10,655 Ex $6798 Gd $4880
Model 451 (disc. 1987). . . . . . NiB $6443 Ex $5670 Gd $3990
Model 451 E (disc. 1989) . . . . NiB $7125 Ex $6225 Gd $4350
Model 451 EL (disc. 1985). . . . . . .NiB $17,787 Ex $14,866 Gd $11,700
Model 451 EELL (disc. 1990). . . . .NiB $15,788 Ex $12,877 Gd $10,777
Model 452 (Intro. 1990) . . . . NiB $29,988 Ex $21,980 Gd $18,799
Model 452 EELL (intro. 1992) . . . . . NiB $41,665 Ex $35,000 Gd $27,889
w/extra bbls, add 30%

MODEL 470 SERIES HAMMERLESS DOUBLE
Gauge: 12 and 20 ga. w/3-inch chambers. 26- or 28-inch bbl. Weight: 5.9 to 6.5 lbs. Low profile, improved box lock action w/single selective trigger. Selected walnut, checkered stock and forend. Metal front bead sight. Scroll-engraved receiver w/gold inlay and silver chrome finish. Imported 1999 to date.

Silver Hawk 12 ga. . . . . NiB $9332 Ex $6880 Gd $5440
Silver Hawk 20 ga. . . . . NiB $9566 Ex $6465 Gd $5566
EL Silver Hawk 12 ga. . . . . .NiB $8310 Ex $7223 Gd $5600
EL Silver Hawk 20 ga. . . . . .NiB $8554 Ex $6133 Gd $5477
EELL (Jubilee II) 12 ga. . . . . .NiB $8366 Ex $6328 Gd $4790
EELL (Jubilee II) 20 ga. . . . . .NiB $9000 Ex $7231 Gd $4889
w/extra bbls., add 30%

MODEL 625 S/S HAMMERLESS DOUBLE
Boxlock. Gauges: 12 or 20. Bbls.: 26-, 28- or 30-inch w/fixed choke combinations. Single selective or double triggers w/extractors. Checkered English-style buttstock and forend. Imported 1984 to 1987.
w/double triggers . . . . NiB $1591 Ex $900 Gd $667
w/single selective trigger. . . . . . NiB $1880 Ex $1067 Gd $700
20 ga., add. $200

MODEL 626 S/S HAMMERLESS DOUBLE
Field Grade side-by-side. Boxlock action w/single selective trigger, extractors and automatic safety. Gauges: 12 (2.75-inch chambers); 20 (3-inch chambers). Bbls.: 26- or 28-inch w/Mobilchoke or various fixed-choke combinations. Weight: 6.75 lbs. (12 ga.). Bright chrome finish. Checkered European walnut buttstock and forend in straight English style. Imported 1985 to 1994.
Model 626 Field (disc. 1988) . . . . . .NiB $1345 Ex $1190 Gd $700
Model 626 Onyx . . . . NiB $1779 Ex $1288 Gd $1006
Model 626 Onyx (3.5-inch
  magnum, disc. 1993) . . . . . . NiB $1798 Ex $1388 Gd $1098
20 ga., add. 50%

MODEL 627 S/S HAMMERLESS DOUBLE
Same as Model 626 S/S except w/engraved sideplates and pistol-grip or straight English-style stock. Imported 1985 to 1994.
Model 627 EL Field . . . . NiB $2370 Ex $2090 Gd $1550
Model 627 EL Sport . . . . NiB $2592 Ex $2210 Gd $1776
Model 627 EELL . . . . NiB $4460 Ex $3978 Gd $2666

MODEL 682 O/U SHOTGUN
Hammerless takedown w/single selective trigger. Gauges: 12, 20, 28, .410. Bbls.: 26- to 34-inch w/fixed chokes or Mobilchoke tubes. Checkered European walnut buttstock/forend in various grades and configurations. Imported 1984 to 2000.
Comp Skeet model . . . . NiB $1566 Ex $1160 Gd $1004
Comp Skeet Deluxe model. . . . . . .NiB $1789 Ex $1440 Gd $1166
Comp Super Skeet . . . . NiB $2599 Ex $2055 Gd $1490
Comp Skeet model, 2-bbl.
  set (disc. 1989). . . . . .NiB $5100 Ex $4256 Gd $2920
Comp Skeet, 4 bbl. set (disc. 1996). . . NiB $5786 Ex $4670 Gd $3241
Sporting Continental. . . . . NiB $1589 Ex $1170 Gd $1097
Sporting Combo . . . . NiB $1778 Ex $1566 Gd $1180

Beretta Model 687EL

Beretta Model 687EEL

Gold Sporting . . . . .NiB $1788 Ex $1266 Gd $1011
Super Sporting . . . . .NiB $1566 Ex $1365 Gd $1291
Comp Trap Gold X . . . . .NiB $2269 Ex $1775 Gd $1231
Comp Trap Top Single (1986-95) . . . . . . .NiB $2177 Ex $1688 Gd $1166
Comp Trap Live Pigeon (1990-98). . . . . . .NiB $2769 Ex $2255 Gd $1568
Comp Mono/Combo Trap Gold X . . . . . . .NiB $2977 Ex $2510 Gd $1765
Comp Mono Trap (1985-88) . . . . .NiB $1867 Ex $1588 Gd $1100
Super Trap Gold X (1991-95) . . . . .NiB $2267 Ex $1880 Gd $1266
Super Trap Combo Gold X (1991-97) . . . .NiB $3166 Ex $2478 Gd $1776
Super Trap Top Single Gold X (1991-95). .NiB $2265 Ex $2099 Gd $1369
Super Trap Unsingle (1992-94) . . . . .NiB $2210 Ex $2050 Gd $1319

MODEL 686 O/U SHOTGUN
Low-profile improved boxlock action. Single selective trigger. Selective automatic ejectors. Gauges: 12, 20, 28 w/3.5- 3- or 2.75-inch chambers, depending upon ga. Bbls.: 26-, 28-, 30-inch w/fixed chokes or Mobilchoke tubes. Weight: 5.75 to 7.5 lbs. Checkered American walnut stock and forearm of various qualities, depending upon model. Receiver finishes also vary, but all have blued bbls. Sideplates to simulate sidelock action on EL models. Imported 1988 to 1995.
Field Onyx. . . . . .NiB $1335 Ex $1108 Gd $733
(3.5-inch Mag., disc.
   1993 & reintro.1996) . . . . .NiB $4370 Ex $2888 Gd $2280
EL Gold Perdiz (1992-97). . . . . .NiB $2077 Ex $1576 Gd $1200
Essential (1994-96). . . . . NiB $1009 Ex $808 Gd $635
Silver Essential (1997-98) . . . . NiB $1180 Ex $966 Gd $680
Silver Pigeon Onyx (intro. 1996) . . . . .NiB $1566 Ex $1254 Gd $870
Silver Perdiz Onyx (disc. 1996) . . . . NiB $1488 Ex $1155 Gd $866
Silver Pigeon/Perdiz Onyx Combo . . . . NiB $1133 Ex $866 Gd $633
L Silver Perdiz (disc. 1994) . . . . NiB $1288 Ex $1007 Gd $766
Skeet Silver Pigeon (1996-98) . . . . NiB $1276 Ex $988 Gd $766
Skeet Silver Perdiz (1994-96) . . . . .NiB $1570 Ex $1288 Gd $944
Skeet Silver Pigeon/Perdiz Combo . . . . . . .NiB $1570 Ex $1288 Gd $944
Sporting Special (1987-93) . . . . .NiB $1798 Ex $1369 Gd $1100
Sporting English (1991-92). . . . . .NiB $1820 Ex $1400 Gd $1188
Sporting Onyx
   w/fixed chokes (1991-92). . .NiB $1743 Ex $1388 Gd $1014
Sporting Onyx
   w/ choke tubes (intro. 1992). .NiB $1344 Ex $1130 Gd $966
Sporting Onyx Gold (disc. 1993) . . . . NiB $1879 Ex $1577 Gd $1188
Sporting Silver Pigeon (intro. 1996) . . . . . . NiB $1598 Ex $1266 Gd $1005
Sporting Silver Perdiz (1993-96) . . . . NiB $1612 Ex $1288 Gd $1130
Sporting Collection Sport (1996-97) . . . . .NiB $1188 Ex $1033 Gd $892
Sporting Combo . . . . .NiB $2667 Ex $2174 Gd $1545
Trap International (1994-95) . . . . NiB $1144 Ex $967 Gd $755
Trap Silver Pigeon (intro. 1997) . . . . NiB $1266 Ex $1057 Gd $798
Trap Top Mono (intro. 1998) . . . . .NiB $1279 Ex $1088 Gd $800

Ultralight Onyx (intro. 1992) . . . . .NiB $1599 Ex $1366 Gd $968
Ultralight Del. Onyx (intro. 1998) . . . . .NiB $2056 Ex $1665 Gd $1156

MODEL 687 O/U SHOTGUN
Same as Model 686 except w/decorative sideplates and varying grades of engraving and game-scene motifs.
L Onyx (disc. 1991) . . . . .NiB $1460 Ex $1233 Gd $865
L Onyx Gold Field (1988-89). . . . . .NiB $1688 Ex $1344 Gd $966
L Onyx Silver Pigeon . . . . .NiB $1288 Ex $1668 Gd $1208
EL Onyx (disc. 1990) . . . . .NiB $2855 Ex $2344 Gd $1629
EL Gold Pigeon . . . . .NiB $3266 Ex $2688 Gd $1863
EL Gold Pigeon small frame . . . . .NiB $3090 Ex $2451 Gd $1761
EL Gold Pigeon Sporting (intro 1993). . . . .NiB $4388 Ex $3571 Gd $2510
EELL Diamond Pigeon . . . . .NiB $4416 Ex $3620 Gd $2560
EELL Diamond Pigeon Skeet. . . . . .NiB $4233 Ex $3548 Gd $2480
EELL Diamond Pigeon Sporting . . . . .NiB $4416 Ex $3578 Gd $2560
EELL Diamond Pigeon X Trap . . . . .NiB $3966 Ex $3133 Gd $2190
EELL Diamond Pigeon Mono Trap . . . . .NiB $4088 Ex $3310 Gd $2366
EELL Diamond Pigeon Trap Combo . . . .NiB $5480 Ex $4766 Gd $3266
EELL Field Combo . . . . .NiB $4570 Ex $3775 Gd $2760
EELL Skeet 4-bbl. set . . . . .NiB $7588 Ex $5977 Gd $3554
EELL Gallery Special . . . . .NiB $7233 Ex $5610 Gd $3798
EELL Gallery Special Combo . . . . NiB $8235 Ex $6799 Gd $4571
EELL Gallery Special pairs . . . . NiB $17,844 Ex $14,560 Gd $10,134
Sporting English (1991-92). . . . . .NiB $2247 Ex $1867 Gd $1359
Sporting Silver Pigeon (intro. 1996). . . . . . .NiB $2079 Ex $1677 Gd $1261
Sporting Silver Perdiz (1993-96) . . . . . .NiB $2255 Ex $1767 Gd $1388

MODEL 1200 SERIES SEMIAUTOLOADING SHOTGUN
Short recoil action. Gauge: 12; 2.75- or 3-inch chamber. Six round magazine. 24-, 26- or 28-inch vent-rib bbl. w/fixed chokes or Mobilchoke tubes. Weight: 7.25 lbs. Matte black finish. Adj. technopolymer stock and forend. Imported 1988 to 1990.
w/fixed choke (disc. 1989) . . . . NiB $466 Ex $359 Gd $266
Riot (disc. 1994) . . . . NiB $476 Ex $368 Gd $277
w/Mobilchoke (disc. 1994) . . . . NiB $741 Ex $577 Gd $400
Riot model . . . . NiB $805 Ex $633 Gd $451
w/Pistol-grip stock, add $65
w/Tritium sights, add $100

MODEL A-301
AUTOLOADING SHOTGUN. . . . . NiB $644 Ex $470 Gd $356
Field Gun. Gas-operated. Scroll-decorated receiver. Gauge: 12 or 20; 2.75-inch chamber in former, 3-inch in latter. Three round magazine. Bbl.: Ventilated rib; 28-inch F or M choke, 26-inch IC. Weight: 6 lbs., 5 oz. – 6 lbs., 14 oz., depending on gauge and bbl. length. Checkered pistol-grip stock/forearm. Imported 1977 to 1982.

Beretta Model A-303

Beretta Model A-390 Field

Beretta Model AL-2

MODEL A-301 MAGNUM. . . . . . .NiB $455 Ex $277 Gd $200
Same as Model A-301 Field Gun except chambered for 12 ga. Three
inch Magnum shells, 30-inch F choke bbl. only, stock w/recoil pad.
Weight: 7.25 lbs.

MODEL A-301 SKEET GUN . . . . .NiB $466 Ex $300 Gd $210
Same as Model A-301 Field Gun except 26-inch bbl. SK choke only,
skeet-style stock, gold-plated trigger.

MODEL A-301 SLUG GUN. . . . .NiB $488 Ex $287 Gd $217
Same as Model A-301 Field Gun except has plain 22-inch bbl., slug
choke, w/rifle sights. Weight: 6 lbs., 14 oz.

MODEL A-301 TRAP GUN . . . . .NiB $466 Ex $287 Gd $233
Same as Model A-301 Field Gun except has 30-inch bbl. in F choke only,
checkered Monte Carlo stock w/recoil pad, gold-plated trigger. Blued bbl.
and receiver. Weight: 7 lbs., 10 oz. Imported 1978 to 1982.

MODEL A-302 SEMIAUTOLOADING SHOTGUN
Similar to gas-operated Model 301. Hammerless, takedown shotgun w/
tubular magazine and Mag-Action that handles both 2.75- and 3-inch
Magnum shells. Gauge: 12 or 20; 2.75- or 3-inch Mag. chambers. Bbl.:
Vent or plain; 22-inch/Slug (12 ga.); 26-inch/IC (12 or 20) 28-inch/M
(20 ga.), 28-inch/Multi-choke (12 or 20 ga.) 30-inch/F (12 ga.). Weight:
6.5 lbs., 20 ga.; 7.25.lbs., 12 ga. Blued/ black finish. Checkered
European walnut, pistol-grip stock and forend. Imported from 1983 to
c. 1987.
Standard model w/fixed choke. . . . .NiB $466 Ex $338 Gd $254
Standard model w/multi-choke . . . . . .NiB $490 Ex $345 Gd $258

MODEL A-302 SUPER LUSSO. . . . . .NiB $1844 Ex $1452 Gd $1166
A custom A-302 in presentation grade w/hand-engraved receiver and
custom select walnut stock.

MODEL A-303 SEMIAUTOLOADER
Similar to Model 302, except w/target specifications in Trap, Skeet
and Youth configurations, and weighs 6.5 to 8 lbs. Imported from
1983 to 1996.
Field and Upland models . . . . . . .NiB $523 Ex $400 Gd $288
Skeet and Trap (disc. 1994) . . . . .NiB $488 Ex $366 Gd $257
Slug model (disc. 1992) . . . . .NiB $453 Ex $377 Gd $260

Sporting Clays . . . . .NiB $600 Ex $453 Gd $279
Super Skeet . . . . .NiB $500 Ex $433 Gd $318
Super Trap. . . . . .NiB $643 Ex $494 Gd $388
Waterfowl/Turkey model (disc. 1992) .NiB $525 Ex $460 Gd $354
w/Mobil choke, add $75

MODEL A-303 YOUTH GUN. . . . . .NiB $498 Ex $376 Gd $277
Locked-breech, gas-operated action. Ga: 12 and 20; 2-round magazine. Bbls.: 24,
26, 28, 30 or 32-inches, vent rib. Weight: 7 lbs. (12 ga.), 6 lbs. (20 ga.). Crossbolt
safety. Length of pull shortened to 12.5 inches. Imported 1988-96.

MODEL AL-390 SEMIAUTOMATIC SHOTGUN
Gas-operated, self-regulating action designed to handle any size load.
Gauges: 12 or 20 w/ 3-inch chamber. Three round magazine. Bbl.: 24,
26, 28 or 30 inches w/vent rib and Mobilchoke tubes. Weight: 7.5 lbs.
Select walnut stock w/adj. comb. Blued or matte black finish. Imported
1992-96. Superseded by AL-390 series.
Standard/Slug models . . . . .NiB $525 Ex $377 Gd $296
Field/Silver Mallard models. . . . .NiB $525 Ex $377 Gd $296
Deluxe/Gold Mallard models . . . .NiB $485 Ex $335 Gd $250
Turkey/Waterfowl model
  (w/matte finish) . . . . .NiB $577 Ex $366 Gd $300
20 ga., add. $75

MODEL AL-390 TARGET
Similar to the Model 390 Field except w/2.75-inch chamber. Skeet:
28-inch ported bbl. w/wide vent rib and fixed choke (SK). Trap: 30- or
32-inch w/Mobilchoke tubes. Weight: 7.5 lbs. Fully adj. buttstock.
Imported from 1993 to 1996.
Sport Trap model . . . . .NiB $599 Ex $367 Gd $290
Sport Skeet model . . . . .NiB $479 Ex $345 Gd $266
Sporting Clays model (unported). . . . . .NiB $700 Ex $579 Gd $421
Super Trap model (ported) . . . . . .NiB $577 Ex $367 Gd $292
Super Skeet model (ported). . . . . .NiB $569 Ex $355 Gd $307
w/ported bbl., add $100
20 ga., add. $75

MODEL AL-1 FIELD GUN. . . . . . . .NiB $566 Ex $349 Gd $279
Same as Model AL-2 gas-operated Field Gun except has bbl. w/o rib,
no engraving on receiver. Imported from 1971 to 1973.

SHOTGUNS

GRADING: **NiB** = New in Box   **Ex** = Excellent or NRA 95%   **Gd** = Good or NRA 68%   **437**

Beretta Model AL-391
Urika Gold Sporting

Beretta Model AL-391
Urika Gold Trap

MODEL AL-2 AUTOLOADING SHOTGUN

Field Gun. Gas-operated. Engraved receiver (1968 version, 12 ga. only, had no engraving). Gauge: 12 or 20. 2.75-inch chamber. Three round magazine. Bbls.: Vent rib; 30-inch F choke, 28-inch F or M choke, 26-inch IC. Weight: 6.5 to 7.25 lbs, depending on ga. and bbl. length. Checkered pistol-grip stock and forearm. Imported from 1968 to 1975.

w/Plain receiver . . . . .NiB $435 Ex $315 Gd $229
w/Engraved receiver . . . . .NiB $633 Ex $500 Gd $378

MODEL AL-2 MAGNUM . . . . . . .NiB $515 Ex $377 Gd $255

Same as Model AL-2 Field Gun except chambered for 12 ga. 3-inch Magnum shells; 30-inch F or 28-inch M choke bbl. only. Weight: About 8 lbs. Imported from 1973 to 1975.

MODEL AL-2 SKEET GUN . . . . . .NiB $466 Ex $321 Gd $234

Same as Model AL-2 Field Gun except has wide rib, 26-inch bbl. in SK choke only, checkered pistol-grip stock and beavertail forearm. Imported 1973 to 1975.

MODEL AL-2 TRAP GUN . . . . . . .NiB $445 Ex $341 Gd $246

Same as Model AL-2 Field Gun except has wide rib, 30 inch bbl. in F choke only, beavertail forearm. Monte Carlo stock w/recoil pad. Weight: About 7.75 lbs. Imported from 1973 to 1975.

MODEL AL-3

Similar to corresponding AL-2 models in design and general specifications. Imported from 1975 to 1976.

Field model . . . . .NiB $466 Ex $331 Gd $244
Magnum model . . . . .NiB $475 Ex $350 Gd $266
Skeet model . . . . .NiB $486 Ex $351 Gd $264
Trap model . . . . .NiB $453 Ex $335 Gd $266

MODEL AL-3 DELUXE TRAP GUN . . . . . NiB $700 Ex $566 Gd $339

Same as standard Model AL-3 Trap Gun except has fully-engraved receiver, gold-plated trigger and safety, stock and forearm of premium-grade European walnut, gold monogram escutcheon inlaid in buttstock. Imported 1975 to 1976.

AL390 FIELD SHOTGUN

Lightweight version of A-390 series. Gauges: 12 or 20 ga. 22- 24-, 26-, 28-, or 30-inch bbl., 41.7 to 47.6 inches overall. Weight: 6.4 to 7.5 lbs. Imported 1992 to 1999.

Field/Silver Mallard model (12 or 20 ga.) . . .NiB $655 Ex $465 Gd $300
Field/Silver Mallard Youth model (20 ga.) . . . . . .NiB $500 Ex $355 Gd $245
Field/Slug (12 ga. only). . . . . .NiB $525 Ex $433 Gd $266
Silver Mallard camo model. . . . . .NiB $533 Ex $379 Gd $295
Silver Mallard model, synthetic stock . . .NiB $566 Ex $430 Gd $349
Gold Mallard (12 or 20 ga.) . . . . .NiB $800 Ex $656 Gd $445
NWTF Special model, camo . . . . .NiB $645 Ex $355 Gd $339
NTWF Special model, synthetic . . . . . . .NiB $600 Ex $440 Gd $322
NWFS Special Youth model. . . . . . . .NiB $590 Ex $367 Gd $292

AL390 SPORT SPORTING SHOTGUN

Similar to Model AL-390 Sport Skeet. Gauges: 12 or 20 ga., 28- or 30-inch bbls. Weight: 6.8 to 8 lbs. Imported from 1995-1999.

Sport Sporting . . . . .NiB $566 Ex $396 Gd $300
Sport Sporting Collection . . . . .NiB $590 Ex $433 Gd $335
Sport Sporting
Youth (20 ga. only) . . . . .NiB $590 Ex $454 Gd $397
Sport Gold Sporting . . . . .NiB $823 Ex $577 Gd $446
EELL Sport
Diamond Sporting . . . . .NiB $2166 Ex $1488 Gd $1094
w/Ported bbl., add $100

AL390 SPORT SKEET SHOTGUN

Gauges: 12 ga. only. 26- or 28-inch bbl. w/3-round mqagazine. Weight: 7.6 to 8 lbs. Matte finish wood and metal. Imported 1995 to 1999.

Sport Skeet. . . . . .NiB $498 Ex $366 Gd $279
Sport Super Skeet . . . . .NiB $576 Ex $377 Gd $301
w/ported bbl., add $125

AL390 SPORT TRAP SHOTGUN

Gauges: 12 ga. only. 30- or 32-inch bbl. w/3-round chamber. Weight: 7.8 to 8.25 lbs. Matte finish wood and metal. Black recoil rubber pad. Imported from 1995 to 1999.

Sport Trap . . . . .NiB $564 Ex $379 Gd $288
Sport Super Trap. . . . . .NiB $688 Ex $512 Gd $360
Multi-choke bbl. (30-inch only), add. $65
w/Ported bbl., add $125

AL391 URIKA AUTOLOADING SHOTGUN

Gauge: 12 and 20 ga. w/3-inch chambers. 28- 30- or 32-inch bbl. Weight: 6.6 to 7.7 lbs. Self-compensating gas valve. Adjustable synthetic and walnut stocks w/ five interchangeable chokes. Imported from 2001 to 2006.

Urika . . . . .NiB $923 Ex $800 Gd $655
Urika synthetic. . . . . .NiB $865 Ex $758 Gd $600
Urika camo
w/Realtree Hardwoods . . . . .NiB $977 Ex $844 Gd $654
Urika
Gold w/black receiver . . . . .NiB $896 Ex $588 Gd $464
Urika Gold
w/silver receiver . . . . .NiB $1196 Ex $974 Gd $799
Urika Youth . . . . .NiB $900 Ex $779 Gd $698
Urika Sporting . . . . .NiB $1088 Ex $965 Gd $600
Urika Gold
Sporting w/black receiver . . . . .NiB $859 Ex $655 Gd $488
Urika
Gold Sporting w/silver receiverNiB $1256 Ex $1011 Gd $733
Urika Trap . . . . .NiB $1047 Ex $798 Gd $633
Urika Gold Trap. . . . . .NiB $1066 Ex $881 Gd $700
Parallel Target .NiB $1066 Ex $881 Gd $700

Beretta Model BL-1

Beretta Model BL3

Beretta Model BL-6

Beretta Model ASEL

MODEL ASE 90 O/U SHOTGUN

Competition-style receiver w/coin-silver finish and gold inlay featuring drop-out trigger group. Gauge: 12; 2.75-inch chamber. Bbls.: 28- or 30-inch w/fixed or Mobilchoke tubes; vent rib. Weight: 8.5 lbs. (30-inch bbl.). Checkered high-grade walnut stock. Imported 1992 to 1994.

Pigeon, Skeet, Trap models . . . . . . NiB $3719 Ex $2466 Gd $1967
Sporting Clays model . . . . NiB $8171 Ex $6559 Gd $4577
Trap Combo model. . . . . . NiB $13,878 Ex $10,798 Gd $8657
Deluxe model (introduced 1996). . .NiB $17,366 Ex $12,988 Gd $9853

MODEL ASE SERIES O/U SHOTGUN

Boxlock. Single non-selective trigger. Selective automatic ejectors. gauges: 12 and 20. Bbls. 26-, 28-, 30-inch; IC and M choke or M and F choke. Weight: about 5.75-7 lbs. Checkered pistol-grip stock and forearm. Receiver w/various grades of engraving. Imported 1947 to 1964.

Model ASE (light scroll engraving) . . . . . . NiB $2366 Ex $1971 Gd $1388
Model ASEL (half coverage engraving) . . . . NiB $3341 Ex $2679 Gd $1882
Model ASEELL (full coverage engraving) . . . . . . NiB $4966 Ex $4054 Gd $2866
For 20 ga. models, add 95%

MODEL BL-1/BL-2 O/U

Boxlock. Plain extractors. Double triggers.12 gauge, 2.75-inch chambers only. Bbls.: 30-and 28-inch M/F choke, 26-inch IC/M choke. Weight: 6.75-7 lbs., depending on bbl. length. Checkered pistol-grip stock and forearm. Imported 1968 to 1973.

Model BL-1 . . . . NiB $478 Ex $339 Gd $227
Model BL-2 (single selective trigger). . . . . . . NiB $596 Ex $487 Gd $356

MODEL BL-2/S . . . . .NiB $554 Ex $451 Gd $307

Similar to Model BL-1, except has selective "Speed-Trigger," vent-rib bbls., 2.75- or 3-inch chambers. Weight: 7-7.5 lbs. Imported 1974 to 1976.

MODEL BL-3 . . . . .NiB $690 Ex $579 Gd $491

Same as Model BL-1, except has deluxe engraved receiver, selective single trigger, vent-rib bbls., 12 or 20 ga., 2.75-inch or 3-inch

chambers in former, 3-inch in latter. Weight: 6-7.5 lbs. depending on ga. and bbl. length. Imported 1968 to 1976.

MODELS BL-4/BL-6

Higher grade versions of Model BL-3 w/more elaborate engraving and fancier wood; Model BL-6 has sideplates. Selective automatic ejectors standard. Imported 1968-76.

Model BL-4 . . . . NiB $966 Ex $779 Gd $633
Model BL-5 . . . . NiB $996 Ex $800 Gd $671
Model BL-6 (1973-76) . . . . NiB $1287 Ex $1108 Gd $977

SERIES BL SKEET GUNS

Models BL-3, BL-4, BL-5 and BL-6 w/standard features of their respective grades plus wider rib and skeet-style stock, 26-inch bbls. SK choked. Weight: 6-7.25 lbs. depending on ga.

Model BL-3 skeet gun . . . . NiB $1166 Ex $877 Gd $588
Model BL-4 skeet gun . . . . NiB $822 Ex $658 Gd $433
Model BL-5 skeet gun . . . . NiB $966 Ex $700 Gd $582
Model BL-6 skeet gun . . . . NiB $1139 Ex $1076 Gd $755

SERIES BL TRAP GUNS

Models BL-3, BL-4, BL-5 and BL-6 w/standard features of their respective grades plus wider rib and Monte Carlo stock w/recoil pad; 30-inch bbls., improved M/F or both F choke. Weight: About 7.5 lbs.

Model BL-3 . . . . NiB $679 Ex $466 Gd $388
Model BL-4 . . . . NiB $733 Ex $566 Gd $452
Model BL-5 . . . . NiB $966 Ex $753 Gd $521
Model BL-6 . . . . NiB $1166 Ex $893 Gd $600

D10 TRIDENT TRAP GUNS NIB $7520 EX $5000 GD $2510

Removeable trigger group. 12 gauge, 3-inch chambers. Bbls.: 30-and 32-inch Optima choke tubes. Weight: 8.8 lbs., depending on bbl. length. Wlanut stock and forearm. Imported 2000 to 2008.

Top Single . . . . .NIB $7520 EX $5000 GD $2510
Bottom Single . . . . .NIB $7520 EX $5000 GD $2510
Combo . . . . NiB $9060 Ex $7200 Gd $4000
Model BL-6 . . . . .NiB $1166 Ex $893 Gd $600

GRADING: **NiB** = New in Box   **Ex** = Excellent or NRA 95%   **Gd** = Good or NRA 68%   **439**

Beretta FS-1 Folding

Beretta Mark II Trap Gun

Beretta S55B

MODEL FS-1
FOLDING SINGLE . . . . .NiB $238 Ex $167 Gd $95
Formerly "Companion." Folds to length of bbl. Hammerless. Underlever. Gauge: 12, 16, 20, 28 or .410. Bbl.: 30-inch in 12 ga., 28-inch in 16 and 20 ga.; 26-inch in 28 and .410 ga.; all F choke. Checkered semipistol-grip stock/forearm. Weight: 4.5-5.5 lbs. depending on ga. Disc. 1971.

MODEL GR-2 HAMMERLESS DOUBLE . . . . . . NiB $956 Ex $788 Gd $641
Boxlock. Plain extractors. Double triggers. Gauges: 12, 20; 2.75-inch chambers in former, 3-inch in latter. Bbls.: Vent rib; 30-inch M/F choke (12 ga. only); 28-inch M/F choke, 26-inch IC/M choke. Weight: 6.5 to 7.5 lbs. depending on ga. and bbl. length. Checkered pistol-grip stock and forearm. Imported 1968 to 1976.

MODEL GR-3 . . . . .NiB $1174 Ex $1021 Gd $751
Same as Model GR-2 except has selective single trigger chambered for 12-ga. Three inch or 2.75-inch shells. Magnum model has 30-inch M/F choke bbl., recoil pad. Weight: about 8 lbs. Imported 1968 to 1976.

MODEL GR-4 . . . . .NiB $1359 Ex $1165 Gd $943
Same as Model GR-2 except has automatic ejectors and selective single trigger, higher grade engraving and wood. 12 ga., 2.75-inch chambers only. Imported 1968 to 1976.

GRADE 100 O/U
SHOTGUN. . . . . .NiB $2134 Ex $1741 Gd $1288
Sidelock. Double triggers. Automatic ejectors. 12 ga. only. Bbls.: 26-, 28-, 30-inch, any standard boring. Weight: About 7.5 lbs. Checkered stock and forend, straight or pistol grip. Disc.

GRADE 200 . . . . .NiB $2780 Ex $2284 Gd $1633
Same general specifications as Grade 00 except higher quality; bores and action parts hard chrome plated. Disc.

MARK II SINGLE-BARREL TRAP GUN . . . . . .NiB $774 Ex $623 Gd $441
Boxlock action similar to that of Series "BL" over-and-unders. Engraved receiver. Automatic ejector. 12 ga. only. 32- or 34-inch bbl. w/wide vent rib. Weight: About 8.5 lbs. Monte Carlo stock w/pistol grip and recoil pad, beavertail forearm. Imported 1972 to 1976.

MODEL S55B O/U
SHOTGUN. . . . . .NiB $672 Ex $490 Gd $336
Boxlock. Plain extractors. Selective single trigger. Gauges: 12, 20; 2.75- or 3-inch chambers in former, 3-inch in latter. Bbls.: vent rib; 30-inch M/F choke or both F choke in 12-ga. Three inch Magnum only; 28-inch M/F choke; 26 inch IC/M choke. Weight: 6.5 to 7.5 lbs. depending on ga. and bbl. length. Checkered pistol-grip stock and forearm. Introduced in 1977. Disc.

MODEL S56E . . . . .NiB $853 Ex $567 Gd $356
Same as Model S55B except has scroll-engraved receiver selective automatic ejectors. Introduced in 1977. Disc.

MODEL S58 SKEET GUN . . . . . . .NiB $855 Ex $621 Gd $443
Same as Model S56E except has 26-inch bbls. of Boehler Antinit Anticorro steel, SK choked, w/wide vent rib; skeet-style stock and forearm. Weight: 7.5 lbs. Introduced in 1977.

MODEL S58 TRAP GUN . . . . .NiB $620 Ex $494 Gd $368
Same as Model S58 Skeet Gun except has 30-inch bbls. bored IM/F Trap, Monte Carlo stock w/recoil pad. Weight: 7 lbs. 10 oz. Introduced in 1977. Disc.

SILVER HAWK FEATHERWEIGHT
HAMMERLESS DOUBLE-BARREL SHOTGUN
Boxlock. Double triggers or non-selective single trigger. Plain extractor. Gauges: 12, 16, 20, 28, 12 Mag. Bbls.: 26- to 32-inch w/high matted

Beretta S682 Gold E Trap

Beretta S682 Gold E Double Trap

rib, all standard choke combinations. Weight: 7 lbs. (12 ga. w/26-inch bbls.). Checkered walnut stock w/beavertail forearm. Disc. 1967.
w/double triggers . . . . NiB $1133 Ex $844 Gd $521
w/single trigger, add. $200

SILVER SNIPE O/U SHOTGUN
Boxlock. Non-selective or selective single trigger. Plain extractor. Gauges: 12, 20, 12 Mag., 20 Mag. Bbls.: 26-, 28-, 30-inch; plain or vent rib; chokes IC/M, M/F, SK number 1 and number 2, F/F. Weight: From about 6 lbs. in 20 ga. to 8.5 lbs. in 12 ga. (Trap gun). Checkered walnut pistol-grip stock, forearm. Imported 1955 to 1967.
w/plain bbl., non-selective trigger. . . . . . NiB $779 Ex $643 Gd $448
w/vent rib bbl., non-selective
   single trigger . . . . .NiB $779 Ex $643 Gd $448
w/selective single trigger, add $100

GOLDEN SNIPE O/U
Same as Silver Snipe (see page 430) except has automatic ejectors, vent rib is standard feature. Imported 1959 to 1967.
w/non-selective single trigger . . . . NiB $1256 Ex $1065 Gd $645

MODEL 57E O/U
Same general specifications as Golden Snipe, but higher quality throughout. Imported 1955 to 1967.
w/non-selective single trigger . . . . NiB $977 Ex $765 Gd $545
w/selective single trigger. . . . . . . NiB $1165 Ex $996 Gd $703

MODEL SL-2 PIGEON SERIES SHOTGUN
Hammerless. Takedown.12 ga. only. Three round magazine. Bbls.: Vent rib; 30-inch F choke, 28-inch M, 26-inch IC. Weight: 7-7.25 lbs., depending on bbl. length. Receiver w/various grades of engraving. Checkered pistol-grip stock and forearm. Imported 1968 to 1971.
Pump shotgun . . . . NiB $553 Ex $442 Gd $308
Silver Pigeon . . . . NiB $466 Ex $367 Gd $377
Gold Pigeon. . . . . NiB $663 Ex $507 Gd $464
Ruby Pigeon. . . . . NiB $863 Ex $638 Gd $477

"SO" SERIES SHOTGUNS
Jubilee Series introduced in 1998. The Beretta Boxlock is made with mechanical works from a single block of hot forged, high- resistance steel. The gun is richly engraved in scroll and game scenes. All engraving is signed by master engravers. High-quality finishing on the inside with high polishing of all internal points. Sidelock. Selective automatic ejectors. Selective single trigger or double triggers. 12 ga. only, 2.75- or 3-inch chambers. Bbls.: Vent rib (wide type on skeet and trap guns); 26-, 27-, 29-, 30-inch; any combination of standard chokes. Weight: 7 to 7.75 lbs., depending on bbl. length, style of stock and density of wood. Stock and forearm of select walnut, finely checkered; straight or pistol-

grip, field, skeet and trap guns have appropriate styles of stock and forearm. Models differ chiefly in quality of wood and grade of engraving. Models SO-3EL, SO-3EELL, SO4 and SO-5 have hand-detachable locks. "SO-4" is used to designate skeet and trap models derived from Model SO-3EL, but with less elaborate engraving. Models SO3EL and SO-3EELL are similar to the earlier SO-4 and SO-5, respectively. Imported 1933 to date.
Jubilee O/U (.410, 12, 16,
   20, 28 ga.) . . . . .NiB $18,766 Ex $15,580 Gd $12,654
Jubilee II Side-by-side. . . . . . . NiB $20,888 Ex $16,876 Gd $13,777
Model SO-2 . . . . NiB $9121 Ex $4760 Gd $3231
Model SO-3 . . . . NiB $7786 Ex $6988 Gd $4766
Model SO-3EL . . . . NiB $10,573 Ex $8227 Gd $5470
Model SO-3EELL . . . . .NiB $12,098 Ex $10,866 Gd $8977
Model SO-4 Field, Skeet or Trap gun . . . . . . .NiB $10,677 Ex $9154 Gd $7110
Model SO-5 Sporting,
   Skeet or Trap model. . . .NiB $12,779 Ex $10,870 Gd $8965
w/extra bbl. set, add. 25%

MODELS SO-6 AND SO-9 PREMIUM GRADE SHOTGUNS
High-grade over/unders in the SO series. Gauges: 12 ga. only (SO-6); 12, 20, 28 and .410 (SO-9). Fixed or Mobilchoke (12 ga. only). Sidelock action. Silver or casehardened receiver (SO-6); English custom hand-engraved scroll or game scenes (SO-9). Supplied w/leather case and accessories. Imported 1990 to date.
SO-6 O/U .NiB $9044 Ex $6987 Gd $4733
Model SO-6 EELL O/U . . . . .NiB $8343 Ex $6865 Gd $6577
Model SO-9 O/U . . . . NiB $50,000 Ex $47,750 Gd $45,000
Model SO-9EELL
   w/custom engraving . . . . . . NiB $110,000 Ex $95,000 Gd $80,000
w/extra bbl. set, add. 25%

MODEL SO6/SO-7 S/S SHOTGUNS
Side-by-side shotgun w/same general specifications as SO Series over/unders except higher grade w/more elaborate engraving, fancier wood.
Model SO-6 (imported 1948-93) . .NiB $7254 Ex $6144 Gd $4988
Model SO-7 (imported 1948-90) . .NiB $8977 Ex $7238 Gd $6144

MODEL TR-1 SINGLE-SHOT
TRAP GUN. . . . . .NiB $355 Ex $279 Gd $125
Hammerless. Underlever action. Engraved frame.12 ga. only. 32-inch bbl. w/vent rib. Weight: About 8.25 lbs. Monte Carlo stock w/pistol grip and recoil pad, beavertail forearm. Imported 1968 to 1971.

MODEL TR-2 . . . . .NiB $364 Ex $231 Gd $156
Same as Model TR-1 except has extended ventilated rib. Imported 1969-73.

Beretta Model SO-2

Beretta Model SO-3

Beretta Model SO-4

Beretta Model SO-5

Beretta Model SO-7

VICTORIA PINTAIL (ES100) SEMIAUTOLOADER

Short Montefeltro-type recoil action. Gauge: 12 w/3-inch chamber. Bbl.: 24-inch slug, 24-, 26- or 28-inch vent rib w/Mobilchoke tubes. Weight: 7 lbs. to 7 lbs., 5 oz. Checkered synthetic or walnut buttstock and forend. Matte finish on both metal and stock. Imported 1993 and 2005.

Field model w/synthetic
  stock (intro. 1998) . . . . .NiB $522 Ex $320 Gd $244
Field model w/walnut stock (disc. 1998). . . . . . NiB $733 Ex $535 Gd $431
Rifled slug model w/synthetic
  stock (intro. 1998) . . . . .NiB $544 Ex $378 Gd $296
Stndard slug model
  w/walnut stock (disc. 1998) . . . .NiB $544 Ex $378 Gd $296
Wetland Camo model (intro. 2000). . . . . NiB $677 Ex $460 Gd $339

BERNARDELLI, VINCENZO —
Gardone V.T. (Brescia), Italy

Previously imported by Armsport, Miam, FL (formerly by Magnum Research, Inc., Quality Arms, Stoeger Industries, Inc. & Action Arms, LTD).

115 SERIES O/U SHOTGUNS

Boxlock w/single trigger and ejectors. 12 ga. only. 25.5-, 26.75-, and 29.5-inch bbls. Concave top and vented middle rib. Anatomical grip stock. Blued or coin-silver finish w/various grades of engraving.

Imported 1985 to 1997.
Standard Model . . . . NiB $1844 Ex $1532 Gd $1176
Hunting Model 115E (disc. 1990) . . . . . . NiB $2247 Ex $1993 Gd $1612
Hunting Model 115L (disc. 1990) . . . . . NiB $2788 Ex $2391 Gd $2095
Hunting Model 115S (disc. 1990) . . . . . NiB $3712 Ex $3122 Gd $2210
Target Model 115 (disc. 1992). . . . . . NiB $1977 Ex $1678 Gd $1440
Target Model 115E (disc. 1992) . . . . . . .NiB $6108 Ex $5388 Gd $3789
Target Model 115L (disc. 1992) . . . . . . .NiB $3855 Ex $3410 Gd $2377
Target Model 115S (disc. 1992) . . . . . . .NiB $6077 Ex $4129 Gd $3755
Trap/Skeet Model 115S
  (imported 1996-97) . . . . . . .NiB $3366 Ex $2581 Gd $1786
Sporting Clays Model 115S
  (imported 1995-97) . . . . . . .NiB $3944 Ex $3216 Gd $2533

BRESCIA
HAMMER DOUBLE . . . . .NiB $1564 Ex $1096 Gd $839
Back-action sidelock. Plain extractors. Double triggers. Gauges: 12, 20. Bbls.: 27.5 or 29.5-inch M/F choke in 12 ga. 25.5-inch IC/M choke in 20 ga.. Weight: From 5.75 to 7 lbs., depending on ga. and bbl. length. English-style stock and forearm, checkered. No longer imported.

ELIO .NiB $1232 Ex $1006 Gd $781
Lightweight game gun, 12 ga. only, w/same general specifications as Standard Gamecock (S. Uberto 1) except weight: About 6 to 6.25 lbs.; has automatic ejectors, fine English-pattern scroll engraving. No longer imported.

Bernardelli Gamecock

Bernardelli Standard Gamecock

Bernardelli Gardone

Bernardelli Italia

Bernardelli Roma 6

GAMECOCK, PREMIER (ROME 3)

Same general specifications as Standard Gamecock (S. Uberto 1) except has sideplates, auto ejectors, single trigger. No longer imported.

Roma 3 (disc. 1989,
  reintroduced 1993-97) . . . . . NiB $1790 Ex $1435 Gd $1108
Roma 3E (disc. 1950) . . . . NiB $1956 Ex $1600 Gd $1119
Roma 3M
  w/single trigger (disc. 1997) . . . .NiB $1956 Ex $1600 Gd $1119

GAMECOCK, STANDARD (S. UBERTO 1) HAMMERLESS

DOUBLE-BARREL SHOTGUN . . . . . .NiB $900 Ex $766 Gd $563
Boxlock. Plain extractors. Double triggers. Gauges: 12, 16, 20; 2.75-inch chambers in 12 and 16, 3-inch in 20 ga. Bbls. 25.5-inch IC/M choke; 27.5-inch M/F choke. Weight: 5.75-6.5 lbs., depending on ga. and bbl. length. English-style straight-grip stock and forearm, checkered. No longer imported.

GARDONE HAMMER DOUBLE . . . . . . NiB $2766 Ex $2261 Gd $1600
Same general specifications as Brescia except for higher grade engraving and wood, but not as high as the Italia. Half-cock safety. Disc. 1956.

HEMINGWAY HAMMERLESS DOUBLE

Boxlock. Single or double triggers w/hinged front. Selective automatic ejectors. Gauges: 12 and 20 w/2.75- or 3-inch chambers, 16 and 28 w/2.75-inch. Bbls.: 23.5- to 28-inch w/fixed chokes. Weight: 6.25 lbs. Checkered English-style European walnut stock. Silvered and engraved receiver.

Standard model . . . . NiB $2288 Ex $1866 Gd $1383
Deluxe model
  w/sideplates (disc. 1993) . . . . . NiB $2698 Ex $2210 Gd $1679
  w/single trigger, add. $125

ITALIA . . . . NiB $1866 Ex $1044 Gd $623
Same general specifications as Brescia except higher grade engraving and wood. Disc. 1986.

ROMA 4 AND ROMA 6

Same as Premier Gamecock (Rome 3) except higher grade engraving and wood, double triggers. Disc. 1997.

Roma 4 (disc. 1989) . . . . NiB $1847 Ex $1412 Gd $1095
Roma 4E (disc. 1997) . . . . NiB $1796 Ex $1370 Gd $1060
Roma 6 (disc. 1989) . . . . NiB $1488 Ex $1233 Gd $1000
Roma 6E (disc. 1997) . . . . NiB $2533 Ex $2000 Gd $1277

ROMA 7, 8, AND 9

Side-by-side. Anson & Deeley boxlock; hammerless. Ejectors; double triggers. 12 ga. Barrels: 27.5-or 29.5-inch. M/F chokes. Fancy hand-checkered European walnut straight or pistol-grip stock, forearm. Elaborately engraved, silver-finished sideplates. Imported 1994 to 1997.

Roma 7 . . . . NiB $3366 Ex $2160 Gd $1500
Roma 8 . . . . NiB $3866 Ex $2571 Gd $1880
Roma 9 . . . . NiB $4665 Ex $3748 Gd $2977

S. UBERTO 2 . . . . .NiB $1460 Ex $1277 Gd $898
Same as Standard Gamecock (S. Uberto 1) except higher grade engraving and wood. Currently imported.

S. UBERTO F.S.

Same as Standard Gamecock except w/higher grade engraving, wood and has auto-ejectors. Disc. 1989, reintro. 1993 to 1997.

Model FS . . . . NiB $1746 Ex $1544 Gd $1100
Model V.B. Incisio . . . . NiB $2169 Ex $1754 Gd $1239
w/single trigger, add. $100

SHOTGUNS

HOLLAND V.B. SERIES SHOTGUNS

Holland & Holland-type sidelock action. Auto-ejectors. Double triggers. 12 ga. only. Bbl. length or choke to custom specification. Silver-finish receiver (Liscio) or engraved coin finish receiver (Incisio). Extra-select wood and game scene engraving (Lusso). Checkered stock (straight or pistol-grip). Imported 1992 to 1997.

Model V.B. Liscio . . . . .NiB $11,650   Ex $10,500   Gd $8675
Model V.B. Incisio . . . . .NiB $12,200   Ex $9779   Gd $6755
Model V.B. Lusso . . . . NiB $9465   Ex $8119   Gd $5231
Model V.B. Extra . . . . NiB $14,766   Ex $10,877   Gd $8669
Model V.B. Gold . . . . NiB $49,600   Ex $44,688   Gd $37,789
w/Engraving Pattern No. 4, add $1250
w/Engraving Pattern No. 12, add $5000
w/Engraving Pattern No. 20, add $9500
w/Single trigger, add $700

Boss Hammerless
Double-Barrel

BOSS & COMPANY — London, England

HAMMERLESS DOUBLE-BARREL

SHOTGUN . . . . .NiB $64,887   Ex $57,955   Gd $35,898
Sidelock. Automatic ejectors. Double triggers, non-selective or selective single trigger. Made in all gauges, bbl. lengths and chokes. Checkered stock and forend, straight or pistol-grip.

HAMMERLESS O/U

SHOTGUN . . . . .NiB $117,650   Ex $94,800   Gd $45,000
Sidelock. Automatic ejectors. Selective single trigger. Made in all gauges, bbl. lengths and chokes. Checkered stock and forend, straight or pistol-grip. Disc.

BREDA MECCANICA BRESCIANA — Brescia, Italy

Formerly ERNESTO BREDA, Milan, Italy. Previously imported by Tristar (Kansas City, MO), Gryphon International (Kansas City, MO) and Diana Imports Co., (San Francisco, CA).

VEGA SPECIAL O/U SHOTGUN . . . . .NiB $676   Ex $543   Gd $410
12 or 20 gauge. Box lock action. Bbl. 26 or 28 inches; single trigger; ejectors. Blue only.

VEGA SPECIAL TRAP . . . . .NiB $966   Ex $733   Gd $590
12 or 20 gauge. Box lock action. Competition triggers and lock. Bbl. 30 or 32 inches; single trigger; ejectors. Blue only.

VEGA LUSSO . . . . .NiB $1765   Ex $1430   Gd $1100
12 gauge only, 3-inch chambers. Scalloped box lock action, single selective trigger, ejectors. Bbl. 26 or 28 inches, ventilated rib. Coin finished receiver with light engraving. Deluxe checkered Circassian walnut stock and forearm. Imported 2001 to 2002.

SIRIO STANDARD . . . . .NiB $2176   Ex $1788   Gd $1354
12 or 20 gauge. Engraved box lock action. Bbl. 26 or 28 inches; single trigger; ejectors. Blue only. Also available in skeet model.

ANDROMEDA SPECIAL . . . . .NiB $755   Ex $665   Gd $525
Side-by-side.12 gauge, single trigger; ejectors, select checkered walnut stock; satin finish on receiver with elaborate engraving.

GOLD SERIES SEMIAUTOMATIC SHOTGUN

12 or (lightweight) 20 gauge, 2.75-inch chamber. Bbl. 25 or 27 inches; ventilated rib standard. Recoil operated
Antares Standard Model . . . . .NiB $543   Ex $421   Gd $336
Argus Model . . . . .NiB $521   Ex $390   Gd $266
Aries Model . . . . .NiB $521   Ex $390   Gd $266

STANDARD GRADE GOLD SERIES . NiB $377   Ex $290   Gd $245
12 gauge, 2-3/4-inch chamber. Recoil operated. Bbl. 25 or 27 inches. Light engraving. Disc.

GRADE 1 .NiB $644   Ex $500   Gd $336
Similar to Standard model but with fancier wood and engraving.

GRADE 2 .NiB $756   Ex $644   Gd $500
Similar to Grade 1 but with more engraving, etc.

GRADE 3 . . . . .NiB $966   Ex $771   Gd $654
Same as Grade 1 but with custom-quality embellishments.

MAGNUM MODEL . . . . .NiB $546   Ex $400   Gd $297
Similar to Standard Grade but with 3-inch chambers.

ALTAIR SPECIAL . . . . .NiB $533   Ex $400   Gd $336
12 gauge, 2.75-inch chamber. Gas-operated. Bbl. 25 or 27 inches, ventilated rib standard. Alloy construction, blue or chrome receiver.

ASTRO . . . . .NiB $1126   Ex $853   Gd $700
12 gauge (disc. 2002) or 20 gauge, 3-inch chamber. Inertia action. Bbl. 22 (slug), 24, 26, 28 or 30 inches; ventilated rib. Black synthetic, Advantage camo, or Circassian walnut stock and forearm. Imported 2001.
Advantage camo model, add $125

ASTROLUX . . . . .NiB $1588   Ex $1344   Gd $1033
Similar to Astro model except has two-tone receiver with engraving and deluxe checkered Circassian walnut stock and forearm. Imported 2001 to 2002.

ERMES SERIES . . . . .NiB $1044   Ex $788   Gd $648
12 gauge, 3-inch chamber. Semiautomatic. Inertia recoil operating system, aluminum alloy receiver, nickeel plated or blue finish on lower receiver. Bbl. 24, 26, or 28 inches. Deluxe checkered Circassian walnut stock and forearm. Imported 2001.
Ermes Silver . . . . .NiB $1287   Ex $1095   Gd $869
Ermes Gold . . . . .NiB $1452   Ex $1138   Gd $1009

MIRA . . . . .NiB $880   Ex $622   Gd $500
12 gauge, 3-inch chamber. Semiautomatic, gas-operated. Aluminum alloy receiver; black or Advantage camo finish. Bbl. 22 (slug), 24, 26, 28 or 30 inches, ventilated rib. Circassian walnut or black synthetic stock and forearm. Imported 2001.
Sporting Clays model, add $50
w/black synthetic stock & forearm, deduct 10%

ARIES 2 . . . . NiB $879 Ex $793 Gd $649
12 gauge, 2-3/4-inch chamber. Semiautomatic, gas-operated. Engraved two-tone receiver. Bbl. 20 or 30 inches, ventilated rib. Deluxe checkered Circassian walnut or black synthetic stock and forearm. Imported 2001 only.

BRETTON-GAUCHER — St. Etienne, France

BABY STANDARD SPRINT O/U . . . . NiB $1088 Ex $855 Gd $687
Inline sliding breech action. 12 or 20 gauge w/2.75-inch chambers. 27.5-inch separated bbls. w/vent rib and choke tubes. Weight: 4.8 to 5 lbs. Engraved alloy receiver. Checkered walnut buttstock and forearm w/satin oil finish. Limited import.

SPRINT DELUXE O/U . . . . NiB $1077 Ex $863 Gd $700
Similar to the Standard Model except w/engraved coin-finished receiver and chambered 12, 16 and 20 ga. Limited import.

FAIR PLAY O/U . . . . NiB $1088 Ex $863 Gd $600
Lightweight action similar to the Sprint Model except w/hinged action that pivots open and is chambered 12 or 20 gauge only. Limited import.

BRNO — Brno and Uherski Brod, Czech Republic (formerly Czechoslovakia)

MODEL 500 O/U SHOTGUN . . . . NiB $900 Ex $777 Gd $568
Hammerless boxlock w/double triggers and ejectors.12 ga. w/2.75-inch chambers. 27.5-inch bbls.. choked M/F. 44 inches overall. Weight: 7 lbs. Etched receiver. Checkered walnut stock w/classic style cheekpiece. Imported from 1987 to 1991.

500 SERIES O/U COMBINATION GUNS
Similar to the 500 Series over/under shotgun above, except w/lower bbl. chambered in rifle calibers and set trigger option. Imported from 1987 to 1995.

Model 502 12 ga./.222 or .243 (disc. 1991)	NiB $2088	Ex $1256	Gd $1077
Model 502 12 ga. .308 or .30-06 (disc. 1991)	NiB $1164	Ex $1038	Gd $772
Model 571 12 ga./6x65R (disc. 1993)	NiB $853	Ex $709	Gd $587
Model 572 12 ga./7x65R (imported since 1992)	NiB $881	Ex $733	Gd $600
Model 584 12 ga./7x57R (imported since 1992)	NiB $1264	Ex $1033	Gd $800
Sport Series 4-bbl. set (disc. 1991)	NiB $3153	Ex $2571	Gd $1863

CZ 581 SOLO O/U SHOTGUN . . . . NiB $966 Ex $738 Gd $561
Hammerless boxlock w/double triggers, ejectors and automatic safety. 12 ga. w/2.75- or 3-inch chambers. 28-inch bbls. choked M/F. Weight: 7.5 lbs. Checkered walnut stock. Disc. 1996.

SUPER SERIES O/U SHOTGUN
Hammerless sidelock w/selective single or double triggers and ejectors. 12 ga. w/2.75- or 3-inch chambers. 27.5-inch bbls. choked M/F. 44.5 inches overall. Weight: 7.25 lbs. Etched or engraved side plates. Checkered European walnut stock w/classic-style cheekpiece. Imported from 1987 to 1991.

Super Series Shotgun (disc. 1992)	NiB $866	Ex $731	Gd $577
Super Series Combo (disc. 1992)	NiB $2021	Ex $1190	Gd $977
Super Ser. 3-bbl. set (disc. 1990)	NiB $1993	Ex $1578	Gd $1266
Super Series engraving, add			$1350

ZH 300 SERIES O/U SHOTGUNS
Hammerless boxlock w/double triggers. Gauge: 12 or 16 w/2.75- or 3-inch chambers. Bbls.: 26, 27.5 or 30 inches; choked M/F. Weight: 7 lbs. Skip-line checkered walnut stock w/classic-style cheekpiece

Imported from 1986-93.

Model 300 (disc. 1993)	NiB $786	Ex $547	Gd $408
Model 301 Field (disc. 1991)	NiB $667	Ex $582	Gd $400
Model 302 Skeet (disc. 1992)	NiB $745	Ex $557	Gd $442
Model 303 Trap (disc. 1992)	NiB $749	Ex $566	Gd $449

ZH 300 SERIES O/U COMBINATION GUNS
Similar to the 300 Series over/under shotgun except lower bbl. chambered in rifle calibers.

Model 300 Combo 8-bbl. Set (disc. 1991)	NiB $3375	Ex $2977	Gd $2500
Model 304 12 ga./7x57R (disc. 1995)	NiB $846	Ex $698	Gd $535
Model 305 12 ga./5.6x52R (disc. 1993)	NiB $921	Ex $769	Gd $544
Model 306 12 ga./5.6x50R (disc. 1993)	NiB $965	Ex $798	Gd $579
Model 307 12 ga./.22 Hornet (Imported since 1995)	NiB $843	Ex $755	Gd $507
Model 324 16 ga./7x57R (disc. 1987)	NiB $880	Ex $742	Gd $509

ZP 149 HAMMERLESS DOUBLE
Sidelock action w/double triggers, automatic ejectors and automatic safety.12 ga. w/2.75- or 3-inch chambers. 28.5-inch bbls. choked M/F. Weight: 7.25 lbs. Checkered walnut buttstock with cheekpiece.

Standard model	NiB $669	Ex $458	Gd $388
Engraved model	NiB $700	Ex $477	Gd $421

BROLIN ARMS, INC. — Pomona, California

FIELD SERIES PUMP SHOTGUN
Slide-action. Gauge: 12 ga. w/3-inch chamber. 24-, 26-, 28- or 30-inch bbl. 44 and 50 inches overall. Weight: 7.3 to 7.6 lbs. Cross-bolt safety. Vent rib bbl. w/screw-in choke tube and bead sights. Non- reflective metal finish. Synthetic or oil-finished wood stock w/swivel studs. Made from 1997 to 1998.

Synthetic stock model	NiB $254	Ex $188	Gd $95
Wood stock model	NiB $200	Ex $129	Gd $75

COMBO MODEL PUMP SHOTGUN
Similar to the Field Model except w/extra 18.5- or 22-inch bbl. w/bead or rifle sight. Made from 1997 to 1998.

Synthetic stock model	NiB $279	Ex $200	Gd $115
Wood stock model	NiB $331	Ex $240	Gd $193

LAWMAN MODEL PUMP SHOTGUN
Similar to the Field Model except has 18.5-inch bbl. w/cylinder bore fixed choke. Weight: 7 lbs. Dual operating bars. Bead, rifle or ghost ring sights. Black synthetic or wood stock. Matte chrome or satin nickel finish. Made from 1997 to 1999.

Synthetic stock model	NiB $217	Ex $151	Gd $90
Wood stock model	NiB $217	Ex $151	Gd $90
w/rifle sights, add			$35
w/ghost ring sights, add			$50
w/satin nickel finish (disc. 1997), add			$50

SLUG MODEL PUMP SHOTGUN
Similar to the Field Model except has 18.5- or 22-inch bbl. w/IC fixed choke or 4-inch extended rifled choke. Rifle or ghost ring sights or optional cantilevered scope mount. Black synthetic or wood stock. Matte blued finish. Made from 1998 to 1999.

Synthetic stock model	NiB $288	Ex $202	Gd $166
Wood stock model	NiB $300	Ex $221	Gd $180
w/rifled bbl., add			$25
w/cantilevered scope mount, add			$50

SHOTGUNS

American Browning Grade I

American Browning Special

TURKEY SPECIAL PUMP SHOTGUN

Similar to the Field Model except has 22-inch vent-rib bbl. w/extended extra-full choke. Rifle or ghost ring sights or optional cantilevered scope mount. Black synthetic or wood stock. Matte blued finish. Made from 1998 to 1999.

Synthetic stock model	NiB $266	Ex $190	Gd $125
Wood stock model	NiB $305	Ex $237	Gd $154
w/cantileveredscope mount, add			$50

BROWNING — Morgan (formerly Ogden), Utah

AMERICAN BROWNING SHOTGUNS

Designated "American" Browning because they were produced in Ilion, New York, the following Remington-made Brownings are almost identical to the Remington Model 11A and Sportsman and the Browning Auto-5. They are the only Browning shotguns manufactured in the U.S. during the 20th century and were made for Browning Arms when production was suspended in Belgium because of WW II.

NOTE: *Fabrique Nationale Herstal (formerly Fabrique Nationale d'Armes de Guerre) of Herstal, Belgium, is the longtime manufacturer of Browning shotguns dating back to 1900. Miroku Firearms Mfg. Co. of Tokyo, Japan, bought into the Browning company and has, since the early 1970s, undertaken some of the production. The following shotguns were manufactured for Browning by these two firms.*

GRADE I AUTOLOADER (AUTO-5)

Recoil-operated autoloader. Similar to the Remington Model 11A except w/different style engraving and identified w/the Browning logo. Gauges: 12, 16 or 20. Plain 26- to 32-inch bbl. w/any standard boring. Two or four shell tubular magazine w/magazine cut-off. Weight: About 6.88 lbs. (20 ga.) to 8 lbs. (12 ga.). Checkered pistol-grip stock and forearm. Made from 1940 to 1949.

American Browning Grade I

Auto-5, 12 or 16 ga.	NiB $856	Ex $744	Gd $400
20 ga., add			20%

SPECIAL 441

Same general specifications as Grade I except supplied w/raised matted rib or vent rib. Disc. 1949.

w/raised matted rib	NiB $894	Ex $756	Gd $435
w/vent rib	NiB $925	Ex $790	Gd $466
20 ga., add			20%

SPECIAL SKEET MODEL . . . . .NiB $815 Ex $645 Gd $477

Same general specifications as Grade I except has 26-inch bbl. w/vent rib and Cutts Compensator. Disc. 1949.

UTILITY FIELD GUN. . . . . .NiB $608 Ex $458 Gd $339

Same general specifications as Grade I except has 28-inch plain bbl. w/ Poly Choke. Disc. 1949.

MODEL 12 PUMP SHOTGUN

Special limited edition Winchester Model 12. Gauge: 20 or 28. Five-round tubular magazine. 26-inch bbl., M choke. 45 inches overall. Weight: about 7 lbs. Grade I has blued receiver, checkered walnut stock w/matte finish. Grade V has engraved receiver, checkered deluxe walnut stock w/high-gloss finish. Made from 1988 to 1992. See illustration next page.

Grade I, 20 ga. 8600 prod.	NiB $866	Ex $569	Gd $449
Grade I, 28 ga.	NiB $1166	Ex $912	Gd $744
Grade V, 20 ga 4000 prod.	NiB $1455	Ex $1187	Gd $879
Grade V, 28 ga	NiB $1768	Ex $1344	Gd $961

MODEL 42 LIMITED Edition SHOTGUN

Special limited edition Winchester Model 42 pump shotgun. Same general specifications as Model 12 except w/smaller frame in .410 ga. and 3-inch chamber. Made from 1991 to 1993.

Grade I			
(6000 produced)	NiB $967	Ex $744	Gd $466
Grade V			
(6000 produced)	NiB $1590	Ex $1156	Gd $863

2000 BUCK SPECIAL . . . . .NiB $588 Ex $467 Gd $355

Same as Field Model except has 24-inch plain bbl. Bored for rifled slug and buckshot, fitted w/rifle sights (open rear, ramp front). 12 ga., 2.75-inch or 3-inch chamber; 20 ga., 2.75-inch chamber. Weight: 12 ga., 7 lbs., 8 oz.; 20 ga., 6 lbs., 10 oz. Made from 1974 to 1981 by FN.

2000 GAS AUTOMATIC SHOTGUN, FIELD MODEL

Gas-operated. Gauge: 12 or 20. 2.75-inch chamber. Four-round magazine. Bbl.: 26-, 28-, 30-inch, any standard choke plain matted bbl. (12 ga. only) or vent rib. Weight: 6 lbs. 11 oz.-7 lbs. 12 oz. depending on ga. and bbl. length. Checkered pistol-grip stock/forearm. Made from 1974 to 1981 by FN; assembled in Portugal.

w/plain matted bbl.	NiB $559	Ex $468	Gd $346

2000 MAGNUM MODEL . . . . . . .NiB $579 Ex $377 Gd $300

Same as Field Model except chambered for 3-inch shells, three-round magazine. Bbl.: 26- (20 ga. only), 28-, 30- or 32-inch (latter two 12 ga. only); any standard choke; vent rib. Weight: 6 lbs., 11 oz.-7 lbs., 13 oz. depending on ga. and bbl. Made from 1974 to 1983 by FN.

Browning Model 12
Limited Editon Grade I

Browning Model 12
Limited Editon Grade V

Browning Model 42
Limited Editon Grade V

Browning M2000 Vent Rib

Browning Model A-500

2000 SKEET MODEL . . . . **NiB $527 Ex $441 Gd $338**
Same as Field Model except has skeet-style stock w/recoil pad, 26-inch
vent-rib bbl., SK choke. 12 or 20 ga., 2.75-inch chamber. Weight: 8 lbs.,
1 oz. (12 ga.); 6 lbs., 12 oz. (20 ga.) Made 1974 to 1981 by FN.

2000 TRAP MODEL . . . . **NiB $527 Ex $441 Gd $338**
Same as Field Model except has Monte Carlo stock w/recoil pad, 30- or
32-inch bbl. w/high-post vent rib and receiver extension, M/I/F chokes. 12 ga.,
2.75-inch chamber. Weight: About 8 lbs., 5 oz. Made 1974 to 1981 by FN.

A-500G GAS-OPERATED SEMIAUTOMATIC
Same general specifications as Browning Model A-500R except gas-
operated. Made 1990 to 1993.
Buck Special . . . . **NiB $590 Ex $466 Gd $339**
Hunting model . . . . **NiB $688 Ex $491 Gd $388**

A-500G SPORTING CLAYS . . . . . . **NiB $663 Ex $490 Gd $388**
Same general specifications as Model A-500G except has matte blued
receiver w/"Sporting Clays" logo. 28- or 30-inch bbl. w/Invector choke
tubes. Made 1992 to 1993.

A-500R SEMIAUTOMATIC
Recoil-operated. Gauge: 12. 26- to 30-inch vent-rib bbls. 24-inch Buck
Special. Invector choke tube system. 2.75- or 3-inch Magnum cartridges. Weight: 7 lbs., 3 oz.-8 lbs., 2 oz. Cross-bolt safety. Gold-plated
trigger. Scroll-engraved receiver. Gloss-finished walnut stock
and forend. Made by FN from 1987 to 1993.

Hunting model . . . . **NiB $677 Ex $476 Gd $388**
Buck Special . . . . **NiB $692 Ex $490 Gd $433**

A-BOLT SERIES SHOTGUN
Bolt-action repeating single-barrel shotgun. 12 ga. only w/3-inch
chambers, 2-round magazine. 22- or 23-inch rifled bbl., w/or
w/o a rifled invector tube. Receiver drilled and tapped for scope
mounts. Bbl. w/ or w/o open sights. Checkered walnut or graph-
ite/fiberglass composite stock. Matte black metal finish. Imported
1995 to 1998.
Stalker model w/
composite stock . . . . **NiB $1365 Ex $1077 Gd $867**
Hunter model w/walnut stock . . . . **NiB $1365 Ex $1077 Gd $867**
w/rifled bbl., add **$200**
w/open sights, add **$75**

AUTOLOADING SHOTGUNS, GRADES II, III & IV
These higher grade models differ from the Standard or Grade I
in general quality, grade of wood, checkering, engraving, etc.,
otherwise specifications are the same. Grade IV guns, sometimes
called Midas Grade, are inlaid w/yellow and green gold. Disc.
in 1940.
Grade II, plain bbl. . . . . **NiB $1698 Ex $1390 Gd $976**
Grade III, plain bbl. . . . . **NiB $1580 Ex $1176 Gd $833**
Grade IV, plain bbl. . . . . **NiB $4469 Ex $3865 Gd $3033**
w/raised, matted rib bbl., add **15%**
w/vent. rib bbl., add **30%**

GRADING: **NiB** = New in Box **Ex** = Excellent or NRA 95% **Gd** = Good or NRA 68%

Browning Automatic-5 Buck Special

Browning Automatic-5 Classic

Browning Automatic-5
Gold Classic

AUTOMATIC-5, LIGHT 20
Same general specifications as Standard Model except lightweight and 20 ga. Bbl.: 26- or 28-inch; plain or vent rib. Weight: About 6.25-6.5 lbs. depending on bbl. Made 1958 to 1976 by FN, since then by Miroku.

FN manu., plain bbl.	NiB $844	Ex $633	Gd $429
FN manu., vent. rib bbl.	NiB $1267	Ex $988	Gd $687
Miroku manu., vent. rib,fixed choke . .	NiB $965	Ex $743	Gd $846
Miroku manu., vent. rib, invectors .	NiB $1065	Ex $844	Gd $600

AUTOMATIC-5, BUCK SPECIAL MODELS
Same as Light 12, Magnum 12, Light 20, Magnum 20, in respective gauges, except 24-inch plain bbl. bored for rifled slug and buckshot, fitted w/rifle sights (open rear, ramp front). Weight: 6.13-8.25 lbs. depending on ga. Made 1964 to 1976 by FN, since then by Miroku.

FN manu., w/plain bbl.	NiB $1276	Ex $889	Gd $567
Miroku manu., ...	NiB $966	Ex $843	Gd $544
w/3-inch mag. rec., add $10%			

AUTOMATIC-5 CLASSIC. . . . . . NiB $1186 Ex $983 Gd $889
Gauge: 12. 5-round capacity. 28-inch vent rib bbl./M choke. 2.75-

inch chamber. Engraved silver-gray receiver. Gold-plated trigger. Crossbolt safety. High-grade, hand-checkered select American walnut stock w/rounded pistol grip. 5,000 issued; made in Japan in 1984, engraved in Belgium.

AUTOMATIC-5 GOLD CLASSIC . . . . NiB $9887 Ex $6690 Gd $4690
Same general specifications as Automatic-5 Classic except engraved receiver inlaid w/gold. Pearl border on stock and forend plus fine-line hand-checkering. Each gun numbered "One of Five Hundred," etc. 500 issued in 1984; made in Belgium.

AUTOMATIC-5, LIGHT 12
12 ga. only. Same general specifications as Standard Model except lightweight (about 7.25 lbs.), has gold-plated trigger. Guns w/rib have striped matting on top of bbl. Fixed chokes or Invector tubes. Made 1948 to 1976 by FN, since then by Miroku.

FN manu., plain bbl.	NiB $889	Ex $655	Gd $498
FN manu., w/raised matte rib	NiB $954	Ex $777	Gd $675
FN manu., vent. rib	NiB $1098	Ex $966	Gd $676
Miroku manu., vent. rib, fixed choke	NiB $889	Ex $667	Gd $487
Miroku manu., vent. rib, Invectors	NiB $1099	Ex $776	Gd $566

AUTOMATIC-5, MAGNUM 12 GAUGE
Same general specifications as Standard Model. Chambered for 3-inch Magnum 12-ga. shells. Bbl.: 28-inch M/F, 30- or 32-inch F/F, plain or vent rib. Weight: 8.5-9 lbs. depending on bbl. Buttstock has recoil pad. Made 1958 to 1976 by FN, since then by Miroku. Fixed chokes or Invector tubes.

FN manu., plain bbl.	NiB $954	Ex $779	Gd $549
FN manu., vent. rib bbl.	NiB $1288	Ex $977	Gd $765
Miroku manu., vent. rib, fixed chokes	NiB $888	Ex $645	Gd $455
Miroku manu., vent. rib, Invectors	NiB $1066	Ex $707	Gd $500

AUTOMATIC-5, MAGNUM 20 GAUGE
Same general specifications as Standard Model except chambered for 3-inch Magnum 20-ga. shell. Bbl.: 26- or 28-inch, plain or vent rib. Weight: 7 lbs., 5 oz.-7 lbs., 7 oz. depending on bbl. Made 1967 to 1976 by FN, since then by Miroku.

FN manu., plain bbl.	NiB $944	Ex $768	Gd $567
FN manu., vent. rib bbl.	NiB $1333	Ex $989	Gd $779
Miroku manu., vent. rib, Invectors .	NiB $989	Ex $766	Gd $590

Browning Auto-5 Sweet Sixteen (New Model)

Browning Model B-80 Upland Special

Browning BPS Hunter

Browning BPS Youth & Ladies Model

SHOTGUNS

AUTOMATIC-5, SKEET MODEL

12 ga. only. Same general specifications as Light 12. Bbl.: 26-or 28-inch, plain or vent rib, SK choke. Weight: 7 lbs., 5 oz.-7 lbs., 10 oz. depending on bbl. Made by FN prior to 1976, since then by Miroku.

FN manu., plain bbl.	NiB $1177	Ex $956	Gd $654
FN manu., vent. rib bbl.	NiB $1769	Ex $1166	Gd $956
Miroku manu., vent. rib bbl.	NiB $987	Ex $766	Gd $554

AUTOMATIC-5 STALKER

Same general specifications as Automatic-5 Light and Magnum models except w/matte blue finish and black graphite fiberglass stock and forearm. Made from 1992 to 1997.

Light model	NiB $966	Ex $831	Gd $664
Magnum model	NiB $1031	Ex $977	Gd $689

AUTOMATIC-5, STANDARD (GRADE I)

Recoil-operated. Gauge: 12 or 16 (16-gauge guns made prior to WW II were chambered for 2-inch shells; standard 16 disc. 1964). Four shell magazine in 5-round model, prewar guns were also available in 3-round model. Bbls.: 26- to 32-inch; plain, raised matted or vent rib; choice of standard chokes. Weight: About 8 lbs., in 12 ga., 7.5 lbs., in 16 ga. Checkered pistol-grip stock and forearm. (Note: Browning Special, disc. about 1940.) Made from 1900 to 1973 by FN.

Grade I, plain bbl.	NiB $844	Ex $677	Gd $544
Grade I (or Browning Special), w/raised matted rib	NiB $977	Ex $778	Gd $580
Grade I (or Browning Special), w/vent. s rib	NiB $977	Ex $778	Gd $580

AUTOMATIC-5, SWEET 16

16 ga. Same general specifications as Standard Model except lightweight (about 6.75 lbs.), has gold plated trigger. Guns w/o VR have striped matting on top of bbl. Made 1937 to 1976 by FN.

w/plain bbl.	NiB $1189	Ex $793	Gd $555
w/raised matted or vent. rib	NiB $1769	Ex $1388	Gd $1012

AUTO-5, SWEET SIXTEEN

NEW MODEL . . . . NiB $1399 Ex $1156 Gd $922
Reissue of popular 16-gauge Hunting Model w/5-round capacity, 2.75-inch chamber, scroll-engraved blued receiver, high-gloss French walnut stock w/rounded pistol grip. 26- or 28-inch vent-rib bbl. F choke tube. Weight: 7 lbs., 5 oz. Reintro. 1987 to 1993. AUTOMATIC-5, TRAP MODEL . . . . NiB $1277 Ex $965 Gd $777

12 ga. only. Same general specifications as Standard Model except has trap-style stock, 30-inch vent-rib bbl. F choke. Weight: 8.5 lbs. Disc. 1971.

MODEL B-80 GAS-OPERATED

AUTOMATIC . . . . NiB $699 Ex $577 Gd $400
Gauge: 12 or 20; 2.75-inch chamber. Four round magazine. Bbl.: 26-, 28- or 30-inch, any standard choke, vent-rib bbl. w/fixed chokes or Invector tubes. Weight: 6 lbs., 12 oz.-8 lbs., 1 oz. depending on ga. and bbl. Checkered pistol-grip stock and forearm. Made 1981 to 1988.

MODEL B-80 PLUS . . . . NiB $765 Ex $605 Gd $466
Same general specifications as Browning Model B-80 except chambered for 3-inch shotshells. Made in 1988.

Browning BPS
Waterfowl – Mossy Oak Shadow Grass

Browning BPS Stalker

MODEL B-80 SUPERLIGHT......NiB $689 Ex $544 Gd $432
Same as Standard Model except weighs 1 lb. less.
MODEL B-80 UPLAND SPECIAL ..... NiB $698 Ex $566 Gd $433
Gauge: 12 or 20. 22-inch vent-rib bbl. Invector choke tube system. 2.75-inch chambers. 42 inches overall. Weight: 5 lbs., 7 oz. (20 ga.); 6 lbs., 10 oz. (12 ga.). German nickel silver sight bead. Crossbolt safety. Checkered walnut straight-grip stock and forend. Disc. 1988.

BPS DEER HUNTER SPECIAL ......NiB $735 Ex $510 Gd $375
Same general specifications as Standard BPS model except has 20.5-inch bbl. w/adj. rifle-style sights. Solid scope mounting system. Checkered walnut stock w/sling swivel studs. Made from 1992 to date.

BPS GAME GUN TURKEY SPECIAL ..... NiB $498 Ex $380 Gd $295
Same general specifications as Standard BPS model except w/matte blue metal finish and satin-finished stock. Chambered for 12 ga. 3-inch only. 20.5-inch bbl. w/extra full invector choke system. Receiver drilled and tapped for scope. Made from 1992 to 2001.

BPS PIGEON GRADE ....NiB $699 Ex $449 Gd $354
Same general specifications as Standard BPS model except w/select grade walnut stock and gold-trimmed receiver. Available in 12 ga. from only w/26- or 28-inch vent-rib bbl. Made 1992 to 1998.

BPS PUMP INVECTOR STALKER
Same general specifications as BPS Pump Shotgun except in 10 and 12 ga. w/Invector choke system, 22-, 26-, 28- or 30-inch bbls.; matte blue metal finish w/matte black stock. Made from 1987 to date.
12 ga. model (3-inch) .... NiB $577 Ex $412 Gd $290
10- & 12 ga. model (3.5-inch)......... NiB $776 Ex $600 Gd $466

BPS PUMP SHOTGUN
Takedown. Gauges: 10, 12 (3.5-inch chamber); 12, 20 and .410 (3-inch) and 28 ga. chambered 2.75-inch. Bbls.: 22-, 24-, 26-, 28-, 30-, or 32-inch; fixed choke or Invector tubes. Weight: 7.5 lbs. (w/28-inch bbl.). Checkered select walnut pistol-grip stock and semi-beavertail forearm, recoil pad. Introduced in 1977 by Miroku.
Magnum Hunter .... NiB $690 Ex $589 Gd $477
Magnum Stalker...................... NiB $690 Ex $589 Gd $477
Magnum Camo .... NiB $779 Ex $644 Gd $546
Hunter.............................. NiB $690 Ex $589 Gd $477
Upland .... NiB $595 Ex $490 Gd $395
Stalker (26, 28- or 30-inch bbl.).......... NiB $566 Ex $477 Gd $375
Stalker 24-inch bbl .... NiB $566 Ex $477 Gd $375
Game Gun - Turkey Special.............. NiB $478 Ex $390 Gd $277
Game Gun - fully rifled bbl............. NiB $700 Ex $622 Gd $490
Hunter 20 ga. .... NiB $600 Ex $497 Gd $400
Upland 20 ga. .... NiB $600 Ex $497 Gd $400
Micro.............................. NiB $488 Ex $397 Gd $300
Hunter 28 ga. .... NiB $590 Ex $480 Gd $400

Bore Hunter .410.................... NiB $644 Ex $564 Gd $433
Buck Spec. (10 or 12 ga., 3.5-inch) .... NiB $700 Ex $566 Gd $470
Buck Spec. (12 or 20 ga.).............. NiB $455 Ex $330 Gd $229
Waterfowl
   (10 or 12 ga., 3.5-inch) ....NiB $700 Ex $566 Gd $470
w/fixed choke, deduct $75

BPS YOUTH AND LADIES' MODEL
Lightweight (6 lbs., 11 oz.) version of BPS Pump Shotgun in 20 ga. w/22-inch bbl. and floating vent rib, F choke (invector) tube. Made 1986 to 2002.
Standard Invector model (disc. 1994)...... NiB $390 Ex $288 Gd $195
Invector Plus model.................. NiB $444 Ex $300 Gd $244

BSA 10 SEMIAUTOMATIC SHOTGUN
Gas-operated short-stroke action. 10 ga.; 3.5-inch chamber. Five round magazine. Bbls.: 26-, 28-or 30-inches w/Invector tubes and vent rib. Weight: 10.5 lbs. Checkered select walnut buttstock and forend. Blued finish. Made 1993 to date. Note: Although intro. as the BSA 10, this model is now marketed as the Gold Series. See separate listing for pricing.

B-SS SIDE-BY-SIDE
Boxlock. Automatic ejectors. Non-selective single trigger (early production) or selective-single trigger (late production). Gauges: 12 or 20 w/3-inch chambers. Bbls.: 26-, 28-, or 30-inches; IC/M, M/F, or F/F chokes; matte solid rib. Weight: 7 to 7.5 lbs. Checkered straight-grip stock and beavertail forearm. Made from 1972 to 1988 by Miroku.
Standard model (early/NSST) .... NiB $1276 Ex $956 Gd $835
Standard model (late/SST) .... NiB $1276 Ex $956 Gd $835
Grade II (antique silver receiver) ...... NiB $3365 Ex $2990 Gd $2455
20 ga. models, add $650

B-SS Side-by-Side Sidelock
Same general specifications as B-SS boxlock models except sidelock version available in 26- or 28-inch bbl. lengths. 26-inch choked IC/M; 28-inch, M/F. Double triggers. Satin-grayed receiver engraved w/rosettes and scrolls. German nickel-silver sight bead. Weight: 6.25 lbs. to 6 lbs., 11 oz. 12 ga. made in 1983; 20 ga. Made in 1984. Disc. 1988.
12 ga. model ....NiB $3865 Ex $3077 Gd $2027
20 ga. model ....NiB $5277 Ex $3388 Gd $2879

B-SS S/S 20 GAUGE SPORTER...... NiB $3241 Ex $2766 Gd $1547
Same as standard B-SS 20 ga. except has selective single trigger, straight-grip stock. Introduced 1977. Disc. 1987.

BT-99 GRADE I SINGLE BBL. TRAP...... NiB $1087 Ex $782 Gd $554
Boxlock. Automatic ejector. 12 ga. only. 32- or 34-inch vent rib bbl., M, IM or F choke. Weight: About 8 lbs. Checkered pistol-grip stock and beavertail forearm, recoil pad. Made 1971 to 1976 by Miroku.

Browning B-SS 20 Gauge Sporter

Browning BT-99 Competition Trap

BT-99 MAX

Boxlock. 12 ga. only w/ejector selector and no safety. 32- or 34-inch ported bbl. w/high post vent rib. Checkered select walnut buttstock and finger-grooved forend w/high luster finish. Engraved receiver w/blued or stainless metal finish. Made 1995 to 1996.
Blued . . . . **NiB $1398 Ex $1110 Gd $790**
Stainless . . . . **NiB $1941 Ex $1590 Gd $1166**

BT-99 PLUS

Similar to the BT-99 Competition except w/Browning Recoil Reduction System. Made 1989 to 1995.
Grade I . . . . **NiB $1869 Ex $1275 Gd $1013**
Pigeon grade . . . . **NiB $1977 Ex $1276 Gd $912**
Signature grade . . . . **NiB $1877 Ex $1233 Gd $888**
Stainless model . . . . **NiB $2106 Ex $1433 Gd $1133**
Golden Clays . . . . **NiB $2926 Ex $2474 Gd $2310**

BT-99 PLUS MICRO . **NiB $1277 Ex $1088 Gd $872**

Same general specifications as BT-99 Plus except scaled down for smaller shooters. 30-inch bbl. w/adj. rib and Browning's recoil reducer system. Made 1991 to 1996.

BT-100 COMPETITION TRAP SPECIAL

Same as BT-99 except has super-high wide rib and standard Monte Carlo or fully adj. stock. Available w/adj. choke or Invector Plus tubes w/optional porting. Made 1976 to 2000.
Grade I w/fixed
  choke (disc. 1992) . . . . **NiB $1867 Ex $1233 Gd $994**
Grade I w/Invectors . . . . **NiB $2077 Ex $1156 Gd $1034**
Grade I stainless (disc. 1994) . . . . . **NiB $2366 Ex $1967 Gd $1256**
Grade I Pigeon Grade (disc. 1994) . . . **NiB $1650 Ex $1290 Gd $1072**

BT-100 SINGLE-SHOT TRAP

Similar to the BT-99 Max, except w/additional stock options and removable trigger group. Made 1995 to 2002.
Grade I blued . . . . **NiB $2044 Ex $1366 Gd $1065**
Stainless . . . . **NiB $2366 Ex $1998 Gd $1387**
Satin finish . . . . **NiB $1490 Ex $1266 Gd $853**
w/adj. comb, add **$150**
w/thumbhole stock, add **$350**
w/replacement trigger assembly, add **$550**
w/fixed choke, deduct **$100**

CITORI O/U HUNTING MODELS

Boxlock. Gauges: 12, 16 (disc. 1989), 20, 28 (disc. 1992) and .410 bore (disc. 1989). Bbl. lengths: 24-, 26-, 28-, or 30-inch w/vent rib. Chambered 2.75-, 3- or 3.5-inch mag. Chokes: IC/M, M/F (Fixed Chokes); Standard Invector, or Invector plus choke systems. Overall length ranges from 41-47 inches. 2.75-, 3- or 3-inch Mag. loads, depending on ga. Weight: 5.75 lbs. to 7 lbs. 13 oz. Single

selective, gold-plated trigger. Medium raised German nickel-silver sight bead. Checkered, rounded pistol-grip walnut stock w/beavertail forend. Invector Chokes and Invector Plus became standard in 1988 and 1995, respectively. Made from 1973 to date by Miroku.
Grade I (disc. 1994) . . . . **NiB $1076 Ex $792 Gd $566**
Grade I - 3.5-inch Mag.(1989 to date) . . **NiB $1076 Ex $792 Gd $566**
Grade II (disc. 1983) . . . . **NiB $1288 Ex $1079 Gd $721**
Grade III (1985-95) . . . . **NiB $2077 Ex $1266 Gd $1091**
Grade V (disc. 1984) . . . . **NiB $2888 Ex $2069 Gd $1243**
Grade VI (1985-95) . . . . **NiB $2888 Ex $2069 Gd $1277**
Sporting Hunter model
  (12 and 20 ga., 1998 to date) **NiB $1387 Ex $1176 Gd $700**
Satin Hunter model
  (12 ga. only, 1998 to date) . . **NiB $1266 Ex $1006 Gd $744**
W/o Invector choke system, deduct **$150**
For 3.5-inch mag., add **$120**
For disc. gauges (16, 28 and .410), add **15%**

CITORI LIGHTNING O/U MODELS

Same general specifications as the Citori Hunting models except w/classic Browning rounded pistol-grip stock. Made from 1988 to date by Miroku.
Grade I . . . . **NiB $1059 Ex $798 Gd $612**
Grade III . . . . **NiB $1969 Ex $1154 Gd $834**
Grade VI . . . . **NiB $3166 Ex $2054 Gd $1152**
Gran Lightning model . . . . **NiB $1998 Ex $1258 Gd $887**
Feather Model (alloy receiver) . . . . . . **NiB $1577 Ex $1159 Gd $1013**
Feather Combo model (2-bbl. set) . . . . **NiB $3500 Ex $2745 Gd $2388**
Privilege model (w/engraved sideplates) . . . . . . **NiB $4855 Ex $3966 Gd $2767**
Micro model, add **10%**
w/o Invector choke
  system, deduct **$250**
28 ga. and .410, add **$15%**

CITORI SKEET GUN

Same as Hunting model except has skeet-style stock and forearm, 26- or 28-inch bbls., both bored SK choke. Available w/either standard vent rib or special target-type, high-post, wide vent rib. Weight (w/26-inch bbls.): 12 ga., 8 lbs., 20 ga., 7 lbs. Made 1974 to date by Miroku.
Grade I . . . . **NiB $1390 Ex $1166 Gd $990**
Grade II . . . . **NiB $1690 Ex $1345 Gd $1125**
Grade III . . . . **NiB $1789 Ex $1433 Gd $1093**
Grade VI (disc. 1995) . . . . **NiB $2345 Ex $1765 Gd $1299**
Golden Clays . . . . **NiB $2866 Ex $1889 Gd $1465**
28 ga. and .410, add **15%**
Grade I, 3-bbl. set (disc. 1996) . . . . . . **NiB $2465 Ex $2079 Gd $1500**
Grade III, 3-bbl. set (disc. 1996) . . . . . **NiB $3577 Ex $2260 Gd $1545**
Grade VI, 3-bbl. set (disc. 1994) . . . . . **NiB $3781 Ex $2477 Gd $2053**

SHOTGUNS

Browning BT-100 Monte Carlo Stock

Browning BT-100 Competition Trap

Browning Citori Lightning

Browning Citori Gran Lightning

Browning Citori Skeet Gun

Golden Clays, 3-bbl. set (disc. 1995) . . . . . . NiB $4376 Ex $3069 Gd $2210
Grade I, 4-bbl. set . . . . NiB $3588 Ex $3066 Gd $2754
Grade III, 4-bbl. set . . . . NiB $4361 Ex $3276 Gd $2390
Grade VI, 4-bbl. set (disc. 1994) . . . . . NiB $4733 Ex $3489 Gd $2466
Golden Clays, 4-bbl. set (disc. 1995) . . . . . . NiB $5656 Ex $3892 Gd $2721

CITORI SPORTING CLAYS
Similar to the standard Citori Lightning model except Classic-style stock with rounded pistol-grip. 30-inch back-bored bbls. with Invector Plus tubes. Receiver with "Lightning Sporting Clays Edition" logo. Made from 1989 to date.
GTI model (disc. 1995) . . . . NiB $1167 Ex $1058 Gd $821
GTI Golden Clays model (1993-94) . . . . . NiB $2455 Ex $1749 Gd $1256
Lightning model (intro. 1989) . . . . NiB $1440 Ex $1102 Gd $866
Lightning Golden Clays (1993-98) . . . . . NiB $2736 Ex $1871 Gd $1319
Lightning Pigeon Grade (1993-94) . . . . NiB $1622 Ex $1188 Gd $887
Micro Citori Lightning model
   (w/low rib) . . . . NiB $1588 Ex $1266 Gd $1006
Special Sporting model (intro. 1989) . NiB $1590 Ex $1268 Gd $1010
Special Sporting
   Golden Clays (1993-98) . . . . NiB $3231 Ex $3110 Gd $2127
Special Sporting Pigeon Grade (1993-94) NiB $1454 Ex $1167 Gd $944
Ultra model
   (intro. 1995) . . . . NiB $1661 Ex $1288 Gd $937
Ultra Golden Clays (intro. 1995) . . . . . . NiB $2134 Ex $1822 Gd $1645
Model 325 (1993-94) . . . . NiB $1292 Ex $1188 Gd $900
Model 325 Golden Clays (1993-94) . . . . . NiB $2545 Ex $1889 Gd $1438

Model 425 Grade I (intro. 1995) . . . . . . NiB $1761 Ex $1216 Gd $1022
Model 425 Golden Clays (intro. 1995) . . . . . . NiB $2665 Ex $2144 Gd $1977
Model 425 WSSF (intro. 1995) . . . . . NiB $1896 Ex $1459 Gd $1256
Model 802 Sporter (ES) Extended
   Swing (intro. 1996) . . . . NiB $1488 Ex $1299 Gd $993
w/2 bbl. set, add $1000
w/adj. stock, add $250
w/high rib, add. $125
w/ported barrels, add $100

CITORI SUPERLIGHT O/U FIELD SHOTGUNS
Similar to the Citori Hunting model except w/straight-grip stock and Schnabel forend tip. Made by Miroku 1982 to date.
Grade I . . . . NiB $1067 Ex $843 Gd $625
Grade III . . . . NiB $2066 Ex $1590 Gd $1167
Grade V (disc. 1985) . . . . NiB $3132 Ex $2398 Gd $2034
Grade VI . . . . NiB $2876 Ex $2334 Gd $1655
w/o Invectors, deduct $300
28 ga. and .410, add 10%

CITORI TRAP GUN
Same as Hunting model except 12 ga. only, has Monte Carlo or fully adjustable stock and beavertail forend, trap-style recoil pad; 20- or 32-inch bbls.; M/F, IM/F, or F/F. Available with either standard vent rib or special target-type, high-post, wide vent rib. Weight: 8 lbs. Made from 1974 to 2001 by Miroku.

Browning Citori Superlight Field Shotgun

Browning Citori Trap

Browning Citori White Lightning Over/Under

Browning Citori Sporting Hunter Over/Under

Browning Gold Hunter

Browning Liége Over/Under Shotgun

SHOTGUNS

Grade I Trap . . . . NiB $1035 Ex $888 Gd $698
Grade I Trap Pigeon grade
  (disc. 1994) . . . . .NiB $1857 Ex $1589 Gd $1134
Grade I Trap Signature grade (disc. 1994) . . . . . . NiB $1756 Ex $1477 Gd $1234
Grade I Plus Trap (disc. 1994) . NiB $2878 Ex $2330 Gd $2099
Grade I Plus Trap
  w/ported bbls. (disc. 1994) . . . .NiB $1979 Ex $1488 Gd $1253
Grade I Plus Trap
  Combo (disc. 1994) . . . . . . .NiB $2773 Ex $2078 Gd $1760
Grade I Plus Trap
  Golden Clays (disc. 1994) . . . NiB $3176 Ex $2465 Gd $2200
Grade II w/HP rib (disc. 1984) . . . . . .NiB $1989 Ex $1423 Gd $1166
Grade III Trap. . . . . .NiB $1958 Ex $1688 Gd $1290
Grade V Trap (disc. 1984) . . . . . NiB $1890 Ex $1656 Gd $1388
Grade VI Trap (disc. 1994). . . . . NiB $2066 Ex $1879 Gd $1488

Grade VI Trap
  Golden Clays (disc. 1994) . .NiB $3000 Ex $2698 Gd $2365

CITORI UPLAND SPECIAL O/U SHOTGUN
A shortened version of the Hunting model fitted with 24-inch bbls. and
straight-grip stock.
12, 20 ga. models. . . . . NiB $1277 Ex $1097 Gd $900
16 ga. (disc. 1989) . . . . NiB $1426 Ex $1266 Gd $954
w/o Inv. Chokes, deduct $150

CITORI WHITE LIGHTNING O/U SHOTGUN
Similar to the standard Citori Lightning model except w/silver nitride
receiver w/scroll and rosette engraving. Satin wood finish w/round pistol grip. Made 1998 to 2001.
12. 20 ga. models. . . . . NiB $1769 Ex $1213 Gd $879
28 ga., .410 models (Intro. 2000). . . . . .NiB $1887 Ex $1369 Gd $1228

GRADING: **NiB** = New in Box   **Ex** = Excellent or NRA 95%   **Gd** = Good or NRA 68%   **453**

CITORI WHITE UPLAND SPECIAL...... NiB $1389 Ex $1168 Gd $879
Similar to the standard Citori Upland model except w/silver nitride receiver w/scroll and rosette engraving. Satin wood finish w/round pistol grip. Made 2000 to 2001.

CYNERY SERIES
Monolock hinge system. Gauges: 12, 20, 28 or .410 bore. Bbl. lengths: 26-, or 28-inch w/vent rib. Chambered 3-inch. Chokes: Invector Plus choke tubes. Overall length ranges from 43-45 inches. Weight: 5 to 6 lbs. Single selective, gold-plated trigger. Wood or composite stock. Silver nitride finish. Made from 2004 to date.
Field grade...................... NiB $2430 Ex $1810 Gd $930
Classic Field grade................ NiB $2360 Ex $1000 Gd $720
Euro Field grade................... NiB $2300 Ex $1500 Gd $760
Feather........................... NiB $2530 Ex $1655 Gd $960
Sporting (made 2004-2007)........ NiB $1900 Ex $1410 Gd $840

DOUBLE AUTOMATIC (STEEL RECEIVER)
Short recoil system. Takedown. 12 ga. only. Two round capacity. Bbls.: 26-, 28-, 30-inches; any standard choke. Checkered pistol-grip stock and forend. Weight: About 7.75 lbs. Made 1955 to 1961.
w/plain bbl.................... NiB $889 Ex $679 Gd $453
w/recessed-rib bbl.......... NiB $1167 Ex $1090 Gd $756

GOLD DEER HUNTER AUTOLOADING SHOTGUN
Similar to the Standard Gold Hunter model except chambered 12 ga. only. 22-inch bbl. W/rifled bore or smooth bore w/5-inch rifled invector tube. Cantilevered scope mount. Made 1997 to 2005.
w/standard finish .... NiB $1000 Ex $766 Gd $591
Field model (w/Mossy Oak finish)...... NiB $956 Ex $619 Gd $495

GOLD HUNTER SERIES
Self-cleaning, gas-operated, short-stroke action. Gauges: 10 or 12 (3.5-inch chamber); 12 or 20 (3-inch chamber). 26-, 28-, or 30-inch bbl. w/ Invector or Invector Plus choke tubes. Checkered walnut stock. Polished or matte black metal finish. Made 1990 to date.
Gold Hunter (Light 10 ga. 3.5-inch
 w/walnut stock) ....NiB $1499 Ex $1277 Gd $1108
Gold Hunter (12 ga. 3.5-inch)........ NiB $977 Ex $790 Gd $559
Gold Hunter (12 or 20 ga. 3-inch)....NiB $1067 Ex $880 Gd $670
Gold Hunter Classic model (12 or 20 ga., 3-inch)......NiB $921 Ex $787 Gd $600
Gold Hunter High Grade Classic
 (12 or 20 ga., 3-inch)......NiB $1690 Ex $1225 Gd $1098
Gold Deer Hunter
 (12 ga. w/22-inch bbl.).......NiB $1078 Ex $884 Gd $643
Gold Turkey Hunter Camo
 (12 ga. /24-inch bbl.).........NiB $987 Ex $699 Gd $534
Gold Waterfowl Hunter
 Camo (12 ga. w/24-inch bbl.)...NiB $987 Ex $699 Gd $534

GOLD STALKER SERIES
Self-cleaning, gas-operated, short-stroke action. Gauges: 10 or 12 (3.5-inch chamber); 12 or 20 (3-inch chamber). 26-, 28-, or 30-inch bbl. w/ Invector or Invector Plus choke tubes. Graphite/fiberglass composite stock. Polished or matte black finish. Made 1998 to 2007.

Gold Stalker Light (10 ga.,
 3.5-inch w/composite stock) NiB $1487 Ex $1269 Gd $1109
Gold Stalker (12 ga. 3.5-inch)....... NiB $1048 Ex $911 Gd $500
Gold Stalker (12 or 20 ga., 3-inch) ..... NiB $898 Ex $654 Gd $521
Gold Stalker Classic
 Model (21 or 20 ga., 3-inch) NiB $1754 Ex $1228 Gd $1067
Gold Deer Stalker
 (12 ga. w/22-inch bbl.).......NiB $855 Ex $529 Gd $380
Gold Turkey Stalker Camo
 (12 ga. w/24-inch bbl.)........NiB $799 Ex $482 Gd $355
Gold Waterfowl Stalker
 Camo (12 ga. w/24-inch bbl.)...NiB $943 Ex $667 Gd $543

Browning Over/Under
Gold Classic

GOLD SPORTING CLAYS SERIES
Similar to Gold Hunter Series except w/2.75-inch chamber and 28- or 30-inch ported bbl. w/Invector Plus chokes. Made 1996 to 2008.
Standard model .... NiB $1132 Ex $821 Gd $677
Sporting Clays (Youth or Ladies).....NiB $1677 Ex $1265 Gd $1071
Sporting Clays w/engraved nickel receiver.......NiB $1793 Ex $1277 Gd $1056

LIEGE O/U SHOTGUN (B26/27)
Boxlock. Automatic ejectors. Non-selective single trigger. 12 ga. only. Bbls.: 26.5-, 28-, or 30-inch; 2.75-inch chambers in 26.5- and 28-inch, 3-inch in 30-inch, IC/M, M/F, or F/F chokes; vent rib. Weight: 7 lbs., 4 oz.to 7 lbs., 14 oz., depending on bbls. Checkered pistol-grip stock and forearm. Made 1973 to 1975 by FN.
Liège (B-26 BAC production) .... NiB $1488 Ex $1161 Gd $988
Liège (B-27 FN prod.,
 Standard Game model)...... NiB $1488 Ex $1161 Gd $988
Deluxe Game model............. NiB $1522 Ex $1269 Gd $1043
Grand Delux Game model .... NiB $1687 Ex $1438 Gd $1210
Deluxe Skeet model .... NiB $1488 Ex $1161 Gd $988
Deluxe Trap model............... NiB $1488 Ex $1161 Gd $988
NRA Sporting................... NiB $1067 Ex $700 Gd $5254

LIGHT SPORTING 802ES ..... NiB $1476 Ex $1211 Gd $989
Over/under. Invector-plus choke tubes. 12 ga. only with 28-inch bbl. Weight: 7 lbs., 5 oz.

LIGHTNING SPORTING CLAYS
Similar to the standard Citori Lightning model except Classic-style stock with rounded pistol grip. 30-inch back-bored bbls. with Invector Plus tubes. Receiver with "Lightning Sporting Clays Edition" logo. Made 1989 to 1994.
Standard model .... NiB $1396 Ex $1178 Gd $909
Pigeon grade .... NiB $1378 Ex $1161 Gd $882

O/U CLASSIC .... NiB $2359 Ex $2091 Gd $1389
Gauge: 20, 2.75-inch chambers. 26-inch blued bbls. choked IC/M. Gold-plated, single selective trigger. Manual, top-tang-mounted safety. Engraved receiver. High grade, select American walnut straight-grip stock with Schnabel forend. Fine-line checkering with pearl borders. High-gloss finish. 5,000 issued in 1986; made in Japan, engraved in Belgium.

O/U GOLD CLASSIC .... NiB $6245 Ex $4890 Gd $3179
Same general specifications as Over/Under Classic except more elaborate engravings, enhanced in gold, including profile of John M. Browning. Fine oil finish. 500 issued; made in 1986 in Belgium.

RECOILLESS TRAP SHOTGUN
The action and bbl. are driven forward when firing to achieve 72 percent less recoil. 12 ga, 2.75-inch chamber. 30-inch bbl. with Invector Plus tubes; adjustable vent rib. 51.63 inches overall. Weight: 9 lbs. Adj. checkered walnut buttstock and forend. Blued finish. Made from 1993 to 1996.Standard model NiB $1088 Ex $865 Gd $644
Micro model (27-inch bbl.) .... NiB $1088 Ex $865 Gd $644
Signature model (27-inch bbl.) .... NiB $1088 Ex $865 Gd $644

SUPERPOSED BICENTENNIAL
COMMEMORATIVE .... NiB $13,650 Ex $12,790 Gd $9779
Special limited edition issued to commemorate U.S. Bicentennial. 51 guns, one for each state in the Union plus one for Washington, D.C. Receiver with sideplates has engraved and gold-inlaid hunter and wild turkey on right side, U.S. flag and bald eagle on left side, together with state markings inlaid in gold, on blued background. Checkered straight-grip stock and Schnabel-style forearm of highly- figured American walnut. Velvet-lined wood presentation case. Made in 1976

Browning Superposed Broadway 12 Trap

Browning Superposed Grade I Lightning

Left Side

Right Side

Browning Superposed Bicentennial

Browning Superposed Grade IV Diana (Postwar)

Browning Superposed Grade V Midas (Postwar)

SHOTGUNS

by FN. Value shown is for gun in new, unfired condition. See illustration next page.

SUPERPOSED
BROADWAY 12 TRAP . . . . . . NiB $2084 Ex $1766 Gd $1460
Same as Standard Trap Gun except has 30- or 32-inch bbls. with wider Broadway rib. Disc. 1976.

SUPERPOSED SHOTGUNS, HUNTING MODELS
Over/under boxlock. Selective automatic ejectors. Selective single trigger; earlier models (worth 25% less) supplied w/double triggers, twin selective triggers or non-selective single trigger. Gauges: 12, 20 (intro. 1949, 3-inch chambers in later production), 28, .410 (latter two ga. intro. 1960). Bbls.: 26.5-, 28-, 30-, 32-inch, raised matted or vent rib, prewar Lightning Model made w/ribbed bbl., postwar version supplied only w/vent rib; any combination of standard chokes. Weight (w/26.5-inch vent-rib bbls.): Standard 12, 7 lbs., 11 oz., Lightning 12, 7 lbs., 6 oz.; Standard 20, 6 lbs., 8 oz.; Lightning 20, 6 lbs., 4 oz.; Lightning 28, 6 lbs., 7 oz.; Lightning .410, 6 lbs., 10 oz. Checkered pistol-grip stock/forearm.

Higher grades (Pigeon, Pointer, Diana, Midas, Grade VI) differ from standard Grade I models in overall quality, engraving, wood and checkering; otherwise, specifications are the same. Midas Grade and Grade VI guns are richly gold inlaid. Made by FN 1928-1976. Prewar models may be considered as disc. in 1940 when Belgium was occupied by Germany. Grade VI offered 1955-1960. Pointer Grade disc. in 1966, Grade I Standard in 1973, Pigeon Grade in 1974. Lightning Grade I, Diana and Midas Grades were not offered after 1976.

Grade I standard weight . . . . . NiB $2390	Ex $1979	Gd $1749
Grade I Lightning . . . . NiB $2209	Ex $1867	Gd $1428
Grade I Lightning, pre-war,		
matted bbl., no rib . . . . NiB $2979	Ex $2255	Gd $1217
Grade II - Pigeon . . . . NiB $4400	Ex $2790	Gd $1966
Grade III - Pointer . . . . NiB $5000	Ex $4155	Gd $3860
Grade IV - Diana . . . . NiB $8250	Ex $6300	Gd $3760
Grade V - Midas. . . . . NiB $7300	Ex $5012	Gd $3690
Grade VI . . . . NiB $10,000	Ex $8292	Gd $6659
For 20 ga., add.			20%
For 28 ga., add.			75%
For .410, add			50%

Values shown are for models w/vent. rib.
w/raised matted rib, deduct 10%

SUPERPOSED LIGHTNING AND SUPERLIGHT MODELS (REISSUE B-25)
Reissue of popular 12-and 20-ga. Superposed shotguns. Lightning

**Browning Superposed Ltd.
Pintail Duck Issue**

models available in 26.5- and 28-inch bbl. lengths w/2.75- or 3-inch chambering, full pistol grip. Superlight models available in 26.5-inch bbl. lengths w/2.75-inch chambering only, and straight-grip stock w/ Schnabel forend. Both have hand-engraved receivers, fine-line checkering, gold-plated single selective trigger, automatic selective ejectors, manual safety. Weight: 6 to 7.5 lbs. Reintroduced 1985.

Grade I, Standard . . . . NiB $2377 Ex $1898 Gd $1344
Grade II, Pigeon . . . . NiB $5696 Ex $3863 Gd $3000
Grade III, Pointer . . . . NiB $8879 Ex $5770 Gd $3760
Grade IV, Diana . . . . NiB $8009 Ex $5679 Gd $3698
Grade V, Midas . . . . .NiB $13,750 Ex $11,299 Gd $10,650
w/extra bbls., add 50%

SUPERPOSED MAGNUM. . . . .NiB $1988 Ex $1572 Gd $1189
Same as Grade I except chambered for 12-ga. 3-inch shells, 30-inch vent-rib bbls., stock w/recoil pad. Weight: About 8.25 lbs. Disc. 1976.

**SUPERPOSED BLACK
DUCK LTD. ISSUE** . . . . NiB $10,390 Ex $8977 Gd $5640
Gauge: 12. Superposed Lightning action. 28-inch vent-rib bbls. Choked M/F. 2.75-inch chambers. Weight: 7 lbs., 6 oz. Gold-inlaid receiver and trigger guard engraved w/black duck scenes. Gold-plated, single selective trigger. Top-tang mounted manual safety. Automatic, selective ejectors. Front and center ivory sights. High-grade, hand-checkered, hand-oiled select walnut stock and forend. 500 issued in 1983.

**SUPERPOSED MALLARD
DUCK LTD. ISSUE** . . . . NiB $10,768 Ex $7322 Gd $5680
Same general specifications as Ltd. Black Duck issue except mallard duck scenes engraved on receiver and trigger guard, dark French walnut stock w/rounded pistol-grip. 500 issued in 1981.

**SUPERPOSED PINTAIL
DUCK LTD. ISSUE** . . . . NiB $10,766 Ex $7298 Gd $5660
Same general specifications as Ltd. Black Duck issue except pintail duck scenes engraved on receiver and trigger guard. Stock is of dark French walnut w/rounded pistol-grip. 500 issued in 1982.

SUPERPOSED, PRESENTATION GRADES
Custom versions of Super-Light, Lightning Hunting, Trap and Skeet Models, w/same general specifications as those of standard guns, but of higher overall quality. The four Presentation grades differ in receiver finish (grayed or blued), engraving gold inlays, wood and checkering. Presentation 4 has side-plates. Made by FN, these models were Intro. in 1977.

Presentation 1 . . . . NiB $3475 Ex $2770 Gd $12967
Presentation 1, gold-inlaid . . . . .NiB $4889 Ex $3388 Gd $2491
Presentation 2 . . . . NiB $4956 Ex $3860 Gd $2709
Presentation 2, gold-inlaid . . . . .NiB $7900 Ex $5275 Gd $4100
Presentation 3, gold-inlaid . . . . .NiB $9975 Ex $7866 Gd $6077
Presentation 4 . . . . NiB $9106 Ex $7320 Gd $5863
Presentation 4, gold-inlaid . . . . . NiB $13,675 Ex $11,960 Gd $9989

SUPERPOSED SKEET GUNS, GRADE I
Same as standard Lightning 12, 20, 28 and .410 Hunting models, except has skeet-style stock and forearm, 26.5- or 28-inch vent-rib bbls. w/SK choke. Available also in All Gauge Skeet Set: Lightning 12 w/one removable forearm and three extra sets of bbls. in 20, 28 and .410 ga. in fitted luggage case. Disc.

1976. (For higher grades see listings for comparable Hunting models)
12 or 20 ga. . . . . NiB $2170 Ex $1690 Gd $1167
28 ga. or .410 . . . . NiB $2566 Ex $2278 Gd $1489
Combo skeet set (all gauges) . . . . .NiB $6549 Ex $6000 Gd $5489

**SUPERPOSED SUPER
LIGHT MODEL**. . . . . NiB $7101 Ex $4877 Gd $4128
Ultralight field gun version of Standard Lightning Model has classic straight-grip stock and slimmer forearm. Available only in 12 and 20 gauges (2.75-inch chambers), w/26.5-inch vent-rib bbls. Weight: 6.5 lbs., (12 ga.); 6 lbs., (20 ga.). Made 1967 to 1976.

SUPERPOSED TRAP GUN . . . . . NiB $5321 Ex $3867 Gd $2998
Same as Grade I except has trap-style stock, beavertail forearm, 30-inch vent-rib bbls., 12 ga. only. Disc. 1976. (For higher grades see listings for comparable hunting models)

TWELVETTE DOUBLE AUTOMATIC
Lightweight version of Double Automatic w/same general specifications except aluminum receiver. Bbl. w/plain matted top or vent rib. Weight: 6.75 to 7 lbs., depending on bbl. Receiver is finished in black w/gold engraving; 1956-1961 receivers were also anodized in gray, brown and green w/silver engraving. Made 1955 to 1971
w/plain bbl. . . . . .NiB $900 Ex $600 Gd $380
w/vent. rib bbl.. . . . . .NiB $1000 Ex $750 Gd $476

CZ (CESKA ZBROJOVKA), INC. — Uhersky Brod, Czech Republic

Imported by CZ-USA, Kansas City, KS.

581 SOLO . . . . .NiB $730 Ex $760 Gd $360
O/U boxlock action with double triggers and ejectors. 12 ga. 2-3/4-inch chambers. Disc. 1995, resumed 1999 to 2005.

ARMARILLO. . . . . .NiB $625 Ex $430 Gd $210
Similar to Durago S/S, double triggers. Made 2005 to 2006.

BOBWHITE . . . . .NiB $778 Ex $500 Gd $260
S/S hammerless boxlock action with double trigger and extractors. 12, 16 or 20 ga. 3-inch chambers. Bbl.: 26 or 28 in. Finish: case hardened. Stock: straight English grip, walnut. Weight: 6 to 7 lbs. Made 2005 to date.

CANVASBACK (103 D) . . . . .NiB $670 Ex $460 Gd $275
O/U boxlock action with single trigger and extractors. 12, 20 ga. 3-inch chambers. Bbl.: 26 or 28 inches, vent. rib, 5 choke tubes, black chrome finish, light engraving. Stock: pistol grip, checkered walnut. Weight: 6.3 to 7.5 lbs. Made 2005 to 2013.
Gold (gold inlays). . . . . .NiB $830 Ex $480 Gd $300
Gold (28 or .410) . . . . add 20%

DURANGO . . . . .NiB $725 Ex $530 Gd $245
S/S hammerless boxlock action with single trigger and extractors. 12 or 20 ga. 3-inch chambers. Bbl.: 20 in. Stock: round knob pistol grip, walnut. Weight: 6 to 6.7 lbs. Made 2005 to 2006.

HAMMER COACH . . . . .NiB $778 Ex $500 Gd $260
S/S boxlock action with double trigger, exposed hammers and extractors. 12 ga. 3-inch chambers. Bbl.: 20 in., fixed choke. Finish: case
hardened. Stock: pistol grip. Weight: 6.7 lbs. Made 2006 to date.
Classic (12, 30-in. bbl.,
  2010-2014). . . . . NiB $963 Ex $580 Gd $300

LIMITED EDITION . . . . NiB $1980 Ex $1520 Gd $800
O/U w/ engraved boxlock action with single gold trigger and ejectors.
12 ga. 3-inch chambers. Bbl.: 28 in., vent. rib. Stock: Cicassin walnut.
50 mfg. Made 2006 to 2009.

MALLARD . . . . .NiB $583 Ex $360 Gd $230
O/U boxlock action with dual triggers and extractors. 12 or 20 ga.
3-inch chambers. Bbl.: 28 inches, vent. rib, 5 choke tubes, coin finish
receiver, black chrom bbl. Stock: prince of whales grip, Turkish walnut. Weight: 6.5 to 7.5 lbs. Made 2005 to date.

REDHEAD PREMIER . . . . .NiB $959 Ex $630 Gd $400
O/U boxlock action with single trigger and ejectors. 12 or 20 ga.
3-inch chambers. Bbl.: 26 or 28 inches, vent. rib, 5 choke tubes,
black chrome bbl. coin finish receiver. Stock: pistol grip, checkered
walnut. Weight: 6.7 to 7.9 lbs. Made 2005 to date.
Mini (28 or .410, 2005-2013). . . .NiB $800 Ex $630 Gd $400
Target (12 ga., 30-in. bbl.) . . . . .NiB $1389 Ex $830 Gd $440

RINGNECK. . . . . .NiB $1022 Ex $680 Gd $360
S/S boxlock action w/ engraved sideplates, single trigger and extractors. 12, 16 or 20 ga. 3-inch chambers. Bbl.: 26 or 28 inches, 5 choke
tubes. Finish: black chrome bbl., case hardened receiver. Stock: pistol
grip, checkered walnut. Weight: 6.3 to 7.1 lbs. Made 2005 to date.
16 ga., add. $200
Mini (28 or .410). . . . . .NiB $1229 Ex $800 Gd $410
Target (12 ga., 30-in. bbl.) . . . . .NiB $1298 Ex $810 Gd $430
Deluxe Custom (20 ga., 28-in. bbl.,
  2006-2012) . . . . .NiB $1700 Ex $1260 Gd $630
Competition (12 ga., 28-in. ported bbl.,
  2010-2011) . . . . .NiB $2730 Ex $1830 Gd $1000

SPORTER STANDARD . . . . . . .NiB $3122 Ex $1630 Gd $800
O/U boxlock action with single trigger and ejectors. 12 ga. 3-inch
chambers. Bbl.: 30 or 32 inches, vent. rib, 6 extended choke tubes,
black chrome bbl., matte black receiver. Stock: pistol grip w/ palm
swell, adj. comb, Grade II Turkish walnut. Weight: 8.7 lbs. Made 2008
to date.

WOODCOCK DELUXE . . . . .NiB $1080 Ex $730 Gd $400
O/U boxlock action with single trigger and ejectors. 12 or 20 ga.
3-inch chambers. Bbl.: 26 or 28 inches, vent. rib, 5 choke tubes,
black chrome bbl. case hardened receiver w/ sideplates. Stock: prince
of whales pistol grip, schnabel forend, walnut. Weight: 6.8 to 7.8 lbs.
Made 2005 to 2010.
Custom (20, 2006-2010). . . . . .NiB $1900 Ex $1330 Gd $710
Target (12 ga., 30-in. brl.) . . . . . .NiB $1389 Ex $830 Gd $440

CENTURY ARMS formerly CENTURY INTERNATIONAL ARMS, INC. — St. Albans, VT, and Boca Raton, FL

ARTHEMIS . . . . .NiB $522 Ex $390 Gd $259
O/U boxlock action with double triggers and extractors. 12, 20, 28 ga.
or .410 bore. 3-inch chambers. 28-inch bbls. Single set trigger, extractors. Checkered wood stock and forearm. Weight: 5.3 to 7.4 lbs. Mfg.
in Turkey by Khan. Disc.

ARTHEMIS O/U . . . . .NiB $475 Ex $310 Gd $245
Gauge: 12, 20, 28, .410. Bbl.: 28 inches, vent. rib, 3-inch chamber.
Single selective trigger, extractors. Stock: Checkered walnut. Weight:
5.3 to 7.4 lbs. Mfg. by PAR. Imported from 2002 to 2009.

CATAMOUNT FURY I . . . . NiB $675 Ex $430 Gd $275
Gas-operated adj. piston, semi-auto w/ detchable 5- or 10-rnd. magazine. Gauge: 12. Bbl.: 20.1 inches, choke tubes. Stock: standard style
checkered synthetic. Mfg. in China. Imported 2013 to date.

CATAMOUNT FURY II . . . . NiB $695 Ex $450 Gd $295
Similar specs as Fury I except synthetic thumbhole stock. Mfg. in China.
Imported 2013 to date.

COACH MODEL. . . . . NiB $325 Ex $200 Gd $140
Side-by-side. Gauge: 12, 20, .410. Bbl.: 20 inches, exposed hammers,
double trigger. Stock: Checkered walnut. Sling swivels. Mfg. in China.

MODEL IJ2. . . . . .NiB $220 Ex $155 Gd $100
Slide-action. Gauge: 12; 2.75-inch or 3-inch chamber. Bbl.: 19 inches,
fixed choke. Ghost ring rear or fiber optic sights. Weight: 7 lbs. Mfg.
in China.

PHANTOM. . . . . .NiB $295 Ex $240 Gd $190
Semi-auto. Gauge: 12. 3-inch chamber. Bbl.: 24, 26 or 28 inches; vent. rib.
Three choke tubes. Stock: Black synthetic. Mfg. in Turkey. Disc.

PW87. .NiB $390 Ex $325 Gd $160
Repro. of Winchester 1887 lever-action. Gauge: 12. 2-3/4-in. chamber.
Bbl.: 19 inches w/ brass bead M choke. Stock: smooth hardwood. Mfg. in
China. Imported from 2013 to date.

SAS-12. . . . . .NiB $250 Ex $185 Gd $100
Semi-auto. Gauge: 12. 2.75-inch chamber. Bbl.: 22 or 23.5 inches.
Detachable 3- or 5-round mag.
Ghost ring rear sight, add $25

ULTRA 87 . . . . .NiB $255 Ex $180 Gd $110
Slide-action. Gauge: 12. Bbl.: 19 inches. Optional heat shield and pistol
grip. Side folding stock. Includes extra 28-inch bbl. Weight: 8.2 lbs.

SHOTGUNS

CHURCHILL — Italy and Spain.
*Imported by Ellett Brothers, Inc., Chapin, SC; previously by Kassnar
Imports, Inc., Harrisburg, PA*

AUTOMATIC SHOTGUN
Gas-operated. Gauge: 12, 2.75- or 3-inch chambers. Five round
magazine w/cutoff. Bbl.: 24-, 25-, 26-, 28-inch w/ICT choke tubes.
Checkered walnut stock w/satin finish. Imported from 1990 to 1994.
Standard model . . . . .NiB $657 Ex $571 Gd $455
Turkey model . . . . .NiB $697 Ex $586 Gd $434

MONARCH O/U SHOTGUN
Hammerless, takedown w/engraved receiver. Selective single or double
triggers. Gauges: 12, 20, 28, .410; 3-inch chambers. Bbls.: 25- or
26-inch (IC/M); 28-inch (M/F). Weight: 6.5-7.5 lbs. Checkered European
walnut buttstock and forend. Made in Italy from 1986 to 1993.
w/double triggers . . . .

Churchill Automatic Shotgun

Churchill Windsor Grade Side-by-Side Shotgun

Churchill Windsor Grade Flyweight Shotgun

E.J. Churchill Premiere

NiB $490 Ex $378 Gd $225
w/single trigger. . . . . **NiB $588 Ex $466 Gd $321**

REGENT O/U SHOTGUNS
Gauges: 12 or 20; 2.75-inch chambers. 27-inch bbls. w/interchangeable choke tubes and wide vent rib. Single selective trigger, selective automatic ejectors. Checkered pistol-grip stock in fancy walnut. Imported from Italy 1984 to 1988 and 1990 to 1994.
Regent V(disc. 1988) . . . . **NiB $987 Ex $680 Gd $590**
Regent VII w/sideplates (disc. 1994) . . . . . . **NiB $873 Ex $779 Gd $544**

REGENT SKEET. . . . . **NiB $873 Ex $779 Gd $544**
12 or 20 ga. w/2.75-inch chambers. Selective automatic ejectors, single-selective trigger. 26-inch over/under bbls. w/vent rib. Weight: 7 lbs. Made in Italy from 1984 to 1988.

REGENT TRAP . . . . **NiB $876 Ex $654 Gd $490**
12-ga. competition shotgun w/2.75-inch chambers. 30-inch over/under bbls. choked IM/F, vent side ribs. Weight: 8 lbs. Selective automatic ejectors, single selective trigger. Checkered Monte Carlo stock w/Supercushion recoil pad. Made in Italy 1984 to 1988.

SPORTING CLAYS O/U . . . . **NiB $945 Ex $800 Gd $575**
Same general specifications as Windsor IV except in 12 ga. only w/28-inch ported bbls. and choke tubes. Selective automatic ejectors. Weight: 7.5 lbs. Made from 1992 to 1994.

WINDSOR O/U SHOTGUNS
Hammerless, boxlock w/engraved receiver, selective single trigger. Extractors or ejectors. Gauges: 12, 20, 28 or .410; 3-inch chambers. Bbls.: 24 to 30 inches w/fixed chokes or choke tubes. Weight: 6 lbs., 3 oz. (Flyweight) to 7 lbs., 10 oz. (12 ga.). Checkered straight (Flyweight) or pistol-grip stock and forend of European walnut. Imported from Italy 1984 to 1993.
Windsor III w/fixed chokes . . . . **NiB $668 Ex $544 Gd $455**
Windsor III w/choke tubes . . . . **NiB $798 Ex $670 Gd $555**
Windsor IV w/fixed chokes (disc. 1993) . . . . . . **NiB $768 Ex $659 Gd $455**
Windsor IV w/choke tubes . . . . **NiB $833 Ex $754 Gd $500**

WINDSOR SIDE-BY-SIDE SHOTGUNS
Boxlock action w/double triggers, ejectors or extractors and automatic safety. Gauges: 10, (3.5-inch chambers); 12, 20, 28, .410 (3-inch chambers), 16 (2.75-inch chambers). Bbls.: 23 to 32 inches w/various fixed choke or choke tube combinations. Weight: 5 lbs., 12 oz. (Flyweight) to 11.5 lbs. (10 ga.). European walnut buttstock and forend. Imported from Spain 1984 to 1990.
Windsor I 10 ga. . . . . **NiB $569 Ex $400 Gd $327**
Windsor I 12 ga. thru .410. . . . . **NiB $569 Ex $400 Gd $327**
Windsor II 12 or 20 ga. . . . . **NiB $569 Ex $400 Gd $327**
Windsor VI 12 or 20 ga. . . . . **NiB $569 Ex $400 Gd $327**

E.J. CHURCHILL, LTD. —
Surrey (previously London), England
The E.J. Churchill shotguns listed below are no longer imported.

PREMIERE QUALITY HAMMERLESS DOUBLE
Sidelock. Automatic ejectors. Double triggers or selective single trigger. Gauges: 12, 16, 20, 28. Bbls.: 25-, 28- 30-, 32-inch; any degree of boring. Weight: 5-8 lbs. depending on ga. and bbl. length. Checkered stock and forend, straight or pistol-grip.
w/double triggers . . . . **NiB $46,775 Ex $36,950 Gd $30,000**
w/single selective trigger, add **$10%**

FIELD MODEL HAMMERLESS DOUBLE
Sidelock Hammerless ejector gun w/same general specifications as Premiere Model but of lower quality.
w/double triggers . . . . **NiB $10,667 Ex $9260 Gd $8110**
w/single selective trigger, add **10%**

PREMIERE QUALITY O/U SHOTGUN

Sidelock. Automatic ejectors. Double triggers or selective single trigger. Gauges: 12, 16, 20, 28. Bbls.: 25-, 28-, 30-, 32-inch, any degree of boring. Weight: 5-8 lbs. depending on ga. and bbl. length. Checkered stock and forend, straight or pistol-grip.

w/double triggers . . . . **NiB $55,000 Ex $38,000 Gd $25,000**
w/selective single trigger, add **10%**
w/raised vent. rib, add **15%**

UTILITY MODEL HAMMERLESS DOUBLE-BARREL

Anson & Deeley boxlock action. Double triggers or single trigger. Gauges: 12, 16, 20, 28, .410. Bbls.: 25-, 28-, 30-, 32-inch, any degree of boring. Weight: 4.5-8 lbs. depending on ga. and bbl. length. Checkered stock and forend, straight or pistol-grip.

w/double triggers . . . . **NiB $7340 Ex $6077 Gd $4340**
w/single selective trigger, add **10%**

XXV PREMIERE

HAMMERLESS DOUBLE . NiB $47,000 Ex $40,000 Gd $35,000
Sidelock. Assisted opening. Automatic ejectors. Double triggers. Gauges: 12, 20. 25-inch bbls. w/narrow, quick-sighting rib; any standard choke combination. English-style straight-grip stock and forearm, checkered.

XXV IMPERIAL . . . . NiB $14,775 Ex $12,700 Gd $9775
Similar to XXV Premiere but no assisted opening feature.

XXV HERCULES . . . . .NiB $10,750 Ex $9450 Gd $6680
Boxlock, otherwise specifications same as for XXV Premiere.

XXV REGAL . . . . NiB $6277 Ex $4988 Gd $3500
Similar to XXV Hercules but w/o assisted opening feature. Gauges: 12, 20, 28, .410.

CLASSIC DOUBLES — Tochigi, Japan
Imported by Classic Doubles International, St. Louis, MO, and previously by Olin as Winchester Models 101 and 23.

MODEL 101 O/U SHOTGUN

Boxlock. Engraved receiver w/single selective trigger, auto ejectors and combination bbl. selector and safety. Gauges: 12, 20, 28 or .410, 2.75-, 3-inch chambers, 25.5- 28- or 30-inch vent-rib bbls. Weight: 6.25 – 7.75 lbs. Checkered French walnut stock. Imported from 1987 to 1990.

Classic I Field. . . . . NiB $1590 Ex $1488 Gd $1033
Classic II Field . . . . NiB $1879 Ex $1540 Gd $1133
Classic Sporter . . . . NiB $2066 Ex $1788 Gd $1233
Classic Sporter combo. . . . . NiB $3475 Ex $2870 Gd $2035
Classic Trap . . . . NiB $1380 Ex $1166 Gd $990
Classic Trap Single . . . . NiB $1435 Ex $1140 Gd $1089
Classic Trap combo. . . . . NiB $2560 Ex $2053 Gd $1498
Classic Skeet . . . . NiB $1765 Ex $1600 Gd $1179
Classic Skeet 2-bbl. set . . . . NiB $2867 Ex $2374 Gd $1790
Classic Skeet 4-bbl. set . . . . NiB $4488 Ex $3972 Gd $2633
ClassicWaterfowler . . . . NiB $1554 Ex $1266 Gd $1031
For Grade II (28 ga.), add $900
For Grade II (.410), add. $300

MODEL 201 SIDE-BY-SIDE SHOTGUN

Boxlock. Single selective trigger, automatic safety, selective ejectors. Gauges: 12 or 20; 3-inch chambers. 26- or 28-inch vent-rib bbl., fixed chokes or internal tubes. Weight: 6 to 7 lbs. Checkered French walnut stock and forearm. Imported 1987 to 1990.

Field model . . . . NiB $2687 Ex $1490 Gd $1264
Skeet model . . . . NiB $2687 Ex $1490 Gd $1264
With internal choke tubes, add $100

MODEL 201

SMALL BORE SET . . . . NiB $4650 Ex $3751 Gd $2975
Same general specifications as the Classic Model 201 except w/ smaller frame, in 28 ga. (IC/M) and .410 (F/M). Weight: 6-6.5 lbs. Imported from 1987 to 1990.

COGSWELL & HARRISON, LTD. —
London, England
AMBASSADOR HAMMERLESS

DOUBLE-BARREL SHOTGUN . . . . . .NiB $6056 Ex $4533 Gd $3718
Boxlock. Sideplates w/game scene or rose scroll engraving. Automatic ejectors. Double triggers. Gauges: 12, 16, 20. Bbls.: 26-28-, 30-inch; any choke combination. Checkered straight-grip stock and forearm. Disc.

AVANT TOUT SERIES HAMMERLESS

DOUBLE-BARREL SHOTGUNS . . . . . . .NiB $2688 Ex $2133 Gd $1954
Boxlock. Sideplates (except Avant Tout III Grade). Automatic ejectors. Double triggers or single trigger (selective or non-selective). Gauges: 12, 16, 20. Bbls.: 25-, 27.5-, 30-inch, any choke combination. Checkered stock and forend, straight grip standard. Made in three models (Avant Tout I or Konor, Avant Tout II or Sandhurst. Avant Tout III or Rex) which differ chiefly in overall quality of engraving, grade of wood, checkering, etc. General specifications are the same. Disc.

Avant Tout I. . . . . NiB $3544 Ex $3160 Gd $2477
Avant Tout II. . . . . NiB $2983 Ex $2786 Gd $1966
Avant Tout III. . . . . NiB $2254 Ex $2090 Gd $1760
w/non-selective single trigger, add $250
w/selective single trigger, add $425

BEST QUALITY HAMMERLESS
SIDELOCK DOUBLE-BARREL SHOTGUN

Hand-detachable locks. Automatic ejectors. Double triggers or single trigger (selective or non-selective). Gauges: 12, 16, 20. Bbls.: 25-, 26-, 28-, 30-inch, any choke combination. Checkered stock and forend, straight grip standard.

Victor model . . . . NiB $6570 Ex $5461 Gd $4130
Primic model (disc.). . . . . NiB $6640 Ex $5521 Gd $4200
w/non-selective single trigger, add $250
w/selective single trigger, add $450

HUNTIC MODEL HAMMERLESS DOUBLE

Sidelock. Automatic ejectors. Double triggers or single trigger (selective or non-selective). Gauges: 12, 16, 20. Bbls.: 25-, 27.5-, 30-inch; any choke combination. Checkered stock and forend, straight grip standard. Disc.

w/double triggers. . . . . NiB $4077 Ex $2986 Gd $1769
w/non-selective single trigger, add $250
w/selective single trigger, add. $400

MARKOR HAMMERLESS DOUBLE

Boxlock. Non-ejector or ejector. Double triggers. Gauges: 12, 16, 20. Bbls.: 27.5 or 30-inch; any choke combination. Checkered stock and forend, straight grip standard. Disc.

Non-ejector . . . . NiB $1784 Ex $1599 Gd $1188
Ejector model, add 20%

REGENCY HAMMERLESS DOUBLE . . . . NiB $4395 Ex $3667 Gd $2971

Anson & Deeley boxlock action. Automatic ejectors. Double triggers. Gauges: 12, 16, 20. Bbls.: 26-, 28-, 30-inch, any choke combination. Checkered straight-grip stock and forearm. Introduced in 1970 to commemorate the firm's bicentennial, this model has deep scroll engraving and the name "Regency" inlaid in gold on the rib. Disc.

SHOTGUNS

COLT'S MFG. CO., INC. — Hartford, Connecticut

Auto Shotguns were made by Franchi and are similar to corresponding models of that manufacturer.

AUTO SHOTGUN — ULTRA LIGHT STANDARD

Recoil-operated. Takedown. Alloy receiver. Gauges: 12, 20. Mag. holds 4 rounds. Bbls.: plain, solid or vent rib, chrome-lined; 26-inch IC or M choke, 28-inch M or F choke, 30-inch F choke, 32-inch F choke. Weight: 12 ga., about 6.25 lbs. Checkered pistol-grip stock and forearm. Made 1964 to 1966.

w/plain bbl. . . . . NiB $400 Ex $297 Gd $200
w/solid rib bbl.. . . . . NiB $450 Ex $344 Gd $250
w/vent. rib bbl. . . . . NiB $450 Ex $344 Gd $250

AUTO SHOTGUN — MAGNUM CUSTOM

Same as Magnum except has engraved receiver, select walnut stock and forearm. Made 1964 to 66.

w/Solid-rib bbl. . . . . NiB $544 Ex $422 Gd $300
w/vent. rib bbl.. . . . . NiB $600 Ex $470 Gd $351

AUTO SHOTGUN — ULTRA LIGHT CUSTOM

Same as Standard Auto except has engraved receiver, select walnut stock and forearm. Made 1964 to 1966.

w/solid-rib bbl.. . . . . NiB $544 Ex $470 Gd $366
w/vent. rib bbl.. . . . . NiB $600 Ex $495 Gd $379

AUTO SHOTGUN — MAGNUM

Same as Standard Auto except steel receiver, chambered for 3-inch Magnum shells, 30- and 32-inch bbls. in 12 ga., 28-inch in 20 ga. Weight: 12 ga., about 8.25 lbs. Made 1964 to 1966.

w/plain bbl. . . . . NiB $552 Ex $447 Gd $332
w/solid-rib bbl. . . . . NiB $622 Ex $470 Gd $356
w/vent. rib bbl. . . . . NiB $644 Ex $500 Gd $371

CUSTOM HAMMERLESS DOUBLE . . . . . NiB $766 Ex $509 Gd $446

Boxlock. Double triggers. Auto ejectors. Gauges: 12 Mag., 16. Bbls.: 26-inch IC/M; 28-inch M/F; 30-inch F/F. Weight: 12 ga., about 7.5 lbs. Checkered pistol-grip stock and beavertail forearm. Made in 1961.

COLTSMAN PUMP

SHOTGUN. . . . . NiB $489 Ex $355 Gd $269

Takedown. Gauges: 12, 16, 20. Magazine holds 4 rounds. Bbls.: 26-inch IC; 28-inch M or F choke; 30-inch F choke. Weight: About 6 lbs. Plain pistol-grip stock and forearm. Made 1961 to 1965 by Manufrance.

CUSTOM PUMP. . . . . NiB $500 Ex $377 Gd $286

Same as Standard Pump shotgun except has checkered stock, vent-rib bbl. Weight: About 6.5 lbs. Made 1961 to 1963 by Manufrance.

SAUER DRILLING. . . . . NiB $4466 Ex $3778 Gd $2360

Three-bbl. combination gun. Boxlock. Set rifle trigger. Tang bbl. selector, automatic rear sight positioner. 12 ga. over .30-06 or .243 rifle bbl. 25-inch bbls., F and M choke. Weight: About 8 lbs. Folding leaf rear sight, blade front w/brass bead. Checkered pistol-grip stock and beavertail forearm, recoil pad. Made 1974 to 1985 by J. P. Sauer & Sohn,

Colt Auto Shotgun
Ultra Light Standard

Colt Custom
Hammerless Double

Colt Standard Pump

Cogswell
& Harrison
Best Quality
Hammerless
Sidelock

Colt-Sauer
Drilling

Charles Daly Over/Under
Field Grade (Postwar)

Eckernförde, Germany.

CONNECTICUT VALLEY CLASSICS — Westport, Connecticut

SPORTER 101 O/U
Gauge: 12; 3-inch chamber. Bbls.: 28-, 30- or 32-inch w/ screw-in tubes. Weight: 7.75 lbs. Engraved stainless or nitrided receiver; blued bbls.

Checkered American black walnut buttstock and forend w/low-luster satin finish. Made from 1993 to 1998.
Classic Sporter . . . . NiB $1966 Ex $1634 Gd $1388
Stainless Classic Sporter . . . . . NiB $2764 Ex $2259 Gd $1744

FIELD O/U
Similar to the standard Classic Sporter over/under model except w/30-inch bbls. only and non-reflective matte blued finish on both bbls. and receiver for Waterfowler; other grades w/different degrees of embellishment; Grade I the lowest and Grade III the highest. Made 1993 to 1998.
Grade I . . . . NiB $2788 Ex $2308 Gd $1683
Grade II . . . . NiB $3166 Ex $2521 Gd $1790
Grade III . . . . NiB $3767 Ex $2866 Gd $1946
Waterfowler . . . . NiB $2581 Ex $2264 Gd $1598

CONNENTO/VENTUR — Formerly imported by Ventura, Seal Beach, California

Model 51 . . . . NiB $456 Ex $361 Gd $295
Gauge: 12, 16, 20, 28 and .410. Double-barrel, box-lock action. Barrels: 26, 28, 30 and 32 inches; various chokes; extractors; and double triggers. Checkered walnut stock. Introduced in 1980, discontinued 1985.
Model 52 . . . . NiB $610 Ex $433 Gd $329
Same as Model 51 except in 10 gauge.

Model 53 . . . . NiB $538 Ex $449 Gd $300
Same as Model 51 except with scalloped receiver, automatic ejectors and optional single selective trigger. Discontinued in 1985.
W/single trigger, add 25%

Model 62 . . . . NiB $1132 Ex $990 Gd $760
Holland & Holland-design sidelock shotgun with various barrel lengths and chokes; automatic ejectors; cocking indicators. Floral engraved receiver, checkered walnut stock. Discontinued in 1982.

Model 64 . . . . NiB $1388 Ex $1054 Gd $877
Same as Model 62 except deluxe finish. Discontinued.

Grade I . . . . NiB $1259 Ex $988 Gd $844
Gauge: 12. Over/under shotgun. Barrels: 32 inches; screw-in choke tubes; high ventilated rib; automatic ejectors; single selective trigger standard. Checkered Monte Carlo walnut stock.

Mark II . . . . NiB $1569 Ex $1236 Gd $1006
Same as Mark I model but with an extra single barrel and fitted leather case.

Mark III . . . . NiB $1788 Ex $1469 Gd $1100
Same as Mark I model but with finely figured walnut stock and engraved metal.

Mark III Combo . . . . NiB $2877 Ex $2243 Gd $2071
Same as Mark III model above but with extra single barrel and fitted leather case.

CHARLES DALY, INC. — New York, New York

The pre-WWII Charles Daly shotguns, w/the exception of the Commander, were manufactured by various firms in Suhl, Germany. The postwar guns, except for the Novamatic series, were produced by Miroku Firearms Mfg. Co., Tokyo. Miroku ceased production in 1976 and the Daly trademark was acquired by Outdoor Sports Headquarters, in Dayton, Ohio. OSHI continued to market O/U shotguns from both Italy and Spain under the Daly logo. Automatic models were produced in Japan for distribution in the USA. In 1996, KBI, Inc. in Harrisburg, PA acquired the Daly trademark and currently imports firearms under that logo.

COMMANDER O/U SHOTGUN
Daly-pattern Anson & Deeley system boxlock action. Automatic ejectors. Double triggers or Miller selective single trigger. Gauges: 12, 16, 20, 28, .410. Bbls.: 26- to 30-inch, IC/M or M/F choke. Weight: 5.25 to 7.25 lbs. depending on ga. and bbl. length. Checkered stock and forend, straight or pistol grip. The two models, 100 and 200, differ in general quality, grade of wood, checkering, engraving, etc.; otherwise specs are the same. Made in Belgium c. 1939.
Model 100 . . . . NiB $665 Ex $500 Gd $397
Model 200 . . . . NiB $866 Ex $703 Gd $511
w/Miller single trigger, add $150

HAMMERLESS DOUBLE-BARREL SHOTGUN
Daly-pattern Anson & Deeley system boxlock action. Automatic ejectors except "Superior Quality" is non-ejector. Double triggers. Gauges: 10, 12, 16, 20, 28, .410. Bbls.: 26- to 32-inch, any combination of chokes. Weight: from 4 to 8.5 lbs. depending on ga. and bbl. length. Checkered pistol-grip stock and forend. The four grades—Regent Diamond, Diamond, Empire, Superior—differ in general quality, grade of wood, checkering, engraving, etc.; otherwise specifications are the same. Disc. about 1933.
Diamond quality . . . . NiB $12,677 Ex $10,445 Gd $7869
Empire quality . . . . NiB $6133 Ex $4632 Gd $3144
Regent Diamond quality . . . . . NiB $14,878 Ex $12,966 Gd $10,077
Superior quality . . . . NiB $1522 Ex $1292 Gd $1000

HAMMERLESS DRILLING
Daly pattern Anson & Deeley system boxlock action. Plain extractors. Double triggers, front single set for rifle bbl. Gauges: 12, 16, 20, .25-20, .25-35, .30-30 rifle bbl. Supplied in various bbl. lengths and weights. Checkered

SHOTGUNS

Charles Daly
Field Semiauto

Charles Daly Field III
Over/Under

pistol-grip stock and forend. Auto rear sight operated by rifle bbl. selector. The three grades — Regent Diamond, Diamond, Superior—differ in general quality, grade of wood, checkering, engraving, etc.; otherwise, specifications are the same. Disc. 1933.

Diamond quality . . . . NiB $7235 Ex $5530 Gd $4200
Regent Diamond quality . . . . . NiB $14,866 Ex $11,977 Gd $9977
Superior quality . . . . NiB $3733 Ex $2988 Gd $2036

HAMMERLESS DOUBLE
EMPIRE GRADE . . . . NiB $1887 Ex $1352 Gd $1091
Boxlock. Plain extractors. Non-selective single trigger. Gauges: 12, 16, 20; 3-inch chambers in 12 and 20, 2.75-inch in 16 ga. Bbls.: vent rib; 26-, 28-, 30-inch (latter in 12 ga. only); IC/M, M/F, F/F. Weight: 6 to 7.75 lbs., depending on ga. and bbls. Checkered pistol-grip stock and beavertail forearm. Made 1968 to 1971.

1974 WILDLIFE COMMEMORATIVE . . . NiB $2466 Ex $2167 Gd $1477
Limited issue of 500 guns. Similar to Diamond Grade over/under. 12-ga. trap and skeet models only. Duck scene engraved on right side of receiver, fine scroll on left side. Made in 1974.

NOVAMATIC LIGHTWEIGHT AUTOLOADER
Same as Breda. Recoil-operated. Takedown. 12 ga., 2.75-inch chamber.

Four-round tubular magazine. Bbls.: Plain vent rib; 26-inch IC or Quick-Choke w/three interchangeable tubes, 28-inch M or F choke. Weight (w/26-inch vent-rib bbl.): 7 lbs., 6 oz. Checkered pistol-grip stock and forearm. Made 1968 by Ernesto Breda, Milan, Italy.
w/plain bbl. . . . . NiB $398 Ex $277 Gd $198
w/vent rib bbl. . . . . NiB $397 Ex $260 Gd $200
w/Quick-Choke, add $50

NOVAMATIC SUPER LIGHTWEIGHT
Lighter version of Novamatic Lightweight. Gauges: 12, 20. Weight (w/26-inch vent-rib bbl.): 12 ga., 6 lbs., 10 oz., 20 ga., 6 lbs. SK choke available in 26-inch vent-rib bbl. 28-inch bbls. in 12 ga. only. Quick-Choke in 20 ga. w/plain bbl. Made 1968 by Ernesto Breda, Milan, Italy.
12 ga., plain bbl. . . . . NiB $387 Ex $288 Gd $198
12 ga., vent. rib bbl. . . . . NiB $387 Ex $288 Gd $198
20 ga., plain bbl. . . . . NiB $543 Ex $433 Gd $315
20 ga., plain bbl. w/Quick-Choke . . . . NiB $388 Ex $335 Gd $217
20 ga., vent. rib bbl. . . . . NiB $433 Ex $290 Gd $200

NOVAMATIC SUPER LIGHTWEIGHT
20 GA. MAGNUM. . . . . NiB $377 Ex $296 Gd $200
Same as Novamatic Super Lightweight 2, except 3-inch chamber, has 3-round magazine, 28-inch vent-rib bbl., F choke.

NOVAMATIC
12 GA. MAGNUM. . . . . NiB $377 Ex $296 Gd $200
Same as Novamatic Lightweight, except chambered for 12-ga. Magnum 3-inch shell. Has 3-round magazine, 30-inch vent rib bbl., F choke, and stock w/recoil pad. Weight: 7.75 lbs.

Post-War Charles Daly shotguns were imported by Sloan's Sporting Goods trading as Charles Daly in New York. In 1976, Outdoor Sports Headquarters acquired the Daly trademark and continued to import European-made shotguns under that logo. In 1996, KBI, Inc., in Harrisburg, PA, acquired the Daly trademark and currently imports firearms under that logo.

NOVAMATIC TRAP GUN . . . . NiB $643 Ex $500 Gd $355
Same as Novamatic Lightweight except has 30-inch vent rib bbl., F choke and Monte Carlo stock w/recoil pad. Weight: 7.75 lbs.

O/U SHOTGUNS (PRE-WWII)
Daly-pattern Anson & Deeley-system boxlock action. Sideplates. Auto ejectors. Double triggers. Gauges: 12, 16, 20. Supplied in various bbl. lengths and weights. Checkered pistol-grip stock and forend. The two grades — Diamond and Empire — differ in general quality, grade of wood, checkering, engraving, etc. — otherwise specifications are the same. Disc. about 1933.
Diamond Quality . . . . NiB $6133 Ex $4965 Gd $3476
Empire Quality . . . . NiB $4771 Ex $3865 Gd $2700

O/U SHOTGUNS (POST-WWII)
Boxlock. Auto ejectors or selective auto/manual ejection. Selective single trigger. Gauges: 12, 12 Magnum (3-inch chambers), 20 (3-inch chambers), 28, .410. Bbls.: Vent rib; 26-, 28-, 30-inch; standard choke combinations. Weight: 6 to 8 lbs. depending on ga. and bbls. Select walnut stock w/pistol grip, fluted forearm checkered; Monte Carlo comb on trap guns; recoil pad on 12-ga. mag. and trap models. The various grades differ in quality of engraving and wood. Made from 1963 to 1976.
Diamond grade . . . . NiB $1588 Ex $1266 Gd $990
Field grade . . . . NiB $933 Ex $800 Gd $576
Superior grade . . . . NiB $1139 Ex $1008 Gd $853
Venture grade . . . . NiB $900 Ex $773 Gd $525

SEXTUPLE MODEL SINGLE-BARREL TRAP GUN
Daly-pattern Anson & Deeley system boxlock action. Six locking bolts. Auto ejector. 12 ga. only. Bbls.: 30-, 32-, 34-inch, vent rib. Weight: 7.5 to 8.25 lbs. Checkered pistol-grip stock and forend. The two models made Empire and

Charles Daly Over/Under
Presentation Grade

Regent Diamond differ in general quality, grade of wood, checkering, engraving, etc., otherwise specifications are the same. Disc. about 1933.

Regent Diamond quality (Linder) . . . . . NiB $2788 Ex $2188 Gd $1886
Empire quality (Linder) . . . . NiB $5300 Ex $4260 Gd $3143
Regent Diamond quality (Sauer) . . . . NiB $3921 Ex $3288 Gd $2876
Empire quality (Sauer). . . . . NiB $2966 Ex $2377 Gd $1677

SINGLE-SHOT TRAP GUN
Daly-pattern Anson & Deeley system boxlock action. Auto ejector. 12 ga. only. Bbls.: 30-, 32-, 34-inch, vent rib. Weight: 7.5 to 8.25 lbs. Checkered pistol-grip stock and forend. This model was made in Empire Quality only. Disc. about 1933.

Empire grade (Linder) . . . . NiB $4765 Ex $3966 Gd $2960
Empire grade (Sauer). . . . . NiB $2477 Ex $2099 Gd $1776

SUPERIOR GRADE SINGLE-SHOT TRAP . NiB $954 Ex $833 Gd $700
Boxlock. Automatic ejector. 12 ga. only. 32- or 34-inch vent-rib bbl., F choke. Weight: About 8 lbs. Monte Carlo stock w/pistol grip and recoil pad, beavertail forearm, checkered. Made 1968 to 1976.

DIAMOND GRADE O/U
Boxlock. Single selective trigger. Selective automatic ejectors. Gauges: 12 and 20, 3-inch chambers (2.75 target grade). Bbls.: 26, 27- or 30-inch w/fixed chokes or screw-in tubes. Weight: 7 lbs. Checkered European walnut stock and forearm w/oil finish. Engraved antique silver receiver and blued bbls. Made from 1984 to 1990.

Standard model . . . . NiB $1088 Ex $900 Gd $670
Skeet model . . . . NiB $1155 Ex $966 Gd $733
Trap model . . . . NiB $1155 Ex $966 Gd $733

DIAMOND GTX DL HUNTER O/U SERIES
Sidelock. Single selective trigger and selective auto ejectors. Gauges: 12, 20, 28 ga. or .410 bore. 26-, 28- and 30-inch bbls w/3-inch chambers (2.75-inch 28 ga.). Choke tubes (12 and 20 ga.), Fixed chokes (28 and 410). Weight: 5-8 lbs. Checkered European walnut stock w/hand-rubbed oil finish and recoil pad. Made from 1997 to 2001.

Diamond GTX DL Hunter . . . . NiB $11,977 Ex $9478 Gd $5800
Diamond GTX EDL Hunter . . . . . NiB $13,778 Ex $10,771 Gd $8987
Diamond GTX Sporting (12 or 20 ga.) . . . . . NiB $5921 Ex $4771 Gd $3380
Diamond GTX Skeet (12 or 20 ga.) . . . . . NiB $5540 Ex $4380 Gd $3100
Diamond GTX Trap (12 ga. only). . . . . . NiB $6144 Ex $4766 Gd $3200

EMPIRE DL HUNTER O/U . . . . . NiB $1456 Ex $1277 Gd $956
Boxlock. Ejectors. Single selective trigger. Gauges:12, 20, 28 ga. and .410 bore. 26- or 28- inch bbls. w/3-inch chambers (2.75-inch 28 ga.). Choke tubes (12 and 20 ga.), Fixed chokes (28 and .410). Engraved coin-silver receiver w/game scene. Imported from 1997 to 1998.

EMPIRE EDL HUNTER SERIES
Similar to Empire DL Hunter except engraved sideplates. Made 1998 to date.

Hunter model. . . . . NiB $1477 Ex $1133 Gd $890
Sporting model. . . . . NiB $1371 Ex $1108 Gd $870

Skeet model . . . . NiB $1388 Ex $1170 Gd $880
Trap model . . . . NiB $1366 Ex $1109 Gd $853
28 ga., add. $110
.410 ga, add. $150
Multi-chokes w/Monte
Carlo stock, add $175

DSS HAMMERLESS DOUBLE . . . . NiB $885 Ex $744 Gd $561
Boxlock. Single selective trigger. Selective automatic ejectors. Gauges: 12 and 20; 3-inch chambers. 26-inch bbls. w/screw-in choke tubes. Weight: 6.75 lbs. Checkered walnut pistol-grip stock and semi-beaver-tail forearm w/recoil pad. Engraved antique silver receiver and blued bbls. Made from 1990. Disc.

FIELD GRADE O/U . . . . NiB $675 Ex $570 Gd $449
Boxlock. Single selective trigger. Extractors. Gauges: 12 and 20; 3-inch chambers. Bbls.: 26-inch, IC/M; 28-inch, M/F. Weight: 6.75 lbs. (12 ga.). Checkered walnut stock and forearm w/semi-gloss finish and recoil pad. Engraved color-casehardened receiver and blued bbls. Made from 1989. Disc.

FIELD SEMIAUTO SHOTGUN . . . . . NiB $622 Ex $476 Gd $377
Recoil-operated. Takedown. 12-ga. and 12-ga. Magnum. Bbls.: 27- and 30-inch; vent rib. Made from 1982 to 1988.

FIELD III O/U SHOTGUN . . . . NiB $679 Ex $580 Gd $445
Boxlock. Plain extractors. Non-selective single trigger. Gauges: 12 or 20. Bbls.: vent rib; 26- and 28-inch; IC/M, M/F. Weight: 6 to 7.75 lbs. depending on ga. and bbls. Chrome-molybdenum steel bbls. Checkered pistol-grip stock and forearm. Made from 1982. Disc.

LUXIE O/U . . . . NiB $900 Ex $733 Gd $529
Similar to the Field Grade except w/selective automatic ejectors and choke tubes. Gauges: 12, 20, 28 and .410. Receiver w/antique silver finish and blued bbls. Made from 1989 to 1994.

MULTI-XII SELF-LOADING SHOTGUN . . . . . . NiB $656 Ex $490 Gd $387
Similar to the gas-operated field semiauto except w/new Multi-Action gas system designed to shoot all loads w/o adjustment. 12 ga. w/3-inch chamber. 27-inch bbl. w/Invector choke tubes, vent rib. Made in Japan from 1987 to 1988.

PRESENTATION
GRADE O/U . . . . NiB $1254 Ex $1009 Gd $770
Purdey boxlock w/double cross-bolt. Gauges: 12 or 20. Engraved receiver w/single selective trigger and auto-ejectors. 27-inch chrome-molybdenum steel, rectified, honed and internally chromed, vent-rib bbls. Hand-checkered deluxe European walnut stock. Made from 1982 to 1986.

SUPERIOR II
SHOTGUN O/U . . . . NiB $1064 Ex $880 Gd $602
Boxlock. Plain extractors. Non-selective single trigger. Gauges: 12 or 20. Bbls.: chrome-molybdenum vent rib 26-, 28-, 30-inch, latter in magnum only, assorted chokes. Silver engraved receiver. Checkered pistol-grip stock and forearm. Made from 1982 to 1988

SHOTGUNS

Davidson Model 63B
Double-Barrel Shotgun

SPORTING CLAYS O/U . . . . NiB $833 Ex $644 Gd $535
Similar to the Field Grade except in 12 ga. only w/ported bbls. and internal choke tubes. Made from 1990 to 1996.

CHIAPPA FIREARMS LTD., — DAYTON, OH
Chiappa owns ARMI SPORT REPLICA FIREARMS MFG. and manufactures Cimarron, Legacy Sports, Taylor's & Co. Imported currently, manufactured in Italy.

MODEL 1887 . . . . NiB $1363 Ex $1295 Gd $400
Lever action. Gauge: 12 ga., 18.5, 22, 24 or 28-inch bbl., choke tubes. Color-casehardened or chrome receiver. Weight: 6.6 lbs. Stock: oil finished smooth walnut. Made from 2009 to date. **DAKOTA ARMS, INC. — Sturgis, South Dakota**

CLASSIC FIELD GRADE
S/S SHOTGUN . . . . NiB $7566 Ex $6548 Gd $4456
Boxlock. Gauge: 20 ga. 27-inch bbl. w/fixed chokes. Double triggers. Selective ejectors. Color-casehardened receiver. Weight: 6 lbs. Checkered English walnut stock and splinter forearm w/hand-rubbed oil finish. Made from 1996 to 1998.

PREMIER GRADE
S/S SHOTGUN . . . . NiB $14,765 Ex $11,466 Gd $9224
Similar to Classic Field Grade model except w/50% engraving coverage. Exhibition grade English walnut stock. Made from 1996 to date.

AMERICAN LEGEND
S/S SHOTGUN . . . . .NiB $16,750 Ex $15,000 Gd $11,550
Limited edition built to customer's specifications. Gauge: 20 ga. 27-inch bbl. Double triggers. Selective ejectors. Fully engraved, coin-silver finished receiver w/gold inlays. Weight: 6 lbs. Hand checkered special-selection English walnut stock and forearm. Made from 1996 to 2005.

DARNE S.A. — Saint-Etienne, France

HAMMERLESS DOUBLE-BARREL SHOTGUNS
Sliding-breech action w/fixed bbls. Auto ejectors. Double triggers. Gauges: 12, 16, 20, 28; also 12 and 20 Magnum w/3-inch chambers. Bbls.: 27.5-inch standard, 25.5- to 31.5-inch lengths available; any standard choke combination. Weight: 5.5 to 7 lbs. depending on ga. and bbl. length. Checkered straight-grip or pistol-grip stock and forearm. The various models differ in grade of engraving and wood. Manufactured from 1881 to 1979.
Model R11 (Bird Hunter) . . . . NiB $7044 Ex $4698 Gd $2677
Model R15 (Pheasant Hunter) . . NiB $14,900 Ex $12,785 Gd $10,000
Model R16 (Magnum) . . . . NiB $3775 Ex $2730 Gd $2167
Model R19 (Quail Hunter) . . . . NiB $22,000 Ex $17,500 Gd $14,275
Model V22 . . . . NiB $31,000 Ex $26,800 Gd $22,975
Model V Hors Série No. 1 . . . . . NiB $77,000 Ex $58,650 Gd $46,790

DAVIDSON GUNS — Manufactured by Fabrica de Armas ILJA, Eibar, Spain; distributed by Davidson Firearms Co., Greensboro, North Carolina

MODEL 63B DOUBLE-BARREL
SHOTGUN . . . . NiB $433 Ex $279 Gd $200
Anson & Deeley boxlock action. Frame engraved and nickel plated. Plain extractors. Auto safety. Double triggers. Gauges: 12, 16, 20, 28, .410. Bbl. lengths: 25 (.410 only), 26, 28, 30 inches (latter 12 ga. only). Chokes: IC/ M, M/F, F/F. Weight: 5 lbs., 11 oz. (.410) to 7 lbs. (12 ga.). Checkered pistol-grip stock and forearm of European walnut. Made in 1963. Disc.

MODEL 63B MAGNUM
Similar to standard Model 63B except chambered for 10 ga. 3.5-inch, 12 and 20 ga. 3-inch Magnum shells; 10 ga. has 32-inch bbls., choked F/F. Weight: 10 lb., 10 oz. Made from 1963. Disc.
12-and 20 ga. magnum . . . . NiB $455 Ex $300 Gd $210
10 ga. magnum . . . . NiB $477 Ex $369 Gd $230

MODEL 69SL DOUBLE-BARREL
SHOTGUN . . . . NiB $455 Ex $400 Gd $270
Sidelock action w/detachable sideplates, engraved and nickel plated. Plain extractors. Auto safety. Double triggers. 12 and 20 ga. Bbls.: 26-inch IC/M, 28-inch M/F. Weight: 12 ga., 7 lbs., 20 ga., 6.5 lbs. Pistol-grip stock and forearm of European walnut, checkered. Made from 1963 to 1976.

MODEL 73 STAGECOACH
HAMMER DOUBLE . . . . NiB $331 Ex $229 Gd $130
Sidelock action w/detachable sideplates and exposed hammers. Plain extractors. Double triggers. Gauges: 12, 20, 3-inch chambers. 20-inch bbls, M/F chokes. Weight: 7 lbs., 12 ga.; 6.5 lbs., 20 ga. Checkered pistol-grip stock and forearm. Made from 1976. Disc.

DIAMOND SHOTGUNS
Currently imported by ADCO Sales, Inc, Woburn, MA. Company established circa 1981, all guns manufactured in Turkey.

GOLD SERIES (SEMIAUTOMATIC) . . . . . . NiB $354 Ex $280 Gd $175
12 gauge, 3-inch chamber. Gas operated. Bbl. 24 (slug) or 28 inches. Ventilated rib with three choke tubes. Semi-humpback design, anodized alloy frame, gold etching. Rotary bolt. Black synthetic or checkered Turkish walnut forearm and stock with recoil pad. Value $50 less for slug version.

IMPERIAL SERIES . . . . NiB $475 Ex $345 Gd $265
Gauge: 12 (3.5-inch) or 20 (3-inch). Bbl.: 24 (12 ga. slug), 26 (20 ga.) or 28 inches; vent. rib, rotary bi-lateral bolt, deluxe checkered stock and forearm. Imported 2003.

Fox Model B

ELITE SERIES . . . . NiB $445 Ex $323 Gd $200
Gauge: 12, 3-inch. Bbl.: 22 (slug), 24, 26 or 28 inches; ventilated rib, deluxe checkered walnut stock and forearm. Imported 2001. Deduct $50 for slug model.

PANTHER SERIES . . . . NiB $415 Ex $338 Gd $200
Gauge: 12, 3-inch. Gas-operated. Black synthetic stock and forearm. Bbl.: 20 (slug or regular) or 28 inches. Imported 2002.
Walnut stock and forearm, add $75
Slug version . . . . deduct $50

MARINER . . . . NiB $338 Ex $198 Gd $110
Gauge: 12, 3-inch. Gas operated. Bbl.: 20 (slug) or 22 inches. Vent. rib. Anodized alloy frame and receiver, satin silver finish. Checkered walnut stock and forearm. Imported 2002.
Slug model, deduct. $50

**GOLD ELITE SERIES
(SLIDE-ACTION).** . . . . NiB $354 Ex $260 Gd $200
12 gauge, 3-inch chamber. Bbl. 24 (slug with open sights), or 28 inches; ventilated rib. Semi-humpback design. Anodized alloy frame, synthetic black or Turkish walnut stock and forearm. Weight: 7 lbs. Imported 2001. Value $40 less for synthetic stock.

EXCEL ARMS OF AMERICA — Gardner, Massachusetts

SERIES 100 O/U SHOTGUN
Gauge: 12. Single selective trigger. Selective auto ejectors. Hand-checkered European walnut stock w/full pistol grip, tulip forend. Black metal finish. Chambered for 2.75-inch shells (Model 103 for 3-inch). Weight: 6. 88 to 7.88 lbs. Disc 1988.
Model 101 w/26-inch bbl., IC/M . . . . . . NiB $465 Ex $367 Gd $266
Model 102 w/28-inch bbl., IC/M . . . . . . NiB $465 Ex $367 Gd $266
Model 103 w/30-inch bbl., M/F. . . . . . . NiB $465 Ex $367 Gd $266
Model 104 w/28-inch bbl., IC/M . . . . . . NiB $465 Ex $367 Gd $266
Model 105, w/28-inch bbl.,
  5 choke tubesNiB $645 Ex $480 Gd $387Model 106, w/28-inch bbl.,
  5 choke tubes . . . . NiB $776 Ex $689 Gd $558
Model 107 Trap, w/30-inch bbl.,
  Full or 5 tubes . . . . NiB $776 Ex $689 Gd $558

**SERIES 200 SIDE-BY-SIDE
SHOTGUN.** . . . . NiB $667 Ex $496 Gd $368
Gauges: 12, 20, 28 and .410. Bbls.: 26-, 27- and 28-inch; various choke combinations. Weight: 7 lbs. average. American or European-style stock and forend. Made from 1985 to 1987.

**SERIES 300 O/U
SHOTGUN.** . . . . NiB $1328 Ex $1133 Gd $1033
Gauge: 12. Bbls.: 26-, 28- and 29-inch. Non-glare black-chrome matte finish. Weight: 7 lbs. average. Selective auto ejectors, engraved receiver. Hand-checkered European walnut stock and forend. Made from 1985 to 1986.

FABARM — Brescia, Italy

Currently imported by Heckler & Koch, Inc., of Sterling, VA (previously by Ithaca Acquisition Corp., St. Lawrence Sales, Inc. and Beeman Precision Arms, Inc.)

See Current listings under "Heckler & Koch."

FIAS — Fabrica Italiana Armi Sabatti Gardone Val Trompia, Italy

GRADE I O/U
Boxlock. Single selective trigger. Gauges: 12, 20, 28, .410; 3-inch chambers. Bbls.: 26-inch IC/M; 28-inch M/F; screw-in choke tubes. Weight: 6.5 to 7.5 lbs. Checkered European walnut stock and forearm. Engraved receiver and blued finish.
12 ga. model . . . . NiB $587 Ex $480 Gd $355
20 ga. model . . . . NiB $633 Ex $512 Gd $367
28 ga. and .410 . . . . NiB $800 Ex $665 Gd $457

FOX — Made by A. H. Fox Gun Co., Philadelphia, Pennsylvania, 1903 to 1930, and since then by Savage Arms, originally of Utica, New York, now of Westfield, Massachusetts. In 1993, Connecticut Manufacturing Co. of New Britain, Connecticut reintroduced selected models.

Values shown are for 12 and 16 ga. doubles made by A. H. Fox. Twenty gauge guns often are valued up to 75% higher. Savage-made Fox models generally bring prices 25% lower. With the exception of Model B, production of Fox shotguns was discontinued about 1942.

MODEL B HAMMERLESS DOUBLE . . . . . . NiB $523 Ex $387 Gd $244
Boxlock. Double triggers. Plain extractor. Gauges: 12, 16, 20, .410. 24- to 30-inch bbls., vent rib on current production; chokes: M/F, C/M, F/F (.410 only). Weight: About 7.5 lbs., 12 ga. Checkered pistol-grip stock and forend. Made about 1940 to 1985.

MODEL B-ST . . . . NiB $644 Ex $475 Gd $350
Same as Model B except has non-selective single trigger. Made from 1955-66.

MODEL B-DE . . . . NiB $645 Ex $476 Gd $351
Same as Model B-ST except frame finished in satin chrome, select walnut buttstock w/checkered pistol grip and beavertail forearm. Made from 1965 to 1966.

MODEL B-DL . . . . NiB $678 Ex $558 Gd $421
Same as Model B-ST except frame finished in satin chrome, select walnut buttstock w/checkered pistol grip side panels, beavertail forearm. Made from 1962 to 1966.

SHOTGUNS

Franchi Model 500
Standard Autoloader

Franchi Model 520 Deluxe

Franchi Model 520
Eldorado Gold

MODEL B-SE . . . . .NiB $922 Ex $700 Gd $531
Same as Model B except has selective ejectors and single trigger. Made
from 1966 to 1989.

HAMMERLESS DOUBLE-BARREL SHOTGUNS
The higher grades have the same general specifications as the standard
Sterlingworth model, w/differences chiefly in workmanship and materi-
als. Higher grade models are stocked in fine select walnut; quantity and
quality of engraving increases w/grade and price. Except for Grade A,
all other grades have auto ejectors.

Grade A . . . . NiB $3160 Ex $1641 Gd $1895
Grade AE . . . . NiB $3598 Ex $2977 Gd $2110
Grade BE . . . . NiB $4962 Ex $3988 Gd $2860
Grade CE . . . . NiB $6200 Ex $5110 Gd $3628
Grade DE . . . . NiB $12,779 Ex $11,360 Gd $10,475
Grade FE . . . . NiB $22,679 Ex $18,960 Gd $13,000
Grade XE . . . . NiB $8634 Ex $7321 Gd $4208
w/Kautzy selective single trigger, add $400
w/vent. rib, add $500
w/beavertail forearm, add $300
20 ga. model, add 60%

SINGLE-BARREL TRAP GUNS
Boxlock. Auto ejector.12 ga. only. 30- or 32-inch vent-rib bbl. Weight:
7.5 to 8 lbs. Trap-style stock and forearm of select walnut, checkered,
recoil pad optional. The four grades differ chiefly in quality of wood
and engraving; Grade M guns, built to order, have finest Circassian
walnut. Stock and receiver are elaborately engraved and inlaid w/gold.
Disc. 1942. Note: In 1932, the Fox Trap Gun was redesigned and those
manufactured after that date have a stock w/full pistol grip and Monte
Carlo comb; at the same time frame was changed to permit the rib line
to extend across it to the rear.
Grade JE . . . . NiB $3990 Ex $2367 Gd $2031
Grade KE . . . . NiB $5366 Ex $4979 Gd $4000
Grade LE . . . . NiB $6778 Ex $4789 Gd $3760
Grade ME . . . . NiB $15,975 Ex $12,880 Gd $9355

"SKEETER" DOUBLE-BARREL
SHOTGUN. . . . . .NiB $4990 Ex $4078 Gd $2855
Boxlock. Gauge: 12 or 20. Bbls.: 28 inches w/full-length vent rib. Weight: Approx.

7 lbs. Buttstock and beavertail forend of select American walnut, finely checkered.
Soft rubber recoil pad and ivory bead sights. Made in early 1930s.
STERLINGWORTH DELUXE
Same general specifications as Sterlingworth except 32-inch bbl. also
available, recoil pad, ivory bead sights.
w/extractors . . . . NiB $2187 Ex $1654 Gd $1100
w/ejectors . . . . NiB $2370 Ex $1979 Gd $1466
20 ga., add. $45%

STERLINGWORTH HAMMERLESS DOUBLE
Boxlock. Double triggers (Fox-Kautzky selective single trigger extra). Plain
extractors (auto ejectors extra). Gauges: 12,16, 20. Bbl. lengths: 26-, 28-,
30-inch; chokes F/F, M/F, C/M (any combination of C to F choke borings was
available at no extra cost). Weight: 12 ga., 6.88 to 8.25 lbs.; 16 ga., 6 to 7
lbs.; 20 ga., 5.75 to 6.75 lbs. Checkered pistol-grip stock and forearm.
w/extractors . . . . NiB $1800 Ex $1489 Gd $1000
w/ejectors . . . . NiB $2170 Ex $1770 Gd $1254
w/selective single trigger, add 25%

STERLINGWORTH SKEET AND UPLAND GUN
Same general specifications as the standard Sterlingworth except has
26- or 28-inch bbls. w/skeet boring only, straight-grip stock. Weight: 7
lbs. (12 ga.).
w/extractors . . . . NiB $2588 Ex $2066 Gd $1489
w/ejectors . . . . NiB $3000 Ex $2469 Gd $1785
20 ga., add. 45%

SUPER HE GRADE . . . . .NiB $5863 Ex $4791 Gd $3310
Long-range gun made in 12 ga. only (chambered for 3-inch shells on
order), 30- or 32-inch full choke bbls., auto ejectors standard. Weight: 8.75
to 9.75 lbs. General specifications same as standard Sterlingworth.

HAMMERLESS DOUBLE-BARREL SHOTGUNS
High-grade doubles similar to the original Fox models. 20 ga. only.
26- 28- or 30-inch bbls. Double triggers automatic safety and ejectors.
Weight: 5.5 to 7 lbs. Custom Circassian walnut stock w/hand-rubbed oil
finish. Custom stock configuration: straight, semi- or full pistol-grip stock
w/traditional pad, hard rubber plate checkered or skeleton butt; Schnabel,
splinter or beavertail forend. Made 1993 to date.
CE grade . . . . NiB $9221 Ex $6855 Gd $4900
XE grade . . . . NiB $9066 Ex $7221 Gd $5054

Franchi 612 Variopress Advantage

Franchi 612 Variopress Sporting

Franchi 612 Variopress

Franchi 620 Variopress Advantage

Franchi 620 Variopress

**Franchi Model 2004
Trap Single Barrel**

stock and forearm. Made from 1976 to 1980.

MODEL 520 DELUXE . . . . NiB $478 Ex $355 Gd $279
Same as Model 500 except higher grade w/engraved receiver. Made from 1975 to 1979.

MODEL 520 ELDORADO GOLD . . . . . NiB $1088 Ex $877 Gd $743
Same as Model 520 except custom grade w/engraved and gold-inlaid receiver, finer quality wood. Intro. 1977.

MODEL 610VS SEMIAUTOMATIC SHOTGUN
Gas-operated Variopress system adjustable to function w/2.75- or 3- inch shells. 12 gauge. Four round magazine. 26- or 28-inch vent rib bbls. w/ Franchoke tubes. Weight: 7 lbs., 2 oz. 47.5 inches overall. Alloy receiver w/ four-lug rotating bolt and loaded chamber indicator. Checkered European walnut buttstock and forearm w/satin finish. Imported from 1997.
Standard model . . . .
NiB $766 Ex $600 Gd $445
Engraved model . . . .
NiB $800 Ex $655 Gd $500

MODEL 612 VARIOPRESS AUTOLOADING SHOTGUN
Gauge: 12 ga. Only. 24- to 28-inch bbl. 45 to 49-inches overall. Weight: 6.8 to 7 lbs. Five round magazine. Bead type sights with C, IC, M chokes. Blued, matte or Advantage camo finish. Imported from 1999 to 2004.
w/satin walnut stock,
   blued finish . . . . .NiB $645 Ex $559 Gd $369
w/synthetic stock,
   matte finish . . . . .NiB $665 Ex $590 Gd $400
w/Advantage
   camo finish . . . . .NiB $800 Ex $645 Gd $449
Defense model. . . . .
NiB $600 Ex $469 Gd $360
Sporting model . . . .
NiB $966 Ex $733 Gd $544

DE grade . . . . NiB $13,788 Ex $11,650 Gd $7900
FE grade . . . . .NiB $18,977 Ex $15,220 Gd $11,760
Exhibition grade . . . . . .NiB $27,480 Ex $22,760 Gd $14,990

LUIGI FRANCHI S.P.A. — Brescia, Italy

MODEL 48/AL ULTRA LIGHT SHOTGUN
Recoil-operated, takedown, hammerless shotgun w/tubular magazine. Gauges: 12 or 20 (2.75-inch); 12-ga. Magnum (3-inch chamber). Bbls.: 24- to 32-inch w/various choke combinations. Weight: 5 lbs., 2 oz. (20 ga.) to 6.25 lbs. (12 ga.). Checkered pistol-grip walnut stock and forend w/high-gloss finish.
Standard model . . . . NiB $779 Ex $554 Gd $430
Hunter or magnum models . . . . . NiB $977 Ex $580 Gd $476

MODEL 500 STANDARD AUTOLOADER . . **NiB $400 Ex $288 Gd $190**
Gas-operated. 12 gauge. Four round magazine. Bbls.: 26-, 28-inch; vent rib; IC, M, IM, F chokes. Weight: About 7 lbs. Checkered pistol-grip

GRADING: **NiB** = New in Box   **Ex** = Excellent or NRA 95%   **Gd** = Good or NRA 68%

SHOTGUNS

MODEL 620 VARIOPRESS AUTOLOADING SHOTGUN
Gauge: 20 ga. Only. 24- 26- or 28-inch bbl. 45 to 49-inches overall. Weight: 5.9 to 6.1 lbs. Five round magazine. Bead type sights with C, IC, M chokes. Satin walnut or Advantage camo stock. Imported from 1999 to 2004.

w/satin walnut stock,
    matte finish . . . . .NiB $655 Ex $498 Gd $367
w/Advantage camo finish. . . . . NiB $790 Ex $554 Gd $421
Youth model
    w/short stock. . . . . NiB $615 Ex $490 Gd $379

MODEL 2003 TRAP O/U . . . . NiB $1355 Ex $1109 Gd $1005
Boxlock. Auto ejectors. Selective single trigger. 12 ga. Bbls.: 30-, 32-inch IM/F, F/F, high-vent rib. Weight (w/30-inch bbl.): 8.25 lbs. Checkered walnut beavertail forearm and stock w/straight or Monte Carlo comb, recoil pad. Luggage-type carrying case. Introduced 1976. Disc.

MODEL 2004 TRAP SINGLE
BARREL TRAP . . . . NiB $1366 Ex $1288 Gd $915
Same as Model 2003 except single bbl., 32- or 34-inch. Full choke. Weight (w/32-inch bbl.): 8.25 lbs. Introduced 1976. Disc.

MODEL 2005 COMBINATION TRAP. . . . . . NiB $1977 Ex $1760 Gd $1233
Model 2004/2005 type gun w/two sets of bbls., single and over/under. Introduced 1976. Disc.

MODEL 2005/3 COMBINATION TRAP . . . . . . NiB $2660 Ex $2175 Gd $1648
Model 2004/2005 type gun w/three sets of bbls., any combination of single and over/under. Introduced 1976. Disc.

MODEL 3000/2 COMBINATION TRAP. . . .NiB $2876 Ex $2599 Gd $1879
Boxlock. Automatic ejectors. Selective single trigger. 12 ga. only. Bbls.: 32-inch over/under choked F/IM, 34-inch underbarrel M choke; high vent rib. Weight (w/32-inch bbls.): 8 lbs., 6 oz. Choice of six different castoff buttstocks. Introduced 1979. Disc.

ALCIONE HAMMERLESS DOUBLE . . . . . NiB $763 Ex $633 Gd $544
Boxlock. Anson & Deeley system action. Auto ejectors. Double triggers. 12 ga. Various bbl. lengths, chokes, weights. Checkered straight-grip stock and forearm. Made from 1940-50.

ALCIONE O/U SHOTGUN
Hammerless, takedown shotgun w/engraved receiver. Selective single trigger and ejectors. 12 ga. w/3-inch chambers. Bbls.: 26-inch (IC/M), 28-inch (M/F). Weight: 6.75 lbs. Checkered French walnut buttstock and forend. Imported from Italy. 1982 to 1989.
Standard model . . . . .NiB $755 Ex $648 Gd $479
SL model (disc. 1986). . . . . . . .NiB $1290 Ex $1077 Gd $800

ALCIONE CLASSIC. . . . . NiB $763 Ex $633 Gd $544
O/U. Boxlock. Auto ejectors. Single select trigger. 12 ga. only. 26- or 28-in. bbl. lengths, choke tubes, 7.5 lbs. blue non-engraved receiver. Checkered stock and forearm. Made from 2004-2005.

ALCIONE FIELD (97-12 IBS) O/U
Similar to the Standard Alcione model except w/nickel-finished receiver. 26- or 28-inch bbls. w/Franchoke tubes. Imported from 1998 to 2005.
Standard Field model . . . . NiB $1263 Ex $1009 Gd $700
SL Field model (w/sideplates, disc.). . . NiB $1296 Ex $1007 Gd $865

ALCIONE SPORT (SL IBS) O/U . . . . . NiB $1567 Ex $1380 Gd $1134
Similar to the Alcione Field model except chambered for 2.75 or 3-inch shells. Ported 29-inch bbls. w/target vent rib and Franchoke tubes.

ALCIONE SX O/U. . . . . NiB $1540 Ex $1060 Gd $700

Franchi Astore 5

Removable engraved sideplates. 12 ga. only. 26- or 28-in. vent rib bbls. w/ choke tubes. Weight: 7.4 lbs. Imported from 2001 to 2005.

ALCIONE TITANIUM O/U . . . . NiB $1540 Ex $1060 Gd $700
Aluminum alloy receiver w/ titanium inserts. Removable sideplates. 12 or 20 ga. 26- or 28-in. vent rib bbls. w/ choke tubes. Weight: 6.8 lbs. Imported from 2002 to 2005.

ALCIONE 2000 SX O/U SHOTGUN. . . . . . NiB $1790 Ex $1388 Gd $1100
Similar to the Standard Alcione model except w/silver finished receiver and gold inlays. 28-inch bbls. w/Franchoke tubes. Weight: 7.25 lbs. Imported from 1996 to 1997.

ARISTOCRAT FIELD MODEL O/U . . . . . NiB $754 Ex $600 Gd $434
Boxlock. Selective auto ejectors. Selective single trigger. 12 ga. Bbls.: 26-inch IC/M; 28- and 30-inch M/F choke, vent rib. Weight (w/26-inch bbls.): 7 lbs. Checkered pistol-grip stock and forearm. Made from 1960 to 1969.

ARISTOCRAT DELUXE AND SUPREME GRADES
Available in Field, Skeet and Trap models w/the same general specifications as standard guns of these types. Deluxe and Supreme Grades are of higher quality, w/stock and forearm of select walnut, elaborate relief engraving on receiver, trigger guard, tang and top lever. Supreme game birds inlaid in gold. Made from 1960 to 1966.
Deluxe grade . . . . NiB $1077 Ex $844 Gd $657
Supreme grade . . . . NiB $1577 Ex $1340 Gd $1098

ARISTOCRAT IMPERIAL AND MONTE CARLO GRADES
Custom guns made in Field, Skeet and Trap models w/the same general specifications as standard for these types. Imperial and Monte Carlo grades are of highest quality w/stock and forearm of select walnut, fine engraving — elaborate on latter grade. Made 1967 to 1969.
Imperial grade . . . . NiB $4134 Ex $2570 Gd $2160
Monte Carlo grade . . . . NiB $3677 Ex $2920 Gd $2100

ARISTOCRAT MAGNUM MODEL . . . . . . NiB $765 Ex $557 Gd $469
Same as Field Model except chambered for 3-inch shells, has 32-inch bbls. choked F/F; stock has recoil pad. Weight: About 8 lbs. Made from 1962 to 1965.

ARISTOCRAT SILVER KING . . . . .NiB $888 Ex $712 Gd $559
Available in Field, Magnum, Meet and Trap models w/the same general specifications as standard guns of these types. Silver King has stock and forearm of select walnut more elaborately engraved silver-finished receiver. Made 1962 to 1969.

ARISTOCRAT SKEET MODEL . . . .NiB $866 Ex $754 Gd $544
Same general specifications as Field Model except made only w/26-inch vent-rib bbls. w/SK chokes No. 1 and No. 2, skeet-style stock and forearm. Weight: About 7.5 lbs. Later production had wider (10mm) rib. Made from 1960 to 1969.

ARISTOCRAT TRAP MODEL . . . . .NiB $877 Ex $754 Gd $561

468

Franchi Falconet Over/Under Buckskin

Franchi Crown Grade

Franchi Diamond Grade

Franchi Eldorado

SHOTGUNS

NiB $1560 Ex $1230 Gd $800
Classic Combo (two bbl. set) . NiB $2330 Ex $1700 Gd $1200
Elite (engraved w/ gold inlays) . NiB $2000 Ex $1500 Gd $830
Sporting (30-in. ported bbls.) . . NiB $1930 Ex $1460 Gd $830

VELOCE O/U . . . . NiB $1250 Ex $1000 Gd $740
Aluminum engraved receiver w/ gold inlays. 20 or 28 ga. 26- or 28-in. vent rib bbls. w/ choke tubes. Pistol or straight deluxe oil finish stock. Weight: 5.5 to 5.8 lbs. Imported from 2001 to 2005.
Grade II (semi pistol grip). . . . . NiB $1760 Ex $1240 Gd $900
Squire (two bbl. set) . . . . NiB $2070 Ex $1500 Gd $910

STANDARD MODEL AUTOLOADER
Recoil operated. Light alloy receiver. Gauges: 12, 20. Four round magazine. Bbls.: 26-, 28-, 30-inch; plain, solid or vent rib, IC/ M, F chokes. Weight: 12 ga., about 6.25 lbs. 20 ga., 5.13 lbs. Checkered pistol-grip stock and forearm. Made from 1950. Disc.
w/plain bbl. . . . . NiB $490 Ex $335 Gd $260
w/solid rib . . . . NiB $550 Ex $512 Gd $339
w/vent rib . . . . NiB $560 Ex $489 Gd $368

CROWN, DIAMOND AND IMPERIAL GRADE
Same general specifications as Standard Model except these are custom guns of the highest quality. Crown Grade has hunting scene engraving, Diamond Grade has silver-inlaid scroll engraving; Imperial Grade has elaborately engraved hunting scenes w/figures inlaid in gold. Stock and forearm of fancy walnut. Made from 1954 to 1975.

Crown grade . . . . NiB $1670 Ex $1496 Gd $1212
Diamond grade . . . . NiB $2044 Ex $1760 Gd $1233
Imperial grade . . . . NiB $2480 Ex $2239 Gd $1799

STANDARD MODEL MAGNUM
Same general specifications as Standard model except has 3-inch chamber, 32-inch (12 ga.) or 28-inch (20 ga.) F choke bbl., recoil pad. Weight: 12 ga., 8.25 lbs.; 20 ga., 6 lbs. Formerly designated "Superange Model." Made from 1954 to 1988.
w/plain bbl. . . . . NiB $500 Ex $412 Gd $286
w/vent rib . . . . NiB $577 Ex $468 Gd $360

DYNAMIC-12
Same general specifications and appearance as Standard Model, except 12 ga. only, has heavier steel receiver. Weight: About 7.25 lbs. Made from 1965 to 1972.
W/plain bbl. . . . . NiB $522 Ex $430 Gd $331
W/vent rib . . . . NiB $550 Ex $433 Gd $330

DYNAMIC-12 SLUG GUN . . . . . . NiB $578 Ex $490 Gd $354
Same as standard gun except 12 ga. only, has heavier steel receiver. Made 1965 to 1972.

DYNAMIC-12 SKEET GUN . . . . . . NiB $677 Ex $549 Gd $456
Same general specifications and appearance as Standard model except has heavier steel receiver, made only in 12 ga. w/26-inch vent-rib bbl., SK choke, stock and forearm of extra fancy walnut. Made from 1965 to 1972.

ELDORADO MODEL . . . . NiB $588 Ex $370 Gd $355
Same general specifications as Standard model except highest grade w/ gold-filled engraving, stock and forearm of select walnut, vent-rib bbl. only. Made 1954 to 1975.

FALCONET INTERNATIONAL
SKEET MODEL . . . . NiB $1163 Ex $977 Gd $800
Similar to Standard Skeet model but higher grade. Made 1970 to 1974.

Same general specifications as Field Model except made only w/30-inch vent-rib bbls., M/F choke, trap-style stock w/recoil pad, beavertail forearm. Later production had Monte Carlo comb, 10mm rib. Made from 1960 to 1969.

ASTORE HAMMERLESS DOUBLE . . . . . NiB $1032 Ex $866 Gd $713
Boxlock. Anson & Deeley system action. Plain extractors. Double triggers. 12 ga. Various bbl. lengths, chokes, weights. Checkered straight-grip stock and forearm. Made 1937 to 1960.

ASTORE II . . . . NiB $1389 Ex $1166 Gd $876
Similar to Astore S but not as high grade. Furnished w/either plain extractors or auto ejectors, double triggers, pistol-grip stock. Bbls.: 27-inch IC/ IM; 28-inch M/F chokes. Currently manufactured for Franchi in Spain.

ASTORE 5 . . . . NiB $2458 Ex $1987 Gd $1466
Same as Astore except has higher grade wood, fine engraving. automatic ejectors, single trigger, 28-inch bbl. M/F or IM/F chokes are standard on current production. Disc.

DE LUXE MODEL PRITI O/U . . . . NiB $400 Ex $320 Gd $210
Boxlock. 12 or 20 ga. only. 26- or 28-in. vent rib bbls. w/ choke tubes. Single trigger. Weight: 7.4 lbs. Imported from 1988 to 1989.

RENAISSANCE FIELD O/U . . . . NiB $1430 Ex $1240 Gd $680
Boxlock. Blued receiver. 12, 20 or 28 ga. 26- or 28-in. vent rib bbls. w/ choke tubes. Oil finish walnut stock w/ Twin Shock recoil pad. Weight: 5.5 to 6.2 lbs. Imported from 2006 to 2010.
Classic (gold trigger & inlays). . . . .

Franchi Hunter Model w/Ventilated Rib

Franchi Black Magic 48/AL Semiautomatic

Franchi LAW-12

Franchi SPAS-12

Franchi Sporting 2000

FALCONET INTERNATIONAL
TRAP MODEL. . . . . .NiB $1165 Ex $980 Gd $803
Similar to Standard model but higher grade; w/straight or Monte Carlo comb stock. Made from 1970 to 1974.

FALCONET O/U FIELD MODELS
Boxlock. Auto ejectors. Selective single trigger. Gauges: 12, 16, 20, 28, .410. Bbls.: 24-, 26-, 28-, 30-inch; vent rib. Chokes: C/IC, IC/M, M/F. Weight: from about 6 lbs. Engraved lightweight alloy receiver, light-colored in Buckskin model, blued in Ebony model, pickled silver in Silver model. Checkered walnut stock and forearm. Made from 1968 to 1975.
Buckskin or Ebony model . . . . . .NiB $655 Ex $460 Gd $449
Silver model . . . . .NiB $655 Ex $460 Gd $449

FALCONET STANDARD SKEET MODEL . . . . . . .NiB $1055 Ex $876 Gd $690
Same general specifications as Field models except made only w/26-inch bbls. w/SK chokes No. 1 and No. 2, wide vent rib, color-casehardened receiver skeet-style stock and forearm. Weight: 12 ga., about 7.75 lbs. Made from 1970 to 1974.

FALCONET STANDARD TRAP MODEL . . . . . . NiB $1366 Ex $965 Gd $744
Same general specifications as Field models except made only in 12 ga. w/30-inch bbls., choked M/F, wide vent rib, color-casehardened receiver, Monte Carlo trap style stock and forearm, recoil pad. Weight: About 8 lbs. Made from 1970 to 1974.

GAS-OPERATED SEMIAUTOMATIC SHOTGUN
Gas-operated, takedown, hammerless shotgun w/tubular magazine. 12 ga. w/2.75-inch chamber. Five round magazine. Bbls.: 24 to 30 inches w/vent rib. Weight: 7.5 lbs. Gold-plated trigger. Checkered pistol-grip stock and forend of European walnut. Imported from Italy 1985 to 1990.
Prestige model . . . . .NiB $677 Ex $456 Gd $449
Elite model . . . . .NiB $688 Ex $571 Gd $388

HAMMERLESS SIDELOCK DOUBLES
Hand-detachable locks. Self-opening action. Auto ejectors. Double triggers or single trigger. Gauges: 12,16, 20. Bbl. lengths, chokes, weights according to customer's specifications. Checkered stock and forend, straight or pistol grip. Made in six grades — Condor, Imperiale, Imperiale S, Imperiale Montecarlo No. 5, Imperiale Montecarlo No.11, Imperiale Montecarlo Extra — which differ chiefly in overall quality, engraving, grade of wood, checkering, etc.; general specifications are the same. Only the Imperial Montecarlo Extra Grade is currently manufactured.
Condor grade. . . . . NiB $7897 Ex $6200 Gd $4978
Imperial, Imperiales grades . . . . NiB $11,776 Ex $9899 Gd $7217
Imperial Monte Carlo
 grades No. 5, 11 . . . . NiB $32,766 Ex $25,777 Gd $21,989
Imperial Monte Carlo Extra grade. . . . . .Custom only. Prices start at $110,000

HUNTER MODEL
Same general specifications as Standard Model except higher grade w/ engraved receiver; w/ribbed bbl. only. Made from 1950 to 1990.

w/solid rib . . . . NiB $500 Ex $390 Gd $322
w/vent rib . . . . NiB $616 Ex $488 Gd $400

HUNTER MODEL MAGNUM . . . . NiB $544 Ex $454 Gd $330
Same as Standard Model Magnum except higher grade w/engraved receiver, vent rib bbl. only. Formerly designated "Wildfowler Model." Made from 1954 to 1973.

PEREGRINE MODEL 400. . . . . NiB $733 Ex $544 Gd $400
Same general specifications as Model 451 except has steel receiver. Weight (w/26.5-inch bbl.): 6 lbs., 15 oz. Made from 1975 to 1978.

PEREGRINE MODEL 451 O/U . . . . NiB $605 Ex $451 Gd $267
Boxlock. Lightweight alloy receiver. Automatic ejectors. Selective single trigger. 12 ga. Bbls.: 26.5-, 28-inch; choked C/IC, IC/M, M/F; vent rib. Weight (w/26.5-inch bbls.): 6 lbs., 1 oz. Checkered pistol-grip stock and forearm. Made from 1975 to 1978.

SKEET GUN . . . . NiB $450 Ex $320 Gd $228
Same general specifications and appearance as Standard Model except made only w/26-inch vent-rib bbl., SK choke. Stock and forearm of extra fancy walnut. Made from 1972 to 1974.

SLUG GUN . . . . NiB $435 Ex $288 Gd $190
Same as Standard Model except has 22-inch plain bbl., Cyl. bore, folding leaf open rear sight, gold bead front sight. Made 1960 to 1990. Disc.

TURKEY GUN . . . . NiB $556 Ex $377 Gd $298
Same as Standard Model Magnum except higher grade w/turkey scene engraved receiver, 12 ga. only, 36-inch matted-rib bbl., Extra Full choke. Made from 1963 to 1965.

BLACK MAGIC 48/AL SEMIAUTOMATIC
Similar to the Franchi Model 48/AL except w/Franchoke screw-in tubes and matte black receiver w/Black Magic logo. Gauge: 12 or 20, 2.75-inch chamber. Bbls.: 24-, 26-, 28-inch w/vent rib; 24-inch rifled slug w/sights. Weight: 5.2 lbs. (20 ga.). Checkered walnut buttstock and forend. Blued finish.
Standard model . . . . NiB $657 Ex $543 Gd $466
Trap model . . . . NiB $722 Ex $596 Gd $500

FALCONET 2000 O/U . . . . NiB $1355 Ex $1121 Gd $967
Boxlock. Single selective trigger. Selective automatic ejectors. Gauge: 12, 2.75-inch chambers. Bbls.: 26-inch w/Franchoke tubes; IC/M/F. Weight: 6 lbs. Checkered walnut stock and forearm. Engraved silver receiver w/gold-plated game scene. Imported from 1992 to 1993.

LAW-12 SHOTGUN . . . . NiB $689 Ex $454 Gd $377
Similar to the SPAS-12 Model except gas-operated semiautomatic action only, ambidextrous safety, decocking lever and adj. sights. Made from 1983 to 1994.

SPAS-12 SHOTGUN
Selective operating system functions as a gas-operated semi-automatic or pump action. Gauge: 12, 2.75-inch chamber. Seven round magazine. Bbl.: 21.5 inches w/cylinder bore and muzzle protector or optional screw-in choke tubes, matte finish. 41 inches overall w/fixed stock. Weight: 8.75 lbs. Blade front sight, aperture rear sight. Folding or black nylon buttstock w/pistol grip and forend, non-reflective anodized finish. Made from 1983 to 1994. Limited importation.
Fixed stock model . . . . NiB $5000 Ex $4500 Gd $2390
Folding stock model . . . . NiB $7000 Ex $6500 Gd $3390
w/choke tubes, add $150

SPORTING 2000 O/U . . . . NiB $1376 Ex $1125 Gd $966
Similar to the Franchi Falconet 2000. Boxlock. Single selective trigger. Selective automatic ejectors. Gauge: 12; 2.75-inch chambers. Ported

(1992-93) or unported 28-inch bbls., w/vent rib. Weight: 7.75 lbs. Blued receiver. Bead front sight. Checkered walnut stock and forearm; plastic composition buttplate. Imported from 1992-93 and 1997 to 1998.

AUGUSTE FRANCOTTE & CIE., S.A. —
Liège, Belgium

Francotte shotguns for many years were distributed in the U.S. by Abercrombie & Fitch of New York City. This firm has used a series of model designations for Francotte guns which do not correspond to those of the manufacturer. Because so many Francotte owners refer to their guns by the A & F model names and numbers, the A & F series is included in a listing separate from that of the standard Francotte numbers.

BOXLOCK HAMMERLESS DOUBLES
Anson & Deeley system. Side clips. Greener crossbolt on models 6886, 8446, 4996 and 9261; square crossbolt on Model 6930, Greener-Scott crossbolt on Model 8537, Purdey bolt on Models 11/18E and 10/18E/628. Auto ejectors. Double triggers. Made in all standard gauges, barrel lengths, chokes, weights. Checkered stock and forend, straight or pistol-grip. The eight models listed vary chiefly in fastenings as described above, finish and engraving, etc.; custom options increase value. Disc.
Model 6886 . . . . NiB $14,688 Ex $13,879 Gd $11,776
Model 8446 (Francotte Special)
  6930, 4996 . . . . NiB $15,889 Ex $14,799 Gd $14,776
Model 8537, 9261 (Francotte Original),
  11/18E . . . . NiB $17,345 Ex $16,221 Gd $14,998
Model 10/18E/628 . . . . NiB $17,998 Ex $16,789 Gd $15,900

BOXLOCK HAMMERLESS DOUBLES – A & F SERIES
Boxlock, Anson & Deeley type. Crossbolt. Sideplate on all except Knockabout Model. Side clips. Auto ejectors. Double triggers. Gauges: 12, 16, 20, 28, .410. Bbls.: 26- to 32-inch in 12 ga.; 26- and 28-inch in other ga.; any boring. Weight: 4.75 to 8 lbs. depending on gauge and barrel length. Checkered stock and forend; straight, half or full pistol grip. The seven grades (No. 45 Eagle Grade, No. 30, No. 25, No. 20, No. 14, Jubilee Model, Knockabout Model) differ chiefly in overall quality, engraving, grade of wood, checkering, etc.; general specifications are the same. Disc.
Jubilee model No. 14 . . . . . . NiB $4200 Ex $2633 Gd $1470
Jubilee model No. 18 . . . . NiB $4687 Ex $3577 Gd $1890
Jubilee model No. 20 . . . . . . NiB $5670 Ex $4122 Gd $2250
Jubilee model No. 25 . . . . . . NiB $6245 Ex $4738 Gd $2290
Jubilee model No. 30 . . . . . . NiB $7832 Ex $6110 Gd $3580
Eagle grade No. 45 . . . . . . .NiB $11,100 Ex $8854 Gd $5220
Knockabout model . . . . NiB $3377 Ex $2688 Gd $1769
20 ga., add. 125%
28 ga. or .410, add. 300%

BOXLOCK HAMMERLESS DOUBLES (W/SIDEPLATES)
Anson & Deeley system. Reinforced frame w/side clips. Purdey-type bolt except on Model 8535, which has Greener crossbolt. Auto ejectors. Double triggers. Made in all standard gauges, bbl. lengths, chokes, weights. Checkered stock and forend, straight or pistol grip. Models 10594, 8535 and 6982 are of equal quality, differing chiefly in style of engraving; Model 9/40E/38321 is a higher grade gun in all details and has fine English-style engraving. Built to customer specifications.
Models 10594, 8535, 6982 . . . .
NiB $6044 Ex $4566 Gd $3177
Model 9/40E/3831 . . . . NiB $6588 Ex $5344 Gd $3889

FINE O/U SHOTGUN . . . . . NiB $10,566 Ex $8978 Gd $6450
Model 9/40.SE. Boxlock, Anson & Deeley system. Auto ejectors. Double

Francotte Model 8446

Francotte Model 10/18E628

Francotte Model 6886

Francotte Model 9261

triggers. Made in all standard gauges; bbl. length, boring to order. Weight: About 6.75 lbs. 12 ga. Checkered stock and forend, straight or pistol grip. Manufactured to customer specifications. Disc 1990.

FINE SIDELOCK
HAMMERLESS DOUBLE . . . . NiB $26,350 Ex $21,789 Gd $15,680
Model 120.HE/328. Automatic ejectors. Double triggers. Made in all standard ga.; bbl. length, boring, weight to order. Checkered stock and forend, straight or pistol-grip. Manufactured to customer specifications. Disc. 1990.

HALF-FINE O/U SHOTGUN . . . . NiB $11,656 Ex $9377 Gd $6275
Model SOB.E/11082. Boxlock, Anson & Deeley system. Auto ejectors. Double triggers. Made in all standard gauges; barrel length, boring to order. Checkered stock and forend, straight or pistol grip. Note: This model is similar to No. 9/40.SE except general quality lower. Disc 1990.

GALEF SHOTGUNS — Manufactured for J. L. Galef & Son, Inc., New York, New York; by M. A. V. I., Gardone F. T., Italy; by Zabala Hermanos, Eiquetta, Spain; and by Antonio Zoli, Gardone V. T., Italy

SILVER SNIPE OVER/UNDER SHOTGUN . . . . . . NiB $699 Ex $598 Gd $445
Boxlock. Plain extractors. Single trigger. Gauges: 12, 20; 3-inch chambers. Bbls: 26-, 28-, 30-inch (latter in 12 ga. only); IC/M, M/F chokes; vent rib. Weight: 12 ga. w/28-inch bbls., 6.5 lbs. Checkered walnut pistol-grip stock and forearm. Introduced by Antonio Zoli in 1968. Disc. See illustration previous page.

GOLDEN SNIPE . . . . NiB $689 Ex $570 Gd $455
Same as Silver Snipe, except has selective automatic ejectors. Made by Antonio Zoli 1968 to date.

MONTE CARLO TRAP
SINGLE-BARREL SHOTGUN . . . . NiB $356 Ex $221 Gd $177
Hammerless. Underlever. Plain extractor. 12 ga. 32-inch bbl., F choke, vent rib.

Weight: About 8.25 lbs. Checkered pistol-grip stock w/Monte Carlo comb and recoil pad, beavertail forearm. Introduced by M. A. V. I. in 1968. Disc.

SILVER HAWK HAMMERLESS DOUBLE . . . . . . NiB $565 Ex $455 Gd $300
Boxlock. Plain extractors. Double triggers. Gauges: 12, 20; 3-inch chambers. Bbls.: 26-, 28-, 30-inch (latter in 12 ga. only); IC/M, M/F chokes. Weight: 12 ga. w/26-inch bbls., 6 lbs. 6 oz. Checkered walnut pistol-grip stock and beavertail forearm. Made by Angelo Zoli 1968 to 1972.

COMPANION FOLDING SINGLE-BARREL SHOTGUN
Hammerless. Underlever. Gauges: 12 Mag., 16, 20 Mag., 28, .410. Bbls.: 26-inch (.410 only), 28-inch (12, 16, 20, 28), 30-inch (12-ga. only); F choke; plain or vent rib. Weight: 4.5 lbs. for .410 to 5 lbs., 9 oz. for 12 ga. Checkered pistol-grip stock and forearm. Made by M. A. V. I. from 1968-83.
w/plain bbl. . . . . NiB $245 Ex $179 Gd $95
w/ventilated rib . . . . NiB $270 Ex $196 Gd $110

ZABALA HAMMERLESS DOUBLE-BARREL SHOTGUN
Boxlock. Plain extractors. Double triggers. Gauges: 10 Mag., 12 Mag., 16, 20 Mag., 28, .410. Bbls.: 22-, 26-, 28-, 30-, 32-inch; IC/IC, IC/M, M/F chokes. Weight: 12 ga. w/28-inch bbls., 7.75 lbs. Checkered walnut pistol-grip stock and beavertail forearm, recoil pad. Made by Zabala from 1972-83.
10 ga. . . . . NiB $355 Ex $270 Gd $200
Other ga. NiB $244 Ex $179 Gd $115

GAMBA — Gardone V. T. (Brescia), Italy

DAYTONA COMPETITION O/U
Boxlock w/Boss-style locking system. Anatomical single trigger; optional adj., single-selective release trigger. Selective automatic ejectors. Gauge: 12 or 20; 2.75- or 3-inch chambers. Bbls.: 26.75-, 28-, 30- or 32-inch choked SK/SK, IM/F or M/F. Weight: 7.5 to 8.5 lbs. Black or chrome receiver w/blued bbls. Checkered select walnut stock and forearm w/oil finish. Imported by Heckler & Koch until 1992.
American Trap model . . . . NiB $2240 Ex $1680 Gd $1021

Galef Silver Snipe Over/Under Shotgun

Galef Companion Folding Single-Barrel Shotgun

Galef Zabala Hammerless Double-Barrel Shotgun

Pigeon, Skeet, Trap models . . . . NiB $1323 Ex $1078 Gd $877 Sporting model . . . . .NiB $5678 Ex $4498 Gd $3123
Sideplate model . . . . .NiB $11,789 Ex $9809 Gd $5977
Engraved models . . . . NiB $13,788 Ex $10,666 Gd $7477
Sidelock model . . . . . .NiB $28,560 Ex $23,778 Gd $19,580

ARMAS GARBI — Eibar, Spain

MODEL 100
SIDELOCK SHOTGUN . . . . . . NiB $5700 Ex $3433 Gd $2433
Gauges: 12, 16, 20 and 28. Bbls.: 25-, 28-, 30-inch. Action: Holland & Holland pattern sidelock; automatic ejectors and double trigger. Weight: 5 lbs., 6 oz. to 7 lbs. 7 oz. English-style straight grip stock w/fine-line hand-checkered butt; classic forend. Made from 1985 to date.

MODEL 101
SIDELOCK SHOTGUN . . . . . . NiB $6788 Ex $4331 Gd $3000
Same general specifications as Model 100 above, except the side-locks are handcrafted w/hand-engraved receiver; select walnut straight-grip stock.

MODEL 102
SIDELOCK SHOTGUN . . . . . . NiB $7175 Ex $4576 Gd $3177
Similar to the Model 101 except w/large scroll engraving. Made from 1985 to 1993.

MODEL 103
HAMMERLESS DOUBLE
Similar to Model 100 except w/Purdey-type, higher grade engraving.
Model 103A Standard . . . . . .NiB $14,675 Ex $11,650 Gd $9967
Model 103A Royal Deluxe . . . . . . NiB $11,870 Ex $9443 Gd $7655
Model 103B . . . . .NiB $21,660 Ex $17,707 Gd $15,990
Model 103B Royal Deluxe . . . . . .NiB $25,677 Ex $22,770 Gd $18,989

MODEL 200
HAMMERLESS DOUBLE . NiB $17,766 Ex $15,221 Gd $11,488
Similar to Model 100 except w/double heavy-duty locks. Continental-style floral and scroll engraving. Checkered deluxe walnut stock and forearm.

GARCIA CORPORATION — Teaneck, New Jersey

BRONCO 22/.410 O/U COMBO . . . . . NiB $300 Ex $197 Gd $100
Swing-out action. Takedown. 18.5-inch bbls.; .22 LR over, .410 ga. under. Weight: 4.5 lbs. One-piece stock and receiver, crackle finish. Intro. In 1976. Disc.

BRONCO .410 SINGLE SHOT . . . . .NiB $233 Ex $120 Gd $90
Swing-out action. Takedown. .410 ga. 18.5-inch bbl. Weight: 3.5 lbs. One-piece stock and receiver, crackle finish. Intro. In 1967. Disc.

GOLDEN EAGLE FIREARMS INC. — Houston, Texas. Manufactured by Nikko Firearms Ltd., Tochigi, Japan

EAGLE MODEL 5000
GRADE I FIELD O/U . . . . NiB $989 Ex $844 Gd $659
Receiver engraved and inlaid w/gold eagle head. Boxlock. Auto ejectors. Selective single trigger. 12, 20 ga.; 2.75- or 3-inch chambers, 12 ga., 3-inch, 20 ga. Bbls.: 26-, 28-, 30-inch (latter only in 12-ga. 3-inch Mag.); IC/M, M/F chokes; vent rib. Weight: 6.25 lbs., 20 ga.; 7.25 lbs., 12 ga.; 8 lbs., 12-ga. Mag. Checkered pistol-grip stock and semi-beavertail forearm. Imported 1975-82. Note: Guns marketed 1975 to 1976 under the Nikko brand name have white receivers; guns made since 1976 are blued.

EAGLE MODEL 5000
GRADE I SKEET . . . . NiB $954 Ex $743 Gd $522
Same as Field model except has 26- or 28-inch bbls. w/wide (11 mm) vent rib, SK choked. Imported from 1975 to 1982.

EAGLE MODEL 5000
GRADE I TRAP . . . . NiB $954 Ex $755 Gd $569
Same as Field model except has 30-, or 32-inch bbls. w/wide (11 mm) vent rib (M/F, IM/F, F/F chokes), trap-style stock w/recoil pad. Imported from 1975 to 1982.

SHOTGUNS

Golden Eagle
Model 5000 Grade II Field

Gorosabel
Model 504 Shotgun

Greener Empire Model
Hammerless

Greener
Far-Killer

EAGLE MODEL 5000
GRADE II FIELD . . . . .NiB $1077 Ex $890 Gd $776
Same as Grade I Field model except higher grade w/fancier wood, more
elaborate engraving and "screaming eagle" inlaid in gold. Imported
from 1975 to 1982.

EAGLE MODEL 5000
GRADE II SKEET . . . . .NiB $1100 Ex $940 Gd $800
Same as Grade I Skeet model except higher grade w/fancier wood,
more elaborate engraving and "screaming eagle" inlaid in gold; inertia
trigger, vent side ribs. Imported from 1975-82.

EAGLE MODEL 5000
GRADE II TRAP . . . . .NiB $1100 Ex $940 Gd $800
Same as Grade I Trap model except higher grade w/fancier wood, more
elaborate engraving and "screaming eagle" inlaid in gold; inertia trigger,
vent side ribs. Imported from 1975 to 1982.

EAGLE MODEL 5000
GRADE III GRANDEE . . . . . . .NiB $2760 Ex $2255 Gd $1798
Best grade, available in Field, Skeet and Trap models w/same general specifications as lower grades. Has sideplates w/game scene
engraving, scroll on frame and bbls., fancy wood (Monte Carlo
comb, full pistol-grip and recoil pad on Trap model). Made from
1976 to 1982.

GOROSABEL — Spain

MODEL 503 SHOTGUN . . . . . . .NiB $1088 Ex $866 Gd $735
Gauges: 12, 16, 20 and .410. Action: Anson & Deely-style boxlock.
Bbls.: 26-, 27-, and 28-inch. Select European walnut, English or pistol
grip, sliver or beavertail forend, hand-checkering. Scalloped frame and
scroll engraving. Intro. 1985; disc.

MODEL 504 SHOTGUN . . . . . . .NiB $1167 Ex $953 Gd $655
Gauge: 12 or 20. Action: Holland & Holland-style sidelock. Bbl.: 26-,
27-, or 28-inch. Select European walnut, English or pistol grip, sliver or
beavertail forend, hand-checkering. Holland-style large scroll engraving. Inro. 1985; disc.

MODEL 505 SHOTGUN . . . . .NiB $1590 Ex $1266 Gd $965
Gauge: 12 or 20. Action: Holland & Holland-style sidelock. Bbls.: 26-,
27-, or 28-inch. Select European walnut, English or pistol grip, silver
or beavertail forend, hand-checkering. Purdey-style fine scroll and rose
engraving. Intro. 1985; disc.

STEPHEN GRANT — Hertfordshire, England

BEST QUALITY SELF-OPENER DOUBLE-BARREL
SHOTGUN . . . . .NiB $19,870 Ex $16,920 Gd $12,612
Sidelock, self-opener. Gauges: 12, 16 and 20. Bbls.: 25 to 30 inches
standard. Highest-grade English or European walnut straight-grip buttstock and forearm w/Greener type lever. Imported by Stoeger in the
1950s.

BEST QUALITY SIDE-LEVER DOUBLE-BARREL
SHOTGUN . . . . .NiB $13,657 Ex $11,770 Gd $9879
Sidelock, self-lever. Gauges: 12, 16 and 20. Bbls.: 25 to 30 inches
standard. Highest-grade English or European walnut straight-grip
buttstock and forearm w/Greener type lever. Imported by Stoeger in
the 1950s.

W. W. GREENER, LTD. — Birmingham, England

EMPIRE MODEL HAMMERLESS DOUBLES
Boxlock. Non-ejector or w/automatic ejectors. Double triggers. 12 ga.
only (2.75-inch or 3-inch chamber). Bbls.: 28- to 32-inch; any choke
combination. Weight: from 7.25 to 7.75 lbs. depending on bbl. length.

Greifelt Grade No. 1 Over-and-Under Shotgun

Greifelt Model 22

Greifelt Model 103E

Greifelt Model 103

12 (2.75-inch or 3-inch), 10, 8. Bbls.: 28-, 30- or 32-inch. Weight: 7.5 to 9 lbs. in 12 ga. Checkered stock, forend; straight or half-pistol grip.

Non-ejector, 12 ga. . . . . NiB $1577 Ex $1122 Gd $909
Ejector, 12 ga. . . . . NiB $3897 Ex $3138 Gd $2217
Non-ejector, 10 or 8 ga. . . . . . NiB $2886 Ex $2231 Gd $1977
Ejector, 10 or 8 ga. . . . . NiB $5500 Ex $4230 Gd $3110

G. P. (GENERAL PURPOSE)
SINGLE BARREL . . . . NiB $444 Ex $358 Gd $229
Greener Improved Martini Lever Action. Takedown. Ejector. 12 ga. only. Bbl. lengths: 26-, 30-, 32-inch. M or F choke. Weight: 6.25 to 6.75 lbs. depending on bbl. length. Checkered straight-grip stock and forearm.

HAMMERLESS EJECTOR DOUBLE-BARREL SHOTGUNS
Boxlock. Auto ejectors. Double triggers, non-selective or selective single trigger. Gauges: 12, 16, 20, 28, .410 (two latter gauges not supplied in Grades DH40 and DH35). Bbls.: 26-, 28-, 30-inch; any choke combination. Weight: From 4.75 to 8 lbs. Depending on ga. and bbl. length. Checkered stock and forend, straight- or half-pistol grip. The Royal, Crown, Sovereign and Jubilee models differ in quality, engraving, grade of wood, checkering, etc. General specifications are the same.

Royal Model Grade DH75 . . . . . . NiB $4170 Ex $3008 Gd $2166
Crown Model Grade DH55 . . . NiB $5166 Ex $3188 Gd $2270
Sovereign Model Grade DH40 . . . . . NiB $5277 Ex $4866 Gd $3900
Jubilee Model Grade DH35 . . . . . NiB $4197 Ex $3145 Gd $2176
w/selective single trigger, add $400
w/non-selective single trigger, add $300
w/vent. rib, add $425
w/single trigger, add $455

GREIFLELT & COMPANY — Suhl, German

GRADE NO. 1 O/U SHOTGUN
Anson & Deeley boxlock, Kersten fastening. Auto ejectors. Double triggers or single trigger. Elaborately engraved. Gauges: 12, 16, 20, 28, .410. Bbls.: 26- to 32-inch, any combination of chokes, vent or solid matted rib. Weight: 4.25 to 8.25 lbs. depending on ga. and bbl. length. Straight- or pistol-grip stock, Purdey-type forend, both checkered. Manufactured prior to World War II.
w/solid matted-rib bbl.,
    except .410 & 28 ga. . . . . . . NiB $3797 Ex $3166 Gd $2280
w/solid matted-rib bbl.,
    .410 & 28 ga . . . . NiB $3844 Ex $3208 Gd $2300
w/ventilated rib, add $125
w/single trigger, add $550

GRADE NO. 3 O/U SHOTGUN
Same general specifications as Grade No. 1 except less fancy engraving. Manufactured prior to World War II.
w/solid matted-rib bbl.,
    except .410 & 28 ga. . . . . . NiB $2987 Ex $2379 Gd $1979
w/solid matted-rib bbl.,
    .410 & 28 ga. . . . . NiB $5187 Ex $4156 Gd $3110
w/ventilated rib, add $125
w/single trigger, add $450
MODEL 22

HAMMERLESS DOUBLE . . . . NiB $2288 Ex $1843 Gd $1244
Anson & Deeley boxlock. Plain extractors. Double triggers. Gauges: 12 and 16. Bbls.: 28- or 30-inch, M/F choke. Checkered stock and forend, pistol grip and cheekpiece standard, English-style stock also supplied. Manufactured since World War II.

Checkered stock and forend, straight- or half-pistol grip. Also furnished in "Empire Deluxe Grade," this model has same general specs, but deluxe finish.

Empire model, non-ejector. . . . . NiB $1887 Ex $1671 Gd $1388
Empire model, ejector. . . . . . . NiB $1955 Ex $1771 Gd $1480
Empire Deluxe model, non-ejector . . . . . NiB $2088 Ex $1933 Gd $1387
Empire Deluxe model, ejector . . . . . . NiB $2677 Ex $2200 Gd $1588

FARKILLER MODEL GRADE F35
HAMMERLESS DOUBLE-BARREL SHOTGUN
Boxlock. Non-ejector or w/automatic ejectors. Double triggers. Gauges:

MODEL 22E
HAMMERLESS DOUBLE . . . . . NiB $2866 Ex $2430 Gd $1832
Same as Model 22 except has automatic ejectors.

MODEL 103
HAMMLERLESS DOUBLE . . . . . NiB $2100 Ex $1821 Gd $1292
Anson & Deeley boxlock. Plain extractors. Double triggers. Gauges: 12 and 16. Bbls.: 28- or 30-inch, M and F choke. Checkered stock and forend, pistol grip and cheekpiece standard, English-style stock also supplied. Manufactured since World War II.

MODEL 103E
HAMMERLESS DOUBLE . . . . . NiB $2200 Ex $1727 Gd $1224
Same as Model 103 except has automatic ejectors.

MODEL 143E O/U SHOTGUN
General specifications same as pre-war Grade No. 1 Over-and-Under, except this model is not supplied in 28 and .410 ga. or w/32-inch bbls. Model 143E is not as high quality as the Grade No. 1 gun. Mfd. Since World War II.
w/raised matted rib,
    double triggers . . . . NiB $2571 Ex $2068 Gd $1563
w/vent. rib, single
    selective trigger . . . . NiB $2860 Ex $2276 Gd $1865

HAMMERLESS DRILLING (THREE-BARREL
COMBINATION GUN) . . . . . . NiB $3677 Ex $3220 Gd $2179
Boxlock. Plain extractors. Double triggers, front single set for rifle bbl. Gauges: 12, 16, 20; rifle bbl. in any caliber adapted to this type of gun. 26-inch bbls. Weight: About 7.5 lbs. Auto rear sight operated by rifle bbl. selector. Checkered stock and forearm, pistol-grip and cheekpiece standard. Manufactured prior to WW II. Note: Value shown is for guns chambered for cartridges readily obtainable. If rifle bbl. is an odd foreign caliber, value will be considerably less.

O/U COMBINATION GUN
Similar in design to this maker's over-and-under shotguns. Gauges: 12, 16, 20, 28, .410; rifle bbl. in any caliber adapted to this type of gun. Bbls.: 24- or 26-inch, solid matted rib. Weight: From 4.75 to 7.25 lbs. Folding rear sight. Manufactured prior to WWII. Note: Values shown are for gauges other than .410 w/rifle bbl. Chambered for a cartridge readily obtainable; if in an odd foreign caliber, value will be considerably less. .410 ga. increases in value by about 50%.
w/non-automatic ejector . . . . . . NiB $5477 Ex $4651 Gd $3822
w/automatic ejector . . . . NiB $6055 Ex $5310 Gd $4430

HARRINGTON & RICHARDSON ARMS —
Gardner, Massachussets
now H&R 1871, Inc.

Formerly Harrington & Richardson Arms Co. of Worcester, Mass. One of the oldest and most distinguished manufacturers of handguns, rifles and shotguns, H&R suspended operations on January 24, 1986. In 1987, New England Firearms was established as an independent company producing selected H&R models under the NEF logo. In 1991, H&R 1871, Inc. was formed from the residual of the parent company and then took over the New England Firearms facility. H&R 1871 produced firearms under both their logo and the NEF brand name until 1999, when the Marlin Firearms Company acquired the assets of H&R 1871.

NO. 3 HAMMERLESS
SINGLE-SHOT SHOTGUN . . . . . . NiB $230 Ex $115 Gd $85
Takedown. Automatic ejector. Gauges: 12, 16, 20, .410. Bbls.: plain, 26- to 32-inch, F choke. Weight: 6.5 to 7.25 lbs. depending on ga.

Harrington & Richardson
No. 3, 5, 6, 7 and 8 shotguns (top to bottom)

and bbl. length. Plain pistol-grip stock and forend. Discontinued 1942.

NO. 5 STANDARD LIGHTWEIGHT
HAMMER SINGLE . . . . NiB $227 Ex $120 Gd $90
Takedown. Auto ejector. Gauges: 24, 28, .410. Bbls.: 26- or 28-inch, F choke. Weight: About 4 to 4.75 lbs. Plain pistol-grip stock/forend. Discontinued 1942.

NO. 6 HEAVY BREECH SINGLE-SHOT
HAMMER SHOTGUN . . . . NiB $244 Ex $135 Gd $90
Takedown. Automatic ejector. Gauges: 10, 12, 16, 20. Bbls.: Plain, 28- to 36-inch, F choke. Weight: About 7 to 7.25 lbs. Plain stock and forend. Discontinued 1942.

Harrington & Richardson
Model 400 Pump

Harrington & Richardson
Model 403 Autoloading

Harrington & Richardson
Model 404C

Harrington & Richardson
Model 440

NO. 7 & 9 BAY STATE SINGLE-SHOT
HAMMER SHOTGUN . . . . **NiB $235 Ex $140 Gd $95**
Takedown. Automatic ejector. Gauges: 12, 16, 20, .410. Bbls.: Plain 26- to 32-inch, F choke. Weight: 5.5 to 6.5 lbs. depending on ga. and bbl. length. Plain pistol-grip stock and forend. Discontinued 1942.

NO. 8 STANDARD SINGLE-SHOT
HAMMER SHOTGUN . . . . **NiB $255 Ex $145 Gd $98**
Takedown. Automatic ejector. Gauges: 12, 16, 20, 24, 28, .410. Bbl.: plain, 26- to 32-inch, F choke. Weight: 5.5 to 6.5 lbs. depending on ga. and bbl. length. Plain pistol-grip stock and forend. Made from 1908 to 1942.

MODEL 348 GAMESTER
BOLT-ACTION SHOTGUN . . . . . **NiB $217 Ex $117 Gd $88**
Takedown. 12 and 16 ga. Two round tubular magazine, 28-inch bbl, F choke. Plain pistol-grip stock. Weight: About 7.5 lbs. Made from 1949 to 1954.

MODEL 349 GAMESTER DELUXE . . . . .**NiB $220 Ex $115 Gd $85**
Same as Model 348 except has 26-inch bbl. W/adj. choke device, recoil pad. Made from 1953 to 1955.

MODEL 351 HUNTSMAN
BOLT-ACTION SHOTGUN . . . . . **NiB $239 Ex $200 Gd $125**
Takedown. 12 and 16 ga. Two round tubular magazine. Pushbutton safety. 26-inch bbl. w/H&R variable choke. Weight: About 6.75 lbs. Monte Carlo stock w/recoil pad. Made from 1956 to 1958.

MODEL 400 PUMP . . . .**NiB $335 Ex $254 Gd $180**
Hammerless. Gauges: 12, 16, 20. Tubular magazine holds 4 shells. 28-inch bbl., F choke. Weight: About 7.25 lbs. Plain pistol-grip stock (recoil pad in 12 and 16 ga.), grooved slide handle. Made from 1955 to 1967.

MODEL 401 . . . .**NiB $335 Ex $240 Gd $190**
Same as Model 400 on previous page, except has H&R variable choke. Made from 1956-63.

MODEL 402 . . . .**NiB $315 Ex $220 Gd $170**
Similar to Model 400 except .410 ga., weight: About 5.5 lbs. Made from 1959-67.

MODEL 403 AUTOLOADING
SHOTGUN. . . . .**NiB $338 Ex $300 Gd $210**
Takedown. .410 ga. Tubular magazine holds four shells. 26-inch bbl., F choke. Weight: About 5.75 lbs. Plain pistol-grip stock and forearm. Made in 1964.

MODEL 404/404C PUMP
SHOTGUN. . . . .**NiB $366 Ex $275 Gd $209**
Boxlock. Plain extractors. Double triggers. Gauges: 12, 20, .410. Bbls.: 28-inch in 12 ga. (M/F choke), 26-inch in 20 ga. (IC/M and .410 (F/F). Weight: 5.5 to 7.25 lbs. Plain walnut-finished hardwood stock and forend on Model 404; 404C checkered. Made in Brazil by Amadeo Rossi from 1969-1972.

MODEL 440 PUMP SHOTGUN . . . . . .**NiB $255 Ex $194 Gd $145**
Hammerless. Gauges: 12, 16, 20. 2.75-inch chamber in 16 ga., 3-inch

Harrington & Richardson
Model 1212 Waterfowl

Harrington & Richardson
Golden Squire — Model 159

Harrington & Richardson
Harrich No. 1

in 12 and 20 ga. Three round magazine. Bbls.: 26-, 28-, 30-inch; IC, M, F choke. Weight: 6.25 lbs. Plain pistol-grip stock and slide handle, recoil pad. Made from 1968-73.

MODEL 442 PUMP SHOTGUN . . . . . NiB $320 Ex $254 Gd $188
Same as Model 440 except has vent rib bbl., checkered stock and forearm, weight: 6.75 lbs. Made from 1969-73.

ULTRA SLUG SERIES . . . . NiB $287 Ex $220 Gd $175
Singel shot 12 or 20 ga w/3-inch chamber w/heavy-wall 24-inch fully rifled bbl. w/scope . Weight: 9 lbs. Walnut-stained Monte Carlo stock, sling swivels, black nylon sling. Made from 1995 to date.

MODEL 1212 FIELD . . . . NiB $435 Ex $321 Gd $250
Boxlock. Plain extractors. Selective single trigger. 12 ga., 2.75-inch chambers. 28-inch bbls., IC/IM, vent rib. Weight: 7 lbs. Checkered walnut pistol-gip stock and fluted forearm. Made 1976-80 by Lanber Arms S. A., Zaldibar (Vizcaya), Spain.

MODEL 1212
WATERFOWL GUN . . . . NiB $544 Ex $368 Gd $277
Same as Field Gun except chambered for 12-ga, 3-inch mag. shells, has 30-inch bbls., M/F chokes, stock and recoil pad, weight: 7.5 lbs. Made from 1976 to 1980.

MODEL 1908
SINGLE-SHOT SHOTGUN . . . . . NiB $244 Ex $177 Gd $100
Takedown. Automatic ejector. Gauges: 12, 16, 24 and 28. Bbls.: 26- to 32-inch, F choke. Weight: 5.25 to 6.5 lbs. depending on ga. and bbl. length. Casehardened receiver. Plain pistol-grip stock. Bead front sight. Made from 1908 to 1934.

MODEL 1908 .410 (12MM)
SINGLE-SHOT SHOTGUN . . . . . NiB $233 Ex $177 Gd $120

Same general specifications as standard Model 1908 except chambered for .410 or 12mm shot cartridge w/bbl. milled down at receiver to give a more pleasing contour.

MODEL 1915 SINGLE-SHOT SHOTGUN
Takedown. Both non-auto and auto-ejectors available. Gauges: 24, 28, .410, 14mm and 12mm. Bbls.: 26- or 28-inch, F choke. Weight: 4 to 4.75 lbs. depending on ga. and bbl. length. Plain black walnut stock w/semi pistol-grip.
24 ga. . . . . NiB $390 Ex $275 Gd $190
28, .410 ga. . . . . NiB $390 Ex $275 Gd $190

FOLDING GUN . . . . NiB $320 Ex $210 Gd $165
Single bbl. hammer shotgun hinged at the front of the frame, the bbl. folds down against the stock. Light Frame model: gauges — 28, 14mm, .410; 22-inch bbl.; weighs about 4.5 lbs. Heavy Frame model: gauges — 12, 16, 20, 28, .410; 26-inch bbl.; weighs from 5.75 to 6.5 lbs. Plain pistol-grip stock and forend. Disc. 1942.

GOLDEN SQUIRE MODEL 159 SINGLE-BARREL
HAMMER SHOTGUN . . . . NiB $265 Ex $170 Gd $121
Hammerless. Side lever. Automatic ejection. Gauges: 12, 20. Bbls: 30-inch in 12 ga., 28-inch in 20 ga., both F choke. Weight: About 6.5 lbs. Straight-grip stock w/recoil pad, forearm w/Schnabel. Made from 1964 to 1966.

GOLDEN SQUIRE JR.
MODEL 459 . . . . NiB $255 Ex $170 Gd $125
Same as Model 159 except gauges 20 and .410, 26-inch bbl., youth stock. Made in 1964.

HARRICH NO. 1 SINGLE-BARREL
TRAP GUN . . . . NiB $1733 Ex $1456 Gd $974
Anson & Deeley-type locking system w/Kersten top locks and double underlocking lugs. Sideplates engraved w/hunting scenes. 12 ga. Bbls.:

Harrington & Richardson
Topper No. 48

Harrington & Richardson
Topper No. 162 — Slug Gun

Harrington & Richardson
Topper Model 198 (098)

Harrington & Richardson
Topper Model 490 —
Greenwing

32-, 34-inch; F choke; high vent rib. Weight: 8.5 lbs. Checkered Monte Carlo stock w/pistol-grip and recoil pad, beavertail forearm, of select walnut. Made in Austria 1971 to 1975.

"TOP RIB"
SINGLE-BARREL SHOTGUN . . . . . . **NiB $335 Ex $265 Gd $190**
Takedown. Auto ejector. Gauges: 12, 16 and 20. Bbls.: 28- to 30-inch, F choke w/full-length matted top rib. Weight: 6.5 to 7 lbs. depending on ga. and bbl. length. Black walnut pistol-grip stock (capped) and forend; both checkered. Flexible rubber buttplate. Made during 1930s.

TOPPER NO. 48 SINGLE-BARREL
HAMMER SHOTGUN . . . .**NiB $280 Ex $195 Gd $145**
Similar to old Model 8 Standard. Takedown. Top lever. Auto ejector. Gauges: 12, 16, 20, .410. Bbls.: plain; 26- to 30-inch; M or F choke. Weight: 5.5 to 6.5 lbs. depending on ga. and bbl. length. Plain pistol-grip stock and forend. Made from 1946 to 1957.

TOPPER MODEL 099 DELUXE . . . . **NiB $244 Ex $155 Gd $110**
Same as Model 158 except has matte nickel finish, semipistol grip walnut-finished American hardwood stock; semibeavertail forearm; 12, 16, 20, and .410 ga. Made from 1982 to 1986.

TOPPER MODEL 148 SINGLE-SHOT
HAMMER SHOTGUN . . . .**NiB $200 Ex $177 Gd $120**
Takedown. Side lever. Auto-ejection. Gauges: 12, 16, 20, .410. Bbls.: 12 ga.,30-, 32- and 36-inch; 16 ga., 28- and 30-inch; 20 and .410

ga., 28-inch; F choke. Weight: 5 to 6.5 lbs. Plain pistol-grip stock and forend, recoil pad. Made from 1958 to 1961.

TOPPER MODEL 158 (058) SINGLE-SHOT
HAMMER SHOTGUN . . . .**NiB $245 Ex $165 Gd $120**
Takedown. Side lever. Automatic ejection. Gauges: 12, 20, .410 (2.75-inch and 3-inch shells); 16 (2.75-inch). bbl. length and choke combinations: 12 ga., 36-inch/F, 32-inch/F, 30-inch/F, 28-inch/F or M; .410, 28-inch/F. Weight: about 5.5 lbs. Plain pistol-grip stock and forend, recoil pad. Made from 1962 to 1981. Note: Designation changed to 058 in 1974.

TOPPER MODEL 162
SLUG GUN . . . . **NiB $300 Ex $221 Gd $165**
Same as Topper Model 158 except has 24-inch bbl., Cyl. bore, w/rifle sights. Made from 1968 to 1986.

TOPPER MODEL 176 10 GA.
MAGNUM . . . . **NiB $280 Ex $185 Gd $145**
Similar to Model 158, but has 36-inch heavy bbl. chambered for 3.5-inch 10- ga. Mag. shells, weight: 10 lbs.; stock w/Monte Carlo comb and recoil pad, longer and fuller forearm. Made from 1977 to 1986.

TOPPER MODEL 188 DELUXE . . . . **NiB $265 Ex $200 Gd $145**
Same as standard Topper Model 148 except has chromed frame, stock and forend in black, red, yellow, blue, green, pink, or purple colored finish. .410 ga. only. Made from 1958 to 1961.

Harrington & Richardson
Topper — Classic Youth

Harrington & Richardson
Topper — Deluxe

TOPPER MODEL 198 (098) DELUXE. . . . . .NiB $244 Ex $180 Gd $130
Same as Model 158 except has chrome-plated frame, black finished stock and forend; 12, 20 and .410 ga. Made 1962 to 1981. Note: Designation changed to 098 in 1974.

TOPPER JR. MODEL 480 . . . . . NiB $236 Ex $165 Gd $100
Similar to No. 48 Topper except has youth-size stock, 26-inch bbl, .410 ga. only. Made from 1958-61.

TOPPER NO. 488 DELUXE . . . . .NiB $254 Ex $179 Gd $115
Same as standard No. 48 Topper except chrome-plated frame, black lacquered stock and forend, recoil pad. Disc. 1957.

TOPPER MODEL 490 . . . . .NiB $245 Ex $185 Gd $135
Same as Model 158 except has youth-size stock (3 inches shorter), 26-inch bbl.; 20 and 28 ga. (M choke), .410 (F). Made 1962 to 1986.

TOPPER MODEL 490 GREENWING . . . . .NiB $266 Ex $190 Gd $140
Same as the Model 490 except has a special high-polished finish. Made from 1981 to 1986.

TOPPER JR. MODEL 580 . . . . . .NiB $210 Ex $166 Gd $100
Same as Model 480 except has colored stocks as on Model 188. Made from 1958 to 1961.

TOPPER MODEL 590 . . . . .NiB $210 Ex $166 Gd $100
Same as Model 490 except has chrome-plated frame, black finished stock and forend. Made from 1962 to 1963.

The following models are manufactured and distributed by the reorganized company of H&R 1871, Inc.

MODEL 098 TOPPER CLASSIC YOUTH . . . . . . NiB $200 Ex $155 Gd $100
Same as Topper Junior except also available in 28 ga. and has checkered American black walnut stock/forend w/satin finish and recoil pad. Made from 1991 to date.

MODEL 098 TOPPER DELUXE. . . . . NiB $200 Ex $155 Gd $100
Same as Model 098 Single Shot Hammer except in 12 ga., 3-inch chamber only. 28-inch bbl.; Mod. choke tube. Made 1992 to date.

MODEL 098 TOPPER
DELUXE RIFLED SLUG GUN . . . . . NiB $217 Ex $125 Gd $95
Same as Topper Deluxe Shotgun except has compensated 24-inch rifled slug bbl. Nickel plated receiver and blued bbl. Black finished hardwood stock. Made from 1996 to date.

MODEL 098 TOPPER HAMMER
SINGLE-SHOT SHOTGUN . . . . .NiB $165 Ex $115 Gd $88
Side lever. Automatic ejector. Gauges: 12, 20 and .410; 3-inch chamber. Bbls.: 28-inch, (12 ga./M); 26-inch, (20 ga./M); 26-inch (.410/F). Weight: 5 to 6 lbs. Satin nickel receiver, blued bbl. Plain pistol-grip stock and semibeavertail forend w/black finish. Re-Intro. 1992.

MODEL 098 TOPPER JUNIOR . . . . . .NiB $200 Ex $129 Gd $90
Same as Model 098 except has youth-size stock and 22-inch bbl. 20 or .410 ga. only. Made 1991 to date.

MODEL .410 TAMER SHOTGUN . . NiB $200 Ex $145 Gd $100
Takedown. Topper-style single-shot, side lever action w/auto ejector. Gauge: .410; 3-inch chamber. 19.5-inch bbl. 33 inches overall. Weight: 5.75 lbs. Black polymer thumbhole stock designed to hold 4 extra shotshells. Matte nickel finish. Made from 1994 to date.

MODEL N.W.T.F. TURKEY MAG
Same as Model 098 Single-Shot Hammer except has 24-inch bbl. chambered 10 or 12 ga. w/3.5-inch chamber w/screw-in choke tube. Weight: 6 lbs. American hardwood stock, Mossy Oak camo finish. Made from 1991 to 1996.
NWTF 10 ga. Turkey Mag (Made 1996) . . . . . . .NiB $200 Ex $125 Gd $90
NWTF 12 ga. Turkey Mag (Made 1991-95). . . . . .NiB $200 Ex $125 Gd $90

MODEL N. W. T. F.
YOUTH TURKEY GUN. . . . . .NiB $195 Ex $115 Gd $88
Same as Model N.W.T.F. Turkey Mag except has 22-inch bbl. chambered in 20 ga. w/3-inch chamber and fixed full choke. Realtree camo finish. Made from 1994 to 1995.

MODEL SB1-920
ULTRA SLUG HUNTER. . . . . .NiB $275 Ex $198 Gd $155
Special 12 ga. action w/12 ga. bbl. blank underbored to 20 ga. to form a fully rifled slug bbl. Gauge: 20 w/3 inch chamber. 24-inch bbl. Weight: 8.5 lbs. Satin nickel receiver, blued bbl. Walnut finished hardwood Monte Carlo stock. Made from 1996 to 1998.

Heckler & Koch Red Lion Mark II

Heckler & Koch Classic Lion Grade I

MODEL ULTRA SLUG HUNTER.....NiB $275 Ex $219 Gd $175
12 or 20 ga. w/3-inch chamber. 22- or 24-inch rifled bbl. Weight: 9 lbs. Matte black receiver and bbl. Walnut finished hardwood Monte Carlo stock. Made from 1997 to date.

MODEL ULTRA SLUG HUNTER DELUXE ...... NiB $335 Ex $210 Gd $155
Similar to Ultra Slug Hunter model except with compensated bbl. Made from 1997 to date.

HECKLER & KOCH FABARM — Oberndorf am Neckar, Germany, and Sterling, Virginia

CLASSIC LION SIDE-BY-SIDE SHOTGUN
12 ga. only. 28- or 30-inch non-ported Tribor bbl. w/3-inch chamber. 46.5 to 48.5-inches overall. Weight: 7 to 7.2 lbs. Five choke tubes; C, IC, M, IM, F. Traditional boxlock design. Oil-finished walnut forearms and stocks w/diamond-cut checkering. Imported from 1999 to date.
Classic Lion Grade I .... NiB $1456 Ex $1288 Gd $890
Classic Lion Grade II ...... NiB $2177 Ex $1766 Gd $1292

CAMO LION SEMI-AUTO SHOTGUN.....NiB $988 Ex $853 Gd $679
12 ga. Only. 24 to 28-inches Tribor bbl. 44.25-48.25-inches overall. Weight: 7-7.2 lbs. 3 inch chamber w/5 choke tubes - C, IC, M, IM, F. Two round mag. Camo covered walnut stock w/rear front bar sights. Imp. 1999 to date.

MAX LION O/U SHOTGUN.....NiB $1977 Ex $1660 Gd $1000
12 or 20 ga. 26- 28- or 30-inch TriBore system bbls. 42.5-47.25-inches overall. Weight: 6.8-7.8 lbs. 3-inch chamber w/5 choke tubes - C, IC, M, IM, F. Single selective adj. trigger and auto ejectors. Side plates w/high-grade stock and rubber recoil pad. Made from 1999 to date.

RED LION MARK II SEMI-AUTO
SHOTGUN.....................NiB $954 Ex $700 Gd $544
12 ga. Only. 24- 26- or 28-inch TriBore system bbls. 44.25 to 48.25-inches overall. Weight: 7 to 7.2 lbs. 3-inch chamber w/five choke tubes- C, IC, M, IM, F. Two round magazine. Matte finish w/ walnut wood stock. Rubber vented recoil pad w/leather cover. Made from 1999 to date.

SILVER LION O/U SHOTGUN. ...... NiB $1388 Ex $1097 Gd $766
12 or 20 ga. 26- 28- or 30-inch TriBore system bbls. 43.25-47.25 inches overall. 3-inch chamber w/5 choke tubes - C, IC, M, IM, F. Single selective trig. and auto ejectors. Wal. stock w/rubber recoil pad. Made from 1999 to date.

SPORTING CLAY LION
SEMI-AUTO SHOTGUN ....NiB $1087 Ex $944 Gd $644
12 ga. only. 28- or 30-inch bbl. w/3-inch chamber and ported Tribore system barrel. Matte finish w/gold plated trigger and carrier release button. Made from 1999 to date.

HERCULES SHOTGUNS

See Listings under "W" for Montgomery Ward.

HEYM — Münnerstadt, Germany

MODEL 22S "SAFETY" SHOTGUN/
RIFLE COMBINATION .... NiB $3798 Ex $2889 Gd $2250
16 and 20 ga. Cal: .22 Mag., .22 Hornet, .222 Rem., .222 Rem. Mag., 5.6x50R Mag., 6.5x57R, 7x57R, .243 Win. 24-inch bbls. 40 inches overall. Weight: About 5.5 lbs. Single-set trigger. Left-side bbl. selector. Integral dovetail base for scope mounting. Arabesque engraving. Walnut stock. Disc. 1993.

MODEL 55 BF SHOTGUN/
RIFLE COMBO .... NiB $7045 Ex $5370 Gd $4398
12, 16 and 20 ga. Calibers: 5.6x50R Mag., 6.5x57R, 7x57R, 7x65R, .243 Win., .308 Win., .30-06. 25-inch bbls., 42 inches overall. Weight: About 6.75 lbs. Black satin-finished, corrosion-resistant bbls. of Krupp special steel. Hand-checkered walnut stock w/long pistol-grip. Hand-engraved leaf scroll. German cheekpiece. Disc. 1988.

J. C. HIGGINS

See Sears, Roebuck & Company.

HUGLU HUNTING FIREARMS — Huglu, Turkey. Imported by Turkish Firearms Corp.

MODEL 101 B 12 AT-DT
COMBO O/U TRAP .... NiB $2387 Ex $1885 Gd $1444
Over/Under boxlock. 12 ga. w/3-inch chambers. Combination 30- or 32-inch top single & O/U bbls. w/fixed chokes or choke tubes. Weight: 8 lbs. Automatic ejectors or extractors. Single selective trigger. Manual safety. Circassian walnut Monte Carlo trap stock w/ palm-swell grip and recoil pad. Silvered frame w/engraving. Imported from 1993 to 1997.

SHOTGUNS

Heym Model 22S
"Safety" Shotgun/Rifle Combination Gun

Heym Model 55
BF Shotgun/Rifle

MODEL 101 B 12 ST O/U TRAP . . . . . NiB $1577 Ex $1377 Gd $937
Same as Model 101 AT-DT except in 32-inch O/U configuration only. Imported from 1994 to 1996.

MODEL 103 B 12 ST O/U
Boxlock. Gauges: 12, 16, 20, 28 or .410. 28-inch bbls. w/fixed chokes. Engraved action w/inlaid game scene and dummy sideplates. Double triggers, extractors and manual safety. Weight: 7.5 lbs. Circassian walnut stock. Imported 1995 to 1996.
Model 103B w/extractors . . . . . . NiB $954 Ex $733 Gd $496
28 ga. and .410, add $125

MODEL 103 C 12 ST O/U
Same general specs as Model 103 B 12 S except w/extractors or ejectors. 12 or 20 ga. w/3-inch chambers. Black receiver w/50% engraving coverage. Imported from 1995 to 1097.
Model 103C w/extractors . . . . NiB $920 Ex $733 Gd $578
Model 103C w/ejectors. . . . . NiB $979 Ex $766 Gd $634

MODEL 103 D 12 ST O/U
Same gen. specs as Mdl. 103 B 12 ST except stand. boxlock. Ext. or eject. 12 or 20 ga. w/3-inch chambers. 80% engraving coverage. Imp. from 1995 to 1997.
Model 103D w/extractors . . . . . . NiB $920 Ex $733 Gd $578
Model 103D w/ejectors . . . . NiB $979 Ex $766 Gd $634

MODEL 103 F 12 ST O/U
Same as Model 103 B except extractors or ejectors. 12 or 20 ga. only. 100% engraving coverage. Imported from 1996 to 1997.
Model 103F w/extractors . . . . . . NiB $1000 Ex $835 Gd $657
Model 103F w/ejectors . . . . NiB $1154 Ex $1010 Gd $745

MODEL 104 A 12 ST O/U
Boxlock. Gauges: 12, 20, 28 or .410. 28-inch bbls. w/fixed chokes or choke tubes. Silvered, engraved receiver w/15% engraving coverage. Double triggers, manual safety and extractors or ejectors. Weight: 7.5 lbs. Circassian walnut stock w/field dimensions. Imported 1995 to 1997.

Model 104A w/extractors . . . . NiB $777 Ex $688 Gd $545
Model 104A w/ejectors. . . . . NiB $790 Ex $700 Gd $600
28 ga. and .410, add $150
w/Choke Tubes, add $75

MODEL 200 SERIES DOUBLE
Boxlock. Gauges: 12, 20, 28, or .410 w/3-inch chambers. 28-inch bbls. w/fixed chokes. Silvered, engraved receiver. Extractors, manual safety, single selective trigger or double triggers. Weight: 7.5 lbs. Circassion walnut stock. Imported from 1995 to 1997.
Model 200 (w/15%
engraving coverage, SST) . . . . . NiB $1033 Ex $878 Gd $633
Model 201 (w/30%
engraving coverage, SST) . . . . NiB $1277 Ex $1100 Gd $955
Model 202 (w/Greener
cross bolt, DT) . . . . NiB $888 Ex $645 Gd $469
28 ga. and .410, add $125

HIGH STANDARD SPORTING ARMS —
East Hartford, Connecticut; formerly High Standard Mfg. Corp. of Hamden, CT

In 1966, High Standard introduced new series of Flite-King Pumps and Supermatic autoloaders, both readily identifiable by the damascened bolt and restyled checkering. To avoid confusion, these models are designated "Series II" in this text. This is not an official factory designation. Operation of this firm was discontinued in 1984.

FLITE-KING FIELD
PUMP—12 GA. . . . . NiB $256 Ex $180 Gd $110
Hammerless. Magazine holds five rounds. Bbls.: 26-inch IC, 28-inch M or F, 30-inch F choke. Weight: 7.25 lbs. Plain pistol-grip stock and slide handle. Made from 1960 to 1966.

FLITE-KING BRUSH—12 GA. . . . . NiB $285 Ex $245 Gd $170
Same as Flite-King Field 2 except has 18- or 20-inch bbl. (cylinder bore) w/rifle sights. Made from 1962 to 1964.

High Standard Flite-King Brush

High Standard Flite-King Deluxe Rib — 12 Gauge

High Standard Flite-King Deluxe Rib — 12 Gauge (Adjustable Choke)

FLITE-KING BRUSH DELUXE . . . . . .NiB $275 Ex $190 Gd $120
Same as Flite-King Brush except has adj. peep rear sight, checkered pistol grip, recoil pad, fluted slide handle, swivels and sling. Not available w/18-inch bbl. Made from 1964 to 1966.

FLITE-KING BRUSH (SERIES II) . . . . . NiB $275 Ex $190 Gd $120
Same as Flite-King Deluxe 12 (II) except has 20-inch bbl., cylinder bore, w/rifle sights. Weight: 7 lbs. Made from 1966 to 1975.

FLITE-KING BRUSH DELUXE (II) . . . . .NiB $290 Ex $200 Gd $135
Same as Flite-King Brush (II) except has adj. peep rear sight, swivels and sling. Made from 1966-75.

FLITE-KING DELUXE 12 GA. (SERIES II)
Hammerless. Five round magazine. 27-inch plain bbls.w/adj. choke. 26-inch IC, 28-inch M or F. 30-inch F choke. Weight: About 7.25 lbs. Checkered pistol-grip stock and forearm, recoil pad. Made from 1966 to 1975.
w/adj. choke . . . . NiB $245 Ex $170 Gd $110
w/fixed choke . . . . NiB $245 Ex $170 Gd $110

FLITE-KING DELUXE
20, 28, .410 GA. (SERIES II) . . . . . NiB $255 Ex $178 Gd $120
Same as Flite-King Deluxe 12 (II) except chambered for 20 and .410 ga. 3-inch shell, 28 ga. 2.75-inch shell w/20- or 28-inch plain bbl. Weight: About 6 lbs. Made from 1966 to 1975.

FLITE-KING DELUXE RIB 12 GA. . . . . .NiB $280 Ex $200 Gd $155
Same as Flite-King Field 12 except vent rib bbl. (28-inch M or F. 30-inch F). Checkered stock and forearm. Made from 1961-66.

FLITE-KING DELUXE RIB 12 GA. (II)
Same as Flite-King Deluxe 12 (II) except has vent rib bbl., available in 27-inch w/adj. choke, 28-inch M or F, 30-inch F choke. Made from 1966 to 1975.
w/adj. choke . . . . .NiB $292 Ex $217 Gd $175
w/fixed choke. . . . . .NiB $292 Ex $217 Gd $175

FLITE-KING DELUXE RIB 20 GA. . . . NiB $265 Ex $198 Gd $125
Same as Flite-King Field 20 except vent-rib bbl. (28 inch M or F), checkered stock and slide handle. Made from 1962 to 1966.

FLITE-KING DELUXE RIB 20, 28, .410 GA. (SERIES II)
Same as Flite-King Deluxe 20, 28, .410 (II) except 20 ga. available w/27-inch adj. choke, 28-inch M or F choke. Weight: about 6.25 lbs. Made from 1966 to 1975.
w/adj. choke . . . . .NiB $265 Ex $198 Gd $125
w/o adj. choke . . . . .NiB $265 Ex $198 Gd $125

FLITE-KING DELUXE SKEET GUN
12 GA. (SERIES II). . . . . .NiB $544 Ex $423 Gd $318
Same as Flite-King Deluxe Rib 12 (II) except available only w/26-inch vent rib bbl., SK choke, recoil pad optional. Made from 1966 to 1975.

FLITE-KING DELUXE SKEET GUN
20, 28, .410 GA. (SERIES II) . . . . . .NiB $454 Ex $39 Gd $243
Same as Flite-King Deluxe Rib 20, 28, .410 (II) except available only w/26-inch vent-rib bbl., SK choke. Made 1966 to 1975.

FLITE-KING DELUXE TRAP
GUN (SERIES II)). . . . . NiB $338 Ex $265 Gd $129
Same as Flite-King Deluxe Rib 12 (II) except available only w/30-inch vent-rib bbl., F choke; trap-style stock. Made from 1966 to 1975.

FLITE-KING FIELD PUMP 20 GA. . . . .NiB $250 Ex $175 Gd $135
Hammerless. Chambered for 3-inch Magnum shells, also handles 2.75-inch. Magazine holds four rounds. Bbls.: 26-inch IC, 28-inch M or F choke. Weight: About 6 lbs. Plain pistol-grip stock and slide handle. Made from 1961 to 1966.

FLITE-KING FIELD PUMP
SHOTGUN 16 GA . . . . NiB $250 Ex $175 Gd $135
Same general specifications as Flite-King 12 except not available in Brush, Skeet and Trap Models or 30-inch bbl. Values same as for 12-ga. guns. Made from 1961 to 1965.

High Standard Flite-King Field
12 Gauge

High Standard Flite-King Field
20 Gauge

High Standard Flite-King Field
Trophy
20 Gauge

High Standard Supermatic Deluxe
12 Gauge (II)

High Standard Supermatic Deluxe
12 Gauge (II) (Adjustable Choke)

FLITE-KING PUMP
SHOTGUN (.410). . . . . .NiB $350 Ex $275 Gd $235
Same general specifications as Flite-King 20 except not available in Special and Trophy Models, or w/other than 26-inch choke bbl. Add $100 to 20 gauge price. Made from 1962 to 1966.

FLITE-KING SKEET
12 GA.. . . . . .NiB $330 Ex $225 Gd $170
Same as Flite-King Deluxe Rib except 26-inch vent rib bbl., w/SK choke. Made from 1962 to 1966.

FLITE-KING SPECIAL 12 GA. . . . . . NiB $250 Ex $175 Gd $135
Same as Flite-King Field 12 except has 27-inch bbl. w/adj. choke. Made from 1960 to 1966.

FLITE-KING SPECIAL 20 GA. . . . . . NiB $250 Ex $175 Gd $135
Same as Flite-King Field 20 except has 27-inch bbl. w/adj. choke. Made from 1961 to 1966.

FLITE-KING TRAP 12 GA.. . . . . . .NiB $330 Ex $225 Gd $140
Same as Flite-King Deluxe Rib 12 except 30-inch vent rib bbl., F choke, special trap stock w/recoil pad. Made from 1962 to 1966.

FLITE-KING TROPHY 12 GA. . . . . NiB $290 Ex $200 Gd $105
Same as Flite-King Deluxe Rib 12 except has 27-inch vent rib bbl. w/adj. choke. Made from 1960 to 1966.

FLITE-KING TROPHY 20 GA. . . . . NiB $290 Ex $200 Gd $105
Same as Flite-King Deluxe Rib 20 except has 27-inch vent rib bbl. w/adj. choke. Made from 1962 to 1966.

SUPERMATIC DEER GUN. . . . . . .NiB $345 Ex $165 Gd $100
Same as Supermatic Field 12 except has 22-inch bbl. (cylinder bore) w/rifle sights, checkered stock and forearm, recoil pad. Weight: 7.75 lbs. Made in 1965.

SUPERMATIC DELUXE 12 GA. (SERIES II)
Gas-operated autoloader. Four round magazine. Bbls.: Plain; 27-inch w/adj. choke (disc. about 1970); 26-inch IC, 28-inch M or F. 30-inch F choke. Weight: About 7.5 lbs. Checkered pistol-grip stock and forearm, recoil pad. Made from 1966 to 1975.
w/adj. choke . . . . .NiB $375 Ex $195 Gd $120
w/vent. rib, add $40

SUPERMATIC DELUXE 20 GA. (SERIES II)
Same as Supermatic Deluxe 12 (II) except chambered for 20 ga. Three inch shell; bbls. available in 27-inch w/adj. choke (disc. about 1970), 26-inch IC, 28-inch M or F choke. Weight: About 7 lbs. Made from 1966 to 1975.
w/adj. choke . . . . .NiB $315 Ex $199 Gd $99
Vent Rib, add $20

SUPERMATIC DELUXE DEER GUN
(SERIES II) . . . . NiB $345 Ex $165 Gd $100
Same as Supermatic Deluxe 12 (II) except has 22-inch bbl., cylinder bore, w/rifle sights. Weight: 7.75 lbs. Made from 1966 to 1974.

SUPERMATIC DELUXE DUCK
12 GA. MAGNUM (SERIES II). . . . . .NiB $335 Ex $227 Gd $140
Same as Supermatic Deluxe 12 (II) except chambered for 3-inch magnum shells, 3-round magazine, 30-inch plain bbl., F choke. Weight: 8 lbs. Made from 1966 to 1974.

High Standard Supermatic Deluxe Deer II

High Standard Supermatic Deluxe Duck Rib

High Standard Supermatic Deluxe Rib

High Standard Supermatic Duck —12 Gauge Magnum

SUPERMATIC DELUXE RIB
12 GA. . . . . .NiB $335 Ex $227 Gd $140
Same as Supermatic Field 12 except vent rib bbl. (28-inch M or F, 30-inch F), checkered stock and forearm. Made from 1961 to 1966.

SUPERMATIC DELUXE RIB 12 GA. (II)
Same as Supermatic Deluxe 12 (II) except has vent rib bbl.; available in 27-inch w/adj. choke, 28-inch M or F, 30-inch F choke. Made from 1966 to 1975.
w/adj. choke . . . . .NiB $335 Ex $227 Gd $140
w/vent. rib, add $50

SUPERMATIC DELUXE RIB
20 GA. . . . . .NiB $377 Ex $265 Gd $180
Same as Supermatic Field 20 except vent rib bbl. (28-inch M or F), checkered stock and forearm. Made from 1963 to 1966.

SUPERMATIC DELUXE RIB 20 GA. (II)
Same as Supermatic Deluxe 20 (II) except has vent rib bbl. Made from 1966 to 1975.
w/adj. choke . . . . .NiB $377 Ex $265 Gd $180
w/vent. rib, add $50

SUPERMATIC DELUXE SKEET GUN
12 GA. (SERIES II). . . . . .NiB $380 Ex $275 Gd $190
Same as Supermatic Deluxe Rib 12 (II) except available only w/26-inch vent rib bbl., SK choke. Made from 1966 to 1975.

SUPERMATIC DELUXE SKEET GUN
20 GA. (SERIES II) . . . . .NiB $370 Ex $285 Gd $200
Same as Supermatic Deluxe Rib 20 (II) except available only w/26-inch vent rib bbl., SK choke. Made from 1966 to 1975.

SUPERMATIC DELUXE
TRAP GUN (SERIES II) . . . . .NiB $315 Ex $239 Gd $177
Same as Supermatic Deluxe Rib 12 (II) except available only w/30-inch vent rib bbl., full choke; trap-style stock. Made 1966 to 1975.

SUPERMATIC DELUXE DUCK RIB
12 GA. MAG. (SERIES II) . . . . . . .NiB $375 Ex $265 Gd $180
Same as Supermatic Deluxe Rib 12 (II) except chambered for 3-inch magnum shells, 3-round magazine; 30-inch vent rib bbl., F choke. Weight: 8 lbs. Made from 1966 to 1975.

SUPERMATIC DUCK 12 GA. MAG. . . . . . NiB $355 Ex $241 Gd $188
Same as Supermatic Field 12 except chambered for 3-inch Magnum shell, 30-inch F choke bbl., recoil pad. Made from 1961 to 1966.

SUPERMATIC TROPHY 12 GA. . . . . NiB $300 Ex $198 Gd $140
Same as Supermatic Deluxe Rib 12 except has 27-inch vent-rib bbl. w/ adj. choke. Made from 1961 to 1966.

SUPERMATIC DUCK RIB 12 GA. MAG. . . . . .NiB $355 Ex $241 Gd $188
Same as Supermatic Duck 12 Magnum except has vent rib bbl., checkered stock and forearm. Made from 1961 to 1966.

SUPERMATIC FIELD AUTOLOADING
SHOTGUN 12 GA. . . . . .NiB $270 Ex $197 Gd $110
Gas-operated. Magazine holds four rounds. Bbls.: 26-inch IC, 28-inch M or F choke, 30-inch F choke. Weight: About 7.5 lbs. Plain pistol-grip stock and forearm. Made from 1960 to 1966.

SUPERMATIC FIELD AUTOLOADING
SHOTGUN 20 GA. . . . . .NiB $290 Ex $217 Gd $156
Gas-operated. Chambered for 3-inch mag. shells, also handles 2.75-inch. Magazine holds three rounds. Bbls.: 26-inch IC, 28-inch M or F choke. Weight: About 7 lbs. Plain pistol-grip stock and forearm. Made from 1963 to 1966.

SUPERMATIC SHADOW AUTOMATIC . . . . . . .NiB $455 Ex $265 Gd $200
Gas-operated. Ga.: 12, 20, 2.75- or 3-inch chamber in 12 ga., 3-inch in 20 ga. Mag. holds four 2.75-inch shells, three 3-inch. Bbls.: Full-size airflow rib; 26-inch (IC or SK choke), 28-inch (M, IM or F), 30-inch (trap or F choke), 12-ga. 3-inch Mag. available only in 30-inch F choke; 20 ga. not available in 30-inch. Weight: 12 ga., 7 lbs. Checkered walnut stock and forearm. Made 1974 to 1975 by Caspoll Int'l., Inc., Tokyo.

High Standard Supermatic Duck Rib — 12 Gauge

High Standard Supermatic Shadow Automatic

High Standard Supermatic Shadow Indy

High Standard Supermatic Shadow Seven

SUPERMATIC SHADOW
INDY O/U . . . . .NiB $935 Ex $770 Gd $500
Boxlock. Fully engraved receiver. Selective auto ejectors. Selective single trigger. 12 ga. 2.75-inch chambers. Bbls.: Full-size airflow rib; 27.5 inch both SK choke, 29.75-inch IM/F or F/F. Weight: W/29.75-inch bbls., 8 lbs. 2 oz. Pistol-grip stock w/recoil pad, ventilated forearm, skip checkering. Made 1974 to 1975 by Caspoll Int'l., Inc., Tokyo.

SUPERMATIC SHADOW SEVEN. . . . . .NiB $755 Ex $533 Gd $400
Same general specifications as Shadow Indy except has conventional vent rib, less elaborate engraving, standard checkering forearm is not vented, no recoil pad. 27.5-inch bbls.; also available in IC/M, M/F choke. Made from 1974 to 1975.

SUPERMATIC SKEET 12 GA. . . . . .NiB $344 Ex $245 Gd $177
Same as Supermatic Deluxe Rib 12 except 26-inch vent-rib bbl. w/SK choke. Made from 1962 to 1966.

SUPERMATIC SKEET 20 GA. . . . . .NiB $390 Ex $277 Gd $217
Same as Supermatic Deluxe Rib 20 except 26-inch vent-rib bbl. w/SK choke. Made from 1964 to 1966.

SUPERMATIC SPECIAL 12 GA. . . . .NiB $290 Ex $190 Gd $145
Same as Supermatic Field 12 except has 27-inch bbl. w/adj. choke. Made from 1960 to 1966.

SUPERMATIC SPECIAL 20 GA. . . . . .NiB $315 Ex $220 Gd $145
Same as Supermatic Field 20 except has 27-inch bbl. w/adj. choke. Made from 1963 to 1966.

SUPERMATIC TRAP 12 GA. . . . . NiB $330 Ex $245 Gd $170
Same as Supermatic Deluxe Rib 12 except 30-inch vent rib bbl., F choke, special trap stock w/recoil pad. Made from 1962 to 1966.

SUPERMATIC TROPHY 20 GA. . . . . NiB $360 Ex $275 Gd $190
Same as Supermatic Deluxe Rib 20 except has 27-inch vent rib bbl. w/ adj. choke. Made from 1963 to 1966.

HOLLAND & HOLLAND, LTD. — London, England
BADMINTON HAMMERLESS DOUBLE-BARREL SHOTGUN, ORIGINAL NO. 2 GRADE
General specifications same as Royal Model except without self-opening action. Made as a game gun or pigeon and wildfowl gun. Introduced in 1902. Disc.
w/double triggers . . . . . .NiB $27,875 Ex $22,500 Gd $18,975
w/single trigger. . . . . . . .NiB $28,875 Ex $24,000 Gd $19,600
20 ga., add. 25%
28 ga., add. 40%
.410, add 65%

CENTENARY MODEL HAMMERLESS DOUBLE-BARREL SHOTGUN
Lightweight (5.5 lbs.). 12 ga. game gun designed for 2-inch shell. Made in four grades — Model Deluxe, Royal, Badminton, Dominion. Values: Add 35% to prices shown for standard guns in those grades. Disc. 1962.

High Standard Supermatic Special

High Standard Supermatic Trophy

Holland & Holland
Royal Model

Holland & Holland Badminton

Holland & Holland Dominion

SHOTGUNS

DOMINION MODEL HAMMERLESS
DOUBLE-BBL. SHOTGUN . . . . . NiB $7355 Ex $6121 Gd $3896
Game Gun. Sidelock. Auto ejectors. Double triggers. Gauges: 12, 16, 20. bbls. 25- to 30-inch, any standard boring. Checkered stock and forend, straight grip standard. Disc. 1967.

DELUXE HAMMERLESS DOUBLE
Same as Royal Model except has special engraving and exhibition grade stock and forearm. Currently manufactured.
w/double triggers . . . . . . NiB $44,579 Ex $41,960 Gd $34,590
w/single trigger . . . . . . NiB $66,800 Ex $53,980 Gd $40,676

NORTHWOOD MODEL HAMMERLESS
DOUBLE-BARREL SHOTGUN. . . . . . NiB $6154 Ex $4944 Gd $4000
Anson & Deeley system boxlock. Auto ejectors. Double triggers. Gauges: 12, 16, 20, 28 in Game Model; 28 ga. not offered in Pigeon Model; Wildfowl Model in 12 ga. only (3-inch chambers available). Bbls.: 28-inch standard in Game and Pigeon Models, 30-inch in

Wildfowl Model; other lengths, any standard choke combination available. Weight: From 5 to 7.75 lbs. depending on ga. and bbls. Checkered straight-grip or pistol-grip stock and forearm. Disc. 1990.

RIVIERA MODEL
PIGEON GUN . . . . NiB $32,877 Ex $25,788 Gd $19,900
Same as Badminton Model but supplied w/two sets of bbls., double triggers. Disc. 1967.

ROYAL MODEL HAMMERLESS DOUBLE
Self-opening. Sidelocks hand-detachable. Auto ejectors. Double triggers or single trigger. Gauges: 12, 16, 20, 28 .410. Built to customer's specifications as to bbl. length, chokes, etc. Made as a Game Gun or Pigeon and Wildfowl Gun, the latter having treble-grip action and side clips. Checkered stock and forend, straight grip standard. Made from 1885, disc. 1951.
w/double triggers . . . . . . NiB $39,900 Ex $31,676 Gd $28,800
w/single trigger . . . . NiB $44,980 Ex $42,600 Gd $36,700

Holland & Holland
Royal Double-Barrel Shotgun

IGA Coach Gun

ROYAL MODEL O/U
Sidelocks, hand-detachable. Auto-ejectors. Double triggers or single trigger. 12 ga. Built to customer's specifications as to bbl. length, chokes, etc. Made as a Game Gun or Pigeon and Wildfowl Gun. Checkered stock and forend, straight grip standard. Note: In 1951 Holland & Holland introduced its New Model Under/Over w/an improved, narrower action body. Disc. 1960.

New model
(double triggers) .... NiB $40,770 Ex $32,550 Gd $21,900
New model
(single trigger) ..... NiB $41,800 Ex $33,750 Gd $22,500
Old model
(double triggers) .... NiB $33,970 Ex $27,600 Gd $20,550
Old model
(single trigger) ..... NiB $36,975 Ex $29,500 Gd $21,880

SINGLE-SHOT SUPER TRAP GUN
Anson & Deeley system boxlock. Auto-ejector. No safety. 12 ga. Bbls.: Wide vent rib, 30- or 32-inch, w/Extra Full choke. Weight: About 8.75 lbs. Monte Carlo stock w/pistol grip and recoil pad, full beavertail forearm. Models differ in grade of engraving and wood used. Disc.

Standard grade .... NiB $4890 Ex $2988 Gd $1598
Deluxe grade .... NiB $7355 Ex $6355 Gd $3559
Exhibition grade .... NiB $9677 Ex $7355 Gd $4977

SPORTING O/U ...... NiB $31,750 Ex $24,776 Gd $17,870
Blitz action. Auto ejectors; single selective trigger. Gauges: 12 or 20 w/2.75-inch chambers. Barrels: 28- to 32-inch w/screw-in choke tubes. Hand-checkered European walnut straight-grip or pistol grip stock, forearm. Made from 1993 to 2003   .

SPORTING O/U
DELUXE .... NiB $38,875 Ex $32,669 Gd $23,670
Same general specs as Sporting O/U except better engraving and select wood. Made from 1993 to date.

HUNTER ARMS COMPANY —
Fulton, New York
FULTON HAMMERLESS DOUBLE-BARREL SHOTGUN
Boxlock. Plain extractors. Double triggers or non-selective single trigger. Gauges: 12 16, 20. Bbls.: 26- to 32-inch various choke combinations.

Weight: about 7 lbs. Checkered pistol-grip stock and forearm. Disc. 1948.
w/double triggers .... NiB $775 Ex $450 Gd $375
w/single trigger .... NiB $990 Ex $700 Gd $555

SPECIAL HAMMERLESS DOUBLE-BARREL SHOTGUN
Boxlock. Plain extractors. Double triggers or non-selective single trigger. Gauges: 12,16, 20. Bbls.: 26- to 30-inch various choke combinations. Weight: 6.5 to 7.25 lbs. depending on bbl. length and ga. Checkered full pistol-grip stock and forearm. Disc. 1948.
w/double triggers .... NiB $933 Ex $655 Gd $500
w/single trigger .... NiB $1155 Ex $820 Gd $600

IGA — Veranopolis, Brazil
Imported by Stoeger Industries, Inc., Accokeek, Maryland.

STANDARD COACH GUN
Side-by-side double. Gauges: 12, 20 and .410. 20-inch bbls. w/3-inch chambers. Fixed chokes (standard model) or screw-in tubes (deluxe model). Weight: 6.5 lbs. Double triggers. Ejector and automatic safety. Blued or nickel finish. Hand-rubbed oil-finished pistol grip stock and forend w/hand checkering (hardwood on standard model or Brazilian walnut (deluxe). Imported from 1983 to 2000.
blued finish .... NiB $400 Ex $295 Gd $200
nickel finish .... NiB $465 Ex $377 Gd $259
engraved stock .... NiB $445 Ex $335 Gd $225
Deluxe Coach Gun (intro. 1997) ...... NiB $400 Ex $290 Gd $195
w/choke tubes, add $75

CONDOR I
O/U, single trigger; Gauges: 12 or 20. 26- or 28-inch bbls. of chrome-molybdenum steel. Chokes: Fixed — M/F or IC/M; screw-in choke tubes (12 and 20 ga.). Three inch chambers. Weight: 6.75 to 7 lbs. Sighting rib w/anti-glare surface. Hand-checkered hardwood pistol-grip stock and forend. Imported from 1983 to 1985.
w/fixed choke. .... NiB $420 Ex $377 Gd $210
w/screw-in tubes .... NiB $510 Ex $441 Gd $350

IGA Turkey S/S Shotgun

IGA Condor Turkey O/U Shotgun

IGA Condor Waterfowl O/U Shotgun

IGA Deluxe Hunter Clay Shotgun

IGA Uplander Side-by-Side Shotgun

CONDOR II . . . . **NiB $477 Ex $365 Gd $290**
Same general specifications as the Condor I O/U except w/ double triggers and fixed chokes only; 26-inch bbls., IC/M; 28-inch bbls., M/F.

CONDOR OUTBACK . . . . **NiB $499 Ex $370 Gd $290**
Same general specifications as the Condor I O/U except w/ 20-inch bbls., IC/M choke tubes, rifle-style sights. Made 2007 to date.

CONDOR SUPREME . . . . **NiB $655 Ex $545 Gd $477**
Same general specifications as Condor I except upgraded w/fine-checkered Brazilian walnut buttstock and forend, a matte-laquered finish, and a massive monoblock that joins the bbls. in a solid one-piece assembly at the breech end. Bbls. w/recessed interchangeable choke tubes formulated for use w/steel shot. Automatic ejectors. Imported from 1995 to 2000.

CONDOR TURKEY MODEL . . . . . **NiB $755 Ex $600 Gd $445**
12 gauge only. 26-inch vent-rib bbls. w/3-inch chambers fitted w/ recessed interchangeable choke tubes. Weight: 8 lbs. Mechanical single trigger. Ejectors and automatic safety. Advantage camouflage on stock and bbls. Made from 1997 to 2000.

CONDOR WATERFOWL MODEL . . . . . . **NiB $770 Ex $605 Gd $475**
Similar to Condor Turkey-Advantage camo model except w/30-inch bbls. Made from 1998 to 2000.

DELUXE HUNTER CLAYS . . . . **NiB $700 Ex $552 Gd $435**
Same general specifications and values as IGA Condor Supreme.

Imported from 1997 to 1999.

DOUBLE DEFENSE . . . . **NIB $499 EX $280 GD $135**
Similar to Coach S/S box lock. Gauges: 12 or 20 ga., 20-inch ported bbls. w/ Picatinny rails. Fixed IC choke; 3-inch chambers. Weight: 6.4 to 7.1 lbs. Single trigger. Matte black finish receiver and pistol-grip wood stock. Imported from 2009 to date.
Non-ported bbl. . . . . **NiB $479 Ex $275 Gd $120**

ERA MODEL 2000 . . . . **NiB $500 Ex $379 Gd $290**
Gauge: 12 w/3-inch chambers. 26- or 28-inch bbls. of chrome-molybdenum steel w/screw-in choke tubes. Extractors. Manual safety. (Mechanical triggers.) Weight: 7 lbs. Checkered Brazilian hardwood stock w/oil finish. Imported from 1992 to 1995.

REUNA SINGLE-SHOT
Visible hammer. Under-lever release. Gauges: 12, 20 and .410; 3-inch chambers. 26- or 28-inch bbls. w/fixed chokes or screw-in choke tubes (12 ga. only). Extractors. Weight: 5.25 to 6.5 lbs. Plain Brazilian hardwood stock and semi-beavertail forend. Imported from 1992 to 1998.
w/fixed choke. . . . . **NiB $210 Ex $155 Gd $90**
w/choke tubes . . . . **NiB $275 Ex $190 Gd $145**

UPLANDER
S/S box lock; Gauges: 12, 20, 28 and .410. 26- or 28-inch bbls. of chrome-molybdenum steel. Various fixed-choke combinations; screw-in choke tubes (12 and 20 ga.). Three inch chambers (2.75-inch in 28 ga.). Weight: 6.25 to 7 lbs. Double triggers. Automatic safety. Matte-

Ithaca Model 37 English Ultra

Ithaca Model 37 Featherlight Standard

Ithaca Model 37 Deerslayer Super Deluxe

Ithaca Model 37 Supreme Grade

finished solid sighting rib. Hand checkered pistol-grip or straight stock and forend w/hand-rubbed, oil-finish. Imported from 1997 to 2000.

Upland w/fixed chokes.	NiB $390	Ex $275	Gd $225
Upland w/screw-in tubes	NiB $420	Ex $345	Gd $290
English model (straight grip)	NiB $500	Ex $395	Gd $290
Ladies model	NiB $477	Ex $365	Gd $300
Supreme model	NiB $610	Ex $477	Gd $325
Youth model	NiB $477	Ex $345	Gd $270

UPLANDER TURKEY MODEL . . . . . NiB $588 Ex $440 Gd $379
12 gauge only. 24-inch solid rib bbls. w/3-inch chambers choked F&F. Weight: 6.75 lbs. Double triggers. Automatic safety. Advantage camouflage on stock and bbls. Made from 1997 to 2000.

ITHACA GUN COMPANY — King Ferry (formerly Ithaca), New York; Ithaca Acquisition Corp./Ithaca Gun Co.

MODEL 37 BICENTENNIAL
COMMEMORATIVE . . . . NiB $645 Ex $553 Gd $445
Limited to issue of 1976. Similar to Model 37 Supreme except has special Bicentennial design etched on receiver, fancy walnut stock and slide handle. Serial numbers U.S.A. 0001 to U.S.A. 1976. Originally issued w/presentation case w/cast-pewter belt buckle. Made in 1976. Best value is for gun in new, unfired condition.

MODEL 37 DEERSLAYER DELUXE
Formerly "Model 87 Deerslayer Deluxe" reintroduced under the original Model 37 designation w/the same specifications. Available w/ smooth bore or rifled bbl. Reintroduced 1996. Disc.

Deluxe model (smoothbore)	NiB $575	Ex $490	Gd $335
Deluxe model (rifled bbl.)	NiB $608	Ex $522	Gd $370

MODEL 37 DEERSLAYER II . . . . . . NiB $608 Ex $522 Gd $370

Gauges: 12 or 20 ga. Five round capacity. 20- or 25-inch rifled bbl. Weight: 7 lbs. Monte Carlo checkered walnut stock and forearm. Receiver drilled and tapped for scope mount. Made 1996 to 2000.

MODEL 37 DEERSLAYER STANDARD . . . . . NiB $355 Ex $280 Gd $225
Same as Model 37 Standard except has 20- or 26-inch bbl. bored for rifled slugs, rifle-type open rear sight and ramp front sight. Weight: 5.75 to 6.5 lbs. depending on ga. and bbl. length. Made from 1959-86.

MODEL 37 DEERSLAYER
SUPER DELUXE . . . . NiB $465 Ex $344 Gd $220
Formerly "Deluxe Deerslayer." Same as Model 37 Standard Deerslayer except has stock and slide handle of fancy walnut. Made 1962 to 1986.

MODEL 37 ENGLISH ULTRALIGHT . . . . . . NiB $635 Ex $500 Gd $400
Same general specifications as Model 37 Ultralite except straight buttstock, 25-inch Hot Forged vent-rib bbl. Made 1984 to 1987.

MODEL 37 FEATHERLIGHT STANDARD GRADE SLIDE-ACTION REPEATING SHOTGUN
Adaptation of the earlier Remington Model 17, a Browning design patented in 1915. Hammerless. Takedown. Gauges: 12, 16 (disc. 1973), 20. Four round magazine. Bbl. lengths: 26-, 28-, 30-inch (the latter in 12 ga. only); standard chokes. Weight: From 5.75 to 7.5 lbs. depending on ga. and bbl. length. Checkered pistol-grip stock and slide handle. Some guns made in the 1950s and 1960s have grooved slide handle; plain or checkered pistol-grip. Made 1937 to 1984.

Standard model w/checkered

pistol grip	NiB $675	Ex $390	Gd $300
w/plain stock	NiB $325	Ex $229	Gd $190
Model 37D Deluxe (1954-77)	NiB $675	Ex $390	Gd $300
Model 37DV Deluxe vent rib (1962-84)	NiB $675	Ex $390	Gd $300
Model 37R Deluxe solid rib (1955-61)	NiB $675	Ex $390	Gd $300
Model 37V Standard vent rib (1962-84)	NiB $315	Ex $244	Gd $148

**Ithaca Model 51
Deluxe Trap**

MODEL 37 FIELD GRADE
MAG. W/TUBES . . . . **NiB $355 Ex $298 Gd $199**
Same general specifications as Model 37 Featherlight except 32-inch bbl. and detachable choke tubes. Vent rib bbl. Made 1984 to 1987.

MODEL 37 CLASSIC. . . . . **NiB $755 Ex $555 Gd $465**
Ggs: 12 or 20 ga. 20- or 28-inch vent rib bbl. w/choke tubes. Knuckle-cut receiver and orig. style "ring-tail" forend. Lim. prod. Made from 1998 to 2005.

MODEL 37 $1000 GRADE
Custom built, elaborately engraved and inlaid w/gold, hand-finished working parts, stock and forend of select figured walnut. General specifications same as standard Model 37. Note: Designated The $1000 Grade prior to World War II. Made 1937 to 1967.
$1000 grade. . . . . **NiB $5988 Ex $4776 Gd $3987**
$5000 grade. . . . . **NiB $5588 Ex $4487 Gd $3960**

MODEL 37 SUPREME GRADE. . . . . . **NiB $955 Ex $588 Gd $535**
Available in Skeet or Trap Gun, similar to Model 37T. Made 1967-86 and 1997. Subtract $225 for newer models.

MODEL 37 ULTRALITE
Same general specifications as Model 37 Featherlight except stream-lined forend, gold trigger, Sid Bell grip cap and vent rib. Weight: 5 to 5.75 lbs. Made from 1984 to 1987.
Standard . . . . **NiB $559 Ex $400 Gd $363**
W/choke tubes, add **$150**

MODEL 37R SOLID RIB GRADE
Same general specifications as the Model 37 Featherlight except has a raised solid rib, adding about .25 pounds of weight. Made 1937 to 1967.
**w/checkered grip
and slide handle.** . . . . **NiB $400 Ex $310 Gd $200**
w/plain stock . . . . **NiB $292 Ex $195 Gd $145**

MODEL 37S SKEET GRADE . . . . . . **NiB $565 Ex $455 Gd $335**
Same general specifications as the Model 37 Featherlight except has vent rib and large extension-type forend; weight: About .5 lb. more. Made from 1937 to 1955.

MODEL 37T TARGET GRADE . . . . .**NiB $545 Ex $376 Gd $255**
Same general specifications as Model 37 Featherlight except has vent-rib bbl., checkered stock and slide handle of fancy walnut (choice of skeet- or trap-style stock). Note: This model replaced Model 37S Skeet and Model 37T Trap. Made from 1955- to 191.

MODEL 37T TRAP GRADE . . . . . . **NiB $545 Ex $376 Gd $255**
Same gen. specs. as Mdl. 37S except has straighter trap-style stock of select walnut, recoil pad; weight: About .5 lb. more. Made from 1937-55.

MODEL 37 TURKEYSLAYER
Gauges: 12 ga. (Standard) or 20 ga. (youth). Slide action. 22-inch bbl. Extended choke tube. Weight: 7 lbs. Advantage camouflage or Realtree pattern. Made from 1996 to 2005.
Standard model . . . .**NiB $425 Ex $260 Gd $190**
Youth model (intro. 1998). . . . . . . **NiB $555 Ex $456 Gd $345**

MODEL 37 WATERFOWLER. . . . . **NiB $490 Ex $375 Gd $260**
12 ga. only w/28-inch bbl. Wetlands camouflage. Made 1998 to 2005.

MODEL 51 DEERSLAYER . . . .**NiB $400 Ex $279 Gd $200**
Same as Model 51 Standard except has 24-inch plain bbl. w/slug boring, rifle sights, recoil pad. Weight: About 7.25 lbs. Made from 1972 to 1984.

MODEL 51 SUPREME SKEET GRADE . . . . . **NiB $525 Ex $390 Gd $270**
Same as Model 51 Standard except 26-inch vent-rib bbl. only, SK choke, skeet-style stock, semi-fancy wood. Weight: About 8 lbs. Made from 1970 to 1987.

MODEL 51 SUPREME TRAP
Same as Model 51 Standard except 12 ga. only, 30-inch bbl. w/broad floating rib, F choke, trap-style stock w/straight or Monte Carlo comb, semifancy wood, recoil pad. Weight: About 8 lbs. Made from 1970 to 1987.
w/straight stock . . . . **NiB $544 Ex $390 Gd $295**
w/Monte Carlo stock, add **$75**

MODEL 51 FEATHERLITE STANDARD
Gas-operated. Gauges: 12, 20. Three round. Bbls.: Plain or vent rib, 30-inch F choke (12 ga. only), 28-inch F or M, 26-inch IC. Weight: 7.25-7.75 lbs. depending on ga. and bbl. Checkered pistol-grip stock, forearm. Made 1970 to 1980. Avail. in 12 and 20 ga., 28-inch M choke only.
w/plain barrel. . . . . **NiB $300 Ex $197 Gd $121**
w/vent rib, add. **$65**

MODEL 51A STANDARD MAGNUM
Same as Model 51 Standard except has 3-inch chamber, handles Magnum shells only; 30-inch bbl. in 12 ga., 28-inch in 20 ga., F or M choke, stock w/recoil pad. Weight: 7.75-8 lbs. Made 1972 to 1982.
w/plain bbl. (disc. 1976). . . . .**NiB $375 Ex $290 Gd $200**
w/camo finish, add. **$65**

MODEL 51A TURKEY GUN . . . . . **NiB $455 Ex $300 Gd $217**
Same general specifications as standard Model 51 Magnum except 26-inch bbl. and matte finish. Disc. 1986.

MODEL 66 LONG TOM . . . . **NiB $210 Ex $155 Gd $100**
Same as Model 66 Standard except has 36-inch F choke bbl., 12 ga. only, checkered stock and recoil pad standard. Made 1969 to 1974.

MODEL 66 STANDARD SUPER SINGLE LEVER
Single shot. Hand-cocked hammer. Gauges: 12 (disc. 1974), 20, .410, 3-inch chambers. Bbls.: 12 ga., 30-inch F choke, 28-inch F or M; 20 ga., 28-inch F or M; .410, 26-inch F. Weight: About 7 lbs. Plain or checkered straight-grip stock, plain forend. Made from 1963 to 1978.
Standard model . . . . **NiB $220 Ex $115 Gd $90**
Vent. rib model (20 ga., 1969-74) . . . . . **NiB $225 Ex $159 Gd $135**
Youth model (1965-78). . . . . **NiB $250 Ex $179 Gd $130**

MODEL 66RS BUCKBUSTER. . . . . **NiB $279 Ex $200 Gd $155**
Same as Model 66 Standard except has 22-inch bbl. cylinder bore w/rifle sights, later version has recoil pad. Originally offered in 12 and 20 ga.; the former was disc. in 1970. Made from 1967 to 1978.

SHOTGUNS

Ithaca
Model 66RS
Buckbuster

Previously issued as the Ithaca Model 37, the Model 87 guns listed below were made available through the Ithaca Acquisition Corp. From 1986-95. Production of the Model 37 resumed under the original logo in 1996.

MODEL 87 DEERLSLAYER SHOTGUN
Gauges: 12 or 20, 3-inch chamber. Bbls.: 18.5-, 20- or 25-inch (w/special or rifled bore). Weight: 6 to 6.75 lbs. Ramp blade front sight, adj. rear. Receiver grooved for scope. Checkered American walnut pistol-grip stock and forearm. Made from 1988 to 1996.

Basic model . . . . NiB $445 Ex $355 Gd $225
Basic Field Combo
  (w/extra 28-inch bbl.). . . . . .NiB $475 Ex $390 Gd $280
Deluxe model . . . . NiB $480 Ex $395 Gd $290
Deluxe Combo
  (w/extra 28-inch bbl.). . . . . .NiB $635 Ex $460 Gd $339
DSPS (8-round model) . . . . NiB $554 Ex $400 Gd $290
Field model . . . . NiB $433 Ex $330 Gd $287
Monte Carlo model . . . . NiB $448 Ex $356 Gd $255
Ultra model (disc. 1991) . . . . . NiB $500 Ex $398 Gd $325

MODEL 87 DEERSLAYER II
RIFLED SHOTGUN . . . . NiB $600 Ex $433 Gd $310
Similar to Standard Deerslayer except w/solid frame construction and 25-inch rifled bbl. Monte Carlo stock. Made 1988 to 1996.

MODEL 87 ULTRALITE
FIELD PUMP SHOTGUN . . . . . . NiB $490 Ex $387 Gd $260
Gauges: 12 and 20; 2.75-inch chambers. 25-inch bbl. w/choke tube. Weight: 5 to 6 lbs. Made from 1988 to 1990.

MODEL 87 FIELD GRADE
Gauge: 12 or 20.; 3-inch chamber. Five round magazine. Fixed chokes or screw-in choke tubes (IC, M, F). Bbls.: 18.5-inch (M&P); 20- and 25-inch (Combo); 26-, 28-, 30-inch vent rib. Weight: 5 to 7 lbs. Made from 1988 to 1996.

Basic field model (disc. 1993) . . NiB $446 Ex $270 Gd $210
Camo model. . . . . NiB $490 Ex $339 Gd $260
Deluxe model. . . . . NiB $505 Ex $340 Gd $280
Deluxe Combo model . . . . NiB $590 Ex $493 Gd $377
English model. . . . . NiB $490 Ex $339 Gd $260
Hand grip model
  (w/polymer pistol-grip). . . . . . . .NiB $533 Ex $425 Gd $315
M&P model (disc. 1995) . . . . . NiB $466 Ex $380 Gd $279
Supreme model. . . . . NiB $720 Ex $589 Gd $400
Turkey model . . . . NiB $445 Ex $365 Gd $256
Ultra Deluxe model (disc. 1992). . . . . .NiB $400 Ex $356 Gd $260

HAMMERLESS DOUBLE-BARREL SHOTGUNS
Boxlock. Plain extractors, auto ejectors standard on the "E" grades. Double triggers, non-selective or selective single trigger extra. Gauges: Magnum 10, 12; 12, 16, 20, 28, .410. Bbls.: 26- to 32-inch, any standard boring. Weight: 5.75 (.410) to 10.5 lbs.

(Magnum 10). Checkered pistol-grip stock and forearm standard. Higher grades differ from Field Grade in quality of workmanship, grade of wood, checkering, engraving, etc.; general specifications are the same. Ithaca doubles made before 1925 (serial number 425,000) the rotary bolt and a stronger frame were adopted. Values shown are for this latter type; earlier models valued about 50% lower. Smaller gauge guns may command up to 75% higher. Disc. 1948.

Field grade . . . . NiB $1088 Ex $900 Gd $677
No. 1 grade . . . . NiB $1377 Ex $1099 Gd $890
No. 2 grade . . . . NiB $2480 Ex $2077 Gd $1100
No. 3 grade . . . . NiB $2456 Ex $1866 Gd $1376
No. 4E grade (ejector) . . . . . NiB $6225 Ex $3688 Gd $2977
No. 5E grade (ejector) . . . . . NiB $5235 Ex $3767 Gd $4400

Extras:
Magnum 10 or 12 ga.
  (in other than the four highest grades), add 20%
Automatic ejectors (grades No. 1, 2, 3,
  w/ejectors designated No. 1E, 2E, 3E), add 35%
Selective single trigger, add. $250
Non-selective single trigger, add $200
Beavertail forend (Field No. 1 or 2), add $200
Beavertail forend (No. 3 or 4), add $200
Beavertail forend (No. 5, 7 or $2000 grade), add $200
Ventilated rib (No. 4, 5, 7 or $2000 grade), add $400
Ventilated rib (lower grades), add $250

LSA-55 TURKEY GUN . . . . NiB $935 Ex $700 Gd $590
Over/under shotgun/rifle combination. Boxlock. Exposed hammer. Plain extractor. Single trigger. 12 ga./222 Rem. 24.5-inch ribbed bbls. (rifle bbl. has muzzle brake). Weight: About 7 lbs. Folding leaf rear sight, bead front sight. Checkered Monte Carlo stock and forearm. Made 1970 to 1977 by Oy Tikkakoski AB, Finland.

MAG-10 AUTOMATIC SHOTGUN
Gas-operated. 10 ga. 3.5-inch Magnum. Three round capacity. 32-inch plain (Standard Grade only) or vent-rib bbl. F choke. Weight: 11 lbs., plain bbl.; 11.5 lbs., vent rib. Standard grade has plain stock and forearm. Deluxe and Supreme Grades have checkering, semi-fancy and fancy wood respectively, and stud swivel. All have recoil pad. Deluxe and Supreme grades made 1974 to 191982. Standard Grade intro. in 1977. All grades disc. 1986.

Camo model. . . . . NiB $735 Ex $555 Gd $379
Deluxe grade . . . . NiB $890 Ex $774 Gd $522
Roadblocker . . . . NiB $855 Ex $740 Gd $533
Standard grade, plain bbl. . . . . . NiB $744 Ex $610 Gd $477
Standard grade
  w/vent. rib . . . . .NiB $844 Ex $633 Gd $530
Standard grade, w/choke tubes . . . . .NiB $988 Ex $755 Gd $544
Supreme grade . . . . NiB $1044 Ex $856 Gd $600

Ithaca Hammerless
Field Grade

Ithaca Hammerless
No. 2

Ithaca Hammerless
No. 4

Ithaca Hammerless
Field Grade

Ithaca Model 5-E

Ithaca Single-Shot Trap
"Dollar Grade"

SINGLE-SHOT TRAP, FLUES AND KNICK MODELS

Boxlock. Hammerless. Ejector. 12 ga. only. Bbl. lengths: 30-, 32-, 34-inch (32-inch only in Victory grade). Vent rib. Weight: About 8 lbs. Checkered pistol-grip stock and forend. Grades differ only in quality of workmanship, engraving, checkering, wood, etc. Flues Model, serial numbers under 400,000, made 1908 to 1921. Triple-bolted Knick Model, serial numbers above 400,000, made since 1921. Victory Model disc. in 1938, No. 7-E in 1964, No. 4-E in 1976, No. 5-E in 1986, Dollar Grade in 1991. Values shown are for Knick Model; Flues models about 50% lower.

Victory grade . . . . NiB $1379 Ex $1100 Gd $925
No. 4-E . . . . NiB $3766 Ex $3470 Gd $1790
No. 5-E . . . . NiB $5000 Ex $4766 Gd $2128
No. 6-E (rare) . . . . NiB $16,980 Ex $14,700 Gd $10,000
No. 7-E (rare) . . . . NiB $7445 Ex $6000 Gd $4655
$2,000 grade . . . . NiB $9,500 Ex $8500 Gd $6650
Pre-war $1000 grade . . . . NiB $10,000 Ex $9577 Gd $6650
Sousa grade (rare) . . . . NiB $14,500+ Ex $12,700+ Gd $9000+

NOTE: *The following Ithaca-Perazzi shotguns were manufactured by Manifattura Armi Perazzi, Brescia, Italy. See also separate Perazzi listings.*

PERAZZI COMPETITION I SKEET . .NiB $14,877 Ex $13,900 Gd $11,270
Boxlock. Auto ejectors. Single trigger. 12 ga. 26.75-inch vent-rib bbls. SK choke w/integral muzzle brake. Weight: About 7.75 lbs. Checkered skeet-style pistol-grip buttstock and forearm; recoil pad. Made from 1969 to 1974.

PERAZZI COMPETITION
TRAP I O/U . . . . .NiB $14,889 Ex $13,679 Gd $11,650
Boxlock. Auto ejectors. Single trigger. 12 ga. 30- or 32-inch vent-rib bbls. IM/F choke. Weight: About 8.5 lbs. Checkered pistol-grip stock, forearm; recoil pad. Made from 1969 to 1974.

PERAZZI COMPETITION I
TRAP SINGLE BARREL . . . . .NiB $11,770 Ex $9455 Gd $7655
Boxlock. Auto ejection. 12 ga. 32- or 34-inch bbl., vent rib, F choke. Weight: 8.5 lbs. Checkered Monte Carlo stock and beavertail forearm, recoil pad. Made from 1973 to 1978.

PERAZZI COMPETITION IV
TRAP GUN . . . . .NiB $13,890 Ex $11,870 Gd $10,000
Boxlock. Auto ejection. 12 ga. 32- or 34-inch bbl. With high, wide vent rib, four interchangeable choke tubes (Extra Full, F, IM, M). Weight: About 8.75 lbs. Checkered Monte Carlo stock and beavertail forearm, recoil pad. Fitted case. Made from 1977 to 1978.

SHOTGUNS

Ithaca-Perazzi
Competition I Skeet

Ithaca-Perazzi
Competition I Trap

Ithaca-Perazzi
Light Game

Ithaca-Perazzi
Mirage Trap

PERAZZI LIGHT GAME
O/U FIELD . . . .**NiB $15,800 Ex $14,790 Gd $13,955**
Boxlock. Auto ejectors. Single trigger. 12 ga. 27.5-inch vent rib bbls., M/F or IC/M choke. Weight: 6.75 lbs. Checkered field-style stock and forearm. Made from 1972 to 74.

PERAZZI MIRAGE . . . .**NiB $6987 Ex $4677 Gd $2700**
Same as Mirage Trap except has 28-inch bbls., M and Extra Full choke, special stock and forearm for live bird shooting. Weight: About 8 lbs. Made from 1973 to 1978.

PERAZZI MIRAGE SKEET . . . . . .**NiB $4350 Ex $3866 Gd $2789**
Same as Mirage Trap except has 28-inch bbls. w/integral muzzle brakes, SK choke, skeet-stype stock and forearm. Weight: About 8 lbs. Made from 1973 to 1978.

PERAZZI MIRAGE TRAP . . . . . **NiB $4365 Ex $3900 Gd $2820**
Same general specifications as MX-8 Trap except has tapered rib. Made from 1973 to 1978.

PERAZZI MT-6 SKEET . . . .**NiB $4233 Ex $3380 Gd $2770**
Same as MT-6 Trap except has 28-inch bbls. w/two skeet choke tubes instead of Extra Full and F, skeet-style stock and forearm. Weight: About 8 lbs. Made from 1976 to 1978.

PERAZZI MT-6 TRAP COMBO . . . . . .**NiB $5377 Ex $4260 Gd $3100**
MT-6 w/extra single under bbl. w/high-rise aluminum vent rib, 32- or 34-inch; seven interchangeable choke tubes (IC through Extra Full). Fitted case. Made from 1977 to 1978.

PERAZZI MT-6
TRAP O/U . . . .**NiB $3700 Ex $2566 Gd $2044**
Boxlock. Auto selective ejectors. Non-selective single trigger. 12 ga. Barrels separated, wide vent rib, 30-or 32-inch, five interchangeable choke tubes (Extra full, F, IM, M, IC). Weight: About 8.5 lbs. Checkered pistol-grip stock/forearm, recoil pad. Fitted case. Made from 1976 to 1978.

PERAZZI MX
8 TRAP COMBO. . . . .**NiB $5688 Ex $4355 Gd $2460**
MX-8 w/extra single bbl., vent rib, 32- or 34-inch, F choke, forearm; two trigger groups included. Made from 1973 to 1978.

PERAZZI MX-8 TRAP
O/U . . . .**NiB $4356 Ex $3879 Gd $2889**
Boxlock. Auto selective ejectors. Non-selective single trigger. 12 ga. Bbls.: High vent rib; 30- or 32-inch, IM/F choke. Weight: 8.25 to 8.5 lbs. Checkered Monte Carlo stock and forearm, recoil pad. Made from 1969 to 1978.

PERAZZI SINGLE-BARREL
TRAP GUN. . . . .**NiB $3350 Ex $2459 Gd $2000**
Boxlock. Auto ejection. 12 ga. 34-inch vent rib bbl., F choke. Weight: Abaout 8.5 lbs. Checkered pistol-grip stock, forearm; recoil pad. Made from 1971 to 1972.

The following Ithaca-SKB shotguns, manufactured by SKB Arms Company, Tokyo, Japan, were distributed in the U.S. by Ithaca Gun Company from 1966-1976. See also listings under SKB.

Ithaca-SKB
Model 100

Ithaca-SKB
Model 280 English

Ithaca-SKB
Model 700 Skeet Grade

Ithaca-SKB
Model 900 Deluxe

SKB MODEL 100 SIDE-BY-SIDE . . . . . .NiB $779 Ex $580 Gd $490
Boxlock. Plain extractors. Selective single trigger. Auto safety. Gauges: 12 and 20; 2.75-inch and 3-inch chambers respectively. Bbls.: 30-inch, F/F (12 ga. only); 28-inch, F/M; 26-inch, IC/M (12 ga. only); 25-inch, IC/M (20 ga. only). Weight: 12 ga., about 7 lbs.; 20 ga., about 6 lbs. Checkered stock and forend. Made 1966 to 1976.

SKB MODEL 150 FIELD GRADE. . . . . .NiB $770 Ex $600 Gd $488
Same as Model 100 except has fancier scroll engraving, beavertail forearm. Made from 1972 to 1974.

SKB 200E FIELD GRADE S/S. . . . . .NiB $1077 Ex $767 Gd $580
Same as Model 100 except auto selective ejectors, engraved and silver-plated frame, gold-plated nameplate and trigger, beavertail forearm. Made from 1966 to 1976.

SKB MODEL 200E SKEET GUN. . . . . .NiB $995 Ex $687 Gd $485
Same as Model 200E Field Grade except 26-inch (12 ga.) and 25-inch (20 ga./2.75-inch chambers) bbls., SK choke; nonautomatic safety and recoil pad. Made from 1966 to 1976.

SKB MODEL 200 ENGLISH. . . . . NiB $1154 Ex $990 Gd $759
Same as Model 200E except has scrolled game scene engraving on frame, English-style straight-grip stock; 30-inch bbls. not available; special quail gun in 20 ga. has 25-inch bbls., both bored IC. Made from 1971 to 1976.

SKB MODEL 300 STANDARD AUTOMATIC SHOTGUN
Recoil-operated. Gauges: 12, 20 (3-inch). Five round capacity. Bbls.: plain or vent rib; 30-inch F choke (12 ga. only), 28-inch F or M, 26-inch IC. Weight: about 7 lbs. Checkered pistol-grip stock and forearm. Made from 1968 to 1972.
w/plain barrel. . . . . .NiB $1088 Ex $765 Gd $490
20 ga, add 30%

SKB MODEL 500
FIELD GRADE O/U . . . . .NiB $665 Ex $455 Gd $323
Boxlock. Auto selective ejectors. Selective single trigger. Non-automatic safety. Gauges: 12 and 20; 2.75-inch and 3-inch chambers respectively. Vent-rib bbls.: 30-inch M/F (12 ga. only); 28-inch M/F; 26-inch IC/M. Weight: 12 ga., about 7.5 lbs; 20 ga., about 6.5 lbs. Checkered stock and forearm. Made from 1966 to 1976.

SKB MODEL 500 MAGNUM . . . . . .NiB $639 Ex $455 Gd $344
Same as Model 500 Field Grade except chambered for 3-inch 12 ga. shells, has 30-inch bbls., IM/F choke. Weight: About 8 lbs. Made 1973 to 1976.

SKB MODEL 600 DOUBLES GUN . . . . . NiB $1096 Ex $766 Gd $500
Same as Model 600 Trap Grade except specially choked for 21-yard first target, 30-yard second. Made from 1973 to 1975.

SKB MODEL 600 FIELD GRADE . . . . . NiB $1100 Ex $775 Gd $525
Same as Model 500 except has silver-plated frame, higher grade wood. Made from 1969 to 1976.

SKB MODEL 600 MAGNUM . . . . . NiB $1125 Ex $800 Gd $550
Same as Model 600 Field Grade except chambered for 3-inch 12 ga. shells; has 30-inch bbls., IM/F choke. Weight: 8.5 lbs. Made from 1969 to 1972.

SKB MODEL 600 SKEET GRADE
Same as Model 500 except also available in 28 and .410 ga., has silver-plated frame, higher grade wood, recoil pad, 26- or 28-inch bbls. (28-inch only in 28 and .410), SK choke. Weight: 7 to 7.75 lbs. depending on ga. and bbl. length. Made from 1966 to 1976.
12 or 20 ga. . . . . .NiB $1155 Ex $830 Gd $575
28 ga. or .410. . . . . .NiB $1500 Ex $1266 Gd $1077

SKB MODEL 600 SKEET SET . . . . . .NiB $2866 Ex $2249 Gd $1545
Model 600 Skeet Grade w/matched set of 20, 28 and .410 ga. bbls., 28-inch, fitted case. Made from 1970-76.

Ithaca-SKB
Century Trap

Ithaca-SKB
Century II Trap

Ithaca-SKB
Model XL300

SKB MODEL 600

TRAP GRADE O/U . . . .**NiB $1055 Ex $700 Gd $533**
Same as Model 500 except 12 ga. only, has silver-plated frame, 30- or 32-inch bbls. choked F/F or F/IM, choice of Monte Carlo or straight stock of higher grade wood, recoil pad. Weight: About 8 lbs. Made from 1966 to 1976.

SKB MODEL 680 ENGLISH . . . .**NiB $1388 Ex $1055 Gd $775**
Same as Model 600 Field Grade except has intricate scroll engraving, English-style straight-grip stock and forearm of extra-fine walnut; 30-inch bbls. not available. Made from 1973 to 1976.

SKB MODEL 700
SKEET COMBO SET . . . .**NiB $3988 Ex $2970 Gd $2175**
Model 700 Skeet Grade w/matched set of 20, 28 and .410 ga. bbls., 28-inch fitted case. Made from 1970 to 1971.

SKB MODEL 700 SKEET GRADE. . . . .**NiB $955 Ex $779 Gd $575**
Same as Model 600 Skeet Grade except not available in 28 and .410 ga., has more elaborate scroll engraving, extra-wide rib, higher grade wood. Made from 1969 to 1975.

SKB MODEL 700 TRAP GRADE . . . . .**NiB $945 Ex $665 Gd $544**
Same as Model 600 Trap Grade except has more elaborate scroll engraving, extra-wide rib, higher grade wood. Made 1969 to 1975.

SKB MODEL 700
DOUBLES GUN . . . .**NiB $866 Ex $744 Gd $559**
Same as Model 700 Trap Grade except choked for 21-yard first target, 30-yard second target. Made from 1973 to 1975.

SKB MODEL 900
DELUXE AUTOMATIC . . . .**NiB $475 Ex $359 Gd $255**
Same as Model 30 except has game scene etched and gold-filled on receiver, vent rib standard. Made 1968 to 1972.

SKB MODEL 900 SLUG GUN . . . . . **NiB $350 Ex $264 Gd $190**
Same as Model 900 Deluxe except has 24-inch plain bbl. w/slug boring, rifle sights. Weight: About 6.5 lbs. Made 1970 to 1972.

SKB CENTURY SINGLE-SHOT
TRAP GUN. . . . .**NiB $689 Ex $500 Gd $356**
Boxlock. Auto ejector. 12 ga. Bbls.: 32- or 34-inch, vent rib, F choke.

Weight: About 8 lbs. Checkered walnut stock w/pistol grip, straight or Monte Carlo comb, recoil pad, beavertail forearm. Made 1973 to 1974.

SKB CENTURY II TRAP . . . .**NiB $700 Ex $495 Gd $400**
Boxlock. Auto ejector. 12 ga. Bbls.: 32- or 34-inch, vent rib, F choke. Weight: 8.25 lbs. Improved version of Century. Same general specifications except has higher comb on checkered stock stock, reverse-taper beavertail forearm w/redesigned locking iron. Made from 1975 to 1976.

SKB MODEL XL300 STANDARD AUTOMATIC
Gas-operated. Gauges: 12, 20 (3-inch). Five round capacity. Bbls.: Plain or vent rib; 30-inch F choke (12 ga. only), 28-inch F or M, 26-inch IC. Weight: 6 to 7.5 lbs. depending on ga. and bbl. Checkered pistol-grip stock, forearm. Made from 1972 to 1976.
w/plain barrel. . . . . .NiB $389 Ex $296 Gd $210
w/ventilated rib . . . . .NiB $365 Ex $283 Gd $205

SKB MODEL XL900
DELUXE AUTOMATIC . . . .**NiB $379 Ex $335 Gd $260**
Same as Model XL300 except has game scene finished in silver on receiver, vent rib standard. Made from 1972 to 1976.

SKB MODEL XL
900 SKEET GRADE . . . .**NiB $490 Ex $377 Gd $315**
Gas-operated. Gauges: 12, 20 (3-inch). Five round tubular magazine. Same as Model XL900 Deluxe except has scrolled receiver finished in black chrome, 26-inch bbl. only, SK choke, skeet-style stock. Weight: 7 or 7.5 lbs. depending on ga. Made from 1972 to 1976.

SKB MODEL XL
900 SLUG GUN . . . .**NiB $445 Ex $377 Gd $290**
Same as Model XL900 Deluxe except has 24-inch plain bbl. w/slug boring, rifle sights. Weight: 6.5 or 7 lbs. depending on ga. Made from 1972 to 1976.

SKB MODEL
XL900 TRAP GRADE. . . . .**NiB $488 Ex $358 Gd $290**
Same as Model XL900 Deluxe except 12 ga. only, has scrolled receiver finished in black chrome, 30-inch bbl. only, IM or F choke, trap style w/straight or Monte Carlo comb, recoil pad. Weight: About 7.75 lbs. Made from 1972 to 1976.

Krieghoff Model 32
Standard Field Gun

Krieghoff Model 32
Single-Shot Trap

IVER JOHNSON ARMS & CYCLE WORKS — Fitchburg, Massachusetts; currently a division of the American Military Arms Corp., Jacksonville, Arkansas

CHAMPION GRADE TOP SNAP
Auto ejector. Gauges: 12,16, 20, 28 and .410. Bbls.: 26- to 36-inch, F choke. Weight: 5.75 to 7.5 lbs. depending on ga. and bbl.length. Plain pistol-grip stock and forend. Extras include checkered stock and forend, pistol-grip cap and knob forend. Known as Model 36. Also made in a Semi-Octagon Breech, Top Matted and Jacketed Breech (extra heavy) models. Made in Champion Lightweight as Model 39 in gauges 24, 28, 32 and .410, .44 and .45 caliber, 12 and 14mm w/same extras. $200; add $100 in the smaller and obsolete gauges. Made from 1909 to 1973.

Standard model . . . . NiB $377 Ex $290 Gd $100
Semi-octagon breech . . . . NiB $466 Ex $351 Gd $229
Top matted rib (disc. 1948). . . . . . NiB $398 Ex $297 Gd $195

HERCULES GRADE HAMMERLESS DOUBLE
Boxlock. (Some made w/false sideplates.) Plain extractors and auto ejectors. Double or Miller single triggers (both selective or non-selective). Gauges: 12, 16, 20 and .410. Bbl. lengths: 26- to 32-inch, all chokes. Weight: 5.75 to 7.75 lbs. depending on ga. and bbl. length. Checkered stock and forend. Straight grip in .410 ga. w/both 2.5- and 3-inch chambers. Extras include Miller single trigger, Jostam Anti-Flinch recoil pad and Lyman ivory sights at extra cost. Disc. 1946.

w/double triggers, extractors . . . . . . NiB $1166 Ex $955 Gd $760
w/double triggers, ejectors, add 30%
w/non-selective single trigger, add $50
w/selective single trigger, add. $50
.410 ga., add 100%

MATTED RIB SINGLE-SHOT HAMMER SHOTGUN
IN SMALLER GAUGES. . . . . .NiB $400 Ex $355 Gd $210
Same general specifications as Champion Grade except has solid matted top rib, checkered stock and forend. Weight: 6 to 6.75 lbs. Disc. 1948.

MODEL 412/422 SILVER SHADOW O/U SHOTGUN
Boxlock. Plain extractors. Double triggers or non-selective single trigger. 12 ga., 3-inch chambers. Bbls.: 26-inch IC/M; 28-inch IC/M, 28-inch M/F; 30-inch both F choke; vent rib. Weight: w/28-inch bbls., 7.5 lbs. Checkered pistol-grip stock/forearm. Made by F. Marocchi, Brescia, Italy from 1973 to 1977.

Model 412 w/double triggers . . . . . NiB $590 Ex $455 Gd $387
Model 422 w/single trigger . . . . . . NiB $754 Ex $600 Gd $445

SKEETER MODEL HAMMERLESS DOUBLE
Boxlock. Plain extractors or selective auto ejectors. Double triggers or Miller single trigger (selective or non-selective). Gauges: 12, 16, 20, 28 and .410. 26- or 28-inch bbls., skeet boring standard. Weight: About 7.5 lbs.; less in smaller gauges. Pistol- or straight-grip stock and beavertail forend, both checkered, of select fancy-figured black walnut. Extras include Miller single trigger, selective or non-selective, Jostam Anti-Flinch recoil pad and Lyman ivory rear sight at additional cost. Disc. 1942.

w/double triggers,
  plain extractors . . . . .NiB $2298 Ex $1987 Gd $1133
w/double triggers,
  automatic ejectors, add 20%
w/non-selective
  single trigger, add 20%
w/selective single
  trigger, add 50%
20 ga,add. 30%
28 ga., add 90%
.410 ga., add 100%

SPECIAL TRAP SINGLE-SHOT
HAMMER SHOTGUN . . . . NiB $500 Ex $365 Gd $298
Auto ejector. 12 ga. only. 32-inch bbl. w/vent rib, F choke. Checkered pistol-grip stock and forend. Weight: about 7.5 lbs. Disc. 1942.

SUPER TRAP HAMMERLESS DOUBLE
Boxlock. Plain extractors. Double trigger or Miller single trigger (selective or non-selective), 12 ga. only, F choke 32-inch bbl., vent rib. Weight: 8.5 lbs. Checkered pistol-grip stock and beavertail forend, recoil pad, Disc. 1942.

w/double triggers . . . . NiB $1756 Ex $1170 Gd $990
w/non-selective single trigger, add $150
w/selective single trigger, add. $150

KBI INC.

See listings under Armscor, Baikal, Charles Daly, Fias, & Omega.

KESSLER ARMS CORP. — Deggendorf, Germany

LEVER-MATIC REPEATING
SHOTGUN . . . . .NiB $335 Ex $227 Gd $179
Lever action. Takedown. Gauges: 12, 16, 20; three-round magazine. Bbls.: 26-, 28-, 30-inch; F choke. Plain pistol-grip stock, recoil pad. Weight: 7 to 7.75 lbs. Disc. 1953.

SHOTGUNS

GRADING: NiB = New in Box   Ex = Excellent or NRA 95%   Gd = Good or NRA 68%

Krieghoff K-80
w/Screw-in Choke
Tubes

Krieghoff K-80
Trap Unsingle

Three Shot Bolt-Action Repeater . . . . . NiB $200 Ex $138 Gd $90
Takedown. Gauges: 12, 16, 20. Two-round detachable box magazine.
Bbls.: 28-inch in 12 and 16 ga.; 26-inch in 20 ga.; F choke. Weight:
6.25 to 7.25 lbs. depending on ga. and bbl. length. Plain one-piece
pistol-grip stock recoil pad. Made from 1951 to 1953.

H. KRIEGHOFF JAGD UND
SPORTWAFFENFABRIK — Ulm (Donau),
Germany

MODEL 32 FOUR-BARREL SKEET SET
Over/under w/four sets of matched bbls.: 12, 20, 28 and .410 ga., in
fitted case. Available in six grades that differ in quality of engraving and
wood. Disc. 1979.

Standard grade	NiB $9344	Ex $7120	Gd $4688
München grade	NiB $10,077	Ex $8767	Gd $6233
San Remo grade	NiB $13,876	Ex $11,990	Gd $10,550
Monte Carlo grade	NiB $20,000	Ex $17,890	Gd $14,650
Crown grade	NiB $27,700	Ex $22,800	Gd $15,660
Super Crown grade	NiB $29,000	Ex $24,770	Gd $17,600
Exhibition grade	NiB $32,000	Ex $28,900	Gd $23,750

MODEL 32 STANDARD GRADE O/U
Similar to prewar Remington Model 23. Boxlock. Auto ejector. Single
trigger. Gauges: 12, 20, 28, .410. Bbls.: Vent rib, 26.5- to 32-inch,
any chokes. Weight: 12 ga. Field gun w/28-inch bbls., about 7.5 lbs.
Checkered pistol-grip stock and forearm of select walnut; available in
field, skeet and trap styles. Made from 1958 to 1981.

w/one set of bbls.	NiB $3125	Ex $2460	Gd $2099
Low-rib two-bbl. trap combo	NiB $4166	Ex $3550	Gd $2779
Vandalia (high-rib) two- bbl. trap combo	NiB $5355	Ex $4288	Gd $3150

MODEL 32 STANDARD GRADE
SINGLE-SHOT TRAP GUN . . . . . NiB $4160 Ex $3277 Gd $3080
Same action as over/under. 28 ga.or .410 bore w/low vent rib on bbl.;
M, IM, or F choke. Checkered Monte Carlo buttstock w/thick cushioned
recoil pad, beavertail forearm. Disc. 1979.

MODEL K-80
Refined and enhanced version of the Mdl. 32. Single selective mech.
trig., adj. for position; release trigger optional. Fixed chokes or screw-in
choke tubes. Interchangeable front bbl. Hangers to adjust point of impact.
Quick-removable stock. Color casehardened or satin grey fin. rec.; alum.
alloy rec. on lightweight models. Avail. in stand. plus 5 engraved grades.
Made from 1980 to date. Standard grade shown except where noted.

SKEET MODELS
Skeet International	NiB $9160	Ex $5375	Gd $3853
Skeet Special	NiB $9277	Ex $6659	Gd $4390

Skeet standard model	NiB $9000	Ex $4788	Gd $3360
Skeet w/choke tubes	NiB $12,776	Ex $9879	Gd $5780

SKEET SETS - Disc. 1999.
Standard grade 2-bbl. set	NiB $12,769	Ex $10,000	Gd $6690
Standard grade 4-bbl. set	NiB $14,879	Ex $11,890	Gd $9877
Bavaria grade 4-bbl. set	NiB $11,900	Ex $9388	Gd $7710
Danube grade 4-bbl. set	NiB $23,998	Ex $20,600	Gd $17,000
Gold Target grade 4-bbl. set.	NiB $31,800	Ex $24,800	Gd $17,955

SPORTING MODELS
Pigeon	NiB $9980	Ex $6654	Gd $4135
Sporting Clays	NiB $9566	Ex $5760	Gd $4400

TRAP MODELS
Trap Combo, add			.30%
Trap Single, add			$600
Trap Standard.	NiB $10,550	Ex $7677	Gd $4612
Trap Unsingle.	NiB $11,880	Ex $9678	Gd $6389
RT models (removable trigger), add			$1500

KRIEGHOFF MODEL KS-5 SINGLE-BARREL TRAP
Boxlock w/no sliding top-latch. Adjustable or optional release trigger.
Gauge: 12; 2.75-inch chamber. Bbl.: 32-, 34-inch w/fixed choke or
screw-in tubes. Weight: 8.5 lbs. Adjustable or Monte Carlo European
walnut stock. Blued or nickel receiver. Made from 1985 to 1999.
Redesigned and streamlined in 1993.

Standard model w/fixed chokes	NiB $2650	Ex $1887	Gd $1109
Standard model w/tubes, add			$250
Special model w/adj.
rib & stock, add			$250
Special model w/adj. rib
& stock, choke tubes, add			$500

TRUMPF DRILLING . . . . . . NiB $14,987 Ex $13,677 Gd $10,880
Boxlock. Steel or Dural receiver. Split extractor or ejector for
shotgun bbls. Double triggers. Gauges: 12, 16, 20; latter w/either
2.75- or 3-inch chambers. Calibers: .243, 6.5x57r5, 7x57r5,
7x65r5, .30-06; other calibers available. 25-inch bbls. w/solid
rib, folding leaf rear sight, post or bead front sight; rifle bbl.
soldered or free floating. Weight: 6.6 to 7.5 lbs. depending on
type of receiver, ga. and caliber. Checkered pistol-grip stock w/
cheekpiece and forearm of figured walnut, sling swivels. Made
from 1953 to 2003.

NEPTUN DRILLING . . . . . NiB $14,988 Ex $11,987 Gd $9000
Same general specifications as Trumpf model except has sidelocks w/
hunting scene engraving. Disc. 2003.

NEPTUN-PRIMUS
DRILLING . . . . NiB $19,800 Ex $16,779 Gd $13,980
Deluxe version of Neptun model; has detachable sidelocks, higher
grade engraving and fancier wood. Disc. 2003.

**Krieghoff
Neptun Drilling**

**Krieghoff ULM
Over/Under**

**TECK O/U
RIFLE-SHOTGUN** . . . . NiB $9788 Ex $5780 Gd $4466
Boxlock. Kersten dble. crossbolt system. Steel or Dural receiver. Split extractor or eject. for shotgun bbl. Single or double triggers. Gauges: 12, 16, 20; latter w/either 2.75- or 3-inch chamber. Cal: .22 Hornet, .222 Rem., .222 Rem. Mag., 7x57r5, 7x64, 7x65r5, .30-30, .300 Win. Mag., .30-06, .308, 9.3x74R. 25-inch bbls. With solid rib, folding leaf rear sight, post or bead front sight; over bbl. is shotgun, under bbl. rifle (later fixed or interchangeable; ext. rifle bbl., $175). Wt: 7.9-9.5 lbs. depending on type of rec. and caliber. Checkered pistol-grip stock w/cheekpiece and semi-beavertail forearm of fig. walnut, sling swivels. Made from 1967 to 2004. Note: This comb. gun is similar in appearance to the same model shotgun.

TECK O/U SHOTGUN . . . . . . NiB $7354 Ex $5678 Gd $4000
Boxlock. Kersten double crossbolt system. Auto ejector. Single or double triggers. Gauges: 12, 16, 20; latter w/either 2.75- or 3-inch chambers. 28-inch vent-rib bbl., M/F choke. Weight: About 7 lbs. Checkered walnut pistol-grip stock and forearm. Made 1967 to 1989.

**ULM O/U
RIFLE-SHOTGUN** . . . . . . NiB $16,228 Ex $12,876 Gd $10,336
Same general specifications as Teck model except has sidelocks w/leaf Arabesque engraving. Made from 1963-2004. Note: This combination gun is similar in appearance to the same model shotgun.

ULM O/U SHOTGUN . . . . . NiB $13,899 Ex $11,679 Gd $8445
Same general specifications as Teck model except has sidelocks w/leaf Arabesque engraving. Made from 1958 to 2004.

ULM-P LIVE PIGEON GUN
Sidelock. Gauge: 12. 28- and 30-inch bbls. Chokes: F/IM. Weight: 8 lbs. Oil-finished, fancy English walnut stock w/semi-beavertail forearm. Light scrollwork engraving. Tapered, vent rib. Made from 1983 to 2004.
Standard. . . . . NiB $19,577 Ex $15,890 Gd $11,088
Dural. . . . . NiB $13,776 Ex $11,087 Gd $9459

ULM-PRIMUS O/U . . . . . NiB $19,779 Ex $17,888 Gd $13,090
Deluxe version of Ulm model; detachable sidelocks, higher grade engraving and fancier wood. Made from 1958 to 2004.

**ULM-PRIMUS O/U
RIFLE-SHOTGUN** . . . . . . NiB $21,870 Ex $18,744 Gd $15,877
Deluxe version of Ulm model; has detachable sidelocks, higher grade engraving and fancier wood. Made 1963 to 2004. Note: This combination gun is similar in appearance to the same model shotgun.

ULM-S SKEET GUN
Sidelock. Gauge: 12. Bbl.: 28-inch. Chokes: Skeet/skeet. Other specifications similar to the Model ULM-P. Made from 1983-86.
Bavaria . . . . NiB $13,789 Ex $11,132 Gd $9000
Standard. . . . . NiB $1188 Ex $9131 Gd $7330

ULM-P O/U LIVE TRAP GUN
Over/under sidelock. Gauge: 12. 30-inch bbl. Tapered vent rib. Chokes: IM/F; optional screw-in choke. Custom grade versions command a higher price. Disc. 1986.
Bavaria . . . . .NiB $18,966 Ex $15,980 Gd $12,776
Standard. . . . . .NiB $15,660 Ex $13,000 Gd $10,100

ULTRA TS RIFLE-SHOTGUN
Deluxe Over/Under combination w/25-inch vent-rib bbls. Chambered 12 ga. only and various rifle calibers for lower bbl. Kickspanner design permits cocking w/thumb safety. Satin receiver. Weight: 6 lbs. Made from 1985 to 1995 Disc.
Ultra O/U combination. . . . . . NiB $4220 Ex $3670 Gd $2800
Ultra B w/selective front trigger. . . . . . .NiB $5589 Ex $4498 Gd $4000

LANBER — Zaldibar, Spain

MODEL 82 O/U SHOTGUN . . . . . NiB $577 Ex $459 Gd $390
Boxlock. Gauge: 12 or 20; 3-inch chambers. 26- or 28-inch vent-rib bbls. w/ejectors and fixed chokes. Weight: 7 lbs., 2 oz. Double or single-selective trigger. Engraved silvered receiver. Checkered European walnut stock and forearm. Imported 1994.

MODEL 87 DELUXE . . . . NiB $875 Ex $760 Gd $555
Over/Under; boxlock. Single selective trigger. 12 or 20 gauge w/3-inch chambers. Barrels: 26- or 28-inch w/choke tubes. Silvered engraved receiver. Imported 1994 only.

MODEL 97 SPORTING CLAYS . . . . . NiB $998 Ex $790 Gd $566
Over/Under; boxlock. Single selective trigger. 12 ga. w/2.75-inch chambers. Bbls: 28-inch w/choke tubes. European walnut stock, forend. Engraved receiver. Imported 1994 only.

MODEL 844 MST MAGNUM O/U . . . . . .NiB $533 Ex $448 Gd $360
Field grade. Gauge: 12. 3-inch Mag. chambers. 30-inch flat vent-rib bbls. Chokes: M/F. Weight: 7 lbs., 7 oz. Single selective trigger. Blued bbls. and engraved receiver. European walnut stock w/hand-checkered pistol grip and forend. Imported from 1984 to 1986.

MODEL 2004 LCH O/U . . . . NiB $669 Ex $490 Gd $370
Field grade. Gauge: 12. 2.75-inch chambers. 28-inch flat vent-rib bbls. 5 interchangeable choke tubes: Cyl, IC, M, IM, F. Weight: About 7 lbs. Single selective trigger. Engraved silver receiver w/fine-line scroll. Walnut stock w/checkered pistol-grip and forend. Rubber recoil pad. Imported from 1984 to 1986.

MODEL 2004 LCH O/U SKEET . . . . . .NiB $855 Ex $659 Gd $544
Same as Model 2004 LCH except 28-inch bbls. w/5 interchangeable choke tubes. Imported from 1984 to 1986.

SHOTGUNS

Lanber Model 82 Field Grade

Laurona Grand Trap — GTO

MODEL 2004
LCH O/U TRAP . . . . **NiB $764 Ex $520 Gd $413**
Gauge: 12. 30-inch vent-rib bbls. Three interchangeable choke tubes: M, IM, F. Manual safety. Other specifications same as Model 2004 LCH O/U. Imported from 1984 to 1986.

CHARLES LANCASTER — London, England

"TWELVE-TWENTY" DOUBLE-BARREL
SHOTGUN. . . . .**NiB $16,788 Ex $14,990 Gd $10,880**
Sidelock, self-opener. Gauge: 12. Bbls.: 24 to 30 inches standard. Weight: About 5.75 lbs. Elaborate metal engraving. Highest quality English or French walnut buttstock and forearm. Imported by Stoeger in the 1950s.

JOSEPH LANG & SONS — London, England

HIGHEST QUALITY
O/U SHOTGUN . . . .**NiB $31,900 Ex $27,678 Gd $20,980**
Sidelock. Gauges: 12, 16, 20, 28 and .410. Bbls.: 25 to 30 inches standard. Highest grade English or French walnut buttstock and forearm. Selective single trigger. Imported by Stoeger in 1950s.

LAURONA — Eibar, Spain

MODEL 300 SERIES
Same general specifications as Model 300 Super Series except supplied w/29-inch over/under bbls. and beavertail forearms. Disc. 1992.
Trap model . . . . **NiB $1377 Ex $1190 Gd $921**
Sporting Clays model . . . . **NiB $1389 Ex $1440 Gd $1000**

SILHOUETTE 300 O/U
Boxlock. Single selective trigger. Selective automatic ejectors. Gauge: 12; 2.75-, 3- or 3.5-inch chambers. 28- or 29-inch vent-rib bbls. w/flush or knurled choke tubes. Weight: 7.75 to 8 lbs. Checkered pistol-grip European walnut stock and beavertail forend. Engraved receiver w/silvered finish and black chrome bbls. Made from 1988 to 1992.
Model 300 Sporting Clays. . . . . **NiB $1498 Ex $1277 Gd $900**
Model 300 Trap, single. . . . . . . **NiB $1577 Ex $1264 Gd $900**
Model 300 Ultra-Magnum. . . . **NiB $1599 Ex $1300 Gd $1055**

SUPER MODEL O/U SHOTGUNS
Boxlock. Single selective or twin single triggers. Selective automatic ejectors. Gauges: 12 or 20; 2.75- or 3-inch chambers. 26-, 28- or 29-inch vent-rib bbls. w/fixed chokes or screw-in choke tubes. Weight: 7 to 7.25 lbs. Checkered pistol-grip European walnut stock. Engraved receiver w/silvered finish and black chrome bbls. Made from 1985 to 1989.
Model 82 Super Game (disc.) . . . . **NiB $688 Ex $500 Gd $395**
Model 83 MG Super Game. . . . . **NiB $1090 Ex $800 Gd $707**
Model 84 S Super Trap. . . . . . . **NiB $1366 Ex $1150 Gd $986**
Model 85 MS Super Game . . . . **NiB $1098 Ex $833 Gd $727**
Model 85 MS 2-bbl. set . . . . . **NiB $2200 Ex $1789 Gd $1340**
Model 85 MS Special Sporting (disc.). **NiB $1390 Ex $1173 Gd $999**
Model 85 MS Super Trap . . . . . **NiB $1386 Ex $1160 Gd $974**
Model 85 MS Pigeon . . . . **NiB $1409 Ex $1190 Gd $1034**
Model 85 MS Super Skeet. . . . **NiB $1409 Ex $1190 Gd $1034**

LEBEAU-COURALLY — Liege, Belgium

BOXLOCK SIDE
BY-SIDE SHOTGUNS . . .**NiB $19,000 Ex $15,870 Gd $10,477**
Gauges: 12, 16, 20 and 28. 26- to 30-inch bbls. Weight: 6.5 lbs. average. Checkered, hand-rubbed, oil-finished, straight-grip stock of French walnut. Classic forend. Made from 1986 to 1988 and 1993.

LEFEVER ARMS COMPANY — Syracuse and Ithaca, New York

Lefever sidelock hammerless double-barrel shotguns were made by Lefever Arms Company of Syracuse, New York from about 1885-1915 (serial numbers 1 to 70,000) when the firm was sold to Ithaca Gun Company of Ithaca, New York. Production of these models was continued at the Ithaca plant until 1919 (serial numbers 70,001 to 72,000). Grades listed are those that appear in the last catalog of the Lefever Gun Company, Syracuse. In 1921, Ithaca introduced the boxlock Lefever Nitro Special double, followed in 1934 by the Lefever Grade A; there also were two single-barrel Lefevers made from 1927-42. Manufacture of Lefever brand shotguns was disc. in 1948. Note: "New Lefever" boxlock shotguns made circa 1904 to 1906 by D. M. Lefever Company, Bowling Green, Ohio, are included in a separate listing.

**Lefever A Grade
Hammerless Double-Barrel Shotgun**

GRADE A HAMMERLESS DOUBLE-BARREL SHOTGUN
Boxlock. Plain extractors or auto ejector. Single or double triggers. Gauges: 12, 16, 20, .410. Bbls.: 26-32 inches, standard chokes. Weight: About 7 lbs. in 12 ga. Checkered pistol-grip stock and forearm. Made from 1934 to 1942.

w/plain extractors, double triggers . . . . .NiB $1198 Ex $955 Gd $773	
w/automatic ejector, add 33%	
w/single trigger, add. 10%	
w/Beavertail Forearm, add $100	
16 ga., add 25%	
20 ga., add 80%	
.410 ga., add 200%	

GRADE A SKEET MODEL
Same as A Grade except standard features include auto ejector, single trigger, beavertail forearm; 26-inch bbls., skeet boring. Disc. 1942.

A Grade Skeet model, 12 ga. . . . . NiB $1699 Ex $1188 Gd $880
16 ga., add 40%
20 ga., add 80%
.410 ga., add 200%

HAMMERLESS SINGLE-SHOT
TRAP GUN. . . . . .NiB $766 Ex $600 Gd $477
Boxlock. Ejector. 12 ga. only. 26- or 32-inch bbl.; Full choke. Weight: About 8 lbs. Checkered pistol-grip stock. Auto ejector; boxlock. Made from 1904 to 1906. Rare.

LONG RANGE HAMMERLESS
SINGLE-BARREL FIELD GUN . . . .NiB $500 Ex $394 Gd $277
Boxlock. Plain extractor. Gauges: 12, 16, 20, .410. Bbl. lengths: 26-32 inches. Weight: 5.5 to 7 lbs. depending on ga. and bbl. length. Checkered pistol-grip stock and forend. Made from 1927to 1942.

NITRO SPECIAL HAMMERLESS DOUBLE
Boxlock. Plain extractors. Single or double triggers. Gauges: 12, 16, 20, .410. Bbls.: 26- to 32-inch, standard chokes. Weight: about 7 lbs. in 12 ga. Checkered pistol-grip stock and forend. Made 1921 to 1948.
Nitro Special w/
 double triggers. . . . . .NiB $855 Ex $522 Gd $377
Nitro Special W/single trigger . . . . NiB $933 Ex $654 Gd $433
16 ga., add 25%
20 ga., add 50%
.410 ga., add 200%

SIDELOCK HAMMERLESS DOUBLES
Plain extractors or auto ejectors. Boxlock. Double triggers or selective single trigger. Gauges: 10, 12, 16, 20. Bbls.: 26-32

inches; standard choke combinations. Weight: 5.75 to 10.5 lbs. depending on ga. and bbl. length. Checkered walnut straight-grip or pistol-grip stock and forearm. Grades differ chiefly in quality of workmanship, engraving, wood, checkering, etc.; general specifications are the same. DS and DSE Grade guns lack the cocking indicators found on all other models. Suffix "E" means model has auto ejector; also standard on A, AA, Optimus, and Thousand Dollar Grade guns.

H grade	NiB $2266	Ex $1770	Gd $1480
HE grade	NiB $3270	Ex $2266	Gd $1780
G grade	NiB $2288	Ex $1998	Gd $1440
GE grade	NiB $3388	Ex $2771	Gd $1880
F grade	NiB $2566	Ex $1966	Gd $1276
FE grade.	NiB $3360	Ex $2770	Gd $1866
E grade	NiB $3790	Ex $2690	Gd $2210
EE grade.	NiB $5750	Ex $3880	Gd $2547
D grade	NiB $4980	Ex $3777	Gd $2869
DE grade	NiB $7132	Ex $4971	Gd $4111
DS grade	NiB $1754	Ex $1530	Gd $1129
DSE grade	NiB $2184	Ex $1788	Gd $1290
C grade	NiB $7443	Ex $4270	Gd $2988
CE grade	NiB $9112	Ex $8445	Gd $6110
B grade	NiB $10,500	Ex $8667	Gd $6330
BE grade	NiB $10,580	Ex $8777	Gd $6580
A grade	NiB $19,880	Ex $17,900	Gd $16,888
AA grade	NiB $28,566	Ex $23,667	Gd $21,876
Optimus grade	NiB $47,900	Ex $42,870	Gd $37,980
Thousand Dollar grade . .	NiB $78,980	Ex $46,888	Gd $36,890
w/single trigger, add. 10%			
10 ga., add 15%			
16 ga., add 45%			
20 ga., add 90%			

D. M. LEFEVER COMPANY —
Bowling Green, Ohio
In 1901, D. M. "Uncle Dan" Lefever, founder of the Lefever Arms Company, withdrew from that firm to organize D. M. Lefever, Sons & Company (later D. M. Lefever Company) to manufacture the "New Lefever" boxlock double- and single-barrel shotguns. These were produced at Bowling Green, Ohio, from about 1904-1906, when Dan Lefever died and the factory closed permanently. Grades listed are those that appear in the last catalog of D. M. Lefever Co.

HAMMERLESS DOUBLE-BARREL SHOTGUNS
"New Lefever." Boxlock. Auto ejector standard on all grades except O Excelsior, which was regularly supplied w/plain extractors (auto ejector offered as an extra). Double triggers or selective single trigger (latter standard on Uncle Dan Grade, extra on all others). Gauges: 12, 16, 20. Bbls.: Any length and choke combination. Weight: 5.5 to 8 lbs. depending on ga. and bbl. length. Checkered walnut straight-grip or pistol-grip stock and forearm. Grades differ chiefly in quality of workmanship, engraving, wood, checkering, etc. General specifications are the same.

SHOTGUNS

O Excelsior grade w/plain
   extractors . . . . NiB $2889 Ex $2255 Gd $1989
O Excelsior grade w/automatic
   ejectors . . . . .NiB $3244 Ex $2990 Gd $2469
No. 9, F grade . . . . NiB $3277 Ex $2929 Gd $2240
No. 8, E grade . . . . NiB $4240 Ex $3888 Gd $2377
No. 7, D grade. . . . . NiB $5277 Ex $4766 Gd $3698
No. 6, C grade . . . . NiB $7000 Ex $4590 Gd $3667
No. 5, B grade . . . . NiB $6722 Ex $4588 Gd $3292
No. 4, AA grade . . . . . . .NiB $10,770 Ex $8857 Gd $5497
Uncle Dan grade . . . . Very rare: $165,000+
w/single trigger, add 10%
16 ga., add 45%
20 ga., add 15%

D. M. LEFEVER SINGLE-BARREL TRAP GUN
Boxlock. Auto ejector. 12 ga. only. Bbls.: 26- to 32 inches, F
choke. Weight: 6.5 to 8 lbs. depending on bbl. length. Checkered
walnut pistol-grip stock and forearm. Made 1904 to 1906.
Extremely rare.

Lefever Sidelock AA Grade

MAGTECH — San Antonio, Texas.
Manufactured by CBC in Brazil.

MODEL 586-2 SLIDE-ACTION SHOTGUN
Gauge: 12; 3-inch chamber. 19-, 26- or 28-inch bbl.; fixed
chokes or integral tubes. 46.5 inches overall. Weight: 8.5 lbs.
Double-action slide bars. Brazilian hardwood stock. Polished
blued finish. Imported 1992 to 1995.
Model 586.2F
   (28-inch bbl., fixed choke) . . NiB $288 Ex $147 Gd $100
Model 586.2P
   (19-inch plain bbl., cyl. bore) . . . . . . NiB $244 Ex $165 Gd $99
Model 586.2 S
   (24-inch bbl., rifle sights, cyl. bore) NiB $290 Ex $155 Gd $125
Model 586.2 VR
   (vent rib w/tubes) . . . . NiB $275 Ex $198 Gd $135

Lefever Sidelock DE Grade

Lefever Sidelock
Thousand Dollar
Grade

MARLIN FIREARMS CO. — North Haven
(formerly New Haven), Connecticut

MODEL 16 VISIBLE HAMMER SLIDE-ACTION REPEATER
Takedown. 16 ga. Five round tubular magazine. Bbls.: 26- or
28-inch, standard chokes. Weight: About 6.25 lbs. Pistol-grip
stock, grooved slide handle; checkering on higher grades.
Difference among grades is in quality of wood, engraving on
Grades C and D. Made from 1904 to 1910.
Grade A . . . . NiB $400 Ex $322 Gd $297
Grade B . . . . NiB $590 Ex $477 Gd $388
Grade C . . . . NiB $722 Ex $466 Gd $388
Grade D. . . . . NiB $1496 Ex $1377 Gd $947

MODEL 17 BRUSH GUN . . . . NiB $389 Ex $297 Gd $190
Same as Model 17 Standard except has 26-inch bbl., cylinder bore.
Weight: About 7 lbs. Made from 1906 to 1908.

MODEL 17 RIOT GUN . . . . . NiB $480 Ex $308 Gd $200
Same as Model 17 Standard except has 20-inch bbl., cylinder bore.
Weight: About 6.88 lbs. Made from 1906 to 1908.

Lefever Sidelock Sideplate BE Grade

Lefever Sidelock Sideplate CE Grade

Lefever Sidelock Optimus Grade

**Magtech Model 586.2
Slide-Action**

**Marlin Model 17
Standard**

**Marlin Model 28B
Hammerless Slide-Action Repeater**

**Marlin Model 30
Visible Hammer Slide-Action
Repeater**

**Marlin Model 43A
Hammerless Slide-Action Repeater**

MODEL 17 STANDARD VISIBLE HAMMER
SLIDE-ACTION REPEATER . . . . . . NiB $422 Ex $290 Gd $188
Solid frame.12 ga. Five round tubular magazine. Bbls.: 30- or 32-inch, F choke. Weight: About 7.5 lbs. Straight-grip stock, grooved slide handle. Made from 1906 to 1908.

MODEL 19 VISIBLE HAMMER SLIDE-ACTION REPEATER
Similar to Model 1898 but improved, lighter weight, w/two extractors, matted sighting groove on receiver top. Weight: About 7 lbs. Made from 1906-07.
Grade A . . . . NiB $466 Ex $390 Gd $277
Grade B . . . . NiB $566 Ex $448 Gd $339
Grade C . . . . NiB $744 Ex $390 Gd $244
Grade D . . . . NiB $1396 Ex $1087 Gd $944

MODEL 21 TRAP VISIBLE HAMMER
SLIDE-ACTION REPEATER
Similar to Model 19 w/same general specifications except has straight-grip stock. Made from 1907 to 1909.
Grade A . . . . NiB $433 Ex $290 Gd $197
Grade B . . . . NiB $580 Ex $450 Gd $344
Grade C . . . . NiB $788 Ex $590 Gd $445
Grade D . . . . NiB $1488 Ex $1116 Gd $977

MODEL 24 VISIBLE HAMMER SLIDE-ACTION REPEATER
Similar to Model 19 but has improved takedown system and auto recoil safety lock, solid matted rib on frame. Weight: About 7.5 lbs. Made from 1908 to 1915.
Grade A . . . . NiB $376 Ex $190 Gd $112
Grade B . . . . NiB $448 Ex $277 Gd $156
Grade C . . . . NiB $766 Ex $500 Gd $410
Grade D . . . . NiB $1500 Ex $1399 Gd $1177

MODEL 26
BRUSH GUN . . . . NiB $388 Ex $270 Gd $135
Same as Model 26 Standard except has 26-inch bbl., cylinder bore. Weight: About 7 lbs. Made from 1909 to 1915.

MODEL 26 RIOT GUN . . . . NiB $360 Ex $266 Gd $131
Same as Model 26 Standard except has 20-inch bbl., cylinder bore. Weight: About 6.88 lbs. Made from 1909 to 1915.

MODEL 26 STANDARD VISIBLE HAMMER
SLIDE-ACTION REPEATER . . . . . . NiB $366 Ex $298 Gd $199
Similar to Model 24 Grade A except solid frame and straight-grip stock. 30- or 32-inch full choke bbl. Weight: About 7.13 lbs. Made from 1909-15.

Marlin Model 43T
Hammerless Slide-Action Repeater

Marlin Model 53
Hammerless Slide-Action

Marlin Model 55
Goose Gun

Marlin Model 55
Humter Bolt-Action Repeater

Marlin Model 55
Swap Gun

MODEL 28 HAMMERLESS SLIDE-ACTION REPEATER
Takedown. 12 ga. Five round tubular magazine. Bbls.: 26-, 28-, 30-, 32-inch, standard chokes; matted-top bbl. except on Model 28D, which has solid matted rib. Weight: About 8 lbs. Pistol-grip stock, grooved slide handle; checkering on higher grades. Grades differ in quality of wood, engraving on Models 28C and 28D. Made 1913 to 1922; all but Model 28A disc. in 1915.

Model 28A	NiB $433	Ex $288	Gd $165
Model 28B	NiB $577	Ex $458	Gd $313
Model 28C	NiB $755	Ex $544	Gd $340
Model 28D	NiB $1480	Ex $1198	Gd $955

MODEL 28T TRAP GUN . . . . NiB $789 Ex $566 Gd $449
Same as Model 28 except has 30-inch matted-rib bbl., Full choke, straight-grip stock w/high-fluted comb of fancy walnut, checkered. Made in 1915.

MODEL 28TS
TRAP GUN . . . . NiB $588 Ex $400 Gd $378
Same as Model 28T except has matted-top bbl., plainer stock. Made in 1915.

MODEL 30 FIELD GUN . . . . NiB $466 Ex $355 Gd $245
Same as Model 30 Grade B except has 25-inch bbl., Mod. choke, straight-grip stock. Made from 1913 to 1914.

MODEL 30 VISIBLE HAMMER SLIDE-ACTION REPEATER
Similar to Model 16 but w/Model 24 improvements. Made from 1910-14. See illustration previous page.

Grade A	NiB $460	Ex $388	Gd $210
Grade B	NiB $660	Ex $433	Gd $309
Grade C	NiB $777	Ex $566	Gd $363
Grade D	NiB $1488	Ex $1177	Gd $1065

MODELS 30A, 30B, 30C, 30D
Same as Model 30; designations were changed in 1915. Also available in 20 ga. w/25- or 28-inch bbl., matted-top bbl. on all grades. Suffixes "A," "B," "C" and "D" correspond to former grades. Made in 1915.

Model 30A	NiB $412	Ex $290	Gd $188
Model 30B	NiB $576	Ex $445	Gd $310
Model 30C	NiB $756	Ex $554	Gd $39
Model 30D	NiB $1421	Ex $1131	Gd $1070

MODEL 31 STANDARD VISIBLE HAMMER
SLIDE-ACTION REPEATER . . . . . . NiB $366 Ex $298 Gd $199
Similar to Model 24 Grade A except solid frame and straight-grip stock. 30- or 32-inch full choke bbl. Weight: About 7.13 lbs. Made from 1909-15.

Model 31A	NiB $476	Ex $355	Gd $254
Model 31B	NiB $598	Ex $455	Gd $389
Model 31C	NiB $766	Ex $644	Gd $490
Model 31D	NiB $1498	Ex $1154	Gd $990

Marlin Model 59
Bolt-Action Single

Marlin Model 60
Single Shot

MODEL 31F FIELD GUN . . . . . . .NiB $488 Ex $366 Gd $271
Same as Model 31B except has 25-inch bbl., M choke, straight- or pistol-grip stock. Made from 1915 to 1917.

**MODEL 42A VISIBLE HAMMER
SLIDE-ACTION REPEATER** . . . . . .NiB $498 Ex $366 Gd $288
Similar to pre-World War I Model 24 Grade A w/same general specifications but not as high quality. Made from 1922-34.

MODEL 43 HAMMERLESS SLIDE-ACTION REPEATER
Similar to pre-World War I Models 28A, 28T and 28TS, w/same general specifications but not as high quality. Made from 1923 to 1930.
Model 43A . . . . .NiB $355 Ex $200 Gd $144
Model 43TS . . . . .NiB $665 Ex $400 Gd $228

MODEL 44 HAMMERLESS SLIDE-ACTION REPEATER
Similar to pre-World War I Model 31A w/same general specifications but not as high quality. 20 ga. only. Model 44A is a standardgrade field gun. Model 44S Special Grade has checkered stock and slide handle of fancy walnut. Made from 1923 to 1935.
Model 44A . . . . .NiB $466 Ex $381 Gd $222
Model 44S . . . . .NiB $622 Ex $476 Gd $338

**MODEL 49 VISIBLE HAMMER SLIDE-
ACTION REPEATING SHOTGUN** .NiB $566 Ex $449 Gd $367
Economy version of Model 42A, offered as a bonus on the purchase of four shares of Marlin stock. About 3000 made 1925 to 1928.

**MODEL 50DL BOLT
ACTION SHOTGUN** . . . . .NiB $388 Ex $229 Gd $131
Gauge: 12 w/3-inch chamber. Two round magazine. 28-inch bbl. w/ modified choke. 48.75 inches overall. Weight: 7.5 lbs. Checkered black synthetic stocks w/ventilated rubber recoil pad. Made 1997 to 1999.

**MODEL 53 HAMMERLESS
SLIDE-ACTION REPEATER** . . . . . .NiB $480 Ex $200 Gd $144
Similar to Model 43A w/same general specifications. Made 1929 to 1930.

MODEL 55 GOOSE GUN
Same as Model 55 Hunter except chambered for 12-ga. 3-inch Magnum shell, has 36-inch bbl., F choke, swivels and sling. Weight: About 8 lbs. Walnut stock (standard model) or checkered black

synthetic stock w/ventilated rubber recoil pad (GDL model). Made from 1962 to 1996.
Model 55 Goose Gun. . . . . .NiB $335 Ex $266 Gd $195
Model 55GDL Goose Gun
 (intro. 1997). . . . . .NiB $398 Ex $297 Gd $239

MODEL 55 HUNTER BOLT-ACTION REPEATER
Takedown. Gauges: 12, 16, 20. Two round clip magazine. 28-inch bbl. (26-inch in 20 ga.), F or adj. choke. Plain pistol-grip stock; 12 ga. has recoil pad. Weight: About 7.25 lbs.; 20 ga., 6.5 lbs. Made 1954 to 1965.
w/plain bbl. . . . . .NiB $120 Ex $70 Gd $50
w/adj. choke . . . . .NiB $155 Ex $99 Gd $75

MODEL 55 SWAMP GUN . . . . . . .NiB $225 Ex $179 Gd $90
Same as Model 55 Hunter except chambered for 12-ga. 3-inch Magnum shell, has shorter 20.5-inch bbl. w/adj. choke, sling swivels and slightly better-quality stock. Weight: About 6.5 lbs. Made from 1963 to 1965.

MODEL 55S SLUG GUN. . . . . .NiB $200 Ex $99 Gd $75
Same as Model 55 Goose Gun except has 24-inch bbl., cylinder bore, rifle sights. Weight: About 7.5 lbs. Made from 1974 to 1979.

**MODEL 59 AUTO-SAFE
BOLT-ACTION SINGLE** . . . . .NiB $244 Ex $176 Gd $95
Takedown. Auto thumb safety, .410 ga. 24-inch bbl., F choke. Weight: About 5 lbs. Plain pistol-grip stock. Made 1959 to 1961.

**MODEL 60 SINGLE-SHOT
SHOTGUN.** . . . . .NiB $210 Ex $145 Gd $95
Visible hammer. Takedown. Boxlock. Automatic ejector. 12 ga. 30- or 32-inch bbl., F choke. Weight: About 6.5 lbs. Pistol-grip stock, beavertail forearm. Note: Only about 600 were produced in 1923.

MODEL 63 HAMMERLESS SLIDE-ACTION REPEATER
Similar to Models 43A and 43T w/same general specifications. Model 63TS Trap Special is same as Model 63T Trap Gun except stock style and dimensions to order. Made from 1931-35.
Model 63A . . . . .NiB $466 Ex $355 Gd $200
Model 63T or 63TS . . . . .NiB $484 Ex $355 Gd $241

MODEL 90 STANDARD O/U SHOTGUN
Hammerless. Boxlock. Double triggers; non-selective single trigger was available as an extra on pre-war guns except .410. Gauges: 12, 16, 20, .410. Bbls.: Plain; 26-, 28- or 30-inch; chokes IC/M or M/F; bbl. design-changed in 1949, eliminating full-length rib between bbls. Weight: 12 ga., about 7.5 lbs.; 16 and 20 ga., about 6.25 lbs. Checkered pistol-grip

Marlin Model 90
Standard Over-and-Under

Marlin Model 120
Magnum Slide-Action Repeater

Marlin Model 410
Lever-Action Repeater

Marlin Model 512
Slugmaster

Marlin Model 55-10
Super Goose 10

Marlin Premier Mark I
Slide-Action Repeater

Marlin Premier Mark IV

Marlin-Glenfield
Model 50 Bolt-Action Repeater

Marocchi Conquista
Sporting Clays

stock and forearm, recoil pad standard on prewar guns. Postwar production: Model 90-DT (double trigger), Model 90-ST (single trigger). Made from 1937 to 1958.

w/double triggers	NiB $566	Ex $400	Gd $245
w/single trigger	NiB $670	Ex $555	Gd $435
Combination model	NiB $2879	Ex $1976	Gd $1777
16 ga., deduct			10%
20 ga., add			15%
.410, add			30%

MODEL 120 MAGNUM
SLIDE-ACTION REPEATER . . . . . .NiB $354 Ex $230 Gd $155
Hammerless. Takedown. 12 ga. (3-inch). Four round tubular magazine. Bbls.: 26-inch vent rib, IC; 28-inch vent rib M choke; 30-inch vent rib, F choke; 38-inch plain, F choke; 40-inch plain, F choke; 26-inch slug bbl. w/rifle sights, IC. Weight: About 7.75 lbs. Checkered pistol-grip stock and forearm, recoil pad. Made from 1971 to 1985.

MODEL 120 SLUG GUN . . . . . . .NiB $344 Ex $265 Gd $175
Same general specifications as Model 120 Magnum except w/20-inch bbl. and about .5 lb. lighter in weight. No vent rib. Adj. rear rifle sights; hooded front sight. Disc. 1990.

MODEL 410 LEVER-ACTION REPEATER
Action similar to that of Marlin Model 93 rifle. Visible hammer. Solid frame. .410 ga. (2.5-inch shell). Five round tubular magazine. 22- or 26-inch bbl., F choke. Weight: About 6 lbs. Plain pistol-grip stock and grooved beavertail forearm. Made from 1929-32.

Model 410 w/22-inch bbl.	NiB $1546	Ex $1463	Gd $1320
Model 410 w/26-inch bbl.	NiB $1470	Ex $1355	Gd $1110
Deluxe model, add			30%

MODEL 512 SLUGMASTER SHOTGUN
Bolt-action repeater. Gauge: 12; 3-inch chamber, 2-round magazine. 21-inch rifled bbl. w/adj. open sight. Weight: 8 lbs. Walnut-finished birch stock (standard model) or checkered black synthetic stock w/ventilated rubber recoil pad (GDL model). Made from 1994 to 1999.

Model 512 Slugmaster	NiB $466	Ex $338	Gd $243
Model 512DL Slugmaster (intro. 1998)	NiB $390	Ex $278	Gd $176
Model 512P Slugmaster w/ported bbl. (intro. 1999)	NiB $447	Ex $366	Gd $260

MODEL 1898 VISIBLE HAMMER SLIDE-ACTION REPEATER
Takedown. 12 ga. Five shell tubular magazine. Bbls.: 26-, 28-, 30-, 32-inch; standard chokes. Weight: About 7.25 lbs. Pistol-grip stock, grooved slide handle; checkering on higher grades. Difference among grades is in quality of wood, engraving on Grades C and D. Made 1898 to 1905. Note: This was the first Marlin shotgun.

Grade A (Field)	NiB $387	Ex $270	Gd $190
Grade B	NiB $558	Ex $400	Gd $294
Grade C	NiB $700	Ex $554	Gd $449
Grade D	NiB $2170	Ex $1799	Gd $954

MODEL 5510 SUPER GOOSE . . . . .NiB $292 Ex $225 Gd $179
Similar to Model 55 Goose Gun except chambered for 10 ga. 3.5-inch Magnum shell, has 34-inch heavy bbl., F choke. Weight: About 10.5 lbs. Made from 1976 to 1985.

PREMIER MARK I
SLIDE-ACTION REPEATER . . . . . .NiB $255 Ex $198 Gd $110
Hammerless. Takedown. 12 ga. Magazine holds 3 shells. Bbls.: 30-inch F choke, 28-inch M, 26-inch IC or SK choke. Weight: About 6 lbs. Plain pistol-grip stock and forearm. Made in France from 1960-63.

PREMIER MARK II & IV
Same action and mechanism as Premier Mark except engraved receiver (Mark IV is more elaborate), checkered stock and forearm, fancier wood, vent rib and similar refinements. Made 1960 to 1963.

Premier Mark II	NiB $356	Ex $265	Gd $200
Premier Mark IV (plain barrel)	NiB $389	Ex $339	Gd $233
Premier Mark IV (vent rib barrel)	NiB $400	Ex $370	Gd $280

GLENFIELD MODEL 50
BOLT-ACTION REPEATER . . . . . .NiB $320 Ex $255 Gd $175
Similar to Model 55 Hunter except chambered for 12-or 20-ga., 3-inch Magnum shell; has 28-inch bbl. in 12 ga., 26-inch in 20 ga., F choke. Made from 1966 to 1974.

GLENFIELD 778 SLIDE-ACTION
REPEATER . . . . .NiB $325 Ex $255 Gd $180
Hammerless. 12 ga. 2.75-inch or 3-inch. Four round tubular magazine. Bbls.: 26-inch IC, 28-inch M, 30-inch F, 38-inch MXR, 20-inch slug bbl. Weight: 7.75 lbs. Checkered pistol-grip. Made from 1979 to 1984.

MAROCCHI — Brescia, Italy
Imported by Precision Sales International of Westfield, MA.

CONQUISTA MODEL O/U SHOTGUN
Boxlock. Gauge: 12; 2.75-inch chambers. 28-, 30- or 32-inch vent rib bbl. Fixed choke or internal tubes. 44.38 to 48 inches overall. Weight: 7.5 to 8.25 lbs. Adj. single-selective trigger. Checkered American walnut stock w/recoil pad. Imported 1994 to 2003.

Lady Sport Grade I	NiB $1978	Ex $1754	Gd $1288
Lady Sport Grade II	NiB $2144	Ex $1788	Gd $1488
Lady Sport Grade III	NiB $3577	Ex $2875	Gd $2290
Skeet Model Grade I	NiB $1895	Ex $1544	Gd $1154
Skeet Model Grade II	NiB $2250	Ex $1863	Gd $1455
Skeet Model Grade III	NiB $3598	Ex $3210	Gd $2240
Sporting Clays Grade I	NiB $1890	Ex $1669	Gd $1275
Sporting Clays Grade II	NiB $2200	Ex $1790	Gd $1376
Sporting Clays Grade III	NiB $3550	Ex $2977	Gd $2169
Trap Model Grade I	NiB $1890	Ex $1588	Gd $1300
Trap Model Grade II	NiB $2170	Ex $1877	Gd $1470
Trap Model Grade III	NiB $3588	Ex $3120	Gd $2260
Left-handed model, add			10%

MAVERICK ARMS, INC. — Eagle Pass, Texas
Ditrubuted by O.F. Mossberg.

MODEL 88 BULLPUP . . . . .NiB $265 Ex $190 Gd $110
Gauge: 12; 3-inch chamber. Bbl.: 18.5-inch w/fixed choke, blued. Weight: 9.5 lbs. Dual safeties: Grip style and crossbolt. Fixed sights in carrying handle. High-impact black synthetic stock; trigger-forward bullpup configuration w/twin pistol-grip design. Made 1990 to 1995.

SHOTGUNS

Maverick Model 88 Pump Shotgun (Vent Rib)

Merkel Model 47E Side-by-Side

MODEL 88 DEER GUN . . . . NiB $377 Ex $241 Gd $176
Crossbolt safety and dual slide bars. Cylinder bore choke. Gauge: 12 only w/3-inch chamber. Bbl.: 24-inch. Weight: 7 lbs. Synthetic stock and forearm. Disc. 1995.

MODEL 88 PUMP SHOTGUN
Gauge: 12; 2.75- or 3-inch chamber. Bbl.: 28 inches/M or 30 inches/F w/fixed choke or screw-in integral tubes; plain or vent rib, blued. Weight: 7.25 lbs. Bead front sight. Black synthetic or wood buttstock and forend; forend grooved. Made from 1989 to date.
Synthetic stock w/plain bbl. . . . . NiB $287 Ex $228 Gd $175
Synthetic stock w/vent-rib bbl. . . . NiB $300 Ex $238 Gd $195
Synthetic Combo w/18.5-in. bbl. . . . NiB $321 Ex $220 Gd $184
Wood stock w/vent-rib bbl./tubes . . . . NiB $300 Ex $225 Gd $179
Wood Combo w/vent-rib bbl./tubes . . . NiB $255 Ex $200 Gd $162

MODEL 88 SECURITY . . . . NiB $275 Ex $190 Gd $145
Crossbolt safety and dual slide bars. Optional heat shield. Cylinder bore choke. Gauge: 12 only w/3-inch chamber. Bbl.: 18.5-inches. Weight: 6 lbs., 8 ozs. Synthetic stock and forearm.
Made from 1993 to date.

MODEL 91 PUMP SHOTGUN
Same as Model 88, except w/2.75-, 3- or 3.5-inch chamber, 28-inch bbl. W/ACCU-F choke, crossbolt safety and synthetic stock only. Made from 1991 to 1995.
Synthetic stock w/plain bbl. . . . . NiB $330 Ex $256 Gd $180
Synthetic stock w/vent-rib bbl. . . . NiB $335 Ex $270 Gd $195

MODEL 95 BOLT-ACTION . . . . . . NiB $255 Ex $190 Gd $140
Modified, fixed choke. Built-in two round magazine. Gauge: 12 only. Bbl.: 25-inch. Weight: 6.75 lbs. Bead sight. Synthetic stock and rubber recoil pad. Made from 1995 to 1997.

MODEL HS12 TACTICAL . . . . NiB $582 Ex $350 Gd $150
O/U boxlock. C or IM choke. Single trigger w/ extractors. Gauge: 12

only. Bbl.: 18.5-in. Weight: 6.25 lbs. Fiber optic sight. Synthetic stock w/ rubber recoil pad. Picatinny rails. Made from 2011 to date.
Thunder Ranch. . . . . NiB $583 Ex $360 Gd $160

MODEL HUNTER FIELD . . . . NiB $518 Ex $275 Gd $130
O/U boxlock. C or IM choke. Single trigger w/ extractors. Gauge: 12 only. Bbl.: 28-in. Weight: 7 lbs. Front bead sight. Synthetic stock w/ rubber recoil pad. Made from 2010 to date.

GEBRÜDER MERKEL — Suhl, Germany
Manufactured by Suhler Jagd-und Sportwaffen GmbH. Imported by GSI, Inc., Trussville, AL, previously by Ames de Chasse.

MODEL 8 HAMMERLESS
DOUBLE. . . . . NiB $1522 Ex $1190 Gd $955
Anson & Deeley boxlock action w/Greener double-bbl. hook lock. Double triggers. Extractors. Automatic safety. Gauges: 12, 16, 20; 2.75- or 3-inch chambers. 26-or 28-inch bbls. w/fixed standard chokes. Checkered European walnut stock, pistol-grip or English-style w/or w/o cheekpiece. Scroll-engraved receiver w/tinted marble finish.

SIDE-BY-SIDE MODEL 47E . . . NiB $4000 Ex $3200 Gd $1890
Hammerless boxlock similar to Model 8 except w/automatic ejectors and cocking indicators. Double hook bolting. Single selective or double triggers. 12, 16 or 20 ga. w/2.75-inch chambers. Standard bbl lengths, choke combos. Hand-checkered European walnut stock, forearm; pistol-grip and cheekpiece or straight English style; sling swivels.

MODEL 47LSC
SPORTING CLAYS S/S . . . . . NiB $3100 Ex $2500 Gd $1789
Anson & Deeley boxlock action w/single-selective adj. trigger, cocking indicators and manual safety. Gauge: 12; 3-inch chambers. 28-inch bbls.w/Briley choke tubes and H&H-style ejectors. Weight:

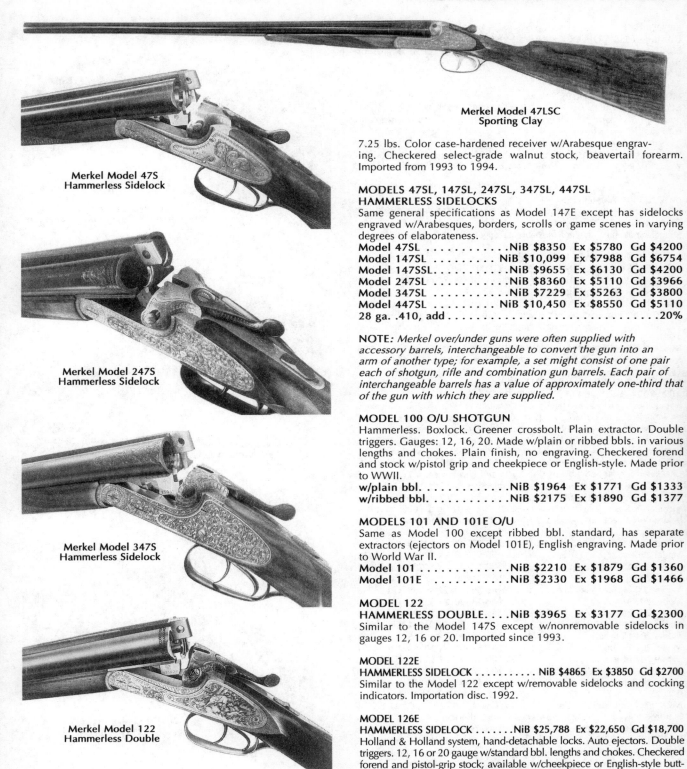

**Merkel Model 47LSC
Sporting Clay**

**Merkel Model 47S
Hammerless Sidelock**

**Merkel Model 247S
Hammerless Sidelock**

**Merkel Model 347S
Hammerless Sidelock**

**Merkel Model 122
Hammerless Double**

7.25 lbs. Color case-hardened receiver w/Arabesque engraving. Checkered select-grade walnut stock, beavertail forearm. Imported from 1993 to 1994.

MODELS 47SL, 147SL, 247SL, 347SL, 447SL
HAMMERLESS SIDELOCKS

Same general specifications as Model 147E except has sidelocks engraved w/Arabesques, borders, scrolls or game scenes in varying degrees of elaborateness.

Model 47SL	NiB $8350	Ex $5780	Gd $4200
Model 147SL	NiB $10,099	Ex $7988	Gd $6754
Model 147SSL	NiB $9655	Ex $6130	Gd $4200
Model 247SL	NiB $8360	Ex $5110	Gd $3966
Model 347SL	NiB $7229	Ex $5263	Gd $3800
Model 447SL	NiB $10,450	Ex $8550	Gd $5110
28 ga. .410, add			20%

NOTE: *Merkel over/under guns were often supplied with accessory barrels, interchangeable to convert the gun into an arm of another type; for example, a set might consist of one pair each of shotgun, rifle and combination gun barrels. Each pair of interchangeable barrels has a value of approximately one-third that of the gun with which they are supplied.*

MODEL 100 O/U SHOTGUN

Hammerless. Boxlock. Greener crossbolt. Plain extractor. Double triggers. Gauges: 12, 16, 20. Made w/plain or ribbed bbls. in various lengths and chokes. Plain finish, no engraving. Checkered forend and stock w/pistol grip and cheekpiece or English-style. Made prior to WWII.

w/plain bbl.	NiB $1964	Ex $1771	Gd $1333
w/ribbed bbl.	NiB $2175	Ex $1890	Gd $1377

MODELS 101 AND 101E O/U

Same as Model 100 except ribbed bbl. standard, has separate extractors (ejectors on Model 101E), English engraving. Made prior to World War II.

Model 101	NiB $2210	Ex $1879	Gd $1360
Model 101E	NiB $2330	Ex $1968	Gd $1466

MODEL 122

HAMMERLESS DOUBLE. . . . .NiB $3965 Ex $3177 Gd $2300
Similar to the Model 147S except w/nonremovable sidelocks in gauges 12, 16 or 20. Imported since 1993.

MODEL 122E

HAMMERLESS SIDELOCK . . . . NiB $4865 Ex $3850 Gd $2700
Similar to the Model 122 except w/removable sidelocks and cocking indicators. Importation disc. 1992.

MODEL 126E

HAMMERLESS SIDELOCK . . . . . . .NiB $25,788 Ex $22,650 Gd $18,700
Holland & Holland system, hand-detachable locks. Auto ejectors. Double triggers. 12, 16 or 20 gauge w/standard bbl. lengths and chokes. Checkered forend and pistol-grip stock; available w/cheekpiece or English-style buttstock. Elaborate game scenes and engraving. Made prior to WW II.

SHOTGUNS

MODEL 127E
HAMMERLESS SIDELOCK . . NiB $24,849 Ex $21,939 Gd $16,374
Similar to the Model 126E except w/elaborate scroll engraving on removable sidelocks w/cocking indicators. Made prior to WW II.

MODEL 128E HAMMERLESS
BOXLOCK DOUBLE . . . . NiB $28,679 Ex $22,167 Gd $16,954
Scalloped Anson & Deeley action w/hinged floorplate and removable sideplates. Auto-ejectors. Double triggers. Elaborate hunting scene or Arabesque engraving. 12, 16 or 20 gauge w/various bbl. lengths and chokes. Checkered forend and stock w/pistol grip and cheekpiece or English-style. Made prior to WW II.

MODEL 130 HAMMERLESS
BOXLOCK DOUBLE . . . . NiB $21,400 Ex $18,560 Gd $16,450
Similar to Model 128E except w/fixed sideplates. Auto ejectors. Double triggers. Elaborate hunting scene or Arabesque engraving. Made prior to WW II.

MODESL 147 & 147E HAMMERLESS
BOXLOCK DOUBLE-BARREL SHOTGUN
Anson & Deeley system w/extractors or auto ejectors. Single selective or double triggers. Gauges: 12, 16, 20 or 28 ga. (Three-inch chambers available in 12 and 20 ga.). Bbls.: 26-inch standard, other lengths available w/any standard choke combination. Weight: 6.5 lbs. Checkered straight-grip stock and forearm. Disc. 1998.

Model 147 w/extractors . . . . . NiB $2588 Ex $2254 Gd $1899
Model 147E w/ejectors . . . . . . NiB $5540 Ex $3770 Gd $2840

Merkel Model 147E
Hammerless Boxlock Double-Barrel Shotgun

MODELS 200, 200E, 201, 201E,
202, 202E & 202EL O/U SHOTGUNS
Hammerless. Boxlock. Kersten double crossbolt. Scalloped frame. Sideplates on Models 202 and 202E. Arabesque or hunting engraving supplied on all except Models 200 and 200E. "E" models have ejectors, others have separate extractors, signal pins, double triggers. Gauges: 12, 16, 20, 24, 28, 32 (last three not available in postwar guns). Ribbed bbls. in various lengths and chokes. Weight: 5.75 to 7.5 lbs. depending on bbl. length and gauge. Checkered forend and stock w/pistol grip and cheekpiece or English-style. The 200, 201, and 202 differ in overall quality, engraving, wood, checkering, etc.; aside from the faux sideplates on Models 202 and 202E, general specifications are the same. Models 200, 201, 202, and 202E, all made before WW II, are disc. Models 201E &202E in production w/revised 2000 series nomenclature.

Model 200 . . . . NiB $2920 Ex $2255 Gd $1730
Model 200E . . . . NiB $3688 Ex $2987 Gd $2116
Model 200 ES Skeet . . . . NiB $4760 Ex $4200 Gd $2977
Model 200ET Trap . . . . NiB $4660 Ex $4189 Gd $3255
Model 200 SC Sporting Clays . . . . NiB $6930 Ex $4599 Gd $3238
Model 201 (disc.) . . . . NiB $3400 Ex $2566 Gd $1888
Model 201E (Pre-WW II) . . . . NiB $7335 Ex $4990 Gd $3288
Model 201E (Post-WW II) . . . . NiB $5100 Ex $3991 Gd $2977
Model 201 ES Skeet . . . . NiB $8100 Ex $6655 Gd $5133
Model 201 ET Trap . . . . NiB $7661 Ex $6255 Gd $4409
Model 202 (disc.) . . . . NiB $8255 Ex $5588 Gd $3577
Model 202E (Pre-WW II) . . . . NiB $8255 Ex $4967 Gd $3886
Model 202E (Post-WWII & 202EL) . . . . . NiB $7091 Ex $5897 Gd $3994

Merkel Model 200E
O/U Shotgun

MODEL 203E SIDELOCK O/U SHOTGUNS
Hammerless action w/hand-detachable sidelocks. Kersten double cross bolt, auto ejectors and double triggers. Gauges: 12 or 20 (16, 24, 28 and 32 disc.). 26.75- or 28-inch vent rib bbls. Arabesque engraving standard or hunting engraving optional on coin-finished receiver. Checkered English or pistol-grip stock and forend.
Model 203E sidelock (disc. 1998) . NiB $10,335 Ex $8556 Gd $5830

Merkel Model 203E
Sidelock O/U Shotgun

Merkel Model
303E
O/U Shotgun

Model 203ES skeet
(imported 1993-97) . . NiB $12,450 Ex $12,330 Gd $10,245
Model 203ET trap
(disc. 1997) . . . . NiB $13,770 Ex $12,560 Gd $10,665

MODEL 204E
O/U SHOTGUN . . . . NiB $8843 Ex $6751 Gd $4766
Similar to Model 203E; has Merkel sidelocks, fine English engraving. Made prior to World War II.

MODEL 210E
SIDE-LOCK O/U SHOTGUN . . NiB $7239 Ex $5340 Gd $3882
Kersten double cross-bolt, scroll-engraved, casehardened receiver. 12, 16 or 20 ga. Double-triggers; pistol-grip stock w/cheekpiece.

MODEL 211E
SIDE-LOCK O/U SHOTGUN . . NiB $6865 Ex $5388 Gd $4488
Same specifications as Model 210E except w/engraved hunting scenes on silver-gray receiver.

MODELS 300, 300E, 301, 301E AND 302 O/U
Merkel-Anson system boxlock. Kersten double crossbolt, two underlugs, scalloped frame, sideplates on Model 302. Arabesque or hunting engraving. "E" models and Model 302 have auto ejectors, others have separate extractors. Signal pins. Double triggers. Gauges: 12, 16, 20, 24, 28, 32. Ribbed bbls. in various lengths and chokes. Checkered forend and stock w/pistol grip and cheekpiece or English-style. Grades 300, 301 and 302 differ in overall quality, engraving, wood, checkering, etc.; aside from the dummy sideplates on Model 302, general specifications are the same. Manufactured prior to World War II.
Model 300 . . . . NiB $5865 Ex $3579 Gd $2988
Model 300E . . . . NiB $8155 Ex $6888 Gd $5224
Model 301 . . . . NiB $6960 Ex $4977 Gd $3200
Model 301E . . . . NiB $8235 Ex $6276 Gd $5004
Model 302 . . . . NiB $14,998 Ex $12,688 Gd $10,097

MODEL 203E SIDELOCK O/U SHOTGUNS
Hammerless action w/hand-detachable sidelocks. Kersten double cross bolt, auto ejectors and double triggers. Gauges: 12 or 20 (16, 24, 28 and 32 disc.). 26.75- or 28-inch vent rib bbls. Arabesque engraving standard or hunting engraving optional on coin-finished receiver. Checkered English or pistol-grip stock and forend.
Model 203E sidelock (disc. 1998) . NiB $10,335 Ex $8556 Gd $5830

MODEL 304E O/U
SHOTGUN . . . . .NiB $24,770 Ex $19,760 Gd $13,010
Special version of the Model 303E-type, but higher quality throughout. This is the top grade Merkel over/under. Currently manufactured. Special order items.

MODELS 400, 400E, 401, 401E O/U
Similar to Model 101 except have Kersten double crossbolt, Arabesque engraving on Models 400 and 400E, hunting engraving on Models 401 and 401E, finer general quality. "E" models have Merkel ejectors, others have separate extractors. Made prior to World War II.
Model 400 . . . . NiB $2190 Ex $1993 Gd $1465
Model 400E . . . . NiB $2433 Ex $2254 Gd $1934
Model 401 . . . . NiB $2798 Ex $2170 Gd $1588
Model 401E . . . . NiB $4366 Ex $3757 Gd $2486

O/U COMBINATION GUNS ("BOCKBÜCHSFLINTEN")
Shotgun bbl. over, rifle bbl. under. Gauges: 12, 16, 20; calibers: 5.6x35 Vierling, 7x57r5, 8x57JR, 8x60R Mag., 9.3x53r5, 9.3x72r5, 9.3x74R and others including domestic calibers from .22 Hornet to .375 H&H. Various bbl. lengths, chokes and weights. Other specifications and values correspond to those of Merkel over/under shotguns listed below. Currently manufactured. Model 210 & 211 series disc. 1992.
Models 410, 410E, 411E (see shotgun models 400, 400E, 401, 401E)
Models 210, 210E, 211, 211E, 212, 212E
(see shotgun models 200, 200E, 201, 201E, 202, 202E)

MODEL 2000EL O/U SHOTGUNS
Kersten double cross-bolt. Gauges: 12 and 20. 26.75- or 28-inch bbls. Weight: 6.4 to 7.28 lbs. Scroll engraved silver-gray receiver. Automatic ejectors and single selective or double triggers. Checkered forend and stock w/pistol grip and cheekpiece or English-style stock w/luxury grade wood. Imported from 1998 to 2005.
Model 2000EL Standard . . . . NiB $5733 Ex $4560 Gd $3288
Model 2000EL Sporter . . . . . . NiB $5980 Ex $4677 Gd $3455

MODEL 2001EL O/U SHOTGUNS
Gauges: 12, 16, 20 and 28; Kersten double cross-bolt lock receiver. 26.75- or 28-inch IC/mod, mod/full bbls. Weight: 6.4 to 7.28 lbs. Three-piece forearm, automatic ejectors and single selective or double triggers. Imported from 1993 to 2005.
Model 2001EL 12 ga. . . . . . . NiB $6566 Ex $5270 Gd $3880
Model 2001EL 16 ga.
(disc. 1997) . . . . .NiB $6400 Ex $5277 Gd $3760
Model 2001EL 20 ga. . . . . . . NiB $6400 Ex $5277 Gd $3760
Model 2001EL 28 ga.
(made 1995) . . . . NiB $7200 Ex $5933 Gd $4200

MODEL 2002EL . . . . NiB $11,990 Ex $8530 Gd $6177
Same specifications as Model 2000EL except hunting scenes w/ Arabesque engraving.

ANSON DRILLINGS
Three-bbl. combination guns; usually made w/double shotgun bbls., over rifle bbl., although "Doppelbüchsdrillingen" were made w/two rifle bbls. over and shotgun bbl. under. Hammerless.Boxlock. Anson & Deeley system. Side clips. Plain extractors. Double triggers. Gauges: 12, 16, 20; rifle calibers: 7x57r5, 8x57JR and 9.3x74R are most common, but other calibers from 5.6mm to 10.75mm available. Bbls.: standard drilling 25.6 inches; short drilling, 21.6 inches. Checkered pistol-grip stock and forend. The three models listed differ chiefly in overall quality, grade of wood, etc.; general specifications are the same. Made prior to WW II.

Miida Model 612
Field Grade O/U

Model 142 Engraved.	NiB $5698	Ex $4887	Gd $3366
Model 142 Standard	NiB $4880	Ex $3688	Gd $2588
Model 145 Field.	NiB $3865	Ex $3200	Gd $2365

MIIDA — Manufactured for Marubeni America Corp., New York, by Olin-Kodensha Co., Tochigi, Japan

MODEL 612 FIELD GRADE O/U. . . NiB $863 Ex $665 Gd $400
Boxlock. Auto ejectors. Selective single trigger. 12 ga. Bbls.: Vent rib; 26-inch, IC/M; 28-inch, M/F choke. Weight: W/26-inch bbl., 6 lbs., 11 oz. Checkered pistol-grip stock and forearm. Made 1972 to 1974.

MODEL 2100 SKEET GUN . . . . . . NiB $954 Ex $749 Gd $488
Similar to Model 612 except has more elaborate engraving on frame (50 percent coverage), skeet-style stock and forearm of select grade wood; 27-inch vent-rib bbls., SK choke. Weight: 7 lbs., 11 oz. Made from 1972 to 1974.

MODEL 2200T TRAP GUN,
MODEL 2200S SKEET GUN . . . . NiB $925 Ex $691 Gd $541
Similar to Model 612 except more elaborate engraving on frame (60 percent coverage), trap- or skeet-style stock and semi-beavertail forearm of fancy walnut, recoil pad on trap stock. Bbls.: Wide vent rib; 29.75-inch, IM/F choke on Trap Gun; 27-inch, SK choke on Skeet Gun. Weight: Trap, 7 lbs., 14 oz.; Skeet, 7 lbs., 11 oz. Made 1972 to 1974.

MODEL 2200 TRAP
& SKEET MODELS . . . . NiB $1088 Ex $766 Gd $594
Same as models 2200T and 2200S except more elaborate engraving on frame (70% coverage). Made from 1972 to 1974.

GRANDEE MODEL GRT/IRS
TRAP/SKEET GUN . . . . NiB $2655 Ex $2390 Gd $1866
Boxlock w/sideplates. Frame, breech ends of bbls., trigger guard and locking lever fully engraved and gold inlaid. Auto ejectors. Selective single trigger. 12 ga. Bbls.: Wide vent rib; 29-inch, F choke on Trap Gun; 27-inch, SK choke on Skeet Gun. Weight: Trap, 7 lbs., 14 oz.; Skeet, 7 lbs., 11 oz. Trap- or skeet-style stock and semi-beavertail forearm of extra fancy wood, recoil pad on trap stock. Made 1972 to 1974.

MITCHELL ARMS — Santa Ana, California

MODEL 9104/9105 PUMP SHOTGUNS
Slide action in Field/Riot configuration. Gauge: 12; 5-round tubular magazine. 20-inch bbl.; fixed choke or screw-in tubes. Weight: 6.5 lbs. Plain walnut stock. Made from 1994 to 1996.
Model 9104 (w/plain bbl.)	NiB $299	Ex $288	Gd $188
Model 9105 (w/rifle sight).	NiB $299	Ex $288	Gd $188
w/choke tubes, add $40			

MODEL 9108/9109 PUMP SHOTGUN
Slide action in Military/Police/Riot configuration. Gauge: 12, 7-round tubular magazine. 20-inch bbl.; fixed choke or screw-in tubes. Weight: 6.5 lbs. Plain walnut stock and grooved slide handle w/brown, green or black finish. Blued metal. Made from 1994 to 1996.
Model 9108 (w/plain bbl.)	NiB $292	Ex $225	Gd $196
Model 9109 (w/rifle sights)	NiB $292	Ex $225	Gd $196
w/choke tubes, add $40			

MODEL 9111/9113 PUMP SHOTGUN
Slide action in Military/Police/Riot configuration. Gauge: 12; 6-round tubular magazine. 18.5-inch bbl.; fixed choke or screw-in tubes. Weight: 6.5 lbs. Synthetic or plain walnut stock and grooved slide handle w/brown, green or black finish. Blued metal. Made from 1994 to 1996.
Model 9111 (w/plain bbl.)	NiB $292	Ex $225	Gd $196
Model 9113 (w/rifle sights)	NiB $292	Ex $225	Gd $196
w/choke tubes, add $40			

MODEL 9114/9114FS
Slide action in Military/Police/Riot configuration. Gauge: 12; 7-round tubular magazine. 20-inch bbl.; fixed choke or screw-in tubes. Weight: 6.5-7 lbs. Synthetic pistol-grip or folding stock. Blued metal. Made from 1994 to 1996.
Model 9114	NiB $345	Ex $245	Gd $169
Model 9114FS	NiB $345	Ex $245	Gd $169

MODEL 9115/9115FS
PUMP SHOTGUN . . . . NiB $366 Ex $240 Gd $159
Slide action in Military/Police/Riot configuration. Gauge: 12; 6-round tubular magazine. 18.5-inch bbl. w/heat-shield handguard. Weight: 7 lbs. Gray synthetic stock and slide handle. Parkerized metal. Made from 1994 to 1996.

MONTGOMERY WARD

See shotgun listings under "W".

MORRONE SHOTGUN — Manufactured by Rhode Island Arms Company, Hope Valley, Rhode Island

STANDARD MODEL 46 O/U . . . NiB $1366 Ex $890 Gd $677
Boxlock. Plain extractors. Non-selective single trigger. Gauges: 12, 20. Bbls.: Plain, vent rib; 26-inch IC/M; 28-inch M/F choke. Weight: About 7 lbs., 12 ga.; 6 lbs., 20 ga. Checkered straight- or pistol-grip stock and forearm. Made 1949-53. Note: Fewer than 500 of these guns were produced, about 50 in 20 ga.. A few had vent-rib bbls. Value shown is for 12 ga. w/plain bbls.. The rare 20 ga. and vent-rib types should bring considerably more.

Mossberg Model 83D

Mossberg Model 85D
Bolt-Action Repeating Shotgun

Mossberg Model 183K

Mossberg Model 185K

Mossberg Model 200K
Slide-Action Repeater

Mossberg Model 395K
Bolt-Action Repeater

O.F. MOSSBERG & SONS, INC. —
North Haven, Connecticut;
Formerly New Haven, Connecticut.

MODEL G4, 70, 73 & 73B . . . . .NiB $150 Ex $85 Gd $50
Single shot. .410 ga. only. Made from 1932 to 1940.

MODEL 83D & 183D . . . . .NiB $217 Ex $121 Gd $95
Bolt action, 3-round. Takedown. .410 ga. only. Two shell fixed top-loading magazine. 23-inch bbl. w/two interchangeable choke tubes (M/F). Later production had 24-inch bbl. Plain one-piece pistol-grip stock. Weight: about 5.5 lbs. Originally designated Model 83D, changed in 1947 to Model 183D. Made from 1940 to 1971.

MODEL 85D & 185D BOLT-ACTION
REPEATING SHOTGUN . . . . .NiB $217 Ex $121 Gd $95
Bolt action. Takedown. 3-round. 20 ga. only. Two-shell detachable box magazine. 25-inch bbl., three interchangeable choke tubes (F, M, IC). Later production had 26-inch bbl. w/F/IC choke tubes. Weight: About 6.25 lbs. Plain one-piece, pistol-grip stock. Originally designated Model 85D, changed in 1947 to Model 185D. Made from 1940 to 1971.

MODEL 183K. . . . . .NiB $240 Ex $131 Gd $100
Same as Model 183D except has 25-inch bbl. w/variable C-Lect-Choke instead of interchangeable choke tubes. Made 1953 to 1986.

MODEL 185K. . . . . .NiB $240 Ex $131 Gd $100
Same as Model 185D except has variable C-Lect-Choke instead of interchangeable choke tubes. Made from 1950 to 1963.

MODEL 190D . . . . .NiB $240 Ex $131 Gd $100
Same as Model 185D except in 16 ga. Weight: About 6 lbs. Made from 1955 to 1971.

Mossberg Mode 500
Accu-Choke

Mossberg Model 500
Camo Pump

Mossberg Model 500
Bullpup Shotgun

MODEL 190K . . . . **NiB $240 Ex $131 Gd $100**
Same as Model 185K except in 16 ga. Takedown. Three round capacity;
2-round magazine. Weight: About 6.75 lbs. Made 1956 to 1963.

MODEL 195D . . . . **NiB $240 Ex $131 Gd $100**
Same as Model 185D except in 12 ga. Takedown. Three round capacity;
2-round magazine. Weight: About 6.75 lbs. Made 1955 to 1971.

MODEL 195K . . . . **NiB $240 Ex $131 Gd $100**
Same as Model 185K except in 12 ga. Takedown. Three round capacity;
2-round magazine. Weight: About 7.5 lbs. Made 1956 to 1963.

MODEL 200D . . . . **NiB $355 Ex $240 Gd $125**
Same as Model 200K except w/two interchangeable choke tubes
instead of C-Lect choke. Made from 1955 to 1959.

MODEL 200K
SLIDE-ACTION REPEATER . . . . **NiB $355 Ex $190 Gd $120**
12 ga. 3-round detachable box magazine. 28-inch bbl. C-Lect choke.
Plain pistol-grip stock. Black nylon slide handle. Weight: About 7.5 lbs.
Made from 1955 to 1959.

MODEL 395K BOLT-ACTION REPEATER . . . **NiB $255 Ex $155 Gd $120**
Takedown. Three round (detachable-clip magazine holds two rounds).12
ga. (3-inch chamber). 28-inch bbl. w/C-Lect-Choke. Weight: About 7.5 lbs.
Monte Carlo stock w/recoil pad. Made 1963 to 1983.

MODEL 385K . . . . **NiB $240 Ex $131 Gd $100**
Same as Model 395K except 20 ga. (3-inch), 26-inch bbl. w/C-Lect-
Choke. Weight: About 6.25 lbs.

Mossberg Model 500
Camper

MODEL 390K . . . . **NiB $240 Ex $131 Gd $100**
Same as Model 395K except 16 ga. (2.75-inch). Made 1963 to 1974.

MODEL 395S SLUGSTER . . . . **NiB $240 Ex $131 Gd $100**
Same as Model 395K except has 24-inch bbl., cylinder bore, rifle
sights, swivels and web sling. Weight: About 7 lbs. Made from
1968 to 1981.

MODEL 500 ACCU-CHOKE SHOTGUN . . . **NiB $290 Ex $231 Gd $125**
Pump-action. Gauge: 12. 24- or 28-inch bbl. Weight: 7.25 lbs.
Checkered walnut-finished wood stock w/ventilated recoil pad.
Available w/synthetic field or Speed-Feed stocks. Drilled and tapped
receivers, swivels and camo sling on camo models. Made from 1987
to date.

Mossberg Model 500
Persuader Law Enforcement

Mossberg Model 500
Mariner

MODEL 500 BANTAM SHOTGUN
Same as Model 500 Sporting Pump except 20 or .410 ga. only. 22-inch w/ACCU-Choke tubes or 24-inch w/F choke; vent rib. Scaled-down checkered hardwood or synthetic stock w/standard or Realtree camo finish. Made from 1990 to 1996 and 1998 to 1999.

Bantam Model (hardwood stock) . . . . . . NiB $255 Ex $198 Gd $130
Bantam Model (synthetic stock) . . . . . . NiB $330 Ex $229 Gd $165
Bantam Model (Realtree camo), add $75

MODEL 500 BULLPUP SHOTGUN . . . . . NiB $722 Ex $486 Gd $344
Pump. Gauge: 12. Six or 8-round capacity. Bbl.: 18.5 to 20 inches. 26.5 and 28.5 inches overall. Weight: About 9.5 lbs. Multiple independent safety systems. Dual pistol grips, rubber recoil pad. Fully enclosed rifle-type sights. Synthetic stock. Ventilated bbl. heat shield. Made from 1987 to 1990.

MODEL 500 CAMO PUMP
Same as Model 500 Sporting Pump except 12 ga. only. Receiver drilled and tapped. QD swivels and camo sling. Special camouflage finish.

Standard model . . . . NiB $390 Ex $255 Gd $200
Combo model (w/ext. Slugster bbl.) . . NiB $409 Ex $270 Gd $220

MODEL 500 CAMPER . . . . NiB $290 Ex $210 Gd $175
Same general specifications as Model 500 Field Grade except .410 bore, 6-round magazine, 18.5-inch plain cylinder bore bbl. Synthetic pistol grip and camo carrying case. Made 1986 to 1990.

MODEL 500 FIELD GRADE HAMMERLESS
SLIDE-ACTION REPEATER
Pre-1977 type. Takedown. Gauges: 12, 16, 20, .410. Three inch chamber (2.75-inch in 16 ga.). Tubular magazine holds five 2.75-inch rounds or four three-inch. Bbls.: Plain- 30-inch regular or heavy Magnum, F choke (12 ga. only); 28-inch, M or F; 26-inch, IC or adj. C-Lect-Choke; 24-inch Slugster, cylinder bore, w/rifle sights. Weight: 5.75 to lbs. Plain pistol-grip stock w/recoil pad, grooved slide handle. After 1973, these guns have checkered stock and slide handles; Models 500AM and 500AS have receivers etched w/game scenes. The latter has swivels and sling. Made from 1962 to 1976.

Model 500A, 12 ga., ... NiB $310 Ex $225 Gd $170
Model 500AM, 12 ga., hvy. Mag. bbl. . . NiB $310 Ex $225 Gd $170
Model 500AK, 12 ga., C-Lect-Choke . . NiB $335 Ex $250 Gd $190
Model 500AS, 12 ga., Slugster . . . . . . NiB $359 Ex $250 Gd $195
Model 500B 16 ga., ... NiB $369 Ex $275 Gd $205
Model 500BK, 16 ga., C-Lect-Choke . . NiB $300 Ex $220 Gd $145
Model 500BS, 16 ga., Slugster . . . . . . NiB $359 Ex $250 Gd $195
Model 500C 20 ga., ... NiB $360 Ex $275 Gd $160
Model 500CK, 20 ga., C-Lect-Choke . . NiB $335 Ex $250 Gd $190
Model 500CS, 20 ga., Slugster . . . . . . NiB $330 Ex $239 Gd $180
Model 500E, .410 ga., ... NiB $300 Ex $220 Gd $140
Model 500EK, .410 ga., C-Lect-Choke . . NiB $350 Ex $275 Gd $165

MODEL 500 "L" SERIES
"L" in model designation. Same as pre-1977 Model 500 Field Grade except not available in 16 ga., has receiver etched w/different game scenes; Accu-Choke w/three interchangeable tubes (IC, M, F) standard, restyled stock and

slide handle. Bbls.: plain or vent rib; 30- or 32-inch, heavy, F choke (12 ga. Magnum and vent rib only); 28-inch, Accu-Choke (12 and 20 ga.); 26-inch F choke (.410 bore only); 18.5-inch (12 ga. only), 24-inch (12 and 20 ga.) Slugster w/rifle sights, cylinder bore. Weight: 6 to 8.5 lbs. Intro. 1977.

Model 500ALD, 12 ga.,
    plain bbl. (disc. 1980) . . . . .NiB $275 Ex $195 Gd $110
Model 500ALDR, 12 ga., vent rib . . . . . . NiB $300 Ex $220 Gd $131
Model 500ALMR, 12 ga.,
    Heavy Duck Gun (disc. 1980) . .NiB $325 Ex $240 Gd $165
Model 500CLD, 20 ga.,
    plain bbl. (disc. 1980) . . . . .NiB $355 Ex $265 Gd $185
Model 500CLDR, 20 ga., vent rib . . . . . . NiB $310 Ex $235 Gd $135
Model 500CLS, 20 ga.,
    Slugster (disc. 1980) . . . . .NiB $355 Ex $265 Gd $185
Model 500EL, .410 ga.,
    plain bbl. (disc. 1980) . . . . .NiB $295 Ex $200 Gd $125
Model 500ELR, .410 ga., vent rib . . . . . . NiB $325 Ex $240 Gd $135

MODEL 500 MARINER SHOTGUN . . . . . NiB $500 Ex $390 Gd $277
Slide action. Gauge: 12. 18.5 or 20-inch bbl. Six round and 8-round respectively. Weight: 7.25 lbs. High-strength synthetic buttstock and forend. Available in extra round-carrying Speed Feed synthetic buttstock. All metal treated for protection against saltwater corrosion. Intro. 1987.

MODEL 500 MUZZLELOADER COMBO. . NiB $390 Ex $275 Gd $190
Same as Model 500 Sporting Pump except w/extra 24-inch rifled .50-caliber muzzleloading bbl. w/ramrod. Made 1991 to 1996.

MODEL 500 PERSUADER LAW ENFORCEMENT
Similar to pre-1977 Model 500 Field Grade except 12 ga. only, 6- or 8-round capacity, has 18.5- or 20-inch plain bbl., cylinder bore, either shotgun or rifle sights, plain pistol-grip stock and grooved slide handle, sling swivels. Special Model 500ATP8-SP has bayonet lug, Parkerized finish. Intro. 1995.

Model 500ATP6, 6-round, 18.5-inch
    bbl., shotgun sights . . . . .NiB $410 Ex $275 Gd $190
Model 500ATP6CN, 6-round,
    nickle finish "Cruiser" pistol-grip. NiB $440 Ex $300 Gd $225
Model 500ATP6N, 6-round, nickel
    finish, 2.75- or 3-inch Mag. shells NiB $410 Ex $275 Gd $190
Model 500ATP6S, 6-round,
    18.5-inch bbl., rifle sights . . . . .NiB $410 Ex $275 Gd $190
Model 500ATP8, 8-round,
    20-inch bbl., shotgun sights . . .NiB $440 Ex $300 Gd $225
Model 500ATP8S, 8-round,
    20-inch bbl., rifle sights . . . . . .NiB $450 Ex $315 Gd $240
Model 500ATP8-SP Spec. Enforcement . . NiB $391 Ex $313 Gd $226
Model 500 Bullpup . . . . NiB $690 Ex $500 Gd $345
Model 500 Intimidator w/laser sight, blued . . NiB $644 Ex $470 Gd $329
Model 500 Intimidator w/laser sight,
    parkerized . . . . .NiB $425 Ex $320 Gd $190
Model 500 Security combo pack . . . . . . NiB $345 Ex $270 Gd $185
Model 500 Cruiser w/pistol grip . . . . NiB $440 Ex $325 Gd $220

GRADING: **NiB** = New in Box   **Ex** = Excellent or NRA 95%   **Gd** = Good or NRA 68%   **515**

Mossberg Model 500
Turkey/Deer Combo

Mossberg Model 590
Military

Mossberg Model 595
Bolt-Action Repeater

MODEL 500 PIGEON GRADE

Same as Model 500 Super Grade except higher quality w/fancy wood, floating vent rib; field gun hunting dog etching, trap and skeet guns have scroll etching. Bbls.: 30-inch, F choke (12 ga. only); 28-inch, M choke; 26-inch, SK choke or C-Lect-Choke. Made from 1971 to 1975.

Model 500APR, 12 ga., field, trap or skeet . NiB $510 Ex $409 Gd $320
Model 500APKR, 12 ga.
  field gun, C-Lect-Choke . . . . . . .NiB $455 Ex $279 Gd $144
Model 500 APTR, 12 ga.,
  Trap gun, Monte Carlo stock . . .NiB $475 Ex $300 Gd $165
Model 500CPR, 20 ga., field or skeet gun . . NiB $365 Ex $279 Gd $180
Model 500EPR, .410 ga.
  field or skeet gun . . . . .NiB $345 Ex $292 Gd $190

MODEL 500 CAMO COMBO SHOTGUN . . NiB $440 Ex $335 Gd $255

Gauges: 12 and 20. 24- and 28-inch bbl. w/adj. rifle sights. Weight: 7 to 7.25 lbs. Available w/blued or camo finish. Drilled and tapped receiver w/sling swivels and camo web sling. Made from 1987 to 1998.

MODEL 500 PUMP SLUGSTER SHOTGUN

Gauges: 12 or 20 w/3-inch chamber. 24-inch smoothbore or rifled bbl. w/adj. rifle sights or intregral scope mount and optional muzzle break (1997 porting became standard). Weight: 7 to 7.25 lbs. Wood or synthetic stock w/standard or Woodland Camo finish. Blued, matte black or Marinecote metal finish. Drilled and tapped receiver w/camo sling and swivels. Made 1987 to date.

Slugster (w/cyl. bore, rifle sights) . . . . NiB $335 Ex $245 Gd $190
Slugster (w/rifled bore, ported) . . . . NiB $415 Ex $335 Gd $240
Slugster (w/rifled bore, unported) . . . . NiB $320 Ex $219 Gd $190
Slugster (w/rifled bore, ported,
  integral scope mount) . . . . .NiB $320 Ex $219 Gd $190
Slugster (w/Marinecote and synthetic stock), add $100
Slugster (w/Truglo fiber optics), add $50

MODEL 500 REGAL SLIDE-ACTION REPEATER

Similar to regular Model 500 except higher quality workmanship throughout. Gauges: 12 and 20. Bbls.: 26- and 28-inch w/various chokes, or Accu-Choke. Weight: 6.75 to 7.5 lbs. Checkered walnut stock and forearm. Made from 1985 to 1987.

Model 500 w/Accu-Choke . . . . . . NiB $320 Ex $219 Gd $190
Model 500 w/fixed choke . . . . . . NiB $300 Ex $200 Gd $165

MODEL 500 SPORTING PUMP

Gauges: 12, 20 or .410, 2.75- or 3-inch chamber. Bbls.: 22 to 28 inches w/fixed choke or screw-in tubes; plain or vent rib. Weight: 6.25 to 7.25 lbs. White bead front sight, brass mid-bead. Checkered hardwood buttstock and forend w/walnut finish.

Standard model . . . . NiB $345 Ex $275 Gd $190
Field combo (w/extra Slugster bbl.) . . . . NiB $440 Ex $325 Gd $240

MODEL 500 SUPER GRADE

Same as pre-1977 Model 500 Field Grade except not made in 16 ga., has vent rib bbl., checkered pistol grip and slide handle. Made from 1965- to 1976.

Model 500AR, 12 ga. . . . . NiB $400 Ex $299 Gd $221
Model 500AMR, 12 ga.,
  heavy magnum bbl. . . . . .NiB $400 Ex $299 Gd $221
Model 500AKR, 12 ga., C-Lect-Choke . . . . . NiB $425 Ex $315 Gd $235
Model 500CR 20 ga. . . . . NiB $400 Ex $299 Gd $221
Model 500CKk, 20 ga., C-Lect-Choke . . . . . NiB $425 Ex $315 Gd $235
Model 500ER, .410 ga. . . . . NiB $400 Ex $299 Gd $221
Model 500EKR, .410 ga., C-Lect-Choke . . . . NiB $425 Ex $315 Gd $235

MODEL 500 TURKEY/DEER COMBO . . . . . . NiB $425 Ex $315 Gd $235

Pump (slide action). Gauge: 12. 20- and 24-inch bbls. Weight: 7.25 lbs. Drilled and tapped receiver, camo sling and swivels. Adj. rifle sights and camo finish. Vent rib. Made from 1987 to 1997.

**Mossberg Model 1000
Junior Autoloading**

**Mossberg Model 5500
Guardian**

MODEL 500 TURKEY GUN. . . . . .NiB $465 Ex $325 Gd $254
Same as Model 500 Camo Pump except w/24-inch ACCU-Choke bbl. w/ extra full choke tube and ghost ring sights. Made 1992 to 1997.

MODEL 500 VIKING PUMP SHOTGUN
Gauges: 12 or 20 w/3-inch chamber. 24-, 26- or 28-inch bbls. available in smoothbore w/Accu-Choke and vent rib or rifled bore w/iron sights and optional muzzle brake (1997 porting became standard). Optional optics: Slug Shooting System (SSS). Weight: 6.9 to 7.2 lbs. Moss-green synthetic stock. Matte black metal finish. Made from 1996 to 1998.
Mdl. 500 Viking
(w/VR & choke tubes, unported) . . . . NiB $300 Ex $225 Gd $144
Mdl. 500 Viking (w/rifled bore, ported) . . NiB $390 Ex $295 Gd $240
Mdl. 500 Viking
  (w/rifled bore, SSS & ported) . . .NiB $390 Ex $295 Gd $240
Mdl. 500 Viking
  (w/rifled bore, unported) . . . . .NiB $300 Ex $225 Gd $144
Mdl. 500 Viking Turkey
  (w/VR, tubes, ported) . . . . .NiB $300 Ex $225 Gd $144

**MODEL 500
WATERFOWL/DEER COMBO** . . . . NiB $455 Ex $350 Gd $285
Same general specifications as the Turkey/Deer combo except w/either 28- or 30-inch bbl. along w/the 24-inch bbl. Made from 1987 to date.

**MODEL 500 ATR SUPER
GRADE TRAP** . . . . NiB $400 Ex $310 Gd $225
Same as pre-1977 Model 500 Field Grade except 12 ga. only w/vent-rib bbl.; 30-inch F choke, checkered Monte Carlo stock w/recoil pad, beavertail slide handle. Made from 1968 to 1971.

**MODEL 500DSPR DUCK STAMP
COMMEMORATIVE** . . . . NiB $600 Ex $465 Gd $300
Limited edition of 1000 to commemorate the Migratory Bird Hunting Stamp program. Same as Model 500DSPR Pigeon Grade 12-Gauge Magnum Heavy Duck Gun w/heavy 30-inch vent-rib bbl., F choke; receiver has special wood duck etching. Gun accompanied by a special wall plaque. Made in 1975.

MODEL 590 BULLPUP . . . . .NiB $745 Ex $449 Gd $335
Same general specifications as the Model 500 Bullpup except 20-inch bbl. and 9-round magazine. Made from 1989 to 1990.

MODEL 590 MARINER PUMP
Same general specifications as the Model 590 Military Security except has Marinecote metal finish and field configuration synthetic stock w/ pistiol-grip conversion included. Made 1989 to 1999.
Model 590 Mariner (w/18.5-inch bbl.). . . NiB $645 Ex $554 Gd $470
Model 590 Mariner (w/20-inch bbl.) . . . . NiB $645 Ex $554 Gd $470
Model 590 Mariner (w/grip conversion), add. $40
Model 590 Mariner (w/ghost ring sight), add $75

MODEL 590 MILITARY SECURITY. . . . . . NiB $544 Ex $389 Gd $290
Same general specifications as the Model 590 Military except there is

no heat shield and gun has short pistol-grip style instead of buttstock. Weight: About 6.75 lbs. Made from 1987 to 1993.

MODEL 590 MILITARY SHOTGUN
Slide-action. Gauge: 12. 9-round capacity. 20-inch bbl. Weight: About 7 lbs. Synthetic or hardwood buttstock and forend. Ventilated bbl. heat shields. Equipped w/bayonet lug. Blued or Parkerized finish. Made from 1987 to date.
Synthetic model, blued . . . . NiB $465 Ex $377 Gd $260
Synthetic model Parkerized . . . . NiB $490 Ex $400 Gd $280
Speedfeed model, blued . . . . NiB $475 Ex $380 Gd $285
Speedfeed model, Parkerized . . . NiB $475 Ex $ 380 Gd $285
Intimidator model
  w/laser sight, blued . . . . .NiB $640 Ex $500 Gd $365
Intimidator model
  w/laser sight, Parkerized . . . . . .NiB $665 Ex $515 Gd $380
For ghost ring sight, add $100

**MODEL 595/595K
BOLT-ACTION REPEATER**. . . . . . .NiB $425 Ex $260 Gd $159
12 ga. only. Four round detachable magazine. 18.5-inch bbl. Weight: About 7 lbs. Walnut finished stock w/recoil pad and sling swivels. Made 1985 to 1986.

MODEL 695 BOLT-ACTION SLUGSTER
Gauge: 12 w/3-inch chamber. Two round detachable magazine. 22-inch fully rifled and ported bbl. w/blade front and folding leaf rear sights. Receiver drilled and tapped for Weaver style scope bases. Available w/1.5x-4.5x scope or fiber optics installed. Weight: 7.5 lbs. Black synthetic stock w/ swivel studs and recoil pad. Made 1996 to 2002.
Model 695 (w/ACCU-choke bbl.) . NiB $300 Ex $220 Gd $175
Model 695
  (w/open sights). . . . . .NiB $380 Ex $296 Gd $207
Model 695
  (w/1.5x-4.5x Bushnell scope) . . . NiB $390 Ex $310 Gd $219
Model 695 (w/Truglo fiber optics) . . .NiB $385 Ex $305 Gd $210
Model 695 OFM Camo. . . . . NiB $355 Ex $280 Gd $196

MODEL 695 BOLT-ACTION TURKEY GUN. NiB $375 Ex $265 Gd $195
Similar to 695 Slugster Model except has smoothbore 22-inch bbl. w/ extra-full turkey Accu-choke tube. Bead front and U-notch rear sights. Full OFM camo finish. Made from 1996 to 2002.

MODEL 712 AUTOLOADING SHOTGUN
Gas-operated, takedown, hammerless shotgun w/5-round (4-round w/3-inch chamber) tubular magazine. 12 ga. Bbls.: 28-inch vent rib or 24-inch plain bbl. Slugster w/rifle sights. Fixed choke or ACCU-choke tube system. Weight: 7.5 lbs. Plain alloy receiver w/top-mounted ambidextrous safety. Checkered. stained hardwood stock w/recoil pad. Imported from Japan 1986 to 1990.
Mdl. 712 w/fixed chokes . . . . NiB $369 Ex $237 Gd $185
Mdl. 712 w/ACCU-Choke tube system . . . . NiB $390 Ex $275 Gd $219
Mdl. 712 Regal w/ACCU-Choke tube system . NiB $390 Ex $275 Gd $219
Mdl. 712 Regal w/ACCU-Choke II tube sys . .NiB $390 Ex $275 Gd $219

SHOTGUNS

MODEL 835 FIELD PUMP SHOTGUN
Similar to the Model 9600 Regal except has walnut-stained hardwood stock and one ACCU-Choke tube only.

Standard model . . . . NiB $365 Ex $220 Gd $154
Turkey model . . . . NiB $365 Ex $220 Gd $154
Combo model (24- & 28-inch bbls.) . . NiB $390 Ex $250 Gd $180

MODEL 835 "NWTF" ULTI-MA SHOTGUN
National Wild Turkey Federation pump-action. Gauge: 12, 3.5-inch chamber. 24-inch vent-rib bbl. w/four ACCU-MAG chokes. Realtree camo finish. QD swivel and post. Made from 1989 to 1993.

Limited Edition model . . . . NiB $470 Ex $366 Gd $239
Special Edition model . . . . NiB $400 Ex $325 Gd $225

MODEL 835 REGAL ULTI-MAG PUMP
Gauge: 12, 3.5-inch chamber. Bbls.: 24- or 28-inch vent-rib w/ACCU-Choke screw-in tubes. Weight: 7.75 lbs. White bead front, brass mid-bead. Checkered hardwood or synthetic stock w/camo finish. Made 1991 to 1996.

Special model . . . . NiB $400 Ex $350 Gd $235
Standard model . . . . NiB $509 Ex $377 Gd $295
Camo Synthetic model . . . . NiB $490 Ex $375 Gd $299
Combo model . . . . NiB $528 Ex $420 Gd $310

MODEL 835 VIKING PUMP SHOTGUN
Gauge: 12 w/3-inch chamber. 28-inch smoothbore bbl. w/Accu-Choke, vent rib and optional muzzle brake (in 1997 porting became standard). Weight: 7.7 lbs. Green synthetic stock. Matte black metal finish. Made from 1996 to 1998.

Model 835 Viking (w/VR and
choke tubes, ported) . . . . .NiB $300 Ex $217 Gd $175
Model 835 Viking (w/VR
and choke tubes, unported) . . . .NiB $445 Ex $270 Gd $210

MODEL 1000 AUTOLOADING SHOTGUN
Gas-operated, takedown, hammerless shotgun w/tubular magazine. Gauges: 12, 20; 2.75- or 3-inch chamber. Bbls.: 22- to 30-inch vent rib w/fixed choke or ACCU-Choke tubes; or 22-inch plain bbl, Slugster w/rifle sights. Weight: 6.5 to 7.5 lbs. Scroll-engraved alloy receiver, crossbolt-type safety. Checkered walnut buttstock and forend. Imported from Japan 1986 to 1987.

Junior model, 20 ga., 22-inch bbl. NiB $555 Ex $435 Gd $320
Standard model w/fixed choke . . . NiB $555 Ex $435 Gd $320
Standard model w/choke tubes . . NiB $555 Ex $435 Gd $320

MODEL 1000 SUPER AUTOLOADING SHOTGUN
Similar to Model 1000, but in 12 ga. only w/3-inch chamber and new gas metering system. Bbls.: 26-, 28- or 30-inch vent rib w/ACCU-Choke tubes.

Standard model w/choke tubes . . NiB $555 Ex $435 Gd $320
Waterfowler model (Parkerized) . . NiB $590 Ex $466 Gd $380

MODEL 1000S SUPER SKEET . . . .NiB $655 Ex $500 Gd $422
Similar to Model 1000 in 12 or 20 ga., except w/all-steel receiver and vented jug-type choke for reduced muzzle jump. Bright-point front sight and brass mid-bead. 1 and 2 oz. forend cap weights.

MODEL 5500 AUTOLOADING SHOTGUN
Gas-operated. Takedown. 12 ga. only. Four round magazine (3-round w/3-inch shells). Bbls.: 18.5- to 30-inch; various chokes. Checkered walnut finished hardwood. Made from 1985 to 1986.

Model 5500 w/ACCU-Choke . . . . NiB $300 Ex $210 Gd $148
Model 5500 modified junior . . . . NiB $300 Ex $210 Gd $148
Model 5500 Slugster. . . . . NiB $355 Ex $209 Gd $155
Model 5500 12 ga. Mag . . . . NiB $335 Ex $254 Gd $190
Model 5500 Guardian . . . . NiB $330 Ex $250 Gd $180

MODEL 5500 MKII AUTOLOADING SHOTGUN
Same as Model 5500 except equipped w/two Accu-Choke bbls.: 26-inch ported for non-Magnum 2.75-inch shells; 28-inch for magnum loads. Made from 1988 to 1993.

Standard model . . . . NiB $330 Ex $209 Gd $135
Camo model . . . . NiB $366 Ex $270 Gd $198
NWTF Mossy Oak model . . . . NiB $415 Ex $330 Gd $225
USST model (1991-92) . . . . NiB $370 Ex $292 Gd $217

MODEL 6000 AUTO SHOTGUN. . NiB $320 Ex $231 Gd $198
Similar to the Model 9200 Regal except has 28-inch vent-rib bbl. w/ mod. ACCU-Choke tube only. Made 1993 only.

MODEL 9200 CAMO SHOTGUN
Similar to the Model 9200 Regal except has synthetic stock and forend and is completely finished in camouflage pattern (incl. bbl.). Made from 1993 to date.

Standard model (OFM camo) . . . . NiB $500 Ex $415 Gd $306
Turkey model (Mossy Oak camo) . . . NiB $475 Ex $429 Gd $360
Turkey model (Shadow Branch camo) . . NiB $615 Ex $490 Gd $376
Comb. model (24 & 28-inch bbls.
w/OFM camo) . . . . .NiB $635 Ex $515 Gd $390

MODEL 9200 CROWN (REGAL) AUTOLOADER
Gauge: 12; 3-inch chamber. Bbls.: 18.5- to 28-inch w/ACCU-Choke tubes; plain or vent rib. Weight: 7.25 to 7.5 lbs. Checkered hardwood buttstock and forend w/walnut finish. Made from 1992 to 2001.

Model 9200 Bantam (w/1-inch shorter stock) . . .NiB $500 Ex $433 Gd $329
Model 9200 w/ACCU-Choke. . . . . NiB $500 Ex $433 Gd $329
Model 9200 w/rifled bbl. . . . . NiB $500 Ex $433 Gd $329
Model 9200 Combo (w/extra Slugster bbl.) . . NiB $550 Ex $493 Gd $379
Model 9200 SP (w/matte blue finish,
18.5-inch bbl.). . . . . .NiB $500 Ex $433 Gd $329

MODEL 9200 PERSUADER . . . . . .NiB $500 Ex $443 Gd $329
Similar to the Model 9200 Regal except has 18.5-inch plain bbl. w/ fixed mod. choke. Parkerized finish. Black synthetic stock w/sling swivels. Made from 1996 to 2001.

MODEL 9200 A1 JUNGLE GUN . . NiB $665 Ex $533 Gd $347
Similar to the Model 9200 Persuader except has mil-spec heavy wall 18.5-inch plain bbl. w/cyl. bore designed for 00 Buck shot. 12 ga. w/2.75-inch chamber. Five round magazine. 38.5 inches overall. Weight: 7 lbs. Black synthetic stock. Parkerized finish. Made from 1998 to 2001.

MODEL 9200 SPECIAL HUNTER . . NiB $555 Ex $435 Gd $365
Similar to the Model 9200 Regal except has 28-inch vent-rib bbl. w/ ACCU-Choke tubes. Parkerized finish. Black synthetic stock. Made from 1998 to 2001.

MODEL 9200 TROPHY
Similar to the Model 9200 Regal except w/24-inch rifled bbl. or 24- or 28-inch vent-rib bbl. w/ACCU-Choke tubes. Checkered walnut stock w/sling swivels. Made from 1992 to 1998.

Trophy (w/vent rib bbl.) . . . . NiB $650 Ex $583 Gd $479
Trophy (w/rifled bbl. & cantilever
scope mount) . . . . .NiB $675 Ex $609 Gd $495
Trophy (w/rifled bbl.
& rifle sights) . . . . .NiB $635 Ex $570 Gd $460

MODEL 9200 USST AUTOLOADER . . NiB $525 Ex $390 Gd $295
Similar to the Model 9200 Regal except has 26-inch vent-rib bbl. w/ACCU-Choke tubes. "United States Shooting Team" engraved on receiver. Made from 1993 to date.

MODEL 9200
VIKING AUTOLOADER . . . . .NiB $425 Ex $330 Gd $290
Gauge: 12 w/3-inch chamber. 28-inch smoothbore bbl. W/Accu-Choke and vent rib. Weight: 7.7 lbs. Green synthetic stock. Matte black metal finish. Made from 1996 to 1998.

Navy Arms Model 83
Bird Hunter O/U

Navy Arms Model 100
Field Hunter Double-Barrel Shotgun

MODEL HS410
HOME SECURITY PUMP SHOTGUN
Gauge: .410; 3-inch chamber. Bbl.: 18.5-inch w/muzzle brake; blued. Weight: 6.25 lbs. Synthetic stock and pistol-grip slide. Optional laser sight. Made from 1990 to date. A similar version of this gun is marketed by Maverick Arms under the same model designation.

Standard model	NiB $345	Ex $270	Gd $195
Laser model	NiB $544	Ex $396	Gd $277

LINE LAUNCHER . . . . NiB $1066 Ex $833 Gd $545
Gauge: 12 w/blank cartridge. Projectile travels from 250 to 275 feet.

"NEW HAVEN BRAND" SHOTGUNS
Promotional models, similar to their standard guns but plainer in finish, are marketed by Mossberg under the "New Haven" brand name. Values generally are about 20 percent lower than for corresponding standard models.

ONYX RESERVE SPORTING . . . . . NiB $760 Ex $580 Gd $370
O/U boxlock, blued engraved receiver. Gauges: 12 only; 3-inch chambers. Bbls.: 28-inch ported vent-rib. Checkered walnut stock and forearm. Made 2010 to 2012.

SILVER RESERVE FIELD . . . . NiB $600 Ex $460 Gd $340
O/U boxlock, gold inlay silver receiver. Gauges: 12, 20, 28 or .410. Bbls.: 26- or 28-in. vent-rib. Checkered walnut stock and forearm. Extractors. Mfg. in Turkey. Imported from 2005 to 2012.

Sporting . . . . NiB $755 Ex $585 Gd $400

SILVER RESERVE II FIELD . . . . NiB $736 Ex $470 Gd $300
O/U boxlock, silver receiver w/ engraving. Gauges: 12, 20, 28 or .410. Bbls.: 26- or 28-in. vent-rib. Checkered black walnut stock and forearm. Extractors or ejectors. Imported from 2012 to date.

Sporting (ported 28-in. bbl.) . . . . NiB $1253 Ex $580 Gd $350
Super Sport (ported 30- or
32-in. bbl.) . . . . NiB $1253 Ex $580 Gd $350

SILVER RESERVE FIELD . . . . NiB $860 Ex $640 Gd $370
S/S boxlock, blued or silver w/ scroll engrved receiver, extractors. Gauges: 12, 20, 28 or .410. Bbls.: 26- or 28-in. Checkered black walnut stock and forearm. Extractors. Made from 2008 to 2012.

Onyx (12 ga., onyx finish) . . . . . . NiB $860 Ex $640 Gd $380

SILVER RESERVE II FIELD . . . . . . NiB $1100 Ex $690 Gd $420
S/S boxlock, blued or silver w/ scroll engrved receiver. Gauges: 12, 20 or 28. Bbls.: 26- or 28-in. Checkered black walnut stock and forearm. Weight: 6.5 to 7.5 lbs. Made from 2012 to date.

NAVY ARMS —
Ridgefield, New Jersey
MODEL 83/93 BIRD HUNTER O/U
Hammerless. Boxlock, engraved receiver. Gauges: 12 and 20; 3-inch chambers. Bbls.: 28-inch chrome lined w/double vent-rib construction. Checkered European walnut stock and forearm. Gold plated triggers. Imported 1984 to 1990.

Model 83 w/extractors	NiB $355	Ex $285	Gd $200
Model 93 w/ejectors	NiB $379	Ex $339	Gd $255

MODEL 95/96 O/U SHOTGUN
Same as the Model 83/93 except w/five interchangeable choke tubes. Imported 1984 to 1990.

Model 95 w/extractors	NiB $448	Ex $355	Gd $210
Model 96 w/ejectors	NiB $555	Ex $376	Gd $280

MODEL 100/150 FIELD HUNTER DOUBLE-BARREL SHOTGUN
Boxlock. Gauges: 12 and 20. Bbls.: 28-inch chrome lined. Checkered European walnut stock and forearm. Imported 1984 to 1990.

Model 100	NiB $460	Ex $390	Gd $288
Model 150 (auto ejectors)	NiB $510	Ex $355	Gd $290

MODEL 100 O/U SHOTGUN . . . . NiB $277 Ex $169 Gd $109
Hammerless, takedown shotgun w/engraved chrome receiver. Single trigger. 12, 20, 28, or .410 ga. w/3-inch chambers. Bbls.: 26-inch (F/F or SK/SK); vent rib. Weight: 6.25 lbs. Checkered European walnut buttstock and forend. Imported 1986 to 1990.

NEW ENGLAND FIREARMS —
Gardner, Massachusetts

In 1987, New England Firearms was established as an independent company producing selected H&R models under the NEF logo after Harrington & Richardson suspended operations on January 24, 1986. In 1991, H&R 1871, Inc. was formed from the residual of the parent H&R company and then took over the New England Firearms facility. H&R 1871 produced firearms under both their logo and the NEF brand name until 1999, when the Marlin Firearms Company acquired the assets of H&R 1871.

NEW ENGLAND FIREARMS NWTF TURKEY SPECIAL
Similar to Turkey and Goose models except 10 or 20 gauge w/22- or 24-inch plain bbl. w/screw-in full-choke tube. Mossy Oak camo finish on entire gun. Made from 1992 to 1996.

GRADING: **NiB** = New in Box   **Ex** = Excellent or NRA 95%   **Gd** = Good or NRA 68%

Noble Model 65

Noble Model 66RCLP
Hammerless Slide-Action Repeating Shotgun

Noble Key Lock Fire Control Mechanism
Supplied with models 66, 166L and 602

Turkey Special 10 ga. . . . . .NiB $265 Ex $177 Gd $98
Turkey Special 20 ga. . . . . .NiB $335 Ex $219 Gd $189

NRA FOUNDATION YOUTH . . . .NiB $190 Ex $155 Gd $100
Smaller scale version of Pardner Model chambered for 20, 28 or .410 w/22- inch plain bbl. High luster blue finish. NRA Foundation logo laser etched on stock. Made from 1999 to 2002.

PARDNER SHOTGUN
Takedown. Side lever. Single bbl. Gauges: 12, 20 and .410 w/3-inch chamber; 16 and 28 w/2.75-inch chamber. 26-, 28- or 32-inch, plain bbl. w/fixed choke. Weight: 5-6 lbs. Bead front sight. Pistol grip-style hardwood stock w/walnut finish. Made from 1988 to date.
Standard model . . . . .NiB $255 Ex $185 Gd $99
Youth model . . . . .NiB $255 Ex $185 Gd $99
Turkey model . . . . .NiB $323 Ex $217 Gd $110
w/32-inch bbl., add $40

PARDNER SPECIAL PURPOSE 10-GA SHOTGUN
Similar to the standard Pardner model except chambered 10 ga. only w/3.5-inch chamber. 24- or 28-inch, plain bbl. w/full choke tube or fixed choke. Weight: 9.5 lbs. Bead front sight. Pistol-grip-style hardwood stock w/camo or matte black finish. Made from 1989 to date.
Special Purpose model w/fixed choke. NiB $315 Ex $220 Gd $125
w/camo finish, add $40
w/choke tube, add $25
w/24-inch bbl. turkey option, add $50

PARDNER SPECIAL PURPOSE
WATERFOWL SINGLE-SHOT . . . .NiB $255 Ex $190 Gd $129
Similar to Special Purpose 10 Ga. model except w/32-inch bbl. Mossy Oak camo stock w/swivel and sling. Made from 1988 to date.

PARDNER TURKEY GUN
Similar to Pardner model except chambered in 12 ga. w/3.0- or 3.5-inch chamber. 24-inch plain bbl. W/turkey full-choke tube or fixed choke. Weight: 9.5 lbs. American hardwood stock w/camo or matte black finish. Made from 1999 to date.
Standard Turkey model . . . . .NiB $200 Ex $110 Gd $85
Camo Turkey model . . . . .NiB $200 Ex $110 Gd $85

SURVIVOR SERIES
Takedown single bbl. shotgun w/side lever release, Automatic ejector and patented transfer-bar safety. Gauges: 12, 20, and .410/.45 ACP w/3-inch chamber. 22-inch bbl. w/modified choke and bead sight. Weight: 6 lbs. Polymer stock and forend w/hollow cavity for storage. Made 1992 to 1993 and 1995 to date.
12 or 20 ga.
  w/blued finish . . . . NiB $220 Ex $144 Gd $98
12 or 20 ga.
  w/nickel finish . . . . NiB $260 Ex $177 Gd $120
.410/.45 LC add $75

TRACKER SLUG GUN
Similar to Pardner model except in 10, 12 or 20 ga. w/24-inch w/ cylinder choke or rifled slug bbl. (Tracker II). Weight: 6 lbs. American hardwood stock w/walnut or camo finish, Schnabel forend, sling swivel studs. Made from 1992 to 2001.
Tracker Slug
  (10 ga.) . . . . NiB $180 Ex $110 Gd $79
Tracker Slug
  (12 or 20 ga.) . . . . NiB $219 Ex $120 Gd $85
Tracker II (rifled bore) . . . . .NiB $219 Ex $120 Gd $85

NIKKO FIREARMS LTD. — Tochigi, Japan

See listings under Golden Eagle Firearms, Inc.

NOBLE MANUFACTURING COMPANY — Haydenville, Massachusetts

Series 602 and 70 are similar in appearance to the corresponding Model 66 guns.

MODEL 40 HAMMERLESS SLIDE-ACTION
REPEATING SHOTGUN . . . . .NiB $255 Ex $190 Gd $130
Solid frame. 12 ga. only. Five round tubular magazine. 28-inch bbl. w/ ventilated Multi-Choke. Weight: About 7.5 lbs. Plain pistol-grip stock, grooved slide handle. Made from 1950 to 1955.

Noble Model 66XL

Noble Model 80
Autoloading Shotgun

Noble Model 166L
Deer Gun

Noble Model 420
Hammerless Double

SHOTGUNS

MODEL 50
SLIDE-ACTION . . . . **NiB $266 Ex $190 Gd $125**
Same as Model 40 except w/o Multi-Choke. M or F choke bbl. Made from 1953 to 1955.

MODEL 60 HAMMERLESS SLIDE-ACTION
REPEATING SHOTGUN . . . . **NiB $325 Ex $255 Gd $159**
Solid frame. 12 and 16 ga. Five round tubular magazine. 28-inch bbl. w/adj. choke. Plain pistol-grip stock w/recoil pad, grooved slide handle. Weight: About 7.5 lbs. Made from 1955 to 1966.

MODEL 65 . . . . **NiB $300 Ex $225 Gd $165**
Same as Model 60 except without adj. choke and recoil pad. M or F choke bbl. Made from 1955 to 1966.

MODEL 66CLP . . . . **NiB $235 Ex $185 Gd $135**
Same as Model 66RCLP except has plain bbl. Introduced in 1967. Disc.

MODEL 66RCLP HAMMERLESS SLIDE-ACTION
REPEATING SHOTGUN . . . . **NiB $339 Ex $235 Gd $176**
Solid frame. Key lock fire control mechanism. Gauges: 12, 16. 3-inch chamber in 12 ga. Five round tubular magazine. 28-inch bbl., vent rib, adj. choke. Weight: About 7.5 lbs. Checkered pistol-grip stock and slide handle, recoil pad. Made from 1967 to 1970.

MODEL 66RLP . . . . **NiB $329 Ex $225 Gd $165**
Same as Model 66RCLP except w/F or M choke. Made from 1967 to 1970.

MODEL 66XL . . . . **NiB $245 Ex $185 Gd $129**
Same as Model 66RCL except has plain bbl., F or M choke, slide handle only checkered, no recoil pad. Made from 1967 to 1970.

MODEL 70CLP HAMMERLESS SLIDE-ACTION
REPEATING SHOTGUN . . . . **NiB $277 Ex $198 Gd $145**
Solid frame. .410 gauge. Magazine holds 5 rounds. 26-inch bbl. w/adj. choke. Weight: About 6 lbs. Checkered buttstock and forearm, recoil pad. Made from 1958 to 1970.

MODEL 70RCLP . . . . **NiB $280 Ex $199 Gd $149**
Same as Model 70CLP except has vent rib. Made 1967 to 1970.

MODEL 70RLP . . . . **NiB $278 Ex $199 Gd $145**
Same as Model 70CLP except has vent rib and no adj. choke. Made from 1967 to 1970.

MODEL 70XL . . . . **NiB $255 Ex $160 Gd $110**
Same as Model 70CLP except without adj. choke and checkering on buttstock. Made from 1958 to 1970.

MODEL 80
AUTOLOADING SHOTGUN. . . . . **NiB $344 Ex $265 Gd $196**
Recoil-operated. .410 ga. Magazine holds three 3-inch shells, four 2.5-inch shells. 26-inch bbl., full choke. Weight: About 6 lbs. Plain pistol-grip stock and fluted forearm. Made from 1964 to 1966.

MODEL 166L DEER GUN . . . . **NiB $355 Ex $270 Gd $199**
Solid frame. Key lock fire control mechanism. 12 ga. 2.75-inch chamber. Five round tubular magazine. 24-inch plain bbl., specially bored for rifled slug. Lyman peep rear sight, post ramp front sight.
Receiver dovetailed for scope mounting. Weight: About 7.25 lbs. Checkered pistol-grip stock and slide handle, swivels and carrying strap. Made from 1967 to 1970.

MODEL 420
HAMMERLESS DOUBLE . . . . **NiB $466 Ex $361 Gd $255**
Boxlock. Plain extractors. Double triggers. Gauges: 12 ga. 3-inch mag.; 16 ga.; 20 ga. 3-inch mag.; .410 ga. Bbls.: 28-inch, except .410 in 26-inch, M/F choke. Weight: About 6.75 lbs. Engraved frame. Checkered walnut stock and forearm. Made from 1958 to 1970.

MODEL 450E
HAMMERLESS DOUBLE . . . . **NiB $490 Ex $376 Gd $290**
Boxlock. Engraved frame. Selective auto ejectors. Double triggers. Gauges: 12, 16, 20. 3-inch chambers in 12 and 20 ga. 28-inch bbls., M/F choke. Weight: About 6 lbs., 14 oz., 12 ga. Checkered

Omega Deluxe Side-by-Side Shotgun

Parker B.H. Grade

Noble Model 450E Hammerless Double

Parker C.H. Grade

pistol-grip stock and beavertail forearm, recoil pad. Made from 1967 to 1970.

MODEL 602CLP . . . . **NiB $366 Ex $255 Gd $235**
Same as Model 602RCLP except has plain barrel. Made from 1958 to 1970.

**MODEL 602RCLP HAMMERLESS SLIDE-ACTION
REPEATING SHOTGUN** . . . . **NiB $355 Ex $255 Gd $190**
Solid frame. Key lock fire control mechanism. 20 ga. 3-inch chamber. Five round tubular magazine. 28-inch bbl., vent rib, adj. choke. Weight: About 6.5 lbs. Checkered pistol-grip stock/slide handle, recoil pad. Made from 1967 to 1970.

MODEL 602RLP . . . . **NiB $315 Ex $233 Gd $157**
Same as Model 602RCLP except without adj. choke, bored F or M choke. Made from 1967 to 1970.

MODEL 602XL . . . . **NiB $285 Ex $177 Gd $145**
Same as Model 602RCL except has plain bbl., F or M choke, slide handle only checkered, no recoil pad. Made from 1958 to 1970.

MODEL 662 . . . . **NiB $308 Ex $244 Gd $165**
Same as Model 602CLP except has aluminum receiver and bbl. Weight: About 4.5 lbs. Made from 1966 to 1970.

OMEGA — Brescia, Italy, and Korea

FOLDING OVER/UNDER STANDARD SHOTGUN
Hammerless Boxlock. Gauges: 12, 20, 28 w/2.75-inch chambers or .410 w/3-inch chambers. Bbls.: 26- or 28-inch vent-rib w/fixed chokes (IC/M, M/F or F/F (.410). Automatic safety. Single trigger. 40.5 inches overall (42.5 inches, 20 ga., 28-inch bbl.). Weight: 6 to 7.5 lbs. Checkered European walnut stock and forearm. Imported from 1984 to 1994.
Standard model (12 ga.) . . . . NiB $475 Ex $355 Gd $298
Standard model (20 ga.) . . . . NiB $475 Ex $355 Gd $298
Standard model (28 ga. & .410) . . . . . . NiB $475 Ex $355 Gd $298

O/U DELUXE SHOTGUN . . . . **NiB $390 Ex $287 Gd $200**
Gauges: 20, 28 and .410. 26- or 28-inch vent-rib bbls. 40.5 inches overall

(42.5 inches, 20 ga., 28-inch bbl.). Chokes: IC/M, M/F or F/F (.410). Weight: About 5.5-6 lbs. Single trigger. Automatic safety. European walnut stock w/checkered pistol grip and tulip forend. Imported from Italy 1984 to 1990.

OMEGA DELUXE
SIDE-BY-SIDE SHOTGUN . . . . **NiB $290 Ex $225 Gd $165**
Same general specifications as the Standard Side-by-Side except has checkered European walnut stock and low bbl. rib. Made in Italy from 1984 to 1989.

STANDARD SIDE-BY-SIDE SHOTGUN, ... **NiB $245 Ex $135 Gd $90**
Gauge: .410. 26-inch bbl. 40.5 inches overall. Choked F/F. Weight: 5.5 lbs. Double trigger. Manual safety. Checkered beechwood stock and semi-pistol grip. Imported from Italy 1984 to 1989.

STANDARD SINGLE-SHOT SHOTGUN
Gauges: 12, 16, 20, 28 and .410. Bbl. lengths: 26-, 28- or 30-inches. Weight: 5 lbs., 4 oz. to 5 lbs., 11 oz. Indonesian walnut stock. Matte-chromed receiver and top lever break. Imported from 1984 to 1987.
Standard fixed . . . . NiB $155 Ex $90 Gd $65
Standard folding . . . . NiB $175 Ex $110 Gd $75
Deluxe folding . . . . NiB $255 Ex $185 Gd $95

DELUXE SINGLE-SHOT SHOTGUN . . . . . **NiB $229 Ex $145 Gd $99**
Same general specifications as the Standard single bbl. except has checkered walnut stock, top lever break, fully-blued receiver, vent rib. Imported from Korea 1984 to 1987.

PARKER BROTHERS — Meriden, Connecticut

This firm was taken over by Remington Arms Company in 1934 and its production facilities moved to Remington's Ilion, New York, plant. In 1984, Winchester took over production until 1999.

HAMMERLESS DOUBLE-BARREL SHOTGUNS
Grades V.H. through A-1 Special. Boxlock. Auto ejectors. Double triggers or selective single trigger. Gauges: 10, 12, 16, 20, 28, .410. Bbls.: 26- to 32-inch, any standard boring. Weight: 6.88-8.5 lbs., 12 ga. Stock and forearm of select walnut, checkered; straight, half-or full-pistol grip.

Parker A-1 Special Grade

Parker A.H. Grade

Parker S.C. Grade

Parker D.H. Grade

Parker
G.H. Grade

Grades differ only in quality of workmanship, grade of wood, engraving, checkering, etc. General specifications are the same for all. Disc. about 1940.

V.H. grade, 12 or 16 ga.	NiB $5733	Ex $4187	Gd $2266
V.H. grade, 20 ga.	NiB $9455	Ex $6077	Gd $3145
V.H. grade, 28 ga.	NiB $28,998	Ex $27,966	Gd $26,778
V.H. grade, .410.	NiB $34,669	Ex $25,766	Gd $21,560
G.H. grade, 12 ga.	NiB $7566	Ex $3998	Gd $2779
G.H. grade, 16 ga.	NiB $8120	Ex $4233	Gd $2988
G.H. grade, 20 ga.	NiB $12,960	Ex $10,679	Gd $7789
G.H. grade, 28 ga.	NiB $33,790	Ex $29,645	Gd $27,889
G.H. grade, .410.	NiB $45,890	Ex $39,955	Gd $27,987
D.H. grade, 12 or 16 ga.	NiB $10,440	Ex $7866	Gd $4350
D.H. grade, 20 ga.	NiB $16,777	Ex $13,790	Gd $11,556
D.H. grade, 28 ga.	NiB $43,088	Ex $39,655	Gd $32,200
D.H. grade, .410.	NiB $72,799	Ex $48,950	Gd $37,788
C.H. grade, 12 or 16 ga.	NiB $17,300	Ex $13,988	Gd $10,996
C.H. grade, 20 ga.	NiB $25,779	Ex $20,099	Gd $17,376
C.H. grade, 28 ga.	NiB $73,588	Ex $60,977	Gd $52,411
B.H. grade, 12 or 16 ga.	NiB $21,689	Ex $18,933	Gd $16,900
B.H. grade, 20 ga.	NiB $31,889	Ex $22,765	Gd $17,766
B.H. grade, 28 ga.	NiB $40,550	Ex $33,980	Gd $24,665
A.H. grade, 12 or 16 ga.	NiB $92,778	Ex $80,000	Gd $66,789
A.H. grade, 20 ga.	NiB $57,778	Ex $40,099	Gd $30,277
A.H. grade, 28 ga.	NiB $104,000	Ex $88,987	Gd $67,033
A.A.H. grade, 12 or 16 ga.	NiB $57,980	Ex $52,077	Gd $37,773
A.A.H. grade, 20 ga.	NiB $83,672	Ex $62,955	Gd $43,900
A.A.H. grade, 28 ga.	NiB $200,000	Ex $175,000	Gd $155,000
A-1 Special grade, 12 or 16 ga.	NiB $100,000	Ex $80,000	Gd $60,000
A-1 Special grade, 20 ga.	NiB $82,000	Ex $65,000	Gd $45,000
A-1 Special grade, 28 ga.	NiB $200,000	Ex $165,000	Gd $110,000

w/selective-single trigger, add **20%**
w/vent. rib, add **35%**
Non-ejector models, deduct **30%**

SINGLE-SHOT TRAP GUNS
Hammerless. Boxlock. Ejector. 12 ga. only. Bbl. lengths: 30-, 32-, 34-inch, any boring, vent rib. Weight: 7.5-8.5 lbs. Stock and forearm of select walnut, checkered; straight, half-or full-pistol grip. The five grades differ only in quality of workmanship, grade of wood, checkering, engraving, etc. General specifications same for all. Disc. about 1940.

S.C. grade	NiB $9355	Ex $7088	Gd $5167
S.B. grade	NiB $11,870	Ex $7279	Gd $6344
S.A. grade	NiB $17,500	Ex $14,223	Gd $11,989
S.A.1 Special (rare)	NiB $42,000	Ex $31,000	Gd $27,000

SKEET GUN
Same as other Parker doubles from Grade V.H.E. up except selective single trigger and beavertail forearm are standard on this model, as are 26-inch bbls., SK choke. Discontinued about 1940. Values are 35 percent higher.

TROJAN HAMMERLESS DOUBLE-BARREL SHOTGUN
Boxlock. Plain extractors. Double trigger or single trigger. Gauges: 12, 16, 20. Bbls.: 30-inch both F choke (12 ga. only) or 28-inch M and F choke. Weight: 6.25-7.75 lbs. Checkered pistol-grip stock and forearm. Disc. 1939.

12 ga.	NiB $5444	Ex $4249	Gd $2677
16 ga.	NiB $6077	Ex $4488	Gd $3210
20 ga.	NiB $6898	Ex $4539	Gd $3556

GRADING: **NiB** = New in Box   **Ex** = Excellent or NRA 95%   **Gd** = Good or NRA 68%

Parker-Hale Model 545A

Parker-Hale Model 645E

Parker Trojan Hammerless
Double-Barrel Shotgun

PARKER REPRODUCTIONS — Middlesex, New Jersey

HAMMERLESS DOUBLE-BARREL SHOTGUNS
Reproduction of the original Parker boxlock. Single selective trigger or double triggers. Selective automatic ejectors. Automatic safety. Gauges: 12, 16, 20, 28 or .410 w/2.75- or 3-inch chambers. Bbls.: 26- or 28-inch w/fixed or internal screw choke tubes SK/SK, IC/M, M/F. Weight: 5.5-7 lbs. Checkered English-style or pistol-grip American walnut stock w/beavertail or splinter forend and checkered skeleton buttplate. Color casehardened receiver with game scenes and scroll engraving. Produced in Japan by Olin Kodensha from 1984-88.

DHE grade, 12 ga.	NiB $4250	Ex $3288	Gd $1366
DHE grade, 12 ga Sporting Clays	NiB $4466	Ex $3890	Gd $2877
DHE grade, 20 ga.	NiB $4866	Ex $3989	Gd $2977
DHE grade, 28 ga.	NiB $5433	Ex $3200	Gd $2366
DHE grade 2-barrel set (16 & 20 ga.)	NiB $6590	Ex $4880	Gd $3588
DHE grade 2-barrel set (28 & .410)	NiB $7377	Ex $5433	Gd $3980
DHE grade 3-barrel set	NiB $10,000	Ex $6566	Gd $5080
B grade Bank Note Lim. Ed., 12 ga.	NiB $5799	Ex $4765	Gd $3499
B grade Bank Note Lim. Ed., 20 ga.	NiB $7352	Ex $6088	Gd $4139
B grade Bank Note Lim. Ed., 28 ga.	NiB $12,000	Ex $9898	Gd $7455
B grade Bank Note Lim. Ed., .410 ga.	NiB $13,900	Ex $10,000	Gd $8894
A-1 Special grade, 12 ga.	NiB $10,877	Ex $8871	Gd $6000
A-1 Special grade, 16 ga.	NiB $12,433	Ex $10,770	Gd $7379
A-1 Special grade, 20 ga.	NiB $10,665	Ex $8932	Gd $6281
A-1 Special grade, 28 ga.	NiB $14,933	Ex $12,966	Gd $9855
A-1 Special gr. 2-barrel set	NiB $13,770	Ex $10,433	Gd $7791
A-1 Special gr. 3-barrel set	NiB $29,650	Ex $23,991	Gd $17,498
A-1 Special gr. custom engraved	NiB $17,888	Ex $14,699	Gd $10,000
A-1 Special gr. custom 2-barrel set	NiB $14,600	Ex $10,553	Gd $7699
w/extra bbl. set, add			$500

PARKER-HALE LIMITED — Manufactured by Ignacio Ugartechea, Spain

MODEL 645A (AMERICAN)
SIDE-BY-SIDE SHOTGUN . . . . NiB $1344 Ex $1116 Gd $844
Gauges: 12, 16 and 20. Boxlock action. 26- and 28-inch bbls. Chokes: IC/M, M/F. Weight: 6 lbs. average. Single non-selective trigger. Automatic safety. Hand-checkered pistol grip walnut stock w/beavertail forend. Raised matted rib. English scroll-design engraved receiver. Discontinued 1990.

MODEL 645E (ENGLISH) SIDE-BY-SIDE SHOTGUN
Same general specifications as the Model 645A except double triggers, straight grip, splinter forend, checkered butt and concave rib. Disc. 1990.

12, 16, 20 ga. with 26- or 28-inch bbl.	NiB $1388	Ex $1166	Gd $898
28, .410 ga. with 27-inch bbl.	NiB $1800	Ex $1490	Gd $1128

MODEL 645E-XXV

12, 16, 20 ga. with 25-inch bbl.	NiB $1288	Ex $1189	Gd $900
28, .410 ga. with 25-inch bbl.	NiB $1698	Ex $1377	Gd $1110

PEDERSEN CUSTOM GUNS — North Haven, Connecticut; div. of O.F. Mossberg & Sons, Inc.

MODEL 1000 O/U HUNTING SHOTGUN
Boxlock. Auto ejectors. Selective single trigger. Gauges: 12, 20. 2.75-inch chambers in 12 ga., 3-inch in 20 ga. Bbls.: Vent rib; 30-inch M/F (12 ga. only); 28-inch IC/M (12 ga. only), M/F; 26-inch IC/M. Checkered pistol-grip stock and forearm. Grade I is the higher quality gun with custom stock dimensions, fancier wood, more elaborate engraving, silver inlays. Made from 1973 to 1975.

Grade I	NiB $2366	Ex $1969	Gd $1449
Grade II	NiB $2210	Ex $1781	Gd $1290

MODEL 1000 MAGNUM
Same as Model 1000 Hunting Gun except chambered for 12-ga. Magnum 3-inch shells, 30-inch bbls., IM/F choke. Made 1973 to 1975.

Grade I	NiB $2809	Ex $2277	Gd $1677
Grade II	NiB $2400	Ex $1900	Gd $1378

MODEL 1000 SKEET GUN
Same as Model 1000 Hunting Gun except has skeet-style stock; 26- and 28-inch bbls. (12 ga. only), SK choke. Made from 1973 to 1975.

Grade I	NiB $2433	Ex $1977	Gd $1698
Grade II	NiB $1998	Ex $1569	Gd $1062

MODEL 1000 TRAP GUN
Same as Model 1000 Hunting Gun except 12 ga. only, has Monte Carlo trap-style stock, 30- or 32-inch bbls., M/F or IM/F choke. Made from 1973 to 1975.

Grade I	NiB $2287	Ex $1862	Gd $1300
Grade II	NiB $1844	Ex $1477	Gd $1106

Pedersen Model 1000 Grade I

Pedersen Model 1000 Grade II

MODEL 1500 O/U
HUNTING SHOTGUN . . . . .NiB $790 Ex $676 Gd $478
Boxlock. Auto ejectors. Selective single trigger. 12 ga. 2.75- or 3-inch chambers. Bbls.: vent rib; 26-inch IC/M; 28- and 30-inch M/F; Magnum has 30-inch, IM/F choke. Weight: 7-7.5 lbs., depending on bbl. length. Checkered pistol-grip stock and forearm. Made from 1973 to 1975.

MODEL 1500 SKEET GUN . . . . . .NiB $833 Ex $690 Gd $569
Same as Model 1500 Hunting Gun except has skeet-style stock, 27-inch bbls., SK choke. Made from 1973 to 1975.

MODEL 1500 TRAP GUN . . . . . . .NiB $788 Ex $648 Gd $520
Same as Model 1500 Hunting Gun except has Monte Carlo trap-style stock, 30- or 32-inch bbls., M/F or IM/F chokes. Made 1973 to 1975.

MODEL 2000 HAMMERLESS DOUBLE
Boxlock. Auto ejectors. Selective single trigger. Gauges: 12, 20. 2.75-inch chambers in 12 ga., 3-inch in 20 ga. Bbls.: Vent rib; 30-inch M/F (12 ga. only); 28-inch M/F, 26-inch IC/M choke. Checkered pistol-grip stock and forearm. Grade I is the higher quality gun w/custom dimensions, fancier wood, more elaborate engraving, silver inlays. Made from 1973 to 1974.
Grade I . . . . NiB $2887 Ex $2260 Gd $1740
Grade II . . . . NiB $2389 Ex $2276 Gd $1578

MODEL 2500
HAMMERLESS DOUBLE . . . . .NiB $780 Ex $655 Gd $356
Boxlock. Auto ejectors. Selective single trigger. Gauges: 12, 20. 2.75-inch chambers in 12 ga., 3-inch in 20 ga. Bbls.: Vent rib; 28-inch M/F; 26-inch IC/M choke. Checkered pistol-grip stock and forearm. Made 1973 to 1974.

MODEL 4000 HAMMERLESS SLIDE-ACTION
REPEATING SHOTGUN . . . . .NiB $597 Ex $440 Gd $375
Custom version of Mossberg Model 500. Full-coverage floral engraving on receiver. Gauges: 12, 20, .410. Three-inch chamber. Bbls.: Vent rib; 26-inch IC or SK choke; 28-inch F or M; 30-inch F. Weight: 6-8 lbs. depending on ga. and bbl. Checkered stock and slide handle of select wood. Made in 1975.

MODEL 4000 TRAP GUN . . . . . . .NiB $590 Ex $466 Gd $265
Same as standard Model 4000 except 12 ga. only, has 30-inch F choke bbl., Monte Carlo trap-style stock w/recoil pad. Made in 1975.

MODEL 4500 . . . . .NiB $500 Ex $390 Gd $335
Same as Model 4000 except has simpler scroll engraving. Made in 1975.

MODEL 4500 TRAP GUN . . . . . . .NiB $525 Ex $420 Gd $366
Same as Model 4000 Trap Gun except has simpler scroll engraving. Made in 1975.

J. C. PENNEY CO., INC. — Dallas, Texas

MODEL 4011
AUTOLOADING SHOTGUN . . . . .NiB $377 Ex $290 Gd $197
Hammerless. Five round magazine. Bbls.: 26-inch IC; 28-inch M or F; 30-inch F choke. Weight: 7.25 lbs. Plain pistol-grip stock and slide handle.

MODEL 6610
SINGLE-SHOT SHOTGUN . . . . . . .NiB $205 Ex $100 Gd $75
Hammerless. Takedown. Auto ejector. Gauges: 12, 16, 20 and .410. Bbl. length: 28-36 inches. Weight: About 6 lbs. Plain pistol-grip stock and forearm.

MODEL 6630
BOLT-ACTION SHOTGUN . . . . . .NiB $254 Ex $179 Gd $115
Takedown. Gauges: 12, 16, 20. Two round clip magazine. 26- and 28-inch bbl. lengths; with or without adj. choke. Plain pistol-grip stock. Weight: About 7.25 lbs.

MODEL 6670
SLIDE-ACTION SHOTGUN . . . . . NiB $260 Ex $188 Gd $140
Hammerless. Gauges: 12, 16, 20, and .410. Three round tubular magazine. Bbls.: 26- to 30-inch; various chokes. Weight: 6.25-7.25 lbs. Walnut finished hardwood stock.

MODEL 6870 SLIDE-ACTION
SHOTGUN. . . . . .NiB $315 Ex $225 Gd $178
Hammerless. Gauges: 12, 16, 20, .410. Four round magazine. Bbls.: Vent rib; 26- to 30-inch, various chokes. Weight: Average 6.5 lbs. Plain pistol-grip stock.

PERAZZI — Manufactured by Manifattura Armi Perazzi, Brescia, Italy

See also listings under Ithaca-Perazzi.

DB81 O/U TRAP . . . . .NiB $5266 Ex $4300 Gd $3450
Gauge: 12; 2.75-inch chambers. 29.5- or 31.5-inch bbls. w/wide vent rib; M/F chokes. Weight: 8 lbs., 6 oz. Detachable and interchangeable trigger with flat V-springs. Bead front sight. Interchangeable and custom-made checkered stock; beavertail forend. Imported 1988 to 1994.

DB81 SINGLE-SHOT TRAP . . .NiB $5300 Ex $4277 Gd $3389
Same general specifications as the DB81 over/under except in single bbl. version w/32- or 34-inch wide vent-rib bbl., F choke. Imported 1988 to 1994.

SHOTGUNS

Perazzi — DB81 Over/Under Trap

Perazzi — Mirage Over/Under Shotgun

Perazzi — MX3 Over/Under Shotgun

Perazzi — MX8 Over/Under Shotgun

GRAND AMERICAN 88 SPECIAL SINGLE TRAP
Same general specifications as MX8 Special Single Trap except w/high ramped rib. Fixed choke or screw-in choke tubes.
Model 88 standard . . . . NiB $4988 Ex $3988 Gd $2777
Model 88 w/interchangeable
  choke tubes . . . . .NiB $4990 Ex $4100 Gd $3099

MIRAGE O/U SHOTGUN
Gauge: 12; 2.75-inch chambers. Bbls.: 27.63-, 29.5- or 31.5-inch vent-rib w/fixed chokes or screw-in choke tubes. Single selective trigger. Weight: 7 to 7.75 lbs. Interchangeable and custom-made checkered buttstock and forend.
Competition Trap,
  Skeet, Pigeon, Sporting . . . .NiB $6400 Ex $5440 Gd $3200
Skeet 4-barrel sets . . . . . NiB $14,680 Ex $12,890 Gd $9800
Competition Special (w/adj. 4-position trigger) add $500

MX-1 O/U SHOTGUN
Similar to Model MX8 except w/ramp-style, tapered rib and modified stock configuration.
Competition Trap, Skeet,
  Pigeon & Sporting . . . . .NiB $6799 Ex $5240 Gd $3390
MXIC (w/choke tubes) . . . . . . NiB $3698 Ex $3288 Gd $2298
MXIB (w/flat low rib) . . . . NiB $3467 Ex $2980 Gd $2098

MX-2 O/U SHOTGUN
Similar to Model MX8 except w/broad high-ramped competition rib.
Competition-Trap, Skeet,
  Pigeon & Sporting . . . . .NiB $6780 Ex $3544 Gd $3589
MX2C (w/choke tubes) . . . . . . NiB $4988 Ex $3998 Gd $2766

MX-3 O/U SHOTGUN
Similar to Model MX8 except w/ramp-style, tapered rib and modified stock configuration.

Competition Trap, Skeet,
  Pigeon & Sporting . . . . NiB $48,988 Ex $42,998 Gd $35,999
Competition Special (w/adj. 4-position trigger) add $400
Game models . . . . NiB $4478 Ex $3659 Gd $2699
Combo O/U plus SB . . . . NiB $5563 Ex $4478 Gd $3380
SB Trap 32- or 34-inch . . . . . NiB $3987 Ex $3166 Gd $2267
Skeet 4-bbl. sets . . . . NiB $12,888 Ex $10,099 Gd $7789
Skeet Special 4-bbl. sets .NiB $13,066 Ex $11,288 Gd $8,996

MX-3 SPECIAL PIGEON SHOTGUN . .NiB $5344 Ex $4276 Gd $3110
Gauge: 12; 2.75-inch chambers. 29.5- or 31.5-inch vent rib bbl.; IC/M and extra full chokes. Weight: 8 lbs., 6 oz. Detachable and interchangeable trigger group w/flat V-springs. Bead front sight. Interchangeable and custom-made checkered stock for live pigeon shoots; splinter forend. Imported 1991 to 1992.

MX-4 O/U SHOTGUN
Similar to Model MX3 in appearance and shares the MX8 locking system. Detachable, adj. 4-position trigger standard. Interchangeable choke tubes optional.
Competition Trap,
  Skeet, Pigeon & Sporting . . .NiB $4487 Ex $4089 Gd $3124
MX4C (w/choke tubes) . . . . . . NiB $5388 Ex $4500 Gd $3787

MX-5 O/U GAME GUN
Similar to Model MX8 except in hunting configuration, chambered in 12 or 20 ga. Non-detachable single selective trigger.
MX5 Standard . . . . NiB $3977 Ex $2886 Gd $2066
MX5C (w/choke tubes) . . . . . . NiB $4264 Ex $3188 Gd $2200

MX-6 AMER.
TRAP SINGLE-BARREL . . . . NiB $4302 Ex $2677 Gd $1988
Single shot. Removable trigger group. 12 ga. Barrels: 32- or 34-inch with fixed or choke tubes. Raised vent rib. Checkered European walnut Monte Carlo stock, beavertail forend. Imported 1995 to 1998.

Perazzi — MX20 Over/Under Game Gun

Perazzi — TMX Single Shot Trap

MX-6 SKEET O/U . . . . NiB $4277 Ex $3100 Gd $2250
Same general specs as MX6 American Trap single barrel except over/under; boxlock. Barrels: 26.75- or 27.50-inch. Imported 1995 to 1998.

MX-6 SPORTING O/U . . . . . . NiB $4277 Ex $3100 Gd $2250
Same specs as MX6 American Trap single barrel except over/under; boxlock. Single selective trigger; external selector. Barrels: 28.38-, 29.50-, or 31.50-inch. Imported 1995 to 1998.

MX-6 TRAP O/U . . . . NiB $4350 Ex $2929 Gd $1877
Same general specs as MX6 American Trap single barrel except over/under; boxlock. Barrels: 29.50-, 30.75-, or 31.50-inch. Imported 1995 to 1998.

MX-7 O/U SHOTGUN . . . . . . NiB $4188 Ex $3755 Gd $2690
Similar to Model MX12 except w/MX3-style receiver and top-mounted trigger selector. Bbls.: 28.73-, 2.5-, 31.5-inch w/vent rib; screw-in choke tubes. Imported 1992 to 1998.

MX-8 O/U SHOTGUN
Gauge: 12, 2.75-inch chambers. Bbls.: 27.63-, 29.5- or 31.5-inch vent-rib w/fixed chokes or screw-in choke tubes. Weight: 7 to 8.5 lbs. Interchangeable and custom-made checkered stock; beavertail forend. Special models have detachable and interchangeable 4-position trigger group w/flat V-springs. Imported 1968 to date.
MX-8 Standard . . . . NiB $8099 Ex $4133 Gd $2377
MX-8 Special (adj. 4-pos. trigger) . . . . NiB $4229 Ex $3378 Gd $2490
MX-8 Special single
 (32-or 34-inch bbl.) . . . . . . NiB $8380 Ex $7121 Gd $4365
MX-8 Special combo . . . . NiB $8009 Ex $6355 Gd $4682

MX-8/20 O/U SHOTGUN . . . NiB $4155 Ex $3370 Gd $2499
Similar to the Model MX8 except w/smaller frame and custom stock. Available in sporting or game configurations with fixed chokes or screw-in tubes. Imported 1993 to date.

MX-9 O/U SHOTGUN . . . . . . NiB $6880 Ex $5672 Gd $4200
Gauge: 12; 2.75-inch chambers. Bbls.: 29.5- or 30.5-inch w/choke tubes and vent side rib. Selective trigger. Checkered walnut stock w/ adj. cheekpiece. Available in single bbl., combo, O/U trap, skeet, pigeon and sporting models. Imported 1993 to 1994.

MX-10 O/U SHOTGUN . . . NiB $8293 Ex $5760 Gd $34,105
Similar to the Model MX9 except w/fixed chokes and different rib configuration. Imported 1993.

MX-10 PIGEON-ELECTROCIBLES O/U. . NiB $8996 Ex $6133 Gd $4400
Over/Under; boxlock. Removable trigger group; external selector. 12 gauge. Barrels: 27.50- or 29.50-inch. Checkered European walnut adjustable stock, beavertail forend. Imported 1995 to date.

MX–11 AMERICAN TRAP COMBO . NiB $5440 Ex $4688 Gd $3277
Over/Under; boxlock. External selector. Removable trigger group; single selective trigger. 12 ga. Bbls: 29-1/2- to 34-inch with fixed or choke tubes; vent rib. European walnut Monte Carlo adjustable stock, beavertail forend. Imported 1995 to date.

**MX-11 AMERICAN TRAP
SINGLE BARREL** . . . . NiB $5155 Ex $4309 Gd $2879
Same general specs as MX11 American Trap combo except 32- or 34-inch single bbl. Imported 1995 to 1996.

MX-11 PIGEON-ELECTROCIBLES O/U . .NiB $5331 Ex $4277 Gd $3100
Same specs as MX11 American Trap combo except 27.50 O/U bbls. Checkered European walnut pistol grip adjustable stock, beavertail forend. Imported 1995 to 1996.

MX-11 SKEET O/U . . . . NiB $5390 Ex $4369 Gd $3122
Same general specs as MX11 American Trap combo except 26.75 or 27.50-inch O/U bbls. Checkered European walnut pistol-grip adjustable stock, beavertail forend. Imported 1995 to 1996.

MX-11 SPORTING O/U . . . . . NiB $5344 Ex $4766 Gd $3409
Same general specs as MX11 American Trap combo except 28.38, 29.50-, or 31.50-inch O/U bbls. Checkered European walnut pistol-grip adjustable stock, beavertail forend. Imported 1995 to 1996.

MX-11 TRAP O/U . . . . NiB $5293 Ex $4266 Gd $3109
Same general specs as MX11 American Trap combo except 29.50,- 30.75- or 31.50-inch O/U bbls. Checkered European walnut pistol-grip adjustable stock, beavertail forend. Imported 1995 to 1996.

MX-12 O/U GAME GUN
Gauge: 12, 2.75-inch chambers. Bbls.: 26-, 27.63-, 28.38- or 29.5-inch, vent rib, fixed chokes or screw-in choke tubes. Non-detachable single selective trigger group w/coil springs. Weight: 7.25 lbs. Interchangeable and custom-made checkered stock; Schnabel forend.
MX12 Standard . . . . NiB $7966 Ex $4312 Gd $3100
MX12C (w/choke tubes) . . . . . NiB $7994 Ex $4366 Gd $3180

**MX-14 AMERICAN TRAP
SINGLE-BARREL** . . . . NiB $6892 Ex $3677 Gd $2573
Single shot. Removable trigger group; unsingle configuration. 12 ga. Bbl: 34-inch with fixed or choke tubes; vent rib. Checkered European walnut Monte Carlo adjustable stock, beavertail forend. Imported 1995 to 1996.

**MX-15 AMERICAN TRAP
SINGLE-BARREL** . . . . NiB $6654 Ex $4138 Gd $2998
Full choke. Detachable trigger group. Gauge: 12 only with 2.75-inch chamber. Bbls: 32 and 34-inch. Weight: 8 lbs., 6 oz.

GRADING: **NiB** = New in Box   **Ex** = Excellent or NRA 95%   **Gd** = Good or NRA 68%

Piotti
Piuma Boxlock Side-by-Side Shotgun

Powell No. 7
Aristocrat Grade Double

MX-20 O/U GAME GUN
Gauges: 20, 28 and .410; 2.75- or 3-inch chambers. 26-inch vent-rib bbls., M/F chokes or screw-in chokes. Auto selective ejectors. Selective single trigger. Weight: 6 lbs., 6 oz. Non-detachable coil-spring trigger. Bead front sight. Interchangeable and custom-made checkered stock w/ Schnabel forend. Imported from 1988 to date.

Standard grade . . . . NiB $5311 Ex $4255 Gd $2987
Standard grade
  w/gold outline . . . . NiB $8991 Ex $7200 Gd $5102
MX20C w/choke tubes . . . . . . NiB $5886 Ex $4480 Gd $3171
SC3 grade . . . . NiB $9766 Ex $7764 Gd $5433
SCO grade . . . . NiB $13,978 Ex $11,888 Gd $9166

MX-28 O/U GAME GUN. . NiB $15,660 Ex $12,987 Gd $9821
Similar to the Model MX12 except chambered in 28 ga. w/26-inch bbls. fitted to smaller frame. Imported from 1993 to date.

MX-410 O/U GAME GUN. . NiB $15,890 Ex $13,298 Gd $10,350
Similar to the Model MX12 except in .410 bore w/3-inch chambers, 26-inch bbls. fitted to smaller frame. Imported from 1993 to date.

TM1 SPECIAL
SINGLE-SHOT TRAP . . . . NiB $3150 Ex $2770 Gd $2000
Gauge: 12- 2.75-inch chambers. 32- or 34-inch bbl. w/wide vent rib; full choke. Weight: 8 lbs., 6 oz. Detachable and interchangeable trigger group with coil springs. Bead front sight. Interchangeable and custom-made stock w/checkered pistol grip and beavertail forend. Imported from 1988 to 1995.

TMX SPECIAL
SINGLE-SHOT TRAP . . . . NiB $3890 Ex $2553 Gd $1966
Same general specifications as Model TM1 Special except w/ultra-high rib. Interchangeable choke tubes optional.

PIOTTI — Brescia, Italy

BOSS O/U . . . . NiB $58,998 Ex $50,000 Gd $35,965
Over/Under; sidelock. Gauges: 12 or 20. Barrels: 26- to 32-inch. Standard chokes. Best quality walnut. Custom-made to customer's specifications. Imported from 1993 to date.

KING NO. 1 SIDELOCK . NiB $35,866 Ex $29,821 Gd $19,670
Gauges: 10, 12, 16, 20, 28 and .410. 25- to 30-inch bbls. (12 ga.), 25- to 28-inch (other ga.). Weight: About 5 lbs. (.410) to 8 lbs. (12 ga.) Holland & Holland pattern sidelock. Double triggers standard. Coin finish or color casehardened. Level file-cut rib. Full-coverage scroll engraving, gold inlays. Hand-rubbed, oil-finished, straight-grip stock with checkered butt, splinter forend.

KING EXTRA SIDE-BY-SIDE
SHOTGUN. . . . . .NiB $77,850 Ex $52,290 Gd $42,777
Same general specifications as the Piotti King No. 1 except has choice of engraving, gold inlays, plus stock is of exhibition-grade wood.

LUNIK SIDE-LOCK
SHOTGUN. . . . . .NiB $35,660 Ex $31,299 Gd $26,000
Same general specifications as the Monte Carlo model except has level, file-cut rib. Renaissance-style, large scroll engraving in relief, gold crown in top lever, gold name, and gold crest in forearm, finely figured wood.

MONTE CARLO
SIDE-LOCK SHOTGUN. . . . NiB $11,488 Ex $9889 Gd $7577
Gauges: 10, 12, 16, 20, 28 or .410. Bbls.: 25- to 30-inch. Holland & Holland pattern sidelock. Weight: 5-8 lbs. Automatic ejectors. Double triggers. Hand-rubbed oil-finished straight-grip stock with checkered butt. Choice of Purdey-style scroll and rosette or Holland & Holland-style large scroll engraving.

PIUMA BOXLOCK
SIDE-BY-SIDE SHOTGUN . NiB $18,667 Ex $12,933 Gd $10,011
Same general specifications as the Monte Carlo model except has Anson & Deeley boxlock action w/demi-bloc bbls., scalloped frame. Standard scroll and rosette engraving. Hand-rubbed, oil-finished straight-grip stock.

WILLIAM POWELL & SON, LTD. — Birmingham, England

NO. 1 BEST GRADE DOUBLE-BARREL
SHOTGUN. . . . . .NiB $42,777 Ex $38,698 Gd $31,033
Sidelock. Gauges: Made to order with 12, 16 and 20 the most common. Bbls.: Made to order in any length but 28 inches was recommended. Highest grade French walnut buttstock and forearm with fine checkering. Metal elaborately engraved. Imported by Stoeger from about 1938 to 1951.

NO. 2 BEST GRADE
DOUBLE-BARREL . . . . .NiB $29,766 Ex $24,761 Gd $16,888
Same general specifications as the Powell No. 1 except plain finish without engraving. Imported by Stoeger from about 1938 to 1951.

NO. 6 CROWN GRADE
DOUBLE-BARREL . . . . .NiB $15,999 Ex $12,733 Gd $10,111
Boxlock. Gauges: Made to order with 12, 16 and 20 the most common. Bbls.: Made to order, but 28 inches was recommended. Highest grade French walnut buttstock and forearm with fine checkering. Metal elaborately engraved. Uses Anson & Deeley locks. Imported by Stoeger from about 1938 to 1951.

NO. 7 ARISTOCRAT GRADE DOUBLE-BARREL
SHOTGUN. . . . . .NiB $9022 Ex $6988 Gd $4766
Same general specifications as the Powell No. 6 Crown Grade Double-Barrel above, except with lower quality wood and metal engraving.

Premier Ambassador
Field Grade

Premier Continental
Field Grade

PRECISION SPORTS SHOTGUNS —
Cortland, New York; manufactured by Ignacio Ugartechea, Spain

600 SERIES AMERICAN HAMMERLESS DOUBLES
Boxlock. Single selective trigger. Selective automatic ejectors. Automatic safety. Gauges: 12, 16, 20, 28, .410; 2.75- or 3-inch chambers. Bbls.: 26-,27- or 28-inch w/raised matte rib; choked IC/M or M/F. Weight: 5.75-7 lbs. Checkered pistol-grip walnut buttstock with beavertail forend. Engraved silvered receiver with blued bbls. Imported from 1986 to 1994.
640A (12, 16, 20 ga. w/extractors) . . . . NiB $1177 Ex $909 Gd $677
640A (28 ga., .410 w/extractors) . . . . NiB $1288 Ex $1067 Gd $779
640 Slug Gun (12 ga. w/extractors) . . NiB $1277 Ex $1059 Gd $723
645A (12, 16, 20 ga. w/ejectors) . . . . . NiB $1177 Ex $909 Gd $677
645A (28 ga., .410, two-bbl. set) . . . . NiB $1488 Ex $1176 Gd $877
645A (20/28 ga. two-bbl. set) . . . . . . NiB $1563 Ex $1253 Gd $919
650A (12 ga. w/extractors, choke tubes) . NiB $1165 Ex $977 Gd $710
655A (12 ga. w/ejectors, choke tubes) . .NiB $1288 Ex $1022 Gd $766

600 SERIES ENGLISH HAMMERLESS DOUBLES
Boxlock. Same general specifications as American 600 series except w/ double triggers and concave rib. Checkered English-style walnut stock w/splinter forend, straight grip and oil finish.
640E (12, 16, 20 ga. w/extractors) . . . . . NiB $956 Ex $790 Gd $622
640E (28 ga., .410 w/extractors) . . . . . . NiB $1088 Ex $900 Gd $644
640 Slug Gun (12 ga. w/extractors) . . NiB $1297 Ex $1044 Gd $780
645E (12, 16, 20 ga. w/ejectors) . . . . . NiB $1300 Ex $1066 Gd $800
645E (28 ga., .410 w/ejectors) . . . . . . NiB $1266 Ex $1022 Gd $776
645E (20/28 ga. two-bbl. set) . . . . . . NiB $1545 Ex $1296 Gd $1000
650E (12 ga. w/extractors, choke tubes) . .NiB $1178 Ex $938 Gd $715
655E (12 ga. w/ejectors, choke tubes) . NiB $1190 Ex $980 Gd $750

MODEL 640M MAGNUM 10 HAMMERLESS DOUBLE
Similar to Model 640E except in 10 ga. w/3.5-inch Mag. chambers. Bbls.: 26-, 30-, 32-inch choked F/F.
Model 640M Big Ten, Turkey . . .NiB $1106 Ex $933 Gd $700
Model 640M Goose Gun . . . . . .NiB $1133 Ex $955 Gd $735

MODEL 645E-XXV HAMMERLESS DOUBLE
Similar to Model 645E except w/25-inch bbl. and Churchill-style rib.
645E-XXV (12, 16, 20 ga. w/ejectors) . . .NiB $1160 Ex $982 Gd $755
645E-XXV (28, .410 ga. w/ejectors) . . . .NiB $1366 Ex $1093 Gd $835

PREMIER SHOTGUNS
Premier shotguns have been produced by various gunmakers in Europe.

**AMBASSADOR MODEL FIELD GRADE HAMMERLESS
DOUBLE-BARREL SHOTGUN** . . . .NiB $544 Ex $466 Gd $377
Sidelock. Plain extractors. Double triggers. Gauges: 12, 16, 20, .410. 3-inch chambers in 20 and .410 ga., 2.75- inch in 12 and 16 ga. Bbls.:

26-inch in .410 ga., 28 inch in other ga.; choked M/F. Weight: 6 lbs., 3 oz.-7 lbs., 3 oz. depending on gauge. Checkered pistol-grip stock and beavertail forearm. Intro. in 1957; disc.

BRUSH KING . . . . .NiB $440 Ex $330 Gd $255
Same as standard Regent model except chambered for 12 (2.75-inch) and 20 ga. (3-inch) only; has 22-inch bbls., IC/M choke, straight-grip stock. Weight: 6 lbs., 3 oz. in 12 ga.; 5 lbs., 12 oz. in 20 ga. Introduced in 1959; disc.

**CONTINENTAL MODEL FIELD GRADE HAMMER
DOUBLE-BARREL SHOTGUN. . . . NiB $577 Ex $426 Gd $300**
Sidelock. Exposed hammers. Plain extractors. Double triggers. Gauges: 12, 16, 20, .410. Three inch chambers in 20 and .410 ga., 2.75-inch in 12 and 16 ga. Bbls.: 26-inch in .410 ga.; 28-inch in other ga.; choked M/F. Weight: 6 lbs., 3 oz.-7 lbs., 3 oz. depending on gauge. Checkered pistol-grip stock and English-style forearm. Introduced in 1957; disc.

**MONARCH SUPREME GRADE HAMMERLESS
DOUBLE-BARREL SHOTGUN. . . .NiB $667 Ex $487 Gd $367**
Boxlock. Auto ejectors. Double triggers. Gauges: 12, 20. 2.75-inch chambers in 12 ga., 3-inch in 20 ga. Bbls.: 28-inch M/F; 26-inch IC/M choke. Weight: 6 lbs., 6 oz., 7 lbs., 2 oz. depending on gauge and bbl. Checkered pistol-grip stock and beavertail forearm of fancy walnut. Introduced in 1959; disc.

**PRESENTATION
CUSTOM GRADE** . . . . .NiB $1488 Ex $1109 Gd $856
Similar to Monarch model but made to order of higher quality with hunting scene engraving, gold and silver inlay, fancier wood. Introduced in 1959; disc.

**REGENT 10 GA.
MAGNUM EXPRESS** . . . . .NiB $665 Ex $431 Gd $345
Same as standard Regent model except chambered for 10-ga. Magnum 3.5-inch shells, has heavier construction, 32-inch bbls. choked F/F, stock with recoil pad. Weight: 11.25 lbs. Introduced in 1957; disc.

**REGENT 12 GA.
MAGNUM EXPRESS** . . . . .NiB $465 Ex $388 Gd $290
Same as standard Regent model except chambered for 12-ga. Magnum 3-inch shells, has 30-inch bbls. choked F and F, stock with recoil pad. Weight: 7.25 lbs. Introduced in 1957; disc.

**REGENT FIELD GRADE
HAMMERLESS
DOUBLE-BARREL SHOTGUN. . . .NiB $477 Ex $355 Gd $271**
Boxlock. Plain extractors. Double triggers. Gauges: 12,16, 20, 28, .410. Three inch chambers in 20 and .410 ga., 2.75-inch in other gauges. Bbls.: 26-inch IC/M, M/F (28 and .410 ga. only); 28-inch M/F; 30-inch M/F (12 ga. only). Weight: 6 lbs., 2 oz.-7 lbs., 4 oz. depending on gauge and bbl. Checkered pistol-grip stock and beavertail forearm. Introduced in 1955; disc.

SHOTGUNS

Purdey Hammerless
Double-Barrel Shotgun

Purdey Over and Under

Purdey Single-Shot Trap

JAMES PURDEY & SONS, LTD. — London, England

HAMMERLESS DOUBLE-BARREL SHOTGUN

Sidelock. Auto ejectors. Single or double triggers. Gauges: 12, 16, 20. Bbls.: 26-, 27-, 28-, 30-inch (latter in 12 ga. only);any boring, any shape or style of rib. Weight: 5.25-5.5 lbs. depending on model, gauge and bbl length. Checkered stock and forearm, straight grip standard, pistol-grip also available. Purdey guns of this type have been made from about 1880 to date. Models include: Game Gun, Featherweight Game Gun, Two-Inch Gun (chambered for 12 ga. 2-inch shells), Pigeon Gun (w/3rd fastening and side clips), values of all models are the same.

With double triggers....NiB $62,700 Ex $54,890 Gd $44,782
With single trigger, add $1000

OVER/UNDER SHOTGUN

Sidelock. Auto ejectors. Single or double triggers. Gauges: 12 16, 20. Bbls.: 26-, 27-, 28-, 30-inch (latter in 12 ga. only); any boring, any style rib. Weight: 6-7.5 pounds depending on gauge and bbl. length. Checkered stock and forend, straight or pistol grip. Prior to WW II, the Purdey Over/Under Gun was made with a Purdey action; since the war James Purdey & Sons have acquired the busi-ness of James Woodward & Sons and all Purdey over/under guns are now built on the Woodward principle. General specifications of both types are the same.
With Purdey action,
  double triggers ....NiB $78,880 Ex $52,609 Gd $24,655
With Woodward action,
  double triggers, add ...., add $3000
  w/single trigger, add 10%

SINGLE-BARREL

TRAP GUN. .... NiB $12,775 Ex $10,560 Gd $8,300
Sidelock. Mechanical features similar to those of the over/under model with Purdey action. 12 ga. only. Built to customer's specifications. Made prior to World War II.

REMINGTON ARMS CO. — Ilion, New York

Eliphalet Remington Jr. began making long arms with his father in 1816. In 1828 they moved their facility to Ilion, N.Y., where it remained a family-run business for decades. As the family began to diminish, other people bought controlling interests and today, still a successful gunmaking company, it is a subsidiary of the DuPont Corporation. Currently owned by the Freedom Group.

MODEL 10A STANDARD GRADE

SLIDE-ACTION REPEATING SHOTGUN ... NiB $420 Ex $335 Gd $255
Hammerless. Takedown. Six-round capacity. 12 ga. only. Five shell tubular magazine. Bbls.: Plain; 26- to 32-inch; choked F, M or Cyl. Weight: About 7.5 lbs. Plain pistol-grip stock, grooved slide handle. Made from 1907 to 1929.

MODEL 11 SPECIAL, TOURNAMENT, EXPERT AND PREMIER GRADE GUNS

These higher grade models differ from the Model 11A in general quality, grade of wood, checkering, engraving, etc. General specifications are the same.

11B Special grade .... NiB $788 Ex $609 Gd $466
11D Tournament grade....... NiB $1388 Ex $1122 Gd $866
11E Expert grade ....NiB $1880 Ex $1455 Gd $1090
11F Premier grade .... NiB $2998 Ex $2356 Gd $1800

MODEL 11A STANDARD GRADE AUTOLOADER

Hammerless Browning type. Five round capacity. Takedown. Gauges: 12, 16, 20. Tubular magazine holds four rounds. Bbls.: Plain, solid or vent rib, lengths from 26-32 inches, F, M, IC, Cyl., SK chokes. Weight: About 8 lbs., 12 ga.; 7.5 lbs., 16 ga.; 7.25 lbs., 20 ga. Checkered pistol grip and forend. Made from 1905 to 1949.
w/plain barrel................NiB $355 Ex $260 Gd $229
w/solid-rib barrel ....NiB $477 Ex $339 Gd $366
w/ventilated-rib barrel .... .NiB $544 Ex $420 Gd $367

Remington Model 11-87
Premier Autoloader

MODEL 11R RIOT GUN . . . . **NiB $445 Ex $300 Gd $195**
Same as Model 11A Standard grade except has 20-inch plain barrel, 12 ga. only. Remington Model 11-48. (See Remington Sportsman-48 Series.)

NOTE: *Model 11-87 bbls. are not interchangable w/ Model 1100 bbls.*

MODEL 11-87 PREMIER AUTOLOADER
Gas-operated. Gauge: 12; 3-in. chamber. Bbl.: 26-, 28- or 30-in. with REMChoke. Weight: 8.13- 8.38 lbs., depending on bbl. length. Checkered walnut w/ satin finish. Made from 1987 to 2006.
Deer Gun w/cant. scope mt... . . . . NiB $855 Ex $654 Gd $477
Premier Skeet (1987-1999) . . . . NiB $740 Ex $535 Gd $420
Premier Standard . . . . NiB $766 Ex $598 Gd $455
Premier Trap (1987-1999) . . . . NiB $844 Ex $707 Gd $510
Left-hand models, add $125

MODEL 11-87 PREMIER SUPER MAGNUM
Gas-operated. Gauge: 12 only, 3-1/2-in. chamber. Bbl.: 28-in. only with extended REMChoke. Weight: 8.4 lbs. Checkered gloss finish walnut stock and forend. Made from 2001 to 2006.
standard . . . . NiB $760 Ex $622 Gd $479
Camo (disc. 2004) . . . . NiB $836 Ex $684 Gd $489

MODEL 11-87 SP (SPECIAL PURPOSE)
Same general specifications as Model 11-87 Premier except with non-reflective wood finish and Parkerized metal. 26-, 28- or 30-in. vent-rib bbl. with REMChoke tubes. Made from 1987 to 1993.
standard . . . . NiB $600 Ex $400 Gd $280
Deer Gun (21-in. bbl., rifle sights) . . . . NiB $690 Ex $445 Gd $295
Magnum (3-1/2-in. chamber) . . . . NiB $730 Ex $450 Gd $300

MODEL 11-87 SPS (SPECIAL PURPOSE SYNTHETIC)
Same general specifications as Model 11-87 SP except with synthetic buttstock and forend. 21-, 26- or 28-inch vent-rib bbl. with REMChoke tubes. Matte black or Mossy Oak camo finish (except NWTF turkey gun). Made from 1990 to 2007.
Deer Gun (21-in. bbl., rifle sights) . . . . . NiB $696 Ex $494 Gd $358
Magnum (3-in., matte black, disc. 2004) . . . NiB $733 Ex $643 Gd $471
Camo (Mossy Oak camo) . . . . NiB $760 Ex $622 Gd $479
Deer Gun w/cant. scope mt. (1987-2005) . . . . NiB $859 Ex $633 Gd $490
NWTF Turkey Gun
  (Brown Trebark, disc. 1993) . . .NiB $775 Ex $690 Gd $510
NWTF Turkey Gun
  (Greenleaf, disc. 1996) . . . . . . .NiB $725 Ex $650 Gd $479
NWTF Turkey
  Gun (Mossy Oak, disc. 1996) . . .NiB $730 Ex $655 Gd $485
NWTF Turkey Gun (Mossy Oak Breakup,
  introduced 1999) . . . . NiB $730 Ex $655 Gd $485
NWTF 20 ga. Turkey Gun
  (Mossy Oak Breakup, 1998 only) NiB $730 Ex $655 Gd $485
Thumbhole Deer Gun (2006-2007) . . . . . NiB $730 Ex $655 Gd $485
SPST Turkey Gun (matte bl.) . . . . NiB $730 Ex $655 Gd $485
Super Magnum
  (3-1/2-in., matte black, disc. 2007) NiB $950 Ex $730 Gd $300
Super Magnum Turkey Camo
  (3-1/2-in., Mossy Oak Breakup, disc. 2007)NiB $950 Ex $730 Gd $300
Waterfowl (Mossy Oak Shadow Grass) NiB $1010 Ex $780 Gd $530

MODEL 11-87 SPORTING CLAYS . . . . . **NiB $866 Ex $700 Gd $509**
Gas-operated. Gauge: 12 only. Bbl.: 26-in. only with extended REMChoke. Weight: 7.5 lbs. Checkered satin finish walnut stock and forend. Made from 1929 to 1999.
NP (nickel plated receiver) . . . . NiB $890 Ex $735 Gd $533

MODEL 11-87 SPORTSMAN
Same general specifications as Model 11-87 Premier except with matte metal finish. 12 or 20 ga. Bbl.: 20- or 21-in. rifled or 26- or 28-in. w/ REMChoke. Weight: 7.3-8.3 lbs. Made from 2005 to date.
Camo (Mossy Oak New Breakup) . . . . NiB $915 Ex $570 Gd $370
Field (wood stock) . . . . NiB $845 Ex $470 Gd $270
ShurShot (synthetic thumbhole stock, cantilever
  scope mount) . . . . NiB $1012 Ex $680 Gd $430
Synthetic (synthetic stock) . . . . NiB $804 Ex $460 Gd $260
Synthetic Deer
  (synthetic stock, cantilever. scope mount) NiB $929 Ex $585 Gd $385

MODEL 11-96 EURO LIGHTWEIGHT
AUTOLOADING SHOTGUN . . . . **NiB $800 Ex $644 Gd $500**
Lightweight version of Model 11-87 w/reprofiled receiver. 12 ga. only w/3-inch chamber. 26- or 28-inch bbl. w/6mm vent rib and REM Choke tubes. Semi-fancy Monte Carlo walnut buttstock and forearm. Weight: 6.8 lbs. w/26-inch bbl. Made in 1996 only.

MODEL 17A STANDARD GRADE SLIDE-ACTION REPEATING SHOTGUN
Hammerless. Takedown. Five round capacity. 20 ga. only. Four round tubular magazine. Bbls.: plain; 26- to 32-inch; choked F, M or Cyl. Weight: About 5.75 lbs. Plain pistol-grip stock, grooved slide handle. Made 1921-33. Note: The present Ithaca Model 37 is an adaptation of this Browning design.
Plain barrel . . . . .NiB $422 Ex $292 Gd $190
Solid rib. . . . . .NiB $490 Ex $400 Gd $290

MODEL 29A STANDARD GRADE
SLIDE-ACTION REPEATING SHOTGUN . **NiB $390 Ex $300 Gd $287**
Hammerless. Takedown. Six round capacity. 12 ga. only. Five round tubular magazine. Bbls.: plain- 26- to 32-inch, choked F, M or Cyl. Weight: About 7.5 lbs. Checkered pistol-grip stock and slide handle. Made from 1929 to 1933.

MODEL 29T TARGET GRADE . . . . **NiB $600 Ex $490 Gd $377**
Same general specifications as Model 29A except has trap-style stock with straight grip, extension slide handle, vent rib bbl. Disc. 1933.

MODEL 31/31L SKEET GRADE
Same general specifications as Model 31A except has 26-inch bbl. with raised solid or vent rib, SK choke, checkered pistol-grip stock and beaver-tail forend. Weight: About 8 lbs., 12 ga. Made from 1932 to 1939.
Model 31 Standard w/raised solid rib . . NiB $477 Ex $290 Gd $200
Model 31 Standard w/ventilated rib . . NiB $566 Ex $408 Gd $335
Model 31L Lightweight w/raised solid rib . . NiB $455 Ex $330 Gd $245
Model 31L Lightweight w/ventilated rib . .NiB $555 Ex $350 Gd $287

SHOTGUNS

Remington Model 11-87 SPS

Remington Model 11-87 SPS Camo

Remington Model 11-87 SP Walnut Stock

Remington Model SP-10 Magnum Camo

MODEL 31D SPECIAL, TOURNAMENT, EXPERT AND PREMIER GRADE GUNS

These higher grade models differ from the Model 31A in general quality, grade of wood, checkering, engraving, etc. General specifications are the same.

Model 31B Special grade . . . . NiB $745 Ex $600 Gd $477
Model 31D Tournament grade . NiB $1688 Ex $1099 Gd $722
Model 31E Expert grade . . . . . NiB $1890 Ex $1266 Gd $977
Model 31F Premier grade . . . NiB $3100 Ex $2013 Gd $1544

MODEL 31S TRAP SPECIAL/31TC TRAP GRADE

Same general specifications as Model 31A except 12 ga. only, has 30- or 32-inch vent-rib bbl., F choke, checkered trap stock with full pistol grip and recoil pad, checkered extension beavertail forend. Weight: About 8 lbs. (Trap Special has solid-rib bbl., half pistol-grip stock with standard walnut forend).

Model 31S Trap Special . . . . NiB $655 Ex $490 Gd $423
Model 31TC Trap grade . . . . NiB $955 Ex $677 Gd $590

MODEL 31A SLIDE-ACTION REPEATER

Hammerless. Takedown. 3- or 5-round capacity. Gauges: 12, 16, 20. Tubular magazine. Bbls.: Plain, solid or vent rib; lengths from 26 -32 inches; F, M, IC, C or SK choke. Weight: About 7.5 lbs.; 12 ga.; 6.75 lbs., 16 ga.; 6.5 lbs., 20 ga. Earlier models have checkered pistol-grip stock and slide handle; later models have plain stock and grooved slide handle. Made from 1931 to 1949.

Model 31A with plain barrel . . . . NiB $479 Ex $366 Gd $244
Model 31A with solid rib barrel . . . NiB $565 Ex $443 Gd $300
Model 31A with vent rib barrel . . NiB $580 Ex $465 Gd $335
Model 31H Hunter
  w/sporting-style stock . . . . NiB $440 Ex $292 Gd $222
Model 31R Riot Gun w/20-
  inch plain bbl., 12 ga. . . . . NiB $509 Ex $388 Gd $287

MODEL 32A STANDARD GRADE O/U

Hammerless. Takedown. Auto ejectors. Early model had double triggers, later built with selective single trigger only. 12 ga. only. Bbls.: Plain, raised matted solid or vent rib; 26-, 28-, 30-, 32-inch; F/M choke standard, option of any combination of F, M, IC, C, SK choke. Weight: About 7.75 lbs. Checkered pistol-grip stock and forend. Made from 1932 to 1942.

w/double triggers . . . . NiB $2165 Ex $1800 Gd $1287
w/selective single trigger. . . . . NiB $2466 Ex $2100 Gd $1533

w/raised solid rib, add 10%
w/ventilated rib, add 20%

MODEL 32 TOURNAMENT, EXPERT AND PREMIER GRADE GUNS

These higher-grade models differ from the Model 32A in general quality, grade of wood, checkering, engraving, etc. General specifications are the same. Made from 1932 to 1942.

Model 32D Tournament grade . . . NiB $4377 Ex $3310 Gd $2560
Model 32E Expert grade . . . . . NiB $4598 Ex $4166 Gd $3000
Model 32F Premier grade . . . NiB $6986 Ex $5809 Gd $3976

MODEL 32 SKEET GRADE . . . . . NiB $2200 Ex $1798 Gd $1433

Same general specifications as Model 32A except 26- or 28-inch bbl., SK choke, beavertail forend, selective single trigger only. Weight: About 7.5 lbs. Made from 1932 to 1942.

MODEL 32TC
TARGET (TRAP) GRADE . . NiB $3233 Ex $2866 Gd $1974

Same general specifications as Model 32A except 30- or 32-inch vent-rib bbl., F choke, trap-style stock with checkered pistol-grip and beavertail forend. Weight: About 8 lbs. Made from 1932 to 1942.

MODEL 89 (1889) . . . . NiB $2133 Ex $1788 Gd $1141

Hammers. Circular action. Gauges: 10, 12, 16, 28- to 32-inch bls.; steel or Damascus twist. Weight 7-10 lbs. Made from 1889 to 1908.

MODEL 90-T SINGLE-SHOT TRAP . . . . NiB $1988 Ex $1790 Gd $1377

Gauge: 12; 2.75-inch chambers. 30-, 32- or 34-inch vent-rib bbl. with fixed chokes or screw-in REMChokes; ported or non-ported. Weight: 8.25 lbs. Checkered American walnut standard or Monte Carlo stock with low-luster finish. Engraved sideplates and drop-out trigger group optional. Made from 1990 to 1997.

MODEL 105 CTI . . . . NiB $1230 Ex $880 Gd $600

Gas-operated, semi-automatic. Titanium and carbon fiber receiver. Gauge: 12; 3-inch chamber. Bbl.: 26- or 28-inch with REMChoke. Weight: 7 lbs., depending on bbl. length. Checkered walnut stock and forend in satin finish. Made from 2006 to 2008.

105 CTi-II (2009 only) . . . . NiB $1230 Ex $880 Gd $600

Remington Model 870
Competition Trap

Remington Model 870
Brushmaster

Remington Model 870
Express Super Magnum

Remington Model 870
Marine Magnum

Remington Model 870
Special Field

MODEL 396 O/U
Boxlock. 12 ga. only w/2.75-inch chamber. 28- and 30-inch blued bbls. w/ Rem chokes. Weight: 7.50 lbs. Nitride-grayed, engraved receiver, trigger guard, tang, hinge pins and forend metal. Engraved sideplates. Checkered satin-finished American walnut stock w/target style forend. Made from 1996 to 1998.

Sporting Clays . . . . NiB $1933 Ex $1658 Gd $1277
396 Skeet. . . . . NiB $1855 Ex $1544 Gd $1153

MODEL 870
"ALL AMERICAN" TRAP GUN . NiB $1277 Ex $1073 Gd $777
Same as Model 870TB except custom grade with engraved receiver, trigger guard and bbl.; Monte Carlo or straight-comb stock and forend of fancy walnut; available only with 30-inch F choke bbl. Made from 1972 to 1977.

MODEL 870 COMPETITION TRAP NiB $766 Ex $555 Gd $439
Based on standard Model 870 receiver except is single-shot with gas-assisted recoil-reducing system, new choke design, a high step-up vent rib and redesigned stock, forend with cut checkering and satin finish. Weight: 8.5 lbs. Made from 1981 to 1987.

MODEL 870 STANDARD . . . . . . .NiB $566 Ex $444 Gd $339
Same as Model 870 Wingmaster Riot Gun except has rifle-type sights.

MODEL 870 BRUSHMASTER DELUXE
Same as Model 870 Standard except available in 20 ga. as well as 12, has cut-checkered, satin-finished American walnut stock and forend, recoil pad.

Right-hand model . . . . NiB $559 Ex $477 Gd $366
Left-hand model . . . . NiB $659 Ex $490 Gd $380

MODEL 870 EXPRESS
Same general specifications Model 870 Wingmaster except has low-luster walnut-finished hardwood stock with pressed checkering and black recoil pad. Gauges: 12, 20 or .410, 3-inch chambers. Bbls.: 26- or 28-inch vent-rib with REMChoke; 25-inch vent-rib with fixed choke (.410 only). Black oxide metal finish. Made from 1987 to date.

12 or 20 ga.. . . . . NiB $355 Ex $290 Gd $200
.410 (w/fixed choke). . . . . .NiB $455 Ex $300 Gd $225
Combo (w/extra 20-inch deer bbl.) NiB $465 Ex $387 Gd $290

MODEL 870 EXPRESS DEER GUN
Same general specifications as Model 870 Express except in 12 ga. only, 20-inch bbl. with fixed IC choke, adj. rifle sights and Monte Carlo stock. Made from 1991 to date.

w/standard barrel . . . . .NiB $433 Ex $297 Gd $200
w/rifled barrel . . . . .NiB $450 Ex $310 Gd $220

MODEL 870 ESM (EXPRESS MAGNUM)
Similar to Model 870 Express except chambered for 12 ga. mag. w/3.5-inch chamber. Bbls.: 23-, 26- or 28-inch vent rib w/REM Choke. Checkered low-luster walnut-finished hardwood, black synthetic or camo buttstock and

Remington Model 870
Special Purpose Deer Gun

Remington Model 870
Wingmaster Field Gun

forearm. Matte black oxide metal finish or full camo finish. Made from 1998 to date.

Model 870 ESM
(w/hardwood stock) . . . . .NiB $455 Ex $310 Gd $225
Model 870 ESM
(w/black synthetic stock) . . .NiB $455 Ex $310 Gd $225
Model 870 ESM
(w/camo synthetic stock) . . . . .NiB $488 Ex $395 Gd $259
Model 870 ESM Synthetic
Turkey (w/synthetic stock) . . . .NiB $488 Ex $395 Gd $259
Model 870 ESM camo
Turkey (w/full camo) . . . . .NiB $488 Ex $395 Gd $259
Model 870 ESM combo
(w/full camo, extra bbl.) . . . . . .NiB $509 Ex $400 Gd $323

**MODEL 870 EXPRESS
SYNTHETIC HOME DEFENSE** . . . .NiB $422 Ex $300 Gd $200
Slide action, hammerless, takedown. 12 ga. only. 18-inch bbl. w/cylinder choke and bead front sight. Positive checkered synthetic stock and forend with non-reflective black finish. Made from 1995 to date.

MODEL 870 EXPRESS TURKEY GUN. NiB $448 Ex $290 Gd $210
Same general specifications as Model 870 Express except has 21-inch vent-rib bbl. and Turkey Extra-Full REMChoke. Made from 1991 to date.

MODEL 870 EXPRESS YOUTH GUN. NiB $391 Ex $248 Gd $181
Same general specifications as Model 870 Express except has scaled-down stock with 12.5-inch pull and 21-inch vent rib bbl. with REMChoke. Made from 1991 to date.

MODEL 870 LIGHTWEIGHT
Same as standard Model 870 but with scaled-down receiver and lightweight mahogany stock; 20 ga. only. 2.75-inch chamber. Bbls.: plain or vent rib; 26-inch, IC; 28-inch, M or F choke. REMChoke available from 1987. Weight 5.75 lbs. w/26-inch plain bbl. American walnut stock and forend with satin or Hi-gloss finish. Made from 1972 to 1994.
w/plain barrel . . . . .NiB $477 Ex $366 Gd $290
w/ventilated rib barrel . . . . .NiB $490 Ex $380 Gd $315
w/REMChoke barrel . . . . .NiB $566 Ex $435 Gd $335

MODEL 870 LIGHTWEIGHT MAGNUM
Same as Model 870 Lightweight but chambered for 20 ga. Magnum 3-inch shell; 28-inch bbl., plain or vent rib, F choke. Weight: 6 lbs. with plain bbl. Made from 1972 to 1994.
w/plain barrel . . . . .NiB $477 Ex $377 Gd $292
w/ventilated rib barrel . . . . .NiB $580 Ex $455 Gd $422

MODEL 870 MAGNUM DUCK GUN
Same as Model 870 Field Gun except has 3-inch chamber 12 and 20 gauge Magnum only. 28- or 30-inch bbl., plain or vent rib, M or F choke, recoil pad. Weight: About 7 or 6.75 lbs. Made from 1964 to date.
w/plain barrel . . . . .NiB $310 Ex $225 Gd $179
w/ventilated rib barrel . . . . .NiB $655 Ex $430 Gd $335

**MODEL 870
MARINE MAGNUM** . . . . .NiB $735 Ex $496 Gd $359
Same general specifications as Model 870 Wingmaster except with 7-round magazine, 18-inch plain bbl. with fixed IC choke, bead front sight and nickel finish. Made from 1992 to date.

**MODEL 870
SA SKEET GUN, SMALL GAUGE** . . . . . .NiB $875 Ex $677 Gd $529
Similar to Wingmaster Model 870SA except chambered for 28 and .410 ga. (2.5-inch chamber for latter); 25-inch vent rib bbl., SK choke. Weight: 6 lbs., 28 ga.; 6.5 lbs., .410. Made from 1969 to 1982.

**MODEL 870 MISSISSIPPI
MAGNUM DUCK GUN** . . . . .NiB $865 Ex $667 Gd $520
Same as Remington Model 870 Magnum duck gun except has 32-inch bbl. "Ducks Unlimited" engraved receiver, Made in 1983.

**MODEL 870
SPECIAL FIELD SHOTGUN** . . . . .NiB $466 Ex $322 Gd $245
Pump action. Hammerless. Gauge: 12 or 20. 21-inch vent-rib bbl. with REMChoke. 41.5 inches overall. Weight: 6-7 lbs. Straight-grip checkered walnut stock and forend. Made from 1987 to 1995.

MODEL 870 SPECIAL PURPOSE DEER GUN
Similar to Special Purpose Magnum except with 20-inch IC choke, rifle sights. Matte black oxide and Parkerized finish. Oil-finished, checkered buttstock and forend with recoil pad. Made from 1986 to date.
Model 870 SP Deer Gun . . . . . . .NiB $744 Ex $488 Gd $333
Model 870 SP Deer Gun,
cant. scope mt. . . . . .NiB $800 Ex $523 Gd $366

**MODEL 870 SPECIAL
PURPOSE MAGNUM** . . . . .NiB $735 Ex $555 Gd $467
Similar to the 870 Magnum duck gun except with 26-, 28- or 30-inch vent rib REMChoke bbl.12 ga. only; 3-inch chamber. Oil-finished field-grade stock with recoil pad, QD swivels and Cordura sling. Made from 1985 to date.

Remington Model 870TC
Wingmaster Trap

MODEL 870SPS MAGNUM
Same general specifications Model 870 Special Purpose Magnum except with synthetic stock and forend. 26- or 28-inch vent-rib bbl. with REMChoke tubes. Matte black or Mossy Oak camo finish. Made from 1991 to date.
70 SPS Mag. (black syn. stock) . . . **NiB $688 Ex $455 Gd $325**
870 SPS-T Camo (Mossy Oak camo) . . . . **NiB $866 Ex $533 Gd $400**

MODEL 870 WINGMASTER FIELD GUN
Same general specifications as Model 870AP except checkered stock and forend. Later models have REMChoke systems in 12 ga. Made from 1964 to date.
w/plain barrel . . . . **NiB $366 Ex $264 Gd $155**
w/ventilated rib barrel . . . . **NiB $665 Ex $439 Gd $266**

MODEL 870 WINGMASTER FIELD GUN, SMALL GAUGE
Same as standard Model 870 except w/scaled-down lightweight receivers. Gauges: 28 and .410. Plain or vent rib 25-inch bbl. choked IC, M or F. Weight: 5.5-6.25 lbs. depending on gauge and bbl. Made 1969 to 1994.
w/plain barrel . . . . **NiB $775 Ex $600 Gd $445**
w/ventilated-rib barrel . . . . **NiB $808 Ex $625 Gd $465**

MODEL 870 WINGMASTER
MAGNUM DELUXE GRADE . . . . **NiB $667 Ex $559 Gd $400**
Same as Model 870 Magnum standard grade except has checkered stock and extension beavertail forearm, bbl. with matted top surface. Disc. in 1963.

MODEL 870 WINGMASTER
MAGNUM STANDARD GRADE . . **NiB $633 Ex $479 Gd $365**
Same as Model 870AP except chambered for 12 ga. 3-inch Magnum, 30-inch F choke bbl., recoil pad. Weight: About 8.25 lbs. Made 1955 to 1963.

MODEL 870 WINGMASTER REMCHOKE SERIES
Slide action, hammerless, takedown with blued all-steel receiver. Gauges: 12, 20; 3-inch chamber. Tubular magazine. Bbls.: 21-, 26-, 28-inch vent-rib with REM Choke. Weight: 7.5 lbs. (12 ga.). Satin-finished, checkered walnut buttstock and forend with recoil pad. Right- or left-hand models. Made from 1986 to date.
Standard model, 12 ga. . . . . **NiB $500 Ex $377 Gd $266**
Standard model, 20 ga. . . . . **NiB $535 Ex $400 Gd $288**
Youth model, 21-inch barrel . . . . . **NiB $500 Ex $377 Gd $321**

MODEL 870ADL WINGMASTER DELUXE GRADE
Same general specifications as Wingmaster Model 870AP except has pistol-grip stock and extension beavertail forend, both finely checkered; matted top surface or vent-rib bbl. Made 1950 to 1963.
w/matted top-surface barrel . . . . . **NiB $488 Ex $365 Gd $288**
w/ventilated-rib barrel . . . . **NiB $509 Ex $412 Gd $300**

MODEL 870AP WINGMASTER STANDARD GRADE
Hammerless. Takedown. Gauges: 12, 16, 20. Tubular magazine holds four rounds. Bbls.: Plain, matted top surface or vent rib; 26-inch IC, 28-inch M or F choke, 30-inch F choke (12 ga. only). Weight: About 7 lbs., 12 ga.; 6.75 lbs., 16 ga.; 6.5 lbs., 20 ga. Plain pistol-grip stock, grooved forend. Made 1950 to 1963.
w/plain barrel . . . . **NiB $359 Ex $300 Gd $209**
w/matted surface barrel . . . . **NiB $435 Ex $335 Gd $225**
w/ventilated rib barrel . . . . **NiB $466 Ex $372 Gd $260**
Left-hand model . . . . **NiB $489 Ex $400 Gd $265**

MODEL 870DL WINGMASTER DELUXE SPECIAL
Same as Model 870ADL except select American walnut stock and forend. Made 1950 to 1963.

w/matted surface barrel . . . . **NiB $665 Ex $445 Gd $310**
w/ventilated-rib barrel . . . . **NiB $715 Ex $477 Gd $349**

MODEL 870D, 870F WINGMASTER
TOURNAMENT AND PREMIER GRADE GUNS
These higher-grade models differ from the Model 870AP in general quality, grade of wood, checkering, engraving, etc. General operating specifications are essentially the same. Made from 1950 to date.
Model 870D Tournament grade . . . . **NiB $3139 Ex $2288 Gd $1660**
Model 870F Premier grade . . . **NiB $6445 Ex $4753 Gd $3465**
Model 870F Premier gr. w/gold inlay . . **NiB $10,098 Ex $7517 Gd $5237**

MODEL 870R
WINGMASTER RIOT GUN . . . . . . **NiB $375 Ex $280 Gd $210**
Same as Model 870AP except 20-inch bbl., IC choke, 12 ga. only.

MODEL 870 SA WINGMASTER SKEET GUN
Same general specifications as Model 870AP except has 26-inch vent-rib bbl., SK choke, ivory bead front sight, metal bead rear sight, pistol-grip stock and extension beavertail forend. Weight: 6.75 to 7.5 lbs. depending on gauge. Made 1950 to 1982.
Model 870SA Skeet grade (disc. 1982) . . . **NiB $677 Ex $395 Gd $288**
Model 870SC Skeet Target
grade (disc. 1980) . . . . **NiB $795 Ex $549 Gd $400**

MODEL 870TB WINGMASTER
TRAP SPECIAL . . . . **NiB $633 Ex $500 Gd $388**
Same general specifications as Model 870AP Wingmaster except has 28- or 30-inch vent rib bbl., F choke, metal bead front sight, no rear sight. "Special" grade trap-style stock and forend, both checkered, recoil pad. Weight: About 8 lbs. Made from 1950 to 1981.

REMINGTON MODEL
870TC TRAP GRADE . . . . **NiB $795 Ex $554 Gd $400**
Same as Model 870 Wingmaster TC except has tournament-grade walnut in stock and forend w/satin finish. Over-bored 30-inch vent rib bbl. w/ 2.75-inch chamber and RemChoke tubes. Reissued in 1996. See separate listing for earlier model.

MODEL 870TC WINGMASTER TRAP GRADE
Same as Model 870TB except higher-grade walnut in stock and forend, has both front and rear sights. Made 1950-79. Model 870 TC reissued in 1996. See separate listing for earlier model.
Model 870 TC Trap (Standard) . . . **NiB $515 Ex $466 Gd $325**
Model 870 TC Trap (Monte Carlo) **NiB $545 Ex $480 Gd $366**

MODEL 878A AUTOMASTER . . . . **NiB $376 Ex $266 Gd $195**
Gas-operated Autoloader. 12 ga., 3-round magazine. Bbls.: 26-inch IC, 28-inch M choke, 30-inch F choke. Weight: About 7 lbs. Plain pistol-grip stock and forearm. Made from 1959-62.

MODEL 887 NITRO MAG. . . . . . . **NiB $445 Ex $285 Gd $200**
Based on Model 870 except has Armorlokt overmolding on metal. 26- or 28-inch bbl. Finish: matte black. Stock: black synthetic. Made from 2009 to date.
Camo Combo . . . . **NiB $728 Ex $700 Gd $300**
Tactical (extended magazine, Picatinny rail, ported extended
   choke tube) . . . . **NiB $534 Ex $340 Gd $230**
Waterfowl Camo
   (Real Tree Advantage Max-4 finish . . **NiB $594 Ex $370 Gd $270**

GRADING: **NiB** = New in Box   **Ex** = Excellent or NRA 95%   **Gd** = Good or NRA 68%

535

SHOTGUNS

Remington Model 1100 Field w/Ventilated Rib

Remington Model 1100 Deer Gun

Remington Model 1100 SA Skeet Gun

NOTE: *New stock checkering patterns and receiver scroll markings were incorporated on all standard Model 1100 field, magnum, skeet and trap models in 1979.*

MODEL 1100 FIELD
Gas-operated. Hammerless. Takedown. Gauges: 12, 16, 20. Bbls.: plain or vent. rib; 30-inch F, 28-inch M or F, 26-inch IC; or REMChoke tubes. Weight: Average 7.25-7.5 lbs. depending on ga. and bbl. length. Checkered walnut pistol-grip stock and forearm in high-gloss finish. Made 1963 to 1988. 16 ga. discontinued 1980.

w/plain barrel	NiB $380	Ex $291	Gd $200
w/ventilated-rib barrel	NiB $422	Ex $356	Gd $239
REMChoke model	NiB $466	Ex $390	Gd $292
REMChoke, Left-hand action	NiB $744	Ex $544	Gd $356

MODEL 1100 CLASSIC FIELD . . . . NiB $675 Ex $480 Gd $310
Similar to Model 1100 Field except 12, 16, 20 or .410 w/ light contoured REMchoke bbl. Non-engraved receiver. Made from 2003 to 2006.

MODEL 1100 DEER GUN . . . . NiB $515 Ex $386 Gd $265
Same as Model 1100 Field Gun except has 22-inch barrel, IC, with rifle-type sights; 12 and 20 ga. only; recoil pad. Weight: About 7.25 lbs. Made from 1963 to 1998.

MODEL 1100 DUCKS UNLIMITED
ATLANTIC COMMEMORATIVE . . NiB $1188 Ex $987 Gd $766
Limited production for one year. Similar specifications to Model 1100 Field except with 32-inch F choke, vent rib bbl. 12-ga. Magnum only. Made in 1982.

MODEL 1100 DUCKS UNLIMITED "THE CHESAPEAKE"
COMMEMORATIVE . . . . NiB $878 Ex $753 Gd $555
Limited edition 1 to 2400. Same general specifications as Model 1100 Field except sequentially numbered with markings "The Chesapeake." 12 ga. Magnum with 30-inch F choke, vent rib bbl. Made in 1981.

MODEL 1100 FIELD GRADE, SMALL BORE
Same as standard Model 1100 but scaled down. Gauges: 28, .410. 25-inch bbl., plain or vent rib; IC, M or F choke. Weight: 6.25-7 lbs. depending on gauge and bbl. Made from 1969 to 1994.

w/plain barrel	NiB $669	Ex $533	Gd $435
w/ventilated rib	NiB $866	Ex $677	Gd $480

MODEL 1100 G3 . . . . NiB $1050 Ex $800 Gd $500
Similar to Model 1100 Field except satin finish steel receiver with titanium PVD coating. 12 or 20 ga.; 3-in. chamber. Bbls.: 26- or 28-in. vent rib w/ ProBore choke tubes. Weight: 6.7-7.6 lbs. depending on bbl. length. Stock: RealWood fiber laminate w/ high gloss finish and checkering. Made from 2006 to 2008.

MODEL 1100 LIGHTWEIGHT
Same as standard Model 1100 but scaled-down receiver and lightweight mahogany stock; 20 ga. only, 2.75-inch chamber. Bbls.: Plain or vent rib; 26-inch IC; 28-inch M and F choke. Weight: 6.25 lbs. Made from 1970 to 1976.

w/plain barrel	NiB $654	Ex $500	Gd $390
w/ventilated rib	NiB $735	Ex $566	Gd $408

MODEL 1100 LIGHTWEIGHT MAGNUM
Same as Model 1100 Lightweight but chambered for 20 gauge Magnum 3-inch shell; 28-inch bbl., plain or vent rib, F choke. Weight: 6.5 lbs. Made from 1977 to 1998.

w/plain barrel	NiB $688	Ex $544	Gd $422
w/ventilated rib	NiB $788	Ex $590	Gd $466
w/choke tubes	NiB $855	Ex $598	Gd $466

MODEL 1100 LT-20 DUCKS UNLIMITED
SPECIAL COMMEMORATIVE . . NiB $1486 Ex $1156 Gd $844
Limited edition 1 to 2400. Same general specifications as Model 1100 Field except sequentially numbered with markings, "The Chesapeake." 20 ga. only. 26-inch IC, vent-rib bbl. Made in 1981.

MODEL 1100 LT-20 SERIES
Same as Model 1100 Field Gun except in 20 ga. with shorter 23-inch vent rib bbl., straight-grip stock. REMChoke series has 21-inch vent rib bbl., choke tubes. Weight: 6.25 lbs. Checkered grip and forearm. Made from 1977 to 1995.

LT-20 Special	NiB $588	Ex $498	Gd $377
LT-20 Deer Gun	NiB $490	Ex $399	Gd $295
LT-20 Youth	NiB $585	Ex $444	Gd $300

MODEL 1100 MAGNUM . . . . NiB $598 Ex $499 Gd $378
Limited production. Similar to the Model 1100 Field except with 26-inch F choke, vent rib bbl. and 3-inch chamber. Made in 1981.

MODEL 1100 MAGNUM DUCK GUN
Same as Model 1100 Field Gun except has 3-inch chamber,12 and 20 ga. Mag. only. 30-inch plain or vent rib bbl. in 12 ga., 28-inch in

Remington Model 1100
Special Field

Remington Model 1100
Tournament Trap

Remington Model 3200
"One of 1000" Skeet

20 ga.; M or F choke. Recoil pad. Weight: About 7.75 lbs. Made from 1963 to 1988.

w/plain barrel . . . . NiB $555   Ex $399   Gd $324
w/ventilated rib barrel . . . . NiB $575   Ex $435   Gd $355

MODEL 1100
ONE OF 3000 FIELD . . . . NiB $1210   Ex $966   Gd $790
Limited edition, numbered 1 to 3000. Similar to Model 1100 Field except with fancy wood and gold-trimmed etched hunting scenes on receiver. 12 gauge with 28-inch Mod., vent rib bbl. Made in 1980.

MODEL 1100 SA SKEET GUN
Same as Model 1100 Field Gun, 12 and 20 ga. except has 26-inch vent-rib bbl., SK choke or with Cutts Compensator. Weight: 7.25-7.5 lbs. Made from 1963 to 1994.

w/skeet-
   choked barrel . . . . NiB $977   Ex $644   Gd $388
w/Cutts Comp, add $200
Left-hand action, add $75

MODEL 1100 SA
LIGHTWEIGHT SKEET . . . . NiB $655   Ex $497   Gd $366
Same as Model 1100 Lightweight except has skeet-style stock and forearm, 26-inch vent-rib bbl., SK choke. Made from 1971 to 1997.

MODEL 1100 SA
SKEET SMALL BORE . . . . NiB $625   Ex $443   Gd $311
Similar to standard Model 1100SA except chambered for 28 and .410 ga. (2.5-inch chamber for latter); 25-inch vent-rib bbl., SK choke. Weight: 6.75 lbs., 28 ga.; 7.25 lbs., .410. Made from 1969 to 1994.

MODEL 1100 SB
LIGHTWEIGHT SKEET . . . . NiB $644   Ex $433   Gd $310
Same as Model 1100SA Lightweight except has select wood. Introduced in 1977.

MODEL 1100
SB SKEET GUN. . . . . NiB $654   Ex $443   Gd $319
Same specifications as Model 1100SA except has select wood. Made from 1963 to 1997.

MODEL 1100
SPECIAL FIELD SHOTGUN . . . . . NiB $600   Ex $492   Gd $388
Gas-operated. Five round capacity. Hammerless. Gauges: 12, 20 or .410. 21- or 23-in. vent-rib bbl. with REMChoke. Weight: 6.5-7.25 lbs. Straight-grip checkered walnut stock and forend. Note: .410 Made from 1983 to 1999.

MODEL 1100 SP MAGNUM
Same as Model 1100 Field except 12 ga. only with 3-inch chambers. Bbls.: 26- or 30-inch F choke; or 26-inch with REM Choke tubes; vent rib. Non-reflective matte black, Parkerized bbl. and receiver. Satin-finished stock and forend. Made 1986.
w/fixed choke . . . . NiB $475   Ex $397   Gd $321
w/REMchoke . . . . NiB $490   Ex $417   Gd $344

MODEL 1100 SPECIAL FIELD
Similar to Model 1100 Field except 12, 20 or .410. Bbls.: 21- and 23-in. vent rib w/ REMChoke tubes (intro. 1987). Weight: Average 7.25-7.5 lbs. depending on ga. and bbl. length. High gloss checkered walnut straight-grip stock and forearm. Made 1983 to 1999.
12 ga. . . . . NiB $525   Ex $350   Gd $200
20 ga. . . . . NiB $690   Ex $540   Gd $400
.410 . . . . NiB $840   Ex $710   Gd $480

MODEL 1100 SYNTHETIC . . . . . . NiB $435   Ex $280   Gd $170
Similar to Model 1100 Field except 12, 16 or 20 ga. Bbls.: 26- or 28-in. vent rib w/ REMChoke tubes. Weight: Average 7-7.5 lbs. depending on ga. and bbl. length. Synthetic stock and forearm. Made 1996 to 2004.
Deer . . . . NiB $500   Ex $280   Gd $170
LT 20 Youth . . . . NiB $440   Ex $270   Gd $160

MODEL 1100 TAC-2 . . . . NiB $800   Ex $580   Gd $400
Similar to Model 1100 Field except 12 ga. only; 2-3/4-in. chamber. Bbls.: 18- or 22-in. vent rib w/ REMChoke tubes, HiViz sights. Weight: 7.5 lbs. depending on bbl. length. Stock: black synthetic SFIV. 6- or 8-rnd. capacity. Made 2006 to date.
Tac-4 (pistol grip) . . . . NiB $870   Ex $650   Gd $240

MODEL 1100 TACTICAL. . . . . NiB $435   Ex $280   Gd $170
Similar to Model 1100 Field except 12 ga. only; 3-in. chamber. Bbls.: 18- or 22-in. vent rib w/ REMChoke tubes, HiViz sights. Weight: 7.5 lbs. depending on bbl. length. Synthetic pistol grip or standard stock and forearm. 6- or 8-rnd. capacity. Disc 2006.

MODEL 1100 TOURNAMENT/PREMIER
These higher grade guns differ from standard models in overall quality, grade of wood, checkering, engraving, gold inlays, etc. General specs are the same. Made 1963 to 1994; 1997 to 1999; 2003.
1100D Tournament . . . . NiB $966   Ex $633   Gd $577
1100F Premier . . . . NiB $1266   Ex $1059   Gd $833
1100F Premier w/ gold inlay NiB $10,332   Ex $7833   Gd $4460

GRADING: **NiB** = New in Box   **Ex** = Excellent or NRA 95%   **Gd** = Good or NRA 68%

Remington Rider No. 9 Single-Shot Shotgun

Remington Sportsman Autoloader

Remington Sportsman — 48A

MODEL 1100
TOURNAMENT SKEET . . . . NiB $977 Ex $738 Gd $490
Similar to Model 1100 Field except with 26-inch bbl. SK choke.
Gauges: 12, LT-20, 28, and .410. Features select walnut stocks and new
cut-checkering patterns. Made from 1979- to 1999.

MODEL 1100TA TRAP GUN . . . . . NiB $529 Ex $417 Gd $330
Similar to Model 1100TB Trap Gun except with regular-grade stocks.
Available in both left- and right-hand versions. Made 1979 to 1986.

MODEL 1100TB TRAP GUN
Same as Model 1100 Field Gun except has special trap stock, straight or
Monte Carlo comb, recoil pad; 30-inch vent-rib bbl., F or M trap choke;
12 ga. only. Weight: 8.25 lbs. Made 1963 to 1979.
Straight stock . . . . NiB $588 Ex $460 Gd $339
Monte Carlo stock . . . . NiB $599 Ex $443 Gd $360

MODEL 1900
HAMMERLESS DOUBLE . . . . . NiB $1889 Ex $1366 Gd $1177
Improved version of Model 1894. Boxlock. Auto ejector. Double triggers. Gauges: 10, 12, 16. Bbls.: 28 to 32 inches. Value shown is for
standard grade with ordnance steel bbls. Made 1900 to 1910.

MODEL 3200 FIELD GRADE . . . . . NiB $1388 Ex $1178 Gd $900
O/U, boxlock. Auto ejectors. Selective single trigger. 12 ga. 2.75-inch
chambers. Bbls.: Vent rib, 26- and 28-inch M/F; 30-inch IC/M. Weight:
About 7.75 lbs. with 26-inch bbls. Checkered pistol-grip stock/forearm.
Made from 1973 to 1978.

MODEL 3200
COMPETITION SKEET GUN . . NiB $1799 Ex $1588 Gd $1165
Same as Model 3200 Skeet Gun except has gilded scrollwork on frame,
engraved forend, latch plate and trigger guard, select fancy wood. Made
from 1973 to 1984.

MODEL 3200
COMPETITION SKEET SET . . . NiB $5733 Ex $4790 Gd $3300
Similar specifications to Model 3200 Field. 12-ga. O/U with additional,
interchangeable bbls. in 20, 28, and .410 ga. Cased. Made from 1980
to 1984.

MODEL 3200
COMPETITION TRAP GUN. . . NiB $1598 Ex $1266 Gd $1177
Same as Model 3200 Trap Gun except has gilded scrollwork on frame,
engraved forend, latch plate and trigger guard, select fancy wood. Made
from 1973 to 1984.

MODEL 3200
FIELD GRADE MAGNUM . . . . NiB $1766 Ex $1588 Gd $1177
Same as Model 3200 Field except chambered for 12 ga. mag. 3-inch
shells 30-inch bbls., M and F or both F choke. Made 1975 to 1984.

MODEL 3200
"ONE OF 1000" SKEET . . . . . . NiB $2088 Ex $1577 Gd $1288
Same as Model 3200 "One of 1000" Trap except has 26- or 28-inch
bbls., SK choke, skeet-style stock and forearm. Made in 1974.

MODEL 3200
"ONE OF 1000" TRAP . . . . . . NiB $2170 Ex $1660 Gd $1375
Limited edition numbered 1 to 1000. Same general specifications as Model
3200 Trap Gun but has frame, trigger guard and forend latch elaborately
engraved (designation "One of 1,000" on frame side), stock and forearm of
high grade walnut. Supplied in carrying case. Made in 1973.

MODEL 3200 SKEET GUN . . . NiB $1779 Ex $1398 Gd $1055
Same as Model 3200 Field Grade except skeet-style stock and full beavertail
forearm, 26- or 28-inch bbls., SK choke. Made from 1973-80.

MODEL 3200
SPECIAL TRAP GUN. . . . . NiB $1598 Ex $1366 Gd $988
Same as Model 3200 Trap Gun except has select fancy-grade wood and
other minor refinements. Made from 1973 to 1984.

MODEL 3200 TRAP GUN . . . . NiB $1499 Ex $1262 Gd $1077
Same as Model 3200 Field Grade except trap-style stock w/Monte Carlo
or straight comb, select wood, beavertail forearm, 30- or 32-inch bbls.
w/ventilated rib, IM/F or F/F chokes. Made 1973 to 1977.

RIDER NO. 9 SINGLE-SHOT . . . . . NiB $555 Ex $433 Gd $335
Improved version of No. 3 Single Barrel Shotgun made in the late
1800s. Semi-hammerless. Gauges 10, 12, 16, 20, 24, 28. 30- to 32-inch
plain bbl. Weight: About 6 lbs. Plain pistol-grip stock and forearm. Auto
ejector. Made from 1902 to 1910.

SP-10 . . . . NiB $1480 Ex $1050 Gd $730
Autoloader. Takedown. Gas-operated with stainless steel piston. 10 ga.,
3.5-inch chamber. Bbls.: 30-inch vent-rib with REMChoke screw-in
tubes. Weight: 11 lbs. Metal bead front. Checkered walnut stock with
satin finish. QD swivels and camo sling. Made from 1989 to 2010.

SP-10 MAGNUM CAMO . . . . . NiB $1560 Ex $1000 Gd $710
Same general specifications as Model SP-10 except has 23- or 26-inch bbl.
Finish: Mossy Oak, Mossy Oak BreakUp, Mossy Oak Obession, Bottomland
or Duck Blind. Stock: standard or thumbhole. Made from 1993 to 2010.

Remington Sportsman
48SC Skeet Target Grade

Remington Sportsman
48A Standard

Remington Sportsman
48A Small Gauge

Synthetic (matte finish) . . . . .NiB $990 Ex $800 Gd $560
Turkey
  (Mossy Oak Obession) . . . . .NiB $1660 Ex $1100 Gd $810
Turkey Combo
  (turkey bbl. and deer bbl.) . . . .NiB $1300 Ex $930 Gd $660
Waterfowl
  (Mossy Oak Duck Blind) . . . .NiB $1570 Ex $1010 Gd $350

SP-10 TURKEY CAMO
NWTF 25TH ANNIVERSARY. . . NiB $1050 Ex $775 Gd $710
Same general specifications as Model SP-10 except limited manufacture for NWTF 25th Anniversary in 1998. Made 1998 only.

PEERLESS O/U . . . . .NiB $1165 Ex $966 Gd $788
Boxlock action and removable, engraved sideplates. Gauge: 12 only with 3-inch chambers. Barrels: 26-, 28-, or 30-inch with vent rib and REMChoke system. Automatic safety and single selective trigger. Weight: 7.25 lbs. to 7.5 lbs. Blued receiver and bbls. Checkered American walnut stock. Made from 1993 to 1998.

SPORTSMAN A STANDARD GRADE AUTOLOADER
Same general specifications as Model 11A except magazine holds two shells. Also available in "B" Special Grade, "D" Tournament Grade, "E" Expert Grade, "F" Premier Grade. Made from 1931 to 1948. Same values as for Model 11A.
48D . . . . .NiB $445 Ex $321 Gd $226

VERSA MAX
Gas operated semi-auto. 12 ga., 3-1/2-in. chambers only. Bbls.: 26- or 28-in. w/ vent rib, HiViz bead, and Pro Bore choke tubes. Finish: matte black. Stock: black synthetic w/ gray checkered insert panels. Made from 2010 to date.
Synthetic . . . . NiB $1427 Ex $900 Gd $530
Synthetic Left Hand . . . . NiB $1497 Ex $970 Gd $600
Waterfowl Camo . . . . NiB $1630 Ex $1100 Gd $660
Waterfowl Pro . . . . NiB $1730 Ex $1120 Gd $670
Wood Tech . . . . NiB $1630 Ex $1100 Gd $660

VERSA MAX
COMPETITION TACTICAL . . . NiB $1699 Ex $1100 Gd $660
Same general specs as Versa Max except has 22-in. bbl. and 8-round capacity. Finish: green cerakote. Made from 2014 to date.

VERSA MAX SPORTSMAN . . . . NiB $1045 Ex $700 Gd $500
Same general specs as Versa Max except w/ 26- or 28-in. bbl. w/ one choke tube, black synthetic stock, matte blue finish. Made from 2013 to date.

Camo . . . . .NiB $1199 Ex $730 Gd $500
Turkey Model . . . . .NiB $1199 Ex $730 Gd $500

VERSA MAX TACTICAL. . . . . NiB $1699 Ex $1100 Gd $660
Same general specs as Versa Max except has 22-in. vent rib bbl. w/ HiViz sights, magazine extension, and Picatinny rail. Finish: black. Made from 2012 to date.
Zombie Gargoyle Green finish .NiB $1627 Ex $1100 Gd $730
Zombie Pink Explosion finish
  (2013 only) . . . . .NiB $1627 Ex $1100 Gd $730

SPORTSMAN SKEET GUN
Same general specifications as the Sportsman A except has 26-inch bbl. (plain, solid or vent rib), SK choke, beavertail forend. Disc. in 1949.
Plain barrel . . . . .NiB $408 Ex $320 Gd $255
Solid-rib barrel . . . . .NiB $408 Ex $320 Gd $255
Ventilated rib barrel . . . . .NiB $475 Ex $355 Gd $290

MODEL 48 MOHAWK SPORTSMAN AUTO
Streamlined receiver. Hammerless. Takedown. Gauges: 12, 16, 20. Tubular magazine holds two rounds. Bbls.: Plain, matted top surface or vent rib; 26-inch IC, 28-inch M or F choke, 30-inch F choke (12 ga. only). Weight: About 7.5 lbs., 12 ga.; 6.25 lbs., 16 ga.; 6.5 lbs., 20 ga. Pistol-grip stock, grooved forend, both checkered. Made from 1949 to 1959.
Plain bbl. . . . . .NiB $376 Ex $270 Gd $198
Matted top-surface bbl. . . . . .NiB $466 Ex $355 Gd $290
Ventilated rib bbl. . . . . .NiB $566 Ex $477 Gd $379

SPORTSMAN MODEL 48 B, D, F,
SELECT, TOURNAMENT & PREMIER GRADE GUNS
These higher grade models differ from the Sportsman-48A in general quality, grade of wood, checkering, engraving, etc. General specifications are the same. Made from 1949 to 1959.
Sportsman-48B Select grade . . . . .NiB $490 Ex $330 Gd $225
Sportsman-48D Tournament grade . NiB $1688 Ex $1178 Gd $988
Sportsman-48F Premier grade . . NiB $6355 Ex $3988 Gd $2500

MODEL 48SA SPORTSMAN SKEET GUN
Same general specifications as Sportsman-48A except has 26-inch bbl. with matted top surface or vent rib, SK choke, ivory bead front sight, metal bead rear sight. Made from 1949 to 1960.
plain barrel . . . . .NiB $377 Ex $279 Gd $200
ventilated rib barrel . . . . .NiB $466 Ex $344 Gd $229
Sportsman-48SC Skeet . . . . .NiB $577 Ex $466 Gd $355
Tournament grade . . . . .NiB $1688 Ex $1299 Gd $1100
Sportsman-48SF Skeet
  Premier grade . . . . .NiB $6220 Ex $4014 Gd $2444

Richland Model 200

Richland Model 202

Richland Model 707 Deluxe

Richland Model 711
Long Range Waterfowl Magnum

MODEL 11-48A RIOT GUN . . . . . NiB $420 Ex $322 Gd $276
Same as Model 11-48A except 20-inch plain barrel and 12 ga. only.
Disc. in 1969.

**MODEL 11-48A STANDARD
GRADE 4-ROUND AUTOLOADER .410 & 28 GAUGE**
Same general specifications as Sportsman-48A except gauge, 3-round
magazine, 25-inch bbl. Weight: About 6.25 lbs. 28 ga. introduced 1952,
.410 in 1954. Disc. in 1969. Values same as shown for Sportsman-48A.

MODEL 11-48A STANDARD GRADE AUTOLOADER
Same general specifications as Sportsman-48A except magazine holds
four rounds, forend not grooved. Also available in Special Grade (11-
48B), Tournament Grade (11-48D) and Premier Grade (11-48F). Made
1949 to 1969. Values same as for Sportsman-48A.

**MODEL 11-48SA SKEET
28 GA. AND .410 . . . . NiB $398 Ex $300 Gd $233**
Same general specifications as Model 11-48A 28 gauge except has
25-inch vent rib bbl., SK choke. 28 ga. introduced 1952, .410 in 1954.

**MODEL 58 SKEET, TARGET, TOURNAMENT
AND PREMIER GRADES**
These higher grade models differ from the Sportsman-58SA in general
quality, grade of wood, checkering, engraving, and other refinements.
General operating and physical specifications are the same.
Sportsman-58C Skeet Gun . . . . . . NiB $544 Ex $397 Gd $322
Sportsman-58D Tournament . . . . .NiB $1656 Ex $1267 Gd $1100
Sportsman-58SF Premier . . . . . NiB $6222 Ex $3566 Gd $2924

SPORTSMAN-58 TOURNAMENT AND PREMIER
These higher grade models differ from the Sportsman-58ADL with vent-
rib bbl. in general quality, grade of wood, checkering, engraving, etc.
General specifications are the same.

Sportsman-58D Tournament . . . . NiB $1099 Ex $824 Gd $590
Sportsman-58F Premier. . . . . . NiB $1889 Ex $1488 Gd $1051

MODEL 58ADL AUTOLOADER
Deluxe grade. Gas-operated. 12 ga. Three round magazine. Bbls.: plain
or vent rib, 26-, 28- or 30-inch; IC, M or F choke, or Remington Special
Skeet choke. Weight: About 7 lbs. Checkered pistol-grip stock and forearm. Made from 1956 to 1964.
plain barrel . . . . NiB $366 Ex $267 Gd $188
ventilated rib barrel . . . . NiB $433 Ex $320 Gd $221

MODEL 58BDL DELUXE SPECIAL GRADE
Same as Model 58ADL except select grade wood.
plain barrel . . . . NiB $544 Ex $422 Gd $338
ventilated rib barrel . . . . NiB $577 Ex $476 Gd $390

**MODEL 58SADL
SKEET GRADE . . . . NiB $588 Ex $432 Gd $338**
Same general specifications as Model 58ADL with vent-rib bbl. except
special skeet stock and forearm.

REVELATION SHOTGUNS

See Western Auto listings.

RICHLAND ARMS COMPANY — Blissfield, Michigan; manufactured in Italy and Spain

**MODEL 200
FIELD GRADE DOUBLE . . . . NiB $400 Ex $294 Gd $179**

Rigby Regal
Side Lock

Hammerless, boxlock, Anson & Deeley-type. Plain extractors. Double triggers. Gauges: 12, 16, 20, 28, .410 (3-inch chambers in 20 and .410; others have 2.75-inch). Bbls.: 28-inch M/F choke, 26-inch IC/M; .410 with 26-inch M/F only; 22-inch IC/M in 20 ga. only. Weight: 6 lbs., 2 oz. to 7 lbs., 4 oz. Checkered walnut stock with cheekpiece, pistol grip, recoil pad; beavertail forend. Made in Spain from 1963 to 1985.

MODEL 202
ALL PURPOSE FIELD GUN . . . . .NiB $554 Ex $348 Gd $245
Hammerless, boxlock, Anson & Deeley-type. Same as Model 200 except has two sets of barrels same gauge. 12 ga.: 30-inch bbls. F/F, 3-inch chambers; 26-inch bbls. IC/M, 2.75-inch chambers. 20 gauge: 28-inch bbls. M/F; 22-inch bbls. IC/M, 3-inch chambers. Made from 1963. Disc.

MODEL 707
DELUXE FIELD GUN . . . . .NiB $433 Ex $266 Gd $180
Hammerless, boxlock, triple bolting system. Plain extractors. Double triggers. Gauges: 12, 2.75-inch chambers; 20, 3-inch chambers. Bbls.: 12 ga., 28-inch M/F, 26-inch IC/M; 20 ga., 30-inch F/F, 28-inch M/F, 26-inch IC/M. Weight: 6 lbs., 4 oz. to 6 lbs., 15 oz. Checkered walnut stock and forend, recoil pad. Made from 1963 to 1972.

MODEL 711 LONG-RANGE WATERFOWL MAGNUM
DOUBLE-BARREL SHOTGUN
Hammerless, boxlock, Anson & Deeley-type, Purdey triple lock. Plain extractors. Double triggers. Auto safety. Gauges: 10, 3.5-inch chambers; 12, 3-inch chambers. Bbls.: 10 ga., 32-inch; 12 ga., 30-inch; F/F. Weight: 10 ga., 11 pounds; 12 ga., 7.75 lbs. Checkered walnut stock and beavertail forend; recoil pad. Made in Spain from 1963 to 1985.
10 ga. magnum . . . . .NiB $545 Ex $356 Gd $280
12 ga. magnum . . . . .NiB $566 Ex $377 Gd $300

MODEL 808
O/U SHOTGUN . . . . .NiB $559 Ex $394 Gd $290
Boxlock. Plain extractors. Non-selective single trigger. 12 ga. only. Bbls. (Vickers steel): 30-inch F/F; 28-inch M/F; 26-inch IC/M. Weight: 6 lbs. to 7 lbs., 3 oz. Checkered walnut stock/forend. Made in Italy from 1963 to 1968.
Premier grade . . . . .NiB $6220 Ex $4014 Gd $2444

JOHN RIGBY & CO. — London, England

HAMMERLESS BOXLOCK DOUBLE-BARREL SHOTGUN
Auto ejectors. Double triggers. Made in all gauges, barrel lengths and chokes. Checkered stock and forend, straight grip standard. Made in two grades: Sackville and Chatsworth. These guns differ in general quality, engraving, etc.; specifications are the same.
Sackville grade . . . . NiB $6450 Ex $4255 Gd $3790
Chatsworth grade . . . . NiB $4779 Ex $4109 Gd $3200

RIZZINI, BATTISTA – 37th Edition

HAMMERLESS SIDELOCK DOUBLE-BARREL SHOTGUN
Auto ejectors. Double triggers. Made in all gauges, barrel lengths and chokes. Checkered stock and forend, straight grip standard. Made in two grades: Regal (best quality) and Sandringham; these guns differ in general quality, engraving, etc., specifications are the same.
Regal grade . . . . . . .NiB $13,677 Ex $11,773 Gd $9892
Sandringham grade. . . . .NiB $11,088 Ex $9000 Gd $5698

RIZZINI, BATTISTA — Marcheno, Italy

Rizzini was purchased by San Swiss AG IN 2002. Imported in the U. S. by SIB Arms, Exeter, New Hampshire; William Larkin Moore & Co., Scottsdale, Arizona; and New England Arms Co., Kittery, Maine.

AURUM O/U . . . . .NiB $2770 Ex $2243 Gd $2016
Gauge: 12, 16 and 20. Boxlock action, light engraving. Case included. Introduced 1996.

AURUM LIGHT . . . . .NiB $4088 Ex $2867 Gd $2390
Similaar to Aurum but 16 gauge only. Imported beginning in 2000.

ARTEMIS . . . . .NiB $2733 Ex $2270 Gd $1966
Similarf to Aurum but with improved engraving and gold inlays.

ARTEMIS DELUXE . . . . NiB $6777 Ex $3861 Gd $3223
Similar to Artemis but with detailed game scene engraving. Available in all gauges

ARTEMIS EL . . . . NiB $17,776 Ex $14,600 Gd $12,980
Same as Artemis Deluxe. Custom gun with superior quality wood and detailed hand engraving. Disc. 2000.

MODEL 780 FIELD . . . . NiB $2140 Ex $1088 Gd $977
Gauge: 10, 12 or 16. Boxlock action, double triggers, extractors, walnut stock and forearm. Disc. 2000.
10 gauge, add $625
Ejector model (S780EL), add $200
Single selective trigger with ejectors, add $250
SST, ejectors and upgraded stock, add $425

MODEL S780 EMEL . . . . .NiB $14,900 Ex $13,655 Gd $11,330
Same as Model 780 Field but with special engraving and hand finished.

MODEL 780 COMPETITION . . . . . . NiB $1488 Ex $1276 Gd $1099
Same as Model 780 Field but with skeet, trap or sporting clays features. Disc.1998.

MODEL 780
SMALL GAUGE SERIES . . . . NiB $1388 Ex $1164 Gd $889
Same as Model 780 Field but in 20, 28, or 36 gauge. Double triggers, ejectors. Disc. 1998.

MODEL 782 EM FIELD . . . . NiB $1566 Ex $1275 Gd $1074
Gauge: 12 or 16. Boxlock action with sideplates, single selective trigger, ejectors and extractors, walnut stock and forearm. Disc. 1998.
Model 782 EM Slug, add $550
Model 782 EML, add. $450

MODEL S782 EMEL . . . . .NiB $14,990 Ex $11,860 Gd $10,066
Same as Model 782 EM Field but specially engraved and hand finished.

SHOTGUNS

Rossi Hammerless Double-Barrel Shotgun

Rossi Overland Hammer Double

Rottweil American Skeet

MODEL S782 EMEL DELUXE ....NiB $13,899 Ex $11,776 Gd $10,066
Gauge: 10, 12, 16, 20, 28, 36 and .410. Barrel:28-inch ventilated rib with choke tubes (except .410); coin-finish engraving; gold inlaids; fine scroll borders; Deluxe English walnut stock. Imported 1994.

MODEL 790 COMPETITION .... NiB $1877 Ex $1687 Gd $1261
Gauge: 12 or 20. Available in trap, skeet or sporting clays models. Black frame outlined with gold line engraving. Disc. 1999.
20 ga. Sporting (sideplates and QD stock), add $1200
Trap model, 20 gauge, subtract $200

MODEL 790 SMALL GAUGE .... NiB $1499 Ex $1179 Gd $1088
Similar to Model 790 Competition but in 20, 29, or 36 guages. Single selective trigger, ejectors. Disc. 2000.

MODEL 790 EL .... NiB $7088 Ex $4977 Gd $3766
Same as Model 790 but hand finished with 18k gold inlays, hand engraving.

MODEL S790 EMEL DELUXE ..... NiB $12,970 Ex $10,088 Gd $8990
Guages: All. Custom gun with 27.5-inch ventilated-rib bbls. choke tubes (except .410); color case-hardened or coin-finished receiver; ornate engraving with Rizzini crest. Stock is deluxe English walnut; leather case included.

MODEL 792 SMALL GAUGE MAGNUM NiB $1791 Ex $1476 Gd $1199
Gauge: 20, 28, or 36. Magnum chambers. Single selective trigger; ejectors; engraved sideplates. Disc. 1998.

MODEL 792 EMEL DELUXE .... NiB $9133 Ex $8093 Gd $6166
Same as Model 793 but hand finished with 18k gold inlays and hand engraving.

MODEL S792 EMEL .... NiB $14,000 Ex $11,980 Gd $10,760
Guages: All. Custom gun with 27.5-inch ventilated-rib bbls. choke tubes (except .410); coin-finished receiver; sideplates with fine game scene engraving and scroll borders; deluxe English walnut stock; leather case included. Imported 1994.

MODEL 2000 TRAP .... NiB $1798 Ex $1448 Gd $1190
Guage: 12 only. Nickel-finished receiver; sideplates; gold trigger; ventilated-rib bbls.. Disc 1998.

MODEL 2000
TRAP EL .... NiB $5477 Ex $4100 Gd $3110
Same as Model 2000 Trap but hand finished with 18k gold inlays and ornate hand engraving.

MODEL 2000-SP .... NiB $3210 Ex $2976 Gd $2241
Guage: 12 only. Bbls.: 26, 29.5, or 32 inches. Over-bored barrels with choke tubes. Engraved sideplates, semi-fancy select QD stock. Case included. Imported 1994 to 1998.

PREMIER SPORTING .... NiB $2669 Ex $2280 Gd $1881
Guages: 12 or 20. Bbls.: 28, 29.5 or 32 inches five chokes per bbl.. Custom built on request. Imported 1994

SPORTING EL .... NiB $3126 Ex $2390 Gd $2177
Same as Premier model but includes multiple chokes and fitted case. Disc. 2000.

UPLAND EL .... NiB $2793 Ex $2277 Gd $1965
Guages: All. Custom gun with 27.5-inch ventilated-rib bbls. choke tubes (except .410); case-hardened receiver; deluxe walnut stock. Hard case included. Imported 1994.

ROSSI — Sao Leopoldo, Brazil

SQUIRE HAMMERLESS DOUBLE-
BARREL SHOTGUN. .... NiB $435 Ex $333 Gd $245
Boxlock. Plain extractors. Double triggers. 12 and 20 ga., .410. Three-inch chambers. Bbls.: 20-, 26-inch IC/M; 28-inch M/F choke. Weight: 7 to 7.5 lbs. Pistol-grip hardwood stock and beavertail forearm, uncheckered. Made 1985 to 1990.

OVERLUND
HAMMER DOUBLE .... NiB $380 Ex $244 Gd $179
Sidelock. Plain extractors. Double triggers. Gauges: 12, .410; 3-inch chambers. Bbls.: 20-inch, IC/M in 12 g.; 26-inch, F/F

Ruger Red Label — 20 Gauge (1982)

Ruger Red Label Over and Under (Stainless)

Sarasqueta Model
3 Hammerless
Boxlock

choke in .410. Weight: 7 lbs. (12 ga.); 6 lbs. (.410). Pistol-grip stock and beavertail forearm, uncheckered. Note: Because of its resemblance to the short-barreled doubles carried by guards riding shotgun on 19th-century stagecoaches, the 12 ga. version originally was called the "Coach Gun." Made 1968 to 1989.

ROTTWEIL SHOTGUNS — Germany

MODEL 72 O/U
SHOTGUN . . . . NiB $1988 Ex $1687 Gd $1277
Hammerless, takedown with engraved receiver. 12 ga.; 2.75-inch chambers. 26.75-inch bbls. with SK/SK chokes. Weight: 7.5 lbs. Interchangeable trigger groups and buttstocks. Checkered French walnut buttstock and forend. Imported from Germany.

MODEL 650 FIELD
O/U SHOTGUN . . . . NiB $888 Ex $675 Gd $544
Breech action. Gauge: 12. 28-inch bbls. Six screw-in choke tubes. Automatic ejectors. Engraved receiver. Checkered pistol grip stock. Made from 1984 to 1986.

AMERICAN SKEET . . . . NiB $2010 Ex $1798 Gd $1288
Boxlock action. Gauge: 12. 27-inch vent-rib bbls. 44.5 inches overall. SK chokes. Weight: 7.5 lbs. Designed for tube sets. Hand-checkered European walnut stock with modified forend. Made from 1984 to 1987.

INTERNATIONAL
TRAP SHOTGUN . . . . NiB $2066 Ex $1799 Gd $1263
Box lock action. Gauge: 12. 30-inch bbls. 48.5 inches overall. Weight: 8 lbs. Choked IM/F. Selective single trigger. Metal bead front sight. Checkered European walnut stock w/pistol grip. Engraved action. Made from 1984 to 1987.

SAIGA — Mfg. by Izhmash in Izhevsk, Russia; last imported by RWC Group in Tullytown, PA

SAIGA-12
AK-style action, gas-operated piston, semi-auto w/ detachable 5-rnd. magazine. 12 or 20 ga. w/ 3-in. chamber. Bbl.: 19- or 22-in. w/ choke tubes (12 ga. only). Stock: black synthetic. Finish: matte black. Weight: 6.7 to 10 lbs. Imported 2002 to 2004, reintroduced 2006 to 2014. Importation banned since 2014 dues US sanctions.

12 or 20 ga. . . . . NiB $780 Ex $500 Gd $300
.410 . . . . NiB $646 Ex $415 Gd $250
Hunting Model (monte carlo style stock
   in wood or synthetic) . . . . NiB $885 Ex $580 Gd $360
Skeletonized Stock . . . . NiB $994 Ex $660 Gd $400
Tactical (AR15 style stock,
   10-rnd. magazine) . . . . NiB $1239 Ex $1115 Gd $734

RUGER — Southport, Connecticut

RED LABEL STANDARD GRADE
O/U boxlock. Auto ejectors. Selective single trigger. 12, 20 or 28 ga. w/2.75- or 3-inch chambers. 26-inch vent-rib bbl., IC/M or SK choke. Single selective trigger. Selective automatic ejectors. Automatic top safety. Standard gold bead front sight. Pistol-grip or English-style American walnut stock and forearm w/hand-cut checkering. The 20 ga. Model was introduced in 1977; 12 ga. version in 1982 and the stainless receiver became standard in 1985. Choke tubes were optional in 1988 and standard in 1990. Weight: 7.0 to 7.5 lbs.

Fixed chokes . . . . NiB $1733 Ex $1388 Gd $1077
Screw-in tube . . . . NiB $1760 Ex $1410 Gd $1100
Grade 1 engraving . . . . NiB $1893 Ex $1421 Gd $1107
Grade 2 engraving . . . . NiB $2298 Ex $2100 Gd $1733
Grade 3 engraving . . . . NiB $2798 Ex $2255 Gd $2100

RED LABEL O/U ALL-WEATHER STAINLESS
Gauges: 12 ga. Only. Bbls.: 26- 28- or 30-inch w/various chokes, fixed or screw-in tubes. Stainless receiver and barrel. Checkered black synthetic stock and forearm. Weight: 7.5 lbs. Made 1999 to 2006.

All-weather stainless model . . . NiB $1387 Ex $1189 Gd $900
w/30-inch bbl., add $200

RED LABEL WOODSIDE
Similar to the Red Label O/U Stainless except in 12 ga. only with wood sideplate extensions. Made from 1995 to 2002. Disc.

Standard. . . . . NiB $1687 Ex $1445 Gd $1110
Engraved . . . . NiB $2389 Ex $1955 Gd $1533

SHOTGUNS

Sarasqueta Models 6E, 11E and 12E

Sauer Model 66 Field Grade II

Sauer Model 66 Field Grade III

RED LABEL SPORTING CLAYS
Similar to the standard Red Label model except chambered 12 or 20 ga. only w/30-inch vent-rib bbls., no side ribs; back-bored w/ screw-in choke tubes (not interchangeable w/other Red Label O/U models). Brass front and mid-rib beads. Made from 1992 to 2011.
Standard. . . . . NiB $1766 Ex $1288 Gd $998
Engraved . . . . NiB $2680 Ex $2110 Gd $1590

RED LABEL "WILDLIFE FOREVER" SPECIAL Edition
Limited edition commemorating the 50th Wildlife Forever anniversary. Similar to the standard Red Label model except chambered 12 ga. only w/engraved receiver enhanced w/gold mallard and pheasant inlays. 300 produced in 1993.
Special edition. . . . . NiB $1690 Ex $1655 Gd $1299
Special edition w/hard case, add. $200

GOLD LABEL . . . . NiB $3650 EX $2288 GD $1060
S/S boxlock. Auto ejectors. Selective single trigger. 12 ga. w/ 3-inch chambers. 28-inch solid-rib bbl., choke tubes. Top safety. Pistol-grip or English-style American walnut stock and forearm w/hand-cut checkering. Stainless receiver. Made from 2002 to 2008.

VICTOR SARASQUETA, S.A. — Eibar, Spain

MODEL 3 HAMMERLESS
BOXLOCK DOUBLE-BARREL SHOTGUN
Plain extractors or auto ejectors. Double triggers. Gauges: 12, 16, 20. Made in various bbl. lengths, chokes and weights. Checkered stock and forend, straight grip standard. Imported from 1985-87.
Model 3, plain extractors . . . . NiB $599 Ex $445 Gd $329
Model 3E, automatic ejectors . . . . NiB $655 Ex $500 Gd $435

HAMMERLESS SIDELOCK DOUBLES
Automatic ejectors (except on Models 4 and 203 which have plain extractors). Double triggers. Gauges: 12, 16, 20. Barrel lengths, chokes and weights made to order. Checkered stock and forend, straight grip standard. Models differ chiefly in overall quality, engraving, grade of wood, checkering, etc.; general specifications are the same. Imported from 1985 to 1987.

Model 4 . . . . NiB $779 Ex $643 Gd $441
Model 4E . . . . NiB $879 Ex $754 Gd $570
Model 203 . . . . NiB $744 Ex $600 Gd $435
Model 203E . . . . NiB $800 Ex $632 Gd $544
Model 6E . . . . NiB $1388 Ex $1108 Gd $700
Model 7E . . . . NiB $1443 Ex $1156 Gd $965
Model 10E . . . . NiB $2588 Ex $2188 Gd $1966
Model 11E . . . . NiB $2800 Ex $2577 Gd $2234
Model 12E . . . . NiB $3110 Ex $2770 Gd $2369

J. P. SAUER & SOHN — Eckernförde, Germany; formerly Suhl, Germany

MODEL 66 O/U FIELD GUN
Purdey-system action with Holland & Holland-type sidelocks. Selective single trigger. Selective auto ejectors. Automatic safety. Available in three grades of engraving. 12 ga. only. Krupp special steel bbls. w/vent rib 28-inch, M/F choke. Weight: About 7.25 lbs. Checkered walnut stock and forend; recoil pad. Made from 1966 to 1975.
Grade I . . . . NiB $2377 Ex $2120 Gd $1798
Grade II . . . . NiB $3256 Ex $2460 Gd $2190
Grade III . . . . NiB $4100 Ex $3712 Gd $2644

MODEL 66 O/U SKEET GUN
Same as Model 66 Field Gun except 26-inch bbls. with wide vent rib, SK choked- skeet-style stock and ventilated beavertail forearm; non-automatic safety. Made from 1966 to 1975.

Grade I	NiB $2312	Ex $2198	Gd $1655
Grade II	NiB $3270	Ex $2980	Gd $2110
Grade III	NiB $3988	Ex $3655	Gd $2980

MODEL 66 O/U TRAP GUN
Same as Model 66 Skeet Gun except has 30-inch bbls. choked F/F or M/F; trap-style stock. Values same as for Skeet model. Made from1966 to 1975.

MODEL 3000E DRILLING
Combination rifle and double barrel shotgun. Blitz action with Greener crossbolt, double underlugs, separate rifle cartridge extractor, front set trigger, firing pin indicators, Greener side safety, sear slide selector locks right shotgun bbl. for firing rifle bbl. Gauge/calibers12 ga. (2.75-inch chambers); .222, .243, .30-06, 7x65R. 25-inch Krupp-Special steel bbls.; M/F choke automatic folding leaf rear rifle sight. Weight: 6.5 to 7.25 lbs. depending on rifle caliber. Checkered walnut stock and forend; pistol grip, Monte Carlo comb and cheekpiece, sling swivels. Standard model with Arabesque engraving; Deluxe model with hunting scenes engraved on action. Currently manufactured. Note: Also see listing under Colt.

Standard model	NiB $4490	Ex $3891	Gd $2776
Deluxe model	NiB $5782	Ex $4669	Gd $3533

ARTEMIS DOUBLE-BARREL SHOTGUN
Holland & Holland-type sidelock with Greener crossbolt double under-lugs, double sear safeties, selective single trigger, selective auto ejectors. Grade I with fine-line engraving, Grade II with full English Arabesque engraving. 12 ga. (2.75-inch chambers). Krupp special steel bbls., 28-inch, M/F choke. Weight: About 6.5 lbs. Checkered walnut pistol-grip stock and beavertail forend; recoil pad. Made from1966 to 1977.

Grade I	NiB $5698	Ex $4766	Gd $4133
Grade II	NiB $6880	Ex $5744	Gd $4500

BBF 54 O/U COMBINATION RIFLE/SHOTGUN
Blitz action with Kersten lock, front set trigger fires rifle bbl., slide-operated sear safety. Gauge/calibers: 16 ga.; .30-30, .30-06, 7x65R, 25-inch Krupp special steel bbls.; shotgun bbl. F choke, folding-leaf rear sight. Weight: About 6 lbs. Checkered walnut stock and forend; pistol grip, mod. Monte Carlo comb and cheekpiece, sling swivels. Standard model with Arabesque engraving; Deluxe model with hunting scenes engraved on action. Currently manufactured.

Standard model	NiB $2977	Ex $2455	Gd $1766
Deluxe model	NiB $3566	Ex $3088	Gd $2655

ROYAL DOUBLE-BARREL SHOTGUNS
Anson & Deeley action (boxlock) with Greener crossbolt, double underlugs, signal pins, selective single trigger, selective auto ejectors, auto safety. Scalloped frame with Arabesque engraving. Krupp special steel bbls. Gauges: 12, 2.75-inch chambers, 20, 3-inch chambers. Bbls.: 30-inch (12 ga. only) and 28-inch, M/F- 26-inch (20 ga. only), IC/M. Weight: 12 ga., about 6.5 lbs.; 20 ga., 6 lbs. Checkered walnut pistol-grip stock and beavertail forend; recoil pad. Made from 1955 to 1977.

Standard model	NiB $1790	Ex $1533	Gd $1206
20 ga. add			20%

SAVAGE ARMS — Westfield, Massachusetts.
Formerly located in Utica, New York. Currently owned by ATK.

MODEL 24C .22/.410 O/U
COMBINATION . . . . NiB $570 Ex $388 Gd $245
Same as Stevens No. 22-.410 with walnut stock and forearm. Made from 1950 to 1965.

**Sauer Model 3000E
Drilling**

**Sauer BBF 54 Combination
Rifle/Shotgun**

**Sauer Royal
Double-Barrel Shotgun**

MODEL 24C
CAMPER'S COMPANION . . . . NiB $675 Ex $466 Gd $290
Same as Model 24FG except made in .22 Magnum/20 ga. only; has 20-inch bbls., shotgun tube Cyl. bore. Weight: 5.75 lbs. Trap in butt provides ammunition storage; comes with carrying case. Made 1972 to 1989.

MODEL 24 FIELD . . . . NiB $498 Ex $277 Gd $190
Same as Models 24DL and 24MDL except frame has black or case-hardened finish. Game scene decoration of frame eliminated in 1974; forearm uncheckered after 1976. Made from 1970 to 1989.

MODEL 24DL . . . . NiB $400 Ex $366 Gd $243
Same general specifications as Model 24S except top-lever opening; satin-chrome-finished frame decorated with game scenes, checkered Monte Carlo stock and forearm. Made from 1962 to 1965.

GRADING: **NiB** = New in Box   **Ex** = Excellent or NRA 95%   **Gd** = Good or NRA 68%   **545**

Savage Model 24
.22-/.410 O/U Combination

Savage Model 24-VS
Camper/Survival/Centerfire Rifle/Shotgun

MODEL 24F-12T TURKEY GUN . .NiB $700 Ex $488 Gd $337
12- or 20-ga. shotgun bbl./.22 Hornet, .223 or .30-30 caliber rifle.
24-inch blued bbls., 3-inch chambers, extra removable F choke tube.
Hammer block safety. Color casehardened frame. DuPont Rynite camo
stock. Swivel studs. Made from 1989 to 2007.

MODEL 24FG FIELD GRADE . . . .NiB $525 Ex $433 Gd $276
Same general specifications as Model 24S except top lever opening.
Made 1972. Disc.

MODEL 24MDL . . . . .NiB $577 Ex $400 Gd $229
Same as Model 24DL except rifle bbl. chambered for 22 WMR. Made
from 1962 to 1969.

MODEL 24MS . . . . .NiB $690 Ex $535 Gd $389
Same as Model 24S except rifle bbl. chambered for 22 WMR. Made
from 1964 to 1971.

**MODEL 24S O/U
COMBINATION . . . . .NiB $477 Ex $339 Gd $225**
Boxlock. Visible hammer. Side lever opening. Plain extractors. Single
trigger. 20 ga. or .410 bore shotgun bbl. under 22 LR bbl., 24-inch. Open
rear sight, ramp front, dovetail for scope mounting. Weight: About 6.75
lbs. Plain pistol-grip stock and forearm. Made from 1964 to 1971.

MODEL 24V. . . . . .NiB $588 Ex $379 Gd $298
Similar to Model 24D except 20 ga. under .222 Rem., .22 Rem., .357
Mag., .22 Hornet or .30-30 rifle bbl. Made from 1967 to 1989.

**MODEL 24-CS CAMPER'S COMPANION
CENTERFIRE RIFLE/SHOTGUN . . .NiB $680 Ex $389 Gd $319**
Caliber: .22 LR over 20 ga. Nickel finish full-length stock and accessory
pistol-grip stock. Overall length: 36 inches with full stock; 26 inches w/
pistol grip. Weight: About 5.75 lbs. Made 1972 to 1988.
.357 Mag./20 ga., add $50

**MODEL 28A STANDARD GRADE
SLIDE-ACTION REPEATING SHOTGUN. . . NiB $445 Ex $398 Gd $300**
Hammerless. Takedown. 12 ga. Five round tubular magazine. Plain bbl., lengths:
26-,28-, 30-, 32-inches, choked C/M/F. Weight: About 7.5 lbs. with 30-inch bbl.
Plain pistol-grip stock, grooved slide handle. Made from 1928 to 1931.

MODEL 28B. . . . . .NiB $366 Ex $287 Gd $245
Raised matted rib; otherwise the same as Model 28A.

MODEL 28D TRAP GRADE. . . . . .NiB $366 Ex $287 Gd $245
Same general specifications as Model 28A except has 30-inch F choke
bbl. w/matted rib, trap-style stock w/checkered pistol grip, checkered
slide handle of select walnut.

**MODEL 30 SOLID FRAME HAMMERLESS
SLIDE-ACTION SHOTGUN. . . . . .NiB $290 Ex $221 Gd $175**
Gauges: 12, 16, 20, .410. 2.75-inch chamber in 16 ga., 3- inch in
other ga. Magazine holds four 2.75-inch shells or three 3-inch shells.
Bbls.: Vent rib; 26-, 28-, 30-inch; IC, M, F choke. Weight: Average
6.25 to 6.75 lbs. depending on ga. Plain pistol-grip stock (checkered
on later production), grooved slide handle. Made from 1958 to 1970.

MODEL 30 TAKEDOWN SLUG GUN. . NiB $255 Ex $175 Gd $125
Same as Model 30FG except 21-inch cyl. bore bbl. with rifle sights.
Made from 1971 to 1979.

MODEL 30AC SOLID FRAME . . . .NiB $379 Ex $288 Gd $179
Same as Model 30 Solid Frame except has 26-inch bbl. with adj. choke;
12 ga. only. Made from 1959 to 1970.

MODEL 30AC TAKEDOWN . . . . .NiB $366 Ex $265 Gd $160
Same as Model 30FG except has 26-inch bbl. with adj. choke; 12 and
20 ga. only. Made from 1971 to 1972.

MODEL 30D TAKEDOWN . . . . . .NiB $277 Ex $200 Gd $167
Deluxe Grade. Same as Model 30FG except has receiver engraved with
game scene, vent rib bbl., recoil pad. Made from 1971. Disc.

**MODEL 30FG TAKEDOWN HAMMERLESS
SLIDE-ACTION SHOTGUN. . . . . . .NiB $265 Ex $180 Gd $95**
Field Grade. Gauges: 12, 20, .410. Three-inch chamber. Magazine
holds four 2.75-inch shells or three 3-inch shells. Bbls.: plain; 26-inch
F choke (.410 ga. only); 28-inch M/F choke; 30-inch F choke (12 ga.
only). Weight: Average 7 to 7.75 lbs. depending on gauge. Checkered
pistol-grip stock, fluted slide handle. Made 1970 to 1979.

MODEL 30L SOLID FRAME . . . . .NiB $300 Ex $241 Gd $176
Same as Model 30 Solid Frame except left-handed model with ejection
port and safety on left side; 12 ga. only. Made 1959 to 1970.

**MODEL 30T SOLID FRAME
TRAP AND DUCK . . . . .NiB $377 Ex $288 Gd $190**
Same as Model 30 Solid Frame except only in 12 ga. w/30-inch F choke
bbl.; has Monte Carlo stock with recoil pad, weight: About 8 lbs. Made
from 1963 to 1970.

**MODEL 30T TAKE DOWN
TRAP GUN. . . . . .NiB $335 Ex $292 Gd $197**
Same as Model 30D except only in 12 ga. w/30-inch F choke bbl.
Monte Carlo stock with recoil pad. Made from 1970 to 1973.

**MODEL 69-RXL SLIDE-ACTION
SHOTGUN. . . . . .NiB $366 Ex $256 Gd $190**
Similar to Model 67 (law enforcement configuration). Hammerless, side
ejection top tang safe for left- or right-hand use. 12 ga. chambered for
2.75- and 3-inch magnum shells. 18.25-inch bbl. Tubular magazine
holds 6 rounds (one less for 3-inch mag). Walnut finish hardwood stock
with recoil pad and grooved operating handle. Weight: About 6.5 lbs.
Made from 1982 to 1989.

Savage 24-C

Savage 24-D

Savage Model 24-F -12T

Savage Model 24-V

Savage Model 30

Savage Model 30 Slug Gun

Savage Model 30-FG

SHOTGUNS

**MODEL 210F BOLT-ACTION
SLUG GUN** . . . . **NiB $490 Ex $377 Gd $290**
Built on Savage 110 action. Gauge: 12 w/3-inch chamber. Two round detachable magazine. 24-inch fully rifled bbl. Receiver drilled and tapped for scope mounts w/no sights. Weight: 7.5 lbs. Checkered black synthetic stock w/swivel studs and recoil pad. Made from 1997 to 2000.

MODEL 210FT BOLT-ACTION SHOTGUN . **NiB $599 Ex $459 Gd $335**
Similar to Model 210F except has smoothbore 24-inch bbl. w/choke tubes. Bead front and U-notch rear sights. Advantage Camo finish. Made from 1997 to 2000.

**MODEL 220 SINGLE-BARREL
SHOTGUN** . . . . **NiB $590 Ex $386 Gd $265**
Hammerless. Takedown. Auto ejector. Gauges: 12,16, 20 .410. Single shot. Bbl. lengths: 12 ga., 28- to 36-inch, 16 ga., 28- to 32-inch; 20 ga., 26- to 32-inch; .410 bore, 26-and 28-inch. F choke. Weight: about 6 lbs. Plain pistol-grip stock and wide forearm. Made 1938 to 1965.

MODEL 220AC. . . . . **NiB $490 Ex $255 Gd $190**
Same as Model 220 except has Savage adj. choke.

GRADING: **NiB** = New in Box   **Ex** = Excellent or NRA 95%   **Gd** = Good or NRA 68%

Savage Model 69-RXL

Savage Model 220

Savage Model 242

MODEL 220L . . . . **NiB $490 Ex $388 Gd $229**
Same general specifications as Model 220 except has side lever opening instead of top lever. Made from 1965 to 1972.

MODEL 220P . . . . **NiB $490 Ex $388 Gd $229**
Same as Model 220 except has PolyChoke bbl., made in 12 ga. with 30-inch bbl., 16 and 20 ga. with 28-inch bbl., no .410 bore; recoil pad.

MODEL 242 O/U SHOTGUN . . . . **NiB $498 Ex $376 Gd $292**
Similar to Model 24D except both bbls. .410 bore, F choke. Weight: About 7 lbs. Made from 1977 to 1980.

MODEL 312 FIELD GRADE O/U . . **NiB $688 Ex $554 Gd $400**
Gauge: 12; 2.75- or 3-inch chambers. 26- or 28-inch bbls. w/vent rib; F/M/IC chokes. 43 or 45 inches overall. Weight: 7 lbs. Internal hammers. Top tang safety. American walnut stock with checkered pistol grip and recoil pad. Made from 1990 to 1993.

MODEL 312 SPORTING CLAYS O/U . . . . **NiB $688 Ex $578 Gd $445**
Same as Model 312 Field Grade except furnished with number 1 and number 2 Skeet tubes and 28-inch bbls. only. Made 1990 to 1993.

MODEL 312 TRAP O/U . . . . **NiB $756 Ex $600 Gd $477**
Same as Model 312 Field Grade except with 30-inch bbls. only, Monte Carlo buttstock, weight: 7.5 lbs. Made from 1990 to 1993.

MODEL 330 O/U SHOTGUN . . . . **NiB $589 Ex $477 Gd $398**
Boxlock. Plain extractors. Selective single trigger. Gauges: 12, 20. 2.75-inch chambers in 12 ga., 3-inch in 20 gauge. Bbls.: 26-inch IC/M; 28-inch M/F; 30-inch M/F choke (12 ga. only). Weight: 6.25 to 7.25 lbs., depending on gauge. Checkered pistol-grip stock and forearm. Made from 1969 to 1978.

MODEL 333 O/U SHOTGUN
Boxlock. Auto ejectors. Selective single trigger. Gauges: 12, 20. 2.75-inch chambers in 12 ga., 3-inch in 20 ga. Bbls.: vent rib; 26-inch SK choke, IC/M; 28-inch M/F; 30-inch M/F choke (12 ga. only). Weight: Average 6.25 to 7.25 lbs. Checkered pistol-grip stock and forearm. Made from 1973 to 1979.

Model 333 12 ga. . . . . **NiB $598 Ex $467 Gd $366**
Model 333 20 ga., add **30%**

MODEL 333T TRAP GUN . . . . . . **NiB $654 Ex $498 Gd $396**
Similar to Model 330 except only in 12 ga. with 30-inch vent-rib bbls., IM/F choke; Monte Carlo stock w/recoil pad. Weight: 7.75 lbs. Made from 1972 to 1979.

MODEL 420 O/U SHOTGUN
Boxlock. Hammerless. Takedown. Automatic safety. Double triggers or non-selective single trigger. Gauges: 12, 16, 20. Bbls.: Plain, 26- to 30-inch (the latter in 12 ga. only); choked M/F, C/IC. Weight with 28-inch bbls.: 12 ga., 7.75 lbs.; 16 ga., 7.5 lbs.; 20 ga., 6.75 lbs. Plain pistol-grip stock and forearm. Made from 1938 to 1942.
With double triggers . . . . **NiB $589 Ex $477 Gd $300**
With single trigger . . . . **NiB $633 Ex $498 Gd $376**

MODEL 430
Same as Model 420 except has matted top bbl., checkered stock of select walnut with recoil pad, checkered forearm. Made from 1938 to 1942.
With double triggers . . . . **NiB $677 Ex $544 Gd $390**
With single trigger . . . . **NiB $677 Ex $559 Gd $443**

MODEL 440 O/U SHOTGUN . . . . **NiB $635 Ex $490 Gd $387**
Boxlock. Plain extractors. Selective single trigger. Gauges: 12, 20. 2.75-inch chambers in 12 ga., 3-inch in 20 ga. Bbls.: Vent rib; 26-inch SK choke, IC/M; 28-inch M/F; 30-inch M/F choke (12 ga. only). Weight: Average 6 to 6.5 lbs. depending on ga. Made from 1968 to 1972.

MODEL 440T TRAP GUN . . . . . . **NiB $598 Ex $488 Gd $392**
Similar to Model 440 except only in 12 ga. with 30-inch bbls., extra-wide vent rib, IM/F choke. Trap-style Monte Carlo stock and semibeavertail forearm of select walnut, recoil pad. Weight: 7.5 lbs. Made from 1969 to 1972.

MODEL 444 DELUXE
O/U SHOTGUN . . . . **NiB $687 Ex $500 Gd $369**
Similar to Model 440 except has auto ejectors, select walnut stock and semi-beavertail forearm. Made from 1969 to 1972.

Savage Model 312
Field Grade O/U

Savage Model 312
Trap O/U

Savage Model 330

Savage Model 333Y

Savage Model 333
20 Gauge

SHOTGUNS

MODEL 550
HAMMERLESS DOUBLE . . . . . . .NiB $355 Ex $290 Gd $200
Boxlock. Auto ejectors. Non-selective single trigger. Gauges: 12, 20. 2.75-inch chamber in 12 ga., 3-inch in 20 ga. Bbls.: Vent rib; 26-inch IC/M; 28-inch M/F; 30-inch M/F choke (12 ga. only). Weight: 7 to 8 lbs. Checkered pistol-grip stock and semi-beavertail forearm. Made 1971 to 1973.

MODEL 720 STANDARD GRADE 5 SHOT AUTOLOADING
SHOTGUN. . . . . .NiB $335 Ex $269 Gd $200
Browning type. Takedown. 12 and 16 ga. Four round tubular magazine. Bbl.: plain; 26- to 32-inch (the latter in 12 ga. only); choked IC, M, F. Weight: About 8.25 lbs., 12 ga. with 30-inch bbl.; 16 ga., about .5 lb. lighter. Checkered pistol-grip stock and forearm. Made from 1930 to 1949.

MODEL 726 UPLAND SPORTER AUTO
SHOTGUN. . . . . .NiB $377 Ex $292 Gd $233
Same as Model 720 except has 2-round magazine capacity. Made from 1931 to 1949.

MODEL 740C
SKEET GUN . . . . .NiB $410 Ex $300 Gd $237
Same as Model 726 except has special skeet stock and full beavertail forearm, equipped with Cutts Compensator. Bbl. length overall with spreader tube is about 24.5 inches. Made from 1936 to 1949.

MODEL 745 LIGHT-WEIGHT
AUTOLOADER. . . . . .NiB $377 Ex $266 Gd $198
Three- or five-round models. Same general specifications as Model 720 except has lightweight alloy receiver, 12 ga.only, 28-inch plain bbl. Weight: About 6.75 lbs. Made from 1940 to 1949.

MODEL 750
AUTO SHOTGUN . . . . .NiB $355 Ex $287 Gd $239
Browning-type autoloader. Takedown. 12 ga. Four round tubular magazine. Bbls.: 28-inch F or M choke; 26-inch IC. Weight: About 7.25 lbs. Checkered walnut pistol-grip stock and grooved forearm. Made from 1960 to 1967.

MODEL 750-AC . . . . .NiB $377 Ex $280 Gd $210
Same as Model 750 except has 26-inch bbl. with adj. choke. Made from 1964 to 1967.

Savage Model 440

Savage Model 440T

Savage Model 550

Savage Model 750

Savage Model 775

Savage Model 775-SC

MODEL 750-SC . . . . **NiB $368 Ex $267 Gd $198**
Same as Model 750 except has 26-inch bbl. with Savage Super Choke.
Made from 1962 to 1963.

**MODEL 755 STANDARD
GRADE AUTOLOADER** . . . . **NiB $389 Ex $297 Gd $245**
Streamlined receiver. Takedown.12 and 16 ga. Four round tubular
magazine (a three-round model with magazine capacity of two
rounds was also produced until 1951). Bbl.: Plain, 30-inch F choke
(12 ga. only), 28-inch F or M, 26-inch IC. Weight: About 8.25 lbs.,
12 ga. Checkered pistol-grip stock and forearm. Made from 1949
to 1958.

MODEL 755-SC . . . . **NiB $389 Ex $297 Gd $245**
Same as Model 755 except has 26-inch bbl. w/recoil-reducing, adj.
Savage Super Choke.

MODEL 775 LIGHTWEIGHT . . . . . **NiB $389 Ex $297 Gd $245**
Same general specifications as Model 755 except has lightweight alloy
receiver, weight: About 6.73 lbs. Made from 1950 to 1965.

MODEL 775-SC . . . . **NiB $410 Ex $300 Gd $255**
Same as Model 775 except has 26-inch bbl. with Savage Super
Choke.

**MODEL 2400 O/U
COMBINATION** . . . . **NiB $775 Ex $577 Gd $450**
Boxlock action similar to that of Model 330. Plain extractors. Selective
single trigger. 12-ga. (2.75-inch chamber) shotgun bbl., F choke over .308
Win. or .222 Rem. rifle bbl.; 23.5-inch; solid matted rib with blade front
sight and folding leaf rear, dovetail for scope mounting. Weight: About
7.5 lbs. Monte Carlo stock w/pistol grip and recoil pad, semibeavertail
forearm, checkered. Made 1975 to 1979 by Valmet.

Savage Model 2400
O/U Combination Gun

SEARS, ROEBUCK & COMPANY — Chicago, Illinois (J. C. Higgins and Ted Williams Models)

Although they do not correspond to specific models below, the names Ted Williams and J. C. Higgins have been used to designate various Sears shotguns at various times.

MODEL 18
BOLT-ACTION REPEATER. . . . . . .NiB $200 Ex $125 Gd $90
Takedown. Three round top-loading magazine. Gauge: .410 only. Bbl.: 25-inch w/variable choke. Weight: About 5.75 lbs.

MODEL 20 SLIDE-ACTION REPEATER .NiB $300 Ex $210 Gd $155
Hammerless. Five round magazine. Bbls.: 26- to 30-inch w/various chokes. Weight: 7.25 lbs. Plain pistol-grip stock and slide handle.

MODEL 21 SLIDE-ACTION REPEATER . . . NiB $320 Ex $235 Gd $190
Same general specifications as the Model 20 except vent rib and adustable choke.

MODEL 30 SLIDE-ACTION REPEATER . NiB $305 Ex $220 Gd $175
Hammerless. Gauges: 12, 16, 20 and .410. Four round magazine. Bbls.: 26- to 30-inch, various chokes. Weight: 6.5 lbs. Plain pistol-grip stock, grooved slide handle.

MODEL 97 SINGLE-SHOT SHOTGUN . . . NiB $165 Ex $100 Gd $79
Takedown. Visible hammer. Automatic ejector. Gauges: 12, 16, 20 and .410. Bbls.: 26- to 36-inch, F choke. Weight: Average 6 lbs. Plain pistol-grip stock and forearm.

MODEL 97-AC SINGLE-SHOT SHOTGUN . . NiB $190 Ex $121 Gd $89
Same general specifications as Model 97 except fancier stock and forearm.

MODEL 101.7 DOUBLE-BARREL
SHOTGUN. . . . . .NiB $335 Ex $229 Gd $175
Boxlock. Double triggers. Gauges: 12, 16, 20, .410. Bbls.: 26- to 32-inch, choked M and F. Weight: From 6 to 7.5 lbs. Plain stock and forend.

MODEL 101.7C DOUBLE-BARREL
SHOTGUN. . . . . .NiB $345 Ex $239 Gd $185
Same general specifications as Model 101.7 except checkered stock and forearm.

MODEL 101.25 BOLT-ACTION SHOTGUN . NiB $220 Ex $125 Gd $90
Takedown. .410 gauge. Five round tubular magazine. 24-inch bbl., F choke. Weight: About 6 lbs. Plain, one-piece pistol-grip stock.

MODEL 101.40 SINGLE-SHOT SHOTGUN . NiB $175 Ex $105 Gd $80
Takedown. Visible hammer. Automatic ejector. Gauges: 12, 16, 20 and .410. Bbls.: 26- to 36-inch, F choke. Weight: Average 6 lbs. Plain pistol-grip stock and forearm.

MODEL 101.1120 BOLT-ACTION REPEATER. .NiB $170 Ex $119 Gd $88
Takedown. .410 ga. 24-inch bbl., F choke. Weight: About 5 lbs. Plain one-piece pistol-grip stock.

MODEL 101.1380
BOLT-ACTION REPEATER . . . . NiB $195 Ex $130 Gd $95
Takedown. Gauges: 12, 16, 20. Two round detachable box magazine. 26-inch bbl., F choke. Weight: About 7 lbs. Plain one-piece pistol-grip stock.

MODEL 101.1610 DOUBLE-BARREL
SHOTGUN. . . . . .NiB $495 Ex $322 Gd $275
Boxlock. Double triggers. Plain extractors. Gauges: 12, 16, 20 and .410. Bbls.: 24- to 30-inch. Various chokes, but mostly M and F. Weight: About 7.5 lbs, 12 ga. Checkered pistol-grip stock and forearm.

MODEL 101.1701 DOUBLE-BARREL
SHOTGUN. . . . . .NiB $420 Ex $335 Gd $240
Same general specifications as Model 101.1610 except satin chrome frame and select walnut stock and forearm.

MODEL 101.5350-D
BOLT-ACTION REPEATER. . . . . . . .NiB $229 Ex $120 Gd $89
Takedown. Gauges: 12, 16, 20. Two round detachable box magazine. 26-inch bbl., F choke. Weight: About 7.25 lbs. Plain one piece pistol-grip stock.

MODEL 101.5410
BOLT-ACTION REPEATER. . . . . . . .NiB $200 Ex $115 Gd $90
Same general specifications as Model 101.5350-D.

SKB ARMS COMPANY — Tokyo, Japan
Imported by G.U. Inc., Omaha, Nebraska

MODEL 385
SIDE-BY-SIDE. . . . . .NiB $2200 Ex $1790 Gd $1176
Boxlock action w/double locking lugs. Gauges: 12, 20 and 28 w/2.75- and 3-inch chambers. 26- or 28-inch bbls. w/Inter-Choke tube system. Single selective trigger. Selective automatic ejectors and automatic safety. Weight: 6 lbs., 10 oz. Silver nitride receiver w/engraved scroll and game scene. Solid rib w/flat matte finish and metal front bead sight. Checkered American walnut English or pistol-grip stock. Imported from 1992.

MODELS 300 AND 400 SIDE-BY-SIDE SHOTGUNS
Similar to Model 200E except higher grade. Models 300 and 400 differ in that the latter has more elaborate engraving and fancier wood.
Model 300 . . . . NiB $1077 Ex $900 Gd $635
Model 400 . . . . NiB $1566 Ex $1309 Gd $1187

MODEL 400 SKEET. . . . . NiB $1566 Ex $1309 Gd $1187
Similar to Model 200E Skeet except higher grade with more elaborate engraving and full fancy wood.

MODEL 480 ENGLISH . . . . . . NiB $1766 Ex $1510 Gd $1377
Similar to Model 280 English except higher grade with more elaborate engraving and full fancy wood.

SHOTGUNS

SKB Model 585 Field

SKB Model 605 Trap

SKB Model 885 Trap

MODEL 500 SERIES O/U SHOTGUN
Boxlock. Gauges: 12 and 20 w/2.75-or 3-inch chambers. Bbls.: 26-, 28- or 30-inch with vent rib; fixed chokes. Weight: 7.5 to 8.5 lbs. Single selective trigger. Selective automatic ejectors. Manual safety. Checkered walnut stock. Blue finish with scroll engraving. Imported 1967 to 1980.
500 Field, 12 ga. . . . . .NiB $1000 Ex $750 Gd $415
500 Field, 20 ga, add. 20%
500 Magnum, 12 ga, add. 25%

MODEL 500 SMALL
GAUGE O/U SHOTGUN . . . . . . .NiB $884 Ex $652 Gd $466
Similar to Model 500 except gauges 28 and .410; has 28-inch vent-rib bbls., M/F chokes. Weight: About 6.5 lbs.

MODEL 505 O/U SHOTGUN
Blued boxlock action. Gauge: 12, 20, 28 and .410. Bbls.: 26-, 28, 30-inch; IC/M, M/F or inner choke tubes. 45.19 inches overall. Weight: 6.6 to 7.4 lbs. Hand checkered walnut stock. Metal bead front sight, ejectors, single selective trigger and ejectors. Introduced 1988.
Standard Field, Skeet or Trap grade. . . NiB $1365 Ex $1188 Gd $765
Standard Two-bbl. Field set . .NiB $1590 Ex $1277 Gd $1006
Skeet grade, three-bbl. set . . .NiB $1904 Ex $1888 Gd $1301
Sporting Clays . . . . .NiB $1189 Ex $977 Gd $668
Trap grade two-bbl. set . . . . .NiB $965 Ex $800 Gd $652

MODEL 585 O/U SHOTGUN
Boxlock. Gauges: 12, 20, 28 and .410; 2.75-or 3-inch chambers. Bbls.: 26-, 28-, 30-, 32- or 34-inch with vent rib; fixed chokes or Inter-choke tubes. Weight: 6.5 to 8.5 lbs. Single selective trigger. Selective automatic ejectors. Manual safety. Checkered walnut stock in standard or Monte Carlo style. Silver nitride finish with engraved game scenes. Made from 1992 to 2008.
Field, Skeet, Trap grades . . . . .NiB $1477 Ex $1211 Gd $933
Field grade, two-bbl. set . . . .NiB $2376 Ex $1969 Gd $1387
Skeet set (20, 28, .410 ga.) . . .NiB $2933 Ex $2460 Gd $1977
Sporting Clays . . . . .NiB $1700 Ex $1390 Gd $1054
Trap Combo (two-bbl. set) . . .NiB $2433 Ex $1976 Gd $1366

MODEL 600 SERIES O/U SHOTGUN
Similar to 500 Series except w/silver nitride receiver. Checkered deluxe walnut stock in both Field and Target Grade configurations . Imported from 1969 to 1980.
600 Field, 12 ga. . . . . .NiB $1093 Ex $773 Gd $540
600 Field, 20 ga. . . . . .NiB $1100 Ex $977 Gd $650
600 Magnum, 12 ga.
3-inch chambers. . . . . .NiB $1100 Ex $977 Gd $650
600 Skeet or Trap grade . . . . .NiB $1154 Ex $1008 Gd $690
600 Trap Doubles model . . . . .NiB $1154 Ex $1008 Gd $690

MODEL 600 SMALL GAUGE. . . .NiB $1210 Ex $945 Gd $650
Same as Model 500 Small Gauge except higher grade with more elaborate engraving and fancier wood.

MODEL 605 SERIES O/U SHOTGUN
Similar to the Model 505 except w/engraved silver nitride receiver and deluxe wood. Introduced 1988.
Field, Skeet, Trap grade . . . . . .NiB $1233 Ex $1026 Gd $779
Skeet three-bbl. set . . . . .NiB $2290 Ex $2003 Gd $1544
Sporting Clays . . . . .NiB $1266 Ex $1033 Gd $780

MODEL 680 ENGLISH O/U SHOTGUN
Similar to 600 Series except w/English style select walnut stock and fine scroll engraving. Imported from 1973 to 1977.
680 English, 12 ga. . . . . .NiB $1477 Ex $1179 Gd $993
680 English, 20 ga. . . . . .NiB $1788 Ex $1165 Gd $1055

MODEL 685 DELUXE O/U
Similar to the 585 Deluxe except with semi-fancy American walnut stock. Gold trigger and jeweled barrel block. Silvered receiver with fine engraving.
Field, Skeet, Trap grade . . . . .NiB $1477 Ex $1319 Gd $1066
Field grade, two-bbl. set . . . .NiB $1977 Ex $1819 Gd $1566
Skeet set . . . . .NiB $1977 Ex $1819 Gd $1566
Sporting Clays . . . . .NiB $1477 Ex $1319 Gd $1066
Trap Combo, two-bbl. set. . . .NiB $2189 Ex $1844 Gd $1360

Sile Field Master II

MODEL 800 SKEET/TRAP O/U
Similar to Model 700 Skeet and Trap except higher grade with more elaborate engraving and fancier wood.

Skeet model . . . . NiB $1329 Ex $1166 Gd $973
Trap model . . . . NiB $1266 Ex $1090 Gd $945

MODEL 880 SKEET/TRAP
Similar to Model 800 Skeet except has sideplates.

Skeet model . . . . NiB $1688 Ex $1470 Gd $1137
Trap model . . . . NiB $1859 Ex $1466 Gd $1123

MODEL 885 DELUXE O/U
Similar to the 685 Deluxe except with engraved sideplates.

Field, Skeet, Trap grade . . . . . NiB $1779 Ex $1456 Gd $1160
Field grade, two-bbl. set . . . . NiB $2665 Ex $2167 Gd $1800
Skeet Set . . . . NiB $1782 Ex $1693 Gd $1366
Sporting Clays . . . . NiB $1834 Ex $1500 Gd $1220
Trap Combo. . . . . NiB $2591 Ex $2277 Gd $1989

The following SKB shotguns were distributed by Ithaca Gun Co. from 1966-76. For specific data, see corresponding listings under Ithaca.

CENTURY SINGLE-BARREL TRAP GUN
The SKB catalog does not differentiate between Century and Century II; however, specifications of current Century are those of Ithaca-SKB Century II.

Century (505). . . . . NiB $966 Ex $831 Gd $634
Century II (605) . . . . NiB $1190 Ex $1006 Gd $798

GAS-OPERATED AUTOMATIC SHOTGUNS
Model XL300 with plain barrel . . . NiB $365 Ex $247 Gd $180
Model XL300 with vent rib . . . . . NiB $400 Ex $365 Gd $217
Model XL900 . . . . NiB $449 Ex $300 Gd $198
Model XL900 Trap . . . . NiB $487 Ex $376 Gd $221
Model XL900 Skeet. . . . . NiB $510 Ex $375 Gd $266
Model XL900 Slug . . . . NiB $488 Ex $370 Gd $259
Model 1300 Upland, Slug. . . . . . . NiB $598 Ex $455 Gd $290
Model 1900 Field, Trap, Slug . . . . NiB $588 Ex $443 Gd $376

SKB OVER/UNDER SHOTGUNS
Model 500 Field . . . . NiB $677 Ex $489 Gd $389
Model 500 Magnum . . . . NiB $690 Ex $500 Gd $421
Model 600 Field . . . . NiB $1070 Ex $883 Gd $600
Model 600 Magnum . . . . NiB $1165 Ex $955 Gd $690
Model 600 Trap . . . . NiB $1190 Ex $975 Gd $710
Model 600 Doubles . . . . NiB $1190 Ex $975 Gd $710
Model 600 Skeet—12 or 20 ga. . . . . . NiB $1190 Ex $975 Gd $710
Model 600 Skeet—28 or .410 . . . . . . NiB $1595 Ex $1266 Gd $1065
Model 600 Skeet Combo. . . . . NiB $2651 Ex $2210 Gd $2085
Model 600 English . . . . NiB $1190 Ex $975 Gd $710
Model 700 Trap . . . . NiB $950 Ex $844 Gd $630
Model 700 Doubles . . . . NiB $877 Ex $600 Gd $490
Model 700 Skeet . . . . NiB $988 Ex $765 Gd $633
Model 700 Skeet Combo. . . . . NiB $2690 Ex $2166 Gd $1650

SKB RECOIL-OPERATED AUTOMATIC SHOTGUNS
Model 300—with plain barrel . . . NiB $477 Ex $370 Gd $269
Model 300—with vent rib . . . . . . NiB $554 Ex $425 Gd $335
Model 900 . . . . NiB $559 Ex $400 Gd $298
Model 900 Slug . . . . NiB $573 Ex $455 Gd $360

SKB SIDE-BY-SIDE DOUBLE-BARREL SHOTGUNS
Model 100. . . . . NiB $795 Ex $650 Gd $425
Model 150. . . . . NiB $795 Ex $650 Gd $425
Model 200E . . . . NiB $1179 Ex $900 Gd $808
Model 200E Skeet . . . . NiB $1179 Ex $900 Gd $808
Model 280 English . . . . NiB $1280 Ex $1006 Gd $922

SIG SAUER — (SIG) Schweizerische Industrie-Gesellschaft, Neuhausen, Switzerland

MODEL SA3 O/U SHOTGUN
Monobloc boxlock action. Single selective trigger. Automatic ejectors. Gauges: 12 or 20 w/3- inch chambers. 26-, 28- or 30-inch vent rib bbls. w/choke tubes. Weight: 6.8 to 7.1 lbs. Checkered select walnut stock and forearm. Satin nickel-finished receiver w/game scene and blued bbls. Imported from 1997-98.

Field model . . . . NiB $1294 Ex $1126 Gd $966
Sporting Clays model . . . . NiB $1500 Ex $1398 Gd $1225

MODEL SA5 O/U SHOTGUN
Similar to SA3 Model except w/detachable sideplates. Gauges: 12 or 20 w/3- inch chambers. 26.5-, 28- or 30-inch vent rib bbls. w/choke tubes. Imported from 1997 to 1999.

Field model . . . . NiB $2288 Ex $2055 Gd $1530
Sporting Clays model . . . . NiB $2455 Ex $2160 Gd $1880

SILE DISTRIBUTORS — New York, New York

FIELD MASTER II O/U SHOTGUN. . . . . NiB $735 Ex $615 Gd $479
Gauge: 12, 3-inch chambers. 28-inch bbl., IC, M, IM, F choke tubes. 45.25 inches overall. Weight: 7.25 lbs. Satin-finished walnut, checkered stock and forend. Introduced 1989.

L.C. SMITH — Made 1890–1945 by Hunter Arms Company, Fulton, New York 1946–51 and 1968–73 and 2004 by Marlin Firearms Company, New Haven, Connecticut

L. C. SMITH DOUBLE-BARREL SHOTGUNS
Values shown are for L. C. Smith doubles made by Hunter. Those of 1946-51 Marlin manufacture generally bring prices about 1/3 lower. Smaller gauge models, especially in the higher grades, command premium prices: Up to 50 percent more for 20 gauge, up to 400 percent for .410.

GRADING: **NiB** = New in Box   **Ex** = Excellent or NRA 95%   **Gd** = Good or NRA 68%

L.C. Smith Crown

L.C. Smith Field

Crown grade, double triggers,
automatic ejectors . . . . . . NiB $11,650 Ex $9000 Gd $7750
Crown grade, selective single trigger,
automatic ejectors . . . . . NiB $12,275 Ex $10,200 Gd $9976
Deluxe grade, selective single trigger,
automatic ejectors . . . NiB $80,000 Ex $65,000 Gd $44,000
Eagle grade, double triggers,
automatic ejectors . . . . .NiB $7450 Ex $6600 Gd $3540
Eagle grade, selective
single trigger . . . . .NiB $8433 Ex $7210 Gd $4450
Field grade, double trigger
plain extractors . . . . .NiB $1877 Ex $1659 Gd $1200
Field grade, double triggers
auto. ej. . . . . .NiB $2400 Ex $2175 Gd $1765
Field grade, non-selective single trigger,
plain extractors . . . . .NiB $1788 Ex $1489 Gd $1016
Field grade, selective single trigger,
automatic ejectors. . . . . . .NiB $2276 Ex $1998 Gd $1688
Ideal grade, double triggers,
plain extractors . . . . .NiB $2698 Ex $2100 Gd $1933
Ideal grade, double triggers,
auto. ej. . . . . .NiB $3355 Ex $2288 Gd $1987
Ideal grade, selective single trigger,
automatic ejectors . . . . . .NiB $2979 Ex $2466 Gd $2132
Monogram grade, selective single trigger,
automatic ejectors . . NiB $17,800 Ex $15,888 Gd $11,880
Olympic grade, selective single trigger,
automatic ejectors . . . . . .NiB $7225 Ex $5179 Gd $3889
Premier grade, selective single trigger
automatic ejectors . . NiB $42,975 Ex $33,670 Gd $25,000
Skeet Special, non-selective single trigger,
automatic ejectors . . . . . .NiB $4055 Ex $3329 Gd $2165
Skeet Special, selective single trigger,
auto ejectors . . . . .NiB $4070 Ex $3360 Gd $2185
.410 ga. . . . . NiB $14,887 Ex $11,965 Gd $9865
Specialty grade, double triggers,
auto ejectors . . . . .NiB $4177 Ex $3688 Gd $3245
Specialty grade, selective single trigger,
automatic ejectors . . . . . . .NiB $3866 Ex $3390 Gd $2788
Trap grade, sel. single trigger,
auto ej. . . . . .NiB $3687 Ex $3255 Gd $2877

L. C. SMITH HAMMERLESS DOUBLE-BARREL SHOTGUNS

Sidelock. Auto ejectors standard on higher grades, extra on Field and Ideal Grades. Double triggers or Hunter single trigger (non-selective or selective). Gauges: 12, 16, 20, .410. Bbls.: 26- to 32-inch, any standard boring. Weight: 6.5 to 8.25 lbs., 12 ga. Checkered stock and forend; choice of straight, half or full pistol grip, beavertail or standard-type forend. Grades differ only in quality of workmanship, wood, checkering, engraving, etc. Same general specifications apply to all. Manufacture of these L. C. Smith guns

was discontinued in 1951. Production of Field Grade 12 ga. was resumed 1968-73. Note: L. C. Smith Shotguns manufactured by the Hunter Arms Co. 1890-13 were designated by numerals to indicate grade with the exception of Pigeon and Monogram.

00 grade . . . . NiB $1577 Ex $1369 Gd $1100
0 grade . . . . NiB $1735 Ex $1575 Gd $1244
1 grade . . . . NiB $2170 Ex $1876 Gd $1390
2 grade . . . . NiB $3533 Ex $2177 Gd $1566
3 grade . . . . NiB $4480 Ex $3066 Gd $2200
Pigeon . . . . NiB $5250 Ex $3688 Gd $2531
4 grade . . . . NiB $6244 Ex $5187 Gd $4966
5 grade . . . . .NiB $10,300 Ex $8879 Gd $6610
Monogram . . . . .NiB $13,975 Ex $11,755 Gd $10,000
A1 . . . . NiB $7225 Ex $4488 Gd $3240
A2. . . . . .NiB $14,779 Ex $11,960 Gd $10,066
A3 . . . . .NiB $42,600 Ex $37,988 Gd $32,776

HAMMERLESS DOUBLE
MODEL 1968 FIELD GRADE. . . .NiB $1165 Ex $980 Gd $644
Re-creation of the original L. C. Smith double. Sidelock. Plain extractors. Double triggers. 12 ga. 28-inch vent-rib bbls., M/F choke. Weight: About 6.75 lbs. Checkered pistol-grip stock and forearm. Made from 1968 to 1973.

HAMMERLESS DOUBLE
MODEL 1968 DELUXE . . . . . . .NiB $1688 Ex $1076 Gd $884
Same as 1968 Field Grade except has Simmons floating vent rib, beavertail forearm. Made from 1971 to 1973.

SINGLE-SHOT TRAP GUNS
Boxlock. Hammerless. Auto ejector.12 gauge only. Bbl. lengths: 32- or 34-inch. Vent rib. Weight: 8 to 8.25 lbs. Checkered pistol-grip stock and forend, recoil pad. Grades vary in quality of workmanship, wood, engraving, etc.; general specifications are the same. Disc. 1951. Note: Values shown are for L. C. Smith single-barrel trap guns made by Hunter. Those of Marlin manufacture generally bring prices about one-third lower.
Olympic grade. . . . . NiB $3188 Ex $2677 Gd $2190
Specialty grade. . . . . NiB $3598 Ex $3200 Gd $2560
Crown grade . . . . NiB $4488 Ex $3900 Gd $2677
Monogram grade . . . . NiB $8865 Ex $6231 Gd $4997
Premier grade. . . . . . . .Very rare (Three or fewer manufactured)
Deluxe grade . . . . .Very rare (Four or fewer manufactured)

NOTE: *Marlin resurrected the L.C. Smith brand from 2005 to 2009 importing O/U and S/S models from manufacturers in Italy and Spain.*

MODEL LC12. . . . . .NiB $860 Ex $800 Gd $560
O/U boxlock. Ejectors. !2 ga. only; 28-in. bbl., vent rib, choke tubes. Stock: fluer-de-lis checkered walnut w/ pistol grip.
LC20 (20 ga.) . . . . .NiB $1000 Ex $875 Gd $580

L.C. Smith 1968 Field Grade

L.C. Smith 1968 Deluxe

L.C. Smith Single-Shot Trap Gun

Smith & Wesson Model 1000 Magnum

Smith & Wesson Model 3000 Slide Action

MODEL LC12 DB . . . . NiB $1400 Ex $1280 Gd $900
S/S boxlock. Ejectors. Detachable side plates. !2 ga. only; 28-in. bbl., vent rib, choke tubes. Stock: fluer-de-lis checkered walnut w/ pistol grip, beavertail forend.
LC20 DB (20 ga.) . . . . NiB $1600 Ex $1480 Gd $1200
LC28 DB (28 ga.) . . . . NiB $1900 Ex $1695 Gd $1395
LC410 DB (.410) . . . . NiB $1900 Ex $1695 Gd $1395

SMITH & WESSON — Springfield, Massachusetts
Howa manufactured, disc. 1984.

MDEL 916 SLIDE-ACTION REPEATER
Hammerless. Solid frame. Gauges: 12, 16, 20. Three inch chamber in 12 and 20 ga. Five round tubular magazine. Bbls.: plain or vent rib; 20-inch C (12 ga., plain only); 26-inch IC- 28-inch M or F; 30-inch F choke (12 ga. only). Weight: With 28-inch plain bbl., 7.25 lbs. Plain pistol-grip stock, fluted slide handle. Made 1972 to 1981.
Plain bbl. . . . . .NiB $225 Ex $170 Gd $110
Ventilated rib bbl. . . . . .NiB $255 Ex $185 Gd $120

MODEL 916T
Same as Model 916 except takedown, 12 ga. only. Not available with 20-inch bbl. Made from 1976 to 1981.
Plain bbl. . . . . .NiB $250 Ex $180 Gd $115
Ventilated rib bbl. . . . . .NiB $275 Ex $200 Gd $140

MODEL 1000 AUTOLOADER . . . .NiB $433 Ex $355 Gd $240
Gas-operated. Takedown. Gauges: 12, 20. 2.75-inch chamber in 12 ga., 3-inch in 20 ga. Four round magazine. Bbls.: Vent rib, 26-inch SK choke, IC; 28-inch M or F; 30-inch F choke (12 ga. only). Weight: With 28-inch bbl., 6.5 lbs. in 20 ga.,7.5 lbs. in 12 ga. Checkered pistol-grip stock and forearm. Made from 1972. Disc.

MODEL 3000
SLIDE ACTION . . . . .NiB $425 Ex $295 Gd $190
Hammerless. 20-ga. Bbls.: 26-inch IC; 28-inch M or F. Chambered for 3-inch magnum and 2.75-inch loads. American walnut stock and forearm. Checkered pistol grip and forearm. Introduced 1982.

MODEL 1000 . . . . .NiB $425 Ex $295 Gd $190
Same as Model 3000 but an earlier version.

MODEL 1000 MAGNUM . . . . . . .NiB $595 Ex $445 Gd $398
Same as standard Model 1000 except chambered for 12 ga. magnum, 3-inch shells; 30-inch bbl. only, M or F choke; stock with recoil pad. Weight: About 8 lbs. Introduced in 1977.

SPRINGFIELD ARMS — Built by Savage Arms Company, Utica, New York

SPRINGFIELD DOUBLE-BARREL
HAMMER SHOTGUN . . . . .NiB $588 Ex $439 Gd $366
Gauges: 12 and 16. Bbls.: 28 to 32 inches. In 12 ga., 32-inch model, both bbls. have F choke. All other gauges and barrel lengths are left barrel, Full; right barrel, Mod. Weight: 7.25 to 8.25 lbs., depending on gauge and bar rel length. Black walnut checkered buttstock and forend. Disc. 1934.

GRADING: **NiB** = New in Box   **Ex** = Excellent or NRA 95%   **Gd** = Good or NRA 68%

SHOTGUNS

Squires Bingham Model 30 Pump Shotgun

SQUIRES BINGHAM CO., INC. — Makati, Rizal, Philippines

MODEL 30
PUM P SHOTGUN . . . .**NiB $366 Ex $255 Gd $175**
Hammerless. 12 ga. Five round magazine. Bbl.: 20-inch Cyl.; 28-inch M; 30-inch F choke. Weight: About 7 lbs. Pulong Dalaga stock and slide handle. Currently manufactured.

J. STEVENS ARMS COMPANY — Chicopee Falls, Massachusetts; division of Savage Arms Corporation

NO. 20 "FAVORITE" SHOTGUN. .NiB $325 Ex $217 Gd $140
Calibers: .22 and .32 shot. Smoothbore bbl. Blade front sight; no rear. Made from 1893 to 1939.

NO. 39 NEW MODEL
POCKET SHOTGUN . . . .**NiB $800 Ex $605 Gd $490**
Gauge: .410. Calibers: .38-40 shot, .44-40 shot. Bbls.: 10, 12, 15 or 18 inches, half-octagonal smoothbore. Shotgun sights. Made 1895 to 1906.

NO. 22-.410 O/U COMBINATION GUN
.22 caliber rifle barrel over .410 ga. shotgun barrel. Visible hammer. Takedown. Single trigger. 24-inch bbls., shotgun bbl. F choke. Weight: About 6 lbs. Open rear sight and ramp front sight of sporting rifle type. Plain pistol-grip stock and forearm; originally supplied with walnut stock and forearm. "Tenite" (plastic) was used in later production. Made 1939 to 1950. Note: This gun is now manufactured as the Savage Model 24.
Wood stock and forearm . . . .**NiB $545 Ex $435 Gd $300**
Tenite stock and forearm . . . .**NiB $525 Ex $460 Gd $345**

MODEL 51 BOLT-ACTION
SHOTGUN. . . . .**NiB $235 Ex $154 Gd $95**
Single shot. Takedown. .410 ga. 24-inch bbl., F choke. Weight: About 4.75 lbs. Plain one-piece pistol-grip stock. checkered on later models. Made from 1962 to 1971.

MODEL 58 BOLT-ACTION
REPEATER . . . .**NiB $254 Ex $165 Gd $120**
Takedown. Gauges: 12, 16, 20. Two round detachable box magazine. 26-inch bbl., F choke. Weight: About 7.25 lbs. Plain one piece pistol-grip stock on early models w/takedown screw on bottom of forend. Made 1933-81. Note: Later production models have 3-inch chamber in 20 ga., checkered stock with recoil pad.

MODEL 58-.410 BOLT-ACTION
REPEATER . . . .**NiB $225 Ex $130 Gd $95**
Takedown. .410 ga. Three round detachable box magazine. 24-inch bbl., F choke. Weight: About 5.5 lbs. Plain one piece pistol-grip stock, checkered on later production. Made from 1937 to 1981.

MODEL 59 BOLT-ACTION
REPEATER . . . .**NiB $255 Ex $190 Gd $135**
Takedown. .410 ga. Five round tubular magazine. 24-inch bbl., F choke. Weight: About 6 lbs. Plain, one piece pistol-grip stock, check-

ered on later production. Made from 1934 to 1973.

MODEL 67 PUMP SHOTGUN
Hammerless, side-ejection solid-steel receiver. Gauges: 12, 20 and .410, 2.75- or 3-inch shells. Bbls.: 21-, 26-, 28- 30-inch with fixed chokes or interchangeable choke tubes, plain or vent rib. Weight: 6.25 to 7.5 lbs. Optional rifle sights. Walnut-finished hardwood stock with corncob-style forend.
Standard model, plain bbl. . . . . . .**NiB $245 Ex $195 Gd $120**
Standard model, vent rib . . . . . .**NiB $255 Ex $205 Gd $125**
Standard model, w/choke tubes . .**NiB $275 Ex $220 Gd $155**
Slug model w/rifle sights . . . .**NiB $255 Ex $205 Gd $125**
Lobo model, matte finish . . . . . .**NiB $255 Ex $205 Gd $125**
Youth model, 20 ga. . . . .**NiB $260 Ex $210 Gd $130**
Camo model. w/choke tubes . . . .**NiB $275 Ex $220 Gd $155**

MODEL 67 WATERFOWL SHOTGUN . . . NiB $335 Ex $200 Gd $135
Hammerless. Gauge: 12. Three round tubular magazine. Walnut finished hardwood stock. Weight: About 7.5 lbs. Made 1972 to 1989.

MODEL 77 SLIDE-ACTION REPEATER. . . . NiB $225 Ex $130 Gd $95
Solid frame. Gauges: 12, 16, 20. Five round tubular magazine. Bbls.: 26-inch IC, 28-inch M or F choke. Weight: About 7.5 lbs. Plain pistol-grip stock with recoil pad, grooved slide handle. Made from 1954 to 1971.

MODEL 77-AC . . . .**NiB $217 Ex $125 Gd $95**
Same as Model 77 except has Savage Super Choke.

MODEL 79-VR SUPER VALUE. . . .NiB $355 Ex $265 Gd $190
Hammerless, side ejection. Bbl.: Chambered for 2.75-inch and 3-inch mag. shells. 12, 20, and .410 ga. vent rib. Walnut finished hardwood stock with checkering on grip. Weight: 6.75-7 lbs. Made 1979 to 1990.

MODEL 94 SINGLE-SHOT SHOTGUN . NiB $165 Ex $95 Gd $70
Takedown. Visible hammer. Auto ejector. Gauges: 12, 16, 20, 28, .410. Bbls.: 26-, 28-, 30-, 32-, 36-inch, F choke. Weight: About 6 lbs. depending on gauge and barrel. Plain pistol-grip stock and forearm. Made from 1939 to 1961.

MODEL 94C. . . . .**NiB $165 Ex $95 Gd $70**
Same as Model 94 except has checkered stock, fluted forearm on late production. Made from 1965 to 1990.

MODEL 94Y YOUTH GUN. . . . .**NiB $165 Ex $95 Gd $70**
Same as Model 94 except made in 20 and .410 ga. only; has 26-inch F choke bbl., 12.5-inch buttstock with recoil pad; checkered pistol grip and fluted forend on late production. Made from 1959 to 1990.

MODEL 95 SINGLE-SHOT SHOTGUN NiB $200 Ex $140 Gd $95
Solid frame. Visible hammer. Plain extractor. 12 ga. Three-inch chamber. Bbls.: 28-inch M- 30-inch F choke. Weight: About 7.25 lbs. Plain pistol-grip stock, grooved forearm. Made 1965 to 1969.

MODEL 107 SINGLE-SHOT
HAMMER SHOTGUN . . . .**NiB $217 Ex $129 Gd $95**
Takedown. Auto ejector. Gauges: 12, 16, 20, .410. Bbl. lengths: 28- and 30-inch (12 and 16 ga.), 28-inch (20 ga.), 26-inch (.410); F choke only.

Stevens Model 51

Stevens Model 58

Stevens Model 58-410

Stevens Model 67 Pump Shotgun

Stevens Model 67 Waterfowl Shotgun

Stevens Model 77

Stevens Model 94C

Stevens Model 95

SHOTGUNS

Stevens Model 94
Youth

Stevens Model 124
Cross-Bolt Repeater

Weight: About 6 lbs., 12 bore ga. Plain pistol-grip stock and forearm. Made from about 1937 to 1953.

MODEL 124
BOLT-ACTION REPEATER . . . . NiB $265 Ex $198 Gd $155
Hammerless. Solid frame. 12 ga. only. Two round tubular magazine. 28-inch bbl.; IC, M or F choke. Weight: About 7 lbs. Tenite stock and forearm. Made from 1947 to 1952.

MODEL 240 O/U SHOTGUN . . . . NiB $448 Ex $375 Gd $270
Visible hammer. Takedown. Double triggers. .410 ga. 26-inch bbls., F choke. Weight: 6 lbs. Tenite (plastic) pistol-grip stock and forearm. Made from 1940 to 1949.

MODEL 258 BOLT-ACTION
REPEATER . . . . .NiB $290 Ex $174 Gd $100
Takedown. 20-gauge. Two round detachable box magazine. 26-inch barrel, Full choke. Weight: About 6.25 lbs. Plain, one piece pistol-grip stock. Made from 1937 to 1965.

MODEL 311 SPRINGFIELD HAMMERLESS DOUBLE
Same general specifications as Stevens Model 530 except earlier production has plain stock and forearm; checkered on current guns. Originally produced as a "Springfield" gun, this model became a part of the Stevens line in 1948 when the Springfield brand name was discontinued. Made from 1931 to 1989.
Pre-WWII . . . . .NiB $675 Ex $450 Gd $325
Post-WWII . . . . .NiB $335 Ex $200 Gd $125

MODEL 311-R
HAMMERLESS DOUBLE . . . . .NiB $300 Ex $225 Gd $145
Same general specifications as Stevens Model 311 except compact design for law enforcement use. Bbls.: 18.25-inch 12 gauge with solid rib, chambered for 2.75 and 3-inch Mag. shells. Double triggers and auto top tang safety. Walnut finished hardwood stock with recoil pad and semi-beavertail forend. Weight: About 6.75 lbs. Made from 1982 to 1989.

MODEL 530
HAMMERLESS DOUBLE . . . . . . .NiB $335 Ex $245 Gd $200
Boxlock. Double triggers. Gauges: 12, 16, 20, .410. Bbl. lengths: 26- to 32-inch; choked M/F, C/M, F/F. Weight: 6 to 7.5 pounds depending on gauge and barrel length. Checkered pistol-grip stock and forearm; some early models with recoil pad. Made from 1936 to 1954.

MODEL 530M . . . . .NiB $339 Ex $255 Gd $210
Same as Model 530 except has Tenite (plastic) stock and forearm. Disc. about 1947.

MODEL 530ST DOUBLE GUN . . .NiB $339 Ex $255 Gd $210
Same as Model 530 except has non-selective single trigger. Disc.

MODEL 620 HAMMERLESS SLIDE-ACTION
REPEATING SHOTGUN . . . . .NiB $400 Ex $255 Gd $180
Takedown. Gauges: 12, 16, 20. Five round tubular magazine. Bbl. lengths: 26-, 28-, 30-, 32-inch; choked F, M IC, C. Weight: About 7.75 lbs., 12 ga.; 7.25 lbs., 16 ga.- 6 lbs., 20 ga. Checkered pistol-grip stock and slide handle. Made from 1927 to 1953.

MODEL 620-C . . . . .NiB $365 Ex $255 Gd $160
Same specifications as Model 620 except equipped with Cutts Compensator and two choke tubes.

MODEL 620-P . . . . .NiB $288 Ex $200 Gd $155
Same specifications as Model 620 equipped with Aero-Dyne PolyChoke and 27-inch bbl.

MODEL 620-PV . . . . .NiB $280 Ex $190 Gd $155
Same specifications as Model 620 except equipped with ventilated PolyChoke and 27-inch bbl.

MODEL 621 . . . . .NiB $359 Ex $210 Gd $155
Same as Model 620 except has raised solid matted-rib barrel. Disc.

MODEL 820 HAMMERLESS
REPEATING SHOTGUN . . . . .NiB $388 Ex $266 Gd $190
Solid frame. 12 gauge only. Five round tubular magazine. 28-inch barrel; IC, M or F choke. Weight: About 7.5 lbs. Plain pistol-grip stock, grooved slide handle. Early models furnished w/Tenite buttstock and forend. Made from 1949 to 1954.

MODEL 820-SC . . . . .NiB $400 Ex $330 Gd $217
Same as Model 820 except has Savage Super Choke.

MODEL 940 SINGLE-
SHOT SHOTGUN. . . . . .NiB $256 Ex $138 Gd $110
Same general specifications as Model 94 except has side lever opening instead of top lever. Made from 1961 to 1970.

MODEL 940Y
YOUTH GUN. . . . . .NiB $265 Ex $155 Gd $115
Same general specifications as Model 94Y except has side lever opening instead of top lever. Made from 1961 to 1970.

Stevens Model 258

Stevens Model 311

Stevens Model 530

Stevens Model 620

Stevens Model 620-P

Stevens Model 820

MODEL 9478 . . . .**NiB $145 Ex $90 Gd $65**
Takedown. Visible hammer. Automatic ejector. Gauges: 12, 20, .410.
Bbls.: 26-, 28-, 30-, 36-inch; Full choke. Weight: Average 6 pounds
depending on gauge and barrel. Plain pistol-grip stock and forearm.
Made from 1978 to 1985.

MODEL 5151 SPRINGFIELD . . . . .**NiB $556 Ex $435 Gd $300**
Same specifications as the Stevens Model 311 except with checkered
grip and forend; equipped with recoil pad and two ivory sights.

STOEGER
See IGA and Tikka shotguns.

TAR-HUNT CUSTOM RIFLES, INC. —
Bloomsburg, Pennsylvania

MODEL RSG-12 MATCHLESS
BOLT-ACTION SLUG GUN. . .**NiB $2366 Ex $2165 Gd $1590**
Similar to Professional model except has McMillan Fibergrain stock
and deluxe blue finish. Made from 1995 to 2004.

MODEL RSG-12 PEERLESS
BOLT-ACTION SLUG GUN. . .**NiB $2944 Ex $2577 Gd $2320**
Similar to Professional model except has McMillan Fibergrain
stock and deluxe NP-3 (Nickel/Teflon) metal finish. Made from
1995 to 2004.

MODEL RSG-12 PROFESSIONAL
BOLT-ACTION SLUG GUN

Bolt action 12 ga. w/2.75-inch chamber, 2-round detachable magazine, 21.5-inch fully rifled bbl. w/ or w/o muzzle brake. Receiver drilled and tapped for scope mounts w/no sights. Weight: 7.75 lbs. 41.5 inches overall. Checkered black McMillan fiberglass stock w/ swivel studs and Pachmayr Deacelerator pad. Made from 1991 to 2004.

RSG-12 model
  w/o muzzle brake (disc. 1993) . . .NiB $2688 Ex $2320 Gd $1997
RSG-12 model
  w/muzzle brake . . . . .NiB $2700 Ex $2375 Gd $2044

MODEL RSG-20 MOUNTAINEER
BOLT ACTION SLUG GUN. . .NiB $2276 Ex $1966 Gd $1433
Similar to Professional model except 20 ga. w/2.75 inch chamber. Black McMillan synthetic stock w/blind magazine. Weight: 6.5 lbs. Made from 1997 to 2004.

TECNI-MEC SHOTGUNS — Italy. Imported by RAHN Gun Work, Inc., Hastings, MI

MODEL SPL 640 FOLDING SHOTGUN
Gauges: 12, 16, 20, 24, 28, 32 and .410 bore. 26-inch bbl. Chokes: IC/IM. Weight: 6.5 lbs. Checkered walnut pistol-grip stock and forend. Engraved receiver. Available with single or double triggers. Imported from 1988 to 1994.

w/single trigger. . . . . .NiB $596 Ex $477 Gd $369
w/double trigger . . . . .NiB $655 Ex $498 Gd $388

THOMPSON/CENTER ARMS — Rochester, New Hampshire, and Springfield, Massachusetts
Purchased by Smith & Wesson in 2006.

CONTENDER
.410 CARBINE . . . . .NiB $500 Ex $387 Gd $279
Gauge: .410 smoothbore. 21-inch vent rib bbl. 34.75 inches overall. Weight: About 5.25 lbs. Bead front sight. Rynite stock and forend. Made 1991 to date.

ENCORE 20 GA. SHOTGUN
Gauge: 20 smoothbore w/rifled slug bbl. or 26-inch vent-rib bbl. w/ three internal screw choke tubes, 38 to 40.5 inches overall. Weight: About 5.25 to 6 lbs. Bead or fiber optic sights. Walnut stock and forend. Made from 1998 to date.

Encore 20 ga.
  w/vent rib . . . . .NiB $485 Ex $390 Gd $275
Encore 20 ga.
  w/rifled slug bbl. . . . . .NiB $522 Ex $421 Gd $300
w/extra bbl., add $325

HUNTER SHOTGUN MODEL . . . .NiB $580 Ex $466 Gd $355
Single shot. Gauge: 10 or 12, 3.5-inch chamber, 25-inch field bbl. with F choke. Weight: 8 lbs. Bead front sight. American black walnut stock with recoil pad. Made from 1987 to 1992.

HUNTER SLUG MODEL . . . . . . .NiB $580 Ex $466 Gd $355
Gauge: 10 (3.5-inch chamber) or 12 (3-inch chamber). Same general specifications as Model '87 Hunter Shotgun except with 22-inch slug (rifled) bbl. and rifle sights. Made from 1987 to 1992.

TIKKA — Manufactured by Sako, Ltd. in Armi Marocchi, Italy

M 07 SHOTGUN/
RIFLE COMBINATION . . . . . . .NiB $1287 Ex $1009 Gd $766
Gauge/caliber: 12/.222 Rem. Shotgun bbl.: About 25 inches; rifled bbl.: About 22.75 inches. 40.66 inches overall. Weight: About 7 lbs. Dovetailed for telescopic sight mounts Single trigger with selector between the bbls. Vent rib. Monte Carlo-style walnut stock with checkered pistol grip and forend. Made from 1965 to 1987.

M 77 O/U SHOTGUN . . . . . . .NiB $1345 Ex $1265 Gd $950
Gauge: 12. 27-inch vent-rib bbls., approx. 44 inches overall, weight: About 7.25 lbs. Bbl. selector. Ejectors. Monte Carlo-style walnut stock with checkered pistol grip and forend; rollover cheekpiece. Made from 1977 to 1987.

M 77K SHOTGUN/ RIFLE
COMBINATION. . . . . .NiB $1733 Ex $1388 Gd $1009
Gauge: 12/70. Calibers: .222 Rem., 5.6x52r5, 6.5x55, 7x57r5, 7x65r5, .308 Win. Vent-rib bbls.: About 25 inches (shotgun); 23 inches (rifle), 42.3 inches overall. Weight: About 7.5 lbs. Double triggers. Monte Carlo-style walnut stock with checkered pistol grip and forend; rollover cheekpiece. Made from 1977 to 1986.

412S/512S SHOOTING SYSTEM
Boxlock action with both under lug and sliding top latch locking mechanism designed to accept interchangeable monobloc barrels, including O/U shotgun, combination and double rifle configurations. Blued or satin nickel receiver w/ cocking indicators. Selective single trigger design w/barrel selector incorporated into the trigger (double triggers available). Blued barrels assemblies w/ extractors or auto ejectors as required. Select American walnut stock with checkered pistol grip and forend. Previously produced in Finland (same as the former Valmet Model 412) but currently manufactured in Italy by joint venture arrangement with Armi Marocchi. From 1990-93, Stoeger Industries imported this model as the 412/S. In 1993 the nomenclature of this shooting system was changed to 512/S. Disc. 1997. Note: For double rifle values, see Tikka Rifles.

MODEL 412S/512S O/U SHOTGUN
Gauge: 12 w/3-inch chambers. 24-, 26-, 28- or 30-inch chrome-lined bbls. w/blued finish and integral stainless steel choke tubes. Weight: 7.25 to 7.5 lbs. Blue or matte nickel receiver. Select American walnut from stock with checkered pistol grip and forend. Imported 1990 to 1997.

Standard Field model . . . . NiB $1145	Ex $989	Gd $766
Standard Trap model . . . . NiB $1277	Ex $1050	Gd $766
Premium Field model . . . . NiB $1688	Ex $1279	Gd $1100
Premium Trap model . . . . NiB $1688	Ex $1279	Gd $1100
Sporting Clays model . . . . NiB $1233	Ex $1054	Gd $866
w/extra O/U shotgun bbl., add. $700		
w/extra O/U combo bbl., add $800		
w/extra O/U rifle bbl., add. $1025		

MODEL 412S/512S OVER/UNDER COMBINATION
Gauge: 12 w/3-inch chamber. Calibers: .222 Rem., .30-06 or .308 Win. Blue or matte nickel receiver, 24-inch chrome-lined bbls. w/extractors and blued finish. Weight: 7.25 to 7.5 lbs. Select American walnut stock with checkered pistol grip and forend. Imported from 1990 to 1997.

Standard Combination model . . . . . .NiB $1598 Ex $1335 Gd $1109
Premium Combination model . . . . . .NiB $1622 Ex $1365 Gd $1135
Extra barrel options, add. $800

TRADITIONS PERFORMANCE FIREARMS —
Importers of shotguns produced by Fausti Stefano of Brescia, Italy, and ATA Firearms, Turkey

FIELD HUNTER MODEL . . . . **NiB $825 Ex $630 Gd $535**
Same as Field I except 12 and 20 gauge, 3-inch chambers, screw-in chokes and extractors.

CLASSIC SERIES, FIELD I O/U . . . . . **NiB $853 Ex $677 Gd $545**
Available in 12, 20, 28 (2 3/4-inch chamber) and .410 gauge, 26- or 28-inch vent rib bbls. W/fixed chokes and extractors. Weight: 6 3/4 to 7 1/4 lbs. Blued finish, silver receiver engraved with game birds. Single, selective trigger. Brass bead front sight. European walnut stock. Overall length 43 to 45 inches. Intro. 2000.

FIELD II MODEL . . . . **NiB $945 Ex $679 Gd $555**
Same as Field I except with screw-in chokes and automatic ejectors.

FIELD III GOLD MODEL . . . . **NiB $1217 Ex $1109 Gd $998**
Same as Field I model except 12 gauge only, high-grade, oil-finish walnut, coin-finish receiver with engraved pheasants and woodcock, deep blue finish on barrels, automatic ejectors and non-slip recoil pad.

SPORTING CLAY II MODEL . . . . . **NiB $1165 Ex $977 Gd $620**
Same as Sporting Clay III model but with European walnut stocks, cut checkering and extended choke tubes. Overall length: 47 inches. Weight: 7 3/4 lbs.

CLASSIC SERIES O/U
SPORTING CLAY III . . . . **NiB $1200 Ex $1095 Gd $985**
Available in 12 and 20 gauge, 3-inch chambers, high grade walnut stock, oil-satin finish, palm swell Schnabel forend. 28- and 30-inch bbls. with 3/8-inch top and middle vent rib, red target front bead sight. Automatic ejectors, extended choke tubes. Weight: 8 1/4 lbs. Intro. 2000.

UPLAND II MODEL . . . . **NiB $1065 Ex $775 Gd $546**
Same as Upland III model except with English walnut straight-grip stock and Schnabel forend, 24- and 26-inch vent rib bbls., floral engraving on blued receiver, automatic ejectors.

UPLAND III MODEL . . . . **NiB $1187 Ex $977 Gd $755**
Same as Sporting Clay III model but round pistol grip and Schnabel forend, blued receiver with engraved upland scene, weight: 7 1/2 lbs.

MAG 350 SERIES TURKEY II O/U . . . . . **NiB $1144 Ex $942 Gd $700**
Magnum 3 1/2-inch chambers in 12 gauge only, 24- and 26-inch bbls., screw-in flush fitting chokes: F and XF. Matte finish, engraved receiver, Mossy Oak or Realtree camo. Intro. 2000.

WATERFOWL II MODEL . . . . **NiB $1159 Ex $910 Gd $715**
Same as Turkey II model except with Advantage Wetlands camo stock and barrels, weight: 8 lbs., overall length 45 inches. Waterfowl model has 28-inch bbls.

MAG HUNTER II . . . . **NiB $1159 Ex $910 Gd $715**
Same as Turkey II model except blued engraved receiver and matte finish walnut stocks, 3 1/2-inch chambers, 28-inch bbls. with screw-in chokes.

ELITE HUNTER . . . . **NiB $1256 Ex $1044 Gd $770**
Same as Elite Field model except 12 and 20 gauge, European walnut stock, beavertail forend, screw-in choke tubes, extractors, three-inch chambers. Blued finish. Vent-rib, tang safety. Weight: 6 1/2 pounds.

ELITE FIELD I DT . . . . **NiB $1006 Ex $853 Gd $600**
Same as Elite Field I except with double triggers, fixed chokes, extractors. Available in 12, 20, 28 (2 3/4-inch chambers) and .410. Bbls: 26 inches, fixed IC/M chokes. Weight: 5 1/2 to 6 1/4 lbs

ELITE FIELD I ST . . . . **NiB $1118 Ex $1065 Gd $790**
Same as Elite Field I except single trigger, fixed chokes, extractors; European walnut stock. Available in 12, 20, 28 (2 3/4-inch chambers) and .410 gauge; fixed IC/M chokes. Weight: 5 3/4 to 6 1/2 lbs.

ELITE FIELD III ST . . . . **NiB $1967 Ex $1689 Gd $1333**
Checkered English walnut straight stock, splinter forend, fixed chokes. Available in 28 and .410 gauge, 26-inch chrome-lined bbls., Cylinder and Modified chokes. Silver trigger guard and receiver with hand-finished engraving of upland game scenes with gold inlays. Automatic ejectors. Brass front sight bead. Weight: About 6 1/2 lbs. Intro. 2000.

AL 2100 SEMI-AUTO SHOTGUNS
FIELD SERIES, WALNUT MODEL . . . . . .**NiB $366 Ex $245 Gd $190**
Gas-operated, 12 and 20 gauge, 3-inch chambers, cut-checkered Turkish walnut stock and forend, blued 26- and 28-inch vent rib bbls., multi-choke system, chrome bore lining. Weight: About 6 lbs. Rifled barrel with cantilever mount available Intro. 2001.

SYNTHETIC STOCK MODEL . . . . . **NiB $350 Ex $290 Gd $225**
Same as the ALS 2100 Walnut model except with synthetic stock, matted finish on receiver and bbl., weight: About 6 lbs.

YOUTH MODEL . . . . **NiB $344 Ex $229 Gd $175**
Same as ALS 2100 Walnut model except with a shorter walnut stock (length of pull: 13 1/2 inches). Available in 12 or 20 gauge with 24-inch vent rib barrel, weight: 5 1/2 to 6 lbs.

HUNTER COMBO MODEL
Same as ALS 2100 Walnut model except comes with two bbls. (28-inch vent rib and 24-inch slug), TruGlo adjustable sights and cantilever mount. Available with Turkish walnut or synthetic stock with matte barrel finish. Weight: 6 1/2 lbs.
Walnut stock. . . . .**NiB $500 Ex $377 Gd $210**
Synthetic stock . . . .**NiB $475 Ex $339 Gd $220**

SLUG HUNTER MODEL . . . . **NiB $355 Ex $245 Gd $190**
Same as ALS 2100 Walnut except with fully-rifled barrel, choice of walnut or synthetic stocks, matte or blue finish; rifle or TruGlo adjustable sights. Weight: About 6 1/4 lbs.

TURKEY HUNTER/
WATERFOWL MODEL . . . . **NiB $375 Ex $265 Gd $220**
Same as ALS 2100 Walnut except with synthetic stock, 3-inch chambers, 26-inch vent rib bbl., screw-in chokes, Mossy Oak or Realtree camo stocks.

HOME SECURITY MODEL . . . . **NiB $335 Ex $260 Gd $190**
Same as ALS 2100 Walnut but with 20-inch cylinder-bore bbl., synthetic stock, 3-inch chambers, six-round capacity with 2 3/4-inch shells. Weight: About 6 lbs.

SHOTGUNS

Valmet Model 412 K
O/U Field Shotgun

Ward Western Field Model 50

Ward Western Field Model 52

TRISTAR SPORTING ARMS — North Kansas City, Missouri

MODEL 1887 LEVER-ACTION REPEATER...... NiB $765 Ex $580 Gd $445
Copy of John Browning's Winchester Model 1887 lever-action shotgun. 12 ga. only. 30-inch bbl. which may be cut down to any desired length of 18 inches or more. Version shown has 20-inch bbl. Imported from 1997 to 1999.

MODEL 300 O/U SHOTGUN .... NiB $465 Ex $335 Gd $199
Similar to the Model 333 except 12 ga. only w/3-inch chambers, 26- or 28-inch vent rib bbls. w/extractors and fixed chokes. Etched receiver w/ double triggers and standard walnut stock. Imported 1994 to 1998.

MODEL 311 SIDE-BY-SIDE SHOTGUN
Boxlock action w/underlug and Greener cross bolt. 12 or 20 ga. w/3-inch chambers, 20, 28- or 30-inch bbls. w/choke tubes or fixed chokes (311R). Double triggers. Extractors. Black chrome finish. Checkered Turkish walnut buttstock and forend. Weight: 6.9 to 7.2 lbs. Imported from 1994 to 1997.
311 Model (w/extractors and choke tubes).. NiB $575 Ex $476 Gd $390
311R Model
  (w/20-inch bbls. and fixed chokes) ... NiB $445 Ex $355 Gd $235

MODEL 330 O/U SHOTGUN
Similar to the Model 333 except 12 ga. only w/3-inch chambers. 26-, 28- or 30-inch vent rib bbls w/extractors or ejectors and fixed chokes or choke tubes. Etched receiver and standard walnut stock. Imported from 1994 to 1999.
330 model (w/ extractor and fixed chokes).. NiB $545 Ex $420 Gd $300
330 D model (w/ejectors and choke tubes) . NiB $733 Ex $567 Gd $488

MODEL 333 O/U SHOTGUN
Boxlock action. 12 or 20 ga. w/3-inch chambers. 26-, 28- or 30-inch vent rib bbls. w/choke tubes. Single selective trigger. Selective automatic ejectors. Engraved receiver w/satin nickel finish. Checkered Turkish fancy walnut buttstock and forend. Weight: 7.5 to 7.75 lbs. Imported from 1994 to 1998.
Field model .... NiB $844 Ex $700 Gd $545
Sporting Clays model (1994-97)....... NiB $900 Ex $755 Gd $580
TRL Ladies Field model........... NiB $800 Ex $675 Gd $550
SCL Ladies Sporting Clays model
  (1994-97)................. NiB $900 Ex $755 Gd $580

SHOTGUNS OF ULM — Ulm, Germany
See listings under Krieghoff.

U.S. REPEATING ARMS CO. — New Haven, Connecticut
See also Winchester shotgun listings.

VALMET — Jyväskylä, Finland

NOTE: *In 1987, Valmet and Sako merged and the Valmet production facilities were moved to Riihimaki, Finland. In 1989 a joint venture agreement was made with Armi Marocchi, and when production began in Italy, the Valmet name was changed to Tikka (Oy Tikkakoski Ab).*

See also Savage Models 330, 333T, 333 and 2400, which were produced by Valmet.

VALMET LION O/U SHOTGUN..... NiB $475 Ex $388 Gd $293
Boxlock. Selective single trigger. Plain extractors. 12 ga. only. Bbls.: 26-inch IC/M; 28-inch M/F, 30-inch M/F, F/F. Weight: About 7 lbs. Checkered pistol-grip stock and forearm. Imported 1947 to 1968.

MODEL 412 S O/U FIELD SHOTGUN... NiB $955 Ex $744 Gd $535
Hammerless. 12-ga., 3-inch chamber, 36-inch bbl., F/F chokes. American walnut Monte Carlo stock. Disc 1989.

MODEL 412 S SHOTGUN RIFLE COMBINATION .... NiB $1135 Ex $956 Gd $745
Similar to model 412 K except bottom bbl. chambered for .222 Rem., .223 Rem., .243 Win., .308 Win. or .30-06. 12-ga. shotgun bbl. with IM choke. Monte Carlo American walnut stock, recoil pad.

MODEL 412 O/U FIELD SHOTGUN............. NiB $866 Ex $723 Gd $587
12-ga. chambered for 2.75-inch shells. 26-inch bbl., IC/M chokes; 28-inch bbl., M/F chokes; 12-ga. chambered for 3-inch shells, 30-inch bbl., M/F chokes. 20-ga. (3-inch shells); 26-inch bbl., IC/M chokes; 28-inch bbl., M/F chokes. American walnut Monte Carlo stock.

Weatherby Model 82
Autoloading Shotgun

MODEL 412 ST SKEET . . . . .NiB $1176 Ex $922 Gd $766
Similar to Model 412 K except skeet stock and chokes. 12 and 20 ga.
Disc. 1989.

MODEL 412 SE TRAP . . . . .NiB $1176 Ex $922 Gd $766
Similar to Model 412 K Field except trap stock, recoil pad. 30-inch
bbls., IM/F chokes. Disc.1989.
w/extra bbl., add. $500

MONTGOMERY WARD — Chicago, Illinois;
Western Field and Hercules Models

*Although they do not correspond to specific models below, the names
Western Field and Hercules have been used to designate various
Montgomery Ward shotguns at various times.*

MODEL 25 SLIDE-ACTION REPEATER . . . . NiB $337 Ex $228 Gd $178
Solid frame. 12 ga. only. Two- or 5-round tubular magazine. 28-inch
bbl., various chokes. Weight: About 7.5 lbs. Plain pistol-grip stock,
grooved slide handle.

MODEL 40 O/U SHOTGUN . . . . . NiB $866 Ex $700 Gd $522
Hammerless. Boxlock. Double triggers. Gauges: 12, l6, 20, .410. Bbls.:
Plain; 26- to 30-inch, various chokes. Checkered pistol-grip stock and
forearm.

MODEL 40N
SLIDE-ACTION REPEATER . . . . . .NiB $329 Ex $233 Gd $179
Same general specifications as Model 25.

(WESTERN FIELD) MODEL 50
PUMPGUN . . . . NiB $300 Ex $244 Gd $178
Solid frame. Gauges: 12 and 16. Two- and 5-round magazine. 26-, 28-
or 30-inch bbl., 48 inches overall w/28-inch bbl. Weight: 7.25 - 7.75
lbs. Metal bead front sight. Walnut stock and grooved forend.

(WESTERN FIELD) MODEL 52
DOUBLE-BARREL SHOTGUN . . . .NiB $388 Ex $277 Gd $191
Hammerless coil-spring action. Gauges: 12, 16, 20 and .410. 26-, 28-,
or 30-inch bbls., 42 to 46 inches overall, depending upon bbl. length.
Weight: 6 (.410 ga. w/26-inch bbl.) to 7.25 lbs. (12 ga. w/30-inch bbls.),
depending upon gauge and bbl. length. Casehardened receiver; blued
bbls. Plain buttstock and forend. Made circa 1954.

MODEL 172 BOLT-ACTION SHOTGUN . . . . NiB $217 Ex $139 Gd $95
Takedown. Two-round detachable clip magazine.12 ga. 28-inch bbl.
with variable choke. Weight: About 7.5 lbs. Monte Carlo stock with
recoil pad.

MODEL 550A SLIDE-ACTION REPEATER . . . . . . NiB $367 Ex $265 Gd $190
Takedown. Gauges: 12, 16, 20, .410. Five-round tubular magazine.
Bbls.: Plain, 26- to 30-inch, various chokes. Weight: 6 (.410 ga. w/26-
inch bbl.) to 8 lbs. (12 ga. w/30-inch bbls.). Plain pistol-grip stock and
grooved slide handle.

MODEL SB300 DOUBLE-BARREL
SHOTGUN . . . . .NiB $376 Ex $298 Gd $220
Same general specifications as Model SD52A.

MODEL SB312 DOUBLE-BARREL SHOTGUN . . . . . . NiB $421 Ex $337 Gd $244
Boxlock. Double triggers. Plain extractors. Gauges: 12, 16, 20, .410.
Bbls.: 24- to 30-inch. Various chokes. Weight: About 7.5 lbs. in 12 ga.;
6.5 lbs in .410 ga. Checkered pistol-grip stock and forearm.

MODEL SD52A DOUBLE-BARREL SHOTGUN . . . . .NiB $344 Ex $255 Gd $200
Boxlock. Double triggers. Plain extractors. Gauges: 12, 16, 20, .410.
Bbls.: 26- to 32-inch, various chokes. Plain forend and pistol-grip buttstock. Weight: 6 (.410 ga., 26-inch bbls.) to 7.5 lbs. (12 ga., 32-inch
bbls.).

WEATHERBY, INC. — Pasa Robles, California

MODEL 82 AUTOLOADING SHOTGUN . . . . . . .NiB $556 Ex $435 Gd $332
Hammerless, gas-operated. 12 ga. only. Bbls.: 22- to 30-inch, various
integral or fixed chokes. Weight: 7.5 lbs. Checkered walnut stock and
forearm. Imported from 1982 to 1989.
BuckMaster Auto Slug
  w/rifle sights (1986-90) . . . . NiB $570 Ex $455 Gd $355
  w/fixed choke, deduct $50

MODEL 92 SLIDE-ACTION
SHOTGUN . . . . .NiB $390 Ex $288 Gd $217
Hammerless, short-stroke action. 12 ga.; 3-inch chamber. Tubular
magazine. Bbls.: 22-, 26-, 28-, 30-inch with fixed choke or IMC choke
tubes; plain or vent rib with rifle sights. Weight: 7.5 lbs. Engraved, matte
black receiver and blued barrel. Checkered high-gloss buttstock and
forend. Imported from Japan 1982 to 1989.
Standard Model 92 . . . . .NiB $330 Ex $261 Gd $195
BuckMaster Pump Slug
  w/rifle sights, (intro. 1986) . . . . . NiB $420 Ex $315 Gd $235

ATHENA O/U SHOTGUN
Engraved boxlock action with Greener crossbolt and sideplates. Gauges:
12, 20, 28 and .410; 2.75- or 3.5-inch chambers. Bbls.: 26-, 28-, 30- or
32-inch with fixed or IMC Multi-choke tubes. Weight: 6.75 to 7.38
lbs. Single selective trigger. Selective auto ejectors. Top tang safety.
Checkered Claro walnut stock and forearm with high-luster finish.
Imported from 1982 to 2002.
Field Model w/IMC multi-chokes,
  12 or 20 ga. . . . . NiB $2177 Ex $1898 Gd $1635
Field Model W/fixed chokes, 28 ga. or .410. .NiB $1976 Ex $1645 Gd $1389
Skeet Model w/fixed chokes, 12 or 20 ga. . . .NiB $1766 Ex $1432 Gd $1255
Skeet Model w/fixed chokes, 28 ga. or .410. .NiB $3320 Ex $2888 Gd $2366
Master Skeet tube set . . . . .NiB $3155 Ex $2776 Gd $2388
Trap Model w/IC tubes . . . . .NiB $2388 Ex $1977 Gd $1677
Grade V (1993 to date) . . . . .NiB $3566 Ex $3100 Gd $2665

SHOTGUNS

Weatherby Model 92
Slide-Action Shotgun

Weatherby Athena
O/U Shotgun

Weatherby Centurion
Automatic Shotgun

Weatherby Olympian Trap
O/U Shotgun

Weatherby Orion
O/U Shotgun

Weatherby Patrician
Deluxe Grade

Weatherby Regency
Trap Gun

CENTURION AUTOMATIC SHOTGUN

Gas-operated. Takedown. 12 ga. 2.75-inch chamber. Three round magazine. Bbls.: Vent ribs; 26-inch SK, IC or M 28-inch M or F; 30-inch Full choke. Weight: With 28-inch bbl., 7 lbs. 10.5 oz. Checkered pistol-grip stock and forearm, recoil pad. Made in Japan from 1972 to 1981.

Field Grade . . . . NiB $398 Ex $288 Gd $219
Trap Gun (30-inch full-choke bbl.) . NiB $435 Ex $377 Gd $235
Deluxe model (etched receiver,
  fancy wood stock) . . . . .NiB $525 Ex $425 Gd $265

OLYMPIAN O/U SHOTGUN

Gauges: 12 and 20. 2.75- (12 ga.) and 3-inch (20 ga.) chambers. Bbls.: 26-, 28-, 30, and 32-inch. Weight: 6.75 - 8.75 lbs. American walnut stock and forend. Disc. 1980.

Field Model . . . . NiB $988 Ex $700 Gd $577
Skeet Model . . . . NiB $1033 Ex $800 Gd $690
Trap Model . . . . NiB $995 Ex $745 Gd $650

ORION O/U SHOTGUN

Boxlock with Greener crossbolt. Gauges: 12, 20, 28 and .410; 2.75- or 3-inch chambers. Bbls.: 26-, 28, 30-, 32- or 34-inch with fixed or IMC Multi-Choke tubes. Weight: 6.5 to 9 lbs. Single selective trigger. Selective auto ejectors. Top tang safety. Checkered, high-gloss pistol-grip Claro walnut stock and forearm. Finish: Grade I, plain blued receive; Grade II, engraved blued receiver; Grade III, silver gray receiver. Imported from 1982 and 2002.

Orion I Field w/IC (12 or 20 ga.) . . . . . . NiB $1456 Ex $1188 Gd $975
Orion II Field w/IC (12 or 20 ga.) . . . . . . NiB $1155 Ex $965 Gd $743
Orion II Classic w/IC (12, 20 or 28 ga.) . NiB $1644 Ex $1388 Gd $1166
Orion II Sporting Clays w/IC (12 ga.) . . . NiB $1997 Ex $1688 Gd $1388
Orion III Field w/IC (12 or 20 ga.) . . . . . NiB $1688 Ex $1397 Gd $1188
Orion III Classic w/IC (12 or 20 ga.) . . . . NiB $1988 Ex $1669 Gd $1367
Orion III English Field w/IC (12 or 20 ga.). .NiB $1733 Ex $1448 Gd $1244
Orion Upland w/IC (12 or 20 ga.) . . . . . . NiB $1376 Ex $1133 Gd $976
Skeet II w/fixed chokes . . . . NiB $1355 Ex $1125 Gd $950
Super Sporting Clays . . . . NiB $1988 Ex $1743 Gd $1129

PATRICIAN SLIDE-ACTION SHOTGUN

Hammerless. Takedown. 12 ga. 2.75-inch chamber. Four round tubular magazine. Bbls.: Vent rib; 26-inch, SK, IC M; 28-inch, M F; 30-inch, F choke. Weight: With 28-inch bbl., 7 lbs., 7 oz. Checkered pistol-grip stock and slide handle, recoil pad. Made in Japan from 1972 to 1982.

Field Grade . . . . NiB $369 Ex $248 Gd $125
Deluxe model (etched receiver,
  fancy grade stock) . . . . .NiB $455 Ex $329 Gd $260
Trap Gun (w/30-inch full-choke bbl.). . . . . . NiB $399 Ex $255 Gd $190

REGENCY FIELD GRADE O/U SHOTGUN .NiB $1387 Ex $1266 Gd $885

Boxlock with sideplates, elaborately engraved. Auto ejectors. Selective single trigger. Gauges: 12, 20. 2.75-inch chamber in 12 ga., 3-inch in 20 ga. Bbls.: Vent rib; 26-inch SK, IC/M, M/F (20 ga. only); 28-inch SK, IC/M, M/F; 30-inch M/F (12 ga only). Weight with 28-inch bbls.: 7 lbs., 6 oz., 12 ga.; 6 lbs., 14 oz., 20 ga. Checkered pistol-grip stock and forearm of fancy walnut. Made in Italy from 1965 to 1982.

REGENCY TRAP GUN . . . . .NiB $990 Ex $823 Gd $688

Similar to Regency Field Grade except has trap-style stock with straight or Monte Carlo comb. Bbls. have vent side ribs and high, wide vent top rib; 30- or 32-inch, M/F, IM/F or F/F chokes. Weight: With 32-inch bbls., 8 lbs. Made in Italy from 1965 to 1982.

WESTERN ARMS CORP. — Ithaca, New York

A division of Ithaca Gun Company

LONG RANGE HAMMERLESS DOUBLE

Boxlock. Plain extractors. Single or double triggers. Gauges: 12, 16, 20, .410. Bbls.: 26- to 32-inch, M/F choke standard. Weight: 7.5 lbs., 12 ga. Plain pistol-grip stock and forend. Made 1929 to 1946.

Double triggers . . . . NiB $398 Ex $244 Gd $165
Single trigger . . . . NiB $400 Ex $295 Gd $188

WESTERN AUTO — Kansas City, Missouri

MODEL 300H SLIDE-ACTION REPEATER . . NiB $435 Ex $300 Gd $255

Gauges: 12,16, 20, .410. Four round tubular magazine. Bbls.: 26- to 30-inch, various chokes. Weight: About 7 lbs. Plain pistol-grip stock, grooved slide handle.

MODEL 310A SLIDE-ACTION REPEATER. . . NiB $366 Ex $270 Gd $200

Takedown. 12 ga. Five round tubular magazine. Bbls.: 28- and 30-inch. Weight: About 7.5 lbs. Plain pistol-grip stock.

MODEL 310B SLIDE-ACTION REPEATER. . . NiB $377 Ex $245 Gd $190

Westley Richards Deluxe Sidelock

Same general specifications as Model 310A except chambered for 16 ga.

MODEL 310C SLIDE-ACTION REPEATER. . . NiB $365 Ex $269 Gd $180

Same general specifications as Model 310A except chambered for 20 ga.

MODEL 310E SLIDE-ACTION REPEATER. . . NiB $425 Ex $366 Gd $229

Same general specifications as Model 310A except chambered for .410 bore.

MODEL 325BK BOLT-ACTION REPEATER . . NiB $276 Ex $190 Gd $125

Takedown. Two round detachable clip magazine. 20 ga. 26-inch bbl. with variable choke. Weight: 6.25 lbs.

WESTERN FIELD

See "W" for listings under Montgomery Ward.

WESTLEY RICHARDS & CO., LTD. —

Birmingham, England

The Pigeon and Wildfowl gun, available in all of the Westley Richards models except the Ovundo, has the same general specifications as the corresponding standard field gun except has magnum action of extra strength and treble bolting, chambered for 12 gauge only (2.75- or 3-inch); 30-inch full choke barrels standard. Weight: About 8 lbs. The manufacturer warns that 12-gauge magnum shells should not be used in their standard weight double-barrel shotguns.

BEST QUALITY BOXLOCK HAMMERLESS DOUBLE-BARRELSHOTGUN

Boxlock. Hand-detachable locks and hinged cover plate. Selective ejectors. Double triggers or selective single trigger. Gauges: 12, 16, 20. Barrel lengths and boring to order. Weight: 5.5 to 6.25 lbs. depending on ga. and bbl. length. Checkered stock and forend, straight or half-pistol grip. Also supplied in Pigeon and Wildfowl models with same values. Made from 1899 to date.

Double triggers . . . . NiB $22,975 Ex $18,990 Gd $14,270
Selective single trigger. . . . . NiB $26,790 Ex $21,998 Gd $14,880

BEST QUALITY SIDELOCK HAMMERLESS DOUBLE-BARREL SHOTGUN

Hand-detachable sidelocks. Selective ejectors. Double triggers or selective single trigger. Gauges: 12, 16, 20, 28, .410. Bbl. lengths and boring to order. Weight: 4.75 to 6.75 lbs., depending on ga. and bbl. length. Checkered stock and forend, straight or half-pistol grip. Also supplied in Pigeon and Wildfowl models with same values. Currently manufactured.

Double triggers . . . . NiB $29,669 Ex $26,766 Gd $22,880
Selective single trigger. . . . . NiB $30,000 Ex $27,898 Gd $24,550

SHOTGUNS

**Westley Richards
Best Quality Sidelock**

**Westley Richards
Deluxe Boxlock**

**Westley Richards
Model E**

**Winchester Model 12 Classic
Limited Edition Grade I**

**Winchester Model 12
Field Gun (1972 Type)**

DELUXE MODEL BOXLOCK
HAMMERLESS DOUBLE-BARREL SHOTGUN
Same general specifications as standard Best Quality gun except higher quality throughout. Has Westley Richards top-projection and treble-bite lever-work, hand-detachable locks. Also supplied in Pigeon and Wildfowl models with same values. Currently manufactured.
w/double trigger . . . . NiB $12,767 Ex $10,433 Gd $8998
w/selective single trigger . . . . NiB $32,880 Ex $30,880 Gd $13,990

DELUXE MODEL SIDELOCK
Same as Best Quality Sidelock except higher grade engraving and wood. Currently manufactured.
w/double triggers . . . . . NiB $27,889 Ex $22,999 Gd $14,887
w/single trigger. . . . . . . NiB $31,998 Ex $26,999 Gd $18,998

MODEL E HAMMERLESS DOUBLE
Anson & Deeley-type boxlock action. Selective ejector or non-ejector. Double triggers. Gauges: 12, 16, 20. Barrel lengths and boring to order. Weight: 5.5 to 7.25 lbs. depending on type, ga. and bbl. length. Checkered stock and forend, straight or half-pistol grip. Also supplied in Pigeon and Wildfowl models with same values. Currently manufactured.
Ejector model . . . . NiB $5388 Ex $4378 Gd $2990
Non-ejector model . . . . NiB $4998 Ex $3788 Gd $3277
OVUNDO (O/U) . . . . .NiB $19,677 Ex $16,999 Gd $12,998

Hammerless. Boxlock. Hand-detachable locks. Dummy sideplates. Selective ejectors. Selective single trigger. 12 ga. Barrel lengths and boring to order. Checkered stock/forend, straight or half-pistol grip. Mfd. before WW II.

TED WILLIAMS
See Sears shotguns.

WINCHESTER —
New Haven, Connecticut

Formerly Winchester Repeating Arms Co., and then mfd. by Winchester-Western Div., Olin Corp., later by U.S. Repeating Arms Company. In 1999, production rights were acquired by Browning Arms Company.

MODEL 12 CLASSIC LIMITED Edition
Gauge: 20; 2.75-inch chamber. Bbl.: 26-inch vent rib; IC. Weight: 7 lbs. Checkered walnut buttstock and forend. Polished blue finish (Grade I) or engraved with gold inlays (Grade IV). Made from 1993 to 1995.
Grade I (4000) . . . . NiB $1100 Ex $889 Gd $656
Grade IV (1000) . . . . NiB $1700 Ex $1308 Gd $998

Winchester Model 12
Pigeon Grade

Winchester Model 12
Standard

Winchester Model 12
Trap w/Monte Carlo Stock

Winchester Model 12
12-4 Engraving

MODEL 12
FEATHERWEIGHT . . . . NiB $688 Ex $577 Gd $555
Same as Model 12 Standard w/plain barrel except has alloy trigger guard. Modified takedown w/redesigned magazine tube, cap and slide handle. 12 ga. only. Bbls.: 26-inch IC; 28-inch M or F; 30-inch F choke. Serial numbers with "F" prefix. Weight: About 6.75 lbs. Made from 1959 to 1962.

MODEL 12 FIELD GUN, 1972 TYPE . . . NiB $800 Ex $685 Gd $522
Same general specifications as Standard Model 12 but 12 ga. only, 26- 28- or 30-inch vent rib bbl., standard chokes. Engine-turned bolt and carrier. Hand-checkered stock/slide handle of semifancy walnut. Made from 1972 to 1975.

MODEL 12 HEAVY DUCK GUN
Same general specifications as Standard Grade except 12 ga. only chambered for 3-inch shells. 30- or 32-inch plain, solid or vent rib bbl. w/full choke only. Three round magazine. Checkered slide handle and pistol-grip walnut buttstock w/recoil pad. Weight: 8.5 to 8.75 lbs. Made from 1935 to 1963.
Plain bbl. ` . . . . NiB $1366 Ex $890 Gd $644
Solid rib (disc. 1959) . . . . NiB $1977 Ex $1288 Gd $876
Vent. rib . . . . NiB $3288 Ex $2810 Gd $2466

MODEL 12 PIGEON GRADE
Deluxe versions of the regular Model 12 Standard or Field Gun, Duck Gun, Skeet Gun and Trap Gun made on special order. This grade has finer finish throughout, hand-smoothed action, engine-turned breech bolt and carrier, stock and extension slide handle of high grade walnut, fancy checkering, stock dimensions to individual specifications. Engraving and carving available at extra cost ranging from about $135 to over $1000. Disc. 1965.

Field Gun, plain bbl.	NiB $4233	Ex $3698	Gd $3166
Field Gun, vent rib	NiB $2255	Ex $1987	Gd $1459
Skeet Gun, matted rib	NiB $2255	Ex $1987	Gd $1459
Skeet Gun, vent rib	NiB $3889	Ex $3350	Gd $3180
Skeet Gun, Cutts Compensator.	NiB $1755	Ex $1398	Gd $1100
Trap Gun, matted rib	NiB $2233	Ex $1966	Gd $1399
Trap Gun, vent rib	NiB $2288	Ex $2190	Gd $2008
16 ga. (Field), add			100%
16 ga. (Skeet), add			100%
20 ga. (Field), add			175%
20 ga. (Skeet), add			175%
28 ga. (Skeet), add			550%

MODEL 12 RIOT GUN . . . . NiB $977 Ex $844 Gd $600
Same general specifications as plain barrel Model 12 Standard except has 20-inch cylinder bore bbl., 12 gauge only. Made from 1918 to 1963.

MODEL 12 SKEET GUN . . . . . NiB $2200 Ex $1977 Gd $1488
Gauges: 12, 16, 20, 28. Five round tubular magazine. 26-inch matted rib bbl., SK choke. Weight: About 7.75 lbs., 12 ga.; 6.75 lbs., other gauges. Bradley red or ivory bead front sight. Winchester 94B middle sight. Checkered pistol-grip stock and extension slide handle. Disc. after WWII.

GRADING: **NiB** = New in Box **Ex** = Excellent or NRA 95% **Gd** = Good or NRA 68%

Winchester Model 21
Custom Grade

Winchester Model 21
Pigeon Grade

**MODEL 12 SKEET GUN,
CUTTS COMPENSATOR** . . . . NiB $1233 Ex $1000 Gd $766
Same general specifications as standard Model 12 Skeet Gun except has plain bbl. fitted with Cutts Compensator, 26 inches overall. Disc. 1954.

MODEL 12 SKEET GUN, PLAIN-BARREL .NiB $2099 Ex $1887 Gd $1650
Same general specifications as standard Model 12 Skeet except w/no rib.

MODEL 12 SKEET GUN, VENT RIB . . . . NiB $4288 Ex $3760 Gd $3290
Same general specifications as standard Model 12 Skeet Gun except has 26-inch bbl. with vent rib, 12 and 20 ga. Disc. in 1965.

MODEL 12 SKEET GUN, 1972 TYPE . . . . . NiB $1288 Ex $909 Gd $663
Same gen. specifications as Standard Model 12 but 12 ga. only. 26-inch vent rib bbl., SK choke. Engine-turned bolt and carrier. Hand-checkered skeet-style stock and slide handle of choice walnut, recoil pad. Made from 1972 to 1975.

MODEL 12 STANDARD GR., MATTED RIB . . . . NiB $835 Ex $579 Gd $443
Same general specifications as plain bbl. Model 12 Standard except has solid raised matted rib. Disc. after World War II.

MODEL 12 STANDARD GR., VENT RIB . . . NiB $866 Ex $571 Gd $400
Same general specifications as plain barrel Model 12 Standard except has vent rib. 26.75- or 30-inch bbl.,12 ga. only. Disc. after World War II.

MODEL 12 STANDARD SLIDE-ACTION REPEATER
Hammerless. Takedown. Gauges: 12, 16, 20, 28. Six round tubular magazine. Plain bbl. Lengths: 26- to 32-inches; choked F to Cyl. Weight: About 7.5 lbs., 12 ga. 30-inch, 6.5 lbs. in other ga. with 28-inch bbl. Plain pistol-grip stock, grooved slide handle. Made from 1912 to 1964.
12 ga., 28-inch bbl., Full choke . . . . NiB $870 Ex $733 Gd $534
16 ga. . . . . NiB $966 Ex $881 Gd $533
20 ga. . . . . NiB $1277 Ex $855 Gd $633
28 ga. . . . . NiB $5767 Ex $3488 Gd $2499

MODEL 12 SUPER PIGEON GRADE . . NiB $4329 Ex $3887 Gd $3176
Custom version of Model 12 with same general specifications as standard models. 12 ga. only. 26-, 28- or 30-inch vent-rib bbl., any standard choke. Engraved receiver. Hand-smoothed and fitted action. Full fancy walnut stock and forearm made to individual order. Made from 1965 to 1972.

MODEL 12 TRAP GUN
Same general specifications as Standard Model 12 except has straighter stock, checkered pistol grip and extension slide handle, recoil pad, 30-inch matted-rib bbl., F choke, 12 ga. only. Disc. after World War II; vent rib model disc. 1965.
Matted rib bbl. . . . . NiB $2210 Ex $1966 Gd $1544
Straight stock, vent rib . . . . . . NiB $2299 Ex $2178 Gd $1933
Monte Carlo stock, vent rib . . . . . . NiB $2175 Ex $2000 Gd $1865

MODEL 12 TRAP GUN, 1972 TYPE. . . . . NiB $1299 Ex $1077 Gd $669
Same general specifications as Standard Model 12 but 12 gauge only. 30-inch vent-rib bbl., F choke. Engine-turned bolt and carrier. Hand-checkered trap-style stock (straight or Monte Carlo comb) and slide handle of select walnut, recoil pad. Intro. in 1972. Disc.

MODEL 20 SINGLE-SHOT HAMMER GUN .NiB $1577 Ex $1266 Gd $1008
Takedown. .410 bore. 2.5-inch chamber. 26-inch bbl., F choke. Checkered pistol-grip stock and forearm. Weight: About 6 lbs. Made from 1919 to 1924.

**ORIGINAL MODEL 21 DOUBLE-BARREL SHOTGUNS
(ORIGINAL PRODUCTION SERIES - 1930 to 1959)**
Hammerless. Boxlock. Automatic safety. Double triggers or selective single trigger, selective or non-selective ejection (all postwar Model 21 shotguns have selective single trigger and selective ejection). Gauges: 12, 16, 20, 28 and .410 bore. Bbls.: Raised matted rib or vent rib; 26-, 28-, 30-, 32-inch, the latter in 12 ga. only; F, IM, M, IC, SK chokes. Weight: 7.5 lbs., 12 ga. w/30-inch bbl.; about 6.5 lbs. 16 or 20 ga. w/28-inch bbl. Checkered pistol- or straight-grip stock, regular or beavertail forend. Made from 1930 to 1959.
Standard Grade, 12 ga. . . . . . NiB $7344 Ex $6100 Gd $4350
Standard Grade, 16. Ga. . . . . . NiB $9000 Ex $5466 Gd $4000
Standard Grade, 20 ga. . . . .NiB $10,008 Ex $6355 Gd $3988
Tournament Grade, 12 ga.
  (1933-34) . . . . .NiB $5733 Ex $5000 Gd $3889
Tournament Grade, 16 ga.
  (1933-34) . . . . .NiB $6893 Ex $6324 Gd $4388
Tournament Grade, 20 ga.
  (1933-34) . . . . NiB $8244 Ex $6887 Gd $4632
Trap Grade, 12 ga. (1940-59) . . . .NiB $5689 Ex $5000 Gd $4277
Trap Grade, 16 ga. (1940-59) . . . .NiB $6044 Ex $4988 Gd $3776
Trap Grade, 20 ga. (1940-59) . . . .NiB $7768 Ex $6322 Gd $3200
Skeet Grade, 12 ga. (1936-59) . . .NiB $5463 Ex $4465 Gd $3100
Skeet Grade, 16 ga. (1936-59) . . .NiB $6200 Ex $4988 Gd $3677
Skeet Grade, 20 ga. (1936-59) . . .NiB $7100 Ex $5998 Gd $4325
Duck Gun, 12 ga., 3-inch (1940-52). .NiB $5980 Ex $4966 Gd $3544
Magnum, 12 ga., 3-inch) (1953-59). .NiB $5688 Ex $4765 Gd $3300
Magnum, 20 ga., 3-inch (1953-59). .NiB $6900 Ex $5779 Gd $4200
Cust. Deluxe grade,
  12 ga. (1993-59) . . . . .NiB $8634 Ex $6892 Gd $4855
Cust. Deluxe grade,
  16 ga., (1933-59) . . . . NiB $10,339 Ex $8833 Gd $6450
Cust. Deluxe grade,
  20 ga. (1933-59) . . . . NiB $11,880 Ex $9893 Gd $6588
Cust. Deluxe grade, 28 ga. (1933-59) Very Rare . . NiB $30,000+
Cust. Deluxe grade, .410 (1933-59) Very Rare . . . NiB $35,000+
Fewer than 100 sm. bore models (28 ga. and .410) were built, which precludes accurate pricing, but projected values could exceed $30,000. Such rare specimens should be authenticated by factory letter and/or independent appraisals.

Winchester Model 23

Winchester Model 24

Winchester Model 25

Winchester Model 36

Winchester Model 37

Winchester Model 37A

Winchester Model 37A
Youth

SHOTGUNS

w/vent. rib,12 ga. models, add	$900
w/vent. rib, 16 ga. models, add	$1825
w/vent. rib, 20 ga. models, add	$1375
w/double triggers & extractors, deduct	30%
w/double triggers, selective ejection, deduct	20%

With Custom Engraving:

No.1 pattern, add	25%
No. 2 pattern, add	35%
No. 3 pattern, add	50%
No. 4 pattern, add	35%
No. 5 pattern, add	65%
No. 6 pattern, add	75%

MODEL 21 CUSTOM, PIGEON, GRAND AMERICAN (CUSTOM SHOP SERIES - PRODUCTION 1959 TO 1981)

Since 1959 the Model 21 has been offered through the Custom Shop in deluxe models. (Custom, Pigeon, Grand American) on special order. General specifications same as for Model 21 standard models except these custom guns have full fancy American walnut stock and forearm with fancy checkering, finely polished and hand-smoothed working parts, etc.; engraving inlays, carved stocks and other extras are available at additional cost. Made 1959 to 1981.

Custom grade, 12 ga. . . . . .NiB $11,980 Ex $9876 Gd $6759
Custom grade, 16 ga. . . . . .NiB $17,544 Ex $13,977 Gd $10,655
Custom grade, 20 ga. . . . . NiB $14,677 Ex $11,877 Gd $8321

GRADING: **NiB** = New in Box   **Ex** = Excellent or NRA 95%   **Gd** = Good or NRA 68%   **569**

Winchester
Model 40 Skeet

Winchester
Model 41 Deluxe

Pigeon grade, 12 ga. . . . . .NiB $17,889	Ex $14,670	Gd $10,300
Pigeon grade, 16 ga. . . . . .NiB $22,889	Ex $18,987	Gd $13,770
Pigeon grade, 20 ga. . . . . .NiB $21,800	Ex $19,880	Gd $14,800
Grand American, 12 ga. . . . . .NiB $25,700	Ex $19,900	Gd $14,600
Grand American, 16 ga. . . . . .NiB $39,600	Ex $31,877	Gd $22,955
Grand American, 20 ga. . . . . .NiB $30,888	Ex $27,888	Gd $20,556
Grand American 3-barrel Set . . . . .NiB $42,750	Ex $35,799	Gd $25,799

Small Bore Models

28 ga. and .410 (fewer than 20 made), ... $35,000+
Fewer than 20 Small Bore models (28 ga. and .410) were built during this period, which precludes accurate pricing, but projected values could exceed $35,000. Such rare specimens should be authenticated by factory letter and/or independent appraisals.

For Custom Shop Engraving from this period:
#1 Pattern, add 10%
#2 Pattern, add 15%
#3 Pattern, add 25%
#4 Pattern, add 35%
#5 Pattern, add 45%
#6 Pattern, add 50%

MODEL 21 U.S.R.A. CUSTOM SERIES (CUSTOM SHOP PRODUCTION 1982 TO DATE*)

Individual model designations for the Model 21 (made from 1931 to 1982) were changed when U. S. Repeating Arms Company assumed production. The new model nomenclature for the Custom/Built catagory, includes: Standard Custom, Special Custom and Grand American — all of which are available on special order through the Custom Shop. General specifications remained the same on these consolidated model variations and included the addition of a Small Bore 2-Barrel Set (28/.410) and a 3-Barrel Set (20/28/.410). Made 1982 to date *Winchester stopped cataloging the Model 21 after 1987. Current manufacture is by Connecticut Shotgun Manufacturing Company with guns marked Model 21.

Standard custom model . . . . .NiB $6988	Ex $5570	Gd $4000
Special Custom model . . . . .NiB $8000	Ex $6500	Gd $4666
Grand American model . . . . .NiB $14,880	Ex $12,980	Gd $9660
Grand American model, 2-bb. set .NiB $48,900	Ex $38,790	Gd $26,998
Grand American, 3-bbl. set . . . . . .NiB $72,877	Ex $59,988	Gd $26,800

The values shown above represent the basic model in each catagory. Since many customers took advantage of the custom built options, individual gun appointments vary and values will need to be adjusted accordingly. For this reason, individual appraisals should be obtained on all subject firearms.

MODEL 23 SIDE-BY-SIDE SHOTGUN

Boxlock. Single trigger. Automatic safety. Gauges: 12, 20, 28, .410. Bbls.: 25.5-, 26-, 28-inch with fixed chokes or Winchoke tubes.

Weight: 5.88 to 7 lbs. Checkered American walnut buttstock and forend. Made in 1979 for Olin at its Olin-Kodensha facility, Japan.

Classic 23 (gold inlay, engraved) . . . . . .NiB $2779	Ex $2466	Gd $2365
Custom 23 (plain receiver, Winchoke). . .NiB $1477	Ex $1155	Gd $966
Heavy Duck 23, Standard . . . . .NiB $2768	Ex $2398	Gd $2077
Lightweight 23, Classic . . . . .NiB $2188	Ex $1808	Gd $1266
Light Duck 23, Standard . . . . .NiB $2987	Ex $2665	Gd $2240
Light Duck 23, 12 ga. Golden Quail . . .NiB $2877	Ex $2549	Gd $2266
Light Duck 23, .410 Golden Quail. . . .NiB $4577	Ex $4328	Gd $3972
Custom Set 23, 20 & 28 ga. . . . . .NiB $6988	Ex $5100	Gd $3766

MODEL 24 HAMMERLESS DOUBLE

Boxlock. Double triggers. Plain extractors. Auto safety. Gauges: 12, 16, 20. Bbls.: 26-inch IC/M; 28-inch M/F (also IC/M in 12 ga. only); 30-inch M and F in 12 ga. only. Weight: About 7.5 lbs., 12 ga. Metal bead front sight. Plain pistol-grip stock, semi-beavertail forearm. Made from 1939 to 1957.

12 ga. model . . . . .NiB $966	Ex $733	Gd $544
16 ga. model . . . . .NiB $1088	Ex $800	Gd $623
20 ga. model . . . . .NiB $1221	Ex $945	Gd $711

MODEL 25 RIOT GUN . . . . .NiB $677 Ex $455 Gd $390
Same as Model 25 Standard except has 20-inch cylinder bore bbl., 12 ga. only. Made from 1949 to 1955.

MODEL 25 7550 . . . . .Ex $404 Gd $358
Hammerless. Solid frame. 12 ga. only. Four round tubular magazine. 28-in. Plain bbl.; IC, M or F choke. Weight: About 7.5 lbs. Metal bead front sight. Plain pistol-grip stock, grooved slide handle. Made from 1949 to 1955.

MODEL 36 SINGLE-SHOT

BOLT ACTION . . . . .NiB $1893 Ex $1688 Gd $1477
Takedown. Uses 9mm Short or Long shot or ball cartridges interchangeably. 18-inch bbl. Plain stock. Weight: About 3 lbs. Made from 1920 to 1927.

MODEL 37 SINGLE-SHOT SHOTGUN

Semi-hammerless. Auto ejection. Takedown. Gauges: 12, 16, 20, 28, .410. Bbl. lengths: 28-, 30-, 32-inch in all gauges except .410; 26- or 28-inch in .410; all barrels plain with F choke. Weight: About 6.5 pounds, 12 ga. Made from 1937 to 1963.

12, 16, 20 ga. models . . . . .NiB $559	Ex $438	Gd $315
Youth model (20 ga. w/red dot indicator). . .NiB $559	Ex $438	Gd $315
.410 model . . . . .NiB $769	Ex $588	Gd $437
28 ga. model ("Red Letter" version) . . . .NiB $2687	Ex $2531	Gd $2033
Other "Red Letter" models, add 20%		
W/32-inch bbl., add 15%		

MODEL 37A SINGLE-SHOT SHOTGUN

Similar to Model 370 except has engraved receiver and gold trigger, checkered pistol-grip stock, fluted forearm; 16 ga. available with 30-inch bbl. only. Made from 1973 to 1980.

Winchester Model 42
Classic Limited Edition

Winchester Model 42
Standard

12, 16 or 20 ga. models . . . . NiB $579 Ex $300 Gd $219
28 ga. model . . . . NiB $2590 Ex $2331 Gd $2268
.410 model . . . . NiB $754 Ex $559 Gd $366
w/32-inch bbl., add $50

MODEL 37A YOUTH . . . . NiB $566 Ex $397 Gd $244
Similar to Model 370 Youth except has engraved receiver and gold trigger, checkered pistol-grip stock, fluted forearm. Made 1973 to 1980.

MODEL 40 STANDARD AUTOLOADER. .NiB $977 Ex $721 Gd $533
Streamlined receiver. Hammerless. Takedown. 12 ga. only. Four round tubular magazine. 28- or 30-inch bbl.; M or F choke. Weight: About 8 lbs. Bead sight on ramp. Plain pistol-grip stock, semi-beavertail forearm. Made from 1940 to 1941.

MODEL 40 SKEET GUN . . . . NiB $1188 Ex $966 Gd $700
Same general specifications as Model 40 Standard except has 24-inch plain bbl. w/Cutts Compensator and screw-in choke tube, checkered forearm and pistol grip, grip cap. Made 1940 to 1941.

MODEL 41 SINGLE-SHOT BOLT ACTION
Takedown. .410 bore. 2.5-inch chamber (chambered for 3-inch shells after 1932). 24-inch bbl., F choke. Plain straight stock standard. Also made in deluxe version. Made from 1920 to 1934.
Standard model . . . . NiB $800 Ex $618 Gd $509
Deluxe model. . . . . NiB $954 Ex $732 Gd $600

MODEL 42 STANDARD GRADE
Hammerless. Takedown. .410 bore (3- or 2.5-inch shell). Tubular magazine holds five 3-inch or six 2.5-inch shells. 26- or 28-inch plain or solid-rib bbl.; cylinder bore, M or F choke. Weight: 5.8 to 6.5 lbs. Plain pistol-grip stock; grooved slide handle. Made from 1933 to 1963.
w/plain bbl. . . . . NiB $2675 Ex $2143 Gd $1609
Model 42 Standard w/solid rib . . NiB $3750 Ex $3396 Gd $3184

MODEL 42 CLASSIC LTD. Edition . NiB $1886 Ex $1599 Gd $1179
Gauge: .410 with 2.75-inch chamber. Bbl.: 26-inch vent rib; F choke. Weight: 7 lbs. Checkered walnut buttstock and forend. Engraved blue with gold inlays. Limited production of 850. Made from 1993.

MODEL 42 DELUXE . . . .NiB $22,700 Ex $19,745 Gd $17,998
Same general specifications as the Model 42 Trap Grade except available w/vent rib after 1955. Finer finish throughout w/hand-smoothed action, engine-turned breech bolt and carrier, stock and extension slide handle of high grade walnut, fancy checkering, stock dimensions to individual specifications. Engraving and carving were offered at extra cost. Made 1940-63.

Note: *Exercise caution on VR models not marked "DELUXE" on the bottom of the receiver. A factory letter will insure that the rib was installed during the initial manufacturing process. Unfortunately, factory authentication is not always possible due to missing or destroyed records. To further complicate this matter, not all VR ribs were installed by Winchester. From 1955-63, both Deluxe and Skeet Grade models were available with Simmons style ribs. After-market rib installations are common.*

MODEL 42 PIGEON GRADE
This higher-grade designation is similar to the Deluxe grade and is available in all configurations. May be identified by engraved Pigeon located at the base of the magazine tube. Most production occurred in the late 1940's. **NOTE:** *To determine the value of any Model 42 Pigeon Grade, add 50% to value listed under the specified Model 42 configuration.*

MODEL 42 SKEET GUN
Same general specifications as Model 42 Standard except has checkered straight or pistol-grip stock and extension slide handle, 26- or 28-inch plain, solid-rib or vent-rib bbl. May be choked F., Mod., Imp. Cyl. or Skeet. Note: Some Model 42 Skeet Guns are chambered for 2.5-inch shells only. Made from 1933 to 1963.
w/plain bbl. . . . . NiB $6277 Ex $4500 Gd $3769
w/solid rib . . . . NiB $6277 Ex $4500 Gd $3769
w/vent. rib . . . . NiB $6833 Ex $5971 Gd $4948
w/ 2.5-inch chamber, add. 35%

MODEL 42 TRAP GRADE
This higher grade designation was available in both field and skeet configurations and is fitted w/deluxe wood w/trap grade checkering pattern and marked "TRAP" on bottom of receiver. Made 1934 to 1939. Superseded by the Deluxe model in 1940.
w/plain bbl. . . . . .NiB $27,977 Ex $24,770 Gd $22,665
w/solid rib . . . . .NiB $27,977 Ex $24,770 Gd $22,665
w/vent. rib . . . . .NiB $27,855 Ex $25,693 Gd $23,449

MODEL 50 FIELD GUN, VENT RIB . . NiB $766 Ex $541 Gd $396
Same as Model 50 Standard except has vent rib.

MODEL 50 SKEET GUN . . . . . NiB $1422 Ex $1269 Gd $1031
Same as Model 50 Standard except has 26-inch vent-rib bbl. with SK choke, skeet-style stock of select walnut.

MODEL 50 STANDARD GRADE . .NiB $779 Ex $500 Gd $388
Non-recoiling bbl. and independent chamber. Gauges: 12 and 20. Two round tubular magazine. Bbl.: 12 ga. — 26-, 28-, 30-inch; 20 ga. — 26-, 28-inch; IC, SK, M, F choke. Checkered pistol-grip stock and forearm. Weight: About 7.75 lbs. Made from 1954 to 1961.

GRADING: **NiB** = New in Box   **Ex** = Excellent or NRA 95%   **Gd** = Good or NRA 68%

Winchester Model 50 Skeet

Winchester Model 1897 Riot Gun

Winchester Model 101

MODEL 50 TRAP GUN . . . . . NiB $1466 Ex $1284 Gd $1066
Same as Model 50 Standard except 12 ga. only, has 30-inch vent-rib bbl. with F choke, Monte Carlo stock of select walnut.

MODEL 59 SEMI-AUTOMATIC . . . . NiB $878 Ex $655 Gd $555
Gauge: 12. Magazine holds two rounds. Alloy receiver. Win-Lite steel and fiberglass bbl.: 26-inch IC, 28-inch M or F choke, 30-inch F choke; also furnished with 26-inch bbl. with Versalite choke (interchangeable F, M, IC tubes; one supplied with gun). Weight: About 6.5 lbs. Checkered pistol-grip stock and forearm. Made 1959 to 1965.

MODEL 1893 . . . . NiB $1100 Ex $930 Gd $600
First pump-action shotgun manufactured by Winchester. Standard Grade. Solid frame. Gauges: 12 black powder shells only. Five-round tubular magazine. Bbl.: Plain; 30 or 32 inches, F choked. Plain pistol-grip stock, grooved slide handle. Appox. 34,000 mfg.Made from 1893 to 1897.

MODEL 1897 BUSH GUN
Takedown or solid frame. Same general specifications as standard Model 1897 except w/ 26-in. cylinder bore bbl. Made 1897 to 1931.
w/solid frame . . . . NiB $995 Ex $700 Gd $554
Takedown model . . . . NiB $1299 Ex $1056 Gd $800

MODEL 1897 RIOT GUN
Takedown or solid frame. Same general specifications as standard Model 1897 except 12 ga. only, 20-inch cylinder bore bbl. Made from 1898 to 1935.
w/solid frame . . . . NiB $1544 Ex $1187 Gd $900
Takedown model . . . . NiB $1390 Ex $1055 Gd $773

MODEL 1897 TRAP, TOURNAMENT & PIGEON GRADES
These higher grade models offer higher overall quality than the standard grade. Made from 1897 to 1939.
Standard Trap grade . . . . NiB $2600 Ex $2208 Gd $1188
Special Trap grade . . . . NiB $1794 Ex $1566 Gd $1180
Tournament grade
  (Black Diamond) . . . . NiB $2971 Ex $2387 Gd $1698
Pigeon grade . . . . NiB $11,000 Ex $9533 Gd $3000

MODEL 1897 TRENCH GUN . NiB $4800 Ex $3693 Gd $2138
Solid frame. Same as Model 1897 Riot Gun except has handguard and is equipped with a bayonet. World War I government issue, from 1917 to 1918.

w/military markings, add **20%**

MODEL 1897 SLIDE-ACTION REPEATER
Standard Grade. Takedown or solid frame. Gauges: 12 and 16. Five-round tubular magazine. Bbl.: Plain; 26 to 32 inches, the latter in 12 ga. only; choked F to Cyl. Weight: About 7.75 lbs. (12 ga. w/28-inch barrel). Plain pistol-grip stock, grooved slide handle. Made from 1897 to 1957.
12 ga. w/solid frame . . . . NiB $1110 Ex $855 Gd $675
16 ga. w/solid frame . . . . NiB $1110 Ex $855 Gd $675
12 ga., takedown model . . . . . . NiB $1356 Ex $1108 Gd $888
16 ga., takedown model . . . . . . NiB $1356 Ex $1108 Gd $888

NOTE: *All Winchester Model 101s are mfd. for Olin Corp. at its Olin-Kodensha facility in Tochigi, Japan. Production for Olin Corp. stopped in Nov. 1987. Importation of Model 101s was continued by Classic Doubles under that logo until 1990. See separate heading for additional data.*

MODEL 101
COMBINATION GUN . . . . . . NiB $2983 Ex $2777 Gd $2369
12-ga. Winchoke bbl. on top and rifle bbl. chambered for .30-06 on bottom (over/under). 25-inch bbls. Engraved receiver. Hand checkered walnut stock and forend. Weight: 8.5 lbs. Mfd. for Olin Corp. in Japan.

MODEL 101 DIAMOND
GRADE TARGET . . . . NiB $1978 Ex $1596 Gd $1180
Similar to Model 101 Standard except silvered frame and Winchoke interchangeable choke tubes. Made from 1981 to 1990.

MODEL 101 O/U FIELD GUN
Boxlock. Engraved receiver. Auto ejectors. Single selective trigger. Combination bbl. selector and safety. Gauges: 12 and 28, 2.75-inch chambers; 20 and .410, 3-inch chambers. Vent rib bbls.: 30- (12 ga. only) and 26.5-inch, IC/M. Weight: 6.25 to 7.75 lbs. depending on gauge and bbl. length. Hand-checkered French walnut and forearm. Made from 1963 to 1981. Gauges other than 12 introduced 1966.
12 and 20 ga. . . . . NiB $1099 Ex $882 Gd $723
28 and .410 ga. . . . . NiB $1622 Ex $1244 Gd $977
12 and 20 ga. mag. . . . . NiB $1288 Ex $1077 Gd $766

MODEL 101 MAGNUM . NiB $1300 Ex $1000 Gd $520
Same specifications as Model 101 Field except w/ 30-in. bbl., 12 or 20 ga. with 3-inch chambers. 25.5-inch bbls. with F/M or F/F choke. Made 1966 to 1981.

Winchester Model 370

Winchester Model 1001
Sporting Clays

Winchester Model 1200
Field Gun

Winchester Model 1200
Field Gun w/Vent Rib

MODEL 101 PIGEON GRADE
Similar to Model 101 Standard except engraved silvered frame and select wood. Winchoke tubes. Made from 1974 to 1987.
12 ga. model . . . . NiB $2200 Ex $1820 Gd $1150
20 ga. model . . . . NiB $2700 Ex $2000 Gd $1500
28 ga. model . . . . NiB $3760 Ex $2920 Gd $1700
.410 model . . . . NiB $3530 Ex $2925 Gd $1700

MODEL 101 PIGEON GRADE LIGHTWEIGHT
Similar to Model 101 Standard except 20 ga. only w/ 27-in. bbl. Receiver engraved w/ gold. Limited production. Made 1995 to 1996.
Two Bbl. Set. . . . . NiB $3600 Ex $2960 Gd $1900

MODEL 101 PIGEON GRADE
SPORTING. . . . . .NiB $2275 Ex $1630 Gd $900
Similar to Model 101 Standard except 12 ga. only w/ 30- or 32-in. ported, wide rib bbl. Silver nitride receiver. Stock: adj. comb, high grade walnut. Made 2009 to 2010.

MODEL 101 QUAIL SPECIAL
Same specifications as small-frame Model 101 except in 28 and .410 ga. with 3-inch chambers. 25.5-inch bbls. with choke tubes (28 ga.) or M/F chokes (.410). Imported from Japan in 1984 to 1987.
12 ga. model . . . . NiB $3155 Ex $2926 Gd $2554
20 ga. . . . . NiB $3599 Ex $3466 Gd $3200
28 ga. model . . . . NiB $5799 Ex $4933 Gd $4200
.410 model . . . . NiB $4733 Ex $4122 Gd $3888

MODEL 101 SKEET . . . . NiB $1200 Ex $830 Gd $600
Same specifications as Model 101 Field except w/ 26.5-in. bbl., 12 or 20 ga. oe 28-in. bbl., 28 ga. or .410. Made 1966 to 1984.
Three Gauge Set
  1974 to 1984) . . . . NiB $3800 Ex $3100 Gd $2000

MODEL 101 TRAP . . . . NiB $1330 Ex $950 Gd $620
Same specifications as Model 101 Field except w/ 30 or 32-in. bbl., 12 ga. only. Standard or wide vent rib. Made 1966 to 1984.

MODEL 370
SINGLE-SHOT SHOTGUN . . . . . . .NiB $245 Ex $200 Gd $99
Visible hammer. Auto ejector. Takedown. Gauges: 12, 16, 20, 28, .410. 2.75-inch chambers in 16 and 28 ga., 3-inch in other ga. Bbls.: 12 ga., 30-, 32- or 36-inch,16 ga; 30- or 32-inch; 20 and 28 ga., 28-inch; .410 bore, 26-inch, all F choke. Weight: 5.5-6.25 lbs. Plain pistol-grip stock and forearm. Made from 1968 to 1973.

MODEL 370 YOUTH MODEL
Same as standard Model 370 except has 26-inch bbl. and 12.5-inch stock with recoil pad; 20 gauge with IM choke, .410 bore with F choke. Made 1968 to 1973.
12, 16 or 20 ga. models . . . . NiB $244 Ex $190 Gd $121
20 ga. model . . . . NiB $300 Ex $221 Gd $165
.410 model . . . . NiB $355 Ex $220 Gd $175

MODEL 1001 O/U SHOTGUN
Boxlock. 12 ga., 2.75- or 3-inch chambers. Bbls.: 28- or 30-inch vent rib; WinPlus choke tubes. Weight: 7-7.75 lbs. Checkered walnut buttstock and forend. Blued finish with scroll engraved receiver. Made from 1993 to 1998.
Field model
  (28-inch bbl., 3-inch) . . . . .NiB $1133 Ex $978 Gd $726
Sporting Clays model . . . . NiB $1166 Ex $1044 Gd $863
Sporting Clays Lite model . . . . . . NiB $1187 Ex $990 Gd $734

MODEL 1200 DEER GUN . . . . . . .NiB $398 Ex $221 Gd $155
Same as standard Model 1200, except has special 22-inch bbl. with rifle-type sights, for rifled slug or buckshot; 12 ga. only. Weight: 6.5 lbs. Made from 1965 to 1974.

Winchester Model 1300
Deer Series — Black Shadow
Synthetic Stock

Winchester Model 1300
Deer Series — Advantage
Full Camo Pattern

Winchester Model 1300
Defender Series — Stainless
Marine Synthetic Stock

MODEL 1200 DEFENDER SERIES
SLIDE-ACTION SECURITY SHOTGUNS

Hammerless. 12 ga. w/3-inch chamber. 18-inch bbl. w/cylinder bore and metal front bead or rifle sights. Four- or 7-round magazine. Weight: 5.5 to 6.75 lbs. 25.6 inches (PG Model) or 38.6 inches overall. Matte blue finish. Synthetic pistol grip or walnut finished hardwood buttstock w/grooved synthetic or hardwood slide handle. NOTE: Even though the 1200 series was introduced in 1964 and was supplanted by the Model 1300 in 1978, the Security series (including the Defender model) was marketed under 1200 series alpha-numeric product codes (G1200DM2R) until 1989. In 1990, the same Defender model was marketed under a 4-digit code (7715) and was then advertised in the 1300 series.

Defender
  w/hardwood stock,bead sight . . .NiB $325 Ex $233 Gd $188
Defender
  w/hardwood stock, rifle sights . .NiB $325 Ex $233 Gd $188
Defender model w/pistol-grip stock. NiB $325 Ex $233 Gd $188
Defender Combo model
  w/extra 28-inch plain bbl. . . . . .NiB $345 Ex $290 Gd $239
Defender Combo model
  w/extra 28-inch vent rib bbl. . . .NiB $425 Ex $344 Gd $239

MODEL 1200 MAGNUM FIELD GUN

Same as standard Model 1200 except chambered for 3-inch 12 and 20 ga. magnum shells; plain or vent-rib bbl., 28- or 30-inch, F choke. Weight: 7.38 to 7.88 lbs. Made from 1964 to 1983.
w/plain bbl. . . . . .NiB $325 Ex $240 Gd $179
w/vent. rib bbl. . . . . .NiB $350 Ex $265 Gd $190
w/recoil reduction system, add $100

MODEL 1200 RANGER
SLIDE-ACTION SHOTGUN . . . . . .NiB $400 Ex $285 Gd $195

Hammerless. 12 and 20 ga.; 3-inch chambers. Walnut finished hardwood stock, ribbed forearm. 28-inch vent-rib bbl.; Winchoke system. Weight: 7.25 lbs. Made from 1982 to 1990 by U. S. Repeating Arms.

MODEL 1200 RANGER YOUTH
SLIDE-ACTION SHOTGUN . . . . . .NiB $400 Ex $285 Gd $195

Same general specifications as standard Ranger Slide-Action except chambered for 20 ga. only, has Four round magazine, recoil pad on buttstock, weight: 6.5 lbs. Mfd. by U. S. Repeating Arms.

MODEL 1200 RANGER SLIDE-ACTION FIELD GUN

Front-locking rotary bolt. Takedown. Four round magazine. Gauges: 12, 16, 20 (2.75-inch chamber). Bbl.: Plain or vent rib; 26-, 28-, 30-inch; IC, M, F choke or with Winchoke (interchangeable tubes IC-M-F). Weight: 6.5 to 7.25 lbs. Checkered pistol-grip stock and fore arm (slide handle), recoil pad; also avail. 1966 to 1970 w/Winchester recoil reduction system (Cycolac stock). Made from 1964 to 1983.
w/plain bbl. . . . . .NiB $400 Ex $285 Gd $195
w/vent. rib bbl. . . . . .NiB $420 Ex $305 Gd $217
w/recoil reduction system, add $100
w/Winchoke, add $50

MODEL 1200 STAINLESS MARINE SERIES SLIDE-ACTION
SECURITY SHOTGUN

Similar to Model 1200 Defender except w/6-round magazine. 18-inch bbl. of ordnance stainless steel w/cylinder bore and rifle sights. Weight: 7 lbs. Bright chrome finish. Synthetic pistol grip or walnut finished hardwood buttstock w/grooved synthetic or hardwood slide handle. Made from 1984 to 1990.
w/hardwood stock . . . . .NiB $325 Ex $235 Gd $175
w/pistol-grip stock . . . . .NiB $325 Ex $235 Gd $175

MODEL 1200 STAINLESS POLICE SERIES SLIDE-ACTION
SECURITY SHOTGUN

Similar to Model 1200 Defender except w/6-round magazine. 18-inch bbl. of ordnance stainless steel w/cylinder bore and rifle sights. Weight: 7 lbs. Matte chrome finish. Synthetic pistol grip or walnut- finished hardwood buttstock w/grooved synthetic or hardwood slide handle. Made from 1984-90.
Police model w/hardwood stock . . NiB $255 Ex $202 Gd $125
Police model w/pistol grip stock . . NiB $255 Ex $202 Gd $125

Winchester Model 1300
Lady Defender — Synthetic Full Stock

Winchester Model 1300
Lady Defender — Synthetic Pistol Grip Stock

Winchester Model 1300
Defender 5-Shot Combo

Winchester Model 1300
Turkey Gun

Winchester Model 1300
XTR w/Winchoke

Winchester Model 1300
Magnum Waterfowl

GRADING: **NiB** = New in Box   **Ex** = Excellent or NRA 95%   **Gd** = Good or NRA 68%

MODEL 1200 TRAP GUN

Same as standard Model 1200 except 12 gauge only. Has 2-round magazine, 30-inch vent-rib bbl., Full choke or 28-inch with Winchoke. Semi-fancy walnut stock, straight Made from 1965-73. Also available 1966 to 1970 w/Winchester recoil reduction system.

w/straight trap stock	NiB $425	Ex $260	Gd $180
w/Monte Carlo stock	NiB $425	Ex $260	Gd $180
w/Recoil reduction system, add			$100
w/Winchoke, add			$50

MODEL 1200 RANGER

COMBINATION SHOTGUN . . . . . NiB $440 Ex $300 Gd $217
Same as Ranger Deer combination except has one 28-inch vent-rib bbl. with M choke and one 18-inch Police Cyl. bore bbl. Made 1987 to 1990.

MODEL 1200 SKEET GUN . . . . . . NiB $450 Ex $310 Gd $225
Same as standard Model 1200 except 12 and 20 ga. only; has 2-round magazine, specially tuned trigger, 26-inch vent-rib bbl. SK choke, semi-fancy walnut stock and forearm. Weight: 7.25 to 7.5 lbs. Made 1965 to 1973. Also avail. 1966 to 1970 with Winchester recoil reduction system (add $50 to value).

MODEL 1300 CAMOPACK . . . . . . NiB $465 Ex $390 Gd $279
Gauge: 12.3-inch Magnum. Four round magazine. Bbls.: 30-and 22-inch with Winchoke system. Weight: 7 lbs. Laminated stock with Win-Cam camouflage green, cut checkering, recoil pad, swivels and sling. Made from 1987-88.

MODEL 1300 DEER SERIES

Similar to standard Model 1300 except 12 or 20 ga. only w/special 22-inch cyl. bore or rifled bbl. and rifle-type sights. Weight: 6.5 lbs. Checkered walnut or synthetic stock w/satin walnut, black or Advantage Full Camo Pattern finish. Matte blue or full-camo metal finish. Made from 1994 to 2006.

w/walnut stock (intro. 1994)	NiB $425	Ex $360	Gd $265
Black Shadow Deer model			
w/synthetic stock (intro. 1994)	NiB $400	Ex $298	Gd $220
Advantage Camo model (1995-98)	NiB $445	Ex $377	Gd $280
Deer Combo			
Deer Combo w/22- and			
28-inch bbls. (1994-98)	NiB $515	Ex $455	Gd $390
W/rifled bbl. (intro. 1996), add			$75

MODEL 1300 DEFENDER SERIES

Gauges: 12 or 20 ga. 18- 24- 28-inch vent rib bbl. w/3-inch chamber. Four-, 7- or 8- round magazine. Weight: 5.6 to 7.4 lbs. Blued, chrome or matte stainless finish. Wood or synthetic stock. Made from 1985 to 2006.

Combo model	NiB $490	Ex $375	Gd $277
Hardwood stock model	NiB $365	Ex $299	Gd $200
Synthetic pistol-grip model	NiB $270	Ex $283	Gd $203
Synthetic stock model	NiB $335	Ex $279	Gd $225
Lady Defender synthetic			
stock (made 1996)	NiB $320	Ex $255	Gd $210
Lady Defender synthetic			
Pistol-grip (made 1996)	NiB $320	Ex $255	Gd $210
Stainless marine			
model w/synthetic stock	NiB $555	Ex $435	Gd $290

MODEL 1300 DELUXE SLIDE-ACTION

Gauges: 12 and 20 w/3-inch chamber. Four round magazine. Bbl.:22, 26 or 28 inch vent rib bbl. w/Winchoke tubes. Weight: 6.5 lbs. Checkered walnut buttstock and forend w/high luster finish. Polished blue metal finish with roll-engraved receiver. Made from 1984 to 2006.

Model 1300 Deluxe			
w/high gloss finish	NiB $500	Ex $390	Gd $292
Model 1300 Ladies/Youth model			
w/22-inch bbl., (disc. 1992)	NiB $455	Ex $360	Gd $258

MODEL 1300 FEATHERWEIGHT SLIDE-ACTION SHOTGUN

Hammerless. Takedown. Four round magazine. Gauges: 12 and 20 (3-inch chambers). Bbls.: 22, 26 or 28 inches w/plain or vent rib w/ Winchoke tubes. Weight: 6.38 to 7 lbs. Checkered walnut buttstock, grooved slide handle. Made from 1978 to 1994.

w/plain bbl.	NiB $400	Ex $365	Gd $290
w/vent. rib	NiB $400	Ex $365	Gd $290
XTR model	NiB $400	Ex $365	Gd $290

MODEL 1300 RANGER SERIES

Gauges: 12 or 20 ga. w/3-inch chamber. Five round magazine. 22-(Rifled), 26- or 28-inch vent-rib bbl. w/Winchoke tubes. Weight: 7.25 lbs. Blued finish. Walnut-finished hardwood buttstock and forend. Made from 1984 to 2006.

Standard model	NiB $377	Ex $366	Gd $270
Combo model	NiB $465	Ex $399	Gd $280
Ranger Deer combo			
(D&T w/rings & bases)	NiB $455	Ex $380	Gd $265
Ranger Ladies/Youth	NiB $366	Ex $255	Gd $190

MODEL 1300 SLIDE-ACTION FIELD GUN

Takedown w/front-locking rotary bolt. Gauges: 12, 20 w/3-inch chamber. Four round magazine. Bbl.: Vent rib; 26-, 28-, 30-inch w/ Win-choke tubes IC-M-F). Weight: 7.25 lbs. Checkered walnut or synthetic stock w/ standard, black or Advantage Full Camo Pattern finish. Matte blue or full-camo metal finish. Made from 1994 to 2006.

Standard Field w/walnut stock	NiB $445	Ex $320	Gd $266
Black Shadow w/black			
synthetic stock	NiB $365	Ex $275	Gd $200
Advantage Camo model	NiB $455	Ex $375	Gd $290

MODEL 1300 SLUG HUNTER SERIES

Similar to standard Model 1300 except chambered 12 ga. only w/ special 22-inch smoothbore w/sabot-rifled choke tube or fully rifled bbl. w/rifle-type sights. Weight: 6.5 lbs. Checkered walnut, hardwood or laminated stock w/satin walnut or WinTuff finish. Matte blue metal finish. Made from 1988 to 1994.

w/hardwood stock	NiB $465	Ex $365	Gd $250
w/laminated stock	NiB $515	Ex $400	Gd $290
w/walnut stock	NiB $500	Ex $380	Gd $265
Whitetails Unlimited model			
w/beavertail forend	NiB $475	Ex $396	Gd $300
w/sabot-rifled choke tubes, add			$50

MODEL 1300 TURKEY SERIES

Gauges: 12 or 20 ga. 22-inch bbl. w/3-inch chamber. Four round magazine. 43 inches overall. Weight: 6.4 to 6.75 lbs. Buttstock and magazine cap, sling studs w/Cordura sling. Drilled and tapped to accept scope base. Checkered walnut, synthetic or laminated wood stock w/low luster finish. Matte blue or full camo finish. Made from 1985 to 2006.

w/Advantage camo	NiB $390	Ex $285	Gd $216
w/Realtree All-Purpose camo	NiB $488	Ex $369	Gd $275
w/Realtre Gray All-Purpose camo	NiB $500	Ex $405	Gd $325
w/Realtree All-Purpose			
camo (matte finish)	NiB $525	Ex $420	Gd $355
w/Black Shadow synthetic stock	NiB $355	Ex $285	Gd $190
w/Win-Cam green laminate stock	NiB $445	Ex $365	Gd $225
Win-Cam combo			
(22- or 30-inch bbl.)	NiB $465	Ex $420	Gd $350
Win-Cam NWTF model			
(22- or 30-inch bbl.)	NiB $525	Ex $375	Gd $285
Win-Cam Youth/Ladies			
model (20 ga.)	NiB $565	Ex $435	Gd $310
Win-Tuf model w/brown			
laminated wood stock	NiB $490	Ex $388	Gd $265

Winchester Model 1400 Field

Winchester Model 1500 w/Plain Barrel

Winchester Model 1500 w/Vent Rib Barrel

MODEL 1300 WATERFOWL SLIDE-ACTION SHOTGUN
Similar to 1300 Standard model except has 28- or 30-inch vent rib bbl. w/Winchoke tubes. Weight: 7 lbs. Matte blue metal finish. Checkered walnut finished hardwood or brown laminated Win-Tuffwood stock w/ camo sling, swivels and recoil pad. Made from 1984 to 1992.
w/hardwood stock . . . . NiB $435 Ex $300 Gd $220
w/laminated stock . . . . NiB $435 Ex $300 Gd $220

MODEL 1300 XTR SLIDE-ACTION . NiB $550 Ex $455 Gd $3209
Hammerless. Takedown. Four shot magazine. Gauges: 12 and 20 (3-inch chambers). Bbl.: Plain or vent rib; 28-inch bbls.; Winchoke (interchangeable tubes IC-M-F). Weight: About 7 lbs. Disc. 2006.

MODEL 1400 AUTOMATIC FIELD GUN
Gas-operated. Front-locking rotary bolt. Takedown. Two round magazine. Gauges: 12, 16, 20 (2.75-inch chamber). Bbl.: Plain or vent rib; 26-, 28-, 30-inch; IC, M, F choke, or with Winchoke (interchangeable tubes IC-M-F). Weight: 6.5 to 7.25 lbs. Checkered pistol-grip stock and forearm, recoil pad, also available with Winchester recoil reduction system (Cycolac stock). Made from 1964 to 1968.
w/plain bbl. . . . . .NiB $355 Ex $244 Gd $190
w/vent. rib bbl. . . . . .NiB $390 Ex $244 Gd $196
w/recoil reduction system, add $125
w/Winchoke, add $50

MODEL 1400 DEER GUN . . . . . . .NiB $369 Ex $255 Gd $190
Same as standard Model 1400 except has special 22-inch bbl. with rifle-type sights, for rifle slug or buckshot; 12 ga. only. Weight: 6.25 lbs. Made from 1965 to 1968.

MODEL 1400
MARK II DEER GUN . . . . .NiB $460 Ex $345 Gd $290
Same general specifications as Model 1400 Deer Gun. Made from 1968-73.

MODEL 1400 MARK II FIELD GUN
Same general specifications as Model 1400 Field Gun, except not chambered for 16 gauge; Winchester Recoil Reduction System not available after 1970. Only 28-inch barrels w/Winchoke offered after 1973. Made from 1968 to 1978.
w/plain bbl. . . . . .NiB $450 Ex $365 Gd $287
w/plain bbl. and Winchoke. . . . . . .NiB $475 Ex $388 Gd $315
w/ vent. rib bbl. . . . . .NiB $544 Ex $390 Gd $290
w/vent. rib bbl. and Winchoke . . .NiB $566 Ex $445 Gd $390

Add for Winchester recoil reduction system $150

MODEL 1400 MARK II
SKEET GUN . . . . .NiB $535 Ex $423 Gd $356
Same general specifications as Model 1400 Skeet Gun. Made from 1968 to 1973.

MODEL 1400 MARK II TRAP GUN
Same general specifications as Model 1400 Trap Gun except also furnished with 28-inch bbl. and Winchoke. Winchester recoil reduction system not available after 1970. Made from 1968 to 1973.
w/straight stock . . . . .NiB $655 Ex $475 Gd $353
w/Monte Carlo stock. . . . . .NiB $657 Ex $525 Gd $400
w/recoil reduction system, add $150
w/Winchoke, add $50

MODEL 1400 MARK II UTILITY SKEET NiB $590 Ex $445 Gd $355
Same general specifications as Model 1400 Mark II Skeet Gun except has stock and forearm of field grade walnut. Made 1970 to 1973.

MODEL 1400 MARK II UTILITY TRAP NiB $590 Ex $445 Gd $355
Same as Model 1400 Mark II Trap Gun except has Monte Carlo stock/ forearm of field grade walnut. Made from 1970 to 1973.

MODEL 1400 RANGER
SEMIAUTOMATIC SHOTGUN . . .NiB $566 Ex $365 Gd $255
Gauges: 12, 20. Two round magazine. 28-inch vent rib bbl. with F choke. Overall length: 48.63 inches. Weight: 7 to 7.25 lbs. Walnut finish, hardwood stock and forearm with cut checkering. Made from 1984 to 1990 by U. S. Repeating Arms.

MODEL 1400 RANGER SEMIAUTOMATIC
DEER SHOTGUN . . . . .NiB $500 Ex $369 Gd $255
Same general specifications as Ranger Semiautomatic except 24.13-inch plain bbl. with rifle sights. Mfd. by U.S. Repeating Arms.

MODEL 1400 SKEET GUN . . . . . .NiB $525 Ex $420 Gd $375
Same as standard Model 1400 except 12 and 20 ga. only, 26-inch vent-rib bbl., SK choke, semi-fancy walnut stock and forearm. Weight: 7.25 to 7.5 lbs. Made from 1965 to 1968. Also available with Winchester recoil reduction system (add $50 to value).

MODEL 1400 TRAP GUN
Same as standard Model 1400 except 12 ga. only with 30-inch vent-rib bbl., F choke. Semi-fancy walnut stock, straight or Monte Carlo trap

SHOTGUNS

Winchester Ranger Deer

Winchester Ranger Slide-Action

Winchester Model 1885
Single-Shot

Winchester Model 1
Field Super-X

Winchester Xpert
96 Field

Winchester Xpert
96 Trap

style. Also available with Winchester recoil reduction system. Weight: About 8.25 lbs. Made from 1965 to 1968.

w/straight stock . . . . .NiB $435 Ex $320 Gd $220
w/Monte Carlo stock. . . . . .NiB $455 Ex $340 Gd $245
w/recoil reduction system, add. $150

MODEL 1500 XTR SEMIAUTOMATIC NiB $465 Ex $300 Gd $290
Gas-operated. Gauges: 12 and 20 (2.75-inch chambers). Bbl.: Plain or vent rib; 28-inch; WinChoke (interchangeable tubes IC-M-F). American walnut stock and forend; checkered grip and forend. Weight: 7.25 lbs. Made from 1978 to 1982.

**MODEL 1885
SINGLE-SHOT SHOTGUN . . .NiB $4377 Ex $3554 Gd $2566**
Falling-block action, same as Model 1885 Rifle. Highwall receiver. Solid frame or takedown. 20 ga. 3-inch chamber. 26-inch bbl.; plain, matted or matted rib; Cyl. bore, M or F choke. Weight: About 5.5 lbs. Straight-grip stock and forearm. Made from 1914 to 1916.

MODEL 1887 LEVER-ACTION SHOTGUN
First of John Browning's patent shotgun designs produced by Winchester. 10 or 12 ga. on casehardened frame fitted w/20-inch blued, cylinder bore or full choke 30- or 32-inch bbl. Plain or checkered walnut stock and forend. Made from 1887 to 1901.

578

10 or 12 ga. Standard model. . . . . . . NiB $4188 Ex $3765 Gd $3287
10 or 12 ga. Deluxe model. . . . . . .NiB $9233 Ex $8977 Gd $6450
10 or 12 ga. Riot Gun . . . . NiB $2770 Ex $2256 Gd $1656
w/.70-150 Ratchet rifled bbl.
   .70 cal. rifle/87 produced) . .NiB $4350 Ex $3000 Gd $2275
w/3 or 4 blade Del. Damascus bbl., add 20%

MODEL 1901 LEVER-ACTION SHOTGUN
Same general specifications as Model 1887, of which this is a redesigned version. 10 ga. only. Made from 1901 to 1920.

Standard model . . . . NiB $4379 Ex $3988 Gd $3500
Deluxe model   . . . . NiB $6100 Ex $4988 Gd $3360

**MODEL 1911 AUTO-
LOADING SHOTGUN . . . . .NiB $755 Ex $655 Gd $500**
Hammerless. Takedown. 12 gauge only. Four round tubular magazine. Bbl.: plain, 26- to 32-inch, standard borings. Weight: About 8.5 lbs. Plain or checkered pistol-grip stock and forearm. Made from 1911 to 1925.

RANGER DEER COMBINATION . .NiB $455 Ex $365 Gd $245
Gauge: 12, 3-inch Magnum. Three round magazine. Bbl.: 24-inch Cyl. bore deer bbl. and 28-inch vent rib bbl. with WinChoke system. Weight: 7.25 lbs. Made from 1987 to 1990.

Woodward
Single-Shot Trap

Woodward O/U
Special Trap Grade

SUPER-X MODEL I AUTO FIELD GUN . . NiB $390 Ex $280 Gd $245
Gas-operated. Takedown.12 ga. 2.75-inch chamber Four round magazine. Bbl.: Vent rib 26-inch IC; 28-inch M or F; 30-inch F choke. Weight: About 7 lbs. Checkered pistol-grip stock. Made 1974 to 1984.

SUPER-X MODEL I SKEET GUN . . NiB $977 Ex $755 Gd $590
Same as Super-X Field Gun except has 26-inch bbl., SK choke, skeet-style stock and forearm of select walnut. Made 1974 to 1984.

SUPER-X MODEL I TRAP GUN
Same as Super-X Field Gun except has 30-inch bbl., IM or F choke, trap-style stock (straight or Monte Carlo comb) and forearm of select walnut, recoil pad. Made from 1974 to 1984.
w/straight stock . . . . NiB $790 Ex $588 Gd $425
w/Monte Carlo stock . . . . NiB $875 Ex $655 Gd $470

XPERT MODEL 96 O/U FIELD GUN . . . . NiB $975 Ex $770 Gd $677
Boxlock action similar to Model 101. Plain receiver. Auto ejectors. Selective single trigger. Gauges: 12, 20. 3-inch chambers. Bbl.: Vent rib; 26-inch IC/M; 28-inch M/F, 30-inch F/F choke (12 ga. only). Weight: 6.25 to 8.25 lbs. depending on ga. and bbls. Checkered pistol-grip stock and forearm. Made from 1976-81 for Olin Corp. at its Olin-Kodensha facility in Japan.

XPERT MODEL 96 SKEET GUN . . . NiB $975 Ex $770 Gd $677
Same as Xpert Field Gun except has 2.75-inch chambers, 27-inch bbls., SK choke, skeet-style stock and forearm. Made 1976 to 1981.

XPERT MODEL 96 TRAP GUN
Same as Xpert Field Gun except 12 ga. only, 2.75-inch chambers, has 30-inch bbls., IM/F or F/F choke, trap-style stock (straight or Monte Carlo comb) with recoil pad. Made from 1976 to 1981.
w/straight stock . . . . NiB $975 Ex $770 Gd $677
w/Monte Carlo stock . . . . NiB $1133 Ex $990 Gd $697

JAMES WOODWARD & SONS —
London, England

James Woodward & Sons was acquired by James Purdey & Sons after World War II.

BEST QUALITY HAMMERLESS DOUBLE
Sidelock. Automatic ejectors. Double triggers or single trigger. Built to order in all standard gauges, bbl. lengths, boring and other specifications. Made as a field gun, pigeon and wildfowl gun, skeet gun or trap gun. Manufactured prior to World War II.
12 ga.
 w/double triggers . . . NiB $30,000 Ex $22,700 Gd $18,900
20 ga.
 w/double triggers . . . NiB $33,000 Ex $26,890 Gd $18,700

28 ga.
 w/double triggers . . . NiB $40,600 Ex $33,560 Gd $25,000
.410 ga.
 w/double triggers . . . . NiB $45,000 Ex $36,900 Gd $25,000
w/selective single trigger, add 10%

BEST QUALITY O/U SHOTGUN
Sidelock. Automatic ejectors. Double triggers or single trigger. Built to order in all standard gauges, bbl. lengths, boring and other specifications, including Special Trap Grade with vent rib. Woodward introduced this type of gun in 1908. Made until World War II.
12 ga.
 w/double triggers . . . NiB $31,660 Ex $25,850 Gd $20,000
20 ga.
 w/double triggers . . . NiB $42,500 Ex $35,980 Gd $25,500
28 ga.
 w/double triggers . . . NiB $55,000 Ex $44,900 Gd $32,000
.410 ga.
.410 w/double triggers . . . NiB $63,000 Ex $49,800 Gd $35,000
w/single trigger, add 10%

BEST QUALITY
SINGLE-SHOT TRAP . . . . NiB $14,860 Ex $12,790 Gd $10,000
Sidelock. Mechanical features of the O/U gun. Vent rib bbl. 12 ga. only. Built to customer's specifications and measurements, including type and amount of checkering, carving and engraving. Made prior to World War II.

ZEPHYR — Manufactured by Victor
Sarasqueta Company, Eibar, Spain

MODEL 1
O/U SHOTGUN . . . . NiB $1341 Ex $1083 Gd $778
Same general specifications as Field Model O/U except with more elaborate engraving, finer wood and checkering. Imported by Stoeger 1930s- to 1951.

MODEL 2
O/U SHOTGUN . . . . NiB $1746 Ex $1393 Gd $994
Sidelock. Auto ejectors. Gauges: 12, 16, 20, 28 and .410. Bbls.: 25 to 30 inches most common. Modest scroll engraving on receiver and sideplates. Checkered, straight-grain select walnut buttstock and forend. Imported by Stoeger 1930s to 1951.

MODEL 3
O/U SHOTGUN . . . . NiB $2369 Ex $1888 Gd $1337
Same general specifications as Zephyr Model 2 O/U except with more elaborate engraving, finer wood and checkering. Imported by Stoeger 1930s to 1951.

SHOTGUNS

Zephyr Crown, Premier and Royal Grades (top to bottom)

MODEL 400E FIELD GRADE DOUBLE-BARREL SHOTGUN
Anson & Deeley boxlock system. Gauges: 12 16, 20, 28 and .410. Bbls.: 25 to 30 inches. Weight: 4.5 lbs. (.410) to 6.25 lbs. (12 ga.). Checkered French walnut buttstock and forearm. Modest scroll engraving on bbls., receiver and trigger guard. Imported by Stoeger 1930s to 1950s.

12, 16 or 20 ga. . . . . NiB $2166 Ex $1388 Gd $1000
28 ga. or .410 . . . . NiB $1877 Ex $1497 Gd $1000
w/selective single trigger, add $250

MODEL 401 E SKEET GRADE DOUBLE-BARREL SHOTGUN
Same general specifications as Field Grade except with beavertail forearm. Bbls.: 25 to 28 inches. Imported by Stoeger 1930s to 1950s.
12, 16 or 20 ga. . . . . NiB $1954 Ex $1600 Gd $1216
28 ga., or .410 . . . . NiB $2144 Ex $1698 Gd $1277
w/selective single trigger, add $450
w/non-selective single trigger, add $300

MODEL 402E DELUXE
DOUBLE-BARREL SHOTGUN NiB $2455 Ex $2089 Gd $1466
Same general specifications as Model 400E Field Grade except for custom refinements. The action was carefully hand-honed for smoother operation; finer, elaborate engraving throughout, plus higher quality wood in stock and forearm. Imported by Stoeger 1930s to 1950s.

CROWN GRADE . . . . NiB $1800 Ex $1498 Gd $1056
Boxlock. Gauges: 12, 16, 20, 28 and .410. Bbls.: 25 to 30 inches standard but any lengths could be ordered. Weight: 6 lbs., 4 oz. (.410) to 7 lbs., 4 oz. (12 ga.). Checkered Spanish walnut stock and beavertail forearm. Receiver engraved with scroll patterns. Imported by Stoeger 1938 to 1951.

FIELD MODEL
O/U SHOTGUN . . . . NiB $988 Ex $745 Gd $566
Anson & Deeley boxlock. Auto ejectors. Gauges: 12, 16 and 20. Bbls.: 25 to 30 inches standard- full-length matt rib. Double triggers. Checkered buttstock and forend. Light scroll engraving on receiver. Imported by Stoeger 1930s to 1951.

HONKER SINGLE-SHOT SHOTGUN . . . . NiB $676 Ex $580 Gd $390
Sidelock. Gauge: 10; 3.5-inch magnum. 36-inch vent rib barrel w/F choke. Weight: 10.5 lbs. Checkered select Spanish walnut buttstock and beavertail forend; recoil pad. Imported by Stoeger 1950s to 1972.

PINEHURST
DOUBLE-BARREL SHOTGUN . . NiB $1388 Ex $1190 Gd $800
Boxlock. Gauges: 12, 16, 20, 28 and .410. Bbls.: 25 to 28 inches most common. Checkered, select walnut buttstock and forend. Selective single trigger and auto ejectors. Imported by Stoeger 1950s to 1972.

PREMIER GRADE
DOUBLE-BARREL SHOTGUN . . . NiB $2870 Ex $2300 Gd $1560
Sidelock. Gauges: 12, 16, 20, 28 and .410. Bbls.: Any length, but 25 to 30 inches most popular. Weight: 4.5 lbs. (.410) to 7 lbs. (12 ga.). Checkered high-grade French walnut buttstock and forend. Imported by Stoeger 1930s to 1951.

ROYAL GRADE
DOUBLE-BARREL SHOTGUN . . . NiB $4388 Ex $2287 Gd $2077
Same general specifications as the Premier Grade except with more elaborate engraving, finer checkering and wood. Imported by Stoeger 1930s to 1951.

STERLINGWORTH II
DOUBLE-BARREL SHOTGUN . . . NiB $1000 Ex $790 Gd $678
Genuine sidelocks with color-casehardened sideplates. Gauges: 12, 16, 20 and .410. Bbls.: 25 to 30 inches. Weight: 6 lbs., 4 oz. (.410) to 7 lbs., 4 oz. (12 ga.). Select Spanish walnut buttstock and beavertail forearm. Light scroll engraving on receiver and sideplates. Automatic, sliding-tang safety. Imported by Stoeger 1950s to 1972.

THUNDERBIRD
DOUBLE-BARREL SHOTGUN . . NiB $1221 Ex $900 Gd $755
Sidelock. Gauges: 12 and 10 Magnum. Bbls.: 32-inch, both F choke. Weight: 8 lbs., 8 oz. (12 ga.), 12 lbs. (10 ga.). Receiver elaborately engraved with waterfowl scenes. Checkered select Spanish walnut buttstock and beavertail forend. Plain extractors, double triggers. Imported by Stoeger 1950 to 1972.

UPLAND KING
DOUBLE-BARREL SHOTGUN . NiB $1290 Ex $1066 Gd $886
Sidelock. Gauges: 12, 16, 20, 28 and .410. Bbls.: 25 to 28 inches most popular. Checkered buttstock and forend of select walnut. Selective single trigger and auto ejectors. Imported by Stoeger 1950 to 1972.

UPLANDER 4E
DOUBLE-BARREL SHOTGUN . . . NiB $900 Ex $688 Gd $525
Same general specifications as the Zephyr Sterlingworth II except with selective auto ejectors and highly polished sideplates. Imported by Stoeger 1951 to 1972.

WOODLANDER II
DOUBLE-BARREL SHOTGUN . . . NiB $645 Ex $465 Gd $377
Boxlock. Gauges: 12, 20 and .410. Bbls.: 25 to 30 inches. Weight: 6 lbs., 4 oz. (.410) to 7 lbs., 4 oz. (12 ga.). Checkered Spanish walnut stock and beavertail forearm. Engraved receiver. Imported by Stoeger 1950 to 1972.

Index

A.A. ARMS
HANDGUNS
AP-9 Series, 15
RIFLES
AR-9 Semiautomatic Carbine, 199
ACCU-TEK
Model AT-9 Auto Pistol, 15
Model AT-25 Auto Pistol, 15
Model AT-32 Auto Pistol, 15
Model AT-40 DA Auto Pistol, 15
Model AT-380 Auto Pistol, 15
Models BL-9, BL 380, 16
Models CP-9, CP-40, CP-45, 16
Model HC-380SS, 16
ACTION ARMS
HANDGUNS
AT-84S DA, 16
AT-84P DA, 16
AT-88P DA, 16
AT-88S DA, 16
RIFLES
Model B Sporter Semi Carbine, 199
Timber Wolf Repeating Rifle, 199
ADAMY, GEBR. JAGDWAFFEN
SHOTGUNS
O/U, S/S, Combination, Drilling, Vierling, 425
ADVANTAGE ARMS
Model 422, 16
AQUIRRE Y ARANZABAL—*See also AyA*
ALDENS SHOTGUN
Model 670 Chieftain Slide Action, 425
ALKARTASUNA
"Ruby" Automatic Pistol, 16
ALPHA ARMS
Alaskan Bolt-Action Rifle, 199
Custom Bolt-Action Rifle, 199
Grand Slam Bolt-Action Rifle, 199
Jaguar Bolt-Action Rifle, 200
AMERICAN ARMS
HANDGUNS
454 SSA Revolver, 17
Bisley SA Revolver, 16
Buckhorn SA Revolver, 17
CX-22 DA Automatic Pistol, 16
EP-380 DA Automatic Pistol, 16
Escort DA Auto Pistol, 16
Mateba Auto Revolver, 16
P-98 DA Automatic Pistol, 16
PK-22 DA Automatic Pistol, 17
PX-22 DA Automatic Pistol, 17
PX-25 DA Automatic Pistol, 17
Regulator SA Revolver, 17
Spectre DA Auto Pistol, 17
Woodmaster SA Auto Pistol, 17
RIFLES
1860 Henry, 200
1866 Winchester, 200
1873 Winchester, 200
SHOTGUNS
Bristol (Sterling) Over/Under, 425
Brittany Hammerless Double, 425
Camper Special, 425
Combo, 425
Derby Hammerless Double, 425
F.S. Series Over/Under, 425
Gentry/York Hammerless Double, 426
Grulla #2 Hammerless Double, 426
Silver I Over/Under, 426
Silver II Over/Under, 426
Silver Lite Over/Under, 426
Silver Skeet/Trap, 426
Silver Sporting Over/Under, 426
Single-Shot Shotgun, 426
Slugger Single-Shot Shotgun, 426
TS/OU 12 Shotgun, 426
TS/SS 10 Hammerless Double, 427
TS/SS 12 Hammerless Double, 427
WS/OU 12 Shotgun, 427
WS/SS 10 Hammerless Double, 427
WT/OU 10 Shotgun, 427
AMERICAN DERRINGER
125th Anniversary, Model 1, 18
Alaskan Survival, Model 4, 18
Cop DA Derringer, 18
Lady Derringer, 18
LM-5 Automatic Pistol, 18
Mini-Cop DA Derringer, 18

Model 1, Stainless, 17
Model 2 Steel "Pen" Pistol, 17
Model 3 Stainless Steel, 17
Model 4 Double Derringer, 17
Model 6, 18
Model 7, 18
Model 8, 18
Model 10, 18
Model 11, 18
Model 25 Automatic Pistol, 18
Model 38 DA Derringer, 18
Semmerling LM-4, 18
Texas Commemorative, 18
AMERICAN FIREARMS
25 Auto Pistol, 19
380 Auto Pistol, 19
AMERICAN SPIRIT FIREARMS
A2 Car Carbine, 200
ASA 24-Inch Match Rifle, 200
ASA A2 Rifle, 200
ASA Bull Barrel Flattop Rifle, 200
ASA Bull Barrel A2 Rifle, 200
ASA Carbine, 200
ASA M4 Rifle, 200
ASA Tactical Rifle, 200
Bull Barrel A2 Invader, 200
DCM Service Rifle, 200
Flattop Car Rifle, 200
Limited Match Rifle, 200
Open Match Rifle, 200
Post-Ban Carbine, 200
AMT (Arcadia Machine & Tool)
HANDGUNS
45 ACP Hardballer, 19
45 ACP Hardballer, Long Slide 19
45 ACP Hardballer Gov't., 19
Automag II Automatic Pistol, 19
Automag III Automatic Pistol, 19
Automag IV Automatic Pistol, 19
Automag V Automatic Pistol, 19
Backup Automatic Pistol, 19
Backup II Automatic Pistol, 20
Backup DAO Auto Pistol, 20
Bull's Eye Target Model, 20
Javelina, 20
Lightning Auto Pistol, 20
On Duty DA Pistol, 20
Skipper Auto Pistol, 20
RIFLES
Bolt Action Repeating Rifle, 200
Bolt Action Single Shot Rifle, 200
Challenger AutoloadingTarget Rifle Series I, II & III, 201
Lightning 25/22 Autoloading Rifle, 201
Lightning Small Game Hunter Series, 201
Magnum Hunter Auto Rifle, 201
ANSCHUTZ, J.G. Jagd und Sportwaffenfabrik—*See also Savage/Anschutz*
HANDGUNS
Exemplar 1416/1451P Bolt-Action Pistol, 20
Exemplar Hornet, 21
Exemplar XIV, 21
Model 64P, 20
RIFLES
Achiever Bolt-Action Rifle, 206
Achiever ST-Super Target, 206
Kadett Bolt-Action Repeating Rifle, 206
Mark 2000 Match, 206
Model 54.18MS, 201
Model 54.18MS-REP Repeating Rifle, 201
Model 64MS Bolt-Action Single-Shot, 201
Model 64MSR Bolt-Action Repeater, 201
Model 64S Bolt-Action Single-Shot, 201
Model 520/61 Semiautomatic, 201
Model 525 Autoloader, 201
Model 1403B, 201
Model 1403D Match SS Target Rifle, 201
Model 1407 ISU Match 54 Rifle, 202
Model 1408-ED Super Running Boar, 202
Model 1411 Match 54 Rifle, 202
Model 1413 Super Match 54 Rifle, 202
Model 1416D, 202
Model 1416D Classic Sporters, 202
Model 1418 Bolt-Action Sporter, 202
Model 1418D Bolt-Action Sporter, 202
Model 1422D Classic/Custom Rifle, 202

Model 1427B Biathlon Rifle, 203
Model 1430D Match, 203
Model 1432 Bolt-Action Sporter, 203
Model 1432D Classic/Custom Rifle, 203
Model 1433 Bolt-Action Sporter, 203
Model 1448D Clay Bird, 203
Model 1449 Youth Sporter, 203
Model 1450B Target Rifle, 203
Model 1451 E/R Sporter/Target, 203
Model 1451D Classic/Custom, 203
Model 1451 ST-R, 204
Model 1516D Classic/Custom Rifle, 204
Models 1516D/1518D Luxus Rifles, 204
Models 1518/1518D Sporting Rifles, 204
Model 1522D Classic/Custom Rifle, 204
Model 1532D Classic/Custom Rifle, 204
Model 1533, 204
Model 1707 Series Repeater, 204
Model 1733D Mannlicher, 205
Model 1740 Monte Carlo Sporter, 205
Model 1743 Monte Carlo Sporter, 205
Model 1903D Match SS Target Rifle, 205
Model 1807 ISU Standard Match, 205
Model 1808ED Super Target, 205
Model 1808MS-R Metallic Silhouette, 205
Model 1810 Super Match II, 205
Model 1811 Prone Match, 205
Model 1813 Super Match, 205
Model 1827 Biathlon Rifle, 205
Model 1907 ISU International Match, 205
Model 1910 International Super M, 205
Model 1911 Prone Match Rifle, 205
Model 1912 Ladies Sporter, 206
Model 1913 Standard Rifle, 206
Model 1913 Super Match Rifle, 206
Model 2007 ISU Standard Rifle, 206
Model 2013 Benchrest (BR-50), 206
Model 2013 Ladies Sporter, 206
Model 2013 Silhouette Rifle, 206
Model 2013 Super Match Rifle, 206
Model BR-50 Bench Rest Rifle, 206
ARMALITE
HANDGUNS
AR-24 Automatic Pistol, 21
AR-24-15C Combat Custom, 21
AR-24K-13 Compact, 21
AR-24K-13 Combat Custom Compact, 21
RIFLES
AR-7 Explorer Custom Rifle, 206
AR-7 Explorer Survival Rifle, 206
AR-10 (A) Semiautomatic Rifle, 207
AR-180 Semiautomatic Rifle, 207
AR-10 (T) Target, 208
AR-50 SS Bolt-Action, 208
M15 Series, 208
SHOTGUNS
AR-17 Golden Gun, 427
ARMI JAGER
RIFLES
AP-74 Commando, 208
AP-74 Semiautomatic Rifle, 208
AP-74 Wood Stock Model, 208
ARMSCOR (Arms Corp.)
HANDGUNS
Model 200DC/TC DA Revolver, 21
Model 202A Revolver, 21
Model 206 Revolver, 21
Model 210 Revolver, 21
Model 1911-A1 Automatic Pistol, 21
Model 1911-A1 Commander, 21
Model 1911-A1 Officer, 21
Model 1911-A1 Medallion Series, 21
RIFLES
Model 20 Auto Rifle, 208
Model 1600 Auto Rifle, 208
Model AK22 Auto Rifle, 208
Model M14 Series, 208
Model M20 Series, 208
Model M1400, 209
Model M1500, 209
Model M1600, 209
Model M1800, 209
Model M2000, 209
SHOTGUNS
Model M-30 Field Pump Shotgun, 427
Model M-30 Riot Pump, 427

INDEX

GRADING: **NiB** = New in Box   **Ex** = Excellent or NRA 95%   **Gd** = Good or NRA 68%

Model M-30 Special Combo, 427
Model M-30 Special Purpose, 427
ARMSPORT SHOTGUNS
1000 Series Hammerless Doubles, 427
Model 1125 Single-Shot Shotgun, 427
Model 2700 Goose Gun, 428
Model 2700 Over/Under Series, 428
Model 2755 Slide-Action Shotgun, 428
Model 2900 Tri-Barrel (Trilling), 428
ARNOLD ARMS
African Safari, 209
Alaskan Trophy, 209
ARRIETA
SHOTGUNS
Boss Round Body, 429
Ligera model, 428
Model 557 Standard, 428
Model 570 Lieja, 428
Model 578 Victoria, 428
Model 590 Regina, 428
Model 595 Principe, 428
Model 600 Imperial, 428
Model 601 Imperial Tyro, 429
Model 801, 429
Model 802, 429
Model 871, 429
Model 871 Extra Finish, 429
Model 872, 429
Model 873, 429
Model 874, 429
Model 875, 429
Model 931, 429
Renaissance Model, 429
A-SQUARE COMPANY
Caesar Bolt-Action Rifle, 209
Genghis Khan Bolt-Action Rifle, 209
Hamilcar Bolt-Action Rifle, 209
Hannibal Bolt-Action Rifle, 209
ASAI AG—See Magnum Research
ASTRA
HANDGUNS
Cadix DA Revolver, 23
Constable DA Auto Pistol, 22
Model 41 DA Revolver, 22
Model 44 DA Revolver, 21
Model 45 DA Revolver, 22
Model 200 Firecat Vest Pocket, 22
Model 202 Firecat Vest Pocket, 22
Model 357 DA Revolver, 21
Model 400 Auto Pistol, 22
Model 600 Mil./Police Type, 22
Model 800 Condor Military, 22
Model 2000 Camper, 22
Model 2000 Cub Pocket, 22
Model 3000 Pocket, 22
Model 3003 Pocket, 22
Model 4000 Falcon, 22
Model A-60 DA, 22
Model A-70 Compact, 22
Model A-75 Decocker, 23
Model A-75 Ultralight, 22
Model A-80, 23
Model A-90 DA, 23
Model A-100 DA, 23
SHOTGUNS
Model 650 Over/Under Shotgun, 429
Model 750 Over/Under Shotgun, 429
AUSTRIAN MILITARY RIFLES
Model 90 Steyr-Mannlicher Carbine, 204
Model 90 Steyr-Mannlicher Rifle, 204
Model 95 Steyr-Mannlicher Carbine, 204
Model 95 Steyr-Mannlicher Service, 204
AUTAUGA ARMS
HANDGUNS
Model 32 DAO, 23
AUTO-ORDNANCE CORPORATION
HANDGUNS
1911 "The General", 23
1911A1 40 S&W Pistol, 23
1911A1 Government Auto Pistol, 23
1927 A-1 Semiautomatic Pistol, 23
ZG-51 Pit Bull, 23
RIFLES
Thompson 27A-1C Lightweight, 211
Thompson 27A-1 Commando, 211
Thompson M1 Semiautomatic, 211
Thompson Model 22-27A-3, 210
Thompson Model 27A-1 Deluxe, 210
Thompson Model 27A-1 Carbine, 211
AYA (Aguirre Y Aranzabal)
SHOTGUNS
Bolero, 430
Contento Over/Under Shotgun, 430
Model 1 Hammerless Double, 429
Model 2 Hammerless Double, 430
Model 4 Hammerless Double, 430

Model 37 Super A, 430
Model 37 Supe, 430
Model 53E, 430
Model 56 Hammerless Double, 430
Model 76 Hammerless Double, 430
Model 76—.410 Gauge, 430
Model 117 Hammerless Double, 430
Matador Hammerless Double, 430
Matador II, 431
Matador III, 431
Model XXV Boxlock, 431
Model XXV Sidelock, 431
BAER, Les
HANDGUNS
1911 Concept Series, 24
1911 Custom Carry Series, 24
1911 Premier Series, 24
1911 Ultimate Master Combat Series, 24
S.R.P. Automatic Pistol, 24
BAIKAL
RIFLES
IZH-18MN Single Shot, 211
MP221 Side By Side, 211
MP161K Semi Automatic, 211
SHOTGUNS
IZH-43 Series Side/Side, 431
Model IZH-18M Single Shot, 431
Model IZH-27 Field Over/Under, 431
Model IZH-27 Over/Under, 431
Model IZH-43 Field Side/Side, 431
MP94 (IZH-94 or SPR94) Combination, 431
BAKER
SHOTGUNS
Batavia Ejector, 431
Batavia Leader Hammerless Double, 431
Batavia Special, 431
Black Beauty, 431
Grade R, 431
Grade S, 432
Paragon, Expert and Deluxe Grades, 432
BALLARD
RIFLES
1-1/2 Hunter's, 211
1-3/4 Far West, 211
No. 5 Pacific, 211
No. 4-1/2 Mid-Range, 211
No. 7 Long-Range, 211
Model 1885 High Wall, 211
BANSNER'S
RIFLES
High Tech Series, 211
Safari Hunter, 211
Ultimate One, 211
World Slam Limited Edition, 211
BARRETT FIREARMS
RIFLES
Model 82 A-1 Semiautomatic Rifle, 212
Model 90 Bolt-Action Rifle, 212
Model 95 Bolt Action, 212
Model 98B Bolt-Action, 212
Model M4468 Semiautomatic, 212
BAUER FIREARMS CORPORATION
25 Automatic Pistol, 24
BAYARD PISTOLS
Model 1908 Pocket, 24
Model 1923 Pocket, 24
Model 1923 Pocket 25, 24
Model 1930 Pocket 25, 24
BEEMAN PRECISION ARMS
HANDGUNS
Mini P08 Automatic Pistol, 25
P08 Automatic Pistol, 24
SP Metallic Silhouette Pistols, 25
RIFLES
Feinwerkbau Model 2600 Series, 212
Weihrauch HW Model 60M Small Bore, 212
Weihrauch HW Model 660 Match, 212
Weihrauch HW Models 60J and 60J-ST, 212
BEHOLLA
Pocket Automatic Pistol, 25
BELGIAN
MILITARY RIFLES
Model 1889 Mauser Military Rifle, 212
Model 1916 Mauser Carbine, 212
Model 1935 Mauser Military Rifle, 212
Model 1936 Mauser Military Rifle, 212
BELKNAP
SHOTGUNS
Model B-63 Single-Shot Shotgun, 432
Model B-63E Single-Shot Shotgun, 432
Model B-64 Slide-Action Shotgun, 432
Model B-65C Autoloading Shotgun, 432
Model B-68 Single-Shot Shotgun, 432
BENELLI
RIFLES
R1 Semi-Automatic, 212

HANDGUNS
Model B-76, 25
Model B-76S, 25
Model B-77, 25
Model B-80, 25
Model B-82, 25
Model MP3S, 25
MP90S World Cup Target Pistol, 25
MP95E Sport Target Pistol, 25
SHOTGUNS
Black Eagle Autoloading Shotgun, 432
Black Eagle Executive, 433
Cordoba, 433
Legacy Autoloading Shotgun, 433
M1 Field Autoloading Shotgun, 433
M1 Super 90 Autoloading Shotgun, 433
M1 Super 90 Defense Autoloader, 433
M1 Super 90 Field, 433
M1 Super 90 Slug Autoloader, 433
M1 Super 90 Sporting Special Autoloader, 433
M2 Autoloader, 433
M3 Super 90 Pump/Autoloader, 433
M4 Tactical Autoloader, 434
Model 121 M1 Military/Police, 432
Montefeltro Super 90 Semiautomatic, 434
Nova Pump Shotgun, 434
SL 121V Semiauto Shotgun, 434
SL 121V Slug Shotgun, 434
SL 123V Semiauto Shotgun, 434
SL 201 Semiautomatic Shotgun, 434
Sport Autoloading Shotgun, 434
Super Black Eagle Autoloading, 434
Ultra Light, 434
Vinci, 434
BENTON & BROWN FIREARMS
Model 93 Bolt-Action Rifle, 212
BERETTA USA
HANDGUNS
Laramie, SA Revolver, 31
Model 20 Double-Action, 26
Model 21 Double-Action, 26
Model 70 Automatic, 26
Model 70S, 26
Model 70T, 26
Model 71, 26
Model 72, 26
Model 76 Auto Target Pistol, 26
Model 81 Double-Action, 26
Model 82 Double-Action, 26
Model 82W, 27
Model 84 Double-Action, 26
Model 84B DA Auto Pistol, 26
Model 84(BB) Double-Action, 26
Model 84 Cheetah 27
Model 85 Double-Action, 27
Model 85B DA, 27
Model 85BB Double-Action, 27
Model 85 Cheetah, 27
Model 85F DA, 27
Model 86 Cheetah DA, 27
Model 87 Cheetah, 27
Model 89 Gold Standard Target, 27
Model 90 DA, 27
Model 90-TWO Type F, 27
Model 92 DA Auto Pistol (1st series), 27
Model 92D, 28
Model 92F Compact, 28
Model 92F Compact L Type M, 28
Model 92F DA, 28
Model 92FS, 29
Model 92FS Brigadier, 28
Model 92FS Centurion, 28
Model 92FS Border Marshal, 28
Model 92G-SD, 29
Model 92G Elite IA, 29
Model 92G Elite II, 29
Model 92S DA (2nd series), 28
Model 92SB-P DA (3rd series), 28
Model 96 DA, 29
Model 96 Stock, 29
Model 101, 29
Model 318 (1934), 29
Model 418, 29
Model 949 Olympic Target, 29
Model 950B, 29
Model 950B Jetfire, 29
Model 950CC, 29
Model 950CC Special, 29
Model 951 (1951) Military, 29
Model 1915, 29
Model 1923, 29
Model 1934, 30
Model 1935, 30
Model 3032 DA Tomcat, 30
Model 8000/8040/8045 Cougar, 30
Model 8000/8040/8045 Mini-Cougar, 30

Model 9000S Subcompact, 30
Stampede, SA Revolver, 31
RIFLES
455 S/S Express Double Rifle, 213
500 Bolt-Action Sporter, 213
501 Bolt-Action Sporter, 213
502 Bolt-Action Sporter, 213
AR-70 Semiautomatic Rifle, 213
Express S686/S689 Sable, 213
Express SSO Over/Under Express Double, 213
Mato, 214
Small Bore Sporting Carbine, 214
SHOTGUNS
D10 Trident, 439
Grade 100 Over/Under Shotgun, 440
Grade 200, 440
Model 57E Over/Under, 434
Model 409PB Hammerless Double, 434
Model 410, 10-Gauge Magnum, 435
Model 410E, 434
Model 411E, 435
Model 424 Hammerless Double, 435
Model 426E, 435
Model 450 Series Hammerless Doubles, 435
Model 470 Series Hammerless Doubel, 435
Model 625 S/S Hammerless Double, 435
Model 626 S/S Hammerless Double, 435
Model 627 S/S Hammerless Double, 435
Model 682 Over/Under Shotgun, 435
Model 686 Over/Under Shotgun, 436
Model 687 Over/Under Shotgun, 436
Model 1200 Series Semiautoloading, 436
Model A-301 Autoloading Shotgun, 436
Model A-301 Magnum, 437
Model A-301 Skeet Gun, 437
Model A-301 Slug Gun, 437
Model A-301 Trap Gun, 437
Model A-302 Semiautoloading, 437
Model A-302 Super Lusso, 437
Model A-303 Semiautoloader, 437
Model A-303 Youth Gun, 437
Model AL-390 Semiautomatic, 437
Model AL-390 Target, 437
Model AL-1 Field Gun, 437
Model AL-2 Autoloading Shotgun, 438
Model AL-2 Magnum, 438
Model AL-2 Skeet Gun, 438
Model AL-2 Trap Gun, 438
Model AL-3 Deluxe Trap Gun, 438
Model AL-3, 438
Model AL390 Field, 438
Model AL390 Sport Skeet, 438
Model AL390 Sport Sporting, 438
Model AL390 Sport Trap, 438
Model AL391 Urika Autoloading, 438
Model ASE 90 Over/Under, 439
Model ASE Series Over/Under Shotgun, 439
Model BL-1/BL-2 Over/Under, 439
Model BL-2/S, 439
Model BL-3, 439
Models BL-4, BL-5 and BL-6, 439
Model BL Series Skeet Guns, 439
Model BL Series Trap Guns, 439
Model FS-1 Folding Single, 439
Golden Snipe Over/Under, 440
Model GR-2 Hammerless Double, 440
Model GR-3, 440
Model GR-4, 440
Mark II Single-Barrel Trap Gun, 440
Model S55B Over/Under Shotgun, 440
Model S56E, 440
Model S58 Skeet Gun, 440
Model S58 Trap Gun, 440
Silver Hawk Featherweight, 440
Silver Snipe Over/Under Shotgun, 441
Model SL-2 Pigeon Series Pump Gun, 441
Model "SO" Series Shotguns, 441
Models SO-6 and SO-9 Premium Grade, 441
Model SO6/SO7 S/S Doubles, 441
Model TR-1 Single-Shot Trap, 441
Model TR-2, 441
Victoria Pintail (ES100), 442
BERNARDELLI, Vincenzo, S.P.A.
HANDGUNS
Model 60 Pocket, 31
Model 68, 31
Model 69 Automatic Target, 31
Model 80, 31
Model 90 Sport Target, 31
Model 100 Target, 31
Model AMR, 31
Model "Baby" Automatic Pistol, 31
Model P010, 31
Model P018 Compact, 31
Model P018 DA, 32

Model P. One DA Auto Pistol, 32
Model P. One Practical VB, 32
Model Sporter, 32
Model USA, 32
Model Vest Pocket, 32
SHOTGUNS
Brescia Hammer Double, 442
Elio Double, 442
Gamecock, Premier (Rome 3), 443
Gamecock, Standard (S. Uberto 1), 443
Gardone Hammer Double, 443
Hemingway Hammerless Double, 443
Holland V.B. Series, 443
Italia, 443
Model 115 Series Over/Under Shotguns, 442
Roma 4 and Roma 6, 443
Roma 7, 8, and 9, 443
S. Uberto 2, 443
S. Uberto F.S., 443
RIFLES
Carbina .22, 214
Express VB, 214
Express 2000, 214
Minerva Express, 214
Model 120, 214
Model 190, 214
Model 2000, 214
BERSA
Model 83, 32
Model 85, 32
Model 86, 33
Model 95, 33
Model 97, 33
Model 223, 33
Model 224, 33
Model 226, 33
Model 383, 33
Model 622, 33
Model 644, 33
Thunder 9, 33
Thunder 22 Auto Pistol (Model 23), 34
Thunder 380, 34
Thunder 380 Plus, 34
BLASER USA
RIFLES
Model R84 Bolt-Action Rifle, 214
Model R93 Classic Series Bolt-Action, 214
Model R93 Safari Series Bolt-Action, 214
BOSS & COMPANY
Hammerless Double-Barrel Shotgun, 444
Hammerless Over/Under Shotgun, 444
BREDA MECCANICA BRESCIANA
Altair Special, 444
Andromeda Special, 444
Astro, 444
Astrolux, 444
Aries 2, 445
Ermes Series, 444
Gold Series Auto, 444
Gold Series Standard, 444
Magnum Model, 444
Mira, 444
Sirio Standard, 444
Vega Lusso, 444
Vega Special O/U, 444
Vega Special Trap, 444
BRETTON SHOTGUNS
Baby Standard Sprint Over/Under, 445
Fair Play Over/Under, 445
Sprint Deluxe Over/Under, 445
BRITISH MILITARY RIFLES
Light Rifle No. 4 Mark I, 215
Rifle No. 1 Mark III, 215
Rifle No. 3 Mark I (Pattern '14), 215
Rifle No. 4 Mark I, 215
Rifle No. 5 Mark I, 215
BRNO
RIFLES—*See also CZ Rifles*
Model I Bolt-Action Sporting Rifle, 215
Model II Bolt-Action Sporting, 215
Model III Bolt-Action Sporting, 215
Model IV Bolt-Action Target, 215
Model V Bolt-Action Sporting, 215
Model 21H Bolt-Action Sporting Rifle, 216
Model 22F, 216
Model 98 Mannlicher, 216
Model 98 Standard, 216
Model ZKB-110 Single-Shot, 216
Model ZKB 689 Bolt-Action Rifle, 216
Model ZKM 611 Semiautomatic Rifle, 216
Hornet Bolt-Action Sporting Rifle, 216
SHOTGUNS
CZ 581 Solo Over/Under Shotgun, 445
Model 500 Over/Under, 445
Model 500 Series Over/Under Combination, 445

Super Series Over/Under Shotgun, 445
ZH 300 Series Over/Under Combination, 445
ZH 300 Series Over/Under, 445
ZP 149 Hammerless Double, 445
BROLIN ARMS
HANDGUNS
Bantam, 34
"Legend Series", 34
"Patriot Series", 34
"Pro-Stock and Pro-Comp", 34
TAC Series, 34
SHOTGUNS
Arms Hawk Pump—Field Series, 445
Arms Hawk Pump—Combo Model, 445
Arms Hawk Pump—Lawman Model, 445
Arms Hawk—Slug Model, 445
Arms Hawk—Turkey Special, 446
BRONCO PISTOL
Model 1918 Pocket, 34
Vest Pocket Auto Pistol, 34
BROWN PRECISION RIFLES
High Country Bolt-Action Sporter, 216
High Country Youth Rifle, 217
Model 7 Super Light Sporter, 216
Pro-Hunter Bolt-Action Rifle, 217
Pro-Varminter Bolt-Action Rifle, 217
Selective Target Model, 217
Tactical Elite Rifle, 217
BROWNING
HANDGUNS
25 Automatic Pistol, 34
32 and 380 Automatic Pistol, 1955 Type, 34
380 Automatic Pistol, 1971 Type, 34
BDA DA Automatic Pistol, 35
BDA-380 DA Automatic Pistol, 35
BDM 9mm DA Automatic Pistol, 35
Buck Mark 22 Automatic Pistol, 35
Buck Mark 22 Camper, 35
Buck Mark 22 Bullseye, 35
Buck Mark 22 Bullseye Target, 35
Buck Mark 22 Challenge, 36
Buck Mark 22 Field, 36
Buck Mark 22 Lite Splash URX, 36
Buck Mark 22 Micro, 36
Buck Mark 22 Micro Plus, 36
Buck Mark 22 Plus, 36
Buck Mark 22 Silhouette, 36
Buck Mark 22 Target 5.5, 36
Buck Mark 22 Unlimited Silhouette, 36
Buck Mark 22 Varmint, 36
Challenger, 37
Challenger II, 37
Challenger III, 37
Hi-Power Automatic Pistol, 37
Hi-Power Capitan, 38
Hi-Power Mark III, 38
Hi-Power Practical, 38
Hi-Power Silver Chrome, 38
Hi-Power 9mm Classic, 38
International Medalist Target Pistol, 38
Medalist Automatic Target Pistol, 39
Nomad Automatic Pistol, 39
Renaissance 9mm, 25 Auto and 380 Auto (1955)
   Engraved Models, 39
RIFLES
BL-22 Lever-Action Repeating Rifle, 223
BLR Lever-Action Repeating Rifle, 223
BLR Lightning Model, 223
BLR Model '81, 224
BPR Pump Rifle, 224
BPR-22 Pump Rifle, 224
F.N. Browning FAL Semiautomatic, 225
High-Power Bolt-Action, Medallion, 224
High-Power Bolt-Action, Olympian, 224
High-Power Bolt-Action, Safari Grade, Medium
   Action, 224
High-Power Bolt-Action, Safari Grade, Short Action,
   224
High-Power Bolt-Action, Safari Grade, Standard
   Action, 224
Model 22 Automatic Rifle, Grade I, 217
Model 22 Automatic Rifle, Grade II, 217
Model 22 Automatic Rifle, Grade III, 217
Model 22 Automatic, Grade VI, 217
Model 52 Bolt-Action Rifle, 217
Model 53 Lever-Action Rifle, 217
Model 65 Grade I Lever-Action Rifle, 218
Model 65 High Grade Rifle, 218
Model 71 Grade I Carbine, 218
Model 71 Grade I Lever-Action Rifle, 218
Model 71 High-Grade Carbine, 218
Model 71 High-Grade Rifle, 218
Model 78 Bicentennial Set, 218
Model 78 Single-Shot Rifle, 218
Model 1885 Single-Shot Rifle, 219

Model 1886 Grade I Lever-Action, 219
Model 1886 High-Grade Lever-Action, 219
Model 1886 Montana Centennial, 219
Model 1895 Grade I Lever-Action, 219
Model 1895 High-Grade Lever-Action, 219
Model A-Bolt 22 Rifle, 220
Model A-Bolt Eclipse Bolt Rifle, 220
Model A-Bolt Euro-Bolt Rifle, 220
Model A-Bolt Hunter-Grade Rifle, 220
Model A-Bolt Medallion-Grade Rifle, 220
Model A-Bolt Stalker Rifle, 222
Model A-Bolt Varmint II Rifle, 222
Model B-92 Lever-Action Rifle, 222
Model BAR Automatic Rifle, Grade I, 222
Model BAR, Grade I, 222
Model BAR, Grade II, 222
Model BAR, Grade III, 222
Model BAR, Grade IV, 222
Model BAR, Grade V, 222
Model BAR Mark II Safari Automatic, 223
Model BAR-22 Automatic Rifle, 223
Model BBR Lightning Rifle, 223
"T-Bolt" T-1 22 Repeating Rifle, 224
"T-Bolt" T-2, 224

SHOTGUNS
A-500G Gas-Operated SA, 447
A-500G Sporting Clays, 447
A-500R Semiautomatic, 447
A-Bolt Series Shotgun, 447
Autoloading, Grade II, III and IV, 447
Automatic-5, Buck Special Models, 448
Automatic-5 Classic, 448
Automatic-5 Gold Classic, 448
Automatic-5, Light 12, 448
Automatic-5, Light 20, 448
Automatic-5, Magnum 12 Gauge, 448
Automatic-5, Magnum 20 Gauge, 448
Automatic-5, Skeet Model, 449
Automatic-5, Stalker, 449
Automatic-5, Standard (Grade I), 449
Automatic-5, Sweet 16, 449
Automatic-5, Sweet Sixteen New Model, 449
Automatic-5, Trap Model, 449
B-80 Gas-Operated, 449
B-80 Plus, 449
B-80 Superlight, 449
B-80 Upland Special, 450
BPS Game Gun Deer Special, 450
BPS Game Gun Turkey Special, 450
BPS Pigeon Grade, 450
BPS Pump Invector Stalker, 450
BPS Pump Shotgun, 450
BPS Youth and Ladies' Model, 450
BSA 10 Semiautomatic Shotgun, 450
B-SS S/S 20 Gauge Sporter, 450
B-SS Side/Side Sidelock, 450
B-SS Side/Side, 450
BT-99 Competition Trap Special, 450
BT-99 Grade I Single Bbl. Trap, 450
BT-99 Max, 450
BT-99 Plus Micro, 451
BT-99 Plus, 451
BT-100 Single-Shot Trap, 451
Citori Hunting Over/Under Models, 451
Citori Lightning Over/Under Models, 451
Citori Skeet Gun, 451
Citori Sporting Clays, 452
Citori Superlight Over/Under Field Shotguns, 452
Citori Trap Gun, 452
Citori Upland Special Over/Under Shotgun, 453
Citori White Lightning Shotgun, 453
Citori White Upland Special, 454
Cynery, 454
Double Automatic (Steel Receiver), 454
Gold Deer Hunter Autoloading, 454
Gold Hunter Series Autoloading, 454
Gold Stalker Series, 454
Gold Sporting Series, 454
Grade I Autoloader, 446
Liège Over/Under Shotgun, 454
Light Sporting 802ES, 454
Lightning Sporting Clays, 454
Special 441, 446
Special Skeet, 446
Model 12 Pump Shotgun, 446
Model 42 Limited Edition Shotgun, 446
Model 2000 Buck Special, 446
Model 2000 Gas Automatic, Field, 446
Model 2000 Magnum Model, 446
Model 2000 Skeet Model, 447
Model 2000 Trap Model, 447
Over/Under Classic, 454
Over/Under Gold Classic, 454
Recoilless Trap Shotgun, 454
Superposed Bicentennial Commemorative, 454

Superposed Broadway 12 Trap, 455
Superposed Hunting Models, 455
Superposed Lightning and Superlight Models, 455
Superposed Magnum, 456
Superposed Ltd. Black Duck Issue, 456
Superposed Ltd. Mallard Duck Issue, 456
Superposed Ltd. Pintail Duck Issue, 456
Superposed, Presentation Grades, 456
Superposed Skeet Guns, Grade I, 456
Superposed Super-Light Model, 456
Superposed Trap Gun, 456
Twelvette Double Automatic, 456
Utility Field Gun, 446

BRYCO ARMS
Models J22, J25, 39
Models M25, M32, M38, 39
Model M48, 39
Model M58, 39
Model M59, 39
Model Nine, 39

BSA GUNS
Centurion Model Match Rifle, 226
CF-2 Bolt-Action Hunting Rifle, 226
CF-2 Stutzen Rifle, 226
CFT Target Rifle, 226
Model 12/15 Martini Heavy, 226
Model 12/15 Martini SS Target Rifle, 226
Model 15 Martini Target Rifle, 226
Majestic Deluxe Featherweight Hunting Rifle, 226
Majestic Deluxe Standard Weight, 226
Martini-International ISU Match, 226
Martini-International Mark V Match, 226
Martini-International Match Rifle—Light Pattern, 226
Martini-International Match Rifle Single-Shot Heavy, 226
Martini-International MK II Match, 226
Martini-International MK III Match, 226
Monarch Deluxe Hunting Rifle, 227
Monarch Deluxe Varmint Rifle, 227
No. 12 Martini Target Rifle, 225
No. 13 Martini SS Target Rifle, 226
No. 13 Sporting Rifle, 226

BUDISCHOWSKY PISTOL
TP-70 DA Automatic, 39

BUSHMASTER FIREARMS
M17S Bullpup, 227
Model XM15 E2S Series, 227

CABELA'S, INC.
1858 Henry Replica, 228
1866 Winchester Replica, 228
1873 Winchester Replica, 228
1873 Sporting Model replica, 228
Cattleman Carbine, 228
Sharps Sporting Rifle, 228

CALICO LIGHT WEAPONS SYSTEMS
HANDGUNS
Model 110, 46
Model M-950, 46
RIFLES
Liberty 50/100 Semiautomatic Rifle, 228
Model M-100 Semiautomatic Series, 228
Model M-105 Semiautomatic Sporter, 228
Model M-900 Semiautomatic Carbine, 228
Model M-951 Tactical Carbine, 228

CANADIAN MILITARY RIFLES
Model 1907 Mark II Ross Military, 228

CENTURY ARMS (CENTURY INTERNATIONAL ARMS)
RIFLES
Centurion M38/M96 Sporter, 228
Centurion M98 Bolt-Action Sporter, 228
Centurion P-14 Sporter, 228
CETME Sporter, 229
Degtyarev DP28, 230
Enfield Sporter No. 4 Bolt-Action Rifle, 229
Gamestalker, 229
G-3 Sporter, 229
GP 1975, 230
GP WASR-10, 229
Golani Sporter, 229
L1A1 FAL Sporter, 229
L1A1/R1A1 Sporter, 229
M-14 Sporter, 229
M-76 Sniper, 230
Model B-82, 229
PAR 1, 230
S.A.R. 1, 229
Sterling SA, 230
Tantal Sporter, 229
Tiger Dragunov, 229
VZ 2008 Sporter, 229
SHOTGUNS
Artemis, 457
Catamount Fury I, 458
Catamount Fury II, 458

Coach, 458
Model IJ2, 458
Phantom, 458
PW87, 458
SAS-12, 458
Ultra 87, 458

CHARLES DALY—*See Daly, Charles*

CHARTER ARMS CORPORATION
HANDGUNS
Bonnie and Clyde Set, 40
Bulldog 357 DA Revolver, 40
Bulldog 44 DA Revolver, 40
Bulldog New Police DA Revolver, 40
Bulldog Police DA Revolver, 41
Bulldog Pug DA Revolver, 41
Bulldog Target DA Revolver, 41
Bulldog Tracker DA Revolver, 41
Explorer II Semiauto Survival Pistol, 41
Model 40, 40
Model 79K, 40
Off-Duty DA Revolver, 42
Pathfinder DA Revolver, 42
Pit Bull DA Revolver, 42
Undercover 32 H&R Magnum or S&W Long, 42
Undercover DA Revolver, 42
Undercover Pocket Police DA Revolver, 42
Undercover Police DA Revolver, 42
Undercoverette DA Revolver, 42
RIFLES
AR-7 Explorer Survival Rifle, 230

CHIAPPA FIREARMS
American Legend S/S Shotgun, 464
Classic Field Grade S/S Shotgun, 464
Model 1887, 464
Premier Grade S/S Shotgun, 464

CHIPMUNK RIFLES
Bolt-Action Single-Shot Rifle, 203

CHURCHILL
RIFLES
Highlander Bolt-Action Rifle, 230
"One of One Thousand" Rifle, 230
Regent Bolt-Action Rifle, 230
SHOTGUNS
Automatic Shotgun, 457
Monarch Over/Under Shotgun, 458
Regent Over/Under Shotguns, 458
Regent Skeet, 458
Regent Trap, 458
Sporting Clays Over/Under, 458
Windsor Over/Under Shotguns, 458
Windsor Side-by-Side Shotguns, 458

CHURCHILL, E.J. Ltd.
Field Model Hammerless Double, 458
Premiere Quality Hammerless Double, 458
Premiere Quality Over/Under, 458
Utility Model Hammerless Double Barrel, 459
XXV Hercules, 459
XXV Imperial, 459
XXV Premiere Hammerless Double, 459
XXV Regal, 459

CIMMARON
HANDGUNS
1872 Open Top Navy/Army, 42
Badlands, 42
El Pistolero Single-Action Revolver, 42
Frontier Six-Shooter, 42
RIFLES
1860 Henry Lever-Action, 230
1866 Yellowboy Carbine, 231
1866 Yellowboy Lever-Action, 230
1873 Lever-Action, 230
1873 Saddle Ring Carbine, 231
1874 Falling Block, 231
1876 Carbine, 232
1876 Centennial Sporting Rifle, 232
1883 Burgess Rifle, 231
1885 Hi-Wall Rifle, 232
1885 Low-Wall Rifle, 232
1892 Rifle, 232
1892 Carbine, 232
Adobe Walls Falling Block Rifle, 231
Civil War Henry Rifle, 231
Lightning Magazine Rifle, 231
Long range Creedmoor, 231
Model 1860 Spencer Rifle, 231
Model 1865 Spencer Repeating Rifle, 231
Model 1871 Rolling Block Baby Carbine, 231
Model 1874 Sporting Rifle, 231
Sharps Rocky Mountain II Model 74, 231
Sharps No. 1 Rifle, 231
CLASSIC DOUBLES
Model 101 Over/Under Shotgun, 459
Model 201 Side-by-Side Shotgun, 459
Model 201 Small Bore Set, 459

CLERKE RECREATION PRODUCTS
Deluxe Hi-Wall, 231
Hi-Wall Single-Shot Rifle, 231
CLIFTON ARMS
Scout Bolt-Action Rifle, 231
COGSWELL & HARRISON, Ltd.
Ambassador Hammerless Double-Barrel Shotgun, 459
Avant Tout Series Hammerless Double-Barrel Shotguns, 459
Best Quality Hammerless Sidelock Double-Barrel, 459
Huntic Model Hammerless Double, 459
Markor Hammerless Double, 459
Regency Hammerless Double, 459
COLT'S MANUFACTURING CO., INC.
SEMI- AUTOMATIC PISTOLS
Model 1900 38, 43
Model 1902 Military 38, 43
Model 1902 Sporting 38, 43
Model 1903 Pocket 32 First Issue, 43
Model 1903 Pocket 32 Second Issue, 43
Model 1903 Pocket 32 Third Issue, 43
Model 1903 Pocket 32 Fourth Issue, 43
Model 1903 Pocket 32 Hammerless, 44
Model 1903 Pocket 38 Hammer, 44
Model 1905 45 Automatic, 44
Model 1905 45 (1907), 44
Model 1908 Pocket 25 Hammerless, 44
Model 1908 Pocket 380, 44
Model 1911 Commercial, 45
Model 1911A1 Commercial, 45
Model 1911 Colt Manufacture, 44
Model 1911 North American, 44
Model 1911 Remington-UMC, 44
Model 1911 Springfield, 44
Model 1911 Navy Model, 44
M1911, Model O, Series 70, WWI repro, 45
M1911A1, Model O, Series 70, WWII repro, 45
1991 Series Government Model, Series 70, Model O, 45
1991 Series Government Model, Series 80, Model O, 45
22 Cadet, 45
22 Sport, 45
22 Target, 45
Ace Automatic Pistol, 45
All American Model 2000, 46
Automatic Caliber .25, 46
Challenger, 46
Commander, 46
Combat Commander, 46
Commander Lightweight, 46
Conversion Unit—45-22, 46
Conversion Unit—22-45, 46
Defender, 46
Delta Elite, 46
Delta Elite (Current), 47
Delta Gold Cup, 47
Gold Cup Mark III National Match, 47
Gold Cup National Match 45, 47
Government Model 1911/1911A1, 47
Huntsman, 47
MK I & II Series '90 Double Eagle Combat Commander, 47
MK II/Series '90 Double Eagle DA, 47
MK II/Series '90 Double Eagle Officer's ACP, 47
MK II/MK III National Match Mid-Range, 47
MK IV/Series '70 Combat Commander, 47
MK IV/Series '70 Gold Cup National Match 45, 48
MK IV/Series '70 Gov't., 48
MK IV/Series '80 380, 48
MK IV/Series '80 Combat Commander, 48
MK IV/Series '80 Combat Government, 48
MK IV/Series '80 Gold Cup National Match, 48
MK IV/Series '80 Government Model, 48
MK IV/Series '80 Lightweight Commander, 48
MK IV/Series '80 Mustang 380, 48
MK IV/Series '80 Mustang Plus II, 49
MK IV/Series '80 Mustang Pocketlite, 49
MK IV/Series '80 Officer's ACP, 49
MK IV/Series '80 SA Lightweight Concealed Carry Officer, 49
MK IV/Series '90 Defender SA Lightweight, 49
MK IV/Series '90 Pony DAO Pistol, 49
MK IV/Series '90 Pony Pocketlite, 49
National Match Automatic Pistol, 49
New Agent, 50
NRA Centennial 45 Gold Cup National Match, 50
Pocket Junior, 50
Super 38, 50
Super Match 38, 50
Targetsman, 50
USMC M45 CQBP, 50
Woodsman Match Target First Issue, 50
Woodsman Match Target, Second Issue, 50
Woodsman Match Target "4.5", 50

Woodsman Sport Model, First Issue, 50
Woodsman Sport Model, Second Issue, 50
Woodsman Target Model, First Issue, 50
Woodsman Target Model, Second Issue, 51
Woodsman Target Model, Third Issue, 51
World War I 50th Anniversary Commemorative Series, 51
World War II 50th Anniversary Commemorative, Series, 51
World War II Commemorative, 51
World War II D-Day Invasion Commemorative, 52
World War II Golden Anniversary V-J Day Tribute, 52
XSE Series Model O, 52
SINGLE-SHOT PISTOLS & DERRINGERS
Camp Perry Model Second Issue, 52
Camp Perry Model Single-Shot Pistol, First Issue, 52
Civil War Centennial, 52
Derringer No. 4 Commemoratives, 52
Derringer No. 4, 52
Lord and Lady Derringers, 53
Rock Island Arsenal Centennial, 53
REVOLVERS
38 DS II, 53
Agent (LW) DA, Second Issue, 53
Agent DA, First Issue, 53
Anaconda DA, 53
Anaconda Titanium DA, 54
Army Special DA, 54
Bankers' Special DA, 54
Bisley Model SA, 54
Buntline Special 45, 54
Cobra DA, Square Butt, 54
Cobra DA, Round Butt, First Issue, 54
Cobra DA, Second Issue, 54
Commando Special DA Revolver, 54
Detective Special DA, First Issue, 54
Detective Special DA, 2nd Issue, 55
Detective Special DA, 3rd Issue, 55
Detective Special DA, 4th Issue, 55
Diamondback DA, 55
DA Army, 55
Frontier Scout, 55
Frontier Scout Commemoratives, 55
1961 Issues:
Kansas Statehood Centennial, 55
Pony Express Centennial, 55
1962 Issues:
Columbus, Ohio, Sesquicentennial, 55
Fort Findlay Cased Pair, 55
Fort Findlay, Ohio, Sesquicentennial, 55
New Mexico Golden Anniversary, 55
West Virginia Statehood Centennial, 55
1963 Issues:
Arizona Territorial Centennial, 55
Battle of Gettysburg Centennial, 55
Carolina Charter Tercentenary, 56
Fort Stephenson, Ohio Sesquicentennial, 56
General John Hunt Morgan Indiana Raid, 56
Idaho Territorial Centennial, 56
1964 Issues:
California Gold Rush, 56
Chamizal Treaty, 56
General Hood Centennial, 56
Montana Territorial Centennial, 56
Nevada "Battle Born", 56
Nevada Statehood Centennial, 56
New Jersey Tercentenary, 56
St. Louis Bicentennial, 56
Wyoming Diamond Jubilee, 56
1965 Issues:
Appomattox Centennial, 56
Forty-Niner Miner, 56
General Meade Campaign, 56
Kansas Cowtown Series—Wichita, 56
Old Fort Des Moines Reconstruction, 56
Oregon Trail, 56
St. Augustine Quadricentennial, 56
1966 Issues:
Colorado Gold Rush, 56
Dakota Territory, 56
Indiana Sesquicentennial, 56
Kansas Cowtown Series—Abilene, 56
Kansas Cowtown Series—Dodge City, 56
Oklahoma Territory, 56
1967 Issues:
Alamo, 56
Kansas Cowtown Series—Coffeyville, 56
Kansas Trail Series—Chisholm Trail, 56
Lawman Series—Bat Masterson, 56
1968 Issues:
Kansas Trail Series—Pawnee Trail, 4
Kansas Trail Series—Santa Fe Trail, 56
Lawman Series—Pat Garrett, 56
Nebraska Centennial, 56

1969 Issues:
Alabama Sesquicentennial, 56
Arkansas Territory Sesquicentennial, 56
California Bicentennial, 56
General Nathan Bedford Forrest, 56
Golden Spike, 56
Kansas Trail Series—Shawnee Trail, 56
Lawman Series—Wild Bill Hickock, 56
1970 Issues:
Kansas Fort Series—Fort Hays, 56
Kansas Fort Series—Fort Larned, 57
Kansas Fort Series—Fort Riley, 57
Lawman Series—Wyatt Earp, 57
Maine Sesquicentennial, 57
Missouri Sesquicentennial, 57
1971 Issues:
Kansas Fort Series—Fort Scott, 57
1972 Issues:
Florida Territory Sesquicentennial, 57
1973 Issues:
Arizona Ranger, 57
King Cobra Revolver, 57
Lawman MK III DA Revolver, 57
Lawman MK V DA Revolver, 57
Magnum Carry DA Revolver, 57
Marine Corps Model (1905) DA Revolver, 57
Model 1877 Lightning Revolver, 57
Metropolitan MK III DA Revolver, 57
New Frontier Buntline Special, 57
New Frontier SA 22 Revolver, 57
New Frontier SA Army Revolver, 57
New Navy (1889) DA, First Issue, 57
New Navy (1892) DA, Second Issue, 58
New Pocket DA Revolver, 58
New Police DA Revolver, 58
New Police Target DA Revolver, 58
New Service DA Revolver, 58
New Service Target, 58
Officers' Model Match, 58
Officers' Model Special, 58
Officers' Model Target DA Revolver, First Issue, 58
Officers' Model Target, Second Issue, 58
Official Police DA Revolver, 59
Official Police MK III DA Revolver, 59
Peacekeeper DA Revolver, 59
Peacemaker 22 Revolver, 59
Peacemaker 22 2nd Amendment Commemorative, 59
Pocket Positive DA Revolver, 59
Police Positive DA, First Issue, 59
Police Positive DA, Second Issue, 59
Police Positive Special DA Revolver, 60
Police Positive Target DA Revolver, 60
Python DA Revolver, 60
Shooting Master DA Revolver, 60
SAA Revolver, 60
SA Army—125th Anniversary, 61
SA Army—Commemorative, 62
1963 Issues:
Arizona Territorial Centennial, 62
West Virginia Statehood Centennial, 62
1964 Issues:
Chamizal Treaty, 62
Colonel Sam Colt Sesquicentennial, 62
Deluxe Presentation, 62
Montana Territorial Centennial, 62
Nevada "Battle Born", 62
Nevada Statehood Centennial, 62
New Jersey Tercentenary, 62
Pony Express Presentation, 62
St. Louis Bicentennial, 62
Wyatt Earp Buntline, 62
1965 Issues:
Appomattox Centennial, 62
Old Fort Des Moines Reconstruction, 62
1966 Issues:
Abercrombie & Fitch Trailblazer—Chicago, 62
Abercrombie & Fitch Trailblazer—New York, 62
Abercrombie & Fitch Trailblazer—San Francisco, 62
California Gold Rush, 62
General Meade, 62
Pony Express Four Square, 62
1967 Issues:
Alamo, 62
Lawman Series—Bat Masterson, 62
1968 Issues:
Lawman Series—Pat Garrett, 62
1969 Issues:
Lawman Series—Wild Bill Hickok, 62
1970 Issues:
Lawman Series—Wyatt Earp, 62
Missouri Sesquicentennial, 62
Texas Ranger, 62
1971 Issues:
NRA Centennial, 62

1975 Issues:
Peacemaker Centennial, 62
Peacemaker Centennial 44-40, 62
Peacemaker Centennial Cased Pair, 62
1979 Issues:
Ned Buntline 45, 62
1986 Issues:
Colt 150th Anniversary, 62
Colt 150th Anniversary (Engraved), 62
SA Cowboy Revolver, 62
SA Sheriff's Model 45, 62
Three-Fifty-Seven DA Revolver, 62
Trooper DA Revolver, 62
Trooper MK III DA Revolver, 63
Trooper MK V Revolver, 63
U.S. Bicentennial Commemorative Set, 63
Viper DA Revolver, 63
RIFLES
1-22 Single-Shot Bolt-Action, 235
22 Autoloader, 235
AR-15 A2 Delta Match H-BAR Rifle, 232
AR-15 A2 Government Model, 233
AR-15 A2 Sporter ll, 233
AR-15 Compact 9mm Carbine, 233
AR-15 Semiautomatic Sporter, 234
AR-15 Sporter Competition H-BAR Rifle, 234
AR-15 Sporter Competition H-BAR (RS), 234
AR-15 Sporter Match Target, 234
AR-15 Sporter Target Rifle, 234
Colt-Sauer Drillings—*see Colt shotgun listings*
Custom Sporting Rifle, 235
Deluxe Rifle, 235
Grand African, 235
Grand Alaskan, 236
Lightning Magazine Rifle - Large Frame, 234
Lightning Magazine Rifle - Medium Frame, 235
Lightning Magazine Rifle - Small Frame, 235
Magnum, 236
Models of 1957 Rifles, 235
Model of 1961, 235
Model of 1961 Standard Rifle, 235
Short Action, 236
Stagecoach 22 Autoloader, 235
Standard Rifle, 235
Sporting Rifle, 236
SHOTGUNS
Auto—Magnum, 460
Auto—Magnum Custom, 460
Auto—Ultra Light Custom, 460
Auto—Ultra Light Standard, 460
Custom Hammerless Double, 460
Custom Pump, 460
Sauer Drilling, 460
Standard Pump Shotgun, 460
COMMANDO CARBINES
Mark III Semiautomatic Carbine, 236
Mark 9, 236
Mark 45, 236
CONNECTICUT VALLEY CLASSICS
Classic Field Over/Under, 461
Classic Sporter Over/Under, 461
CONNENTO/VENTUR
Model 51, 461
Model 52, 461
Model 53, 461
Model 62, 461
Model 64, 461
Mark I, 461
Mark II, 461
Mark III, 461
Mark III Combo, 461
CONTINENTAL RIFLES
Double Rifle, 236
COONAN ARMS
Model 357 Magnum Cadet Compact, 63
Model 357 Magnum Auto, 63
COOPER ARMS
Model 21, 237
Model 22, 237
Model 22 Pro Varmint, 237
Model 36 TRP-1 Series, 237
Model 36CF Bolt-Action Rifle, 237
Model 36RF Bolt-Action Rifle, 237
Model 38 Single Shot, 237
Model 40 Classic Bolt-Action Rifle, 237
CUMBERLAND MOUNTAIN ARMS
Plateau Rifle, 237
CZ
PISTOLS
CZ 2075 RAMI P, 64
CZ 40, 64
CZ P-01, 63
CZ P-07 Duty, 64
CZ VZ 61 Skorpion, 65
Model 27, 64

Model 38, 64
Model 50, 64
Model 52, 64
Model 70, 64
Model 75 DA Auto, 64
Model 75 Shadow, 64
Model 75 SP-01 Phantom, 64
Model 75 B, 64
Model 82 DA, 64
Model 83 DA, 64
Model 85 Automatic DA, 65
Model 85 Combat DA, 65
Model 97B DA, 65
Model 100 DA, 65
Model 1945 DA Pocket, 65
Model Duo Pocket, 65
RIFLES
511 Semi-Automatic, 238
550 Bolt-Action Series, 238
ZKK 600 Bolt-Action Rifle, 237
ZKK 601 Bolt-Action Rifle, 237
ZKK 602 Bolt-Action Rifle, 237
ZKM 452 Bolt-Action Repeating Rifle, 238
ZKM 527 Bolt-Action Rifle, 238
ZKM 537 Sporter Bolt-Action Rifle, 238
SHOTGUNS
581 Solo O/U Shotgun, 456
Armarillo S/S Shotgun, 456
Bobwhite S/S Shotgun, 456
Canvasback (103 D) O/U Shotgun, 456
Durango S/S Shotgun, 457
Hammer Coach S/S Shotgun, 457
Hammer Classic S/S Shotgun, 457
Limited Edition O/U Shotgun, 457
Mallard O/U Shotgun, 457
Redhead Premier O/U Shotgun, 457
Ringneck S/S Shotgun, 457
Sporter Standard O/U Shotgun, 457
Woodcock Deluxe O/U Shotgun, 457
CZECHOSLOVAKIAN RIFLES
Model 1924 (VZ24) Mauser Military, 238
Model 1933 (VZ33) Mauser Military Carbine, 239
DAEWOO PISTOLS
PISTOLS
Model DH40, 66
Model DH45, 66
Model DP51, 66
Model DP52, 66
RIFLES
DR200 SA Semiautomatic Sporter, 239
DR300 SA Semiautomatic Sporter, 239
DAISY RIFLES
V/L Collector's Kit, 239
V/L Presentation Grade, 239
V/L Standard Rifle, 239
DAKOTA/E.M.F.
Bisley SA Revolver, 66
Hartford SA Revolver, 66
Model 1873 SA Revolver, 66
Model 1875 Outlaw SA Revolver, 66
Model 1890 Remington Police, 66
Sheriff's Model SA Revolver, 66
Target SA Revolver, 66
DAKOTA ARMS
RIFLES
Model 10 Single-Shot Rifle, 239
Model 22 Bolt-Action Sporter Rifle, 240
Model 76 African Bolt-Action Rifle, 240
Model 76 Alpine Bolt-Action Rifle, 240
Model 76 Traveler Series, 240
Model 76 Classic Bolt-Action Rifle, 240
Model 76 Longbow Tactical Rifle, 240
Model 76 Safari Bolt-Action Rifle, 240
Model 76 Varmint Bolt-Action Rifle, 240
Model 97 Hunter Bolt-Action Series, 240
Model 97 Varmint Hunter Bolt-Action, 241
SHOTGUNS
American Legend S/S Shotgun, 464
Classic Field Grade S/S Shotgun, 464
Premium Grade S/S Shotgun, 464
DALY, CHARLES
HANDGUNS
Model M1911 Field FS Auto, 66
RIFLES
Bolt Action Rifle, 241
Empire Combination Gun, 241
Empire Grade Auto Rifle, 241
Empire Grade Bolt-Action Rifle, 241
Field Grade Auto Rifle, 241
Field Grade Bolt-Action Rifle (RF), 241
Field Grade Hunter Bolt-Action Rifle, 241
Hammerless Drilling: See Listing under Charles Daly
Shotguns Hornet Rifle, 241
Mauser 98, 241
Mini-Mauser 98, 241

Semiautomatic Rifle, 241
Superior Combination Gun, 241
Superior Grade Bolt-Action Rifle, 241
True Youth Bolt-Action Rifle, 241
SHOTGUNS
1974 Wildlife Commemorative, 462
Commander Over/Under Shotgun, 461
Diamond Grade Over/Under, 463
Diamond GTX DL Hunter Over/Under Series, 463
DSS Hammerless Double, 463
Empire DL Hunter Over/Under, 463
Empire EDL Hunter Series, 463
Field Grade Over/Under, 463
Field Semiauto Shotgun, 463
Field III Over/Under Shotgun, 463
Hammerless Double-Barrel Shotgun, 461
Hammerless Drilling, 461
Hammerless Double—Empire Grade, 462
Luxie Over/Under, 463
Multi-XII Self-loading Shotgun, 463
Novamatic Lightweight Autoloader, 462
Novamatic Super Lightweight 20-Gauge Magnum, 462
Novamatic Super Lightweight, 462
Novamatic 12-Gauge Magnum, 462
Novamatic Trap Gun, 462
Over/Under Shotguns (Prewar), 462
Over/Under Shotguns (Postwar), 462
Sextuple Single-Barrel Trap Gun, 462
Single-Shot Trap Gun, 463
Sporting Clays Over/Under, 464
Superior Grade SS Trap, 463
Over/Under Presentation Grade, 463
Over/Under Superior II Shotgun, 463
DAN WESSON—*See Wesson Firearms*
DARNE S.A.
Hammerless Double-Barrel Shotguns, 464
DAVIDSON GUNS
Model 63B Double-Barrel Shotgun, 464
Model 63B Magnum, 464
Model 69SL Double-Barrel Shotgun, 464
Model 73 Stagecoach, 464
DAVIS INDUSTRIES HANDGUNS
Long Bore Derringer, 67
Model D Derringer, 67
Model P-32, 67
Model P-380, 67
DESERT INDUSTRIES HANDGUNS
Double Deuce, 67
Two-Bit Special Pistol, 67
DETONICS HANDGUNS
Combat Master, 67
Pocket 9, 67
Scoremaster, 67
Service Master, 67
Service Master II, 67
DIAMOND
Elite Series, 464
Gold Elite Series, 464
Gold Series, 464
Imperial Series, 464
Mariner, 464
Panther Series, 464
DOWNSIZER HANDGUNS
Model WSP DAO Pistol, 67
DPMS Firearms
Panther Carbine, 242
Panther 22, 242
Panther LR-308, 242
Panther LR-30S, 242
Panther LR-243, 242
Panther CSAT Tactical, 242
Panther Raptr, 242
Panther Repr, 242
Prairie Panther, 242
DREYSE PISTOLS
Model 1907 Automatic Pistol, 67
Vest Pocket Automatic Pistol, 68
DWM PISTOL
Pocket Automatic Pistol, 68
EAGLE ARMS RIFLES
Model EA-15 Carbine, 242
Model EA-15 Golden Eagle Match, 242
Model EA-15 Semiautomatic Rifle, 242
ED BROWN
"Class A Ltd" SA Automatic Pistol, 68
"Classic Custom" SA Automatic Pistol, 68
"Special Forces" SA Automatic Pistol, 68
EMF COMPANY RIFLES
Model AP74 Paratrooper, 243
Model AP-74 Semiautomatic Carbine, 243
Model AP74-W Sporter Carbine, 243
Model 1860 Henry Rifle, 243
Model 1866 Yellow Boy Carbine, 243
Model 1866 Yellow Boy Rifle, 243
Model 1873 Sporting Rifle Carbine, 243

Model 1873 Sporting Rifle, 243
ENFIELD REVOLVER
(British Service) No. 2 MK 1 Revolver, 68
ENTERPRISE ARMS PISTOLS
Boxer SA Automatic Pistol, 68
"Elite" SA Automatic Pistol, 68
"Medalist" SA Automatic Pistol, 68
"Tactical" SA Automatic Pistol, 68
"TSM" SA Automatic Pistol, 68
ERMA-WERKE
HANDGUNS
Model ER-772 Match Revolver, 68
Model ER-773 Match Revolver, 69
Model ER-777 Match Revolver, 69
Model ESP-85A Competition Pistol, 69
Model KGP68 Automatic Pistol, 69
Model KGP69 Automatic Pistol, 69
RIFLES
Model EG72 Pump Action Repeater, 243
Model EG73, 243
Model EG712 Lever-Action Repeating Carbine, 243
Model EGM1, 244
Model EM1 22 Semi Carbine, 244
EUROPEAN AMERICAN ARMORY
HANDGUNS
Big Bore Bounty Hunter SA Revolver, 70
European Model Auto Pistol, 69
EA22 Target, 70
Bounty Hunter SA Revolver, 70
FAB 92 Auto Pistol, 70
Standard Grade Revolver, 70
Tactical Grade Revolver, 70
Windicator Target Revolver, 70
Witness DA Auto Pistol, 70
Witness Carry Comp, 70
Witness Compact Witness (L Series), 70
Witness Subcompact DA Auto Pistol, 71
Witness Limited Class Auto Pistol, 71
Witness Target Pistols, 71
RIFLES
Model HW 660, 244
Model HW Bolt-Action Single-Shot Target Rifle, 244
Model Sabitti SP1822, 244
EXCEL ARMS OF AMERICA
Series 100-107 Over/Under Shotguns, 465
Series 200 Side-by-Side Shotgun, 465
Series 300 Over/Under Shotgun, 465
FABARM SHOTGUNS—See Heckler & Koch
FABRIQUE NATIONALE HERSTAL
Deluxe Mauser Bolt-Action Sporting Rifle, 245
Deluxe Mauser—Presentation Grade, 245
FAL/FNC/LAR Semiautomatic, 245
Models 1924, 1934/30 and 1930 Mauser Military
Rifles, 244
Model 1949 Semiautomatic Military, 245
Model 1950 Mauser Military Rifle, 245
Supreme Mauser Sporting, 245
Supreme Magnum Mauser, 245
FAS PISTOLS
Model 601 Match Target Pistol, 71
Model 602 Match Target Pistol, 71
Model 603 Match Target Pistol, 71
Model 607 Match Target Pistol, 71
FEATHER INDUSTRIES—See also Mitchell Arms
HANDGUNS
Guardian Angel Derringer, 71
RIFLES
Model AT-9 Semiautomatic Rifle, 245
Model AT-22, 245
Model F2 SA Carbine, 245
Model F9 SA Carbine, 245
FEG (FEGYVERGYAN)
Mark II AP-22 DA Automatic Pistol, 71
Mark II AP-380 DA Automatic Pistol, 71
Mark II APK-380 DA Automatic Pistol, 71
Model GKK-9 (92C) Auto Pistol, 72
Model GKK-45 Auto Pistol, 72
Model MBK-9HP Auto Pistol, 72
Model PA-63 Auto Pistol, 72
Model PJK-9HP Auto Pistol, 72
Model PSP-25 Auto Pistol, 72
Model SMC-22 Auto Pistol, 72
Model SMC-380 Auto Pistol, 72
Model SMC-918 Auto Pistol, 72
FIALA OUTFITTERS
Repeating Pistol, 72
FIAS
Grade I Over/Under, 465
F.I.E. CORPORATION
HANDGUNS
Arminius DA Standard Revolver, 72
Buffalo Scout SA Revolver, 73
Hombre SA Revolver, 73
Little Ranger SA Revolver, 73
Model A27BW "The Best" Semiauto, 72

Model TZ75 DA Semiautomatic, 73
Super Titan II, 73
Texas Ranger Single-Action Revolver, 73
Titan II Semiautomatic, 73
Titan Tiger Double-Action Revolver, 73
Yellow Rose SA Revolver, 73
FINNISH LION RIFLES
Champion Free Rifle, 245
Match Rifle, 245
Standard ISU Target Rifle, 245
Standard Target Rifle, 245
FIREARMS INTERNATIONAL
Model D Automatic Pistol, 73
Regent DA Revolver, 74
FN BROWNING PISTOLS
6.35mm Pocket Auto Pistol, 74
Baby Auto Pistol, 75
Model 1900 Pocket Auto Pistol, 74
Model 1903 Military Auto Pistol, 74
Model 1910 Pocket Auto Pistol, 74
Model 1922 (10/22) Police/Military Auto, 74
Model 1935 Military Hi-Power Pistols, 74
FOREHAND & WADSWORTH—See listings of comparable Harrington & Richardson and Iver Johnson Revolvers for values.
FORJAS TAURUS S.A.—See Taurus
FORT WORTH FIREARMS
Citation, 76
Match Master Standard, 75
Match master Dovetail, 75
Match Master Deluxe, 75
Olympic, 76
Sharpshooter, 76
Sport King, 76
Trophy, 76
Victor, 76
FOX SHOTGUNS
CMC Hammerless Double-Barrel, 466
Hammerless Double-Barrel Shot Guns, 466
Model B Hammerless Double, 465
Model B-DE, 465
Model B-DL, 465
Model B-SE, 466
Model B-ST, 466
Single-Barrel Trap Guns, 466
"Skeeter" Double-Barrel, 466
Sterlingworth Deluxe, 466
Sterlingworth Hammerless Double, 466
Sterlingworth Skeet and Upland Game Gun, 466
Super HE Grade, 466
FRANCAIS Le PISTOLS
Army Model Automatic Pistol, 76
Policeman Model Automatic Pistol, 76
Staff Officer Model Automatic Pistol, 76
FRANCHI, Luigi, S.P.A.
RIFLES
Centennial Automatic Rifle, 245
SHOTGUNS
Alcione Classic O/U, 468
Alcione Hammerless Double, 468
Alcione Over/Under, 468
Alcione Field (97-12 IBS) Over/Under, 469
Alcione Sport (SL IBS) Over/Under, 469
Alcione SX O/U, 469
Alcione Titanium O/U, 469
Alcione 2000 SX Over/Under Shotgun, 469
Aristocrat Deluxe and Supreme, 469
Aristocrat Field Model Over/Under, 469
Aristocrat Imperial and Monte Carlo, 469
Aristocrat Magnum Model, 469
Aristocrat Silver King, 469
Aristocrat Skeet Model, 469
Aristocrat Trap Model, 469
Astore 2, 469
Astore 5, 469
Astore Hammerless Double, 469
Black Magic 48/AL Semiautomatic, 469
Crown, Diamond and Imperial, 469
De Luxe Model Priti O/U, 469
Dynamic-12 Skeet Gun, 469
Dynamic-12 Slug Gun, 469
Dynamic-12, 469
Eldorado Model, 469
Falconet 2000 Over/Under Gun, 471
Falconet International Skeet Model, 469
Falconet International Trap Model, 470
Falconet Over/Under Field Models, 470
Falconet Standard Skeet Model, 470
Falconet Standard Trap Model, 470
Gas-Operated Semiautomatic, 470
Hammerless Sidelock Doubles, 470
Hunter Model, 470
Hunter Model Magnum, 471
LAW-12 Shotgun, 471
Model 48/AL Ultra Light Shotgun, 467

Model 500 Standard Autoloader, 467
Model 520 Deluxe, 467
Model 520 Eldorado Gold, 467
Model 610VS Semiautomatic, 467
Model 612 Variopress, 467
Model 620 Variopress, 468
Model 2003 Trap Over/Under, 468
Model 2004 Trap Single Barrel, 468
Model 2005 Combination Trap, 468
Model 2005/3 Combination Trap, 468
Model 3000/2 Combination Trap, 468
Peregrine Model 400, 471
Peregrine Model 451, 471
Renaissance Classic O/U, 469
Renaissance Elite O/U, 469
Renaissance Field O/U, 469
Renaissance Sporting O/U, 469
Skeet Gun, 471
Slug Gun, 471
SPAS-12 Shotgun, 471
Sporting 2000 Over/Under, 471
Standard Model Autoloader, 469
Standard Model Magnum, 469
Turkey Gun, 471
Veloce O/U, 469
Veloce Grade II O/U, 469
Veloce Squire O/U, 469
FRANCOTTE
RIFLES
Bolt-Action Rifle, 246
Boxlock Mountain Rifle, 246
Double Rifle, 246
SHOTGUNS
Boxlock Hammerless Doubles, 471
Model 6886, 471
Model 8446, 6930, 471
Model 8537, 9261, 471
Model 10/18E/628, 471
Boxlock Hammerless—A & F Series, 471
Jubilee Model No. 14, 471
Jubilee Model No. 18, 471
Jubilee Model No. 20, 471
Jubilee Model No. 25, 471
Jubilee Model No. 30, 471
No. 45 Eagle Grade, 471
Knockabout Model, 471
Boxlock Hammerles Doubles (Sideplates), 471
Models 10594, 8535, 6982, 471
Model 9/40E/38321, 471
Fine Over/Under Shotgun, 471
Fine Sidelock Hammerless Double, 472
Half-Fine Over/Under Shotgun, 472
FREEDOM ARMS
REVOLVERS
Model 1997 Premier Grade SA Revolver, 76
Model 83 Field Grade SA Revolver, 76
Model 83 Field Grade Hunter Pack SA Revolver, 76
Model 83 Premier Grade SA Revolver, 76
Model 83 Premier Grade Hunter Pack SA Revolver, 76
Model 83 Rimfire Grade SA Revolver, 76
Model 83 Silhouette Grade (Rimfire) SA Revolver, 76
Model 83 Silhouette Grade (Centerfire)
SA Revolver, 76
Model U.S. Deputy Marshal SA Revolver, 76
Model FA-L-22LR Mini-Revolver, 77
Model FA-S-22LR Mini-Revolver, 77
Model FA-S-22M Mini-Revolver, 77
FRENCH MILITARY PISTOLS
PISTOLS
Model 1935A Automatic Pistol, 77
Model 1935S Automatic Pistol, 77
Model 1950 Automatic Pistol, 77
Model MAB F1 Automatic Pistol, 77
Model MAB P-15 Automatic Pistol, 77
Model MAB P-8 Automatic Pistol, 77
RIFLES
Model 1936 MAS Military Rifle, 246
FROMMER PISTOLS
Baby Pocket Automatic Pistol, 77
Lilliput Pocket Automatic Pistol, 77
Stop Pocket Automatic Pistol, 77
GALEF SHOTGUNS
SHOTGUNS
Companion Folding Single-Barrel, 472
Golden Snipe, 472
Monte Carlo Trap Single-Barrel, 472
Silver Hawk Hammerless Double, 472
Silver Snipe Over/Under Shotgun, 472
Zabala Hammerless Double-Barrel, 472
GALENA HANDGUNS
Acceleratror, 78
AMT Backup, 77
Automag II, 77
Automag III, 78
Automag IV, 78

Automag 440, 78
Commando, 78
Hardballer, 78
Longslide, 78
GALESI PISTOLS
Automatic Pistol, 78
Model 6 Pocket Automatic Pistol, 78
Model 9 Pocket Automatic Pistol, 78
GALIL RIFLES
AR Semiautomatic Rifle, 246
Model 223 AR, 246
Model 308 AR, 246
Model 223 ARM, 246
Model 308 ARM, 246
Sporter Semiautomatic Rifle, 246
GAMBA S. p. A., SHOTGUN
Daytona Competition Over/Under, 472
GARBI, ARMAS
Model 100 Sidelock Shotgun, 473
Model 101 Sidelock Shotgun, 473
Model 102 Sidelock Shotgun, 473
Model 103 Hammerless Double, 473
Model 200 Hammerless Double, 473
GARCIA CORPORATION
RIFLES
Bronco 22 Single-Shot Rifle, 241
SHOTGUNS
Bronco .410 Single Shot, 473
Bronco 22/.410 Over/Under Combination, 473
GERMAN MILITARY RIFLES
Model 24T (Gew. 24T) Mauser Rifle, 247
Model 29/40 (Gew. 29/40) Mauser Rifle, 247
Model 33/40 (Gew. 33/40) Mauser Rifle, 247
Models 41and 41-W (Gew. 41, Gew. 41-W)
Semiautomatic Military Rifles, 247
Model 43 (Gew. 43, Kar. 43) Semiauto Military, 247
Model 1888 (Gew. 88) Mauser-Mannlicher
Service, 247
Model 1888 (Kar. 88) Mauser-Mannlicher Carbine, 247
Model 1898 (Gew. 98) Mauser Military, 248
Model 1898A (Kar. 98A) Mauser Carbine, 248
Model 1898B (Kar. 98B) Mauser Carbine, 248
Model 1898K (Kar. 98K) Mauser Carbine, 248
Model VK 98 People's Rifle ("Volksaewehr"), 248
GÉVARM RIFLE
E-1 Autoloading Rifle, 249
GLISENTI PISTOL
Brixia Model, 78
Model 1910 Italian Service Automatic, 78
Sosso Model, 78
GLOCK
Desert Storm Commemorative, 80
Model 17 DA Automatic Pistol, 78
Model 17L Competition, 78
Model 19 Compact, 79
Model 20 DA Auto Pistol, 79
Model 21 Automatic Pistol, 79
Model 22 Automatic Pistol, 79
Model 23 Automatic Pistol, 79
Model 24 Automatic Pistol, 79
Model 26 DA Automatic Pistol, 79
Model 27 DA Auto Pistol, 79
Model 29 DA Auto Pistol, 79
Model 30 DA Auto Pistol, 79
Model 31 DA Auto Pistol, 79
Model 32 DA Auto Pistol, 79
Model 33 DA Auto Pistol, 80
Model 34 Auto Pistol, 80
Model 35 Auto Pistol, 80
Model 36 DA Auto Pistol, 80
Model 37, 80
Model 38 Compact, 80
Model 39 Sub-Compact, 80
Model 41, 80
Model 42 Sub-Compact, 80
GOLDEN EAGLE
RIFLES
Model 7000 Grade I African, 249
Model 7000 Big Game Series, 249
SHOTGUNS
Eagle Model 5000 Grade I Trap, 474
Eagle Model 5000 Grade II Field, 474
Model 5000 Grade I Field Over/Under, 473
Model 5000 Grade I Skeet, 473
Model 5000 Grade II Skeet, 474
Model 5000 Grade II Trap, 474
Model 5000 Grade III Grandee, 474
GOROSABEL SHOTGUNS
Model 503, 474
Model 504, 474
Model 505, 474
GRANT, STEPHEN SHOTGUNS
Best Quality Self-Opener Double-Barrel, 474
Best Quality Side-Lever Double-Barrel, 474
GREAT WESTERN ARMS

Deputy Model, 80
Double Barrel Derringer, 80
Fast Draw Model, 80
SA Frontier Revolver, 80
Sheriff's Model, 80
Target Model, 80
GREENER, Ltd., SHOTGUNS
Empire Model Hammerless Doubles, 474
Far-Killer Model Grade FH35 Hammerless Double-
Barrel Shotgun, 475
G. P. (General Purpose) Single Barrel, 475
Hammerless Ejector Double-Barrel, 475
GREIFELT & COMPANY
RIFLES
Sport Model 22 Hornet Bolt-Action, 249
SHOTGUNS
Grade No. 1 Over/Under, 475
Grade No. 3 Over/Under, 475
Hammerless Drilling (Three Barrel Combination
Gun), 475
Model 22 Hammerless Double, 475
Model 22E Hammerless Double, 476
Model 103 Hammlerless Double, 476
Model 103E Hammerless Double, 476
Model 143E Over/Under, 476
Over-and-Under Combination Gun, 476
GRENDEL
Model P-10 Automatic Pistol, 80
Model P-12 DA Automatic Pistol, 80
Model P-30 Automatic Pistol, 81
Model P-31 Automatic Pistol, 81
GUNSITE
"Advanced Tactical" SA Auto Pistol, 81
"Custom Carry" SA Auto Pistol, 81
GUSTAF RIFLES
Deluxe, 249
Grand Prix Single-Shot Target Rifle, 249
Model 2000 Bolt-Action Rifle, 249
Monte Carlo Standard Bolt-Action Sporting Rifle, 249
Special, 249
Sporter, 249
Standard, 250
Trofé, 250
HAENEL
'88 Mauser Sporter, 250
Mauser-Mannlicher Bolt-Action Sporting Rifle, 250
H&R 1871—*See Harrington & Richardson*
HÄMMERLI
HANDGUNS
Hämmerli-Walther Olympia Model 200,
1952-Type, 84
Hämmerli-Walther Olympia Model 200,
1958-Type, 84
Hämmerli-Walther Olympia Model 202, 84
Hämmerli-Walther Olympia Model 205, 84
International Model 206 Auto Pistol, 83
International Model 207, 83
International Model 209 Auto Pistol, 83
International Model 210, 83
Model 33MP Free Pistol, 81
Model 100 Free Pistol, 81
Model 101, 81
Model 102, 81
Model 103, 81
Model 104, 81
Model 105, 81
Model 106, 81
Model 107, 81
Model 120 Heavy Barrel, 82
Model 120-1 Single-Shot Free Pistol, 82
Model 120-2, 82
Model 152 Electronic Pistol, 82
Models 150/151 Free Pistols, 82
Models 160/162 Free Pistols, 82
Model 208 Standard Auto Pistol, 82
Model 208S Target Pistol, 82
Model 211, 82
Model 212 Hunter's Pistol, 83
Model 215, 83
Model 230-1 Rapid Fire Auto Pistol, 83
Model 230-2, 83
Model 232 Rapid Fire Auto Pistol, 83
Model 280 Target Auto Pistol, 84
Model P240 Target Pistol, 84
Walther Olympia Model 201, 84
Walther Olympia Model 203, 84
Walther Olympia Model 204, 84
Virginian SA Revolver, 84
RIFLES
Model 45 Smallbore Bolt-Action Single-Shot Match
Rifle, 250
Model 54 Smallbore Match Rifle, 250
Model 508 Free Rifle, 250
Model 506 Smallbore Match Rifle, 250
Model Olympia 300 Meter Bolt-Action Single-Shot

Free Rifle, 250
Tanner 300 Meter Free Rifle, 251
HARRINGTON & RICHARDSON
AUTOMATIC/SINGLE-SHOT PISTOLS
SL 25 Pistol, 85
SL 32 Pistol, 85
USRA Model Single-Shot Target Pistol, 85
REVOLVERS
22 Special DA, 85
American DA, 90
Automatic Ejecting DA Revolver, 90
Bobby DA, 90
Defender 38 DA, 90
Expert Model DA, 90
Hammerless DA, Large Frame, 90
Hammerless DA, Small Frame, 90
Hunter Model DA, 90
Model 4 (1904) DA, 85
Model 5 (1905) DA, 85
Model 6 (1906) DA, 85
Model 199 Sportsman SA Revolver, 86
Model 504 DA, 86
Model 532 DA, 86
Model 586 DA, 86
Model 603 Target, 86
Model 604 Target, 86
Model 622/623 DA, 86
Model 632/633 Guardsman DA Revolver, 86
Model 649/650 DA, 86
Model 666 DA, 86
Model 676 DA, 86
Model 686 DA, 86
Model 732/733 DA, 87
Model 826 DA, 87
Model 829/830 DA, 87
Model 832/833 DA, 87
Model 900/901 DA, 87
Model 903 Target, 87
Model 904 Target, 87
Model 905 Target, 88
Model 922 DA Revolver, First Issue, 88
Model 922/923 DA Revolver, Second Issue, 88
Model 925 Defender, 88
Model 926 DA, 88
Model 929/930 Sidekick DA Revolver, 89
Model 939/940 Ultra Sidekick DA Revolver, 89
Model 949/950 Forty-Niner DA Revolver, 89
Model 976 DA, 89
Model 999 Sportsman DA Revolver, First Issue, 89
Model 999 Sportsman DA Revolver, Second Issue, 89
Model 999 Sportsman DA Revolver (New), 89
New Defender DA, 90
Premier DA, 90
STR 022 Blank Revolver, 90
STR 032 Blank Revolver, 90
Target Model DA, 91
Trapper Model DA, 91
Ultra Sportsman, 91
Vest Pocket DA, 91
Young America DA, 91
RIFLES
Custer Memorial Issue, 256
Model 60 Reising, 251
Model 65 Military, 251
Model 150 Leatherneck, 251
Model 151, 251
Model 155 Single Shot, 251
Model 157 Single Shot, 252
Model 158 Topper Jet, 252
Model 158C, 253
Model 163 Mustang, 253
Model 165 Leatherneck, 253
Model 171, 253
Model 171 Deluxe, 253
Model 172, 253
Model 173, 254
Model 174, 254
Model 178, 254
Model 250 Sportster Bolt-Action, 254
Model 251, 254
Model 265 "Reg'lar" Bolt-Action, 254
Model 300 Ultra Bolt-Action, 254
Model 301 Carbine, 254
Model 308, 255
Model 317 Ultra Wildcat Bolt-Action, 255
Model 317P Presentation Grade, 255
Model 330 Hunter's Rifle, 255
Model 333, 255
Model 340, 255
Model 360 Ultra, 255
Model 361, 255
Model 369 Ace, 256
Model 370 Ultra Medalist, 256
Model 422, 256
Model 450, 256

Model 451 Medalist Bolt-Action Target Rifle, 256
Model 465 Targeteer Special, 256
Model 707, 256
Model 707 Deluxe, 256
Model 750 Pioneer, 256
Model 751, 256
Model 755 Sahara, 256
Model 760 Single Shot, 256
Model 765 Pioneer, 256
Model 800 Lynx, 256
Model 852 Fieldsman, 256
Model 865 Plainsman, 256
Model 866, 256
Model 1873 100th Anniversary (1871-1971)
  Commemorative Officer's Springfield Rep., 256
Model 5200 Match Rifle, 256
Model 5200 Sporter, 256
Targeteer Jr., 256
Ultra Single-Shot Rifle, 256

SHOTGUNS
Folding Gun, 478
Golden Squire Jr. Model 459, 478
Golden Squire Model 159 Single-Barrel Hammer, 478
Harrich No. 1 Single-Barrel Trap Gun, 478
Model 098 Topper Classic Youth, 480
Model 098 Topper Deluxe, 480
Model 098 Topper Deluxe Rifled Slug Gun, 480
Model 098 Topper Hammer Single-Shot Shotgun, 480
Model 098 Topper Junior, 480
Model 348 Gamester Bolt-Action, 477
Model 349 Gamester Deluxe, 477
Model 351 Huntsman Bolt-Action, 477
Model 400 Pump, 477
Model 401, 477
Model 402, 477
Model 403, 477
Model 404/404C, 477
Model .410 Tamer Shotgun, 480
Model 440 Pump, 477
Model 442, 478
Model 1212 Field, 478
Model 1212 Waterfowl Gun, 478
Model 1908 .410 (12mm) Single-Shot, 478
Model 1908 Single-Shot Shotgun, 478
Model 1915 Single-Shot Shotgun, 478
Model N. W. T. F. Turkey Mag, 480
Model N. W. T. F. Youth Turkey Gun, 480
No. 3 Hammerless Single-Shot, 476
No. 5 Standard Lightweight Hammer Single, 476
No. 6 Heavy Breech Single-Shot Hammer
  Shotgun, 476
No. 7 or 9 Bay State Single-Shot Hammer
  Shotgun, 477
No. 8 Standard Single-Shot Hammer Shotgun, 477
"Top Rib" Single-Barrel Shotgun, 479
Topper No. 48 Single-Barrel Hammer, 479
Topper Model 099 Deluxe, 479
Topper Model 148 Single-Shot Hammer Shotgun, 479
Topper Model 158 (058) Single-Shot Hammer, 479
Topper Model 162 Slug Gun, 479
Topper Model 176 10 Gauge Magnum, 479
Topper Model 188 Deluxe, 480
Topper Model 198 (098) Deluxe, 480
Topper Model 490, 480
Topper Jr. Model 480, 480
Topper No. 488 Deluxe, 480
Topper Model 490 Greenwing, 480
Topper Jr. Model 580, 480
Topper Model 590, 480
Ultra Slug Hunter, 481
Ultra Slug Hunter Deluxe, 481
Ultra Slug Series, 478

HARRIS GUNWORKS
Signature Alaskan Bolt-Action, 257
Signature Classic Sporter, 257
Signature Mountain Rifle, 257
Signature Super Varminter, 258
Signature Talon Safari, 258

HARTFORD ARMS & EQUIPMENT
Automatic Target Pistol, 92
Repeating Pistol, 92
Single-Shot Target Pistol, 92

HASKELL MANUFACTURING—*See listing under*
Hi-Point

HAWES FIREARMS
Deputy Denver Marshal, 92
Deputy Marshal SA Revolver, 92
Deputy Montana Marshal, 92
Deputy Silver City Marshal, 92
Deputy Texas Marshal, 92
Favorite Single-Shot Target Pistol, 92
Sauer Chief Marshal SA Target Revolver, 93
Sauer Federal Marshal, 93
Sauer Montana Marshal, 93
Sauer Silver City Marshal, 93

Sauer Texas Marshal, 93
Sauer Western Marshal SA Revolver, 94

HECKLER & KOCH
  HANDGUNS
  Model HK4 DA Auto Pistol, 94
  Model Mark 23 DA Auto Pistol, 94
  Model P7K3 DA Auto Pistol, 94
  Model P7M8, 94
  Model P7M10, 94
  Model P7M13, 95
  Model P7 (PSP) Auto Pistol, 95
  Model P9S DA Automatic Pistol, 95
  Model P9S Target Competition Kit, 95
  Model SP89, 95
  Model USP Auto Pistol, 95
  Model USP9 Compact, 96
  Model USP40 Compact, 96
  Model USP45 Compact, 96
  Model USP Expert, 96
  Model USP Tactical, 96
  Model VP'70Z Auto Pistol, 97
  RIFLES
  Model 911 Semiauto, 258
  Model HK91 A-2 Semiauto, 258
  Model HK91 A-3 Semiauto, 258
  Model HK93 Semiautomatic, 258
  Model HK94 Semiautomatic Carbine, 258
  Model HK300 Semiautomatic, 258
  Model HK630 Semiautomatic, 258
  Model HK770 Semiautomatic, 258
  Model HK940 Semiautomatic, 258
  Model HK PSG-1 Marksman Rifle, 258
  Model SL8-1, 259
  Model SR-9 Semiauto, 259
  Model SR-9 Target Rifle, 259
  Model USC Carbine Rifle, 259
  SHOTGUNS
  Classic Lion Side by Side, 481
  Camo Lion Semi-Auto, 481
  Max Lion Over/Under, 481
  Red Lion Mark II Semi Auto, 481
  Silver Lion Over/Under, 481
  Sporting Clay Lion Semi Auto, 481

HELWAN PISTOLS—*See listings under Interarms*
HENRY REPEATING ARMS
  RIFLES
  .30-30 Lever Action, 259
  Acu-Bolt, 259
  "Big Boy" Lever Action, 259
  Lever Action, 259
  Mini Bolt, 259
  Pump Action, 259
  U.S. Survival .22 Semi-Automatic, 259

HERCULES RIFLES/SHOTGUN—*See listings under "W"*
for Montgomery Ward
HERITAGE MANUFACTURING
Model H-25 Auto Pistol, 97
Rough Rider SA Revolver, 97
Sentry DA Revolver, 97
Stealth DA Auto Pistol, 97

HEROLD RIFLE
Repeating Sporting Rifle, 259
HEYM
  RIFLES
  Express Bolt-Action Rifle, 260
  Model 55B Over/Under Double Rifle, 259
  Model 88B Double Rifle, 260
  SR-20 Alpine, Safari and Trophy Series, 260
  SR-20 Bolt-Action Rifle, 260
  SR-20 Classic Bolt-Action Rifle, 260
  SHOTGUNS
  Model 22S "Safety" Shotgun/Rifle Combination, 481
  Model 55 BF Shotgun/Rifle Combo, 481

HIGGINS, J.C.—*See Sears, Roebuck & Company*
HI-POINT FIREARMS
  PISTOLS
  Model CF-380 Polymer, 97
  Model JS-40/JC-40 (Iberia), 97
  Model JS-45/JH-45 (Haskell), 97
  Model JS-9mm Auto Pistol, 97
  Model JS-9mm Comp Pistol (Stallard), 97
  Model JS-9mm/C-9mm Compact Pistol (Beemiller), 97
  RIFLES
  Model 995 Carbine, 260

HIGH STANDARD SPORTING ARMS
  AUTOMATIC PISTOLS
  Field-King Automatic Pistol—First Model, 98
  Field-King Automatic Pistol—Second Model, 98
  Flite-King Automatic Pistol—First Model, 99
  Flite-King AutomaticPistol—Second Model, 99
  Model A Automatic Pistol, 98
  Model B Automatic Pistol, 98
  Model C Automatic Pistol, 98
  Model D Automatic Pistol, 98
  Model Dura-Matic Automatic Pistol, 98

Model E Automatic Pistol, 98
Model G-380 Automatic Pistol, 99
Model G-B Automatic Pistol, 99
Model G-D Automatic Pistol, 99
Model G-E Automatic Pistol, 99
Model H-A Automatic Pistol, 99
Model H-B Automatic Pistol, 99
Model H-D Automatic Pistol, 99
Model H-DM Automatic Pistol, 99
Model H-E Automatic Pistol, 99
Olympic Automatic—First Model (G-O), 100
Olympic Automatic—Second Model, 100
Olympic Automatic Pistol—Third Model, 100
Olympic Commemorative, 100
Olympic I.S.U., 100
Olympic I.S.U. Military, 100
Olympic Military, 100
Sharpshooter Automatic Pistol, 100
Sport-King Automatic—First Model, 101
Sport-King Automatic Pistol—Third Model, 101
Sport-King Automatic Pistol—Second Model, 101
Sport-King Lightweight, 101
Supermatic Automatic Pistol, 101
Supermatic Citation, 101
Supermatic Citation Military, 102
Supermatic Tournament, 102
Supermatic Tournament Military, 102
Supermatic Trophy Military, 102
Supermatic Trophy, 102
Victor Automatic Pistol, 102

DERRINGER
Derringer, 103
REVOLVERS
Camp Gun, 103
Double-Nine DA Revolver—Aluminum Frame, 103
Double-Nine Deluxe, 103
Double-Nine—Steel Frame, 103
Durango, 103
High Sierra DA Revolver, 103
Hombre, 103
Kit Gun DA Revolver, 103
Longhorn—Aluminum Frame, 104
Longhorn—Steel Frame, 104
Natchez, 104
Posse, 104
Sentinel DA Revolver, 104
Sentinel Deluxe, 104
Sentinel Imperial, 105
Sentinel 1 DA Revolver, 105
Sentinel Mark II DA Revolver, 105
Sentinel Mark III, 105
Sentinel Mark IV, 105
Sentinel Snub, 105

RIFLES
Hi-Power Deluxe Rifle, 260
Sport King Pump Rifle, 260
Hi-Power Field Bolt-Action Rifle, 260
Sport-King Autoloading Carbine, 261
Sport-King Deluxe Autoloader, 261
Sport-King Field Autoloader, 261
Sport-King Special Autoloader, 261

SHOTGUNS
Flite-King Brush—12 Ga., 482
Flite-King Brush Deluxe, 483
Flite-King Brush (Series II), 483
Flite-King Brush Deluxe (Series II), 483
Flite King Deluxe—12 Ga (Series II), 483
Flite-King Deluxe—20, 28, .410 Ga (Series II), 483
Flite-King Deluxe Rib—12 Ga., 483
Flite-King Deluxe Rib—12 Ga. (II), 483
Flite-King Deluxe Rib—20 Ga., 483
Flite-King Deluxe Rib—20, 28, .410 Ga. (Series II),
  483
Flite-King Deluxe Skeet Gun (Series II), 483
Flite-King Deluxe Skeet Gun—20, 28, .410 Ga.
  (Series II), 483
Flite-King Deluxe Trap Gun (II), 483
Flite-King Field Pump—12 Ga., 482
Flite-King Field Pump—16 Ga., 483
Flite-King Field Pump—20 Ga., 483
Flite-King Pump—.410 Ga., 484
Flite-King Skeet—12 Ga., 484
Flite-King Special—12 Ga., 484
Flite-King Special—20 Ga., 484
Flite-King Trap—12 Ga., 484
Flite-King Trophy—12 Ga., 484
Flite-King Trophy—20 Ga., 484
Supermatic Deer Gun, 484
Supermatic Deluxe—12 Ga. (Series II), 484
Supermatic Deluxe—20 Ga. (Series II), 484
Supermatic Deluxe Deer Gun (Series II), 484
Supermatic Duck—12 Ga. Mag., 484
Supermatic Deluxe Rib—12 Ga., 485
Supermatic Deluxe Rib—20 Ga., 485
Supermatic Deluxe Rib—20 Ga. (Series II), 485

INDEX

Supermatic Deluxe Skeet Gun—12 Ga. (Series II), 485
Supermatic Deluxe Skeet Gun—20 Ga. (Series II), 485
Supermatic Deluxe Trap Gun (Series II), 485
Supermatic Duck Rib—12 Ga. Magnum (Series II), 485
Supermatic Duck Rib—12 Ga. Magnum, 485
Supermatic Trophy—12 Ga., 485
Supermatic Field Autoloading Shotgun—12 Ga., 485
Supermatic Field Autoloading Shotgun—20 Ga., 485
Supermatic Shadow Automatic, 485
Supermatic Shadow Indy Over/Under, 486
Supermatic Shadow Seven, 486
Supermatic Skeet—12 Ga., 486
Supermatic Skeet—20 Ga., 486
Supermatic Special—12 Ga., 486
Supermatic Special—20 Ga., 486
Supermatic Trap—12 Ga., 486
Supermatic Trophy—20 Ga., 486

HIGH STANDARD MANUFACTURING COMPANY
PISTOLS
10X Automatic Pistol, 106
Citation MS Auto Pistol, 106
Olympic I.S.U. Automatic Pistol, 105
Sport King Auto Pistol, 105
Supermatic Citation Auto Pistol, 105
Supermatic Tournament, 106
Supermatic Trophy, 106
Victor Automatic, 106

HOLLAND & HOLLAND
RIFLES
Best Quality Magazine Rifle, 261
Deluxe Magazine Rifle, 261
No. 2 Model Hammerless Ejector Double Rifle, 261
Royal Deluxe Double Rifle, 261
Royal Hammerless Ejector Rifle, 261
SHOTGUNS
Badminton Model Hammerless Double-Barrel
  Originally No. 2 Grade, 486
Centenary Model Hammerless Double-Barrel, 486
Dominion Model Hammerless Double-Barrel, 487
Model Deluxe Hammerless Double, 487
Northwood Model Hammerless Double-Barrel, 487
Riviera Model Pigeon Gun, 487
Royal Hammerless Double, 487
Royal Model Over/Under, 488
Single-Shot Super Trap Gun, 488
Sporting Over/Under, 488
Sporting Over/Under Deluxe, 488

HOPKINS & ALLEN ARMS—See listings of comparable
Harrington & Richardson and Iver Johnson models
for values

HOWA RIFLES—See also Mossberg (1500) Smith &
Wesson (1500 & 1700) and Weatherby (Vanguard)
Model 1500 Hunter, 262
Model 1500 PCS, 262
Model 1500 Lightning Bolt-Action Rifle, 262
Model 1500 Realtree Camo Rifle, 262
Model 1500 Trophy/Varmint Bolt-Action Rifle, 262
Model 1500 Woodgrain Lightning Rifle, 262

H-S PRECISION
Pro-Series, 262

HUGLU
Model 101 B12 AT-DT Combo Over/Under Trap, 481
Model 101 B12 ST Over/Under Trap, 482
Model 103 B12 ST Over/Under, 482
Model 103 C12 ST Over/Under, 482
Model 103 D12 ST Over/Under, 482
Model 103 F12 ST Over/Under, 482
Model 104 A12 ST Over/Under, 482
Model 200 Series Double, 482
Model 200, 482
Model 201, 482
Model 202, 482

HUNGARIAN MILITARY RIFLES
Model 1935M Mannlicher Military Rifle, 262
Model 1943M (German Gew. 98/40) Mannlicher
  Military Rifle, 262

HUNTER ARMS COMPANY
SHOTGUNS
Fulton Hammerless Double-Barrel, 488
Special Hammerless Double-Barrel, 488

HUSQVARNA Vapenfabrik A.B.
1950 Hi-Power Sporting Rifle, 263
1951 Hi-Power Rifle, 263
Model 456 Lightweight Full-Stock Sporter, 263
Model 8000 Imperial Grade Rifle, 263
Model 9000 Crown Grade Rifle, 263
Series 1000 Super Grade, 263
Series 1100 Deluxe Model Hi-Power, 263
Series 3000 Crown Grade, 263
Series 3100 Crown Grade, 263
Series 4000 Lightweight Rifle, 263
Series 4100 Lightweight Rifle, 263
Series 6000 Imperial Custom Grade, 263
Series 7070 Imperial Monte Carlo Lightweight, 263
Series P-3000 Presentation Rifle, 263

IGA SHOTGUNS
Coach Gun, 488
Condor I Over/Under Single-Trigger, 488
Condor II Over/Under Double-Trigger, 489
Condor Outback, 489
Condor Supreme, 489
Condor Turkey Model Over/Under Shotgun, 489
Condor Waterfowl Model, 489
Deluxe Hunter Clay Shotgun, 489
Double Defense, 489
ERA 2000 Over/Under Shotgun, 489
Reuna Single-Shot Shotgun, 489
Uplander Side/Side Shotgun, 489
Uplander Turkey Model S/S Double, 490

INGRAM (Military Armament Corp.)—See listings
under M.A.C.

INTERARMS—See also Bersa Pistol
REVOLVERS
Interarms/Helwan Brigadier, 106
Virginian Dragoon SA Revolver, 106
Virginian Revolver Silhouette Model, 106
Virginian SA Revolver, 106
RIFLES
African Series, 264
Mark X Alaskan, 264
Mark X Bolt-Action Sporter Series, 264
Mark X Cavalier, 264
Mark X Continental Mannlicher Style Carbine, 264
Mark X Lightweight Sporter, 264
Mark X Marquis Mannlicher Style Carbine, 264
Mini-Mark X Bolt-Action Rifle, 264
Mark X Viscount, 264

INTRATEC U.S.A.
Category 9 DAO Semiautomatic, 106
Category 40 DAO Semiautomatic, 106
Category 45 DAO Semiautomatic, 106
Model ProTec 25 DA Semiautomatic, 107
Model Tec-9 Semiautomatic, 107
Model Tec-9M Semiautomatic, 107
Model Tec-22T Semiautomatic, 107
Tec-38 Derringer, 107

IVER JOHNSON FIREARMS—See Johnson's Arms

ISRAEL ARMS
Bul-M5 Locked Breech SA, 107
GAL Model (5000) Auto Pistol, 107
Golan Model (2500) Auto Pistol, 107
Kareen MK II (1500) Auto Pistol, 107
Kareen MK II Compact Auto Pistol, 107

ITALIAN MILITARY
Model 38 Military Rifle, 264

ITHACA GUN COMPANY
BSA CF-2 BA Repeating Rifle, 266
Model 49 Saddlegun Lever-Action, 265
Model 49 Saddlegun—Deluxe, 265
Model 49 Saddlegun—Magnum, 265
Model 49 Saddlegun—Presentation, 265
Model 49 Saddlegun—St. Louis Bicentennial, 265
Model 49R Saddlegun Repeating Rifle, 265
Model 49 Youth Saddlegun, 266
Model 72 Saddlegun—Deluxe, 266
Model 72 Repeating Carbine, 266
Model LSA-65 BA Standard Grade, 266
Model LSA-65 Deluxe, 266
Model X5-C Lightning Autoloader, 266
Model X5-T Lightning Autoloader Tubular Repeating
  Rifle, 266
Model X-15 Lightning Autoloader, 266
SHOTGUNS
Hammerless Double-Barrel, 492
LSA-55 Turkey Gun, 492
Mag-10 Automatic Shotgun, 492
Model 37 Bicentennial Commemorative, 490
Model 37 Deerslayer Deluxe, 490
Model 37 Deerslayer II, 490
Model 37 Deerslayer Standard, 490
Model 37 Deerslayer Super Deluxe, 490
Model 37 English Ultra, 490
Model 37 Featherlight Standard, 490
Model 37 Field Grade Magnum w/Tubes, 491
Model 37 New Classic, 491
Model 37 Supreme Grade, 491
Model 37 Thousand Dollar Grade, 491
Model 37 Turkeyslayer, 491
Model 37T Target Grade, 491
Model 37T Trap Grade, 491
Model 37S Skeet Grade, 491
Model 37R Solid Rib Grade, 491
Model 37 Ultralite, 491
Model 37 Waterfowler, 491
Model 51 Deerslayer, 491
Model 51 Deluxe Skeet Grade, 491
Model 51 Deluxe Trap Grade, 491
Model 51 Standard Automatic, 491
Model 51 Standard Magnum, 491
Model 51A Turkey Gun, 491

Model 66 Long Tom, 491
Model 66 Standard Super Single Lever, 491
Model 66RS Buckbuster, 491
Model 87 Deerslayer II Rifled, 492
Model 87 Deerslayer Shotgun, 492
Model 87 Field Grade, 492
Model 87 Ultralite Field Pump, 492
Perazzi Competition I Skeet, 493
Perazzi Competition Trap I Over/Under, 493
Perazzi Competition I Trap Single Barrel, 493
Perazzi Competition IV Trap Gun, 493
Perazzi Light Game Over/Under Field, 494
Perazzi Mirage Live Bird, 494
Perazzi Mirage Skeet, 494
Perazzi Mirage Trap, 494
Perazzi MT-6 Skeet, 494
Perazzi MT-6 Trap Combo, 494
Perazzi MT-6 Trap Over/Under, 494
Perazzi MX-8 Trap Combo, 494
Perazzi MX-8 Trap Over/Under, 494
Perazzi Single-Barrel Trap Gun, 494
Single-Shot Trap, Flues and Knick, 493
SKB Model 100 Side-by-side, 495
SKB Model 150 Field Grade, 495
SKB Model 200E Field Grade S/S, 495
SKB Model 200E Skeet Gun, 495
SKB Model 280 English, 495
SKB Model 300 Standard Automatic, 495
SKB Model 500 Field Grade Over/Under, 495
SKB Model 500 Magnum, 495
SKB Model 600 Doubles Gun, 495
SKB Model 600 Field Grade, 495
SKB Model 600 Magnum, 495
SKB Model 600 Skeet Combo Set, 495
SKB Model 600 Skeet Grade, 495
SKB Model 600 Trap Grade Over/Under, 496
SKB Model 680 English, 496
SKB Model 700 Doubles Gun, 496
SKB Model 700 Skeet Set, 496
SKB Model 700 Skeet Grade, 496
SKB Model 700 Trap Grade, 496
SKB Model 900 Deluxe Automatic, 496
SKB Model 900 Slug Gun, 496
SKB Century II, 496
SKB Century Single-Shot Trap Gun, 496
SKB Model XL300 Standard Automatic, 496
SKB Model XL900 Deluxe Automatic, 496
SKB Model XL900 Skeet Grade, 496
SKB Model XL900 Slug Gun, 496
SKB Model XL900 Trap Grade, 496

JAPANESE MILITARY
PISTOLS
Model 14 (1925) Automatic Pistol, 107
Model 26 DAO Revolver, 107
Model 94 (1934) Automatic Pistol, 108
Nambu Model 1914 Automatic Pistol, 108
RIFLES
Model 38 Arisaka Carbine, 267
Model 38 Arisaka Service Rifle, 267
Model 44 Cavalry Carbine, 267
Model 99 Service Rifle, 267

JARRETT CUSTOM RIFLES
Model No. 2 Walkabout, 267
Model No. 3 Custom, 267
Model No. 4 Professional Hunter, 267

JENNINGS FIREARMS—See additional listings under
Bryco Arms
Model J Auto Pistol, 108

JOHNSON AUTOMATICS
Model 1941 Semiauto Military Rifle, 267
Sporting Rifle Prototype, 267

JOHNSON'S, IVER ARMS & CYCLE WORKS
AUTOMATIC PISTOLS
9mm DA, 108
Compact 25 ACP, 108
Enforcer, 108
PP30 Super Enforcer Automatic, 108
Pony Automatic Pistol, 108
TP-22 D, 109
TP25 DA Pocket, 109
Trailsman, 109
REVOLVERS
American Bulldog, 110
Armsworth Model 855 SA, 110
Cadet DA Revolver, 110
Cattleman, 110
Cattleman Buckhorn SA, 111
Cattleman Buntline SA, 111
Cattleman Trail Blazer, 111
Champion 22 Target SA, 111
Deluxe Target, 111
Model 55 Target DA, 109
Model 55-S, 109
Model 56 Blank, 109
Model 57A Target DA, 109

Model 66 Trailsman DA, 109
Model 67 Viking DA, 110
Model 67S Viking Snub, 110
Model 1900 DA, 110
Model 1900 Target DA, 110
Protector Sealed 8 DA, 111
Rookie DA, 111
Safety Hammer DA, 111
Safety Hammerless DA, 111
Sidewinder "S", 112
Sidewinder DA, 112
Sportsman DA, 112
Supershot 22 DA, 112
Supershot 9-Shot DA, 112
Supershot Model 844, 112
Supershot Sealed 8 DA, 112
Swing Out DA, 112
Target 9-Shot DA, 112
Target Sealed 8 DA, 112
Trigger-Cocking SA Target, 112
RIFLES
Li'l Champ Bolt-Action Rifle, 267
Model M-1 Semiautomatic Carbine, 268
Model PM.30 Semiautomatic Carbine, 268
Model SC30FS Semiautomatic Carbine, 268
Survival Semiautomatic Carbine, 268
Trailblazer Semiauto Rifle, 268
Model X Bolt-Action Rifle, 268
Model XX (2X) Bolt-Action Rifle, 268
SHOTGUNS
Champion Grade Single-Shot Hammmer Shotgun, 497
Hercules Grade Hammerless Double, 497
Matted Rib Single-Shot Hammer, 497
Silver Shadow Over/Under Shotgun, 497
Skeeter Model Hammerless Double, 497
Special Trap Single-Shot Hammer Shotgun, 497
Super Trap Hammerless Double, 497
KAHR ARMS
CW series DAO Auto Pistol, 113
CM series DAO Auto Pistol, 113
E9 DAO Auto Pistol, 113
Model K9 DAO, 112
Model K40 DAO, 112
Model MK9 DAO, 112
MK Micro series DAO Auto Pistol, 113
T series DAO Auto Pistol, 113
TP series DAO Auto Pistol, 113
KBI—*See listing under Armscor, Baikal, Charles Daly,*
FEG, Fias, Liberty I.M.I., and Omega Arms
HANDGUNS
Model PSP-25, 113
RIFLES
Super Classic, 268
SHOTGUNS—*See listing under Armscore, Baikal,*
Charles Daly and Omega Arms
K.D.F.
Model K15 Bolt-Action Rifle, 268
KEL-TEC CNC INDUSTRIES
HANDGUNS
Model P-11 DAO, 113
P-32, 113
P-3AT, 113
P-40, 113
PLR-16, 113
PLR-22, 113
PF-9, 113
PMR-30, 113
RIFLES
Sub-Series Semiautomatic Rifles, 269
Sub-2000, 269
SU-16A, 269
KESSLER ARMS
Lever-Matic Repeating Shotgun, 497
Three Shot Bolt-Action Repeater, 498
KIMBER MANUFACTURING
HANDGUNS
Model Classic 45, 113
Series II Models, 114
RIFLES
Model 82 Bolt-Action Rifle, 269
Model 82C Classic Bolt-Action Rifle, 269
Model 84 Bolt-Action Rifle, 270
Model 89 Big-Game Rifle, 270
KNIGHT'S ARMAMENT COMPANY
SR-15 Match Rifle, 271
SR-15 M-5, 271
SR-15 M-4, 271
SR-25 Match Rifle, 271
SR-25, 271
SR-25 Sporter Rifle, 271
SR-50 Long Range Precision, 271
KONGSBERG RIFLES
Model 393 Classic Sporter, 271
Model 393 Deluxe Sporter, 271
Model 393 Thumbhole Sporter, 271

KORTH PISTOLS
Combat, Sport, Target, 114
Semiautomatic Pistol, 114
KRICO RIFLES
Bolt-Action Sporting Rifle, 273
Carbine, 273
Model 260 Semiautomatic Rifle, 271
Model 300 Bolt-Action Rifle, 271
Model 311 Small-Bore Rifle, 272
Model 320 Bolt-Action Sporter, 272
Model 340 Metallic Silhouette, 272
Model 360 S2 Biathlon Rifle, 272
Model 360S Biathlon Rifle, 272
Model 400 Bolt-Action Rifle, 272
Model 420 Bolt-Action Rifle, 272
Model 440 S Bolt-Action Rifle, 272
Model 500 Match Rifle, 272
Model 600 Bolt-Action Rifle, 272
Model 620 Bolt-Action Rifle, 272
Model 640 Super Sniper Bolt-Action Repeating, 272
Model 640 Varmint Rifle, 272
Model 707 Bolt-Action Rifle, 273
Model 720 Bolt-Action Rifle, 273
Special Varmint Rifle, 273
KRIEGHOFF, H. Jagd und Sportwaffenfabrik
RIFLES
Teck Over/Under Rifle, 273
Ulm Over/Under Rifle, 273
ULM-Primus Over/Under Rifle, 274
SHOTGUNS
Model 32 Four-Barrel Skeet Set, 498
Model 32 Standard Grade Over/Under, 498
Model 32 Standard Grade Single-Shot Trap Gun, 498
Model K-80, 498
SKEET MODELS
Skeet International, 498
Skeet Special, 498
Skeet Standard Model, 498
Skeet Choke Tubes, 498
SKEET SETS
Bavaria Grade 4-Bbl. Set, 498
Danube Grade 4-Bbl. Set, 498
Gold Target Grade 4-Bbl. Set, 498
Standard Grade 2-Bbl. Set, 498
Standard Grade 4-Bbl. Set, 498
SPORTING MODELS
Pigeon, 498
Sporting, 498
TRAP MODELS
Krieghoff Model KS-5 Single-Barrel Trap, 498
Neptun Drilling, 498
Neptun-Primus Drilling, 498
RT Models, 498
Teck Over/Under Rifle-Shotgun, 499
Teck Over/Under Shotgun, 499
Trap Combo, 498
Trap Single, 498
Trap Standard, 498
Trap Unsingle, 498
Trumpf Drilling, 499
Ulm Over/Under Rifle-Shotgun, 499
Ulm Over/Under Shotgun, 499
U-P Live Pigeon Gun, 499
U-P Over/Under Live Trap Gun, 499
Ulm-Primus Over/Under Rifle-Shotgun, 499
Ulm-Primus Over/Under, 499
ULM-S Skeet Gun, 499
Ultra Over/Under Live Trap Gun, 499
L.A.R. MANUFACTURING
HANDGUNS
Mark I Grizzly Win. Mag., 114
Mark IV Grizzly, 114
Mark V, 114
RIFLES
Big Boar Competitor Bolt-Action Rifle, 274
LAKEFIELD ARMS—*See also listing under Savage or*
production since 1994
Model 64B Semiautomatic Rifle, 274
Model 90B Bolt-Action Target Rifle, 274
Model 91T/91TR Bolt-Action Target Rifle, 274
Model 92S Target Rifle, 274
Model 93M Bolt Action, 274
Mark I Bolt-Action Rifle, 274
Mark II Bolt-Action Rifle, 274
LAHTI PISTOLS
Automatic Pistol, 114
LANBER SHOTGUNS
Model 82 Over/Under Shotgun, 499
Model 87 Deluxe, 499
Model 97 Sporting Clays, 499
Model 844 MST Magnum Over/Under, 499
Model 2004 LCH Over/Under, 499
Model 2004 LCH Over/Under Skeet, 499
Model 2004 LCH Over/Under Trap, 500

LANCASTER SHOTGUN
"Twelve-Twenty" Double-Barrel, 500
LANG & SONS
Highest Quality Over/Under Shotgun, 500
LASERAIM TECHNOLOGIES
Series I SA, 115
Series II SA, 115
Series III SA, 115
Velocity Series SA, 115
LAURONA
RIFLE
Model 2000X Over/Under Express, 274
SHOTGUNS
Grand Trap Combo, 500
Model GTO, 500
Model GTU, 500
Silhouette 300 Over/Under
Model 300 Sporting Clays, 500
Model 300 Trap, 500
Model 300 Trap, Single, 500
Model 300 Ultra-Magnum, 500
Super Model Over/Under
Model 82 Super Game, 500
Model 83 MG Super Game, 500
Model 84 S Super Trap, 500
Model 85 MG 2-Bbl. Set, 500
Model 85 MG Super Game, 500
Model 85 MS Pigeon, 500
Model 85 MS Special Sporting, 500
Model 85 MS Super Trap, 500
Model 85 S Super Skeet, 500
LEBEAU-COURALLY SHOTGUNS
Boxlock Side-by-Side, 500
LEFEVER ARMS COMPANY
A Grade Hammerless Doubel-Barrel, 501
A Grade Skeet Model, 501
Hammerless Single-Shot Trap Gun, 501
Long Range Hammerless Single-Barrel Field Gun, 501
Nitro Special Hammerless Double, 501
Sidelock Hammerless Doubles:
A Grade, 501
AA Grade, 501
B Grade, 501
BE Grade, 501
C Grade, 501
CE Grade, 501
D Grade, 501
DE Grade, 501
DS Grade, 501
DSE Grade, 501
E Grade, 501
EE Grade, 501
F Grade, 501
FE Grade, 501
G Grade, 501
GE Grade, 501
H Grade, 501
HE Grade, 501
Optimus Grade, 501
Thousand Dollar Grade, 501
LEFEVER COMPANY, D.M.
Hammerless Double-Barrel Shotguns:
No. 4, AA Grade, 502
No. 5, B Grade, 502
No. 6, C Grade, 502
No. 7, C Grade, 502
No. 8, E Grade, 502
No. 9, F Grade, 502
Uncle Dan Grade, 502
Single-Barrel Trap Gun, 502
O/Excelsior with Plain Extractors, 502
O/Excelsior with Auto Extractors, 502
LIGNOSE PISTOLS
Model 2 Pocket, 115
Einhand Model 2A Pocket, 115
Einhand Model 3A Pocket, 115
LLAMA HANDGUNS
AUTOMATIC PISTOLS
BE-XI Deluxe, 116
Compact Frame, 116
Duo-Tone Large Frame, 117
Duo-Tone Small Frame, 117
G-IIIA Deluxe, 117
Large-Frame Automatic Pistol (IXA), 117
M-82 DA, 117
M-87 Comp, 117
MICRO-MAX SA, 117
MINI-MAX II SA, 117
MINI-MAX SA, 117
MAX-I SA, 117
MAX-II SA, 118
Model IIIA, 116
Models IIIA, XA, XV Deluxe, 116
Models VIII, IXA, XI Deluxe, 116
Model IXA, 116

INDEX

Model VIII, 116
Model XA, 116
Model XI, 116
Model XV, 116
Models BE-IIIA, BE-XA, BE-XV, 116
Models BE-VIII, BE-IXA,
Models CE-IIIA, CE-XA, CE-XV, 116
Models CE-VIII, CE-IXA, CE-XI, 116
Models C-IIIA, C-XA, C-XV, 116
Models C-VIII, C-IXA, C-XI, 116
Omni 9mm Double-Action, 118
Omni 45 Double-Action, 118
Single-Action, 118
Small-Frame, 118
REVOLVERS
Comanche I Double-Action, 118
Comanche II, 118
Comanche III Chrome, 118
Comanche III Double-Action, 118
Martial Double-Action, 118
Martial Double-Action Deluxe, 118
Super Comanche IV DA, 119
Super Comanche V DA, 119
LORCIN ENGINEERING
Model L-22 Semiautomatic, 119
Model L-25, LT-25 Semiautomatic, 119
Model L-32 Semiautomatic, 119
Model L-380 Semiautomatic, 119
Model L9MM Semiautomatic, 119
Over/Under Derringer, 119
LUGER PISTOLS
1900 American Eagle, 119
1900 Commercial, 119
1900 Swiss, 119
1902 American Eagle, 119
1902 Carbine, 119
1902 Cartridge Counter, 119
1902 Commercial, 119
1902 American Eagle, 119
1902 American Eagle Cartridge Counter, 119
1904 GL "Baby", 120
1904 Naval (Reworked), 120
1906 (11.35), 120
1906 American Eagle (7.65), 120
1906 American Eagle (9mm), 120
1906 Bern (7.65mm), 120
1906 Brazilian (7.65mm), 120
1906 Brazilian (9mm), 120
1906 Commercial, 120
1906 Dutch, 120
1906 Loewe and Company, 120
1906 Naval, 120
1906 Naval Commercial, 120
1906 Portuguese Army, 120
1906 Portuguese Naval, 120
1906 Russian, 120
1906 Swiss, 120
1906 Swiss (Rework), 120
1906 Swiss Police, 120
1908 Bulgarian, 120
1908 Commercial, 120
1908 Erfurt Military, 120
1908 Military, 121
1908 Naval, 121
1908 Naval (Commercial), 121
1914 Erfurt Artillery, 121
1914 Erfurt Military, 121
1914 Naval, 121
1914-1918 DWM Artillery, 121
1914-1918 DWM Military, 121
1920 Carbine, 121
1920 Navy Carbine, 121
1920 Commercial, 121
1920 Police, 121
1923 Commerical, 121
1923 Dutch Commerical, 121
1923 Krieghoff Commercial, 121
1923 Safe and Loaded, 121
1923 Stoeger, 122
1926 "Baby" Prototype, 122
1929 Swiss, 122
1934 BYF, 122
1934 Krieghoff Commercial (Side Frame), 122
1934 Krieghoff S, 122
1934 Mauser (Oberndorf), 122
1934 Mauser Banner (Military), 122
1934 Mauser Commercial, 122
1934 Mauser Dutch, 122
1934 Mauser Latvian, 122
1934 Mauser S/42 (Dated), 122
1934 Simson-S Toggle, 122
42 Mauser Banner (BYF), 122
Abercrombie and Fitch, 122
Dutch Royal Air Force, 123
DWM (G Date), 123

DWM and Erfurt, 123
Krieghoff (Grip Safety), 123
Krieghoff 36, 123
Krieghoff-Dated 1936-1945, 123
Mauser Banner (Grip Safety), 123
Mauser Banner (Swiss Proof), 123
Mauser Banner 42 (Dated), 123
Mauser Freise, 123
Russian Commercial, 123
S/42, 123
Simson and Company, 123
Vickers-Dutch, 123
LUNA
PISTOLS
Model 200 Free Pistol, 123
RIFLES
Single-Shot Target Rifle, 274
M.A.C. (MILITARY ARMAMENT CORP.)
Ingram Model 10, 123
Ingram Model 10A1S, 124
Ingram Model 11, 124
MAGNUM RESEARCH
HANDGUNS
Baby Eagle Semiautomatic, 124
Baby Eagle II Semiautomatic, 124
BFR Long Cylinder Revolver, 124
BFR Short Cylinder Revolver, 124
Desert Eagle Mk VII Semiautomatic, 124
Desert Eagle Mark XIX, 124
Micro Desert Eagle, 125
(ASAI) Model One Pro 45 Pistol, 125
Mountain Eagle Semiautomatic, 125
SSP-91 Lone Eagle Pistol, 125
RIFLES
Mountain Eagle BA Rifle Series, 274
MAGTECH
RIFLES
Model MT 122.2/R Bolt-Action, 275
Model MT 122.2/S Bolt-Action, 275
Model MT 122.2T Bolt-Action, 275
SHOTGUNS
Model 586.2 Slide-Action, 502
   Model 586.2 F, 502
   Model 586.2 P, 502
   Model 586.2 S, 502
   Model 586.2 VR, 502
MANNLICHER SPORTING RIFLES
Carbine Model, 1961-MCA, 277
High Velocity Bolt-Action Sporting, 277
M72 Model L/M Carbine, 277
M72 Model L/M Rifle, 278
M72 Model S Rifle, 278
M72 Model S/T Rifle, 278
Model L Carbine, 276
Model L Rifle, 276
Model L Varmint Rifle, 276
Model Luxus Bolt-Action Rifle, 276
Model M Carbine, 276
Model M Professional Rifle, 276
Model M Rifle, 276
Model S Rifle, 276
Model SL Carbine, 276
Model SL Rifle, 276
Model SL Varmint Rifle, 276
Model SSG Match Target Rifle, 276
Model S/T Rifle, 276
Model 1903 Bolt-Action Sporting, 276
Model 1905 Carbine, 276
Model 1908 Carbine, 276
Model 1910 Carbine, 276
Model 1924 Carbine, 276
Model 1950 Bolt-Action Sporting Rifle, 276
Model 1950 Carbine, 277
Model 1950 6.5 Carbine, 277
Model 1952 Improved Sporting Rifle, 277
Model 1952 Improved Carbine, 277
Model 1952 Improved 6.5 Carbine, 277
Model 1956 Custom Carbine, 277
Model SBS Forester Rifle, 278
Model SBS Pro-Hunter Rifle, 278
Rifle, Model 1961-MCA, 277
MARLIN FIREARMS
RIFLES
Model 9 Semiautomatic Carbine, 278
Model 15Y/15YN, 278
Model 18 Baby SA Repeater, 278
Model 20 SA Repeating Rifle, 279
Model 25 Bolt-Action, 279
Model 25 Slide-Action Repeater, 279
Model 25M Bolt Action W/Scope, 279
Model 25MB Midget Magnum, 279
Model 25MG/25MN/25N/25NC Bolt-Action Rifle, 279
Model 27 SA Repeating Rifle, 280
Model 27S, 280
Model 29 Slide-Action Repeater, 280

Model 30AS Lever-Action, 280
Model 32 Slide-Action Repeater, 280
Model 36 LA Repeating Carbine, 280
Model 36 Sporting Carbine, 281
Model 36A/36A-DL Repeating Rifle, 281
Model 37A SA Repeating, 281
Model 38 SA Repeating Rifle, 281
Model 39 Carbine, 281
Model 39 90th Anniversary Carbine, 281
Model 39 Century Ltd., 281
Model 39 Lever-Action Repeater, 281
Model 39A, 281
Model 39A 90th Anniversary Rifle, 281
Model 39A Article II Rifle, 281
Model 39A/39AS Rifle, 282
Model 39A "Mountie" Repeating Rifle, 282
Model 39A Octagon, 282
Model 39D, 282
Model 39M Article II Carbine, 282
Model Golden 39M, 282
Model 39M "Mountie" Carbine, 282
Model 39TDS Carbine, 282
Model 45, 283
Model 49/49DL Autoloading Rifle, 283
Model 50/50E Autoloading Rifle, 283
Model 56 Levermatic Rifle, 283
Model 57 Levermatic Rifle, 283
Model 57M Levermatic, 283
Model 60 Semiautomatic Rifle, 283
Model 60C Self-Loading Rifle, 283
Model 60SS Semiautomatic Rifle, 283
Model 62 Levermatic Rifle, 283
Model 65 BA Single-Shot Rifle, 283
Model 70HC Semiautomatic, 283
Model 70P Semiautomatic, 283
Model 70PSS Semiautomatic, 283
Model 75C Semiautomatic, 284
Model 80 BA Repeating Rifle, 284
Model 80C/80DL BA Repeater, 284
Model 81/81E Bolt-Action Repeater, 284
Model 81C/81DL BA Repeater, 284
Model 88-C/88-DL Autoloading, 284
Model 89-C/89-DL Autoloading Rifle, 285
Model 92 LA Repeating Rifle, 285
Model 93 LA Repeating Rifle, 285
Model 93 Musket, 285
Model 93/93SC Carbine, 285
Model 94 LA Cowboy Series, 285
Model 94 LA Repeating Rifle, 285
Model 97 LA Repeating Rifle, 285
Model 98 Autoloading Rifle, 285
Model 99 Autoloading Rifle, 285
Model 99C, 285
Model 99DL, 285
Model 99M1 Carbine, 286
Model 100 BA Single-Shot Rifle, 286
Model 100SB, 286
Model 100 Tom Mix Special, 287
Model 101, 287
Model 101 DL, 287
Model 122 SS Junior Target Rifle, 287
Model 322 Bolt-Action Varmint Rifle, 287
Model 336 Cowboy, 287
Model 336 Marauder, 287
Model 336M, 287
Model 336 Micro Groove Zipper, 287
Model 336 Octagon, 287
Model 336AS, 287
Model 336 Sporting Carbine, 287
Model 336 Zane Grey Century, 287
Model 336A Lever-Action Rifle, 287
Model 336A-DL, 287
Model 336C Lever-Action Carbine, 287
Model 336CS W/Scope, 287
Model 336DT Deluxe Texan, 287
Model 336T Texan Carbine, 287
Model 336TS, 288
Model 444 LA Repeating Rifle, 288
Model 444 Sporter, 288
Model 444P, 288
Model 444SS, 288
Model 455 Bolt-Action Sporter, 288
Model 780 BA Repeater Series, 288
Model 795 SL, 288
Model 880 BA Repeater Series, 288
Model 922 Magnum SL Rifle, 289
Model 980 22 Magnum, 289
Model 989 Autoloading Rifle, 289
Model 989M2 Carbine, 289
Model 990 Semiautomatic, 289
Model 995 Semiautomatic, 290
Model 1870-1970 Centennial Matched Pair, 290
Model 1892 Lever-Action Rifle, 290
Model 1893 Lever-Action Rifle, 290
Model 1894 Lever-Action Rifle, 290

Model 1894 Carbine, 291
Model 1894CL Classic, 291
Model 1894CS Lever-Action Rifle, 291
Model 1894M Lever-Action, 291
Model 1894S Lever-Action, 291
Model 1895 45-70 Repeater, 292
Model 1895 Lever-Action Repeater, 292
Model 1895G (Guide Gun) Lever-Action, 292
Model 1895M Lever-Action, 292
Model 1895SS Lever-Action, 292
Model 1897 Lever-Action Rifle (See Marlin Model 97)
Model 1897 Cowboy Lever-Action, 293
Model 1936 Lever-Action Carbine (See Marlin Model 36)
Model 2000 Target Rifle, 293
Model 7000, 293
Model A-1 Autoloading Rifle, 293
Model A-1C Autoloading Rifle, 293
Model A-1DL, 293
Model A-1E, 294
Model MR-7 Bolt-Action Rifle, 294
Model 10, 294
Model 20, 294
Model 30, 294
Model 30A, 294
Model 36G, 294
Model 60, 294
Model 70, 294
Model 80G, 294
Model 81G, 295
Model 99G, 289
Model 101G, 295
Model 989G Autoloading Rifle, 295
SHOTGUNS
Model 16 Visible Hammer Slide-Action, 502
Model 17 Brush Gun, 502
Model 17 Riot Gun, 502
Model 17 Standard Visible Hammer Slide-Action, 503
Model 19 Visible Hammer Slide-Action Repeater, 503
Model 21 Trap Visible Hammer Slide-Action Repeater, 503
Model 24 Visible Hammer Slide-Action Repeater, 503
Model 26 Brush Gun, 503
Model 26 Riot Gun, 503
Model 26 Standard Visible Hammer Slide-Action Repeater, 503
Model 28 Hammerless Slide-Action Repeater, 504
Model 28T Trap Gun, 504
Model 28TS Trap Gun, 504
Model 30 Field Gun, 504
Model 30 Visible Hammer Slide-Action Repeater, 504
Models 30A, 30B, 30C, 30D, 504
Model 31 Hammerless Slide-Action Repeater, 504
Model 31F Field Gun, 505
Model 42A Visible Hammer Slide-Action Repeater, 505
Model 43 Hammerless Slide-Action Repeater, 505
Model 44 Hammerless Slide-Action Repeater, 505
Model 49 Visible Hammer Slide-Action Repeating, 505
Model 50DL Bolt Action Shotgun, 505
Model 53 Hammerless Slide-Action Repeater, 505
Model 55 Goose Gun, 505
Model 55 Hunter Bolt-Action Repeater, 505
Model 55 Swamp Gun, 505
Model 55S Slug Gun, 505
Model 59 Auto-Safe Bolt-Action Single, 505
Model 60 Single-Shot Shotgun, 505
Model 63 Hammerless Slide-Action Repeater, 505
Model 90 Standard Over/Under Shotgun, 505
Model 120 Magnum Slide-Action, 507
Model 120 Slug Gun, 507
Model 410 Lever-Action Repeater, 507
Model 512 Slugmaster Shotgun, 507
Model 1898 Visible Hammer Slide-Action Repeater, 507
Model 55-10 Super Goose 10, 507
Premier Mark I Slide-Action Repeater, 507
Premier Mark II and IV, 507
Model 50 Bolt-Action, 507
Model 778 Slide-Action Repeater, 507
MAROCCHI SHOTGUNS
Conquista Model Over/Under, 507
    Lady Sport Garde I, 507
    Lady Sport Grade II, 507
    Lady Sport Grade III, 507
    Skeet Model Grade I, 507
    Skeet Model Grade II, 507
    Skeet Model Grade III, 507
    Sporting Clays Grade I, 507
    Sporting Clays Grade II, 507
    Sporting Clays Grade III, 507
    Trap Model Grade I, 507
    Trap Model Grade II, 507
    Trap Model Grade III, 507
    Left-Handed Model, 507

MAUSER
PISTOLS
Luger Lange Pistole 08, 126
Model 80-SA, 125
Model 90 DA, 125
Model 90 DAC Compact, 125
Model 1898 (1896) Military, 125
Model HSC DA, 125
Parabellum Luger, 126
Pocket Model 1910, 126
Pocket Model 1914, 126
Pocket Model 1934, 126
WTP Model I, 126
WTP Model II, 126
RIFLES
PRE-WORLD WAR I MODELS
Bolt-Action Sporting Carbine, 296
Bolt-Action Sporting Rifle, 296
Bolt-Action Sporting Rifle, Military "Type C", 296
Bolt-Action Sporting Rifle, Short "Type K", 296
PRE-WORLD WAR II MODELS
Model DSM34 Bolt-Action Single-Shot Sporting, 296
Model EL320 BA - SS Sporting Rifle, 296
Model EN310 BA - SS Sporting Rifle, 296
Model ES340 BA - SS Target Rifle, 296
Model ES340B BA - SS Target Rifle, 296
Model ES350 BA - SS Target Rifle, 296
Model ES350B BA - SS Target Rifle, 296
Model KKW BA - SS Target Rifle, 296
Model M410 Bolt-Action Repeating Sporting Rifle, 296
Model MM410B Bolt-Action Repeating Sporting Rifle, 297
Model MS350B Target Rifle, 297
Model MS420 Sporting Rifle, 297
Model MS420B Target Rifle, 297
Standard Model Rifle, 297
Type "A" Bolt-Action Sporting Rifle, 297
Type "A" BA Sporting Rifle, Magnum, 297
Type "A" BA Sporting Rifle, Short, 297
Type "B" Bolt-Action Sporting Rifle, 297
Type "K" BA Sporting Rifle, 297
Type "M" BA Sporting Carbine, 297
Type "S" BA Sporting Carbine, 298
POST-WORLD WAR II Models
Model 66S Standard Sporting Rifle, 298
Model 66S Deluxe Sporter, 298
Model 66S Ultra, 298
Model 66SG Big Game, 298
Model 66SH High Performance, 299
Model 66SP Super Match Target, 299
Model 66ST Carbine, 299
Model 83 Bolt-Action Rifle, 299
Model 96, 299
Model 99 Classic Bolt-Action Rifle, 299
Model 107 Bolt-Action Rifle, 299
Model 201/201 Luxus BA Rifle, 299
Model 2000 Bolt-Action Sporting Rifle, 300
Model 2000 Classic DA Sporting Rifle, 300
Model 3000 Bolt-Action Sporting Rifle, 300
Model 3000 Magnum, 300
Model 4000 Varmint Rifle, 300
MAVERICK ARMS SHOTGUNS
Model 88 Bullpup, 507
Model 88 Deer Gun, 508
Model 88 Pump Shotgun, 508
Model 88 Security, 508
Model 91 Pump Shotgun, 508
Model 95 Bolt Action, 508
Model HS12 Tactical O/U, 508
Model HS12 Tactical Thunder Ranch O/U, 508
Model Hunter Field O/U, 508
McMILLAN—See listing under Harris Gunworks
MERKEL
RIFLES
Over/Under Rifles ("Bock-Doppelbüchsen"), 300
Model 210, 300
Model 210E, 300
Model 213, 300
Model 240E1, 300
Model 313E, 300
Model 320E, 300
Model 321, 300
Model 321E, 300
Model 322, 300
Model 323E, 300
Model 324, 300
SHOTGUNS
Anson Drillings, 511
Model 8 Hammerless Double, 508
Model 47E Side-by-Side, 508
Model 47LSC Sporting Clays S/S, 508
Models 47SL, 147SL, 247SL, 347S, 447S Hammerless Sidelocks, 509
Models 100 Over/Under, 509
Models 101 and 101E Over/Unders, 509

Model 122 Hammerless Double, 509
Model 122E Hammerless Sidelock, 509
Model 126E Hammerless Sidelock, 509
Model 127E Hammerless Sidelock, 510
Model 128E Hammerless Sidelock Double, 510
Model 130 Hammerless Boxlock Double, 510
Model 147, 147E Hammerless Boxlock Double-Barrel, 510
Models 200, 200E, 201, 201E, 202 and 202E, 510
Model 203E Sidelock Over/Under Shotguns, 510
Model 204E Over/Under Shotgun, 510
Model 210E Sidelock Over/Under Shotgun, 511
Model 211E Sidelock Over/Under Shotgun, 511
Models 300, 300E, 301, 301E and 302 Over/Under, 511
Model 303EL Over/Under Shotgun, 511
Model 304E Over/Under Shotgun, 511
Models 400, 400E, 401, 401E, 511
Over/Under Combination ("Bock-Büchsflinten"), 511
Model 2000EL Over/Under Shotguns, 511
Model 2001EL Over/Under Shotguns, 511
Model 2002EL, 511
MERWIN
First Model Frontier Army, 126
Second Model Frontier Army, 126
Second Model Pocket Army, 126
Third Model Frontier Army, 126
Third Model Frontier Army DA, 126
Third Model Pocket Army, 126
Third Model Pocket Army DA, 126
Fourth Model Pocket Army, 126
Fourth Model Pocket Army DA, 126
First Pocket Model, 126
Second Pocket Model, 127
Third Pocket Model, 127
Third Pocket Model w/Trigger Guard, 127
Small Frame Pocket Model, 127
Small Frame Pocket Model 32, 127
Tip-Up Model 32, 127
MEXICAN MILITARY RIFLE
Model 1936, 300
MIIDA SHOTGUNS
Grandee Model GRT/IRS Trap/Skeet Gun, 512
Model 612 Field Grade Over/Under, 512
Model 2100 Skeet Gun, 512
Model 2200T Trap Gun, Model 2200S Skeet Gun, 512
MIDLAND RIFLES
Model 2100, 301
Model 2600, 301
Model 2700, 301
Model 2800, 301
MITCHELL ARMS
HANDGUNS
Alpha Model, 127
American Eagle, 127
Citation II, 127
Model 1911 Gold Signature, 127
Model Guardian Angel Derringer, 128
Model Guardian II, 128
Model Guardian III, 128
Model Titan II DA, 128
Model Titan III DA, 128
Olympic I.S.U., 127
Sharpshooter, 127
SA Sport King II, 127
SA Army Revolver, 127
Trophy II, 127
Victor II, 128
RIFLES
AK-22, 301
CAR-15 22 Semiautomatic Rifle, 301
Galil 22 Semiautomatic Rifle, 301
M-16A 22 Semiautomatic Rifle, 301
MAS 22 Semiautomatic Rifle, 301
Model 15/22 Semiautomatic, 301
Model 9300 Series, 301
Model 9302, 301
Model 9303, 301
Model 9304, 301
Model 9305, 301
PPS Semiautomatic Rifle, 301
SHOTGUNS
Model 9104/9105 Pump Shotguns, 512
Model 9108/9109 Pump Shotgun, 512
Model 9111/9113 Pump Shotgun, 512
Model 9114/9114FS, 512
Model 9115/9115FS Pump Shotgun, 512
MKE PISTOL
Kirikkale DA, 128
MOA CORPORATION
Maximum Carbine Pistol, 128
Maximum Single-Shot, 128
MONTGOMERY WARD—See shotgun listings under "W"

MORRONE SHOTGUN
Standard Model 46 Over-and-Under, 512
MOSSBERG & SONS
PISTOLS
Brownie "Pepperbox" Pistol, 129
RIFLES
Model 10, 301
Model 14, 301
Model 20, 301
Model 25/25A, 301
Model 26B/26C, 302
Model 30, 302
Model 34, 302
Model 35 Target Grade, 302
Model 35A, 302
Model 35A-LS, 302
Model 35B, 302
Model 40, 302
Model 42, 302
Model 42A/L42A, 302
Model 42B/42C, 302
Model 42M, 303
Model 43/L43, 303
Model 43B, 303
Model 44, 304
Model 44B, 304
Model 44US Bolt-Action Repeater, 304
Model 45, 304
Model 45A, L45A, 45AC, 304
Model 45B/45C, 304
Model 46, 304
Model 46A, 46A-LS, L46A-LS, 304
Model 46B, 305
Model 46BT, 305
Model 46C, 305
Model 46M, 305
Model 50, 305
Model 51, 305
Model 51M, 305
Model 140B, 305
Model 140K, 305
Model 142-A, 305
Model 142K, 306
Model 144, 306
Model 144LS, 306
Model 146B , 306
Model 151K, 306
Model 151M, 306
Model 152, 306
Model 152K, 306
Model 320B Boy Scout Target, 306
Model 320K Hammerless, 306
Model 321B, 306
Model 321K, 306
Model 333, 306
Model 340B Target Sporter, 306
Model 340K Hammerless, 306
Model 340M, 306
Model 341, 308
Model 342K Hammerless, 308
Model 346B, 308
Model 346K Hammerless, 308
Model 350K, 308
Model 351C, 308
Model 351K, 308
Model 352K, 308
Model 353, 308
Model 377 Plinkster, 309
Model 380, 309
Model 400 Palomino, 309
Model 402 Palomino, 309
Model 430, 309
Model 432 Western-Style, 309
Model 472 Brush Gun, 310
Model 472 Lever-Action Carbine, 310
Model 472 One in Five Thousand, 310
Model 472 Rifle, 310
Model 479, 310
Model 620K Hammerless, 310
Model 620K-A, 310
Model 640K Chuckster Hammerless, 310
Model 640KS, 310
Model 640M, 310
Model 642K Carbine, 310
Model 800 Centerfire, 311
Model 800D Super Grade, 311
Model 800M, 311
Model 800VT Varmint/Target, 311
Model 810 Centerfire, 311
Model 1500 Mountaineer Grade I Centerfire, 311
Model 1500 Varmint, 312
Model 1700LS Classic Hunter, 312
Model B, 312
Model K Slide Action, 312
Model L, 312

Models L42A, L43, L45A, L46A-LS, 312
Model M Slide Action, 312
Model R, 312
SHOTGUNS
Line Launhcer, 519
Model G4, 70, 73 & 73B, 513
Model 83D or 183D, 513
Model 85D or 185D Bolt-Action Repeating
  Shotgun, 513
Model 183K, 513
Model 185K, 513
Model 190D, 513
Model 190K, 514
Model 195D, 514
Model 195K, 514
Model 200D, 514
Model 200K Slide-Action Repeater, 514
Model 385K, 514
Model 390K, 514
Model 395K Bolt-Action Repeater, 514
Model 395S Slugster, 514
Model 500 Accu-Choke Shotgun, 514
Model 500 Bantam Shotgun, 515
Model 500 Bullpup Shotgun, 515
Model 500 Camo Pump, 515
Model 500 Camper, 515
Model 500 Field Grade Hammerless Slide Action, 515
Model 500 "L" Series, 515
Model 500 Mariner Shotgun, 515
Model 500 Muzzleloader Combo, 515
Model 500 Persuader Law Enforcement Shotgun, 515
Model 500 Pigeon Grade, 515
Model 500 Camo Combo Shotgun, 516
Model 500 Pump Slugster Shotgun, 516
Model 500 Regal Slide-Action Repeater, 516
Model 500 Sporting Pump, 516
Model 500 Super Grade, 516
Model 500 Turkey/Deer Combo, 516
Model 500 Turkey Gun, 517
Model 500 Viking Pump Shotgun, 517
Model 500 Waterfowl/Deer Combo, 517
Model 500ATR Super Grade Trap, 517
Model 500DSPR Duck Stamp Commemorative, 517
Model 590 Mariner Pump, 517
Model 590 Bullpup, 517
Model 590 Military Security, 517
Model 590 Military Shotgun, 517
Model 595 Bolt-Action Repeater, 517
Model 6000 Auto Shotgun, 517
Model 695 Bolt Action Slugster, 517
Model 695 Bolt Action Turkey Gun, 517
Model 712 Autoloading Shotgun, 517
Model 835 "NWTF" Ulti-Mag, 518
Model 835 Field Pump Shotgun, 518
Model 835 Regal Ulti-Mag Pump, 518
Model 835 Viking Pump Shotgun, 518
Model 1000 Autoloading Shotgun, 518
Model 1000 Super Autoloading, 518
Model 1000S Super Skeet, 518
Model 5500 Autoloading Shotgun, 518
Model 5500 MKII Autoloading, 518
Model 6000 Auto Shotgun, 518
Model 9200 A1 Jungle gun, 518
Model 9200 Camo Shotgun, 518
Model 9200 Crown (Regal) Autoloader, 518
Model 9200 Persuader, 518
Model 9200 Special Hunter, 518
Model 9200 Trophy, 518
Model 9200 USST Autoloader, 518
Model 9200 Viking Autoloader, 518
Model HS410 Home Security Pump Shotgun, 519
"New Haven Brand" Shotguns, 519
Onlyx Reserse Sporting S/S, 519
Onyx Reserse Sporting O/U, 519
Silver Reserse Field O/U, 519
Silver Reserse Sporting O/U, 519
Silver Reserse II Field O/U, 519
Silver Reserse II Sport O/U, 519
Silver Reserse II Super Sport O/U, 519
Silver Reserse Field S/S, 519
Silver Reserse II Field S/S, 519
MUSGRAVE RIFLES
Premier NR5 BA Hunting Rifle, 312
RSA NR1 BA - SS Target Rifle, 313
Valiant NR6 Hunting Rifle, 313
MUSKETEER RIFLES
Mauser Sporter, 313
NAMBU PISTOLS—*See listings under Japanese Military
Pistols*
NAVY ARMS COMPANY
PISTOLS/REVOLVERS
Buntline Frontier, 129
Frontier SA Revolver, 129
Frontier Target Model, 129
Luger (Standard) Automatic, 130

Model 1873 SA Revolver, 129
Model 1875 SA Revolver, 129
Model 1875 Schofield Revolver, 129
Rolling Block Single-Shot Pistol, 130
TT-Olympia Pistol, 130
RIFLES
45-70 Mauser Carbine, 313
45-70 Mauser Rifle, 313
Model 1873 Carbine, 313
Model 1873 Winchester Border Rifle, 313
Model 1873 Sporting Carbine/Rifle, 313
Model 1873 Lever-Action Rifle, 313
Model 1873 Trappers, 313
Model 1874 Sharps Cavalry Carbine, 313
Model 1874 Sharps Sniper Rifle, 313
ENGRAVED ModelS
Grade "A", 313
Grade "B", 313
Grade "C", 313
Henry Lever-Action Rifle, 313
Martini Target Rifle, 313
Revolving Carbine, 313
Rolling Block Baby Carbine, 313
Rolling Block Buffalo Carbine, 313
Rolling Block Buffalo Rifle, 314
Rolling Block Creedmoor Rifle, 314
Yellowboy Carbine, 314
Yellowboy Lever-Action Repeater, 314
Yellowboy Trapper's Model, 315
SHOTGUNS
Model 83/93 Bird Hunter Over/Under, 519
Model 95/96 Over/Under Shotgun, 519
Model 100 Over/Under Shotgun, 519
Model 100/150 Field Hunter Double-Barrel
  Shotgun, 519
NEW ENGLAND FIREARMS
REVOLVERS
Lady Ultra Revolver, 130
Model R73 Revolver, 130
Model R92 Revolver, 130
Model 832 Starter Pistol, 130
Ultra Revolver, 130
RIFLES
Handi-Rifle, 315
Super-Light Handi-Rifle, 315
Sportster, 315
Survivor, 315
SHOTGUNS
NWTF Turkey Special, 519
NRA Foundation Youth, 520
Pardner Shotgun, 520
Pardner Special Purpose 10 Ga., 520
Pardner Special Purpose Waterfowl Single-Shot, 520
Pardner Turkey Gun, 520
Survivor Series, 520
Tracker Slug Guns, 520
NEWTON SPORTING RIFLES
Buffalo Sporting Rifle, 315
Mauser Sporting Rifle, 315
Standard Model Sporting Rifle First Type, 315
NIKKO FIREARMS—*See listings under Golden Eagle
Firearms*
NOBLE MFG.
RIFLES
Model 10 Bolt-Action, 316
Model 20 Bolt-Action, 316
Model 33 Slide-Action Repeater, 316
Model 33A, 316
Model 222 Bolt-Action SS, 316
Model 236 SA Repeating Rifle, 316
Model 278 Lever-Action Rifle, 316
SHOTGUNS
Model 40 Hammerless Slide-Action, 520
Model 50 Slide-Action, 521
Model 60 Hammerless Slide-Action, 521
Model 65, 521
Model 66CLP, 521
Model 66RCLP Hammerless Slide-Action Repeating
  Shotgun, 521
Model 66RLP, 521
Model 66XL, 521
Model 70CLP Hammerless Slide-Action Repeating
  Shotgun, 521
Model 70RCLP, 521
Model 70RLP, 521
Model 70XL, 521
Model 80 Autoloading Shotgun, 521
Model 166L Deer Gun, 521
Model 420 Hammerless Double, 521
Model 450E Hammerless Double, 521
Model 602CLP, 522
Model 602RCLP Hammerless Slide-Action Repeating
  Shotgun, 522
Model 602RLP, 522
Model 602XL, 522

Model 662, 522
NORINCO
Model 81S/AK Semiautomatic Rifle, 316
Model 84S/AK Semiautomatic Rifle, 317
Model AK-47 Thumbhole Sporter, 317
Model Mak 90/91 Sport, 317
NORTH AMERICAN ARMS
Black Widow Revolver, 131
Guardian DAO Pistol, 131
Mini-Master Target Revolver, 131
Model 22LR, 130
Model 22S Mini Revolver, 130
Model 450 Magnum Express, 130
NORWEGIAN MILITARY PISTOLS
Model 1912, 131
Model 1914, 131
OLYMPIC ARMS
HANDGUNS
OA-93 AR Semiautomatic Pistol, 131
OA-96 AR Semiautomatic Pistol, 131
RIFLES
Bolt-Action Sake, 317
CAR 97, 317
FAR-15, 317
GI-16, 317
GI-20, 317
K3B Carbine, 317
K4B/K4B68, 318
K4B-A4, 318
K7 Eliminator, 318
K8 Target Match, 318
K8-Mag, 318
K9/K10/K40/K45, 318
K9GL/K40GL, 318
K16, 318
K-30 (.30 carbine), 318
K68, 318
K74, 318
LTF Tactical Rifle, 317
OA-93 Carbine, 317
OA-93PT, 317
PCR Series:
PCR-1/Ultra Match, 317
PCR-2/MultiMatch ML-1, 317
PCR-3/MultiMatch ML-2, 317
PCR-4/AR-15 Match, 317
PCR-5/CAR-15 (223 Rem.), 317
PCR-5/CAR-15 (9mm, 40S&W, 45ACP), 317
PCR-6/A-2 (7.62x39mm), 317
Survivor 1, 317
Ultra CSR Tactical, 317
OMEGA SHOTGUNS
Folding Over/Under, 522
Over/Under Shotgun, Deluxe, 522
Side-by-Side Shotgun, Deluxe, 522
Side-by-Side Shotgun, Standard, 522
Single-Shot Shotgun, Deluxe, 522
Single-Shot Shotgun, Standard, 522
ORTGIES PISTOLS
Pocket Automatic Pistol, 131
Vest Pocket Automatic Pistol, 131
PARA-ORDNANCE
Limited Edition Series, 131
Model P-10 SA, 131
P-12 Compact, 131
P-13 Auto Pistol, 132
P-14 Auto Pistol, 132
P-15 Auto Pistol, 132
P-16 SA, 132
P-18 SA, 132
PXT Single Stack Series, 132
PXT High Capacity Series, 132
PARKER BROTHERS SHOTGUNS
Hammerless Double-Barrel Shotguns, 522
G.H. Grades, 523
A-1 Grades, 523
A.H. Grades, 523
A.A.H. Grades, 523
B.H. Grades, 523
C.H. Grades, 523
D.H. Grades, 523
Single-Shot Trap Guns, 523
S.A-1 Special, 523
S.A.A. Grade, 523
S.A. Grade, 523
S.B. Grade, 523
S.C Grade, 523
Skeet Gun, 523
Trojan Hammerless Double-Barrel Shotguns, 523
PARKER REPRODUCTIONS
Hammerless Double-Barrel Shotguns, 524
A-1 Special Grades, 524
B Grades, 524
DHE Grades, 524

PARKER-HALE LIMITED
RIFLES
Model 81 African, 318
Model 81 Classic Bolt-Action Rifle, 318
Model 85 Sniper Rifle, 318
Model 87 BA Repeating Target Rifle, 318
Model 1000 Standard Rifle, 319
Model 1100 Lightweight BA Rifle, 319
Model 1100M African Magnum Rifle, 319
Model 1200 Super BA Sporting Rifle, 319
Model 1200 Super Clip BA Rifle, 319
Model 1200 Super Magnum, 319
Model 1200P Presentation, 319
Model 1200V Varmint, 319
Model 1300C Scout, 319
Model 2100 Midland Bolt Action Rifle, 319
Model 2707 Lightweight, 319
Model 2800 Midland, 319
SHOTGUNS
Model 645A (American) Side-by-Side, 524
Model 645E (English) Side-by-Side, 524
Model 645E-XXV, 524
PEDERSEN CUSTOM GUNS
RIFLES
Model 3000 Grade I Bolt-Action Rifle, 319
Model 3000 Grade II, 319
Model 3000 Grade III, 320
Model 4700 Custom Deluxe LA Rifle, 320
SHOTGUNS
Model 1000 Over/Under Hunting, 524
Model 1000 Magnum, 524
Model 1000 Skeet Gun, 524
Model 1000 Trap Gun, 524
Model 1500 Over/Under Hunting Shotgun, 525
Model 1500 Skeet Gun, 525
Model 1500 Trap Gun, 525
Model 2000 Hammerless Double, 525
Model 2500 Hammerless Double, 525
Model 4000 BA Hammerless SA Repeating SG, 525
Model 4000 Trap Gun, 525
Model 4500, 525
Model 4500 Trap Gun, 525
PENNEY, J.C. COMPANY
RIFLES
Model 2025 Bolt-Action Repeater, 320
Model 2035 Bolt-Action Repeater, 320
Model 2935 Lever-Action Rifle, 320
Model 6400 BA Centerfire Rifle, 320
Model 6660 Autoloading Rifle, 320
SHOTGUNS
Model 4011 Autoloading Shotgun, 525
Model 6610 Single-Shot Shotgun, 525
Model 6630 Bolt-Action Shotgun, 525
Model 6670 Slide-Action Shotgun, 525
Model 6870 Slide-Action Shotgun, 525
PHOENIX ARMS
Model HP22/HP25 SA, 132
Model HP Rangemaster Deluxe Target SA, 132
Model HP Rangemaster Target SA, 132
Model "Raven" SA, 132
PERAZZI SHOTGUNS—*See also listings under Ithaca-Perazzi*
DB81 Over/Under Trap, 525
DB81 Single-Shot Trap, 525
Grand American 88 Special Single Trap, 526
Mirage Over/Under Shotgun, 526
MX1 Over/Under Shotgun, 526
MX2 Over/Under Shotgun, 526
MX3 Over/Under Shotgun, 526
MX3 Special Pigeon Shotgun, 526
MX4 Over/Under Shotgun, 526
MX5 Over/Under Game Gun, 526
MX6 American Trap Single Barrel, 526
MX6 Skeet Over/Under, 527
MX6 Sporting Over/Under, 527
MX6 Trap Over/Under, 527
MX7 Over/Under Shotgun, 527
MX8 Over/Under Shotgun, 527
MX8/20 Over/Under Shotgun, 527
MX9 Over/Under Shotgun, 527
MX10 Over/Under Shotgun, 527
MX10 Pigeon-Electrocibles Over/Under, 527
MX11 American Trap Combo, 527
MX11 American Trap Single Barrel, 527
MX11 Pigeon-Electrocibles Over/Under, 527
MX11 Skeet Over/Under, 527
MX11 Sporting Over/Under, 527
MX11 Trap Over/Under, 527
MX12 Over/Under Game Gun, 527
MX14 American Trap Single-Barrel, 527
MX15 American Trap Single-Barrel, 527
MX20 Over/Under Game Gun, 528
MX28 Over/Under Game Gun, 528
MX410 Over/Under Game Gun, 528
TM1 Special Single-Shot Trap, 528

TMX Special Single-Shot Trap, 528
PIOTTI SHOTGUNS
Boss Over/Under, 528
King No. 1 Sidelock, 528
King Extra Side-by-Side Shotgun, 528
Lunik Sidelock Shotgun, 528
Monte Carlo Sidelock Shotgun, 528
Piuma Boxlock Side-by-Side, 528
PLAINFIELD MACHINE COMPANY
HANDGUNS
Model 71, 133
Model 72, 133
RIFLES
M-1 Carbine, 320
M-1 Carbine, Commando Model, 320
M-1 Carbine, Military Sporter, 320
M-1 Deluxe Sporter, 320
POLISH MILITARY PISTOLS
Model P-64, 133
Model P-83 WANAD, 133
POLISH MILITARY RIFLES
Model 1898 (Karabin 98, K98) Mauser, 320
Model 1898 (Karabin 98, WZ98A) M Military, 320
Model 1929 (Karabin 29, WZ29) M Military, 320
POWELL, William & Sons, Ltd.
RIFLES
Double-Barrel Rifle, 321
Bolt-Action Rifle, 321
SHOTGUNS
No. 1 Best Grade Double-Barrel, 528
No. 2 Best Grade Double, 528
No. 6 Crown Grade Double, 528
No. 7 Aristocrat Grade Double, 528
PRECISION SPORTS SHOTGUNS
Sports 600 Series American Hammerless Doubles:
Model 640A American Series Slug Gun, 529
Models 640A American Series, 529
Models 645A American Series, 529
Model 650A American Series, 529
Model 655A American Series, 529
Sports 600 Series English Hammerless Doubles:
Models 640E English Series, 529
Model 640E English Series Slug Gun, 529
Models 645E English Series, 529
Model 650E English Series, 529
Model 655E English Series, 529
Sports Model 640M Magnum 10 Hammerless, 529
Sports Model 645E-XXV Hammerless Double, 529
PREMIER SHOTGUNS
Ambassador Model Field Grade Hammerless DB, 529
Brush King, 529
Continental Model Field Grade Hammer DB, 529
Monarch Supreme Grade Hammerless DB, 529
Presentation Custom Grade, 529
Regent 10-Gauge Magnum Express, 529
Regent 12-Gauge Magnum Express, 529
Regent Model Field Grade Hammerless, 529
PROFESSIONAL ORDNANCE
Model Carbon-15 Type 20, 133
Model Carbon-15 Type 97, 133
PTR 91, INC
RIFLES
Model PTR-91F Semi-Automatic, 321
PUMA
RIFLES
Model 1886 Lever Action, 321
Model 92 Lever Action, 321
PPS/22, 321
PURDEY, James & Sons
RIFLES
Bolt-Action Rifle, 321
Double Rifle, 321
SHOTGUNS
Hammerless Double-Barrel Shotgun, 530
Over/Under Shotgun, 530
Single-Barrel Trap Gun, 530
RADOM PISTOL
P-35 Automatic Pistol, 133
RANDALL FIREARMS
Model A111, 134
Model A112, 134
Model A121, 134
Model A211, 134
Model A232, 134
Model A331, 134
Model B111, 134
Model B131, 134
Model B311, 134
Model B312 LeMay, 134
Model B331, 134
RAPTOR ARMS COMPANY
Bolt-Action Rifles, 321
RECORD-MATCH PISTOLS
Model 200 Free Pistol, 134
Model 210 Free Pistol, 134

INDEX

REISING ARMS
Target Automatic Pistol, 134
REMINGTON ARMS COMPANY
HANDGUNS
Model 51 Automatic Pistol, 134
Model 95 Double Derringer, 134
New Model Single-Shot Target Pistol, 135
Model XP-100 Custom Pistol, 135
Model XP-100 Silhouette, 135
Model XP-100 Single-Shot Pistol, 135
Model XP-100 Varmint Special, 135
Model XP-100R Custom Repeater, 135
DERRINGERS
Eliot's Single-Shot, 135
Eliot's Four-Shot, 135
Eliot's Five-Shot, 135
Model 1866 Navy Rolling Block, 135
Model 1870 Navy Rolling Block, 135
Model 1890 Single-Action Revolver, 135
Model 1911 UMC, 135
Model 1911A1 Rand, 135
Over and Under, 135
Rider's magazine, 135
Vest Pocket, 135
Zig-Zag, 135
RIFLES
Remington Single-Shot Rifles:
No. 1 Sporting Rifle, 322
No. 1-1/2 Sporting Rifle, 322
No. 2 Sporting Rifle, 322
No. 3 Creedmoor and Scheutzen Rifles, 322
No. 3 High Power Rifle, 322
No. 3 Sporting Rifle, 322
No. 4 Single-Shot Rifle, 322
No. 4S Military Model 22 Single-Shot Rifle, 322
No. 5 Special Single-Shot Rifle, 322
No. 6 Takedown Rifle, 322
No. 7 Target and Sporting Rifle, 322
Model 33 Bolt-Action Single-Shot Rifle, 323
Model 33 NRA Junior Target Rifle, 323
Model 40X Centerfire Rifle, 323
Model 40X Heavyweight Bolt-Action Target, 323
Model 40X Sporter, 323
Model 40X Standard Barrel, 323
Model 40XB Centerfire Match Rifle, 323
Model 40XB Rangemaster Centerfire, 323
Model 40XB Rangemaster Rimfire Match Rifle, 323
Model 40XB Varmint Special Rifle, 323
Model 40XBBR Bench Rest Rifle, 323
Model 40XC National Match Course Rifle, 324
Model 40XR Custom Sporter Rifle, 324
Model 40XR Rimfire Position Rifle, 324
Model 41A Targetmaster Bolt-Action SS Rifle, 324
Model 41AS, 324
Model 41P, 324
Model 41SB, 324
Model 510A Targetmaster Bolt-Action SS Rifle, 324
Model 510P, 324
Model 510X-SB, 324
Model 510X Bolt-Action Single-Shot Rifle, 325
Model 514 Bolt-Action Single-Shot, 325
Model 514BC Boy's Carbine, 325
Model 514P, 325
Model 540X Rimfire Target Rifle, 325
Model 540XR Position Rifle, 325
Model 540XRJR, 325
Model 580 Bolt-Action Single-Shot, 325
Model 580BR Boy's Rifle, 325
Model 580SB Smooth Bore, 325
International Free Rifle, 325
International Match Free Rifle, 325
Nylon 10 Bolt-Action Single-Shot, 326
Bolt-Action Repeating Rifles:
Model Seven (7) CF Bolt-Action Rifle, 326
Model Seven (7) FS Rifle, 326
Model Seven (7) KS Rifle, 326
Model Seven (7) LS Rifle, 326
Model Seven (7) LSS Rifle, 326
Model Seven (7) MS Custom Rifle, 326
Model Seven (7) SS Rifle, 326
Model Seven (7) Youth Rifle, 326
Model 30A Bolt-Action Express Rifle, 326
Model 30R Carbine, 326
Model 30S Sporting Rifle, 326
Model 34 Bolt-Action Repeater, 326
Model 34 NRA Target Rifle, 326
Model 37 Rangemaster Bolt-Action Target (I), 327
Model 37 Rangemaster Bolt-Action Target (II), 327
Model 40XB Centerfire Repeater, 327
Model 788 Sportsman Bolt-Action Rifle, 327
Model 341A Sportsmaster Bolt-Action Repeater, 327
Model 341P, 328
Model 341SB, 328
Model 511A Scoremaster BA Box, 328
Model 511P, 328

Model 511X Bolt-Action Repeater, 328
Model 512A Sportsmaster BA Repeater, 328
Model 512P, 328
Model 512X Bolt-Action Repeater, 328
Model 513S Bolt-Action Rifle, 328
Model 513TR Matchmaster Bolt-Action Target, 328
Model 521TL Junior Target Bolt-Action Repeater, 328
Model 522 Viper, 328
Model 541-S Custom Sporter, 328
Model 541-T Bolt-Action Rifle, 328
Model 581 Clip Repeater, 329
Model 581-S Bolt-Action Rifle, 329
Model 582 Tubular Repeater, 329
Model 591 Bolt-Action Clip Repeater, 329
Model 592 Tubular Repeater, 329
Model 600 Bolt-Action Carbine, 329
Model 600 Magnum, 329
Model 600 Montana Territorial Centennial, 329
Model 660 Magnum, 329
Model 660 STP, 329
Model 700 ADL Centerfire Rifle, 329
Model 700 APR, 329
Model 700 AS, 329
Model 700 AWR, 331
Model 700 BDL European Rifle, 331
Model 700 BDL Centerfire Rifle, 331
Model 700 BDL SS, 331
Model 700 BDL Varmint Special, 331
Model 700 Classic, 331
Model 700 Custom Bolt-Action Rifle, 331
Model 700 CS Custom Bolt Action, 331
Model 700 FS, 331
Model 700 KS Custom MTN Rifle, 331
Model 700 LS Bolt-Action Rifle, 333
Model 700 LSS, 333
Model 700 MTN Rifle, 333
Model 700 RS, 333
Model 700 Safari Grade, 333
Model 700 Sendero, 334
Model 700 VLS (Varmint Laminated Stock), 334
Model 700 VS, 334
Model 720A Bolt-Action High Power, 334
Model 721A Standard Grade Bolt-Action
High-Power, 334
Model 721A Magnum Standard Grade, 334
Model 721ADL/BDL Magnum, 334
Model 722A Standard Grade Sporter, 334
Model 722 ADL Deluxe Grade, 334
Model 722 BDL Deluxe Special, 334
Model 725 Kodiak Magnum Rifle, 334
Model 725 ADL Repeating Rifle, 334
Model 788 Centerfire, 334
Nylon 11 Bolt-Action Rifle, 335
Nylon 12 Bolt-Action Rifle, 335
Slide- and Lever-Action Rifles:
Model Six (6), 335
Model Six (6) Slide-Action Repeater, Peerless
Grade, 335
Model Six (6) Slide-Action Repeater, Premier
Grade, 335
Model 12A, 12B, 12C, 12CS, 335
Model 14A High Power, 335
Model 14R Carbine, 335
Model 14.5 Carbine, 335
Model 14.5 Rifle, 335
Model 25A, 335
Model 25R Carbine, 335
Model 121A Fieldmaster, 335
Model 121S, 335
Model 121SB, 335
Model 141A Gamemaster, 336
Model 572A Fieldmaster, 336
Model 572BDL Deluxe, 336
Model 572SB Smooth Bore, 336
Model 760 Bicentennial Commemorative, 336
Model 760 Carbine, 336
Model 760 Gamemaster Standard Grade, 336
Model 760ADL Deluxe Grade, 336
Model 760BDL Custom Deluxe, 336
Model 760D Peerless Grade, 336
Model 760F Premier Grade, 337
Model 7600 Slide-Action Carbine, 337
Model 7600 Slide-Action Rifle, 337
Model 7600 Special Purpose, 337
Nylon 76, 337
Sportsman 76, 337
Semiautomatic Rifles:
Model Four (4), 338
Model Four Diamond Anniversary Ltd. Edition, 338
Model 8A, 338
Model 16, 338
Model 24A, 338
Model 81A Woodsmaster, 338
Model 141A Speedmaster, 338
Model 550A, 338

Model 550P, 338
Model 550-2G, 338
Model 552A Speedmaster, 338
Model 552BDL Deluxe, 338
Model 552C Carbine, 338
Model 552GS Gallery Special, 338
Model 740A Woodsmaster, 338
Model 740ADL/BDL Deluxe, 338
Model 742 Bicentennial Commemorative, 338
Model 742 Canadian Centennial, 338
Model 742 Carbine, 338
Model 742 Woodsmaster, 338
Model 742BDL Custom Deluxe, 338
Model 742D Peerless Grade, 339
Model 742F Premier Grade, 339
Model 7400 Autoloader, 339
Model 7400 Carbine, 339
Model 7400 Special Purpose, 339
Nylon 66 Apache Black, 339
Nylon 66 Bicentennial Commemorative, 339
Nylon 66 Mohawk Brown Autoloader, 339
Nylon 66MB Autoloading Rifle, 339
Nylon 77 Clip Repeater, 339
Sportsman 74 Autoloading Rifle, 339
SHOTGUNS
Model 10A Standard Grade Slide-Action Repeating
Shotgun, 530
Model 11 Special, Tournament, Expert and Premier
Grade Guns, 530
Model 11A Standard Grade Autoloader, 530
Model 11R Riot Gun, 531
Model 14A Riot Gun, 540
Model 11-48A Standard Grade 4-Shot Autoloader, 540
Model 11-48A Standard Grade 5-Shot Autoloader, 540
Model 11-48SA .410 & 28 Ga. Skeet, 540
Model 11-87 Premier Autoloader, 531
Model 11-87 Special Purpose Magnum, 531
Model 11-87 SPS Magnum, 531
Model 11-96 EURO Lightweight, 531
Model 17A Standard Grade Slide-Action, 531
Model 29A Standard Grade Slide-Action, 531
Model 29T Target Grade, 531
Model 31 and 31L Skeet Grade, 531
Model 31 Special, Tournament, Expert and Premier
Grade Guns, 532
Model 31A Slide-Action Repeater, 532
Model 31S Trap Special/31TC Trap Grade, 532
Model 32 Skeet Grade, 532
Model 32BBR Bench Rest Rifle, 532
Model 32 Tournament, Expert and Premier Grade
Guns, 532
Model 32A Standard Grade Over/Under, 532
Model 32TC Target (Trap) Grade, 532
Model 89 (1989), 532
Model 90-T Single-Shot Trap, 532
Model 105 CTi Autoloader, 532
Model 396 Over/Under, 533
Model 870 "All American" Trap Gun, 533
Model 870 Competition Trap, 533
Model 870 Deer Gun Brushmaster Deluxe, 533
Model 870 Deer Gun Standard, 533
Model 870 Express Deer Gun, 533
Model 870 Express Super Magnum, 533
Model 870 Express Synthetic Home Defense, 534
Model 870 Express Turkey Gun, 534
Model 870 Express Youth Gun, 534
Model 870 Express, 534
Model 870 Lightweight Magnum, 534
Model 870 Lightweight, 534
Model 870 Magnum Duck Gun, 534
Model 870 Marine Magnum, 534
Model 870 Mississippi Magnum Duck Gun, 534
Model 870 SA Skeet Gun, Small Bore, 534
Model 870 Special Field Shotgun, 534
Model 870 Special Purpose Deer Gun, 534
Model 870 Special Purpose Magnum, 534
Model 870SPS Magnum, 535
Model 870 Wingmaster Field Gun, 535
Model 870 Wingmaster Field Gun, Small Bore, 535
Model 870 Wingmaster Magnum Deluxe Grade, 535
Model 870 Wingmaster Magnum Standard Grade, 535
Model 870 Wingmaster REM Choke Series, 535
Model 870ADL Wingmaster Deluxe Grade, 535
Model 870AP Wingmaster Standard Grade, 535
Model 870BDL Wingmaster Deluxe Special, 535
Model 870D, 870F Wingmaster Tournament and
Premier Grade, 535
Model 870R Wingmaster Riot Gun, 535
Model 870SA Wingmaster Skeet Gun, 535
Model 870TB Wingmaster Trap Special, 535
Model 870TC Trap Grade, 535
Model 870TC Wingmaster Trap Grade, 535
Model 878A Automaster, 535
Model 887 Nitro Mag, 535
Model 887 Nitro Mag Camo Combo, 536
Model 887 Nitro Mag Tactical, 536

Model 887 Nitro Mag Waterfowl, 536
Model 1100 Automatic Field Gun, 536
Model 1100 Deer Gun, 536
Model 1100 Ducks Unlimited "The Chesapeake" Commemorative, 536
Model 1100 Ducks Unlimited Atlantic Commemorative, 536
Model 1100 Field Grade, Small Bore, 536
Model 1100 G3, 536
Model 1100 Lightweight Magnum, 536
Model 1100 Lightweight, 536
Model 1100 LT-20 Ducks Unlimited Special Commemorative, 536
Model 1100 LT-20 Series, 536
Model 1100 Magnum, 536
Model 1100 Magnum Duck Gun, 536
Model 1100 "One of 3000" Field, 537
Model 1100 SA Lightweight Skeet, 537
Model 1100 SA Skeet Gun, 537
Model 1100 SA Skeet Small Bore, 537
Model 1100 SB Lightweight Skeet, 537
Model 1100 SB Skeet Gun, 537
Model 1100 SP Magnum, 537
Model 1100 Special Field Shotgun, 537
Model 1100 Tournament and Premier, 537
Model 1100 Tournament Skeet, 538
Model 1100TA Trap Gun, 538
Model 1100TB Trap Gun, 538
Model 1900 Hammerless Double, 538
Model 3200 Competition Skeet Gun, 538
Model 3200 Competition Skeet Set, 538
Model 3200 Competition Trap Gun, 538
Model 3200 Field Grade Magnum, 538
Model 3200 Field Grade Over/Under, 538
Model 3200 "One of 1000" Skeet, 538
Model 3200 "One of 1000" Trap, 538
Model 3200 Skeet Gun, 538
Model 3200 Special Trap Gun, 538
Model 3200 Trap Gun, 538
Peerless Over/Under, 539
Rider No. 9 Single-Shot Shotgun, 538
SP-10 Magnum Autoloader, 538
SP-10 Magnum Camo, 538
SP-10 Magnum Turkey Combo, 539
Sportsman A Standard Grade Autoloader, 539
Sportsman Skeet Gun, 539
Sportsman-48 B, D, F Special, Tournament and Premier Grade, 539
Sportsman-48A Standard Grade 3-Shot Autoloader, 539
Sportsman-48SA Skeet Gun, 539
Sportsman-58 Skeet Target, Tournament & Premier Grades, 540
Sportsman-58 Tournament and Premier, 540
Sportsman-58ADL Autoloader, 540
Sportsman-58BDL Deluxe Special Grade, 540
Sportsman-58SA Skeet Grade, 540
Versa Max, 539
Versa Max Competition Tactical, 539
Versa Max Sportsman, 539
Versa Max Tactical, 539
REVELATION SHOTGUNS—*See Western Auto listings*
RG REVOLVERS
Model 23, 136
Model 38S, 136
RICHLAND ARMS COMPANY
Model 200 Field Grade Double, 540
Model 202 All-Purpose Field Gun, 541
Model 707 Deluxe Field Gun, 541
Model 711 Long Range Waterfowl Magnum, 541
Model 808 Over/Under Gun, 541
RIGBY, John & Company
RIFLES
Model 278 Lightweight Magazine Rifle, 340
Model 278 Magazine Sporting Rifle, 340
Model 350 Magnum Magazine Sporting Rifle, 340
Model 416 Big Game Magazine Sporting Rifle, 340
Best Quality Hammerless Ejector, 340
Second Quality Hammerless Ejector, 340
Third Quality Hammerless Ejector, 340
SHOTGUNS
Hammerless Box Lock Double Barrel Shotguns, 541
Hammerless Side Lock Double-Barrel Shotguns, 541
RIZZINI, BATTISTA
SHOTGUNS
Aurum O/U, 541
Aurum Light, 541
Artemis, 541
Artemis Deluxe, 541
Artemis EL, 541
Model 780, 541
Model 780 Competition, 541
Model 780 Small Guage Series, 541
Model 782, 541
Model 790, 542

Model 790 Competition, 542
Model 790 EL, 542
Model 790 EMEL Deluxe, 542
Model 790 Small Guage, 542
Model 792, 542
Model 792 EMEL Deluxe, 542
Model 792 Small Guage Magnum, 542
Model S780 EMEL, 542
Model S782 EMEL, 542
Model S782 EMEL Deluxe, 542
Model S790 EMEL, 542
Model S792 EMEL, 542
Model 2000-SP, 542
Model 2000 Trap, 542
Model 2000 Trap EL, 542
Premier Sporting, 542
Sporting EL, 542
Upland EL, 542
ROSS RIFLE CO
Model 1910 Bolt-Action Sporting Rifle, 340
ROSSI, Amadeo, S.A.
REVOLVERS
Model 31 DA, 136
Model 51 DA, 136
Model 68, 136
Model 84 DA, 136
Model 85, 136
Model 88 DA, 136
Model 88/2 DA, 136
Model 89 DA, 136
Model 94 DA, 136
Model 95 (951), 136
Models 351/352 Revolvers, 136
Models 461/462 Revolvers, 136
Model 511 DA, 136
Model 515 DA, 136
Model 518 DA, 136
Model 677 DA, 136
Model 720 DA, 136
Model 841 DA, 136
Model 851 DA, 136
Model 877 DA, 136
Model 941 DA, 136
Model 951 DA, 136
Model 971 DA, 136
Model 971 VRC DA, 137
Cyclops DA, 137
DA Revolver, 137
Sportsman's 22, 137
RIFLES
62 Gallery Model SAC Carbine, 340
62 Gallery Model Magnum, 340
62 Gallery Model Slide-Action Repeater, 341
Lever-Action 65/92 Carbine, 341
SHOTGUNS
Hammerless Double-Barrel Shotgun, 542
Overland Hammer Double, 542
ROTTWEIL SHOTGUNS
Model 72 Over/Under Shotgun, 543
Model 650 Field Over/Under Shotgun, 543
American Skeet, 543
International Trap Shotgun, 543
RUBY PISTOL
7.65mm Automatic Pistol, 137
RUGER
AUTOMATIC/SINGLE-SHOT PISTOLS
22 Charger Automatic, 137
Hawkeye Single-Shot Pistol, 137
Mark I Target Model, 138
Mark II Automatic Pistol, 138
Mark II 22/45 Automatic Pistol, 138
Mark II Bull Barrel Model, 138
Mark II Government Model, 138
Mark II Target Model, 138
Mark III Automatic Pistol, 138
Mark III Target Automatic Pistol, 138
Mark III 22/45 Automatic Pistol, 139
Model LCP Automatic Pistol, 139
Model LC9 Pistol, 139
Model LC380 Pistol, 139
Model P-85 Automatic Pistol, 139
Model P-89 Automatic Pistol, 139
Model P-89 DAC/DAO Auto Pistols, 139
Model P-90, KP90 DA, 139
Model KP-91 DA Automatic Pistol, 139
Model P-93D Auto Pistol, 140
Model P-94 Automatic Pistol, 140
Model P-95PR Automatic Pistol, 140
Model P-97D Automatic Pistol, 140
Model P-345 Automatic Pistol, 140
Model P-944, 140
Model SR22, 140
Model SR9, 140
Model SR9C, 140
Model SR40, 140

Model SR40C, 140
Model SR45, 140
Model SR1911, 140
Standard Model Automatic Pistol, 140
REVOLVERS
Bearcat SA (Old Model), 140
Bisley SA Revolver, Large Frame, 141
Bisley Single-Six Revolver, Small Frame, 141
Blackhawk SA Flat-Top (Old Model) Revolver, 141
Blackhawk SA Convertible, 141
Blackhawk SA Revolver, 141
GP-100 DA, 141
GP-100 Match Champion, 141
LCR DAO Revolver, 141
New Model Bearcat, 141
New Model Blackhawk Convertible, 142
New Model Blackhawk SA, 141
New Model Blackhaw Bisley, 141
New Model Blackhawk Convertible, 142
New Model Super Single-Six SSM, 142
New Model Super Blackhawk SA, 142
New Model Super Blackhawk Bisley, 142
New Model Super Single-Six Convertible, 142
New Model Vaquero, 143
New Model Vaquero Bisley, 143
Police Service-Six, 143
Redhawk DA Revolver, 143
Super Redhawk DA, 143
Security-Six DA Revolver, 143
Single-Six SA Revolver (Old Model), 143
Single-Six Lightweight, 144
Single-Nine, 144
Single-Ten, 144
SP101 DA, 144
Speed-Six DA, 144
Super Blackhawk SA 44 Mag. Revolver (Old Model), 144
Vaquero SA, 144
Vaquero Bisley, 144
RIFLES
American Rifle, 347
American Rifle Rimfire, 347
Guide Gun, 347
Mini-14 Ranch Rifle, 344
Mini-14 Semiautomatic Rifle, 343
Mini-14 Target, 344
Mini-14 Tactical, 344
Mini-Thirty (30) Autoloader, 344
Model 10/22 Autoloading Carbine, 343
Model 44 Autoloading Carbine, 343
Model 77 Bolt-Action Rifle, 345
Model 77 Mark II All-Weather Rifle, 345
Model 77 Mark II Bolt-Action Rifle, 347
Model 77 Gunsite Scout, 347
Model 77/22 Hornet Bolt-Action Rifle, 347
Model 77/22 Rimfire Bolt-Action Rifle, 347
Model 77/44 Bolt-Action, 347
Model 99/44 Deerfield, 343
Model HM77 Hawkeye, 347
Number One (1) Light Sporter, 341
Number One (1) Medium Sporter, 341
Number One (1) "North Americans" Presentation Rifle, 341
Number One (1) RSI International Single-Shot Rifle, 341
Number One (1) Special Varminter, 341
Number One (1) Standard Rifle, 341
Number One (1) Tropical Rifle, 341
Number Three (3) Single-Shot Carbine, 343
PC Series Semiautomatic Carbines, 344
SR-556/SR-556 Carbine, 345
SR-762 Carbine, 345
SHOTGUNS
Gold Label Side-by-side, 544
Red Label Plain Grade Over/Under, 543
Red Label Over/Under All Weather Stainless, 543
Red Label "Woodside" Over/Under, 543
Red Label Sporting Clays Over/Under Stainless, 544
Red Label Special Edition - Wildlife Forever, 544
RUSSIAN
SERVICE PISTOLS
Model 30 Tokarev Service, 144
Model PM Makarov, 145
MILITARY RIFLES
Model 1891 Mosin Military Rifle, 349
Tokarev Model 40 Semiautomatic Military Rifle, 349
SAIGA
SHOTGUNS
Saiga-12, 543
Saiga .410, 543
Saiga Hunting Model, 543
Saiga Skeletonized Stock, 543
Saiga Tactical, 543
SAKO
HANDGUNS

22-32 Olympic Pistol, 145
RIFLES
Classic Bolt-Action Rifle, 350
Deluxe Grade AI, 351
Deluxe Grade AII, 351
Deluxe Grade AIII, 351
Deluxe Lightweight Bolt-Action Rifle, 351
Fiberclass Bolt-Action Rifle, 351
Finnbear Carbine, 351
Finnbear Sporter, 351
Finnfire Bolt-Action Rifle, 351
Finnwolf Lever-Action Rifle, 351
Finsport 2707, 352
Forester Carbine, 352
Forester Heavy Barrel, 352
Forester Sporter, 352
Golden Anniversary Model, 352
High-Power Mauser Sporting Rifle, 352
Hunter Lightweight Bolt-Action Rifle, 352
Laminated Stock Bolt-Action Rifles, 352
Magnum Mauser, 352
Mannlicher-Style Carbine, 352
Model 72, 349
Model 73 Lever-Action Rifle, 349
Model 74 Carbine, 349
Model 74 Heavy Barrel Rifle, Long Action, 350
Model 74 Heavy Barrel Rifle, Medium Action, 350
Model 74 Heavy Barrel Rifle, Short Action, 350
Model 74 Super Sporter, Long Action, 350
Model 74 Super Sporter, Medium Action, 350
Model 74 Super Sporter, Short Action, 350
Model 75 Deluxe, 350
Model 75 Hunter, 350
Model 75 Stainless Synthetic, 350
Model 75 Varmint Rifle, 350
Model 78 Super Hornet Sporter, 350
Model 78 Super Rimfire Sporter, 350
Safari Grade, 352
Sporter Deluxe, 344
Standard Grade AI, 352
Standard Grade AII, 352
Standard Grade AIII, 353
Super Deluxe Rifle, 353
TRG Bolt-Action Target Rifle, 353
TRG-S Bolt-Action Rifle, 353
Vixen Carbine, 353
Vixen Heavy Barrel, 353
Vixen Sporter, 353
SARASQUETA, S. A.
Model 3 Hammerless Boxlock Double-Barrel SG, 544
Hammerless Sidelock Doubles, 544
Model 4 & 4E, 544
Model 6E, 544
Model 7E, 544
Model 10E, 544
Model 11E, 544
Model 12E, 544
Model 203 & 203E, 544
SAUER HANDGUNS—*See listings under Hawes and Sig Sauer*
1913 Pocket, 145
1930 Pocket, 145
Model 38H DA, 145
Pocket 25, 145
Single-Action Revolvers—*See Listings under Hawes*
SAUER, J.P., & Sohn
RIFLES
Mauser Bolt-Action Sporting Rifle, 353
Model S-90 Bolt-Action Rifles, 353
Model 200 Bolt-Action Rifles, 353
Model 202 Bolt-Action Rifles, 353
SHOTGUNS
Artemis Double-Barrel Shotgun, 545
BBF 54 Over/Under Combination Rifle/Shotgun, 545
Model 66 Over/Under Field Gun, 544
Model 66 Over/Under Skeet Gun, 545
Model 66 Over/Under Trap Gun, 545
Model 3000E Drilling, 545
Royal Double-Barrel Shotguns, 545
SAVAGE ARMS
PISTOLS
Model 101 SA, 145
Model 501/502 "Striker" Series Pistols, 145
Model 510/516 "Striker" Series Pistols, 146
Model 1907, 145
Model 1915, 146
Model 1917, 146
U.S. Army Test Model 1910, 146
RIFLES
Model 3 Bolt-Action Single-Shot Rifle, 353
Model 3S, 354
Model 3ST, 354
Model 4 Bolt-Action Repeater, 354
Model 4M, 354
Model 4S, 354

Model 5 Bolt-Action Repeater, 354
Model 5S, 354
Model 6 Autoloading Rifle, 354
Model 6S, 354
Model 7 Autoloading Rifle, 354
Model 7S, 355
Model 19 Bolt-Action Target Rifle, 355
Model 19 NRA Bolt-Action Match Rifle, 355
Model 19H, 355
Model 19L, 355
Model 19M, 355
Model 20-1926 Hi-Power, 355
Model 23A Bolt-Action Sporting Rifle, 355
Model 23AA, 355
Model 23B, 355
Model 23C, 355
Model 23D, 355
Model 25 Slide-Action Repeater, 355
Model 29 Slide-Action Repeater, 355
Model 40 Bolt-Action Sporting Rifle, 356
Model 45 Super Sporter, 356
Model 60 Autoloading Rifle, 356
Model 63K Key Lock Bolt-Action Single-Shot Rifle, 356
Model 63KM, 356
Model 64F Autoloading Rifle, 356
Model 64G Autoloading Rifle, 356
Model 71 "Stevens Favorite" Single-Shot Lever-Action Rifle, 356
Model 90 Autoloading Carbine, 356
Model 93F Bolt-Action Rifle, 356
Model 93G Bolt-Action Rifle, 356
Model 99A Bolt-Action Rifle, 356
Model 99A (II), 357
Model 99B, 357
Model 99C, 357
Model 99CD, 357
Model 99DE Citation Grade, 357
Model 99DL Deluxe, 357
Model 99E Carbine (I), 358
Model 99E Carbine (II), 358
Model 99EG (I), 358
Model 99EG (II), 358
Model 99F Featherweight (I), 358
Model 99F Featherweight (II), 358
Model 99G, 358
Model 99H Carbine, 359
Model 99K, 359
Model 99PE Presentation Grade, 359
Model 99R (I), 359
Model 99R (II), 359
Model 99RS (I), 361
Model 99RS (II), 361
Model 99T, 361
Model 99-358, 361
Model 110 Sporter Bolt-Action Rifle, 361
Model 110B Bolt-Action Rifle, 361
Model 110BL, 361
Model 110C, 361
Model 110CL, 361
Model 110CY Youth/Ladies Rifle, 361
Model 110D, 361
Model 110DL, 361
Model 110E, 362
Model 110EL, 362
Model 110F/110K Bolt-Action Rifle, 362
Model 110FM Sierra Ultra Light, 362
Model 110FP Police Rifle, 362
Model 110G Bolt-Action Rifle, 362
Model 110GV Varmint Rifle, 362
Model 110M Magnum, 362
Model 110MC, 362
Model 110P Premier Grade, 362
Model 110PE Presentation Grade, 362
Model 110PEL Presentation Grade, 363
Model 110PL Premier Grade, 363
Model 110S/110V, 363
Model 111 Chieftain Bolt-Action Rifle, 363
Models 111F, 111FC, 111FNS Classic Hunters, 363
Models 111G, 111GC, 111GNS Class Hunters, 363
Model 112BV, 112BVSS Heavy Varmint Rifles, 363
Model 112FV, 112FVS, 112 FVSS Varmint Rifles, 363
Model 112V Varmint Rifle, 363
Model 114C, 114CE, 114CU Rifles, 364
Model 116FSK Kodiak Rifle, 364
Model 116SE, 116US Rifles, 364
Models 116FSAK, 116FCSAK Bolt-Action, 364
Models 116FSC, 116FSS Bolt-Action Rifles, 364
Model 170 Pump-Action Centerfire Rifle, 364
Model 170C Carbine, 364
Model 219 Single-Shot Rifle, 364
Model 221-229 Utility Guns, 364
Model 340 Bolt-Action Repeater, 364
Model 340S Deluxe, 365
Model 342, 365
Model 342S Deluxe, 365

Model Anniversary 1895 Lever Action, 365
Model 1903 Slide-Action Repeater, 365
Model 1904 Bolt-Action Single-Shot Rifle, 365
Model 1905 Bolt-Action Single-Shot Rifle, 366
Model 1909 Slide-Action Repeater, 366
Model 1912 Autoloading Rifle, 366
Model 1914 Slide-Action Repeater, 366
Model 1920 Hi-Power Bolt-Action Rifle, 366
Model 10 Bolt Action Target Rifle, 366
Model Mark 10D, 366
Model 54 Custom Sporter, 366
Model 54M, 366
Model 64 Bolt-Action Target Rifle, 366
Model 153 Bolt-Action Sporter, 366
Model 153S, 366
Model 164 Custom Sporter, 366
Model 164M, 366
Model 184 Sporter, 366
Model 34 Bolt-Action Repeater, 366
Model 34M, 366
Model 35, 367
Model 35M, 367
Model 46 Bolt Action, 367
Model 65 Bolt-Action Rifle, 367
Model 65M, 367
Model 72 Crackshot Single-Shot Lever-Action, 367
Model 73 Bolt-Action Single-Shot, 367
Model 73Y Youth Model, 367
Model 74 Little Favorite, 367
Model 80 Autoloading Rifle, 367
Model 88 Autoloading Rifle, 367
Model 89 Single-Shot Lever-Action Carbine, 367
Model 987-T Autoloading Rifle, 367
"Stevens Favorite", 367
SHOTGUNS
Model 24 22-.410 Over/Under Combination, 545
Model 24C Camper's Companion, 545
Model 24D, 545
Model 24DL, 545
Model 24F-12T Turkey Gun, 546
Model 24FG Field Grade, 546
Model 24MDL, 546
Model 24MS, 546
Model 24S Over/Under Combination, 546
Model 24V, 546
Model 24-VS Camper/Survival/Centerfire Rifle/SG, 546
Model 28A Standard Grade Slide-Action Repeating, 546
Model 28B, 546
Model 28D Trap Grade, 546
Model 30 Solid Frame Hammerless Slide-Action, 546
Model 30 Takedown Slug Gun, 546
Model 30AC Solid Frame, 546
Model 30AC Takedown, 546
Model 30ACL Solid Frame, 546
Model 30D Takedown, 546
Model 30FG Takedown Hammerless Slide-Action, 546
Model 30L Solid Frame, 546
Model 30T Solid Frame Trap and Duck, 546
Model 30T Takedown Trap Gun, 546
Model 69-RXL Slide-Action Shotgun, 546
Model 210F Bolt Action Slug Gun, 547
Model 210FT Bolt Action Shotgun, 547
Model 220 Single-Barrel Shotgun, 547
Model 220AC, 547
Model 220L, 548
Model 220P, 548
Model 242 Over/Under Shotgun, 548
Model 312 Field Grade Over/Under, 548
Model 312 Sporting Clays Over/Under, 548
Model 312 Trap Over/Under, 548
Model 330 Over/Under Shotgun, 548
Model 333 Over/Under Shotgun, 548
Model 333T Trap Gun, 548
Model 420 Over/Under Shotgun, 548
Model 430, 548
Model 440 Over/Under Shotgun, 548
Model 440T Trap Gun, 548
Model 444 Deluxe Over/Under Shotgun, 548
Model 550 Hammerless Double, 549
Model 720 Standard Grade 5-Shot Autoloading, 549
Model 726 Upland Sporter Grade, 549
Model 740C Skeet Gun, 549
Model 745 Lightweight Autoloader, 549
Model 750 Automatic Shotgun, 549
Model 750-AC, 549
Model 750-SC, 550
Model 755 Standard Grade Autoloader, 550
Model 755-SC, 550
Model 775 Lightweight, 550
Model 775-SC, 550
Model 2400 Over/Under Combination, 550

SCHILLING
'88 Mauser Sporter, 367

Mauser-Mannlicher Bolt Action Sporting Rifle, 367
SCHULTZ & LARSEN GEVAERFABRIK
Free Rifle Model 54, 367
Match Rifle No. 47, 367
Model 54J Sporting Rifle, 367
SEARS, ROEBUCK & COMPANY
HANDGUNS
J.C. Higgins Model 80, 146
J.C. Higgins Model 88 DA Revolver, 146
J.C. Higgins Ranger DA Revolver, 147
RIFLES
Model 2C Bolt-Action Rifle, 367
Model 42 Bolt-Action Repeater, 367
Model 42DL Bolt-Action Repeater, 368
Model 44DL Lever-Action Rifle, 368
Model 53 Bolt-Action Rifle, 368
Model 54 Lever-Action Rifle, 368
Model 103 Series Bolt-Action Repeater, 368
Model 103.2 Bolt-Action Repeater, 369
SHOTGUNS
Model 18 Bolt-Action Repeater, 551
Model 20 Slide-Action Repeater, 551
Model 21 Slide-Action Repeater, 551
Model 30 Slide-Action Repeater, 551
Model 97 Single-Shot Shotgun, 551
Model 97-AC Single-Shot Shotgun, 551
Model 101.1120 Bolt-Action Repeater, 551
Model 101.1380 Bolt-Action Repeater, 551
Model 101.1610 Double-Barrel, 551
Model 101.1701 Double-Barrel, 551
Model 101.25 Bolt-Action Shotgun, 551
Model 101.40 Single-Shot Shotgun, 551
Model 101.5350-D Bolt-Action Repeater, 551
Model 101.5410 Bolt-Action Repeater, 551
Model 101.7 Double-Barrel, 551
Model 101.7C Double-Barrel, 551
SKB ARMS COMPANY
Models 300 and 400 Side-by-Side Doubles, 551
Model 385 Side-by-Side, 551
Model 400 Skeet, 551
Model 480 English, 551
Model 500 Series Over/Under, 552
Model 500 Small Gauge Over/Under, 552
Model 505 Over/Under Shotgun, 552
Model 585 Deluxe Over/Under Shotgun, 552
Model 600 Small Gauge, 552
Model 600 Over/Under Series, 552
Model 605 Trap Over/Under Shotgun, 552
Model 680 English Over/Under, 552
Model 685 Deluxe Over/Under, 552
Model 800 Skeet/Trap Over/Under, 553
Model 880 Skeet/Trap, 553
Model 885 Deluxe Over/Under, 553
Century Single-Barrel Trap Gun, 553
Gas-operated Automatic Shotguns, 553:
Model XL300
Model XL300 w/Plain Barrel
Model XL300 w/Vent Rib
Model XL900
Model XL900 Skeet
Model XL900 Slug
Model XL900 Trap
Model 1300 Upland, Slug
Model 1900 Field, Trap, Slug
Over/Under Shotguns, 553
Model 500 Field
Model 500 Magnum
Model 600 Doubles
Model 600 English
Model 600 Field
Model 600 Magnum
Model 600 Skeet 12 Or 20 Gauge
Model 600 Skeet 28 Or .410 Gauge
Model 600 Skeet Combo
Model 600 Trap
Model 700 Doubles
Model 700 Skeet
Model 700 Skeet Combo
Model 700 Trap
Recoil-Operated Automatic Shotguns, 553:
Model 300
Model 900
Side-by-Side Double-Barrel Shotguns, 553:
Model 100
Model 150
Model 200E
Model 200E Skeet
Model 280 English
SECURITY IND. OF AMERICA
Model PM357 DA Revolver, 147
Model PPM357 DA Revolver, 147
Model PSS38 DA Revolver, 147
SEDGLEY
HANDGUNS
Baby Hammerless Ejector Revolver, 147

RIFLES
Springfield Sporter, 368
Springfield Left-Hand Sporter, 368
Sedgley Springfield Mannlicher-Type Sporter, 368
SEECAMP
Model LWS 25 DAO Pistol, 147
Model LWS 32 DAO Pistol, 147
SHERIDAN PRODUCTS
Knockabout Single-Shot Pistol, 147
SHILEN RIFLES
DGA Benchrest Rifle, 368
DGA Sporter, 368
DGA Varminter, 368
SHILOH RIFLE MFG
Sharps Model 1874 Business Rifle, 369
Sharps Model 1874 Long Range Express Rifle, 369
Sharps Model 1874 Montana Roughrider, 369
Sharps Model 1874 Saddle Rifle, 369
Sharps Model 1874 Sporting Rifle No. 1, 369
Sharps Model 1874 Sporting Rifle No. 3, 369
SHOTGUNS OF ULM—*See listings under Krieghoff*
SIG PISTOLS
P210-1 Automatic Pistol, 147
P210-2, 147
P210-5 Target Pistol, 147
P210-6 Target Pistol, 147
P210 22 Conversion Unit, 147
SIG SAUER
HANDGUNS
Model P220 DA/DAO, 148
Model P220 Sport Automatic, 148
Model P225 DA Automatic, 148
Model P226 DA/DAO Automatic, 148
Model P228 DA Automatic, 148
Model P229 DA/DAO Automatic, 148
Model P229 Sport Automatic, 148
Model P230 DA, 148
Model P232 DA/DAO Automatic, 149
Model P239 DA/DAO Automatic, 149
RIFLES
SIG551-A1
SIG556 Classic, 370
SIG556R, 370
SSG 3000, 370
Tactical 2, 370
SHOTGUNS
Model SA3 Over/Under Shotgun, 553
Model SA5 Over/Under Shotgun, 553
SIG SWISS AMT
AMT Semiautomatic Rifle, 369
AMT Sporting Rifle, 369
PE57 Semiautomatic Rifle, 369
SILE SHOTGUNS
Field Master II Over/Under Shotgun, 553
SMITH, L.C.
SHOTGUNS
Double-Barrel Shotguns, 553:
Crown Grade, 554
Deluxe Grade, 554
Eagle Grade, 554
Field Grade, 554
Ideal Grade, 554
Monogram Grade, 554
Olympic Grade, 554
Premier Grade, 554
Skeet Special, 554
Specialty Grade, 554
Trap Grade, 554
Hammerless Double-Barrel Shotguns, 554:
0 Grade
00 Grade
1 Grade
2 Grade
3 Grade
4 Grade
5 Grade
A1, 542
A2, 542
A3, 542
Monogram
Hammerless Double Model 1968 Deluxe, 554
Hammerless Double Model 1968 Field Grade, 554
Single-Shot Trap Guns, 554
Marlin Import, 554:
Model LC12 O/U, 554
Model LC20 O/U, 554
Model LC12 DB S/S, 555
Model LC20 DB S/S, 555
Model LC28 DB S/S, 555
Model LC410 DB S/S, 555
SMITH & WESSON
AUTOMATIC/SINGLE-SHOT PISTOLS
Model 22 Sport Series, 149
Model 22A Semi-Automatic Target Pistol, 149
Model 32 Automatic Pistol, 149

Model 35 (1913) Automatic Pistol, 149
Model 39 9mm DA Auto Pistol, 149
Model 41 22 Automatic Pistol, 149
Model 46 22 Auto Pistol, 150
Model 52 38 Master Auto, 150
Model 59 9mm DA Auto, 151
Model 61 Escort Pocket, 151
Model 410 Auto Pistol, 151
Model 411 Auto Pistol, 151
Model 422 SA Auto Pistol, 151
Model 439 9mm Automatic, 151
Model 457 Compact Auto Pistol, 151
Model 459 DA Automatic, 151
Model 469 9mm Automatic, 151
Model 539 DA Automatic, 151
Model 559 DA Automatic, 151
Model 622 SA Auto Pistol, 151
Model 639 Automatic, 151
Model 645 DA Automatic, 152
Model 659 9mm Automatic, 152
Model 669 Automatic, 152
Model 745 Automatic Pistol, 152
Model 908/909/910 Auto Pistols, 152
Model 915 Auto Pistol, 153
Model 1000 Series DA Auto, 153
Model 2206 SA Automatic Pistol, 153
Model 2213 Sportsman Auto, 153
Model 2214 Sportsman Auto, 153
Model 3904/3906 DA Auto Pistol, 153
Model 3913/3914 DA Automatic, 153
Model 3953/3954 DA Auto Pistol, 154
Model 4000 Series DA Auto, 154
Model 4013/4014 DA Automatic, 154
Model 4053/4054 DA Auto Pistol, 154
Model 4500 Series DA Automatic, 154
Model 5900 Series DA Automatic, 155
Model 6900 Compact Series, 155
M&P9 C.O.R.E. Automatic Pistol, 155
M&P9 Pro Series Automatic Pistol, 155
M&P40 Automatic Pistol, 155
M&P40 Pro Series Automatic Pistol, 155
M&P45 Automatic Pistol, 155
M&P357 Automatic Pistol, 155
M&P Bodyguard Automatic Pistol, 155
M&P Shield Automatic Pistol, 156
Model 1891 Target Pistol, First Model, 156
Model 1891 Target Pistol, Second Model, 156
Perfected Single-Shot Target Pistol, 156
Sigma SW380 Automatic Pistol, 156
Sigma SW9 Series Automatic Pistol, 156
Straight Line Single-Shot Target Pistol, 156
SW40 Series Automatic Pistol, 156
REVOLVERS
K-22 Masterpiece DA, 170
K-22 Outdoorsman DA, 170
K32 and K38 Heavy Masterpieces, 170
K-32 Target DA, 170
Ladysmith (Model M Hand Ejector), 170
Model 1 Hand Ejector, 156
Model 10 38 Military & Police DA, 157
Model 10 38 Military & Police\Heavy Barrel, 157
Model 12/13 (Air Force Model) DA, 157
Model 12 38 M & P Airweight, 157
Model 13 357 Military/Police, 157
Models 14 (K38) and 16 (K32) Masterpiece, 157
Models 15 (38) & 18 (22) Combat Masterpiece DA, 157
Model 15 Classic Series, 157
Model 17 K-22 Masterpiece DA, 157
Model 17 Classic Series, 157
Model 18, 157
Model 18 Classic Series, 157
Model 19 357 Combat Magnum DA, 158
Model 20 38/44 Heavy Duty DA, 158
Model 21 1950 44 Military DA, 158
Model 22 1950 Army DA, 158
Model 22 Classics Series, 158
Model 22 Classics Series Model of 1917, 158
Model 22/32 Kit Gun, 158
Model 22/32 Target DA, 158
Model 23 38/44 Outdoorsman DA, 159
Model 24 1950 44 Target DA, 159
Model 24-6 Classics Series, 160
Model 25 1955 45 Target DA, 160
Model 25 Classics Series, 160
Model 26 1950 45 Light Target DA, 160
Model 27 357 Magnum DA, 160
MOdel 27 Classics Series, 160
Model 28 Highway Patrolman, 160
Model 29 44 Magnum DA, 160
MOdel 29 Classics Series, 161
Model 30 32 Hand Ejector DA, 161
Models 31 & 33 Regulation Police DA, 161
Model 32 Double-Action, 161
Model 32 Terrier DA, 161

Model 32-20 Military & Police DA, 161
Model 34 DA Revolver, 161
Model 35 1953 22/32 Target, 161
Model 36 Chief's Special DA, 162
Model 37 Airweight Chief's Special, 162
Model 38 Bodyguard Airweight DA, 162
Model 38 DA Revolver, 162
Model 38 Hand Ejector DA, 162
Model 38 Military & Police Target DA, 162
Model 38 Perfected DA, 162
Model 40 Centennial DA Hammerless Revolver, 162
Model 42 Centennial Airweight, 162
Model 42 Classics Series, 162
Model 43 1955 22/32 Kit Gun Airweight, 162
Model 44 1926 Military DA, 163
Model 44 and 38 DA Revolvers, 163
Model 44 Hand Ejector DA, 163
Model 44 Hand Ejector, Second Model DA, 164
Model 48 (K-22) Masterpiece M.R.F. DA, 164
Model 48 Classics Series, 164
Model 49 Bodyguard, 164
Model 51 1960 22/32 Kit Gun, 164
Model 53 22 Rem. Jet DA, 164
Model 57 41 Magnum DA, 164
Model 57 Classics Series, 164
Model 58 41 Military & Police DA, 164
Model 58 Classic Series, 164
Model 60 Stainless DA, 164
Model 63 (1977) Kit Gun DA, 164
Model 64 38 M&P Stainless, 164
Model 65 357 Military/Police Stainless, 164
Model 66 357 Combat Magnum Stainless, 165
Model 67 38 Combat Masterpiece Stainless, 165
Model 68 38 Combat Masterpiece Stainless, 165
Model 125th Anniversary Commemorative, 165
Model 242 Airlite TI Centennial, 165
Model 310 Nightguard, 165
Model 315 Nightguard, 165
Model 317 Airlite DA, 165
Model 325 Nightguard, 165
Model 325 PD-Airlite SC, 166
Model 327 Nightguard, 166
Model 327 PD-Airlite SC, 166
Model 329 PD-Airlite SC, 166
Model 331 Airlite TI Chiefs Special, 166
Model 332 Airlite TI Centennial, 166
Model 337 Airlite TI Chiefs Special, 166
Model 337 Airlite TI Kit Gun, 166
Model 337 Airlight PD Airlite TI, 166
Model 340 Airlite SC Centennial, 166
Model 340 PD Airlite SC Centennial, 166
Model 340 M&P Centennial, 166
Model 342 Airlite TI Centennial, 166
Model 342 PD Airlite TI Centennial, 166
Model 351 PD Airlite SC Chiefs Special, 166
Model 351 PD Airlite Centennial, 166
Model 357 PD, 166
Model 357 Nightguard, 166
Model 360 Airlite SC Chiefs Special, 166
Model 360 PD Airlite SC Chiefs Special, 166
Model 360 M&P Chiefs Special, 166
Model 386 Airlite SC Mountain Lite, 166
Model 386 PD Airlite SC, 166
Model 386 SC/S, 166
Model 386 Nightguard, 167
Model 386 XL Hunter Airlite SC, 167
Model 396 Airlite TI Mountain Life, 167
Model 396 Nightguard, 167
Model 431 Airweight, 167
Model 431 Centennial Airweight, 167
Model 438 Airweight, 167
Model 442 Airweight Centennial, 167
Model 469 V/XVR, 167
Model 500, 167
Model 586 Distinguished Combat Magnum, 167
Model 610 Classic DA, 167
Model 617K-22 Masterpiece DA, 167
Model 619, 168
Model 620, 168
Model 624 Double-Action, 168
Model 625 DA, 168
Model 625 JM, 168
Model 627 DA, 168
Model 629 DA, 168
Model 631 DA, 168
Model 632 Centennial DA, 168
Model 637 Chiefs Special Airweight DA, 168
Model 638 Bodyguard Airweight DA, 168
Model 640 Centennial DA, 168
Model 642 Centennial Airweight DA, 168
Model 648 DA, 169
Model 649 Bodyguard DA, 169
Model 650 Revolver, 169
Model 651 Stainless DA, 169
Model 657 Revolver, 169

Model 681, 169
Model 686, 169
Model 686 Plus, 169
Model 696, 169
Model 940 Centennial DA, 170
Model 1891 SA, 170
Model 1917 Army DA Revolver, 170
No. 3 SA (New Model), 156
No. 3 SA Frontier, 156
No. 3 SA Target, 156
Regulation Police DA (I Frame), 170
Regulation Police Target DA, 170
Safety Hammerless Revolver, 170
Texas Ranger Commemorative, 171
RIFLES
Model 1500, 370
Model 1500DL Deluxe, 370
Model 1700 LS "Classic Hunter", 370
Model A Bolt-Action Rifle, 370
Model B, 371
Model C, 371
Model D, 371
Model E, 371
SHOTGUNS
Model 916 Slide-Action Repeater, 555
Model 916T, 555
Model 1000 Autoloader, 555
Model 1000 Magnum, 555
Model 1000P, 555
Model 3000 Slide Action, 555
SPHINX ENGINEERING
Model AT-380 DA Pistol, 171
Model AT2000S DA Automatic Pistol, 171
Model AT2000C/2000CS Competitor, 171
Model AT2000GM/GMS Grand Master, 172
SPRINGFIELD
PISTOLS
Firecat Automatic Pistol, 173
Model M1911 Series Auto Pistol, 172
Model 1911-A1 Government, 172
Model 1911-A1 (Pre '90 Series), 172
Model 1911-A1 (Custom Load Series), 172
Model 1911-A1 PDP Series, 172
Model M1911-A1 Champion, 172
Model M1911-A1 Compact, 172
Model M1911-A1 Ultra Compact, 172
Model 1911-A1 TRP Operator, 173
Model 1911-A1 Long Slide Custom Loaded, 173
Panther Automatic Pistol, 173
P9 DA Combat Series, 173
P9 Competition Series, 174
XD Series, 174
XD(M) Series, 174
RIFLES
BM-59 Semiautomatic Rifle, 371
M-1 Garand Semiautomatic Rifle, 371
Match M1A, 371
Model M-6 Scout Rifle/Shotgun Combo, 372
Model SAR-8 Sporter Rifle, 372
Model SAR-48, SAR-4800, 372
Standard M1A Semiautomatic, 371
SPRINGFIELD ARMS
Double-Barrel Hammer Shotgun, 555
SPRINGFIELD RIFLES—See Stevens-Springfield Rifles
and U.S. Military Rifles
SQUIRES BINGHAM
RIFLES
Model 14D Deluxe Bolt-Action Repeating, 372
Model 15, 372
Model M16 Semiautomatic Rifle, 372
Model M20D Deluxe, 372
SHOTGUNS
Model 30 Pump Shotgun, 556
STALLARD ARMS—See listings under Hi-Point
STAG ARMS
Model 1, 372
Model 2, 372
Model 3, 372
Model 4, 373
Model 5, 373
Model 6, 373
Model 7, 373
Model 8, 373
Model 9, 373
STANDARD ARMS COMPANY
Model G Automatic Rifle, 373
Model M Hand-Operated Rifle, 373
STAR
PISTOLS
Model 30M DA Auto Pistol, 174
Model 30PK DA Auto Pistol, 174
Model 31 PK DA Auto Pistol, 175
Model 31P DA Auto Pistol, 175
Model A Automatic Pistol, 175
Models AS, BS, PS, 175

Model B, 175
Model BKM, 175
Model BKS Starlight, 175
Model BM Automatic Pistol, 175
Model CO Pocket Automatic Pistol, 175
Model CU Starlet Pocket Pistol, 175
Model F Automatic Pistol, 175
Model F Olympic Rapid-Fire, 175
Model FM, 175
Model FR, 175
Model FRS, 175
Model FS, 175
Model H, 176
Model HK Lancer Automatic Pistol, 176
Model HN Automatic Pistol, 176
Model I Automatic Pistol, 176
Model IN, 176
Model M Military Automatic Pistol, 176
Models M40, M43, M4 Firestar Auto Pistols, 176
Megastar Automatic Pistol, 176
Model P, 176
Model PD Automatic Pistol, 176
Model S, 176
Model SL Automatic Pistol, 176
Model Starfire DK Automatic Pistol, 176
Models Super A, Super B, Super, Super M,
 Super P, 176
Models Super SL, Super S, 177
Model Super SM Automatic Pistol, 177
Model Super Target Model, 177
Ultrastar DA Automatic Pistol, 177
RIFLES
Rolling Block Carbine, 373
STENDA-WERKE PISTOL
Pocket Automatic Pistol, 177
STERLING ARMS CORPORATION
HANDGUNS
Model 283 Target 300 Auto Pistol, 177
Model 284 Target 300L, 177
Model 285 Husky, 178
Model 286 Trapper, 178
Model 287 PPL-380 Automatic Pistol, 178
Model 300 Automatic Pistol, 178
Model 300S, 178
Model 302, 178
Model 302S, 178
Model 400 DA Automatic Pistol, 178
Model 400S, 178
Model 450 DA Auto Pistol, 178
Model PPL-22 Automatic Pistol, 178
RIFLES
Mark 6 Semiautomatic Carbine, 373
STEVENS ARMS COMPANY
PISTOLS
No. 10 Single-Shot Target Pistol, 178
No. 35 Offhand Model Single-Shot, 178
Offhand No. 35 Single-Shot, 178
No. 36 Single Shot, 178
No. 37 Single Shot, 178
No. 38 Single Shot, 179
No. 41 Tip-Up, 179
RIFLES
Buckhorn Model 053 Bolt-Action Single-Shot, 375
Buckhorn Model 53, 375
Buckhorn 055, 376
Buckhorn Model 056 Bolt-Action, 376
Buckhorn Model 56, 376
Buckhorn No. 057, 376
Buckhorn No. 57, 376
Buckhorn Model 066 Bolt-Action Repeating, 376
Buckhorn Model 66, 376
Buckhorn No. 076 Autoloading Rifle, 376
Buckhorn No. 76, 376
Crack Shot No. 26 Single-Shot Rifle, 376
Crack Shot No. 26.5, 376
Favorite No. 17 Single-Shot Rifle, 376
Favorite No. 18, 377
Favorite No. 19, 377
Favorite No. 20, 377
Favorite No. 27, 377
Favorite No. 28, 377
Favorite No. 29, 377
Model 15, 373
Model 15Y Youth's Rifle, 373
Model 66 Bolt-Action Repeating Rifle, 374
Model 87 Autoloading Rifle, 374
Model 322 Hi-Power Bolt-Action Carbine, 375
Model 322-S, 375
Model 325 Hi-Power Bolt-Action Carbine, 375
Model 325-S, 375
Model 416 Bolt-Action Target Rifle, 375
No. 12 Marksman Single-Shot Rifle, 373
No. 14 Little Scout Single-Shot Rifle, 373
No. 14.5 Little Scout Single-Shot Rifle, 373
No. 44 Ideal Single-Shot Rifle, 373

No. 44.5 Ideal Single-Shot Rifle, 374
Nos. 45 to 54 Ideal Single-Shot Rifles, 374
No. 70 Visible Loading Slide-Action, 374
No. 414 Armory Model Single-Shot Rifle, 375
No. 419 Junior Target Model, 375
Walnut Hill No. 417-0 Single-Shot Target Rifle, 377
Walnut Hill No. 417-1, 377
Walnut Hill No. 417-2, 377
Walnut Hill No. 417-3, 377
Walnut Hill No. 417.5 Single-Shot Rifle, 377
Walnut Hill No. 418 Single-Shot Rifle, 377
SHOTGUNS
Model 51 Bolt-Action Shotgun, 556
Model 58 Bolt-Action Repeater, 556
Model 58-.410 Bolt-Action Repeater, 556
Model 59 Bolt-Action Repeater, 556
Model 67 Pump Shotgun, 556
Model 67 Waterfowl Shotgun, 556
Model 77 Slide-Action Repeater, 556
Model 77-AC, 556
Model 79-VR Super Value, 556
Model 94 Single-Shot Shotgun, 556
Model 94C, 556
Model 94Y Youth Gun, 556
Model 95 Single-Shot Shotgun, 556
Model 107 Single-Shot Hammer, 556
Model 124 Cross Bolt Repeater, 558
Model 240 Over/Under Shotgun, 558
Model 258 Bolt-Action Repeater, 558
Model 311 R Hammerless Double, 558
Model 311 Springfield Hammerless Double, 558
Model 530 Hammerless Double, 558
Model 530M, 558
Model 530ST Double Gun, 558
Model 620 Hammerless Slide-Action Repeating, 558
Model 620-C, 558
Model 620-P, 558
Model 620-PV, 558
Model 621, 558
Model 820 Hammerless Slide-Action Repeating, 558
Model 820-SC, 558
Model 940 Single-Shot Shotgun, 558
Model 940Y Youth Gun, 558
Model 5151 Springfield, 559
Model 9478, 559
No. 20 "Favorite" Shotgun, 556
No. 22-.410 Over/Under Combination, 556
No. 39 New Model Pocket Shotgun, 556
STEVENS-SPRINGFIELD
Model 15 Single-Shot Bolt-Action Rifle, 377
Model 82 Bolt-Action Single-Shot Rifle, 377
Model 83 Bolt-Action Single-Shot Rifle, 378
Model 84, 378
Model 84-S (084), 378
Model 85, 378
Model 85-S (085), 378
Model 86 Bolt-Action, 378
Model 86-S (086), 378
Model 87-S (087), 378
STEYR PISTOLS
GB Semiautomatic Pistol, 179
M12 Automatic Pistol, 179
STEYR-DAIMLER-PUCH A.G.—See also listings under
Mannlicher
AUG-SA Semiautomatic Rifle, 379
Small Bore Carbine, 379
STOEGER—See IGA and TIKKA Shotguns
LUGERS
American Eagle Luger, 179
Standard Luger 22 Automatic Pistol, 179
Steel Frame Luger 22 Auto Pistol, 179
Target Luger 22 Automatic Pistol, 180
RIFLES
Hornet Rifle, 379
SURVIVAL ARM
AR-7 Explorer, 379
TAR-HUNT SHOTGUNS
Model RSG-12 Matchless Bolt Action Slug, 559
Model RSG-12 Peerless Bolt Action Slug, 559
Model RSG-12 Professional Bolt Action Slug, 560
Model RSG-20 Mountaineer Bolt Action Slug, 560
TARGA PISTOLS
Model GT26S Auto Pistol, 180
Model GT32 Auto Pistol, 180
Model GT380 Automatic Pistol, 180
Model GT380XE Automatic Pistol, 180
TAURUS S.A.
Model Gaucho, 180
MOdel 17C, 180
Model 17IB, 180
Model 17 Tracker, 181
Model 21T Tracker, 181
Model 22H Raging Hornet, 181
Model 30C Raging Thirty Hunter, 181
Model 44 DA Revolver, 181

Model 44C Tracker, 181
Model 45-410 "The Judge", 181
Model 45-410 "The Judge" Public Defender, 181
Model 65 DA Revolver, 181
Model 66 DA Revolver, 181
Model 73 DA Revolver, 181
Model 74 Target Grade DA Revolver, 181
Model 80 DA Revolver, 181
Model 82 Heavy Barrel, 181
Model 83 Heavy Barrel Target Grade, 181
Model 84 Target Grade Revolver, 182
Model 85 DA Revolver, 182
Model 85PLYB2 "Protector Ply", 182
Model 86 Custom Custom Target DA Revolver, 182
Model 94 Target Grade, 182
Model 96 Target Scout, 182
Model 431 DA Revolver, 182
Model 441 DA Revolver, 182
Model 445 DA Revolver, 182
Model 454 DA Raging Bull Revolver, 182
Model 669/669VR DA Revolver, 182
Model 741/761 DA Revolver, 183
Model 941 Target Revolver, 183
Model 22 Ply, 183
Model 25 Ply, 183
Model PT 22 DA Automatic Pistol, 183
Model PT-24/7, 183
Model PT-24/7 Pro Full Size, 183
Model PT-24/7 G2, 183
Model PT-24/7 OSS, 183
Model PT 25 DA Automatic Pistol, 183
Model PT-58 Semiautomatic Pistol, 183
Model PT-92AF Semiautomatic Pistol, 184
Model PT-92AFC Compact Pistol, 184
Model PT 99AF Semiautomatic Pistol, 184
Model PT 100 DA Automatic Pistol, 184
Model PT 101 DA Automatic Pistol, 184
Model PT 111 Millennium DAO Pistol, 179
Model PT 908 Semiautomatic Pistol, 184
Model PT 911 Compact Semiautomatic Pistol, 184
Model PT 938 Compact Semiautomatic Pistol, 184
Model PT 940 Compact Semiautomatic Pistol, 184
Model PT 945 Compact Semiautomatic Pistol, 184
TECNI-MEC SHOTGUNS
Model SPL 640 Folding Shotgun, 560
TEXAS ARMS
Defender Derringer, 184
TEXAS LONGHORN ARMS
"The Jezebel" Pistol, 185
Sesquicentennial SA Revolver, 185
SA Revolver Cased Set, 185
South Texas Army Limited Edition SA Revolver, 185
Texas Border Special SA Revolver, 185
West Texas Flat Top Target SA Revolver, 185
THOMPSON PISTOL
Model 27A-5 Semiautomatic Pistol, 185
THOMPSON/CENTER ARMS
HANDGUNS
Contender Single-Shot Pistol, 185
Contender Bull Barrel, 185
Contender Internal Choke Model, 185
Contender Octagon Barrel, 186
Contender Stainless, 186
Contender Super 14/16, 186
Contender TC Alloy II, 186
Encore Single-Shot Pistol, 186
G2 Contender Single-Shot Pistol, 186
Pro-Hunter Single-Shot Pistol, 186
RIFLES
Contender Carbine, 379
Contender Carbine Survival System, 379
Encore Rifle, 380
Encore Katahdin, 380
Pro Hunter Rifle, 380
Hotshot (Camo Stock), 380
Stainless Contender Carbine, 380
TCR '83 Aristocrat Model, 380
TCR '87 Hunter Rifle, 380
Dimension, 380
Icon, 380
Icon Precision Hunter, 380
Icon Warlord, 381
Venture, 381
Venture Predator, 381
Silver Lynx, 381
Model R-55 Classic, 381
SHOTGUNS
Contender .410 Ga. Carbine, 560
Encore 20 Ga., 560
Model '87 Hunter Shotgun, 560
Model '87 Hunter Slug, 560

TIKKA
RIFLES

Battue Model, 383
Continental Model, 384
LSA55 Deluxe, 382
LSA55 Sporter, 382
LSA55 Standard Bolt-Action Repeater, 382
LSA65 Deluxe, 382
LSA65 Standard, 382
Model M55, 382
Model M65, 382
Model M65 Wildboar, 383
Model 412S Double Rifle, 382
Model 512S Double Rifle, 382
New Generation Rifles, 383
Premium Grade Rifle, 383
Sporter Model, 384
T3 Hunter, 381
T3 Laminated Stainless, 381
T3 Lite, 381
T3 Lite Stainless, 381
T3 Tactical, 381
T3 Varmint, 381
T3 Varmint Stainless, 382
Whitetail Bolt-Action Rifle Series, 383
Whitetail Hunter Model, 384
SHOTGUNS
M 07 Shotgun/Rifle Combination, 560
M 77 Over/Under Shotgun, 560
M 77K Shotgun/Rifle Combination, 560
Model 412S/512S Shooting System, 560
Model 412S/512S Over/Under, 560
Model 412S/512S Over/Under Combination, 560
TRADITIONS PERFORMANCE ARMS
SHOTGUNS
ALS 2100 SA Field Series, Walnut Stock, 561
ALS 2100 SA Field Series, Synthetic Stock, 561
ALS 2100 SA Field Series, Youth Model, 561
ALS 2100 SA Field Series, Hunter Combo Stock, 561
ALS 2100 SA Field Series, Slug Hunter Model, 561
ALS 2100 SA Field Series, Turkey Hunter Waterfowl
Model, 561
ALS 2100 SA Field Series, Home Security Model, 561
Classic Series, Field I Over/Under, 561
Model Field Hunter, 561
Model Field II, 561
Model Filed III Gold Model, 561
Model Classic Series Over/Under Sporting Clay III, 561
Model Sporting Clay II, 561
Model Upland III, 561
Model Upland II, 561
Model Mag 350 Series Turkey II Over/Under, 561
Model Waterfowl II, 561
Model Mag Hunter II, 561
Model Elite III ST Double-Barrel, 561
Model Elite Hunter ST Double-Barrel, 561
Model Elite Field I ST Double-Barrel, 561
Model Elite Field I DT Double-Barrel, 561
TRISTAR SPORTING ARMS
Model 1887 Lever-Action Repeater, 562
Model 300 Over/Under Shotgun, 562
Model 311 Side/Side Shotgun, 562
Model 330 Over/Under Shotgun, 562
Model 333 Over/Under Shotgun, 562
UBERTI
HANDGUNS
Model 1871 Rolling Block Target Pistol, 186
Model 1873 Cattleman SA Revolver, 186
Model 1875 Remington Outlaw, 186
Model 1890 Remington Police, 186
RIFLES
Henry Rifle, 384
Model 1866 Sporting Rifle, 384
Model 1873 Sporting Rifle, 384
Model 1875 Army Target, 384
Rolling Block Baby Carbine, 384
ULM SHOTGUNS—See listings under Kreghoff
ULTRA-HI PRODUCTS CO.
Model 2200 Single-Shot Bolt-Action Rifle, 385
ULTRA LIGHT ARMS
HANDGUNS
Model 20 Series Pistols, 187
RIFLES
Model 20 Bolt-Action Rifle, 385
Model 20S Bolt-Action Rifle, 385
Model 24 Bolt-Action Rifle, 385
Model 28 Bolt-Action Rifle, 385
Model 40 Bolt-Action Rifle, 385
U.S. ARMS CORPORATION
Abilene SA Revolver, 188
U.S. MILITARY RIFLES
Carbine, Caliber 30, M1, 387
M2 22 Springfield Target Rifle, 387
Model 1898 Krag-Jorgensen Carbine, 385
Model 1898 Krag-Jorgensen Military Rifle, 385
Model 1903 Mark I Springfield, 386
Model 1903 National Match Springfield, 386

INDEX

Model 1903 Springfield Military Rifle, 386
Model 1903 Springfield Sporter, 386
Model 1903 Style T Springfield Match Rifle, 386
Model 1903 Type A Springfield Free Rifle, 386
Model 1903 Type B Springfield Free Rifle, 386
Model 1903-A1 Springfield, 386
Model 1903-A3 Springfield, 387
Model 1917 Enfield Military Rifle, 387
Model 1922-M1 22 Springfield Target Rifle, 387
Rifle, Caliber 30, M1 (Garand) Mil. Rifle, 387
Rifle, Caliber 30, M1, National Match, 387
U.S. REPEATING ARMS CO.—See Winchester Rifle
listings
UNITED STATES FIRE ARMS MFG CO.
HANDGUNS
1910 Commercial Model, 188
1911 Military Model, 188
Single Action Army Revolver Premium Grade, 188
UNIQUE PISTOLS
PISTOLS
Kriegs Model L Automatic Pistol, 187
Model B/CF Automatic Pistol, 187
Model D2, 187
Model D6 Automatic Pistol, 187
Model DES/32U Rapid Fire Pistol, 187
Model DES/69-U Target Pistol, 187
Model DES/VO Rapid Fire Match, 187
Model L Automatic Pistol, 187
Model Mikros Pocket, 187
Model RR Automatic Pistol, 188
Model 2000-U Match Pistol, 188
RIFLES
T66 Match Rifle, 385
UNIVERSAL FIREARMS
Enforcer (3000) Semiautomatic Pistol, 188
RIFLES
Deluxe Carbine, 387
Standard M-1 Carbine, 388
UZI
PISTOLS
Semiautomatic Pistol, 188
"Eagle" Series Semiautomatic DA Pistol, 188
RIFLES
Semiautomatic Model B Carbine, 388
Semiautomatic Mini Carbine, 388
VALMET OY
RIFLES
Hunter Semiautomatic Rifle, 388
M-62S Semiautomatic Rifle, 388
M-71S, 388
M-76 Semiautomatic Rifle, 388
M-78 Semiautomatic Rifle, 388
M-82 Semiautomatic Carbine, 388
Model 412 S Double Rifle, 388
SHOTGUNS—See also SAVAGE
Lion Over/Under Shotgun, 562
Model 412 Over/Under Field Shotgun, 562
Model 412 S Over/Under Field Shotgun, 562
Model 412 S Shotgun/Rifle Combination, 562
Model 412 ST Skeet, 563
Model 412 SE Trap, 563
VICKERS LTD.
Empire Model, 388
Jubilee Model Single-Shot Target Rifle, 388
VOERE
VEC-91 Lightning Bolt-Action Rifle, 389
VOERE, VOELTER & COMPANY
Model 1007 Biathlon Repeater, 389
Model 1013 Bolt-Action Repeater, 389
Model 2107 Bolt-Action Repeater, 390
WALTHER
PISTOLS
Commercial Model (Post-War), 190, 191
Commercial Model (U.S. Production 1986-2001), 191
Commericial Model with Crown "N" Proof, 190
Commercial Model with Eagle Proof (Prewar), 191
Hämmerli-Walther Olympia 200, 1952 Type, 194
Mauser Contract Pistols (Late 1942-44), 190
Model 1 Automatic Pistol, 189
Model 2 Automatic Pistol, 189
Model 3 Automatic Pistol, 189
Model 4 Automatic Pistol, 189
Model 5 Automatic Pistol, 189
Model 6 Automatic Pistol, 189
Model 7 Automatic Pistol, 189
Model 8 Automatic Pistol, 189
Model 8 Lightweight, 189
Model 9 Vest Pocket, 189
Model PP 7.65mm Presentation, 191
Model Free Pistol, 192
Model GSP Target Automatic Pistol, 192
Model HP Double-Action Automatic, 189
Model OSP Rapid Fire Target Pistol, 192
Model P4 (P38-IV) DA Pistol, 193
Model P5 Compact Pistol, 193

Model P5 DA Pistol, 193
Model P38 (P1) DA Automatic, 193
Model P38 Deluxe Engraved Pistol, 193
Model P38K, 193
Model P 88 DA Automatic Pistol, 193
Model P 88 DA Compact, 193
Model P99 DA Automatic Pistol, 193
Model PP DA Automatic Pistol, 190
Model PP Deluxe Engraved, 190
Model PP Lightweight, 191
Model PP Sport, 190
Model PP Super DA Pistol, 191
Model PPK 7.65mm Presentation, 192
Model PPK Deluxe Engraved, 191
Model PPK Double-Action, 191
Model PPK Lightweight, 192
Model PPK/S DA Automatic Pistol, 192
Model PPK/S Deluxe Engraved, 192
Model TPH DA Pocket Pistol, 194
Olympia Funfkampf Automatic, 190
Olympia Hunting Automatic, 190
Olympia Rapid Fire Automatic, 190
Olympia Sport Automatic, 190
P38 Military DA Automatic, 190
Self-Loading Sport Pistol, 190
Spreewerke Contract Pistols (Late 1942-45), 190
Walther Contract Pistols (Late 1940-44), 190
Wartime Model with Eagle "N" Proof, 190, 191
RIFLES
Model 1 Autoloading Rifle (Light), 388
Model 2 Autoloading Rifle, 388
Model V Bolt-Action Single-Shot Rifle, 389
Model V Meisterbüchse (Champion), 389
Olympic Bolt-Action Match Rifle, 389
Post WWII Models
Model GX-1 Free Rifle, 389
Model KKJ Sporter, 389
Model KKJ-HO, 389
Model KKJ-MA, 389
Model KKM International Match Rifle, 389
Model KKM-S, 389
Model SSV Varmint Rifle, 390
Moving Target Match Rifle, 389
Model U.I.T. Special Match Rifle, 390
Model U.I.T. Super Match Rifle, 390
Prone 400 Target Rifle, 390
WARD, Montgomery
RIFLES
Model 14M-497B Western Field Bolt-Action, 391
Model M771 Western Field Lever-Action Rifle, 391
Model M772 Western Field Lever-Action Rifle, 391
Model M775 Bolt-Action Rifle, 391
Model M776 Bolt-Action Rifle, 391
Model M778 Lever-Action, 391
Model M780 Bolt-Action Rifle, 391
Model M782 Bolt-Action Rifle, 391
Model M808, 391
Model M832 Bolt-Action Rifle, 391
Model M836, 392
Model M865 Lever-Action Carbine, 392
Model M894 Autoloading Carbine, 392
Model M-SD57, 392
SHOTGUNS
Model 25 Slide-Action Repeater, 563
Model 40 Over/Under Shotgun, 563
Model 40N Slide-Action Repeater, 563
Model 172 Bolt-Action Shotgun, 563
Model 550A Slide-Action Repeater, 563
Model SB300 Double-Barrel, 563
Model SB312 Double-Barrel, 563
Model SD52A Double-Barrel, 563
(Western Field) Model 50 Pumpgun, 563
(Western Field) Model 52 Double-Barrel Shotgun, 563
WARNER PISTOL
Infallible Pocket Automatic Pistol, 194
WEATHERBY
RIFLES
Crown Custom Rifle, 391
Deluxe 378 Magnum Rifle, 392
Deluxe Magnum Rifle, 392
Deluxe Rifle, 392
Fiberguard Rifle, 392
Fibermark Rifle, 392
Mark V Accumark Bolt Action Repeating, 392
Mark V Accumark Light Weight Rifle, 392
Mark V Classicmark I Rifle, 393
Mark V Classicmark II Rifle, 393
Mark V Deluxe Bolt-Action Sporting Rifle, 393
Mark V Deluxe Rifle, 393
Mark V Euromark Bolt-Action Rifle, 393
Mark V Lazermark Rifle, 393
Mark V Safari Grade Rifle, 393
Mark V Sporter Rifle, 393
Mark V Light Weight Sporter Rifle, 394
Mark V Stainless Rifle, 394

Mark V (LW) Stainless Rifle2, 394
Mark V SLS Rifle, 394
Mark V Synthetic Rifle, 394
Mark V Ultra Light Weight Rifle, 394
Mark XXII Deluxe 22 Automatic Sporter Clip-fed, 394
Mark XXII, Tubular Magazine Model, 394
Vanguard (I) Bolt-Action Sporting Rifle, 394
Vanguard Classic I Rifle, 394
Vanguard Classic II Rifle, 394
Vanguard VGX Deluxe, 394
Varmintmaster Bolt-Action Rifle, 394
Weathermark Alaskan Rifle, 395
Weathermark Rifle, 395
SHOTGUNS
Athena Over/Under Shotgun, 563
Centurion Automatic Shotgun, 564
Model 82 Autoloading Shotgun, 563
Model 92 Slide-Action Shotgun, 563
Olympian Over/Under Shotgun, 564
Orion Over/Under Shotgun, 565
Patrician Slide-Action Shotgun, 565
Regency Field Grade Over/Under Shotgun, 565
Regency Trap Gun, 565
WEBLEY & SCOTT LTD.
Model 9mm Military & Police, 194
Model 25 Hammer, 194
Model 25 Hammerless, 194
Mark I 455, 194
Mark III 38 Military & Police Revolver, 194
Mark IV 22 Caliber Target Revolver, 194
Mark IV 38 Military & Police Revolver, 194
Mark VI No. 1 British Service Revolver, 194
Mark VI 22 Target Revolver, 194
Metropolitan Police Automatic Pistol, 195
RIC Model DA Revolver, 195
"Semiautomatic" Single-Shot Pistol, 195
Single-Shot Target Pistol, 195
Webley-Fosbery Automatic Revolver, 195
WEIHRAUCH
Model HW 60 Target Rifle, 394
Model HW 66 Bolt-Action Rifle, 394
Model HW 660 Match Bolt-Action Rifle, 395
WESSON FIREARMS
Commander Classic Bobtail, 66
Global, 66
Hunter Pacs, 196
Patriot, 66
Pointman Seven, 66
Model 8 Service, 195
Model 8-2 Service, 195
Model 9 Target, 195
Model 9-2 Target, 195
Model 9-2H Heavy Barrel, 195
Model 9-2HV Vent Rib Heavy Barrel, 195
Model 9-2V Vent Rib, 195
Model 11 Service DA Revolver, 195
Model 12 Target, 195
Model 14 Service DA Revolver, 195
Model 14-2 Service DA Revolver, 195
Model 15 Target, 196
Model 15-2 Target, 196
Model 15-2H Heavy Barrel, 196
Model 15-2HV Vent Rib Heavy Barrel, 196
Model 15-2V Vent Rib, 196
WESTERN ARMS
SHOTGUN
Long Range Hammerless Double, 565
WESTERN AUTO
Model 300H Slide-Action Repeater, 565
Model 310A Slide-Action Repeater, 565
Model 310B Slide-Action Repeater, 565
Model 310C Slide-Action Repeater, 565
Model 310E Slide-Action Repeater, 565
Model 325BK Bolt-Action Repeater, 565
WESTERN FIELD RIFLES—See listings under "W" for
Montgomry Wards
WESTLEY RICHARDS & CO
RIFLES
Best Quality Double Rifle, 395
Best Quality Magazine Rifle, 395
SHOTGUNS
Best Quality Boxlock Hammerless Double-Barrel, 565
Best Quality Sidelock Hammerless Double-Barrel, 565
Model Deluxe Boxlock Hammerless Double-Barrel,
566
Model Deluxe Sidelock, 566
Model E Hammerless Double, 566
Ovundo (Over/Under), 566
WHITNEY FIREARMS COMPANY
Wolverine Automatic Pistol, 196
WICHITA ARMS
PISTOLS
Classic Pistol, 196
Hunter Pistol, 197
International Pistol, 197

MK-40 Silhouette Pistol, 197
Silhouette Pistol (WSP), 197
RIFLES
Model WCR Classic Bolt-Action Rifle, 395
Model WSR Silhouette Bolt-Action Rifle, 395
Model WMR Stainless Magnum Bolt-Action Rifle, 395
Model WVR Varmint Rifle, 396
WICKLIFFE RIFLES
'76 Commemorative Model, 395
'76 Deluxe Model, 395
'76 Standard Model Single-Shot Rifle, 395
Stinger Model, 396
Traditionalist Model, 396
WILKINSON ARMS
PISTOLS
"Linda" Semiautomatic Pistol, 197
"Sherry" Semiautomatic Pistol, 197
"Diane" Semiautomatic Pistol, 197
RIFLES
Terry Carbine, 396
WILLIAMS TED RIFLES—See Sears, Roebuck and
Company
WINCHESTER RIFLES
Model 1873 Lever-Action Carbine, 397
Model 1873 Lever-Action Rifle, 397
Model 1873 One of One Thousand, 397
Model 1873 Special Sporting Rifle, 397
Model 1885 Single-Shot Rifle, 397
Model 1885 High-Wall Sporting Rifle, 397
Model 1885 Low-Wall Sporting Rifle, 397
Model 1885 Scheutzen Rifle, 397
Model 1885 Special Sporting Rifle, 397
Model 1885 Single-Shot Musket, 397
Model 1885 Single-Shot "Winder" Musket, 397
Model 1886 Lever-Action Rifle, 397
Model 1886 Saddle-Ring Carbine, 398
Model 1890 Slide-Action Rifle, 398
Model 1892 Lever-Action Rifle, 398
Model 1892 Saddle-Ring Carbine, 398
Model 1894 Lever-Action Rifle, 398
Model 1894 Lever-Action Deluxe, 400
Model 1894 Saddle-Ring Carbine, 400
Model 1894 Lever-Action Rifle, 400
Model 1894 Standard Carbine, 400
Model 1895 Lever-Action Carbine, 400
Model 1895 Lever-Action Rifle, 400
Model 1897 Lee Bolt-Action Rifle, 400
Model 1900 Bolt-Action Single-Shot Rifle, 400
Model 1902 Bolt-Action Single-Shot Rifle, 400
Model 1903 Self-Loading Rifle, 400
Model 1904 Bolt-Action Single-Shot Rifle, 400
Model 1904 99 Thumb-Trigger Bolt-Action Single-Shot
Rifle, 400
Model 1905 Self-Loading Rifle, 400
Model 1906 Slide-Action Repeater, 400
Model 1907 Self-Loading Rifle, 400
Model 1910 Self-Loading Rifle, 400
Model 43 Bolt-Action Sporting Rifle, 400
Model 43 Special Grade, 401
Model 47 Bolt-Action Single-Shot Rifle, 401
Model 52 Bolt-Action Target Rifle, 401
Model 52 Heavy Barrel, 401
Model 52 International Match Rifle, 401
Model 52 International Prone, 401
Model 52 Sporting Rifle, 401
Model 52-B Bolt-Action Rifle, 401
Model 52-B Bull Gun/Heavy Barrel, 401
Model 52-C Bolt-Action Rifle, 402
Model 52-D Bolt-Action Target Rifle, 402
Model 53 Lever-Action Repeater, 402
Model 54 Bolt-Action High Power Sporting (I), 402
Model 54 Bolt-Action High Power Sporting (II), 403
Model 54 Carbine (I), 403
Model 54 Carbine (II), 403
Model 54 National Match Rifle, 403
Model 54 Sniper's Match Rifle, 403
Model 54 Sniper's Rifle, 403
Model 54 Super Grade, 403
Model 54 Target Rifle, 403
Model 55 "Automatic" Single-Shot, 403
Model 55 Lever-Action Repeater, 403
Model 56 Bolt-Action Sporting Rifle, 403
Model 57 Bolt-Action Rifle, 404
Model 58 Bolt-Action Single-Shot, 404
Model 59 Bolt-Action Single-Shot, 404
Model 60, 60A Bolt-Action Single-Shot, 404
Model 60A Target Rifle, 404
Model 61 Hammerless Slide-Action Repeater, 404
Model 61 Magnum, 404
Model 62 Visible Hammer, 406
Model 63 Self-Loading Rifle, 406
Model 64 219 Zipper, 406
Model 64 Deluxe Deer Rifle, 406

Model 64 Lever-Action Repeater, 406
Model 65 Lever-Action Repeater, 406
Model 65 218 Bee, 406
Model 67 Bolt-Action Single-Shot Rifle, 406
Model 67 Boy's Rifle, 406
Model 68 Bolt-Action Single-Shot, 406
Model 69 Bolt-Action Rifle, 406
Model 69A Bolt-Action Rifle, 407
Model 70, 407
PRE-1964 MODEL 70 (1982 TO DATE)
Model 70 African Rifle, 407
Model 70 Alaskan, 408
Model 70 Bull Gun, 408
Model 70 Featherweight Sporter, 408
Model 70 National Match Rifle, 408
Model 70 Standard Grade, 408
Model 70 Super Grade Featherweight, 409
Model 70 Super Grade, 409
Model 70 Target Rifle, 409
Model 70 Target Heavyweight, 409
Model 70 Target Bull Barrel, 409
Model 70 Varmint Rifle, 409
Model 70 Westerner, 409
1964-TYPE MODEL 70:
Model 70 African, 409
Model 70 Deluxe, 409
Model 70 International Army Match Rifle, 409
Model 70 Magnum, 409
Model 70 Mannlicher, 409
Model 70 Standard, 409
Model 70 Target, 409
Model 70 Varmint, 409
1972-TYPE MODEL 70:
Model 70 African, 410
Model 70 Classic SM, 410
Model 70 Classic Sporter Stainless, 410
Model 70 Classic Sporter, 410
Model 70 Custom Sharpshooter, 411
Model 70 Custom Sporting Sharpshooter, 411
Model 70 Featherweight Classic, 411
Model 70 Golden 50th Anniversary Edition Bolt-
Action Rifle, 411
Model 70 International Army Match, 411
Model 70 Lightweight, 411
Model 70 Magnum, 411
Model 70 Standard, 411
Model 70 Standard Carbine, 411
Model 70 Sporter DBM, 411
Model 70 Stainless Sporter SSM, 411
Model 70 Classic Super Grade, 411
Model 70 Target, 411
Model 70 Ultra Match, 412
Model 70 Varmint (Heavy Barrel), 412
Model 70 Win-Cam Rifle, 412
Model 70 Winlite Bolt-Action Rifle, 412
Model 70 Win-Tuff Bolt-Action Rifle, 412
Model 70 XTR Featherweight, 412
Model 70 XTR Sporter Magnum, 412
Model 70 XTR Sporter Rifle, 411
Model 70 XTR Sporter Varmint, 412
Model 70A, 412
Model 70A Magnum, 412
Model 70 Ultimate Classic Bolt-Action Rifle, 412
Model 70 Laminated Stainless Bolt-Action, 412
WINCHESTER MODEL 70 CHARACTERISTICS:
Model 70 First Model, 412
Model 70 Second Model, 412
Model 70 Third Model, 413
Model 70 Fourth Model, 413
Model 70 Fifth Model, 413
POST-1964 WINCHESTER:
1964 Winchester Model 70, 413
1966 Winchester Model 70, 413
1972 Winchester Model 70, 413
1978 Winchester Model 70, 413
Model 70 Black Shadow, 414
Model 70 Classic Camo Bolt-Action Rifle, 414
Model 70 Classic Compact Bolt-Action Rifle, 414
Model 70 Classic Laredo Range Hunter, 414
Model 70 Coyote, 414
Model 70 Ranger, 415
Model 70 Ranger Compact, 415
Model 70 Stealth, 415
Model 71 Lever-Action Repeater, 415
Model 72 Bolt-Action Repeater, 415
Model 73 Lever-Action Repeater, 415
Model 74 Self-Loading Rifle, 415
Model 75 Sporting Rifle, 415
Model 75 Target Rifle, 416
Model 77 Semiautomatic Rifle, Clip Type, 416
Model 77 Tubular Magazine Type, 416
Model 86 Carbine and Rifle, 416
Model 88 Carbine, 416

Model 88 Lever-Action Rifle, 416
Model 92 Grade 1 Lever-Action Rifle, 416
Model 94 Antique Carbine, 417
Model 94 Carbine, 417
Model 94 Classic Carbine, 417
Model 94 Classic Rifle, 417
Model 94 Deluxe Carbine, 417
Model 94 Long Barrel Rifle, 417
Model 94 Trapper, 417
Model 94 Win-Tuff Rifle, 417
Model 94 Wrangler Carbine, 417
Model 94 XTR Big Bore, 417
Model 94 XTR Lever-Action Rifle, 417
MODEL 94 COMMEMORATIVES:
Model 94 Alaskan Purchase Centennial
Commemorative Carbine, 420
Model 94 Antlered Game, 417
Model 94 Bicentennial '76 Carbine, 417
Model 94 Buffalo Bill Commemorative, 418
Canadian Centennial '67 Commemorative, 418
Centennial '66 Commemorative, 418
Model 94 Cheyenne Commemorative, 418
Model 94 Chief Crazy Horse Commemorative, 418
Model 94 Colt Commemorative Carbine Set, 418
Model 94 Cowboy Commemorative Carbine, 418
Model 94 Golden Spike Commemorative Carbine, 419
Model 94 Illinois Sesquicentennial Com. Carbine, 419
Model 94 John Wayne Commemorative Carbine, 420
Model 94 Legendary Frontiersmen
Commemorative, 419
Model 94 Legendary Lawmen Commemorative, 419
Model 94 Lone Star Commemorative, 419
Model 94 Nebraska Centennial Commem.
Carbine, 419
Model 94 NRA Centennial Matched Set, 419
Model 94 NRA Centennial Musket, 419
Model 94 NRA Centennial Rifle, 419
Model 94 Oliver F. Winchester Commemorative, 420
Model 94 Texas Ranger Association Carbine, 419
Model 94 Texas Ranger Commemorative Carbine, 419
Model 94 Theodore Roosevelt Commemorative Rifle/
Carbine, 419
Model 94 Trapper, 419
Model 94 Wells Fargo & Co. Commemorative
Carbine, 420
Model 94 Wrangler Carbine, 420
Model 94 Wyoming Diamond Jubilee Commemorative
Carbine, 420
Model 100 Autoloading Rifle, 420
Model 100 Carbine, 420
Model 121 Deluxe, 420
Model 121 Standard Bolt-Action Single Shot, 420
Model 121 Youth, 420
Model 131 Bolt-Action Repeater, 420
Model 135, 420
Model 141 Bolt-Action Tubular Repeater, 420
Model 145, 420
Model 150 Lever-Action Carbine, 420
Model 190 Carbine, 420
Model 190 Semiautomatic Rifle, 421
Model 250 Deluxe Rifle, 421
Model 250 Standard Lever-Action Rifle, 421
Model 255 Deluxe Rifle, 421
Model 255 Standard Rifle, 421
Model 270 Deluxe Rifle, 421
Model 270 Standard Slide-Action Rifle, 421
Model 278 Deluxe Rifle, 421
Model 278 Standard Rifle, 421
Model 290 Deluxe Rifle, 421
Model 290 Standard Semiautmatic Rifle, 421
Model 310 Bolt-Action Single Shot, 421
Model 320 Bolt-Action Repeater, 421
Model 490 Semiautomatic Rifle, 421
Model 670 Bolt-Action Sporting Rifle, 422
Model 670 Carbine, 422
Model 670 Magnum, 422
Model 770 Bolt-Action Sporting Rifle, 422
Model 770 Magnum, 422
Model 9422 Lever-Action Rimfire Rifles, 422
Double Xpress Rifle, 423
Ranger Youth Bolt-Action Carbine, 423
Ranger Lever-Action Carbine, 423
Ranger Bolt-Action Carbine, 423
Super X (SXR), 423
Wildcat, 423
Model 1892 Grade I Lever-Action Rifle, 423
Model 1892 Grade II Lever-Action Rifle, 423
SHOTGUNS
Model 12 Classic Limited Edition, 566
Model 12 Featherweight, 567
Model 12 Field Gun, 1972 Type, 567
Model 12 Heavy Duck Gun, 567
Model 12 Pigeon Grade, 567

Model 12 Riot Gun, 567
Model 12 Skeet Gun, 567
Model 12 Skeet Gun, 1972 Type, 568
Model 12 Skeet Gun, Cutts Compensator, 568
Model 12 Skeet Gun, Plain Barrel, 568
Model 12 Skeet Gun, Vent Rib, 568
Model 12 Standard Gr., Matted Rib, 568
Model 12 Standard Gr., Vent Rib, 568
Model 12 Standard Slide-Action Repeater, 568
Model 12 Super Pigeon Grade, 568
Model 12 Trap Gun, 568
Model 12 Trap Gun, 1972 Type, 568
Model 20 Single-Shot Hammer Gun, 568
Model 21 Original Double-Barrel Shotguns, 568
    Standard Grades
    Tournament Grades
    Trap Grades
    Skeet Grades
    Duck Gun
    Magnum Gun
    Custom Built/Deluxe Models
Model 21 Custom, Pigeon, Grand American, 569
Model 21 U.S.R.A. Custom Built Series, 570
Model 23 Side-by-Side Shotgun, 570
Model 24 Hammerless Double, 570
Model 25 Riot Gun, 570
Model 25 Slide-Action Repeater, 570
Model 36 Single-Shot Bolt Action, 570
Model 37 Single-Shot Shotgun, 570
Model 37A Single Shot Shotgun, 570
Model 37A Youth, 571
Model 40 Skeet Gun, 571
Model 40 Standard Autoloader Gun, 571
Model 41 Single-Shot Bolt Action, 571
Model 42 Classic Ltd. Edition, 571
Model 42 Deluxe, 571
Model 42 Pigeon Grade, 571
Model 42 Skeet Gun, 571
Model 42 Standard, 571
Model 42 Trap Grade, 571
Model 50 Field Gun, Vent Rib, 571
Model 50 Skeet Gun, 571
Model 50 Standard Grade, 571
Model 50 Trap Gun, 572
Model 59 Autoloading Shotgun, 572
Model 97 Bush Gun, 572
Model 97 Riot Gun, 572
Model 97 Slide-Action Repeater, 572
Model 97 Trap, Tournamen & Pigeon, 572
Model 97 Trench Gun, 572

Model 101 Combination Gun, 572
Model 101 Diamond Grade Target, 572
Model 101 Field Gun Over/Under, 572
Model 101 Magnum, 572
Model 101 Pigeon Grade, 573
Model 101 Pigeon Grade Lightweight, 573
Model 101 Pigeon Grade Sporting, 573
Model 101 Skeet, 573
Model 101 Trap, 573
Model 101 Quail Special Over/Under, 573
Model 370 Single-Shot Shotgun, 573
Model 370 Youth, 573
Model 1001 Over/Under Shotgun, 573
Model 1200 Deer Gun, 573
Model 1200 Defender Series Slide-Action Security
  Shotguns, 574
Model 1200 Field Gun Magnum, 574
Model 1200 Ranger Slide-Action, 574
Model 1200 Ranger Youth Slide-Action Shotgun, 574
Model 1200 Slide-Action Field Gun, 574
Model 1200 Stainless Marine Series Slide-Action
  Security Shotgun, 574
Model 1200 Stainless Police Series Slide-Action
  Security Shotgun, 574
Model 1200 Trap Gun, 576
Model 1200 Ranger Combination, 576
Model 1200 Skeet Gun, 576
Model 1300 CamoPack, 576
Model 1300 Deer Series, 576
Model 1300 Defender Series, 576
Model 1300 Deluxe Slide-Action, 576
Model 1300 Featherweight Slide-Action Shotgun, 576
Model 1300 Ranger Series, 576
Model 1300 Slide-Action Field Gun, 576
Model 1300 Slug Hunter Series, 576
Model 1300 Turkey Series, 576
Model 1300 Waterfowl Slide-Action Shotgun, 577
Model 1300 XTR Slide-Action, 577
Model 1400 Automatic Field Gun, 577
Model 1400 Deer Gun, 577
Model 1400 Mark II Deer Gun, 577
Model 1400 Mark II Field Gun, 577
Model 1400 Mark II Skeet Gun, 577
Model 1400 Mark II Trap Gun, 577
Model 1400 Mark II Utility Skeet, 577
Model 1400 Mark II Utility Trap, 577
Model 1400 Ranger Semiautomatic Deer Shotgun, 577
Model 1400 Ranger Semiautomatic Shotgun, 577
Model 1400 Skeet Gun, 577
Model 1400 Trap Gun, 577

Model 1500 XTR Semiautomatic, 578
Model 1885 Single-Shot Shotgun, 578
Model 1887 Lever-Action Shotgun, 578
Model 1893 Pump-Action Shotgun, 572
Model 1901 Lever-Action, 578
Model 1911 Autoloading, 578
Ranger Deer Combination, 578
Super-X Model I Auto Field Gun, 579
Super-X Model I Skeet Gun, 579
Super-X Model I Trap Gun, 579
Xpert Model 96 Over/Under Field Gun, 579
Xpert Model 96 Skeet Gun, 579
Xpert Model 96 Trap Gun, 579
WOODWARD & SONS
  Best Quality Hammerless Double, 579
  Best Quality Over/Under Shotgun, 579
  Best Quality Single-Shot Trap, 579
WINSLOW ARMS COMPANY
  Bolt-Action Sporting Rifle, 423
ZEPHYR
  RIFLES
  Double Rifle, 423
  SHOTGUNS
  Crown Grade, 580
  Field Model Over/Under Shotgun, 580
  Honker Single-Shot Shotgun, 580
  Model 1 Over/Under Shotgun, 579
  Model 2 Over/Under Shotgun, 579
  Model 3 Over/Under Shotgun, 579
  Model 400E Field Grade Double-Barrel Shotgun, 580
  Model 401E Skeet Grade Double-Barrel Shotgun, 580
  Model 402E Deluxe Double-Barrel Shotgun, 580
  Pinehurst Double-Barrel Shotgun, 580
  Premier Grade Double-Barrel, 580
  Royal Grade Double-Barrel, 580
  Sterlingworth II Double-Barrel, 580
  Thunderbird Double-Barrel, 580
  Upland King Double-Barrel, 580
  Uplander 4E Double-Barrel, 580
  Woodlander II Double-Barrel, 580